C# 10 IN A NUTSHELL

THE DEFINITIVE REFERENCE

Joseph Albahari

Beijing · Boston · Farnham · Sebastopol · Tokyo

C# 10 in a Nutshell

by Joseph Albahari

Published by O'Reilly Media, Inc., 1005 Gravenstein Highway North, Sebastopol, CA 95472.

O'Reilly books may be purchased for educational, business, or sales promotional use. Online editions are also available for most titles (*http://oreilly.com*). For more information, contact our corporate/institutional sales department: 800-998-9938 or *corporate@oreilly.com*.

Acquisitions Editor: Amanda Quinn	**Indexer:** WordCo Indexing Services, Inc.
Development Editor: Corbin Collins	**Interior Designer:** David Futato
Production Editor: Kristen Brown	**Cover Designer:** Karen Montgomery
Copyeditor: Charles Roumeliotis	**Illustrator:** Kate Dullea
Proofreader: Piper Editorial Consulting, LLC	

February 2022:   First Edition

Revision History for the First Edition

2022-02-08:   First Release

See *http://oreilly.com/catalog/errata.csp?isbn=9781098121952* for release details.

978-1-098-12195-2

[LSI]

Table of Contents

Preface

C# 10 represents the ninth major update to Microsoft's flagship programming language, positioning C# as a language with unusual flexibility and breadth. At one end, it offers high-level abstractions such as query expressions and asynchronous continuations, whereas at the other end, it allows low-level efficiency through constructs such as custom value types and optional pointers.

The price of this growth is that there's more than ever to learn. Although tools such as Microsoft's IntelliSense—and online references—are excellent in helping you on the job, they presume an existing map of conceptual knowledge. This book provides exactly that map of knowledge in a concise and unified style—free of clutter and long introductions.

Like the past seven editions, *C# 10 in a Nutshell* is organized around concepts and use cases, making it friendly both to sequential reading and to random browsing. It also plumbs significant depths while assuming only basic background knowledge, making it accessible to intermediate as well as advanced readers.

This book covers C#, the Common Language Runtime (CLR), and the .NET 6 Base Class Library (BCL). We've chosen this focus to allow space for difficult and advanced topics without compromising depth or readability. Features recently added to C# are flagged so that you can also use this book as a reference for C# 9, C# 8, and C# 7.

Intended Audience

This book targets intermediate to advanced audiences. No prior knowledge of C# is required, but some general programming experience is necessary. For the beginner, this book complements, rather than replaces, a tutorial-style introduction to programming.

This book is an ideal companion to any of the vast array of books that focus on an applied technology such as ASP.NET Core or Windows Presentation Foundation

(WPF). *C# 10 in a Nutshell* covers the areas of the language and .NET that such books omit, and vice versa.

If you're looking for a book that skims every .NET technology, this is not for you. This book is also unsuitable if you want to learn about APIs specific to mobile device development.

How This Book Is Organized

Chapters 2 through 4 concentrate purely on C#, starting with the basics of syntax, types, and variables, and finishing with advanced topics such as unsafe code and preprocessor directives. If you're new to the language, you should read these chapters sequentially.

The remaining chapters focus on .NET 6's Base Class Libraries (BCLs), covering such topics as Language-Integrated Query (LINQ), XML, collections, concurrency, I/O and networking, memory management, reflection, dynamic programming, attributes, cryptography, and native interoperability. You can read most of these chapters randomly, except for Chapters 5 and 6, which lay a foundation for subsequent topics. You're also best off reading the three chapters on LINQ in sequence, and some chapters assume some knowledge of concurrency, which we cover in Chapter 14.

What You Need to Use This Book

The examples in this book require .NET 6. You will also find Microsoft's .NET documentation useful to look up individual types and members (which is available online).

Although it's possible to write source code in a simple text editor and build your program from the command line, you'll be much more productive with a *code scratchpad* for instantly testing code snippets, plus an *integrated development environment* (IDE) for producing executables and libraries.

For a Windows code scratchpad, download LINQPad 7 from *www.linqpad.net* (free). LINQPad fully supports C# 10 and is maintained by the author.

For a Windows IDE, download Visual Studio 2022 (*https://visualstudio.micro soft.com*): any edition is suitable for what's taught in this book. For a cross-platform IDE, download Visual Studio Code.

 All code listings for all chapters are available as interactive (editable) LINQPad samples. You can download the entire lot in a single click: at the bottom left, click the LINQPad's Samples tab, click "Download more samples," and then choose "C# 10 in a Nutshell."

Conventions Used in This Book

The book uses basic UML notation to illustrate relationships between types, as shown in Figure P-1. A slanted rectangle means an abstract class; a circle means an interface. A line with a hollow triangle denotes inheritance, with the triangle pointing to the base type. A line with an arrow denotes a one-way association; a line without an arrow denotes a two-way association.

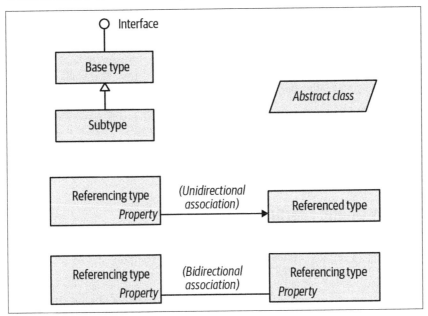

Figure P-1. Sample diagram

The following typographical conventions are used in this book:

Italic
> Indicates new terms, URIs, filenames, and directories

`Constant width`
> Indicates C# code, keywords and identifiers, and program output

`Constant width bold`
> Shows a highlighted section of code

`Constant width italic`
> Shows text that should be replaced with user-supplied values

Using Code Examples

Supplemental material (code examples, exercises, etc.) is available for download at *http://www.albahari.com/nutshell*.

This book is here to help you get your job done. In general, you may use the code in this book in your programs and documentation. You do not need to contact us for permission unless you're reproducing a significant portion of the code. For example, writing a program that uses several chunks of code from this book does not require permission. Selling or distributing examples from O'Reilly books *does* require permission. Answering a question by citing this book and quoting example code does not require permission (although we appreciate attribution). Incorporating a significant amount of example code from this book into your product's documentation *does* require permission.

We appreciate, but generally do not require, attribution. An attribution usually includes the title, author, publisher, and ISBN. For example: "*C# 10 in a Nutshell* by Joseph Albahari (O'Reilly). Copyright 2022 Joseph Albahari, 978-1-098-12195-2."

If you feel your use of code examples falls outside fair use or the permission given here, feel free to contact us at *permissions@oreilly.com*.

O'Reilly Online Learning

 For more than 40 years, *O'Reilly Media* has provided technology and business training, knowledge, and insight to help companies succeed.

Our unique network of experts and innovators share their knowledge and expertise through books, articles, and our online learning platform. O'Reilly's online learning platform gives you on-demand access to live training courses, in-depth learning paths, interactive coding environments, and a vast collection of text and video from O'Reilly and 200+ other publishers. For more information, visit *http://oreilly.com*.

How to Contact Us

Please address comments and questions concerning this book to the publisher:

O'Reilly Media, Inc.
1005 Gravenstein Highway North
Sebastopol, CA 95472
800-998-9938 (in the United States or Canada)
707-829-0515 (international or local)
707-829-0104 (fax)

We have a web page for this book, where we list errata, examples, and any additional information. You can access this page at *https://oreil.ly/c-sharp-nutshell-10*.

Email *bookquestions@oreilly.com* to comment or ask technical questions about this book.

For news and information about our books and courses, visit *http://oreilly.com*.

Find us on Facebook: *http://facebook.com/oreilly*

Follow us on Twitter: *http://twitter.com/oreillymedia*

Watch us on YouTube: *http://youtube.com/oreillymedia*

Acknowledgments

Since its first incarnation in 2007, this book has relied on input from some superb technical reviewers. For their input into recent editions, I'd like to extend particular thanks to Stephen Toub, Paulo Morgado, Fred Silberberg, Vitek Karas, Aaron Robinson, Jan Vorlicek, Sam Gentile, Rod Stephens, Jared Parsons, Matthew Groves, Dixin Yan, Lee Coward, Bonnie DeWitt, Wonseok Chae, Lori Lalonde, and James Montemagno.

And for their input into earlier editions, I'm most grateful to Eric Lippert, Jon Skeet, Stephen Toub, Nicholas Paldino, Chris Burrows, Shawn Farkas, Brian Grunkemeyer, Maoni Stephens, David DeWinter, Mike Barnett, Melitta Andersen, Mitch Wheat, Brian Peek, Krzysztof Cwalina, Matt Warren, Joel Pobar, Glyn Griffiths, Ion Vasilian, Brad Abrams, and Adam Nathan.

I appreciate that many of the technical reviewers are accomplished individuals at Microsoft, and I particularly thank you for taking the time to raise this book to the next quality bar.

I want to thank Ben Albahari and Eric Johannsen, who contributed to previous editions, and the O'Reilly team—particularly my efficient and responsive editor Corbin Collins. Finally, my deepest thanks to my wonderful wife, Li Albahari, whose presence kept me happy throughout the project.

Introducing C# and .NET

C# is a general-purpose, type-safe, object-oriented programming language. The goal of the language is programmer productivity. To this end, C# balances simplicity, expressiveness, and performance. The chief architect of the language since its first version is Anders Hejlsberg (creator of Turbo Pascal and architect of Delphi). The C# language is platform neutral and works with a range of platform-specific runtimes.

Object Orientation

C# is a rich implementation of the object-orientation paradigm, which includes *encapsulation*, *inheritance*, and *polymorphism*. Encapsulation means creating a boundary around an *object* to separate its external (public) behavior from its internal (private) implementation details. Following are the distinctive features of C# from an object-oriented perspective:

Unified type system
> The fundamental building block in C# is an encapsulated unit of data and functions called a *type*. C# has a *unified type system* in which all types ultimately share a common base type. This means that all types, whether they represent business objects or are primitive types such as numbers, share the same basic functionality. For example, an instance of any type can be converted to a string by calling its ToString method.

Classes and interfaces
> In a traditional object-oriented paradigm, the only kind of type is a class. In C#, there are several other kinds of types, one of which is an *interface*. An interface is like a class that cannot hold data. This means that it can define only *behavior* (and not *state*), which allows for multiple inheritance as well as a separation between specification and implementation.

Properties, methods, and events
> In the pure object-oriented paradigm, all functions are *methods*. In C#, methods are only one kind of *function member*, which also includes *properties* and *events* (there are others, too). Properties are function members that encapsulate a piece of an object's state, such as a button's color or a label's text. Events are function members that simplify acting on object state changes.

Although C# is primarily an object-oriented language, it also borrows from the *functional programming* paradigm; specifically:

Functions can be treated as values
> Using *delegates*, C# allows functions to be passed as values to and from other functions.

C# supports patterns for purity
> Core to functional programming is avoiding the use of variables whose values change, in favor of declarative patterns. C# has key features to help with those patterns, including the ability to write unnamed functions on the fly that "capture" variables (*lambda expressions*) and the ability to perform list or reactive programming via *query expressions*. C# also provides *records*, which make it easy to write *immutable* (read-only) types.

Type Safety

C# is primarily a *type-safe* language, meaning that instances of types can interact only through protocols they define, thereby ensuring each type's internal consistency. For instance, C# prevents you from interacting with a *string* type as though it were an *integer* type.

More specifically, C# supports *static typing*, meaning that the language enforces type safety at *compile time*. This is in addition to type safety being enforced at *runtime*.

Static typing eliminates a large class of errors before a program is even run. It shifts the burden away from runtime unit tests onto the compiler to verify that all the types in a program fit together correctly. This makes large programs much easier to manage, more predictable, and more robust. Furthermore, static typing allows tools such as IntelliSense in Visual Studio to help you write a program because it knows for a given variable what type it is, and hence what methods you can call on that variable. Such tools can also identify everywhere in your program that a variable, type, or method is used, allowing for reliable refactoring.

> C# also allows parts of your code to be dynamically typed via the `dynamic` keyword. However, C# remains a predominantly statically typed language.

C# is also called a *strongly typed language* because its type rules are strictly enforced (whether statically or at runtime). For instance, you cannot call a function that's designed to accept an integer with a floating-point number, unless you first *explicitly* convert the floating-point number to an integer. This helps prevent mistakes.

Memory Management

C# relies on the runtime to perform automatic memory management. The Common Language Runtime has a garbage collector that executes as part of your program, reclaiming memory for objects that are no longer referenced. This frees programmers from explicitly deallocating the memory for an object, eliminating the problem of incorrect pointers encountered in languages such as C++.

C# does not eliminate pointers: it merely makes them unnecessary for most programming tasks. For performance-critical hotspots and interoperability, pointers and explicit memory allocation is permitted in blocks that are marked unsafe.

Platform Support

C# has runtimes that support the following platforms:

- Windows Desktop 7-11 (for rich-client, web, server, and command-line applications)
- macOS (for rich-client, web, and command-line applications)
- Linux and macOS (for web and command-line applications)
- Android and iOS (for mobile applications)
- Windows 10 devices (Xbox, Surface Hub, and HoloLens)

There is also a technology called *Blazor* that can compile C# to web assembly that runs in a browser.

CLRs, BCLs, and Runtimes

Runtime support for C# programs consists of a *Common Language Runtime* and a *Base Class Library*. A runtime can also include a higher-level *application layer* that contains libraries for developing rich-client, mobile, or web applications (see Figure 1-1). Different runtimes exist to allow for different kinds of applications, as well as different platforms.

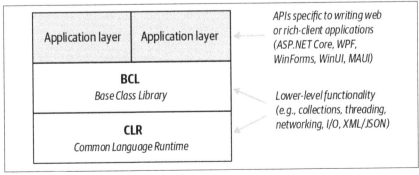

Figure 1-1. Runtime architecture

Common Language Runtime

A *Common Language Runtime* (CLR) provides essential runtime services such as automatic memory management and exception handling. (The word "common" refers to the fact that the same runtime can be shared by other *managed* programming languages, such as F#, Visual Basic, and Managed C++.)

C# is called a *managed language* because it compiles source code into managed code, which is represented in *Intermediate Language* (IL). The CLR converts the IL into the native code of the machine, such as X64 or X86, usually just prior to execution. This is referred to as *Just-in-Time (JIT) compilation*. Ahead-of-time compilation is also available to improve startup time with large assemblies or resource-constrained devices (and to satisfy iOS app store rules when developing mobile apps).

The container for managed code is called an *assembly*. An assembly contains not only IL but also type information (*metadata*). The presence of metadata allows assemblies to reference types in other assemblies without needing additional files.

 You can examine and disassemble the contents of an assembly with Microsoft's *ildasm* tool. And with tools such as ILSpy or JetBrain's dotPeek, you can go further and decompile the IL to C#. Because IL is higher level than native machine code, the decompiler can do quite a good job of reconstructing the original C#.

A program can query its own metadata (*reflection*) and even generate new IL at runtime (*reflection.emit*).

Base Class Library

A CLR always ships with a set of assemblies called a *Base Class Library* (BCL). A BCL provides core functionality to programmers, such as collections, input/output, text processing, XML/JSON handling, networking, encryption, interop, concurrency, and parallel programming.

A BCL also implements types that the C# language itself requires (for features such as enumeration, querying, and asynchrony) and lets you explicitly access features of the CLR, such as reflection and memory management.

Runtimes

A *runtime* (also called a *framework*) is a deployable unit that you download and install. A runtime consists of a CLR (with its BCL), plus an optional *application layer* specific to the kind of application that you're writing—web, mobile, rich client, etc. (If you're writing a command-line console application or a non-UI library, you don't need an application layer.)

When writing an application, you *target* a particular runtime, which means that your application uses and depends on the functionality that the runtime provides.

Your choice of runtime also determines which platforms your application will support.

The following table lists the major runtime options:

Application layer	CLR/BCL	Program type	Runs on...
ASP.NET	.NET 6	Web	Windows, Linux, macOS
Windows Desktop	.NET 6	Windows	Windows 7–10+
MAUI (early 2022)	.NET 6	Mobile, desktop	iOS, Android, macOS, Windows 10+
WinUI 3 (early 2022)	.NET 6	Win10	Windows 10+ desktop
UWP	.NET Core 2.2	Win10 + Win10 devices	Windows 10+ desktop & devices
(Legacy) .NET Framework	.NET Framework	Web, Windows	Windows 7–10+

Figure 1-2 shows this information graphically and also serves as a guide to what's covered in the book.

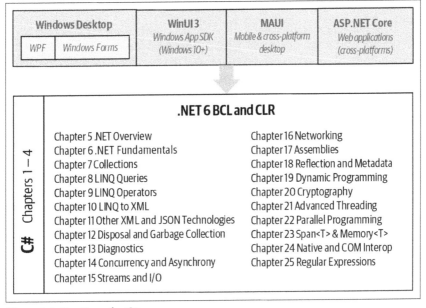

Figure 1-2. Runtimes for C#

.NET 6

.NET 6 is Microsoft's flagship open-source runtime. You can write web and console applications that run on Windows, Linux, and macOS; rich-client applications that run on Windows 7 through 11 and macOS; and mobile apps that run on iOS and Android. This book focuses on the .NET 6 CLR and BCL.

Unlike .NET Framework, .NET 6 is not preinstalled on Windows machines. If you try to run a .NET 6 application without the correct runtime being present, a message will appear directing you to a web page where you can download the runtime. You can avoid this by creating a *self-contained* deployment, which includes the parts of the runtime required by the application.

 .NET 6's predecessor was .NET 5, whose predecessor was .NET Core 3. (Microsoft removed "Core" from the name and skipped version 4.) The reason for skipping a version was to avoid confusion with *.NET Framework* 4.x.

This means that assemblies compiled under .NET Core versions 1, 2, and 3 (and .NET 5) will, in most cases, run without modification under .NET 6. In contrast, assemblies compiled under (any version of) .NET Framework are usually incompatible with .NET 6.

The .NET 6 BCL and CLR are very similar to .NET 5 (and .NET Core 3), with their differences centering mostly on performance and deployment.

MAUI

MAUI (Multi-platform App UI, early 2022) is designed for creating mobile apps for iOS and Android, as well as cross-platform desktop apps for macOS and Windows. MAUI is an evolution of Xamarin, and allows a single project to target multiple platforms.

UWP and WinUI 3

Universal Windows Platform (UWP) is designed for writing immersive touch-first applications that run on Windows 10+ desktop and devices (Xbox, Surface Hub, and HoloLens). UWP apps are sandboxed and ship via the Windows Store. UWP is preinstalled with Windows 10. It uses a version of the .NET Core 2.2 CLR/BCL, and it's unlikely that this dependency will be updated. Instead, Microsoft has released a successor called *WinUI 3*, as part of the *Windows App SDK*.

The Windows App SDK works with the latest .NET, integrates better with the .NET desktop APIs, and can run outside a sandbox. However, it does not yet support devices such as Xbox or HoloLens.

.NET Framework

.NET Framework is Microsoft's original Windows-only runtime for writing web and rich-client applications that run (only) on Windows desktops/servers. No major new releases are planned, although Microsoft will continue to support and maintain the current 4.8 release due to the wealth of existing applications.

With the .NET Framework, the CLR/BCL is integrated with the application layer. Applications written in .NET Framework can be recompiled under .NET 6, although they usually require some modification. Some features of .NET Framework are not present in .NET 6 (and vice versa).

.NET Framework is preinstalled with Windows and is automatically patched via Windows Update. When you target .NET Framework 4.8, you can use the features of C# 7.3 and earlier.

The word ".NET" has long been used as an umbrella term for any technology that includes the word ".NET" (.NET Framework, .NET Core, .NET Standard, and so on).

This means that Microsoft's renaming of .NET Core to .NET has created an unfortunate ambiguity. In this book, we'll refer to the new .NET as *.NET 5+*. And to refer to .NET Core and its successors, we'll use the phrase ".NET Core and .NET 5+."

To add to the confusion, .NET (5+) is a framework, yet it's very different from the *.NET Framework*. Hence, we'll use the term *runtime* in preference to *framework*, where possible.

Niche Runtimes

There are also the following niche runtimes:

- The .NET Micro Framework is for running .NET code on highly resource-constrained embedded devices (under one megabyte).
- Unity is a game development platform that allows game logic to be scripted with C#.

It's also possible to run managed code within SQL Server. With SQL Server CLR integration, you can write custom functions, stored procedures, and aggregations in C# and then call them from SQL. This works in conjunction with .NET Framework and a special "hosted" CLR that enforces a sandbox to protect the integrity of the SQL Server process.

A Brief History of C#

The following is a reverse chronology of the new features in each C# version, for the benefit of readers who are already familiar with an older version of the language.

What's New in C# 10

C# 10 ships with Visual Studio 2022, and is used when you target .NET 6.

File-scoped namespaces

In the common case that all types in a file are defined in a single namespace, a *file-scoped namespace* declaration in C# 10 reduces clutter and eliminates an unnecessary level of indentation:

```
namespace MyNamespace;  // Applies to everything that follows in the file.

class Class1 {}         // inside MyNamespace
class Class2 {}         // inside MyNamespace
```

The global using directive

When you prefix a using directive with the global keyword, it applies the directive to all files in the project:

```
global using System;
global using System.Collection.Generic;
```

This lets you avoid repeating the same directives in every file. global using directives work with using static.

Additionally, .NET 6 projects now support *implicit global using directives*: if the ImplicitUsings element is set to true in the project file, the most commonly used namespaces are automatically imported (based on the SDK project type). See "The global using Directive (C# 10)" on page 88 for more detail.

Nondestructive mutation for anonymous types

C# 9 introduced the with keyword, to perform nondestructive mutation on records. In C# 10, the with keyword also works with anonymous types:

```
var a1 = new { A = 1, B = 2, C = 3, D = 4, E = 5 };
var a2 = a1 with { E = 10 };
Console.WriteLine (a2);        // { A = 1, B = 2, C = 3, D = 4, E = 10 }
```

New deconstruction syntax

C# 7 introduced the deconstruction syntax for tuples (or any type with a Deconstruct method). C# 10 takes this syntax further, letting you mix assignment and declaration in the same deconstruction:

```
var point = (3, 4);
double x = 0;
(x, double y) = point;
```

Field initializers and parameterless constructors in structs

From C# 10, you can include field initializers and parameterless constructors in structs (see "Structs" on page 129). These execute only when the constructor is called explicitly, and so can easily be bypassed—for instance, via the default keyword. This feature was introduced primarily for the benefit of struct records.

Record structs

Records were first introduced in C# 9, where they acted as a compiled-enhanced class. In C# 10, records can also be structs:

```
record struct Point (int X, int Y);
```

The rules are otherwise similar: *record structs* have much the same features as *class structs* (see "Records" on page 211). An exception is that the compiler-generated properties on record structs are writable, unless you prefix the record declaration with the readonly keyword.

Lambda expression enhancements

The syntax around lambda expressions has been enhanced in a number of ways. First, implicit typing (var) is permitted:

```
var greeter = () => "Hello, world";
```

The implicit type for a lambda expression is an Action or Func delegate, so greeter, in this case, is of type Func<string>. You must explicitly state any parameter types:

```
var square = (int x) => x * x;
```

Second, a lambda expression can specify a return type:

```
var sqr = int (int x) => x;
```

This is primarily to improve compiler performance with complex nested lambdas.

Third, you can pass a lambda expression into a method parameter of type object, Delegate, or Expression:

```
M1 (() => "test");   // Implicitly typed to Func<string>
M2 (() => "test");   // Implicitly typed to Func<string>
M3 (() => "test");   // Implicitly typed to Expression<Func<string>>

void M1 (object x) {}
void M2 (Delegate x) {}
void M3 (Expression x) {}
```

Finally, you can apply attributes to a lambda expression's compile-generated target method (as well as its parameters and return value):

```
Action a = [Description("test")] () => { };
```

See "Applying Attributes to Lambda Expressions (C# 10)" on page 228 for more detail.

Nested property patterns

The following simplified syntax is legal in C# 10 for nested property pattern matching (see "Property Patterns" on page 225):

```
var obj = new Uri ("https://www.linqpad.net");
if (obj is Uri { Scheme.Length: 5 }) ...
```

This is equivalent to:

```
if (obj is Uri { Scheme: { Length: 5 }}) ...
```

CallerArgumentExpression

A method parameter to which you apply the [CallerArgumentExpression] attribute captures an argument expression from the call site:

```
Print (Math.PI * 2);

void Print (double number,
            [CallerArgumentExpression("number")] string expr = null)
    => Console.WriteLine (expr);

// Output: Math.PI * 2
```

This feature is intended primarily for validation and assertion libraries (see "Caller-ArgumentExpression (C# 10)" on page 231).

Other new features

The #line directive has been enhanced in C# 10 to allow a column and range to be specified.

Interpolated strings in C# 10 can be constants, as long as the interpolated values are constants.

Records can seal the ToString() method in C# 10.

C#'s definite assignment analysis has been improved so that expressions such as the following work:

```
if (foo?.TryParse ("123", out var number) ?? false)
    Console.WriteLine (number);
```

(Prior to C# 10, the compiler would generate an error: "Use of unassigned local variable 'number'.")

What's New in C# 9.0

C# 9.0 shipped with Visual Studio 2019, and is used when you target .NET 5.

Top-level statements

With *top-level statements* (see "Top-Level Statements" on page 35), you can write a program without the baggage of a Main method and Program class:

```
using System;
Console.WriteLine ("Hello, world");
```

Top-level statements can include methods (which act as local methods). You can also access command-line arguments via the "magic" args variable and return a value to the caller. Top-level statements can be followed by type and namespace declarations.

Init-only setters

An *init-only setter* (see "Init-only setters" on page 108) in a property declaration uses the init keyword instead of the set keyword:

```
class Foo { public int ID { get; init; } }
```

This behaves like a read-only property, except that it can also be set via an object initializer:

```
var foo = new Foo { ID = 123 };
```

This makes it possible to create immutable (read-only) types that can be populated via an object initializer instead of a constructor, and helps to avoid the antipattern of constructors that accept a large number of optional parameters. Init-only setters also allow for *nondestructive mutation* when used in *records*.

Records

A *record* (see "Records" on page 211) is a special kind of class that's designed to work well with immutable data. Its most special feature is that it supports *nondestructive mutation* via a new keyword (with):

```
Point p1 = new Point (2, 3);
Point p2 = p1 with { Y = 4 };    // p2 is a copy of p1, but with Y set to 4
Console.WriteLine (p2);          // Point { X = 2, Y = 4 }

record Point
{
   public Point (double x, double y) => (X, Y) = (x, y);

   public double X { get; init; }
   public double Y { get; init; }
}
```

In simple cases, a record can also eliminate the boilerplate code of defining properties and writing a constructor and deconstructor. We can replace our Point record definition with the following, without loss of functionality:

```
record Point (double X, double Y);
```

Like tuples, records exhibit structural equality by default. Records can subclass other records and can include the same constructs that classes can include. The compiler implements records as classes at runtime.

Pattern-matching improvements

The *relational pattern* (see "Patterns" on page 222) allows the <, >, <=, and >= operators to appear in patterns:

```
string GetWeightCategory (decimal bmi) => bmi switch {
   < 18.5m => "underweight",
   < 25m => "normal",
   < 30m => "overweight",
   _ => "obese" };
```

With *pattern combinators*, you can combine patterns via three new keywords (and, or, and not):

```
bool IsVowel (char c) => c is 'a' or 'e' or 'i' or 'o' or 'u';
```

```
bool IsLetter (char c) => c is >= 'a' and <= 'z'
                            or >= 'A' and <= 'Z';
```

As with the && and || operators, and has higher precedence than or. You can override this with parentheses.

The not combinator can be used with the *type pattern* to test whether an object is (not) a type:

```
if (obj is not string) ...
```

Target-typed new expressions

When constructing an object, C# 9 lets you omit the type name when the compiler can infer it unambiguously:

```
System.Text.StringBuilder sb1 = new();
System.Text.StringBuilder sb2 = new ("Test");
```

This is particularly useful when the variable declaration and initialization are in different parts of your code:

```
class Foo
{
  System.Text.StringBuilder sb;
  public Foo (string initialValue) => sb = new (initialValue);
}
```

And in the following scenario:

```
MyMethod (new ("test"));
void MyMethod (System.Text.StringBuilder sb) { ... }
```

see "Target-Typed new Expressions" on page 69 for more information.

Interop improvements

C# 9 introduced *function pointers* (see "Function Pointers" on page 248 and "Callbacks with Function Pointers" on page 967). Their main purpose is to allow unmanaged code to call static methods in C# without the overhead of a delegate instance, with the ability to bypass the P/Invoke layer when the arguments and return types are *blittable* (represented identically on each side).

C# 9 also introduced the nint and nuint native-sized integer types (see "Native-Sized Integers" on page 246), which map at runtime to System.IntPtr and System.UIntPtr. At compile time, they behave like numeric types with support for arithmetic operations.

Other new features

Additionally, C# 9 now lets you do the following:

- Override a method or read-only property such that it returns a more derived type (see "Covariant return types" on page 120)

- Apply attributes to local functions (see "Attributes" on page 227)

- Apply the `static` keyword to lambda expressions or local functions to ensure that you don't accidentally capture local or instance variables (see "Static lambdas" on page 177)

- Make any type work with the `foreach` statement, by writing a `GetEnumerator` extension method

- Define a *module initializer* method that executes once when an assembly is first loaded, by applying the `[ModuleInitializer]` attribute to a (static void parameterless) method

- Use a "discard" (underscore symbol) as a lambda expression argument

- Write *extended partial methods* that are mandatory to implement—enabling scenarios such as Roslyn's new *source generators* (see "Extended partial methods" on page 114)

- Apply an attribute to methods, types, or modules to prevent local variables from being initialized by the runtime (see "[SkipLocalsInit]" on page 248)

What's New in C# 8.0

C# 8.0 first shipped with Visual Studio 2019, and is still used today when you target .NET Core 3 or .NET Standard 2.1.

Indices and ranges

Indices and *ranges* simplify working with elements or portions of an array (or the low-level types `Span<T>` and `ReadOnlySpan<T>`).

Indices let you refer to elements relative to the *end* of an array by using the `^` operator. `^1` refers to the last element, `^2` refers to the second-to-last element, and so on:

```
char[] vowels = new char[] {'a','e','i','o','u'};
char lastElement  = vowels [^1];   // 'u'
char secondToLast = vowels [^2];   // 'o'
```

Ranges let you "slice" an array by using the `..` operator:

```
char[] firstTwo =  vowels [..2];    // 'a', 'e'
char[] lastThree = vowels [2..];    // 'i', 'o', 'u'
char[] middleOne = vowels [2..3]    // 'i'
char[] lastTwo =   vowels [^2..];   // 'o', 'u'
```

C# implements indexes and ranges with the help of the `Index` and `Range` types:

```
Index last = ^1;
Range firstTwoRange = 0..2;
char[] firstTwo = vowels [firstTwoRange];   // 'a', 'e'
```

You can support indices and ranges in your own classes by defining an indexer with a parameter type of Index or Range:

```
class Sentence
{
  string[] words = "The quick brown fox".Split();

  public string this   [Index index] => words [index];
  public string[] this [Range range] => words [range];
}
```

For more information, see "Indices" on page 56.

Null-coalescing assignment

The ??= operator assigns a variable only if it's null. Instead of

```
if (s == null) s = "Hello, world";
```

you can now write this:

```
s ??= "Hello, world";
```

Using declarations

If you omit the brackets and statement block following a using statement, it becomes a *using declaration*. The resource is then disposed when execution falls outside the *enclosing* statement block:

```
if (File.Exists ("file.txt"))
{
  using var reader = File.OpenText ("file.txt");
  Console.WriteLine (reader.ReadLine());
  ...
}
```

In this case, reader will be disposed when execution falls outside the if statement block.

Read-only members

C# 8 lets you apply the readonly modifier to a struct's *functions*, ensuring that if the function attempts to modify any field, a compile-time error is generated:

```
struct Point
{
  public int X, Y;
  public readonly void ResetX() => X = 0;  // Error!
}
```

If a readonly function calls a non-readonly function, the compiler generates a warning (and defensively copies the struct to avoid the possibility of a mutation).

Static local methods

Adding the `static` modifier to a local method prevents it from seeing the local variables and parameters of the enclosing method. This helps to reduce coupling and enables the local method to declare variables as it pleases, without risk of colliding with those in the containing method.

Default interface members

C# 8 lets you add a default implementation to an interface member, making it optional to implement:

```
interface ILogger
{
  void Log (string text) => Console.WriteLine (text);
}
```

This means that you can add a member to an interface without breaking implementations. Default implementations must be called explicitly through the interface:

```
((ILogger)new Logger()).Log ("message");
```

Interfaces can also define static members (including fields), which can be accessed from code inside default implementations:

```
interface ILogger
{
  void Log (string text) => Console.WriteLine (Prefix + text);
  static string Prefix = "";
}
```

Or from outside the interface unless restricted via an accessibility modifier on the static interface member (such as `private`, `protected`, or `internal`):

```
ILogger.Prefix = "File log: ";
```

Instance fields are prohibited. For more details, see "Default Interface Members" on page 139.

Switch expressions

From C# 8, you can use `switch` in the context of an *expression*:

```
string cardName = cardNumber switch     // assuming cardNumber is an int
{
  13 => "King",
  12 => "Queen",
  11 => "Jack",
  _ => "Pip card"    // equivalent to 'default'
};
```

For more examples, see "Switch expressions" on page 82.

Tuple, positional, and property patterns

C# 8 supports three new patterns, mostly for the benefit of switch statements/expressions (see "Patterns" on page 222). *Tuple patterns* let you switch on multiple values:

```
int cardNumber = 12; string suite = "spades";
string cardName = (cardNumber, suite) switch
{
  (13, "spades") => "King of spades",
  (13, "clubs") => "King of clubs",
  ...
};
```

Positional patterns allow a similar syntax for objects that expose a deconstructor, and *property patterns* let you match on an object's properties. You can use all of the patterns both in switches and with the is operator. The following example uses a *property pattern* to test whether obj is a string with a length of 4:

```
if (obj is string { Length:4 }) ...
```

Nullable reference types

Whereas *nullable value types* bring nullability to value types, *nullable reference types* do the opposite and bring (a degree of) *non-nullability* to reference types, with the purpose of helping to avoid NullReferenceExceptions. Nullable reference types introduce a level of safety that's enforced purely by the compiler in the form of warnings or errors when it detects code that's at risk of generating a NullReferenceException.

Nullable reference types can be enabled either at the project level (via the Nullable element in the *.csproj* project file) or in code (via the #nullable directive). After it's enabled, the compiler makes non-nullability the default: if you want a reference type to accept nulls, you must apply the ? suffix to indicate a *nullable reference type*:

```
#nullable enable    // Enable nullable reference types from this point on

string s1 = null;   // Generates a compiler warning! (s1 is non-nullable)
string? s2 = null;  // OK: s2 is nullable reference type
```

Uninitialized fields also generate a warning (if the type is not marked as nullable), as does dereferencing a nullable reference type, if the compiler thinks a NullReferenceException might occur:

```
void Foo (string? s) => Console.Write (s.Length);  // Warning (.Length)
```

To remove the warning, you can use the *null-forgiving operator* (!):

```
void Foo (string? s) => Console.Write (s!.Length);
```

For a full discussion, see "Nullable Reference Types" on page 200.

Asynchronous streams

Prior to C# 8, you could use `yield return` to write an *iterator*, or `await` to write an *asynchronous function*. But you couldn't do both and write an iterator that awaits, yielding elements asynchronously. C# 8 fixes this through the introduction of *asynchronous streams*:

```
async IAsyncEnumerable<int> RangeAsync (
  int start, int count, int delay)
{
  for (int i = start; i < start + count; i++)
  {
    await Task.Delay (delay);
    yield return i;
  }
}
```

The `await foreach` statement consumes an asynchronous stream:

```
await foreach (var number in RangeAsync (0, 10, 100))
  Console.WriteLine (number);
```

For more information, see "Asynchronous Streams" on page 650.

What's New in C# 7.x

C# 7.x was first shipped with Visual Studio 2017. C# 7.3 is still used today by Visual Studio 2019 when you target .NET Core 2, .NET Framework 4.6 to 4.8, or .NET Standard 2.0.

C# 7.3

C# 7.3 made minor improvements to existing features, such as enabling use of the equality operators with tuples, improving overload resolution, and offering the ability to apply attributes to the backing fields of automatic properties:

```
[field:NonSerialized]
public int MyProperty { get; set; }
```

C# 7.3 also built on C# 7.2's advanced low-allocation programming features, with the ability to reassign *ref locals*, no requirement to pin when indexing `fixed` fields, and field initializer support with `stackalloc`:

```
int* pointer  = stackalloc int[] {1, 2, 3};
Span<int> arr = stackalloc []    {1, 2, 3};
```

Notice that stack-allocated memory can be assigned directly to a `Span<T>`. We describe spans—and why you would use them—in Chapter 23.

C# 7.2

C# 7.2 added a new `private protected` modifier (the *intersection* of `internal` and `protected`), the ability to follow named arguments with positional ones when calling methods, and `readonly` structs. A `readonly` struct enforces that all fields are readonly, to aid in declaring intent and to allow the compiler more optimization freedom:

```
readonly struct Point
{
    public readonly int X, Y;    // X and Y must be readonly
}
```

C# 7.2 also added specialized features to help with micro-optimization and low-allocation programming: see "The in modifier" on page 64, "Ref Locals" on page 67, "Ref Returns" on page 68, and "Ref Structs" on page 131).

C# 7.1

From C# 7.1, you can omit the type when using the default keyword, if the type can be inferred:

```
decimal number = default;    // number is decimal
```

C# 7.1 also relaxed the rules for switch statements (so that you can pattern-match on generic type parameters), allowed a program's Main method to be asynchronous, and allowed tuple element names to be inferred:

```
var now = DateTime.Now;
var tuple = (now.Hour, now.Minute, now.Second);
```

Numeric literal improvements

Numeric literals in C# 7 can include underscores to improve readability. These are called *digit separators* and are ignored by the compiler:

```
int million = 1_000_000;
```

Binary literals can be specified with the 0b prefix:

```
var b = 0b1010_1011_1100_1101_1110_1111;
```

Out variables and discards

C# 7 makes it easier to call methods that contain out parameters. First, you can now declare *out variables* on the fly (see "Out variables and discards" on page 64):

```
bool successful = int.TryParse ("123", out int result);
Console.WriteLine (result);
```

And when calling a method with multiple out parameters, you can *discard* ones you're uninterested in with the underscore character:

```
SomeBigMethod (out _, out _, out _, out int x, out _, out _, out _);
Console.WriteLine (x);
```

Type patterns and pattern variables

You can also introduce variables on the fly with the is operator. These are called *pattern variables* (see "Introducing a pattern variable" on page 118):

```
void Foo (object x)
{
  if (x is string s)
    Console.WriteLine (s.Length);
}
```

The switch statement also supports type patterns, so you can switch on *type* as well as constants (see "Switching on types" on page 81). You can specify conditions with a when clause and also switch on the null value:

```
switch (x)
{
  case int i:
    Console.WriteLine ("It's an int!");
    break;
  case string s:
    Console.WriteLine (s.Length);    // We can use the s variable
    break;
  case bool b when b == true:       // Matches only when b is true
    Console.WriteLine ("True");
    break;
  case null:
    Console.WriteLine ("Nothing");
    break;
}
```

Local methods

A *local method* is a method declared within another function (see "Local methods" on page 98):

```
void WriteCubes()
{
  Console.WriteLine (Cube (3));
  Console.WriteLine (Cube (4));
  Console.WriteLine (Cube (5));

  int Cube (int value) => value * value * value;
}
```

Local methods are visible only to the containing function and can capture local variables in the same way that lambda expressions do.

More expression-bodied members

C# 6 introduced the expression-bodied "fat-arrow" syntax for methods, read-only properties, operators, and indexers. C# 7 extends this to constructors, read/write properties, and finalizers:

```
public class Person
{
  string name;

  public Person (string name) => Name = name;
```

```
public string Name
{
  get => name;
  set => name = value ?? "";
}

~Person () => Console.WriteLine ("finalize");
}
```

Deconstructors

C# 7 introduces the *deconstructor* pattern (see "Deconstructors" on page 102). Whereas a constructor typically takes a set of values (as parameters) and assigns them to fields, a *deconstructor* does the reverse and assigns fields back to a set of variables. We could write a deconstructor for the Person class in the preceding example as follows (exception handling aside):

```
public void Deconstruct (out string firstName, out string lastName)
{
  int spacePos = name.IndexOf (' ');
  firstName = name.Substring (0, spacePos);
  lastName = name.Substring (spacePos + 1);
}
```

Deconstructors are called with the following special syntax:

```
var joe = new Person ("Joe Bloggs");
var (first, last) = joe;              // Deconstruction
Console.WriteLine (first);            // Joe
Console.WriteLine (last);             // Bloggs
```

Tuples

Perhaps the most notable improvement to C# 7 is explicit *tuple* support (see "Tuples" on page 207). Tuples provide a simple way to store a set of related values:

```
var bob = ("Bob", 23);
Console.WriteLine (bob.Item1);   // Bob
Console.WriteLine (bob.Item2);   // 23
```

C#'s new tuples are syntactic sugar for using the System.ValueTuple<...> generic structs. But thanks to compiler magic, tuple elements can be named:

```
var tuple = (name:"Bob", age:23);
Console.WriteLine (tuple.name);    // Bob
Console.WriteLine (tuple.age);     // 23
```

With tuples, functions can return multiple values without resorting to out parameters or extra type baggage:

```
static (int row, int column) GetFilePosition() => (3, 10);

static void Main()
{
  var pos = GetFilePosition();
```

```
    Console.WriteLine (pos.row);      // 3
    Console.WriteLine (pos.column);   // 10
  }
```

Tuples implicitly support the deconstruction pattern, so you can easily *deconstruct* them into individual variables:

```
static void Main()
{
  (int row, int column) = GetFilePosition();   // Creates 2 local variables
  Console.WriteLine (row);      // 3
  Console.WriteLine (column);   // 10
}
```

throw expressions

Prior to C# 7, throw was always a statement. Now it can also appear as an expression in expression-bodied functions:

```
public string Foo() => throw new NotImplementedException();
```

A throw expression can also appear in a ternary conditional expression:

```
string Capitalize (string value) =>
  value == null ? throw new ArgumentException ("value") :
  value == "" ? "" :
  char.ToUpper (value[0]) + value.Substring (1);
```

What's New in C# 6.0

C# 6.0, which shipped with Visual Studio 2015, features a new-generation compiler, completely written in C#. Known as project "Roslyn," the new compiler exposes the entire compilation pipeline via libraries, allowing you to perform code analysis on arbitrary source code. The compiler itself is open source, and the source code is available at *github.com/dotnet/roslyn*.

In addition, C# 6.0 features several minor but significant enhancements, aimed primarily at reducing code clutter.

The *null-conditional* ("Elvis") operator (see "Null Operators" on page 74) avoids having to explicitly check for null before calling a method or accessing a type member. In the following example, result evaluates to null instead of throwing a NullReferenceException:

```
System.Text.StringBuilder sb = null;
string result = sb?.ToString();      // result is null
```

Expression-bodied functions (see "Methods" on page 98) allow methods, properties, operators, and indexers that comprise a single expression to be written more tersely, in the style of a lambda expression:

```
public int TimesTwo (int x) => x * 2;
public string SomeProperty => "Property value";
```

Property initializers (Chapter 3) let you assign an initial value to an automatic property:

```
public DateTime TimeCreated { get; set; } = DateTime.Now;
```

Initialized properties can also be read-only:

```
public DateTime TimeCreated { get; } = DateTime.Now;
```

Read-only properties can also be set in the constructor, making it easier to create immutable (read-only) types.

Index initializers (Chapter 4) allow single-step initialization of any type that exposes an indexer:

```
var dict = new Dictionary<int,string>()
{
  [3] = "three",
  [10] = "ten"
};
```

String interpolation (see "String Type" on page 52) offers a succinct alternative to `string.Format`:

```
string s = $"It is {DateTime.Now.DayOfWeek} today";
```

Exception filters (see "try Statements and Exceptions" on page 181) let you apply a condition to a catch block:

```
string html;
try
{
  html = await new HttpClient().GetStringAsync ("http://asef");
}
catch (WebException ex) when (ex.Status == WebExceptionStatus.Timeout)
{
  ...
}
```

The `using static` (see "Namespaces" on page 87) directive lets you import all the static members of a type so that you can use those members unqualified:

```
using static System.Console;
...
WriteLine ("Hello, world");   // WriteLine instead of Console.WriteLine
```

The `nameof` (Chapter 3) operator returns the name of a variable, type, or other symbol as a string. This avoids breaking code when you rename a symbol in Visual Studio:

```
int capacity = 123;
string x = nameof (capacity);   // x is "capacity"
string y = nameof (Uri.Host);   // y is "Host"
```

And finally, you're now allowed to `await` inside `catch` and `finally` blocks.

What's New in C# 5.0

C# 5.0's big new feature was support for *asynchronous functions* via two new keywords, async and await. Asynchronous functions enable *asynchronous continuations*, which make it easier to write responsive and thread-safe rich-client applications. They also make it easy to write highly concurrent and efficient I/O-bound applications that don't tie up a thread resource per operation. We cover asynchronous functions in detail in Chapter 14.

What's New in C# 4.0

C# 4.0 introduced four major enhancements:

Dynamic binding (Chapters 4 and 19) defers *binding*—the process of resolving types and members—from compile time to runtime and is useful in scenarios that would otherwise require complicated reflection code. Dynamic binding is also useful when interoperating with dynamic languages and COM components.

Optional parameters (Chapter 2) allow functions to specify default parameter values so that callers can omit arguments, and *named arguments* allow a function caller to identify an argument by name rather than position.

Type variance rules were relaxed in C# 4.0 (Chapters 3 and 4), such that type parameters in generic interfaces and generic delegates can be marked as *covariant* or *contravariant*, allowing more natural type conversions.

COM interoperability (Chapter 24) was enhanced in C# 4.0 in three ways. First, arguments can be passed by reference without the ref keyword (particularly useful in conjunction with optional parameters). Second, assemblies that contain COM interop types can be *linked* rather than *referenced*. Linked interop types support type equivalence, avoiding the need for *Primary Interop Assemblies* and putting an end to versioning and deployment headaches. Third, functions that return COM Variant types from linked interop types are mapped to dynamic rather than object, eliminating the need for casting.

What's New in C# 3.0

The features added to C# 3.0 were mostly centered on *Language-Integrated Query* (LINQ) capabilities. LINQ enables queries to be written directly within a C# program and checked *statically* for correctness, and query both local collections (such as lists or XML documents) or remote data sources (such as a database). The C# 3.0 features added to support LINQ comprised implicitly typed local variables, anonymous types, object initializers, lambda expressions, extension methods, query expressions, and expression trees.

Implicitly typed local variables (var keyword, Chapter 2) let you omit the variable type in a declaration statement, allowing the compiler to infer it. This reduces clutter as well as allows *anonymous types* (Chapter 4), which are simple classes created on the fly that are commonly used in the final output of LINQ queries. You can also implicitly type arrays (Chapter 2).

Object initializers (Chapter 3) simplify object construction by allowing you to set properties inline after the constructor call. Object initializers work with both named and anonymous types.

Lambda expressions (Chapter 4) are miniature functions created by the compiler on the fly; they are particularly useful in "fluent" LINQ queries (Chapter 8).

Extension methods (Chapter 4) extend an existing type with new methods (without altering the type's definition), making static methods feel like instance methods. LINQ's query operators are implemented as extension methods.

Query expressions (Chapter 8) provide a higher-level syntax for writing LINQ queries that can be substantially simpler when working with multiple sequences or range variables.

Expression trees (Chapter 8) are miniature code Document Object Models (DOMs) that describe lambda expressions assigned to the special type `Expression<TDelegate>`. Expression trees make it possible for LINQ queries to execute remotely (e.g., on a database server) because they can be introspected and translated at runtime (e.g., into an SQL statement).

C# 3.0 also added automatic properties and partial methods.

Automatic properties (Chapter 3) cut the work in writing properties that simply `get`/`set` a private backing field by having the compiler do that work automatically. *Partial methods* (Chapter 3) let an autogenerated partial class provide customizable hooks for manual authoring that "melt away" if unused.

What's New in C# 2.0

The big new features in C# 2 were generics (Chapter 3), nullable value types (Chapter 4), iterators (Chapter 4), and anonymous methods (the predecessor to lambda expressions). These features paved the way for the introduction of LINQ in C# 3.

C# 2 also added support for partial classes and static classes, and a host of minor and miscellaneous features such as the namespace alias qualifier, friend assemblies, and fixed-size buffers.

The introduction of generics required a new CLR (CLR 2.0), because generics maintain full type fidelity at runtime.

2

C# Language Basics

In this chapter, we introduce the basics of the C# language.

Almost all of the code listings in this book are available as interactive samples in LINQPad. Working through these samples in conjunction with the book accelerates learning in that you can edit the samples and instantly see the results without needing to set up projects and solutions in Visual Studio.

To download the samples, in LINQPad, click the Samples tab, and then click "Download more samples." LINQPad is free— go to *http://www.linqpad.net*.

A First C# Program

Following is a program that multiplies 12 by 30 and prints the result, 360, to the screen. The double forward slash indicates that the remainder of a line is a *comment*:

```
int x = 12 * 30;               // Statement 1
System.Console.WriteLine (x);  // Statement 2
```

Our program consists of two *statements*. Statements in C# execute sequentially and are terminated by a semicolon. The first statement computes the *expression* 12 * 30 and stores the result in a *variable*, named x, whose type is a 32-bit integer (int). The second statement calls the WriteLine *method* on a *class* called Console, which is defined in a *namespace* called System. This prints the variable x to a text window on the screen.

A method performs a function; a class groups function members and data members to form an object-oriented building block. The Console class groups members that handle command-line input/output (I/O) functionality, such as the WriteLine method. A class is a kind of *type*, which we examine in "Type Basics" on page 30.

At the outermost level, types are organized into *namespaces*. Many commonly used types—including the Console class—reside in the System namespace. The .NET libraries are organized into nested namespaces. For example, the System.Text namespace contains types for handling text, and System.IO contain types for input/output.

Qualifying the Console class with the System namespace on every use adds clutter. The using directive lets you avoid this clutter by *importing* a namespace:

```
using System;                    // Import the System namespace

int x = 12 * 30;
Console.WriteLine (x);      // No need to specify System.
```

A basic form of code reuse is to write higher-level functions that call lower-level functions. We can *refactor* our program with a reusable *method* called FeetToInches that multiplies an integer by 12, as follows:

```
using System;

Console.WriteLine (FeetToInches (30));      // 360
Console.WriteLine (FeetToInches (100));     // 1200

int FeetToInches (int feet)
{
  int inches = feet * 12;
  return inches;
}
```

Our method contains a series of statements surrounded by a pair of braces. This is called a *statement block*.

A method can receive *input* data from the caller by specifying *parameters* and *output* data back to the caller by specifying a *return type*. Our FeetToInches method has a parameter for inputting feet, and a return type for outputting inches:

```
int FeetToInches (int feet)
...
```

The *literals* 30 and 100 are the *arguments* passed to the FeetToInches method.

If a method doesn't receive input, use empty parentheses. If it doesn't return anything, use the void keyword:

```
using System;
SayHello();

void SayHello()
{
  Console.WriteLine ("Hello, world");
}
```

Methods are one of several kinds of functions in C#. Another kind of function we used in our example program was the * *operator*, which performs multiplication. There are also *constructors, properties, events, indexers*, and *finalizers*.

Compilation

The C# compiler compiles source code (a set of files with the *.cs* extension) into an *assembly*. An assembly is the unit of packaging and deployment in .NET. An assembly can be either an *application* or a *library*. A normal console or Windows application has an *entry point*, whereas a library does not. The purpose of a library is to be called upon (*referenced*) by an application or by other libraries. .NET itself is a set of libraries (as well as a runtime environment).

Each of the programs in the preceding section began directly with a series of statements (called *top-level statements*). The presence of top-level statements implicitly creates an entry point for a console or Windows application. (Without top-level statements, a *Main method* denotes an application's entry point—see "Custom Types" on page 31.)

> Unlike .NET Framework, .NET 6 assemblies never have an *.exe* extension. The *.exe* that you see after building a .NET 6 application is a platform-specific native loader responsible for starting your application's *.dll* assembly.
>
> .NET 6 also allows you to create a self-contained deployment that includes the loader, your assemblies, and the .NET runtime—all in a single *.exe* file.

The dotnet tool (*dotnet.exe* on Windows) helps you to manage .NET source code and binaries from the command line. You can use it to both build and run your program, as an alternative to using an integrated development environment (IDE) such as Visual Studio or Visual Studio Code.

You can obtain the dotnet tool either by installing the .NET 6 SDK or by installing Visual Studio. Its default location is *%ProgramFiles%\dotnet* on Windows or */usr/bin/dotnet* on Ubuntu Linux.

To compile an application, the dotnet tool requires a *project file* as well as one or more C# files. The following command *scaffolds* a new console project (creates its basic structure):

```
dotnet new Console -n MyFirstProgram
```

This creates a subfolder called *MyFirstProgram* containing a project file called *MyFirstProgram.csproj* and a C# file called *Program.cs* that prints "Hello world".

To build and run your program, run the following command from the *MyFirstProgram* folder:

```
dotnet run MyFirstProgram
```

Or, if you just want to build without running:

```
dotnet build MyFirstProgram.csproj
```

The output assembly will be written to a subdirectory under *bin\debug*.

We explain assemblies in detail in Chapter 17.

Syntax

C# syntax is inspired by C and C++ syntax. In this section, we describe C#'s elements of syntax, using the following program:

```
using System;

int x = 12 * 30;
Console.WriteLine (x);
```

Identifiers and Keywords

Identifiers are names that programmers choose for their classes, methods, variables, and so on. Here are the identifiers in our example program, in the order in which they appear:

```
System    x    Console    WriteLine
```

An identifier must be a whole word, essentially made up of Unicode characters starting with a letter or underscore. C# identifiers are case sensitive. By convention, parameters, local variables, and private fields should be in *camel case* (e.g., myVariable), and all other identifiers should be in *Pascal case* (e.g., MyMethod).

Keywords are names that mean something special to the compiler. There are two keywords in our example program, using and int.

Most keywords are *reserved*, which means that you can't use them as identifiers. Here is the full list of C# reserved keywords:

abstract	do	in	protected	throw
as	double	int	public	true
base	else	interface	readonly	try
bool	enum	internal	record	typeof
break	event	is	ref	uint
byte	explicit	lock	return	ulong
case	extern	long	sbyte	unchecked
catch	false	namespace	sealed	unsafe
char	finally	new	short	ushort
checked	fixed	null	sizeof	using
class	float	object	stackalloc	virtual
const	for	operator	static	void
continue	foreach	out	string	volatile
decimal	goto	override	struct	while
default	if	params	switch	
delegate	implicit	private	this	

If you really want to use an identifier that clashes with a reserved keyword, you can do so by qualifying it with the @ prefix; for instance:

```
int using = 123;     // Illegal
int @using = 123;    // Legal
```

The @ symbol doesn't form part of the identifier itself. So, @myVariable is the same as myVariable.

Contextual keywords

Some keywords are *contextual*, meaning that you also can use them as identifiers—without an @ symbol:

add	dynamic	join	on	value
alias	equals	let	or	var
and	from	managed	orderby	with
ascending	get	nameof	partial	when
async	global	nint	remove	where
await	group	not	select	yield
by	init	notnull	set	
descending	into	nuint	unmanaged	

With contextual keywords, ambiguity cannot arise within the context in which they are used.

Literals, Punctuators, and Operators

Literals are primitive pieces of data lexically embedded into the program. The literals we used in our example program are 12 and 30.

Punctuators help demarcate the structure of the program. An example is the semicolon, which terminates a statement. Statements can wrap multiple lines:

```
Console.WriteLine
    (1 + 2 + 3 + 4 + 5 + 6 + 7 + 8 + 9 + 10);
```

An *operator* transforms and combines expressions. Most operators in C# are denoted with a symbol, such as the multiplication operator, *. We discuss operators in more detail later in this chapter. These are the operators we used in our example program:

```
=  *  .  ()
```

A period denotes a member of something (or a decimal point with numeric literals). Parentheses are used when declaring or calling a method; empty parentheses are used when the method accepts no arguments. (Parentheses also have other purposes that you'll see later in this chapter.) An equals sign performs *assignment*. (The double equals sign, ==, performs equality comparison, as you'll see later.)

Comments

C# offers two different styles of source-code documentation: *single-line comments* and *multiline comments*. A single-line comment begins with a double forward slash and continues until the end of the line; for example:

```
int x = 3;    // Comment about assigning 3 to x
```

A multiline comment begins with /* and ends with */; for example:

```
int x = 3;    /* This is a comment that
                 spans two lines */
```

Comments can embed XML documentation tags, which we explain in "XML Documentation" on page 252.

Type Basics

A *type* defines the blueprint for a value. In this example, we use two literals of type int with values 12 and 30. We also declare a *variable* of type int whose name is x:

```
int x = 12 * 30;
Console.WriteLine (x);
```

 Because most of the code listings in this book require types from the System namespace, we will omit "using System" from now on, unless we're illustrating a concept relating to namespaces.

A *variable* denotes a storage location that can contain different values over time. In contrast, a *constant* always represents the same value (more on this later):

```
const int y = 360;
```

All values in C# are *instances* of a type. The meaning of a value and the set of possible values a variable can have are determined by its type.

Predefined Type Examples

Predefined types are types that are specially supported by the compiler. The int type is a predefined type for representing the set of integers that fit into 32 bits of memory, from -2^{31} to $2^{31} - 1$, and is the default type for numeric literals within this range. You can perform functions such as arithmetic with instances of the int type, as follows:

```
int x = 12 * 30;
```

Another predefined C# type is string. The string type represents a sequence of characters, such as ".NET" or "http://oreilly.com". You can work with strings by calling functions on them, as follows:

```
string message = "Hello world";
string upperMessage = message.ToUpper();
Console.WriteLine (upperMessage);          // HELLO WORLD
```

```
int x = 2022;
message = message + x.ToString();
Console.WriteLine (message);                    // Hello world2022
```

In this example, we called x.ToString() to obtain a string representation of the integer x. You can call ToString() on a variable of almost any type.

The predefined bool type has exactly two possible values: true and false. The bool type is commonly used with an if statement to conditionally branch execution flow:

```
bool simpleVar = false;
if (simpleVar)
  Console.WriteLine ("This will not print");

int x = 5000;
bool lessThanAMile = x < 5280;
if (lessThanAMile)
  Console.WriteLine ("This will print");
```

In C#, predefined types (also referred to as built-in types) are recognized with a C# keyword. The System namespace in .NET contains many important types that are not predefined by C# (e.g., DateTime).

Custom Types

Just as we can write our own methods, we can write our own types. In this next example, we define a custom type named UnitConverter—a class that serves as a blueprint for unit conversions:

```
UnitConverter feetToInchesConverter = new UnitConverter (12);
UnitConverter milesToFeetConverter  = new UnitConverter (5280);

Console.WriteLine (feetToInchesConverter.Convert(30));     // 360
Console.WriteLine (feetToInchesConverter.Convert(100));    // 1200

Console.WriteLine (feetToInchesConverter.Convert(
               milesToFeetConverter.Convert(1)));          // 63360

public class UnitConverter
{
  int ratio;                                // Field

  public UnitConverter (int unitRatio)      // Constructor
  {
     ratio = unitRatio;
  }

  public int Convert (int unit)             // Method
  {
     return unit * ratio;
```

```
    }
}
```

 In this example, our class definition appears in the same file as our top-level statements. This is legal—as long as the top-level statements appear first—and is acceptable when writing small test programs. With larger programs, the standard approach is to put the class definition in a separate file such as *UnitConverter.cs*.

Members of a type

A type contains *data members* and *function members*. The data member of UnitConverter is the *field* called ratio. The function members of UnitConverter are the Convert method and the UnitConverter's *constructor*.

Symmetry of predefined types and custom types

A beautiful aspect of C# is that predefined types and custom types have few differences. The predefined int type serves as a blueprint for integers. It holds data—32 bits—and provides function members that use that data, such as ToString. Similarly, our custom UnitConverter type acts as a blueprint for unit conversions. It holds data—the ratio—and provides function members to use that data.

Constructors and instantiation

Data is created by *instantiating* a type. Predefined types can be instantiated simply by using a literal such as 12 or "Hello world". The new operator creates instances of a custom type. We created and declared an instance of the UnitConverter type with this statement:

```
UnitConverter feetToInchesConverter = new UnitConverter (12);
```

Immediately after the new operator instantiates an object, the object's *constructor* is called to perform initialization. A constructor is defined like a method, except that the method name and return type are reduced to the name of the enclosing type:

```
public UnitConverter (int unitRatio) { ratio = unitRatio; }
```

Instance versus static members

The data members and function members that operate on the *instance* of the type are called *instance members*. The UnitConverter's Convert method and the int's ToString method are examples of instance members. By default, members are instance members.

Data members and function members that don't operate on the instance of the type can be marked as static. To refer to a static member from outside its type, you specify its *type* name rather than an *instance*. An example is the WriteLine method of the Console class. Because this is static, we call Console.WriteLine() and not new Console().WriteLine().

(The Console class is actually declared as a *static class*, which means that *all* of its members are static, and you can never create instances of a Console.)

In the following code, the instance field Name pertains to an instance of a particular Panda, whereas Population pertains to the set of all Panda instances. We create two instances of the Panda, print their names, and then print the total population:

```
Panda p1 = new Panda ("Pan Dee");
Panda p2 = new Panda ("Pan Dah");

Console.WriteLine (p1.Name);      // Pan Dee
Console.WriteLine (p2.Name);      // Pan Dah

Console.WriteLine (Panda.Population);   // 2

public class Panda
{
  public string Name;             // Instance field
  public static int Population;   // Static field

  public Panda (string n)         // Constructor
  {
    Name = n;                     // Assign the instance field
    Population = Population + 1;   // Increment the static Population field
  }
}
```

Attempting to evaluate p1.Population or Panda.Name will generate a compile-time error.

The public keyword

The public keyword exposes members to other classes. In this example, if the Name field in Panda was not marked as public, it would be private and could not be accessed from outside the class. Marking a member public is how a type communicates: "Here is what I want other types to see—everything else is my own private implementation details." In object-oriented terms, we say that the public members *encapsulate* the private members of the class.

Defining namespaces

Particularly with larger programs, it makes sense to organize types into namespaces. Here's how to define the Panda class inside a namespace called Animals:

```
using System;
using Animals;

Panda p = new Panda ("Pan Dee");
Console.WriteLine (p.Name);

namespace Animals
{
  public class Panda
```

```
    {
      ...
    }
}
```

In this example, we also *imported* the `Animals` namespace so that our top-level statements could access its types without qualification. Without that import, we'd need to do this:

```
Animals.Panda p = new Animals.Panda ("Pan Dee");
```

We cover namespaces in detail at the end of this chapter (see "Namespaces" on page 87).

Defining a Main method

All of our examples, so far, have used top-level statements (a feature introduced in C# 9).

Without top-level statements, a simple console or Windows application looks like this:

```
using System;

class Program
{
  static void Main()    // Program entry point
  {
    int x = 12 * 30;
    Console.WriteLine (x);
  }
}
```

In the absence of top-level statements, C# looks for a static method called `Main`, which becomes the entry point. The `Main` method can be defined inside any class (and only one `Main` method can exist). Should your `Main` method need to access private members of a particular class, defining a `Main` method inside that class can be simpler than using top-level statements.

The `Main` method can optionally return an integer (rather than `void`) in order to return a value to the execution environment (where a nonzero value typically indicates an error). The `Main` method can also optionally accept an array of strings as a parameter (that will be populated with any arguments passed to the executable). For example:

```
static int Main (string[] args) {...}
```

 An array (such as `string[]`) represents a fixed number of elements of a particular type. Arrays are specified by placing square brackets after the element type. We describe them in "Arrays" on page 54.

(The `Main` method can also be declared `async` and return a `Task` or `Task<int>` in support of asynchronous programming, which we cover in Chapter 14.)

Top-Level Statements

Top-level statements (introduced in C# 9) let you avoid the baggage of a static `Main` method and a containing class. A file with top-level statements comprises three parts, in this order:

1. (Optionally) `using` directives

2. A series of statements, optionally mixed with method declarations

3. (Optionally) Type and namespace declarations

For example:

```
using System;                            // Part 1

Console.WriteLine ("Hello, world");      // Part 2
void SomeMethod1() { ... }               // Part 2
Console.WriteLine ("Hello again!");      // Part 2
void SomeMethod2() { ... }               // Part 2

class SomeClass { ... }                  // Part 3
namespace SomeNamespace { ... }          // Part 3
```

Because the CLR doesn't explicitly support top-level statements, the compiler translates your code into something like this:

```
using System;                            // Part 1

static class Program$  // Special compiler-generated name
{
    static void Main$ (string[] args)  // Compiler-generated name
    {
        Console.WriteLine ("Hello, world");      // Part 2
        void SomeMethod1() { ... }               // Part 2
        Console.WriteLine ("Hello again!");      // Part 2
        void SomeMethod2() { ... }               // Part 2
    }
}

class SomeClass { ... }                  // Part 3
namespace SomeNamespace { ... }          // Part 3
```

Notice that everything in Part 2 is wrapped inside the main method. This means that `SomeMethod1` and `SomeMethod2` act as *local methods*. We discuss the full implications in "Local methods" on page 98, the most important being that local methods (unless declared as `static`) can access variables declared within the containing method:

```
int x = 3;
LocalMethod();

void LocalMethod() { Console.WriteLine (x); }   // We can access x
```

Another consequence is that top-level methods cannot be accessed from other classes or types.

Top-level statements can optionally return an integer value to the caller and access a "magic" variable of type string[] called args, corresponding to command-line arguments passed by the caller.

As a program can have only one entry point, there can be at most one file with top-level statements in a C# project.

Types and Conversions

C# can convert between instances of compatible types. A conversion always creates a new value from an existing one. Conversions can be either *implicit* or *explicit*: implicit conversions happen automatically, and explicit conversions require a *cast*. In the following example, we *implicitly* convert an int to a long type (which has twice the bit capacity of an int) and *explicitly* cast an int to a short type (which has half the bit capacity of an int):

```
int x = 12345;        // int is a 32-bit integer
long y = x;           // Implicit conversion to 64-bit integer
short z = (short)x;   // Explicit conversion to 16-bit integer
```

Implicit conversions are allowed when both of the following are true:

- The compiler can guarantee that they will always succeed.
- No information is lost in conversion.[1]

Conversely, *explicit* conversions are required when one of the following is true:

- The compiler cannot guarantee that they will always succeed.
- Information might be lost during conversion.

(If the compiler can determine that a conversion will *always* fail, both kinds of conversion are prohibited. Conversions that involve generics can also fail in certain conditions—see "Type Parameters and Conversions" on page 152.)

 The *numeric conversions* that we just saw are built into the language. C# also supports *reference conversions* and *boxing conversions* (see Chapter 3) as well as *custom conversions* (see "Operator Overloading" on page 239). The compiler doesn't enforce the aforementioned rules with custom conversions, so it's possible for badly designed types to behave otherwise.

---

1 A minor caveat is that very large long values lose some precision when converted to double.

Value Types Versus Reference Types

All C# types fall into the following categories:

- Value types
- Reference types
- Generic type parameters
- Pointer types

 In this section, we describe value types and reference types. We cover generic type parameters in "Generics" on page 145 and pointer types in "Unsafe Code and Pointers" on page 243.

Value types comprise most built-in types (specifically, all numeric types, the char type, and the bool type) as well as custom struct and enum types.

Reference types comprise all class, array, delegate, and interface types. (This includes the predefined string type.)

The fundamental difference between value types and reference types is how they are handled in memory.

Value types

The content of a *value type* variable or constant is simply a value. For example, the content of the built-in value type, int, is 32 bits of data.

You can define a custom value type with the struct keyword (see Figure 2-1):

```
public struct Point { public int X; public int Y; }
```

Or more tersely:

```
public struct Point { public int X, Y; }
```

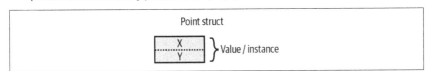

Figure 2-1. A value-type instance in memory

The assignment of a value-type instance always *copies* the instance; for example:

```
Point p1 = new Point();
p1.X = 7;

Point p2 = p1;            // Assignment causes copy

Console.WriteLine (p1.X); // 7
Console.WriteLine (p2.X); // 7
```

```
p1.X = 9;                    // Change p1.X

Console.WriteLine (p1.X);  // 9
Console.WriteLine (p2.X);  // 7
```

Figure 2-2 shows that p1 and p2 have independent storage.

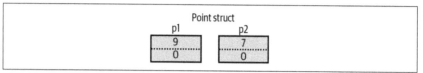

Figure 2-2. Assignment copies a value-type instance

Reference types

A reference type is more complex than a value type, having two parts: an *object* and the *reference* to that object. The content of a reference-type variable or constant is a reference to an object that contains the value. Here is the Point type from our previous example rewritten as a class rather than a struct (shown in Figure 2-3):

```
public class Point { public int X, Y; }
```

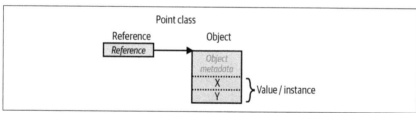

Figure 2-3. A reference-type instance in memory

Assigning a reference-type variable copies the reference, not the object instance. This allows multiple variables to refer to the same object—something not ordinarily possible with value types. If we repeat the previous example, but with Point now a class, an operation to p1 affects p2:

```
Point p1 = new Point();
p1.X = 7;

Point p2 = p1;               // Copies p1 reference

Console.WriteLine (p1.X);  // 7
Console.WriteLine (p2.X);  // 7

p1.X = 9;                    // Change p1.X

Console.WriteLine (p1.X);  // 9
Console.WriteLine (p2.X);  // 9
```

Figure 2-4 shows that p1 and p2 are two references that point to the same object.

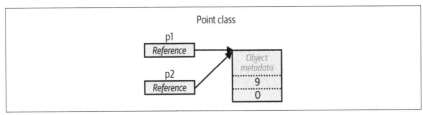

Figure 2-4. Assignment copies a reference

Null

A reference can be assigned the literal null, indicating that the reference points to no object:

```
Point p = null;
Console.WriteLine (p == null);    // True

// The following line generates a runtime error
// (a NullReferenceException is thrown):
Console.WriteLine (p.X);
```

class Point {...}

 In "Nullable Reference Types" on page 200, we describe a feature of C# that helps to reduce accidental NullReference Exception errors.

In contrast, a value type cannot ordinarily have a null value:

```
Point p = null;   // Compile-time error
int x = null;     // Compile-time error
```

struct Point {...}

 C# also has a construct called *nullable value types* for representing value-type nulls. For more information, see "Nullable Value Types" on page 194.

Storage overhead

Value-type instances occupy precisely the memory required to store their fields. In this example, Point takes 8 bytes of memory:

```
struct Point
{
  int x;  // 4 bytes
  int y;  // 4 bytes
}
```

Technically, the CLR positions fields within the type at an address that's a multiple of the fields' size (up to a maximum of 8 bytes). Thus, the following actually consumes 16 bytes of memory (with the 7 bytes following the first field "wasted"):

```
struct A { byte b; long l; }
```

You can override this behavior by applying the StructLayout attribute (see "Mapping a Struct to Unmanaged Memory" on page 973).

Reference types require separate allocations of memory for the reference and object. The object consumes as many bytes as its fields, plus additional administrative overhead. The precise overhead is intrinsically private to the implementation of the .NET runtime, but at minimum, the overhead is 8 bytes, used to store a key to the object's type as well as temporary information such as its lock state for multithreading and a flag to indicate whether it has been fixed from movement by the garbage collector. Each reference to an object requires an extra 4 or 8 bytes, depending on whether the .NET runtime is running on a 32- or 64-bit platform.

Predefined Type Taxonomy

The predefined types in C# are as follows:

Value types

- Numeric

    — Signed integer (sbyte, short, int, long)

    — Unsigned integer (byte, ushort, uint, ulong)

    — Real number (float, double, decimal)

- Logical (bool)
- Character (char)

Reference types

- String (string)
- Object (object)

Predefined types in C# alias .NET types in the System namespace. There is only a syntactic difference between these two statements:

```
int i = 5;
System.Int32 i = 5;
```

The set of predefined *value* types excluding decimal are known as *primitive types* in the CLR. Primitive types are so called because they are supported directly via instructions in compiled code, and this usually translates to direct support on the underlying processor; for example:

```
                        // Underlying hexadecimal representation
int i = 7;              // 0x7
bool b = true;          // 0x1
char c = 'A';           // 0x41
float f = 0.5f;         // uses IEEE floating-point encoding
```

The System.IntPtr and System.UIntPtr types are also primitive (see Chapter 24).

Numeric Types

C# has the predefined numeric types shown in Table 2-1.

Table 2-1. Predefined numeric types in C#

C# type	System type	Suffix	Size	Range
Integral—signed				
sbyte	SByte		8 bits	-2^7 to 2^7-1
short	Int16		16 bits	-2^{15} to $2^{15}-1$
int	Int32		32 bits	-2^{31} to $2^{31}-1$
long	Int64	L	64 bits	-2^{63} to $2^{63}-1$
nint	IntPtr		32/64 bits	
Integral—unsigned				
byte	Byte		8 bits	0 to 2^8-1
ushort	UInt16		16 bits	0 to $2^{16}-1$
uint	UInt32	U	32 bits	0 to $2^{32}-1$
ulong	UInt64	UL	64 bits	0 to $2^{64}-1$
unint	UIntPtr		32/64 bits	
Real				
float	Single	F	32 bits	$\pm\,(\sim10^{-45}$ to $10^{38})$
double	Double	D	64 bits	$\pm\,(\sim10^{-324}$ to $10^{308})$
decimal	Decimal	M	128 bits	$\pm\,(\sim10^{-28}$ to $10^{28})$

Of the *integral* types, int and long are first-class citizens and are favored by both C# and the runtime. The other integral types are typically used for interoperability or when space efficiency is paramount. The nint and nuint native-sized integer types (introduced in C# 9) are most useful in helping with pointer arithmetic, so we will describe these in a later chapter (see "Native-Sized Integers" on page 246).

Of the *real* number types, float and double are called *floating-point types*[2] and are typically used for scientific and graphical calculations. The decimal type is typically used for financial calculations, for which base-10-accurate arithmetic and high precision are required.

 From .NET 5, there is a 16-bit floating point type called Half. This is intended mainly for interoperating with graphics card processors and does not have native support in most CPUs. Half is not a primitive CLR type and does not have special language support in C#.

Numeric Literals

Integral-type literals can use decimal or hexadecimal notation; hexadecimal is denoted with the 0x prefix. For example:

```
int x = 127;
long y = 0x7F;
```

You can insert an underscore anywhere within a numeric literal to make it more readable:

```
int million = 1_000_000;
```

You can specify numbers in binary with the 0b prefix:

```
var b = 0b1010_1011_1100_1101_1110_1111;
```

Real literals can use decimal and/or exponential notation:

```
double d = 1.5;
double million = 1E06;
```

Numeric literal type inference

By default, the compiler *infers* a numeric literal to be either double or an integral type:

- If the literal contains a decimal point or the exponential symbol (E), it is a double.

- Otherwise, the literal's type is the first type in this list that can fit the literal's value: int, uint, long, and ulong.

For example:

```
Console.WriteLine (    1.0.GetType());  // Double  (double)
Console.WriteLine (   1E06.GetType());  // Double  (double)
Console.WriteLine (      1.GetType());  // Int32   (int)
```

---

2 Technically, decimal is a floating-point type, too, although it's not referred to as such in the C# language specification.

```
Console.WriteLine ( 0xF0000000.GetType()); // UInt32  (uint)
Console.WriteLine (0x100000000.GetType()); // Int64   (long)
```

Numeric suffixes

Numeric suffixes explicitly define the type of a literal. Suffixes can be either lower-case or uppercase, and are as follows:

Category	C# type	Example
F	float	float f = 1.0F;
D	double	double d = 1D;
M	decimal	decimal d = 1.0M;
U	uint	uint i = 1U;
L	long	long i = 1L;
UL	ulong	ulong i = 1UL;

The suffixes U and L are rarely necessary because the uint, long, and ulong types can nearly always be either *inferred* or *implicitly converted* from int:

```
long i = 5;     // Implicit lossless conversion from int literal to long
```

The D suffix is technically redundant in that all literals with a decimal point are inferred to be double. And you can always add a decimal point to a numeric literal:

```
double x = 4.0;
```

The F and M suffixes are the most useful and should always be applied when specifying float or decimal literals. Without the F suffix, the following line would not compile, because 4.5 would be inferred to be of type double, which has no implicit conversion to float:

```
float f = 4.5F;
```

The same principle is true for a decimal literal:

```
decimal d = -1.23M;     // Will not compile without the M suffix.
```

We describe the semantics of numeric conversions in detail in the following section.

Numeric Conversions

Converting between integral types

Integral type conversions are *implicit* when the destination type can represent every possible value of the source type. Otherwise, an *explicit* conversion is required; for example:

```
int x = 12345;        // int is a 32-bit integer
long y = x;           // Implicit conversion to 64-bit integral type
short z = (short)x;   // Explicit conversion to 16-bit integral type
```

Converting between floating-point types

A `float` can be implicitly converted to a `double` given that a `double` can represent every possible value of a `float`. The reverse conversion must be explicit.

Converting between floating-point and integral types

All integral types can be implicitly converted to all floating-point types:

```
int i = 1;
float f = i;
```

The reverse conversion must be explicit:

```
int i2 = (int)f;
```

 When you cast from a floating-point number to an integral type, any fractional portion is truncated; no rounding is performed. The static class `System.Convert` provides methods that round while converting between various numeric types (see Chapter 6).

Implicitly converting a large integral type to a floating-point type preserves *magnitude* but can occasionally lose *precision*. This is because floating-point types always have more magnitude than integral types but can have less precision. Rewriting our example with a larger number demonstrates this:

```
int i1 = 100000001;
float f = i1;          // Magnitude preserved, precision lost
int i2 = (int)f;       // 100000000
```

Decimal conversions

All integral types can be implicitly converted to the decimal type given that a decimal can represent every possible C# integral-type value. All other numeric conversions to and from a decimal type must be explicit because they introduce the possibility of either a value being out of range or precision being lost.

Arithmetic Operators

The arithmetic operators (+, -, *, /, %) are defined for all numeric types except the 8- and 16-bit integral types:

```
+    Addition
-    Subtraction
*    Multiplication
/    Division
%    Remainder after division
```

Increment and Decrement Operators

The increment and decrement operators (++, --, respectively) increment and decrement numeric types by 1. The operator can either follow or precede the variable, depending on whether you want its value *before* or *after* the increment/decrement; for example:

```
int x = 0, y = 0;
Console.WriteLine (x++);   // Outputs 0; x is now 1
Console.WriteLine (++y);   // Outputs 1; y is now 1
```

Specialized Operations on Integral Types

The *integral types* are int, uint, long, ulong, short, ushort, byte, and sbyte.

Division

Division operations on integral types always eliminate the remainder (round toward zero). Dividing by a variable whose value is zero generates a runtime error (a DivideByZeroException):

```
int a = 2 / 3;      // 0

int b = 0;
int c = 5 / b;      // throws DivideByZeroException
```

Dividing by the *literal* or *constant* 0 generates a compile-time error.

Overflow

At runtime, arithmetic operations on integral types can overflow. By default, this happens silently—no exception is thrown, and the result exhibits "wraparound" behavior, as though the computation were done on a larger integer type and the extra significant bits discarded. For example, decrementing the minimum possible int value results in the maximum possible int value:

```
int a = int.MinValue;
a--;
Console.WriteLine (a == int.MaxValue); // True
```

Overflow check operators

The checked operator instructs the runtime to generate an OverflowException rather than overflowing silently when an integral-type expression or statement exceeds the arithmetic limits of that type. The checked operator affects expressions with the ++, --, +, - (binary and unary), *, /, and explicit conversion operators between integral types. Overflow checking incurs a small performance cost.

> The checked operator has no effect on the double and float types (which overflow to special "infinite" values, as you'll see soon) and no effect on the decimal type (which is always checked).

You can use checked around either an expression or a statement block:

```
int a = 1000000;
int b = 1000000;

int c = checked (a * b);    // Checks just the expression.

checked                     // Checks all expressions
{                           // in statement block.
    ...
    c = a * b;
    ...
}
```

You can make arithmetic overflow checking the default for all expressions in a program by selecting the "checked" option at the project level (in Visual Studio, go to Advanced Build Settings). If you then need to disable overflow checking just for specific expressions or statements, you can do so with the unchecked operator. For example, the following code will not throw exceptions—even if the project's "checked" option is selected:

```
int x = int.MaxValue;
int y = unchecked (x + 1);
unchecked { int z = x + 1; }
```

Overflow checking for constant expressions

Regardless of the "checked" project setting, expressions evaluated at compile time are always overflow-checked—unless you apply the unchecked operator:

```
int x = int.MaxValue + 1;                // Compile-time error
int y = unchecked (int.MaxValue + 1);    // No errors
```

Bitwise operators

C# supports the following bitwise operators:

Operator	Meaning	Sample expression	Result
~	Complement	~0xfU	0xfffffff0U
&	And	0xf0 & 0x33	0x30
|	Or	0xf0 | 0x33	0xf3
^	Exclusive Or	0xff00 ^ 0x0ff0	0xf0f0
<<	Shift left	0x20 << 2	0x80
>>	Shift right	0x20 >> 1	0x10

From .NET 6, additional bitwise operations are exposed via a new class called BitOperations in the System.Numerics namespace (see "BitOperations" on page 320).

8- and 16-Bit Integral Types

The 8- and 16-bit integral types are byte, sbyte, short, and ushort. These types lack their own arithmetic operators, so C# implicitly converts them to larger types as required. This can cause a compile-time error when trying to assign the result back to a small integral type:

```
short x = 1, y = 1;
short z = x + y;        // Compile-time error
```

In this case, x and y are implicitly converted to int so that the addition can be performed. This means that the result is also an int, which cannot be implicitly cast back to a short (because it could cause loss of data). To make this compile, you must add an explicit cast:

```
short z = (short) (x + y);   // OK
```

Special Float and Double Values

Unlike integral types, floating-point types have values that certain operations treat specially. These special values are NaN (Not a Number), +∞, −∞, and −0. The float and double classes have constants for NaN, +∞, and −∞, as well as other values (MaxValue, MinValue, and Epsilon); for example:

```
Console.WriteLine (double.NegativeInfinity);   // -Infinity
```

The constants that represent special values for double and float are as follows:

Special value	Double constant	Float constant
NaN	double.NaN	float.NaN
+∞	double.PositiveInfinity	float.PositiveInfinity
−∞	double.NegativeInfinity	float.NegativeInfinity
−0	−0.0	−0.0f

Dividing a nonzero number by zero results in an infinite value:

```
Console.WriteLine ( 1.0 /  0.0);        //  Infinity
Console.WriteLine (-1.0 /  0.0);        // -Infinity
Console.WriteLine ( 1.0 / -0.0);        // -Infinity
Console.WriteLine (-1.0 / -0.0);        //  Infinity
```

Dividing zero by zero, or subtracting infinity from infinity, results in a NaN:

```
Console.WriteLine ( 0.0 /  0.0);        //  NaN
Console.WriteLine ((1.0 /  0.0) - (1.0 / 0.0));   //  NaN
```

When using ==, a NaN value is never equal to another value, even another NaN value:

```
Console.WriteLine (0.0 / 0.0 == double.NaN);     // False
```

To test whether a value is NaN, you must use the `float.IsNaN` or `double.IsNaN` method:

```
Console.WriteLine (double.IsNaN (0.0 / 0.0));   // True
```

When using `object.Equals`, however, two NaN values are equal:

```
Console.WriteLine (object.Equals (0.0 / 0.0, double.NaN));   // True
```

 NaNs are sometimes useful in representing special values. In Windows Presentation Foundation (WPF), `double.NaN` represents a measurement whose value is "Automatic." Another way to represent such a value is with a nullable type (Chapter 4); another is with a custom struct that wraps a numeric type and adds an additional field (Chapter 3).

`float` and `double` follow the specification of the IEEE 754 format types, supported natively by almost all processors. You can find detailed information on the behavior of these types at *http://www.ieee.org*.

double Versus decimal

`double` is useful for scientific computations (such as computing spatial coordinates). `decimal` is useful for financial computations and values that are "human-made" rather than the result of real-world measurements. Here's a summary of the differences:

Category	double	decimal
Internal representation	Base 2	Base 10
Decimal precision	15–16 significant figures	28–29 significant figures
Range	$\pm(\sim 10^{-324}$ to $\sim 10^{308})$	$\pm(\sim 10^{-28}$ to $\sim 10^{28})$
Special values	+0, −0, +∞, −∞, and NaN	None
Speed	Native to processor	Non-native to processor (about 10 times slower than double)

Real Number Rounding Errors

`float` and `double` internally represent numbers in base 2. For this reason, only numbers expressible in base 2 are represented precisely. Practically, this means most literals with a fractional component (which are in base 10) will not be represented precisely; for example:

```
float x = 0.1f;  // Not quite 0.1
Console.WriteLine (x + x + x + x + x + x + x + x + x + x);   // 1.0000001
```

This is why `float` and `double` are bad for financial calculations. In contrast, `decimal` works in base 10 and so can precisely represent numbers expressible in base 10 (as well as its factors, base 2 and base 5). Because real literals are in base 10, `decimal` can precisely represent numbers such as 0.1. However, neither double nor decimal can precisely represent a fractional number whose base 10 representation is recurring:

```
decimal m = 1M / 6M;        // 0.1666666666666666666666667M
double  d = 1.0 / 6.0;      // 0.16666666666666666
```

This leads to accumulated rounding errors:

```
decimal notQuiteWholeM = m+m+m+m+m+m;  // 1.0000000000000000000000000002M
double  notQuiteWholeD = d+d+d+d+d+d;  // 0.99999999999999989
```

which break equality and comparison operations:

```
Console.WriteLine (notQuiteWholeM == 1M);   // False
Console.WriteLine (notQuiteWholeD < 1.0);   // True
```

Boolean Type and Operators

C#'s bool type (aliasing the System.Boolean type) is a logical value that can be assigned the literal true or false.

Although a Boolean value requires only one bit of storage, the runtime will use one byte of memory because this is the minimum chunk that the runtime and processor can efficiently work with. To avoid space inefficiency in the case of arrays, .NET provides a BitArray class in the System.Collections namespace that is designed to use just one bit per Boolean value.

bool Conversions

No casting conversions can be made from the bool type to numeric types, or vice versa.

Equality and Comparison Operators

== and != test for equality and inequality of any type but always return a bool value.[3] Value types typically have a very simple notion of equality:

```
int x = 1;
int y = 2;
int z = 1;
Console.WriteLine (x == y);      // False
Console.WriteLine (x == z);      // True
```

For reference types, equality, by default, is based on *reference*, as opposed to the actual *value* of the underlying object (more on this in Chapter 6):

```
Dude d1 = new Dude ("John");
Dude d2 = new Dude ("John");
Console.WriteLine (d1 == d2);    // False
Dude d3 = d1;
```

---

3 It's possible to *overload* these operators (Chapter 4) such that they return a non-bool type, but this is almost never done in practice.

```
Console.WriteLine (d1 == d3);        // True

public class Dude
{
  public string Name;
  public Dude (string n) { Name = n; }
}
```

The equality and comparison operators, ==, !=, <, >, >=, and <=, work for all numeric types, but you should use them with caution with real numbers (as we saw in "Real Number Rounding Errors" on page 48). The comparison operators also work on enum type members by comparing their underlying integral-type values. We describe this in "Enums" on page 140.

We explain the equality and comparison operators in greater detail in "Operator Overloading" on page 239, "Equality Comparison" on page 324, and "Order Comparison" on page 335.

Conditional Operators

The && and || operators test for *and* and *or* conditions. They are frequently used in conjunction with the ! operator, which expresses *not*. In the following example, the UseUmbrella method returns true if it's rainy or sunny (to protect us from the rain or the sun), as long as it's not also windy (umbrellas are useless in the wind):

```
static bool UseUmbrella (bool rainy, bool sunny, bool windy)
{
  return !windy && (rainy || sunny);
}
```

The && and || operators *short-circuit* evaluation when possible. In the preceding example, if it is windy, the expression (rainy || sunny) is not even evaluated. Short-circuiting is essential in allowing expressions such as the following to run without throwing a NullReferenceException:

```
if (sb != null && sb.Length > 0) ...
```

The & and | operators also test for *and* and *or* conditions:

```
return !windy & (rainy | sunny);
```

The difference is that they *do not short-circuit*. For this reason, they are rarely used in place of conditional operators.

 Unlike in C and C++, the & and | operators perform (non-short-circuiting) Boolean comparisons when applied to bool expressions. The & and | operators perform *bitwise* operations only when applied to numbers.

Conditional operator (ternary operator)

The *conditional operator* (more commonly called the *ternary operator* because it's the only operator that takes three operands) has the form q ? a : b; thus, if condition q is true, a is evaluated, otherwise b is evaluated:

```
static int Max (int a, int b)
{
  return (a > b) ? a : b;
}
```

The conditional operator is particularly useful in LINQ expressions (Chapter 8).

Strings and Characters

C#'s char type (aliasing the System.Char type) represents a Unicode character and occupies 2 bytes (UTF-16). A char literal is specified within single quotes:

```
char c = 'A';      // Simple character
```

Escape sequences express characters that cannot be expressed or interpreted literally. An escape sequence is a backslash followed by a character with a special meaning; for example:

```
char newLine = '\n';
char backSlash = '\\';
```

Table 2-2 shows the escape sequence characters.

Table 2-2. Escape sequence characters

Char	Meaning	Value
\'	Single quote	0x0027
\"	Double quote	0x0022
\\	Backslash	0x005C
\0	Null	0x0000
\a	Alert	0x0007
\b	Backspace	0x0008
\f	Form feed	0x000C
\n	New line	0x000A
\r	Carriage return	0x000D
\t	Horizontal tab	0x0009
\v	Vertical tab	0x000B

The \u (or \x) escape sequence lets you specify any Unicode character via its four-digit hexadecimal code:

```
char copyrightSymbol = '\u00A9';
char omegaSymbol     = '\u03A9';
char newLine         = '\u000A';
```

Char Conversions

An implicit conversion from a char to a numeric type works for the numeric types that can accommodate an unsigned short. For other numeric types, an explicit conversion is required.

String Type

C#'s string type (aliasing the System.String type, covered in depth in Chapter 6) represents an immutable (unmodifiable) sequence of Unicode characters. A string literal is specified within double quotes:

```
string a = "Heat";
```

 string is a reference type rather than a value type. Its equality operators, however, follow value-type semantics:

```
string a = "test";
string b = "test";
Console.Write (a == b);  // True
```

The escape sequences that are valid for char literals also work inside strings:

```
string a = "Here's a tab:\t";
```

The cost of this is that whenever you need a literal backslash, you must write it twice:

```
string a1 = "\\\\server\\fileshare\\helloworld.cs";
```

To avoid this problem, C# allows *verbatim* string literals. A verbatim string literal is prefixed with @ and does not support escape sequences. The following verbatim string is identical to the preceding one:

```
string a2 = @"\\server\fileshare\helloworld.cs";
```

A verbatim string literal can also span multiple lines:

```
string escaped  = "First Line\r\nSecond Line";
string verbatim = @"First Line
Second Line";

// True if your text editor uses CR-LF line separators:
Console.WriteLine (escaped == verbatim);
```

You can include the double-quote character in a verbatim literal by writing it twice:

```
string xml = @"<customer id=""123""></customer>";
```

String concatenation

The + operator concatenates two strings:

```
string s = "a" + "b";
```

One of the operands might be a nonstring value, in which case ToString is called on that value:

```
string s = "a" + 5;   // a5
```

Using the + operator repeatedly to build up a string is inefficient: a better solution is to use the System.Text.StringBuilder type (described in Chapter 6).

String interpolation

A string preceded with the $ character is called an *interpolated string*. Interpolated strings can include expressions enclosed in braces:

```
int x = 4;
Console.Write ($"A square has {x} sides");   // Prints: A square has 4 sides
```

Any valid C# expression of any type can appear within the braces, and C# will convert the expression to a string by calling its ToString method or equivalent. You can change the formatting by appending the expression with a colon and a *format string* (format strings are described in "String.Format and composite format strings" on page 276):

```
string s = $"255 in hex is {byte.MaxValue:X2}";   // X2 = 2-digit hexadecimal
// Evaluates to "255 in hex is FF"
```

Should you need to use a colon for another purpose (such as a ternary conditional operator, which we'll cover later), you must wrap the entire expression in parentheses:

```
bool b = true;
Console.WriteLine ($"The answer in binary is {(b ? 1 : 0)}");
```

Interpolated strings must complete on a single line, unless you also specify the verbatim string operator:

```
int x = 2;
// Note that $ must appear before @ prior to C# 8:
string s = $@"this interpolation spans {
x} lines";
```

To include a brace literal in an interpolated string, repeat the desired brace character.

String comparisons

string does not support < and > operators for comparisons. You must use the string's CompareTo method, described in Chapter 6.

Constant interpolated strings (C# 10)

From C# 10, interpolated strings can be constants, as long as the interpolated values are constants:

```
const string greeting = "Hello";
const string message = $"{greeting}, world";
```

Arrays

An array represents a fixed number of variables (called *elements*) of a particular type. The elements in an array are always stored in a contiguous block of memory, providing highly efficient access.

An array is denoted with square brackets after the element type:

```
char[] vowels = new char[5];    // Declare an array of 5 characters
```

Square brackets also *index* the array, accessing a particular element by position:

```
vowels[0] = 'a';
vowels[1] = 'e';
vowels[2] = 'i';
vowels[3] = 'o';
vowels[4] = 'u';
Console.WriteLine (vowels[1]);    // e
```

This prints "e" because array indexes start at 0. You can use a for loop statement to iterate through each element in the array. The for loop in this example cycles the integer i from 0 to 4:

```
for (int i = 0; i < vowels.Length; i++)
  Console.Write (vowels[i]);          // aeiou
```

The Length property of an array returns the number of elements in the array. After an array has been created, you cannot change its length. The System.Collec tion namespace and subnamespaces provide higher-level data structures, such as dynamically sized arrays and dictionaries.

An *array initialization expression* lets you declare and populate an array in a single step:

```
char[] vowels = new char[] {'a','e','i','o','u'};
```

Or simply:

```
char[] vowels = {'a','e','i','o','u'};
```

All arrays inherit from the System.Array class, providing common services for all arrays. These members include methods to get and set elements regardless of the array type. We describe them in "The Array Class" on page 355.

Default Element Initialization

Creating an array always preinitializes the elements with default values. The default value for a type is the result of a bitwise zeroing of memory. For example, consider creating an array of integers. Because `int` is a value type, this allocates 1,000 integers in one contiguous block of memory. The default value for each element will be 0:

```
int[] a = new int[1000];
Console.Write (a[123]);          // 0
```

Value types versus reference types

Whether an array element type is a value type or a reference type has important performance implications. When the element type is a value type, each element value is allocated as part of the array, as shown here:

```
Point[] a = new Point[1000];
int x = a[500].X;                // 0

public struct Point { public int X, Y; }
```

Had `Point` been a class, creating the array would have merely allocated 1,000 null references:

```
Point[] a = new Point[1000];
int x = a[500].X;                         // Runtime error, NullReferenceException

public class Point { public int X, Y; }
```

To avoid this error, we must explicitly instantiate 1,000 `Point`s after instantiating the array:

```
Point[] a = new Point[1000];
for (int i = 0; i < a.Length; i++) // Iterate i from 0 to 999
    a[i] = new Point();            // Set array element i with new point
```

An array *itself* is always a reference type object, regardless of the element type. For instance, the following is legal:

```
int[] a = null;
```

Indices and Ranges

Indices and *ranges* (introduced in C# 8) simplify working with elements or portions of an array.

Indices and ranges also work with the CLR types `Span<T>` and `ReadOnlySpan<T>` (see Chapter 23).

You can also make your own types work with indices and ranges, by defining an indexer of type `Index` or `Range` (see "Indexers" on page 109).

Indices

Indices let you refer to elements relative to the *end* of an array, with the ^ operator. ^1 refers to the last element, ^2 refers to the second-to-last element, and so on:

```
char[] vowels = new char[] {'a','e','i','o','u'};
char lastElement  = vowels [^1];    // 'u'
char secondToLast = vowels [^2];    // 'o'
```

(^0 equals the length of the array, so vowels[^0] generates an error.)

C# implements indices with the help of the Index type, so you can also do the following:

```
Index first = 0;
Index last = ^1;
char firstElement = vowels [first];    // 'a'
char lastElement = vowels [last];      // 'u'
```

Ranges

Ranges let you "slice" an array by using the .. operator:

```
char[] firstTwo =  vowels [..2];    // 'a', 'e'
char[] lastThree = vowels [2..];    // 'i', 'o', 'u'
char[] middleOne = vowels [2..3];   // 'i'
```

The second number in the range is *exclusive*, so ..2 returns the elements *before* vowels[2].

You can also use the ^ symbol in ranges. The following returns the last two characters:

```
char[] lastTwo = vowels [^2..];    // 'o', 'u'
```

C# implements ranges with the help of the Range type, so you can also do the following:

```
Range firstTwoRange = 0..2;
char[] firstTwo = vowels [firstTwoRange];    // 'a', 'e'
```

Multidimensional Arrays

Multidimensional arrays come in two varieties: *rectangular* and *jagged*. Rectangular arrays represent an *n*-dimensional block of memory, and jagged arrays are arrays of arrays.

Rectangular arrays

Rectangular arrays are declared using commas to separate each dimension. The following declares a rectangular two-dimensional array for which the dimensions are 3 by 3:

```
int[,] matrix = new int[3,3];
```

The GetLength method of an array returns the length for a given dimension (starting at 0):

```
for (int i = 0; i < matrix.GetLength(0); i++)
  for (int j = 0; j < matrix.GetLength(1); j++)
    matrix[i,j] = i * 3 + j;
```

You can initialize a rectangular array with explicit values. The following code creates an array identical to the previous example:

```
int[,] matrix = new int[,]
{
  {0,1,2},
  {3,4,5},
  {6,7,8}
};
```

Jagged arrays

Jagged arrays are declared using successive square brackets to represent each dimension. Here is an example of declaring a jagged two-dimensional array for which the outermost dimension is 3:

```
int[][] matrix = new int[3][];
```

 Interestingly, this is new int[3][] and not new int[] [3]. Eric Lippert has written *an excellent article* (*http://alba hari.com/jagged*) on why this is so.

The inner dimensions aren't specified in the declaration because, unlike a rectangular array, each inner array can be an arbitrary length. Each inner array is implicitly initialized to null rather than an empty array. You must manually create each inner array:

```
for (int i = 0; i < matrix.Length; i++)
{
  matrix[i] = new int[3];                    // Create inner array
  for (int j = 0; j < matrix[i].Length; j++)
    matrix[i][j] = i * 3 + j;
}
```

You can initialize a jagged array with explicit values. The following code creates an array identical to the previous example with an additional element at the end:

```
int[][] matrix = new int[][]
{
  new int[] {0,1,2},
  new int[] {3,4,5},
  new int[] {6,7,8,9}
};
```

Simplified Array Initialization Expressions

There are two ways to shorten array initialization expressions. The first is to omit the new operator and type qualifications:

```
char[] vowels = {'a','e','i','o','u'};

int[,] rectangularMatrix =
{
  {0,1,2},
  {3,4,5},
  {6,7,8}
};

int[][] jaggedMatrix =
{
  new int[] {0,1,2},
  new int[] {3,4,5},
  new int[] {6,7,8,9}
};
```

The second approach is to use the var keyword, which instructs the compiler to implicitly type a local variable:

```
var i = 3;            // i is implicitly of type int
var s = "sausage";    // s is implicitly of type string

// Therefore:

var rectMatrix = new int[,]    // rectMatrix is implicitly of type int[,]
{
  {0,1,2},
  {3,4,5},
  {6,7,8}
};

var jaggedMat = new int[][]    // jaggedMat is implicitly of type int[][]
{
  new int[] {0,1,2},
  new int[] {3,4,5},
  new int[] {6,7,8,9}
};
```

Implicit typing can be taken one stage further with arrays: you can omit the type qualifier after the new keyword and have the compiler *infer* the array type:

```
var vowels = new[] {'a','e','i','o','u'};    // Compiler infers char[]
```

For this to work, the elements must all be implicitly convertible to a single type (and at least one of the elements must be of that type, and there must be exactly one best type), as in the following example:

```
var x = new[] {1,10000000000};    // all convertible to long
```

Bounds Checking

All array indexing is bounds checked by the runtime. An IndexOutOfRange Exception is thrown if you use an invalid index:

```
int[] arr = new int[3];
arr[3] = 1;                       // IndexOutOfRangeException thrown
```

Array bounds checking is necessary for type safety and simplifies debugging.

 Generally, the performance hit from bounds checking is minor, and the Just-in-Time (JIT) compiler can perform optimizations, such as determining in advance whether all indexes will be safe before entering a loop, thus avoiding a check on each iteration. In addition, C# provides "unsafe" code that can explicitly bypass bounds checking (see "Unsafe Code and Pointers" on page 243).

Variables and Parameters

A variable represents a storage location that has a modifiable value. A variable can be a *local variable*, *parameter* (*value*, *ref*, *out*, or *in*), *field* (*instance* or *static*), or *array element*.

The Stack and the Heap

The stack and the heap are the places where variables reside. Each has very different lifetime semantics.

Stack

The stack is a block of memory for storing local variables and parameters. The stack logically grows and shrinks as a method or function is entered and exited. Consider the following method (to avoid distraction, input argument checking is ignored):

```
static int Factorial (int x)
{
  if (x == 0) return 1;
  return x * Factorial (x-1);
}
```

This method is recursive, meaning that it calls itself. Each time the method is entered, a new int is allocated on the stack, and each time the method exits, the int is deallocated.

Heap

The heap is the memory in which *objects* (i.e., reference-type instances) reside. Whenever a new object is created, it is allocated on the heap, and a reference to that object is returned. During a program's execution, the heap begins filling up as new objects are created. The runtime has a garbage collector that periodically deallocates objects from the heap, so your program does not run out of memory. An object is eligible for deallocation as soon as it's not referenced by anything that's itself "alive."

In the following example, we begin by creating a StringBuilder object referenced by the variable ref1 and then write out its content. That StringBuilder object is then immediately eligible for garbage collection because nothing subsequently uses it.

Then, we create another `StringBuilder` referenced by variable `ref2` and copy that reference to `ref3`. Even though `ref2` is not used after that point, `ref3` keeps the same `StringBuilder` object alive—ensuring that it doesn't become eligible for collection until we've finished using `ref3`:

```
using System;
using System.Text;

StringBuilder ref1 = new StringBuilder ("object1");
Console.WriteLine (ref1);
// The StringBuilder referenced by ref1 is now eligible for GC.

StringBuilder ref2 = new StringBuilder ("object2");
StringBuilder ref3 = ref2;
// The StringBuilder referenced by ref2 is NOT yet eligible for GC.

Console.WriteLine (ref3);        // object2
```

Value-type instances (and object references) live wherever the variable was declared. If the instance was declared as a field within a class type, or as an array element, that instance lives on the heap.

 You can't explicitly delete objects in C#, as you can in C++. An unreferenced object is eventually collected by the garbage collector.

The heap also stores static fields. Unlike objects allocated on the heap (which can be garbage-collected), these live until the process ends.

Definite Assignment

C# enforces a definite assignment policy. In practice, this means that outside of an `unsafe` or interop context, you can't accidentally access uninitialized memory. Definite assignment has three implications:

- Local variables must be assigned a value before they can be read.
- Function arguments must be supplied when a method is called (unless marked as optional; see "Optional parameters" on page 65).
- All other variables (such as fields and array elements) are automatically initialized by the runtime.

For example, the following code results in a compile-time error:

```
int x;
Console.WriteLine (x);        // Compile-time error
```

Fields and array elements are automatically initialized with the default values for their type. The following code outputs 0 because array elements are implicitly assigned to their default values:

```
int[] ints = new int[2];
Console.WriteLine (ints[0]);     // 0
```

The following code outputs 0, because fields are implicitly assigned a default value (whether instance or static):

```
Console.WriteLine (Test.X);   // 0

class Test { public static int X; }   // field
```

Default Values

All type instances have a default value. The default value for the predefined types is the result of a bitwise zeroing of memory:

Type	Default value
Reference types (and nullable value types)	null
Numeric and enum types	0
char type	'\0'
bool type	false

You can obtain the default value for any type via the default keyword:

```
Console.WriteLine (default (decimal));   // 0
```

You can optionally omit the type when it can be inferred:

```
decimal d = default;
```

The default value in a custom value type (i.e., struct) is the same as the default value for each field defined by the custom type.

Parameters

A method may have a sequence of parameters. Parameters define the set of arguments that must be provided for that method. In the following example, the method Foo has a single parameter named p, of type int:

```
Foo (8);                       // 8 is an argument
static void Foo (int p) {...}   // p is a parameter
```

You can control how parameters are passed with the ref, in, and out modifiers:

Parameter modifier	Passed by	Variable must be definitely assigned
(None)	Value	Going in
ref	Reference	Going in
in	Reference (read-only)	Going in
out	Reference	Going out

Passing arguments by value

By default, arguments in C# are *passed by value*, which is by far the most common case. This means that a copy of the value is created when passed to the method:

```
int x = 8;
Foo (x);                     // Make a copy of x
Console.WriteLine (x);       // x will still be 8

static void Foo (int p)
{
  p = p + 1;                 // Increment p by 1
  Console.WriteLine (p);     // Write p to screen
}
```

Assigning p a new value does not change the contents of x, because p and x reside in different memory locations.

Passing a reference-type argument by value copies the *reference* but not the object. In the following example, Foo sees the same StringBuilder object we instantiated (sb) but has an independent *reference* to it. In other words, sb and fooSB are separate variables that reference the same StringBuilder object:

```
StringBuilder sb = new StringBuilder();
Foo (sb);
Console.WriteLine (sb.ToString());    // test

static void Foo (StringBuilder fooSB)
{
  fooSB.Append ("test");
  fooSB = null;
}
```

Because fooSB is a *copy* of a reference, setting it to null doesn't make sb null. (If, however, fooSB was declared and called with the ref modifier, sb *would* become null.)

The ref modifier

To *pass by reference*, C# provides the ref parameter modifier. In the following example, p and x refer to the same memory locations:

```
int x = 8;
Foo (ref  x);                // Ask Foo to deal directly with x
Console.WriteLine (x);       // x is now 9

static void Foo (ref int p)
{
  p = p + 1;                 // Increment p by 1
  Console.WriteLine (p);     // Write p to screen
]
```

Now assigning p a new value changes the contents of x. Notice how the `ref` modifier is required both when writing and when calling the method.[4] This makes it very clear what's going on.

The `ref` modifier is essential in implementing a swap method (in "Generics" on page 145, we show how to write a swap method that works with any type):

```
string x = "Penn";
string y = "Teller";
Swap (ref x, ref y);
Console.WriteLine (x);    // Teller
Console.WriteLine (y);    // Penn

static void Swap (ref string a, ref string b)
{
  string temp = a;
  a = b;
  b = temp;
}
```

 A parameter can be passed by reference or by value, regardless of whether the parameter type is a reference type or a value type.

The out modifier

An out argument is like a `ref` argument except for the following:

- It need not be assigned before going into the function.
- It must be assigned before it comes *out* of the function.

The out modifier is most commonly used to get multiple return values back from a method; for example:

```
string a, b;
Split ("Stevie Ray Vaughn", out a, out b);
Console.WriteLine (a);                    // Stevie Ray
Console.WriteLine (b);                    // Vaughn

void Split (string name, out string firstNames, out string lastName)
{
  int i = name.LastIndexOf (' ');
  firstNames = name.Substring (0, i);
  lastName = name.Substring (i + 1);
}
```

Like a `ref` parameter, an out parameter is passed by reference.

---

4 An exception to this rule is when calling Component Object Model (COM) methods. We discuss this in Chapter 25.

Out variables and discards

You can declare variables on the fly when calling methods with out parameters. We can replace the first two lines in our preceding example with this:

```
Split ("Stevie Ray Vaughan", out string a, out string b);
```

When calling methods with multiple out parameters, sometimes you're not interested in receiving values from all the parameters. In such cases, you can "discard" the ones in which you're uninterested by using an underscore:

```
Split ("Stevie Ray Vaughan", out string a, out _);   // Discard 2nd param
Console.WriteLine (a);
```

In this case, the compiler treats the underscore as a special symbol, called a *discard*. You can include multiple discards in a single call. Assuming SomeBigMethod has been defined with seven **out** parameters, we can ignore all but the fourth, as follows:

```
SomeBigMethod (out _, out _, out _, out int x, out _, out _, out _);
```

For backward compatibility, this language feature will not take effect if a real underscore variable is in scope:

```
string _;
Split ("Stevie Ray Vaughan", out string a, out _);
Console.WriteLine (_);     // Vaughan
```

Implications of passing by reference

When you pass an argument by reference, you alias the storage location of an existing variable rather than create a new storage location. In the following example, the variables x and y represent the same instance:

```
class Test
{
  static int x;

  static void Main() { Foo (out x); }

  static void Foo (out int y)
  {
    Console.WriteLine (x);        // x is 0
    y = 1;                        // Mutate y
    Console.WriteLine (x);        // x is 1
  }
}
```

The in modifier

An in parameter is similar to a ref parameter except that the argument's value cannot be modified by the method (doing so generates a compile-time error). This modifier is most useful when passing a large value type to the method because it allows the compiler to avoid the overhead of copying the argument prior to passing it in while still protecting the original value from modification.

Overloading solely on the presence of `in` is permitted:

```
void Foo (   SomeBigStruct a) { ... }
void Foo (in SomeBigStruct a) { ... }
```

To call the second overload, the caller must use the `in` modifier:

```
SomeBigStruct x = ...;
Foo (x);       // Calls the first overload
Foo (in x);    // Calls the second overload
```

When there's no ambiguity,

```
void Bar (in SomeBigStruct a) { ... }
```

use of the `in` modifier is optional for the caller:

```
Bar (x);      // OK (calls the 'in' overload)
Bar (in x);   // OK (calls the 'in' overload)
```

To make this example meaningful, `SomeBigStruct` would be defined as a struct (see "Structs" on page 129).

The params modifier

The `params` modifier, if applied to the last parameter of a method, allows the method to accept any number of arguments of a particular type. The parameter type must be declared as an (single-dimensional) array, as shown in the following example:

```
int total = Sum (1, 2, 3, 4);
Console.WriteLine (total);              // 10

// The call to Sum above is equivalent to:
int total2 = Sum (new int[] { 1, 2, 3, 4 });

int Sum (params int[] ints)
{
  int sum = 0;
  for (int i = 0; i < ints.Length; i++)
    sum += ints [i];                    // Increase sum by ints[i]
  return sum;
}
```

If there are zero arguments in the `params` position, a zero-length array is created.

You can also supply a `params` argument as an ordinary array. The first line in our example is semantically equivalent to this:

```
int total = Sum (new int[] { 1, 2, 3, 4 } );
```

Optional parameters

Methods, constructors, and indexers (Chapter 3) can declare *optional parameters*. A parameter is optional if it specifies a *default value* in its declaration:

```
void Foo (int x = 23) { Console.WriteLine (x); }
```

You can omit optional parameters when calling the method:

```
Foo();     // 23
```

The *default argument* of 23 is actually *passed* to the optional parameter x—the compiler bakes the value 23 into the compiled code at the *calling* side. The preceding call to Foo is semantically identical to

```
Foo (23);
```

because the compiler simply substitutes the default value of an optional parameter wherever it is used.

 Adding an optional parameter to a public method that's called from another assembly requires recompilation of both assemblies—just as though the parameter were mandatory.

The default value of an optional parameter must be specified by a constant expression, a parameterless constructor of a value type, or a default expression. Optional parameters cannot be marked with ref or out.

Mandatory parameters must occur *before* optional parameters in both the method declaration and the method call (the exception is with params arguments, which still always come last). In the following example, the explicit value of 1 is passed to x, and the default value of 0 is passed to y:

```
Foo (1);    // 1, 0

void Foo (int x = 0, int y = 0) { Console.WriteLine (x + ", " + y); }
```

You can do the converse (pass a default value to x and an explicit value to y) by combining optional parameters with *named arguments*.

Named arguments

Rather than identifying an argument by position, you can identify an argument by name:

```
Foo (x:1, y:2);  // 1, 2

void Foo (int x, int y) { Console.WriteLine (x + ", " + y); }
```

Named arguments can occur in any order. The following calls to Foo are semantically identical:

```
Foo (x:1, y:2);
Foo (y:2, x:1);
```

A subtle difference is that argument expressions are evaluated in the order in which they appear at the *calling* site. In general, this makes a difference only with interdependent side-effecting expressions such as the following, which writes 0, 1:

```
int a = 0;
Foo (y: ++a, x: --a);   // ++a is evaluated first
```

Of course, you would almost certainly avoid writing such code in practice!

You can mix named and positional arguments:

```
Foo (1, y:2);
```

However, there is a restriction: positional arguments must come before named arguments unless they are used in the correct position. So, you could call Foo like this:

```
Foo (x:1, 2);       // OK. Arguments in the declared positions
```

But not like this:

```
Foo (y:2, 1);       // Compile-time error. y isn't in the first position
```

Named arguments are particularly useful in conjunction with optional parameters. For instance, consider the following method:

```
void Bar (int a = 0, int b = 0, int c = 0, int d = 0) { ... }
```

You can call this supplying only a value for d, as follows:

```
Bar (d:3);
```

This is particularly useful when calling COM APIs, which we discuss in detail in Chapter 24.

Ref Locals

A somewhat esoteric feature of C# is that you can define a local variable that *references* an element in an array or field in an object (from C# 7):

```
int[] numbers = { 0, 1, 2, 3, 4 };
ref int numRef = ref numbers [2];
```

In this example, numRef is a *reference* to numbers[2]. When we modify numRef, we modify the array element:

```
numRef *= 10;
Console.WriteLine (numRef);         // 20
Console.WriteLine (numbers [2]);    // 20
```

The target for a ref local must be an array element, field, or local variable; it cannot be a *property* (Chapter 3). *Ref locals* are intended for specialized micro-optimization scenarios and are typically used in conjunction with *ref returns*.

Ref Returns

The Span<T> and ReadOnlySpan<T> types that we describe in Chapter 23 use ref returns to implement a highly efficient indexer. Outside such scenarios, ref returns are not commonly used, and you can consider them a micro-optimization feature.

You can return a *ref local* from a method. This is called a *ref return*:

```
class Program
{
  static string x = "Old Value";

  static ref string GetX() => ref x;    // This method returns a ref

  static void Main()
  {
    ref string xRef = ref GetX();        // Assign result to a ref local
    xRef = "New Value";
    Console.WriteLine (x);               // New Value
  }
}
```

If you omit the ref modifier on the calling side, it reverts to returning an ordinary value:

```
string localX = GetX();  // Legal: localX is an ordinary non-ref variable.
```

You also can use ref returns when defining a property or indexer:

```
static ref string Prop => ref x;
```

Such a property is implicitly writable, despite there being no set accessor:

```
Prop = "New Value";
```

You can prevent such modification by using ref readonly:

```
static ref readonly string Prop => ref x;
```

The ref readonly modifier prevents modification while still enabling the performance gain of returning by reference. The gain would be very small in this case, because x is of type string (a reference type): no matter how long the string, the only inefficiency that you can hope to avoid is the copying of a single 32- or 64-bit *reference*. Real gains can occur with custom value types (see "Structs" on page 129), but only if the struct is marked as readonly (otherwise, the compiler will perform a defensive copy).

Attempting to define an explicit set accessor on a *ref return* property or indexer is illegal.

var—Implicitly Typed Local Variables

It is often the case that you declare and initialize a variable in one step. If the compiler is able to infer the type from the initialization expression, you can use the keyword var in place of the type declaration; for example:

```
var x = "hello";
var y = new System.Text.StringBuilder();
var z = (float)Math.PI;
```

This is precisely equivalent to the following:

```
string x = "hello";
System.Text.StringBuilder y = new System.Text.StringBuilder();
float z = (float)Math.PI;
```

Because of this direct equivalence, implicitly typed variables are statically typed. For example, the following generates a compile-time error:

```
var x = 5;
x = "hello";    // Compile-time error; x is of type int
```

 var can decrease code readability when you can't deduce the type purely by looking at the variable declaration; for example:

```
Random r = new Random();
var x = r.Next();
```

What type is x?

In "Anonymous Types" on page 205, we will describe a scenario in which the use of var is mandatory.

Target-Typed new Expressions

Another way to reduce lexical repetition is with *target-typed* new *expressions* (from C# 9):

```
System.Text.StringBuilder sb1 = new();
System.Text.StringBuilder sb2 = new ("Test");
```

This is precisely equivalent to:

```
System.Text.StringBuilder sb1 = new System.Text.StringBuilder();
System.Text.StringBuilder sb2 = new System.Text.StringBuilder ("Test");
```

The principle is that you can call new without specifying a type name if the compiler is able to unambiguously infer it. Target-typed new expressions are particularly useful when the variable declaration and initialization are in different parts of your code. A common example is when you want to initialize a field in a constructor:

```
class Foo
{
  System.Text.StringBuilder sb;

  public Foo (string initialValue)
  {
```

```
      sb = new (initialValue);
    }
  }
```

Target-typed new expressions are also helpful in the following scenario:

```
MyMethod (new ("test"));

void MyMethod (System.Text.StringBuilder sb) { ... }
```

Expressions and Operators

An *expression* essentially denotes a value. The simplest kinds of expressions are constants and variables. Expressions can be transformed and combined using operators. An *operator* takes one or more input *operands* to output a new expression.

Here is an example of a *constant expression*:

```
12
```

We can use the * operator to combine two operands (the literal expressions 12 and 30), as follows:

```
12 * 30
```

We can build complex expressions because an operand can itself be an expression, such as the operand (12 * 30) in the following example:

```
1 + (12 * 30)
```

Operators in C# can be classed as *unary*, *binary*, or *ternary*, depending on the number of operands they work on (one, two, or three). The binary operators always use *infix* notation in which the operator is placed *between* the two operands.

Primary Expressions

Primary expressions include expressions composed of operators that are intrinsic to the basic plumbing of the language. Here is an example:

```
Math.Log (1)
```

This expression is composed of two primary expressions. The first expression performs a member lookup (with the . operator), and the second expression performs a method call (with the () operator).

Void Expressions

A void expression is an expression that has no value, such as this:

```
Console.WriteLine (1)
```

Because it has no value, you cannot use a void expression as an operand to build more complex expressions:

```
1 + Console.WriteLine (1)      // Compile-time error
```

Assignment Expressions

An assignment expression uses the = operator to assign the result of another expression to a variable; for example:

```
x = x * 5
```

An assignment expression is not a void expression—it has a value of whatever was assigned, and so can be incorporated into another expression. In the following example, the expression assigns 2 to x and 10 to y:

```
y = 5 * (x = 2)
```

You can use this style of expression to initialize multiple values:

```
a = b = c = d = 0
```

The *compound assignment operators* are syntactic shortcuts that combine assignment with another operator:

```
x *= 2     // equivalent to x = x * 2
x <<= 1    // equivalent to x = x << 1
```

(A subtle exception to this rule is with *events*, which we describe in Chapter 4: the += and -= operators here are treated specially and map to the event's add and remove accessors.)

Operator Precedence and Associativity

When an expression contains multiple operators, *precedence* and *associativity* determine the order of their evaluation. Operators with higher precedence execute before operators with lower precedence. If the operators have the same precedence, the operator's associativity determines the order of evaluation.

Precedence

The following expression

```
1 + 2 * 3
```

is evaluated as follows because * has a higher precedence than +:

```
1 + (2 * 3)
```

Left-associative operators

Binary operators (except for assignment, lambda, and null-coalescing operators) are *left-associative*; in other words, they are evaluated from left to right. For example, the following expression

```
8 / 4 / 2
```

is evaluated as follows:

```
( 8 / 4 ) / 2   // 1
```

You can insert parentheses to change the actual order of evaluation:

```
8 / ( 4 / 2 )    // 4
```

Right-associative operators

The *assignment operators* as well as the lambda, null-coalescing, and conditional operators are *right-associative*; in other words, they are evaluated from right to left. Right associativity allows multiple assignments, such as the following, to compile:

```
x = y = 3;
```

This first assigns 3 to y and then assigns the result of that expression (3) to x.

Operator Table

Table 2-3 lists C#'s operators in order of precedence. Operators in the same category have the same precedence. We explain user-overloadable operators in "Operator Overloading" on page 239.

Table 2-3. C# operators (categories in order of precedence)

Category	Operator symbol	Operator name	Example	User-overloadable
Primary	.	Member access	x.y	No
	?. and ?[]	Null-conditional	x?.y or x?[0]	No
	! (postfix)	Null-forgiving	x!.y or x![0]	No
	-> (unsafe)	Pointer to struct	x->y	No
	()	Function call	x()	No
	[]	Array/index	a[x]	Via indexer
	++	Post-increment	x++	Yes
	--	Post-decrement	x--	Yes
	new	Create instance	new Foo()	No
	stackalloc	Stack allocation	stackalloc(10)	No
	typeof	Get type from identifier	typeof(int)	No
	nameof	Get name of identifier	nameof(x)	No
	checked	Integral overflow check on	checked(x)	No
	unchecked	Integral overflow check off	unchecked(x)	No
	default	Default value	default(char)	No
Unary	await	Await	await myTask	No

Category	Operator symbol	Operator name	Example	User-overloadable
	`sizeof`	Get size of struct	`sizeof(int)`	No
	+	Positive value of	`+x`	Yes
	–	Negative value of	`-x`	Yes
	!	Not	`!x`	Yes
	~	Bitwise complement	`~x`	Yes
	++	Pre-increment	`++x`	Yes
	--	Pre-decrement	`--x`	Yes
	( )	Cast	`(int)x`	No
	^	Index from end	`array[^1]`	No
	* (unsafe)	Value at address	`*x`	No
	& (unsafe)	Address of value	`&x`	No
Range	.. ..^	Range of indices	`x..y` `x..^y`	No

Switch & with	`switch`	Switch expression	`num switch {`
			`1 => true,`
			`_ => false`
			`}`
				No

	`with`	With expression	`rec with` `{ X = 123 }`	No
Multiplicative	*	Multiply	`x * y`	Yes
	/	Divide	`x / y`	Yes
	%	Remainder	`x % y`	Yes
Additive	+	Add	`x + y`	Yes
	–	Subtract	`x - y`	Yes
Shift	<<	Shift left	`x << 1`	Yes
	>>	Shift right	`x >> 1`	Yes
Relational	<	Less than	`x < y`	Yes
	>	Greater than	`x > y`	Yes
	<=	Less than or equal to	`x <= y`	Yes
	>=	Greater than or equal to	`x >= y`	Yes
	`is`	Type is or is subclass of	`x is y`	No
	`as`	Type conversion	`x as y`	No
Equality	==	Equals	`x == y`	Yes

Category	Operator symbol	Operator name	Example	User-overloadable
	!=	Not equals	x != y	Yes
Logical And	&	And	x & y	Yes
Logical Xor	^	Exclusive Or	x ^ y	Yes
Logical Or	|	Or	x | y	Yes
Conditional And	&&	Conditional And	x && y	Via &
Conditional Or	||	Conditional Or	x || y	Via |
Null coalescing	??	Null coalescing	x ?? y	No
Conditional	?:	Conditional	isTrue ? thenThis : elseThis	No
Assignment and lambda	=	Assign	x = y	No
	*=	Multiply self by	x *= 2	Via *
	/=	Divide self by	x /= 2	Via /
	%=	Remainder & assign to self	x %= 2	
	+=	Add to self	x += 2	Via +
	-=	Subtract from self	x -= 2	Via -
	<<=	Shift self left by	x <<= 2	Via <<
	>>=	Shift self right by	x >>= 2	Via >>
	&=	And self by	x &= 2	Via &
	^=	Exclusive-Or self by	x ^= 2	Via ^
	|=	Or self by	x |= 2	Via |
	??=	Null-coalescing assignment	x ??= 0	No
	=>	Lambda	x => x + 1	No

Null Operators

C# provides three operators to make it easier to work with nulls: the *null-coalescing operator*, the *null-coalescing assignment operator*, and the *null-conditional operator*.

Null-Coalescing Operator

The ?? operator is the *null-coalescing operator*. It says, "If the operand to the left is non-null, give it to me; otherwise, give me another value." For example:

```
string s1 = null;
string s2 = s1 ?? "nothing";   // s2 evaluates to "nothing"
```

If the lefthand expression is non-null, the righthand expression is never evaluated. The null-coalescing operator also works with nullable value types (see "Nullable Value Types" on page 194).

Null-Coalescing Assignment Operator

The `??=` operator (introduced in C# 8) is the *null-coalescing assignment operator*. It says, "If the operand to the left is null, assign the right operand to the left operand." Consider the following:

```
myVariable ??= someDefault;
```

This is equivalent to:

```
if (myVariable == null) myVariable = someDefault;
```

The `??=` operator is particularly useful in implementing lazily calculated properties. We'll cover this topic later, in "Calculated Fields and Lazy Evaluation" on page 217.

Null-Conditional Operator

The `?.` operator is the *null-conditional* or "Elvis" operator (after the Elvis emoticon). It allows you to call methods and access members just like the standard dot operator except that if the operand on the left is null, the expression evaluates to null instead of throwing a `NullReferenceException`:

```
System.Text.StringBuilder sb = null;
string s = sb?.ToString();  // No error; s instead evaluates to null
```

The last line is equivalent to the following:

```
string s = (sb == null ? null : sb.ToString());
```

Null-conditional expressions also work with indexers:

```
string foo = null;
char? c = foo?[1];  // c is null
```

Upon encountering a null, the Elvis operator short-circuits the remainder of the expression. In the following example, s evaluates to null, even with a standard dot operator between `ToString()` and `ToUpper()`:

```
System.Text.StringBuilder sb = null;
string s = sb?.ToString().ToUpper();  // s evaluates to null without error
```

Repeated use of Elvis is necessary only if the operand immediately to its left might be null. The following expression is robust to both x being null and x.y being null:

```
x?.y?.z
```

It is equivalent to the following (except that x.y is evaluated only once):

```
x == null ? null
        : (x.y == null ? null : x.y.z)
```

The final expression must be capable of accepting a null. The following is illegal:

```
System.Text.StringBuilder sb = null;
int length = sb?.ToString().Length;    // Illegal : int cannot be null
```

We can fix this with the use of nullable value types (see "Nullable Value Types" on page 194). If you're already familiar with nullable value types, here's a preview:

```
int? length = sb?.ToString().Length;    // OK: int? can be null
```

You can also use the null-conditional operator to call a void method:

```
someObject?.SomeVoidMethod();
```

If someObject is null, this becomes a "no-operation" rather than throwing a Null ReferenceException.

You can use the null-conditional operator with the commonly used type members that we describe in Chapter 3, including *methods, fields, properties*, and *indexers*. It also combines well with the *null-coalescing operator*:

```
System.Text.StringBuilder sb = null;
string s = sb?.ToString() ?? "nothing";    // s evaluates to "nothing"
```

Statements

Functions comprise statements that execute sequentially in the textual order in which they appear. A *statement block* is a series of statements appearing between braces (the {} tokens).

Declaration Statements

A variable declaration introduces a new variable, optionally initializing it with an expression. You may declare multiple variables of the same type in a comma-separated list:

```
string someWord = "rosebud";
int someNumber = 42;
bool rich = true, famous = false;
```

A constant declaration is like a variable declaration except that it cannot be changed after it has been declared, and the initialization must occur with the declaration (see "Constants" on page 96):

```
const double c = 2.99792458E08;
c += 10;                          // Compile-time Error
```

Local variables

The scope of a local variable or local constant extends throughout the current block. You cannot declare another local variable with the same name in the current block or in any nested blocks:

```
int x;
{
  int y;
  int x;          // Error - x already defined
```

```
}
{
  int y;              // OK - y not in scope
}
Console.Write (y);  // Error - y is out of scope
```

 A variable's scope extends in *both directions* throughout its code block. This means that if we moved the initial declaration of x in this example to the bottom of the method, we'd get the same error. This is in contrast to C++ and is somewhat peculiar, given that it's not legal to refer to a variable or constant before it's declared.

Expression Statements

Expression statements are expressions that are also valid statements. An expression statement must either change state or call something that might change state. Changing state essentially means changing a variable. Following are the possible expression statements:

- Assignment expressions (including increment and decrement expressions)
- Method call expressions (both void and nonvoid)
- Object instantiation expressions

Here are some examples:

```
// Declare variables with declaration statements:
string s;
int x, y;
System.Text.StringBuilder sb;

// Expression statements
x = 1 + 2;                  // Assignment expression
x++;                        // Increment expression
y = Math.Max (x, 5);        // Assignment expression
Console.WriteLine (y);      // Method call expression
sb = new StringBuilder();   // Assignment expression
new StringBuilder();        // Object instantiation expression
```

When you call a constructor or a method that returns a value, you're not obliged to use the result. However, unless the constructor or method changes state, the statement is completely useless:

```
new StringBuilder();    // Legal, but useless
new string ('c', 3);    // Legal, but useless
x.Equals (y);           // Legal, but useless
```

Selection Statements

C# has the following mechanisms to conditionally control the flow of program execution:

- Selection statements (if, switch)
- Conditional operator (?:)
- Loop statements (while, do-while, for, foreach)

This section covers the simplest two constructs: the if statement and the switch statement.

The if statement

An if statement executes a statement if a bool expression is true:

```
if (5 < 2 * 3)
  Console.WriteLine ("true");        // true
```

The statement can be a code block:

```
if (5 < 2 * 3)
{
  Console.WriteLine ("true");
  Console.WriteLine ("Let's move on!");
}
```

The else clause

An if statement can optionally feature an else clause:

```
if (2 + 2 == 5)
  Console.WriteLine ("Does not compute");
else
  Console.WriteLine ("False");       // False
```

Within an else clause, you can nest another if statement:

```
if (2 + 2 == 5)
  Console.WriteLine ("Does not compute");
else
  if (2 + 2 == 4)
    Console.WriteLine ("Computes");    // Computes
```

Changing the flow of execution with braces

An else clause always applies to the immediately preceding if statement in the statement block:

```
if (true)
  if (false)
    Console.WriteLine();
```

```
    else
      Console.WriteLine ("executes");
```

This is semantically identical to the following:

```
if (true)
{
  if (false)
    Console.WriteLine();
  else
    Console.WriteLine ("executes");
}
```

We can change the execution flow by moving the braces:

```
if (true)
{
  if (false)
    Console.WriteLine();
}
else
  Console.WriteLine ("does not execute");
```

With braces, you explicitly state your intention. This can improve the readability of nested if statements—even when not required by the compiler. A notable exception is with the following pattern:

```
void TellMeWhatICanDo (int age)
{
  if (age >= 35)
    Console.WriteLine ("You can be president!");
  else if (age >= 21)
    Console.WriteLine ("You can drink!");
  else if (age >= 18)
    Console.WriteLine ("You can vote!");
  else
    Console.WriteLine ("You can wait!");
}
```

Here, we've arranged the if and else statements to mimic the "elseif" construct of other languages (and C#'s #elif preprocessor directive). Visual Studio's auto-formatting recognizes this pattern and preserves the indentation. Semantically, though, each if statement following an else statement is functionally nested within the else clause.

The switch statement

switch statements let you branch program execution based on a selection of possible values that a variable might have. switch statements can result in cleaner code than multiple if statements because switch statements require an expression to be evaluated only once:

```
void ShowCard (int cardNumber)
{
  switch (cardNumber)
```

```
    {
      case 13:
        Console.WriteLine ("King");
        break;
      case 12:
        Console.WriteLine ("Queen");
        break;
      case 11:
        Console.WriteLine ("Jack");
        break;
      case -1:                          // Joker is -1
        goto case 12;                   // In this game joker counts as queen
      default:                          // Executes for any other cardNumber
        Console.WriteLine (cardNumber);
        break;
    }
  }
```

This example demonstrates the most common scenario, which is switching on *constants*. When you specify a constant, you're restricted to the built-in integral types; the bool, char, and enum types; and the string type.

At the end of each case clause, you must specify explicitly where execution is to go next, with some kind of jump statement (unless your code ends in an infinite loop). Here are the options:

- break (jumps to the end of the switch statement)
- goto case *x* (jumps to another case clause)
- goto default (jumps to the default clause)
- Any other jump statement—namely, return, throw, continue, or goto *label*

When more than one value should execute the same code, you can list the common cases sequentially:

```
switch (cardNumber)
{
  case 13:
  case 12:
  case 11:
    Console.WriteLine ("Face card");
    break;
  default:
    Console.WriteLine ("Plain card");
    break;
}
```

This feature of a switch statement can be pivotal in terms of producing cleaner code than multiple if-else statements.

Switching on types

 Switching on a type is a special case of switching on a *pattern*. A number of other patterns have been introduced in recent versions of C#; see "Patterns" on page 222 for a full discussion.

You can also switch on *types* (from C# 7):

```
TellMeTheType (12);
TellMeTheType ("hello");
TellMeTheType (true);

void TellMeTheType (object x)    // object allows any type.
{
  switch (x)
  {
    case int i:
      Console.WriteLine ("It's an int!");
      Console.WriteLine ($"The square of {i} is {i * i}");
      break;
    case string s:
      Console.WriteLine ("It's a string");
      Console.WriteLine ($"The length of {s} is {s.Length}");
      break;
    default:
      Console.WriteLine ("I don't know what x is");
      break;
  }
}
```

(The object type allows for a variable of any type; we discuss this fully in "Inheritance" on page 115 and "The object Type" on page 125.)

Each *case* clause specifies a type upon which to match, and a variable upon which to assign the typed value if the match succeeds (the "pattern" variable). Unlike with constants, there's no restriction on what types you can use.

You can predicate a case with the when keyword:

```
switch (x)
{
  case bool b when b == true:     // Fires only when b is true
    Console.WriteLine ("True!");
    break;
  case bool b:
    Console.WriteLine ("False!");
    break;
}
```

The order of the case clauses can matter when switching on type (unlike when switching on constants). This example would give a different result if we reversed the two cases (in fact, it would not even compile, because the compiler would determine that the second case is unreachable). An exception to this rule is the default clause, which is always executed last, regardless of where it appears.

If you want to switch on a type, but are uninterested in its value, you can use a *discard* (_):

```
case DateTime _:
    Console.WriteLine ("It's a DateTime");
```

You can stack multiple case clauses. The Console.WriteLine in the following code will execute for any floating-point type greater than 1,000:

```
switch (x)
{
  case float f when f > 1000:
  case double d when d > 1000:
  case decimal m when m > 1000:
    Console.WriteLine ("We can refer to x here but not f or d or m");
    break;
}
```

In this example, the compiler lets us consume the pattern variables f, d, and m, *only* in the when clauses. When we call Console.WriteLine, its unknown which one of those three variables will be assigned, so the compiler puts all of them out of scope.

You can mix and match constants and patterns in the same switch statement. And you can also switch on the null value:

```
case null:
    Console.WriteLine ("Nothing here");
    break;
```

Switch expressions

From C# 8, you can use switch in the context of an *expression*. Assuming that cardNumber is of type int, the following illustrates its use:

```
string cardName = cardNumber switch
{
  13 => "King",
  12 => "Queen",
  11 => "Jack",
  _ => "Pip card"    // equivalent to 'default'
};
```

Notice that the switch keyword appears *after* the variable name and that the case clauses are expressions (terminated by commas) rather than statements. Switch expressions are more compact than their switch statement counterparts, and you can use them in LINQ queries (Chapter 8).

If you omit the default expression (_) and the switch fails to match, an exception is thrown.

You can also switch on multiple values (the *tuple* pattern):

```
int cardNumber = 12;
string suite = "spades";
```

```
string cardName = (cardNumber, suite) switch
{
  (13, "spades") => "King of spades",
  (13, "clubs") => "King of clubs",
  ...
};
```

Many more options are possible through the use of *patterns* (see "Patterns" on page 222).

Iteration Statements

C# enables a sequence of statements to execute repeatedly with the while, do-while, for, and foreach statements.

while and do-while loops

while loops repeatedly execute a body of code while a bool expression is true. The expression is tested *before* the body of the loop is executed. For example, the following writes 012:

```
int i = 0;
while (i < 3)
{
  Console.Write (i);
  i++;
}
```

do-while loops differ in functionality from while loops only in that they test the expression *after* the statement block has executed (ensuring that the block is always executed at least once). Here's the preceding example rewritten with a do-while loop:

```
int i = 0;
do
{
  Console.WriteLine (i);
  i++;
}
while (i < 3);
```

for loops

for loops are like while loops with special clauses for *initialization* and *iteration* of a loop variable. A for loop contains three clauses as follows:

```
for (initialization-clause; condition-clause; iteration-clause)
  statement-or-statement-block
```

Here's what each clause does:

Initialization clause
    Executed before the loop begins; used to initialize one or more *iteration* variables

Condition clause
    The bool expression that, while true, will execute the body

Iteration clause
    Executed *after* each iteration of the statement block; used typically to update the iteration variable

For example, the following prints the numbers 0 through 2:

```
for (int i = 0; i < 3; i++)
  Console.WriteLine (i);
```

The following prints the first 10 Fibonacci numbers (in which each number is the sum of the previous two):

```
for (int i = 0, prevFib = 1, curFib = 1; i < 10; i++)
{
  Console.WriteLine (prevFib);
  int newFib = prevFib + curFib;
  prevFib = curFib; curFib = newFib;
}
```

Any of the three parts of the for statement can be omitted. You can implement an infinite loop such as the following (though while(true) can be used, instead):

```
for (;;)
  Console.WriteLine ("interrupt me");
```

foreach loops

The foreach statement iterates over each element in an enumerable object. Most of the .NET types that represent a set or list of elements are enumerable. For example, both an array and a string are enumerable. Here is an example of enumerating over the characters in a string, from the first character through to the last:

```
foreach (char c in "beer")    // c is the iteration variable
  Console.WriteLine (c);
```

Here's the output:

```
b
e
e
r
```

We define enumerable objects in "Enumeration and Iterators" on page 189.

Jump Statements

The C# jump statements are break, continue, goto, return, and throw.

Jump statements obey the reliability rules of try statements (see "try Statements and Exceptions" on page 181). This means that:

- A jump out of a try block always executes the try's finally block before reaching the target of the jump.

- A jump cannot be made from the inside to the outside of a finally block (except via throw).

The break statement

The break statement ends the execution of the body of an iteration or switch statement:

```
int x = 0;
while (true)
{
  if (x++ > 5)
    break;      // break from the loop
}
// execution continues here after break
...
```

The continue statement

The continue statement forgoes the remaining statements in a loop and makes an early start on the next iteration. The following loop skips even numbers:

```
for (int i = 0; i < 10; i++)
{
  if ((i % 2) == 0)       // If i is even,
    continue;             // continue with next iteration

  Console.Write (i + " ");
}

OUTPUT: 1 3 5 7 9
```

The goto statement

The goto statement transfers execution to another label within a statement block. The form is as follows:

```
goto statement-label;
```

Or, when used within a switch statement:

```
goto case case-constant;     // (Only works with constants, not patterns)
```

A *label* is a placeholder in a code block that precedes a statement, denoted with a colon suffix. The following iterates the numbers 1 through 5, mimicking a for loop:

```
int i = 1;
startLoop:
if (i <= 5)
{
  Console.Write (i + " ");
  i++;
  goto startLoop;
}

OUTPUT: 1 2 3 4 5
```

The goto case *case-constant* transfers execution to another case in a switch block (see "The switch statement" on page 79).

The return statement

The return statement exits the method and must return an expression of the method's return type if the method is nonvoid:

```
decimal AsPercentage (decimal d)
{
  decimal p = d * 100m;
  return p;                 // Return to the calling method with value
}
```

A return statement can appear anywhere in a method (except in a finally block) and can be used more than once.

The throw statement

The throw statement throws an exception to indicate an error has occurred (see "try Statements and Exceptions" on page 181):

```
if (w == null)
    throw new ArgumentNullException (...);
```

Miscellaneous Statements

The using statement provides an elegant syntax for calling Dispose on objects that implement IDisposable, within a finally block (see "try Statements and Exceptions" on page 181 and "IDisposable, Dispose, and Close" on page 557).

C# overloads the using keyword to have independent meanings in different contexts. Specifically, the using *directive* is different from the using *statement*.

The lock statement is a shortcut for calling the Enter and Exit methods of the Monitor class (see Chapters 14 and 23).

Namespaces

A *namespace* is a domain for type names. Types are typically organized into hierarchical namespaces, making them easier to find and preventing conflicts. For example, the RSA type that handles public key encryption is defined within the following namespace:

```
System.Security.Cryptography
```

A namespace forms an integral part of a type's name. The following code calls RSA's Create method:

```
System.Security.Cryptography.RSA rsa =
    System.Security.Cryptography.RSA.Create();
```

 Namespaces are independent of assemblies, which are *.dll* files that serve as units of deployment (described in Chapter 17).

Namespaces also have no impact on member visibility—public, internal, private, and so on.

The namespace keyword defines a namespace for types within that block; for example:

```
namespace Outer.Middle.Inner
{
  class Class1 {}
  class Class2 {}
}
```

The dots in the namespace indicate a hierarchy of nested namespaces. The code that follows is semantically identical to the preceding example:

```
namespace Outer
{
  namespace Middle
  {
    namespace Inner
    {
      class Class1 {}
      class Class2 {}
    }
  }
}
```

You can refer to a type with its *fully qualified name*, which includes all namespaces from the outermost to the innermost. For example, we could refer to Class1 in the preceding example as Outer.Middle.Inner.Class1.

Types not defined in any namespace are said to reside in the *global namespace*. The global namespace also includes top-level namespaces, such as Outer in our example.

File-Scoped Namespaces (C# 10)

Often, you will want all the types in a file to be defined in one namespace:

```
namespace MyNamespace
{
  class Class1 {}
  class Class2 {}
}
```

From C# 10, you can accomplish this with a *file-scoped namespace*:

```
namespace MyNamespace;   // Applies to everything that follows in the file.

class Class1 {}          // inside MyNamespace
class Class2 {}          // inside MyNamespace
```

File-scoped namespaces reduce clutter and eliminate an unnecessary level of indentation.

The using Directive

The using directive *imports* a namespace, allowing you to refer to types without their fully qualified names. The following imports the previous example's Outer.Mid dle.Inner namespace:

```
using Outer.Middle.Inner;

Class1 c;     // Don't need fully qualified name
```

 It's legal (and often desirable) to define the same type name in different namespaces. However, you'd typically do so only if it was unlikely for a consumer to want to import both namespaces at once. A good example is the TextBox class, which is defined both in System.Windows.Controls (WPF) and System.Windows.Forms (Windows Forms).

A using directive can be nested within a namespace itself to limit the scope of the directive.

The global using Directive (C# 10)

From C# 10, if you prefix a using directive with the global keyword, the directive will apply to all files in the project or compilation unit:

```
global using System;
global using System.Collection.Generic;
```

This lets you centralize common imports and avoid repeating the same directives in every file.

global using directives must precede nonglobal directives and cannot appear inside namespace declarations. The global directive can be used with using static.

Implicit global usings

From .NET 6, project files allow for implicit global using directives. If the ImplicitUsings element is set to true in the project file (the default for new projects), the following namespaces are automatically imported:

```
System
System.Collections.Generic
System.IO
System.Linq
System.Net.Http
System.Threading
System.Threading.Tasks
```

Additional namespaces are imported, based on the project SDK (Web, Windows Forms, WPF, and so on).

using static

The using static directive imports a *type* rather than a namespace. All static members of the imported type can then be used without qualification. In the following example, we call the Console class's static WriteLine method without needing to refer to the type:

```
using static System.Console;

WriteLine ("Hello");
```

The using static directive imports all accessible static members of the type, including fields, properties, and nested types (Chapter 3). You can also apply this directive to enum types (Chapter 3), in which case their members are imported. So, if we import the following enum type

```
using static System.Windows.Visibility;
```

we can specify Hidden instead of Visibility.Hidden:

```
var textBox = new TextBox { Visibility = Hidden };    // XAML-style
```

Should an ambiguity arise between multiple static imports, the C# compiler is not smart enough to infer the correct type from the context and will generate an error.

Rules Within a Namespace

Name scoping

Names declared in outer namespaces can be used unqualified within inner namespaces. In this example, Class1 does not need qualification within Inner:

```
namespace Outer
{
  class Class1 {}

  namespace Inner
```

```
    {
      class Class2 : Class1  {}
    }
  }
```

If you want to refer to a type in a different branch of your namespace hierarchy, you can use a partially qualified name. In the following example, we base SalesReport on Common.ReportBase:

```
namespace MyTradingCompany
{
  namespace Common
  {
    class ReportBase {}
  }
  namespace ManagementReporting
  {
    class SalesReport : Common.ReportBase  {}
  }
}
```

Name hiding

If the same type name appears in both an inner and an outer namespace, the inner name wins. To refer to the type in the outer namespace, you must qualify its name:

```
namespace Outer
{
  class Foo { }

  namespace Inner
  {
    class Foo { }

    class Test
    {
      Foo f1;          // = Outer.Inner.Foo
      Outer.Foo f2;    // = Outer.Foo
    }
  }
}
```

 All type names are converted to fully qualified names at compile time. Intermediate Language (IL) code contains no unqualified or partially qualified names.

Repeated namespaces

You can repeat a namespace declaration, as long as the type names within the namespaces don't conflict:

```
namespace Outer.Middle.Inner
{
  class Class1 {}
}
```

```
namespace Outer.Middle.Inner
{
  class Class2 {}
}
```

We can even break the example into two source files such that we could compile each class into a different assembly.

Source file 1:

```
namespace Outer.Middle.Inner
{
  class Class1 {}
}
```

Source file 2:

```
namespace Outer.Middle.Inner
{
  class Class2 {}
}
```

Nested using directives

You can nest a using directive within a namespace. This allows you to scope the using directive within a namespace declaration. In the following example, Class1 is visible in one scope but not in another:

```
namespace N1
{
  class Class1 {}
}

namespace N2
{
  using N1;

  class Class2 : Class1 {}
}

namespace N2
{
  class Class3 : Class1 {}    // Compile-time error
}
```

Aliasing Types and Namespaces

Importing a namespace can result in type-name collision. Rather than importing the entire namespace, you can import just the specific types that you need, giving each type an alias:

```
using PropertyInfo2 = System.Reflection.PropertyInfo;
class Program { PropertyInfo2 p; }
```

An entire namespace can be aliased, as follows:

```
using R = System.Reflection;
class Program { R.PropertyInfo p; }
```

Advanced Namespace Features

Extern

Extern aliases allow your program to reference two types with the same fully qualified name (i.e., the namespace and type name are identical). This is an unusual scenario and can occur only when the two types come from different assemblies. Consider the following example.

Library 1, compiled to *Widgets1.dll*:

```
namespace Widgets
{
  public class Widget {}
}
```

Library 2, compiled to *Widgets2.dll*:

```
namespace Widgets
{
  public class Widget {}
}
```

Application, which references *Widgets1.dll* and *Widgets2.dll*:

```
using Widgets;

Widget w = new Widget();
```

The application cannot compile, because `Widget` is ambiguous. Extern aliases can resolve the ambiguity. The first step is to modify the application's *.csproj* file, assigning a unique alias to each reference:

```
<ItemGroup>
  <Reference Include="Widgets1">
    <Aliases>W1</Aliases>
  </Reference>
  <Reference Include="Widgets2">
    <Aliases>W2</Aliases>
  </Reference>
</ItemGroup>
```

The second step is to use the `extern alias` directive:

```
extern alias W1;
extern alias W2;

W1.Widgets.Widget w1 = new W1.Widgets.Widget();
W2.Widgets.Widget w2 = new W2.Widgets.Widget();
```

Namespace alias qualifiers

As we mentioned earlier, names in inner namespaces hide names in outer namespaces. However, sometimes even the use of a fully qualified type name does not resolve the conflict. Consider the following example:

```
namespace N
{
  class A
  {
    static void Main() => new A.B();     // Instantiate class B
    public class B {}                    // Nested type
  }
}

namespace A
{
  class B {}
}
```

The `Main` method could be instantiating either the nested class `B` or the class `B` within the namespace `A`. The compiler always gives higher precedence to identifiers in the current namespace, in this case the nested `B` class.

To resolve such conflicts, a namespace name can be qualified, relative to one of the following:

- The global namespace—the root of all namespaces (identified with the contextual keyword `global`)
- The set of extern aliases

The `::` token performs namespace alias qualification. In this example, we qualify using the global namespace (this is most commonly seen in autogenerated code to avoid name conflicts):

```
namespace N
{
  class A
  {
    static void Main()
    {
      System.Console.WriteLine (new A.B());
      System.Console.WriteLine (new global::A.B());
    }

    public class B {}
  }
}

namespace A
{
  class B {}
}
```

Here is an example of qualifying with an alias (adapted from the example in "Extern"):

```
extern alias W1;
extern alias W2;

W1::Widgets.Widget w1 = new W1::Widgets.Widget();
W2::Widgets.Widget w2 = new W2::Widgets.Widget();
```

3

Creating Types in C#

In this chapter, we delve into types and type members.

Classes

A *class* is the most common kind of reference type. The simplest possible class declaration is as follows:

```
class YourClassName
{
}
```

A more complex class optionally has the following:

Preceding the keyword class	*Attributes* and *class modifiers*. The non-nested class modifiers are `public`, `internal`, `abstract`, `sealed`, `static`, `unsafe`, and `partial`.
Following Your ClassName	*Generic type parameters* and *constraints*, a *base class*, and *interfaces*.
Within the braces	*Class members* (these are *methods, properties, indexers, events, fields, constructors, overloaded operators, nested types*, and a *finalizer*).

This chapter covers all of these constructs except attributes, operator functions, and the `unsafe` keyword, which are covered in Chapter 4. The following sections enumerate each of the class members.

Fields

A *field* is a variable that is a member of a class or struct; for example:

```
class Octopus
{
  string name;
  public int Age = 10;
}
```

Fields allow the following modifiers:

Static modifier	`static`
Access modifiers	`public internal private protected`
Inheritance modifier	`new`
Unsafe code modifier	`unsafe`
Read-only modifier	`readonly`
Threading modifier	`volatile`

There are two popular naming conventions for private fields: camel-cased (e.g., `firstName`) and camel-cased with an underscore (`_firstName`). The latter convention lets you instantly distinguish private fields from parameters and local variables.

The readonly modifier

The `readonly` modifier prevents a field from being modified after construction. A read-only field can be assigned only in its declaration or within the enclosing type's constructor.

Field initialization

Field initialization is optional. An uninitialized field has a default value (`0`, `'\0'`, `null`, `false`). Field initializers run before constructors:

```
public int Age = 10;
```

A field initializer can contain expressions and call methods:

```
static readonly string TempFolder = System.IO.Path.GetTempPath();
```

Declaring multiple fields together

For convenience, you can declare multiple fields of the same type in a comma-separated list. This is a convenient way for all the fields to share the same attributes and field modifiers:

```
static readonly int legs = 8,
                    eyes = 2;
```

Constants

A *constant* is evaluated statically at compile time, and the compiler literally substitutes its value whenever used (rather like a macro in C++). A constant can be `bool`, `char`, `string`, any of the built-in numeric types, or an enum type.

A constant is declared with the `const` keyword and must be initialized with a value. For example:

```
public class Test
{
  public const string Message = "Hello World";
}
```

A constant can serve a similar role to a `static readonly` field, but it is much more restrictive—both in the types you can use and in field initialization semantics. A constant also differs from a `static readonly` field in that the evaluation of the constant occurs at compile time; thus

```
public static double Circumference (double radius)
{
  return 2 * System.Math.PI * radius;
}
```

is compiled to:

```
public static double Circumference (double radius)
{
  return 6.2831853071795862 * radius;
}
```

It makes sense for `PI` to be a constant because its value is predetermined at compile time. In contrast, a `static readonly` field's value can potentially differ each time the program is run:

```
static readonly DateTime StartupTime = DateTime.Now;
```

A `static readonly` field is also advantageous when exposing to other assemblies a value that might change in a later version. For instance, suppose that assembly X exposes a constant as follows:

```
public const decimal ProgramVersion = 2.3;
```

If assembly Y references X and uses this constant, the value 2.3 will be baked into assembly Y when compiled. This means that if X is later recompiled with the constant set to 2.4, Y will still use the old value of 2.3 *until* Y *is recompiled*. A `static readonly` field avoids this problem.

Another way of looking at this is that any value that might change in the future is not constant by definition; thus, it should not be represented as one.

Constants can also be declared local to a method:

```
void Test()
{
  const double twoPI = 2 * System.Math.PI;
  ...
}
```

Nonlocal constants allow the following modifiers:

Access modifiers   `public internal private protected`
Inheritance modifier   `new`

Methods

A method performs an action in a series of statements. A method can receive *input* data from the caller by specifying *parameters*, and *output* data back to the caller by specifying a *return type*. A method can specify a `void` return type, indicating that it doesn't return any value to its caller. A method can also output data back to the caller via `ref`/`out` parameters.

A method's *signature* must be unique within the type. A method's signature comprises its name and parameter types in order (but not the parameter *names*, nor the return type).

Methods allow the following modifiers:

Static modifier   `static`
Access modifiers   `public internal private protected`
Inheritance modifiers   `new virtual abstract override sealed`
Partial method modifier   `partial`
Unmanaged code modifiers   `unsafe extern`
Asynchronous code modifier   `async`

Expression-bodied methods

A method that comprises a single expression, such as

```
int Foo (int x) { return x * 2; }
```

can be written more tersely as an *expression-bodied method*. A fat arrow replaces the braces and `return` keyword:

```
int Foo (int x) => x * 2;
```

Expression-bodied functions can also have a void return type:

```
void Foo (int x) => Console.WriteLine (x);
```

Local methods

You can define a method within another method:

```
void WriteCubes()
{
  Console.WriteLine (Cube (3));
  Console.WriteLine (Cube (4));
  Console.WriteLine (Cube (5));
```

```
    int Cube (int value) => value * value * value;
}
```

The local method (Cube, in this case) is visible only to the enclosing method (Write Cubes). This simplifies the containing type and instantly signals to anyone looking at the code that Cube is used nowhere else. Another benefit of local methods is that they can access the local variables and parameters of the enclosing method. This has a number of consequences, which we describe in detail in "Capturing Outer Variables" on page 176.

Local methods can appear within other function kinds, such as property accessors, constructors, and so on. You can even put local methods inside other local methods and inside lambda expressions that use a statement block (Chapter 4). Local methods can be iterators (Chapter 4) or asynchronous (Chapter 14).

Static local methods

Adding the static modifier to a local method (from C# 8) prevents it from seeing the local variables and parameters of the enclosing method. This helps to reduce coupling and prevents the local method from accidentally referring to variables in the containing method.

Local methods and top-level statements

Any methods that you declare in top-level statements are treated as local methods. This means that (unless marked as static) they can access the variables in the top-level statements:

```
int x = 3;
Foo();

void Foo() => Console.WriteLine (x);
```

Overloading methods

 Local methods cannot be overloaded. This means that methods declared in top-level statements (which are treated as local methods) cannot be overloaded.

A type can *overload* methods (define multiple methods with the same name) as long as the signatures are different. For example, the following methods can all coexist in the same type:

```
void Foo (int x) {...}
void Foo (double x) {...}
void Foo (int x, float y) {...}
void Foo (float x, int y) {...}
```

However, the following pairs of methods cannot coexist in the same type, because the return type and the params modifier are not part of a method's signature:

```
void  Foo (int x) {...}
float Foo (int x) {...}             // Compile-time error

void  Goo (int[] x) {...}
void  Goo (params int[] x) {...} // Compile-time error
```

Whether a parameter is pass-by-value or pass-by-reference is also part of the signature. For example, Foo(int) can coexist with either Foo(ref int) or Foo(out int). However, Foo(ref int) and Foo(out int) cannot coexist:

```
void Foo (int x) {...}
void Foo (ref int x) {...}    // OK so far
void Foo (out int x) {...}    // Compile-time error
```

Instance Constructors

Constructors run initialization code on a class or struct. A constructor is defined like a method, except that the method name and return type are reduced to the name of the enclosing type:

```
Panda p = new Panda ("Petey");   // Call constructor

public class Panda
{
  string name;               // Define field
  public Panda (string n)    // Define constructor
  {
    name = n;                // Initialization code (set up field)
  }
}
```

Instance constructors allow the following modifiers:

Access modifiers	public internal private protected
Unmanaged code modifiers	unsafe extern

Single-statement constructors can also be written as expression-bodied members:

```
public Panda (string n) => name = n;
```

Overloading constructors

A class or struct may overload constructors. To avoid code duplication, one constructor can call another, using the this keyword:

```
using System;

public class Wine
{
  public decimal Price;
  public int Year;
  public Wine (decimal price) { Price = price; }
```

```
    public Wine (decimal price, int year) : this (price) { Year = year; }
}
```

When one constructor calls another, the *called constructor* executes first.

You can pass an *expression* into another constructor, as follows:

```
    public Wine (decimal price, DateTime year) : this (price, year.Year) { }
```

The expression itself cannot make use of the this reference, for example, to call an instance method. (This is enforced because the object has not been initialized by the constructor at this stage, so any methods that you call on it are likely to fail.) It can, however, call static methods.

Implicit parameterless constructors

For classes, the C# compiler automatically generates a parameterless public constructor if and only if you do not define any constructors. However, as soon as you define at least one constructor, the parameterless constructor is no longer automatically generated.

Constructor and field initialization order

We previously saw that fields can be initialized with default values in their declaration:

```
    class Player
    {
      int shields = 50;    // Initialized first
      int health = 100;    // Initialized second
    }
```

Field initializations occur *before* the constructor is executed, and in the declaration order of the fields.

Nonpublic constructors

Constructors do not need to be public. A common reason to have a nonpublic constructor is to control instance creation via a static method call. The static method could be used to return an object from a pool rather than creating a new object, or to return various subclasses based on input arguments:

```
    public class Class1
    {
      Class1() {}                            // Private constructor
      public static Class1 Create (...)
      {
        // Perform custom logic here to return an instance of Class1
        ...
      }
    }
```

Deconstructors

A deconstructor (also called a *deconstructing method*) acts as an approximate opposite to a constructor: whereas a constructor typically takes a set of values (as parameters) and assigns them to fields, a deconstructor does the reverse and assigns fields back to a set of variables.

A deconstruction method must be called Deconstruct and have one or more out parameters, such as in the following class:

```
class Rectangle
{
  public readonly float Width, Height;

  public Rectangle (float width, float height)
  {
    Width = width;
    Height = height;
  }

  public void Deconstruct (out float width, out float height)
  {
    width = Width;
    height = Height;
  }
}
```

The following special syntax calls the deconstructor:

```
var rect = new Rectangle (3, 4);
(float width, float height) = rect;          // Deconstruction
Console.WriteLine (width + " " + height);    // 3 4
```

The second line is the deconstructing call. It creates two local variables and then calls the Deconstruct method. Our deconstructing call is equivalent to the following:

```
float width, height;
rect.Deconstruct (out width, out height);
```

Or:

```
rect.Deconstruct (out var width, out var height);
```

Deconstructing calls allow implicit typing, so we could shorten our call to this:

```
(var width, var height) = rect;
```

Or simply this:

```
var (width, height) = rect;
```

You can use C#'s discard symbol (_) if you're uninterested in one or more variables:

```
var (_, height) = rect;
```

This better indicates your intention than declaring a variable that you never use.

If the variables into which you're deconstructing are already defined, omit the types altogether:

```
float width, height;
(width, height) = rect;
```

This is called a *deconstructing assignment*. You can use a deconstructing assignment to simplify your class's constructor:

```
public Rectangle (float width, float height) =>
  (Width, Height) = (width, height);
```

You can offer the caller a range of deconstruction options by overloading the Deconstruct method.

The Deconstruct method can be an extension method (see "Extension Methods" on page 202). This is a useful trick if you want to deconstruct types that you did not author.

From C# 10, you can mix and match existing and new variables when deconstructing:

```
double x1 = 0;
(x1, double y2) = rect;
```

Object Initializers

To simplify object initialization, any accessible fields or properties of an object can be set via an *object initializer* directly after construction. For example, consider the following class:

```
public class Bunny
{
  public string Name;
  public bool LikesCarrots;
  public bool LikesHumans;

  public Bunny () {}
  public Bunny (string n) { Name = n; }
}
```

Using object initializers, you can instantiate Bunny objects as follows:

```
// Note parameterless constructors can omit empty parentheses
Bunny b1 = new Bunny { Name="Bo", LikesCarrots=true, LikesHumans=false };
Bunny b2 = new Bunny ("Bo")     { LikesCarrots=true, LikesHumans=false };
```

The code to construct b1 and b2 is precisely equivalent to the following:

```
Bunny temp1 = new Bunny();     // temp1 is a compiler-generated name
temp1.Name = "Bo";
temp1.LikesCarrots = true;
temp1.LikesHumans = false;
Bunny b1 = temp1;

Bunny temp2 = new Bunny ("Bo");
temp2.LikesCarrots = true;
temp2.LikesHumans = false;
Bunny b2 = temp2;
```

The temporary variables are to ensure that if an exception is thrown during initialization, you can't end up with a half-initialized object.

Object Initializers Versus Optional Parameters

Instead of using object initializers, we could make Bunny's constructor accept optional parameters:

```
public Bunny (string name,
              bool likesCarrots = false,
              bool likesHumans = false)
{
  Name = name;
  LikesCarrots = likesCarrots;
  LikesHumans = likesHumans;
}
```

This would allow us to construct a Bunny as follows:

```
Bunny b1 = new Bunny (name: "Bo",
                      likesCarrots: true);
```

Historically, this approach could be advantageous in that it allowed us to make Bunny's fields (or *properties*, which we'll explain shortly) read-only. Making fields or properties read-only is good practice when there's no valid reason for them to change throughout the life of the object. However, as we'll see soon in our discussion on properties, the init modifier that was introduced in C# 9 lets us achieve this goal with object initializers.

Optional parameters have two drawbacks. The first is that while their use in constructors allows for read-only types, they don't (easily) allow for *nondestructive mutation*. (We'll cover nondestructive mutation—and the solution to this problem—in "Records" on page 211.)

The second drawback of optional parameters is that when used in public libraries, they hinder backward compatibility. This is because the act of adding an optional parameter at a later date breaks the assembly's *binary compatibility* with existing consumers. (This is particularly important when a library is published on NuGet: the problem becomes intractable when a consumer references packages A and B, if A and B each depend on incompatible versions of L.)

The difficulty is that each optional parameter value is baked into the *calling site*. In other words, C# translates our constructor call into this:

```
Bunny b1 = new Bunny ("Bo", true, false);
```

This is problematic if we instantiate the Bunny class from another assembly and later modify Bunny by adding another optional parameter—such as likesCats. Unless the referencing assembly is also recompiled, it will continue to call the (now nonexistent) constructor with three parameters and fail at runtime. (A subtler problem is that if we changed the value of one of the optional parameters, callers in other assemblies would continue to use the old optional value until they were recompiled.)

The this Reference

The this reference refers to the instance itself. In the following example, the Marry method uses this to set the partner's mate field:

```
public class Panda
{
  public Panda Mate;

  public void Marry (Panda partner)
  {
    Mate = partner;
    partner.Mate = this;
  }
}
```

The this reference also disambiguates a local variable or parameter from a field; for example:

```
public class Test
{
  string name;
  public Test (string name) { this.name = name; }
}
```

The this reference is valid only within nonstatic members of a class or struct.

Properties

Properties look like fields from the outside, but internally they contain logic, like methods do. For example, you can't tell by looking at the following code whether CurrentPrice is a field or a property:

```
Stock msft = new Stock();
msft.CurrentPrice = 30;
msft.CurrentPrice -= 3;
Console.WriteLine (msft.CurrentPrice);
```

A property is declared like a field but with a get/set block added. Here's how to implement CurrentPrice as a property:

```
public class Stock
{
  decimal currentPrice;              // The private "backing" field

  public decimal CurrentPrice        // The public property
  {
    get { return currentPrice; }
    set { currentPrice = value; }
  }
}
```

get and set denote property *accessors*. The get accessor runs when the property
is read. It must return a value of the property's type. The set accessor runs when
the property is assigned. It has an implicit parameter named value of the property's
type that you typically assign to a private field (in this case, currentPrice).

Although properties are accessed in the same way as fields, they differ in that they
give the implementer complete control over getting and setting its value. This control enables the implementer to choose whatever internal representation is needed
without exposing the internal details to the user of the property. In this example, the
set method could throw an exception if value was outside a valid range of values.

 Throughout this book, we use public fields extensively to keep
the examples free of distraction. In a real application, you
would typically favor public properties over public fields in
order to promote encapsulation.

Properties allow the following modifiers:

Static modifier	static
Access modifiers	public internal private protected
Inheritance modifiers	new virtual abstract override sealed
Unmanaged code modifiers	unsafe extern

Read-only and calculated properties

A property is read-only if it specifies only a get accessor, and it is write-only if it
specifies only a set accessor. Write-only properties are rarely used.

A property typically has a dedicated backing field to store the underlying data.
However, a property can also be computed from other data:

```
decimal currentPrice, sharesOwned;

public decimal Worth
{
  get { return currentPrice * sharesOwned; }
}
```

Expression-bodied properties

You can declare a read-only property, such as the one in the preceding example, more tersely as an *expression-bodied property*. A fat arrow replaces all the braces and the get and return keywords:

```
public decimal Worth => currentPrice * sharesOwned;
```

With a little extra syntax, set accessors can also be expression-bodied:

```
public decimal Worth
{
  get => currentPrice * sharesOwned;
  set => sharesOwned = value / currentPrice;
}
```

Automatic properties

The most common implementation for a property is a getter and/or setter that simply reads and writes to a private field of the same type as the property. An *automatic property* declaration instructs the compiler to provide this implementation. We can improve the first example in this section by declaring CurrentPrice as an automatic property:

```
public class Stock
{
  ...
  public decimal CurrentPrice { get; set; }
}
```

The compiler automatically generates a private backing field of a compiler-generated name that cannot be referred to. The set accessor can be marked private or protected if you want to expose the property as read-only to other types. Automatic properties were introduced in C# 3.0.

Property initializers

You can add a *property initializer* to automatic properties, just as with fields:

```
public decimal CurrentPrice { get; set; } = 123;
```

This gives CurrentPrice an initial value of 123. Properties with an initializer can be read-only:

```
public int Maximum { get; } = 999;
```

Just as with read-only fields, read-only automatic properties can also be assigned in the type's constructor. This is useful in creating *immutable* (read-only) types.

get and set accessibility

The get and set accessors can have different access levels. The typical use case for this is to have a public property with an internal or private access modifier on the setter:

```
public class Foo
{
  private decimal x;
  public decimal X
  {
    get          { return x;  }
    private set { x = Math.Round (value, 2); }
  }
}
```

Notice that you declare the property itself with the more permissive access level (public, in this case) and add the modifier to the accessor you want to be *less* accessible.

Init-only setters

From C# 9, you can declare a property accessor with init instead of set:

```
public class Note
{
  public int Pitch     { get; init; } = 20;    // "Init-only" property
  public int Duration { get; init; } = 100;   // "Init-only" property
}
```

These *init-only* properties act like read-only properties, except that they can also be set via an object initializer:

```
var note = new Note { Pitch = 50 };
```

After that, the property cannot be altered:

```
note.Pitch = 200;  // Error - init-only setter!
```

Init-only properties cannot even be set from inside their class, except via their property initializer, the constructor, or another init-only accessor.

The alternative to init-only properties is to have read-only properties that you populate via a constructor:

```
public class Note
{
  public int Pitch     { get; }
  public int Duration { get; }

  public Note (int pitch = 20, int duration = 100)
  {
    Pitch = pitch; Duration = duration;
  }
}
```

Should the class be part of a public library, this approach makes versioning difficult, in that adding an optional parameter to the constructor at a later date breaks binary compatibility with consumers (whereas adding a new init-only property breaks nothing).

Init-only properties have another significant advantage, which is that they allow for nondestructive mutation when used in conjunction with records (see "Records" on page 211).

As with ordinary set accessors, init-only accessors can provide an implementation:

```
public class Note
{
  readonly int _pitch;
  public int Pitch { get => _pitch; init => _pitch = value; }
  ...
```

Notice that the _pitch field is read-only: init-only setters are permitted to modify readonly fields in their own class. (Without this feature, _pitch would need to be writable, and the class would fail at being internally immutable.)

Changing a property's accessor from init to set (or vice versa) is a *binary breaking change*: anyone that references your assembly will need to recompile their assembly.

This should not be an issue when creating wholly immutable types, in that your type will never require properties with a (writable) set accessor.

CLR property implementation

C# property accessors internally compile to methods called get_*XXX* and set_*XXX*:

```
public decimal get_CurrentPrice {...}
public void set_CurrentPrice (decimal value) {...}
```

An init accessor is processed like a set accessor, but with an extra flag encoded into the set accessor's "modreq" metadata (see "Init-only properties" on page 794).

Simple nonvirtual property accessors are *inlined* by the Just-in-Time (JIT) compiler, eliminating any performance difference between accessing a property and a field. Inlining is an optimization in which a method call is replaced with the body of that method.

Indexers

Indexers provide a natural syntax for accessing elements in a class or struct that encapsulate a list or dictionary of values. Indexers are similar to properties but are accessed via an index argument rather than a property name. The string class has an indexer that lets you access each of its char values via an int index:

```
string s = "hello";
Console.WriteLine (s[0]); // 'h'
Console.WriteLine (s[3]); // 'l'
```

The syntax for using indexers is like that for using arrays, except that the index argument(s) can be of any type(s).

Indexers have the same modifiers as properties (see "Properties" on page 105) and can be called null-conditionally by inserting a question mark before the square bracket (see "Null Operators" on page 74):

```
string s = null;
Console.WriteLine (s?[0]);  // Writes nothing; no error.
```

Implementing an indexer

To write an indexer, define a property called this, specifying the arguments in square brackets:

```
class Sentence
{
  string[] words = "The quick brown fox".Split();

  public string this [int wordNum]      // indexer
  {
    get { return words [wordNum];  }
    set { words [wordNum] = value; }
  }
}
```

Here's how we could use this indexer:

```
Sentence s = new Sentence();
Console.WriteLine (s[3]);      // fox
s[3] = "kangaroo";
Console.WriteLine (s[3]);      // kangaroo
```

A type can declare multiple indexers, each with parameters of different types. An indexer can also take more than one parameter:

```
public string this [int arg1, string arg2]
{
  get { ... }  set { ... }
}
```

If you omit the set accessor, an indexer becomes read-only, and you can use expression-bodied syntax to shorten its definition:

```
public string this [int wordNum] => words [wordNum];
```

CLR indexer implementation

Indexers internally compile to methods called get_Item and set_Item, as follows:

```
public string get_Item (int wordNum) {...}
public void set_Item (int wordNum, string value) {...}
```

Using indices and ranges with indexers

You can support indices and ranges (see "Indices and ranges" on page 13) in your own classes by defining an indexer with a parameter type of Index or Range.

We could extend our previous example by adding the following indexers to the
Sentence class:

```
public string this [Index index] => words [index];
public string[] this [Range range] => words [range];
```

This then enables the following:

```
Sentence s = new Sentence();
Console.WriteLine (s [^1]);           // fox
string[] firstTwoWords = s [..2];     // (The, quick)
```

Static Constructors

A static constructor executes once per *type* rather than once per *instance*. A type can
define only one static constructor, and it must be parameterless and have the same
name as the type:

```
class Test
{
   static Test() { Console.WriteLine ("Type Initialized"); }
}
```

The runtime automatically invokes a static constructor just prior to the type being
used. Two things trigger this:

- Instantiating the type
- Accessing a static member in the type

The only modifiers allowed by static constructors are unsafe and extern.

If a static constructor throws an unhandled exception (Chapter 4), that type becomes *unusable* for the life of the
application.

From C# 9, you can also define *module initializers*, which
execute once per assembly (when the assembly is first loaded).
To define a module initializer, write a static void method
and then apply the [ModuleInitializer] attribute to that
method:

```
[System.Runtime.CompilerServices.ModuleInitializer]
internal static void InitAssembly()
{
   ...
}
```

Static constructors and field initialization order

Static field initializers run just *before* the static constructor is called. If a type has
no static constructor, static field initializers will execute just prior to the type being
used—or *anytime earlier* at the whim of the runtime.

Static field initializers run in the order in which the fields are declared. The following example illustrates this. X is initialized to 0, and Y is initialized to 3:

```
class Foo
{
  public static int X = Y;    // 0
  public static int Y = 3;    // 3
}
```

If we swap the two field initializers around, both fields are initialized to 3. The next example prints 0 followed by 3 because the field initializer that instantiates a Foo executes before X is initialized to 3:

```
Console.WriteLine (Foo.X);    // 3

class Foo
{
  public static Foo Instance = new Foo();
  public static int X = 3;

  Foo() => Console.WriteLine (X);    // 0
}
```

If we swap the two lines in boldface, the example prints 3 followed by 3.

Static Classes

A class marked static cannot be instantiated or subclassed, and must be composed solely of static members. The System.Console and System.Math classes are good examples of static classes.

Finalizers

Finalizers are class-only methods that execute before the garbage collector reclaims the memory for an unreferenced object. The syntax for a finalizer is the name of the class prefixed with the ~ symbol:

```
class Class1
{
  ~Class1()
  {
    ...
  }
}
```

This is actually C# syntax for overriding Object's Finalize method, and the compiler expands it into the following method declaration:

```
protected override void Finalize()
{
  ...
  base.Finalize();
}
```

We discuss garbage collection and finalizers fully in Chapter 12.

Finalizers allow the following modifier:

Unmanaged code modifier   `unsafe`

You can write single-statement finalizers using expression-bodied syntax:

```
~Class1() => Console.WriteLine ("Finalizing");
```

Partial Types and Methods

Partial types allow a type definition to be split—typically across multiple files. A common scenario is for a partial class to be autogenerated from some other source (such as a Visual Studio template or designer), and for that class to be augmented with additional hand-authored methods:

```
// PaymentFormGen.cs - auto-generated
partial class PaymentForm { ... }

// PaymentForm.cs - hand-authored
partial class PaymentForm { ... }
```

Each participant must have the `partial` declaration; the following is illegal:

```
partial class PaymentForm {}
class PaymentForm {}
```

Participants cannot have conflicting members. A constructor with the same parameters, for instance, cannot be repeated. Partial types are resolved entirely by the compiler, which means that each participant must be available at compile time and must reside in the same assembly.

You can specify a base class on one or more partial class declarations, as long as the base class, if specified, is the same. In addition, each participant can independently specify interfaces to implement. We cover base classes and interfaces in "Inheritance" on page 115 and "Interfaces" on page 134.

The compiler makes no guarantees with regard to field initialization order between partial type declarations.

Partial methods

A partial type can contain *partial methods*. These let an autogenerated partial type provide customizable hooks for manual authoring; for example:

```
partial class PaymentForm     // In auto-generated file
{
  ...
  partial void ValidatePayment (decimal amount);
}

partial class PaymentForm     // In hand-authored file
{
  ...
```

```
  partial void ValidatePayment (decimal amount)
  {
    if (amount > 100)
      ...
  }
}
```

A partial method consists of two parts: a *definition* and an *implementation*. The definition is typically written by a code generator, and the implementation is typically manually authored. If an implementation is not provided, the definition of the partial method is compiled away (as is the code that calls it). This allows autogenerated code to be liberal in providing hooks without having to worry about bloat. Partial methods must be void and are implicitly private. They cannot include out parameters.

Extended partial methods

Extended partial methods (from C# 9) are designed for the reverse code generation scenario, where a programmer defines hooks that a code generator implements. An example of where this might occur is with *source generators*, a Roslyn feature that lets you feed the compiler an assembly that automatically generates portions of your code.

A partial method declaration is *extended* if it begins with an accessibility modifier:

```
public partial class Test
{
  public partial void M1();    // Extended partial method
  private partial void M2();   // Extended partial method
}
```

The presence of the accessibility modifier doesn't just affect accessibility: it tells the compiler to treat the declaration differently.

Extended partial methods *must* have implementations; they do not melt away if unimplemented. In this example, both M1 and M2 must have implementations because they each specify accessibility modifiers (public and private).

Because they cannot melt away, extended partial methods can return any type and can include out parameters:

```
public partial class Test
{
  public partial bool IsValid (string identifier);
  internal partial bool TryParse (string number, out int result);
}
```

The nameof operator

The nameof operator returns the name of any symbol (type, member, variable, and so on) as a string:

```
int count = 123;
string name = nameof (count);        // name is "count"
```

Its advantage over simply specifying a string is that of static type checking. Tools such as Visual Studio can understand the symbol reference, so if you rename the symbol in question, all of its references will be renamed, too.

To specify the name of a type member such as a field or property, include the type as well. This works with both static and instance members:

```
string name = nameof (StringBuilder.Length);
```

This evaluates to Length. To return StringBuilder.Length, you would do this:

```
nameof (StringBuilder) + "." + nameof (StringBuilder.Length);
```

Inheritance

A class can *inherit* from another class to extend or customize the original class. Inheriting from a class lets you reuse the functionality in that class instead of building it from scratch. A class can inherit from only a single class but can itself be inherited by many classes, thus forming a class hierarchy. In this example, we begin by defining a class called Asset:

```
public class Asset
{
  public string Name;
}
```

Next, we define classes called Stock and House, which will inherit from Asset. Stock and House get everything an Asset has, plus any additional members that they define:

```
public class Stock : Asset   // inherits from Asset
{
  public long SharesOwned;
}

public class House : Asset   // inherits from Asset
{
  public decimal Mortgage;
}
```

Here's how we can use these classes:

```
Stock msft = new Stock { Name="MSFT",
                         SharesOwned=1000 };

Console.WriteLine (msft.Name);        // MSFT
Console.WriteLine (msft.SharesOwned); // 1000

House mansion = new House { Name="Mansion",
                            Mortgage=250000 };
```

```
Console.WriteLine (mansion.Name);      // Mansion
Console.WriteLine (mansion.Mortgage);  // 250000
```

The *derived classes*, Stock and House, inherit the Name field from the *base class*, Asset.

A derived class is also called a *subclass*.

A base class is also called a *superclass*.

Polymorphism

References are *polymorphic*. This means a variable of type *x* can refer to an object that subclasses *x*. For instance, consider the following method:

```
public static void Display (Asset asset)
{
    System.Console.WriteLine (asset.Name);
}
```

This method can display both a Stock and a House because they are both Assets:

```
Stock msft     = new Stock ... ;
House mansion = new House ... ;

Display (msft);
Display (mansion);
```

Polymorphism works on the basis that subclasses (Stock and House) have all the features of their base class (Asset). The converse, however, is not true. If Display was modified to accept a House, you could not pass in an Asset:

```
Display (new Asset());      // Compile-time error

public static void Display (House house)        // Will not accept Asset
{
    System.Console.WriteLine (house.Mortgage);
}
```

Casting and Reference Conversions

An object reference can be:

- Implicitly *upcast* to a base class reference
- Explicitly *downcast* to a subclass reference

Upcasting and downcasting between compatible reference types performs *reference conversions*: a new reference is (logically) created that points to the *same* object. An upcast always succeeds; a downcast succeeds only if the object is suitably typed.

Upcasting

An upcast operation creates a base class reference from a subclass reference:

```
Stock msft = new Stock();
Asset a = msft;              // Upcast
```

After the upcast, variable a still references the same Stock object as variable msft. The object being referenced is not itself altered or converted:

```
Console.WriteLine (a == msft);       // True
```

Although a and msft refer to the identical object, a has a more restrictive view on that object:

```
Console.WriteLine (a.Name);          // OK
Console.WriteLine (a.SharesOwned);   // Compile-time error
```

The last line generates a compile-time error because the variable a is of type Asset, even though it refers to an object of type Stock. To get to its SharesOwned field, you must *downcast* the Asset to a Stock.

Downcasting

A downcast operation creates a subclass reference from a base class reference:

```
Stock msft = new Stock();
Asset a = msft;                           // Upcast
Stock s = (Stock)a;                       // Downcast
Console.WriteLine (s.SharesOwned);        // <No error>
Console.WriteLine (s == a);               // True
Console.WriteLine (s == msft);            // True
```

As with an upcast, only references are affected—not the underlying object. A downcast requires an explicit cast because it can potentially fail at runtime:

```
House h = new House();
Asset a = h;              // Upcast always succeeds
Stock s = (Stock)a;       // Downcast fails: a is not a Stock
```

If a downcast fails, an InvalidCastException is thrown. This is an example of *runtime type checking* (we elaborate on this concept in "Static and Runtime Type Checking" on page 127).

The as operator

The as operator performs a downcast that evaluates to null (rather than throwing an exception) if the downcast fails:

```
Asset a = new Asset();
Stock s = a as Stock;        // s is null; no exception thrown
```

This is useful when you're going to subsequently test whether the result is null:

```
if (s != null) Console.WriteLine (s.SharesOwned);
```

Without such a test, a cast is advantageous, because if it fails, a more helpful exception is thrown. We can illustrate by comparing the following two lines of code:

```
long shares = ((Stock)a).SharesOwned;    // Approach #1
long shares = (a as Stock).SharesOwned;  // Approach #2
```

If a is not a Stock, the first line throws an InvalidCastException, which is an accurate description of what went wrong. The second line throws a NullReferenceException, which is ambiguous. Was a not a Stock, or was a null?

Another way of looking at it is that with the cast operator, you're saying to the compiler, "I'm *certain* of a value's type; if I'm wrong, there's a bug in my code, so throw an exception!" Whereas with the as operator, you're uncertain of its type and want to branch according to the outcome at runtime.

The as operator cannot perform *custom conversions* (see "Operator Overloading" on page 239), and it cannot do numeric conversions:

```
long x = 3 as long;    // Compile-time error
```

The as and cast operators will also perform upcasts, although this is not terribly useful because an implicit conversion will do the job.

The is operator

The is operator tests whether a variable matches a *pattern*. C# supports several kinds of patterns, the most important being a *type pattern*, where a type name follows the is keyword.

In this context, the is operator tests whether a reference conversion would succeed—in other words, whether an object derives from a specified class (or implements an interface). It is often used to test before downcasting:

```
if (a is Stock)
    Console.WriteLine (((Stock)a).SharesOwned);
```

The is operator also evaluates to true if an *unboxing conversion* would succeed (see "The object Type" on page 125). However, it does not consider custom or numeric conversions.

The is operator works with many other patterns introduced in recent versions of C#. For a full discussion, see "Patterns" on page 222.

Introducing a pattern variable

You can introduce a variable while using the is operator:

```
if (a is Stock s)
    Console.WriteLine (s.SharesOwned);
```

This is equivalent to the following:

```
Stock s;
if (a is Stock)
{
  s = (Stock) a;
  Console.WriteLine (s.SharesOwned);
}
```

The variable that you introduce is available for "immediate" consumption, so the following is legal:

```
if (a is Stock s && s.SharesOwned > 100000)
  Console.WriteLine ("Wealthy");
```

And it remains in scope outside the is expression, allowing this:

```
if (a is Stock s && s.SharesOwned > 100000)
  Console.WriteLine ("Wealthy");
Else
  s = new Stock();   // s is in scope

Console.WriteLine (s.SharesOwned);  // Still in scope
```

Virtual Function Members

A function marked as virtual can be *overridden* by subclasses wanting to provide a specialized implementation. Methods, properties, indexers, and events can all be declared virtual:

```
public class Asset
{
  public string Name;
  public virtual decimal Liability => 0;   // Expression-bodied property
}
```

(Liability => 0 is a shortcut for { get { return 0; } }. For more details on this syntax, see "Expression-bodied properties" on page 107.)

A subclass overrides a virtual method by applying the override modifier:

```
public class Stock : Asset
{
  public long SharesOwned;
}

public class House : Asset
{
  public decimal Mortgage;
  public override decimal Liability => Mortgage;
}
```

By default, the Liability of an Asset is 0. A Stock does not need to specialize this behavior. However, the House specializes the Liability property to return the value of the Mortgage:

```
House mansion = new House { Name="McMansion", Mortgage=250000 };
Asset a = mansion;
Console.WriteLine (mansion.Liability);  // 250000
Console.WriteLine (a.Liability);        // 250000
```

The signatures, return types, and accessibility of the virtual and overridden methods must be identical. An overridden method can call its base class implementation via the base keyword (we cover this in "The base Keyword" on page 122).

 Calling virtual methods from a constructor is potentially dangerous because authors of subclasses are unlikely to know, when overriding the method, that they are working with a partially initialized object. In other words, the overriding method might end up accessing methods or properties that rely on fields not yet initialized by the constructor.

Covariant return types

From C# 9, you can override a method (or property get accessor) such that it returns a *more derived* (subclassed) type. For example:

```
public class Asset
{
  public string Name;
  public virtual Asset Clone() => new Asset { Name = Name };
}

public class House : Asset
{
  public decimal Mortgage;
  public override House Clone() => new House
                            { Name = Name, Mortgage = Mortgage };
}
```

This is permitted because it does not break the contract that Clone must return an Asset: it returns a House, which *is* an Asset (and more).

Prior to C# 9, you had to override methods with the identical return type:

```
public override Asset Clone() => new House { ... }
```

This still does the job, because the overridden Clone method instantiates a House rather than an Asset. However, to treat the returned object as a House, you must then perform a downcast:

```
House mansion1 = new House { Name="McMansion", Mortgage=250000 };
House mansion2 = (House) mansion1.Clone();
```

Abstract Classes and Abstract Members

A class declared as *abstract* can never be instantiated. Instead, only its concrete *subclasses* can be instantiated.

Abstract classes are able to define *abstract members*. Abstract members are like virtual members except that they don't provide a default implementation. That implementation must be provided by the subclass unless that subclass is also declared abstract:

```
public abstract class Asset
{
    // Note empty implementation
    public abstract decimal NetValue { get; }
}

public class Stock : Asset
{
    public long SharesOwned;
    public decimal CurrentPrice;

    // Override like a virtual method.
    public override decimal NetValue => CurrentPrice * SharesOwned;
}
```

Hiding Inherited Members

A base class and a subclass can define identical members. For example:

```
public class A      { public int Counter = 1; }
public class B : A  { public int Counter = 2; }
```

The Counter field in class B is said to *hide* the Counter field in class A. Usually, this happens by accident, when a member is added to the base type *after* an identical member was added to the subtype. For this reason, the compiler generates a warning and then resolves the ambiguity as follows:

- References to A (at compile time) bind to A.Counter.
- References to B (at compile time) bind to B.Counter.

Occasionally, you want to hide a member deliberately, in which case you can apply the new modifier to the member in the subclass. The new modifier *does nothing more than suppress the compiler warning that would otherwise result*:

```
public class A      { public     int Counter = 1; }
public class B : A { public new int Counter = 2; }
```

The new modifier communicates your intent to the compiler—and other programmers—that the duplicate member is not an accident.

C# overloads the new keyword to have independent meanings in different contexts. Specifically, the new *operator* is different from the new *member modifier*.

new versus override

Consider the following class hierarchy:

```
public class BaseClass
{
  public virtual void Foo()  { Console.WriteLine ("BaseClass.Foo"); }
}

public class Overrider : BaseClass
{
  public override void Foo() { Console.WriteLine ("Overrider.Foo"); }
}

public class Hider : BaseClass
{
  public new void Foo()     { Console.WriteLine ("Hider.Foo"); }
}
```

The differences in behavior between Overrider and Hider are demonstrated in the following code:

```
Overrider over = new Overrider();
BaseClass b1 = over;
over.Foo();                        // Overrider.Foo
b1.Foo();                          // Overrider.Foo

Hider h = new Hider();
BaseClass b2 = h;
h.Foo();                           // Hider.Foo
b2.Foo();                          // BaseClass.Foo
```

Sealing Functions and Classes

An overridden function member can *seal* its implementation with the sealed keyword to prevent it from being overridden by further subclasses. In our earlier virtual function member example, we could have sealed House's implementation of Liability, preventing a class that derives from House from overriding Liability, as follows:

```
public sealed override decimal Liability { get { return Mortgage; } }
```

You can also apply the sealed modifier to the class itself, to prevent subclassing. Sealing a class is more common than sealing a function member.

Although you can seal a function member against overriding, you can't seal a member against being *hidden*.

The base Keyword

The base keyword is similar to the this keyword. It serves two essential purposes:

- Accessing an overridden function member from the subclass

- Calling a base-class constructor (see the next section)

In this example, House uses the base keyword to access Asset's implementation of Liability:

```
public class House : Asset
{
  ...
  public override decimal Liability => base.Liability + Mortgage;
}
```

With the base keyword, we access Asset's Liability property *nonvirtually*. This means that we will always access Asset's version of this property—regardless of the instance's actual runtime type.

The same approach works if Liability is *hidden* rather than *overridden*. (You can also access hidden members by casting to the base class before invoking the function.)

Constructors and Inheritance

A subclass must declare its own constructors. The base class's constructors are *accessible* to the derived class but are never automatically *inherited*. For example, if we define Baseclass and Subclass as follows:

```
public class Baseclass
{
  public int X;
  public Baseclass () { }
  public Baseclass (int x) { this.X = x; }
}

public class Subclass : Baseclass { }
```

the following is illegal:

```
Subclass s = new Subclass (123);
```

Subclass must hence "redefine" any constructors it wants to expose. In doing so, however, it can call any of the base class's constructors via the base keyword:

```
public class Subclass : Baseclass
{
  public Subclass (int x) : base (x) { }
}
```

The base keyword works rather like the this keyword except that it calls a constructor in the base class.

Base-class constructors always execute first; this ensures that *base* initialization occurs before *specialized* initialization.

Implicit calling of the parameterless base-class constructor

If a constructor in a subclass omits the base keyword, the base type's *parameterless* constructor is implicitly called:

```
public class BaseClass
{
  public int X;
  public BaseClass() { X = 1; }
}

public class Subclass : BaseClass
{
  public Subclass() { Console.WriteLine (X); }  // 1
}
```

If the base class has no accessible parameterless constructor, subclasses are forced to use the base keyword in their constructors.

Constructor and field initialization order

When an object is instantiated, initialization takes place in the following order:

1. From subclass to base class:

   a. Fields are initialized.

   b. Arguments to base-class constructor calls are evaluated.

2. From base class to subclass:

   a. Constructor bodies execute.

For example:

```
public class B
{
  int x = 1;           // Executes 3rd
  public B (int x)
  {
    ...                // Executes 4th
  }
}
public class D : B
{
  int y = 1;           // Executes 1st
  public D (int x)
    : base (x + 1)     // Executes 2nd
  {
    ...                // Executes 5th
  }
}
```

Overloading and Resolution

Inheritance has an interesting impact on method overloading. Consider the following two overloads:

```
static void Foo (Asset a) { }
static void Foo (House h) { }
```

When an overload is called, the most specific type has precedence:

```
House h = new House (...);
Foo(h);                    // Calls Foo(House)
```

The particular overload to call is determined statically (at compile time) rather than at runtime. The following code calls Foo(Asset), even though the runtime type of a is House:

```
Asset a = new House (...);
Foo(a);                    // Calls Foo(Asset)
```

 If you cast Asset to dynamic (Chapter 4), the decision as to which overload to call is deferred until runtime and is then based on the object's actual type:

```
Asset a = new House (...);
Foo ((dynamic)a);   // Calls Foo(House)
```

The object Type

object (System.Object) is the ultimate base class for all types. Any type can be upcast to object.

To illustrate how this is useful, consider a general-purpose *stack*. A stack is a data structure based on the principle of *LIFO*—"last in, first out." A stack has two operations: *push* an object on the stack, and *pop* an object off the stack. Here is a simple implementation that can hold up to 10 objects:

```
public class Stack
{
  int position;
  object[] data = new object[10];
  public void Push (object obj)   { data[position++] = obj;  }
  public object Pop()             { return data[--position]; }
}
```

Because Stack works with the object type, we can Push and Pop instances of *any type* to and from the Stack:

```
Stack stack = new Stack();
stack.Push ("sausage");
string s = (string) stack.Pop();   // Downcast, so explicit cast is needed

Console.WriteLine (s);             // sausage
```

`object` is a reference type, by virtue of being a class. Despite this, value types, such as `int`, can also be cast to and from `object`, and so be added to our stack. This feature of C# is called *type unification* and is demonstrated here:

```
stack.Push (3);
int three = (int) stack.Pop();
```

When you cast between a value type and `object`, the CLR must perform some special work to bridge the difference in semantics between value and reference types. This process is called *boxing* and *unboxing*.

 In "Generics" on page 145, we describe how to improve our `Stack` class to better handle stacks with same-typed elements.

Boxing and Unboxing

Boxing is the act of converting a value-type instance to a reference-type instance. The reference type can be either the `object` class or an interface (which we visit later in the chapter).[1] In this example, we box an `int` into an object:

```
int x = 9;
object obj = x;             // Box the int
```

Unboxing reverses the operation by casting the object back to the original value type:

```
int y = (int)obj;           // Unbox the int
```

Unboxing requires an explicit cast. The runtime checks that the stated value type matches the actual object type, and throws an `InvalidCastException` if the check fails. For instance, the following throws an exception because `long` does not exactly match `int`:

```
object obj = 9;             // 9 is inferred to be of type int
long x = (long) obj;        // InvalidCastException
```

The following succeeds, however:

```
object obj = 9;
long x = (int) obj;
```

As does this:

```
object obj = 3.5;           // 3.5 is inferred to be of type double
int x = (int) (double) obj; // x is now 3
```

In the last example, `(double)` performs an *unboxing*, and then `(int)` performs a *numeric conversion*.

---

1 The reference type can also be `System.ValueType` or `System.Enum` (Chapter 6).

Boxing conversions are crucial in providing a unified type system. The system is not perfect, however: we'll see in "Generics" on page 145 that variance with arrays and generics supports only *reference conversions* and not *boxing conversions*:

```
object[] a1 = new string[3];   // Legal
object[] a2 = new int[3];      // Error
```

Copying semantics of boxing and unboxing

Boxing *copies* the value-type instance into the new object, and unboxing *copies* the contents of the object back into a value-type instance. In the following example, changing the value of i doesn't change its previously boxed copy:

```
int i = 3;
object boxed = i;
i = 5;
Console.WriteLine (boxed);   // 3
```

Static and Runtime Type Checking

C# programs are type-checked both statically (at compile time) and at runtime (by the CLR).

Static type checking enables the compiler to verify the correctness of your program without running it. The following code will fail because the compiler enforces static typing:

```
int x = "5";
```

Runtime type checking is performed by the CLR when you downcast via a reference conversion or unboxing:

```
object y = "5";
int z = (int) y;          // Runtime error, downcast failed
```

Runtime type checking is possible because each object on the heap internally stores a little type token. You can retrieve this token by calling the GetType method of object.

The GetType Method and typeof Operator

All types in C# are represented at runtime with an instance of System.Type. There are two basic ways to get a System.Type object:

- Call GetType on the instance.
- Use the typeof operator on a type name.

GetType is evaluated at runtime; typeof is evaluated statically at compile time (when generic type parameters are involved, it's resolved by the JIT compiler).

System.Type has properties for such things as the type's name, assembly, base type, and so on:

```
Point p = new Point();
Console.WriteLine (p.GetType().Name);          // Point
Console.WriteLine (typeof (Point).Name);       // Point
Console.WriteLine (p.GetType() == typeof(Point)); // True
Console.WriteLine (p.X.GetType().Name);        // Int32
Console.WriteLine (p.Y.GetType().FullName);    // System.Int32

public class Point { public int X, Y; }
```

System.Type also has methods that act as a gateway to the runtime's reflection model, described in Chapter 18.

The ToString Method

The ToString method returns the default textual representation of a type instance. This method is overridden by all built-in types. Here is an example of using the int type's ToString method:

```
int x = 1;
string s = x.ToString();      // s is "1"
```

You can override the ToString method on custom types as follows:

```
Panda p = new Panda { Name = "Petey" };
Console.WriteLine (p);   // Petey

public class Panda
{
  public string Name;
  public override string ToString() => Name;
}
```

If you don't override ToString, the method returns the type name.

 When you call an *overridden* object member such as ToString directly on a value type, boxing doesn't occur. Boxing then occurs only if you cast:

```
int x = 1;
string s1 = x.ToString();      // Calling on nonboxed value
object box = x;
string s2 = box.ToString();  // Calling on boxed value
```

Object Member Listing

Here are all the members of object:

```
public class Object
{
  public Object();

  public extern Type GetType();
```

```
public virtual bool Equals (object obj);
public static bool Equals  (object objA, object objB);
public static bool ReferenceEquals (object objA, object objB);

public virtual int GetHashCode();

public virtual string ToString();

protected virtual void Finalize();
protected extern object MemberwiseClone();
}
```

We describe the Equals, ReferenceEquals, and GetHashCode methods in "Equality Comparison" on page 324.

Structs

A *struct* is similar to a class, with the following key differences:

- A struct is a value type, whereas a class is a reference type.

- A struct does not support inheritance (other than implicitly deriving from object, or more precisely, System.ValueType).

A struct can have all of the members that a class can, except for a finalizer. And because it cannot be subclassed, members cannot be marked as virtual, abstract, or protected.

 Prior to C# 10, structs were further prohibited from defining fields initializers and parameterless constructors. Although this prohibition has now been relaxed—primarily for the benefit of record structs (see "Records" on page 211)—it's worth thinking carefully before defining these constructs, as they can result in confusing behavior that we'll describe in "Struct Construction Semantics" on page 129.

A struct is appropriate when value-type semantics are desirable. Good examples of structs are numeric types, where it is more natural for assignment to copy a value rather than a reference. Because a struct is a value type, each instance does not require instantiation of an object on the heap; this results in useful savings when creating many instances of a type. For instance, creating an array of value type elements requires only a single heap allocation.

Because structs are value types, an instance cannot be null. The default value for a struct is an empty instance, with all fields empty (set to their default values).

Struct Construction Semantics

Unlike with classes, every field in a struct must be explicitly assigned in the constructor (or field initializer). For example:

```
struct Point
{
  int x, y;
  public Point (int x, int y) { this.x = x; this.y = y; }   // OK
}
```

If we added the following constructor, the struct would not compile, because y would remain unassigned:

```
public Point (int x)       { this.x = x; }   // Not OK
```

The default constructor

In addition to any constructors that you define, a struct always has an implicit parameterless constructor that performs a bitwise-zeroing of its fields (setting them to their default values):

```
Point p = new Point();       // p.x and p.y will be 0
struct Point { int x, y; }
```

Even when you define a parameterless constructor of your own, the implicit parameterless constructor still exists and can be accessed via the default keyword:

```
Point p1 = new Point();       // p1.x and p1.y will be 1
Point p2 = default;           // p2.x and p2.y will be 0

struct Point
{
  int x = 1;
  int y;
  public Point() => y = 1;
}
```

In this example, we initialized x to 1 via a field initializer, and we initialized y to 1 via the parameterless constructor. And yet with the default keyword, we were still able to create a Point that bypassed both initializations. The default constructor can be accessed other ways, too, as the following example illustrates:

```
var points = new Point[10];   // Each point in the array will be (0,0)
var test = new Test();        // test.p will be (0,0)

class Test { Point p; }
```

 Having what amounts to two parameterless constructors can be a source of confusion and is arguably a good reason to avoid defining field initializers and explicit parameterless constructors in structs.

A good strategy with structs is to design them such that their default value is a valid state, thereby making initialization redundant. For example, rather than this:

```
struct WebOptions { public string Protocol { get; set; } = "https"; }
```

consider the following:

```
struct WebOptions
{
  string protocol;
  public string Protocol { get => protocol ?? "https";
                            set => protocol = value;    }
}
```

Read-Only Structs and Functions

You can apply the `readonly` modifier to a struct to enforce that all fields are readonly; this aids in declaring intent as well as affording the compiler more optimization freedom:

```
readonly struct Point
{
  public readonly int X, Y;   // X and Y must be readonly
}
```

If you need to apply `readonly` at a more granular level, you can apply the `readonly` modifier (from C# 8) to a struct's *functions*. This ensures that if the function attempts to modify any field, a compile-time error is generated:

```
struct Point
{
  public int X, Y;
  public readonly void ResetX() => X = 0;  // Error!
}
```

If a `readonly` function calls a non-`readonly` function, the compiler generates a warning (and defensively copies the struct to avoid the possibility of a mutation).

Ref Structs

Ref structs were introduced in C# 7.2 as a niche feature primarily for the benefit of the `Span<T>` and `ReadOnlySpan<T>` structs that we describe in Chapter 23 (and the highly optimized `Utf8JsonReader` that we describe in Chapter 11). These structs help with a micro-optimization technique that aims to reduce memory allocations.

Unlike reference types, whose instances always live on the heap, value types live *in-place* (wherever the variable was declared). If a value type appears as a parameter or local variable, it will reside on the stack:

```
void SomeMethod()
{
  Point p;   // p will reside on the stack
}
struct Point { public int X, Y; }
```

But if a value type appears as a field in a class, it will reside on the heap:

```
class MyClass
{
  Point p;   // Lives on heap, because MyClass instances live on the heap
}
```

Similarly, arrays of structs live on the heap, and boxing a struct sends it to the heap.

Adding the `ref` modifier to a struct's declaration ensures that it can only ever reside on the stack. Attempting to use a *ref struct* in such a way that it could reside on the heap generates a compile-time error:

```
var points = new Point [100];          // Error: will not compile!

ref struct Point { public int X, Y; }
class MyClass     { Point P;        }   // Error: will not compile!
```

Ref structs were introduced mainly for the benefit of the Span<T> and ReadOnly Span<T> structs. Because Span<T> and ReadOnlySpan<T> instances can exist only on the stack, it's possible for them to safely wrap stack-allocated memory.

Ref structs cannot partake in any C# feature that directly or indirectly introduces the possibility of existing on the heap. This includes a number of advanced C# features that we describe in Chapter 4, namely lambda expressions, iterators, and asynchronous functions (because, behind the scenes, these features all create hidden classes with fields). Also, ref structs cannot appear inside non-ref structs, and they cannot implement interfaces (because this could result in boxing).

Access Modifiers

To promote encapsulation, a type or type member can limit its *accessibility* to other types and other assemblies by adding one of five *access modifiers* to the declaration:

public
> Fully accessible. This is the implicit accessibility for members of an enum or interface.

internal
> Accessible only within the containing assembly or friend assemblies. This is the default accessibility for non-nested types.

private
> Accessible only within the containing type. This is the default accessibility for members of a class or struct.

protected
> Accessible only within the containing type or subclasses.

protected internal
> The *union* of protected and internal accessibility. A member that is protected internal is accessible in two ways.

`private protected` *(from C# 7.2)*

The *intersection* of `protected` and `internal` accessibility. A member that is `private protected` is accessible only within the containing type, or subclasses *that reside in the same assembly* (making it *less* accessible than `protected` or `internal` alone).

Examples

`Class2` is accessible from outside its assembly; `Class1` is not:

```
class Class1 {}                  // Class1 is internal (default)
public class Class2 {}
```

`ClassB` exposes field x to other types in the same assembly; `ClassA` does not:

```
class ClassA { int x;        } // x is private (default)
class ClassB { internal int x; }
```

Functions within `Subclass` can call `Bar` but not `Foo`:

```
class BaseClass
{
  void Foo()           {}      // Foo is private (default)
  protected void Bar() {}
}

class Subclass : BaseClass
{
  void Test1() { Foo(); }      // Error - cannot access Foo
  void Test2() { Bar(); }      // OK
}
```

Friend Assemblies

You can expose `internal` members to other *friend* assemblies by adding the `System.Runtime.CompilerServices.InternalsVisibleTo` assembly attribute, specifying the name of the friend assembly as follows:

```
[assembly: InternalsVisibleTo ("Friend")]
```

If the friend assembly has a strong name (see Chapter 17), you must specify its *full* 160-byte public key:

```
[assembly: InternalsVisibleTo ("StrongFriend, PublicKey=0024f000048c...")]
```

You can extract the full public key from a strongly named assembly with a LINQ query (we explain LINQ in detail in Chapter 8):

```
string key = string.Join ("",
  Assembly.GetExecutingAssembly().GetName().GetPublicKey()
    .Select (b => b.ToString ("x2")));
```

The companion sample in LINQPad invites you to browse to an assembly and then copies the assembly's full public key to the clipboard.

Accessibility Capping

A type caps the accessibility of its declared members. The most common example of capping is when you have an `internal` type with `public` members. For example, consider this:

```
class C { public void Foo() {} }
```

C's (default) `internal` accessibility caps Foo's accessibility, effectively making Foo `internal`. A common reason Foo would be marked `public` is to make for easier refactoring should C later be changed to `public`.

Restrictions on Access Modifiers

When overriding a base class function, accessibility must be identical on the overridden function; for example:

```
class BaseClass              { protected virtual  void Foo() {} }
class Subclass1 : BaseClass { protected override void Foo() {} }  // OK
class Subclass2 : BaseClass { public    override void Foo() {} }  // Error
```

(An exception is when overriding a `protected internal` method in another assembly, in which case the override must simply be `protected`.)

The compiler prevents any inconsistent use of access modifiers. For example, a subclass itself can be less accessible than a base class, but not more:

```
internal class A {}
public class B : A {}        // Error
```

Interfaces

An interface is similar to a class, but only *specifies behavior* and does not hold state (data). Consequently:

- An interface can define only functions and not fields.

- Interface members are *implicitly abstract*. (Although nonabstract functions are permitted from C# 8, this is considered a special case, which we describe in "Default Interface Members" on page 139.)

- A class (or struct) can implement *multiple* interfaces. In contrast, a class can inherit from only a *single* class, and a struct cannot inherit at all (aside from deriving from `System.ValueType`).

An interface declaration is like a class declaration, but it (typically) provides no implementation for its members because its members are implicitly abstract. These members will be implemented by the classes and structs that implement the interface. An interface can contain only functions, that is, methods, properties, events, and indexers (which noncoincidentally are precisely the members of a class that can be abstract).

As defined in System.Collections, here is the definition of the IEnumerator interface:

```
public interface IEnumerator
{
  bool MoveNext();
  object Current { get; }
  void Reset();
}
```

Interface members are always implicitly public and cannot declare an access modifier. Implementing an interface means providing a public implementation for all of its members:

```
internal class Countdown : IEnumerator
{
  int count = 11;
  public bool MoveNext() => count-- > 0;
  public object Current => count;
  public void Reset() { throw new NotSupportedException(); }
}
```

You can implicitly cast an object to any interface that it implements:

```
IEnumerator e = new Countdown();
while (e.MoveNext())
  Console.Write (e.Current);       // 109876543210
```

> Even though Countdown is an internal class, its members that implement IEnumerator can be called publicly by casting an instance of Countdown to IEnumerator. For instance, if a public type in the same assembly defined a method as follows:
>
> ```
> public static class Util
> {
>   public static object GetCountDown() => new CountDown();
> }
> ```
>
> a caller from another assembly could do this:
>
> ```
> IEnumerator e = (IEnumerator) Util.GetCountDown();
> e.MoveNext();
> ```
>
> If IEnumerator were itself defined as internal, this wouldn't be possible.

Extending an Interface

Interfaces can derive from other interfaces; for instance:

```
public interface IUndoable             { void Undo(); }
public interface IRedoable : IUndoable { void Redo(); }
```

IRedoable "inherits" all the members of IUndoable. In other words, types that implement IRedoable must also implement the members of IUndoable.

Explicit Interface Implementation

Implementing multiple interfaces can sometimes result in a collision between member signatures. You can resolve such collisions by *explicitly implementing* an interface member. Consider the following example:

```
interface I1 { void Foo(); }
interface I2 { int Foo(); }

public class Widget : I1, I2
{
  public void Foo()
  {
    Console.WriteLine ("Widget's implementation of I1.Foo");
  }

  int I2.Foo()
  {
    Console.WriteLine ("Widget's implementation of I2.Foo");
    return 42;
  }
}
```

Because I1 and I2 have conflicting Foo signatures, Widget explicitly implements I2's Foo method. This lets the two methods coexist in one class. The only way to call an explicitly implemented member is to cast to its interface:

```
Widget w = new Widget();
w.Foo();                    // Widget's implementation of I1.Foo
((I1)w).Foo();              // Widget's implementation of I1.Foo
((I2)w).Foo();              // Widget's implementation of I2.Foo
```

Another reason to explicitly implement interface members is to hide members that are highly specialized and distracting to a type's normal use case. For example, a type that implements ISerializable would typically want to avoid flaunting its ISerializable members unless explicitly cast to that interface.

Implementing Interface Members Virtually

An implicitly implemented interface member is, by default, sealed. It must be marked virtual or abstract in the base class in order to be overridden:

```
public interface IUndoable { void Undo(); }

public class TextBox : IUndoable
{
  public virtual void Undo() => Console.WriteLine ("TextBox.Undo");
}

public class RichTextBox : TextBox
{
  public override void Undo() => Console.WriteLine ("RichTextBox.Undo");
}
```

Calling the interface member through either the base class or the interface calls the subclass's implementation:

```
RichTextBox r = new RichTextBox();
r.Undo();                        // RichTextBox.Undo
((IUndoable)r).Undo();           // RichTextBox.Undo
((TextBox)r).Undo();             // RichTextBox.Undo
```

An explicitly implemented interface member cannot be marked virtual, nor can it be overridden in the usual manner. It can, however, be *reimplemented*.

Reimplementing an Interface in a Subclass

A subclass can reimplement any interface member already implemented by a base class. Reimplementation hijacks a member implementation (when called through the interface) and works whether or not the member is virtual in the base class. It also works whether a member is implemented implicitly or explicitly—although it works best in the latter case, as we will demonstrate.

In the following example, TextBox implements IUndoable.Undo explicitly, and so it cannot be marked as virtual. To "override" it, RichTextBox must reimplement IUndoable's Undo method:

```
public interface IUndoable { void Undo(); }

public class TextBox : IUndoable
{
  void IUndoable.Undo() => Console.WriteLine ("TextBox.Undo");
}

public class RichTextBox : TextBox, IUndoable
{
  public void Undo() => Console.WriteLine ("RichTextBox.Undo");
}
```

Calling the reimplemented member through the interface calls the subclass's implementation:

```
RichTextBox r = new RichTextBox();
r.Undo();                  // RichTextBox.Undo    Case 1
((IUndoable)r).Undo();     // RichTextBox.Undo    Case 2
```

Assuming the same RichTextBox definition, suppose that TextBox implemented Undo *implicitly*:

```
public class TextBox : IUndoable
{
  public void Undo() => Console.WriteLine ("TextBox.Undo");
}
```

This would give us another way to call Undo, which would "break" the system, as shown in Case 3:

```
RichTextBox r = new RichTextBox();
r.Undo();                        // RichTextBox.Undo    Case 1
```

```
((IUndoable)r).Undo();    // RichTextBox.Undo      Case 2
((TextBox)r).Undo();      // TextBox.Undo         Case 3
```

Case 3 demonstrates that reimplementation hijacking is effective only when a member is called through the interface and not through the base class. This is usually undesirable in that it can create inconsistent semantics. This makes reimplementation most appropriate as a strategy for overriding *explicitly* implemented interface members.

Alternatives to interface reimplementation

Even with explicit member implementation, interface reimplementation is problematic for a couple of reasons:

- The subclass has no way to call the base class method.
- The base class author might not anticipate that a method would be reimplemented and might not allow for the potential consequences.

Reimplementation can be a good last resort when subclassing hasn't been anticipated. A better option, however, is to design a base class such that reimplementation will never be required. There are two ways to achieve this:

- When implicitly implementing a member, mark it `virtual` if appropriate.
- When explicitly implementing a member, use the following pattern if you anticipate that subclasses might need to override any logic:

```
public class TextBox : IUndoable
{
  void IUndoable.Undo()          => Undo();     // Calls method below
  protected virtual void Undo() => Console.WriteLine ("TextBox.Undo");
}

public class RichTextBox : TextBox
{
  protected override void Undo() => Console.WriteLine("RichTextBox.Undo");
}
```

If you don't anticipate any subclassing, you can mark the class as `sealed` to preempt interface reimplementation.

Interfaces and Boxing

Converting a struct to an interface causes boxing. Calling an implicitly implemented member on a struct does not cause boxing:

```
interface I { void Foo();        }
struct S : I { public void Foo() {} }

...
S s = new S();
s.Foo();          // No boxing.
```

```
I i = s;            // Box occurs when casting to interface.
i.Foo();
```

Default Interface Members

From C# 8, you can add a default implementation to an interface member, making it optional to implement:

```
interface ILogger
{
  void Log (string text) => Console.WriteLine (text);
}
```

This is advantageous if you want to add a member to an interface defined in a popular library without breaking (potentially thousands of) implementations.

Default implementations are always explicit, so if a class implementing ILogger fails to define a Log method, the only way to call it is through the interface:

```
class Logger : ILogger { }
...
((ILogger)new Logger()).Log ("message");
```

This prevents a problem of multiple implementation inheritance: if the same default member is added to two interfaces that a class implements, there is never an ambiguity as to which member is called.

Interfaces can also now define static members (including fields), which can be accessed from code inside default implementations:

```
interface ILogger
{
  void Log (string text) =>
    Console.WriteLine (Prefix + text);

  static string Prefix = "";
}
```

Because interface members are implicitly public, you can also access static members from the outside:

```
ILogger.Prefix = "File log: ";
```

You can restrict this by adding an accessibility modifier to the static interface member (such as private, protected, or internal).

Instance fields are (still) prohibited. This is in line with the principle of interfaces, which is to define *behavior*, not *state*.

Enums

An *enum* is a special value type that lets you specify a group of named numeric constants. For example:

```
public enum BorderSide { Left, Right, Top, Bottom }
```

We can use this enum type as follows:

```
BorderSide topSide = BorderSide.Top;
bool isTop = (topSide == BorderSide.Top);   // true
```

Each enum member has an underlying integral value. These are by default:

- Underlying values are of type int.

- The constants 0, 1, 2... are automatically assigned in the declaration order of the enum members.

You can specify an alternative integral type, as follows:

```
public enum BorderSide : byte { Left, Right, Top, Bottom }
```

You can also specify an explicit underlying value for each enum member:

```
public enum BorderSide : byte { Left=1, Right=2, Top=10, Bottom=11 }
```

 The compiler also lets you explicitly assign *some* of the enum members. The unassigned enum members keep incrementing from the last explicit value. The preceding example is equivalent to the following:

```
public enum BorderSide : byte
  { Left=1, Right, Top=10, Bottom }
```

Enum Conversions

You can convert an enum instance to and from its underlying integral value with an explicit cast:

```
int i = (int) BorderSide.Left;
BorderSide side = (BorderSide) i;
bool leftOrRight = (int) side <= 2;
```

You can also explicitly cast one enum type to another. Suppose that Horizontal Alignment is defined as follows:

```
public enum HorizontalAlignment
{
  Left = BorderSide.Left,
  Right = BorderSide.Right,
  Center
}
```

A translation between the enum types uses the underlying integral values:

```
HorizontalAlignment h = (HorizontalAlignment) BorderSide.Right;
// same as:
HorizontalAlignment h = (HorizontalAlignment) (int) BorderSide.Right;
```

The numeric literal 0 is treated specially by the compiler in an enum expression and does not require an explicit cast:

```
BorderSide b = 0;     // No cast required
if (b == 0) ...
```

There are two reasons for the special treatment of 0:

- The first member of an enum is often used as the "default" value.

- For *combined enum* types, 0 means "no flags."

Flags Enums

You can combine enum members. To prevent ambiguities, members of a combinable enum require explicitly assigned values, typically in powers of two:

```
[Flags]
enum BorderSides { None=0, Left=1, Right=2, Top=4, Bottom=8 }
```

or:

```
enum BorderSides { None=0, Left=1, Right=1<<1, Top=1<<2, Bottom=1<<3 }
```

To work with combined enum values, you use bitwise operators such as | and &. These operate on the underlying integral values:

```
BorderSides leftRight = BorderSides.Left | BorderSides.Right;

if ((leftRight & BorderSides.Left) != 0)
  Console.WriteLine ("Includes Left");      // Includes Left

string formatted = leftRight.ToString();    // "Left, Right"

BorderSides s = BorderSides.Left;
s |= BorderSides.Right;
Console.WriteLine (s == leftRight);   // True

s ^= BorderSides.Right;               // Toggles BorderSides.Right
Console.WriteLine (s);                // Left
```

By convention, the Flags attribute should always be applied to an enum type when its members are combinable. If you declare such an enum without the Flags attribute, you can still combine members, but calling ToString on an enum instance will emit a number rather than a series of names.

By convention, a combinable enum type is given a plural rather than singular name.

For convenience, you can include combination members within an enum declaration itself:

```
[Flags]
enum BorderSides
{
  None=0,
  Left=1, Right=1<<1, Top=1<<2, Bottom=1<<3,
  LeftRight = Left | Right,
  TopBottom = Top  | Bottom,
  All       = LeftRight | TopBottom
}
```

Enum Operators

The operators that work with enums are:

```
=   ==   !=   <   >   <=   >=   +   -   ^   &   |   ~
+=   -=   ++  --   sizeof
```

The bitwise, arithmetic, and comparison operators return the result of processing the underlying integral values. Addition is permitted between an enum and an integral type, but not between two enums.

Type-Safety Issues

Consider the following enum:

```
public enum BorderSide { Left, Right, Top, Bottom }
```

Because an enum can be cast to and from its underlying integral type, the actual value it can have might fall outside the bounds of a legal enum member:

```
BorderSide b = (BorderSide) 12345;
Console.WriteLine (b);              // 12345
```

The bitwise and arithmetic operators can produce similarly invalid values:

```
BorderSide b = BorderSide.Bottom;
b++;                               // No errors
```

An invalid BorderSide would break the following code:

```
void Draw (BorderSide side)
{
  if      (side == BorderSide.Left)  {...}
  else if (side == BorderSide.Right) {...}
  else if (side == BorderSide.Top)   {...}
  else                               {...} // Assume BorderSide.Bottom
}
```

One solution is to add another else clause:

```
  ...
  else if (side == BorderSide.Bottom) ...
  else throw new ArgumentException ("Invalid BorderSide: " + side, "side");
```

Another workaround is to explicitly check an enum value for validity. The static Enum.IsDefined method does this job:

```
BorderSide side = (BorderSide) 12345;
Console.WriteLine (Enum.IsDefined (typeof (BorderSide), side));   // False
```

Unfortunately, Enum.IsDefined does not work for flagged enums. However, the following helper method (a trick dependent on the behavior of Enum.ToString()) returns true if a given flagged enum is valid:

```
for (int i = 0; i <= 16; i++)
{
  BorderSides side = (BorderSides)i;
  Console.WriteLine (IsFlagDefined (side) + " " + side);
}

bool IsFlagDefined (Enum e)
{
  decimal d;
  return !decimal.TryParse(e.ToString(), out d);
```

```
    }

[Flags]
public enum BorderSides { Left=1, Right=2, Top=4, Bottom=8 }
```

Nested Types

A *nested type* is declared within the scope of another type:

```
public class TopLevel
{
  public class Nested { }             // Nested class
  public enum Color { Red, Blue, Tan } // Nested enum
}
```

A nested type has the following features:

- It can access the enclosing type's private members and everything else the enclosing type can access.
- You can declare it with the full range of access modifiers rather than just public and internal.
- The default accessibility for a nested type is private rather than internal.
- Accessing a nested type from outside the enclosing type requires qualification with the enclosing type's name (like when accessing static members).

For example, to access Color.Red from outside our TopLevel class, we'd need to do this:

```
TopLevel.Color color = TopLevel.Color.Red;
```

All types (classes, structs, interfaces, delegates, and enums) can be nested within either a class or a struct.

Here is an example of accessing a private member of a type from a nested type:

```
public class TopLevel
{
  static int x;
  class Nested
  {
    static void Foo() { Console.WriteLine (TopLevel.x); }
  }
}
```

Here is an example of applying the protected access modifier to a nested type:

```
public class TopLevel
{
  protected class Nested { }
}

public class SubTopLevel : TopLevel
{
```

```
  static void Foo() { new TopLevel.Nested(); }
}
```

Here is an example of referring to a nested type from outside the enclosing type:

```
public class TopLevel
{
  public class Nested { }
}

class Test
{
  TopLevel.Nested n;
}
```

Nested types are used heavily by the compiler itself when it generates private classes that capture state for constructs such as iterators and anonymous methods.

 If the sole reason for using a nested type is to avoid cluttering a namespace with too many types, consider using a nested namespace instead. A nested type should be used because of its stronger access control restrictions, or when the nested class must access private members of the containing class.

Generics

C# has two separate mechanisms for writing code that is reusable across different types: *inheritance* and *generics*. Whereas inheritance expresses reusability with a base type, generics express reusability with a "template" that contains "placeholder" types. Generics, when compared to inheritance, can *increase type safety* and *reduce casting and boxing*.

 C# generics and C++ templates are similar concepts, but they work differently. We explain this difference in "C# Generics Versus C++ Templates" on page 157.

Generic Types

A generic type declares *type parameters*—placeholder types to be filled in by the consumer of the generic type, which supplies the *type arguments*. Here is a generic type Stack<T>, designed to stack instances of type T. Stack<T> declares a single type parameter T:

```
public class Stack<T>
{
  int position;
  T[] data = new T[100];
  public void Push (T obj)  => data[position++] = obj;
  public T Pop()            => data[--position];
}
```

We can use Stack<T> as follows:

```
var stack = new Stack<int>();
stack.Push (5);
stack.Push (10);
int x = stack.Pop();        // x is 10
int y = stack.Pop();        // y is 5
```

Stack<int> fills in the type parameter T with the type argument int, implicitly creating a type on the fly (the synthesis occurs at runtime). Attempting to push a string onto our Stack<int> would, however, produce a compile-time error. Stack<int> effectively has the following definition (substitutions appear in bold, with the class name hashed out to avoid confusion):

```
public class ###
{
  int position;
  int[] data = new int[100];
  public void Push (int obj)  => data[position++] = obj;
  public int Pop()            => data[--position];
}
```

Technically, we say that Stack<T> is an *open type*, whereas Stack<int> is a *closed type*. At runtime, all generic type instances are closed—with the placeholder types filled in. This means that the following statement is illegal:

```
var stack = new Stack<T>();   // Illegal: What is T?
```

However, it's legal if it's within a class or method that itself defines T as a type parameter:

```
public class Stack<T>
{
  ...
  public Stack<T> Clone()
  {
    Stack<T> clone = new Stack<T>();   // Legal
    ...
  }
}
```

Why Generics Exist

Generics exist to write code that is reusable across different types. Suppose that we need a stack of integers, but we don't have generic types. One solution would be to hardcode a separate version of the class for every required element type (e.g., IntStack, StringStack, etc.). Clearly, this would cause considerable code duplication. Another solution would be to write a stack that is generalized by using object as the element type:

```
public class ObjectStack
{
  int position;
  object[] data = new object[10];
```

```
    public void Push (object obj) => data[position++] = obj;
    public object Pop()           => data[--position];
}
```

An `ObjectStack`, however, wouldn't work as well as a hardcoded `IntStack` for specifically stacking integers. An `ObjectStack` would require boxing and downcasting that could not be checked at compile time:

```
// Suppose we just want to store integers here:
ObjectStack stack = new ObjectStack();

stack.Push ("s");               // Wrong type, but no error!
int i = (int)stack.Pop();       // Downcast - runtime error
```

What we need is both a general implementation of a stack that works for all element types as well as a way to easily specialize that stack to a specific element type for increased type safety and reduced casting and boxing. Generics give us precisely this by allowing us to parameterize the element type. `Stack<T>` has the benefits of both `ObjectStack` and `IntStack`. Like `ObjectStack`, `Stack<T>` is written once to work *generally* across all types. Like `IntStack`, `Stack<T>` is *specialized* for a particular type—the beauty is that this type is T, which we substitute on the fly.

`ObjectStack` is functionally equivalent to `Stack<object>`.

Generic Methods

A generic method declares type parameters within the signature of a method.

With generic methods, many fundamental algorithms can be implemented in a general-purpose way. Here is a generic method that swaps the contents of two variables of any type T:

```
static void Swap<T> (ref T a, ref T b)
{
  T temp = a;
  a = b;
  b = temp;
}
```

`Swap<T>` is called as follows:

```
int x = 5;
int y = 10;
Swap (ref x, ref y);
```

Generally, there is no need to supply type arguments to a generic method, because the compiler can implicitly infer the type. If there is ambiguity, generic methods can be called with type arguments as follows:

```
Swap<int> (ref x, ref y);
```

Within a generic *type*, a method is not classed as generic unless it *introduces* type parameters (with the angle bracket syntax). The Pop method in our generic stack merely uses the type's existing type parameter, T, and is not classed as a generic method.

Methods and types are the only constructs that can introduce type parameters. Properties, indexers, events, fields, constructors, operators, and so on cannot declare type parameters, although they can partake in any type parameters already declared by their enclosing type. In our generic stack example, for instance, we could write an indexer that returns a generic item:

```
public T this [int index] => data [index];
```

Similarly, constructors can partake in existing type parameters but not *introduce* them:

```
public Stack<T>() { }    // Illegal
```

Declaring Type Parameters

Type parameters can be introduced in the declaration of classes, structs, interfaces, delegates (covered in Chapter 4), and methods. Other constructs, such as properties, cannot *introduce* a type parameter, but they can *use* one. For example, the property Value uses T:

```
public struct Nullable<T>
{
  public T Value { get; }
}
```

A generic type or method can have multiple parameters:

```
class Dictionary<TKey, TValue> {...}
```

To instantiate:

```
Dictionary<int,string> myDict = new Dictionary<int,string>();
```

Or:

```
var myDict = new Dictionary<int,string>();
```

Generic type names and method names can be overloaded as long as the number of type parameters is different. For example, the following three type names do not conflict:

```
class A        {}
class A<T>     {}
class A<T1,T2> {}
```

By convention, generic types and methods with a *single* type parameter typically name their parameter T, as long as the intent of the parameter is clear. When using *multiple* type parameters, each parameter is prefixed with T but has a more descriptive name.

typeof and Unbound Generic Types

Open generic types do not exist at runtime: they are closed as part of compilation. However, it is possible for an *unbound* generic type to exist at runtime—purely as a `Type` object. The only way to specify an unbound generic type in C# is via the `typeof` operator:

```
class A<T> {}
class A<T1,T2> {}
...

Type a1 = typeof (A<>);    // Unbound type (notice no type arguments).
Type a2 = typeof (A<,>);   // Use commas to indicate multiple type args.
```

Open generic types are used in conjunction with the Reflection API (Chapter 18).

You can also use the `typeof` operator to specify a closed type:

```
Type a3 = typeof (A<int,int>);
```

Or, you can specify an open type (which is closed at runtime):

```
class B<T> { void X() { Type t = typeof (T); } }
```

The default Generic Value

You can use the `default` keyword to get the default value for a generic type parameter. The default value for a reference type is `null`, and the default value for a value type is the result of bitwise-zeroing the value type's fields:

```
static void Zap<T> (T[] array)
{
  for (int i = 0; i < array.Length; i++)
    array[i] = default(T);
}
```

From C# 7.1, you can omit the type argument for cases in which the compiler is able to infer it. We could replace the last line of code with this:

```
    array[i] = default;
```

Generic Constraints

By default, you can substitute a type parameter with any type whatsoever. *Constraints* can be applied to a type parameter to require more specific type arguments. These are the possible constraints:

```
where T : base-class   // Base-class constraint
where T : interface    // Interface constraint
where T : class        // Reference-type constraint
where T : class?       // (see "Nullable Reference Types" in Chapter 1)
where T : struct       // Value-type constraint (excludes Nullable types)
where T : unmanaged    // Unmanaged constraint
where T : new()        // Parameterless constructor constraint
where U : T            // Naked type constraint
```

```
where T : notnull       // Non-nullable value type, or (from C# 8)
                        // a non-nullable reference type
```

In the following example, GenericClass<T,U> requires T to derive from (or be identical to) SomeClass and implement Interface1, and requires U to provide a parameterless constructor:

```
class      SomeClass {}
interface Interface1 {}

class GenericClass<T,U> where T : SomeClass, Interface1
                        where U : new()
{...}
```

You can apply constraints wherever type parameters are defined, in both methods and type definitions.

A *base-class constraint* specifies that the type parameter must subclass (or match) a particular class; an *interface constraint* specifies that the type parameter must implement that interface. These constraints allow instances of the type parameter to be implicitly converted to that class or interface. For example, suppose that we want to write a generic Max method, which returns the maximum of two values. We can take advantage of the generic interface defined in the System namespace called IComparable<T>:

```
public interface IComparable<T>   // Simplified version of interface
{
  int CompareTo (T other);
}
```

CompareTo returns a positive number if this is greater than other. Using this interface as a constraint, we can write a Max method as follows (to avoid distraction, null checking is omitted):

```
static T Max <T> (T a, T b) where T : IComparable<T>
{
  return a.CompareTo (b) > 0 ? a : b;
}
```

The Max method can accept arguments of any type implementing IComparable<T> (which includes most built-in types such as int and string):

```
int z = Max (5, 10);            // 10
string last = Max ("ant", "zoo"); // zoo
```

The *class constraint* and *struct constraint* specify that T must be a reference type or (non-nullable) value type. A great example of the struct constraint is the Sys tem.Nullable<T> struct (we discuss this class in depth in "Nullable Value Types" on page 194):

```
struct Nullable<T> where T : struct {...}
```

The *unmanaged constraint* (introduced in C# 7.3) is a stronger version of a struct constraint: T must be a simple value type or a struct that is (recursively) free of any reference types.

The *parameterless constructor constraint* requires T to have a public parameterless constructor. If this constraint is defined, you can call new() on T:

```
static void Initialize<T> (T[] array) where T : new()
{
  for (int i = 0; i < array.Length; i++)
    array[i] = new T();
}
```

The *naked type constraint* requires one type parameter to derive from (or match) another type parameter. In this example, the method FilteredStack returns another Stack, containing only the subset of elements where the type parameter U is of the type parameter T:

```
class Stack<T>
{
  Stack<U> FilteredStack<U>() where U : T {...}
}
```

Subclassing Generic Types

A generic class can be subclassed just like a nongeneric class. The subclass can leave the base class's type parameters open, as in the following example:

```
class Stack<T>                    {...}
class SpecialStack<T> : Stack<T> {...}
```

Or, the subclass can close the generic type parameters with a concrete type:

```
class IntStack : Stack<int>  {...}
```

A subtype can also introduce fresh type arguments:

```
class List<T>                      {...}
class KeyedList<T,TKey> : List<T> {...}
```

Technically, *all* type arguments on a subtype are fresh: you could say that a subtype closes and then reopens the base type arguments. This means that a subclass can give new (and potentially more meaningful) names to the type arguments that it reopens:

```
class List<T> {...}
class KeyedList<TElement,TKey> : List<TElement> {...}
```

Self-Referencing Generic Declarations

A type can name *itself* as the concrete type when closing a type argument:

```
public interface IEquatable<T> { bool Equals (T obj); }

public class Balloon : IEquatable<Balloon>
```

```
{
  public string Color { get; set; }
  public int CC { get; set; }

  public bool Equals (Balloon b)
  {
    if (b == null) return false;
    return b.Color == Color && b.CC == CC;
  }
}
```

The following are also legal:

```
class Foo<T> where T : IComparable<T> { ... }
class Bar<T> where T : Bar<T> { ... }
```

Static Data

Static data is unique for each closed type:

```
Console.WriteLine (++Bob<int>.Count);     // 1
Console.WriteLine (++Bob<int>.Count);     // 2
Console.WriteLine (++Bob<string>.Count);  // 1
Console.WriteLine (++Bob<object>.Count);  // 1

class Bob<T> { public static int Count; }
```

Type Parameters and Conversions

C#'s cast operator can perform several kinds of conversion, including:

- Numeric conversion

- Reference conversion

- Boxing/unboxing conversion

- Custom conversion (via operator overloading; see Chapter 4)

The decision as to which kind of conversion will take place happens at *compile time*, based on the known types of the operands. This creates an interesting scenario with generic type parameters, because the precise operand types are unknown at compile time. If this leads to ambiguity, the compiler generates an error.

The most common scenario is when you want to perform a reference conversion:

```
StringBuilder Foo<T> (T arg)
{
  if (arg is StringBuilder)
    return (StringBuilder) arg;   // Will not compile
  ...
}
```

Without knowledge of T's actual type, the compiler is concerned that you might have intended this to be a *custom conversion*. The simplest solution is to instead use the as operator, which is unambiguous because it cannot perform custom conversions:

```
StringBuilder Foo<T> (T arg)
{
  StringBuilder sb = arg as StringBuilder;
  if (sb != null) return sb;
  ...
}
```

A more general solution is to first cast to object. This works because conversions to/from object are assumed not to be custom conversions, but reference or boxing/unboxing conversions. In this case, StringBuilder is a reference type, so it must be a reference conversion:

```
return (StringBuilder) (object) arg;
```

Unboxing conversions can also introduce ambiguities. The following could be an unboxing, numeric, or custom conversion:

```
int Foo<T> (T x) => (int) x;      // Compile-time error
```

The solution, again, is to first cast to object and then to int (which then unambiguously signals an unboxing conversion in this case):

```
int Foo<T> (T x) => (int) (object) x;
```

Covariance

Assuming A is convertible to B, X has a covariant type parameter if X<A> is convertible to X<B>.

With C#'s notion of covariance (and contravariance), "convertible" means convertible via an *implicit reference conversion*— such as A *subclassing* B, or A *implementing* B. Numeric conversions, boxing conversions, and custom conversions are not included.

For instance, type IFoo<T> has a covariant T if the following is legal:

```
IFoo<string> s = ...;
IFoo<object> b = s;
```

Interfaces permit covariant type parameters (as do delegates; see Chapter 4), but classes do not. Arrays also allow covariance (A[] can be converted to B[] if A has an implicit reference conversion to B) and are discussed here for comparison.

Covariance and contravariance (or simply "variance") are advanced concepts. The motivation behind introducing and enhancing variance in C# was to allow generic interface and generic types (in particular, those defined in .NET, such as IEnumerable<T>) to work more as you'd expect. You can benefit from this without understanding the details behind covariance and contravariance.

Variance is not automatic

To ensure static type safety, type parameters are not automatically variant. Consider the following:

```
class Animal {}
class Bear : Animal {}
class Camel : Animal {}

public class Stack<T>    // A simple Stack implementation
{
  int position;
  T[] data = new T[100];
  public void Push (T obj)  => data[position++] = obj;
  public T Pop()            => data[--position];
}
```

The following fails to compile:

```
Stack<Bear> bears = new Stack<Bear>();
Stack<Animal> animals = bears;             // Compile-time error
```

That restriction prevents the possibility of runtime failure with the following code:

```
animals.Push (new Camel());      // Trying to add Camel to bears
```

Lack of covariance, however, can hinder reusability. Suppose, for instance, that we wanted to write a method to Wash a stack of animals:

```
public class ZooCleaner
{
  public static void Wash (Stack<Animal> animals) {...}
}
```

Calling Wash with a stack of bears would generate a compile-time error. One workaround is to redefine the Wash method with a constraint:

```
class ZooCleaner
{
  public static void Wash<T> (Stack<T> animals) where T : Animal { ... }
}
```

We can now call Wash as follows:

```
Stack<Bear> bears = new Stack<Bear>();
ZooCleaner.Wash (bears);
```

Another solution is to have Stack<T> implement an interface with a covariant type parameter, as you'll see shortly.

Arrays

For historical reasons, array types support covariance. This means that B[] can be cast to A[] if B subclasses A (and both are reference types):

```
Bear[] bears = new Bear[3];
Animal[] animals = bears;      // OK
```

The downside of this reusability is that element assignments can fail at runtime:

```
animals[0] = new Camel();      // Runtime error
```

Declaring a covariant type parameter

Type parameters on interfaces and delegates can be declared covariant by marking them with the out modifier. This modifier ensures that, unlike with arrays, covariant type parameters are fully type-safe.

We can illustrate this with our Stack<T> class by having it implement the following interface:

```
public interface IPoppable<out T> { T Pop(); }
```

The out modifier on T indicates that T is used only in *output positions* (e.g., return types for methods). The out modifier flags the type parameter as *covariant* and allows us to do this:

```
var bears = new Stack<Bear>();
bears.Push (new Bear());
// Bears implements IPoppable<Bear>. We can convert to IPoppable<Animal>:
IPoppable<Animal> animals = bears;   // Legal
Animal a = animals.Pop();
```

The conversion from bears to animals is permitted by the compiler—by virtue of the type parameter being covariant. This is type-safe because the case the compiler is trying to avoid—pushing a Camel onto the stack—can't occur, because there's no way to feed a Camel *into* an interface where T can appear only in *out*put positions.

> Covariance (and contravariance) in interfaces is something that you typically *consume*: it's less common that you need to *write* variant interfaces.

> Curiously, method parameters marked as out are not eligible for covariance, due to a limitation in the CLR.

We can leverage the ability to cast covariantly to solve the reusability problem described earlier:

```
public class ZooCleaner
{
  public static void Wash (IPoppable<Animal> animals) { ... }
}
```

> The IEnumerator<T> and IEnumerable<T> interfaces described in Chapter 7 have a covariant T. This allows you to cast IEnumerable<string> to IEnumerable<object>, for instance.

The compiler will generate an error if you use a covariant type parameter in an *input* position (e.g., a parameter to a method or a writable property).

Covariance (and contravariance) works only for elements with *reference conversions*—not *boxing conversions*. (This applies both to type parameter variance and array variance.) So, if you wrote a method that accepted a parameter of type IPoppable<object>, you could call it with IPoppable<string> but not IPoppable<int>.

Contravariance

We previously saw that, assuming that A allows an implicit reference conversion to B, a type X has a covariant type parameter if X<A> allows a reference conversion to X<B>. *Contravariance* is when you can convert in the reverse direction—from X<B> to X<A>. This is supported if the type parameter appears only in *input* positions and is designated with the in modifier. Extending our previous example, suppose the Stack<T> class implements the following interface:

```
public interface IPushable<in T> { void Push (T obj); }
```

We can now legally do this:

```
IPushable<Animal> animals = new Stack<Animal>();
IPushable<Bear> bears = animals;    // Legal
bears.Push (new Bear());
```

No member in IPushable *outputs* a T, so we can't get into trouble by casting animals to bears (there's no way to Pop, for instance, through that interface).

Our Stack<T> class can implement both IPushable<T> and IPoppable<T>—despite T having opposing variance annotations in the two interfaces! This works because you must exercise variance through the interface and not the class; therefore, you must commit to the lens of either IPoppable or IPushable before performing a variant conversion. This lens then restricts you to the operations that are legal under the appropriate variance rules.

This also illustrates why *classes* do not allow variant type parameters: concrete implementations typically require data to flow in both directions.

To give another example, consider the following interface, defined in the System namespace:

```
public interface IComparer<in T>
{
  // Returns a value indicating the relative ordering of a and b
  int Compare (T a, T b);
}
```

Because the interface has a contravariant T, we can use an IComparer<**object**> to compare two *strings*:

```
var objectComparer = Comparer<object>.Default;
// objectComparer implements IComparer<object>
IComparer<string> stringComparer = objectComparer;
int result = stringComparer.Compare ("Brett", "Jemaine");
```

Mirroring covariance, the compiler will report an error if you try to use a contravariant type parameter in an output position (e.g., as a return value or in a readable property).

C# Generics Versus C++ Templates

C# generics are similar in application to C++ templates, but they work very differently. In both cases, a synthesis between the producer and consumer must take place in which the placeholder types of the producer are filled in by the consumer. However, with C# generics, producer types (i.e., open types such as List<T>) can be compiled into a library (such as *mscorlib.dll*). This works because the synthesis between the producer and the consumer that produces closed types doesn't actually happen until runtime. With C++ templates, this synthesis is performed at compile time. This means that in C++ you don't deploy template libraries as *.dlls*—they exist only as source code. It also makes it difficult to dynamically inspect, let alone create, parameterized types on the fly.

To dig deeper into why this is the case, consider again the Max method in C#:

```
static T Max <T> (T a, T b) where T : IComparable<T>
  => a.CompareTo (b) > 0 ? a : b;
```

Why couldn't we have implemented it like this?

```
static T Max <T> (T a, T b)
  => (a > b ? a : b);              // Compile error
```

The reason is that Max needs to be compiled once and work for all possible values of T. Compilation cannot succeed because there is no single meaning for > across all values of T—in fact, not every T even has a > operator. In contrast, the following code shows the same Max method written with C++ templates. This code will be compiled separately for each value of T, taking on whatever semantics > has for a particular T and failing to compile if a particular T does not support the > operator:

```
template <class T> T Max (T a, T b)
{
  return a > b ? a : b;
}
```

4

Advanced C#

In this chapter, we cover advanced C# topics that build on concepts explored in Chapters 2 and 3. You should read the first four sections sequentially; you can read the remaining sections in any order.

Delegates

A *delegate* is an object that knows how to call a method.

A *delegate type* defines the kind of method that *delegate instances* can call. Specifically, it defines the method's *return type* and its *parameter types*. The following defines a delegate type called `Transformer`:

```
delegate int Transformer (int x);
```

`Transformer` is compatible with any method with an `int` return type and a single `int` parameter, such as this:

```
int Square (int x) { return x * x; }
```

Or, more tersely:

```
int Square (int x) => x * x;
```

Assigning a method to a delegate variable creates a delegate *instance*:

```
Transformer t = Square;
```

You can invoke a delegate instance in the same way as a method:

```
int answer = t(3);    // answer is 9
```

Here's a complete example:

```
Transformer t = Square;       // Create delegate instance
int result = t(3);            // Invoke delegate
Console.WriteLine (result);   // 9

int Square (int x) => x * x;
```

```
delegate int Transformer (int x);    // Delegate type declaration
```

A delegate instance literally acts as a delegate for the caller: the caller invokes the delegate, and then the delegate calls the target method. This indirection decouples the caller from the target method.

The statement

```
Transformer t = Square;
```

is shorthand for:

```
Transformer t = new Transformer (Square);
```

 Technically, we are specifying a *method group* when we refer to Square without brackets or arguments. If the method is overloaded, C# will pick the correct overload based on the signature of the delegate to which it's being assigned.

The expression

```
t(3)
```

is shorthand for:

```
t.Invoke(3)
```

 A delegate is similar to a *callback*, a general term that captures constructs such as C function pointers.

Writing Plug-In Methods with Delegates

A delegate variable is assigned a method at runtime. This is useful for writing plug-in methods. In this example, we have a utility method named Transform that applies a transform to each element in an integer array. The Transform method has a delegate parameter, which you can use for specifying a plug-in transform:

```
int[] values = { 1, 2, 3 };
Transform (values, Square);     // Hook in the Square method

foreach (int i in values)
  Console.Write (i + " ");      // 1   4   9

void Transform (int[] values, Transformer t)
{
  for (int i = 0; i < values.Length; i++)
    values[i] = t (values[i]);
}

int Square (int x) => x * x;
int Cube (int x) => x * x * x;

delegate int Transformer (int x);
```

We can change the transformation just by changing Square to Cube in the second line of code.

Our Transform method is a *higher-order function* because it's a function that takes a function as an argument. (A method that *returns* a delegate would also be a higher-order function.)

Instance and Static Method Targets

A delegate's target method can be a local, static, or instance method. The following illustrates a static target method:

```
Transformer t = Test.Square;
Console.WriteLine (t(10));      // 100

class Test { public static int Square (int x) => x * x; }

delegate int Transformer (int x);
```

The following illustrates an instance target method:

```
Test test = new Test();
Transformer t = test.Square;
Console.WriteLine (t(10));      // 100

class Test { public int Square (int x) => x * x; }

delegate int Transformer (int x);
```

When an *instance* method is assigned to a delegate object, the latter maintains a reference not only to the method but also to the *instance* to which the method belongs. The System.Delegate class's Target property represents this instance (and will be null for a delegate referencing a static method). Here's an example:

```
MyReporter r = new MyReporter();
r.Prefix = "%Complete: ";
ProgressReporter p = r.ReportProgress;
p(99);                                  // %Complete: 99
Console.WriteLine (p.Target == r);      // True
Console.WriteLine (p.Method);           // Void ReportProgress(Int32)
r.Prefix = "";
p(99);                                  // 99

public delegate void ProgressReporter (int percentComplete);

class MyReporter
{
  public string Prefix = "";

  public void ReportProgress (int percentComplete)
    => Console.WriteLine (Prefix + percentComplete);
}
```

Because the instance is stored in the delegate's Target property, its lifetime is extended to (at least as long as) the delegate's lifetime.

Multicast Delegates

All delegate instances have *multicast* capability. This means that a delegate instance can reference not just a single target method but also a list of target methods. The + and += operators combine delegate instances:

```
SomeDelegate d = SomeMethod1;
d += SomeMethod2;
```

The last line is functionally the same as the following:

```
d = d + SomeMethod2;
```

Invoking d will now call both SomeMethod1 and SomeMethod2. Delegates are invoked in the order in which they are added.

The - and -= operators remove the right delegate operand from the left delegate operand:

```
d -= SomeMethod1;
```

Invoking d will now cause only SomeMethod2 to be invoked.

Calling + or += on a delegate variable with a null value works, and it is equivalent to assigning the variable to a new value:

```
SomeDelegate d = null;
d += SomeMethod1;        // Equivalent (when d is null) to d = SomeMethod1;
```

Similarly, calling -= on a delegate variable with a single matching target is equivalent to assigning null to that variable.

 Delegates are *immutable*, so when you call += or -=, you're in fact creating a *new* delegate instance and assigning it to the existing variable.

If a multicast delegate has a nonvoid return type, the caller receives the return value from the last method to be invoked. The preceding methods are still called, but their return values are discarded. For most scenarios in which multicast delegates are used, they have void return types, so this subtlety does not arise.

 All delegate types implicitly derive from System.Multicast Delegate, which inherits from System.Delegate. C# compiles +, -, +=, and -= operations made on a delegate to the static Combine and Remove methods of the System.Delegate class.

Multicast delegate example

Suppose that you wrote a method that took a long time to execute. That method could regularly report progress to its caller by invoking a delegate. In this example, the HardWork method has a ProgressReporter delegate parameter, which it invokes to indicate progress:

```
public delegate void ProgressReporter (int percentComplete);

public class Util
{
  public static void HardWork (ProgressReporter p)
  {
    for (int i = 0; i < 10; i++)
    {
      p (i * 10);                                // Invoke delegate
      System.Threading.Thread.Sleep (100);  // Simulate hard work
    }
  }
}
```

To monitor progress, we can create a multicast delegate instance p, such that progress is monitored by two independent methods:

```
ProgressReporter p = WriteProgressToConsole;
p += WriteProgressToFile;
Util.HardWork (p);

void WriteProgressToConsole (int percentComplete)
  => Console.WriteLine (percentComplete);

void WriteProgressToFile (int percentComplete)
  => System.IO.File.WriteAllText ("progress.txt",
                                  percentComplete.ToString());
```

Generic Delegate Types

A delegate type can contain generic type parameters:

```
public delegate T Transformer<T> (T arg);
```

With this definition, we can write a generalized Transform utility method that works on any type:

```
int[] values = { 1, 2, 3 };
Util.Transform (values, Square);     // Hook in Square
foreach (int i in values)
  Console.Write (i + " ");           // 1   4   9

int Square (int x) => x * x;

public class Util
{
  public static void Transform<T> (T[] values, Transformer<T> t)
  {
    for (int i = 0; i < values.Length; i++)
      values[i] = t (values[i]);
  }
}
```

The Func and Action Delegates

With generic delegates, it becomes possible to write a small set of delegate types that are so general they can work for methods of any return type and any (reasonable) number of arguments. These delegates are the Func and Action delegates, defined in the System namespace (the in and out annotations indicate *variance*, which we cover in the context of delegates shortly):

```
delegate TResult Func <out TResult>                 ();
delegate TResult Func <in T, out TResult>           (T arg);
delegate TResult Func <in T1, in T2, out TResult>   (T1 arg1, T2 arg2);
... and so on, up to T16

delegate void Action                                ();
delegate void Action <in T>                         (T arg);
delegate void Action <in T1, in T2>                 (T1 arg1, T2 arg2);
... and so on, up to T16
```

These delegates are extremely general. The Transformer delegate in our previous example can be replaced with a Func delegate that takes a single argument of type T and returns a same-typed value:

```
public static void Transform<T> (T[] values, Func<T,T> transformer)
{
  for (int i = 0; i < values.Length; i++)
    values[i] = transformer (values[i]);
}
```

The only practical scenarios not covered by these delegates are ref/out and pointer parameters.

 When C# was first introduced, the Func and Action delegates did not exist (because generics did not exist). It's for this historical reason that much of .NET uses custom delegate types rather than Func and Action.

Delegates Versus Interfaces

A problem that you can solve with a delegate can also be solved with an interface. For instance, we can rewrite our original example with an interface called ITransformer instead of a delegate:

```
int[] values = { 1, 2, 3 };
Util.TransformAll (values, new Squarer());
foreach (int i in values)
  Console.WriteLine (i);

public interface ITransformer
{
  int Transform (int x);
}

public class Util
{
```

```
public static void TransformAll (int[] values, ITransformer t)
{
  for (int i = 0; i < values.Length; i++)
    values[i] = t.Transform (values[i]);
}
}

class Squarer : ITransformer
{
  public int Transform (int x) => x * x;
}
```

A delegate design might be a better choice than an interface design if one or more of
these conditions are true:

- The interface defines only a single method.
- Multicast capability is needed.
- The subscriber needs to implement the interface multiple times.

In the ITransformer example, we don't need to multicast. However, the interface
defines only a single method. Furthermore, our subscriber might need to implement
ITransformer multiple times, to support different transforms, such as square or
cube. With interfaces, we're forced into writing a separate type per transform
because a class can implement ITransformer only once. This is quite cumbersome:

```
int[] values = { 1, 2, 3 };
Util.TransformAll (values, new Cuber());
foreach (int i in values)
  Console.WriteLine (i);

class Squarer : ITransformer
{
  public int Transform (int x) => x * x;
}

class Cuber : ITransformer
{
  public int Transform (int x) => x * x * x;
}
```

Delegate Compatibility

Type compatibility

Delegate types are all incompatible with one another, even if their signatures are the
same:

```
D1 d1 = Method1;
D2 d2 = d1;                          // Compile-time error

void Method1() { }
```

```
delegate void D1();
delegate void D2();
```

 The following, however, is permitted:

```
D2 d2 = new D2 (d1);
```

Delegate instances are considered equal if they have the same method targets:

```
D d1 = Method1;
D d2 = Method1;
Console.WriteLine (d1 == d2);        // True

void Method1() { }
delegate void D();
```

Multicast delegates are considered equal if they reference the same methods *in the same order.*

Parameter compatibility

When you call a method, you can supply arguments that have more specific types than the parameters of that method. This is ordinary polymorphic behavior. For the same reason, a delegate can have more specific parameter types than its method target. This is called *contravariance*. Here's an example:

```
StringAction sa = new StringAction (ActOnObject);
sa ("hello");

void ActOnObject (object o) => Console.WriteLine (o);   // hello

delegate void StringAction (string s);
```

(As with type parameter variance, delegates are variant only for *reference conversions.*)

A delegate merely calls a method on someone else's behalf. In this case, the String Action is invoked with an argument of type string. When the argument is then relayed to the target method, the argument is implicitly upcast to an object.

 The standard event pattern is designed to help you utilize contravariance through its use of the common EventArgs base class. For example, you can have a single method invoked by two different delegates, one passing a MouseEventArgs and the other passing a KeyEventArgs.

Return type compatibility

If you call a method, you might get back a type that is more specific than what you asked for. This is ordinary polymorphic behavior. For the same reason, a delegate's target method might return a more specific type than described by the delegate. This is called *covariance*:

```
ObjectRetriever o = new ObjectRetriever (RetriveString);
object result = o();
Console.WriteLine (result);      // hello

string RetriveString() => "hello";

delegate object ObjectRetriever();
```

ObjectRetriever expects to get back an object, but an object *subclass* will also do: delegate return types are *covariant*.

Generic delegate type parameter variance

In Chapter 3, we saw how generic interfaces support covariant and contravariant type parameters. The same capability exists for delegates, too.

If you're defining a generic delegate type, it's good practice to do the following:

- Mark a type parameter used only on the return value as covariant (out).

- Mark any type parameters used only on parameters as contravariant (in).

Doing so allows conversions to work naturally by respecting inheritance relationships between types.

The following delegate (defined in the System namespace) has a covariant TResult:

```
delegate TResult Func<out TResult>();
```

This allows:

```
Func<string> x = ...;
Func<object> y = x;
```

The following delegate (defined in the System namespace) has a contravariant T:

```
delegate void Action<in T> (T arg);
```

This allows:

```
Action<object> x = ...;
Action<string> y = x;
```

Events

When using delegates, two emergent roles commonly appear: *broadcaster* and *subscriber*.

The *broadcaster* is a type that contains a delegate field. The broadcaster decides when to broadcast, by invoking the delegate.

The *subscribers* are the method target recipients. A subscriber decides when to start and stop listening by calling += and -= on the broadcaster's delegate. A subscriber does not know about, or interfere with, other subscribers.

Events are a language feature that formalizes this pattern. An event is a construct that exposes just the subset of delegate features required for the broadcaster/subscriber model. The main purpose of events is to *prevent subscribers from interfering with one another.*

The easiest way to declare an event is to put the event keyword in front of a delegate member:

```
// Delegate definition
public delegate void PriceChangedHandler (decimal oldPrice,
                                           decimal newPrice);

public class Broadcaster
{
  // Event declaration
  public event PriceChangedHandler PriceChanged;
}
```

Code within the Broadcaster type has full access to PriceChanged and can treat it as a delegate. Code outside of Broadcaster can perform only += and -= operations on the PriceChanged event.

How Do Events Work on the Inside?

Three things happen under the hood when you declare an event as follows:

```
public class Broadcaster
{
  public event PriceChangedHandler PriceChanged;
}
```

First, the compiler translates the event declaration into something close to the following:

```
PriceChangedHandler priceChanged;   // private delegate
public event PriceChangedHandler PriceChanged
{
  add    { priceChanged += value; }
  remove { priceChanged -= value; }
}
```

The add and remove keywords denote explicit *event accessors*—which act rather like property accessors. We describe how to write these later.

Second, the compiler looks *within* the Broadcaster class for references to Price Changed that perform operations other than += or -= and redirects them to the underlying priceChanged delegate field.

Third, the compiler translates += and -= operations on the event to calls to the event's add and remove accessors. Interestingly, this makes the behavior of += and -= unique when applied to events: unlike in other scenarios, it's not simply a shortcut for + and - followed by an assignment.

Consider the following example. The Stock class fires its PriceChanged event every time the Price of the Stock changes:

```
public delegate void PriceChangedHandler (decimal oldPrice,
                                           decimal newPrice);
public class Stock
{
  string symbol;
  decimal price;

  public Stock (string symbol) => this.symbol = symbol;

  public event PriceChangedHandler PriceChanged;

  public decimal Price
  {
    get => price;
    set
    {
      if (price == value) return;      // Exit if nothing has changed
      decimal oldPrice = price;
      price = value;
      if (PriceChanged != null)        // If invocation list not
        PriceChanged (oldPrice, price); // empty, fire event.
    }
  }
}
```

If we remove the event keyword from our example so that PriceChanged becomes an ordinary delegate field, our example would give the same results. However, Stock would be less robust insomuch as subscribers could do the following things to interfere with one another:

- Replace other subscribers by reassigning PriceChanged (instead of using the += operator)
- Clear all subscribers (by setting PriceChanged to null)
- Broadcast to other subscribers by invoking the delegate

Standard Event Pattern

In almost all cases for which events are defined in the .NET libraries, their definition adheres to a standard pattern designed to provide consistency across library and user code. At the core of the standard event pattern is System.EventArgs, a predefined .NET class with no members (other than the static Empty field). EventArgs is a base class for conveying information for an event. In our Stock example, we would subclass EventArgs to convey the old and new prices when a PriceChanged event is fired:

```
public class PriceChangedEventArgs : System.EventArgs
{
  public readonly decimal LastPrice;
  public readonly decimal NewPrice;

  public PriceChangedEventArgs (decimal lastPrice, decimal newPrice)
  {
    LastPrice = lastPrice;
    NewPrice = newPrice;
  }
}
```

For reusability, the EventArgs subclass is named according to the information it contains (rather than the event for which it will be used). It typically exposes data as properties or as read-only fields.

With an EventArgs subclass in place, the next step is to choose or define a delegate for the event. There are three rules:

- It must have a void return type.

- It must accept two arguments: the first of type object and the second a subclass of EventArgs. The first argument indicates the event broadcaster, and the second argument contains the extra information to convey.

- Its name must end with EventHandler.

.NET defines a generic delegate called System.EventHandler<> to help with this:

```
public delegate void EventHandler<TEventArgs> (object source, TEventArgs e)
```

Before generics existed in the language (prior to C# 2.0), we would have had to instead write a custom delegate as follows:

```
public delegate void PriceChangedHandler
  (object sender, PriceChangedEventArgs e);
```

For historical reasons, most events within the .NET libraries use delegates defined in this way.

The next step is to define an event of the chosen delegate type. Here, we use the generic EventHandler delegate:

```
public class Stock
{
  ...
  public event EventHandler<PriceChangedEventArgs> PriceChanged;
}
```

Finally, the pattern requires that you write a protected virtual method that fires the event. The name must match the name of the event, prefixed with the word *On*, and then accept a single EventArgs argument:

```
public class Stock
{
  ...

  public event EventHandler<PriceChangedEventArgs> PriceChanged;

  protected virtual void OnPriceChanged (PriceChangedEventArgs e)
  {
    if (PriceChanged != null) PriceChanged (this, e);
  }
}
```

 To work robustly in multithreaded scenarios (Chapter 14), you need to assign the delegate to a temporary variable before testing and invoking it:

```
var temp = PriceChanged;
if (temp != null) temp (this, e);
```

We can achieve the same functionality without the temp variable with the null-conditional operator:

```
PriceChanged?.Invoke (this, e);
```

Being both thread-safe and succinct, this is the best general way to invoke events.

This provides a central point from which subclasses can invoke or override the event (assuming the class is not sealed).

Here's the complete example:

```
using System;

Stock stock = new Stock ("THPW");
stock.Price = 27.10M;
// Register with the PriceChanged event
stock.PriceChanged += stock_PriceChanged;
stock.Price = 31.59M;

void stock_PriceChanged (object sender, PriceChangedEventArgs e)
{
  if ((e.NewPrice - e.LastPrice) / e.LastPrice > 0.1M)
    Console.WriteLine ("Alert, 10% stock price increase!");
}

public class PriceChangedEventArgs : EventArgs
{
  public readonly decimal LastPrice;
  public readonly decimal NewPrice;

  public PriceChangedEventArgs (decimal lastPrice, decimal newPrice)
  {
    LastPrice = lastPrice; NewPrice = newPrice;
  }
}

public class Stock
```

Advanced C#

```
{
  string symbol;
  decimal price;

  public Stock (string symbol) => this.symbol = symbol;

  public event EventHandler<PriceChangedEventArgs> PriceChanged;

  protected virtual void OnPriceChanged (PriceChangedEventArgs e)
  {
    PriceChanged?.Invoke (this, e);
  }

  public decimal Price
  {
    get => price;
    set
    {
      if (price == value) return;
      decimal oldPrice = price;
      price = value;
      OnPriceChanged (new PriceChangedEventArgs (oldPrice, price));
    }
  }
}
```

The predefined nongeneric EventHandler delegate can be used when an event doesn't carry extra information. In this example, we rewrite Stock such that the PriceChanged event is fired after the price changes, and no information about the event is necessary, other than it happened. We also make use of the EventArgs.Empty property to avoid unnecessarily instantiating an instance of EventArgs:

```
public class Stock
{
  string symbol;
  decimal price;

  public Stock (string symbol) { this.symbol = symbol; }

  public event EventHandler PriceChanged;

  protected virtual void OnPriceChanged (EventArgs e)
  {
    PriceChanged?.Invoke (this, e);
  }

  public decimal Price
  {
    get { return price; }
    set
    {
      if (price == value) return;
      price = value;
```

```
        OnPriceChanged (EventArgs.Empty);
      }
    }
  }
```

Event Accessors

An event's *accessors* are the implementations of its += and -= functions. By default, accessors are implemented implicitly by the compiler. Consider this event declaration:

```
public event EventHandler PriceChanged;
```

The compiler converts this to the following:

- A private delegate field

- A public pair of event accessor functions (add_PriceChanged and remove_PriceChanged) whose implementations forward the += and -= operations to the private delegate field

You can take over this process by defining *explicit* event accessors. Here's a manual implementation of the PriceChanged event from our previous example:

```
private EventHandler priceChanged;        // Declare a private delegate

public event EventHandler PriceChanged
{
  add    { priceChanged += value; }
  remove { priceChanged -= value; }
}
```

This example is functionally identical to C#'s default accessor implementation (except that C# also ensures thread safety around updating the delegate via a lock-free compare-and-swap algorithm; see *http://albahari.com/threading*). By defining event accessors ourselves, we instruct C# not to generate default field and accessor logic.

With explicit event accessors, you can apply more complex strategies to the storage and access of the underlying delegate. There are three scenarios for which this is useful:

- When the event accessors are merely relays for another class that is broadcasting the event.

- When the class exposes many events, for which most of the time very few subscribers exist, such as a Windows control. In such cases, it is better to store the subscriber's delegate instances in a dictionary because a dictionary will contain less storage overhead than dozens of null delegate field references.

- When explicitly implementing an interface that declares an event.

Here is an example that illustrates the last point:

```
public interface IFoo { event EventHandler Ev; }

class Foo : IFoo
{
  private EventHandler ev;

  event EventHandler IFoo.Ev
  {
    add     { ev += value; }
    remove { ev -= value; }
  }
}
```

The add and remove parts of an event are compiled to add_*XXX* and remove_*XXX* methods.

Event Modifiers

Like methods, events can be virtual, overridden, abstract, or sealed. Events can also be static:

```
public class Foo
{
  public static event EventHandler<EventArgs> StaticEvent;
  public virtual event EventHandler<EventArgs> VirtualEvent;
}
```

Lambda Expressions

A *lambda expression* is an unnamed method written in place of a delegate instance. The compiler immediately converts the lambda expression to either of the following:

- A delegate instance.

- An *expression tree*, of type Expression<TDelegate>, representing the code inside the lambda expression in a traversable object model. This allows the lambda expression to be interpreted later at runtime (see "Building Query Expressions" on page 442).

In the following example, x => x * x is a lambda expression:

```
Transformer sqr = x => x * x;
Console.WriteLine (sqr(3));     // 9

delegate int Transformer (int i);
```

Internally, the compiler resolves lambda expressions of this type by writing a private method and then moving the expression's code into that method.

A lambda expression has the following form:

```
(parameters) => expression-or-statement-block
```

For convenience, you can omit the parentheses if and only if there is exactly one parameter of an inferable type.

In our example, there is a single parameter, x, and the expression is x * x:

```
x => x * x;
```

Each parameter of the lambda expression corresponds to a delegate parameter, and the type of the expression (which may be void) corresponds to the return type of the delegate.

In our example, x corresponds to parameter i, and the expression x * x corresponds to the return type int, therefore being compatible with the Transformer delegate:

```
delegate int Transformer (int i);
```

A lambda expression's code can be a *statement block* instead of an expression. We can rewrite our example as follows:

```
x => { return x * x; };
```

Lambda expressions are used most commonly with the Func and Action delegates, so you will most often see our earlier expression written as follows:

```
Func<int,int> sqr = x => x * x;
```

Here's an example of an expression that accepts two parameters:

```
Func<string,string,int> totalLength = (s1, s2) => s1.Length + s2.Length;
int total = totalLength ("hello", "world");   // total is 10;
```

If you do not need to use the parameters, you can *discard* them with an underscore (from C# 9):

```
Func<string,string,int> totalLength = (_,_) => ...
```

Here's an example of an expression that takes zero arguments:

```
Func<string> greetor = () => "Hello, world";
```

From C# 10, the compiler permits implicit typing with lambda expressions that can be resolved via the Func and Action delegates, so we can shorten this statement to:

```
var greeter = () => "Hello, world";
```

Explicitly Specifying Lambda Parameter and Return Types

The compiler can usually *infer* the type of lambda parameters contextually. When this is not the case, you must specify the type of each parameter explicitly. Consider the following two methods:

```
void Foo<T> (T x)        {}
void Bar<T> (Action<T> a) {}
```

The following code will fail to compile, because the compiler cannot infer the type of x:

```
Bar (x => Foo (x));      // What type is x?
```

We can fix this by explicitly specifying x's type as follows:

```
Bar ((int x) => Foo (x));
```

This particular example is simple enough that it can be fixed in two other ways:

```
Bar<int> (x => Foo (x));    // Specify type parameter for Bar
Bar<int> (Foo);            // As above, but with method group
```

The following example illustrates another use for explicit parameter types (from C# 10):

```
var sqr = (int x) => x * x;
```

The compiler infers sqr to be of type Func<int,int>. (Without specifying int, implicit typing would fail: the compiler would know that sqr should be Func<T,T>, but it wouldn't know what T should be.)

From C# 10, you can also specify the lambda return type:

```
var sqr = int (int x) => x;
```

Specifying a return type can improve compiler performance with complex nested lambdas.

Capturing Outer Variables

A lambda expression can reference any variables that are accessible where the lambda expression is defined. These are called *outer variables*, and can include local variables, parameters, and fields:

```
int factor = 2;
Func<int, int> multiplier = n => n * factor;
Console.WriteLine (multiplier (3));          // 6
```

Outer variables referenced by a lambda expression are called *captured variables*. A lambda expression that captures variables is called a *closure*.

Variables can also be captured by anonymous methods and local methods. The rules for captured variables, in these cases, are the same.

Captured variables are evaluated when the delegate is actually *invoked*, not when the variables were *captured*:

```
int factor = 2;
Func<int, int> multiplier = n => n * factor;
factor = 10;
Console.WriteLine (multiplier (3));          // 30
```

Lambda expressions can themselves update captured variables:

```
int seed = 0;
Func<int> natural = () => seed++;
Console.WriteLine (natural());        // 0
Console.WriteLine (natural());        // 1
Console.WriteLine (seed);             // 2
```

Captured variables have their lifetimes extended to that of the delegate. In the following example, the local variable seed would ordinarily disappear from scope when Natural finished executing. But because seed has been *captured*, its lifetime is extended to that of the capturing delegate, natural:

```
static Func<int> Natural()
{
  int seed = 0;
  return () => seed++;        // Returns a closure
}

static void Main()
{
  Func<int> natural = Natural();
  Console.WriteLine (natural());        // 0
  Console.WriteLine (natural());        // 1
}
```

A local variable *instantiated* within a lambda expression is unique per invocation of the delegate instance. If we refactor our previous example to instantiate seed *within* the lambda expression, we get a different (in this case, undesirable) result:

```
static Func<int> Natural()
{
  return() => { int seed = 0; return seed++; };
}

static void Main()
{
  Func<int> natural = Natural();
  Console.WriteLine (natural());        // 0
  Console.WriteLine (natural());        // 0
}
```

> Capturing is internally implemented by "hoisting" the captured variables into fields of a private class. When the method is called, the class is instantiated and lifetime-bound to the delegate instance.

Static lambdas

When you capture local variables, parameters, instance fields, or the this reference, the compiler may need to create and instantiate a private class to store a reference to the captured data. This incurs a small performance cost, because memory must be allocated (and subsequently collected). In situations where performance is critical, one micro-optimization strategy is to minimize the load on the garbage collector by ensuring that code hot paths incur few or no allocations.

From C# 9, you can ensure that a lambda expression, local function, or anonymous method doesn't capture state by applying the static keyword. This can be useful in micro-optimization scenarios to prevent unintentional memory allocations. For example, we can apply the static modifier to a lambda expression as follows:

```
Func<int, int> multiplier = static n => n * 2;
```

If we later try to modify the lambda expression such that it captures a local variable, the compiler will generate an error:

```
int factor = 2;
Func<int, int> multiplier = static n => n * factor;  // will not compile
```

The lambda itself evaluates to a delegate instance, which requires a memory allocation. However, if the lambda doesn't capture variables, the compiler will reuse a single cached instance across the life of the application, so there will be no cost in practice.

This feature can also be used with local methods. In the following example, the Multiply method cannot access the factor variable:

```
void Foo()
{
  int factor = 123;
  static int Multiply (int x) => x * 2;   // Local static method
}
```

Of course, the Multiply method could still explicitly allocate memory by calling new. What this protects us from is a potential allocation by *stealth*. Applying static here is also arguably useful as a documentation tool, indicating a reduced level of coupling.

Static lambdas can still access static variables and constants (because these do not require a closure).

The static keyword acts merely as a *check*; it has no effect on the IL that the compiler produces. Without the static keyword, the compiler does not generate a closure unless it needs to (and even then, it has tricks to mitigate the cost).

Capturing iteration variables

When you capture the iteration variable of a for loop, C# treats that variable as though it were declared *outside* the loop. This means that the *same* variable is captured in each iteration. The following program writes 333 instead of 012:

```
Action[] actions = new Action[3];

for (int i = 0; i < 3; i++)
  actions [i] = () => Console.Write (i);

foreach (Action a in actions) a();      // 333
```

Each closure (shown in boldface) captures the same variable, i. (This actually makes sense when you consider that i is a variable whose value persists between loop iterations; you can even explicitly change i within the loop body if you want.) The consequence is that when the delegates are later invoked, each delegate sees i's value at the time of *invocation*—which is 3. We can illustrate this better by expanding the for loop, as follows:

```
Action[] actions = new Action[3];
int i = 0;
actions[0] = () => Console.Write (i);
i = 1;
actions[1] = () => Console.Write (i);
i = 2;
actions[2] = () => Console.Write (i);
i = 3;
foreach (Action a in actions) a();     // 333
```

The solution, if we want to write 012, is to assign the iteration variable to a local variable that's scoped *within* the loop:

```
Action[] actions = new Action[3];
for (int i = 0; i < 3; i++)
{
   int loopScopedi = i;
   actions [i] = () => Console.Write (loopScopedi);
}
foreach (Action a in actions) a();     // 012
```

Because loopScopedi is freshly created on every iteration, each closure captures a *different* variable.

 Prior to C# 5.0, foreach loops worked in the same way. This caused considerable confusion: unlike with a for loop, the iteration variable in a foreach loop is immutable, and so you would expect it to be treated as local to the loop body. The good news is that it's now fixed, and you can safely capture a foreach loop's iteration variable without surprises.

Lambda Expressions Versus Local Methods

The functionality of local methods (see "Local methods" on page 19) overlaps with that of lambda expressions. Local methods have the following three advantages:

- They can be recursive (they can call themselves) without ugly hacks.
- They avoid the clutter of specifying a delegate type.
- They incur slightly less overhead.

Local methods are more efficient because they avoid the indirection of a delegate (which costs some CPU cycles and a memory allocation). They can also access local variables of the containing method without the compiler having to "hoist" the captured variables into a hidden class.

However, in many cases you *need* a delegate—most commonly when calling a higher-order function, that is, a method with a delegate-typed parameter:

```
public void Foo (Func<int,bool> predicate) { ... }
```

(You can see plenty more of these in Chapter 8.) In such cases, you need a delegate anyway, and it's in precisely these cases that lambda expressions are usually terser and cleaner.

Anonymous Methods

Anonymous methods are a C# 2.0 feature that was mostly subsumed by C# 3.0's lambda expressions. An anonymous method is like a lambda expression, but it lacks the following features:

- Implicitly typed parameters
- Expression syntax (an anonymous method must always be a statement block)
- The ability to compile to an expression tree, by assigning to Expression<T>

An anonymous method uses the delegate keyword followed (optionally) by a parameter declaration and then a method body. For example:

```
Transformer sqr = delegate (int x) {return x * x;};
Console.WriteLine (sqr(3));                          // 9

delegate int Transformer (int i);
```

The first line is semantically equivalent to the following lambda expression:

```
Transformer sqr =      (int x) => {return x * x;};
```

Or simply:

```
Transformer sqr =         x  => x * x;
```

Anonymous methods capture outer variables in the same way lambda expressions do, and can be preceded by the static keyword to make them behave like static lambdas.

 A unique feature of anonymous methods is that you can omit the parameter declaration entirely—even if the delegate expects it. This can be useful in declaring events with a default empty handler:

```
public event EventHandler Clicked = delegate { };
```

This avoids the need for a null check before firing the event. The following is also legal:

```
// Notice that we omit the parameters:
Clicked += delegate { Console.WriteLine ("clicked"); };
```

try Statements and Exceptions

A try statement specifies a code block subject to error-handling or cleanup code. The try *block* must be followed by one or more catch *blocks* and/or a finally *block*, or both. The catch block executes when an error is thrown in the try block. The finally block executes after execution leaves the try block (or, if present, the catch block) to perform cleanup code, regardless of whether an exception was thrown.

A catch block has access to an Exception object that contains information about the error. You use a catch block to either compensate for the error or *rethrow* the exception. You rethrow an exception if you merely want to log the problem or if you want to rethrow a new, higher-level exception type.

A finally block adds determinism to your program: the CLR endeavors to always execute it. It's useful for cleanup tasks such as closing network connections.

A try statement looks like this:

```
try
{
  ... // exception may get thrown within execution of this block
}
catch (ExceptionA ex)
{
  ... // handle exception of type ExceptionA
}
catch (ExceptionB ex)
{
  ... // handle exception of type ExceptionB
}
finally
{
  ... // cleanup code
}
```

Consider the following program:

```
int y = Calc (0);
Console.WriteLine (y);

int Calc (int x) => 10 / x;
```

Because x is zero, the runtime throws a DivideByZeroException, and our program terminates. We can prevent this by catching the exception as follows:

```
try
{
  int y = Calc (0);
  Console.WriteLine (y);
}
catch (DivideByZeroException ex)
{
  Console.WriteLine ("x cannot be zero");
```

```
        }
    Console.WriteLine ("program completed");

    int Calc (int x) => 10 / x;
```

Here's the output:

```
x cannot be zero
program completed
```

 This is a simple example to illustrate exception handling. We could deal with this particular scenario better in practice by checking explicitly for the divisor being zero before calling `Calc`.

Checking for preventable errors is preferable to relying on try/catch blocks because exceptions are relatively expensive to handle, taking hundreds of clock cycles or more.

When an exception is thrown within a `try` statement, the CLR performs a test:

Does the `try` *statement have any compatible* `catch` *blocks?*

- If so, execution jumps to the compatible `catch` block, followed by the `finally` block (if present), and then execution continues normally.

- If not, execution jumps directly to the `finally` block (if present), then the CLR looks up the call stack for other `try` blocks; if found, it repeats the test.

If no function in the call stack takes responsibility for the exception, the program terminates.

The catch Clause

A `catch` clause specifies what type of exception to catch. This must either be `System.Exception` or a subclass of `System.Exception`.

Catching `System.Exception` catches all possible errors. This is useful in the following circumstances:

- Your program can potentially recover regardless of the specific exception type.
- You plan to rethrow the exception (perhaps after logging it).
- Your error handler is the last resort, prior to termination of the program.

More typically, though, you catch *specific exception types* to avoid having to deal with circumstances for which your handler wasn't designed (e.g., an `OutOfMemoryException`).

You can handle multiple exception types with multiple `catch` clauses (again, this example could be written with explicit argument checking rather than exception handling):

```
class Test
{
  static void Main (string[] args)
  {
    try
    {
      byte b = byte.Parse (args[0]);
      Console.WriteLine (b);
    }
    catch (IndexOutOfRangeException)
    {
      Console.WriteLine ("Please provide at least one argument");
    }
    catch (FormatException)
    {
      Console.WriteLine ("That's not a number!");
    }
    catch (OverflowException)
    {
      Console.WriteLine ("You've given me more than a byte!");
    }
  }
}
```

Only one catch clause executes for a given exception. If you want to include a safety net to catch more general exceptions (such as System.Exception), you must put the more-specific handlers *first*.

An exception can be caught without specifying a variable, if you don't need to access its properties:

```
catch (OverflowException)   // no variable
{
  ...
}
```

Furthermore, you can omit both the variable and the type (meaning that all exceptions will be caught):

```
catch { ... }
```

Exception filters

You can specify an *exception filter* in a catch clause by adding a when clause:

```
catch (WebException ex) when (ex.Status == WebExceptionStatus.Timeout)
{
  ...
}
```

If a WebException is thrown in this example, the Boolean expression following the when keyword is then evaluated. If the result is false, the catch block in question is ignored and any subsequent catch clauses are considered. With exception filters, it can be meaningful to catch the same exception type again:

```
catch (WebException ex) when (ex.Status == WebExceptionStatus.Timeout)
{ ... }
catch (WebException ex) when (ex.Status == WebExceptionStatus.SendFailure)
{ ... }
```

The Boolean expression in the when clause can be side-effecting, such as a method that logs the exception for diagnostic purposes.

The finally Block

A finally block always executes—regardless of whether an exception is thrown and whether the try block runs to completion. You typically use finally blocks for cleanup code.

A finally block executes after any of the following:

- A catch block finishes (or throws a new exception).

- The try block finishes (or throws an exception for which there's no catch block).

- Control leaves the try block because of a jump statement (e.g., return or goto).

The only things that can defeat a finally block are an infinite loop or the process ending abruptly.

A finally block helps add determinism to a program. In the following example, the file that we open *always* gets closed, regardless of whether:

- The try block finishes normally.

- Execution returns early because the file is empty (EndOfStream).

- An IOException is thrown while reading the file.

```
void ReadFile()
{
  StreamReader reader = null;    // In System.IO namespace
  try
  {
    reader = File.OpenText ("file.txt");
    if (reader.EndOfStream) return;
    Console.WriteLine (reader.ReadToEnd());
  }
  finally
  {
    if (reader != null) reader.Dispose();
  }
}
```

In this example, we closed the file by calling Dispose on the StreamReader. Calling Dispose on an object, within a finally block, is a standard convention and is supported explicitly in C# through the using statement.

The using statement

Many classes encapsulate unmanaged resources, such as file handles, graphics handles, or database connections. These classes implement System.IDisposable, which defines a single parameterless method named Dispose to clean up these resources. The using statement provides an elegant syntax for calling Dispose on an IDisposable object within a finally block.

Thus,

```
using (StreamReader reader = File.OpenText ("file.txt"))
{
  ...
}
```

is precisely equivalent to the following:

```
{
  StreamReader reader = File.OpenText ("file.txt");
  try
  {
    ...
  }
  finally
  {
    if (reader != null)
      ((IDisposable)reader).Dispose();
  }
}
```

using declarations

If you omit the brackets and statement block following a using statement (C# 8+), it becomes a *using declaration*. The resource is then disposed when execution falls outside the *enclosing* statement block:

```
if (File.Exists ("file.txt"))
{
  using var reader = File.OpenText ("file.txt");
  Console.WriteLine (reader.ReadLine());
  ...
}
```

In this case, reader will be disposed when execution falls outside the if statement block.

Throwing Exceptions

Exceptions can be thrown either by the runtime or in user code. In this example, Display throws a System.ArgumentNullException:

```
try { Display (null); }
catch (ArgumentNullException ex)
{
  Console.WriteLine ("Caught the exception");
```

```
  }

  void Display (string name)
  {
    if (name == null)
      throw new ArgumentNullException (nameof (name));

    Console.WriteLine (name);
  }
```

 Because null-checking an argument and throwing an ArgumentNullException is such a common code path, there's actually a shortcut for it, from .NET 6:

```
void Display (string name)
{
  ArgumentNullException.ThrowIfNull (name);
  Console.WriteLine (name);
}
```

Notice that we didn't need to specify the name of the parameter. We'll explain why later, in "CallerArgumentExpression (C# 10)" on page 231.

throw expressions

throw can also appear as an expression in expression-bodied functions:

```
public string Foo() => throw new NotImplementedException();
```

A throw expression can also appear in a ternary conditional expression:

```
string ProperCase (string value) =>
  value == null ? throw new ArgumentException ("value") :
  value == "" ? "" :
  char.ToUpper (value[0]) + value.Substring (1);
```

Rethrowing an exception

You can capture and rethrow an exception as follows:

```
try { ... }
catch (Exception ex)
{
  // Log error
  ...
  throw;          // Rethrow same exception
}
```

 If we replaced throw with throw ex, the example would still work, but the StackTrace property of the newly propagated exception would no longer reflect the original error.

Rethrowing in this manner lets you log an error without *swallowing* it. It also lets you back out of handling an exception should circumstances turn out to be beyond what you expected. The other common scenario is to rethrow a more specific exception type:

```
try
{
  ... // Parse a DateTime from XML element data
}
catch (FormatException ex)
{
  throw new XmlException ("Invalid DateTime", ex);
}
```

Notice that when we constructed XmlException, we passed in the original exception, ex, as the second argument. This argument populates the InnerException property of the new exception and aids debugging. Nearly all types of exception offer a similar constructor.

Rethrowing a *less*-specific exception is something you might do when crossing a trust boundary, so as not to leak technical information to potential hackers.

Key Properties of System.Exception

The most important properties of System.Exception are the following:

StackTrace
: A string representing all the methods that are called from the origin of the exception to the catch block.

Message
: A string with a description of the error.

InnerException
: The inner exception (if any) that caused the outer exception. This, itself, can have another InnerException.

> All exceptions in C# are runtime exceptions—there is no equivalent to Java's compile-time checked exceptions.

Common Exception Types

The following exception types are used widely throughout the CLR and .NET libraries. You can throw these yourself or use them as base classes for deriving custom exception types:

System.ArgumentException
: Thrown when a function is called with a bogus argument. This generally indicates a program bug.

System.ArgumentNullException
: Subclass of ArgumentException that's thrown when a function argument is (unexpectedly) null.

System.ArgumentOutOfRangeException
: Subclass of `ArgumentException` that's thrown when a (usually numeric) argument is too big or too small. For example, this is thrown when passing a negative number into a function that accepts only positive values.

System.InvalidOperationException
: Thrown when the state of an object is unsuitable for a method to successfully execute, regardless of any particular argument values. Examples include reading an unopened file or getting the next element from an enumerator for which the underlying list has been modified partway through the iteration.

System.NotSupportedException
: Thrown to indicate that a particular functionality is not supported. A good example is calling the `Add` method on a collection for which `IsReadOnly` returns `true`.

System.NotImplementedException
: Thrown to indicate that a function has not yet been implemented.

System.ObjectDisposedException
: Thrown when the object upon which the function is called has been disposed.

Another commonly encountered exception type is `NullReferenceException`. The CLR throws this exception when you attempt to access a member of an object whose value is `null` (indicating a bug in your code). You can throw a `NullReferenceException` directly (for testing purposes) as follows:

```
throw null;
```

The TryXXX Method Pattern

When writing a method, you have a choice, when something goes wrong, to return some kind of failure code or throw an exception. In general, you throw an exception when the error is outside the normal workflow—or if you expect that the immediate caller won't be able to cope with it. Occasionally, though, it can be best to offer both choices to the consumer. An example of this is the `int` type, which defines two versions of its `Parse` method:

```
public int Parse     (string input);
public bool TryParse (string input, out int returnValue);
```

If parsing fails, `Parse` throws an exception; `TryParse` returns `false`.

You can implement this pattern by having the *XXX* method call the `TryXXX` method as follows:

```
public return-type XXX (input-type input)
{
  return-type returnValue;
  if (!TryXXX (input, out returnValue))
    throw new YYYException (...)
```

```
        return returnValue;
    }
```

Alternatives to Exceptions

As with int.TryParse, a function can communicate failure by sending an error code back to the calling function via a return type or parameter. Although this can work with simple and predictable failures, it becomes clumsy when extended to all errors, polluting method signatures and creating unnecessary complexity and clutter. It also cannot generalize to functions that are not methods, such as operators (e.g., the division operator) or properties. An alternative is to place the error in a common place where all functions in the call stack can see it (e.g., a static method that stores the current error per thread). This, though, requires each function to participate in an error-propagation pattern, which is cumbersome and, ironically, itself error prone.

Enumeration and Iterators

Enumeration

An *enumerator* is a read-only, forward-only cursor over a *sequence of values*. C# treats a type as an enumerator if it does any of the following:

- Has a public parameterless method named MoveNext and property called Current

- Implements System.Collections.Generic.IEnumerator<T>

- Implements System.Collections.IEnumerator

The foreach statement iterates over an *enumerable* object. An enumerable object is the logical representation of a sequence. It is not itself a cursor, but an object that produces cursors over itself. C# treats a type as enumerable if it does any of the following (the check is performed in this order):

- Has a public parameterless method named GetEnumerator that returns an enumerator

- Implements System.Collections.Generic.IEnumerable<T>

- Implements System.Collections.IEnumerable

- (From C# 9) Can bind to an *extension method* named GetEnumerator that returns an enumerator (see "Extension Methods" on page 202)

The enumeration pattern is as follows:

```
class Enumerator    // Typically implements IEnumerator or IEnumerator<T>
{
    public IteratorVariableType Current { get {...} }
    public bool MoveNext() {...}
```

```
    }

    class Enumerable    // Typically implements IEnumerable or IEnumerable<T>
    {
        public Enumerator GetEnumerator() {...}
    }
```

Here is the high-level way of iterating through the characters in the word *beer* using a foreach statement:

```
    foreach (char c in "beer")
        Console.WriteLine (c);
```

Here is the low-level way of iterating through the characters in *beer* without using a foreach statement:

```
    using (var enumerator = "beer".GetEnumerator())
        while (enumerator.MoveNext())
        {
            var element = enumerator.Current;
            Console.WriteLine (element);
        }
```

If the enumerator implements IDisposable, the foreach statement also acts as a using statement, implicitly disposing the enumerator object.

Chapter 7 explains the enumeration interfaces in further detail.

Collection Initializers

You can instantiate and populate an enumerable object in a single step:

```
    using System.Collections.Generic;
    ...

    List<int> list = new List<int> {1, 2, 3};
```

The compiler translates this to the following:

```
    using System.Collections.Generic;
    ...

    List<int> list = new List<int>();
    list.Add (1);
    list.Add (2);
    list.Add (3);
```

This requires that the enumerable object implements the System.Collec
tions.IEnumerable interface, and that it has an Add method that has the appropriate number of parameters for the call. You can similarly initialize dictionaries (see
"Dictionaries" on page 372) as follows:

```
    var dict = new Dictionary<int, string>()
    {
        { 5, "five" },
```

```
    { 10, "ten" }
  };
```

Or, more succinctly:

```
var dict = new Dictionary<int, string>()
{
  [3] = "three",
  [10] = "ten"
};
```

The latter is valid not only with dictionaries but with any type for which an indexer exists.

Iterators

Whereas a foreach statement is a *consumer* of an enumerator, an iterator is a *producer* of an enumerator. In this example, we use an iterator to return a sequence of Fibonacci numbers (where each number is the sum of the previous two):

```
using System;
using System.Collections.Generic;

foreach (int fib in Fibs(6))
  Console.Write (fib + "  ");
}

IEnumerable<int> Fibs (int fibCount)
{
  for (int i = 0, prevFib = 1, curFib = 1; i < fibCount; i++)
  {
    yield return prevFib;
    int newFib = prevFib+curFib;
    prevFib = curFib;
    curFib = newFib;
  }
}

OUTPUT: 1  1  2  3  5  8
```

Whereas a return statement expresses, "Here's the value you asked me to return from this method," a yield return statement expresses, "Here's the next element you asked me to yield from this enumerator." On each yield statement, control is returned to the caller, but the callee's state is maintained so that the method can continue executing as soon as the caller enumerates the next element. The lifetime of this state is bound to the enumerator such that the state can be released when the caller has finished enumerating.

The compiler converts iterator methods into private classes that implement IEnumerable<T> and/or IEnumerator<T>. The logic within the iterator block is "inverted" and spliced into the MoveNext method and Current property on the compiler-written enumerator class. This means that when you call an iterator method, all you're doing is instantiating the compiler-written class; none of your code actually runs! Your code runs only when you start enumerating over the resultant sequence, typically with a foreach statement.

Iterators can be local methods (see "Local methods" on page 19).

Iterator Semantics

An iterator is a method, property, or indexer that contains one or more yield statements. An iterator must return one of the following four interfaces (otherwise, the compiler will generate an error):

```
// Enumerable interfaces
System.Collections.IEnumerable
System.Collections.Generic.IEnumerable<T>

// Enumerator interfaces
System.Collections.IEnumerator
System.Collections.Generic.IEnumerator<T>
```

An iterator has different semantics, depending on whether it returns an *enumerable* interface or an *enumerator* interface. We describe this in Chapter 7.

Multiple yield statements are permitted:

```
foreach (string s in Foo())
  Console.WriteLine(s);          // Prints "One","Two","Three"

IEnumerable<string> Foo()
{
  yield return "One";
  yield return "Two";
  yield return "Three";
}
```

yield break

A return statement is illegal in an iterator block; instead you must use the yield break statement to indicate that the iterator block should exit early, without return-ing more elements. We can modify Foo as follows to demonstrate:

```
IEnumerable<string> Foo (bool breakEarly)
{
  yield return "One";
  yield return "Two";

  if (breakEarly)
    yield break;
```

```
  yield return "Three";
}
```

Iterators and try/catch/finally blocks

A yield return statement cannot appear in a try block that has a catch clause:

```
IEnumerable<string> Foo()
{
  try { yield return "One"; }    // Illegal
  catch { ... }
}
```

Nor can yield return appear in a catch or finally block. These restrictions are due to the fact that the compiler must translate iterators into ordinary classes with MoveNext, Current, and Dispose members, and translating exception-handling blocks would create excessive complexity.

You can, however, yield within a try block that has (only) a finally block:

```
IEnumerable<string> Foo()
{
  try { yield return "One"; }    // OK
  finally { ... }
}
```

The code in the finally block executes when the consuming enumerator reaches the end of the sequence or is disposed. A foreach statement implicitly disposes the enumerator if you break early, making this a safe way to consume enumerators. When working with enumerators explicitly, a trap is to abandon enumeration early without disposing it, circumventing the finally block. You can avoid this risk by wrapping explicit use of enumerators in a using statement:

```
string firstElement = null;
var sequence = Foo();
using (var enumerator = sequence.GetEnumerator())
  if (enumerator.MoveNext())
    firstElement = enumerator.Current;
```

Composing Sequences

Iterators are highly composable. We can extend our example, this time to output even Fibonacci numbers only:

```
using System;
using System.Collections.Generic;

foreach (int fib in EvenNumbersOnly (Fibs(6)))
  Console.WriteLine (fib);

IEnumerable<int> Fibs (int fibCount)
{
  for (int i = 0, prevFib = 1, curFib = 1; i < fibCount; i++)
```

```
    {
      yield return prevFib;
      int newFib = prevFib+curFib;
      prevFib = curFib;
      curFib = newFib;
    }
  }

  IEnumerable<int> EvenNumbersOnly (IEnumerable<int> sequence)
  {
    foreach (int x in sequence)
      if ((x % 2) == 0)
        yield return x;
  }
```

Each element is not calculated until the last moment—when requested by a Move
Next() operation. Figure 4-1 shows the data requests and data output over time.

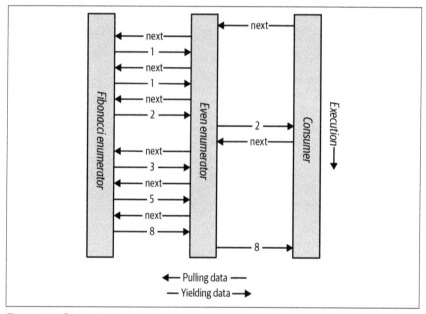

Figure 4-1. Composing sequences

The composability of the iterator pattern is extremely useful in LINQ; we discuss
the subject again in Chapter 8.

Nullable Value Types

Reference types can represent a nonexistent value with a null reference. Value types,
however, cannot ordinarily represent null values:

```
string s = null;      // OK, Reference Type
int i = null;         // Compile Error, Value Type cannot be null
```

To represent null in a value type, you must use a special construct called a *nullable type*. A nullable type is denoted with a value type followed by the ? symbol:

```
int? i = null;                   // OK, Nullable Type
Console.WriteLine (i == null);   // True
```

Nullable<T> Struct

T? translates into System.Nullable<T>, which is a lightweight immutable structure, having only two fields, to represent Value and HasValue. The essence of System .Nullable<T> is very simple:

```
public struct Nullable<T> where T : struct
{
  public T Value {get;}
  public bool HasValue {get;}
  public T GetValueOrDefault();
  public T GetValueOrDefault (T defaultValue);

  ...
}
```

The code

```
int? i = null;
Console.WriteLine (i == null);            // True
```

translates to the following:

```
Nullable<int> i = new Nullable<int>();
Console.WriteLine (! i.HasValue);         // True
```

Attempting to retrieve Value when HasValue is false throws an InvalidOperation Exception. GetValueOrDefault() returns Value if HasValue is true; otherwise, it returns new T() or a specified custom default value.

The default value of T? is null.

Implicit and Explicit Nullable Conversions

The conversion from T to T? is implicit, while the conversion from T? to T is explicit:

```
int? x = 5;       // implicit
int y = (int)x;   // explicit
```

The explicit cast is directly equivalent to calling the nullable object's Value property. Hence, an InvalidOperationException is thrown if HasValue is false.

Boxing and Unboxing Nullable Values

When T? is boxed, the boxed value on the heap contains T, not T?. This optimization is possible because a boxed value is a reference type that can already express null.

C# also permits the unboxing of nullable value types with the as operator. The result will be null if the cast fails:

```
object o = "string";
int? x = o as int?;
Console.WriteLine (x.HasValue);    // False
```

Operator Lifting

The Nullable<T> struct does not define operators such as <, >, or even ==. Despite this, the following code compiles and executes correctly:

```
int? x = 5;
int? y = 10;
bool b = x < y;        // true
```

This works because the compiler borrows or "lifts" the less-than operator from the underlying value type. Semantically, it translates the preceding comparison expression into this:

```
bool b = (x.HasValue && y.HasValue) ? (x.Value < y.Value) : false;
```

In other words, if both x and y have values, it compares via int's less-than operator; otherwise, it returns false.

Operator lifting means that you can implicitly use T's operators on T?. You can define operators for T? in order to provide special-purpose null behavior, but in the vast majority of cases, it's best to rely on the compiler automatically applying systematic nullable logic for you. Here are some examples:

```
int? x = 5;
int? y = null;

// Equality operator examples
Console.WriteLine (x == y);    // False
Console.WriteLine (x == null); // False
Console.WriteLine (x == 5);    // True
Console.WriteLine (y == null); // True
Console.WriteLine (y == 5);    // False
Console.WriteLine (y != 5);    // True

// Relational operator examples
Console.WriteLine (x < 6);     // True
Console.WriteLine (y < 6);     // False
Console.WriteLine (y > 6);     // False

// All other operator examples
Console.WriteLine (x + 5);     // 10
Console.WriteLine (x + y);     // null (prints empty line)
```

The compiler performs null logic differently depending on the category of operator. The following sections explain these different rules.

Equality operators (== and !=)

Lifted equality operators handle nulls just like reference types do. This means that two null values are equal:

```
Console.WriteLine (      null ==      null);  // True
Console.WriteLine ((bool?)null == (bool?)null);  // True
```

Further:

- If exactly one operand is null, the operands are unequal.
- If both operands are non-null, their Values are compared.

Relational operators (<, <=, >=, >)

The relational operators work on the principle that it is meaningless to compare null operands. This means comparing a null value to either a null or a non-null value returns false:

```
bool b = x < y;    // Translation:

bool b = (x.HasValue && y.HasValue)
         ? (x.Value < y.Value)
         : false;

// b is false (assuming x is 5 and y is null)
```

All other operators (+, −, *, /, %, &, |, ^, <<, >>, +, ++, --, !, ~)

These operators return null when any of the operands are null. This pattern should be familiar to SQL users:

```
int? c = x + y;    // Translation:

int? c = (x.HasValue && y.HasValue)
         ? (int?) (x.Value + y.Value)
         : null;

// c is null (assuming x is 5 and y is null)
```

An exception is when the & and | operators are applied to bool?, which we discuss shortly.

Mixing nullable and non-nullable operators

You can mix and match nullable and non-nullable value types (this works because there is an implicit conversion from T to T?):

```
int? a = null;
int b = 2;
int? c = a + b;    // c is null - equivalent to a + (int?)b
```

bool? with & and | Operators

When supplied operands of type bool?, the & and | operators treat null as an *unknown value*. So, null | true is true because:

- If the unknown value is false, the result would be true.
- If the unknown value is true, the result would be true.

Similarly, null & false is false. This behavior should be familiar to SQL users. The following example enumerates other combinations:

```
bool? n = null;
bool? f = false;
bool? t = true;
Console.WriteLine (n | n);    // (null)
Console.WriteLine (n | f);    // (null)
Console.WriteLine (n | t);    // True
Console.WriteLine (n & n);    // (null)
Console.WriteLine (n & f);    // False
Console.WriteLine (n & t);    // (null)
```

Nullable Value Types and Null Operators

Nullable value types work particularly well with the ?? operator (see "Null-Coalescing Operator" on page 74), as illustrated in this example:

```
int? x = null;
int y = x ?? 5;        // y is 5

int? a = null, b = 1, c = 2;
Console.WriteLine (a ?? b ?? c);  // 1 (first non-null value)
```

Using ?? on a nullable value type is equivalent to calling GetValueOrDefault with an explicit default value except that the expression for the default value is never evaluated if the variable is not null.

Nullable value types also work well with the null-conditional operator (see "Null-Conditional Operator" on page 75). In the following example, length evaluates to null:

```
System.Text.StringBuilder sb = null;
int? length = sb?.ToString().Length;
```

We can combine this with the null-coalescing operator to evaluate to zero instead of null:

```
int length = sb?.ToString().Length ?? 0;  // Evaluates to 0 if sb is null
```

Scenarios for Nullable Value Types

One of the most common scenarios for nullable value types is to represent unknown values. This frequently occurs in database programming, where a class is mapped to a table with nullable columns. If these columns are strings (e.g., an

EmailAddress column on a Customer table), there is no problem because string is a reference type in the CLR, which can be null. However, most other SQL column types map to CLR struct types, making nullable value types very useful when mapping SQL to the CLR:

```
// Maps to a Customer table in a database
public class Customer
{
  ...
  public decimal? AccountBalance;
}
```

A nullable type can also be used to represent the backing field of what's sometimes called an *ambient property*. An ambient property, if null, returns the value of its parent:

```
public class Row
{
  ...
  Grid parent;
  Color? color;

  public Color Color
  {
    get { return color ?? parent.Color; }
    set { color = value == parent.Color ? (Color?)null : value; }
  }
}
```

Alternatives to Nullable Value Types

Before nullable value types were part of the C# language (i.e., before C# 2.0), there were many strategies to deal with them, examples of which still appear in the .NET libraries for historical reasons. One of these strategies is to designate a particular non-null value as the "null value"; an example is in the string and array classes. String.IndexOf returns the magic value of –1 when the character is not found:

```
int i = "Pink".IndexOf ('b');
Console.WriteLine (i);          // -1
```

However, Array.IndexOf returns –1 only if the index is 0-bounded. The more general formula is that IndexOf returns one less than the lower bound of the array. In the next example, IndexOf returns 0 when an element is not found:

```
// Create an array whose lower bound is 1 instead of 0:

Array a = Array.CreateInstance (typeof (string),
                                new int[] {2}, new int[] {1});
a.SetValue ("a", 1);
a.SetValue ("b", 2);
Console.WriteLine (Array.IndexOf (a, "c"));  // 0
```

Nominating a "magic value" is problematic for several reasons:

- It means that each value type has a different representation of null. In contrast, nullable value types provide one common pattern that works for all value types.

- There might be no reasonable designated value. In the previous example, −1 could not always be used. The same is true for our earlier example representing an unknown account balance.

- Forgetting to test for the magic value results in an incorrect value that might go unnoticed until later in execution—when it pulls an unintended magic trick. Forgetting to test HasValue on a null value, however, throws an InvalidOpera tionException on the spot.

- The ability for a value to be null is not captured in the *type*. Types communicate the intention of a program, allow the compiler to check for correctness, and enable a consistent set of rules enforced by the compiler.

Nullable Reference Types

Whereas *nullable value types* bring nullability to value types, *nullable reference types* (C# 8+) do the opposite. When enabled, they bring (a degree of) *non-nullability* to reference types, with the purpose of helping to avoid NullReferenceExceptions.

Nullable reference types introduce a level of safety that's enforced purely by the compiler, in the form of warnings when it detects code that's at risk of generating a NullReferenceException.

To enable nullable reference types, you must either add the Nullable element to your .csproj project file (if you want to enable it for the entire project):

```
<PropertyGroup>
  <Nullable>enable</Nullable>
</PropertyGroup>
```

or/and use the following directives in your code, in the places where it should take effect:

```
#nullable enable    // enables nullable reference types from this point on
#nullable disable   // disables nullable reference types from this point on
#nullable restore   // resets nullable reference types to project setting
```

After being enabled, the compiler makes non-nullability the default: if you want a reference type to accept nulls without the compiler generating a warning, you must apply the ? suffix to indicate a *nullable reference type*. In the following example, s1 is non-nullable, whereas s2 is nullable:

```
#nullable enable    // Enable nullable reference types

string s1 = null;   // Generates a compiler warning!
string? s2 = null;  // OK: s2 is nullable reference type
```

Because nullable reference types are compile-time constructs, there's no runtime difference between string and string?. In contrast, nullable value types introduce something concrete into the type system, namely the Nullable<T> struct.

The following also generates a warning because x is not initialized:

```
class Foo { string x; }
```

The warning disappears if you initialize x, either via a field initializer or via code in the constructor.

The Null-Forgiving Operator

The compiler also warns you upon dereferencing a nullable reference type, if it thinks a NullReferenceException might occur. In the following example, accessing the string's Length property generates a warning:

```
void Foo (string? s) => Console.Write (s.Length);
```

You can remove the warning with the *null-forgiving operator* (!):

```
void Foo (string? s) => Console.Write (s!.Length);
```

Our use of the null-forgiving operator in this example is dangerous in that we could end up throwing the very NullReferenceException we were trying to avoid in the first place. We could fix it as follows:

```
void Foo (string? s)
{
  if (s != null) Console.Write (s.Length);
}
```

Notice now that we don't need the null-forgiving operator. This is because the compiler performs *static flow analysis* and is smart enough to infer—at least in simple cases—when a dereference is safe and there's no chance of a NullReference Exception.

The compiler's ability to detect and warn is not bulletproof, and there are also limits to what's possible in terms of coverage. For instance, it's unable to know whether an array's elements have been populated, and so the following does not generate a warning:

```
var strings = new string[10];
Console.WriteLine (strings[0].Length);
```

Separating the Annotation and Warning Contexts

Enabling nullable reference types via the #nullable enable directive (or the <Nullable>enable</Nullable> project setting) does two things:

- It enables the *nullable annotation context*, which tells the compiler to treat all reference-type variable declarations as non-nullable unless suffixed by the ? symbol.

- It enables the *nullable warning context*, which tells the compiler to generate warnings upon encountering code at risk of throwing a `NullReference Exception`.

It can sometimes be useful to separate these two concepts and enable *just* the annotation context, or (less usefully) *just* the warning context:

```
#nullable enable annotations    // Enable the annotation context
// OR:
#nullable enable warnings        // Enable the warning context
```

(The same trick works with #nullable `disable` and #nullable `restore`.)

You can also do it via the project file:

```
<Nullable>annotations</Nullable>
<!-- OR -->
<Nullable>warnings</Nullable>
```

Enabling just the annotation context for a particular class or assembly can be a good first step in introducing nullable reference types into a legacy codebase. By correctly annotating public members, your class or assembly can act as a "good citizen" to other classes or assemblies—so that *they* can benefit fully from nullable reference types—without having to deal with warnings in your own class or assembly.

Treating Nullable Warnings as Errors

In greenfield projects, it makes sense to fully enable the nullable context from the outset. You might want to take the additional step of treating nullable warnings as errors so that your project cannot compile until all null warnings have been resolved:

```
<PropertyGroup>
  <Nullable>enable</Nullable>
  <WarningsAsErrors>CS8600;CS8602;CS8603</WarningsAsErrors>
</PropertyGroup>
```

Extension Methods

Extension methods allow an existing type to be extended with new methods without altering the definition of the original type. An extension method is a static method of a static class, where the `this` modifier is applied to the first parameter. The type of the first parameter will be the type that is extended:

```
public static class StringHelper
{
  public static bool IsCapitalized (this string s)
  {
```

```
      if (string.IsNullOrEmpty(s)) return false;
      return char.IsUpper (s[0]);
  }
}
```

The IsCapitalized extension method can be called as though it were an instance method on a string, as follows:

```
Console.WriteLine ("Perth".IsCapitalized());
```

An extension method call, when compiled, is translated back into an ordinary static method call:

```
Console.WriteLine (StringHelper.IsCapitalized ("Perth"));
```

The translation works as follows:

```
arg0.Method (arg1, arg2, ...);              // Extension method call
StaticClass.Method (arg0, arg1, arg2, ...); // Static method call
```

Interfaces can be extended, too:

```
public static T First<T> (this IEnumerable<T> sequence)
{
  foreach (T element in sequence)
    return element;

  throw new InvalidOperationException ("No elements!");
}
...
Console.WriteLine ("Seattle".First());   // S
```

Extension Method Chaining

Extension methods, like instance methods, provide a tidy way to chain functions. Consider the following two functions:

```
public static class StringHelper
{
  public static string Pluralize (this string s) {...}
  public static string Capitalize (this string s) {...}
}
```

x and y are equivalent, and both evaluate to "Sausages", but x uses extension methods, whereas y uses static methods:

```
string x = "sausage".Pluralize().Capitalize();
string y = StringHelper.Capitalize (StringHelper.Pluralize ("sausage"));
```

Ambiguity and Resolution

Namespaces

An extension method cannot be accessed unless its class is in scope, typically by its namespace being imported. Consider the extension method IsCapitalized in the following example:

```
using System;

namespace Utils
{
  public static class StringHelper
  {
    public static bool IsCapitalized (this string s)
    {
      if (string.IsNullOrEmpty(s)) return false;
      return char.IsUpper (s[0]);
    }
  }
}
```

To use IsCapitalized, the following application must import Utils to avoid a compile-time error:

```
namespace MyApp
{
  using Utils;

  class Test
  {
    static void Main() => Console.WriteLine ("Perth".IsCapitalized());
  }
}
```

Extension methods versus instance methods

Any compatible instance method will always take precedence over an extension method. In the following example, Test's Foo method will always take precedence, even when called with an argument x of type int:

```
class Test
{
  public void Foo (object x) { }    // This method always wins
}

static class Extensions
{
  public static void Foo (this Test t, int x) { }
}
```

The only way to call the extension method in this case is via normal static syntax, in other words, Extensions.Foo(...).

Extension methods versus extension methods

If two extension methods have the same signature, the extension method must be called as an ordinary static method to disambiguate the method to call. If one extension method has more specific arguments, however, the more specific method takes precedence.

To illustrate, consider the following two classes:

```
static class StringHelper
{
  public static bool IsCapitalized (this string s) {...}
}
static class ObjectHelper
{
  public static bool IsCapitalized (this object s) {...}
}
```

The following code calls StringHelper's IsCapitalized method:

```
bool test1 = "Perth".IsCapitalized();
```

Classes and structs are considered more specific than interfaces.

Demoting an extension method

An interesting scenario can arise when Microsoft adds an extension method to a .NET runtime library that conflicts with an extension method in some existing third-party library. As the author of the third-party library, you might want to "withdraw" your extension method, but without removing it, and without breaking binary compatibility with existing consumers.

Fortunately, this is easy to accomplish, simply by removing the this keyword from your extension method's definition. This demotes your extension method to an ordinary static method. The beauty of this solution is that any assembly that was compiled against your old library will continue to work (and bind to *your* method, as before). This is because extension method calls are converted to static method calls during compilation.

Consumers will be affected by your demotion only when they recompile, at which time calls to your former extension method will now bind to Microsoft's version (if the namespace has been imported). Should the consumer still want to call your method, they can do so by invoking it as a static method.

Anonymous Types

An anonymous type is a simple class created by the compiler on the fly to store a set of values. To create an anonymous type, use the new keyword followed by an object initializer, specifying the properties and values the type will contain; for example:

```
var dude = new { Name = "Bob", Age = 23 };
```

The compiler translates this to (approximately) the following:

```
internal class AnonymousGeneratedTypeName
{
  private string name;  // Actual field name is irrelevant
  private int    age;   // Actual field name is irrelevant

  public AnonymousGeneratedTypeName (string name, int age)
  {
    this.name = name; this.age = age;
```

```
    }

    public string  Name { get { return name; } }
    public int     Age  { get { return age;  } }

    // The Equals and GetHashCode methods are overridden (see Chapter 6).
    // The ToString method is also overridden.
}
...

var dude = new AnonymousGeneratedTypeName ("Bob", 23);
```

You must use the var keyword to reference an anonymous type because it doesn't have a name.

The property name of an anonymous type can be inferred from an expression that is itself an identifier (or ends with one); thus

```
int Age = 23;
var dude = new { Name = "Bob", Age, Age.ToString().Length };
```

is equivalent to the following:

```
var dude = new { Name = "Bob", Age = Age, Length = Age.ToString().Length };
```

Two anonymous type instances declared within the same assembly will have the same underlying type if their elements are named and typed identically:

```
var a1 = new { X = 2, Y = 4 };
var a2 = new { X = 2, Y = 4 };
Console.WriteLine (a1.GetType() == a2.GetType());   // True
```

Additionally, the Equals method is overridden to perform *structural equality comparison* (comparison of the data):

```
Console.WriteLine (a1.Equals (a2));   // True
```

whereas the equality operator (==) performs referential comparison:

```
Console.WriteLine (a1 == a2);         // False
```

You can create arrays of anonymous types as follows:

```
var dudes = new[]
{
  new { Name = "Bob", Age = 30 },
  new { Name = "Tom", Age = 40 }
};
```

A method cannot (usefully) return an anonymously typed object, because it is illegal to write a method whose return type is var:

```
var Foo() => new { Name = "Bob", Age = 30 };  // Not legal!
```

Instead, you must use object or dynamic, and then whoever calls Foo must rely on dynamic binding, with loss of static type safety (and IntelliSense in Visual Studio):

```
dynamic Foo() => new { Name = "Bob", Age = 30 };  // No static type safety.
```

Anonymous types are immutable, so instances cannot be modified after creation. However, from C# 10, you can use the with keyword to create a copy with variations (*nondestructive mutation*):

```
var a1 = new { A = 1, B = 2, C = 3, D = 4, E = 5 };
var a2 = a1 with { E = 10 };
Console.WriteLine (a2);      // { A = 1, B = 2, C = 3, D = 4, E = 10 }
```

Anonymous types are particularly useful when writing LINQ queries (see Chapter 8).

Tuples

Like anonymous types, tuples provide a simple way to store a set of values. The main purpose of tuples is to safely return multiple values from a method without resorting to out parameters (something you cannot do with anonymous types).

 Tuples do almost everything that anonymous types do and more. Their one disadvantage—as you'll see soon—is runtime type erasure with named elements.

The simplest way to create a *tuple literal* is to list the desired values in parentheses. This creates a tuple with *unnamed* elements, which you refer to as Item1, Item2, and so on:

```
var bob = ("Bob", 23);    // Allow compiler to infer the element types

Console.WriteLine (bob.Item1);    // Bob
Console.WriteLine (bob.Item2);    // 23
```

Tuples are *value types*, with *mutable* (read/write) elements:

```
var joe = bob;              // joe is a *copy* of bob
joe.Item1 = "Joe";          // Change joe's Item1 from Bob to Joe
Console.WriteLine (bob);    // (Bob, 23)
Console.WriteLine (joe);    // (Joe, 23)
```

Unlike with anonymous types, you can specify a *tuple type* explicitly. Just list each of the element types in parentheses:

```
(string,int) bob  = ("Bob", 23);
```

This means that you can usefully return a tuple from a method:

```
(string,int) person = GetPerson(); // Could use 'var' instead if we want
Console.WriteLine (person.Item1);  // Bob
Console.WriteLine (person.Item2);  // 23

(string,int) GetPerson() => ("Bob", 23);
```

Tuples play well with generics, so the following types are all legal:

```
Task<(string,int)>
Dictionary<(string,int),Uri>
IEnumerable<(int id, string name)>   // See below for naming elements
```

Naming Tuple Elements

You can optionally give meaningful names to elements when creating tuple literals:

```
var tuple = (name:"Bob", age:23);

Console.WriteLine (tuple.name);    // Bob
Console.WriteLine (tuple.age);     // 23
```

You can do the same when specifying *tuple types*:

```
var person = GetPerson();
Console.WriteLine (person.name);   // Bob
Console.WriteLine (person.age);    // 23

(string name, int age) GetPerson() => ("Bob", 23);
```

Note that you can still treat the elements as unnamed and refer to them as Item1, Item2, etc. (although Visual Studio hides these fields from IntelliSense).

Element names are automatically *inferred* from property or field names:

```
var now = DateTime.Now;
var tuple = (now.Day, now.Month, now.Year);
Console.WriteLine (tuple.Day);               // OK
```

Tuples are type compatible with one another if their element types match up (in order). Their element names need not:

```
(string name, int age, char sex)  bob1 = ("Bob", 23, 'M');
(string age,  int sex, char name) bob2 = bob1;   // No error!
```

Our particular example leads to confusing results:

```
Console.WriteLine (bob2.name);     // M
Console.WriteLine (bob2.age);      // Bob
Console.WriteLine (bob2.sex);      // 23
```

Type erasure

We stated previously that the C# compiler handles anonymous types by building custom classes with named properties for each of the elements. With tuples, C# works differently and uses a preexisting family of generic structs:

```
public struct ValueTuple<T1>
public struct ValueTuple<T1,T2>
public struct ValueTuple<T1,T2,T3>
...
```

Each of the ValueTuple<> structs has fields named Item1, Item2, and so on.

Hence, (string,int) is an alias for ValueTuple<string,int>, and this means that named tuple elements have no corresponding property names in the underlying types. Instead, the names exist only in the source code, and in the imagination of the compiler. At runtime, the names mostly disappear, so if you decompile a program that refers to named tuple elements, you'll see references to just Item1,

Item2, and so on. Further, when you examine a tuple variable in a debugger after having assigned it to an `object` (or Dump it in LINQPad), the element names are not there. And for the most part, you cannot use *reflection* (Chapter 18) to determine a tuple's element names at runtime.

We said that the names *mostly* disappear because there's an exception. With methods/properties that return named tuple types, the compiler emits the element names by applying a custom attribute called `TupleElementNamesAttribute` (see "Attributes" on page 227) to the member's return type. This allows named elements to work when calling methods in a different assembly (for which the compiler does not have the source code).

ValueTuple.Create

You can also create tuples via a factory method on the (nongeneric) `ValueTuple` type:

```
ValueTuple<string,int> bob1 = ValueTuple.Create ("Bob", 23);
(string,int)            bob2 = ValueTuple.Create ("Bob", 23);
(string name, int age) bob3 = ValueTuple.Create ("Bob", 23);
```

Deconstructing Tuples

Tuples implicitly support the deconstruction pattern (see "Deconstructors" on page 20), so you can easily *deconstruct* a tuple into individual variables. Consider the following:

```
var bob = ("Bob", 23);

string name = bob.Item1;
int age = bob.Item2;
```

With the tuple's deconstructor, you can simplify the code to this:

```
var bob = ("Bob", 23);

(string name, int age) = bob;   // Deconstruct the bob tuple into
                                // separate variables (name and age).
Console.WriteLine (name);
Console.WriteLine (age);
```

The syntax for deconstruction is confusingly similar to the syntax for declaring a tuple with named elements. The following highlights the difference:

```
(string name, int age)      = bob;   // Deconstructing a tuple
(string name, int age) bob2 = bob;   // Declaring a new tuple
```

Here's another example, this time when calling a method and with type inference (`var`):

```
var (name, age, sex) = GetBob();
Console.WriteLine (name);    // Bob
Console.WriteLine (age);     // 23
Console.WriteLine (sex);     // M

string, int, char) GetBob() => ( "Bob", 23, 'M');
```

You can also deconstruct directly into fields and properties, which provides a nice shortcut for populating multiple fields or properties in a constructor:

```
class Point
{
  public readonly int X, Y;
  public Point (int x, int y) => (X, Y) = (x, y);
}
```

Equality Comparison

As with anonymous types, the Equals method performs structural equality comparison. This means that it compares the underlying *data* rather than the *reference*:

```
var t1 = ("one", 1);
var t2 = ("one", 1);
Console.WriteLine (t1.Equals (t2));    // True
```

In addition, ValueTuple<> overloads the == and != operators:

```
Console.WriteLine (t1 == t2);    // True (from C# 7.3)
```

Tuples also override the GetHashCode method, making it practical to use tuples as keys in dictionaries. We cover equality comparison in detail in "Equality Comparison" on page 324, and dictionaries in Chapter 7.

The ValueTuple<> types also implement IComparable (see "Order Comparison" on page 335), making it possible to use tuples as a sorting key.

The System.Tuple classes

You'll find another family of generic types in the System namespace called Tuple (rather than ValueTuple). These were introduced back in 2010 and were defined as classes (whereas the ValueTuple types are structs). Defining tuples as classes was in retrospect considered a mistake: in the scenarios in which tuples are commonly used, structs have a slight performance advantage (in that they avoid unnecessary memory allocations), with almost no downside. Hence, when Microsoft added language support for tuples in C# 7, it ignored the existing Tuple types in favor of the new ValueTuple. You might still come across the Tuple classes in code written prior to C# 7. They have no special language support and are used as follows:

```
Tuple<string,int> t = Tuple.Create ("Bob", 23);   // Factory method
Console.WriteLine (t.Item1);    // Bob
Console.WriteLine (t.Item2);    // 23
```

Records

A *record* is a special kind of class or struct that's designed to work well with immutable (read-only) data. Its most useful feature is *nondestructive mutation*; however, records are also useful in creating types that just combine or hold data. In simple cases, they eliminate boilerplate code while honoring the equality semantics most suitable for immutable types.

Records are purely a C# compile-time construct. At runtime, the CLR sees them just as classes or structs (with a bunch of extra "synthesized" members added by the compiler).

Background

Writing immutable types (whose fields cannot be modified after initialization) is a popular strategy for simplifying software and reducing bugs. It's also a core aspect of functional programming, where mutable state is avoided and functions are treated as data. LINQ is inspired by this principle.

In order to "modify" an immutable object, you must create a new one and copy over the data while incorporating your modifications (this is called *nondestructive mutation*). In terms of performance, this is not as inefficient as you might expect, because a *shallow copy* will always suffice (a *deep copy*, where you also copy subobjects and collections, is unnecessary when data is immutable). But in terms of coding effort, implementing nondestructive mutation can be very inefficient, especially when there are many properties. Records solve this problem via a language-supported pattern.

A second issue is that programmers—particularly *functional programmers*—sometimes use immutable types just to combine data (without adding behavior). Defining such types is more work than it should be, requiring a constructor to assign each parameter to each property (a deconstructor may also be useful). With records, the compiler can do this work for you.

Finally, one of the consequences of an object being immutable is that its identity cannot change, which means that it's more useful for such types to implement *structural equality* than *referential equality*. Structural equality means that two instances are the same if their data is the same (as with tuples). Records give you structural equality by default—regardless of whether the underlying type is a class or struct—without any boilerplate code.

Defining a Record

A record definition is like a class or struct definition, and can contain the same kinds of members, including fields, properties, methods, and so on. Records can implement interfaces, and (class-based) records can subclass other (class-based) records.

By default, the underlying type of a record is a class:

```
record Point { }          // Point is a class
```

From C# 10, the underlying type of a record can also be a struct:

```
record struct Point { }   // Point is a struct
```

(record class is also legal and has the same meaning as record.)

A simple record might contain just a bunch of init-only properties and perhaps a constructor:

```
record Point
{
  public Point (double x, double y) => (X, Y) = (x, y);

  public double X { get; init; }
  public double Y { get; init; }
}
```

Our constructor employs a shortcut that we described in the preceding section.

```
(X, Y) = (x, y);
```

is equivalent (in this case) to the following:

```
{ this.X = x; this.Y = y; }
```

Upon compilation, C# transforms the record definition into a class (or struct) and performs the following additional steps:

- It writes a protected *copy constructor* (and a hidden *Clone* method) to facilitate nondestructive mutation.

- It overrides/overloads the equality-related functions to implement structural equality.

- It overrides the ToString() method (to expand the record's public properties, as with anonymous types).

The preceding record declaration expands into something like this:

```
class Point
{
  public Point (double x, double y) => (X, Y) = (x, y);

  public double X { get; init; }
  public double Y { get; init; }

  protected Point (Point original)    // "Copy constructor"
  {
    this.X = original.X; this.Y = original.Y
  }

  // This method has a strange compiler-generated name:
  public virtual Point <Clone>$() => new Point (this);   // Clone method
```

```
// Additional code to override Equals, ==, !=, GetHashCode, ToString()
// ...
}
```

 While there's nothing to stop you from putting *optional parameters* into the constructor, a good pattern (at least in public libraries) is to leave them out of the constructor and expose them purely as init-only properties:

```
new Foo (123, 234) { Optional2 = 345 };

record Foo
{
  public Foo (int required1, int required2) { ... }

  public int Required1 { get; init; }
  public int Required2 { get; init; }

  public int Optional1 { get; init; }
  public int Optional2 { get; init; }
}
```

The advantage of this pattern is that you can safely add init-only properties later without breaking binary compatibility with consumers who have compiled against older versions of your assembly.

Parameter lists

A record definition can also include a *parameter list*:

```
record Point (double X, double Y)
{
  // You can optionally define additional class members here...
}
```

Parameters can include the in and params modifiers, but not out or ref. If a parameter list is specified, the compiler performs the following extra steps:

- It writes an init-only property per parameter.
- It writes a *primary constructor* to populate the properties.
- It writes a deconstructor.

Mutability with Record Structs

When you define a parameter list in a record struct, the compiler emits writable properties instead of init-only properties, unless you prefix the record declaration with readonly:

```
readonly record struct Point (double X, double Y);
```

The rationale is that in typical use cases, the safety benefits of immutability arise not from a *struct* being immutable but from its *home* being immutable. In the following example, we are unable to mutate field X, even though X is writable:

```
var test = new Immutable();
test.Field.X++;  // Prohibited, because Field is readonly
test.Prop.X++;   // Prohibited, because Prop is {get;} only

class Immutable
{
  public readonly Mutable Field;
  public Mutable Prop { get; }
}

struct Mutable { public int X, Y; }
```

And while we could do the following:

```
var test = new Immutable();
Mutable m = test.Prop;
m.X++;
```

all that we would achieve is to mutate a local variable (a *copy* of test.Prop). Mutating a local variable can be a useful optimization and doesn't invalidate the benefits of an immutable type system.

Conversely, if we made Field a writable field, and Prop a writable property, we could simply replace their contents—regardless of how the Mutable struct was declared.

This means that if we declare our Point record simply as

```
record Point (double X, double Y);
```

the compiler will end up generating (almost) exactly what we listed in the preceding expansion. A minor difference is that the parameter names in the primary constructor will end up as X and Y instead of x and y:

```
public Point (double X, double Y)   // "Primary constructor"
{
  this.X = X; this.Y = Y;
}
```

 Also, due to being a *primary constructor*, parameters X and Y become magically available to any field or property initializers in your record. We discuss the subtleties of this later, in "Primary Constructors" on page 219.

Another difference, when you define a parameter list, is that the compiler also generates a deconstructor:

```
public void Deconstruct (out double X, out double Y)   // Deconstructor
{
  X = this.X; Y = this.Y;
}
```

Records with parameter lists can be subclassed using the following syntax:

```
record Point3D (double X, double Y, double Z) : Point (X, Y);
```

The compiler then emits a primary constructor as follows:

```
class Point3D : Point
{
  public double Z { get; init; }

  public Point3D (double X, double Y, double Z) : base (X, Y)
    => this.Z = Z;
}
```

 Parameter lists offer a nice shortcut when you need a class that simply groups together a bunch of values (a *product type* in functional programming), and can also be useful for prototyping. As we'll see later, they're not so helpful when you need to add logic to the init accessors (such as argument validation).

Nondestructive Mutation

The most important step that the compiler performs with all records is to write a *copy constructor* (and a hidden *Clone* method). This enables nondestructive mutation via the with keyword:

```
Point p1 = new Point (3, 3);
Point p2 = p1 with { Y = 4 };
Console.WriteLine (p2);        // Point { X = 3, Y = 4 }

record Point (double X, double Y);
```

In this example, p2 is a copy of p1, but with its Y property set to 4. The benefit is more apparent when there are more properties:

```
Test t1 = new Test (1, 2, 3, 4, 5, 6, 7, 8);
Test t2 = t1 with { A = 10, C = 30 };
Console.WriteLine (t2);

record Test (int A, int B, int C, int D, int E, int F, int G, int H);
```

Here's the output:

```
Test { A = 10, B = 2, C = 30, D = 4, E = 5, F = 6, G = 7, H = 8 }
```

Nondestructive mutation occurs in two phases:

1. First, the *copy constructor* clones the record. By default, it copies each of the record's underlying fields, creating a faithful replica while bypassing (the overhead of) any logic in the init accessors. All fields are included (public and private, as well as the hidden fields that back automatic properties).

2. Then, each property in the *member initializer list* is updated (this time using the init accessors).

The compiler translates:

```
Test t2 = t1 with { A = 10, C = 30 };
```

into something functionally equivalent to the following:

```
Test t2 = new Test(t1);   // Use copy constructor to clone t1 field by field
t2.A = 10;                // Update property A
t2.C = 30;                // Update property C
```

(The same code would not compile if you wrote it explicitly because A and C are init-only properties. Furthermore, the copy constructor is *protected*; C# works around this by invoking it via a public hidden method that it writes into the record called <Clone>$.)

If necessary, you can define your own *copy constructor*. C# will then use your definition instead of writing one itself:

```
protected Point (Point original)
{
    this.X = original.X; this.Y = original.Y;
}
```

Writing a custom copy constructor might be useful if your record contains mutable subobjects or collections that you wish to clone, or if there are computed fields that you wish to clear. Unfortunately, you can only *replace*, not *enhance*, the default implementation.

> When subclassing another record, the copy constructor is responsible for copying only its own fields. To copy the base record's fields, delegate to the base:
>
> ```
> protected Point (Point original) : base (original)
> {
>     ...
> }
> ```

Property Validation

With explicit properties, you can write validation logic into the init accessors. In the following example, we ensure that X can never be NaN (Not a Number):

```
record Point
{
    // Notice that we assign x to the X property (and not the _x field):
    public Point (double x, double y) => (X, Y) = (x, y);

    double _x;
    public double X
    {
        get => _x;
        init
        {
            if (double.IsNaN (value))
                throw new ArgumentException ("X Cannot be NaN");
            _x = value;
        }
    }
}
```

```
    public double Y { get; init; }
}
```

Our design ensures that validation occurs both during construction and when the object is nondestructively mutated:

```
Point p1 = new Point (2, 3);
Point p2 = p1 with { X = double.NaN };   // throws an exception
```

Recall that the automatically generated *copy constructor* copies over all fields and automatic properties. This means that the generated copy constructor will now look like this:

```
protected Point (Point original)
{
    _x = original._x; Y = original.Y;
}
```

Notice that the copying of the _x field circumvents the X property accessor. However, this cannot break anything, because it's faithfully copying an object that will have already been safely populated via X's init accessor.

Calculated Fields and Lazy Evaluation

A popular functional programming pattern that works well with immutable types is *lazy evaluation*, where a value is not computed until required, and is then cached for reuse. Suppose, for instance, that we want to define a property in our Point record that returns the distance from the origin (0, 0):

```
record Point (double X, double Y)
{
    public double DistanceFromOrigin => Math.Sqrt (X*X + Y*Y);
}
```

Let's now try to refactor this to avoid the cost of recomputing DistanceFromOrigin every time the property is accessed. We'll start by removing the property list and defining X, Y, and DistanceFromOrigin as read-only properties. Then we can calculate the latter in the constructor:

```
record Point
{
    public double X { get; }
    public double Y { get; }
    public double DistanceFromOrigin { get; }

    public Point (double x, double y) =>
        (X, Y, DistanceFromOrigin) = (x, y, Math.Sqrt (x*x + y*y));
}
```

This works, but it doesn't allow for nondestructive mutation (changing X and Y to init-only properties would break the code because DistanceFromOrigin would become stale after the init accessors execute). It's also suboptimal in that the calculation is always performed, regardless of whether the DistanceFromOrigin property

```

<div style="writing-mode: vertical">Advanced C#</div>
```

is ever read. The optimal solution is to cache its value in a field and populate it *lazily* (on first use):

```
record Point
{
  ...

  double? _distance;
  public double DistanceFromOrigin
  {
    get
    {
      if (_distance == null)
        _distance = Math.Sqrt (X*X + Y*Y);

      return _distance.Value;
    }
  }
}
```

 Technically, we *mutate* _distance in this code. It's still fair, though, to call Point an immutable type. Mutating a field purely to populate a lazy value does not invalidate the principles or benefits of immutability, and can even be masked through the use of the Lazy<T> type that we describe in Chapter 21.

With C#'s *null-coalescing assignment operator* (??=) we can reduce the entire property declaration to one line of code:

```
public double DistanceFromOrigin => _distance ??= Math.Sqrt (X*X + Y*Y);
```

(This says, return _distance if it's non-null; otherwise return Math.Sqrt (X*X + Y*Y) while assigning it to _distance.)

To make this work with init-only properties, we need one further step, which is to clear the cached _distance field when X or Y is updated via the init accessor. Here's the complete code:

```
record Point
{
  public Point (double x, double y) => (X, Y) = (x, y);

  double _x, _y;
  public double X { get => _x; init { _x = value; _distance = null; } }
  public double Y { get => _y; init { _y = value; _distance = null; } }

  double? _distance;
  public double DistanceFromOrigin => _distance ??= Math.Sqrt (X*X + Y*Y);
}
```

Point can now be mutated nondestructively:

```
Point p1 = new Point (2, 3);
Console.WriteLine (p1.DistanceFromOrigin);   // 3.605551275463989
```

```
Point p2 = p1 with { Y = 4 };
Console.WriteLine (p2.DistanceFromOrigin);   // 4.47213595499958
```

A nice bonus is that the autogenerated copy constructor copies over the cached _distance field. This means that should a record have other properties that aren't involved in the calculation, a nondestructive mutation of those properties wouldn't trigger an unnecessary loss of the cached value. If you don't care for this bonus, an alternative to clearing the cached value in the init accessors is to write a custom copy constructor that ignores the cached field. This is more concise because it works with parameter lists, and the custom copy constructor can leverage the deconstructor:

```
record Point (double X, double Y)
{
   double? _distance;
   public double DistanceFromOrigin => _distance ??= Math.Sqrt (X*X + Y*Y);

   protected Point (Point other) => (X, Y) = other;
}
```

Note that with either solution, the addition of lazy calculated fields breaks the default structural equality comparison (because such fields may or may not be populated), although we'll see shortly that it's relatively easy to fix.

Primary Constructors

When you define a record with a parameter list, the compiler generates property declarations automatically, as well as a *primary constructor* (and a deconstructor). As we've seen, this works well in simple cases, and in more complex cases you can omit the parameter list and write the property declarations and constructor manually.

C# also offers a mildly useful intermediate option—if you're willing to deal with the curious semantics of primary constructors—which is to define a parameter list while writing some or all of the property declarations yourself:

```
record Student (string ID, string LastName, string GivenName)
{
   public string ID { get; } = ID;
}
```

In this case, we "took over" the ID property definition, defining it as read-only (instead of init-only), preventing it from partaking in nondestructive mutation. If you never need to nondestructively mutate a particular property, making it read-only lets you store computed data in the record without having to code up a refresh mechanism.

Notice that we needed to include a *property initializer* (in boldface):

```
public string ID { get; } = ID;
```

When you "take over" a property declaration, you become responsible for initializing its value; the primary constructor no longer does this automatically. Note that the ID in boldface refers to the *primary constructor parameter*, not the ID property.

With record structs, it's legal to redefine a property as a field:

```
record struct Student (string ID)
{
    public string ID = ID;
}
```

A unique feature of primary constructors is that their parameters (ID, LastName, and GivenName in this case) are magically visible to all field and property initializers. We can illustrate this by extending our example as follows:

```
record Student (string ID, string LastName, string FirstName)
{
    public string ID { get; } = ID;
    readonly int _enrollmentYear = int.Parse (ID.Substring (0, 4));
}
```

Again, the ID in boldface refers to the primary constructor parameter, not the property. (The reason for there not being an ambiguity is that it's illegal to access properties from initializers.)

In this example, we calculated _enrollmentYear from the first four digits of the ID. While it's safe to store this in a read-only field (because the ID property is read-only and so cannot be nondestructively mutated), this code would not work so well in the real world. This is because without an explicit constructor, there's no central place in which to validate ID and throw a meaningful exception should it be invalid (a common requirement).

Validation is also a good reason for needing to write explicit init-only accessors (as we discussed in "Property Validation" on page 216). Unfortunately, primary constructors do not play well in this scenario. To illustrate, consider the following record, where an init accessor performs a null validation check:

```
record Person (string Name)
{
    string _name = Name;
    public string Name
    {
        get  => _name;
        init => _name = value ?? throw new ArgumentNullException ("Name");
    }
}
```

Because Name is not an automatic property, it cannot define an initializer. The best we can do is put the initializer on the backing field (in boldface). Unfortunately, doing so bypasses the null check:

```
var p = new Person (null);    // Succeeds! (bypasses the null check)
```

The difficulty is that there's no way to assign a primary constructor parameter to a property without writing the constructor ourselves. While there are workarounds (such as factoring the init validation logic into a separate static method that we call twice), the simplest workaround is to avoid the parameter list altogether and write an ordinary constructor manually (and deconstructor, should you need it):

```
record Person
{
    public Person (string name) => Name = name;  // Assign to *PROPERTY*

    string _name;
    public string Name { get => _name; init => ... }
}
```

Records and Equality Comparison

Just as with structs, anonymous types, and tuples, records provide structural equality out of the box, meaning that two records are equal if their fields (and automatic properties) are equal:

```
var p1 = new Point (1, 2);
var p2 = new Point (1, 2);
Console.WriteLine (p1.Equals (p2));   // True

record Point (double X, double Y);
```

The *equality operator* also works with records (as it does with tuples):

```
Console.WriteLine (p1 == p2);         // True
```

The default equality implementation for records is unavoidably fragile. In particular, it breaks if the record contains lazy values, transient values, arrays, or collection types (which require special handling for equality comparison). Fortunately, it's relatively easy to fix (should you need equality to work), and doing so is less work than adding full equality behavior to classes or structs.

Unlike with classes and structs, you do not (and cannot) override the object.Equals method; instead, you define a public Equals method with the following signature:

```
record Point (double X, double Y)
{
    double _someOtherField;
    public virtual bool Equals (Point other) =>
        other != null && X == other.X && Y == other.Y;
}
```

The Equals method must be virtual (not override), and it must be *strongly typed* such that it accepts the actual record type (Point in this case, not object). Once you get the signature right, the compiler will automatically patch in your method.

In our example, we changed the equality logic such that we compare only X and Y (and ignore _someOtherField).

Should you subclass another record, you can call the base.Equals method:

```
public virtual bool Equals (Point other) => base.Equals (other) && ...
```

As with any type, if you take over equality comparison, you should also override GetHashCode(). A nice feature of records is that you don't overload != or ==; nor do you implement IEquatable<T>: this is all done for you. We cover this topic of equality comparison fully in "Equality Comparison" on page 324.

Patterns

In Chapter 3, we demonstrated how to use the is operator to test whether a reference conversion will succeed:

```
if (obj is string)
    Console.WriteLine (((string)obj).Length);
```

Or, more concisely:

```
if (obj is string s)
    Console.WriteLine (s.Length);
```

This employs one kind of pattern called a *type pattern*. The is operator also supports other patterns that were introduced in recent versions of C#, such as the *property pattern*:

```
if (obj is string { Length:4 })
    Console.WriteLine ("A string with 4 characters");
```

Patterns are supported in the following contexts:

- After the is operator (*variable* is *pattern*)
- In switch statements
- In switch expressions

We've already covered the type pattern (and briefly, the tuple pattern) in "Switching on types" on page 81 and "The is operator" on page 118. In this section, we cover more advanced patterns that were introduced in recent versions of C#.

Some of the more specialized patterns are intended for use in switch statements/expressions. Here, they reduce the need for when clauses and let you use switches where you couldn't previously.

> The patterns in this section are mild-to-moderately useful in some scenarios. Remember that you can always replace highly patterned switch expressions with simple if statements— or, in some cases, the ternary conditional operator—often without much extra code.

var Pattern

The *var pattern* is a variation of the *type pattern* whereby you replace the type name with the var keyword. The conversion always succeeds, so its purpose is merely to let you reuse the variable that follows:

```
bool IsJanetOrJohn (string name) =>
  name.ToUpper() is var upper && (upper == "JANET" || upper == "JOHN");
```

This is equivalent to:

```
bool IsJanetOrJohn (string name)
{
  string upper = name.ToUpper();
  return upper == "JANET" || upper == "JOHN";
}
```

The ability to introduce and reuse an intermediate variable (upper, in this case) in an expression-bodied method is convenient. Unfortunately, it tends to be useful only when the method in question has a bool return type.

Constant Pattern

The constant pattern lets you match directly to a constant, and is useful when working with the object type:

```
void Foo (object obj)
{
  if (obj is 3) ...
}
```

This expression in boldface is equivalent to the following:

```
obj is int && (int)obj == 3
```

(Being a static operator, C# won't let you use == to compare an object directly to a constant, because the compiler needs to know the types in advance.)

On its own, this pattern is only marginally useful in that there's a reasonable alternative:

```
if (3.Equals (obj)) ...
```

As we'll see soon, the constant pattern can become more useful with *pattern combinators*.

Relational Patterns

From C# 9, you can use the <, >, <=, and >= operators in patterns:

```
if (x is > 100) Console.WriteLine ("x is greater than 100");
```

This becomes meaningfully useful in a switch:

```
string GetWeightCategory (decimal bmi) => bmi switch
{
  < 18.5m => "underweight",
  < 25m => "normal",
  < 30m => "overweight",
  _ => "obese"
};
```

Relational patterns become even more useful in conjunction with *pattern combinators*.

 The relational pattern also works when the variable has a compile-time type of object, but you have to be extremely careful with your use of numeric constants. In the following example, the last line prints False because we are attempting to match a decimal value to an integer literal:

```
object obj = 2m;                      // obj is decimal
Console.WriteLine (obj is < 3m);  // True
Console.WriteLine (obj is < 3);   // False
```

Pattern Combinators

From C# 9, you can use the and, or, and not keywords to combine patterns:

```
bool IsJanetOrJohn (string name) => name.ToUpper() is "JANET" or "JOHN";

bool IsVowel (char c) => c is 'a' or 'e' or 'i' or 'o' or 'u';

bool Between1And9 (int n) => n is >= 1 and <= 9;

bool IsLetter (char c) => c is >= 'a' and <= 'z'
                               or >= 'A' and <= 'Z';
```

As with the && and || operators, and has higher precedence than or. You can override this with parentheses.

A nice trick is to combine the not combinator with the *type pattern* to test whether an object is (not) a type:

```
if (obj is not string) ...
```

This looks nicer than:

```
if (!(obj is string)) ...
```

Tuple and Positional Patterns

The *tuple pattern* (introduced in C# 8) matches tuples:

```
var p = (2, 3);
Console.WriteLine (p is (2, 3));    // True
```

You can use this to switch on multiple values:

```
int AverageCelsiusTemperature (Season season, bool daytime) =>
  (season, daytime) switch
  {
    (Season.Spring, true) => 20,
    (Season.Spring, false) => 16,
    (Season.Summer, true) => 27,
    (Season.Summer, false) => 22,
    (Season.Fall, true) => 18,
    (Season.Fall, false) => 12,
    (Season.Winter, true) => 10,
```

```
      (Season.Winter, false) => -2,
      _ => throw new Exception ("Unexpected combination")
};

enum Season { Spring, Summer, Fall, Winter };
```

The tuple pattern can be considered a special case of the *positional pattern* (C# 8+), which matches any type that exposes a Deconstruct method (see "Deconstructors" on page 20). In the following example, we leverage the Point record's compiler-generated deconstructor:

```
var p = new Point (2, 2);
Console.WriteLine (p is (2, 2));  // True

record Point (int X, int Y);      // Has compiler-generated deconstructor
```

You can deconstruct as you match, using the following syntax:

```
Console.WriteLine (p is (var x, var y) && x == y);   // True
```

Here's a switch expression that combines a type pattern with a positional pattern:

```
string Print (object obj) => obj switch
{
  Point (0, 0)                    => "Empty point",
  Point (var x, var y) when x == y => "Diagonal"
  ...
};
```

Property Patterns

A property pattern (C# 8+) matches on one or more of an object's property values. We gave a simple example previously in the context of the is operator:

```
if (obj is string { Length:4 }) ...
```

However, this doesn't save much over the following:

```
if (obj is string s && s.Length == 4) ...
```

With switch statements and expressions, property patterns are more useful. Consider the System.Uri class, which represents a URI. It has properties that include Scheme, Host, Port, and IsLoopback. In writing a firewall, we could decide whether to allow or block a URI by employing a switch expression that uses property patterns:

```
bool ShouldAllow (Uri uri) => uri switch
{
  { Scheme: "http",  Port: 80  } => true,
  { Scheme: "https", Port: 443 } => true,
  { Scheme: "ftp",   Port: 21  } => true,
  { IsLoopback: true           } => true,
  _ => false
};
```

You can nest properties, making the following clause legal:

```
{ Scheme: { Length: 4 }, Port: 80 } => true,
```

which, from C# 10, can be simplified to:

```
{ Scheme.Length: 4, Port: 80 } => true,
```

You can use other patterns inside property patterns, including the relational pattern:

```
{ Host: { Length: < 1000 }, Port: > 0 } => true,
```

More elaborate conditions can be expressed with a when clause:

```
{ Scheme: "http" } when string.IsNullOrWhiteSpace (uri.Query) => true,
```

You can also combine the property pattern with the type pattern:

```
bool ShouldAllow (object uri) => uri switch
{
  Uri { Scheme: "http",  Port: 80  } => true,
  Uri { Scheme: "https", Port: 443 } => true,
  ...
```

As you might expect with type patterns, you can introduce a variable at the end of a clause and then consume that variable:

```
Uri { Scheme: "http", Port: 80 } httpUri => httpUri.Host.Length < 1000,
```

You can also use that variable in a when clause:

```
Uri { Scheme: "http", Port: 80 } httpUri
                    when httpUri.Host.Length < 1000 => true,
```

A somewhat bizarre twist with property patterns is that you can also introduce variables at the *property* level:

```
{ Scheme: "http", Port: 80, Host: string host } => host.Length < 1000,
```

Implicit typing is permitted, so you can substitute string with var. Here's a complete example:

```
bool ShouldAllow (Uri uri) => uri switch
{
  { Scheme: "http",  Port: 80, Host: var host } => host.Length < 1000,
  { Scheme: "https", Port: 443            } => true,
  { Scheme: "ftp",   Port: 21             } => true,
  { IsLoopback: true                      } => true,
  _ => false
};
```

It's difficult to invent examples for which this saves more than a few characters. In our case, the alternative is actually shorter:

```
{ Scheme: "http", Port: 80 } => uri.Host.Length < 1000 => ...
```

Or:

```
{ Scheme: "http", Port: 80, Host: { Length: < 1000 } } => ...
```

Attributes

You're already familiar with the notion of attributing code elements of a program with modifiers, such as `virtual` or `ref`. These constructs are built into the language. *Attributes* are an extensible mechanism for adding custom information to code elements (assemblies, types, members, return values, parameters, and generic type parameters). This extensibility is useful for services that integrate deeply into the type system, without requiring special keywords or constructs in the C# language.

A good scenario for attributes is *serialization*—the process of converting arbitrary objects to and from a particular format for storage or transmission. In this scenario, an attribute on a field can specify the translation between C#'s representation of the field and the format's representation of the field.

Attribute Classes

An attribute is defined by a class that inherits (directly or indirectly) from the abstract class `System.Attribute`. To attach an attribute to a code element, specify the attribute's type name in square brackets, before the code element. For example, the following attaches the `ObsoleteAttribute` to the `Foo` class:

```
[ObsoleteAttribute]
public class Foo {...}
```

This particular attribute is recognized by the compiler and will cause compiler warnings if a type or member marked as obsolete is referenced. By convention, all attribute types end in the word *Attribute*. C# recognizes this and allows you to omit the suffix when attaching an attribute:

```
[Obsolete]
public class Foo {...}
```

`ObsoleteAttribute` is a type declared in the `System` namespace as follows (simplified for brevity):

```
public sealed class ObsoleteAttribute : Attribute {...}
```

The .NET libraries include many predefined attributes. We describe how to write your own attributes in Chapter 18.

Named and Positional Attribute Parameters

Attributes can have parameters. In the following example, we apply `XmlTypeAttribute` to a class. This attribute instructs the XML serializer (in `System.Xml.Serialization`) as to how an object is represented in XML and accepts several *attribute parameters*. The following attribute maps the `CustomerEntity` class to an XML element named `Customer`, which belongs to the `http://oreilly.com` namespace:

```
[XmlType ("Customer", Namespace="http://oreilly.com")]
public class CustomerEntity { ... }
```

Attribute parameters fall into one of two categories: *positional* or *named*. In the preceding example, the first argument is a positional parameter; the second is a named parameter. Positional parameters correspond to parameters of the attribute type's public constructors. Named parameters correspond to public fields or public properties on the attribute type.

When specifying an attribute, you must include positional parameters that correspond to one of the attribute's constructors. Named parameters are optional.

In Chapter 18, we describe the valid parameter types and rules for their evaluation.

Applying Attributes to Assemblies and Backing Fields

Implicitly, the target of an attribute is the code element it immediately precedes, which is typically a type or type member. You can also attach attributes, however, to an assembly. This requires that you explicitly specify the attribute's target. Here is how you can use the `AssemblyFileVersion` attribute to attach a version to the assembly:

```
[assembly: AssemblyFileVersion ("1.2.3.4")]
```

From C# 7.3, you can use the `field:` prefix to apply an attribute to the backing fields of an automatic property. This can be useful in controlling serialization:

```
[field:NonSerialized]
public int MyProperty { get; set; }
```

Applying Attributes to Lambda Expressions (C# 10)

From C# 10, you can apply attributes to the method, parameters, and return value of a lambda expression:

```
Action<int> a = [Description ("Method")]
                [return: Description ("Return value")]
                ([Description ("Parameter")]int x) => Console.Write (x);
```

This is useful when working with frameworks—such as ASP.NET—that rely on you placing attributes on methods that you write. With this feature, you can avoid having to create named methods for simple operations.

These attributes are applied to the compiler-generated method to which the delegate points. In Chapter 18, we'll describe how to reflect over attributes in code. For now, here's the extra code you need to resolve that indirection:

```
var methodAtt = a.GetMethodInfo().GetCustomAttributes();
var paramAtt = a.GetMethodInfo().GetParameters()[0].GetCustomAttributes();
var returnAtt = a.GetMethodInfo().ReturnParameter.GetCustomAttributes();
```

To avoid syntactical ambiguity when applying attributes to a parameter on a lambda expression, parentheses are always required. Attributes are not permitted on expression-tree lambdas.

Specifying Multiple Attributes

You can specify multiple attributes for a single code element. You can list each attribute either within the same pair of square brackets (separated by a comma) or in separate pairs of square brackets (or a combination of the two). The following three examples are semantically identical:

```
[Serializable, Obsolete, CLSCompliant(false)]
public class Bar {...}

[Serializable] [Obsolete] [CLSCompliant(false)]
public class Bar {...}

[Serializable, Obsolete]
[CLSCompliant(false)]
public class Bar {...}
```

Caller Info Attributes

You can tag optional parameters with one of three *caller info attributes*, which instruct the compiler to feed information obtained from the caller's source code into the parameter's default value:

- [CallerMemberName] applies the caller's member name.
- [CallerFilePath] applies the path to the caller's source code file.
- [CallerLineNumber] applies the line number in the caller's source code file.

The Foo method in the following program demonstrates all three:

```
using System;
using System.Runtime.CompilerServices;

class Program
{
  static void Main() => Foo();

  static void Foo (
    [CallerMemberName] string memberName = null,
    [CallerFilePath] string filePath = null,
    [CallerLineNumber] int lineNumber = 0)
  {
    Console.WriteLine (memberName);
    Console.WriteLine (filePath);
    Console.WriteLine (lineNumber);
  }
}
```

Assuming that our program resides in *c:\source\test\Program.cs*, the output would be:

```
Main
c:\source\test\Program.cs
6
```

As with standard optional parameters, the substitution is done at the *calling site*. Hence, our Main method is syntactic sugar for this:

```
static void Main() => Foo ("Main", @"c:\source\test\Program.cs", 6);
```

Caller info attributes are useful for logging—and for implementing patterns such as firing a single change notification event whenever any property on an object changes. In fact, there's a standard interface for this in the System.ComponentModel namespace, called INotifyPropertyChanged:

```
public interface INotifyPropertyChanged
{
  event PropertyChangedEventHandler PropertyChanged;
}

public delegate void PropertyChangedEventHandler
  (object sender, PropertyChangedEventArgs e);

public class PropertyChangedEventArgs : EventArgs
{
  public PropertyChangedEventArgs (string propertyName);
  public virtual string PropertyName { get; }
}
```

Notice that PropertyChangedEventArgs requires the name of the property that changed. By applying the [CallerMemberName] attribute, however, we can implement this interface and invoke the event without ever specifying property names:

```
public class Foo : INotifyPropertyChanged
{
  public event PropertyChangedEventHandler PropertyChanged = delegate { };

  void RaisePropertyChanged ([CallerMemberName] string propertyName = null)
    => PropertyChanged (this, new PropertyChangedEventArgs (propertyName));

  string customerName;
  public string CustomerName
  {
    get => customerName;
    set
    {
      if (value == customerName) return;
      customerName = value;
      RaisePropertyChanged();
      // The compiler converts the above line to:
      // RaisePropertyChanged ("CustomerName");
    }
  }
}
```

CallerArgumentExpression (C# 10)

A method parameter to which you apply the [CallerArgumentExpression] attribute captures an argument expression from the call site:

```
Print (Math.PI * 2);

void Print (double number,
            [CallerArgumentExpression("number")] string expr = null)
  => Console.WriteLine (expr);

// Output: Math.PI * 2
```

The compiler feeds in the calling expression's source code literally, including comments:

```
Print (Math.PI /*(n)*/ * 2);

// Output:  Math.PI /*(n)*/ * 2
```

The main application for this feature is when writing validation and assertion libraries. In the following example, an exception is thrown, whose message includes the text "2 + 2 == 5". This aids in debugging:

```
Assert (2 + 2 == 5);

void Assert (bool condition,
             [CallerArgumentExpression ("condition")] string message = null)
{
  if (!condition) throw new Exception ("Assertion failed: " + message);
}
```

Another example is the static ThrowIfNull method on the ArgumentNullException class. This method was introduced in .NET 6 and is defined as follows:

```
public static void ThrowIfNull (object argument,
  [CallerArgumentExpression("argument")] string paramName = null)
{
  if (argument == null)
    throw new ArgumentNullException (paramName);
}
```

It is used as follows:

```
void Print (string message)
{
  ArgumentNullException.ThrowIfNull (message);

  ...
}
```

You can use [CallerArgumentExpression] multiple times, to capture multiple argument expressions.

Dynamic Binding

Dynamic binding defers *binding*—the process of resolving types, members, and operators—from compile time to runtime. Dynamic binding is useful when at compile time *you* know that a certain function, member, or operation exists, but the *compiler* does not. This commonly occurs when you are interoperating with dynamic languages (such as IronPython) and COM as well as for scenarios in which you might otherwise use reflection.

A dynamic type is declared with the contextual keyword `dynamic`:

```
dynamic d = GetSomeObject();
d.Quack();
```

A dynamic type tells the compiler to relax. We expect the runtime type of d to have a Quack method. We just can't prove it statically. Because d is dynamic, the compiler defers binding Quack to d until runtime. To understand what this means requires distinguishing between *static binding* and *dynamic binding*.

Static Binding Versus Dynamic Binding

The canonical binding example is mapping a name to a specific function when compiling an expression. To compile the following expression, the compiler needs to find the implementation of the method named Quack:

```
d.Quack();
```

Let's suppose that the static type of d is Duck:

```
Duck d = ...
d.Quack();
```

In the simplest case, the compiler does the binding by looking for a parameterless method named Quack on Duck. Failing that, the compiler extends its search to methods taking optional parameters, methods on base classes of Duck, and extension methods that take Duck as its first parameter. If no match is found, you'll get a compilation error. Regardless of what method is bound, the bottom line is that the binding is done by the compiler, and the binding utterly depends on statically knowing the types of the operands (in this case, d). This makes it *static binding*.

Now let's change the static type of d to object:

```
object d = ...
d.Quack();
```

Calling Quack gives us a compilation error, because although the value stored in d can contain a method called Quack, the compiler cannot know it, because the only information it has is the type of the variable, which in this case is object. But let's now change the static type of d to dynamic:

```
dynamic d = ...
d.Quack();
```

A dynamic type is like object—it's equally nondescriptive about a type. The difference is that it lets you use it in ways that aren't known at compile time. A dynamic object binds at runtime based on its runtime type, not its compile-time type. When the compiler sees a dynamically bound expression (which in general is an expression that contains any value of type dynamic), it merely packages up the expression such that the binding can be done later at runtime.

At runtime, if a dynamic object implements IDynamicMetaObjectProvider, that interface is used to perform the binding. If not, binding occurs in almost the same way as it would have had the compiler known the dynamic object's runtime type. These two alternatives are called *custom binding* and *language binding*.

Custom Binding

Custom binding occurs when a dynamic object implements IDynamicMetaObject Provider (IDMOP). Although you can implement IDMOP on types that you write in C#, and that is useful to do, the more common case is that you have acquired an IDMOP object from a dynamic language that is implemented in .NET on the Dynamic Language Runtime (DLR), such as IronPython or IronRuby. Objects from those languages implicitly implement IDMOP as a means by which to directly control the meanings of operations performed on them.

We discuss custom binders in greater detail in Chapter 19, but for now, let's write a simple one to demonstrate the feature:

```
using System;
using System.Dynamic;

dynamic d = new Duck();
d.Quack();              // Quack method was called
d.Waddle();             // Waddle method was called

public class Duck : DynamicObject
{
  public override bool TryInvokeMember (
    InvokeMemberBinder binder, object[] args, out object result)
  {
    Console.WriteLine (binder.Name + " method was called");
    result = null;
    return true;
  }
}
```

The Duck class doesn't actually have a Quack method. Instead, it uses custom binding to intercept and interpret all method calls.

Language Binding

Language binding occurs when a dynamic object does not implement IDynamic MetaObjectProvider. It is useful when working around imperfectly designed types or inherent limitations in the .NET type system (we explore more scenarios in

Chapter 19). A typical problem when using numeric types is that they have no common interface. We have seen that we can bind methods dynamically; the same is true for operators:

```
int x = 3, y = 4;
Console.WriteLine (Mean (x, y));

dynamic Mean (dynamic x, dynamic y) => (x + y) / 2;
```

The benefit is obvious—you don't need to duplicate code for each numeric type. However, you lose static type safety, risking runtime exceptions rather than compile-time errors.

 Dynamic binding circumvents static type safety but not runtime type safety. Unlike with reflection (Chapter 18), you can't circumvent member accessibility rules with dynamic binding.

By design, language runtime binding behaves as similarly as possible to static binding, had the runtime types of the dynamic objects been known at compile time. In our previous example, the behavior of our program would be identical if we hardcoded Mean to work with the int type. The most notable exception in parity between static and dynamic binding is for extension methods, which we discuss in "Uncallable Functions" on page 238.

 Dynamic binding also incurs a performance hit. Because of the DLR's caching mechanisms, however, repeated calls to the same dynamic expression are optimized—allowing you to efficiently call dynamic expressions in a loop. This optimization brings the typical overhead for a simple dynamic expression on today's hardware down to less than 100 ns.

RuntimeBinderException

If a member fails to bind, a RuntimeBinderException is thrown. You can think of this like a compile-time error at runtime:

```
dynamic d = 5;
d.Hello();                    // throws RuntimeBinderException
```

The exception is thrown because the int type has no Hello method.

Runtime Representation of Dynamic

There is a deep equivalence between the dynamic and object types. The runtime treats the following expression as true:

```
typeof (dynamic) == typeof (object)
```

This principle extends to constructed types and array types:

```
typeof (List<dynamic>) == typeof (List<object>)
typeof (dynamic[]) == typeof (object[])
```

Like an object reference, a dynamic reference can point to an object of any type (except pointer types):

```
dynamic x = "hello";
Console.WriteLine (x.GetType().Name);  // String

x = 123;  // No error (despite same variable)
Console.WriteLine (x.GetType().Name);  // Int32
```

Structurally, there is no difference between an object reference and a dynamic reference. A dynamic reference simply enables dynamic operations on the object it points to. You can convert from `object` to `dynamic` to perform any dynamic operation you want on an `object`:

```
object o = new System.Text.StringBuilder();
dynamic d = o;
d.Append ("hello");
Console.WriteLine (o);  // hello
```

> Reflecting on a type exposing (public) dynamic members reveals that those members are represented as annotated objects; for example
>
> ```
> public class Test
> {
>     public dynamic Foo;
> }
> ```
>
> is equivalent to:
>
> ```
> public class Test
> {
>     [System.Runtime.CompilerServices.DynamicAttribute]
>     public object Foo;
> }
> ```
>
> This allows consumers of that type to know that `Foo` should be treated as dynamic while allowing languages that don't support dynamic binding to fall back to `object`.

Dynamic Conversions

The dynamic type has implicit conversions to and from all other types:

```
int i = 7;
dynamic d = i;
long j = d;      // No cast required (implicit conversion)
```

For the conversion to succeed, the runtime type of the dynamic object must be implicitly convertible to the target static type. The preceding example worked because an `int` is implicitly convertible to a `long`.

The following example throws a `RuntimeBinderException` because an `int` is not implicitly convertible to a `short`:

```
int i = 7;
dynamic d = i;
short j = d;     // throws RuntimeBinderException
```

var Versus dynamic

The var and dynamic types bear a superficial resemblance, but the difference is deep:

- var says, "Let the *compiler* figure out the type."
- dynamic says, "Let the *runtime* figure out the type."

To illustrate:

```
dynamic x = "hello";   // Static type is dynamic; runtime type is string
var y = "hello";       // Static type is string; runtime type is string
int i = x;             // Runtime error      (cannot convert string to int)
int j = y;             // Compile-time error (cannot convert string to int)
```

The static type of a variable declared with var can be dynamic:

```
dynamic x = "hello";
var y = x;             // Static type of y is dynamic
int z = y;             // Runtime error (cannot convert string to int)
```

Dynamic Expressions

Fields, properties, methods, events, constructors, indexers, operators, and conversions can all be called dynamically.

Trying to consume the result of a dynamic expression with a void return type is prohibited—just as with a statically typed expression. The difference is that the error occurs at runtime:

```
dynamic list = new List<int>();
var result = list.Add (5);         // RuntimeBinderException thrown
```

Expressions involving dynamic operands are typically themselves dynamic because the effect of absent type information is cascading:

```
dynamic x = 2;
var y = x * 3;         // Static type of y is dynamic
```

There are a couple of obvious exceptions to this rule. First, casting a dynamic expression to a static type yields a static expression:

```
dynamic x = 2;
var y = (int)x;        // Static type of y is int
```

Second, constructor invocations always yield static expressions—even when called with dynamic arguments. In this example, x is statically typed to a StringBuilder:

```
dynamic capacity = 10;
var x = new System.Text.StringBuilder (capacity);
```

In addition, there are a few edge cases for which an expression containing a dynamic argument is static, including passing an index to an array and delegate creation expressions.

Dynamic Calls Without Dynamic Receivers

The canonical use case for dynamic involves a dynamic *receiver*. This means that a dynamic object is the receiver of a dynamic function call:

```
dynamic x = ...;
x.Foo();          // x is the receiver
```

However, you can also call statically known functions with dynamic arguments. Such calls are subject to dynamic overload resolution and can include the following:

- Static methods

- Instance constructors

- Instance methods on receivers with a statically known type

In the following example, the particular Foo that gets dynamically bound is dependent on the runtime type of the dynamic argument:

```
class Program
{
  static void Foo (int x)    => Console.WriteLine ("int");
  static void Foo (string x) => Console.WriteLine ("string");

  static void Main()
  {
    dynamic x = 5;
    dynamic y = "watermelon";

    Foo (x);    // int
    Foo (y);    // string
  }
}
```

Because a dynamic receiver is not involved, the compiler can statically perform a basic check to see whether the dynamic call will succeed. It checks whether a function with the correct name and number of parameters exists. If no candidate is found, you get a compile-time error:

```
class Program
{
  static void Foo (int x)    => Console.WriteLine ("int");
  static void Foo (string x) => Console.WriteLine ("string");

  static void Main()
  {
    dynamic x = 5;
    Foo (x, x);       // Compiler error - wrong number of parameters
    Fook (x);         // Compiler error - no such method name
  }
}
```

Static Types in Dynamic Expressions

It's obvious that dynamic types are used in dynamic binding. It's not so obvious that static types are also used—wherever possible—in dynamic binding. Consider the following:

```
class Program
{
  static void Foo (object x, object y) { Console.WriteLine ("oo"); }
  static void Foo (object x, string y) { Console.WriteLine ("os"); }
  static void Foo (string x, object y) { Console.WriteLine ("so"); }
  static void Foo (string x, string y) { Console.WriteLine ("ss"); }

  static void Main()
  {
    object o = "hello";
    dynamic d = "goodbye";
    Foo (o, d);              // os
  }
}
```

The call to Foo (o,d) is dynamically bound because one of its arguments, d, is dynamic. But because o is statically known, the binding—even though it occurs dynamically—will make use of that. In this case, overload resolution will pick the second implementation of Foo due to the static type of o and the runtime type of d. In other words, the compiler is "as static as it can possibly be."

Uncallable Functions

Some functions cannot be called dynamically. You cannot call the following:

- Extension methods (via extension method syntax)
- Members of an interface, if you need to cast to that interface to do so
- Base members hidden by a subclass

Understanding why this is so is useful in understanding dynamic binding.

Dynamic binding requires two pieces of information: the name of the function to call and the object upon which to call the function. However, in each of the three uncallable scenarios, an *additional type* is involved, which is known only at compile time. As of this writing, there's no way to specify these additional types dynamically.

When calling extension methods, that additional type is implicit. It's the static class on which the extension method is defined. The compiler searches for it given the using directives in your source code. This makes extension methods compile-time-only concepts because using directives melt away upon compilation (after they've done their job in the binding process in mapping simple names to namespace-qualified names).

When calling members via an interface, you specify that additional type via an implicit or explicit cast. There are two scenarios for which you might want to do this: when calling explicitly implemented interface members and when calling interface members implemented in a type internal to another assembly. We can illustrate the former with the following two types:

```
interface IFoo   { void Test();        }
class Foo : IFoo { void IFoo.Test() {} }
```

To call the Test method, we must cast to the IFoo interface. This is easy with static typing:

```
IFoo f = new Foo();   // Implicit cast to interface
f.Test();
```

Now consider the situation with dynamic typing:

```
IFoo f = new Foo();
dynamic d = f;
d.Test();                 // Exception thrown
```

The implicit cast shown in bold tells the *compiler* to bind subsequent member calls on f to IFoo rather than Foo—in other words, to view that object through the lens of the IFoo interface. However, that lens is lost at runtime, so the DLR cannot complete the binding. The loss is illustrated as follows:

```
Console.WriteLine (f.GetType().Name);    // Foo
```

A similar situation arises when calling a hidden base member: you must specify an additional type via either a cast or the base keyword—and that additional type is lost at runtime.

 Should you need to invoke interface members dynamically, a workaround is to use the Uncapsulator open source library, available on NuGet and GitHub. Uncapsulator was written by the author to address this problem, and leverages *custom binding* to provide a better dynamic than dynamic:

```
IFoo f = new Foo();
dynamic uf = f.Uncapsulate();
uf.Test();
```

Uncapsulator also lets you cast to base types and interfaces by name, dynamically call static members, and access nonpublic members of a type.

Operator Overloading

You can overload operators to provide more natural syntax for custom types. Operator overloading is most appropriately used for implementing custom structs that represent fairly primitive data types. For example, a custom numeric type is an excellent candidate for operator overloading.

The following symbolic operators can be overloaded:

+ (unary)	- (unary)	!	~	++
--	+	-	*	/
%	&	|	^	<<
>>	==	!=	>	<
>=	<=			

The following operators are also overloadable:

- Implicit and explicit conversions (with the `implicit` and `explicit` keywords)
- The `true` and `false` *operators* (not *literals*)

The following operators are indirectly overloaded:

- The compound assignment operators (e.g., +=, /=) are implicitly overridden by overriding the noncompound operators (e.g., +, /).
- The conditional operators && and || are implicitly overridden by overriding the bitwise operators & and |.

Operator Functions

You overload an operator by declaring an *operator function*. An operator function has the following rules:

- The name of the function is specified with the `operator` keyword followed by an operator symbol.
- The operator function must be marked `static` and `public`.
- The parameters of the operator function represent the operands.
- The return type of an operator function represents the result of an expression.
- At least one of the operands must be the type in which the operator function is declared.

In the following example, we define a struct called `Note` representing a musical note and then overload the + operator:

```
public struct Note
{
  int value;
  public Note (int semitonesFromA) { value = semitonesFromA; }
  public static Note operator + (Note x, int semitones)
  {
    return new Note (x.value + semitones);
```

```
    }
}
```

This overload allows us to add an int to a Note:

```
Note B = new Note (2);
Note CSharp = B + 2;
```

Overloading an operator automatically overloads the corresponding compound assignment operator. In our example, because we overrode +, we can use += too:

```
CSharp += 2;
```

Just as with methods and properties, C# allows operator functions comprising a single expression to be written more tersely with expression-bodied syntax:

```
public static Note operator + (Note x, int semitones)
                        => new Note (x.value + semitones);
```

Overloading Equality and Comparison Operators

Equality and comparison operators are sometimes overridden when writing structs, and in rare cases when writing classes. Special rules and obligations come with overloading the equality and comparison operators, which we explain in Chapter 6. A summary of these rules is as follows:

Pairing
> The C# compiler enforces operators that are logical pairs to both be defined. These operators are (== !=), (< >), and (<= >=).

Equals *and* GetHashCode
> In most cases, if you overload (==) and (!=), you must override the Equals and GetHashCode methods defined on object to get meaningful behavior. The C# compiler will give a warning if you do not do this. (See "Equality Comparison" on page 324 for more details.)

IComparable *and* IComparable<T>
> If you overload (< >) and (<= >=), you should implement IComparable and IComparable<T>.

Custom Implicit and Explicit Conversions

Implicit and explicit conversions are overloadable operators. These conversions are typically overloaded to make converting between strongly related types (such as numeric types) concise and natural.

To convert between weakly related types, the following strategies are more suitable:

- Write a constructor that has a parameter of the type to convert from.
- Write To*XXX* and (static) From*XXX* methods to convert between types.

As explained in the discussion on types, the rationale behind implicit conversions is that they are guaranteed to succeed and not lose information during the conversion. Conversely, an explicit conversion should be required either when runtime circumstances will determine whether the conversion will succeed or if information might be lost during the conversion.

In this example, we define conversions between our musical Note type and a double (which represents the frequency in hertz of that note):

```
...
// Convert to hertz
public static implicit operator double (Note x)
  => 440 * Math.Pow (2, (double) x.value / 12 );

// Convert from hertz (accurate to the nearest semitone)
public static explicit operator Note (double x)
  => new Note ((int) (0.5 + 12 * (Math.Log (x/440) / Math.Log(2) ) ));
...

Note n = (Note)554.37;   // explicit conversion
double x = n;            // implicit conversion
```

Following our own guidelines, this example might be better implemented with a ToFrequency method (and a static From Frequency method) instead of implicit and explicit operators.

Custom conversions are ignored by the as and is operators:

```
Console.WriteLine (554.37 is Note);   // False
Note n = 554.37 as Note;              // Error
```

Overloading true and false

The true and false operators are overloaded in the extremely rare case of types that are Boolean "in spirit" but do not have a conversion to bool. An example is a type that implements three-state logic: by overloading true and false, such a type can work seamlessly with conditional statements and operators—namely, if, do, while, for, &&, ||, and ?:. The System.Data.SqlTypes.SqlBoolean struct provides this functionality:

```
SqlBoolean a = SqlBoolean.Null;
if (a)
  Console.WriteLine ("True");
else if (!a)
  Console.WriteLine ("False");
else
  Console.WriteLine ("Null");

OUTPUT:
Null
```

The following code is a reimplementation of the parts of SqlBoolean necessary to demonstrate the true and false operators:

```
public struct SqlBoolean
{
  public static bool operator true (SqlBoolean x)
    => x.m_value == True.m_value;

  public static bool operator false (SqlBoolean x)
    => x.m_value == False.m_value;

  public static SqlBoolean operator ! (SqlBoolean x)
  {
    if (x.m_value == Null.m_value)  return Null;
    if (x.m_value == False.m_value) return True;
    return False;
  }

  public static readonly SqlBoolean Null =  new SqlBoolean(0);
  public static readonly SqlBoolean False = new SqlBoolean(1);
  public static readonly SqlBoolean True =  new SqlBoolean(2);

  private SqlBoolean (byte value) { m_value = value; }
  private byte m_value;
}
```

Unsafe Code and Pointers

C# supports direct memory manipulation via pointers within blocks of code marked unsafe and compiled with the /unsafe compiler option. Pointer types are primarily useful for interoperability with C APIs, but you also can use them for accessing memory outside the managed heap or for performance-critical hotspots.

Pointer Basics

For every value type or reference type *V*, there is a corresponding pointer type *V**. A pointer instance holds the address of a variable. Pointer types can be (unsafely) cast to any other pointer type. Following are the main pointer operators:

Operator	Meaning
&	The *address-of* operator returns a pointer to the address of a variable.
*	The *dereference* operator returns the variable at the address of a pointer.
->	The *pointer-to-member* operator is a syntactic shortcut, in which x->y is equivalent to (*x).y.

In keeping with C, adding (or subtracting) an integer offset to a pointer generates another pointer. Subtracting one pointer from another generates a 64-bit integer (on both 64-bit and 32-bit platforms).

Unsafe Code

By marking a type, type member, or statement block with the unsafe keyword, you're permitted to use pointer types and perform C style pointer operations on memory within that scope. Here is an example of using pointers to quickly process a bitmap:

```
unsafe void BlueFilter (int[,] bitmap)
{
  int length = bitmap.Length;
  fixed (int* b = bitmap)
  {
    int* p = b;
    for (int i = 0; i < length; i++)
      *p++ &= 0xFF;
  }
}
```

Unsafe code can run faster than a corresponding safe implementation. In this case, the code would have required a nested loop with array indexing and bounds checking. An unsafe C# method can also be faster than calling an external C function given that there is no overhead associated with leaving the managed execution environment.

The fixed Statement

The fixed statement is required to pin a managed object, such as the bitmap in the previous example. During the execution of a program, many objects are allocated and deallocated from the heap. To avoid unnecessary waste or fragmentation of memory, the garbage collector moves objects around. Pointing to an object is futile if its address could change while referencing it, so the fixed statement tells the garbage collector to "pin" the object and not move it around. This can have an impact on the efficiency of the runtime, so you should use fixed blocks only briefly, and you should avoid heap allocation within the fixed block.

Within a fixed statement, you can get a pointer to any value type, an array of value types, or a string. In the case of arrays and strings, the pointer will actually point to the first element, which is a value type.

Value types declared inline within reference types require the reference type to be pinned, as follows:

```
Test test = new Test();
unsafe
{
  fixed (int* p = &test.X)   // Pins test
  {
    *p = 9;
  }
  Console.WriteLine (test.X);
}

class Test { public int X; }
```

We describe the fixed statement further in "Mapping a Struct to Unmanaged Memory" on page 973.

The Pointer-to-Member Operator

In addition to the & and * operators, C# also provides the C++ style -> operator, which you can use on structs:

```
Test test = new Test();
unsafe
{
  Test* p = &test;
  p->X = 9;
  System.Console.WriteLine (test.X);
}

struct Test { public int X; }
```

The stackalloc Keyword

You can allocate memory in a block on the stack explicitly by using the stackalloc keyword. Because it is allocated on the stack, its lifetime is limited to the execution of the method, just as with any other local variable (whose life hasn't been extended by virtue of being captured by a lambda expression, iterator block, or asynchronous function). The block can use the [ ] operator to index into memory:

```
int* a = stackalloc int [10];
for (int i = 0; i < 10; ++i)
   Console.WriteLine (a[i]);
```

In Chapter 23, we describe how you can use Span<T> to manage stack-allocated memory without using the unsafe keyword:

```
Span<int> a = stackalloc int [10];
for (int i = 0; i < 10; ++i)
   Console.WriteLine (a[i]);
```

Fixed-Size Buffers

The fixed keyword has another use, which is to create fixed-size buffers within structs (this can be useful when calling an unmanaged function; see Chapter 24):

```
new UnsafeClass ("Christian Troy");

unsafe struct UnsafeUnicodeString
{
  public short Length;
  public fixed byte Buffer[30];    // Allocate block of 30 bytes
}

unsafe class UnsafeClass
{
  UnsafeUnicodeString uus;

  public UnsafeClass (string s)
  {
    uus.Length = (short)s.Length;
```

```
    fixed (byte* p = uus.Buffer)
      for (int i = 0; i < s.Length; i++)
        p[i] = (byte) s[i];
  }
}
```

Fixed-size buffers are not arrays: if Buffer were an array, it would consist of a reference to an object stored on the (managed) heap, rather than 30 bytes within the struct itself.

The fixed keyword is also used in this example to pin the object on the heap that contains the buffer (which will be the instance of UnsafeClass). Hence, fixed means two different things: fixed in *size* and fixed in *place*. The two are often used together, in that a fixed-size buffer must be fixed in place to be used.

void*

A *void pointer* (void*) makes no assumptions about the type of the underlying data and is useful for functions that deal with raw memory. An implicit conversion exists from any pointer type to void*. A void* cannot be dereferenced, and arithmetic operations cannot be performed on void pointers. Here's an example:

```
short[] a = { 1, 1, 2, 3, 5, 8, 13, 21, 34, 55 };
unsafe
{
  fixed (short* p = a)
  {
    //sizeof returns size of value-type in bytes
    Zap (p, a.Length * sizeof (short));
  }
}
foreach (short x in a)
  System.Console.WriteLine (x);    // Prints all zeros

unsafe void Zap (void* memory, int byteCount)
{
  byte* b = (byte*)memory;
  for (int i = 0; i < byteCount; i++)
    *b++ = 0;
}
```

Native-Sized Integers

The nint and nuint *native-sized* integer types (introduced in C# 9) are sized to match the address space of the process at runtime (in practice, 32 or 64 bits). Native-sized integers can improve efficiency, overflow safety, and convenience when performing pointer arithmetic.

The gain in efficiency arises because when you subtract two pointers in C#, the result is always a 64-bit integer (long), which is inefficient on 32-bit platforms. By first casting the pointers to nint, the result of a subtraction is also nint (which will be 32 bits on a 32-bit platform):

```
unsafe nint AddressDif (char* x, char* y) => (nint)x - (nint)y;
```

The gain in overflow safety and convenience arises when you need a type to represent an offset in memory or a buffer length. This is because the historical alternative to using nint/nuint has been to repurpose System.IntPtr and System.UIntPtr, types whose intended purpose is to wrap operating system handles or address pointers, allowing interop outside an unsafe context. Although they are natively sized, these types have limited support for arithmetic—and the support they have is always unchecked (so overflows fail silently).

In contrast, native-sized integers behave much like standard integers, with full support for arithmetic operations and overflow checking:

```
nint x = 123, y = 234;
checked
{
  nint sum = x + y, product = x * y;
  Console.WriteLine (product);
}
```

Native-sized integers can be assigned 32-bit integer constants (but not 64-bit integer constants, because these might overflow at runtime). You can use an explicit cast to convert to or from other integral types.

At runtime, nint and nuint map to the IntPtr and UIntPtr structs, so you can convert between them without casting (an *identity conversion*):

```
nint x = 123;
IntPtr p = x;
nint y = p;
```

For reasons described previously, nint/nuint are not merely shortcuts for IntPtr/ UIntPtr, despite their runtime equivalence. Specifically, the compiler treats a variable of type nint/nuint as a *numeric type*, allowing you to perform arithmetic operations not implemented by IntPtr and UIntPtr (and with checked blocks honored).

A nint/nuint variable is like an IntPtr/UIntPtr wearing a special hat. This hat is recognized by the compiler to mean "please treat me as a safe numeric type."

This multi-hat behavior is unique to native-sized integers. For example, int acts as a pure *synonym* for System.Int32, and the two can be freely interchanged.

This nonequivalence means that both constructs are useful:

- nint/nuint are useful for representing a memory offset or buffer length.
- IntPtr/UIntPtr are useful for wrapping handles and pointers for interop.

Using the types in this manner also correctly signals your intention.

A good example of the real-world use of `nint` and `nuint` is in the implementation of `Buffer.MemoryCopy`. You can see this in the .NET source code for *Buffer.cs* on GitHub or by decompiling the method in ILSpy. A simplified version has also been included in the LINQPad samples for *C# 10 in a Nutshell*.

Function Pointers

A *function pointer* (from C# 9) is like a delegate, but without the indirection of a delegate instance; instead, it points directly to a method. A function pointer can point only to static methods, lacks multicast capability, and requires an `unsafe` context (because it bypasses runtime type safety). Its main purpose is to simplify and optimize interop with unmanaged APIs (see "Callbacks from Unmanaged Code" on page 967).

A function pointer type is declared as follows (with the return type appearing last):

```
delegate*<int, char, string, void>   // (void refers to the return type)
```

This matches a function with this signature:

```
void SomeFunction (int x, char y, string z)
```

The & operator creates a function pointer from a method group. Here's a complete example:

```
unsafe
{
  delegate*<string, int> functionPointer = &GetLength;
  int length = functionPointer ("Hello, world");

  static int GetLength (string s) => s.Length;
}
```

In this example, `functionPointer` is not an *object* upon which you can call a method such as `Invoke` (or with a reference to a `Target` object). Instead, it's a variable that points directly to the target method's address in memory:

```
Console.WriteLine ((IntPtr)functionPointer);
```

Like any other pointer, it's not subject to runtime type checking. The following treats our function's return value as a `decimal` (which, being longer than an `int`, means that we incorporate some random memory into the output):

```
var pointer2 = (delegate*<string, decimal>) (IntPtr) functionPointer;
Console.WriteLine (pointer2 ("Hello, unsafe world"));
```

[SkipLocalsInit]

When C# compiles a method, it emits a flag that instructs the runtime to initialize the method's local variables to their default values (by zeroing the memory). From C# 9, you can ask the compiler not to emit this flag by applying the

[SkipLocalInit] attribute to a method (in the System.Runtime.CompilerServices namespace):

```
[SkipLocalsInit]
void Foo() ...
```

You can also apply this attribute to a type—which is equivalent to applying it to all of the type's methods—or even an entire module (the container for an assembly):

```
[module: System.Runtime.CompilerServices.SkipLocalsInit]
```

In normal safe scenarios, [SkipLocalsInit] has little effect on functionality or performance, because C#'s definite assignment policy requires that you explicitly assign local variables before they can be read. This means that the JIT optimizer is likely to emit the same machine code, whether or not the attribute is applied.

In an unsafe context, however, use of [SkipLocalsInit] can usefully save the CLR from the overhead of initializing value-typed local variables, creating a small performance gain with methods that make extensive use of the stack (through a large stackalloc). The following example prints uninitialized memory when [SkipLocalsInit] is applied (instead of all zeros):

```
[SkipLocalsInit]
unsafe void Foo()
{
    int local;
    int* ptr = &local;
    Console.WriteLine (*ptr);

    int* a = stackalloc int [100];
    for (int i = 0; i < 100; ++i) Console.WriteLine (a [i]);
}
```

Interestingly, you can achieve the same result in a "safe" context through the use of Span<T>:

```
[SkipLocalsInit]
void Foo()
{
    Span<int> a = stackalloc int [100];
    for (int i = 0; i < 100; ++i) Console.WriteLine (a [i]);
}
```

Consequently, use of [SkipLocalsInit] requires that you compile your assembly with the *unsafe* option—even if none of your methods are marked as unsafe.

Preprocessor Directives

Preprocessor directives supply the compiler with additional information about regions of code. The most common preprocessor directives are the conditional directives, which provide a way to include or exclude regions of code from compilation:

```
#define DEBUG
class MyClass
{
  int x;
  void Foo()
  {
    #if DEBUG
    Console.WriteLine ("Testing: x = {0}", x);
    #endif
  }
  ...
}
```

In this class, the statement in Foo is compiled as conditionally dependent upon the presence of the DEBUG symbol. If we remove the DEBUG symbol, the statement is not compiled. You can define preprocessor symbols within a source file (as we have done) or at a project level in the *.csproj* file:

```
<PropertyGroup>
  <DefineConstants>DEBUG;ANOTHERSYMBOL</DefineConstants>
</PropertyGroup>
```

With the #if and #elif directives, you can use the ||, &&, and ! operators to perform *or*, *and*, and *not* operations on multiple symbols. The following directive instructs the compiler to include the code that follows if the TESTMODE symbol is defined and the DEBUG symbol is not defined:

```
#if TESTMODE && !DEBUG
  ...
```

Keep in mind, however, that you're not building an ordinary C# expression, and the symbols upon which you operate have absolutely no connection to *variables*—static or otherwise.

The #error and #warning symbols prevent accidental misuse of conditional directives by making the compiler generate a warning or error given an undesirable set of compilation symbols. Table 4-1 lists the preprocessor directives.

Table 4-1. Preprocessor directives

Preprocessor directive	Action
#define *symbol*	Defines *symbol*
#undef *symbol*	Undefines *symbol*
#if *symbol* [*operator symbol2*]...	*symbol* to test
	operators are ==, !=, &&, and ||, followed by #else, #elif, and #endif
#else	Executes code to subsequent #endif
#elif *symbol* [*operator symbol2*]	Combines #else branch and #if test

Preprocessor directive	Action
`#endif`	Ends conditional directives
`#warning` *text*	*text* of the warning to appear in compiler output
`#error` *text*	*text* of the error to appear in compiler output
`#error version`	Reports the compiler version and exits
`#pragma warning [disable | restore]`	Disables/restores compiler warning(s)
`#line [ number ["file"] | hidden]`	*number* specifies the line in source code (a column can also be specified from C# 10); *file* is the filename to appear in computer output; `hidden` instructs debuggers to skip over code from this point until the next `#line` directive
`#region` *name*	Marks the beginning of an outline
`#endregion`	Ends an outline region
`#nullable` *option*	See "Nullable reference types" on page 16

Conditional Attributes

An attribute decorated with the `Conditional` attribute will be compiled only if a given preprocessor symbol is present:

```
// file1.cs
#define DEBUG
using System;
using System.Diagnostics;
[Conditional("DEBUG")]
public class TestAttribute : Attribute {}

// file2.cs
#define DEBUG
[Test]
class Foo
{
  [Test]
  string s;
}
```

The compiler will incorporate the `[Test]` attributes only if the DEBUG symbol is in scope for *file2.cs*.

Pragma Warning

The compiler generates a warning when it spots something in your code that seems unintentional. Unlike errors, warnings don't ordinarily prevent your application from compiling.

Compiler warnings can be extremely valuable in spotting bugs. Their usefulness, however, is undermined when you get *false* warnings. In a large application, maintaining a good signal-to-noise ratio is essential if the "real" warnings are to be noticed.

To this effect, the compiler allows you to selectively suppress warnings by using the #pragma warning directive. In this example, we instruct the compiler not to warn us about the field Message not being used:

```
public class Foo
{
  static void Main() { }

  #pragma warning disable 414
  static string Message = "Hello";
  #pragma warning restore 414
}
```

Omitting the number in the #pragma warning directive disables or restores all warning codes.

If you are thorough in applying this directive, you can compile with the /warnaserror switch—this instructs the compiler to treat any residual warnings as errors.

XML Documentation

A *documentation comment* is a piece of embedded XML that documents a type or member. A documentation comment comes immediately before a type or member declaration and starts with three slashes:

```
/// <summary>Cancels a running query.</summary>
public void Cancel() { ... }
```

Multiline comments can be done like this:

```
/// <summary>
/// Cancels a running query
/// </summary>
public void Cancel() { ... }
```

Or like this (notice the extra star at the start):

```
/**
    <summary> Cancels a running query. </summary>
*/
public void Cancel() { ... }
```

If you add the following option to your *.csproj* file

```
<PropertyGroup>
  <DocumentationFile>SomeFile.xml</DocumentationFile>
</PropertyGroup>
```

the compiler extracts and collates documentation comments into the specified XML file. This has two main uses:

- If placed in the same folder as the compiled assembly, tools such as Visual Studio and LINQPad automatically read the XML file and use the information to provide IntelliSense member listings to consumers of the assembly of the same name.

- Third-party tools (such as Sandcastle and NDoc) can transform the XML file into an HTML help file.

Standard XML Documentation Tags

Here are the standard XML tags that Visual Studio and documentation generators recognize:

`<summary>`

> `<summary>...</summary>`

Indicates the tool tip that IntelliSense should display for the type or member, typically a single phrase or sentence.

`<remarks>`

> `<remarks>...</remarks>`

Additional text that describes the type or member. Documentation generators pick this up and merge it into the bulk of a type's or member's description.

`<param>`

> `<param name="name">...</param>`

Explains a parameter on a method.

`<returns>`

> `<returns>...</returns>`

Explains the return value for a method.

`<exception>`

> `<exception [cref="type"]>...</exception>`

Lists an exception that a method can throw (`cref` refers to the exception type).

`<example>`

> `<example>...</example>`

Denotes an example (used by documentation generators). This usually contains both description text and source code (source code is typically within a `<c>` or `<code>` tag).

`<c>`

> `<c>...</c>`

Indicates an inline code snippet. This tag is usually used within an `<example>` block.

`<code>`

```
<code>...</code>
```

Indicates a multiline code sample. This tag is usually used within an `<example>` block.

`<see>`

```
<see cref="member">...</see>
```

Inserts an inline cross-reference to another type or member. HTML documentation generators typically convert this to a hyperlink. The compiler emits a warning if the type or member name is invalid. To refer to generic types, use curly braces; for example, `cref="Foo{T,U}"`.

`<seealso>`

```
<seealso cref="member">...</seealso>
```

Cross-references another type or member. Documentation generators typically write this into a separate "See Also" section at the bottom of the page.

`<paramref>`

```
<paramref name="name"/>
```

References a parameter from within a `<summary>` or `<remarks>` tag.

`<list>`

```
<list type=[ bullet | number | table ]>
  <listheader>
    <term>...</term>
    <description>...</description>
  </listheader>
  <item>
    <term>...</term>
    <description>...</description>
  </item>
</list>
```

Instructs documentation generators to emit a bulleted, numbered, or table-style list.

`<para>`

```
<para>...</para>
```

Instructs documentation generators to format the contents into a separate paragraph.

`<include>`

```
<include file='filename' path='tagpath[@name="id"]'>...</include>
```

Merges an external XML file that contains documentation. The path attribute denotes an XPath query to a specific element in that file.

User-Defined Tags

Little is special about the predefined XML tags recognized by the C# compiler, and you are free to define your own. The only special processing done by the compiler is on the `<param>` tag (in which it verifies the parameter name and that all the parameters on the method are documented) and the `cref` attribute (in which it verifies that the attribute refers to a real type or member and expands it to a fully qualified type or member ID). You can also use the `cref` attribute in your own tags; it is verified and expanded just as it is in the predefined `<exception>`, `<permission>`, `<see>`, and `<seealso>` tags.

Type or Member Cross-References

Type names and type or member cross-references are translated into IDs that uniquely define the type or member. These names are composed of a prefix that defines what the ID represents and a signature of the type or member. Following are the member prefixes:

XML type prefix	ID prefixes applied to...
N	Namespace
T	Type (class, struct, enum, interface, delegate)
F	Field
P	Property (includes indexers)
M	Method (includes special methods)
E	Event
!	Error

The rules describing how the signatures are generated are well documented, although fairly complex.

Here is an example of a type and the IDs that are generated:

```
// Namespaces do not have independent signatures
namespace NS
{
  /// T:NS.MyClass
  class MyClass
  {
    /// F:NS.MyClass.aField
    string aField;

    /// P:NS.MyClass.aProperty
    short aProperty {get {...} set {...}}

    /// T:NS.MyClass.NestedType
    class NestedType {...};

    /// M:NS.MyClass.X()
```

```
   void X() {...}

   /// M:NS.MyClass.Y(System.Int32,System.Double@,System.Decimal@)
   void Y(int p1, ref double p2, out decimal p3) {...}

   /// M:NS.MyClass.Z(System.Char[ ],System.Single[0:,0:])
   void Z(char[ ] p1, float[,] p2) {...}

   /// M:NS.MyClass.op_Addition(NS.MyClass,NS.MyClass)
   public static MyClass operator+(MyClass c1, MyClass c2) {...}

   /// M:NS.MyClass.op_Implicit(NS.MyClass)~System.Int32
   public static implicit operator int(MyClass c) {...}

   /// M:NS.MyClass.#ctor
   MyClass() {...}

   /// M:NS.MyClass.Finalize
   ~MyClass() {...}

   /// M:NS.MyClass.#cctor
   static MyClass() {...}
   }
}
```

5

.NET Overview

Almost all of the capabilities of the .NET 6 runtime are exposed via a vast set of managed types. These types are organized into hierarchical namespaces and packaged into a set of assemblies.

Some of the .NET types are used directly by the CLR and are essential for the managed hosting environment. These types reside in an assembly called *System.Private.CoreLib.dll* and include C#'s built-in types as well as the basic collection classes, and types for stream processing, serialization, reflection, threading, and native interoperability.

System.Private.CoreLib.dll replaces .NET Framework's *mscorlib.dll*. Many places in the official documentation still refer to mscorlib.

At a level above this are additional types that "flesh out" the CLR-level functionality, providing features such as XML, JSON, networking, and Language-Integrated Query. These constitute the Base Class Library (BCL). Sitting above this are *application layers*, which provide APIs for developing particular kinds of applications such as web or rich client.

In this chapter, we provide the following:

- An overview of the BCL (which we cover in the rest of the book)
- A high-level summary of the application layers

What's New in .NET 6

In .NET 6, the Base Class Library has numerous new features. In particular:

- New `DateOnly`/`TimeOnly` structs cleanly capture a date or time for scenarios such as recording a birthday or alarm time (see "DateOnly and TimeOnly" on page 292).

- A new `BitOperations` static class provides access to low-level base-2 numeric operations (see "BitOperations" on page 320).

- The following new LINQ methods have been added: `Chunk`, `DistinctBy`, `UnionBy`, `IntersectBy`, `ExceptBy`, `MinBy`, and `MaxBy` (see Chapter 9). `Take` also now accepts a `Range` variable.

- The new `JsonNode` API provides a fluent writable DOM whose types don't require disposal (see "JsonNode" on page 551. `Utf8JsonWriter` also now has a `WriteRawValue` method.

- The new `RandomAccess` class provides performant thread-safe file I/O operations.

- The new `NullabilityInfoContext` class in `System.Reflection` queries nullability annotations (see "NullabilityContextInfo" on page 794).

- The `RandomNumberGenerator` class in `System.Security.Cryptography` now has a static `GetBytes(int)` method that returns an array of random bytes in one operation. There are also new methods to simplify encryption and decryption (see "Encrypting in Memory" on page 856).

- A new `ForEachAsync` method on the `Parallel` class limits asynchronous concurrency (see "Parallel.ForEachAsync" on page 882). `Task` also now has a `WaitAsync` method, which applies a timeout to any asynchronous operation, and there's a new timer designed to work with `await` (see "PeriodicTimer" on page 902).

- The new `NativeMemory` class provides a lightweight wrapper around low-level memory allocation operations such as malloc.

.NET 6 also features numerous performance improvements to the runtime and enhanced support for Windows ARM64 and Apple M1/M2 processors.

In the application layers, the biggest change is in the introduction of MAUI (Multiplatform App UI, early 2022), which replaces Xamarin for cross-platform mobile development. MAUI also supports cross-platform desktop application development for macOS and Windows, and targets a unified .NET 6 CLR/BCL. UWP also has a successor, Windows App SDK (with WinUI 3 as its presentation layer), and a new technology has emerged called Blazor Desktop for writing HTML-based desktop and mobile applications.

.NET Standard

The wealth of public libraries that are available on NuGet wouldn't be as valuable if they supported only .NET 6. When writing a library, you'll often want to support a variety of platforms and runtime versions. To achieve that goal without creating a separate build for each runtime, you must target the lowest common denominator. This is relatively easy if you wish to support only .NET 6's direct predecessors: for example, if you target .NET Core 3.0, your library will run on .NET Core 3.0, .NET Core 3.1, and .NET 5+.

The situation becomes messier if you also want to support .NET Framework or Xamarin. This is because each of these runtimes has a CLR and BCL with overlapping features—no one runtime is a pure subset of the others.

.NET Standard solves this problem by defining artificial subsets that work across an entire range of legacy runtimes. By targeting .NET Standard, you can easily write libraries with extensive reach.

 .NET Standard is not a runtime; it's merely a specification describing a minimum baseline of functionality (types and members) that guarantees compatibility with a certain set of runtimes. The concept is similar to C# interfaces: .NET Standard is like an interface that concrete types (runtimes) can implement.

.NET Standard 2.0

The most useful version is *.NET Standard 2.0*. A library that targets .NET Standard 2.0 instead of a specific runtime will run without modification on most modern and legacy runtimes that are still in use today, including:

- .NET Core 2.0+ (including .NET 5 and .NET 6)
- UWP 10.0.16299+
- Mono 5.4+ (the CLR/BCL used by older versions of Xamarin)
- .NET Framework 4.6.1+

To target .NET Standard 2.0, add the following to your *.csproj* file:

```
<PropertyGroup>
  <TargetFramework>netstandard2.0</TargetFramework>
<PropertyGroup>
```

Most of the APIs described in this book are supported by .NET Standard 2.0.

.NET Standard 2.1

NET Standard 2.1 is a superset of .NET Standard 2.0 that supports (only) the following platforms:

- .NET Core 3+
- Mono 6.4+

.NET Standard 2.1 is not supported by any version of .NET Framework (and not even by UWP), making it much less useful than .NET Standard 2.0.

The following APIs, in particular, are available in .NET Standard 2.1 (but not .NET Standard 2.0):

- Span<T> (Chapter 23)
- Reflection.Emit (Chapter 18)
- ValueTask<T> (Chapter 14)

Older .NET Standards

There are also older .NET Standards, most notably 1.1, 1.2, 1.3, and 1.6. A higher-numbered standard is always a strict superset of a lower-numbered standard. For instance, if you write a library that targets .NET Standard 1.6, you will support not only recent versions of the major runtimes but also .NET Core 1.0. And if you target .NET Standard 1.3, you support everything we've already mentioned plus .NET Framework 4.6.0. The table that follows elaborates:

If you target...	You also support...
Standard 1.6	.NET Core 1.0
Standard 1.3	Above plus .NET 4.6.0
Standard 1.2	Above plus .NET 4.5.1, Windows Phone 8.1, WinRT for Windows 8.1
Standard 1.1	Above plus .NET 4.5.0, Windows Phone 8.0, WinRT for Windows 8.0

> The 1.x standards lack thousands of APIs that are present in 2.0, including much of what we describe in this book. This can make targeting a 1.x standard significantly more challenging, especially if you need to integrate existing code or libraries.

You can also think of .NET Standard as a lowest common denominator. In the case of .NET Standard 2.0, the runtimes that implement it have a similar BCL, so the lowest common denominator is big and useful. However, if you also want compatibility with .NET Core 1.0 (with its significantly cut-down BCL), the lowest common denominator—.NET Standard 1.x—becomes much smaller and less useful.

.NET Framework and .NET 6 Compatibility

Because .NET Framework has existed for so long, it's not uncommon to encounter libraries that are available *only* for .NET Framework (with no .NET Standard, .NET Core, or .NET 6 equivalent). To help mitigate this situation, .NET 5+ and .NET Core projects are permitted to reference .NET Framework assemblies, with the following provisos:

- An exception is thrown should the .NET Framework assembly call an API that's unsupported.

- Nontrivial dependencies might (and often do) fail to resolve.

In practice, it's most likely to work in simple cases, such as an assembly that wraps an unmanaged DLL.

Runtime and C# Language Versions

By default, your project's runtime version determines which C# language version is used:

- For .NET 6, it's C# 10.

- For .NET 5, it's C# 9.

- For .NET Core 3.x, Xamarin, and .NET Standard 2.1, it's C# 8.

- For .NET Core 2.x, .NET Framework, and .NET Standard 2.0 and below, it's C# 7.3.

This is because later versions of C# rely on types that are available only in later runtimes.

You can override the language version in your project file with the `<LangVersion>` element. Using an older runtime (such as .NET 5) with a later language version (such as C# 10) means that the language features that rely on newer .NET types will not work (although in some cases, you can define those types yourself).

Reference Assemblies

When you target .NET Standard, your project implicitly references an assembly called *netstandard.dll*, which contains all of the allowable types and members for your chosen version of .NET Standard. This is called a *reference assembly* because it exists only for the benefit of the compiler and contains no compiled code. At runtime, the "real" assemblies are identified through assembly redirection attributes (the choice of assemblies will depend on which runtime and platform the assembly eventually runs on).

Interestingly, a similar thing happens when you target .NET 6. Your project implicitly references a set of reference assemblies whose types mirror what's in the runtime assemblies for the chosen .NET version. This helps with versioning and cross-platform compatibility, and also allows you to target a different .NET version than what is installed on your machine.

The CLR and BCL

System Types

The most fundamental types live directly in the System namespace. These include C#'s built-in types; the Exception base class; the Enum, Array, and Delegate base classes; and Nullable, Type, DateTime, TimeSpan, and Guid. The System namespace also includes types for performing mathematical functions (Math), generating random numbers (Random), and converting between various types (Convert and BitConverter).

Chapter 6 describes these types as well as the interfaces that define standard protocols used across .NET for such tasks as formatting (IFormattable) and order comparison (IComparable).

The System namespace also defines the IDisposable interface and the GC class for interacting with the garbage collector, which we cover in Chapter 12.

Text Processing

The System.Text namespace contains the StringBuilder class (the editable or *mutable* cousin of string) and the types for working with text encodings, such as UTF-8 (Encoding and its subtypes). We cover this in Chapter 6.

The System.Text.RegularExpressions namespace contains types that perform advanced pattern-based search-and-replace operations; we describe these in Chapter 25.

Collections

.NET offers a variety of classes for managing collections of items. These include both list- and dictionary-based structures; they work in conjunction with a set of standard interfaces that unify their common characteristics. All collection types are defined in the following namespaces, covered in Chapter 7:

```
System.Collections               // Nongeneric collections
System.Collections.Generic       // Generic collections
System.Collections.Specialized   // Strongly typed collections
System.Collections.ObjectModel   // Bases for your own collections
System.Collections.Concurrent    // Thread-safe collections (Chapter 22)
```

Querying

Language-Integrated Query (LINQ) allows you to perform type-safe queries over local and remote collections (e.g., SQL Server tables) and is described in Chapters 8 through 10. A big advantage of LINQ is that it presents a consistent querying API across a variety of domains. The essential types reside in the following namespaces:

```
System.Linq              // LINQ to Objects and PLINQ
System.Linq.Expressions  // For building expressions manually
System.Xml.Linq          // LINQ to XML
```

XML and JSON

XML and JSON are widely supported in .NET. Chapter 10 focuses entirely on LINQ to XML—a lightweight XML Document Object Model (DOM) that can be constructed and queried through LINQ. Chapter 11 covers the performant low-level XML reader/writer classes, XML schemas and stylesheets, and types for working with JSON:

```
System.Xml                // XmlReader, XmlWriter
System.Xml.Linq           // The LINQ to XML DOM
System.Xml.Schema         // Support for XSD
System.Xml.Serialization  // Declarative XML serialization for .NET types
System.Xml.XPath          // XPath query language
System.Xml.Xsl            // Stylesheet support

System.Text.Json          // JSON reader/writer and DOM
```

In the online supplement at *http://www.albahari.com/nutshell*, we cover the JSON serializer.

Diagnostics

In Chapter 13, we cover logging and assertion and describe how to interact with other processes, write to the Windows event log, and handle performance monitoring. The types for this are defined in and under System.Diagnostics.

Concurrency and Asynchrony

Many modern applications need to deal with more than one thing happening at a time. Since C# 5.0, this has become easier through asynchronous functions and high-level constructs such as tasks and task combinators. Chapter 14 explains all of this in detail, after starting with the basics of multithreading. Types for working with threads and asynchronous operations are in the System.Threading and System.Threading.Tasks namespaces.

Streams and Input/Output

.NET provides a stream-based model for low-level input/output (I/O). Streams are typically used to read and write directly to files and network connections, and can be chained or wrapped in decorator streams to add compression or encryption functionality. Chapter 15 describes the stream architecture as well as the specific support for working with files and directories, compression, pipes, and memory-mapped files. The Stream and I/O types are defined in and under the System.IO

namespace, and the Windows Runtime (WinRT) types for file I/O are in and under
`Windows.Storage`.

Networking

You can directly access most standard network protocols such as HTTP, TCP/IP,
and SMTP via the types in `System.Net`. In Chapter 16, we demonstrate how to
communicate using each of these protocols, starting with simple tasks such as
downloading from a web page and finishing with using TCP/IP directly to retrieve
POP3 email. Here are the namespaces we cover:

```
System.Net
System.Net.Http        // HttpClient
System.Net.Mail        // For sending mail via SMTP
System.Net.Sockets     // TCP, UDP, and IP
```

Assemblies, Reflection, and Attributes

The assemblies into which C# programs compile comprise executable instructions
(stored as IL) and metadata, which describes the program's types, members, and
attributes. Through reflection, you can inspect this metadata at runtime and do such
things as dynamically invoke methods. With `Reflection.Emit`, you can construct
new code on the fly.

In Chapter 17, we describe the makeup of assemblies and how to dynamically load
and isolate them. In Chapter 18, we cover reflection and attributes—describing
how to inspect metadata, dynamically invoke functions, write custom attributes,
emit new types, and parse raw IL. The types for using reflection and working with
assemblies reside in the following namespaces:

```
System
System.Reflection
System.Reflection.Emit
```

Dynamic Programming

In Chapter 19, we look at some of the patterns for dynamic programming and uti-
lizing the Dynamic Language Runtime (DLR). We describe how to implement the
Visitor pattern, write custom dynamic objects, and interoperate with IronPython.
The types for dynamic programming are in `System.Dynamic`.

Cryptography

.NET provides extensive support for popular hashing and encryption protocols.
In Chapter 20, we cover hashing, symmetric and public-key encryption, and the
Windows Data Protection API. The types for this are defined in:

```
System.Security
System.Security.Cryptography
```

Advanced Threading

C#'s asynchronous functions make concurrent programming significantly easier because they lessen the need for lower-level techniques. However, there are still times when you need signaling constructs, thread-local storage, reader/writer locks, and so on. Chapter 21 explains this in depth. Threading types are in the System.Threading namespace.

Parallel Programming

In Chapter 22, we cover in detail the libraries and types for leveraging multicore processors, including APIs for task parallelism, imperative data parallelism, and functional parallelism (PLINQ).

Span<T> and Memory<T>

To help with micro-optimizing performance hotspots, the CLR provides a number of types to help you program in such a way as to reduce the load on the memory manager. Two of the key types are Span<T> and Memory<T>, which we describe in Chapter 23.

Native and COM Interoperability

You can interoperate with both native and Component Object Model (COM) code. Native interoperability allows you to call functions in unmanaged DLLs, register callbacks, map data structures, and interoperate with native data types. COM interoperability allows you to call COM types (on Windows machines) and expose .NET types to COM. The types that support these functions are in System.Runtime.Inter opServices, and we cover them in Chapter 24.

Regular Expressions

In Chapter 25, we cover how you can use regular expressions to match character patterns in strings.

Serialization

.NET provides several systems for saving and restoring objects to a binary or text representation. Such systems can be used for communication as well as for saving and restoring objects to a file. In the online supplement at *http://www.alba-hari.com/nutshell*, we cover all four serialization engines: the binary serializer, the (newly updated) JSON serializer, the XML serializer, and the data contract serializer.

The Roslyn Compiler

The C# compiler itself is written in C#—the project is called "Roslyn," and the libraries are available as NuGet packages. With these libraries, you can utilize the compiler's functionality in many ways besides compiling source code to an assembly, such as writing code analysis and refactoring tools. We cover Roslyn in the online supplement, at *http://www.albahari.com/nutshell*.

Application Layers

User interface (UI)–based applications can be divided into two categories: *thin client*, which amounts to a website, and *rich client*, which is a program the end user must download and install on a computer or mobile device.

For writing thin-client applications in C#, there's ASP.NET Core, which runs on Windows, Linux, and macOS. ASP.NET Core is also designed for writing web APIs.

For rich-client applications, there is a choice of APIs:

- The Windows Desktop layer includes the WPF and Windows Forms APIs, and runs on Windows 7/8/10/11 desktop.

- UWP lets you write Windows Store apps that run on Windows 10+ desktop and devices.

- WinUI 3 (Windows App SDK) is a recent successor to UWP that runs on Windows 10+ desktop.

- MAUI (formerly Xamarin) runs on iOS and Android mobile devices. MAUI also allows for cross-platform desktop applications that target macOS and Windows.

There are also third-party libraries, such as Avalonia, which offer cross-platform UI support.

ASP.NET Core

ASP.NET Core is a lightweight modular successor to ASP.NET and is suitable for creating web sites, REST-based web APIs, and microservices. It can also run in conjunction with two popular single-page-application frameworks: React and Angular.

ASP.NET supports the popular *Model-View-Controller* (MVC) pattern, as well as a newer technology called Blazor, where client-side code is written in C# instead of JavaScript.

ASP.NET Core runs on Windows, Linux, and macOS and can self-host in a custom process. Unlike its .NET Framework predecessor (ASP.NET), ASP.NET Core is not dependent on System.Web and the historical baggage of web forms.

As with any thin-client architecture, ASP.NET Core offers the following general advantages over rich clients:

- There is zero deployment at the client end.
- The client can run on any platform that supports a web browser.
- Updates are easily deployed.

Windows Desktop

The Windows Desktop application layer offers a choice of two UI APIs for writing rich-client applications: WPF and Windows Forms. Both APIs run on Windows Desktop/Server 7 through 11.

WPF

WPF was introduced in 2006 and has been enhanced ever since. Unlike its predecessor, Windows Forms, WPF explicitly renders controls using DirectX, with the following benefits:

- It supports sophisticated graphics, such as arbitrary transformations, 3D rendering, multimedia, and true transparency. Skinning is supported through styles and templates.
- Its primary measurement unit is not pixel based, so applications display correctly at any DPI setting.
- It has extensive and flexible layout support, which means that you can localize an application without danger of elements overlapping.
- Its use of DirectX makes rendering fast and able to take advantage of graphics hardware acceleration.
- It offers reliable data binding.
- UIs can be described declaratively in XAML files that can be maintained independent of the "code-behind" files—this helps to separate appearance from functionality.

WPF takes some time to learn due to its size and complexity. The types for writing WPF applications are in the System.Windows namespace and all subnamespaces except for System.Windows.Forms.

Windows Forms

Windows Forms is a rich-client API that shipped with the first version of .NET Framework in 2000. Compared to WPF, Windows Forms is a relatively simple technology that provides most of the features you need for writing a typical Windows application. It also has significant relevancy in maintaining legacy applications. But compared to WPF, it has numerous drawbacks, most of which stem from it being a wrapper over GDI+ and the Win32 control library:

- Although it provides mechanisms for DPI-awareness, it's still too easy to write applications that break on clients whose DPI settings differ from the developer's.

- The API for drawing nonstandard controls is GDI+, which, although reasonably flexible, is slow in rendering large areas (and without double buffering, might flicker).

- Controls lack true transparency.

- Most controls are noncompositional. For instance, you can't put an image control inside a tab control header. Customizing list views, combo boxes, and tab controls in a way that would be trivial with WPF is time consuming and painful in Windows Forms.

- Dynamic layout is difficult to correctly implement reliably.

The last point is an excellent reason to favor WPF over Windows Forms—even if you're writing a business application that needs just a UI and not a "user experience." The layout elements in WPF, such as Grid, make it easy to assemble labels and text boxes such that they always align—even after language-changing localization—without messy logic and without any flickering. Further, you don't need to bow to the lowest common denominator in screen resolution—WPF layout elements have been designed from the outset to adapt properly to resizing.

On the positive side, Windows Forms is relatively simple to learn and still has a good number of third-party controls.

The Windows Forms types are in the System.Windows.Forms (in *System.Windows.Forms.dll*) and System.Drawing (in *System.Drawing.dll*) namespaces. The latter also contains the GDI+ types for drawing custom controls.

UWP and WinUI 3

UWP is a rich-client API for writing touch-first UIs that target Windows 10+ desktop and devices. The word "Universal" refers to its ability to run on a range of Windows 10 devices, including Xbox, Surface Hub, and HoloLens. However, it's not compatible with earlier versions of Windows, including Windows 7 and Windows 8/8.1.

The UWP API uses XAML and is somewhat similar to WPF. Here are its key differences:

- The primary mode of distribution for UWP apps is the Windows Store.

- UWP apps run in a sandbox to lessen the threat of malware, which means that they cannot perform tasks such as reading or writing arbitrary files, and they cannot run with administrative elevation.

- UWP relies on WinRT types that are part of the operating system (Windows), not the managed runtime. This means that when writing apps, you must nominate a Windows *version range* (such as Windows 10 build 17763 to Windows 10 build 18362). This means that you either need to target an old API or require that your customers install the latest Windows update.

Because of the limitations created by these differences, UWP never succeeded in matching the popularity of WPF and Windows Forms. To address this, Microsoft has introduced a new technology to supersede UWP called Windows App SDK (with a UI layer called WinUI 3).

The Windows App SDK transfers the WinRT APIs from the operating system to the runtime, thereby exposing a fully managed interface and removing the necessity to target a specific operating system version range. It also does the following:

- Integrates better with the Windows Desktop APIs (Windows Forms and WPF)
- Allows you to write applications that run outside the Windows Store sandbox
- Runs atop the latest .NET (instead of being tied to .NET Core 2.2, as is the case with UWP)

The Windows App SDK, however, does not support Xbox or HoloLens at the time of writing.

MAUI

MAUI (early 2022) is the new incarnation of Xamarin, and lets you develop mobile apps in C# that target iOS and Android (as well as cross-platform desktop apps that target macOS and Windows).

The CLR/BCL that runs on iOS and Android is called Mono (a derivation of the open-source Mono runtime). Historically, Mono hasn't been fully compatible with .NET, and libraries that ran on both Mono and .NET would target .NET Standard. With MAUI, Mono's public interface has merged with .NET 6, making Mono, in effect, an *implementation* of .NET 6.

Features new to MAUI include a unified project interface, hot reloading, support for Blazor Desktop and hybrid apps, and improved performance and startup times. See *https://github.com/dotnet/maui* for more information.

6

.NET Fundamentals

Many of the core facilities that you need when programming are provided not by the C# language but by types in the .NET BCL. In this chapter, we cover types that help with fundamental programming tasks, such as virtual equality comparison, order comparison, and type conversion. We also cover the basic .NET types, such as String, DateTime, and Enum.

The types in this section reside in the System namespace, with the following exceptions:

- StringBuilder is defined in System.Text, as are the types for *text encodings*.

- CultureInfo and associated types are defined in System.Globalization.

- XmlConvert is defined in System.Xml.

String and Text Handling

Char

A C# char represents a single Unicode character and aliases the System.Char struct. In Chapter 2, we described how to express char literals:

```
char c = 'A';
char newLine = '\n';
```

System.Char defines a range of static methods for working with characters, such as ToUpper, ToLower, and IsWhiteSpace. You can call these through either the System.Char type or its char alias:

```
Console.WriteLine (System.Char.ToUpper ('c'));    // C
Console.WriteLine (char.IsWhiteSpace ('\t'));     // True
```

ToUpper and ToLower honor the end user's locale, which can lead to subtle bugs. The following expression evaluates to false in Turkey:

```
char.ToUpper ('i') == 'I'
```

The reason is because in Turkey, char.ToUpper ('i') is 'İ' (notice the dot on top!). To avoid this problem, System.Char (and System.String) also provides culture-invariant versions of ToUpper and ToLower ending with the word *Invariant*. These always apply English culture rules:

```
Console.WriteLine (char.ToUpperInvariant ('i'));    // I
```

This is a shortcut for:

```
Console.WriteLine (char.ToUpper ('i', CultureInfo.InvariantCulture))
```

For more on locales and culture, see "Formatting and Parsing" on page 297.

Most of char's remaining static methods are related to categorizing characters. Table 6-1 lists these.

Table 6-1. Static methods for categorizing characters

Static method	Characters included	Unicode categories included
IsLetter	A–Z, a–z, and letters of other alphabets	UpperCaseLetter LowerCaseLetter TitleCaseLetter ModifierLetter OtherLetter
IsUpper	Uppercase letters	UpperCaseLetter
IsLower	Lowercase letters	LowerCaseLetter
IsDigit	0–9 plus digits of other alphabets	DecimalDigitNumber
IsLetterOrDigit	Letters plus digits	(IsLetter, IsDigit)
IsNumber	All digits plus Unicode fractions and Roman numeral symbols	DecimalDigitNumber LetterNumber OtherNumber
IsSeparator	Space plus all Unicode separator characters	LineSeparator ParagraphSeparator
IsWhiteSpace	All separators plus \n, \r, \t, \f, and \v	LineSeparator ParagraphSeparator
IsPunctuation	Symbols used for punctuation in Western and other alphabets	DashPunctuation ConnectorPunctuation InitialQuotePunctuation FinalQuotePunctuation
IsSymbol	Most other printable symbols	MathSymbol ModifierSymbol OtherSymbol
IsControl	Nonprintable "control" characters below 0x20, such as \r, \n, \t, \0, and characters between 0x7F and 0x9A	(None)

For more granular categorization, char provides a static method called GetUnicode Category; this returns a UnicodeCategory enumeration whose members are shown in the rightmost column of Table 6-1.

 By explicitly casting from an integer, it's possible to produce a char outside the allocated Unicode set. To test a character's validity, call char.GetUnicodeCategory: if the result is UnicodeCategory.OtherNotAssigned, the character is invalid.

A char is 16 bits wide—enough to represent any Unicode character in the *Basic Multilingual Plane*. To go beyond this, you must use surrogate pairs: we describe the methods for doing this in "Text Encodings and Unicode" on page 281.

String

A C# string (== System.String) is an immutable (unchangeable) sequence of characters. In Chapter 2, we described how to express string literals, perform equality comparisons, and concatenate two strings. This section covers the remaining functions for working with strings, exposed through the static and instance members of the System.String class.

Constructing strings

The simplest way to construct a string is to assign a literal, as we saw in Chapter 2:

```
string s1 = "Hello";
string s2 = "First Line\r\nSecond Line";
string s3 = @"\\server\fileshare\helloworld.cs";
```

To create a repeating sequence of characters, you can use string's constructor:

```
Console.Write (new string ('*', 10));      // **********
```

You can also construct a string from a char array. The ToCharArray method does the reverse:

```
char[] ca = "Hello".ToCharArray();
string s = new string (ca);             // s = "Hello"
```

string's constructor is also overloaded to accept various (unsafe) pointer types, in order to create strings from types such as char*.

Null and empty strings

An empty string has a length of zero. To create an empty string, you can use either a literal or the static string.Empty field; to test for an empty string, you can either perform an equality comparison or test its Length property:

```
string empty = "";
Console.WriteLine (empty == "");            // True
Console.WriteLine (empty == string.Empty);  // True
Console.WriteLine (empty.Length == 0);      // True
```

Because strings are reference types, they can also be null:

```
string nullString = null;
Console.WriteLine (nullString == null);        // True
Console.WriteLine (nullString == "");          // False
Console.WriteLine (nullString.Length == 0);    // NullReferenceException
```

The static `string.IsNullOrEmpty` method is a useful shortcut for testing whether a given string is either null or empty.

Accessing characters within a string

A string's indexer returns a single character at the given index. As with all functions that operate on strings, this is zero-indexed:

```
string str  = "abcde";
char letter = str[1];        // letter == 'b'
```

`string` also implements `IEnumerable<char>`, so you can `foreach` over its characters:

```
foreach (char c in "123") Console.Write (c + ",");     // 1,2,3,
```

Searching within strings

The simplest methods for searching within strings are `StartsWith`, `EndsWith`, and `Contains`. These all return `true` or `false`:

```
Console.WriteLine ("quick brown fox".EndsWith ("fox"));      // True
Console.WriteLine ("quick brown fox".Contains ("brown"));    // True
```

`StartsWith` and `EndsWith` are overloaded to let you specify a `StringComparison` enum or a `CultureInfo` object to control case and culture sensitivity (see "Ordinal versus culture comparison" on page 278). The default is to perform a case-sensitive match using rules applicable to the current (localized) culture. The following instead performs a case-insensitive search using the *invariant* culture's rules:

```
"abcdef".StartsWith ("aBc", StringComparison.InvariantCultureIgnoreCase)
```

The `Contains` method doesn't offer the convenience of this overload, although you can achieve the same result with the `IndexOf` method.

`IndexOf` is more powerful: it returns the first position of a given character or substring (or –1 if the substring isn't found):

```
Console.WriteLine ("abcde".IndexOf ("cd"));    // 2
```

`IndexOf` is also overloaded to accept a `startPosition` (an index from which to begin searching) as well as a `StringComparison` enum:

```
Console.WriteLine ("abcde abcde".IndexOf ("CD", 6,
                   StringComparison.CurrentCultureIgnoreCase));     // 8
```

`LastIndexOf` is like `IndexOf`, but it works backward through the string.

`IndexOfAny` returns the first matching position of any one of a set of characters:

```
Console.Write ("ab,cd ef".IndexOfAny (new char[] {' ', ','} ));      // 2
Console.Write ("pas5w0rd".IndexOfAny ("0123456789".ToCharArray() )); // 3
```

`LastIndexOfAny` does the same in the reverse direction.

Manipulating strings

Because `String` is immutable, all the methods that "manipulate" a string return a new one, leaving the original untouched (the same goes for when you reassign a string variable).

`Substring` extracts a portion of a string:

```
string left3 = "12345".Substring (0, 3);     // left3 = "123";
string mid3  = "12345".Substring (1, 3);     // mid3 = "234";
```

If you omit the length, you get the remainder of the string:

```
string end3  = "12345".Substring (2);         // end3 = "345";
```

`Insert` and `Remove` insert or remove characters at a specified position:

```
string s1 = "helloworld".Insert (5, ", ");   // s1 = "hello, world"
string s2 = s1.Remove (5, 2);                 // s2 = "helloworld";
```

`PadLeft` and `PadRight` pad a string to a given length with a specified character (or a space if unspecified):

```
Console.WriteLine ("12345".PadLeft (9, '*')); // ****12345
Console.WriteLine ("12345".PadLeft (9));      //     12345
```

If the input string is longer than the padding length, the original string is returned unchanged.

`TrimStart` and `TrimEnd` remove specified characters from the beginning or end of a string; `Trim` does both. By default, these functions remove whitespace characters (including spaces, tabs, new lines, and Unicode variations of these):

```
Console.WriteLine ("  abc \t\r\n ".Trim().Length);   // 3
```

`Replace` replaces all (nonoverlapping) occurrences of a particular character or substring:

```
Console.WriteLine ("to be done".Replace (" ", " | ") ); // to | be | done
Console.WriteLine ("to be done".Replace (" ", "")    ); // tobedone
```

`ToUpper` and `ToLower` return uppercase and lowercase versions of the input string. By default, they honor the user's current language settings; `ToUpperInvariant` and `ToLowerInvariant` always apply English alphabet rules.

Splitting and joining strings

Split divides a string into pieces:

```
string[] words = "The quick brown fox".Split();

foreach (string word in words)
  Console.Write (word + "|");      // The|quick|brown|fox|
```

By default, Split uses whitespace characters as delimiters; it's also overloaded to accept a params array of char or string delimiters. Split also optionally accepts a StringSplitOptions enum, which has an option to remove empty entries: this is useful when words are separated by several delimiters in a row.

The static Join method does the reverse of Split. It requires a delimiter and string array:

```
string[] words = "The quick brown fox".Split();
string together = string.Join (" ", words);      // The quick brown fox
```

The static Concat method is similar to Join but accepts only a params string array and applies no separator. Concat is exactly equivalent to the + operator (the compiler, in fact, translates + to Concat):

```
string sentence     = string.Concat ("The", " quick", " brown", " fox");
string sameSentence = "The" + " quick" + " brown" + " fox";
```

String.Format and composite format strings

The static Format method provides a convenient way to build strings that embed variables. The embedded variables (or values) can be of any type; the Format simply calls ToString on them.

The master string that includes the embedded variables is called a *composite format string*. When calling string.Format, you provide a composite format string followed by each of the embedded variables:

```
string composite = "It's {0} degrees in {1} on this {2} morning";
string s = string.Format (composite, 35, "Perth", DateTime.Now.DayOfWeek);

// s == "It's 35 degrees in Perth on this Friday morning"
```

(And that's Celsius!)

We can use interpolated string literals to the same effect (see "String Type" on page 52). Just precede the string with the $ symbol and put the expressions in braces:

```
string s = $"It's hot this {DateTime.Now.DayOfWeek} morning";
```

Each number in curly braces is called a *format item*. The number corresponds to the argument position and is optionally followed by:

- A comma and a *minimum width* to apply
- A colon and a *format string*

The minimum width is useful for aligning columns. If the value is negative, the data is left-aligned; otherwise, it's right-aligned:

```
string composite = "Name={0,-20} Credit Limit={1,15:C}";

Console.WriteLine (string.Format (composite, "Mary", 500));
Console.WriteLine (string.Format (composite, "Elizabeth", 20000));
```

Here's the result:

```
Name=Mary              Credit Limit=      $500.00
Name=Elizabeth         Credit Limit=   $20,000.00
```

Here's the equivalent without using `string.Format`:

```
string s = "Name=" + "Mary".PadRight (20) +
           " Credit Limit=" + 500.ToString ("C").PadLeft (15);
```

The credit limit is formatted as currency by virtue of the `"C"` format string. We describe format strings in detail in "Formatting and Parsing" on page 297.

Comparing Strings

In comparing two values, .NET differentiates the concepts of *equality comparison* and *order comparison*. Equality comparison tests whether two instances are semantically the same; order comparison tests which of two (if any) instances comes first when arranging them in ascending or descending sequence.

 Equality comparison is not a *subset* of order comparison; the two systems have different purposes. It's legal, for instance, to have two unequal values in the same ordering position. We resume this topic in "Equality Comparison" on page 324.

For string equality comparison, you can use the `==` operator or one of `string`'s `Equals` methods. The latter are more versatile because they allow you to specify options such as case insensitivity.

 Another difference is that `==` does not work reliably on strings if the variables are cast to the `object` type. We explain why this is so in "Equality Comparison" on page 324.

For string order comparison, you can use either the `CompareTo` instance method or the static `Compare` and `CompareOrdinal` methods. These return a positive or negative number, or zero, depending on whether the first value comes after, before, or alongside the second.

Before going into the details of each, we need to examine .NET's underlying string comparison algorithms.

Ordinal versus culture comparison

There are two basic algorithms for string comparison: *ordinal* and *culture sensitive.* Ordinal comparisons interpret characters simply as numbers (according to their numeric Unicode value); culture-sensitive comparisons interpret characters with reference to a particular alphabet. There are two special cultures: the "current culture," which is based on settings picked up from the computer's control panel, and the "invariant culture," which is the same on every computer (and closely matches American culture).

For equality comparison, both ordinal and culture-specific algorithms are useful. For ordering, however, culture-specific comparison is nearly always preferable: to order strings alphabetically, you need an alphabet. Ordinal relies on the numeric Unicode point values, which happen to put English characters in alphabetical order —but even then, not exactly as you might expect. For example, assuming case sensitivity, consider the strings "Atom", "atom", and "Zamia". The invariant culture puts them in the following order:

    "atom", "Atom", "Zamia"

Ordinal arranges them instead as follows:

    "Atom", "Zamia", "atom"

This is because the invariant culture encapsulates an alphabet, which considers uppercase characters adjacent to their lowercase counterparts (aAbBcCdD...). The ordinal algorithm, however, puts all the uppercase characters first and then all lowercase characters (A...Z, a...z). This is essentially a throwback to the ASCII character set invented in the 1960s.

String equality comparison

Despite ordinal's limitations, string's == operator always performs *ordinal case-sensitive* comparison. The same goes for the instance version of string.Equals when called without arguments; this defines the "default" equality comparison behavior for the string type.

The ordinal algorithm was chosen for string's == and Equals functions because it's both highly efficient and *deterministic.* String equality comparison is considered fundamental and is performed far more frequently than order comparison.

A "strict" notion of equality is also consistent with the general use of the == operator.

The following methods allow culture-aware or case-insensitive comparisons:

    public bool Equals(string value, StringComparison comparisonType);

    public static bool Equals (string a, string b,
                               StringComparison comparisonType);

The static version is advantageous in that it still works if one or both of the strings are null. StringComparison is an enum defined as follows:

```
public enum StringComparison
{
  CurrentCulture,            // Case-sensitive
  CurrentCultureIgnoreCase,
  InvariantCulture,          // Case-sensitive
  InvariantCultureIgnoreCase,
  Ordinal,                   // Case-sensitive
  OrdinalIgnoreCase
}
```

For example:

```
Console.WriteLine (string.Equals ("foo", "FOO",
                   StringComparison.OrdinalIgnoreCase));   // True

Console.WriteLine ("ü" == "û");                            // False

Console.WriteLine (string.Equals ("ü", "û",
                   StringComparison.CurrentCulture));      // ?
```

(The result of the third example is determined by the computer's current language settings.)

String order comparison

String's CompareTo instance method performs *culture-sensitive, case-sensitive* order comparison. Unlike the == operator, CompareTo does not use ordinal comparison: for ordering, a culture-sensitive algorithm is much more useful. Here's the method's definition:

```
public int CompareTo (string strB);
```

 The CompareTo instance method implements the generic IComparable interface, a standard comparison protocol used across the .NET libraries. This means string's CompareTo defines the default ordering behavior of strings in such applications as sorted collections, for instance. For more information on IComparable, see "Order Comparison" on page 335.

For other kinds of comparison, you can call the static Compare and CompareOrdinal methods:

```
public static int Compare (string strA, string strB,
                           StringComparison comparisonType);

public static int Compare (string strA, string strB, bool ignoreCase,
                           CultureInfo culture);

public static int Compare (string strA, string strB, bool ignoreCase);

public static int CompareOrdinal (string strA, string strB);
```

The last two methods are simply shortcuts for calling the first two methods.

All of the order comparison methods return a positive number, a negative number, or zero depending on whether the first value comes after, before, or alongside the second value:

```
Console.WriteLine ("Boston".CompareTo ("Austin"));    // 1
Console.WriteLine ("Boston".CompareTo ("Boston"));    // 0
Console.WriteLine ("Boston".CompareTo ("Chicago"));   // -1
Console.WriteLine ("ü".CompareTo ("ü"));              // 0
Console.WriteLine ("foo".CompareTo ("FOO"));          // -1
```

The following performs a case-insensitive comparison using the current culture:

```
Console.WriteLine (string.Compare ("foo", "FOO", true));   // 0
```

By supplying a CultureInfo object, you can plug in any alphabet:

```
// CultureInfo is defined in the System.Globalization namespace

CultureInfo german = CultureInfo.GetCultureInfo ("de-DE");
int i = string.Compare ("Müller", "Muller", false, german);
```

StringBuilder

The StringBuilder class (System.Text namespace) represents a mutable (editable) string. With a StringBuilder, you can Append, Insert, Remove, and Replace substrings without replacing the whole StringBuilder.

StringBuilder's constructor optionally accepts an initial string value as well as a starting size for its internal capacity (default is 16 characters). If you go beyond this, StringBuilder automatically resizes its internal structures to accommodate (at a slight performance cost) up to its maximum capacity (default is int.MaxValue).

A popular use of StringBuilder is to build up a long string by repeatedly calling Append. This approach is much more efficient than repeatedly concatenating ordinary string types:

```
StringBuilder sb = new StringBuilder();
for (int i = 0; i < 50; i++) sb.Append(i).Append(",");
```

To get the final result, call ToString():

```
Console.WriteLine (sb.ToString());

0,1,2,3,4,5,6,7,8,9,10,11,12,13,14,15,16,17,18,19,20,21,22,23,24,25,26,
27,28,29,30,31,32,33,34,35,36,37,38,39,40,41,42,43,44,45,46,47,48,49,
```

AppendLine performs an Append that adds a new line sequence ("\r\n" in Windows). AppendFormat accepts a composite format string, just like String.Format.

In addition to the Insert, Remove, and Replace methods (Replace works like string's Replace), StringBuilder defines a Length property and a writable indexer for getting/setting individual characters.

To clear the contents of a `StringBuilder`, either instantiate a new one or set its `Length` to zero.

Setting a `StringBuilder`'s `Length` to zero doesn't shrink its *internal* capacity. So, if the `StringBuilder` previously contained one million characters, it will continue to occupy around two megabytes of memory after zeroing its `Length`. If you want to release the memory, you must create a new `StringBuilder` and allow the old one to drop out of scope (and be garbage collected).

Text Encodings and Unicode

A *character set* is an allocation of characters, each with a numeric code, or *code point*. There are two character sets in common use: Unicode and ASCII. Unicode has an address space of approximately one million characters, of which about 100,000 are currently allocated. Unicode covers most spoken world languages as well as some historical languages and special symbols. The ASCII set is simply the first 128 characters of the Unicode set, which covers most of what you see on a US-style keyboard. ASCII predates Unicode by 30 years and is still sometimes used for its simplicity and efficiency: each character is represented by one byte.

The .NET type system is designed to work with the Unicode character set. ASCII is implicitly supported, though, by virtue of being a subset of Unicode.

A *text encoding* maps characters from their numeric code point to a binary representation. In .NET, text encodings come into play primarily when dealing with text files or streams. When you read a text file into a string, a *text encoder* translates the file data from binary into the internal Unicode representation that the `char` and `string` types expect. A text encoding can restrict what characters can be represented as well as affect storage efficiency.

There are two categories of text encoding in .NET:

- Those that map Unicode characters to another character set
- Those that use standard Unicode encoding schemes

The first category contains legacy encodings such as IBM's EBCDIC and 8-bit character sets with extended characters in the upper-128 region that were popular prior to Unicode (identified by a code page). The ASCII encoding is also in this category: it encodes the first 128 characters and drops everything else. This category contains the *nonlegacy* GB18030 as well, which is the mandatory standard for applications written in China—or sold to China—since 2000.

In the second category are UTF-8, UTF-16, and UTF-32 (and the obsolete UTF-7). Each differs in space efficiency. UTF-8 is the most space-efficient for most kinds of text: it uses *between one and four bytes* to represent each character. The first 128 characters require only a single byte, making it compatible with ASCII. UTF-8 is the most popular encoding for text files and streams (particularly on the internet), and it is the default for stream input/output (I/O) in .NET (in fact, it's the default for almost everything that implicitly uses an encoding).

UTF-16 uses one or two 16-bit words to represent each character. This is what .NET uses internally to represent characters and strings. Some programs also write files in UTF-16.

UTF-32 is the least space-efficient: it maps each code point directly to 32 bits, so every character consumes four bytes. UTF-32 is rarely used for this reason. It does, however, make random access very easy because every character takes an equal number of bytes.

Obtaining an Encoding object

The Encoding class in System.Text is the common base type for classes that encapsulate text encodings. There are several subclasses—their purpose is to encapsulate families of encodings with similar features. The most common encodings can be obtained through dedicated static properties on Encoding:

Encoding name	Static property on Encoding
UTF-8	Encoding.UTF8
UTF-16	Encoding.Unicode (*not* UTF16)
UTF-32	Encoding.UTF32
ASCII	Encoding.ASCII

You can obtain other encodings by calling Encoding.GetEncoding with a standard Internet Assigned Numbers Authority (IANA) Character Set name:

```
// In .NET 5+ and .NET Core, you must first call RegisterProvider:
Encoding.RegisterProvider (CodePagesEncodingProvider.Instance);

Encoding chinese = Encoding.GetEncoding ("GB18030");
```

The static GetEncodings method returns a list of all supported encodings along with their standard IANA names:

```
foreach (EncodingInfo info in Encoding.GetEncodings())
  Console.WriteLine (info.Name);
```

The other way to obtain an encoding is to directly instantiate an encoding class. Doing so allows you to set various options via constructor arguments, including:

- Whether to throw an exception if an invalid byte sequence is encountered when decoding. The default is false.

- Whether to encode/decode UTF-16/UTF-32 with the most significant bytes first (*big endian*) or the least significant bytes first (*little endian*). The default is *little endian*, the standard on the Windows operating system.

- Whether to emit a byte-order mark (a prefix that indicates *endianness*).

Encoding for file and stream I/O

The most common application for an `Encoding` object is to control how text is read and written to a file or stream. For example, the following writes "Testing..." to a file called *data.txt* in UTF-16 encoding:

```
System.IO.File.WriteAllText ("data.txt", "Testing...", Encoding.Unicode);
```

If you omit the final argument, `WriteAllText` applies the ubiquitous UTF-8 encoding.

UTF-8 is the default text encoding for all file and stream I/O.

We resume this subject in Chapter 15, in "Stream Adapters" on page 687.

Encoding to byte arrays

You can also use an `Encoding` object to go to and from a byte array. The `GetBytes` method converts from `string` to `byte[]` with the given encoding; `GetString` converts from `byte[]` to `string`:

```
byte[] utf8Bytes  = System.Text.Encoding.UTF8.GetBytes    ("0123456789");
byte[] utf16Bytes = System.Text.Encoding.Unicode.GetBytes ("0123456789");
byte[] utf32Bytes = System.Text.Encoding.UTF32.GetBytes   ("0123456789");

Console.WriteLine (utf8Bytes.Length);    // 10
Console.WriteLine (utf16Bytes.Length);   // 20
Console.WriteLine (utf32Bytes.Length);   // 40

string original1 = System.Text.Encoding.UTF8.GetString    (utf8Bytes);
string original2 = System.Text.Encoding.Unicode.GetString (utf16Bytes);
string original3 = System.Text.Encoding.UTF32.GetString   (utf32Bytes);

Console.WriteLine (original1);        // 0123456789
Console.WriteLine (original2);        // 0123456789
Console.WriteLine (original3);        // 0123456789
```

UTF-16 and surrogate pairs

Recall that .NET stores characters and strings in UTF-16. Because UTF-16 requires one or two 16-bit words per character, and a `char` is only 16 bits in length, some Unicode characters require two `char`s to represent. This has a couple of consequences:

- A string's `Length` property can be greater than its real character count.
- A single `char` is not always enough to fully represent a Unicode character.

Most applications ignore this because nearly all commonly used characters fit into a section of Unicode called the *Basic Multilingual Plane* (BMP), which requires only one 16-bit word in UTF-16. The BMP covers several dozen world languages and includes more than 30,000 Chinese characters. Excluded are characters of some ancient languages, symbols for musical notation, and some less-common Chinese characters.

If you need to support two-word characters, the following static methods in char convert a 32-bit code point to a string of two chars and back again:

```
string ConvertFromUtf32 (int utf32)
int    ConvertToUtf32   (char highSurrogate, char lowSurrogate)
```

Two-word characters are called *surrogates*. They are easy to spot because each word is in the range 0xD800 to 0xDFFF. You can use the following static methods in char to assist:

```
bool IsSurrogate     (char c)
bool IsHighSurrogate (char c)
bool IsLowSurrogate  (char c)
bool IsSurrogatePair (char highSurrogate, char lowSurrogate)
```

The StringInfo class in the System.Globalization namespace also provides a range of methods and properties for working with two-word characters.

Characters outside the BMP typically require special fonts and have limited operating system support.

Dates and Times

The following immutable structs in the System namespace do the job of representing dates and times: DateTime, DateTimeOffset, TimeSpan, DateOnly, and TimeOnly. C# doesn't define any special keywords that map to these types.

TimeSpan

A TimeSpan represents an interval of time—or a time of the day. In the latter role, it's simply the "clock" time (without the date), which is equivalent to the time since midnight, assuming no daylight saving transition. A TimeSpan has a resolution of 100 ns, has a maximum value of about 10 million days, and can be positive or negative.

There are three ways to construct a TimeSpan:

- Through one of the constructors
- By calling one of the static From... methods
- By subtracting one DateTime from another

Here are the constructors:

```
public TimeSpan (int hours, int minutes, int seconds);
public TimeSpan (int days, int hours, int minutes, int seconds);
public TimeSpan (int days, int hours, int minutes, int seconds,
                                                   int milliseconds);
public TimeSpan (long ticks);   // Each tick = 100ns
```

The static From... methods are more convenient when you want to specify an interval in just a single unit, such as minutes, hours, and so on:

```
public static TimeSpan FromDays (double value);
public static TimeSpan FromHours (double value);
public static TimeSpan FromMinutes (double value);
public static TimeSpan FromSeconds (double value);
public static TimeSpan FromMilliseconds (double value);
```

For example:

```
Console.WriteLine (new TimeSpan (2, 30, 0));      // 02:30:00
Console.WriteLine (TimeSpan.FromHours (2.5));      // 02:30:00
Console.WriteLine (TimeSpan.FromHours (-2.5));     // -02:30:00
```

TimeSpan overloads the < and > operators as well as the + and - operators. The following expression evaluates to a TimeSpan of 2.5 hours:

```
TimeSpan.FromHours(2) + TimeSpan.FromMinutes(30);
```

The next expression evaluates to one second short of 10 days:

```
TimeSpan.FromDays(10) - TimeSpan.FromSeconds(1);   // 9.23:59:59
```

Using this expression, we can illustrate the integer properties Days, Hours, Minutes, Seconds, and Milliseconds:

```
TimeSpan nearlyTenDays = TimeSpan.FromDays(10) - TimeSpan.FromSeconds(1);

Console.WriteLine (nearlyTenDays.Days);          // 9
Console.WriteLine (nearlyTenDays.Hours);         // 23
Console.WriteLine (nearlyTenDays.Minutes);       // 59
Console.WriteLine (nearlyTenDays.Seconds);       // 59
Console.WriteLine (nearlyTenDays.Milliseconds);  // 0
```

In contrast, the Total... properties return values of type double describing the entire time span:

```
Console.WriteLine (nearlyTenDays.TotalDays);          // 9.99998842592593
Console.WriteLine (nearlyTenDays.TotalHours);         // 239.999722222222
Console.WriteLine (nearlyTenDays.TotalMinutes);       // 14399.9833333333
Console.WriteLine (nearlyTenDays.TotalSeconds);       // 863999
Console.WriteLine (nearlyTenDays.TotalMilliseconds);  // 863999000
```

The static Parse method does the opposite of ToString, converting a string to a TimeSpan. TryParse does the same but returns false rather than throwing an exception if the conversion fails. The XmlConvert class also provides TimeSpan/string conversion methods that follow standard XML formatting protocols.

The default value for a TimeSpan is TimeSpan.Zero.

TimeSpan can also be used to represent the time of the day (the elapsed time since midnight). To obtain the current time of day, call `DateTime.Now.TimeOfDay`.

DateTime and DateTimeOffset

`DateTime` and `DateTimeOffset` are immutable structs for representing a date and, optionally, a time. They have a resolution of 100 ns and a range covering the years 0001 through 9999.

`DateTimeOffset` is functionally similar to `DateTime`. Its distinguishing feature is that it also stores a Coordinated Universal Time (UTC) offset; this allows more meaningful results when comparing values across different time zones.

 An excellent article on the rationale behind the introduction of `DateTimeOffset` is available online (*https://oreil.ly/-sNh3*), titled "A Brief History of DateTime," by Anthony Moore.

Choosing between DateTime and DateTimeOffset

`DateTime` and `DateTimeOffset` differ in how they handle time zones. A `DateTime` incorporates a three-state flag indicating whether the `DateTime` is relative to the following:

- The local time on the current computer
- UTC (the modern equivalent of Greenwich Mean Time)
- Unspecified

A `DateTimeOffset` is more specific—it stores the offset from UTC as a `TimeSpan`:

```
July 01 2019 03:00:00 -06:00
```

This influences equality comparisons, which is the main factor in choosing between `DateTime` and `DateTimeOffset`. Specifically:

- `DateTime` ignores the three-state flag in comparisons and considers two values equal if they have the same year, month, day, hour, minute, and so on.
- `DateTimeOffset` considers two values equal if they refer to the *same point in time*.

 Daylight Saving Time can make this distinction important even if your application doesn't need to handle multiple geographic time zones.

So, `DateTime` considers the following two values different, whereas `DateTimeOffset` considers them equal:

```
July 01 2019 09:00:00 +00:00 (GMT)
July 01 2019 03:00:00 -06:00 (local time, Central America)
```

In most cases, `DateTimeOffset`'s equality logic is preferable. For example, in calculating which of two international events is more recent, a `DateTimeOffset` implicitly gives the correct answer. Similarly, a hacker plotting a Distributed Denial of Service attack would reach for a `DateTimeOffset`! To do the same with `DateTime` requires standardizing on a single time zone (typically UTC) throughout your application. This is problematic for two reasons:

- To be friendly to the end user, UTC `DateTime`s require explicit conversion to local time prior to formatting.
- It's easy to forget and incorporate a local `DateTime`.

`DateTime` is better, though, at specifying a value relative to the local computer at runtime—for example, if you want to schedule an archive at each of your international offices for next Sunday, at 3 A.M. local time (when there's the least amount of activity). Here, `DateTime` would be more suitable because it would respect each site's local time.

Internally, `DateTimeOffset` uses a short integer to store the UTC offset in minutes. It doesn't store any regional information, so there's nothing present to indicate whether an offset of +08:00, for instance, refers to Singapore time or Perth time.

We revisit time zones and equality comparison in more depth in "DateOnly and TimeOnly" on page 292.

SQL Server 2008 introduced direct support for `DateTimeOff` set through a new data type of the same name.

Constructing a DateTime

`DateTime` defines constructors that accept integers for the year, month, and day—and, optionally, the hour, minute, second, and millisecond:

```
public DateTime (int year, int month, int day);

public DateTime (int year, int month, int day,
                 int hour, int minute, int second, int millisecond);
```

If you specify only a date, the time is implicitly set to midnight (0:00).

The `DateTime` constructors also allow you to specify a `DateTimeKind`—an enum with the following values:

```
Unspecified, Local, Utc
```

This corresponds to the three-state flag described in the preceding section. `Unspecified` is the default, and it means that the `DateTime` is time-zone-agnostic. `Local` means relative to the local time zone on the current computer. A local `DateTime` does not include information about *which particular time zone* it refers to, or, unlike `DateTimeOffset`, the numeric offset from UTC.

A `DateTime`'s `Kind` property returns its `DateTimeKind`.

`DateTime`'s constructors are also overloaded to accept a `Calendar` object, as well. This allows you to specify a date using any of the `Calendar` subclasses defined in `System.Globalization`:

```
DateTime d = new DateTime (5767, 1, 1,
                           new System.Globalization.HebrewCalendar());

Console.WriteLine (d);     // 12/12/2006 12:00:00 AM
```

(The formatting of the date in this example depends on your computer's control panel settings.) A `DateTime` always uses the default Gregorian calendar—this example, a one-time conversion, takes place during construction. To perform computations using another calendar, you must use the methods on the `Calendar` subclass itself.

You can also construct a `DateTime` with a single *ticks* value of type `long`, where *ticks* is the number of 100 ns intervals from midnight 01/01/0001.

For interoperability, `DateTime` provides the static `FromFileTime` and `FromFile TimeUtc` methods for converting from a Windows file time (specified as a `long`) and `FromOADate` for converting from an OLE automation date/time (specified as a `double`).

To construct a `DateTime` from a string, call the static `Parse` or `ParseExact` method. Both methods accept optional flags and format providers; `ParseExact` also accepts a format string. We discuss parsing in greater detail in "Formatting and Parsing" on page 297.

Constructing a DateTimeOffset

`DateTimeOffset` has a similar set of constructors. The difference is that you also specify a UTC offset as a `TimeSpan`:

```
public DateTimeOffset (int year, int month, int day,
                       int hour, int minute, int second,
                       TimeSpan offset);

public DateTimeOffset (int year, int month, int day,
                       int hour, int minute, int second, int millisecond,
                       TimeSpan offset);
```

The `TimeSpan` must amount to a whole number of minutes; otherwise an exception is thrown.

`DateTimeOffset` also has constructors that accept a `Calendar` object, a `long` *ticks* value, and static `Parse` and `ParseExact` methods that accept a string.

You can construct a `DateTimeOffset` from an existing `DateTime` either by using these constructors:

```
public DateTimeOffset (DateTime dateTime);
public DateTimeOffset (DateTime dateTime, TimeSpan offset);
```

or with an implicit cast:

```
DateTimeOffset dt = new DateTime (2000, 2, 3);
```

> The implicit cast from `DateTime` to `DateTimeOffset` is handy because most of the .NET BCL supports `DateTime`—not `DateTimeOffset`.

If you don't specify an offset, it's inferred from the `DateTime` value using these rules:

- If the `DateTime` has a `DateTimeKind` of `Utc`, the offset is zero.
- If the `DateTime` has a `DateTimeKind` of `Local` or `Unspecified` (the default), the offset is taken from the current local time zone.

To convert in the other direction, `DateTimeOffset` provides three properties that return values of type `DateTime`:

- The `UtcDateTime` property returns a `DateTime` in UTC time.
- The `LocalDateTime` property returns a `DateTime` in the current local time zone (converting it if necessary).
- The `DateTime` property returns a `DateTime` in whatever zone it was specified, with a `Kind` of `Unspecified` (i.e., it returns the UTC time plus the offset).

The current DateTime/DateTimeOffset

Both `DateTime` and `DateTimeOffset` have a static `Now` property that returns the current date and time:

```
Console.WriteLine (DateTime.Now);           // 11/11/2019 1:23:45 PM
Console.WriteLine (DateTimeOffset.Now);     // 11/11/2019 1:23:45 PM -06:00
```

`DateTime` also provides a `Today` property that returns just the date portion:

```
Console.WriteLine (DateTime.Today);         // 11/11/2019 12:00:00 AM
```

The static `UtcNow` property returns the current date and time in UTC:

```
Console.WriteLine (DateTime.UtcNow);        // 11/11/2019 7:23:45 AM
Console.WriteLine (DateTimeOffset.UtcNow);  // 11/11/2019 7:23:45 AM +00:00
```

The precision of all these methods depends on the operating system and is typically in the 10 to 20 ms region.

Working with dates and times

DateTime and DateTimeOffset provide a similar set of instance properties that return various date/time elements:

```
DateTime dt = new DateTime (2000, 2, 3,
                            10, 20, 30);

Console.WriteLine (dt.Year);         // 2000
Console.WriteLine (dt.Month);        // 2
Console.WriteLine (dt.Day);          // 3
Console.WriteLine (dt.DayOfWeek);    // Thursday
Console.WriteLine (dt.DayOfYear);    // 34

Console.WriteLine (dt.Hour);         // 10
Console.WriteLine (dt.Minute);       // 20
Console.WriteLine (dt.Second);       // 30
Console.WriteLine (dt.Millisecond);  // 0
Console.WriteLine (dt.Ticks);        // 630851700300000000
Console.WriteLine (dt.TimeOfDay);    // 10:20:30  (returns a TimeSpan)
```

DateTimeOffset also has an Offset property of type TimeSpan.

Both types provide the following instance methods to perform computations (most accept an argument of type double or int):

```
AddYears  AddMonths   AddDays
AddHours  AddMinutes  AddSeconds  AddMilliseconds  AddTicks
```

These all return a new DateTime or DateTimeOffset, and they take into account such things as leap years. You can pass in a negative value to subtract.

The Add method adds a TimeSpan to a DateTime or DateTimeOffset. The + operator is overloaded to do the same job:

```
TimeSpan ts = TimeSpan.FromMinutes (90);
Console.WriteLine (dt.Add (ts));
Console.WriteLine (dt + ts);            // same as above
```

You can also subtract a TimeSpan from a DateTime/DateTimeOffset and subtract one DateTime/DateTimeOffset from another. The latter gives you a TimeSpan:

```
DateTime thisYear = new DateTime (2015, 1, 1);
DateTime nextYear = thisYear.AddYears (1);
TimeSpan oneYear = nextYear - thisYear;
```

Formatting and parsing DateTimes

Calling ToString on a DateTime formats the result as a *short date* (all numbers) followed by a *long time* (including seconds). For example:

```
11/11/2019 11:50:30 AM
```

The operating system's control panel, by default, determines such things as whether the day, month, or year comes first; the use of leading zeros; and whether 12- or 24-hour time is used.

Calling `ToString` on a `DateTimeOffset` is the same, except that the offset is also returned:

```
11/11/2019 11:50:30 AM -06:00
```

The `ToShortDateString` and `ToLongDateString` methods return just the date portion. The long date format is also determined by the control panel; an example is "Wednesday, 11 November 2015." `ToShortTimeString` and `ToLongTimeString` return just the time portion, such as 17:10:10 (the former excludes seconds).

These four just-described methods are actually shortcuts to four different *format strings*. `ToString` is overloaded to accept a format string and provider, allowing you to specify a wide range of options and control how regional settings are applied. We describe this in "Formatting and Parsing" on page 297.

 `DateTimes` and `DateTimeOffsets` can be misparsed if the culture settings differ from those in force when formatting takes place. You can avoid this problem by using `ToString` in conjunction with a format string that ignores culture settings (such as "o"):

```
DateTime dt1 = DateTime.Now;
string cannotBeMisparsed = dt1.ToString ("o");
DateTime dt2 = DateTime.Parse (cannotBeMisparsed);
```

The static `Parse`/`TryParse` and `ParseExact`/`TryParseExact` methods do the reverse of `ToString`, converting a string to a `DateTime` or `DateTimeOffset`. These methods are also overloaded to accept a format provider. The `Try*` methods return `false` instead of throwing a `FormatException`.

Null DateTime and DateTimeOffset values

Because `DateTime` and `DateTimeOffset` are structs, they are not intrinsically nullable. When you need nullability, there are two ways around this:

- Use a `Nullable` type (i.e., `DateTime?` or `DateTimeOffset?`).

- Use the static field `DateTime.MinValue` or `DateTimeOffset.MinValue` (the *default values* for these types).

A nullable type is usually the best approach because the compiler helps to prevent mistakes. `DateTime.MinValue` is useful for backward compatibility with code written prior to C# 2.0 (when nullable value types were introduced).

 Calling `ToUniversalTime` or `ToLocalTime` on a `DateTime.Min Value` can result in it no longer being `DateTime.MinValue` (depending on which side of GMT you are on). If you're right on GMT (England, outside daylight saving), the problem won't arise at all because local and UTC times are the same. This is your compensation for the English winter!

DateOnly and TimeOnly

The DateOnly and TimeOnly structs (from .NET 6) exist for when you *only* want to represent a date or time.

DateOnly is similar to DateTime, but without a time component. DateOnly also lacks DateTimeKind; in effect, it's always Unspecified and has no concept of Local or Utc. The historical alternative to DateOnly was to use DateTime with a zero time (midnight). The difficulty with this approach is that equality comparisons fail when a non-zero time finds its way into your code.

TimeOnly is similar to DateTime, but without a date component. TimeOnly is intended for capturing the time of day and is suitable for applications such as recording alarm times or opening hours.

DateTime and Time Zones

DateTime is simplistic in its handling of time zones. Internally, it stores a DateTime using two pieces of information:

- A 62-bit number, indicating the number of ticks since 1/1/0001

- A 2-bit enum, indicating the DateTimeKind (Unspecified, Local, or Utc)

When you compare two DateTime instances, only their *ticks* values are compared; their DateTimeKinds are ignored:

```
DateTime dt1 = new DateTime (2000, 1, 1, 10, 20, 30, DateTimeKind.Local);
DateTime dt2 = new DateTime (2000, 1, 1, 10, 20, 30, DateTimeKind.Utc);
Console.WriteLine (dt1 == dt2);        // True
DateTime local = DateTime.Now;
DateTime utc = local.ToUniversalTime();
Console.WriteLine (local == utc);      // False
```

The instance methods ToUniversalTime/ToLocalTime convert to universal/local time. These apply the computer's current time zone settings and return a new DateTime with a DateTimeKind of Utc or Local. No conversion happens if you call ToUniversalTime on a DateTime that's already Utc, or ToLocalTime on a DateTime that's already Local. You will get a conversion, however, if you call ToUniversal Time or ToLocalTime on a DateTime that's Unspecified.

You can construct a DateTime that differs from another only in Kind with the static DateTime.SpecifyKind method:

```
DateTime d = new DateTime (2015, 12, 12);  // Unspecified
DateTime utc = DateTime.SpecifyKind (d, DateTimeKind.Utc);
Console.WriteLine (utc);                // 12/12/2015 12:00:00 AM
```

DateTimeOffset and Time Zones

Internally, `DateTimeOffset` comprises a `DateTime` field whose value is always in UTC, and a 16-bit integer field for the UTC offset in minutes. Comparisons look only at the (UTC) `DateTime`; the `Offset` is used primarily for formatting.

The `ToUniversalTime`/`ToLocalTime` methods return a `DateTimeOffset` representing the same point in time but with a UTC or local offset. Unlike with `DateTime`, these methods don't affect the underlying date/time value, only the offset:

```
DateTimeOffset local = DateTimeOffset.Now;
DateTimeOffset utc   = local.ToUniversalTime();

Console.WriteLine (local.Offset);    // -06:00:00 (in Central America)
Console.WriteLine (utc.Offset);      // 00:00:00

Console.WriteLine (local == utc);               // True
```

To include the `Offset` in the comparison, you must use the `EqualsExact` method:

```
Console.WriteLine (local.EqualsExact (utc));    // False
```

TimeZoneInfo

The `TimeZoneInfo` class provides information on time zone names, UTC offsets, and Daylight Saving Time rules.

TimeZone

The static `TimeZone.CurrentTimeZone` method returns a `TimeZone`:

```
TimeZone zone = TimeZone.CurrentTimeZone;
Console.WriteLine (zone.StandardName);   // Pacific Standard Time
Console.WriteLine (zone.DaylightName);   // Pacific Daylight Time
```

The `GetDaylightChanges` method returns specific Daylight Saving Time information for a given year:

```
DaylightTime day = zone.GetDaylightChanges (2019);
Console.WriteLine (day.Start.ToString ("M"));   // 10 March
Console.WriteLine (day.End.ToString ("M"));     // 03 November
Console.WriteLine (day.Delta);                  // 01:00:00
```

TimeZoneInfo

The static `TimeZoneInfo.Local` method returns a `TimeZoneInfo` object based on the current local settings. The following demonstrates the result if run in California:

```
TimeZoneInfo zone = TimeZoneInfo.Local;
Console.WriteLine (zone.StandardName);   // Pacific Standard Time
Console.WriteLine (zone.DaylightName);   // Pacific Daylight Time
```

The `IsDaylightSavingTime` and `GetUtcOffset` methods work as follows:

```
DateTime dt1 = new DateTime (2019, 1, 1);   // DateTimeOffset works, too
DateTime dt2 = new DateTime (2019, 6, 1);
Console.WriteLine (zone.IsDaylightSavingTime (dt1));   // True
Console.WriteLine (zone.IsDaylightSavingTime (dt2));   // False
Console.WriteLine (zone.GetUtcOffset (dt1));   // -08:00:00
Console.WriteLine (zone.GetUtcOffset (dt2));   // -07:00:00
```

You can obtain a `TimeZoneInfo` for any of the world's time zones by calling `Find SystemTimeZoneById` with the zone ID. We'll switch to Western Australia for reasons that will soon become clear:

```
TimeZoneInfo wa = TimeZoneInfo.FindSystemTimeZoneById
                  ("W. Australia Standard Time");

Console.WriteLine (wa.Id);                        // W. Australia Standard Time
Console.WriteLine (wa.DisplayName);               // (GMT+08:00) Perth
Console.WriteLine (wa.BaseUtcOffset);             // 08:00:00
Console.WriteLine (wa.SupportsDaylightSavingTime);    // True
```

The `Id` property corresponds to the value passed to `FindSystemTimeZoneById`. The static `GetSystemTimeZones` method returns all world time zones; hence, you can list all valid zone ID strings as follows:

```
foreach (TimeZoneInfo z in TimeZoneInfo.GetSystemTimeZones())
  Console.WriteLine (z.Id);
```

> You can also create a custom time zone by calling `Time ZoneInfo.CreateCustomTimeZone`. Because `TimeZoneInfo` is immutable, you must pass in all the relevant data as method arguments.
>
> You can serialize a predefined or custom time zone to a (semi) human-readable string by calling `ToSerialized String`—and deserialize it by calling `TimeZoneInfo.FromSer ializedString`.

The static `ConvertTime` method converts a `DateTime` or `DateTimeOffset` from one time zone to another. You can include either just a destination `TimeZoneInfo`, or both source and destination `TimeZoneInfo` objects. You can also convert directly from or to UTC with the methods `ConvertTimeFromUtc` and `ConvertTimeToUtc`.

For working with Daylight Saving Time, `TimeZoneInfo` provides the following additional methods:

- `IsInvalidTime` returns `true` if a `DateTime` is within the hour (or delta) that's skipped when the clocks move forward.

- `IsAmbiguousTime` returns `true` if a `DateTime` or `DateTimeOffset` is within the hour (or delta) that's repeated when the clocks move back.

- `GetAmbiguousTimeOffsets` returns an array of `TimeSpans` representing the valid offset choices for an ambiguous `DateTime` or `DateTimeOffset`.

You can't obtain simple dates from a `TimeZoneInfo` indicating the start and end of Daylight Saving Time. Instead, you must call `GetAdjustmentRules`, which returns a declarative summary of all daylight saving rules that apply to all years. Each rule has a `DateStart` and `DateEnd` indicating the date range within which the rule is valid:

```
foreach (TimeZoneInfo.AdjustmentRule rule in wa.GetAdjustmentRules())
  Console.WriteLine ("Rule: applies from " + rule.DateStart +
                                    " to " + rule.DateEnd);
```

Western Australia first introduced Daylight Saving Time in 2006, *midseason* (and then rescinded it in 2009). This required a special rule for the first year; hence, there are two rules:

```
Rule: applies from 1/01/2006 12:00:00 AM to 31/12/2006 12:00:00 AM
Rule: applies from 1/01/2007 12:00:00 AM to 31/12/2009 12:00:00 AM
```

Each `AdjustmentRule` has a `DaylightDelta` property of type `TimeSpan` (this is one hour in almost every case) and properties called `DaylightTransitionStart` and `DaylightTransitionEnd`. The latter two are of type `TimeZoneInfo.Transition Time`, which has the following properties:

```
public bool IsFixedDateRule { get; }
public DayOfWeek DayOfWeek { get; }
public int Week { get; }
public int Day { get; }
public int Month { get; }
public DateTime TimeOfDay { get; }
```

A transition time is somewhat complicated in that it needs to represent both fixed and floating dates. An example of a floating date is "the last Sunday in March." Here are the rules for interpreting a transition time:

1. If, for an end transition, `IsFixedDateRule` is true, Day is 1, Month is 1, and `TimeOfDay` is `DateTime.MinValue`, there is no end to Daylight Saving Time in that year (this can happen only in the southern hemisphere, upon the initial introduction of daylight saving time to a region).

2. Otherwise, if `IsFixedDateRule` is true, the Month, Day, and `TimeOfDay` properties determine the start or end of the adjustment rule.

3. Otherwise, if `IsFixedDateRule` is false, the Month, DayOfWeek, Week, and `TimeOfDay` properties determine the start or end of the adjustment rule.

In the last case, Week refers to the week of the month, with "5" meaning the last week. We can demonstrate this by enumerating the adjustment rules for our wa time zone:

```
foreach (TimeZoneInfo.AdjustmentRule rule in wa.GetAdjustmentRules())
{
  Console.WriteLine ("Rule: applies from " + rule.DateStart +
                                    " to " + rule.DateEnd);

  Console.WriteLine ("   Delta: " + rule.DaylightDelta);
```

```
Console.WriteLine ("   Start: " + FormatTransitionTime
                               (rule.DaylightTransitionStart, false));

Console.WriteLine ("   End:   " + FormatTransitionTime
                               (rule.DaylightTransitionEnd, true));
Console.WriteLine();
}
```

In `FormatTransitionTime`, we honor the rules just described:

```
static string FormatTransitionTime (TimeZoneInfo.TransitionTime tt,
                                    bool endTime)
{
  if (endTime && tt.IsFixedDateRule
            && tt.Day == 1 && tt.Month == 1
            && tt.TimeOfDay == DateTime.MinValue)
    return "-";

  string s;
  if (tt.IsFixedDateRule)
    s = tt.Day.ToString();
  else
    s = "The " +
        "first second third fourth last".Split() [tt.Week - 1] +
        " " + tt.DayOfWeek + " in";

  return s + " " + DateTimeFormatInfo.CurrentInfo.MonthNames [tt.Month-1]
           + " at " + tt.TimeOfDay.TimeOfDay;
}
```

Daylight Saving Time and DateTime

If you use a `DateTimeOffset` or a UTC `DateTime`, equality comparisons are unimpeded by the effects of Daylight Saving Time. But with local `DateTimes`, daylight saving can be problematic.

We can summarize the rules as follows:

- Daylight saving affects local time but not UTC time.
- When the clocks turn back, comparisons that rely on time moving forward will break if (and only if) they use local `DateTimes`.
- You can always reliably round-trip between UTC and local times (on the same computer)—even as the clocks turn back.

The `IsDaylightSavingTime` tells you whether a given local `DateTime` is subject to Daylight Saving Time. UTC times always return `false`:

```
Console.Write (DateTime.Now.IsDaylightSavingTime());      // True or False
Console.Write (DateTime.UtcNow.IsDaylightSavingTime());   // Always False
```

Assuming dto is a `DateTimeOffset`, the following expression does the same:

```
dto.LocalDateTime.IsDaylightSavingTime
```

The end of Daylight Saving Time presents a particular complication for algorithms that use local time, because when the clocks go back, the same hour (or more precisely, `Delta`) repeats itself.

You can reliably compare any two `DateTimes` by first calling `ToUniversalTime` on each. This strategy fails if (and only if) exactly one of them has a `DateTimeKind` of `Unspecified`. This potential for failure is another reason for favoring `DateTimeOffset`.

Formatting and Parsing

Formatting means converting *to* a string; parsing means converting *from* a string. The need to format or parse arises frequently in programming, in a variety of situations. Hence, .NET provides a variety of mechanisms:

`ToString` *and* `Parse`
These methods provide default functionality for many types.

Format providers
These manifest as additional `ToString` (and `Parse`) methods that accept a *format string* and/or a *format provider*. Format providers are highly flexible and culture-aware. .NET includes format providers for the numeric types and `DateTime/DateTimeOffset`.

`XmlConvert`
This is a static class with methods that format and parse while honoring XML standards. `XmlConvert` is also useful for general-purpose conversion when you need culture independence or you want to preempt misparsing. `XmlConvert` supports the numeric types, `bool`, `DateTime`, `DateTimeOffset`, `TimeSpan`, and `Guid`.

Type converters
These target designers and XAML parsers.

In this section, we discuss the first two mechanisms, focusing particularly on format providers. We then describe `XmlConvert`, type converters, and other conversion mechanisms.

ToString and Parse

The simplest formatting mechanism is the `ToString` method. It gives meaningful output on all simple value types (`bool`, `DateTime`, `DateTimeOffset`, `TimeSpan`, `Guid`, and all the numeric types). For the reverse operation, each of these types defines a static `Parse` method:

```
string s = true.ToString();     // s = "True"
bool b = bool.Parse (s);        // b = true
```

If the parsing fails, a FormatException is thrown. Many types also define a Try Parse method, which returns false if the conversion fails rather than throwing an exception:

```
bool failure = int.TryParse ("qwerty", out int i1);
bool success = int.TryParse ("123", out int i2);
```

If you don't care about the output and want to test only whether parsing would succeed, you can use a discard:

```
bool success = int.TryParse ("123", out int _);
```

If you anticipate an error, calling TryParse is faster and more elegant than calling Parse in an exception handling block.

The Parse and TryParse methods on DateTime(Offset) and the numeric types respect local culture settings; you can change this by specifying a CultureInfo object. Specifying invariant culture is often a good idea. For instance, parsing "1.234" into a double gives us 1234 in Germany:

```
Console.WriteLine (double.Parse ("1.234"));     // 1234  (In Germany)
```

This is because in Germany, the period indicates a thousands separator rather than a decimal point. Specifying *invariant culture* fixes this:

```
double x = double.Parse ("1.234", CultureInfo.InvariantCulture);
```

The same applies when calling ToString():

```
string x = 1.234.ToString (CultureInfo.InvariantCulture);
```

Format Providers

Sometimes, you need more control over how formatting and parsing take place. There are dozens of ways to format a DateTime(Offset), for instance. Format providers allow extensive control over formatting and parsing, and are supported for numeric types and date/times. Format providers are also used by user interface controls for formatting and parsing.

The gateway to using a format provider is IFormattable. All numeric types—and DateTime(Offset)—implement this interface:

```
public interface IFormattable
{
    string ToString (string format, IFormatProvider formatProvider);
}
```

The first argument is the *format string*; the second is the *format provider*. The format string provides instructions; the format provider determines how the instructions are translated. For example:

```
NumberFormatInfo f = new NumberFormatInfo();
f.CurrencySymbol = "$$";
Console.WriteLine (3.ToString ("C", f));          // $$ 3.00
```

Here, "C" is a format string that indicates *currency*, and the NumberFormatInfo object is a format provider that determines how currency—and other numeric representations—are rendered. This mechanism allows for globalization.

All format strings for numbers and dates are listed in "Standard Format Strings and Parsing Flags" on page 303.

If you specify a null format string or provider, a default is applied. The default format provider is CultureInfo.CurrentCulture, which, unless reassigned, reflects the computer's runtime control panel settings. For example, on this computer:

```
Console.WriteLine (10.3.ToString ("C", null));  // $10.30
```

For convenience, most types overload ToString such that you can omit a null provider:

```
Console.WriteLine (10.3.ToString ("C"));      // $10.30
Console.WriteLine (10.3.ToString ("F4"));     // 10.3000 (Fix to 4 D.P.)
```

Calling ToString on a DateTime(Offset) or a numeric type with no arguments is equivalent to using a default format provider, with an empty format string.

.NET defines three format providers (all of which implement IFormatProvider):

```
NumberFormatInfo
DateTimeFormatInfo
CultureInfo
```

All enum types are also formattable, though there's no special IFormatProvider class.

Format providers and CultureInfo

Within the context of format providers, CultureInfo acts as an indirection mechanism for the other two format providers, returning a NumberFormatInfo or DateTimeFormatInfo object applicable to the culture's regional settings.

In the following example, we request a specific culture (*en*glish language in Great Britain):

```
CultureInfo uk = CultureInfo.GetCultureInfo ("en-GB");
Console.WriteLine (3.ToString ("C", uk));       // £3.00
```

This executes using the default NumberFormatInfo object applicable to the en-GB culture.

The next example formats a DateTime with invariant culture. Invariant culture is always the same, regardless of the computer's settings:

```
DateTime dt = new DateTime (2000, 1, 2);
CultureInfo iv = CultureInfo.InvariantCulture;
Console.WriteLine (dt.ToString (iv));          // 01/02/2000 00:00:00
Console.WriteLine (dt.ToString ("d", iv));      // 01/02/2000
```

 Invariant culture is based on American culture, with the following differences:

- The currency symbol is ☼ instead of $.

- Dates and times are formatted with leading zeros (though still with the month first).

- Time uses the 24-hour format rather than an AM/PM designator.

Using NumberFormatInfo or DateTimeFormatInfo

In the next example, we instantiate a `NumberFormatInfo` and change the group separator from a comma to a space. We then use it to format a number to three decimal places:

```
NumberFormatInfo f = new NumberFormatInfo ();
f.NumberGroupSeparator = " ";
Console.WriteLine (12345.6789.ToString ("N3", f));   // 12 345.679
```

The initial settings for a `NumberFormatInfo` or `DateTimeFormatInfo` are based on the invariant culture. Sometimes, however, it's more useful to choose a different starting point. To do this, you can `Clone` an existing format provider:

```
NumberFormatInfo f = (NumberFormatInfo)
                CultureInfo.CurrentCulture.NumberFormat.Clone();
```

A cloned format provider is always writable—even if the original was read-only.

Composite formatting

Composite format strings allow you to combine variable substitution with format strings. The static `string.Format` method accepts a composite format string (we illustrated this in "String.Format and composite format strings" on page 276):

```
string composite = "Credit={0:C}";
Console.WriteLine (string.Format (composite, 500));   // Credit=$500.00
```

The `Console` class itself overloads its `Write` and `WriteLine` methods to accept composite format strings, allowing us to shorten this example slightly:

```
Console.WriteLine ("Credit={0:C}", 500);   // Credit=$500.00
```

You can also append a composite format string to a `StringBuilder` (via `Append Format`), and to a `TextWriter` for I/O (see Chapter 15).

`string.Format` accepts an optional format provider. A simple application for this is to call `ToString` on an arbitrary object while passing in a format provider:

```
string s = string.Format (CultureInfo.InvariantCulture, "{0}", someObject);
```

This is equivalent to the following:

```
string s;
if (someObject is IFormattable)
  s = ((IFormattable)someObject).ToString (null,
                                      CultureInfo.InvariantCulture);
else if (someObject == null)
  s = "";
else
  s = someObject.ToString();
```

Parsing with format providers

There's no standard interface for parsing through a format provider. Instead, each participating type overloads its static `Parse` (and `TryParse`) method to accept a format provider and, optionally, a `NumberStyles` or `DateTimeStyles` enum.

`NumberStyles` and `DateTimeStyles` control how parsing works: they let you specify such things as whether parentheses or a currency symbol can appear in the input string (by default, the answer to both questions is *no*). For example:

```
int error = int.Parse ("(2)");   // Exception thrown

int minusTwo = int.Parse ("(2)", NumberStyles.Integer |
                          NumberStyles.AllowParentheses);   // OK

decimal fivePointTwo = decimal.Parse ("£5.20", NumberStyles.Currency,
                          CultureInfo.GetCultureInfo ("en-GB"));
```

The next section lists all `NumberStyles` and `DateTimeStyles` members as well as the default parsing rules for each type.

IFormatProvider and ICustomFormatter

All format providers implement `IFormatProvider`:

```
public interface IFormatProvider { object GetFormat (Type formatType); }
```

The purpose of this method is to provide indirection—this is what allows `Culture Info` to defer to an appropriate `NumberFormatInfo` or `DateTimeInfo` object to do the work.

By implementing `IFormatProvider`—along with `ICustomFormatter`—you can also write your own format provider that works in conjunction with existing types. `ICustomFormatter` defines a single method, as follows:

```
string Format (string format, object arg, IFormatProvider formatProvider);
```

The following custom format provider writes numbers as words:

```
public class WordyFormatProvider : IFormatProvider, ICustomFormatter
{
  static readonly string[] _numberWords =
```

```
"zero one two three four five six seven eight nine minus point".Split();

IFormatProvider _parent;    // Allows consumers to chain format providers

public WordyFormatProvider () : this (CultureInfo.CurrentCulture) { }
public WordyFormatProvider (IFormatProvider parent) => _parent = parent;

public object GetFormat (Type formatType)
{
  if (formatType == typeof (ICustomFormatter)) return this;
  return null;
}

public string Format (string format, object arg, IFormatProvider prov)
{
  // If it's not our format string, defer to the parent provider:
  if (arg == null || format != "W")
    return string.Format (_parent, "{0:" + format + "}", arg);

  StringBuilder result = new StringBuilder();
  string digitList = string.Format (CultureInfo.InvariantCulture,
                                    "{0}", arg);
  foreach (char digit in digitList)
  {
    int i = "0123456789-.".IndexOf (digit),
                            StringComparison.InvariantCulture);
    if (i == -1) continue;
    if (result.Length > 0) result.Append (' ');
    result.Append (_numberWords[i]);
  }
  return result.ToString();
}
}
```

Notice that in the Format method, we used string.Format—with Invariant Culture—to convert the input number to a string. It would have been simpler just to call ToString() on arg, but then CurrentCulture would have been used instead. The reason for needing the invariant culture is evident a few lines later:

```
int i = "0123456789-.".IndexOf (digit),
                        StringComparison.InvariantCulture);
```

It's critical here that the number string comprises only the characters 0123456789-. and not any internationalized versions of these.

Here's an example of using WordyFormatProvider:

```
double n = -123.45;
IFormatProvider fp = new WordyFormatProvider();
Console.WriteLine (string.Format (fp, "{0:C} in words is {0:W}", n));

// -$123.45 in words is minus one two three point four five
```

You can use custom format providers only in composite format strings.

Standard Format Strings and Parsing Flags

The standard format strings control how a numeric type or `DateTime/DateTime Offset` is converted to a string. There are two kinds of format strings:

Standard format strings

> With these, you provide general guidance. A standard format string consists of a single letter, followed, optionally, by a digit (whose meaning depends on the letter). An example is `"C"` or `"F2"`.

Custom format strings

> With these, you micromanage every character with a template. An example is `"0:#.000E+00"`.

Custom format strings are unrelated to custom format providers.

Numeric Format Strings

Table 6-2 lists all standard numeric format strings.

Table 6-2. Standard numeric format strings

Letter	Meaning	Sample input	Result	Notes
G or g	"General"	`1.2345, "G"`	1.2345	Switches to exponential notation
		`0.00001, "G"`	1E-05	for small or large numbers.
		`0.00001, "g"`	1e-05	G3 limits precision to three digits
		`1.2345, "G3"`	1.23	in *total* (before + after point).
		`12345, "G3"`	1.23E04	
F	Fixed point	`2345.678, "F2"`	2345.68	F2 rounds to two decimal places.
		`2345.6, "F2"`	2345.60	
N	Fixed point with *group separator* ("Numeric")	`2345.678, "N2"`	2,345.68	As above, with group (1,000s) separator (details from format provider).
		`2345.6, "N2"`	2,345.60	
D	Pad with leading zeros	`123, "D5"`	00123	For integral types only. D5 pads left to five digits; does not truncate.
		`123, "D1"`	123	
E or e	Force exponential notation	`56789, "E"`	5.678900E+004	Six-digit default precision.
		`56789, "e"`	5.678900e+004	
		`56789, "E2"`	5.68E+004	
C	Currency	`1.2, "C"`	$1.20	C with no digit uses default number of D.P. from format provider.
		`1.2, "C4"`	$1.2000	
P	Percent	`.503, "P"`	50.30%	Uses symbol and layout from format provider. Decimal places can optionally be overridden.
		`.503, "P0"`	50%	

Letter	Meaning	Sample input	Result	Notes
X or x	Hexadecimal	47, "X" 47, "x" 47, "X4"	2F 2f 002F	X for uppercase hex digits; x for lowercase hex digits. Integrals only.
R or G9/G17	Round-trip	1f / 3f, "R"	0.333333**43**	Use R for BigInteger, G17 for double, or G9 for float.

Supplying no numeric format string (or a null or blank string) is equivalent to using the "G" standard format string followed by no digit. This exhibits the following behavior:

- Numbers smaller than 10^{-4} or larger than the type's precision are expressed in exponential (scientific) notation.

- The two decimal places at the limit of float or double's precision are rounded away to mask the inaccuracies inherent in conversion to decimal from their underlying binary form.

 The automatic rounding just described is usually beneficial and goes unnoticed. However, it can cause trouble if you need to round-trip a number; in other words, convert it to a string and back again (maybe repeatedly) while preserving value equality. For this reason, the R, G17, and G9 format strings exist to circumvent this implicit rounding.

Table 6-3 lists custom numeric format strings.

Table 6-3. Custom numeric format strings

Specifier	Meaning	Sample input	Result	Notes
#	Digit placeholder	12.345, ".##" 12.345, ".####"	12.35 12.345	Limits digits after D.P.
0	Zero placeholder	12.345, ".00" 12.345, ".0000" 99, "000.00"	12.35 12.3450 099.00	As above, but also pads with zeros before and after D.P.
.	Decimal point			Indicates D.P. Actual symbol comes from NumberFormatInfo.
,	Group separator	1234, "#,###,###" 1234, "0,000,000"	1,234 0,001,234	Symbol comes from Number FormatInfo.
, (as above)	Multiplier	1000000, "#," 1000000, "#,,"	1000 1	If comma is at end or before D.P., it acts as a multiplier—dividing result by 1,000, 1,000,000, etc.

Specifier	Meaning	Sample input	Result	Notes
%	Percent notation	0.6, "00%"	60%	First multiplies by 100 and then substitutes percent symbol obtained from NumberFormatInfo.
E0, e0, E+0, e+0 E-0, e-0	Exponent notation	1234, "0E0" 1234, "0E+0" 1234, "0.00E00" 1234, "0.00e00"	1E3 1E+3 1.23E03 1.23e03	
\	Literal character quote	50, @"\#0"	#50	Use in conjunction with an @ prefix on the string—or use \\.
'xx''xx'	Literal string quote	50, "0 '...'"	50 ...	
;	Section separator	15, "#;(#);zero"	15	(If positive.)
		-5, "#;(#);zero"	(5)	(If negative.)
		0, "#;(#);zero"	zero	(If zero.)
Any other char	Literal	35.2, "$0 . 00c"	$35 . 20c	

NumberStyles

Each numeric type defines a static `Parse` method that accepts a `NumberStyles` argument. `NumberStyles` is a flags enum that lets you determine how the string is read as it's converted to a numeric type. It has the following combinable members:

```
AllowLeadingWhite    AllowTrailingWhite
AllowLeadingSign     AllowTrailingSign
AllowParentheses     AllowDecimalPoint
AllowThousands       AllowExponent
AllowCurrencySymbol  AllowHexSpecifier
```

`NumberStyles` also defines these composite members:

```
None  Integer  Float  Number  HexNumber  Currency  Any
```

Except for `None`, all composite values include `AllowLeadingWhite` and `Allow TrailingWhite`. Figure 6-1 shows their remaining makeup, with the most useful three emphasized.

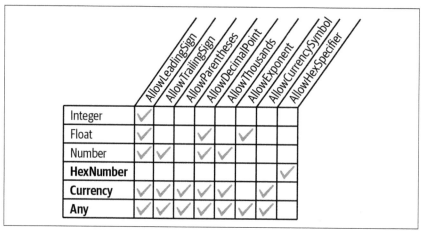

Figure 6-1. Composite NumberStyles

When you call `Parse` without specifying any flags, the defaults illustrated in Figure 6-2 are applied.

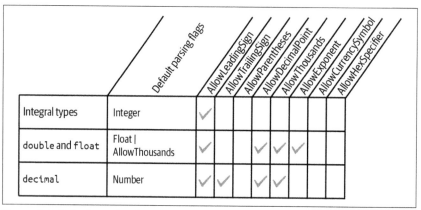

Figure 6-2. Default parsing flags for numeric types

If you don't want the defaults shown in Figure 6-2, you must explicitly specify `NumberStyles`:

```
int thousand = int.Parse ("3E8", NumberStyles.HexNumber);
int minusTwo = int.Parse ("(2)", NumberStyles.Integer |
                          NumberStyles.AllowParentheses);
double aMillion = double.Parse ("1,000,000", NumberStyles.Any);
decimal threeMillion = decimal.Parse ("3e6", NumberStyles.Any);
decimal fivePointTwo = decimal.Parse ("$5.20", NumberStyles.Currency);
```

Because we didn't specify a format provider, this example works with your local currency symbol, group separator, decimal point, and so on. The next example is hardcoded to work with the euro sign and a blank group separator for currencies:

```
NumberFormatInfo ni = new NumberFormatInfo();
ni.CurrencySymbol = "€";
ni.CurrencyGroupSeparator = " ";
double million = double.Parse ("€1 000 000", NumberStyles.Currency, ni);
```

Date/Time Format Strings

Format strings for `DateTime`/`DateTimeOffset` can be divided into two groups based
on whether they honor culture and format provider settings. Table 6-4 lists those
that do; Table 6-5 lists those that don't. The sample output comes from formatting
the following `DateTime` (with *invariant culture*, in the case of Table 6-4):

```
new DateTime (2000, 1, 2,  17, 18, 19);
```

Table 6-4. Culture-sensitive date/time format strings

Format string	Meaning	Sample output
d	Short date	`01/02/2000`
D	Long date	`Sunday, 02 January 2000`
t	Short time	`17:18`
T	Long time	`17:18:19`
f	Long date + short time	`Sunday, 02 January 2000 17:18`
F	Long date + long time	`Sunday, 02 January 2000 17:18:19`
g	Short date + short time	`01/02/2000 17:18`
G (default)	Short date + long time	`01/02/2000 17:18:19`
m, M	Month and day	`02 January`
y, Y	Year and month	`January 2000`

Table 6-5. Culture-insensitive date/time format strings

Format string	Meaning	Sample output	Notes
o	Round-trippable	`2000-01-02T17:18:19.0000000`	Will append time zone information unless `DateTimeKind` is `Unspecified`.
r, R	RFC 1123 standard	`Sun, 02 Jan 2000 17:18:19 GMT`	You must explicitly convert to UTC with `DateTime.ToUniversalTime`.
s	Sortable; ISO 8601	`2000-01-02T17:18:19`	Compatible with text-based sorting.
u	"Universal" sortable	`2000-01-02 17:18:19Z`	Similar to above; must explicitly convert to UTC.
U	UTC	`Sunday, 02 January 2000 17:18:19`	Long date + short time, converted to UTC.

The format strings "r", "R", and "u" emit a suffix that implies UTC; yet they don't automatically convert a local to a UTC DateTime (so you must do the conversion yourself). Ironically, "U" automatically converts to UTC but doesn't write a time zone suffix! In fact, "o" is the only format specifier in the group that can write an unambiguous DateTime without intervention.

DateTimeFormatInfo also supports custom format strings: these are analogous to numeric custom format strings. The list is extensive and is available online in Microsoft's documentation (*https://oreil.ly/kUSCm*). Here's an example of a custom format string:

```
yyyy-MM-dd HH:mm:ss
```

Parsing and misparsing DateTimes

Strings that put the month or day first are ambiguous and can easily be misparsed—particularly if you have global customers. This is not a problem in user interface controls, because the same settings are in force when parsing as when formatting. But when writing to a file, for instance, day/month misparsing can be a real problem. There are two solutions:

- Always state the same explicit culture when formatting and parsing (e.g., invariant culture).

- Format DateTime and DateTimeOffsets in a manner *independent* of culture.

The second approach is more robust—particularly if you choose a format that puts the four-digit year first: such strings are much more difficult to misparse by another party. Further, strings formatted with a *standards-compliant* year-first format (such as "o") can parse correctly alongside locally formatted strings—rather like a "universal donor." (Dates formatted with "s" or "u" have the further benefit of being sortable.)

To illustrate, suppose that we generate a culture-insensitive DateTime string s as follows:

```
string s = DateTime.Now.ToString ("o");
```

The "o" format string includes milliseconds in the output. The following custom format string gives the same result as "o" but without milliseconds:

```
yyyy-MM-ddTHH:mm:ss K
```

We can reparse this in two ways. ParseExact demands strict compliance with the specified format string:

```
DateTime dt1 = DateTime.ParseExact (s, "o", null);
```

(You can achieve a similar result with XmlConvert's ToString and ToDateTime methods.)

Parse, however, implicitly accepts both the "o" format and the CurrentCulture format:

```
DateTime dt2 = DateTime.Parse (s);
```

This works with both DateTime and DateTimeOffset.

 ParseExact is usually preferable if you know the format of the string that you're parsing. It means that if the string is incorrectly formatted, an exception will be thrown—which is usually better than risking a misparsed date.

DateTimeStyles

DateTimeStyles is a flags enum that provides additional instructions when calling Parse on a DateTime(Offset). Here are its members:

```
None,
AllowLeadingWhite, AllowTrailingWhite, AllowInnerWhite,
AssumeLocal, AssumeUniversal, AdjustToUniversal,
NoCurrentDateDefault, RoundTripKind
```

There is also a composite member, AllowWhiteSpaces:

```
AllowWhiteSpaces = AllowLeadingWhite | AllowTrailingWhite | AllowInnerWhite
```

The default is None. This means that extra whitespace is normally prohibited (whitespace that's part of a standard DateTime pattern is exempt).

AssumeLocal and AssumeUniversal apply if the string doesn't have a time zone suffix (such as Z or +9:00). AdjustToUniversal still honors time zone suffixes but then converts to UTC using the current regional settings.

If you parse a string comprising a time but no date, today's date is applied by default. If you apply the NoCurrentDateDefault flag, however, it instead uses 1st January 0001.

Enum Format Strings

In "Enums" on page 140, we described formatting and parsing enum values. Table 6-6 lists each format string and the result of applying it to the following expression:

```
Console.WriteLine (System.ConsoleColor.Red.ToString (formatString));
```

Table 6-6. Enum format strings

Format string	Meaning	Sample output	Notes
G or g	"General"	Red	Default
F or f	Treat as though Flags attribute were present	Red	Works on combined members even if enum has no Flags attribute
D or d	Decimal value	12	Retrieves underlying integral value
X or x	Hexadecimal value	0000000C	Retrieves underlying integral value

Other Conversion Mechanisms

In the previous two sections, we covered format providers—.NET's primary mechanism for formatting and parsing. Other important conversion mechanisms are scattered through various types and namespaces. Some convert to and from string, and some do other kinds of conversions. In this section, we discuss the following topics:

- The Convert class and its functions:
    - Real to integral conversions that round rather than truncate
    - Parsing numbers in base 2, 8, and 16
    - Dynamic conversions
    - Base-64 translations
- XmlConvert and its role in formatting and parsing for XML
- Type converters and their role in formatting and parsing for designers and XAML
- BitConverter, for binary conversions

Convert

.NET calls the following types *base types*:

- bool, char, string, System.DateTime, and System.DateTimeOffset
- All the C# numeric types

The static Convert class defines methods for converting every base type to every other base type. Unfortunately, most of these methods are useless: either they throw exceptions or they are redundant alongside implicit casts. Among the clutter, however, are some useful methods, listed in the following sections.

All base types (explicitly) implement IConvertible, which defines methods for converting to every other base type. In most cases, the implementation of each of these methods simply calls a method in Convert. On rare occasions, it can be useful to write a method that accepts an argument of type IConvertible.

Rounding real to integral conversions

In Chapter 2, we saw how implicit and explicit casts allow you to convert between numeric types. In summary:

- Implicit casts work for nonlossy conversions (e.g., int to double).
- Explicit casts are required for lossy conversions (e.g., double to int).

Casts are optimized for efficiency; hence, they *truncate* data that won't fit. This can be a problem when converting from a real number to an integer, because often you want to *round* rather than truncate. Convert's numerical conversion methods address just this issue—they always *round*:

```
double d = 3.9;
int i = Convert.ToInt32 (d);    // i == 4
```

Convert uses *banker's rounding*, which snaps midpoint values to even integers (this prevents positive or negative bias). If banker's rounding is a problem, first call Math.Round on the real number: this accepts an additional argument that allows you to control midpoint rounding.

Parsing numbers in base 2, 8, and 16

Hidden among the To(*integral-type*) methods are overloads that parse numbers in another base:

```
int thirty = Convert.ToInt32 ("1E", 16);    // Parse in hexadecimal
uint five  = Convert.ToUInt32 ("101", 2);   // Parse in binary
```

The second argument specifies the base. It can be any base you like—as long as it's 2, 8, 10, or 16!

Dynamic conversions

Occasionally, you need to convert from one type to another, but you don't know what the types are until runtime. For this, the Convert class provides a ChangeType method:

```
public static object ChangeType (object value, Type conversionType);
```

The source and target types must be one of the "base" types. ChangeType also accepts an optional IFormatProvider argument. Here's an example:

```
Type targetType = typeof (int);
object source = "42";
```

```
object result = Convert.ChangeType (source, targetType);

Console.WriteLine (result);             // 42
Console.WriteLine (result.GetType());   // System.Int32
```

An example of when this might be useful is in writing a deserializer that can work with multiple types. It can also convert any enum to its integral type (see "Enums" on page 140).

A limitation of ChangeType is that you cannot specify a format string or parsing flag.

Base-64 conversions

Sometimes, you need to include binary data such as a bitmap within a text document, such as an XML file or email message. Base 64 is a ubiquitous means of encoding binary data as readable characters, using 64 characters from the ASCII set.

Convert's ToBase64String method converts from a byte array to base 64; From Base64String does the reverse.

XmlConvert

If you're dealing with data that's originated from or destined for an XML file, XmlConvert (in the System.Xml namespace) provides the most suitable methods for formatting and parsing. The methods in XmlConvert handle the nuances of XML formatting without needing special format strings. For instance, true in XML is "true" and not "True." The .NET BCL internally uses XmlConvert extensively. XmlConvert is also good for general-purpose culture-independent serialization.

The formatting methods in XmlConvert are all provided as overloaded ToString methods; the parsing methods are called ToBoolean, ToDateTime, and so on:

```
string s = XmlConvert.ToString (true);       // s = "true"
bool isTrue = XmlConvert.ToBoolean (s);
```

The methods that convert to and from DateTime accept an XmlDateTimeSerializa tionMode argument. This is an enum with the following values:

```
Unspecified, Local, Utc, RoundtripKind
```

Local and Utc cause a conversion to take place when formatting (if the DateTime is not already in that time zone). The time zone is then appended to the string:

```
2010-02-22T14:08:30.9375          // Unspecified
2010-02-22T14:07:30.9375+09:00    // Local
2010-02-22T05:08:30.9375Z         // Utc
```

Unspecified strips away any time-zone information embedded in the DateTime (i.e., DateTimeKind) before formatting. RoundtripKind honors the DateTime's Date TimeKind—so when it's reparsed, the resultant DateTime struct will be exactly as it was originally.

Type Converters

Type converters are designed to format and parse in design-time environments. They also parse values in Extensible Application Markup Language (XAML) documents—as used in Windows Presentation Foundation (WPF).

In .NET, there are more than 100 type converters—covering such things as colors, images, and URIs. In contrast, format providers are implemented for only a handful of simple value types.

Type converters typically parse strings in a variety of ways—without needing hints. For instance, in a WPF application in Visual Studio, if you assign a control a background color by typing `"Beige"` into the appropriate property window, `Color`'s type converter figures out that you're referring to a color name and not an RGB string or system color. This flexibility can sometimes make type converters useful in contexts outside of designers and XAML documents.

All type converters subclass `TypeConverter` in `System.ComponentModel`. To obtain a `TypeConverter`, call `TypeDescriptor.GetConverter`. The following obtains a `Type Converter` for the `Color` type (in the `System.Drawing` namespace):

```
TypeConverter cc = TypeDescriptor.GetConverter (typeof (Color));
```

Among many other methods, `TypeConverter` defines methods to `ConvertToString` and `ConvertFromString`. We can call these as follows:

```
Color beige  = (Color) cc.ConvertFromString ("Beige");
Color purple = (Color) cc.ConvertFromString ("#800080");
Color window = (Color) cc.ConvertFromString ("Window");
```

By convention, type converters have names ending in *Converter* and are usually in the same namespace as the type they're converting. A type links to its converter via a `TypeConverterAttribute`, allowing designers to pick up converters automatically.

Type converters can also provide design-time services such as generating standard value lists for populating a drop-down list in a designer or assisting with code serialization.

BitConverter

Most base types can be converted to a byte array, by calling `BitConverter.GetBytes`:

```
foreach (byte b in BitConverter.GetBytes (3.5))
  Console.Write (b + " ");                    // 0 0 0 0 0 0 12 64
```

`BitConverter` also provides methods, such as `ToDouble`, for converting in the other direction.

The `decimal` and `DateTime(Offset)` types are not supported by `BitConverter`. You can, however, convert a `decimal` to an `int` array by calling `decimal.GetBits`. To go the other way around, `decimal` provides a constructor that accepts an `int` array.

In the case of `DateTime`, you can call `ToBinary` on an instance—this returns a `long` (upon which you can then use `BitConverter`). The static `DateTime.FromBinary` method does the reverse.

Globalization

There are two aspects to *internationalizing* an application: *globalization* and *localization*.

Globalization is concerned with three tasks (in decreasing order of importance):

1. Making sure that your program doesn't *break* when run in another culture
2. Respecting a local culture's formatting rules; for instance, when displaying dates
3. Designing your program so that it picks up culture-specific data and strings from satellite assemblies that you can later write and deploy

Localization means concluding that last task by writing satellite assemblies for specific cultures. You can do this *after* writing your program (we cover the details in "Resources and Satellite Assemblies" on page 752).

.NET helps you with the second task by applying culture-specific rules by default. We've already seen how calling `ToString` on a `DateTime` or number respects local formatting rules. Unfortunately, this makes it easy to fail the first task and have your program break because you're expecting dates or numbers to be formatted according to an assumed culture. The solution, as we've seen, is either to specify a culture (such as the invariant culture) when formatting and parsing or to use culture-independent methods such as those in `XmlConvert`.

Globalization Checklist

We've already covered the important points in this chapter. Here's a summary of the essential work required:

- Understand Unicode and text encodings (see "Text Encodings and Unicode" on page 281).
- Be mindful that methods such as `ToUpper` and `ToLower` on `char` and `string` are culture sensitive: use `ToUpperInvariant`/`ToLowerInvariant` unless you want culture sensitivity.
- Favor culture-independent formatting and parsing mechanisms for `DateTime` and `DateTimeOffsets` such as `ToString("o")` and `XmlConvert`.
- Otherwise, specify a culture when formatting/parsing numbers or date/times (unless you *want* local-culture behavior).

Testing

You can test against different cultures by reassigning Thread's `CurrentCulture` property (in `System.Threading`). The following changes the current culture to Turkey:

```
Thread.CurrentThread.CurrentCulture = CultureInfo.GetCultureInfo ("tr-TR");
```

Turkey is a particularly good test case because:

- `"i".ToUpper() != "I"` and `"I".ToLower() != "i"`.
- Dates are formatted as day.month.year (note the period separator).
- The decimal point indicator is a comma instead of a period.

You can also experiment by changing the number and date formatting settings in the Windows Control Panel: these are reflected in the default culture (`Culture Info.CurrentCulture`).

`CultureInfo.GetCultures()` returns an array of all available cultures.

 Thread and `CultureInfo` also support a `CurrentUICulture` property. This is concerned more with localization, which we cover in Chapter 17.

Working with Numbers

Conversions

We covered numeric conversions in previous chapters and sections; Table 6-7 summarizes all of the options.

Table 6-7. Summary of numeric conversions

Task	Functions	Examples

e	Parse
	TryParse
		`double d = double.Parse ("3.5");`
		`int i;`
		`bool ok = int.TryParse ("3", out i);`

Parsing from base 2, 8, or 16	Convert.ToIntegral	`int i = Convert.ToInt32 ("1E", 16);`
Formatting to hexadecimal	ToString ("X")	`string hex = 45.ToString ("X");`
Lossless numeric conversion	Implicit cast	`int i = 23;` `double d = i;`
Truncating numeric conversion	Explicit cast	`double d = 23.5;` `int i = (int) d;`

Task	Functions	Examples
Rounding numeric conversion (real to integral)	Convert.ToIntegral	double d = 23.5; int i = Convert.ToInt32 (d);

Math

Table 6-8 lists the key members of the static Math class. The trigonometric functions accept arguments of type double; other methods such as Max are overloaded to operate on all numeric types. The Math class also defines the mathematical constants E (*e*) and PI.

Table 6-8. Methods in the static Math class

Category	Methods
Rounding	Round, Truncate, Floor, Ceiling
Maximum/minimum	Max, Min
Absolute value and sign	Abs, Sign
Square root	Sqrt
Raising to a power	Pow, Exp
Logarithm	Log, Log10
Trigonometric	Sin, Cos, Tan, Sinh, Cosh, Tanh, Asin, Acos, Atan

The Round method lets you specify the number of decimal places with which to round as well as how to handle midpoints (away from zero, or with banker's rounding). Floor and Ceiling round to the nearest integer: Floor always rounds down, and Ceiling always rounds up—even with negative numbers.

Max and Min accept only two arguments. If you have an array or sequence of numbers, use the Max and Min extension methods in System.Linq.Enumerable.

BigInteger

The BigInteger struct is a specialized numeric type. It resides in the System.Numerics namespace and allows you to represent an arbitrarily large integer without any loss of precision.

C# doesn't provide native support for BigInteger, so there's no way to represent BigInteger literals. You can, however, implicitly convert from any other integral type to a BigInteger:

```
BigInteger twentyFive = 25;     // implicit conversion from integer
```

To represent a bigger number, such as one googol (10^{100}), you can use one of BigInteger's static methods, such as Pow (raise to the power):

```
BigInteger googol = BigInteger.Pow (10, 100);
```

Alternatively, you can Parse a string:

```
BigInteger googol = BigInteger.Parse ("1".PadRight (101, '0'));
```

Calling ToString() on this prints every digit:

```
Console.WriteLine (googol.ToString()); // 10000000000000000000000000000000
0000000000000000000000000000000000000000000000000000000000000000000000
```

You can perform potentially lossy conversions between BigInteger and the standard numeric types by using the explicit cast operator:

```
double g2 = (double) googol;        // Explicit cast
BigInteger g3 = (BigInteger) g2;    // Explicit cast
Console.WriteLine (g3);
```

The output from this demonstrates the loss of precision:

```
99999999999999997336168804116691 2...
```

BigInteger overloads all the arithmetic operators including remainder (%) as well as the comparison and equality operators.

You can also construct a BigInteger from a byte array. The following code generates a 32-byte random number suitable for cryptography and then assigns it to a BigInteger:

```
// This uses the System.Security.Cryptography namespace:
RandomNumberGenerator rand = RandomNumberGenerator.Create();
byte[] bytes = new byte [32];
rand.GetBytes (bytes);
var bigRandomNumber = new BigInteger (bytes);    // Convert to BigInteger
```

The advantage of storing such a number in a BigInteger over a byte array is that you get value-type semantics. Calling ToByteArray converts a BigInteger back to a byte array.

Half

The Half struct is a 16-bit floating point type and was introduced with .NET 5. Half is intended mainly for interoperating with graphics card processors and does not have native support in most CPUs.

You can convert between Half and float or double via an explicit cast:

```
Half h = (Half) 123.456;
Console.WriteLine (h);     // 123.44  (note loss of precision)
```

There are no arithmetic operations defined for this type, so you must convert to another type such as float or double in order to perform calculations.

Half has a range of –65500 to 65500:

```
Console.WriteLine (Half.MinValue);    // -65500
Console.WriteLine (Half.MaxValue);    // 65500
```

Note the loss of precision at the maximum range:

```
Console.WriteLine ((Half)65500);    // 65500
Console.WriteLine ((Half)65490);    // 65500
Console.WriteLine ((Half)65480);    // 65470
```

Complex

The Complex struct is another specialized numeric type that represents complex numbers with real and imaginary components of type double. Complex resides in the namespace (along with BigInteger).

To use Complex, instantiate the struct, specifying the real and imaginary values:

```
var c1 = new Complex (2, 3.5);
var c2 = new Complex (3, 0);
```

There are also implicit conversions from the standard numeric types.

The Complex struct exposes properties for the real and imaginary values as well as the phase and magnitude:

```
Console.WriteLine (c1.Real);       // 2
Console.WriteLine (c1.Imaginary);  // 3.5
Console.WriteLine (c1.Phase);      // 1.05165021254837
Console.WriteLine (c1.Magnitude);  // 4.03112887414927
```

You can also construct a Complex number by specifying magnitude and phase:

```
Complex c3 = Complex.FromPolarCoordinates (1.3, 5);
```

The standard arithmetic operators are overloaded to work on Complex numbers:

```
Console.WriteLine (c1 + c2);    // (5, 3.5)
Console.WriteLine (c1 * c2);    // (6, 10.5)
```

The Complex struct exposes static methods for more advanced functions, including the following:

- Trigonometric (Sin, Asin, Sinh, Tan, etc.)
- Logarithms and exponentiations
- Conjugate

Random

The Random class generates a pseudorandom sequence of random bytes, integers, or doubles.

To use Random, you first instantiate it, optionally providing a seed to initiate the random number series. Using the same seed guarantees the same series of numbers (if run under the same CLR version), which is sometimes useful when you want reproducibility:

```
Random r1 = new Random (1);
Random r2 = new Random (1);
Console.WriteLine (r1.Next (100) + ", " + r1.Next (100));      // 24, 11
Console.WriteLine (r2.Next (100) + ", " + r2.Next (100));      // 24, 11
```

If you don't want reproducibility, you can construct Random with no seed; in that case, it uses the current system time to make one up.

Because the system clock has limited granularity, two Random instances created close together (typically within 10 ms) will yield the same sequence of values. A common trap is to instantiate a new Random object every time you need a random number rather than reusing the *same* object.

A good pattern is to declare a single static Random instance. In multithreaded scenarios, however, this can cause trouble because Random objects are not thread-safe. We describe a workaround in "Thread-Local Storage" on page 898.

Calling Next(n) generates a random integer between 0 and $n-1$. NextDouble generates a random double between 0 and 1. NextBytes fills a byte array with random values.

Random is not considered random enough for high-security applications such as cryptography. For this, .NET provides a *cryptographically strong* random number generator, in the System.Security.Cryptography namespace. Here's how to use it:

```
var rand = System.Security.Cryptography.RandomNumberGenerator.Create();
byte[] bytes = new byte [32];
rand.GetBytes (bytes);         // Fill the byte array with random numbers.
```

The downside is that it's less flexible: filling a byte array is the only means of obtaining random numbers. To obtain an integer, you must use BitConverter:

```
byte[] bytes = new byte [4];
rand.GetBytes (bytes);
int i = BitConverter.ToInt32 (bytes, 0);
```

BitOperations

The `System.Numerics.BitOperations` class (from .NET 6) exposes the following methods to help with base-2 operations:

`IsPow2`
> Returns true if a number is a power of 2

`LeadingZeroCount/TrailingZeroCount`
> Returns the number of leading zeros, when formatted as a base-2 32-bit or 64-bit unsigned integer

`Log2`
> Returns the integer base-2 log of an unsigned integer

`PopCount`
> Returns the number of bits set to 1 in an unsigned integer

`RotateLeft/RotateRight`
> Performs a bitwise left/right rotation

`RoundUpToPowerOf2`
> Rounds an unsigned integer up to the closest power of 2

Enums

In Chapter 3, we described C#'s enum type and showed how to combine members, test equality, use logical operators, and perform conversions. .NET extends C#'s support for enums through the `System.Enum` type. This type has two roles:

- Providing type unification for all `enum` types
- Defining static utility methods

Type unification means that you can implicitly cast any enum member to a `System.Enum` instance:

```
Display (Nut.Macadamia);    // Nut.Macadamia
Display (Size.Large);       // Size.Large

void Display (Enum value)
{
  Console.WriteLine (value.GetType().Name + "." + value.ToString());
}

enum Nut  { Walnut, Hazelnut, Macadamia }
enum Size { Small, Medium, Large }
```

The static utility methods on `System.Enum` are primarily related to performing conversions and obtaining lists of members.

Enum Conversions

There are three ways to represent an enum value:

- As an enum member
- As its underlying integral value
- As a string

In this section, we describe how to convert between each.

Enum to integral conversions

Recall that an explicit cast converts between an enum member and its integral value.
An explicit cast is the correct approach if you know the enum type at compile time:

```
[Flags]
public enum BorderSides { Left=1, Right=2, Top=4, Bottom=8 }
...
int i = (int) BorderSides.Top;          // i == 4
BorderSides side = (BorderSides) i;     // side == BorderSides.Top
```

You can cast a System.Enum instance to its integral type in the same way. The trick is
to first cast to an object and then the integral type:

```
static int GetIntegralValue (Enum anyEnum)
{
  return (int) (object) anyEnum;
}
```

This relies on you knowing the integral type: the method we just wrote would crash
if passed an enum whose integral type was long. To write a method that works with
an enum of any integral type, you can take one of three approaches. The first is to call
Convert.ToDecimal:

```
static decimal GetAnyIntegralValue (Enum anyEnum)
{
  return Convert.ToDecimal (anyEnum);
}
```

This works because every integral type (including ulong) can be converted to
decimal without loss of information. The second approach is to call Enum.GetUnder
lyingType in order to obtain the enum's integral type, and then call Convert.Change
Type:

```
static object GetBoxedIntegralValue (Enum anyEnum)
{
  Type integralType = Enum.GetUnderlyingType (anyEnum.GetType());
  return Convert.ChangeType (anyEnum, integralType);
}
```

This preserves the original integral type, as the following example shows:

```
object result = GetBoxedIntegralValue (BorderSides.Top);
Console.WriteLine (result);                        // 4
Console.WriteLine (result.GetType());              // System.Int32
```

 Our GetBoxedIntegralType method in fact performs no value
conversion; rather, it *reboxes* the same value in another type.
It translates an integral value in *enum-type* clothing to an integral value in *integral-type* clothing. We describe this further in
"How Enums Work" on page 323.

The third approach is to call Format or ToString specifying the "d" or "D" format
string. This gives you the enum's integral value as a string, and it is useful when
writing custom serialization formatters:

```
static string GetIntegralValueAsString (Enum anyEnum)
{
  return anyEnum.ToString ("D");     // returns something like "4"
}
```

Integral to enum conversions

Enum.ToObject converts an integral value to an enum instance of the given type:

```
object bs = Enum.ToObject (typeof (BorderSides), 3);
Console.WriteLine (bs);                        // Left, Right
```

This is the dynamic equivalent of the following:

```
BorderSides bs = (BorderSides) 3;
```

ToObject is overloaded to accept all integral types as well as object. (The latter
works with any boxed integral type.)

String conversions

To convert an enum to a string, you can either call the static Enum.Format method or
call ToString on the instance. Each method accepts a format string, which can be
"G" for default formatting behavior, "D" to emit the underlying integral value as a
string, "X" for the same in hexadecimal, or "F" to format combined members of an
enum without the Flags attribute. We listed examples of these in "Standard Format
Strings and Parsing Flags" on page 303.

Enum.Parse converts a string to an enum. It accepts the enum type and a string that
can include multiple members:

```
BorderSides leftRight = (BorderSides) Enum.Parse (typeof (BorderSides),
                                       "Left, Right");
```

An optional third argument lets you perform case-insensitive parsing. An Argument
Exception is thrown if the member is not found.

Enumerating Enum Values

Enum.GetValues returns an array comprising all members of a particular enum type:

```
foreach (Enum value in Enum.GetValues (typeof (BorderSides)))
    Console.WriteLine (value);
```

Composite members such as LeftRight = Left | Right are included, too.

Enum.GetNames performs the same function but returns an array of *strings*.

 Internally, the CLR implements GetValues and GetNames by reflecting over the fields in the enum's type. The results are cached for efficiency.

How Enums Work

The semantics of enums are enforced largely by the compiler. In the CLR, there's no runtime difference between an enum instance (when unboxed) and its underlying integral value. Further, an enum definition in the CLR is merely a subtype of System.Enum with static integral-type fields for each member. This makes the ordinary use of an enum highly efficient, with a runtime cost matching that of integral constants.

The downside of this strategy is that enums can provide *static* but not *strong* type safety. We saw an example of this in Chapter 3:

```
[Flags] public enum BorderSides { Left=1, Right=2, Top=4, Bottom=8 }
...
BorderSides b = BorderSides.Left;
b += 1234;                         // No error!
```

When the compiler is unable to perform validation (as in this example), there's no backup from the runtime to throw an exception.

What we said about there being no runtime difference between an enum instance and its integral value might seem at odds with the following:

```
[Flags] public enum BorderSides { Left=1, Right=2, Top=4, Bottom=8 }
...
Console.WriteLine (BorderSides.Right.ToString());      // Right
Console.WriteLine (BorderSides.Right.GetType().Name);  // BorderSides
```

Given the nature of an enum instance at runtime, you'd expect this to print 2 and Int32! The reason for its behavior is down to some more compile-time trickery. C# explicitly *boxes* an enum instance before calling its virtual methods—such as ToString or GetType. And when an enum instance is boxed, it gains a runtime wrapping that references its enum type.

The Guid Struct

The Guid struct represents a globally unique identifier: a 16-byte value that, when generated, is almost certainly unique in the world. Guids are often used for keys of various sorts, in applications and databases. There are 2^{128} or 3.4×10^{38} unique Guids.

The static `Guid.NewGuid` method generates a unique `Guid`:

```
Guid g = Guid.NewGuid ();
Console.WriteLine (g.ToString()); // 0d57629c-7d6e-4847-97cb-9e2fc25083fe
```

To instantiate an existing value, you use one of the constructors. The two most useful constructors are:

```
public Guid (byte[] b);    // Accepts a 16-byte array
public Guid (string g);    // Accepts a formatted string
```

When represented as a string, a `Guid` is formatted as a 32-digit hexadecimal number, with optional hyphens after the 8th, 12th, 16th, and 20th digits. The whole string can also be optionally wrapped in brackets or braces:

```
Guid g1 = new Guid ("{0d57629c-7d6e-4847-97cb-9e2fc25083fe}");
Guid g2 = new Guid ("0d57629c7d6e484797cb9e2fc25083fe");
Console.WriteLine (g1 == g2);  // True
```

Being a struct, a `Guid` honors value-type semantics; hence, the equality operator works in the preceding example.

The `ToByteArray` method converts a `Guid` to a byte array.

The static `Guid.Empty` property returns an empty `Guid` (all zeros). This is often used in place of `null`.

Equality Comparison

Until now, we've assumed that the `==` and `!=` operators are all there is to equality comparison. The issue of equality, however, is more complex and subtler, sometimes requiring the use of additional methods and interfaces. This section explores the standard C# and .NET protocols for equality, focusing particularly on two questions:

- When are `==` and `!=` adequate—and inadequate—for equality comparison, and what are the alternatives?

- How and when should you customize a type's equality logic?

But before exploring the details of equality protocols and how to customize them, we first must look at the preliminary concept of value versus referential equality.

Value Versus Referential Equality

There are two kinds of equality:

Value equality
    Two values are *equivalent* in some sense.

Referential equality
    Two references refer to *exactly the same object*.

Unless overridden:

- Value types use *value equality.*
- Reference types use *referential equality.* (This is overridden with anonymous types and records.)

Value types, in fact, can use *only* value equality (unless boxed). A simple demonstration of value equality is to compare two numbers:

```
int x = 5, y = 5;
Console.WriteLine (x == y);   // True (by virtue of value equality)
```

A more elaborate demonstration is to compare two DateTimeOffset structs. The following prints True because the two DateTimeOffsets refer to the *same point in time* and so are considered equivalent:

```
var dt1 = new DateTimeOffset (2010, 1, 1, 1, 1, 1, TimeSpan.FromHours(8));
var dt2 = new DateTimeOffset (2010, 1, 1, 2, 1, 1, TimeSpan.FromHours(9));
Console.WriteLine (dt1 == dt2);   // True
```

DateTimeOffset is a struct whose equality semantics have been tweaked. By default, structs exhibit a special kind of value equality called *structural equality* in which two values are considered equal if all of their members are equal. (You can see this by creating a struct and calling its Equals method; more on this later.)

Reference types exhibit referential equality by default. In the following example, f1 and f2 are not equal, despite their objects having identical content:

```
class Foo { public int X; }
...
Foo f1 = new Foo { X = 5 };
Foo f2 = new Foo { X = 5 };
Console.WriteLine (f1 == f2);   // False
```

In contrast, f3 and f1 are equal because they reference the same object:

```
Foo f3 = f1;
Console.WriteLine (f1 == f3);   // True
```

Later in this section, we explain how you can *customize* reference types to exhibit value equality. An example of this is the Uri class in the System namespace:

```
Uri uri1 = new Uri ("http://www.linqpad.net");
Uri uri2 = new Uri ("http://www.linqpad.net");
Console.WriteLine (uri1 == uri2);              // True
```

The string class exhibits similar behavior:

```
var s1 = "http://www.linqpad.net";
var s2 = "http://" + "www.linqpad.net";
Console.WriteLine (s1 == s2);        // True
```

Standard Equality Protocols

There are three standard protocols that types can implement for equality comparison:

- The == and != operators
- The virtual Equals method in object
- The IEquatable<T> interface

In addition, there are the *pluggable* protocols and the IStructuralEquatable interface, which we describe in Chapter 7.

== and !=

We've already seen in many examples how the standard == and != operators perform equality/inequality comparisons. The subtleties with == and != arise because they are *operators*; thus, they are statically resolved (in fact, they are implemented as static functions). So, when you use == or !=, C# makes a *compile-time* decision as to which type will perform the comparison, and no virtual behavior comes into play. This is normally desirable. In the following example, the compiler hardwires == to the int type because x and y are both int:

```
int x = 5;
int y = 5;
Console.WriteLine (x == y);      // True
```

But in the next example, the compiler wires the == operator to the object type:

```
object x = 5;
object y = 5;
Console.WriteLine (x == y);      // False
```

Because object is a class (and so a reference type), object's == operator uses *referential equality* to compare x and y. The result is false because x and y each refer to different boxed objects on the heap.

The virtual Object.Equals method

To correctly equate x and y in the preceding example, we can use the virtual Equals method. Equals is defined in System.Object and so is available to all types:

```
object x = 5;
object y = 5;
Console.WriteLine (x.Equals (y));      // True
```

Equals is resolved at runtime—according to the object's actual type. In this case, it calls Int32's Equals method, which applies *value equality* to the operands, returning true. With reference types, Equals performs referential equality comparison by default; with structs, Equals performs structural comparison by calling Equals on each of its fields.

Hence, Equals is suitable for equating two objects in a type-agnostic fashion. The
following method equates two objects of any type:

```
public static bool AreEqual (object obj1, object obj2)
  => obj1.Equals (obj2);
```

There is one case, however, in which this fails. If the first argument is null, you get
a NullReferenceException. Here's the fix:

```
public static bool AreEqual (object obj1, object obj2)
{
  if (obj1 == null) return obj2 == null;
  return obj1.Equals (obj2);
}
```

Or, more succinctly:

```
public static bool AreEqual (object obj1, object obj2)
  => obj1 == null ? obj2 == null : obj1.Equals (obj2);
```

The static object.Equals method

The object class provides a static helper method that does the work of AreEqual in
the preceding example. Its name is Equals—just like the virtual method—but there's
no conflict because it accepts *two* arguments:

```
public static bool Equals (object objA, object objB)
```

This provides a null-safe equality comparison algorithm for when the types are
unknown at compile time:

```
object x = 3, y = 3;
Console.WriteLine (object.Equals (x, y));   // True
x = null;
Console.WriteLine (object.Equals (x, y));   // False
y = null;
Console.WriteLine (object.Equals (x, y));   // True
```

A useful application is when writing generic types. The following code will not compile if object.Equals is replaced with the == or != operator:

```
class Test <T>
{
  T _value;
  public void SetValue (T newValue)
  {
    if (!object.Equals (newValue, _value))
    {
      _value = newValue;
      OnValueChanged();
    }
  }
  protected virtual void OnValueChanged() { ... }
}
```

Operators are prohibited here because the compiler cannot bind to the static method of an unknown type.

> A more elaborate way to implement this comparison is with the EqualityComparer<T> class. This has the advantage of preventing boxing:
>
> ```
> if (!EqualityComparer<T>.Default.Equals (newValue, _value))
> ```
>
> We discuss EqualityComparer<T> in more detail in Chapter 7 (see "Plugging in Equality and Order" on page 388).

The static object.ReferenceEquals method

Occasionally, you need to force referential equality comparison. The static object.ReferenceEquals method does just that:

```
Widget w1 = new Widget();
Widget w2 = new Widget();
Console.WriteLine (object.ReferenceEquals (w1, w2));      // False

class Widget { ... }
```

You might want to do this because it's possible for Widget to override the virtual Equals method such that w1.Equals(w2) would return true. Further, it's possible for Widget to overload the == operator so that w1==w2 would also return true. In such cases, calling object.ReferenceEquals guarantees normal referential equality semantics.

Another way to force referential equality comparison is to cast the values to object and then apply the == operator.

The IEquatable<T> interface

A consequence of calling object.Equals is that it forces boxing on value types. This is undesirable in highly performance-sensitive scenarios because boxing is relatively expensive compared to the actual comparison. A solution was introduced in C# 2.0, with the IEquatable<T> interface:

```
public interface IEquatable<T>
{
  bool Equals (T other);
}
```

The idea is that IEquatable<T>, when implemented, gives the same result as calling object's virtual Equals method—but more quickly. Most basic .NET types implement IEquatable<T>. You can use IEquatable<T> as a constraint in a generic type:

```
class Test<T> where T : IEquatable<T>
{
  public bool IsEqual (T a, T b)
  {
    return a.Equals (b);     // No boxing with generic T
  }
}
```

If we remove the generic constraint, the class would still compile, but a.Equals(b) would instead bind to the slower object.Equals (slower assuming T was a value type).

When Equals and == are not equal

We said earlier that it's sometimes useful for == and Equals to apply different definitions of equality. For example:

```
double x = double.NaN;
Console.WriteLine (x == x);          // False
Console.WriteLine (x.Equals (x));    // True
```

The double type's == operator enforces that one NaN can never equal anything else—even another NaN. This is most natural from a mathematical perspective, and it reflects the underlying CPU behavior. The Equals method, however, is obliged to apply *reflexive* equality; in other words:

x.Equals (x) must *always* return true.

Collections and dictionaries rely on Equals behaving this way; otherwise, they could not find an item they previously stored.

Having Equals and == apply different definitions of equality is actually quite rare with value types. A more common scenario is with reference types; this happens when the author customizes `Equals` so that it performs value equality while leaving `==` to perform (default) referential equality. The `StringBuilder` class does exactly that:

```
var sb1 = new StringBuilder ("foo");
var sb2 = new StringBuilder ("foo");
Console.WriteLine (sb1 == sb2);         // False (referential equality)
Console.WriteLine (sb1.Equals (sb2));   // True  (value equality)
```

Let's now look at how to customize equality.

Equality and Custom Types

Recall default equality comparison behavior:

- Value types use *value equality*.
- Reference types use *referential equality* unless overridden (as is the case with anonymous types and records).

Further:

- A struct's `Equals` method applies *structural value equality* by default (i.e., it compares each field in the struct).

Sometimes, it makes sense to override this behavior when writing a type. There are two cases for doing so:

- To change the meaning of equality
- To speed up equality comparisons for structs

Changing the meaning of equality

Changing the meaning of equality makes sense when the default behavior of `==` and `Equals` is unnatural for your type and is *not what a consumer would expect*. An example is `DateTimeOffset`, a struct with two private fields: a UTC `DateTime` and a numeric integer offset. If you were writing this type, you'd probably want to ensure that equality comparisons considered only the UTC `DateTime` field and not the offset field. Another example is numeric types that support `NaN` values such as `float` and `double`. If you were implementing such types yourself, you'd want to ensure that `NaN`-comparison logic was supported in equality comparisons.

With classes, it's sometimes more natural to offer *value equality* as the default instead of *referential equality*. This is often the case with small classes that hold a simple piece of data, such as `System.Uri` (or `System.String`).

With records, the compiler automatically implements structural equality (by comparing each field). Sometimes, however, this will include fields that you don't want to compare, or objects that require special comparison logic, such as collections.

The process of overriding equality with records is slightly different because records follow a special pattern that's designed to play well with its rules for inheritance.

Speeding up equality comparisons with structs

The default *structural equality* comparison algorithm for structs is relatively slow. Taking over this process by overriding Equals can improve performance by a factor of five. Overloading the == operator and implementing IEquatable<T> allows unboxed equality comparisons, and this can speed things up by a factor of five again.

 Overriding equality semantics for reference types doesn't benefit performance. The default algorithm for referential equality comparison is already very fast because it simply compares two 32- or 64-bit references.

There's another, rather peculiar case for customizing equality, and that's to improve a struct's hashing algorithm for better performance in a hashtable. This comes as a result of the fact that equality comparison and hashing are joined at the hip. We examine hashing in a moment.

How to override equality semantics

To override equality with classes or structs, here are the steps:

1. Override GetHashCode() and Equals().

2. (Optionally) overload != and ==.

3. (Optionally) implement IEquatable<T>.

The process is different (and simpler) with records because the compiler already overrides the equality methods and operators in line with its own special pattern. If you want to intervene, you must conform to this pattern, which means writing an Equals method with a signature like this:

```
record Test (int X, int Y)
{
  public virtual bool Equals (Test t) => t != null && t.X == X && t.Y == Y;
}
```

Notice that Equals is virtual (not override) and accepts the actual record type (Test in this case, and not object). The compiler will recognize that your method has the "correct" signature and will patch it in.

You must also override GetHashCode(), just as you would with classes or structs. You don't need to (and shouldn't) overload != and ==, or implement IEquatable<T>, because this is already done for you.

Overriding GetHashCode

It might seem odd that System.Object—with its small footprint of members—defines a method with a specialized and narrow purpose. GetHashCode is a virtual method in Object that fits this description; it exists primarily for the benefit of just the following two types:

```
System.Collections.Hashtable
System.Collections.Generic.Dictionary<TKey,TValue>
```

These are *hashtables*—collections for which each element has a key used for storage and retrieval. A hashtable applies a very specific strategy for efficiently allocating elements based on their key. This requires that each key have an Int32 number, or *hash code*. The hash code need not be unique for each key but should be as varied as possible for good hashtable performance. Hashtables are considered important enough that GetHashCode is defined in System.Object—so that every type can emit a hash code.

 We describe hashtables in detail in Chapter 7.

Both reference and value types have default implementations of GetHashCode, meaning that you don't need to override this method—*unless you override* Equals. (And if you override GetHashCode, you will almost certainly want to also override Equals.)

Here are the other rules for overriding object.GetHashCode:

- It must return the same value on two objects for which Equals returns true (hence, GetHashCode and Equals are overridden together).
- It must not throw exceptions.
- It must return the same value if called repeatedly on the same object (unless the object has *changed*).

For maximum performance in hashtables, you should write GetHashCode so as to minimize the likelihood of two different values returning the same hashcode. This gives rise to the third reason for overriding Equals and GetHashCode on structs, which is to provide a more efficient hashing algorithm than the default. The default implementation for structs is at the discretion of the runtime and can be based on every field in the struct.

In contrast, the default GetHashCode implementation for *classes* is based on an internal object token, which is unique for each instance in the CLR's current implementation.

If an object's hashcode changes after it's been added as a key to a dictionary, the object will no longer be accessible in the dictionary. You can preempt this by basing hashcode calculations on immutable fields.

We provide a complete example illustrating how to override `GetHashCode` shortly.

Overriding Equals

The axioms for `object.Equals` are as follows:

- An object cannot equal `null` (unless it's a nullable type).
- Equality is *reflexive* (an object equals itself).
- Equality is *commutative* (if `a.Equals(b)`, then `b.Equals(a)`).
- Equality is *transitive* (if `a.Equals(b)` and `b.Equals(c)`, then `a.Equals(c)`).
- Equality operations are repeatable and reliable (they don't throw exceptions).

Overloading == and !=

In addition to overriding `Equals`, you can optionally overload the equality and inequality operators. This is nearly always done with structs because the consequence of not doing so is that the == and != operators will simply not work on your type.

With classes, there are two ways to proceed:

- Leave == and != alone—so that they apply referential equality.
- Overload == and != in line with `Equals`.

The first approach is most common with custom types—especially *mutable* types. It ensures that your type follows the expectation that == and != should exhibit referential equality with reference types, and this prevents confusing consumers. We saw an example earlier:

```
var sb1 = new StringBuilder ("foo");
var sb2 = new StringBuilder ("foo");
Console.WriteLine (sb1 == sb2);       // False (referential equality)
Console.WriteLine (sb1.Equals (sb2)); // True  (value equality)
```

The second approach makes sense with types for which a consumer would never want referential equality. These are typically immutable—such as the `string` and `System.Uri` classes—and are sometimes good candidates for `structs`.

Although it's possible to overload != such that it means something other than !(==), this is almost never done in practice, except in cases such as comparing `float.NaN`.

Implementing IEquatable<T>

For completeness, it's also good to implement IEquatable<T> when overriding Equals. Its results should always match those of the overridden object's Equals method. Implementing IEquatable<T> comes at no programming cost if you structure your Equals method implementation as in the example that follows in a moment.

An example: the Area struct

Imagine that we need a struct to represent an area whose width and height are interchangeable. In other words, 5 × 10 is equal to 10 × 5. (Such a type would be suitable in an algorithm that arranges rectangular shapes.)

Here's the complete code:

```
public struct Area : IEquatable <Area>
{
  public readonly int Measure1;
  public readonly int Measure2;

  public Area (int m1, int m2)
  {
    Measure1 = Math.Min (m1, m2);
    Measure2 = Math.Max (m1, m2);
  }

  public override bool Equals (object other)
      => other is Area a && Equals (a);     // Calls method below

  public bool Equals (Area other)           // Implements IEquatable<Area>
    => Measure1 == other.Measure1 && Measure2 == other.Measure2;

  public override int GetHashCode()
    => HashCode.Combine (Measure1, Measure2);

  public static bool operator == (Area a1, Area a2) => a1.Equals (a2);

  public static bool operator != (Area a1, Area a2) => !a1.Equals (a2);
}
```

From C# 10, you can shortcut the process with records. By declaring this as a record struct, you can remove all the code following the constructor.

In implementing GetHashCode, we used .NET's HashCode.Combine function to produce a composite hashcode. (Before that function existed, a popular approach was to multiply each value by some prime number and then add them together.)

Here's a demonstration of the Area struct:

```
Area a1 = new Area (5, 10);
Area a2 = new Area (10, 5);
```

```
Console.WriteLine (a1.Equals (a2));    // True
Console.WriteLine (a1 == a2);          // True
```

Pluggable equality comparers

If you want a type to take on different equality semantics just for a specific scenario, you can use a pluggable IEqualityComparer. This is particularly useful in conjunction with the standard collection classes, and we describe it in the following chapter, in "Plugging in Equality and Order" on page 388.

Order Comparison

As well as defining standard protocols for equality, C# and .NET define two standard protocols for determining the order of one object relative to another:

- The IComparable interfaces (IComparable and IComparable<T>)
- The > and < operators

The IComparable interfaces are used by general-purpose sorting algorithms. In the following example, the static Array.Sort method works because System.String implements the IComparable interfaces:

```
string[] colors = { "Green", "Red", "Blue" };
Array.Sort (colors);
foreach (string c in colors) Console.Write (c + " ");   // Blue Green Red
```

The < and > operators are more specialized, and they are intended mostly for numeric types. Because they are statically resolved, they can translate to highly efficient bytecode, suitable for computationally intensive algorithms.

.NET also provides pluggable ordering protocols, via the IComparer interfaces. We describe these in the final section of Chapter 7.

IComparable

The IComparable interfaces are defined as follows:

```
public interface IComparable      { int CompareTo (object other); }
public interface IComparable<in T> { int CompareTo (T other);      }
```

The two interfaces represent the same functionality. With value types, the generic type-safe interface is faster than the nongeneric interface. In both cases, the CompareTo method works as follows:

- If a comes after b, a.CompareTo(b) returns a positive number.
- If a is the same as b, a.CompareTo(b) returns 0.
- If a comes before b, a.CompareTo(b) returns a negative number.

For example:

```
Console.WriteLine ("Beck".CompareTo ("Anne"));    // 1
Console.WriteLine ("Beck".CompareTo ("Beck"));    // 0
Console.WriteLine ("Beck".CompareTo ("Chris"));   // -1
```

Most of the base types implement both IComparable interfaces. These interfaces are also sometimes implemented when writing custom types. We provide an example shortly.

IComparable versus Equals

Consider a type that both overrides Equals and implements the IComparable interfaces. You'd expect that when Equals returns true, CompareTo should return 0. And you'd be right. But here's the catch:

> When Equals returns false, CompareTo can return what it likes (as long as it's internally consistent)!

In other words, equality can be "fussier" than comparison, but not vice versa (violate this and sorting algorithms will break). So, CompareTo can say, "All objects are equal," whereas Equals says, "But some are more equal than others!"

A great example of this is System.String. String's Equals method and == operator use *ordinal* comparison, which compares the Unicode point values of each character. Its CompareTo method, however, uses a less fussy *culture-dependent* comparison. On most computers, for instance, the strings "ü" and "ü" are different according to Equals but the same according to CompareTo.

In Chapter 7, we discuss the pluggable ordering protocol, IComparer, which allows you to specify an alternative ordering algorithm when sorting or instantiating a sorted collection. A custom IComparer can further extend the gap between CompareTo and Equals—a case-insensitive string comparer, for instance, will return 0 when comparing "A" and "a". The reverse rule still applies, however: CompareTo can never be fussier than Equals.

> When implementing the IComparable interfaces in a custom type, you can avoid running afoul of this rule by writing the first line of CompareTo as follows:
>
> ```
> if (Equals (other)) return 0;
> ```
>
> After that, it can return what it likes, as long as it's consistent!

< and >

Some types define < and > operators. For instance:

```
bool after2010 = DateTime.Now > new DateTime (2010, 1, 1);
```

You can expect the < and > operators, when implemented, to be functionally consistent with the IComparable interfaces. This is standard practice across .NET.

It's also standard practice to implement the IComparable interfaces whenever < and > are overloaded, although the reverse is not true. In fact, most .NET types that implement IComparable *do not* overload < and >. This differs from the situation with equality for which it's normal to overload == when overriding Equals.

Typically, > and < are overloaded only when:

- A type has a strong intrinsic concept of "greater than" and "less than" (versus IComparable's broader concepts of "comes before" and "comes after").
- There is only one way, *or context*, in which to perform the comparison.
- The result is invariant across cultures.

System.String doesn't satisfy the last point: the results of string comparisons can vary according to language. Hence, string doesn't support the > and < operators:

```
bool error = "Beck" > "Anne";      // Compile-time error
```

Implementing the IComparable Interfaces

In the following struct representing a musical note, we implement the IComparable interfaces as well as overloading the < and > operators. For completeness, we also override Equals/GetHashCode and overload == and !=:

```
public struct Note : IComparable<Note>, IEquatable<Note>, IComparable
{
  int _semitonesFromA;
  public int SemitonesFromA { get { return _semitonesFromA; } }

  public Note (int semitonesFromA)
  {
    _semitonesFromA = semitonesFromA;
  }

  public int CompareTo (Note other)             // Generic IComparable<T>
  {
    if (Equals (other)) return 0;    // Fail-safe check
    return _semitonesFromA.CompareTo (other._semitonesFromA);
  }

  int IComparable.CompareTo (object other)       // Nongeneric IComparable
  {
    if (!(other is Note))
      throw new InvalidOperationException ("CompareTo: Not a note");
    return CompareTo ((Note) other);
  }

  public static bool operator < (Note n1, Note n2)
    => n1.CompareTo (n2) < 0;

  public static bool operator > (Note n1, Note n2)
    => n1.CompareTo (n2) > 0;

  public bool Equals (Note other)    // for IEquatable<Note>
    => _semitonesFromA == other._semitonesFromA;
```

```
public override bool Equals (object other)
{
  if (!(other is Note)) return false;
  return Equals ((Note) other);
}

public override int GetHashCode() => _semitonesFromA.GetHashCode();

public static bool operator == (Note n1, Note n2) => n1.Equals (n2);

public static bool operator != (Note n1, Note n2) => !(n1 == n2);
}
```

Utility Classes

Console

The static Console class handles standard input/output for console-based applications. In a command-line (console) application, the input comes from the keyboard via Read, ReadKey, and ReadLine, and the output goes to the text window via Write and WriteLine. You can control the window's position and dimensions with the properties WindowLeft, WindowTop, WindowHeight, and WindowWidth. You can also change the BackgroundColor and ForegroundColor properties and manipulate the cursor with the CursorLeft, CursorTop, and CursorSize properties:

```
Console.WindowWidth = Console.LargestWindowWidth;
Console.ForegroundColor = ConsoleColor.Green;
Console.Write ("test... 50%");
Console.CursorLeft -= 3;
Console.Write ("90%");      // test... 90%
```

The Write and WriteLine methods are overloaded to accept a composite format string (see String.Format in "String and Text Handling" on page 271). However, neither method accepts a format provider, so you're stuck with CultureInfo .CurrentCulture. (The workaround, of course, is to explicitly call string.Format.)

The Console.Out property returns a TextWriter. Passing Console.Out to a method that expects a TextWriter is a useful way to get that method to write to the Console for diagnostic purposes.

You can also redirect the Console's input and output streams via the SetIn and SetOut methods:

```
// First save existing output writer:
System.IO.TextWriter oldOut = Console.Out;

// Redirect the console's output to a file:
using (System.IO.TextWriter w = System.IO.File.CreateText
                                ("e:\\output.txt"))
{
  Console.SetOut (w);
```

```
    Console.WriteLine ("Hello world");
}

// Restore standard console output
Console.SetOut (oldOut);
```

In Chapter 15, we describe how streams and text writers work.

 When running WPF or Windows Forms applications under Visual Studio, the Console's output is automatically redirected to Visual Studio's output window (in debug mode). This can make Console.Write useful for diagnostic purposes; although in most cases, the Debug and Trace classes in the System.Diagnostics namespace are more appropriate (see Chapter 13).

Environment

The static System.Environment class provides a range of useful properties:

Files and folders
   CurrentDirectory, SystemDirectory, CommandLine

Computer and operating system
   MachineName, ProcessorCount, OSVersion, NewLine

User logon
   UserName, UserInteractive, UserDomainName

Diagnostics
   TickCount, StackTrace, WorkingSet, Version

You can obtain additional folders by calling GetFolderPath; we describe this in "File and Directory Operations" on page 699.

You can access OS environment variables (what you see when you type **set** at the command prompt) with the following three methods: GetEnvironmentVariable, GetEnvironmentVariables, and SetEnvironmentVariable.

The ExitCode property lets you set the return code—for when your program is called from a command or batch file—and the FailFast method terminates a program immediately, without performing cleanup.

The Environment class available to Windows Store apps offers just a limited number of members (ProcessorCount, NewLine, and FailFast).

Process

The Process class in System.Diagnostics allows you to launch a new process. (In Chapter 13, we describe how you can also use it to interact with other processes running on the computer.)

For security reasons, the Process class is not available to Windows Store apps, and you cannot start arbitrary processes. Instead, you must use the Windows.System.Launcher class to "launch" a URI or file to which you have access. For example,

```
Launcher.LaunchUriAsync (new Uri ("http://albahari.com"));

var file = await KnownFolders.DocumentsLibrary
                              .GetFileAsync ("foo.txt");
Launcher.LaunchFileAsync (file);
```

opens the URI or file, using whatever program is associated with the URI scheme or file extension. Your program must be in the foreground for this to work.

The static Process.Start method has several overloads; the simplest accepts a simple filename with optional arguments:

```
Process.Start ("notepad.exe");
Process.Start ("notepad.exe", "e:\\file.txt");
```

The most flexible overload accepts a ProcessStartInfo instance. With this, you can capture and redirect the launched process's input, output, and error output (if you leave UseShellExecute as false). The following captures the output of calling ipconfig:

```
ProcessStartInfo psi = new ProcessStartInfo
{
  FileName = "cmd.exe",
  Arguments = "/c ipconfig /all",
  RedirectStandardOutput = true,
  UseShellExecute = false
};
Process p = Process.Start (psi);
string result = p.StandardOutput.ReadToEnd();
Console.WriteLine (result);
```

If you don't redirect output, Process.Start executes the program in parallel to the caller. If you want to wait for the new process to complete, you can call WaitForExit on the Process object, with an optional timeout.

Redirecting output and error streams

With UseShellExecute false (the default in .NET), you can capture the standard input, output, and error streams and then write/read these streams via the Standard Input, StandardOutput, and StandardError properties.

A difficulty arises when you need to redirect both the standard output and standard error streams, in that you can't usually know in which order to read data from each (because you don't know in advance how the data will be interleaved). The solution is to read from both streams at once, which you can accomplish by reading from (at least) one of the streams *asynchronously*. Here's how to do this:

- Handle the `OutputDataReceived` and/or `ErrorDataReceived` events. These events fire when output/error data is received.

- Call `BeginOutputReadLine` and/or `BeginErrorReadLine`. This enables the aforementioned events.

The following method runs an executable while capturing both the output and error streams:

```
(string output, string errors) Run (string exePath, string args = "")
{
  using var p = Process.Start (new ProcessStartInfo (exePath, args)
  {
    RedirectStandardOutput = true,
    RedirectStandardError = true,
    UseShellExecute = false,
  });

  var errors = new StringBuilder ();

  // Read from the error stream asynchronously...
  p.ErrorDataReceived += (sender, errorArgs) =>
  {
    if (errorArgs.Data != null) errors.AppendLine (errorArgs.Data);
  };
  p.BeginErrorReadLine ();

  // ...while we read from the output stream synchronously:
  string output = p.StandardOutput.ReadToEnd();

  p.WaitForExit();
  return (output, errors.ToString());
}
```

UseShellExecute

In .NET 5+ (and .NET Core), the default for `UseShellEx` `ecute` is false, whereas in .NET Framework, it was true. Because this is a breaking change, it's worth checking all calls to `Process.Start` when porting code from .NET Framework.

The `UseShellExecute` flag changes how the CLR starts the process. With `UseShell` `Execute` true, you can do the following:

- Specify a path to a file or document rather than an executable (resulting in the operating system opening the file or document with its associated application)

- Specify a URL (resulting in the operating system navigating to that URL in the default web browser)

- (Windows only) Specify a *Verb* (such as "runas", to run the process with administrative elevation)

The drawback is that you cannot redirect the input or output streams. Should you need to do so—while launching a file or document—a workaround is to set UseShellExecute to false and invoke the command-line process (cmd.exe) with the "/c" switch, as we did earlier when calling *ipconfig*.

Under Windows, UseShellExecute instructs the CLR to use the Windows *ShellExecute* function instead of the *CreateProcess* function. Under Linux, UseShellExecute instructs the CLR to call *xdg-open*, *gnome-open*, or *kfmclient*.

AppContext

The static System.AppContext class exposes two useful properties:

- BaseDirectory returns the folder in which the application started. This folder is important for assembly resolution (finding and loading dependencies) and locating configuration files (such as *appsettings.json*).

- TargetFrameworkName tells you the name and version of the .NET runtime that the application targets (as specified in its *.runtimeconfig.json* file). This might be older than the runtime actually in use.

In addition, the AppContext class manages a global string-keyed dictionary of Boolean values, intended to offer library writers a standard mechanism for allowing consumers to switch new features on or off. This untyped approach makes sense with experimental features that you want to keep undocumented to the majority of users.

The consumer of a library requests that you enable a feature as follows:

```
AppContext.SetSwitch ("MyLibrary.SomeBreakingChange", true);
```

Code within that library can then check for that switch as follows:

```
bool isDefined, switchValue;
isDefined = AppContext.TryGetSwitch ("MyLibrary.SomeBreakingChange",
                                     out switchValue);
```

TryGetSwitch returns false if the switch is undefined; this lets you distinguish an undefined switch from one whose value is set to false, should this be necessary.

> Ironically, the design of TryGetSwitch illustrates how not to write APIs. The out parameter is unnecessary, and the method should instead return a nullable bool whose value is true, false, or null for undefined. This would then enable the following use:
>
> ```
> bool switchValue = AppContext.GetSwitch ("...") ?? false;
> ```

7

Collections

.NET provides a standard set of types for storing and managing collections of objects. These include resizable lists, linked lists, sorted and unsorted dictionaries, and arrays. Of these, only arrays form part of the C# language; the remaining collections are just classes you instantiate like any other.

We can divide the types in the .NET BCL for collections into the following categories:

- Interfaces that define standard collection protocols
- Ready-to-use collection classes (lists, dictionaries, etc.)
- Base classes for writing application-specific collections

This chapter covers each of these categories, with an additional section on the types used in determining element equality and order.

The collection namespaces are as follows:

Namespace	Contains
`System.Collections`	Nongeneric collection classes and interfaces
`System.Collections.Specialized`	Strongly typed nongeneric collection classes
`System.Collections.Generic`	Generic collection classes and interfaces
`System.Collections.ObjectModel`	Proxies and bases for custom collections
`System.Collections.Concurrent`	Thread-safe collections (see Chapter 22)

Enumeration

In computing, there are many different kinds of collections, ranging from simple data structures, such as arrays or linked lists, to more complex ones, such as red/black trees and hashtables. Although the internal implementation and external characteristics of these data structures vary widely, the ability to traverse the contents of the collection is an almost universal need. The .NET BCL supports this need via a pair of interfaces (IEnumerable and IEnumerator, and their generic counterparts) that allow different data structures to expose a common traversal API. These are part of a larger set of collection interfaces illustrated in Figure 7-1.

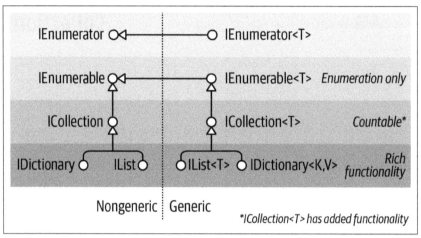

Figure 7-1. Collection interfaces

IEnumerable and IEnumerator

The IEnumerator interface defines the basic low-level protocol by which elements in a collection are traversed—or enumerated—in a forward-only manner. Its declaration is as follows:

```
public interface IEnumerator
{
  bool MoveNext();
  object Current { get; }
  void Reset();
}
```

MoveNext advances the current element or "cursor" to the next position, returning false if there are no more elements in the collection. Current returns the element at the current position (usually cast from object to a more specific type). MoveNext must be called before retrieving the first element—this is to allow for an empty collection. The Reset method, if implemented, moves back to the start, allowing the collection to be enumerated again. Reset exists mainly for Component Object Model (COM) interoperability; calling it directly is generally avoided because it's not universally supported (and is unnecessary in that it's usually just as easy to instantiate a new enumerator).

Collections do not usually *implement* enumerators; instead, they *provide* enumerators, via the interface IEnumerable:

```
public interface IEnumerable
{
  IEnumerator GetEnumerator();
}
```

By defining a single method retuning an enumerator, IEnumerable provides flexibility in that the iteration logic can be farmed out to another class. Moreover, it means
that several consumers can enumerate the collection at once without interfering
with one another. You can think of IEnumerable as "IEnumeratorProvider," and it is
the most basic interface that collection classes implement.

The following example illustrates low-level use of IEnumerable and IEnumerator:

```
string s = "Hello";

// Because string implements IEnumerable, we can call GetEnumerator():
IEnumerator rator = s.GetEnumerator();

while (rator.MoveNext())
{
  char c = (char) rator.Current;
  Console.Write (c + ".");
}

// Output:  H.e.l.l.o.
```

However, it's rare to call methods on enumerators directly in this manner because
C# provides a syntactic shortcut: the foreach statement. Here's the same example
rewritten using foreach:

```
string s = "Hello";       // The String class implements IEnumerable

foreach (char c in s)
  Console.Write (c + ".");
```

IEnumerable<T> and IEnumerator<T>

IEnumerator and IEnumerable are nearly always implemented in conjunction with
their extended generic versions:

```
public interface IEnumerator<T> : IEnumerator, IDisposable
{
  T Current { get; }
}

public interface IEnumerable<T> : IEnumerable
{
  IEnumerator<T> GetEnumerator();
}
```

By defining a typed version of Current and GetEnumerator, these interfaces
strengthen static type safety, avoid the overhead of boxing with value-type elements,
and are more convenient to the consumer. Arrays automatically implement IEnumer
able<T> (where T is the member type of the array).

Thanks to the improved static type safety, calling the following method with an array of characters will generate a compile-time error:

```
void Test (IEnumerable<int> numbers) { ... }
```

It's a standard practice for collection classes to publicly expose IEnumerable<T> while "hiding" the nongeneric IEnumerable through explicit interface implementation. This is so that if you directly call GetEnumerator(), you get back the type-safe generic IEnumerator<T>. There are times, though, when this rule is broken for reasons of backward compatibility (generics did not exist prior to C# 2.0). A good example is arrays—these must return the nongeneric (the nice way of putting it is "classic") IEnumerator to prevent breaking earlier code. To get a generic IEnumerator<T>, you must cast to expose the explicit interface:

```
int[] data = { 1, 2, 3 };
var rator = ((IEnumerable <int>)data).GetEnumerator();
```

Fortunately, you rarely need to write this sort of code, thanks to the foreach statement.

IEnumerable<T> and IDisposable

IEnumerator<T> inherits from IDisposable. This allows enumerators to hold references to resources such as database connections—and ensure that those resources are released when enumeration is complete (or abandoned partway through). The foreach statement recognizes this detail and translates the following:

```
foreach (var element in somethingEnumerable) { ... }
```

into the logical equivalent of this:

```
using (var rator = somethingEnumerable.GetEnumerator())
  while (rator.MoveNext())
  {
    var element = rator.Current;
    ...
  }
```

When to Use the Nongeneric Interfaces

Given the extra type safety of the generic collection interfaces such as IEnumerable<T>, the question arises: do you ever need to use the nongeneric IEnumerable (or ICollection or IList)?

In the case of IEnumerable, you must implement this interface in conjunction with IEnumerable<T>—because the latter derives from the former. However, it's very rare that you actually implement these interfaces from scratch: in nearly all cases, you can take the higher-level approach of using iterator methods, Collection<T>, and LINQ.

So, what about as a consumer? In nearly all cases, you can manage entirely with the generic interfaces. The nongeneric interfaces are still occasionally useful, though, in their ability to provide type unification for collections across all element types. The following method, for instance, counts elements in any collection *recursively*:

```
public static int Count (IEnumerable e)
{
  int count = 0;
  foreach (object element in e)
  {
    var subCollection = element as IEnumerable;
    if (subCollection != null)
      count += Count (subCollection);
    else
      count++;
  }
  return count;
}
```

Because C# offers covariance with generic interfaces, it might seem valid to have this method instead accept IEnumerable<object>. This, however, would fail with value-type elements and with legacy collections that don't implement IEnumerable<T>—an example is ControlCollection in Windows Forms.

(On a slight tangent, you might have noticed a potential bug in our example: *cyclic* references will cause infinite recursion and crash the method. We could fix this most easily with the use of a HashSet (see "HashSet<T> and SortedSet<T>" on page 370).

The using block ensures disposal—more on IDisposable in Chapter 12.

Implementing the Enumeration Interfaces

You might want to implement IEnumerable or IEnumerable<T> for one or more of the following reasons:

- To support the foreach statement
- To interoperate with anything expecting a standard collection
- To meet the requirements of a more sophisticated collection interface
- To support collection initializers

To implement IEnumerable/IEnumerable<T>, you must provide an enumerator. You can do this in one of three ways:

- If the class is "wrapping" another collection, by returning the wrapped collection's enumerator
- Via an iterator using yield return
- By instantiating your own IEnumerator/IEnumerator<T> implementation

You can also subclass an existing collection: Collection<T> is designed just for this purpose (see "Customizable Collections and Proxies" on page 378). Yet another approach is to use the LINQ query operators, which we cover in Chapter 8.

Returning another collection's enumerator is just a matter of calling GetEnumerator on the inner collection. However, this is viable only in the simplest scenarios in which the items in the inner collection are exactly what are required. A more flexible approach is to write an iterator, using C#'s yield return statement. An *iterator* is a C# language feature that assists in writing collections, in the same way the foreach statement assists in consuming collections. An iterator automatically handles the implementation of IEnumerable and IEnumerator—or their generic versions. Here's a simple example:

```
public class MyCollection : IEnumerable
{
  int[] data = { 1, 2, 3 };

  public IEnumerator GetEnumerator()
  {
    foreach (int i in data)
      yield return i;
  }
}
```

Notice the "black magic": GetEnumerator doesn't appear to return an enumerator at all! Upon parsing the yield return statement, the compiler writes a hidden nested enumerator class behind the scenes and then refactors GetEnumerator to instantiate and return that class. Iterators are powerful and simple (and are used extensively in the implementation of LINQ-to-Object's standard query operators).

Keeping with this approach, we can also implement the generic interface IEnumerable<T>:

```
public class MyGenCollection : IEnumerable<int>
{
  int[] data = { 1, 2, 3 };

  public IEnumerator<int> GetEnumerator()
  {
    foreach (int i in data)
      yield return i;
  }

  // Explicit implementation keeps it hidden:
  IEnumerator IEnumerable.GetEnumerator() => GetEnumerator();
}
```

Because IEnumerable<T> inherits from IEnumerable, we must implement both the generic and the nongeneric versions of GetEnumerator. In accordance with standard practice, we've implemented the nongeneric version explicitly. It can simply call the generic GetEnumerator because IEnumerator<T> inherits from IEnumerator.

The class we've just written would be suitable as a basis from which to write a more sophisticated collection. However, if we need nothing above a simple IEnumerable<T> implementation, the yield return statement allows for an easier variation. Rather than writing a class, you can move the iteration logic into a method returning a generic IEnumerable<T> and let the compiler take care of the rest. Here's an example:

```
public static IEnumerable <int> GetSomeIntegers()
{
  yield return 1;
  yield return 2;
  yield return 3;
}
```

Here's our method in use:

```
foreach (int i in Test.GetSomeIntegers())
  Console.WriteLine (i);
```

The final approach in writing GetEnumerator is to write a class that implements IEnumerator directly. This is exactly what the compiler does behind the scenes, in resolving iterators. (Fortunately, it's rare that you'll need to go this far yourself.) The following example defines a collection that's hardcoded to contain the integers 1, 2, and 3:

```
public class MyIntList : IEnumerable
{
  int[] data = { 1, 2, 3 };

  public IEnumerator GetEnumerator() => new Enumerator (this);

  class Enumerator : IEnumerator       // Define an inner class
  {                                    // for the enumerator.
    MyIntList collection;
    int currentIndex = -1;

    public Enumerator (MyIntList items) => this.collection = items;

    public object Current
    {
      get
      {
        if (currentIndex == -1)
          throw new InvalidOperationException ("Enumeration not started!");
        if (currentIndex == collection.data.Length)
          throw new InvalidOperationException ("Past end of list!");
        return collection.data [currentIndex];
      }
    }

    public bool MoveNext()
```

```
  {
    if (currentIndex >= collection.data.Length - 1) return false;
    return ++currentIndex < collection.data.Length;
  }

  public void Reset() => currentIndex = -1;
  }
}
```

 Implementing Reset is optional—you can instead throw a NotSupportedException.

Note that the first call to MoveNext should move to the first (and not the second) item in the list.

To get on par with an iterator in functionality, we must also implement IEnumerator<T>. Here's an example with bounds checking omitted for brevity:

```
class MyIntList : IEnumerable<int>
{
  int[] data = { 1, 2, 3 };

  // The generic enumerator is compatible with both IEnumerable and
  // IEnumerable<T>. We implement the nongeneric GetEnumerator method
  // explicitly to avoid a naming conflict.

  public IEnumerator<int> GetEnumerator() => new Enumerator(this);
  IEnumerator IEnumerable.GetEnumerator() => new Enumerator(this);

  class Enumerator : IEnumerator<int>
  {
    int currentIndex = -1;
    MyIntList collection;

    public Enumerator (MyIntList items) => this.items = items;

    public int Current => collection.data [currentIndex];
    object IEnumerator.Current => Current;

    public bool MoveNext() => ++currentIndex < collection.data.Length;

    public void Reset() => currentIndex = -1;

    // Given we don't need a Dispose method, it's good practice to
    // implement it explicitly, so it's hidden from the public interface.
    void IDisposable.Dispose() {}
  }
}
```

The example with generics is faster because IEnumerator<int>.Current doesn't require casting from int to object and so avoids the overhead of boxing.

The ICollection and IList Interfaces

Although the enumeration interfaces provide a protocol for forward-only iteration over a collection, they don't provide a mechanism to determine the size of the collection, access a member by index, search, or modify the collection. For such functionality, .NET defines the ICollection, IList, and IDictionary interfaces. Each comes in both generic and nongeneric versions; however, the nongeneric versions exist mostly for legacy support.

Figure 7-1 showed the inheritance hierarchy for these interfaces. The easiest way to summarize them is as follows:

IEnumerable<T> *(and* IEnumerable)
    Provides minimum functionality (enumeration only)

ICollection<T> *(and* ICollection)
    Provides medium functionality (e.g., the Count property)

IList<T>/IDictionary<K,V> *and their nongeneric versions*
    Provide maximum functionality (including "random" access by index/key)

It's rare that you'll need to *implement* any of these interfaces. In nearly all cases when you need to write a collection class, you can instead subclass Collection<T> (see "Customizable Collections and Proxies" on page 378). LINQ provides yet another option that covers many scenarios.

The generic and nongeneric versions differ in ways over and above what you might expect, particularly in the case of ICollection. The reasons for this are mostly historical: because generics came later, the generic interfaces were developed with the benefit of hindsight, leading to a different (and better) choice of members. For this reason, ICollection<T> does not extend ICollection, IList<T> does not extend IList, and IDictionary<TKey, TValue> does not extend IDictionary. Of course, a collection class itself is free to implement both versions of an interface if beneficial (which it often is).

Another, subtler reason for IList<T> not extending IList is that casting to IList<T> would then return an interface with both Add(T) and Add(object) members. This would effectively defeat static type safety because you could call Add with an object of any type.

This section covers ICollection<T>, IList<T>, and their nongeneric versions; "Dictionaries" on page 372 covers the dictionary interfaces.

There is no *consistent* rationale in the way the words *col-lection* and *list* are applied throughout the .NET libraries. For instance, because IList<T> is a more functional version of ICollection<T>, you might expect the class List<T> to be correspondingly more functional than the class Collec tion<T>. This is not the case. It's best to consider the terms *collection* and *list* as broadly synonymous, except when a specific type is involved.

ICollection<T> and ICollection

ICollection<T> is the standard interface for countable collections of objects. It provides the ability to determine the size of a collection (Count), determine whether an item exists in the collection (Contains), copy the collection into an array (ToArray), and determine whether the collection is read-only (IsReadOnly). For writable collections, you can also Add, Remove, and Clear items from the collection. And because it extends IEnumerable<T>, it can also be traversed via the foreach statement:

```
public interface ICollection<T> : IEnumerable<T>, IEnumerable
{
  int Count { get; }

  bool Contains (T item);
  void CopyTo (T[] array, int arrayIndex);
  bool IsReadOnly { get; }

  void Add(T item);
  bool Remove (T item);
  void Clear();
}
```

The nongeneric ICollection is similar in providing a countable collection, but it doesn't provide functionality for altering the list or checking for element membership:

```
public interface ICollection : IEnumerable
{
    int Count { get; }
    bool IsSynchronized { get; }
    object SyncRoot { get; }
    void CopyTo (Array array, int index);
}
```

The nongeneric interface also defines properties to assist with synchronization (Chapter 14)—these were dumped in the generic version because thread safety is no longer considered intrinsic to the collection.

Both interfaces are fairly straightforward to implement. If implementing a read-only ICollection<T>, the Add, Remove, and Clear methods should throw a NotSuppor tedException.

These interfaces are usually implemented in conjunction with either the IList or the IDictionary interface.

IList<T> and IList

IList<T> is the standard interface for collections indexable by position. In addition to the functionality inherited from ICollection<T> and IEnumerable<T>, it provides the ability to read or write an element by position (via an indexer) and insert/remove by position:

```
public interface IList<T> : ICollection<T>, IEnumerable<T>, IEnumerable
{
  T this [int index] { get; set; }
  int IndexOf (T item);
  void Insert (int index, T item);
  void RemoveAt (int index);
}
```

The IndexOf methods perform a linear search on the list, returning −1 if the specified item is not found.

The nongeneric version of IList has more members because it inherits less from ICollection:

```
public interface IList : ICollection, IEnumerable
{
  object this [int index] { get; set }
  bool IsFixedSize { get; }
  bool IsReadOnly { get; }
  int  Add      (object value);
  void Clear();
  bool Contains (object value);
  int  IndexOf  (object value);
  void Insert   (int index, object value);
  void Remove   (object value);
  void RemoveAt (int index);
}
```

The Add method on the nongeneric IList interface returns an integer—this is the index of the newly added item. In contrast, the Add method on ICollection<T> has a void return type.

The general-purpose List<T> class is the quintessential implementation of both IList<T> and IList. C# arrays also implement both the generic and nongeneric ILists (although the methods that add or remove elements are hidden via explicit interface implementation and throw a NotSupportedException if called).

An `ArgumentException` is thrown if you try to access a multidimensional array via `IList`'s indexer. This is a trap when writing methods such as the following:

```
public object FirstOrNull (IList list)
{
  if (list == null || list.Count == 0) return null;
  return list[0];
}
```

This might appear bulletproof, but it will throw an exception if called with a multidimensional array. You can test for a multidimensional array at runtime with this expression (more on this in Chapter 19):

```
list.GetType().IsArray && list.GetType().GetArrayRank()>1
```

IReadOnlyCollection<T> and IReadOnlyList<T>

.NET also defines collection and list interfaces that expose just the members required for read-only operations:

```
public interface IReadOnlyCollection<out T> : IEnumerable<T>, IEnumerable
{
  int Count { get; }
}

public interface IReadOnlyList<out T> : IReadOnlyCollection<T>,
                                        IEnumerable<T>, IEnumerable
{
  T this[int index] { get; }
}
```

Because the type parameter for these interfaces is used only in output positions, it's marked as *covariant*. This allows a list of cats, for instance, to be treated as a read-only list of animals. In contrast, T is not marked as covariant with `ICollection<T>` and `IList<T>`, because T is used in both input and output positions.

These interfaces represent a read-only *view* of a collection or list; the underlying implementation might still be writable. Most of the writable (*mutable*) collections implement both the read-only and read/write interfaces.

In addition to letting you work with collections covariantly, the read-only interfaces allow a class to publicly expose a read-only view of a private writable collection. We demonstrate this—along with a better solution—in "ReadOnlyCollection<T>" on page 383.

`IReadOnlyList<T>` maps to the Windows Runtime type `IVectorView<T>`.

The Array Class

The Array class is the implicit base class for all single and multidimensional arrays, and it is one of the most fundamental types implementing the standard collection interfaces. The Array class provides type unification, so a common set of methods is available to all arrays, regardless of their declaration or underlying element type.

Because arrays are so fundamental, C# provides explicit syntax for their declaration and initialization, which we described in Chapters 2 and 3. When an array is declared using C#'s syntax, the CLR implicitly subtypes the Array class —synthesizing a *pseudotype* appropriate to the array's dimensions and element types. This pseudotype implements the typed generic collection interfaces, such as IList<string>.

The CLR also treats array types specially upon construction, assigning them a contiguous space in memory. This makes indexing into arrays highly efficient, but prevents them from being resized later on.

Array implements the collection interfaces up to IList<T> in both their generic and nongeneric forms. IList<T> itself is implemented explicitly, though, to keep Array's public interface clean of methods such as Add or Remove, which throw an exception on fixed-length collections such as arrays. The Array class does actually offer a static Resize method, although this works by creating a new array and then copying over each element. As well as being inefficient, references to the array elsewhere in the program will still point to the original version. A better solution for resizable collections is to use the List<T> class (described in the following section).

An array can contain value-type or reference-type elements. Value-type elements are stored in place in the array, so an array of three long integers (each 8 bytes) will occupy 24 bytes of contiguous memory. A reference type element, however, occupies only as much space in the array as a reference (4 bytes in a 32-bit environment or 8 bytes in a 64-bit environment). Figure 7-2 illustrates the effect, in memory, of the following program:

```
StringBuilder[] builders = new StringBuilder [5];
builders [0] = new StringBuilder ("builder1");
builders [1] = new StringBuilder ("builder2");
builders [2] = new StringBuilder ("builder3");

long[] numbers = new long [3];
numbers [0] = 12345;
numbers [1] = 54321;
```

Collections

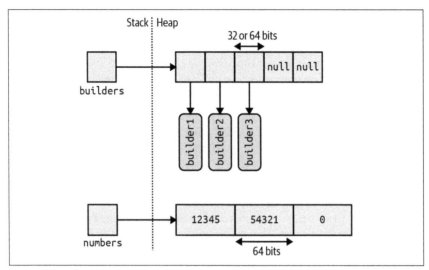

Figure 7-2. Arrays in memory

Because `Array` is a class, arrays are always (themselves) reference types—regardless of the array's element type. This means that the statement `arrayB = arrayA` results in two variables that reference the same array. Similarly, two distinct arrays will always fail an equality test, unless you employ a *structural equality comparer*, which compares every element of the array:

```
object[] a1 = { "string", 123, true };
object[] a2 = { "string", 123, true };

Console.WriteLine (a1 == a2);                          // False
Console.WriteLine (a1.Equals (a2));                    // False

IStructuralEquatable se1 = a1;
Console.WriteLine (se1.Equals (a2,
  StructuralComparisons.StructuralEqualityComparer));  // True
```

Arrays can be duplicated by calling the `Clone` method: `arrayB = arrayA.Clone()`. However, this results in a shallow clone, meaning that only the memory represented by the array itself is copied. If the array contains value-type objects, the values themselves are copied; if the array contains reference type objects, just the references are copied (resulting in two arrays whose members reference the same objects). Figure 7-3 demonstrates the effect of adding the following code to our example:

```
StringBuilder[] builders2 = builders;
StringBuilder[] shallowClone = (StringBuilder[]) builders.Clone();
```

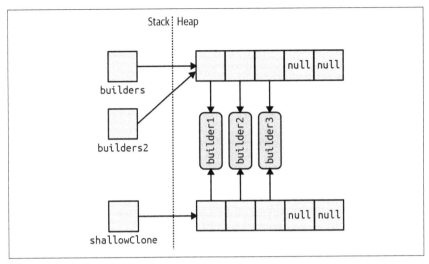

Figure 7-3. Shallow-cloning an array

To create a deep copy—for which reference type subobjects are duplicated—you must loop through the array and clone each element manually. The same rules apply to other .NET collection types.

Although `Array` is designed primarily for use with 32-bit indexers, it also has limited support for 64-bit indexers (allowing an array to theoretically address up to 2^{64} elements) via several methods that accept both `Int32` and `Int64` parameters. These overloads are useless in practice because the CLR does not permit any object—including arrays—to exceed two gigabytes in size (whether running on a 32- or 64-bit environment).

 Many of the methods on the `Array` class that you expect to be instance methods are in fact static methods. This is an odd design decision, and means that you should check for both static and instance methods when looking for a method on `Array`.

Construction and Indexing

The easiest way to create and index arrays is through C#'s language constructs:

```
int[] myArray = { 1, 2, 3 };
int first = myArray [0];
int last = myArray [myArray.Length - 1];
```

Alternatively, you can instantiate an array dynamically by calling `Array.Create Instance`. This allows you to specify element type and rank (number of dimensions) at runtime as well as allowing nonzero-based arrays through specifying a lower bound. Nonzero-based arrays are not compatible with the .NET Common

Language Specification (CLS) and should not be exposed as public members in a library that might be consumed by a program written in F# or Visual Basic.

The GetValue and SetValue methods let you access elements in a dynamically created array (they also work on ordinary arrays):

```
// Create a string array 2 elements in length:
Array a = Array.CreateInstance (typeof(string), 2);
a.SetValue ("hi", 0);                       //  → a[0] = "hi";
a.SetValue ("there", 1);                    //  → a[1] = "there";
string s = (string) a.GetValue (0);         //  → s = a[0];

// We can also cast to a C# array as follows:
string[] cSharpArray = (string[]) a;
string s2 = cSharpArray [0];
```

Zero-indexed arrays created dynamically can be cast to a C# array of a matching or compatible type (compatible by standard array-variance rules). For example, if Apple subclasses Fruit, Apple[] can be cast to Fruit[]. This leads to the issue of why object[] was not used as the unifying array type rather than the Array class. The answer is that object[] is incompatible with both multidimensional and value-type arrays (and nonzero-based arrays). An int[] array cannot be cast to object[]. Hence, we require the Array class for full type unification.

GetValue and SetValue also work on compiler-created arrays, and they are useful when writing methods that can deal with an array of any type and rank. For multidimensional arrays, they accept an *array* of indexers:

```
public object GetValue (params int[] indices)
public void    SetValue (object value, params int[] indices)
```

The following method prints the first element of any array, regardless of rank:

```
void WriteFirstValue (Array a)
{
  Console.Write (a.Rank + "-dimensional; ");

  // The indexers array will automatically initialize to all zeros, so
  // passing it into GetValue or SetValue will get/set the zero-based
  // (i.e., first) element in the array.

  int[] indexers = new int[a.Rank];
  Console.WriteLine ("First value is " + a.GetValue (indexers));
}

void Demo()
{
  int[]  oneD = { 1, 2, 3 };
  int[,] twoD = { {5,6}, {8,9} };

  WriteFirstValue (oneD);    // 1-dimensional; first value is 1
  WriteFirstValue (twoD);    // 2-dimensional; first value is 5
}
```

For working with arrays of unknown type but known rank, generics provide an easier and more efficient solution:

```
void WriteFirstValue<T> (T[] array)
{
  Console.WriteLine (array[0]);
}
```

SetValue throws an exception if the element is of an incompatible type for the array.

When an array is instantiated, whether via language syntax or Array.CreateIn stance, its elements are automatically initialized. For arrays with reference type elements, this means writing nulls; for arrays with value-type elements, this means calling the value-type's default constructor (effectively "zeroing" the members). The Array class also provides this functionality on demand via the Clear method:

```
public static void Clear (Array array, int index, int length);
```

This method doesn't affect the size of the array. This is in contrast to the usual use of Clear (such as in ICollection<T>.Clear) whereby the collection is reduced to zero elements.

Enumeration

Arrays are easily enumerated with a foreach statement:

```
int[] myArray = { 1, 2, 3};
foreach (int val in myArray)
  Console.WriteLine (val);
```

You can also enumerate using the static Array.ForEach method, defined as follows:

```
public static void ForEach<T> (T[] array, Action<T> action);
```

This uses an Action delegate, with this signature:

```
public delegate void Action<T> (T obj);
```

Here's the first example rewritten with Array.ForEach:

```
Array.ForEach (new[] { 1, 2, 3 }, Console.WriteLine);
```

Length and Rank

Array provides the following methods and properties for querying length and rank:

```
public int  GetLength      (int dimension);
public long GetLongLength  (int dimension);

public int  Length         { get; }
public long LongLength      { get; }

public int GetLowerBound (int dimension);
public int GetUpperBound (int dimension);

public int Rank { get; }     // Returns number of dimensions in array
```

GetLength and GetLongLength return the length for a given dimension (0 for a single-dimensional array), and Length and LongLength return the total number of elements in the array—all dimensions included.

GetLowerBound and GetUpperBound are useful with nonzero indexed arrays. Get UpperBound returns the same result as adding GetLowerBound to GetLength for any given dimension.

Searching

The Array class offers a range of methods for finding elements within a one-dimensional array:

BinarySearch *methods*
> For rapidly searching a sorted array for a particular item

IndexOf/LastIndex *methods*
> For searching unsorted arrays for a particular item

Find/FindLast/FindIndex/FindLastIndex/FindAll/Exists/TrueForAll
> For searching unsorted arrays for item(s) that satisfy a given Predicate<T>

None of the array searching methods throws an exception if the specified value is not found. Instead, if an item is not found, methods returning an integer return –1 (assuming a zero-indexed array), and methods returning a generic type return the type's default value (e.g., 0 for an int, or null for a string).

The binary search methods are fast, but they work only on sorted arrays and require that the elements be compared for *order* rather than simply *equality*. To this effect, the binary search methods can accept an IComparer or IComparer<T> object to arbitrate on ordering decisions (see "Plugging in Equality and Order" on page 388). This must be consistent with any comparer used in originally sorting the array. If no comparer is provided, the type's default ordering algorithm will be applied based on its implementation of IComparable / IComparable<T>.

The IndexOf and LastIndexOf methods perform a simple enumeration over the array, returning the position of the first (or last) element that matches the given value.

The predicate-based searching methods allow a method delegate or lambda expression to arbitrate on whether a given element is a "match." A predicate is simply a delegate accepting an object and returning true or false:

```
public delegate bool Predicate<T> (T object);
```

In the following example, we search an array of strings for a name containing the letter "a":

```
string[] names = { "Rodney", "Jack", "Jill" };
string match = Array.Find (names, ContainsA);
Console.WriteLine (match);     // Jack
```

```
ContainsA (string name) { return name.Contains ("a"); }
```

Here's the same code shortened with a lambda expression:

```
string[] names = { "Rodney", "Jack", "Jill" };
string match = Array.Find (names, n => n.Contains ("a"));      // Jack
```

FindAll returns an array of all items satisfying the predicate. In fact, it's equivalent to Enumerable.Where in the System.Linq namespace, except that FindAll returns an array of matching items rather than an IEnumerable<T> of the same.

Exists returns true if any array member satisfies the given predicate, and is equivalent to Any in System.Linq.Enumerable.

TrueForAll returns true if all items satisfy the predicate, and is equivalent to All in System.Linq.Enumerable.

Sorting

Array has the following built-in sorting methods:

```
// For sorting a single array:

public static void Sort<T> (T[] array);
public static void Sort    (Array array);

// For sorting a pair of arrays:

public static void Sort<TKey,TValue> (TKey[] keys, TValue[] items);
public static void Sort              (Array keys, Array items);
```

Each of these methods is additionally overloaded to also accept the following:

```
int index                    // Starting index at which to begin sorting
int length                   // Number of elements to sort
IComparer<T> comparer        // Object making ordering decisions
Comparison<T> comparison     // Delegate making ordering decisions
```

The following illustrates the simplest use of Sort:

```
int[] numbers = { 3, 2, 1 };
Array.Sort (numbers);                        // Array is now { 1, 2, 3 }
```

The methods accepting a pair of arrays work by rearranging the items of each array in tandem, basing the ordering decisions on the first array. In the next example, both the numbers and their corresponding words are sorted into numerical order:

```
int[] numbers = { 3, 2, 1 };
string[] words = { "three", "two", "one" };
Array.Sort (numbers, words);

// numbers array is now { 1, 2, 3 }
// words   array is now { "one", "two", "three" }
```

`Array.Sort` requires that the elements in the array implement `IComparable` (see "Order Comparison" on page 335). This means that most built-in C# types (such as integers, as in the preceding example) can be sorted. If the elements are not intrinsically comparable or you want to override the default ordering, you must provide `Sort` with a custom `comparison` provider that reports on the relative position of two elements. There are ways to do this:

- Via a helper object that implements `IComparer` /`IComparer<T>` (see "Plugging in Equality and Order" on page 388)
- Via a `Comparison` delegate:

  ```
  public delegate int Comparison<T> (T x, T y);
  ```

The `Comparison` delegate follows the same semantics as `IComparer<T>.CompareTo`: if x comes before y, a negative integer is returned; if x comes after y, a positive integer is returned; if x and y have the same sorting position, 0 is returned.

In the following example, we sort an array of integers such that the odd numbers come first:

```
int[] numbers = { 1, 2, 3, 4, 5 };
Array.Sort (numbers, (x, y) => x % 2 == y % 2 ? 0 : x % 2 == 1 ? -1 : 1);

// numbers array is now { 1, 3, 5, 2, 4 }
```

 As an alternative to calling `Sort`, you can use LINQ's `OrderBy` and `ThenBy` operators. Unlike `Array.Sort`, the LINQ operators don't alter the original array, instead emitting the sorted result in a fresh `IEnumerable<T>` sequence.

Reversing Elements

The following `Array` methods reverse the order of all—or a portion of—elements in an array:

```
public static void Reverse (Array array);
public static void Reverse (Array array, int index, int length);
```

Copying

`Array` provides four methods to perform shallow copying: `Clone`, `CopyTo`, `Copy`, and `ConstrainedCopy`. The former two are instance methods; the latter two are static methods.

The `Clone` method returns a whole new (shallow-copied) array. The `CopyTo` and `Copy` methods copy a contiguous subset of the array. Copying a multidimensional rectangular array requires you to map the multidimensional index to a linear index. For example, the middle square (`position[1,1]`) in a 3 × 3 array is represented with the index 4, from the calculation: 1 * 3 + 1. The source and destination ranges can overlap without causing a problem.

ConstrainedCopy performs an *atomic* operation: if all of the requested elements cannot be successfully copied (due to a type error, for instance), the operation is rolled back.

Array also provides an AsReadOnly method that returns a wrapper that prevents elements from being reassigned.

Converting and Resizing

Array.ConvertAll creates and returns a new array of element type TOutput, calling the supplied Converter delegate to copy over the elements. Converter is defined as follows:

```
public delegate TOutput Converter<TInput,TOutput> (TInput input)
```

The following converts an array of floats to an array of integers:

```
float[] reals = { 1.3f, 1.5f, 1.8f };
int[] wholes = Array.ConvertAll (reals, r => Convert.ToInt32 (r));

// wholes array is { 1, 2, 2 }
```

The Resize method works by creating a new array and copying over the elements, returning the new array via the reference parameter. However, any references to the original array in other objects will remain unchanged.

> The System.Linq namespace offers an additional buffet of extension methods suitable for array conversion. These methods return an IEnumerable<T>, which you can convert back to an array via Enumerable's ToArray method.

Lists, Queues, Stacks, and Sets

.NET provides a basic set of concrete collection classes that implement the interfaces described in this chapter. This section concentrates on the *list-like* collections (versus the *dictionary-like* collections, which we cover in "Dictionaries" on page 372). As with the interfaces we discussed previously, you usually have a choice of generic or nongeneric versions of each type. In terms of flexibility and performance, the generic classes win, making their nongeneric counterparts redundant except for backward compatibility. This differs from the situation with collection interfaces, for which the nongeneric versions are still occasionally useful.

Of the classes described in this section, the generic List class is the most commonly used.

List<T> and ArrayList

The generic List and nongeneric ArrayList classes provide a dynamically sized array of objects and are among the most commonly used of the collection classes. ArrayList implements IList, whereas List<T> implements both IList and IList<T> (and the read-only version, IReadOnlyList<T>). Unlike with arrays, all interfaces are implemented publicly, and methods such as Add and Remove are exposed and work as you would expect.

Internally, List<T> and ArrayList work by maintaining an internal array of objects, replaced with a larger array upon reaching capacity. Appending elements is efficient (because there is usually a free slot at the end), but inserting elements can be slow (because all elements after the insertion point must be shifted to make a free slot), as can removing elements (especially near the start). As with arrays, searching is efficient if the BinarySearch method is used on a list that has been sorted, but it is otherwise inefficient because each item must be individually checked.

 List<T> is up to several times faster than ArrayList if T is a value type, because List<T> avoids the overhead of boxing and unboxing elements.

List<T> and ArrayList provide constructors that accept an existing collection of elements: these copy each element from the existing collection into the new List<T> or ArrayList:

```
public class List<T> : IList<T>, IReadOnlyList<T>
{
  public List ();
  public List (IEnumerable<T> collection);
  public List (int capacity);

  // Add+Insert
  public void Add          (T item);
  public void AddRange     (IEnumerable<T> collection);
  public void Insert       (int index, T item);
  public void InsertRange  (int index, IEnumerable<T> collection);

  // Remove
  public bool Remove       (T item);
  public void RemoveAt     (int index);
  public void RemoveRange  (int index, int count);
  public int  RemoveAll    (Predicate<T> match);

  // Indexing
  public T this [int index] { get; set; }
  public List<T> GetRange (int index, int count);
  public Enumerator<T> GetEnumerator();

  // Exporting, copying and converting:
  public T[] ToArray();
  public void CopyTo (T[] array);
  public void CopyTo (T[] array, int arrayIndex);
  public void CopyTo (int index, T[] array, int arrayIndex, int count);
  public ReadOnlyCollection<T> AsReadOnly();
  public List<TOutput> ConvertAll<TOutput> (Converter <T,TOutput>
                                                  converter);
  // Other:
  public void Reverse();              // Reverses order of elements in list.
  public int Capacity { get;set; }   // Forces expansion of internal array.
```

```
    public void TrimExcess();         // Trims internal array back to size.
    public void Clear();              // Removes all elements, so Count=0.
}

public delegate TOutput Converter <TInput, TOutput> (TInput input);
```

In addition to these members, List<T> provides instance versions of all of Array's searching and sorting methods.

The following code demonstrates List's properties and methods (for examples on searching and sorting, see "The Array Class" on page 355):

```
var words = new List<string>();     // New string-typed list

words.Add ("melon");
words.Add ("avocado");
words.AddRange (new[] { "banana", "plum" } );
words.Insert (0, "lemon");                          // Insert at start
words.InsertRange (0, new[] { "peach", "nashi" });  // Insert at start

words.Remove ("melon");
words.RemoveAt (3);                        // Remove the 4th element
words.RemoveRange (0, 2);                   // Remove first 2 elements

// Remove all strings starting in 'n':
words.RemoveAll (s => s.StartsWith ("n"));

Console.WriteLine (words [0]);                      // first word
Console.WriteLine (words [words.Count - 1]);        // last word
foreach (string s in words) Console.WriteLine (s);  // all words
List<string> subset = words.GetRange (1, 2);        // 2nd->3rd words

string[] wordsArray = words.ToArray();     // Creates a new typed array

// Copy first two elements to the end of an existing array:
string[] existing = new string [1000];
words.CopyTo (0, existing, 998, 2);

List<string> upperCaseWords = words.ConvertAll (s => s.ToUpper());
List<int> lengths = words.ConvertAll (s => s.Length);
```

The nongeneric ArrayList class requires clumsy casts—as the following example demonstrates:

```
ArrayList al = new ArrayList();
al.Add ("hello");
string first = (string) al [0];
string[] strArr = (string[]) al.ToArray (typeof (string));
```

Such casts cannot be verified by the compiler; the following compiles successfully but then fails at runtime:

```
int first = (int) al [0];     // Runtime exception
```

An `ArrayList` is functionally similar to `List<object>`. Both are useful when you need a list of mixed-type elements that share no common base type (other than `object`). A possible advantage of choosing an `ArrayList`, in this case, would be if you need to deal with the list using reflection (Chapter 19). Reflection is easier with a nongeneric `ArrayList` than a `List<object>`.

If you import the `System.Linq` namespace, you can convert an `ArrayList` to a generic `List` by calling `Cast` and then `ToList`:

```
ArrayList al = new ArrayList();
al.AddRange (new[] { 1, 5, 9 } );
List<int> list = al.Cast<int>().ToList();
```

`Cast` and `ToList` are extension methods in the `System.Linq.Enumerable` class.

LinkedList<T>

`LinkedList<T>` is a generic doubly linked list (see Figure 7-4). A doubly linked list is a chain of nodes in which each references the node before, the node after, and the actual element. Its main benefit is that an element can always be inserted efficiently anywhere in the list because it just involves creating a new node and updating a few references. However, finding where to insert the node in the first place can be slow because there's no intrinsic mechanism to index directly into a linked list; each node must be traversed, and binary-chop searches are not possible.

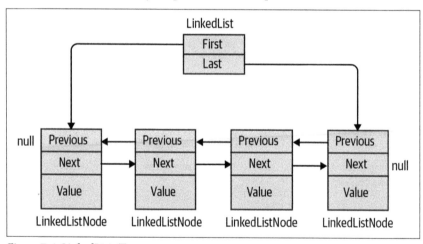

Figure 7-4. LinkedList<T>

`LinkedList<T>` implements `IEnumerable<T>` and `ICollection<T>` (and their nongeneric versions), but not `IList<T>` because access by index is not supported. List nodes are implemented via the following class:

```
public sealed class LinkedListNode<T>
{
  public LinkedList<T> List { get; }
  public LinkedListNode<T> Next { get; }
  public LinkedListNode<T> Previous { get; }
  public T Value { get; set; }
}
```

When adding a node, you can specify its position either relative to another node or at the start/end of the list. LinkedList<T> provides the following methods for this:

```
public void AddFirst(LinkedListNode<T> node);
public LinkedListNode<T> AddFirst (T value);

public void AddLast (LinkedListNode<T> node);
public LinkedListNode<T> AddLast (T value);

public void AddAfter (LinkedListNode<T> node, LinkedListNode<T> newNode);
public LinkedListNode<T> AddAfter (LinkedListNode<T> node, T value);

public void AddBefore (LinkedListNode<T> node, LinkedListNode<T> newNode);
public LinkedListNode<T> AddBefore (LinkedListNode<T> node, T value);
```

Similar methods are provided to remove elements:

```
public void Clear();

public void RemoveFirst();
public void RemoveLast();

public bool Remove (T value);
public void Remove (LinkedListNode<T> node);
```

LinkedList<T> has internal fields to keep track of the number of elements in the list as well as the head and tail of the list. These are exposed in the following public properties:

```
public int Count { get; }                    // Fast
public LinkedListNode<T> First { get; }      // Fast
public LinkedListNode<T> Last { get; }       // Fast
```

LinkedList<T> also supports the following searching methods (each requiring that the list be internally enumerated):

```
public bool Contains (T value);
public LinkedListNode<T> Find (T value);
public LinkedListNode<T> FindLast (T value);
```

Finally, LinkedList<T> supports copying to an array for indexed processing and obtaining an enumerator to support the foreach statement:

```
public void CopyTo (T[] array, int index);
public Enumerator<T> GetEnumerator();
```

Here's a demonstration on the use of `LinkedList<string>`:

```
var tune = new LinkedList<string>();
tune.AddFirst ("do");                            // do
tune.AddLast ("so");                             // do - so

tune.AddAfter (tune.First, "re");                // do - re- so
tune.AddAfter (tune.First.Next, "mi");           // do - re - mi- so
tune.AddBefore (tune.Last, "fa");                // do - re - mi - fa- so

tune.RemoveFirst();                              // re - mi - fa - so
tune.RemoveLast();                               // re - mi - fa

LinkedListNode<string> miNode = tune.Find ("mi");
tune.Remove (miNode);                            // re - fa
tune.AddFirst (miNode);                          // mi- re - fa

foreach (string s in tune) Console.WriteLine (s);
```

Queue<T> and Queue

`Queue<T>` and `Queue` are first-in, first-out (FIFO) data structures, providing methods to `Enqueue` (add an item to the tail of the queue) and `Dequeue` (retrieve and remove the item at the head of the queue). A `Peek` method is also provided to return the element at the head of the queue without removing it, as well as a `Count` property (useful in checking that elements are present before dequeuing).

Although queues are enumerable, they do not implement `IList<T>`/`IList`, because members cannot be accessed directly by index. A `ToArray` method is provided, however, for copying the elements to an array from which they can be randomly accessed:

```
public class Queue<T> : IEnumerable<T>, ICollection, IEnumerable
{
  public Queue();
  public Queue (IEnumerable<T> collection);    // Copies existing elements
  public Queue (int capacity);                 // To lessen auto-resizing
  public void Clear();
  public bool Contains (T item);
  public void CopyTo (T[] array, int arrayIndex);
  public int Count { get; }
  public T Dequeue();
  public void Enqueue (T item);
  public Enumerator<T> GetEnumerator();        // To support foreach
  public T Peek();
  public T[] ToArray();
  public void TrimExcess();
}
```

The following is an example of using `Queue<int>`:

```
var q = new Queue<int>();
q.Enqueue (10);
q.Enqueue (20);
```

```
int[] data = q.ToArray();         // Exports to an array
Console.WriteLine (q.Count);      // "2"
Console.WriteLine (q.Peek());     // "10"
Console.WriteLine (q.Dequeue());  // "10"
Console.WriteLine (q.Dequeue());  // "20"
Console.WriteLine (q.Dequeue());  // throws an exception (queue empty)
```

Queues are implemented internally using an array that's resized as required—much like the generic List class. The queue maintains indexes that point directly to the head and tail elements; therefore, enqueuing and dequeuing are extremely quick operations (except when an internal resize is required).

Stack<T> and Stack

Stack<T> and Stack are last-in, first-out (LIFO) data structures, providing methods to Push (add an item to the top of the stack) and Pop (retrieve and remove an element from the top of the stack). A nondestructive Peek method is also provided, as is a Count property and a ToArray method for exporting the data for random access:

```
public class Stack<T> : IEnumerable<T>, ICollection, IEnumerable
{
  public Stack();
  public Stack (IEnumerable<T> collection);   // Copies existing elements
  public Stack (int capacity);                // Lessens auto-resizing
  public void Clear();
  public bool Contains (T item);
  public void CopyTo (T[] array, int arrayIndex);
  public int Count { get; }
  public Enumerator<T> GetEnumerator();       // To support foreach
  public T Peek();
  public T Pop();
  public void Push (T item);
  public T[] ToArray();
  public void TrimExcess();
}
```

The following example demonstrates Stack<int>:

```
var s = new Stack<int>();
s.Push (1);                        //                Stack = 1
s.Push (2);                        //                Stack = 1,2
s.Push (3);                        //                Stack = 1,2,3
Console.WriteLine (s.Count);       // Prints 3
Console.WriteLine (s.Peek());      // Prints 3,  Stack = 1,2,3
Console.WriteLine (s.Pop());       // Prints 3,  Stack = 1,2
Console.WriteLine (s.Pop());       // Prints 2,  Stack = 1
Console.WriteLine (s.Pop());       // Prints 1,  Stack = <empty>
Console.WriteLine (s.Pop());       // throws exception
```

Stacks are implemented internally with an array that's resized as required, as with Queue<T> and List<T>.

BitArray

A `BitArray` is a dynamically sized collection of compacted `bool` values. It is more memory efficient than both a simple array of `bool` and a generic `List` of `bool` because it uses only one bit for each value, whereas the `bool` type otherwise occupies one byte for each value.

`BitArray`'s indexer reads and writes individual bits:

```
var bits = new BitArray(2);
bits[1] = true;
```

There are four bitwise operator methods (`And`, `Or`, `Xor`, and `Not`). All but the last accept another `BitArray`:

```
bits.Xor (bits);              // Bitwise exclusive-OR bits with itself
Console.WriteLine (bits[1]);   // False
```

HashSet<T> and SortedSet<T>

`HashSet<T>` and `SortedSet<T>` have the following distinguishing features:

- Their `Contains` methods execute quickly using a hash-based lookup.
- They do not store duplicate elements and silently ignore requests to add duplicates.
- You cannot access an element by position.

`SortedSet<T>` keeps elements in order, whereas `HashSet<T>` does not.

The commonality of the `HashSet<T>` and `SortedSet<T>` types is captured by the interface `ISet<T>`. From .NET 5, these classes also implement an interface called `IReadOnlySet<T>`, which is also implemented by the immutable set types (see "Immutable Collections" on page 384).

`HashSet<T>` is implemented with a hashtable that stores just keys; `SortedSet<T>` is implemented with a red/black tree.

Both collections implement `ICollection<T>` and offer methods that you would expect, such as `Contains`, `Add`, and `Remove`. In addition, there's a predicate-based removal method called `RemoveWhere`.

The following constructs a `HashSet<char>` from an existing collection, tests for membership, and then enumerates the collection (notice the absence of duplicates):

```
var letters = new HashSet<char> ("the quick brown fox");

Console.WriteLine (letters.Contains ('t'));   // true
Console.WriteLine (letters.Contains ('j'));   // false

foreach (char c in letters) Console.Write (c);   // the quickbrownfx
```

(The reason we can pass a string into HashSet<char>'s constructor is that string implements IEnumerable<char>.)

The really interesting methods are the set operations. The following set operations are *destructive* in that they modify the set:

```
public void UnionWith          (IEnumerable<T> other);    // Adds
public void IntersectWith      (IEnumerable<T> other);    // Removes
public void ExceptWith         (IEnumerable<T> other);    // Removes
public void SymmetricExceptWith (IEnumerable<T> other);   // Removes
```

whereas the following methods simply query the set and so are nondestructive:

```
public bool IsSubsetOf         (IEnumerable<T> other);
public bool IsProperSubsetOf   (IEnumerable<T> other);
public bool IsSupersetOf       (IEnumerable<T> other);
public bool IsProperSupersetOf (IEnumerable<T> other);
public bool Overlaps           (IEnumerable<T> other);
public bool SetEquals          (IEnumerable<T> other);
```

UnionWith adds all the elements in the second set to the original set (excluding duplicates). IntersectWith removes the elements that are not in both sets. We can extract all of the vowels from our set of characters as follows:

```
var letters = new HashSet<char> ("the quick brown fox");
letters.IntersectWith ("aeiou");
foreach (char c in letters) Console.Write (c);      // euio
```

ExceptWith removes the specified elements from the source set. Here, we strip all vowels from the set:

```
var letters = new HashSet<char> ("the quick brown fox");
letters.ExceptWith ("aeiou");
foreach (char c in letters) Console.Write (c);      // th qckbrwnfx
```

SymmetricExceptWith removes all but the elements that are unique to one set or the other:

```
var letters = new HashSet<char> ("the quick brown fox");
letters.SymmetricExceptWith ("the lazy brown fox");
foreach (char c in letters) Console.Write (c);      // quicklazy
```

Note that because HashSet<T> and SortedSet<T> implement IEnumerable<T>, you can use another type of set (or collection) as the argument to any of the set operation methods.

SortedSet<T> offers all the members of HashSet<T>, plus the following:

```
public virtual SortedSet<T> GetViewBetween (T lowerValue, T upperValue)
public IEnumerable<T> Reverse()
public T Min { get; }
public T Max { get; }
```

SortedSet<T> also accepts an optional IComparer<T> in its constructor (rather than an *equality comparer*).

Here's an example of loading the same letters into a `SortedSet<char>`:

```
var letters = new SortedSet<char> ("the quick brown fox");
foreach (char c in letters) Console.Write (c);    // bcefhiknoqrtuwx
```

Following on from this, we can obtain the letters in the set between *f* and *i* as follows:

```
foreach (char c in letters.GetViewBetween ('f', 'i'))
   Console.Write (c);                                   //  fhi
```

Dictionaries

A *dictionary* is a collection in which each element is a key/value pair. Dictionaries are most commonly used for lookups and sorted lists.

.NET defines a standard protocol for dictionaries, via the interfaces `IDictionary` and `IDictionary<TKey,TValue>`, as well as a set of general-purpose dictionary classes. The classes each differ in the following regard:

- Whether items are stored in sorted sequence
- Whether items can be accessed by position (index) as well as by key
- Whether generic or nongeneric
- Whether it's fast or slow to retrieve items by key from a large dictionary

Table 7-1 summarizes each of the dictionary classes and how they differ in these respects.

The performance times are in milliseconds and based on performing 50,000 operations on a dictionary with integer keys and values on a 1.5 GHz PC. (The differences in performance between generic and nongeneric counterparts using the same underlying collection structure are due to boxing, and show up only with value-type elements.)

Table 7-1. Dictionary classes

Type	Internal structure	Retrieve by index?	Memory overhead (avg. bytes per item)	Speed: random insertion	Speed: sequential insertion	Speed: retrieval by key
Unsorted						
Dictionary <K,V>	Hashtable	No	22	30	30	20
Hashtable	Hashtable	No	38	50	50	30
ListDictionary	Linked list	No	36	50,000	50,000	50,000
OrderedDictionary	Hashtable + array	Yes	59	70	70	40

Type	Internal structure	Retrieve by index?	Memory overhead (avg. bytes per item)	Speed: random insertion	Speed: sequential insertion	Speed: retrieval by key
Sorted						
SortedDictionary <K,V>	Red/black tree	No	20	130	100	120
SortedList <K,V>	2xArray	Yes	2	3,300	30	40
SortedList	2xArray	Yes	27	4,500	100	180

In Big-O notation, retrieval time by key is as follows:

- O(1) for Hashtable, Dictionary, and OrderedDictionary
- O(log n) for SortedDictionary and SortedList
- O(n) for ListDictionary (and nondictionary types such as List<T>)

n is the number of elements in the collection.

IDictionary<TKey,TValue>

IDictionary<TKey,TValue> defines the standard protocol for all key/value-based collections. It extends ICollection<T> by adding methods and properties to access elements based on a key of arbitrary type:

```
public interface IDictionary <TKey, TValue> :
  ICollection <KeyValuePair <TKey, TValue>>, IEnumerable
{
    bool ContainsKey (TKey key);
    bool TryGetValue (TKey key, out TValue value);
    void Add       (TKey key, TValue value);
    bool Remove    (TKey key);

    TValue this [TKey key]      { get; set; }  // Main indexer - by key
    ICollection <TKey> Keys     { get; }       // Returns just keys
    ICollection <TValue> Values { get; }       // Returns just values
}
```

 There's also an interface called IReadOnlyDiction ary<TKey,TValue>, which defines the read-only subset of dictionary members.

To add an item to a dictionary, you either call Add or use the index's set accessor— the latter adds an item to the dictionary if the key is not already present (or updates the item if it is present). Duplicate keys are forbidden in all dictionary implementations, so calling Add twice with the same key throws an exception.

To retrieve an item from a dictionary, use either the indexer or the `TryGetValue` method. If the key doesn't exist, the indexer throws an exception, whereas `TryGet Value` returns `false`. You can test for membership explicitly by calling `Contains Key`; however, this incurs the cost of two lookups if you then subsequently retrieve the item.

Enumerating directly over an `IDictionary<TKey,TValue>` returns a sequence of `KeyValuePair` structs:

```
public struct KeyValuePair <TKey, TValue>
{
  public TKey Key     { get; }
  public TValue Value { get; }
}
```

You can enumerate over just the keys or values via the dictionary's `Keys/Values` properties.

We demonstrate the use of this interface with the generic `Dictionary` class in the following section.

IDictionary

The nongeneric `IDictionary` interface is the same in principle as `IDiction ary<TKey,TValue>`, apart from two important functional differences. It's important to be aware of these differences, because `IDictionary` appears in legacy code (including the .NET BCL itself in places):

- Retrieving a nonexistent key via the indexer returns null (rather than throwing an exception).

- `Contains` tests for membership rather than `ContainsKey`.

Enumerating over a nongeneric `IDictionary` returns a sequence of `Dictionary Entry` structs:

```
public struct DictionaryEntry
{
  public object Key   { get; set; }
  public object Value { get; set; }
}
```

Dictionary<TKey,TValue> and Hashtable

The generic `Dictionary` class is one of the most commonly used collections (along with the `List<T>` collection). It uses a hashtable data structure to store keys and values, and it is fast and efficient.

> The nongeneric version of `Dictionary<TKey,TValue>` is called `Hashtable`; there is no nongeneric class called `Dictio nary`. When we refer simply to `Dictionary`, we mean the generic `Dictionary<TKey,TValue>` class.

`Dictionary` implements both the generic and nongeneric `IDictionary` interfaces, the generic `IDictionary` being exposed publicly. `Dictionary` is, in fact, a "textbook" implementation of the generic `IDictionary`.

Here's how to use it:

```
var d = new Dictionary<string, int>();

d.Add("One", 1);
d["Two"] = 2;      // adds to dictionary because "two" not already present
d["Two"] = 22;     // updates dictionary because "two" is now present
d["Three"] = 3;

Console.WriteLine (d["Two"]);            // Prints "22"
Console.WriteLine (d.ContainsKey ("One"));   // true (fast operation)
Console.WriteLine (d.ContainsValue (3));     // true (slow operation)
int val = 0;
if (!d.TryGetValue ("onE", out val))
  Console.WriteLine ("No val");          // "No val" (case sensitive)

// Three different ways to enumerate the dictionary:

foreach (KeyValuePair<string, int> kv in d)      //  One; 1
  Console.WriteLine (kv.Key + "; " + kv.Value);  //  Two; 22
                                                 //  Three; 3

foreach (string s in d.Keys) Console.Write (s);  // OneTwoThree
Console.WriteLine();
foreach (int i in d.Values) Console.Write (i);   // 1223
```

Its underlying hashtable works by converting each element's key into an integer hashcode—a pseudo-unique value—and then applying an algorithm to convert the hashcode into a hash key. This hash key is used internally to determine which "bucket" an entry belongs to. If the bucket contains more than one value, a linear search is performed on the bucket. A good hash function does not strive to return strictly unique hashcodes (which would usually be impossible); it strives to return hashcodes that are evenly distributed across the 32-bit integer space. This prevents the scenario of ending up with a few very large (and inefficient) buckets.

A dictionary can work with keys of any type, providing it's able to determine equality between keys and obtain hashcodes. By default, equality is determined via the key's `object.Equals` method, and the pseudo-unique hashcode is obtained via the key's `GetHashCode` method. You can change this behavior either by overriding these methods or by providing an `IEqualityComparer` object when constructing the dictionary. A common application of this is to specify a case-insensitive equality comparer when using string keys:

```
var d = new Dictionary<string, int> (StringComparer.OrdinalIgnoreCase);
```

We discuss this further in "Plugging in Equality and Order" on page 388.

As with many other types of collections, you can improve the performance of a dictionary slightly by specifying the collection's expected size in the constructor, avoiding or lessening the need for internal resizing operations.

The nongeneric version is named `Hashtable` and is functionally similar apart from differences stemming from it exposing the nongeneric `IDictionary` interface discussed previously.

The downside to `Dictionary` and `Hashtable` is that the items are not sorted. Furthermore, the original order in which the items were added is not retained. As with all dictionaries, duplicate keys are not allowed.

 When the generic collections were introduced back in 2005, the CLR team chose to name them according to what they represent (`Dictionary`, `List`) rather than how they are internally implemented (`Hashtable`, `ArrayList`). Although this is good because it gives them the freedom to later change the implementation, it also means that the *performance contract* (often the most important criteria in choosing one kind of collection over another) is no longer captured in the name.

OrderedDictionary

An `OrderedDictionary` is a nongeneric dictionary that maintains elements in the same order that they were added. With an `OrderedDictionary`, you can access elements both by index and by key.

 An `OrderedDictionary` is not a *sorted* dictionary.

An `OrderedDictionary` is a combination of a `Hashtable` and an `ArrayList`. This means that it has all the functionality of a `Hashtable`, plus functions such as `RemoveAt` and an integer indexer. It also exposes `Keys` and `Values` properties that return elements in their original order.

This class was introduced in .NET 2.0, yet, peculiarly, there's no generic version.

ListDictionary and HybridDictionary

`ListDictionary` uses a singly linked list to store the underlying data. It doesn't provide sorting, although it does preserve the original entry order of the items. `ListDictionary` is extremely slow with large lists. Its only real "claim to fame" is its efficiency with very small lists (fewer than 10 items).

`HybridDictionary` is a `ListDictionary` that automatically converts to a `Hashtable` upon reaching a certain size, to address `ListDictionary`'s problems with performance. The idea is to get a low memory footprint when the dictionary is small and good performance when the dictionary is large. However, given the overhead in converting from one to the other—and the fact that a `Dictionary` is not excessively heavy or slow in either scenario—you wouldn't suffer unreasonably by using a Dictionary to begin with.

Both classes come only in nongeneric form.

Sorted Dictionaries

The .NET BCL provides two dictionary classes internally structured such that their content is always sorted by key:

- SortedDictionary<TKey,TValue>
- SortedList<TKey,TValue>[1]

(In this section, we abbreviate <TKey,TValue> to <,>.)

SortedDictionary<,> uses a red/black tree: a data structure designed to perform consistently well in any insertion or retrieval scenario.

SortedList<,> is implemented internally with an ordered array pair, providing fast retrieval (via a binary-chop search) but poor insertion performance (because existing values need to be shifted to make room for a new entry).

SortedDictionary<,> is much faster than SortedList<,> at inserting elements in a random sequence (particularly with large lists). SortedList<,>, however, has an extra ability: to access items by index as well as by key. With a sorted list, you can go directly to the *n*th element in the sorting sequence (via the indexer on the Keys/Values properties). To do the same with a SortedDictionary<,>, you must manually enumerate over *n* items. (Alternatively, you could write a class that combines a sorted dictionary with a list class.)

None of the three collections allows duplicate keys (as is the case with all dictionaries).

The following example uses reflection to load all of the methods defined in System.Object into a sorted list keyed by name and then enumerates their keys and values:

```
// MethodInfo is in the System.Reflection namespace

var sorted = new SortedList <string, MethodInfo>();

foreach (MethodInfo m in typeof (object).GetMethods())
  sorted [m.Name] = m;

foreach (string name in sorted.Keys)
  Console.WriteLine (name);
```

[1] There's also a functionally identical nongeneric version of this called SortedList.

```
foreach (MethodInfo m in sorted.Values)
  Console.WriteLine (m.Name + " returns a " + m.ReturnType);
```

Here's the result of the first enumeration:

```
Equals
GetHashCode
GetType
ReferenceEquals
ToString
```

Here's the result of the second enumeration:

```
Equals returns a System.Boolean
GetHashCode returns a System.Int32
GetType returns a System.Type
ReferenceEquals returns a System.Boolean
ToString returns a System.String
```

Notice that we populated the dictionary through its indexer. If we instead used the Add method, it would throw an exception because the object class upon which we're reflecting overloads the Equals method, and you can't add the same key twice to a dictionary. By using the indexer, the later entry overwrites the earlier entry, preventing this error.

 You can store multiple members of the same key by making each value element a list:

```
SortedList <string, List<MethodInfo>>
```

Extending our example, the following retrieves the MethodInfo whose key is "GetHashCode", just as with an ordinary dictionary:

```
Console.WriteLine (sorted ["GetHashCode"]);       // Int32 GetHashCode()
```

So far, everything we've done would also work with a SortedDictionary<,>. The following two lines, however, which retrieve the last key and value, work only with a sorted list:

```
Console.WriteLine (sorted.Keys [sorted.Count - 1]);       // ToString
Console.WriteLine (sorted.Values[sorted.Count - 1].IsVirtual);  // True
```

Customizable Collections and Proxies

The collection classes discussed in previous sections are convenient in that you can directly instantiate them, but they don't allow you to control what happens when an item is added to or removed from the collection. With strongly typed collections in an application, you sometimes need this control; for instance:

- To fire an event when an item is added or removed
- To update properties because of the added or removed item

- To detect an "illegal" add/remove operation and throw an exception (for example, if the operation violates a business rule)

The .NET BCL provides collection classes for this exact purpose, in the `System.Col`
`lections.ObjectModel` namespace. These are essentially proxies or wrappers that
implement `IList<T>` or `IDictionary<,>` by forwarding the methods through to an
underlying collection. Each `Add`, `Remove`, or `Clear` operation is routed via a virtual
method that acts as a "gateway" when overridden.

Customizable collection classes are commonly used for publicly exposed collections; for instance, a collection of controls exposed publicly on a `System`
`.Windows.Form` class.

Collection<T> and CollectionBase

The `Collection<T>` class is a customizable wrapper for `List<T>`.

As well as implementing `IList<T>` and `IList`, it defines four additional virtual
methods and a protected property as follows:

```
public class Collection<T> :
  IList<T>, ICollection<T>, IEnumerable<T>, IList, ICollection, IEnumerable
{
  // ...

  protected virtual void ClearItems();
  protected virtual void InsertItem (int index, T item);
  protected virtual void RemoveItem (int index);
  protected virtual void SetItem (int index, T item);

  protected IList<T> Items { get; }
}
```

The virtual methods provide the gateway by which you can "hook in" to change or
enhance the list's normal behavior. The protected `Items` property allows the implementer to directly access the "inner list"—this is used to make changes internally
without the virtual methods firing.

The virtual methods need not be overridden; they can be left alone until there's a
requirement to alter the list's default behavior. The following example demonstrates
the typical "skeleton" use of `Collection<T>`:

```
Zoo zoo = new Zoo();
zoo.Animals.Add (new Animal ("Kangaroo", 10));
zoo.Animals.Add (new Animal ("Mr Sea Lion", 20));
foreach (Animal a in zoo.Animals) Console.WriteLine (a.Name);

public class Animal
{
  public string Name;
  public int Popularity;

  public Animal (string name, int popularity)
```

```
  {
    Name = name; Popularity = popularity;
  }
}

public class AnimalCollection : Collection <Animal>
{
  // AnimalCollection is already a fully functioning list of animals.
  // No extra code is required.
}

public class Zoo    // The class that will expose AnimalCollection.
{                   // This would typically have additional members.

  public readonly AnimalCollection Animals = new AnimalCollection();
}
```

As it stands, AnimalCollection is no more functional than a simple List<Animal>; its role is to provide a base for future extension. To illustrate, let's now add a Zoo property to Animal so that it can reference the Zoo in which it lives and override each of the virtual methods in Collection<Animal> to maintain that property automatically:

```
public class Animal
{
  public string Name;
  public int Popularity;
  public Zoo Zoo { get; internal set; }
  public Animal(string name, int popularity)
  {
    Name = name; Popularity = popularity;
  }
}

public class AnimalCollection : Collection <Animal>
{
  Zoo zoo;
  public AnimalCollection (Zoo zoo) { this.zoo = zoo; }

  protected override void InsertItem (int index, Animal item)
  {
    base.InsertItem (index, item);
    item.Zoo = zoo;
  }
  protected override void SetItem (int index, Animal item)
  {
    base.SetItem (index, item);
    item.Zoo = zoo;
  }
  protected override void RemoveItem (int index)
  {
    this [index].Zoo = null;
    base.RemoveItem (index);
  }
  protected override void ClearItems()
```

```
    {
      foreach (Animal a in this) a.Zoo = null;
      base.ClearItems();
    }
  }

  public class Zoo
  {
    public readonly AnimalCollection Animals;
    public Zoo() { Animals = new AnimalCollection (this); }
  }
```

Collection<T> also has a constructor accepting an existing IList<T>. Unlike with other collection classes, the supplied list is *proxied* rather than *copied*, meaning that subsequent changes will be reflected in the wrapping Collection<T> (although *without* Collection<T>'s virtual methods firing). Conversely, changes made via the Collection<T> will change the underlying list.

CollectionBase

CollectionBase is the nongeneric version of Collection<T>. This provides most of the same features as Collection<T> but is clumsier to use. Instead of the template methods InsertItem, RemoveItem, SetItem, and ClearItem, Collection Base has "hook" methods that double the number of methods required: OnInsert, OnInsertComplete, OnSet, OnSetComplete, OnRemove, OnRemoveComplete, OnClear, and OnClearComplete. Because CollectionBase is nongeneric, you must also implement typed methods when subclassing it—at a minimum, a typed indexer and Add method.

KeyedCollection<TKey,TItem> and DictionaryBase

KeyedCollection<TKey,TItem> subclasses Collection<TItem>. It both adds and subtracts functionality. What it adds is the ability to access items by key, much like with a dictionary. What it subtracts is the ability to proxy your own inner list.

A keyed collection has some resemblance to an OrderedDictionary in that it combines a linear list with a hashtable. However, unlike OrderedDictionary, it doesn't implement IDictionary and doesn't support the concept of a key/value *pair*. Keys are obtained instead from the items themselves: via the abstract GetKeyForItem method. This means that enumerating a keyed collection is just like enumerating an ordinary list.

You can best think of KeyedCollection<TKey,TItem> as Collection<TItem> plus fast lookup by key.

Because it subclasses Collection<>, a keyed collection inherits all of Collec tion<>'s functionality, except for the ability to specify an existing list in construction. The additional members it defines are as follows:

```
public abstract class KeyedCollection <TKey, TItem> : Collection <TItem>
```

```
// ...

    protected abstract TKey GetKeyForItem(TItem item);
    protected void ChangeItemKey(TItem item, TKey newKey);

    // Fast lookup by key - this is in addition to lookup by index.
    public TItem this[TKey key] { get; }

    protected IDictionary<TKey, TItem> Dictionary { get; }
}
```

GetKeyForItem is what the implementer overrides to obtain an item's key from the underlying object. The ChangeItemKey method must be called if the item's key property changes, in order to update the internal dictionary. The Dictionary property returns the internal dictionary used to implement the lookup, which is created when the first item is added. This behavior can be changed by specifying a creation threshold in the constructor, delaying the internal dictionary from being created until the threshold is reached (in the interim, a linear search is performed if an item is requested by key). A good reason not to specify a creation threshold is that having a valid dictionary can be useful in obtaining an ICollection<> of keys, via the Dictionary's Keys property. This collection can then be passed on to a public property.

The most common use for KeyedCollection<,> is in providing a collection of items accessible both by index and by name. To demonstrate this, let's revisit the zoo, this time implementing AnimalCollection as a KeyedCollection<string, Animal>:

```
public class Animal
{
    string name;
    public string Name
    {
        get { return name; }
        set {
            if (Zoo != null) Zoo.Animals.NotifyNameChange (this, value);
            name = value;
        }
    }
    public int Popularity;
    public Zoo Zoo { get; internal set; }

    public Animal (string name, int popularity)
    {
        Name = name; Popularity = popularity;
    }
}

public class AnimalCollection : KeyedCollection <string, Animal>
{
    Zoo zoo;
    public AnimalCollection (Zoo zoo) { this.zoo = zoo; }
```

```
internal void NotifyNameChange (Animal a, string newName) =>
  this.ChangeItemKey (a, newName);

protected override string GetKeyForItem (Animal item) => item.Name;

// The following methods would be implemented as in the previous example
protected override void InsertItem (int index, Animal item)...
protected override void SetItem (int index, Animal item)...
protected override void RemoveItem (int index)...
protected override void ClearItems()...
}

public class Zoo
{
  public readonly AnimalCollection Animals;
  public Zoo() { Animals = new AnimalCollection (this); }
}
```

The following code demonstrates its use:

```
Zoo zoo = new Zoo();
zoo.Animals.Add (new Animal ("Kangaroo", 10));
zoo.Animals.Add (new Animal ("Mr Sea Lion", 20));
Console.WriteLine (zoo.Animals [0].Popularity);           // 10
Console.WriteLine (zoo.Animals ["Mr Sea Lion"].Popularity);  // 20
zoo.Animals ["Kangaroo"].Name = "Mr Roo";
Console.WriteLine (zoo.Animals ["Mr Roo"].Popularity);    // 10
```

DictionaryBase

The nongeneric version of KeyedCollection is called DictionaryBase. This legacy class takes a very different approach in that it implements IDictionary and uses clumsy hook methods like CollectionBase: OnInsert, OnInsertComplete, OnSet, OnSetComplete, OnRemove, OnRemoveComplete, OnClear, and OnClearComplete (and additionally, OnGet). The primary advantage of implementing IDictionary over taking the KeyedCollection approach is that you don't need to subclass it in order to obtain keys. But since the very purpose of DictionaryBase is to be subclassed, it's no advantage at all. The improved model in KeyedCollection is almost certainly due to the fact that it was written some years later, with the benefit of hindsight. DictionaryBase is best considered useful for backward compatibility.

ReadOnlyCollection<T>

ReadOnlyCollection<T> is a wrapper, or *proxy*, that provides a read-only view of a collection. This is useful in allowing a class to publicly expose read-only access to a collection that the class can still update internally.

A read-only collection accepts the input collection in its constructor, to which it maintains a permanent reference. It doesn't take a static copy of the input collection, so subsequent changes to the input collection are visible through the read-only wrapper.

To illustrate, suppose that your class wants to provide read-only public access to a list of strings called Names. We could do this as follows:

```
public class Test
{
  List<string> names = new List<string>();
  public IReadOnlyList<string> Names => names;
}
```

Although Names returns a read-only interface, the consumer can still downcast at runtime to List<string> or IList<string> and then call Add, Remove, or Clear on the list. ReadOnlyCollection<T> provides a more robust solution:

```
public class Test
{
  List<string> names = new List<string>();
  public ReadOnlyCollection<string> Names { get; private set; }

  public Test() => Names = new ReadOnlyCollection<string> (names);

  public void AddInternally() => names.Add ("test");
}
```

Now, only members within the Test class can alter the list of names:

```
Test t = new Test();

Console.WriteLine (t.Names.Count);      // 0
t.AddInternally();
Console.WriteLine (t.Names.Count);      // 1

t.Names.Add ("test");                   // Compiler error
((IList<string>) t.Names).Add ("test"); // NotSupportedException
```

Immutable Collections

We just described how ReadOnlyCollection<T> creates a read-only view of a collection. Restricting the ability to write (*mutate*) a collection—or any other object—simplifies software and reduces bugs.

The *immutable collections* extend this principle, by providing collections that cannot be modified at all after initialization. Should you need to add an item to an immutable collection, you must instantiate a new collection, leaving the old one untouched.

Immutability is a hallmark of *functional programming* and has the following benefits:

- It eliminates a large class of bugs associated with changing state.
- It vastly simplifies parallelism and multithreading, by preventing most of the thread-safety problems that we describe in Chapters 14, 22, and 23.
- It makes code easier to reason about.

The disadvantage of immutability is that when you need to make a change, you must create a whole new object. This incurs a performance hit, although there are mitigating strategies that we discuss in this section, including the ability to reuse portions of the original structure.

The immutable collections are part of .NET (in .NET Framework, they are available via the *System.Collections.Immutable* NuGet package). All collections are defined in the System.Collections.Immutable namespace:

Type	Internal structure
ImmutableArray<T>	Array
ImmutableList<T>	AVL tree
ImmutableDictionary<K,V>	AVL tree
ImmutableHashSet<T>	AVL tree
ImmutableSortedDictionary<K,V>	AVL tree
ImmutableSortedSet<T>	AVL tree
ImmutableStack<T>	Linked list
ImmutableQueue<T>	Linked list

The ImmutableArray<T> and ImmutableList<T> types are both immutable versions of List<T>. Both do the same job but with different performance characteristics that we discuss in "Immutable Collections and Performance" on page 387.

The immutable collections expose a public interface similar to their mutable counterparts. The key difference is that the methods that appear to alter the collection (such as Add or Remove) don't alter the original collection; instead they return a new collection with the requested item added or removed.

 Immutable collections prevent the adding and removing of items; they don't prevent the items *themselves* from being mutated. To get the full benefits of immutability, you need to ensure that only immutable items end up in an immutable collection.

Creating Immutable Collections

Each immutable collection type offers a Create<T>() method, which accepts optional initial values and returns an initialized immutable collection:

```
ImmutableArray<int> array = ImmutableArray.Create<int> (1, 2, 3);
```

Each collection also offers a CreateRange<T> method, which does the same job as Create<T>; the difference is that its parameter type is IEnumerable<T> instead of params T[].

You can also create an immutable collection from an existing IEnumerable<T>, using appropriate extension methods (ToImmutableArray, ToImmutableList, ToImmutableDictionary, and so on):

```
var list = new[] { 1, 2, 3 }.ToImmutableList();
```

Manipulating Immutable Collections

The Add method returns a new collection containing the existing elements plus the new one:

```
var oldList = ImmutableList.Create<int> (1, 2, 3);

ImmutableList<int> newList = oldList.Add (4);

Console.WriteLine (oldList.Count);    // 3  (unaltered)
Console.WriteLine (newList.Count);    // 4
```

The Remove method operates in the same fashion, returning a new collection with the item removed.

Repeatedly adding or removing elements in this manner is inefficient, because a new immutable collection is created for each add or remove operation. A better solution is to call AddRange (or RemoveRange), which accepts an IEnumerable<T> of items, which are all added or removed in one go:

```
var anotherList = oldList.AddRange (new[] { 4, 5, 6 });
```

The immutable list and array also defines Insert and InsertRange methods to insert elements at a particular index, a RemoveAt method to remove at an index, and RemoveAll, which removes based on a predicate.

Builders

For more complex initialization needs, each immutable collection class defines a *builder* counterpart. Builders are classes that are functionally equivalent to a mutable collection, with similar performance characteristics. After the data is initialized, calling .ToImmutable() on a builder returns an immutable collection:

```
ImmutableArray<int>.Builder builder = ImmutableArray.CreateBuilder<int>();
builder.Add (1);
builder.Add (2);
builder.Add (3);
builder.RemoveAt (0);
ImmutableArray<int> myImmutable = builder.ToImmutable();
```

You also can use builders to *batch* multiple updates to an existing immutable collection:

```
var builder2 = myImmutable.ToBuilder();
builder2.Add (4);        // Efficient
builder2.Remove (2);     // Efficient
...                      // More changes to builder...
```

```
// Return a new immutable collection with all the changes applied:
ImmutableArray<int> myImmutable2 = builder2.ToImmutable();
```

Immutable Collections and Performance

Most of the immutable collections use an *AVL tree* internally, which allows the add/remove operations to reuse portions of the original internal structure rather than having to re-create the entire thing from scratch. This reduces the overhead of add/remove operations from potentially *huge* (with large collections) to just *moderately large*, but it comes at the cost of making read operations slower. The end result is that most immutable collections are slower than their mutable counterparts for both reading and writing.

The most seriously affected is `ImmutableList<T>`, which for both read and add operations is 10 to 200 times slower than `List<T>` (depending on the size of the list). This is why `ImmutableArray<T>` exists: by using an array inside, it avoids the overhead for read operations (for which it's comparable in performance to an ordinary mutable array). The flipside is that it's *much* slower than (even) `Immu``tableList<T>` for add operations because none of the original structure can be reused.

Hence, `ImmutableArray<T>` is desirable when you want unimpeded *read*-performance and don't expect many subsequent calls to `Add` or `Remove` (without using a builder):

Type	Read performance	Add performance
`ImmutableList<T>`	Slow	Slow
`ImmutableArray<T>`	Very fast	Very slow

 Calling `Remove` on an `ImmutableArray` is more expensive than calling `Remove` on a `List<T>`—even in the worst-case scenario of removing the first element—because allocating the new collection places additional load on the garbage collector.

Although the immutable collections as a whole incur a potentially significant performance cost, it's important to keep the overall magnitude in perspective. An `Add` operation on an `ImmutableList` with a million elements is still likely to occur in less than a microsecond on a typical laptop, and a read operation, in less than 100 nanoseconds. And, if you need to perform write-operations in a loop, you can avoid the accumulated cost with a builder.

The following factors also work to mitigate the costs:

- Immutability allows for easy concurrency and parallelization (Chapter 23), so you can employ all available cores. Parallelizing with mutable state easily leads to errors and requires the use of locks or concurrent collections, both of which hurt performance.

- With immutability, you don't need to "defensively copy" collections or data structures to guard against unexpected change. This was a factor in favoring the use of immutable collections in writing recent portions of Visual Studio.

- In most typical programs, few collections have enough items for the difference to matter.

In addition to Visual Studio, the well-performing Microsoft Roslyn toolchain was built with immutable collections, demonstrating how the benefits can outweigh the costs.

Plugging in Equality and Order

In the sections "Equality Comparison" on page 324 and "Order Comparison" on page 335, we described the standard .NET protocols that make a type equatable, hashable, and comparable. A type that implements these protocols can function correctly in a dictionary or sorted list "out of the box." More specifically:

- A type for which `Equals` and `GetHashCode` return meaningful results can be used as a key in a `Dictionary` or `Hashtable`.

- A type that implements `IComparable` /`IComparable<T>` can be used as a key in any of the *sorted* dictionaries or lists.

A type's default equating or comparison implementation typically reflects what is most "natural" for that type. Sometimes, however, the default behavior is not what you want. You might need a dictionary whose `string` type key is treated without respect to case. Or you might want a sorted list of customers, sorted by each customer's postcode. For this reason, .NET also defines a matching set of "plug-in" protocols. The plug-in protocols achieve two things:

- They allow you to switch in alternative equating or comparison behavior.

- They allow you to use a dictionary or sorted collection with a key type that's not intrinsically equatable or comparable.

The plug-in protocols consist of the following interfaces:

`IEqualityComparer` *and* `IEqualityComparer<T>`

- Performs plug-in *equality comparison and hashing*
- Recognized by `Hashtable` and `Dictionary`

`IComparer` *and* `IComparer<T>`

- Performs plug-in *order comparison*
- Recognized by the sorted dictionaries and collections; also, `Array.Sort`

Each interface comes in both generic and nongeneric forms. The IEqualityCom
parer interfaces also have a default implementation in a class called Equality
Comparer.

In addition, there are interfaces called IStructuralEquatable and IStructuralCom
parable, which allow for the option of structural comparisons on classes and arrays.

IEqualityComparer and EqualityComparer

An equality comparer switches in nondefault equality and hashing behavior, primarily for the Dictionary and Hashtable classes.

Recall the requirements of a hashtable-based dictionary. It needs answers to two
questions for any given key:

- Is it the same as another?
- What is its integer hashcode?

An equality comparer answers these questions by implementing the IEquality
Comparer interfaces:

```
public interface IEqualityComparer<T>
{
   bool Equals (T x, T y);
   int GetHashCode (T obj);
}

public interface IEqualityComparer        // Nongeneric version
{
   bool Equals (object x, object y);
   int GetHashCode (object obj);
}
```

To write a custom comparer, you implement one or both of these interfaces (implementing both gives maximum interoperability). Because this is somewhat tedious,
an alternative is to subclass the abstract EqualityComparer class, defined as follows:

```
public abstract class EqualityComparer<T> : IEqualityComparer,
                                            IEqualityComparer<T>
{
  public abstract bool Equals (T x, T y);
  public abstract int GetHashCode (T obj);

  bool IEqualityComparer.Equals (object x, object y);
  int IEqualityComparer.GetHashCode (object obj);

  public static EqualityComparer<T> Default { get; }
}
```

EqualityComparer implements both interfaces; your job is simply to override the
two abstract methods.

The semantics for `Equals` and `GetHashCode` follow the same rules for `object`
`.Equals` and `object.GetHashCode`, described in Chapter 6. In the following example, we define a `Customer` class with two fields and then write an equality comparer
that matches both the first and last names:

```
public class Customer
{
  public string LastName;
  public string FirstName;

  public Customer (string last, string first)
  {
    LastName = last;
    FirstName = first;
  }
}
public class LastFirstEqComparer : EqualityComparer <Customer>
{
  public override bool Equals (Customer x, Customer y)
    => x.LastName == y.LastName && x.FirstName == y.FirstName;

  public override int GetHashCode (Customer obj)
    => (obj.LastName + ";" + obj.FirstName).GetHashCode();
}
```

To illustrate how this works, let's create two customers:

```
Customer c1 = new Customer ("Bloggs", "Joe");
Customer c2 = new Customer ("Bloggs", "Joe");
```

Because we've not overridden `object.Equals`, normal reference type equality
semantics apply:

```
Console.WriteLine (c1 == c2);            // False
Console.WriteLine (c1.Equals (c2));      // False
```

The same default equality semantics apply when using these customers in a
`Dictionary` without specifying an equality comparer:

```
var d = new Dictionary<Customer, string>();
d [c1] = "Joe";
Console.WriteLine (d.ContainsKey (c2));        // False
```

Now, with the custom equality comparer:

```
var eqComparer = new LastFirstEqComparer();
var d = new Dictionary<Customer, string> (eqComparer);
d [c1] = "Joe";
Console.WriteLine (d.ContainsKey (c2));        // True
```

In this example, we would have to be careful not to change the customer's `First`
`Name` or `LastName` while it was in use in the dictionary; otherwise, its hashcode
would change and the `Dictionary` would break.

EqualityComparer<T>.Default

Calling `EqualityComparer<T>.Default` returns a general-purpose equality comparer that you can use as an alternative to the static `object.Equals` method. The advantage is that it first checks whether T implements `IEquatable<T>`, and if so, it calls that implementation instead, avoiding the boxing overhead. This is particularly useful in generic methods:

```
static bool Foo<T> (T x, T y)
{
  bool same = EqualityComparer<T>.Default.Equals (x, y);
  ...
```

ReferenceEqualityComparer.Instance (.NET 5+)

From .NET 5, `ReferenceEqualityComparer.Instance` returns an equality comparer that always applies referential equality. In the case of value types, its `Equals` method always returns false.

IComparer and Comparer

Comparers are used to switch in custom ordering logic for sorted dictionaries and collections.

Note that a comparer is useless to the unsorted dictionaries such as `Dictionary` and `Hashtable`—these require an `IEqualityComparer` to get hashcodes. Similarly, an equality comparer is useless for sorted dictionaries and collections.

Here are the `IComparer` interface definitions:

```
public interface IComparer
{
  int Compare(object x, object y);
}
public interface IComparer <in T>
{
  int Compare(T x, T y);
}
```

As with equality comparers, there's an abstract class that you can subtype instead of implementing the interfaces:

```
public abstract class Comparer<T> : IComparer, IComparer<T>
{
  public static Comparer<T> Default { get; }

  public abstract int Compare (T x, T y);       // Implemented by you
  int IComparer.Compare (object x, object y);   // Implemented for you
}
```

The following example illustrates a class that describes a wish as well as a comparer that sorts wishes by priority:

```
class Wish
{
  public string Name;
  public int Priority;

  public Wish (string name, int priority)
  {
    Name = name;
    Priority = priority;
  }
}

class PriorityComparer : Comparer<Wish>
{
  public override int Compare (Wish x, Wish y)
  {
    if (object.Equals (x, y)) return 0;      // Optimization
    if (x == null) return -1;
    if (y == null) return 1;
    return x.Priority.CompareTo (y.Priority);
  }
}
```

The object.Equals check ensures that we can never contradict the Equals method. Calling the static object.Equals method in this case is better than calling x.Equals because it still works if x is null!

Here's how our PriorityComparer is used to sort a List:

```
var wishList = new List<Wish>();
wishList.Add (new Wish ("Peace", 2));
wishList.Add (new Wish ("Wealth", 3));
wishList.Add (new Wish ("Love", 2));
wishList.Add (new Wish ("3 more wishes", 1));

wishList.Sort (new PriorityComparer());
foreach (Wish w in wishList) Console.Write (w.Name + " | ");

// OUTPUT: 3 more wishes | Love | Peace | Wealth |
```

In the next example, SurnameComparer allows you to sort surname strings in an order suitable for a phonebook listing:

```
class SurnameComparer : Comparer <string>
{
  string Normalize (string s)
  {
    s = s.Trim().ToUpper();
    if (s.StartsWith ("MC")) s = "MAC" + s.Substring (2);
    return s;
  }

  public override int Compare (string x, string y)
    => Normalize (x).CompareTo (Normalize (y));
}
```

Here's `SurnameComparer` in use in a sorted dictionary:

```
var dic = new SortedDictionary<string,string> (new SurnameComparer());
dic.Add ("MacPhail", "second!");
dic.Add ("MacWilliam", "third!");
dic.Add ("McDonald", "first!");

foreach (string s in dic.Values)
  Console.Write (s + " ");                    // first! second! third!
```

StringComparer

`StringComparer` is a predefined plug-in class for equating and comparing strings, allowing you to specify language and case sensitivity. `StringComparer` implements both `IEqualityComparer` and `IComparer` (and their generic versions), so you can use it with any type of dictionary or sorted collection.

Because `StringComparer` is abstract, you obtain instances via its static properties. `StringComparer.Ordinal` mirrors the default behavior for string equality comparison and `StringComparer.CurrentCulture` for order comparison. Here are all of its static members:

```
public static StringComparer CurrentCulture { get; }
public static StringComparer CurrentCultureIgnoreCase { get; }
public static StringComparer InvariantCulture { get; }
public static StringComparer InvariantCultureIgnoreCase { get; }
public static StringComparer Ordinal { get; }
public static StringComparer OrdinalIgnoreCase { get; }
public static StringComparer Create (CultureInfo culture,
                                     bool ignoreCase);
```

In the following example, an ordinal case-insensitive dictionary is created such that `dict["Joe"]` and `dict["JOE"]` mean the same thing:

```
var dict = new Dictionary<string, int> (StringComparer.OrdinalIgnoreCase);
```

In the next example, an array of names is sorted, using Australian English:

```
string[] names = { "Tom", "HARRY", "sheila" };
CultureInfo ci = new CultureInfo ("en-AU");
Array.Sort<string> (names, StringComparer.Create (ci, false));
```

The final example is a culture-aware version of the `SurnameComparer` we wrote in the previous section (to compare names suitable for a phonebook listing):

```
class SurnameComparer : Comparer<string>
{
  StringComparer strCmp;

  public SurnameComparer (CultureInfo ci)
  {
    // Create a case-sensitive, culture-sensitive string comparer
    strCmp = StringComparer.Create (ci, false);
  }
```

Collections

```
string Normalize (string s)
{
  s = s.Trim();
  if (s.ToUpper().StartsWith ("MC")) s = "MAC" + s.Substring (2);
  return s;
}

public override int Compare (string x, string y)
{
  // Directly call Compare on our culture-aware StringComparer
  return strCmp.Compare (Normalize (x), Normalize (y));
}
}
```

IStructuralEquatable and IStructuralComparable

As we discussed in Chapter 6, structs implement *structural comparison* by default:
two structs are equal if all of their fields are equal. Sometimes, however, structural
equality and order comparison are useful as plug-in options on other types, as
well—such as arrays. The following interfaces help with this:

```
public interface IStructuralEquatable
{
  bool Equals (object other, IEqualityComparer comparer);
  int GetHashCode (IEqualityComparer comparer);
}

public interface IStructuralComparable
{
  int CompareTo (object other, IComparer comparer);
}
```

The IEqualityComparer/IComparer that you pass in are applied to each individual
element in the composite object. We can demonstrate this by using arrays. In
the following example, we compare two arrays for equality, first using the default
Equals method, then using IStructuralEquatable's version:

```
int[] a1 = { 1, 2, 3 };
int[] a2 = { 1, 2, 3 };
IStructuralEquatable se1 = a1;
Console.Write (a1.Equals (a2));                                      // False
Console.Write (se1.Equals (a2, EqualityComparer<int>.Default));     // True
```

Here's another example:

```
string[] a1 = "the quick brown fox".Split();
string[] a2 = "THE QUICK BROWN FOX".Split();
IStructuralEquatable se1 = a1;
bool isTrue = se1.Equals (a2, StringComparer.InvariantCultureIgnoreCase);
```

8

LINQ Queries

LINQ, or Language Integrated Query, is a set of language and runtime features for writing structured type-safe queries over local object collections and remote data sources.

LINQ enables you to query any collection implementing IEnumerable<T>, whether an array, list, or XML Document Object Model (DOM), as well as remote data sources, such as tables in an SQL Server database. LINQ offers the benefits of both compile-time type checking and dynamic query composition.

This chapter describes the LINQ architecture and the fundamentals of writing queries. All core types are defined in the System.Linq and System.Linq.Expressions namespaces.

> The examples in this and the following two chapters are preloaded into an interactive querying tool called LINQPad. You can download LINQPad from *http://www.linqpad.net*.

Getting Started

The basic units of data in LINQ are *sequences* and *elements*. A sequence is any object that implements IEnumerable<T>, and an element is each item in the sequence. In the following example, names is a sequence, and "Tom", "Dick", and "Harry" are elements:

```
string[] names = { "Tom", "Dick", "Harry" };
```

We call this a *local sequence* because it represents a local collection of objects in memory.

A *query operator* is a method that transforms a sequence. A typical query operator accepts an *input sequence* and emits a transformed *output sequence*. In the Enumera ble class in System.Linq, there are around 40 query operators—all implemented as static extension methods. These are called *standard query operators*.

Queries that operate over local sequences are called *local* queries or *LINQ-to-objects* queries.

LINQ also supports sequences that can be dynamically fed from a remote data source such as an SQL Server database. These sequences additionally implement the IQueryable<T> interface and are supported through a matching set of standard query operators in the Queryable class. We discuss this further in "Interpreted Queries" on page 424.

A query is an expression that, when enumerated, transforms sequences with query operators. The simplest query comprises one input sequence and one operator. For instance, we can apply the Where operator on a simple array to extract those strings whose length is at least four characters, as follows:

```
string[] names = { "Tom", "Dick", "Harry" };
IEnumerable<string> filteredNames = System.Linq.Enumerable.Where
                                    (names, n => n.Length >= 4);
foreach (string n in filteredNames)
  Console.WriteLine (n);

Dick
Harry
```

Because the standard query operators are implemented as extension methods, we can call Where directly on names, as though it were an instance method:

```
IEnumerable<string> filteredNames = names.Where (n => n.Length >= 4);
```

For this to compile, you must import the System.Linq namespace. Here's a complete example:

```
using System;
using System.Collections.Generic;
using System.Linq;

string[] names = { "Tom", "Dick", "Harry" };

IEnumerable<string> filteredNames = names.Where (n => n.Length >= 4);
foreach (string name in filteredNames) Console.WriteLine (name);

Dick
Harry
```

We could further shorten our code by implicitly typing filteredNames:

```
var filteredNames = names.Where (n => n.Length >= 4);
```

This can hinder readability, however, outside of an IDE, where there are no tool tips to help. For this reason, we make less use of implicit typing in this chapter than you might in your own projects.

Most query operators accept a lambda expression as an argument. The lambda expression helps guide and shape the query. In our example, the lambda expression is as follows:

```
n => n.Length >= 4
```

The input argument corresponds to an input element. In this case, the input argument n represents each name in the array and is of type string. The Where operator requires that the lambda expression return a bool value, which if true, indicates that the element should be included in the output sequence. Here's its signature:

```
public static IEnumerable<TSource> Where<TSource>
  (this IEnumerable<TSource> source, Func<TSource,bool> predicate)
```

The following query extracts all names that contain the letter "a":

```
IEnumerable<string> filteredNames = names.Where (n => n.Contains ("a"));

foreach (string name in filteredNames)
  Console.WriteLine (name);        // Harry
```

So far, we've built queries using extension methods and lambda expressions. As you'll see shortly, this strategy is highly composable in that it allows the chaining of query operators. In this book, we refer to this as *fluent syntax*.[1] C# also provides another syntax for writing queries, called *query expression* syntax. Here's our preceding query written as a query expression:

```
IEnumerable<string> filteredNames = from n in names
                                    where n.Contains ("a")
                                    select n;
```

Fluent syntax and query syntax are complementary. In the following two sections, we explore each in more detail.

Fluent Syntax

Fluent syntax is the most flexible and fundamental. In this section, we describe how to chain query operators to form more complex queries—and show why extension methods are important to this process. We also describe how to formulate lambda expressions for a query operator and introduce several new query operators.

Chaining Query Operators

In the preceding section, we showed two simple queries, each comprising a single query operator. To build more complex queries, you append additional query operators to the expression, creating a chain. To illustrate, the following query extracts all strings containing the letter "a," sorts them by length, and then converts the results to uppercase:

---

1 The term is based on Eric Evans and Martin Fowler's work on fluent interfaces.

```
using System;
using System.Collections.Generic;
using System.Linq;

string[] names = { "Tom", "Dick", "Harry", "Mary", "Jay" };

IEnumerable<string> query = names
  .Where    (n => n.Contains ("a"))
  .OrderBy (n => n.Length)
  .Select  (n => n.ToUpper());

foreach (string name in query) Console.WriteLine (name);

JAY
MARY
HARRY
```

 The variable, n, in our example, is privately scoped to each of the lambda expressions. We can reuse the identifier n for the same reason that we can reuse the identifier c in the following method:

```
void Test()
{
  foreach (char c in "string1") Console.Write (c);
  foreach (char c in "string2") Console.Write (c);
  foreach (char c in "string3") Console.Write (c);
}
```

Where, OrderBy, and Select are standard query operators that resolve to extension methods in the Enumerable class (if you import the System.Linq namespace).

We already introduced the Where operator, which emits a filtered version of the input sequence. The OrderBy operator emits a sorted version of its input sequence; the Select method emits a sequence in which each input element is transformed or *projected* with a given lambda expression (n.ToUpper(), in this case). Data flows from left to right through the chain of operators, so the data is first filtered, then sorted, and then projected.

 A query operator never alters the input sequence; instead, it returns a new sequence. This is consistent with the *functional programming* paradigm from which LINQ was inspired.

Here are the signatures of each of these extension methods (with the OrderBy signature slightly simplified):

```
public static IEnumerable<TSource> Where<TSource>
  (this IEnumerable<TSource> source, Func<TSource,bool> predicate)

public static IEnumerable<TSource> OrderBy<TSource,TKey>
  (this IEnumerable<TSource> source, Func<TSource,TKey> keySelector)

public static IEnumerable<TResult> Select<TSource,TResult>
  (this IEnumerable<TSource> source, Func<TSource,TResult> selector)
```

When query operators are chained as in this example, the output sequence of one operator is the input sequence of the next. The complete query resembles a production line of conveyor belts, as illustrated in Figure 8-1.

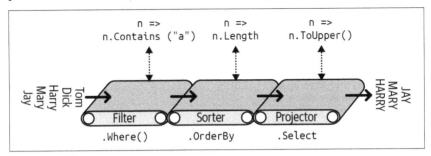

Figure 8-1. Chaining query operators

We can construct the identical query *progressively*, as follows:

```
// You must import the System.Linq namespace for this to compile:

IEnumerable<string> filtered   = names   .Where   (n => n.Contains ("a"));
IEnumerable<string> sorted     = filtered.OrderBy (n => n.Length);
IEnumerable<string> finalQuery = sorted  .Select  (n => n.ToUpper());
```

finalQuery is compositionally identical to the query we constructed previously. Further, each intermediate step also comprises a valid query that we can execute:

```
foreach (string name in filtered)
  Console.Write (name + "|");        // Harry|Mary|Jay|

Console.WriteLine();
foreach (string name in sorted)
  Console.Write (name + "|");        // Jay|Mary|Harry|

Console.WriteLine();
foreach (string name in finalQuery)
  Console.Write (name + "|");        // JAY|MARY|HARRY|
```

Why extension methods are important

Instead of using extension method syntax, you can use conventional static method syntax to call the query operators:

```
IEnumerable<string> filtered = Enumerable.Where (names,
                                    n => n.Contains ("a"));
IEnumerable<string> sorted = Enumerable.OrderBy (filtered, n => n.Length);
IEnumerable<string> finalQuery = Enumerable.Select (sorted,
                                    n => n.ToUpper());
```

This is, in fact, how the compiler translates extension method calls. Shunning extension methods comes at a cost, however, if you want to write a query in a single statement as we did earlier. Let's revisit the single-statement query—first in extension method syntax:

```
IEnumerable<string> query = names.Where  (n => n.Contains ("a"))
                                .OrderBy (n => n.Length)
                                .Select  (n => n.ToUpper());
```

Its natural linear shape reflects the left-to-right flow of data and also keeps lambda expressions alongside their query operators (*infix* notation). Without extension methods, the query loses its *fluency*:

```
IEnumerable<string> query =
  Enumerable.Select (
    Enumerable.OrderBy (
      Enumerable.Where (
        names, n => n.Contains ("a")
      ), n => n.Length
    ), n => n.ToUpper()
  );
```

Composing Lambda Expressions

In previous examples, we fed the following lambda expression to the Where operator:

```
n => n.Contains ("a")     // Input type = string, return type = bool.
```

A lambda expression that takes a value and returns a bool is called a *predicate*.

The purpose of the lambda expression depends on the particular query operator. With the Where operator, it indicates whether an element should be included in the output sequence. In the case of the OrderBy operator, the lambda expression maps each element in the input sequence to its sorting key. With the Select operator, the lambda expression determines how each element in the input sequence is transformed before being fed to the output sequence.

A lambda expression in a query operator always works on individual elements in the input sequence—not the sequence as a whole.

The query operator evaluates your lambda expression upon demand, typically once per element in the input sequence. Lambda expressions allow you to feed your own logic into the query operators. This makes the query operators versatile as well as being simple under the hood. Here's a complete implementation of Enumera ble.Where, exception handling aside:

```
public static IEnumerable<TSource> Where<TSource>
  (this IEnumerable<TSource> source, Func<TSource,bool> predicate)
{
  foreach (TSource element in source)
    if (predicate (element))
      yield return element;
}
```

Lambda expressions and Func signatures

The standard query operators utilize generic Func delegates. Func is a family of general-purpose generic delegates in the System namespace, defined with the following intent:

> The type arguments in Func appear in the same order they do in lambda expressions.

Hence, Func<TSource,bool> matches a TSource=>bool lambda expression: one that accepts a TSource argument and returns a bool value.

Similarly, Func<TSource,TResult> matches a TSource=>TResult lambda expression.

The Func delegates are listed in "Lambda Expressions" on page 174.

Lambda expressions and element typing

The standard query operators use the following type parameter names:

Generic type letter	Meaning
TSource	Element type for the input sequence
TResult	Element type for the output sequence (if different from TSource)
TKey	Element type for the *key* used in sorting, grouping, or joining

TSource is determined by the input sequence. TResult and TKey are typically *inferred from your lambda expression*.

For example, consider the signature of the Select query operator:

```
public static IEnumerable<TResult> Select<TSource,TResult>
  (this IEnumerable<TSource> source, Func<TSource,TResult> selector)
```

Func<TSource,TResult> matches a TSource=>TResult lambda expression: one that maps an *input element* to an *output element*. TSource and TResult can be different types, so the lambda expression can change the type of each element. Further, the lambda expression *determines the output sequence type*. The following query uses Select to transform string type elements to integer type elements:

```
string[] names = { "Tom", "Dick", "Harry", "Mary", "Jay" };
IEnumerable<int> query = names.Select (n => n.Length);

foreach (int length in query)
  Console.Write (length + "|");    // 3|4|5|4|3|
```

The compiler can *infer* the type of TResult from the return value of the lambda expression. In this case, n.Length returns an int value, so TResult is inferred to be int.

The Where query operator is simpler and requires no type inference for the output because input and output elements are of the same type. This makes sense because the operator merely filters elements; it does not *transform* them:

```
public static IEnumerable<TSource> Where<TSource>
    (this IEnumerable<TSource> source, Func<TSource,bool> predicate)
```

Finally, consider the signature of the OrderBy operator:

```
// Slightly simplified:
public static IEnumerable<TSource> OrderBy<TSource,TKey>
    (this IEnumerable<TSource> source, Func<TSource,TKey> keySelector)
```

Func<TSource,TKey> maps an input element to a *sorting key*. TKey is inferred from your lambda expression and is separate from the input and output element types. For instance, we could choose to sort a list of names by length (int key) or alphabetically (string key):

```
string[] names = { "Tom", "Dick", "Harry", "Mary", "Jay" };
IEnumerable<string> sortedByLength, sortedAlphabetically;
sortedByLength       = names.OrderBy (n => n.Length);   // int key
sortedAlphabetically = names.OrderBy (n => n);          // string key
```

 You can call the query operators in Enumerable with traditional delegates that refer to methods instead of lambda expressions. This approach is effective in simplifying certain kinds of local queries—particularly with LINQ to XML—and is demonstrated in Chapter 10. It doesn't work with IQuerya ble<T>-based sequences, however (e.g., when querying a database), because the operators in Queryable require lambda expressions in order to emit expression trees. We discuss this later in "Interpreted Queries" on page 424.

Natural Ordering

The original ordering of elements within an input sequence is significant in LINQ. Some query operators rely on this ordering, such as Take, Skip, and Reverse.

The Take operator outputs the first x elements, discarding the rest:

```
int[] numbers  = { 10, 9, 8, 7, 6 };
IEnumerable<int> firstThree = numbers.Take (3);     // { 10, 9, 8 }
```

The Skip operator ignores the first x elements and outputs the rest:

```
IEnumerable<int> lastTwo    = numbers.Skip (3);     // { 7, 6 }
```

Reverse does exactly as it says:

```
IEnumerable<int> reversed   = numbers.Reverse();    // { 6, 7, 8, 9, 10 }
```

With local queries (LINQ-to-objects), operators such as Where and Select preserve the original ordering of the input sequence (as do all other query operators, except for those that specifically change the ordering).

Other Operators

Not all query operators return a sequence. The *element* operators extract one element from the input sequence; examples are First, Last, and ElementAt:

```
int[] numbers     = { 10, 9, 8, 7, 6 };
int firstNumber   = numbers.First();                        // 10
int lastNumber    = numbers.Last();                         // 6
int secondNumber  = numbers.ElementAt(1);                   // 9
int secondLowest  = numbers.OrderBy(n=>n).Skip(1).First();  // 7
```

Because these operators return a single element, you don't usually call further query operators on their result unless that element itself is a collection.

The *aggregation* operators return a scalar value, usually of numeric type:

```
int count = numbers.Count();        // 5;
int min = numbers.Min();            // 6;
```

The *quantifiers* return a bool value:

```
bool hasTheNumberNine = numbers.Contains (9);         // true
bool hasMoreThanZeroElements = numbers.Any();         // true
bool hasAnOddElement = numbers.Any (n => n % 2 != 0); // true
```

Some query operators accept two input sequences. Examples are Concat, which appends one sequence to another, and Union, which does the same but with duplicates removed:

```
int[] seq1 = { 1, 2, 3 };
int[] seq2 = { 3, 4, 5 };
IEnumerable<int> concat = seq1.Concat (seq2);   // { 1, 2, 3, 3, 4, 5 }
IEnumerable<int> union  = seq1.Union (seq2);    // { 1, 2, 3, 4, 5 }
```

The joining operators also fall into this category. Chapter 9 covers all of the query operators in detail.

Query Expressions

C# provides a syntactic shortcut for writing LINQ queries, called *query expressions*. Contrary to popular belief, a query expression is not a means of embedding SQL into C#. In fact, the design of query expressions was inspired primarily by *list comprehensions* from functional programming languages such as LISP and Haskell, although SQL had a cosmetic influence.

 In this book, we refer to query expression syntax simply as *query syntax.*

In the preceding section, we wrote a fluent-syntax query to extract strings containing the letter "a," sorted by length and converted to uppercase. Here's the same thing in query syntax:

```
using System;
using System.Collections.Generic;
using System.Linq;

string[] names = { "Tom", "Dick", "Harry", "Mary", "Jay" };

IEnumerable<string> query =
  from    n in names
  where   n.Contains ("a")      // Filter elements
  orderby n.Length              // Sort elements
  select  n.ToUpper();          // Translate each element (project)

foreach (string name in query) Console.WriteLine (name);

JAY
MARY
HARRY
```

Query expressions always start with a `from` clause and end with either a `select` or `group` clause. The `from` clause declares a *range variable* (in this case, n), which you can think of as traversing the input sequence—rather like `foreach`. Figure 8-2 illustrates the complete syntax as a railroad diagram.

 To read this diagram, start at the left and then proceed along the track as if you were a train. For instance, after the mandatory `from` clause, you can optionally include an `orderby`, `where`, `let`, or `join` clause. After that, you can either continue with a `select` or `group` clause, or go back and include another `from`, `orderby`, `where`, `let`, or `join` clause.

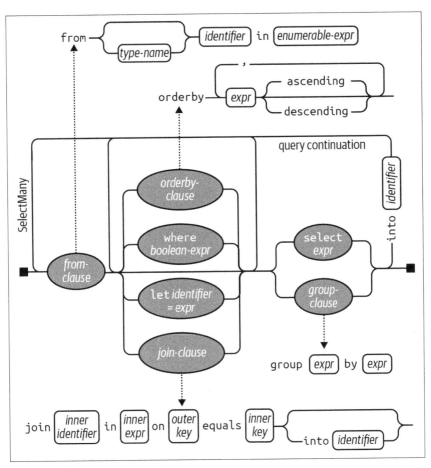

Figure 8-2. Query syntax

The compiler processes a query expression by translating it into fluent syntax. It does this in a fairly mechanical fashion—much like it translates foreach statements into calls to GetEnumerator and MoveNext. This means that anything you can write in query syntax you can also write in fluent syntax. The compiler (initially) translates our example query into the following:

```
IEnumerable<string> query = names.Where  (n => n.Contains ("a"))
                                 .OrderBy (n => n.Length)
                                 .Select  (n => n.ToUpper());
```

The Where, OrderBy, and Select operators then resolve using the same rules that would apply if the query were written in fluent syntax. In this case, they bind to extension methods in the Enumerable class because the System.Linq namespace is imported and names implements IEnumerable<string>. The compiler doesn't specifically favor the Enumerable class, however, when translating query expressions. You can think of the compiler as mechanically injecting the words "Where,"

"OrderBy," and "Select" into the statement and then compiling it as though you had typed the method names yourself. This offers flexibility in how they resolve. The operators in the database queries that we write in later sections, for instance, will bind instead to extension methods in Queryable.

If we remove the using System.Linq directive from our program, the query would not compile, since the Where, OrderBy, and Select methods would have nowhere to bind. Query expressions cannot compile unless you import System.Linq or another namespace with an implementation of these query methods.

Range Variables

The identifier immediately following the from keyword syntax is called the *range variable*. A range variable refers to the current element in the sequence on which the operation is to be performed.

In our examples, the range variable n appears in every clause in the query. And yet, the variable actually enumerates over a *different* sequence with each clause:

```
from    n in names          // n is our range variable
where   n.Contains ("a")    // n = directly from the array
orderby n.Length            // n = subsequent to being filtered
select  n.ToUpper()         // n = subsequent to being sorted
```

This becomes clear when we examine the compiler's mechanical translation to fluent syntax:

```
names.Where   (n => n.Contains ("a"))    // Locally scoped n
     .OrderBy (n => n.Length)            // Locally scoped n
     .Select  (n => n.ToUpper())         // Locally scoped n
```

As you can see, each instance of n is scoped privately to its own lambda expression.

Query expressions also let you introduce new range variables via the following clauses:

- let
- into
- An additional from clause
- join

We cover these later in this chapter in "Composition Strategies" on page 418 as well as in Chapter 9, in "Projecting" on page 449 and "Joining" on page 449.

Query Syntax Versus SQL Syntax

Query expressions look superficially like SQL, yet the two are very different. A LINQ query boils down to a C# expression, and so follows standard C# rules. For example, with LINQ, you cannot use a variable before you declare it. In SQL, you can reference a table alias in the SELECT clause before defining it in a FROM clause.

A subquery in LINQ is just another C# expression and so requires no special syntax. Subqueries in SQL are subject to special rules.

With LINQ, data logically flows from left to right through the query. With SQL, the order is less well structured with regard to data flow.

A LINQ query comprises a conveyor belt or *pipeline* of operators that accept and emit sequences whose element order can matter. An SQL query comprises a *network* of clauses that work mostly with *unordered sets*.

Query Syntax Versus Fluent Syntax

Query and fluent syntax each have advantages.

Query syntax is simpler for queries that involve any of the following:

- A let clause for introducing a new variable alongside the range variable
- SelectMany, Join, or GroupJoin, followed by an outer range variable reference

(We describe the let clause in "Composition Strategies" on page 418; we describe SelectMany, Join, and GroupJoin in Chapter 9.)

The middle ground is queries that involve the simple use of Where, OrderBy, and Select. Either syntax works well; the choice here is largely personal.

For queries that comprise a single operator, fluent syntax is shorter and less cluttered.

Finally, there are many operators that have no keyword in query syntax. These require that you use fluent syntax—at least in part. This means any operator outside of the following:

```
Where, Select, SelectMany
OrderBy, ThenBy, OrderByDescending, ThenByDescending
GroupBy, Join, GroupJoin
```

Mixed-Syntax Queries

If a query operator has no query-syntax support, you can mix query syntax and fluent syntax. The only restriction is that each query-syntax component must be complete (i.e., start with a from clause and end with a select or group clause).

Assuming this array declaration

```
string[] names = { "Tom", "Dick", "Harry", "Mary", "Jay" };
```

the following example counts the number of names containing the letter "a":

```
int matches = (from n in names where n.Contains ("a") select n).Count();
// 3
```

The next query obtains the first name in alphabetical order:

```
string first = (from n in names orderby n select n).First();    // Dick
```

The mixed-syntax approach is sometimes beneficial in more complex queries. With these simple examples, however, we could stick to fluent syntax throughout without penalty:

```
int matches = names.Where (n => n.Contains ("a")).Count();    // 3
string first = names.OrderBy (n => n).First();                // Dick
```

 There are times when mixed-syntax queries offer by far the highest "bang for the buck" in terms of function and simplicity. It's important not to unilaterally favor either query or fluent syntax; otherwise, you'll be unable to write mixed-syntax queries when they are the best option.

Where applicable, the remainder of this chapter shows key concepts in both fluent and query syntax.

Deferred Execution

An important feature of most query operators is that they execute not when constructed but when *enumerated* (in other words, when MoveNext is called on its enumerator). Consider the following query:

```
var numbers = new List<int> { 1 };

IEnumerable<int> query = numbers.Select (n => n * 10);    // Build query

numbers.Add (2);                          // Sneak in an extra element

foreach (int n in query)
    Console.Write (n + "|");              // 10|20|
```

The extra number that we sneaked into the list *after* constructing the query is included in the result because it's not until the foreach statement runs that any filtering or sorting takes place. This is called *deferred* or *lazy* execution and is the same as what happens with delegates:

```
Action a = () => Console.WriteLine ("Foo");
// We've not written anything to the Console yet. Now let's run it:
a(); // Deferred execution!
```

All standard query operators provide deferred execution, with the following exceptions:

- Operators that return a single element or scalar value, such as First or Count

- The following *conversion operators*:

    ```
    ToArray, ToList, ToDictionary, ToLookup, ToHashSet
    ```

These operators cause immediate query execution because their result types have no mechanism to provide deferred execution. The Count method, for instance, returns a simple integer, which doesn't then get enumerated. The following query is executed immediately:

```
int matches = numbers.Where (n => n <= 2).Count();    // 1
```

Deferred execution is important because it decouples query *construction* from query *execution*. This allows you to construct a query in several steps and also makes database queries possible.

 Subqueries provide another level of indirection. Everything in a subquery is subject to deferred execution, including aggregation and conversion methods. We describe this in "Subqueries" on page 414.

Reevaluation

Deferred execution has another consequence: a deferred execution query is reevaluated when you reenumerate:

```
var numbers = new List<int>() { 1, 2 };

IEnumerable<int> query = numbers.Select (n => n * 10);
foreach (int n in query) Console.Write (n + "|");    // 10|20|

numbers.Clear();
foreach (int n in query) Console.Write (n + "|");    // <nothing>
```

There are a couple of reasons why reevaluation is sometimes disadvantageous:

- Sometimes, you want to "freeze" or cache the results at a certain point in time.
- Some queries are computationally intensive (or rely on querying a remote database), so you don't want to unnecessarily repeat them.

You can defeat reevaluation by calling a conversion operator such as ToArray or ToList. ToArray copies the output of a query to an array; ToList copies to a generic List<T>:

```
var numbers = new List<int>() { 1, 2 };

List<int> timesTen = numbers
  .Select (n => n * 10)

  .ToList();                   // Executes immediately into a List<int>

numbers.Clear();
Console.WriteLine (timesTen.Count);    // Still 2
```

Captured Variables

If your query's lambda expressions *capture* outer variables, the query will honor the value of those variables at the time the query *runs*:

```
int[] numbers = { 1, 2 };

int factor = 10;
IEnumerable<int> query = numbers.Select (n => n * factor);
factor = 20;
foreach (int n in query) Console.Write (n + "|");    // 20|40|
```

This can be a trap when building up a query within a for loop. For example, suppose that we want to remove all vowels from a string. The following, although inefficient, gives the correct result:

```
IEnumerable<char> query = "Not what you might expect";

query = query.Where (c => c != 'a');
query = query.Where (c => c != 'e');
query = query.Where (c => c != 'i');
query = query.Where (c => c != 'o');
query = query.Where (c => c != 'u');

foreach (char c in query) Console.Write (c);  // Nt wht y mght xpct
```

Now watch what happens when we refactor this with a for loop:

```
IEnumerable<char> query = "Not what you might expect";
string vowels = "aeiou";

for (int i = 0; i < vowels.Length; i++)
  query = query.Where (c => c != vowels[i]);

foreach (char c in query) Console.Write (c);
```

An IndexOutOfRangeException is thrown upon enumerating the query because, as we saw in Chapter 4 (see "Capturing Outer Variables" on page 176), the compiler scopes the iteration variable in the for loop as if it were declared *outside* the loop. Hence, each closure captures the *same* variable (i) whose value is 5 when the query is actually enumerated. To solve this, you must assign the loop variable to another variable declared *inside* the statement block:

```
for (int i = 0; i < vowels.Length; i++)
{
  char vowel = vowels[i];
  query = query.Where (c => c != vowel);
}
```

This forces a fresh local variable to be captured on each loop iteration.

> Another way to solve the problem is to replace the for loop with a foreach loop:
>
> ```
> foreach (char vowel in vowels)
>   query = query.Where (c => c != vowel);
> ```

How Deferred Execution Works

Query operators provide deferred execution by returning *decorator* sequences.

Unlike a traditional collection class such as an array or linked list, a decorator sequence (in general) has no backing structure of its own to store elements. Instead, it wraps another sequence that you supply at runtime, to which it maintains a permanent dependency. Whenever you request data from a decorator, it in turn must request data from the wrapped input sequence.

 The query operator's transformation constitutes the "decoration." If the output sequence performed no transformation, it would be a *proxy* rather than a decorator.

Calling `Where` merely constructs the decorator wrapper sequence, which holds a reference to the input sequence, the lambda expression, and any other arguments supplied. The input sequence is enumerated only when the decorator is enumerated.

Figure 8-3 illustrates the composition of the following query:

```
IEnumerable<int> lessThanTen = new int[] { 5, 12, 3 }.Where (n => n < 10);
```

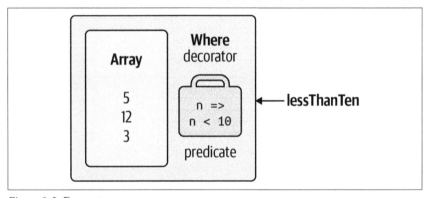

Figure 8-3. Decorator sequence

When you enumerate `lessThanTen`, you are, in effect, querying the array through the `Where` decorator.

The good news—should you ever want to write your own query operator—is that implementing a decorator sequence is easy with a C# iterator. Here's how you can write your own `Select` method:

```
public static IEnumerable<TResult> MySelect<TSource,TResult>
  (this IEnumerable<TSource> source, Func<TSource,TResult> selector)
{
  foreach (TSource element in source)
    yield return selector (element);
}
```

This method is an iterator by virtue of the yield return statement. Functionally, it's a shortcut for the following:

```
public static IEnumerable<TResult> MySelect<TSource,TResult>
  (this IEnumerable<TSource> source, Func<TSource,TResult> selector)
{
  return new SelectSequence (source, selector);
}
```

where *SelectSequence* is a (compiler-written) class whose enumerator encapsulates the logic in the iterator method.

Hence, when you call an operator such as Select or Where, you're doing nothing more than instantiating an enumerable class that decorates the input sequence.

Chaining Decorators

Chaining query operators creates a layering of decorators. Consider the following query:

```
IEnumerable<int> query = new int[] { 5, 12, 3 }.Where   (n => n < 10)
                                              .OrderBy (n => n)
                                              .Select  (n => n * 10);
```

Each query operator instantiates a new decorator that wraps the previous sequence (rather like a Russian nesting doll). Figure 8-4 illustrates the object model of this query. Note that this object model is fully constructed prior to any enumeration.

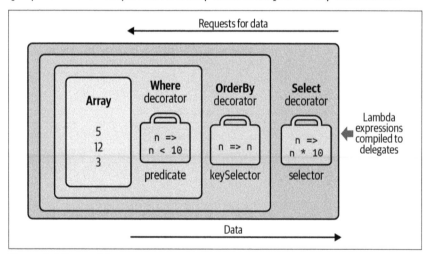

Figure 8-4. Layered decorator sequences

When you enumerate query, you're querying the original array, transformed through a layering or chain of decorators.

Adding ToList onto the end of this query would cause the preceding operators to execute immediately, collapsing the whole object model into a single list.

Figure 8-5 shows the same object composition in Unified Modeling Language (UML) syntax. Select's decorator references the OrderBy decorator, which references Where's decorator, which references the array. A feature of deferred execution is that you build the identical object model if you compose the query progressively:

```
IEnumerable<int>
    source    = new int[] { 5, 12, 3 },
    filtered  = source   .Where   (n => n < 10),
    sorted    = filtered .OrderBy (n => n),
    query     = sorted   .Select  (n => n * 10);
```

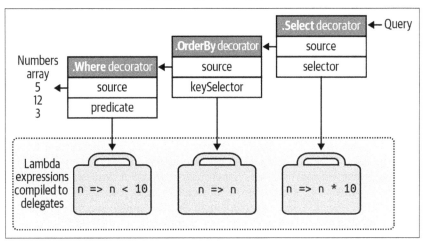

Figure 8-5. UML decorator composition

How Queries Are Executed

Here are the results of enumerating the preceding query:

```
foreach (int n in query) Console.WriteLine (n);
```

30
50

Behind the scenes, the foreach calls GetEnumerator on Select's decorator (the last or outermost operator), which kicks off everything. The result is a chain of enumerators that structurally mirrors the chain of decorator sequences. Figure 8-6 illustrates the flow of execution as enumeration proceeds.

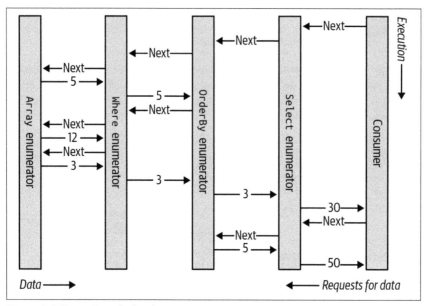

Figure 8-6. Execution of a local query

In the first section of this chapter, we depicted a query as a production line of conveyor belts. Extending this analogy, we can say a LINQ query is a lazy production line, where the conveyor belts roll elements only upon *demand*. Constructing a query constructs a production line—with everything in place—but with nothing rolling. Then, when the consumer requests an element (enumerates over the query), the rightmost conveyor belt activates; this in turn triggers the others to roll—as and when input sequence elements are needed. LINQ follows a demand-driven *pull* model, rather than a supply-driven *push* model. This is important—as you'll see later—in allowing LINQ to scale to querying SQL databases.

Subqueries

A *subquery* is a query contained within another query's lambda expression. The following example uses a subquery to sort musicians by their last name:

```
string[] musos =
  { "David Gilmour", "Roger Waters", "Rick Wright", "Nick Mason" };

IEnumerable<string> query = musos.OrderBy (m => m.Split().Last());
```

m.Split converts each string into a collection of words, upon which we then call the Last query operator. m.Split().Last is the subquery; query references the *outer query*.

Subqueries are permitted because you can put any valid C# expression on the right-hand side of a lambda. A subquery is simply another C# expression. This means that the rules for subqueries are a consequence of the rules for lambda expressions (and the behavior of query operators in general).

 The term *subquery*, in the general sense, has a broader meaning. For the purpose of describing LINQ, we use the term only for a query referenced from within the lambda expression of another query. In a query expression, a subquery amounts to a query referenced from an expression in any clause except the `from` clause.

A subquery is privately scoped to the enclosing expression and can reference parameters in the outer lambda expression (or range variables in a query expression).

`m.Split().Last` is a very simple subquery. The next query retrieves all strings in an array whose length matches that of the shortest string:

```
string[] names = { "Tom", "Dick", "Harry", "Mary", "Jay" };

IEnumerable<string> outerQuery = names
  .Where (n => n.Length == names.OrderBy (n2 => n2.Length)
                                .Select  (n2 => n2.Length).First());

// Tom, Jay
```

Here's the same thing as a query expression:

```
IEnumerable<string> outerQuery =
  from   n in names
  where  n.Length ==
           (from n2 in names orderby n2.Length select n2.Length).First()
  select n;
```

Because the outer range variable (n) is in scope for a subquery, we cannot reuse n as the subquery's range variable.

A subquery is executed whenever the enclosing lambda expression is evaluated. This means that a subquery is executed upon demand, at the discretion of the outer query. You could say that execution proceeds from the *outside in*. Local queries follow this model literally; interpreted queries (e.g., database queries) follow this model *conceptually*.

LINQ Queries

The subquery executes as and when required, to feed the outer query. As Figures 8-7 and 8-8 illustrate, the subquery in our example (the top conveyor belt in Figure 8-7) executes once for every outer loop iteration.

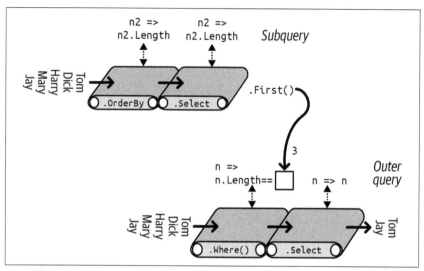

Figure 8-7. Subquery composition

We can express our preceding subquery more succinctly as follows:

```
IEnumerable<string> query =
  from  n in names
  where n.Length == names.OrderBy (n2 => n2.Length).First().Length
  select n;
```

With the Min aggregation function, we can simplify the query further:

```
IEnumerable<string> query =
  from  n in names
  where n.Length == names.Min (n2 => n2.Length)
  select n;
```

In "Interpreted Queries" on page 424, we describe how remote sources such as SQL tables can be queried. Our example makes an ideal database query because it would be processed as a unit, requiring only one round trip to the database server. This query, however, is inefficient for a local collection because the subquery is recalculated on each outer loop iteration. We can avoid this inefficiency by running the subquery separately (so that it's no longer a subquery):

```
int shortest = names.Min (n => n.Length);

IEnumerable<string> query = from  n in names
                            where n.Length == shortest
                            select n;
```

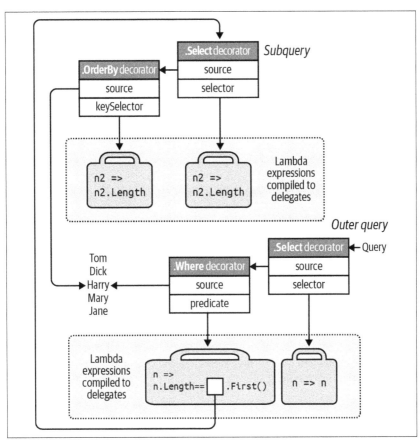

Figure 8-8. UML subquery composition

 Factoring out subqueries in this manner is nearly always desirable when querying local collections. An exception is when the subquery is *correlated*, meaning that it references the outer range variable. We explore correlated subqueries in "Projecting" on page 449.

Subqueries and Deferred Execution

An element or aggregation operator such as First or Count in a subquery doesn't force the *outer* query into immediate execution—deferred execution still holds for the outer query. This is because subqueries are called *indirectly*—through a delegate in the case of a local query, or through an expression tree in the case of an interpreted query.

An interesting case arises when you include a subquery within a Select expression. In the case of a local query, you're actually *projecting a sequence of queries*—each itself subject to deferred execution. The effect is generally transparent, and it serves to further improve efficiency. We revisit `Select` subqueries in some detail in Chapter 9.

Composition Strategies

In this section, we describe three strategies for building more complex queries:

- Progressive query construction
- Using the `into` keyword
- Wrapping queries

All are *chaining* strategies and produce identical runtime queries.

Progressive Query Building

At the start of the chapter, we demonstrated how you could build a fluent query progressively:

```
var filtered  = names    .Where   (n => n.Contains ("a"));
var sorted    = filtered .OrderBy (n => n);
var query     = sorted   .Select  (n => n.ToUpper());
```

Because each of the participating query operators returns a decorator sequence, the resultant query is the same chain or layering of decorators that you would get from a single-expression query. There are a couple of potential benefits, however, to building queries progressively:

- It can make queries easier to write.
- You can add query operators *conditionally*. For example,

    ```
    if (includeFilter) query = query.Where (...)
    ```

  is more efficient than

    ```
    query = query.Where (n => !includeFilter || <expression>)
    ```

  because it avoids adding an extra query operator if `includeFilter` is false.

A progressive approach is often useful in query comprehensions. Imagine that we want to remove all vowels from a list of names and then present in alphabetical order those whose length is still more than two characters. In fluent syntax, we could write this query as a single expression—by projecting *before* we filter:

```
IEnumerable<string> query = names
  .Select  (n => n.Replace ("a", "").Replace ("e", "").Replace ("i", "")
                  .Replace ("o", "").Replace ("u", ""))
  .Where   (n => n.Length > 2)
  .OrderBy (n => n);

// Dck
// Hrry
// Mry
```

Rather than calling string's Replace method five times, we could remove vowels from a string more efficiently with a regular expression:

```
n => Regex.Replace (n, "[aeiou]", "")
```

string's Replace method has the advantage, though, of also working in database queries.

Translating this directly into a query expression is troublesome because the select clause must come after the where and orderby clauses. And if we rearrange the query so as to project last, the result would be different:

```
IEnumerable<string> query =
  from    n in names
  where   n.Length > 2
  orderby n
  select  n.Replace ("a", "").Replace ("e", "").Replace ("i", "")
             .Replace ("o", "").Replace ("u", "");

// Dck
// Hrry
// Jy
// Mry
// Tm
```

Fortunately, there are a number of ways to get the original result in query syntax. The first is by querying progressively:

```
IEnumerable<string> query =
  from    n in names
  select n.Replace ("a", "").Replace ("e", "").Replace ("i", "")
             .Replace ("o", "").Replace ("u", "");

query = from n in query where n.Length > 2 orderby n select n;

// Dck
// Hrry
// Mry
```

The into Keyword

 The into keyword is interpreted in two very different ways by query expressions, depending on context. The meaning we're describing now is for signaling *query continuation* (the other is for signaling a GroupJoin).

The into keyword lets you "continue" a query after a projection and is a shortcut for progressively querying. With into, we can rewrite the preceding query as follows:

```
IEnumerable<string> query =
  from    n in names
  select n.Replace ("a", "").Replace ("e", "").Replace ("i", "")
             .Replace ("o", "").Replace ("u", "")
  into noVowel
    where noVowel.Length > 2 orderby noVowel select noVowel;
```

LINQ Queries

The only place you can use into is after a select or group clause. into "restarts" a query, allowing you to introduce fresh where, orderby, and select clauses.

 Although it's easiest to think of into as restarting a query from the perspective of a query expression, it's *all one query* when translated to its final fluent form. Hence, there's no intrinsic performance hit with into. Nor do you lose any points for its use!

The equivalent of into in fluent syntax is simply a longer chain of operators.

Scoping rules

All range variables are out of scope following an into keyword. The following will not compile:

```
var query =
  from n1 in names
  select n1.ToUpper()
  into n2                          // Only n2 is visible from here on.
    where n1.Contains ("x")        // Illegal: n1 is not in scope.
    select n2;
```

To see why, consider how this maps to fluent syntax:

```
var query = names
  .Select (n1 => n1.ToUpper())
  .Where  (n2 => n1.Contains ("x"));     // Error: n1 no longer in scope
```

The original name (n1) is lost by the time the Where filter runs. Where's input sequence contains only uppercase names, so it cannot filter based on n1.

Wrapping Queries

A query built progressively can be formulated into a single statement by wrapping one query around another. In general terms,

```
var tempQuery = tempQueryExpr
var finalQuery = from ... in tempQuery ...
```

can be reformulated as:

```
var finalQuery = from ... in (tempQueryExpr)
```

Wrapping is semantically identical to progressive query building or using the into keyword (without the intermediate variable). The end result in all cases is a linear chain of query operators. For example, consider the following query:

```
IEnumerable<string> query =
  from   n in names
  select n.Replace ("a", "").Replace ("e", "").Replace ("i", "")
          .Replace ("o", "").Replace ("u", "");

query = from n in query where n.Length > 2 orderby n select n;
```

Reformulated in wrapped form, it's the following:

```
IEnumerable<string> query =
  from n1 in
  (
    from   n2 in names
    select n2.Replace ("a", "").Replace ("e", "").Replace ("i", "")
              .Replace ("o", "").Replace ("u", "")
  )
  where n1.Length > 2 orderby n1 select n1;
```

When converted to fluent syntax, the result is the same linear chain of operators as in previous examples:

```
IEnumerable<string> query = names
  .Select  (n => n.Replace ("a", "").Replace ("e", "").Replace ("i", "")
                  .Replace ("o", "").Replace ("u", ""))
  .Where   (n => n.Length > 2)
  .OrderBy (n => n);
```

(The compiler does not emit the final .Select (n => n), because it's redundant.)

Wrapped queries can be confusing because they resemble the *subqueries* we wrote earlier. Both have the concept of an inner and outer query. When converted to fluent syntax, however, you can see that wrapping is simply a strategy for sequentially chaining operators. The end result bears no resemblance to a subquery, which embeds an inner query within the *lambda expression* of another.

Returning to a previous analogy: when wrapping, the "inner" query amounts to the *preceding conveyor belts*. In contrast, a subquery rides above a conveyor belt and is activated upon demand through the conveyor belt's lambda worker (as illustrated in Figure 8-7).

Projection Strategies

Object Initializers

So far, all of our select clauses have projected scalar element types. With C# object initializers, you can project into more complex types. For example, suppose, as a first step in a query, we want to strip vowels from a list of names while still retaining the original versions alongside, for the benefit of subsequent queries. We can write the following class to assist:

```
class TempProjectionItem
{
  public string Original;    // Original name
  public string Vowelless;   // Vowel-stripped name
}
```

We then can project into it with object initializers:

```
string[] names = { "Tom", "Dick", "Harry", "Mary", "Jay" };

IEnumerable<TempProjectionItem> temp =
  from n in names
  select new TempProjectionItem
  {
    Original  = n,
    Vowelless = n.Replace ("a", "").Replace ("e", "").Replace ("i", "")
                 .Replace ("o", "").Replace ("u", "")
  };
```

The result is of type `IEnumerable<TempProjectionItem>`, which we can subsequently query:

```
IEnumerable<string> query = from   item in temp
                            where  item.Vowelless.Length > 2
                            select item.Original;
// Dick
// Harry
// Mary
```

Anonymous Types

Anonymous types allow you to structure your intermediate results without writing special classes. We can eliminate the `TempProjectionItem` class in our previous example with anonymous types:

```
var intermediate = from n in names

  select new
  {
    Original = n,
    Vowelless = n.Replace ("a", "").Replace ("e", "").Replace ("i", "")
                 .Replace ("o", "").Replace ("u", "")
  };

IEnumerable<string> query = from   item in intermediate
                            where  item.Vowelless.Length > 2
                            select item.Original;
```

This gives the same result as the previous example, but without needing to write a one-off class. The compiler does the job instead, generating a temporary class with fields that match the structure of our projection. This means, however, that the intermediate query has the following type:

```
IEnumerable <random-compiler-generated-name>
```

The only way we can declare a variable of this type is with the `var` keyword. In this case, `var` is more than just a clutter reduction device; it's a necessity.

We can write the entire query more succinctly with the `into` keyword:

```
var query = from n in names
  select new
  {
    Original = n,
    Vowelless = n.Replace ("a", "").Replace ("e", "").Replace ("i", "")
                 .Replace ("o", "").Replace ("u", "")
  }
  into temp
  where temp.Vowelless.Length > 2
  select temp.Original;
```

Query expressions provide a shortcut for writing this kind of query: the let keyword.

The let Keyword

The let keyword introduces a new variable alongside the range variable.

With let, we can write a query extracting strings whose length, excluding vowels, exceeds two characters, as follows:

```
string[] names = { "Tom", "Dick", "Harry", "Mary", "Jay" };

IEnumerable<string> query =
  from n in names
  let vowelless = n.Replace ("a", "").Replace ("e", "").Replace ("i", "")
                   .Replace ("o", "").Replace ("u", "")
  where vowelless.Length > 2
  orderby vowelless
  select n;        // Thanks to let, n is still in scope.
```

The compiler resolves a let clause by projecting into a temporary anonymous type that contains both the range variable and the new expression variable. In other words, the compiler translates this query into the preceding example.

let accomplishes two things:

- It projects new elements alongside existing elements.
- It allows an expression to be used repeatedly in a query without being rewritten.

The let approach is particularly advantageous in this example because it allows the select clause to project either the original name (n) or its vowel-removed version (vowelless).

You can have any number of let statements before or after a where statement (see Figure 8-2). A let statement can reference variables introduced in earlier let statements (subject to the boundaries imposed by an into clause). let *reprojects* all existing variables transparently.

A let expression need not evaluate to a scalar type: sometimes it's useful to have it evaluate to a subsequence, for instance.

Interpreted Queries

LINQ provides two parallel architectures: *local* queries for local object collections and *interpreted* queries for remote data sources. So far, we've examined the architecture of local queries, which operate over collections implementing IEnumerable<T>. Local queries resolve to query operators in the Enumerable class (by default), which in turn resolve to chains of decorator sequences. The delegates that they accept—whether expressed in query syntax, fluent syntax, or traditional delegates—are fully local to Intermediate Language (IL) code, just like any other C# method.

By contrast, interpreted queries are *descriptive*. They operate over sequences that implement IQueryable<T>, and they resolve to the query operators in the Querya ble class, which emit *expression trees* that are interpreted at runtime. These expression trees can be translated, for instance, to SQL queries, allowing you to use LINQ to query a database.

The query operators in Enumerable can actually work with IQueryable<T> sequences. The difficulty is that the resultant queries always execute locally on the client. This is why a second set of query operators is provided in the Queryable class.

To write interpreted queries, you need to start with an API that exposes sequences of type IQueryable<T>. An example is Microsoft's *Entity Framework Core* (EF Core), which allows you to query a variety of databases, including SQL Server, Oracle, MySQL, PostgreSQL, and SQLite.

It's also possible to generate an IQueryable<T> wrapper around an ordinary enumerable collection by calling the AsQueryable method. We describe AsQueryable in "Building Query Expressions" on page 442.

IQueryable<T> is an extension of IEnumerable<T> with additional methods for constructing expression trees. Most of the time you can ignore the details of these methods; they're called indirectly by the runtime. "Building Query Expressions" on page 442 covers IQueryable<T> in more detail.

To illustrate, let's create a simple customer table in SQL Server and populate it with a few names using the following SQL script:

```
create table Customer
(
  ID int not null primary key,
  Name varchar(30)
)
insert Customer values (1, 'Tom')
insert Customer values (2, 'Dick')
insert Customer values (3, 'Harry')
insert Customer values (4, 'Mary')
insert Customer values (5, 'Jay')
```

With this table in place, we can write an interpreted LINQ query in C# that uses EF
Core to retrieve customers whose name contains the letter "a," as follows:

```
using System;
using System.Linq;
using Microsoft.EntityFrameworkCore;

using var dbContext = new NutshellContext();

IQueryable<string> query = from c in dbContext.Customers
  where   c.Name.Contains ("a")
  orderby c.Name.Length
  select  c.Name.ToUpper();

foreach (string name in query) Console.WriteLine (name);

public class Customer
{
  public int ID { get; set; }
  public string Name { get; set; }
}

// We'll explain the following class in more detail in the next section.
public class NutshellContext : DbContext
{
  public virtual DbSet<Customer> Customers { get; set; }

  protected override void OnConfiguring (DbContextOptionsBuilder builder)
    => builder.UseSqlServer ("...connection string...");

  protected override void OnModelCreating (ModelBuilder modelBuilder)
    => modelBuilder.Entity<Customer>().ToTable ("Customer")
                                      .HasKey (c => c.ID);
}
```

EF Core translates this query into the following SQL:

```
SELECT UPPER([c].[Name])
FROM [Customers] AS [c]
WHERE CHARINDEX(N'a', [c].[Name]) > 0
ORDER BY CAST(LEN([c].[Name]) AS int)
```

Here's the end result:

```
// JAY
// MARY
// HARRY
```

How Interpreted Queries Work

Let's examine how the preceding query is processed.

First, the compiler converts query syntax to fluent syntax. This is done exactly as with local queries:

```
IQueryable<string> query = dbContext.customers
                    .Where   (n => n.Name.Contains ("a"))
                    .OrderBy (n => n.Name.Length)
                    .Select  (n => n.Name.ToUpper());
```

Next, the compiler resolves the query operator methods. Here's where local and interpreted queries differ—interpreted queries resolve to query operators in the Queryable class instead of the Enumerable class.

To see why, we need to look at the dbContext.Customers variable, the source upon which the entire query builds. dbContext.Customers is of type DbSet<T>, which implements IQueryable<T> (a subtype of IEnumerable<T>). This means that the compiler has a choice in resolving Where: it could call the extension method in Enumerable or the following extension method in Queryable:

```
public static IQueryable<TSource> Where<TSource> (this
    IQueryable<TSource> source, Expression <Func<TSource,bool>> predicate)
```

The compiler chooses Queryable.Where because its signature is a *more specific match*.

Queryable.Where accepts a predicate wrapped in an Expression<TDelegate> type. This instructs the compiler to translate the supplied lambda expression—in other words, n=>n.Name.Contains("a")—to an *expression tree* rather than a compiled delegate. An expression tree is an object model based on the types in System.Linq.Expressions that can be inspected at runtime (so that EF Core can later translate it to an SQL statement).

Because Queryable.Where also returns IQueryable<T>, the same process follows with the OrderBy and Select operators. Figure 8-9 illustrates the end result. In the shaded box, there is an *expression tree* describing the entire query, which can be traversed at runtime.

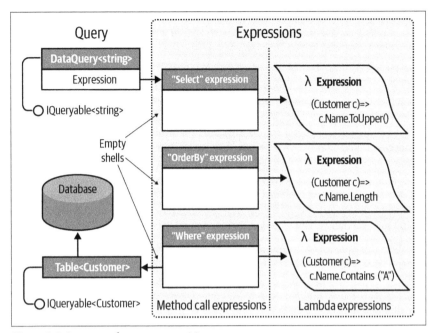

Figure 8-9. Interpreted query composition

Execution

Interpreted queries follow a deferred execution model—just like local queries. This means that the SQL statement is not generated until you start enumerating the query. Further, enumerating the same query twice results in the database being queried twice.

Under the hood, interpreted queries differ from local queries in how they execute. When you enumerate over an interpreted query, the outermost sequence runs a program that traverses the entire expression tree, processing it as a unit. In our example, EF Core translates the expression tree to an SQL statement, which it then executes, yielding the results as a sequence.

To work, EF Core needs to understand the schema of the database. It does this by leveraging conventions, code attributes, and a fluent configuration API. We'll explore this in detail later in the chapter.

We said previously that a LINQ query is like a production line. However, when you enumerate an IQueryable conveyor belt, it doesn't start up the whole production line, like with a local query. Instead, just the IQueryable belt starts up, with a special enumerator that calls upon a production manager. The manager reviews the entire production line—which consists not of compiled code but of *dummies* (method call expressions) with instructions pasted to their *foreheads* (expression trees). The manager then traverses all the expressions, in this case transcribing them to a single piece of paper (an SQL statement), which it then executes, feeding the results back to the consumer. Only one belt turns; the rest of the production line is a network of empty shells, existing just to describe what needs to be done.

This has some practical implications. For instance, with local queries, you can write your own query methods (fairly easily, with iterators) and then use them to supplement the predefined set. With remote queries, this is difficult and even undesirable. If you wrote a MyWhere extension method accepting IQueryable<T>, it would be like putting your own dummy into the production line. The production manager wouldn't know what to do with your dummy. Even if you intervened at this stage, your solution would be hardwired to a particular provider, such as EF Core, and would not work with other IQueryable implementations. Part of the benefit of having a standard set of methods in Queryable is that they define a *standard vocabulary* for querying *any* remote collection. As soon as you try to extend the vocabulary, you're no longer interoperable.

Another consequence of this model is that an IQueryable provider might be unable to cope with some queries—even if you stick to the standard methods. EF Core is limited by the capabilities of the database server; some LINQ queries have no SQL translation. If you're familiar with SQL, you'll have a good intuition for what these are, although at times you'll need to experiment to see what causes a runtime error; it can be surprising what *does* work!

Combining Interpreted and Local Queries

A query can include both interpreted and local operators. A typical pattern is to have the local operators on the *outside* and the interpreted components on the *inside*; in other words, the interpreted queries feed the local queries. This pattern works well when querying a database.

For instance, suppose that we write a custom extension method to pair up strings in a collection:

```
public static IEnumerable<string> Pair (this IEnumerable<string> source)
{
  string firstHalf = null;
  foreach (string element in source)
    if (firstHalf == null)
      firstHalf = element;
    else
    {
      yield return firstHalf + ", " + element;
      firstHalf = null;
    }
}
```

We can use this extension method in a query that mixes EF Core and local operators:

```
using var dbContext = new NutshellContext ();
IEnumerable<string> q = dbContext.Customers
  .Select (c => c.Name.ToUpper())
```

```
        .OrderBy (n => n)
        .Pair()                          // Local from this point on.
        .Select ((n, i) => "Pair " + i.ToString() + " = " + n);

    foreach (string element in q) Console.WriteLine (element);

    // Pair 0 = DICK, HARRY
    // Pair 1 = JAY, MARY
```

Because dbContext.Customers is of a type implementing IQueryable<T>, the Select operator resolves to Queryable.Select. This returns an output sequence also of type IQueryable<T>, so the OrderBy operator similarly resolves to Queryable.OrderBy. But the next query operator, Pair, has no overload accepting IQueryable<T>—only the less specific IEnumerable<T>. So, it resolves to our local Pair method—wrapping the interpreted query in a local query. Pair also returns IEnumerable, so the Select that follows resolves to another local operator.

On the EF Core side, the resulting SQL statement is equivalent to this:

```
SELECT UPPER([c].[Name]) FROM [Customers] AS [c] ORDER BY UPPER([c].[Name])
```

The remaining work is done locally. In effect, we end up with a local query (on the outside) whose source is an interpreted query (the inside).

AsEnumerable

Enumerable.AsEnumerable is the simplest of all query operators. Here's its complete definition:

```
public static IEnumerable<TSource> AsEnumerable<TSource>
            (this IEnumerable<TSource> source)
{
    return source;
}
```

Its purpose is to cast an IQueryable<T> sequence to IEnumerable<T>, forcing subsequent query operators to bind to Enumerable operators instead of Queryable operators. This causes the remainder of the query to execute locally.

To illustrate, suppose that we had a MedicalArticles table in SQL Server and wanted to use EF Core to retrieve all articles on influenza whose abstract contained fewer than 100 words. For the latter predicate, we need a regular expression:

```
Regex wordCounter = new Regex (@"\b(\w|[-'])+\b");

using var dbContext = new NutshellContext ();

var query = dbContext.MedicalArticles
    .Where (article => article.Topic == "influenza" &&
                    wordCounter.Matches (article.Abstract).Count < 100);
```

The problem is that SQL Server doesn't support regular expressions, so EF Core will throw an exception, complaining that the query cannot be translated to SQL. We can solve this by querying in two steps: first retrieving all articles on influenza through an EF Core query, and then filtering *locally* for abstracts of fewer than 100 words:

```
Regex wordCounter = new Regex (@"\b(\w|[-'])+\b");

using var dbContext = new NutshellContext ();

IEnumerable<MedicalArticle> efQuery = dbContext.MedicalArticles
  .Where (article => article.Topic == "influenza");

IEnumerable<MedicalArticle> localQuery = efQuery
  .Where (article => wordCounter.Matches (article.Abstract).Count < 100);
```

Because efQuery is of type IEnumerable<MedicalArticle>, the second query binds to the local query operators, forcing that part of the filtering to run on the client.

With AsEnumerable, we can do the same in a single query:

```
Regex wordCounter = new Regex (@"\b(\w|[-'])+\b");

using var dbContext = new NutshellContext ();

var query = dbContext.MedicalArticles
  .Where (article => article.Topic == "influenza")

  .AsEnumerable()
  .Where (article => wordCounter.Matches (article.Abstract).Count < 100);
```

An alternative to calling AsEnumerable is to call ToArray or ToList. The advantage of AsEnumerable is that it doesn't force immediate query execution, nor does it create any storage structure.

Moving query processing from the database server to the client can hurt performance, especially if it means retrieving more rows. A more efficient (though more complex) way to solve our example would be to use SQL CLR integration to expose a function on the database that implemented the regular expression.

We further demonstrate combined interpreted and local queries in Chapter 10.

EF Core

Throughout this and Chapter 9, we use EF Core to demonstrate interpreted queries. Let's now examine the key features of this technology.

EF Core Entity Classes

EF Core lets you use any class to represent data, as long as it contains a public property for each column that you want to query.

For instance, we could define the following entity class to query and update a *Customers* table in the database:

```
public class Customer
{
  public int ID { get; set; }
  public string Name { get; set; }
}
```

DbContext

After defining entity classes, the next step is to subclass DbContext. An instance of that class represents your sessions working with the database. Typically, your DbContext subclass will contain one DbSet<T> property for each entity in your model:

```
public class NutshellContext : DbContext
{
  public DbSet<Customer> Customers { get; set; }
  ... properties for other tables ...

}
```

A DbContext object does three things:

- It acts as a factory for generating DbSet<> objects that you can query.
- It keeps track of any changes that you make to your entities so that you can write them back (see "Change Tracking" on page 437).
- It provides virtual methods that you can override to configure the connection and model.

Configuring the connection

By overriding the OnConfiguring method, you can specify the database provider and connection string:

```
public class NutshellContext : DbContext
{
  ...
  protected override void OnConfiguring (DbContextOptionsBuilder
                                          optionsBuilder) =>
    optionsBuilder.UseSqlServer
      (@"Server=(local);Database=Nutshell;Trusted_Connection=True");
}
```

In this example, the connection string is specified as a string literal. Production applications would typically retrieve it from a configuration file such as *appsettings.json*.

UseSqlServer is an extension method defined in an assembly that's part of the *Microsoft.EntityFramework.SqlServer* NuGet package. Packages are available for other database providers, including Oracle, MySQL, PostgreSQL, and SQLite.

If you're using ASP.NET, you can allow its dependency injection framework to preconfigure `optionsBuilder`; in most cases, this lets you avoid overriding `OnConfiguring` altogether. To enable this, define a constructor on `DbContext` as follows:

```
public NutshellContext (DbContextOptions<NutshellContext>
                        options)
    : base(options) { }
```

If you do choose to override `OnConfiguring` (perhaps to provide a configuration if your `DbContext` is used in another scenario), you can check whether options have already been configured as follows:

```
protected override void OnConfiguring (
  DbContextOptionsBuilder optionsBuilder)
{
  if (!optionsBuilder.IsConfigured)
  {
    ...
  }
}
```

In the `OnConfiguring` method, you can enable other options, including lazy loading (see "Lazy loading" on page 440).

Configuring the Model

By default, EF Core is *convention based*, meaning that it infers the database schema from your class and property names.

You can override the defaults using the *fluent api* by overriding `OnModelCreating` and calling extension methods on the `ModelBuilder` parameter. For example, we can explicitly specify the database table name for our `Customer` entity as follows:

```
protected override void OnModelCreating (ModelBuilder modelBuilder) =>
  modelBuilder.Entity<Customer>()
    .ToTable ("Customer");   // Table is called 'Customer'
```

Without this code, EF Core would map this entity to a table named "Customers" rather than "Customer", because we have a `DbSet<Customer>` property in our `DbContext` called `Customers`:

```
public DbSet<Customer> Customers { get; set; }
```

The following code maps all of your entities to table names that match the entity *class name* (which is typically singular) rather than the `DbSet<T>` *property name* (which is typically plural):

```
protected override void OnModelCreating (ModelBuilder
                                            modelBuilder)
{
  foreach (IMutableEntityType entityType in
          modelBuilder.Model.GetEntityTypes())
  {
    modelBuilder.Entity (entityType.Name)
      .ToTable (entityType.ClrType.Name);
  }
}
```

The fluent API offers an expanded syntax for configuring columns. In the next example, we use two popular methods:

- `HasColumnName`, which maps a property to a differently named column
- `IsRequired`, which indicates that a column is not nullable

```
protected override void OnModelCreating (ModelBuilder modelBuilder) =>
  modelBuilder.Entity<Customer> (entity =>
  {
      entity.ToTable ("Customer");
      entity.Property (e => e.Name)
          .HasColumnName ("Full Name")   // Column name is 'Full Name'
          .IsRequired();                 // Column is not nullable
  });
```

Table 8-1 lists some of the most important methods in the fluent API.

Instead of using the fluent API, you can configure your model by applying special attributes to your entity classes and properties ("data annotations"). This approach is less flexible in that the configuration must be fixed at compile-time, and is less powerful in that there are some options that can be configured only via the fluent API.

Table 8-1. Fluent API model configuration methods

Method	Purpose	Example

ToTable	Specify the database table name for a given entity	`builder`
		`    .Entity<Customer>()`
		`    .ToTable("Customer");`

HasColumnName	Specify the column name for a given property	`builder.Entity<Customer>()`
		`    .Property(c => c.Name)`
		`    .HasColumnName("Full Name");`

HasKey	Specify a key (usually that deviates from convention)	`builder.Entity<Customer>()` `    .HasKey(c => c.CustomerNr);`

LINQ Queries

Method	Purpose	Example

IsRequired	Specify that the property requires a value (is not nullable)	```
		builder.Entity<Customer>()
		    .Property(c => c.Name)
		    .IsRequired();
		``

HasMaxLength	Specify the maximum length of a variable-length type (usually a string) whose width can vary	```
		builder.Entity<Customer>()
		    .Property(c => c.Name)
		    .HasMaxLength(60);
		``

HasColumnType	Specify the database data type for a column	```
		builder.Entity<Purchase>()
		    .Property(p => p.Description)
		    .HasColumnType("varchar(80)");
		``

Ignore	Ignore a type	``` builder.Ignore<Products>(); ```
Ignore	Ignore a property of a type	``` builder.Entity<Customer>() .Ignore(c => c.ChatName); ```

HasIndex	Specify a property (or combination of properties) should serve in the database as an index	```
		// Compound index:
		builder.Entity<Purchase>()
		    .HasIndex(p =>
		        new { p.Date, p.Price });
		
		// Unique index on one property
		builder
		    .Entity<MedicalArticle>()
		    .HasIndex(a => a.Topic)
		    .IsUnique();
		``

HasOne	See "Navigation Properties" on page 438	```
		builder.Entity<Purchase>()
		    .HasOne(p => p.Customer)
		    .WithMany(c => c.Purchases);
		``

HasMany	See "Navigation Properties" on page 438	```
		builder.Entity<Customer>()
		    .HasMany(c => c.Purchases)
		    .WithOne(p => p.Customer);
		``

Creating the database

EF Core supports a *code-first* approach, which means that you can start by defining entity classes and then ask EF Core to create the database. The easiest way to do the latter is to call the following method on a DbContext instance:

```
dbContext.Database.EnsureCreated();
```

A better approach, however, is to use EF Core's *migrations* feature, which not only creates the database but configures it such that EF Core can automatically update the schema in the future when your entity classes change. You can enable migrations in Visual Studio's Package Manager Console and ask it to create the database with the following commands:

```
Install-Package Microsoft.EntityFrameworkCore.Tools
Add-Migration InitialCreate
Update-Database
```

The first command installs tools to manage EF Core from within Visual Studio. The second command generates a special C# class known as a code migration that contains instructions to create the database. The final command runs those instructions against the database connection string specified in the project's application configuration file.

Using DbContext

After you've defined Entity classes and subclassed DbContext, you can instantiate your DbContext and query the database, as follows:

```
using var dbContext = new NutshellContext();
Console.WriteLine (dbContext.Customers.Count());
// Executes "SELECT COUNT(*) FROM [Customer] AS [c]"
```

You can also use your DbContext instance to write to the database. The following code inserts a row into the Customer table:

```
using var dbContext = new NutshellContext();
Customer cust = new Customer()
{
  Name = "Sara Wells"
};
dbContext.Customers.Add (cust);
dbContext.SaveChanges();    // Writes changes back to database
```

The following queries the database for the customer that was just inserted:

```
using var dbContext = new NutshellContext();
Customer cust = dbContext.Customers
  .Single (c => c.Name == "Sara Wells")
```

The following updates that customer's name and writes the change to the database:

```
cust.Name = "Dr. Sara Wells";
dbContext.SaveChanges();
```

The Single operator is ideal for retrieving a row by primary key. Unlike First, it throws an exception if more than one element is returned.

Object Tracking

A DbContext instance keeps track of all the entities it instantiates, so it can feed the same ones back to you whenever you request the same rows in a table. In other words, a context in its lifetime will never emit two separate entities that refer to the same row in a table (where a row is identified by primary key). This capability is called *object tracking*.

To illustrate, suppose the customer whose name is alphabetically first also has the lowest ID. In the following example, a and b will reference the same object:

```
using var dbContext = new NutshellContext ();

Customer a = dbContext.Customers.OrderBy (c => c.Name).First();
Customer b = dbContext.Customers.OrderBy (c => c.ID).First();
```

Disposing DbContext

Although DbContext implements IDisposable, you can (in general) get away without disposing instances. Disposing forces the context's connection to dispose—but this is usually unnecessary because EF Core closes connections automatically whenever you finish retrieving results from a query.

Disposing a context prematurely can actually be problematic because of lazy evaluation. Consider the following:

```
IQueryable<Customer> GetCustomers (string prefix)
{
  using (var dbContext = new NutshellContext ())
    return dbContext.Customers
                .Where (c => c.Name.StartsWith (prefix));
}
...
foreach (Customer c in GetCustomers ("a"))
  Console.WriteLine (c.Name);
```

This will fail because the query is evaluated when we enumerate it—which is *after* disposing its DbContext.

There are some caveats, though, on not disposing contexts:

- It relies on the connection object releasing all unmanaged resources on the Close method. Even though this holds true with SqlConnection, it's theoretically possible for a third-party connection to keep resources open if you call Close but not Dispose (though this would arguably violate the contract defined by IDbConnection.Close).

- If you manually call GetEnumerator on a query (instead of using foreach) and then fail to either dispose the enumerator or consume the sequence, the connection will remain open. Disposing the DbContext provides a backup in such scenarios.

- Some people feel that it's tidier to dispose contexts (and all objects that implement IDisposable).

If you want to explicitly dispose contexts, you must pass a DbContext instance into methods such as GetCustomers to avoid the problem described. In scenarios such as ASP.NET Core MVC where the context instance is provided via dependency injection (DI), the DI infrastructure will manage the context lifetime. It will be created when a unit of work (such as an HTTP request processed in the controller) begins and disposed when that unit of work ends.

Consider what happens when EF Core encounters the second query. It starts by querying the database—and obtaining a single row. It then reads the primary key of this row and performs a lookup in the context's entity cache. Seeing a match, it returns the existing object *without updating any values*. So, if another user had just updated that customer's Name in the database, the new value would be ignored. This is essential for avoiding unexpected side effects (the Customer object could be in use elsewhere) and also for managing concurrency. If you had altered properties on the Customer object and not yet called SaveChanges, you wouldn't want your properties automatically overwritten.

 You can disable object tracking by chaining the AsNo Tracking extension method to your query or by setting ChangeTracker.QueryTrackingBehavior on the context to QueryTrackingBehavior.NoTracking. No-tracking queries are useful when data is used read-only as it improves performance and reduces memory use.

To get fresh information from the database, you must either instantiate a new context or call the Reload method, as follows:

```
dbContext.Entry (myCustomer).Reload();
```

The best practice is to use a fresh DbContext instance per unit of work so that the need to manually reload an entity is rare.

Change Tracking

When you change a property value in an entity loaded via DbContext, EF Core recognizes the change and updates the database accordingly upon calling SaveChanges. To do that, it creates a snapshot of the state of entities loaded through your DbContext subclass and compares the current state to the original one when SaveChanges is called (or when you manually query change tracking, as you'll see in a moment). You can enumerate the tracked changes in a DbContext as follows:

```
foreach (var e in dbContext.ChangeTracker.Entries())
{
  Console.WriteLine ($"{e.Entity.GetType().FullName} is {e.State}");
  foreach (var m in e.Members)
    Console.WriteLine (
      $"  {m.Metadata.Name}: '{m.CurrentValue}' modified: {m.IsModified}");
}
```

When you call SaveChanges, EF Core uses the information in the ChangeTracker to construct SQL statements that will update the database to match the changes in your objects, issuing insert statements to add new rows, update statements to modify data, and delete statements to remove rows that were removed from the object graph in your DbContext subclass. Any TransactionScope is honored; if none is present, it wraps all statements in a new transaction.

You can optimize change tracking by implementing INotifyPropertyChanged and, optionally, INotifyPropertyChanging in your entities. The former allows EF Core to avoid the overhead of comparing modified with original entities; the latter allows EF Core to avoid storing the original values altogether. After implementing these interfaces, call the HasChangeTrackingStrategy method on the ModelBuilder when configuring the model in order to activate the optimized change tracking.

Navigation Properties

Navigation properties allow you to do the following:

- Query related tables without having to manually join
- Insert, remove, and update related rows without explicitly updating foreign keys

For example, suppose that a customer can have a number of purchases. We can represent a one-to-many relationship between *Customer* and *Purchase* with the following entities:

```
public class Customer
{
  public int ID { get; set; }
  public string Name { get; set; }

  // Child navigation property, which must be of type ICollection<T>:
  public virtual List<Purchase> Purchases {get;set;} = new List<Purchase>();
}

public class Purchase
{
  public int ID { get; set; }
  public DateTime Date { get; set; }
  public string Description { get; set; }
  public decimal Price { get; set; }
  public int CustomerID? { get; set; }      // Foreign key field

  public Customer Customer { get; set; }     // Parent navigation property
}
```

EF Core is able to infer from these entities that CustomerID is a foreign key to the *Customer* table, because the name "CustomerID" follows a popular naming convention. If we were to ask EF Core to create a database from these entities, it would create a foreign key constraint between Purchase.CustomerID and Customer.ID.

 If EF Core is unable to infer the relationship, you can configure it explicitly in the OnModelCreating method as follows:

```
modelBuilder.Entity<Purchase>()
  .HasOne (e => e.Customer)
  .WithMany (e => e.Purchases)
  .HasForeignKey (e => e.CustomerID);
```

With these navigation properties set up, we can write queries such as this:

```
var customersWithPurchases = Customers.Where (c => c.Purchases.Any());
```

We cover how to write such queries in detail in Chapter 9.

Adding and removing entities from navigation collections

When you add new entities to a collection navigation property, EF Core automatically populates the foreign keys upon calling SaveChanges:

```
Customer cust = dbContext.Customers.Single (c => c.ID == 1);

Purchase p1 = new Purchase { Description="Bike",  Price=500 };
Purchase p2 = new Purchase { Description="Tools", Price=100 };

cust.Purchases.Add (p1);
cust.Purchases.Add (p2);

dbContext.SaveChanges();
```

In this example, EF Core automatically writes 1 into the CustomerID column of each of the new purchases and writes the database-generated ID for each purchase to Purchase.ID.

When you remove an entity from a collection navigation property and call Save Changes, EF Core will either clear the foreign key field or delete the corresponding row from the database, depending on how the relationship has been configured or inferred. In this case, we've defined Purchase.CustomerID as a nullable integer (so that we can represent purchases without a customer, or cash transactions), so removing a purchase from a customer would clear its foreign key field rather than deleting it from the database.

Loading navigation properties

When EF Core populates an entity, it does not (by default) populate its navigation properties:

```
using var dbContext = new NutshellContext();
var cust = dbContext.Customers.First();
Console.WriteLine (cust.Purchases.Count);    // Always 0
```

One solution is to use the Include extension method, which instructs EF Core to *eagerly* load navigation properties:

```
var cust = dbContext.Customers
  .Include (c => c.Purchases)
  .Where (c => c.ID == 2).First();
```

Another solution is to use a projection. This technique is particularly useful when you need to work with only some of the entity properties, because it reduces data transfer:

```
var custInfo = dbContext.Customers
  .Where (c => c.ID == 2)
  .Select (c => new
    {
      Name = c.Name,
```

```
    Purchases = c.Purchases.Select (p => new { p.Description, p.Price })
    })
  .First();
```

Both of these techniques inform EF Core what data you require so that it can be fetched in a single database query. It's also possible to manually instruct EF Core to populate a navigation property as needed:

```
dbContext.Entry (cust).Collection (b => b.Purchases).Load();
// cust.Purchases is now populated.
```

This is called *explicit loading*. Unlike the preceding approaches, this generates an extra round trip to the database.

Lazy loading

Another approach for loading navigation properties is called *lazy loading*. When enabled, EF Core populates navigation properties on demand by generating a proxy class for each of your entity classes that intercepts attempts to access unloaded navigation properties. For this to work, each navigation property must be virtual, and the class it's defined in must be inheritable (not sealed). Also, the context must not have been disposed when the lazy load occurs, so that an additional database request can be performed.

You can enable lazy loading in the OnConfiguring method of your DbContext subclass, as follows:

```
protected override void OnConfiguring (DbContextOptionsBuilder
                                       optionsBuilder)
{
  optionsBuilder
    .UseLazyLoadingProxies()
    ...
}
```

(You will also need to add a reference to the Microsoft.EntityFramework Core.Proxies NuGet package.)

The cost of lazy loading is that EF Core must make an additional request to the database each time you access an unloaded navigation property. If you make many such requests, performance can suffer as a result of excessive round-tripping.

With lazy loading enabled, the runtime type of your classes is a proxy derived from your entity class. For example:

```
using var dbContext = new NutshellContext();
var cust = dbContext.Customers.First();
Console.WriteLine (cust.GetType());
// Castle.Proxies.CustomerProxy
```

Deferred Execution

EF Core queries are subject to deferred execution, just like local queries. This allows you to build queries progressively. There is one aspect, however, in which EF Core has special deferred execution semantics, and that is when a subquery appears within a Select expression.

With local queries, you get double-deferred execution, because from a functional perspective, you're selecting a sequence of *queries*. So, if you enumerate the outer result sequence but never enumerate the inner sequences, the subquery will never execute.

With EF Core, the subquery is executed at the same time as the main outer query. This prevents excessive round-tripping.

For example, the following query executes in a single round trip upon reaching the first foreach statement:

```
using var dbContext = new NutshellContext ();

var query = from c in dbContext.Customers
            select
                from p in c.Purchases
                select new { c.Name, p.Price };

foreach (var customerPurchaseResults in query)
  foreach (var namePrice in customerPurchaseResults)
    Console.WriteLine ($"{ namePrice.Name} spent { namePrice.Price}");
```

Any navigation properties that you explicitly project are fully populated in a single round trip:

```
var query = from c in dbContext.Customers
            select new { c.Name, c.Purchases };

foreach (var row in query)
  foreach (Purchase p in row.Purchases)   // No extra round-tripping
    Console.WriteLine (row.Name + " spent " + p.Price);
```

But if we enumerate a navigation property without first having either eagerly loaded or projected, deferred execution rules apply. In the following example, EF Core executes another Purchases query on each loop iteration (assuming lazy loading is enabled):

```
foreach (Customer c in dbContext.Customers.ToArray())
  foreach (Purchase p in c.Purchases)    // Another SQL round-trip
    Console.WriteLine (c.Name + " spent " + p.Price);
```

This model is advantageous when you want to *selectively* execute the inner loop, based on a test that can be performed only on the client:

```
foreach (Customer c in dbContext.Customers.ToArray())
  if (myWebService.HasBadCreditHistory (c.ID))
    foreach (Purchase p in c.Purchases)   // Another SQL round trip
      Console.WriteLine (c.Name + " spent " + p.Price);
```

Note the use of `ToArray` in the previous two queries. By default, SQL Server cannot initiate a new query while the results of the current query are still being processed. Calling `ToArray` materializes the customers so that additional queries can be issued to retrieve purchases per customer. It is possible to configure SQL Server to allow multiple active result sets (MARS) by appending `;MultipleActiveResultSets=True` to the database connection string. Use MARS with caution as it can mask a chatty database design that could be improved by eager loading and/or projecting the required data.

(In Chapter 9, we explore `Select` subqueries in more detail, in "Projecting" on page 449.)

Building Query Expressions

So far in this chapter, when we've needed to dynamically compose queries, we've done so by conditionally chaining query operators. Although this is adequate in many scenarios, sometimes you need to work at a more granular level and dynamically compose the lambda expressions that feed the operators.

In this section, we assume the following `Product` class:

```
public class Product
{
  public int ID { get; set; }
  public string Description { get; set; }
  public bool Discontinued { get; set; }
  public DateTime LastSale { get; set; }
}
```

Delegates Versus Expression Trees

Recall that:

- Local queries, which use `Enumerable` operators, take delegates.
- Interpreted queries, which use `Queryable` operators, take expression trees.

We can see this by comparing the signature of the `Where` operator in `Enumerable` and `Queryable`:

```
public static IEnumerable<TSource> Where<TSource> (this
  IEnumerable<TSource> source, Func<TSource,bool> predicate)

public static IQueryable<TSource> Where<TSource> (this
  IQueryable<TSource> source, Expression<Func<TSource,bool>> predicate)
```

When embedded within a query, a lambda expression looks identical whether it binds to `Enumerable`'s operators or `Queryable`'s operators:

```
IEnumerable<Product> q1 = localProducts.Where (p => !p.Discontinued);
IQueryable<Product>  q2 = sqlProducts.Where  (p => !p.Discontinued);
```

When you assign a lambda expression to an intermediate variable, however, you must be explicit about whether to resolve to a delegate (i.e., Func<>) or an expression tree (i.e., Expression<Func<>>). In the following example, predicate1 and predicate2 are not interchangeable:

```
Func <Product, bool> predicate1 = p => !p.Discontinued;
IEnumerable<Product> q1 = localProducts.Where (predicate1);

Expression <Func <Product, bool>> predicate2 = p => !p.Discontinued;
IQueryable<Product> q2 = sqlProducts.Where (predicate2);
```

Compiling expression trees

You can convert an expression tree to a delegate by calling Compile. This is of particular value when writing methods that return reusable expressions. To illustrate, let's add a static method to the Product class that returns a predicate evaluating to true if a product is not discontinued and has sold in the past 30 days:

```
public class Product
{
  public static Expression<Func<Product, bool>> IsSelling()
  {
    return p => !p.Discontinued && p.LastSale > DateTime.Now.AddDays (-30);
  }
}
```

The method just written can be used both in interpreted and local queries, as follows:

```
void Test()
{
  var dbContext = new NutshellContext();
  Product[] localProducts = dbContext.Products.ToArray();

  IQueryable<Product> sqlQuery =
    dbContext.Products.Where (Product.IsSelling());

  IEnumerable<Product> localQuery =
    localProducts.Where (Product.IsSelling().Compile());
}
```

.NET does not provide an API to convert in the reverse direction, from a delegate to an expression tree. This makes expression trees more versatile.

AsQueryable

The AsQueryable operator lets you write whole *queries* that can run over either local or remote sequences:

```
IQueryable<Product> FilterSortProducts (IQueryable<Product> input)
{
  return from p in input
         where ...
```

```
        orderby ...
        select p;
}

void Test()
{
  var dbContext = new NutshellContext();
  Product[] localProducts = dbContext.Products.ToArray();

  var sqlQuery   = FilterSortProducts (dbContext.Products);
  var localQuery = FilterSortProducts (localProducts.AsQueryable());
  ...
}
```

AsQueryable wraps IQueryable<T> clothing around a local sequence so that subsequent query operators resolve to expression trees. When you later enumerate over the result, the expression trees are implicitly compiled (at a small performance cost), and the local sequence enumerates as it would ordinarily.

Expression Trees

We said previously that an implicit conversion from a lambda expression to Expression<TDelegate> causes the C# compiler to emit code that builds an expression tree. With some programming effort, you can do the same thing manually at runtime—in other words, dynamically build an expression tree from scratch. The result can be cast to an Expression<TDelegate> and used in EF Core queries or compiled into an ordinary delegate by calling Compile.

The Expression DOM

An expression tree is a miniature code DOM. Each node in the tree is represented by a type in the System.Linq.Expressions namespace. Figure 8-10 illustrates these types.

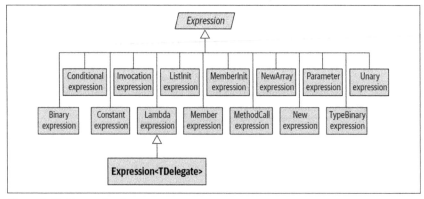

Figure 8-10. Expression types

The base class for all nodes is the (nongeneric) Expression class. The generic Expression<TDelegate> class actually means "typed lambda expression" and might have been named LambdaExpression<TDelegate> if it wasn't for the clumsiness of this:

```
LambdaExpression<Func<Customer,bool>> f = ...
```

Expression<T>'s base type is the (nongeneric) LambdaExpression class. Lamdba Expression provides type unification for lambda expression trees: any typed Expression<T> can be cast to a LambdaExpression.

The thing that distinguishes LambdaExpressions from ordinary Expressions is that lambda expressions have *parameters*.

To create an expression tree, don't instantiate node types directly; rather, call static methods provided on the Expression class, such as Add, And, Call, Constant, LessThan, and so on.

Figure 8-11 shows the expression tree that the following assignment creates:

```
Expression<Func<string, bool>> f = s => s.Length < 5;
```

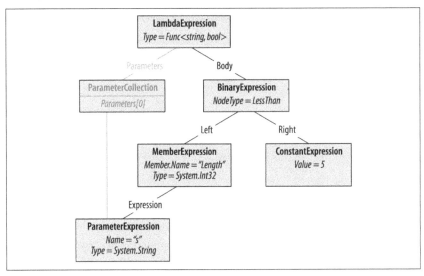

Figure 8-11. Expression tree

We can demonstrate this as follows:

```
Console.WriteLine (f.Body.NodeType);                    // LessThan
Console.WriteLine (((BinaryExpression) f.Body).Right);  // 5
```

Let's now build this expression from scratch. The principle is that you start from the bottom of the tree and work your way up. The bottommost thing in our tree is a ParameterExpression, the lambda expression parameter called "s" of type string:

```
ParameterExpression p = Expression.Parameter (typeof (string), "s");
```

The next step is to build the MemberExpression and ConstantExpression. In the former case, we need to access the Length *property* of our parameter, "s":

```
MemberExpression stringLength = Expression.Property (p, "Length");
ConstantExpression five = Expression.Constant (5);
```

Next is the LessThan comparison:

```
BinaryExpression comparison = Expression.LessThan (stringLength, five);
```

The final step is to construct the lambda expression, which links an expression Body to a collection of parameters:

```
Expression<Func<string, bool>> lambda
  = Expression.Lambda<Func<string, bool>> (comparison, p);
```

A convenient way to test our lambda is by compiling it to a delegate:

```
Func<string, bool> runnable = lambda.Compile();

Console.WriteLine (runnable ("kangaroo"));      // False
Console.WriteLine (runnable ("dog"));           // True
```

 The easiest way to determine which expression type to use is to examine an existing lambda expression in the Visual Studio debugger.

We continue this discussion online, at *http://www.albahari.com/expressions*.

9

LINQ Operators

This chapter describes each of the LINQ query operators. As well as serving as a reference, two of the sections, "Projecting" on page 449 and "Joining" on page 449, cover a number of conceptual areas:

- Projecting object hierarchies
- Joining with `Select`, `SelectMany`, `Join`, and `GroupJoin`
- Query expressions with multiple range variables

All of the examples in this chapter assume that a `names` array is defined as follows:

```
string[] names = { "Tom", "Dick", "Harry", "Mary", "Jay" };
```

Examples that query a database assume that a variable called `dbContext` is instantiated as

```
var dbContext = new NutshellContext();
```

where `NutshellContext` is defined as follows:

```
public class NutshellContext : DbContext
{
  public DbSet<Customer> Customers { get; set; }
  public DbSet<Purchase> Purchases { get; set; }

  protected override void OnModelCreating(ModelBuilder modelBuilder)
  {
    modelBuilder.Entity<Customer>(entity =>
    {
      entity.ToTable("Customer");
      entity.Property(e => e.Name).IsRequired();  // Column is not nullable
    });
    modelBuilder.Entity<Purchase>(entity =>
    {
      entity.ToTable("Purchase");
      entity.Property(e => e.Date).IsRequired();
```

```
      entity.Property(e => e.Description).IsRequired();
    });
  }
}

public class Customer
{
  public int ID { get; set; }
  public string Name { get; set; }

  public virtual List<Purchase> Purchases { get; set; }
    = new List<Purchase>();
}

public class Purchase
{
  public int ID { get; set; }
  public int? CustomerID { get; set; }
  public DateTime Date { get; set; }
  public string Description { get; set; }
  public decimal Price { get; set; }

  public virtual Customer Customer { get; set; }
}
```

 All of the examples in this chapter are preloaded into LINQ-Pad, along with a sample database with a matching schema. You can download LINQPad from *http://www.linqpad.net*.

Here are corresponding SQL Server table definitions:

```
CREATE TABLE Customer (
  ID int NOT NULL IDENTITY PRIMARY KEY,
  Name nvarchar(30) NOT NULL
)

CREATE TABLE Purchase (
  ID int NOT NULL IDENTITY PRIMARY KEY,
  CustomerID int NOT NULL REFERENCES Customer(ID),
  Date datetime NOT NULL,
  Description nvarchar(30) NOT NULL,
  Price decimal NOT NULL
)
```

Overview

In this section, we provide an overview of the standard query operators. They fall into three categories:

- Sequence in, sequence out (sequence→sequence)

- Sequence in, single element or scalar value out

- Nothing in, sequence out (*generation* methods)

We first present each of the three categories and the query operators they include, and then we take up each individual query operator in detail.

Sequence→Sequence

Most query operators fall into this category—accepting one or more sequences as input and emitting a single output sequence. Figure 9-1 illustrates those operators that restructure the shape of the sequences.

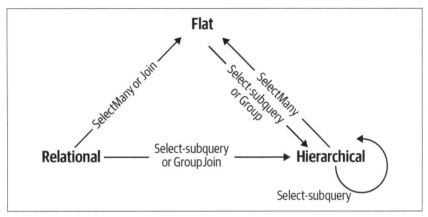

Figure 9-1. Shape-changing operators

Filtering

`IEnumerable<TSource> →IEnumerable<TSource>`

Returns a subset of the original elements.

```
Where, Take, TakeLast, TakeWhile, Skip, SkipLast, SkipWhile,
Distinct, DistinctBy
```

Projecting

`IEnumerable<TSource>→IEnumerable<TResult>`

Transforms each element with a lambda function. `SelectMany` flattens nested sequences; `Select` and `SelectMany` perform inner joins, left outer joins, cross joins, and non-equi joins with EF Core.

```
Select, SelectMany
```

Joining

`IEnumerable<TOuter>, IEnumerable<TInner>→IEnumerable<TResult>`

Meshes elements of one sequence with another. `Join` and `GroupJoin` operators are designed to be efficient with local queries and support inner and left outer joins. The `Zip` operator enumerates two sequences in step, applying a function over each

LINQ Operators

element pair. Rather than naming the type arguments TOuter and TInner, the Zip operator names them TFirst and TSecond:

IEnumerable<TFirst>, IEnumerable<TSecond>→IEnumerable<TResult>

> Join, GroupJoin, Zip

Ordering

IEnumerable<TSource>→IOrderedEnumerable<TSource>

Returns a reordering of a sequence.

> OrderBy, OrderByDescending, ThenBy, ThenByDescending, Reverse

Grouping

IEnumerable<TSource>→IEnumerable<IGrouping<TKey,TElement>>

IEnumerable<TSource>→IEnumerable<TElement[]>

Groups a sequence into subsequences.

> GroupBy, Chunk

Set operators

IEnumerable<TSource>, IEnumerable<TSource>→IEnumerable<TSource>

Takes two same-typed sequences and returns their commonality, sum, or difference.

> Concat, Union, UnionBy, Intersect, IntersectBy, Except, ExceptBy

Conversion methods: Import

IEnumerable→IEnumerable<TResult>

> OfType, Cast

Conversion methods: Export

IEnumerable<TSource>→An array, list, dictionary, lookup, or sequence

> ToArray, ToList, ToDictionary, ToLookup, AsEnumerable, AsQueryable

Sequence→Element or Value

The following query operators accept an input sequence and emit a single element or value.

Element operators

IEnumerable<TSource>→TSource

Picks a single element from a sequence.

```
First, FirstOrDefault, Last, LastOrDefault, Single, SingleOrDefault,
ElementAt, ElementAtOrDefault, MinBy, MaxBy, DefaultIfEmpty
```

Aggregation methods

`IEnumerable<TSource>`→*scalar*

Performs a computation across a sequence, returning a scalar value (typically a number).

```
Aggregate, Average, Count, LongCount, Sum, Max, Min
```

Quantifiers

`IEnumerable<TSource>`→*bool*

An aggregation returning `true` or `false`.

```
All, Any, Contains, SequenceEqual
```

Void→Sequence

In the third and final category are query operators that produce an output sequence from scratch.

Generation methods

`void`→`IEnumerable<TResult>`

Manufactures a simple sequence.

```
Empty, Range, Repeat
```

Filtering

`IEnumerable<TSource>`→`IEnumerable<TSource>`

Method	Description	SQL equivalents
Where	Returns a subset of elements that satisfy a given condition	WHERE
Take	Returns the first count elements and discards the rest	WHERE ROW_NUMBER()... *or* TOP *n* subquery
Skip	Ignores the first count elements and returns the rest	WHERE ROW_NUMBER()... *or* NOT IN (SELECT TOP *n*...)
TakeLast	Takes only the last count elements	Exception thrown
SkipLast	Takes only the last count elements	Exception thrown
TakeWhile	Emits elements from the input sequence until the predicate is false	Exception thrown

Method	Description	SQL equivalents
`SkipWhile`	Ignores elements from the input sequence until the predicate is false, and then emits the rest	Exception thrown
`Distinct,` `DistinctBy`	Returns a sequence that excludes duplicates	`SELECT DISTINCT...`

The "SQL equivalents" column in the reference tables in this chapter do not necessarily correspond to what an `IQueryable` implementation such as EF Core will produce. Rather, it indicates what you'd typically use to do the same job if you were writing the SQL query yourself. Where there is no simple translation, the column is left blank. Where there is no translation at all, the column reads "Exception thrown."

`Enumerable` implementation code, when shown, excludes checking for null arguments and indexing predicates.

With each of the filtering methods, you always end up with either the same number or fewer elements than you started with. You can never get more! The elements are also identical when they come out; they are not transformed in any way.

Where

Argument	Type
Source sequence	`IEnumerable<TSource>`
Predicate	`TSource => bool or (TSource,int) => bool`[a]

[a] Prohibited with LINQ to SQL and Entity Framework

Query syntax

```
where bool-expression
```

Enumerable.Where implementation

The internal implementation of `Enumerable.Where`, null checking aside, is functionally equivalent to the following:

```
public static IEnumerable<TSource> Where<TSource>
  (this IEnumerable<TSource> source, Func <TSource, bool> predicate)
{
  foreach (TSource element in source)
    if (predicate (element))
      yield return element;
}
```

Overview

Where returns the elements from the input sequence that satisfy the given predicate. For instance:

```
string[] names = { "Tom", "Dick", "Harry", "Mary", "Jay" };
IEnumerable<string> query = names.Where (name => name.EndsWith ("y"));

// Harry
// Mary
// Jay
```

In query syntax:

```
IEnumerable<string> query = from n in names
                            where n.EndsWith ("y")
                            select n;
```

A where clause can appear more than once in a query and be interspersed with let, orderby, and join clauses:

```
from n in names
where n.Length > 3
let u = n.ToUpper()
where u.EndsWith ("Y")
select u;

// HARRY
// MARY
```

Standard C# scoping rules apply to such queries. In other words, you cannot refer to a variable prior to declaring it with a range variable or a let clause.

Indexed filtering

Where's predicate optionally accepts a second argument, of type int. This is fed with the position of each element within the input sequence, allowing the predicate to use this information in its filtering decision. For example, the following skips every second element:

```
IEnumerable<string> query = names.Where ((n, i) => i % 2 == 0);

// Tom
// Harry
// Jay
```

An exception is thrown if you use indexed filtering in EF Core.

SQL LIKE comparisons in EF Core

The following methods on string translate to SQL's LIKE operator:

```
Contains, StartsWith, EndsWith
```

For instance, c.Name.Contains ("abc") translates to customer.Name LIKE '%abc%' (or more accurately, a parameterized version of this). Contains lets you compare only against a locally evaluated expression; to compare against another column, you must use the EF.Functions.Like method:

```
... where EF.Functions.Like (c.Description, "%" + c.Name + "%")
```

EF.Functions.Like also lets you perform more complex comparisons (e.g., LIKE 'abc%def%').

< and > string comparisons in EF Core

You can perform *order* comparison on strings with string's CompareTo method; this maps to SQL's < and > operators:

```
dbContext.Purchases.Where (p => p.Description.CompareTo ("C") < 0)
```

WHERE x IN (…, …, …) in EF Core

With EF Core, you can apply the Contains operator to a local collection within a filter predicate. For instance:

```
string[] chosenOnes = { "Tom", "Jay" };

from c in dbContext.Customers
where chosenOnes.Contains (c.Name)
...
```

This maps to SQL's IN operator. In other words:

```
WHERE customer.Name IN ("Tom", "Jay")
```

If the local collection is an array of entities or nonscalar types, EF Core might instead emit an EXISTS clause.

Take, TakeLast, Skip, and SkipLast

Argument	Type
Source sequence	IEnumerable<TSource>
Number of elements to take or skip	int

Take emits the first *n* elements and discards the rest; Skip discards the first *n* elements and emits the rest. The two methods are useful together when implementing a web page allowing a user to navigate through a large set of matching records. For instance, suppose that a user searches a book database for the term "mercury", and there are 100 matches. The following returns the first 20:

```
IQueryable<Book> query = dbContext.Books
  .Where   (b => b.Title.Contains ("mercury"))
  .OrderBy (b => b.Title)
  .Take (20);
```

The next query returns books 21 to 40:

```
IQueryable<Book> query = dbContext.Books
  .Where   (b => b.Title.Contains ("mercury"))
  .OrderBy (b => b.Title)
  .Skip (20).Take (20);
```

EF Core translates Take and Skip to the ROW_NUMBER function in SQL Server 2005, or a TOP *n* subquery in earlier versions of SQL Server.

The TakeLast and SkipLast methods take or skip the last *n* elements.

From .NET 6, the Take method is overloaded to accept a Range variable. This overload can subsume the functionality of all four methods; for instance, Take(5..) is equivalent to Skip(5), and Take(..^5) is equivalent to SkipLast(5).

TakeWhile and SkipWhile

Argument	Type
Source sequence	IEnumerable<TSource>
Predicate	TSource => bool or (TSource,int) => bool

TakeWhile enumerates the input sequence, emitting each item until the given predicate is false. It then ignores the remaining elements:

```
int[] numbers      = { 3, 5, 2, 234, 4, 1 };
var takeWhileSmall = numbers.TakeWhile (n => n < 100);   // { 3, 5, 2 }
```

SkipWhile enumerates the input sequence, ignoring each item until the given predicate is false. It then emits the remaining elements:

```
int[] numbers      = { 3, 5, 2, 234, 4, 1 };
var skipWhileSmall = numbers.SkipWhile (n => n < 100);   // { 234, 4, 1 }
```

TakeWhile and SkipWhile have no translation to SQL and throw an exception if used in an EF Core query.

Distinct and DistinctBy

Distinct returns the input sequence, stripped of duplicates. You can optionally pass in a custom equality comparer. The following returns distinct letters in a string:

```
char[] distinctLetters = "HelloWorld".Distinct().ToArray();
string s = new string (distinctLetters);                  // HeloWrd
```

We can call LINQ methods directly on a string because string implements IEnumerable<char>.

The DistinctBy method was introduced in .NET 6 and lets you specify a key selector to be applied before performing equality comparison. The result of the following expression is {1,2,3}:

```
new[] { 1.0, 1.1, 2.0, 2.1, 3.0, 3.1 }.DistinctBy (n => Math.Round (n, 0))
```

Projecting

IEnumerable<TSource>→ IEnumerable<TResult>

Method	Description	SQL equivalents
Select	Transforms each input element with the given lambda expression	SELECT
SelectMany	Transforms each input element, and then flattens and concatenates the resultant subsequences	INNER JOIN, LEFT OUTER JOIN, CROSS JOIN

 When querying a database, Select and SelectMany are the most versatile joining constructs; for local queries, Join and GroupJoin are the most *efficient* joining constructs.

Select

Argument	Type
Source sequence	IEnumerable<TSource>
Result selector	TSource => TResult or (TSource,int) => TResult[a]

[a] Prohibited with EF Core

Query syntax

```
select projection-expression
```

Enumerable implementation

```
public static IEnumerable<TResult> Select<TSource,TResult>
  (this IEnumerable<TSource> source, Func<TSource,TResult> selector)
{
  foreach (TSource element in source)
    yield return selector (element);
}
```

Overview

With Select, you always get the same number of elements that you started with. Each element, however, can be transformed in any manner by the lambda function.

The following selects the names of all fonts installed on the computer (from System.Drawing):

```
IEnumerable<string> query = from f in FontFamily.Families
                            select f.Name;
```

```
foreach (string name in query) Console.WriteLine (name);
```

In this example, the `select` clause converts a `FontFamily` object to its name. Here's the lambda equivalent:

```
IEnumerable<string> query = FontFamily.Families.Select (f => f.Name);
```

`Select` statements are often used to project into anonymous types:

```
var query =
  from f in FontFamily.Families
  select new { f.Name, LineSpacing = f.GetLineSpacing (FontStyle.Bold) };
```

A projection with no transformation is sometimes used with query syntax to satisfy the requirement that the query end in a `select` or `group` clause. The following selects fonts supporting strikeout:

```
IEnumerable<FontFamily> query =
  from f in FontFamily.Families
  where f.IsStyleAvailable (FontStyle.Strikeout)
  select f;

foreach (FontFamily ff in query) Console.WriteLine (ff.Name);
```

In such cases, the compiler omits the projection when translating to fluent syntax.

Indexed projection

The `selector` expression can optionally accept an integer argument, which acts as an indexer, providing the expression with the position of each input in the input sequence. This works only with local queries:

```
string[] names = { "Tom", "Dick", "Harry", "Mary", "Jay" };

IEnumerable<string> query = names
  .Select ((s,i) => i + "=" + s);      // { "0=Tom", "1=Dick", ... }
```

Select subqueries and object hierarchies

You can nest a subquery in a `select` clause to build an object hierarchy. The following example returns a collection describing each directory under `Path.Get TempPath()`, with a subcollection of files under each directory:

```
string tempPath = Path.GetTempPath();
DirectoryInfo[] dirs = new DirectoryInfo (tempPath).GetDirectories();

var query =
  from d in dirs
  where (d.Attributes & FileAttributes.System) == 0
  select new
  {
    DirectoryName = d.FullName,
    Created = d.CreationTime,
```

```
      Files = from f in d.GetFiles()
               where (f.Attributes & FileAttributes.Hidden) == 0
               select new { FileName = f.Name, f.Length, }
    };

  foreach (var dirFiles in query)
  {
    Console.WriteLine ("Directory: " + dirFiles.DirectoryName);
    foreach (var file in dirFiles.Files)
      Console.WriteLine ("   " + file.FileName + " Len: " + file.Length);
  }
```

The inner portion of this query can be called a *correlated subquery*. A subquery is correlated if it references an object in the outer query—in this case, it references d, the directory being enumerated.

 A subquery inside a Select allows you to map one object hierarchy to another, or map a relational object model to a hierarchical object model.

With local queries, a subquery within a Select causes double-deferred execution. In our example, the files aren't filtered or projected until the inner foreach statement enumerates.

Subqueries and joins in EF Core

Subquery projections work well in EF Core, and you can use them to do the work of SQL-style joins. Here's how we retrieve each customer's name along with their high-value purchases:

```
var query =
  from c in dbContext.Customers
  select new {
              c.Name,
              Purchases = (from p in dbContext.Purchases
                           where p.CustomerID == c.ID && p.Price > 1000
                           select new { p.Description, p.Price })
                           .ToList()
             };

foreach (var namePurchases in query)
{
  Console.WriteLine ("Customer: " + namePurchases.Name);
  foreach (var purchaseDetail in namePurchases.Purchases)
    Console.WriteLine ("   - $$$: " + purchaseDetail.Price);
}
```

 Note the use of ToList in the subquery. EF Core 3 cannot create queryables from the subquery result when that subquery references the DbContext. This issue is being tracked by the EF Core team and might be resolved in a future release.

This style of query is ideally suited to interpreted queries. The outer query and subquery are processed as a unit, preventing unnecessary round-tripping. With local queries, however, it's inefficient because every combination of outer and inner elements must be enumerated to get the few matching combinations. A better choice for local queries is `Join` or `GroupJoin`, described in the following sections.

This query matches up objects from two disparate collections, and it can be thought of as a "join." The difference between this and a conventional database join (or subquery) is that we're not flattening the output into a single two-dimensional result set. We're mapping the relational data to hierarchical data, rather than to flat data.

Here's the same query simplified by using the `Purchases` collection navigation property on the `Customer` entity:

```
from c in dbContext.Customers
select new
{
  c.Name,
  Purchases = from p in c.Purchases      // Purchases is List<Purchase>
              where p.Price > 1000
              select new { p.Description, p.Price }
};
```

(EF Core 3 does not require `ToList` when performing the subquery on a navigation property.)

Both queries are analogous to a left outer join in SQL in the sense that we get all customers in the outer enumeration, regardless of whether they have any purchases. To emulate an inner join—whereby customers without high-value purchases are excluded—we would need to add a filter condition on the purchases collection:

```
from c in dbContext.Customers
where c.Purchases.Any (p => p.Price > 1000)
select new {
            c.Name,
            Purchases = from p in c.Purchases
                        where p.Price > 1000
                        select new { p.Description, p.Price }
          };
```

This is slightly untidy, however, in that we've written the same predicate (`Price > 1000`) twice. We can avoid this duplication with a `let` clause:

```
from c in dbContext.Customers
let highValueP = from p in c.Purchases
                 where p.Price > 1000
                 select new { p.Description, p.Price }
where highValueP.Any()
select new { c.Name, Purchases = highValueP };
```

This style of query is flexible. By changing Any to Count, for instance, we can modify the query to retrieve only customers with at least two high-value purchases:

```
...
where highValueP.Count() >= 2
select new { c.Name, Purchases = highValueP };
```

Projecting into concrete types

In the examples so far, we've instantiated anonymous types in the output. It can also be useful to instantiate (ordinary) named classes, which you populate with object initializers. Such classes can include custom logic and can be passed between methods and assemblies without using type information.

A typical example is a custom business entity. A custom business entity is simply a class that you write with some properties but is designed to hide lower-level (database-related) details. You might exclude foreign key fields from business-entity classes, for instance. Assuming that we wrote custom entity classes called Customer Entity and PurchaseEntity, here's how we could project into them:

```
IQueryable<CustomerEntity> query =
  from c in dbContext.Customers
  select new CustomerEntity
  {
    Name = c.Name,
    Purchases =
      (from p in c.Purchases
       where p.Price > 1000
       select new PurchaseEntity {
                                    Description = p.Description,
                                    Value = p.Price
                                  }
      ).ToList()
  };

// Force query execution, converting output to a more convenient List:
List<CustomerEntity> result = query.ToList();
```

 When created to transfer data between tiers in a program or between separate systems, custom business entity classes are often called data transfer objects (DTO). DTOs contain no business logic.

Notice that so far, we've not had to use a Join or SelectMany statement. This is because we're maintaining the hierarchical shape of the data, as illustrated in Figure 9-2. With LINQ, you can often avoid the traditional SQL approach of flattening tables into a two-dimensional result set.

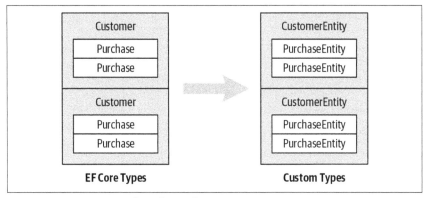

Figure 9-2. Projecting an object hierarchy

SelectMany

Argument	Type
Source sequence	`IEnumerable<TSource>`
Result selector	`TSource => IEnumerable<TResult>` or `(TSource,int) => IEnumerable<TResult>`[a]

[a] Prohibited with EF Core

Query syntax

```
from identifier1 in enumerable-expression1
from identifier2 in enumerable-expression2
...
```

Enumerable implementation

```
public static IEnumerable<TResult> SelectMany<TSource,TResult>
  (IEnumerable<TSource> source,
   Func <TSource,IEnumerable<TResult>> selector)
{
  foreach (TSource element in source)
    foreach (TResult subElement in selector (element))
      yield return subElement;
}
```

Overview

`SelectMany` concatenates subsequences into a single flat output sequence.

Recall that for each input element, `Select` yields exactly one output element. In contrast, `SelectMany` yields *0..n* output elements. The *0..n* elements come from a subsequence or child sequence that the lambda expression must emit.

LINQ Operators

You can use SelectMany to expand child sequences, flatten nested collections, and join two collections into a flat output sequence. Using the conveyor belt analogy, SelectMany funnels fresh material onto a conveyor belt. With SelectMany, each input element is the *trigger* for the introduction of fresh material. The fresh material is emitted by the selector lambda expression and must be a sequence. In other words, the lambda expression must emit a *child sequence* per input *element*. The final result is a concatenation of the child sequences emitted for each input element.

Starting with a simple example, suppose that we have the following array of names,

```
string[] fullNames = { "Anne Williams", "John Fred Smith", "Sue Green" };
```

that we want to convert to a single flat collection of words—in other words:

```
"Anne", "Williams", "John", "Fred", "Smith", "Sue", Green"
```

SelectMany is ideal for this task, because we're mapping each input element to a variable number of output elements. All we must do is come up with a selector expression that converts each input element to a child sequence. string.Split does the job nicely: it takes a string and splits it into words, emitting the result as an array:

```
string testInputElement = "Anne Williams";
string[] childSequence  = testInputElement.Split();

// childSequence is { "Anne", "Williams" };
```

So, here's our SelectMany query and the result:

```
IEnumerable<string> query = fullNames.SelectMany (name => name.Split());

foreach (string name in query)
  Console.Write (name + "|");   // Anne|Williams|John|Fred|Smith|Sue|Green|
```

 If you replace SelectMany with Select, you get the same results in hierarchical form. The following emits a sequence of string *arrays*, requiring nested foreach statements to enumerate:

```
IEnumerable<string[]> query =
  fullNames.Select (name => name.Split());

foreach (string[] stringArray in query)
  foreach (string name in stringArray)
    Console.Write (name + "|");
```

The benefit of SelectMany is that it yields a single *flat* result sequence.

SelectMany is supported in query syntax and is invoked by having an *additional generator*—in other words, an extra from clause in the query. The from keyword has two meanings in query syntax. At the start of a query, it introduces the original range variable and input sequence. *Anywhere else* in the query, it translates to SelectMany. Here's our query in query syntax:

```
IEnumerable<string> query =
  from fullName in fullNames
  from name in fullName.Split()     // Translates to SelectMany
  select name;
```

Note that the additional generator introduces a new range variable—in this case, name. The old range variable stays in scope, however, and we can subsequently access both.

Multiple range variables

In the preceding example, both name and fullName remain in scope until the query either ends or reaches an into clause. The extended scope of these variables is *the* killer scenario for query syntax over fluent syntax.

To illustrate, we can take the preceding query and include fullName in the final projection:

```
IEnumerable<string> query =
  from fullName in fullNames
  from name in fullName.Split()
  select name + " came from " + fullName;
```

Anne came from Anne Williams
Williams came from Anne Williams
John came from John Fred Smith
...

Behind the scenes, the compiler must pull some tricks to let you access both variables. A good way to appreciate this is to try writing the same query in fluent syntax. It's tricky! It becomes yet more difficult if you insert a where or orderby clause before projecting:

```
from fullName in fullNames
from name in fullName.Split()
orderby fullName, name
select name + " came from " + fullName;
```

The problem is that SelectMany emits a flat sequence of child elements—in our case, a flat collection of words. The original "outer" element from which it came (fullName) is lost. The solution is to "carry" the outer element with each child, in a temporary anonymous type:

```
from fullName in fullNames
from x in fullName.Split().Select (name => new { name, fullName } )
orderby x.fullName, x.name
select x.name + " came from " + x.fullName;
```

The only change here is that we're wrapping each child element (name) in an anonymous type that also contains its fullName. This is similar to how a let clause is resolved. Here's the final conversion to fluent syntax:

```
IEnumerable<string> query = fullNames
  .SelectMany (fName => fName.Split()
                        .Select (name => new { name, fName } ))
  .OrderBy (x => x.fName)
  .ThenBy  (x => x.name)
  .Select  (x => x.name + " came from " + x.fName);
```

Thinking in query syntax

As we just demonstrated, there are good reasons to use query syntax if you need multiple range variables. In such cases, it helps to not only use query syntax but also to think directly in its terms.

There are two basic patterns when writing additional generators. The first is *expanding and flattening subsequences*. To do this, you call a property or method on an existing range variable in your additional generator. We did this in the previous example:

```
from fullName in fullNames
from name in fullName.Split()
```

Here, we've expanded from enumerating full names to enumerating words. An analogous EF Core query is when you expand collection navigation properties. The following query lists all customers along with their purchases:

```
IEnumerable<string> query = from c in dbContext.Customers
                            from p in c.Purchases
                            select c.Name + " bought a " + p.Description;
```

```
Tom bought a Bike
Tom bought a Holiday
Dick bought a Phone
Harry bought a Car
...
```

Here, we've expanded each customer into a subsequence of purchases.

The second pattern is performing a *cartesian product*, or *cross join*, in which every element of one sequence is matched with every element of another. To do this, introduce a generator whose selector expression returns a sequence unrelated to a range variable:

```
int[] numbers = { 1, 2, 3 };  string[] letters = { "a", "b" };

IEnumerable<string> query = from n in numbers
                            from l in letters
                            select n.ToString() + l;
```

```
// RESULT: { "1a", "1b", "2a", "2b", "3a", "3b" }
```

This style of query is the basis of SelectMany-style *joins*.

Joining with SelectMany

You can use `SelectMany` to join two sequences simply by filtering the results of a cross product. For instance, suppose that we want to match players for a game. We could start as follows:

```
string[] players = { "Tom", "Jay", "Mary" };

IEnumerable<string> query = from name1 in players
                            from name2 in players
                            select name1 + " vs " + name2;

//RESULT: { "Tom vs Tom", "Tom vs Jay", "Tom vs Mary",
//          "Jay vs Tom", "Jay vs Jay", "Jay vs Mary",
//          "Mary vs Tom", "Mary vs "Jay", "Mary vs Mary" }
```

The query reads "For every player, reiterate every player, selecting player 1 versus player 2." Although we got what we asked for (a cross join), the results are not useful until we add a filter:

```
IEnumerable<string> query = from name1 in players
                            from name2 in players
                            where name1.CompareTo (name2) < 0
                            orderby name1, name2
                            select name1 + " vs " + name2;

//RESULT: { "Jay vs Mary", "Jay vs Tom", "Mary vs Tom" }
```

The filter predicate constitutes the *join condition*. Our query can be called a *non-equi join* because the join condition doesn't use an equality operator.

SelectMany in EF Core

`SelectMany` in EF Core can perform cross joins, non-equi joins, inner joins, and left outer joins. You can use `SelectMany` with both predefined associations and ad hoc relationships—just as with `Select`. The difference is that `SelectMany` returns a flat rather than a hierarchical result set.

An EF Core cross join is written just as in the preceding section. The following query matches every customer to every purchase (a cross join):

```
var query = from c in dbContext.Customers
            from p in dbContext.Purchases
            select c.Name + " might have bought a " + p.Description;
```

More typically, though, you'd want to match customers to only their own purchases. You achieve this by adding a `where` clause with a joining predicate. This results in a standard SQL-style equi-join:

```
var query = from c in dbContext.Customers
            from p in dbContext.Purchases
            where c.ID == p.CustomerID
            select c.Name + " bought a " + p.Description;
```

This translates well to SQL. In the next section, we see how it extends to support outer joins. Reformulating such queries with LINQ's Join operator actually makes them *less* extensible—LINQ is opposite to SQL in this sense.

If you have collection navigation properties in your entities, you can express the same query by expanding the subcollection instead of filtering the cross product:

```
from c in dbContext.Customers
from p in c.Purchases
select new { c.Name, p.Description };
```

The advantage is that we've eliminated the joining predicate. We've gone from filtering a cross product to expanding and flattening.

You can add where clauses to such a query for additional filtering. For instance, if we want only customers whose names started with "T", we could filter as follows:

```
from c in dbContext.Customers
where c.Name.StartsWith ("T")
from p in c.Purchases
select new { c.Name, p.Description };
```

This EF Core query would work equally well if the where clause were moved one line down because the same SQL is generated in both cases. If it is a local query, however, moving the where clause down would make it less efficient. With local queries, you should filter *before* joining.

You can introduce new tables into the mix with additional from clauses. For instance, if each purchase had purchase item child rows, you could produce a flat result set of customers with their purchases, each with their purchase detail lines as follows:

```
from c in dbContext.Customers
from p in c.Purchases
from pi in p.PurchaseItems
select new { c.Name, p.Description, pi.Detail };
```

Each from clause introduces a new *child* table. To include data from a *parent* table (via a navigation property), you don't add a from clause—you simply navigate to the property. For example, if each customer has a salesperson whose name you want to query, just do this:

```
from c in dbContext.Customers
select new { Name = c.Name, SalesPerson = c.SalesPerson.Name };
```

You don't use SelectMany in this case because there's no subcollection to flatten. Parent navigation properties return a single item.

Outer joins with SelectMany

We saw previously that a `Select` subquery yields a result analogous to a left outer join:

```
from c in dbContext.Customers
select new {
            c.Name,
            Purchases = from p in c.Purchases
                        where p.Price > 1000
                        select new { p.Description, p.Price }
            };
```

In this example, every outer element (customer) is included, regardless of whether the customer has any purchases. But suppose that we rewrite this query with `SelectMany` so that we can obtain a single flat collection rather than a hierarchical result set:

```
from c in dbContext.Customers
from p in c.Purchases
where p.Price > 1000
select new { c.Name, p.Description, p.Price };
```

In the process of flattening the query, we've switched to an inner join: customers are now included only for whom one or more high-value purchases exist. To get a left outer join with a flat result set, we must apply the `DefaultIfEmpty` query operator on the inner sequence. This method returns a sequence with a single null element if its input sequence has no elements. Here's such a query, price predicate aside:

```
from c in dbContext.Customers
from p in c.Purchases.DefaultIfEmpty()
select new { c.Name, p.Description, Price = (decimal?) p.Price };
```

This works perfectly with EF Core, returning all customers—even if they have no purchases. But if we were to run this as a local query, it would crash because when p is null, `p.Description` and `p.Price` throw a `NullReferenceException`. We can make our query robust in either scenario, as follows:

```
from c in dbContext.Customers
from p in c.Purchases.DefaultIfEmpty()
select new {
            c.Name,
            Descript = p == null ? null : p.Description,
            Price = p == null ? (decimal?) null : p.Price
            };
```

Let's now reintroduce the price filter. We cannot use a where clause as we did before, because it would execute *after* `DefaultIfEmpty`:

```
from c in dbContext.Customers
from p in c.Purchases.DefaultIfEmpty()
where p.Price > 1000...
```

The correct solution is to splice the Where clause *before* DefaultIfEmpty with a subquery:

```
from c in dbContext.Customers
from p in c.Purchases.Where (p => p.Price > 1000).DefaultIfEmpty()
select new {
            c.Name,
            Descript = p == null ? null : p.Description,
            Price = p == null ? (decimal?) null : p.Price
          };
```

EF Core translates this to a left outer join. This is an effective pattern for writing such queries.

 If you're used to writing outer joins in SQL, you might be tempted to overlook the simpler option of a Select subquery for this style of query in favor of the awkward but familiar SQL-centric flat approach. The hierarchical result set from a Select subquery is often better suited to outer join–style queries because there are no additional nulls to deal with.

Joining

Method	Description	SQL equivalents
Join	Applies a lookup strategy to match elements from two collections, emitting a flat result set	INNER JOIN
GroupJoin	Similar to Join, but emits a *hierarchical* result set	INNER JOIN, LEFT OUTER JOIN
Zip	Enumerates two sequences in step (like a zipper), applying a function over each element pair	Exception thrown

Join and GroupJoin

IEnumerable<TOuter>, IEnumerable<TInner>→IEnumerable<TResult>

Join arguments

Argument	Type
Outer sequence	IEnumerable<TOuter>
Inner sequence	IEnumerable<TInner>
Outer key selector	TOuter => TKey
Inner key selector	TInner => TKey
Result selector	(TOuter,TInner) => TResult

GroupJoin arguments

Argument	Type
Outer sequence	`IEnumerable<TOuter>`
Inner sequence	`IEnumerable<TInner>`
Outer key selector	`TOuter => TKey`
Inner key selector	`TInner => TKey`
Result selector	`(TOuter,IEnumerable<TInner>) => TResult`

Query syntax

```
from outer-var in outer-enumerable
join inner-var in inner-enumerable on outer-key-expr equals inner-key-expr
  [ into identifier ]
```

Overview

Join and GroupJoin mesh two input sequences into a single output sequence. Join emits flat output; GroupJoin emits hierarchical output.

Join and GroupJoin provide an alternative strategy to Select and SelectMany. The advantage of Join and GroupJoin is that they execute efficiently over local in-memory collections because they first load the inner sequence into a keyed lookup, avoiding the need to repeatedly enumerate over every inner element. The disadvantage is that they offer the equivalent of inner and left outer joins only; cross joins and non-equi joins must still be done using Select/SelectMany. With EF Core queries, Join and GroupJoin offer no real benefits over Select and SelectMany.

Table 9-1 summarizes the differences between each of the joining strategies.

Table 9-1. Joining strategies

Strategy	Result shape	Local query efficiency	Inner joins	Left outer joins	Cross joins	Non-equi joins
Select + SelectMany	Flat	Bad	Yes	Yes	Yes	Yes
Select + Select	Nested	Bad	Yes	Yes	Yes	Yes
Join	Flat	Good	Yes	—	—	—
GroupJoin	Nested	Good	Yes	Yes	—	—
GroupJoin + SelectMany	Flat	Good	Yes	Yes	—	—

LINQ
Operators

Join

The `Join` operator performs an inner join, emitting a flat output sequence.

The following query lists all customers alongside their purchases without using a navigation property:

```
IQueryable<string> query =
  from c in dbContext.Customers
  join p in dbContext.Purchases on c.ID equals p.CustomerID
  select c.Name + " bought a " + p.Description;
```

The results match what we would get from a `SelectMany`-style query:

```
Tom bought a Bike
Tom bought a Holiday
Dick bought a Phone
Harry bought a Car
```

To see the benefit of `Join` over `SelectMany`, we must convert this to a local query. We can demonstrate this by first copying all customers and purchases to arrays and then querying the arrays:

```
Customer[] customers = dbContext.Customers.ToArray();
Purchase[] purchases = dbContext.Purchases.ToArray();
var slowQuery = from c in customers
                from p in purchases where c.ID == p.CustomerID
                select c.Name + " bought a " + p.Description;

var fastQuery = from c in customers
                join p in purchases on c.ID equals p.CustomerID
                select c.Name + " bought a " + p.Description;
```

Although both queries yield the same results, the `Join` query is considerably faster because its implementation in `Enumerable` preloads the inner collection (`purchases`) into a keyed lookup.

The query syntax for `join` can be written in general terms, as follows:

```
join inner-var in inner-sequence on outer-key-expr equals inner-key-expr
```

Join operators in LINQ differentiate between the *outer sequence* and *inner sequence*. Syntactically:

- The *outer sequence* is the input sequence (`customers`, in this case).

- The *inner sequence* is the new collection you introduce (`purchases`, in this case).

`Join` performs inner joins, meaning customers without purchases are excluded from the output. With inner joins, you can swap the inner and outer sequences in the query and still get the same results:

```
from p in purchases                                // p is now outer
join c in customers on p.CustomerID equals c.ID    // c is now inner
...
```

You can add further join clauses to the same query. If each purchase, for instance, has one or more purchase items, you could join the purchase items, as follows:

```
from c in customers
join p in purchases on c.ID equals p.CustomerID        // first join
join pi in purchaseItems on p.ID equals pi.PurchaseID  // second join
...
```

purchases acts as the *inner* sequence in the first join and as the *outer* sequence in the second join. You could obtain the same results (inefficiently) using nested foreach statements, as follows:

```
foreach (Customer c in customers)
  foreach (Purchase p in purchases)
    if (c.ID == p.CustomerID)
      foreach (PurchaseItem pi in purchaseItems)
        if (p.ID == pi.PurchaseID)
          Console.WriteLine (c.Name + "," + p.Price + "," + pi.Detail);
```

In query syntax, variables from earlier joins remain in scope—just as they do with SelectMany-style queries. You're also permitted to insert where and let clauses in between join clauses.

Joining on multiple keys

You can join on multiple keys with anonymous types, as follows:

```
from x in sequenceX
join y in sequenceY on new { K1 = x.Prop1, K2 = x.Prop2 }
                equals new { K1 = y.Prop3, K2 = y.Prop4 }
...
```

For this to work, the two anonymous types must be structured identically. The compiler then implements each with the same internal type, making the joining keys compatible.

Joining in fluent syntax

The following query syntax join

```
from c in customers
join p in purchases on c.ID equals p.CustomerID
select new { c.Name, p.Description, p.Price };
```

in fluent syntax is as follows:

```
customers.Join (                      // outer collection
    purchases,                        // inner collection
    c => c.ID,                        // outer key selector
    p => p.CustomerID,                // inner key selector
    (c, p) => new
        { c.Name, p.Description, p.Price }    // result selector
);
```

LINQ
Operators

The result selector expression at the end creates each element in the output sequence. If you have additional clauses prior to projecting, such as orderby in this example:

```
from c in customers
join p in purchases on c.ID equals p.CustomerID
orderby p.Price
select c.Name + " bought a " + p.Description;
```

you must manufacture a temporary anonymous type in the result selector in fluent syntax. This keeps both c and p in scope following the join:

```
customers.Join (                    // outer collection
        purchases,                  // inner collection
        c => c.ID,                  // outer key selector
        p => p.CustomerID,          // inner key selector
        (c, p) => new { c, p } )    // result selector
    .OrderBy (x => x.p.Price)
    .Select  (x => x.c.Name + " bought a " + x.p.Description);
```

Query syntax is usually preferable when joining; it's less fiddly.

GroupJoin

GroupJoin does the same work as Join, but instead of yielding a flat result, it yields a hierarchical result, grouped by each outer element. It also allows left outer joins. GroupJoin is not currently supported in EF Core.

The query syntax for GroupJoin is the same as for Join, but is followed by the into keyword.

Here's the most basic example, using a local query:

```
Customer[] customers = dbContext.Customers.ToArray();
Purchase[] purchases = dbContext.Purchases.ToArray();

IEnumerable<IEnumerable<Purchase>> query =
  from c in customers
  join p in purchases on c.ID equals p.CustomerID
  into custPurchases
  select custPurchases;   // custPurchases is a sequence
```

 An into clause translates to GroupJoin only when it appears directly after a join clause. After a select or group clause, it means *query continuation*. The two uses of the into keyword are quite different, although they have one feature in common: they both introduce a new range variable.

The result is a sequence of sequences, which we could enumerate as follows:

```
foreach (IEnumerable<Purchase> purchaseSequence in query)
  foreach (Purchase p in purchaseSequence)
    Console.WriteLine (p.Description);
```

This isn't very useful, however, because purchaseSequence has no reference to the customer. More commonly, you'd do this:

```
from c in customers
join p in purchases on c.ID equals p.CustomerID
into custPurchases
select new { CustName = c.Name, custPurchases };
```

This gives the same results as the following (inefficient) Select subquery:

```
from c in customers
select new
{
  CustName = c.Name,
  custPurchases = purchases.Where (p => c.ID == p.CustomerID)
};
```

By default, GroupJoin does the equivalent of a left outer join. To get an inner join—whereby customers without purchases are excluded—you need to filter on custPurchases:

```
from c in customers join p in purchases on c.ID equals p.CustomerID
into custPurchases
where custPurchases.Any()
select ...
```

Clauses after a group-join into operate on *subsequences* of inner child elements, not *individual* child elements. This means that to filter individual purchases, you'd need to call Where *before* joining:

```
from c in customers
join p in purchases.Where (p2 => p2.Price > 1000)
  on c.ID equals p.CustomerID
into custPurchases ...
```

You can construct lambda queries with GroupJoin as you would with Join.

Flat outer joins

You run into a dilemma if you want both an outer join and a flat result set. GroupJoin gives you the outer join; Join gives you the flat result set. The solution is to first call GroupJoin, then DefaultIfEmpty on each child sequence, and then finally SelectMany on the result:

```
from c in customers
join p in purchases on c.ID equals p.CustomerID into custPurchases
from cp in custPurchases.DefaultIfEmpty()
select new
{
  CustName = c.Name,
  Price = cp == null ? (decimal?) null : cp.Price
};
```

DefaultIfEmpty emits a sequence with a single null value if a subsequence of purchases is empty. The second from clause translates to SelectMany. In this role, it *expands and flattens* all the purchase subsequences, concatenating them into a single sequence of purchase *elements*.

Joining with lookups

The Join and GroupJoin methods in Enumerable work in two steps. First, they load the inner sequence into a *lookup*. Second, they query the outer sequence in combination with the lookup.

A *lookup* is a sequence of groupings that can be accessed directly by key. Another way to think of it is as a dictionary of sequences—a dictionary that can accept many elements under each key (sometimes called a *multidictionary*). Lookups are read-only and defined by the following interface:

```
public interface ILookup<TKey,TElement> :
   IEnumerable<IGrouping<TKey,TElement>>, IEnumerable
{
  int Count { get; }
  bool Contains (TKey key);
  IEnumerable<TElement> this [TKey key] { get; }
}
```

 The joining operators—like other sequence-emitting operators—honor deferred or lazy execution semantics. This means the lookup is not built until you begin enumerating the output sequence (and then the *entire* lookup is built right then).

You can create and query lookups manually as an alternative strategy to using the joining operators when dealing with local collections. There are a couple of benefits to doing so:

- You can reuse the same lookup over multiple queries—as well as in ordinary imperative code.

- Querying a lookup is an excellent way of understanding how Join and Group Join work.

The ToLookup extension method creates a lookup. The following loads all purchases into a lookup—keyed by their CustomerID:

```
ILookup<int?,Purchase> purchLookup =
   purchases.ToLookup (p => p.CustomerID, p => p);
```

The first argument selects the key; the second argument selects the objects that are to be loaded as values into the lookup.

Reading a lookup is rather like reading a dictionary except that the indexer returns a *sequence* of matching items rather than a *single* matching item. The following enumerates all purchases made by the customer whose ID is 1:

```
foreach (Purchase p in purchLookup [1])
   Console.WriteLine (p.Description);
```

With a lookup in place, you can write SelectMany/Select queries that execute as efficiently as Join/GroupJoin queries. Join is equivalent to using SelectMany on a lookup:

```
from c in customers
from p in purchLookup [c.ID]
select new { c.Name, p.Description, p.Price };

Tom  Bike      500
Tom  Holiday   2000
Dick Bike      600
Dick Phone     300
...
```

Adding a call to DefaultIfEmpty makes this into an outer join:

```
from c in customers
from p in purchLookup [c.ID].DefaultIfEmpty()
 select new {
            c.Name,
            Descript = p == null ? null : p.Description,
            Price = p == null ? (decimal?) null : p.Price
         };
```

GroupJoin is equivalent to reading the lookup inside a projection:

```
from c in customers
select new {
           CustName = c.Name,
           CustPurchases = purchLookup [c.ID]
         };
```

Enumerable implementations

Here's the simplest valid implementation of Enumerable.Join, null checking aside:

```
public static IEnumerable <TResult> Join
                              <TOuter,TInner,TKey,TResult> (
   this IEnumerable <TOuter>       outer,
   IEnumerable <TInner>            inner,
   Func <TOuter,TKey>             outerKeySelector,
   Func <TInner,TKey>             innerKeySelector,
   Func <TOuter,TInner,TResult>   resultSelector)
{
  ILookup <TKey, TInner> lookup = inner.ToLookup (innerKeySelector);
  return
    from outerItem in outer
    from innerItem in lookup [outerKeySelector (outerItem)]
    select resultSelector (outerItem, innerItem);
}
```

GroupJoin's implementation is like that of Join but simpler:

```
public static IEnumerable <TResult> GroupJoin
                              <TOuter,TInner,TKey,TResult> (
    this IEnumerable <TOuter>       outer,
    IEnumerable <TInner>            inner,
    Func <TOuter,TKey>              outerKeySelector,
    Func <TInner,TKey>              innerKeySelector,
    Func <TOuter,IEnumerable<TInner>,TResult>  resultSelector)
{
    ILookup <TKey, TInner> lookup = inner.ToLookup (innerKeySelector);
    return
      from outerItem in outer
      select resultSelector
        (outerItem, lookup [outerKeySelector (outerItem)]);
}
```

The Zip Operator

IEnumerable<TFirst>, IEnumerable<TSecond>→IEnumerable<TResult>

The Zip operator enumerates two sequences in step (like a zipper), returning a sequence based on applying a function over each element pair. For instance, the following:

```
int[] numbers = { 3, 5, 7 };
string[] words = { "three", "five", "seven", "ignored" };
IEnumerable<string> zip = numbers.Zip (words, (n, w) => n + "=" + w);
```

produces a sequence with the following elements:

```
3=three
5=five
7=seven
```

Extra elements in either input sequence are ignored. Zip is not supported by EF Core.

Ordering

IEnumerable<TSource>→IOrderedEnumerable<TSource>

Method	Description	SQL equivalents
OrderBy, ThenBy	Sorts a sequence in ascending order	ORDER BY ...
OrderByDescending, ThenByDescending	Sorts a sequence in descending order	ORDER BY ... DESC
Reverse	Returns a sequence in reverse order	Exception thrown

Ordering operators return the same elements in a different order.

OrderBy, OrderByDescending, ThenBy, and ThenByDescending

OrderBy and OrderByDescending arguments

Argument	Type
Input sequence	IEnumerable<TSource>
Key selector	TSource => TKey

Return type = IOrderedEnumerable<TSource>

ThenBy and ThenByDescending arguments

Argument	Type
Input sequence	IOrderedEnumerable<TSource>
Key selector	TSource => TKey

Query syntax

```
orderby expression1 [descending] [, expression2 [descending] ... ]
```

Overview

OrderBy returns a sorted version of the input sequence, using the keySelector expression to make comparisons. The following query emits a sequence of names in alphabetical order:

```
IEnumerable<string> query = names.OrderBy (s => s);
```

The following sorts names by length:

```
IEnumerable<string> query = names.OrderBy (s => s.Length);

// Result: { "Jay", "Tom", "Mary", "Dick", "Harry" };
```

The relative order of elements with the same sorting key (in this case, Jay/Tom and Mary/Dick) is indeterminate—unless you append a ThenBy operator:

```
IEnumerable<string> query = names.OrderBy (s => s.Length).ThenBy (s => s);

// Result: { "Jay", "Tom", "Dick", "Mary", "Harry" };
```

ThenBy reorders only elements that had the same sorting key in the preceding sort. You can chain any number of ThenBy operators. The following sorts first by length, then by the second character, and finally by the first character:

```
names.OrderBy (s => s.Length).ThenBy (s => s[1]).ThenBy (s => s[0]);
```

Here's the equivalent in query syntax:

```
from s in names
orderby s.Length, s[1], s[0]
select s;
```

 The following variation is *incorrect*—it will actually order first by s[1] and then by s.Length (or in the case of a database query, it will order *only* by s[1] and discard the former ordering):

```
from s in names
orderby s.Length
orderby s[1]
...
```

LINQ also provides OrderByDescending and ThenByDescending operators, which do the same things, emitting the results in reverse order. The following EF Core query retrieves purchases in descending order of price, with those of the same price listed alphabetically:

```
dbContext.Purchases.OrderByDescending (p => p.Price)
                    .ThenBy (p => p.Description);
```

In query syntax:

```
from p in dbContext.Purchases
orderby p.Price descending, p.Description
select p;
```

Comparers and collations

In a local query, the key selector objects themselves determine the ordering algorithm via their default IComparable implementation (see Chapter 7). You can override the sorting algorithm by passing in an IComparer object. The following performs a case-insensitive sort:

```
names.OrderBy (n => n, StringComparer.CurrentCultureIgnoreCase);
```

Passing in a comparer is not supported in query syntax or in any way by EF Core. When querying a database, the comparison algorithm is determined by the participating column's collation. If the collation is case sensitive, you can request a case-insensitive sort by calling ToUpper in the key selector:

```
from p in dbContext.Purchases
orderby p.Description.ToUpper()
select p;
```

IOrderedEnumerable and IOrderedQueryable

The ordering operators return special subtypes of IEnumerable<T>. Those in Enumerable return IOrderedEnumerable<TSource>; those in Queryable return IOrderedQueryable<TSource>. These subtypes allow a subsequent ThenBy operator to refine rather than replace the existing ordering.

The additional members that these subtypes define are not publicly exposed, so they present like ordinary sequences. The fact that they are different types comes into play when building queries progressively:

```
IOrderedEnumerable<string> query1 = names.OrderBy (s => s.Length);
IOrderedEnumerable<string> query2 = query1.ThenBy (s => s);
```

If we instead declare query1 of type IEnumerable<string>, the second line would not compile—ThenBy requires an input of type IOrderedEnumerable<string>. You can avoid worrying about this by implicitly typing range variables:

```
var query1 = names.OrderBy (s => s.Length);
var query2 = query1.ThenBy (s => s);
```

Implicit typing can create problems of its own, though. The following will not compile:

```
var query = names.OrderBy (s => s.Length);
query = query.Where (n => n.Length > 3);        // Compile-time error
```

The compiler infers query to be of type IOrderedEnumerable<string>, based on OrderBy's output sequence type. However, the Where on the next line returns an ordinary IEnumerable<string>, which cannot be assigned back to query. You can work around this either with explicit typing or by calling AsEnumerable() after OrderBy:

```
var query = names.OrderBy (s => s.Length).AsEnumerable();
query = query.Where (n => n.Length > 3);                     // OK
```

The equivalent in interpreted queries is to call AsQueryable.

Grouping

Method	Description	SQL equivalents
GroupBy	Groups a sequence into subsequences	GROUP BY
Chunk	Groups a sequence into arrays of a fixed size	

GroupBy

IEnumerable<TSource>→IEnumerable<IGrouping<TKey,TElement>>

Argument	Type
Input sequence	IEnumerable<TSource>
Key selector	TSource => TKey
Element selector (optional)	TSource => TElement
Comparer (optional)	IEqualityComparer<TKey>

Query syntax

```
group element-expression by key-expression
```

Overview

GroupBy organizes a flat input sequence into sequences of *groups*. For example, the following organizes all of the files in *Path.GetTempPath()* by extension:

```
string[] files = Directory.GetFiles (Path.GetTempPath());

IEnumerable<IGrouping<string,string>> query =
  files.GroupBy (file => Path.GetExtension (file));
```

Or, with implicit typing:

```
var query = files.GroupBy (file => Path.GetExtension (file));
```

Here's how to enumerate the result:

```
foreach (IGrouping<string,string> grouping in query)
{
  Console.WriteLine ("Extension: " + grouping.Key);
  foreach (string filename in grouping)
    Console.WriteLine ("   - " + filename);
}

Extension: .pdf
 -- chapter03.pdf
 -- chapter04.pdf
Extension: .doc
 -- todo.doc
 -- menu.doc
 -- Copy of menu.doc
...
```

Enumerable.GroupBy works by reading the input elements into a temporary dictionary of lists so that all elements with the same key end up in the same sublist. It then emits a sequence of *groupings*. A grouping is a sequence with a Key property:

```
public interface IGrouping <TKey,TElement> : IEnumerable<TElement>,
                                             IEnumerable
{
  TKey Key { get; }    // Key applies to the subsequence as a whole
}
```

By default, the elements in each grouping are untransformed input elements unless you specify an elementSelector argument. The following projects each input element to uppercase:

```
files.GroupBy (file => Path.GetExtension (file), file => file.ToUpper());
```

An elementSelector is independent of the keySelector. In our case, this means that the Key on each grouping is still in its original case:

Extension: .pdf
```
-- CHAPTER03.PDF
-- CHAPTER04.PDF
```
Extension: .doc
```
-- TODO.DOC
```

Note that the subcollections are not emitted in alphabetical order of key. GroupBy merely *groups*; it does not *sort*. In fact, it preserves the original ordering. To sort, you must add an OrderBy operator:

```
files.GroupBy (file => Path.GetExtension (file), file => file.ToUpper())
     .OrderBy (grouping => grouping.Key);
```

GroupBy has a simple and direct translation in query syntax:

```
group element-expr by key-expr
```

Here's our example in query syntax:

```
from file in files
group file.ToUpper() by Path.GetExtension (file);
```

As with select, group "ends" a query—unless you add a query continuation clause:

```
from file in files
group file.ToUpper() by Path.GetExtension (file) into grouping
orderby grouping.Key
select grouping;
```

Query continuations are often useful in a group by query. The next query filters out groups that have fewer than five files in them:

```
from file in files
group file.ToUpper() by Path.GetExtension (file) into grouping
where grouping.Count() >= 5
select grouping;
```

 A where after a group by is equivalent to HAVING in SQL. It applies to each subsequence or grouping as a whole rather than the individual elements.

Sometimes, you're interested purely in the result of an aggregation on a grouping and so can abandon the subsequences:

```
string[] votes = { "Dogs", "Cats", "Cats", "Dogs", "Dogs" };

IEnumerable<string> query = from vote in votes
                            group vote by vote into g
                            orderby g.Count() descending
                            select g.Key;

string winner = query.First();    // Dogs
```

GroupBy in EF Core

Grouping works in the same way when querying a database. If you have navigation properties set up, you'll find, however, that the need to group arises less frequently than with standard SQL. For instance, to select customers with at least two purchases, you don't need to group; the following query does the job nicely:

```
from c in dbContext.Customers
where c.Purchases.Count >= 2
select c.Name + " has made " + c.Purchases.Count + " purchases";
```

An example of when you might use grouping is to list total sales by year:

```
from p in dbContext.Purchases
group p.Price by p.Date.Year into salesByYear
select new {
            Year       = salesByYear.Key,
            TotalValue = salesByYear.Sum()
          };
```

LINQ's grouping is more powerful than SQL's GROUP BY in that you can fetch all detail rows without any aggregation:

```
from p in dbContext.Purchases
group p by p.Date.Year
Date.Year
```

However, this doesn't work in EF Core. An easy workaround is to call .AsEnumerable() just before grouping so that the grouping happens on the client. This is no less efficient as long as you perform any filtering *before* grouping so that you only fetch the data you need from the server.

Another departure from traditional SQL comes in there being no obligation to project the variables or expressions used in grouping or sorting.

Grouping by multiple keys

You can group by a composite key, using an anonymous type:

```
from n in names
group n by new { FirstLetter = n[0], Length = n.Length };
```

Custom equality comparers

You can pass a custom equality comparer into GroupBy, in a local query, to change the algorithm for key comparison. Rarely is this required, though, because changing the key selector expression is usually sufficient. For instance, the following creates a case-insensitive grouping:

```
group n by n.ToUpper()
```

Chunk

`IEnumerable<TSource>→IEnumerable<TElement[]>`

Argument	Type
Input sequence	`IEnumerable<TSource>`
`size`	`int`

Introduced in .NET 6, Chunk groups a sequence into chunks of a given size (or fewer, if there aren't enough elements):

```
foreach (int[] chunk in new[] { 1, 2, 3, 4, 5, 6, 7, 8 }.Chunk (3))
  Console.WriteLine (string.Join (", ", chunk));
```

Output:

```
1, 2, 3
4, 5, 6
7, 8
```

Set Operators

`IEnumerable<TSource>, IEnumerable<TSource>→IEnumerable<TSource>`

Method	Description	SQL equivalents
`Concat`	Returns a concatenation of elements in each of the two sequences	`UNION ALL`
`Union, UnionBy`	Returns a concatenation of elements in each of the two sequences, excluding duplicates	`UNION`
`Intersect, IntersectBy`	Returns elements present in both sequences	`WHERE ... IN (...)`
`Except, ExceptBy`	Returns elements present in the first but not the second sequence	`EXCEPT` or `WHERE ... NOT IN (...)`

Concat, Union, and UnionBy

Concat returns all the elements of the first sequence, followed by all the elements of the second. Union does the same but removes any duplicates:

```
int[] seq1 = { 1, 2, 3 }, seq2 = { 3, 4, 5 };

IEnumerable<int>
  concat = seq1.Concat (seq2),   // { 1, 2, 3, 3, 4, 5 }
  union  = seq1.Union  (seq2);   // { 1, 2, 3, 4, 5 }
```

Specifying the type argument explicitly is useful when the sequences are differently typed but the elements have a common base type. For instance, with the reflection API (Chapter 18), methods and properties are represented with `MethodInfo` and

PropertyInfo classes, which have a common base class called MemberInfo. We can concatenate methods and properties by stating that base class explicitly when calling Concat:

```
MethodInfo[] methods = typeof (string).GetMethods();
PropertyInfo[] props = typeof (string).GetProperties();
IEnumerable<MemberInfo> both = methods.Concat<MemberInfo> (props);
```

In the next example, we filter the methods before concatenating:

```
var methods = typeof (string).GetMethods().Where (m => !m.IsSpecialName);
var props = typeof (string).GetProperties();
var both = methods.Concat<MemberInfo> (props);
```

This example relies on interface type parameter variance: methods is of type IEnumerable<MethodInfo>, which requires a covariant conversion to IEnumerable <MemberInfo>. It's a good illustration of how variance makes things work more like you'd expect.

UnionBy (introduced in .NET 6) takes a keySelector, which is used in determining whether an element is a duplicate. In the following example, we perform a case-insensitive union:

```
string[] seq1 = { "A", "b", "C" };
string[] seq2 = { "a", "B", "c" };
var union = seq1.UnionBy (seq2, x => x.ToUpperInvariant());
// union is { "A", "b", "C" }
```

In this case, the same thing can be accomplished with Union, if we supply an equality comparer:

```
var union = seq1.Union (seq2, StringComparer.InvariantCultureIgnoreCase);
```

Intersect, Intersect By, Except, and ExceptBy

Intersect returns the elements that two sequences have in common. Except returns the elements in the first input sequence that are *not* present in the second:

```
int[] seq1 = { 1, 2, 3 }, seq2 = { 3, 4, 5 };

IEnumerable<int>
  commonality = seq1.Intersect (seq2),   // { 3 }
  difference1 = seq1.Except    (seq2),   // { 1, 2 }
  difference2 = seq2.Except    (seq1);   // { 4, 5 }
```

Enumerable.Except works internally by loading all of the elements in the first collection into a dictionary and then removing from the dictionary all elements present in the second sequence. The equivalent in SQL is a NOT EXISTS or NOT IN subquery:

```
SELECT number FROM numbers1Table
WHERE number NOT IN (SELECT number FROM numbers2Table)
```

The `IntersectBy` and `ExceptBy` methods (from .NET 6) let you specify a key selector that's applied before performing equality comparison (see the discussion on `UnionBy` in the preceding section).

Conversion Methods

LINQ deals primarily in sequences; in other words, collections of type `IEnumerable<T>`. The conversion methods convert to and from other types of collections:

Method	Description
OfType	Converts `IEnumerable` to `IEnumerable<T>`, discarding wrongly typed elements
Cast	Converts `IEnumerable` to `IEnumerable<T>`, throwing an exception if there are any wrongly typed elements
ToArray	Converts `IEnumerable<T>` to `T[]`
ToList	Converts `IEnumerable<T>` to `List<T>`
ToDictionary	Converts `IEnumerable<T>` to `Dictionary<TKey,TValue>`
ToLookup	Converts `IEnumerable<T>` to `ILookup<TKey,TElement>`
AsEnumerable	Upcasts to `IEnumerable<T>`
AsQueryable	Casts or converts to `IQueryable<T>`

OfType and Cast

`OfType` and `Cast` accept a nongeneric `IEnumerable` collection and emit a generic `IEnumerable<T>` sequence that you can subsequently query:

```
ArrayList classicList = new ArrayList();          // in System.Collections
classicList.AddRange ( new int[] { 3, 4, 5 } );
IEnumerable<int> sequence1 = classicList.Cast<int>();
```

`Cast` and `OfType` differ in their behavior when encountering an input element that's of an incompatible type. `Cast` throws an exception; `OfType` ignores the incompatible element. Continuing the preceding example:

```
DateTime offender = DateTime.Now;
classicList.Add (offender);
IEnumerable<int>
  sequence2 = classicList.OfType<int>(), // OK - ignores offending DateTime
  sequence3 = classicList.Cast<int>();   // Throws exception
```

The rules for element compatibility exactly follow those of C#'s `is` operator, and therefore consider only reference conversions and unboxing conversions. We can see this by examining the internal implementation of `OfType`:

```
public static IEnumerable<TSource> OfType <TSource> (IEnumerable source)
{
  foreach (object element in source)
    if (element is TSource)
```

```
      yield return (TSource)element;
  }
```

`Cast` has an identical implementation, except that it omits the type compatibility test:

```
public static IEnumerable<TSource> Cast <TSource> (IEnumerable source)
{
  foreach (object element in source)
    yield return (TSource)element;
}
```

A consequence of these implementations is that you cannot use `Cast` to perform numeric or custom conversions (for these, you must perform a `Select` operation instead). In other words, `Cast` is not as flexible as C#'s cast operator:

```
int i = 3;
long l = i;           // Implicit numeric conversion int->long
int i2 = (int) l;     // Explicit numeric conversion long->int
```

We can demonstrate this by attempting to use `OfType` or `Cast` to convert a sequence of `int`s to a sequence of `long`s:

```
int[] integers = { 1, 2, 3 };

IEnumerable<long> test1 = integers.OfType<long>();
IEnumerable<long> test2 = integers.Cast<long>();
```

When enumerated, `test1` emits zero elements and `test2` throws an exception. Examining `OfType`'s implementation, it's fairly clear why. After substituting `TSource`, we get the following expression:

```
(element is long)
```

This returns `false` for an `int` element, due to the lack of an inheritance relationship.

> The reason that `test2` throws an exception when enumerated is more subtle. Notice in `Cast`'s implementation that `element` is of type `object`. When `TSource` is a value type, the CLR assumes this is an *unboxing conversion* and synthesizes a method that reproduces the scenario described in the section "Boxing and Unboxing" on page 126:
>
> ```
> int value = 123;
> object element = value;
> long result = (long) element;  // exception
> ```
>
> Because the `element` variable is declared of type `object`, an object-to-`long` cast is performed (an unboxing) rather than an `int`-to-`long` numeric conversion. Unboxing operations require an exact type match, so the object-to-`long` unbox fails when given an `int`.

As we suggested previously, the solution is to use an ordinary `Select`:

```
IEnumerable<long> castLong = integers.Select (s => (long) s);
```

`OfType` and `Cast` are also useful in downcasting elements in a generic input sequence. For instance, if you have an input sequence of type IEnumerable<Fruit>, `OfType<Apple>` would return just the apples. This is particularly useful in LINQ to XML (see Chapter 10).

`Cast` has query syntax support: simply precede the range variable with a type:

```
from TreeNode node in myTreeView.Nodes
...
```

ToArray, ToList, ToDictionary, ToHashSet, and ToLookup

`ToArray`, `ToList`, and `ToHashSet` emit the results into an array, List<T> or Hash Set<T>. When they execute, these operators force the immediate enumeration of the input sequence. For examples, refer to "Deferred Execution" on page 408 in Chapter 8.

`ToDictionary` and `ToLookup` accept the following arguments:

Argument	Type
Input sequence	IEnumerable<TSource>
Key selector	TSource => TKey
Element selector (optional)	TSource => TElement
Comparer (optional)	IEqualityComparer<TKey>

`ToDictionary` also forces immediate execution of a sequence, writing the results to a generic `Dictionary`. The `keySelector` expression you provide must evaluate to a unique value for each element in the input sequence; otherwise, an exception is thrown. In contrast, `ToLookup` allows many elements of the same key. We described lookups in "Joining with lookups" on page 474.

AsEnumerable and AsQueryable

`AsEnumerable` upcasts a sequence to IEnumerable<T>, forcing the compiler to bind subsequent query operators to methods in `Enumerable` instead of `Queryable`. For an example, see "Combining Interpreted and Local Queries" on page 428.

`AsQueryable` downcasts a sequence to IQueryable<T> if it implements that interface. Otherwise, it instantiates an IQueryable<T> wrapper over the local query.

LINQ
Operators

Element Operators

```
IEnumerable<TSource>→ TSource
```

Method	Description	SQL equivalents
First, FirstOrDefault	Returns the first element in the sequence, optionally satisfying a predicate	SELECT TOP 1 ... ORDER BY ...
Last, LastOrDefault	Returns the last element in the sequence, optionally satisfying a predicate	SELECT TOP 1 ... ORDER BY ... DESC
Single, SingleOrDefault	Equivalent to First/FirstOrDefault, but throws an exception if there is more than one match	
ElementAt, ElementAtOrDefault	Returns the element at the specified position	Exception thrown
MinBy, MaxBy	Returns the element with the smallest or largest value	Exception thrown
DefaultIfEmpty	Returns a single-element sequence whose value is default(TSource) if the sequence has no elements	OUTER JOIN

Methods ending in "OrDefault" return default(TSource) rather than throwing an exception if the input sequence is empty or if no elements match the supplied predicate.

default(TSource) is null for reference type elements, false for the bool type, and zero for numeric types.

First, Last, and Single

Argument	Type
Source sequence	IEnumerable<TSource>
Predicate (optional)	TSource => bool

The following example demonstrates First and Last:

```
int[] numbers   = { 1, 2, 3, 4, 5 };
int first       = numbers.First();                    // 1
int last        = numbers.Last();                     // 5
int firstEven   = numbers.First  (n => n % 2 == 0);   // 2
int lastEven    = numbers.Last   (n => n % 2 == 0);   // 4
```

The following demonstrates First versus FirstOrDefault:

```
int firstBigError  = numbers.First          (n => n > 10);   // Exception
int firstBigNumber = numbers.FirstOrDefault (n => n > 10);   // 0
```

To prevent an exception, `Single` requires exactly one matching element; `SingleOr Default` requires one *or zero* matching elements:

```
int onlyDivBy3 = numbers.Single (n => n % 3 == 0);   // 3
int divBy2Err  = numbers.Single (n => n % 2 == 0);   // Error: 2 & 4 match

int singleError = numbers.Single          (n => n > 10);   // Error
int noMatches   = numbers.SingleOrDefault (n => n > 10);   // 0
int divBy2Error = numbers.SingleOrDefault (n => n % 2 == 0);  // Error
```

`Single` is the "fussiest" in this family of element operators. `FirstOrDefault` and `LastOrDefault` are the most tolerant.

In EF Core, `Single` is often used to retrieve a row from a table by primary key:

```
Customer cust = dataContext.Customers.Single (c => c.ID == 3);
```

ElementAt

Argument	Type
Source sequence	IEnumerable<TSource>
Index of element to return	int

`ElementAt` picks the *n*th element from the sequence:

```
int[] numbers  = { 1, 2, 3, 4, 5 };
int third      = numbers.ElementAt (2);          // 3
int tenthError = numbers.ElementAt (9);          // Exception
int tenth      = numbers.ElementAtOrDefault (9); // 0
```

`Enumerable.ElementAt` is written such that if the input sequence happens to implement `IList<T>`, it calls `IList<T>`'s indexer. Otherwise, it enumerates *n* times and then returns the next element. `ElementAt` is not supported in EF Core.

MinBy and MaxBy

`MinBy` and `MaxBy` (introduced in .NET 6) return the element with the smallest or largest value, as determined by a `keySelector`:

```
string[] names = { "Tom", "Dick", "Harry", "Mary", "Jay" };
Console.WriteLine (names.MaxBy (n => n.Length));   // Harry
```

In contrast, `Min` and `Max` (which we will cover in the following section) return the smallest or largest value itself:

```
Console.WriteLine (names.Max  (n => n.Length));   // 5
```

If two or more elements share a minimum/maximum value, `MinBy`/`MaxBy` returns the first:

```
Console.WriteLine (names.MinBy (n => n.Length));   // Tom
```

If the input sequence is empty, MinBy and MaxBy return null if the element type is nullable (or throw an exception if the element type is not nullable).

DefaultIfEmpty

DefaultIfEmpty returns a sequence containing a single element whose value is default(TSource) if the input sequence has no elements; otherwise, it returns the input sequence unchanged. You use this in writing flat outer joins: see "Outer joins with SelectMany" on page 467 and "Flat outer joins" on page 473.

Aggregation Methods

IEnumerable<TSource>→*scalar*

Method	Description	SQL equivalents
Count, LongCount	Returns the number of elements in the input sequence, optionally satisfying a predicate	COUNT (...)
Min, Max	Returns the smallest or largest element in the sequence	MIN (...), MAX (...)
Sum, Average	Calculates a numeric sum or average over elements in the sequence	SUM (...), AVG (...)
Aggregate	Performs a custom aggregation	Exception thrown

Count and LongCount

Argument	Type
Source sequence	IEnumerable<TSource>
Predicate (optional)	TSource => bool

Count simply enumerates over a sequence, returning the number of items:

```
int fullCount = new int[] { 5, 6, 7 }.Count();    // 3
```

The internal implementation of Enumerable.Count tests the input sequence to see whether it happens to implement ICollection<T>. If it does, it simply calls ICollec tion<T>.Count; otherwise, it enumerates over every item, incrementing a counter.

You can optionally supply a predicate:

```
int digitCount = "pa55w0rd".Count (c => char.IsDigit (c));    // 3
```

LongCount does the same job as Count but returns a 64-bit integer, allowing for sequences of greater than two billion elements.

Min and Max

Argument	Type
Source sequence	IEnumerable<TSource>
Result selector (optional)	TSource => TResult

Min and Max return the smallest or largest element from a sequence:

```
int[] numbers = { 28, 32, 14 };
int smallest = numbers.Min();  // 14;
int largest  = numbers.Max();  // 32;
```

If you include a selector expression, each element is first projected:

```
int smallest = numbers.Max (n => n % 10);  // 8;
```

A selector expression is mandatory if the items themselves are not intrinsically comparable—in other words, if they do not implement IComparable<T>:

```
Purchase runtimeError = dbContext.Purchases.Min ();               // Error
decimal? lowestPrice = dbContext.Purchases.Min (p => p.Price);  // OK
```

A selector expression determines not only how elements are compared, but also the final result. In the preceding example, the final result is a decimal value, not a purchase object. To get the cheapest purchase, you need a subquery:

```
Purchase cheapest = dbContext.Purchases
  .Where (p => p.Price == dbContext.Purchases.Min (p2 => p2.Price))
  .FirstOrDefault();
```

In this case, you could also formulate the query without an aggregation by using an OrderBy followed by FirstOrDefault.

Sum and Average

Argument	Type
Source sequence	IEnumerable<TSource>
Result selector (optional)	TSource => TResult

Sum and Average are aggregation operators that are used in a similar manner to Min and Max:

```
decimal[] numbers  = { 3, 4, 8 };
decimal sumTotal   = numbers.Sum();        // 15
decimal average    = numbers.Average();    // 5   (mean value)
```

The following returns the total length of each of the strings in the names array:

```
int combinedLength = names.Sum (s => s.Length);  // 19
```

LINQ
Operators

Sum and Average are fairly restrictive in their typing. Their definitions are hard-wired to each of the numeric types (int, long, float, double, decimal, and their nullable versions). In contrast, Min and Max can operate directly on anything that implements IComparable<T>—such as a string, for instance.

Further, Average always returns either decimal, float, or double, according to the following table:

Selector type	Result type
decimal	decimal
float	float
int, long, double	double

This means that the following does not compile ("cannot convert double to int"):

```
int avg = new int[] { 3, 4 }.Average();
```

But this will compile:

```
double avg = new int[] { 3, 4 }.Average();   // 3.5
```

Average implicitly upscales the input values to prevent loss of precision. In this example, we averaged integers and got 3.5 without needing to resort to an input element cast:

```
double avg = numbers.Average (n => (double) n);
```

When querying a database, Sum and Average translate to the standard SQL aggregations. The following query returns customers whose average purchase was more than $500:

```
from c in dbContext.Customers
where c.Purchases.Average (p => p.Price) > 500
select c.Name;
```

Aggregate

Aggregate allows you to specify a custom accumulation algorithm for implementing unusual aggregations. Aggregate is not supported in EF Core and is somewhat specialized in its use cases. The following demonstrates how Aggregate can do the work of Sum:

```
int[] numbers = { 1, 2, 3 };
int sum = numbers.Aggregate (0, (total, n) => total + n);   // 6
```

The first argument to Aggregate is the *seed*, from which accumulation starts. The second argument is an expression to update the accumulated value, given a fresh element. You can optionally supply a third argument to project the final result value from the accumulated value.

Most problems for which `Aggregate` has been designed can be solved as easily with a `foreach` loop—and with more familiar syntax. The advantage of using `Aggregate` is that with large or complex aggregations, you can automatically parallelize the operation with PLINQ (see Chapter 22).

Unseeded aggregations

You can omit the seed value when calling `Aggregate`, in which case the first element becomes the *implicit* seed, and aggregation proceeds from the second element. Here's the preceding example, *unseeded*:

```
int[] numbers = { 1, 2, 3 };
int sum = numbers.Aggregate ((total, n) => total + n);   // 6
```

This gives the same result as before, but we're actually doing a *different calculation*. Before, we were calculating $0 + 1 + 2 + 3$; now we're calculating $1 + 2 + 3$. We can better illustrate the difference by multiplying instead of adding:

```
int[] numbers = { 1, 2, 3 };
int x = numbers.Aggregate (0, (prod, n) => prod * n);   // 0*1*2*3 = 0
int y = numbers.Aggregate (   (prod, n) => prod * n);   //   1*2*3 = 6
```

As you'll see in Chapter 22, unseeded aggregations have the advantage of being parallelizable without requiring the use of special overloads. However, there are some traps with unseeded aggregations.

Traps with unseeded aggregations

The unseeded aggregation methods are intended for use with delegates that are *commutative* and *associative*. If used otherwise, the result is either *unintuitive* (with ordinary queries) or *nondeterministic* (in the case that you parallelize the query with PLINQ). For example, consider the following function:

```
(total, n) => total + n * n
```

This is neither commutative nor associative. (For example, $1 + 2 * 2 \mathrel{!=} 2 + 1 * 1$.) Let's see what happens when we use it to sum the square of the numbers 2, 3, and 4:

```
int[] numbers = { 2, 3, 4 };
int sum = numbers.Aggregate ((total, n) => total + n * n);   // 27
```

Instead of calculating

```
2*2 + 3*3 + 4*4    // 29
```

it calculates:

```
2 + 3*3 + 4*4    // 27
```

We can fix this in a number of ways. First, we could include 0 as the first element:

```
int[] numbers = { 0, 2, 3, 4 };
```

Not only is this inelegant, but it will still give incorrect results if parallelized—because PLINQ uses the function's assumed associativity by selecting *multiple* elements as seeds. To illustrate, if we denote our aggregation function as follows:

```
f(total, n) => total + n * n
```

LINQ to Objects would calculate this:

```
f(f(f(0, 2),3),4)
```

whereas PLINQ might do this:

```
f(f(0,2),f(3,4))
```

with the following result:

```
First partition:   a = 0 + 2*2  (= 4)
Second partition:  b = 3 + 4*4  (= 19)
Final result:      a + b*b  (= 365)
OR EVEN:           b + a*a  (= 35)
```

There are two good solutions. The first is to turn this into a seeded aggregation with 0 as the seed. The only complication is that with PLINQ, we'd need to use a special overload in order for the query not to execute sequentially (see "Optimizing PLINQ" on page 919).

The second solution is to restructure the query such that the aggregation function is commutative and associative:

```
int sum = numbers.Select (n => n * n).Aggregate ((total, n) => total + n);
```

Of course, in such simple scenarios you can (and should) use the Sum operator instead of Aggregate:

```
int sum = numbers.Sum (n => n * n);
```

You can actually go quite far just with Sum and Average. For instance, you can use Average to calculate a root-mean-square:

```
Math.Sqrt (numbers.Average (n => n * n))
```

You can even calculate standard deviation:

```
double mean = numbers.Average();
double sdev = Math.Sqrt (numbers.Average (n =>
               {
                   double dif = n - mean;
                   return dif * dif;
               }));
```

Both are safe, efficient, and fully parallelizable. In Chapter 22, we give a practical example of a custom aggregation that can't be reduced to Sum or Average.

Quantifiers

IEnumerable<TSource>→*bool*

Method	Description	SQL equivalents
Contains	Returns true if the input sequence contains the given element	WHERE ... IN (...)
Any	Returns true if any elements satisfy the given predicate	WHERE ... IN (...)
All	Returns true if all elements satisfy the given predicate	WHERE (...)
SequenceEqual	Returns true if the second sequence has identical elements to the input sequence	

Contains and Any

The Contains method accepts an argument of type TSource; Any accepts an optional *predicate*.

Contains returns true if the given element is present:

```
bool hasAThree = new int[] { 2, 3, 4 }.Contains (3);      // true;
```

Any returns true if the given expression is true for at least one element. We can rewrite the preceding query with Any as follows:

```
bool hasAThree = new int[] { 2, 3, 4 }.Any (n => n == 3);  // true;
```

Any can do everything that Contains can do, and more:

```
bool hasABigNumber = new int[] { 2, 3, 4 }.Any (n => n > 10);  // false;
```

Calling Any without a predicate returns true if the sequence has one or more elements. Here's another way to write the preceding query:

```
bool hasABigNumber = new int[] { 2, 3, 4 }.Where (n => n > 10).Any();
```

Any is particularly useful in subqueries and is used often when querying databases; for example:

```
from c in dbContext.Customers
where c.Purchases.Any (p => p.Price > 1000)
select c
```

All and SequenceEqual

All returns true if all elements satisfy a predicate. The following returns customers whose purchases are less than $100:

```
dbContext.Customers.Where (c => c.Purchases.All (p => p.Price < 100));
```

SequenceEqual compares two sequences. To return true, each sequence must have identical elements, in the identical order. You can optionally provide an equality comparer; the default is EqualityComparer<T>.Default.

Generation Methods

void→IEnumerable<TResult>

Method	Description
Empty	Creates an empty sequence
Repeat	Creates a sequence of repeating elements
Range	Creates a sequence of integers

Empty, Repeat, and Range are static (nonextension) methods that manufacture simple local sequences.

Empty

Empty manufactures an empty sequence and requires just a type argument:

```
foreach (string s in Enumerable.Empty<string>())
  Console.Write (s);                          // <nothing>
```

In conjunction with the ?? operator, Empty does the reverse of DefaultIfEmpty. For example, suppose that we have a jagged array of integers and we want to get all the integers into a single flat list. The following SelectMany query fails if any of the inner arrays is null:

```
int[][] numbers =
{
  new int[] { 1, 2, 3 },
  new int[] { 4, 5, 6 },
  null                   // this null makes the query below fail.
};

IEnumerable<int> flat = numbers.SelectMany (innerArray => innerArray);
```

Empty in conjunction with ?? fixes the problem:

```
IEnumerable<int> flat = numbers
  .SelectMany (innerArray => innerArray ?? Enumerable.Empty <int>());

foreach (int i in flat)
  Console.Write (i + " ");     // 1 2 3 4 5 6
```

Range and Repeat

Range accepts a starting index and count (both integers):

```
foreach (int i in Enumerable.Range (5, 3))
  Console.Write (i + " ");                     // 5 6 7
```

Repeat accepts an element to repeat, and the number of repetitions:

```
foreach (bool x in Enumerable.Repeat (true, 3))
  Console.Write (x + " ");                     // True True True
```

10

LINQ to XML

.NET provides a number of APIs for working with XML data. The primary choice for general-purpose XML document processing is *LINQ to XML*. LINQ to XML comprises a lightweight, LINQ-friendly XML document object model (DOM), plus a set of supplementary query operators.

In this chapter, we concentrate entirely on LINQ to XML. In Chapter 11, we cover the forward-only XML reader/writer, and in the online supplement (*http://www.albahari.com/nutshell*), we cover the types for working with schemas and stylesheets. .NET also includes the legacy XmlDocument-based DOM, which we don't cover.

The LINQ to XML DOM is extremely well designed and highly performant. Even without LINQ, the LINQ to XML DOM is valuable as a lightweight façade over the low-level XmlReader and XmlWriter classes.

All LINQ to XML types are defined in the System.Xml.Linq namespace.

Architectural Overview

This section starts with a very brief introduction to the concept of a DOM, and then explains the rationale behind LINQ to XML's DOM.

What Is a DOM?

Consider the following XML file:

```
<?xml version="1.0" encoding="utf-8"?>
<customer id="123" status="archived">
  <firstname>Joe</firstname>
  <lastname>Bloggs</lastname>
</customer>
```

As with all XML files, we start with a *declaration* and then a root *element*, whose name is customer. The customer element has two *attributes*, each with a name (id and status) and value ("123" and "archived"). Within customer, there are two child elements, firstname and lastname, each having simple text content ("Joe" and "Bloggs").

Each of these constructs—declaration, element, attribute, value, and text content—can be represented with a class. And if such classes have collection properties for storing child content, we can assemble a *tree* of objects to fully describe a document. This is called a *Document Object Model*, or DOM.

The LINQ to XML DOM

LINQ to XML comprises two things:

- An XML DOM, which we call the *X-DOM*
- A set of about 10 supplementary query operators

As you might expect, the X-DOM consists of types such as XDocument, XElement, and XAttribute. Interestingly, the X-DOM types are not tied to LINQ—you can load, instantiate, update, and save an X-DOM without ever writing a LINQ query.

Conversely, you could use LINQ to query a DOM created of the older W3C-compliant types. However, this would be frustrating and limiting. The distinguishing feature of the X-DOM is that it's *LINQ-friendly*, meaning:

- It has methods that emit useful IEnumerable sequences upon which you can query.
- Its constructors are designed such that you can build an X-DOM tree through a LINQ projection.

X-DOM Overview

Figure 10-1 shows the core X-DOM types. The most frequently used of these types is XElement. XObject is the root of the *inheritance* hierarchy; XElement and XDocument are roots of the *containership* hierarchy.

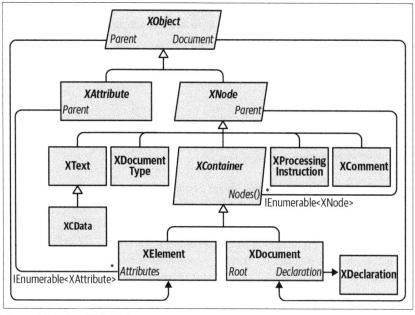

Figure 10-1. Core X-DOM types

Figure 10-2 shows the X-DOM tree created from the following code:

```
string xml = @"<customer id='123' status='archived'>
                <firstname>Joe</firstname>
                <lastname>Bloggs<!--nice name--></lastname>
               </customer>";

XElement customer = XElement.Parse (xml);
```

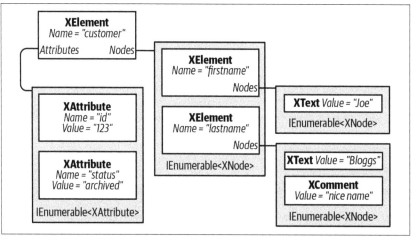

Figure 10-2. A simple X-DOM tree

XObject is the abstract base class for all XML content. It defines a link to the Parent element in the containership tree as well as an optional XDocument.

XNode is the base class for most XML content excluding attributes. The distinguishing feature of XNode is that it can sit in an ordered collection of mixed-type XNodes. For instance, consider the following XML:

```
<data>
  Hello world
  <subelement1/>
  <!--comment-->
  <subelement2/>
</data>
```

Within the parent element <data>, there's first an XText node (Hello world), then an XElement node, then an XComment node, and then a second XElement node. In contrast, an XAttribute will tolerate only other XAttributes as peers.

Although an XNode can access its parent XElement, it has no concept of *child* nodes: this is the job of its subclass XContainer. XContainer defines members for dealing with children and is the abstract base class for XElement and XDocument.

XElement introduces members for managing attributes—as well as a Name and Value. In the (fairly common) case of an element having a single XText child node, the Value property on XElement encapsulates this child's content for both get and set operations, cutting unnecessary navigation. Thanks to Value, you can mostly avoid working directly with XText nodes.

XDocument represents the root of an XML tree. More precisely, it *wraps* the root XElement, adding an XDeclaration, processing instructions, and other root-level "fluff." Unlike with the W3C DOM, its use is optional: you can load, manipulate, and save an X-DOM without ever creating an XDocument! The nonreliance on XDocument also means that you can efficiently and easily move a node subtree to another X-DOM hierarchy.

Loading and Parsing

Both XElement and XDocument provide static Load and Parse methods to build an X-DOM tree from an existing source:

- Load builds an X-DOM from a file, URI, Stream, TextReader, or XmlReader.
- Parse builds an X-DOM from a string.

For example:

```
XDocument fromWeb = XDocument.Load ("http://albahari.com/sample.xml");

XElement fromFile = XElement.Load (@"e:\media\somefile.xml");

XElement config = XElement.Parse (
  @"<configuration>
```

```
    <client enabled='true'>
      <timeout>30</timeout>
    </client>
  </configuration>");
```

In later sections, we describe how to traverse and update an X-DOM. As a quick preview, here's how to manipulate the config element we just populated:

```
foreach (XElement child in config.Elements())
  Console.WriteLine (child.Name);                      // client

XElement client = config.Element ("client");

bool enabled = (bool) client.Attribute ("enabled");  // Read attribute
Console.WriteLine (enabled);                          // True
client.Attribute ("enabled").SetValue (!enabled);    // Update attribute

int timeout = (int) client.Element ("timeout");      // Read element
Console.WriteLine (timeout);                          // 30
client.Element ("timeout").SetValue (timeout * 2);   // Update element

client.Add (new XElement ("retries", 3));            // Add new element

Console.WriteLine (config);      // Implicitly call config.ToString()
```

Here's the result of that last Console.WriteLine:

```
<configuration>
  <client enabled="false">
    <timeout>60</timeout>
    <retries>3</retries>
  </client>
</configuration>
```

 XNode also provides a static ReadFrom method that instantiates and populates any type of node from an XmlReader. Unlike Load, it stops after reading one (complete) node, so you can continue to read manually from the XmlReader afterward.

You can also do the reverse and use an XmlReader or XmlWriter to read or write an XNode, via its CreateReader and CreateWriter methods.

We describe XML readers and writers and how to use them with the X-DOM in Chapter 11.

Saving and Serializing

Calling ToString on any node converts its content to an XML string—formatted with line breaks and indentation as we just saw. (You can disable the line breaks and indentation by specifying SaveOptions.DisableFormatting when calling ToString.)

XElement and XDocument also provide a Save method that writes an X-DOM to a file, Stream, TextWriter, or XmlWriter. If you specify a file, an XML declaration is automatically written. There is also a `WriteTo` method defined in the `XNode` class, which accepts just an `XmlWriter`.

We describe in more detail the handling of XML declarations when saving in "Documents and Declarations" on page 515.

Instantiating an X-DOM

Rather than using the `Load` or `Parse` methods, you can build an X-DOM tree by manually instantiating objects and adding them to a parent via `XContainer`'s `Add` method.

To construct an `XElement` and `XAttribute`, simply provide a name and value:

```
XElement lastName = new XElement ("lastname", "Bloggs");
lastName.Add (new XComment ("nice name"));

XElement customer = new XElement ("customer");
customer.Add (new XAttribute ("id", 123));
customer.Add (new XElement ("firstname", "Joe"));
customer.Add (lastName);

Console.WriteLine (customer.ToString());
```

Here's the result:

```
<customer id="123">
  <firstname>Joe</firstname>
  <lastname>Bloggs<!--nice name--></lastname>
</customer>
```

A value is optional when constructing an `XElement`—you can provide just the element name and add content later. Notice that when we did provide a value, a simple string sufficed—we didn't need to explicitly create and add an `XText` child node. The X-DOM does this work automatically, so you can deal simply with "values."

Functional Construction

In our preceding example, it's difficult to glean the XML structure from the code. X-DOM supports another mode of instantiation, called *functional construction* (from functional programming). With functional construction, you build an entire tree in a single expression:

```
XElement customer =
  new XElement ("customer", new XAttribute ("id", 123),
    new XElement ("firstname", "joe"),
    new XElement ("lastname", "bloggs",
      new XComment ("nice name")
    )
  );
```

This has two benefits. First, the code resembles the shape of the XML. Second, it can be incorporated into the select clause of a LINQ query. For example, the following query projects from an EF Core entity class into an X-DOM:

```
XElement query =
  new XElement ("customers",
    from c in dbContext.Customers.AsEnumerable()
    select
      new XElement ("customer", new XAttribute ("id", c.ID),
        new XElement ("firstname", c.FirstName),
        new XElement ("lastname", c.LastName,
          new XComment ("nice name")
        )
      )
  );
```

We examine this further later in this chapter in "Projecting into an X-DOM" on page 525.

Specifying Content

Functional construction is possible because the constructors for XElement (and XDocument) are overloaded to accept a params object array:

```
public XElement (XName name, params object[] content)
```

The same holds true for the Add method in XContainer:

```
public void Add (params object[] content)
```

Hence, you can specify any number of child objects of any type when building or appending an X-DOM. This works because *anything* counts as legal content. To see how, we need to examine how each content object is processed internally. Here are the decisions made by XContainer, in order:

1. If the object is null, it's ignored.

2. If the object is based on XNode or XStreamingElement, it's added as is to the Nodes collection.

3. If the object is an XAttribute, it's added to the Attributes collection.

4. If the object is a string, it's wrapped in an XText node and added to Nodes.[1]

5. If the object implements IEnumerable, it's enumerated, and the same rules are applied to each element.

6. Otherwise, the object is converted to a string, wrapped in an XText node, and then added to Nodes.[2]

---

[1] The X-DOM actually optimizes this step internally by storing simple text content in a string. The XTEXT node is not actually created until you call Nodes( ) on the XContainer.

Everything ends up in one of two buckets: Nodes or Attributes. Furthermore, any object is valid content because it can always ultimately call ToString on it and treat it as an XText node.

 Before calling ToString on an arbitrary type, XContainer first tests whether it is one of the following types:

```
float, double, decimal, bool,
DateTime, DateTimeOffset, TimeSpan
```

If so, it calls an appropriate typed ToString method on the XmlConvert helper class instead of calling ToString on the object itself. This ensures that the data is round-trippable and compliant with standard XML formatting rules.

Automatic Deep Cloning

When a node or attribute is added to an element (whether via functional construction or an Add method), the node or attribute's Parent property is set to that element. A node can have only one parent element: if you add an already parented node to a second parent, the node is automatically *deep-cloned*. In the following example, each customer has a separate copy of address:

```
var address = new XElement ("address",
                  new XElement ("street", "Lawley St"),
                  new XElement ("town", "North Beach")
              );
var customer1 = new XElement ("customer1", address);
var customer2 = new XElement ("customer2", address);

customer1.Element ("address").Element ("street").Value = "Another St";
Console.WriteLine (
  customer2.Element ("address").Element ("street").Value);   // Lawley St
```

This automatic duplication keeps X-DOM object instantiation free of side effects—another hallmark of functional programming.

Navigating and Querying

As you might expect, the XNode and XContainer classes define methods and properties for traversing the X-DOM tree. Unlike a conventional DOM, however, these functions don't return a collection that implements IList<T>. Instead, they return either a single value or a *sequence* that implements IEnumerable<T>—upon which you are then expected to execute a LINQ query (or enumerate with a foreach). This allows for advanced queries as well as simple navigation tasks—using familiar LINQ query syntax.

---

2 See footnote 1.

Element and attribute names are case sensitive in the X-DOM, just as they are in XML.

Child Node Navigation

Return type	Members	Works on
XNode	FirstNode { get; }	XContainer
	LastNode { get; }	XContainer
IEnumerable<XNode>	Nodes()	XContainer*
	DescendantNodes()	XContainer*
	DescendantNodesAndSelf()	XElement*
XElement	Element (XName)	XContainer
IEnumerable<XElement>	Elements()	XContainer*
	Elements (XName)	XContainer*
	Descendants()	XContainer*
	Descendants (XName)	XContainer*
	DescendantsAndSelf()	XElement*
	DescendantsAndSelf (XName)	XElement*
bool	HasElements { get; }	XElement

Functions marked with an asterisk in the third column of this and other tables also operate on *sequences* of the same type. For instance, you can call Nodes on either an XContainer or a sequence of XContainer objects. This is possible because of extension methods defined in System.Xml.Linq—the supplementary query operators we talked about in the overview.

FirstNode, LastNode, and Nodes

FirstNode and LastNode give you direct access to the first or last child node; Nodes returns all children as a sequence. All three functions consider only direct descendants:

```
var bench = new XElement ("bench",
            new XElement ("toolbox",
              new XElement ("handtool", "Hammer"),
              new XElement ("handtool", "Rasp")
            ),
            new XElement ("toolbox",
              new XElement ("handtool", "Saw"),
              new XElement ("powertool", "Nailgun")
            ),
            new XComment ("Be careful with the nailgun")
          );
```

```
foreach (XNode node in bench.Nodes())
    Console.WriteLine (node.ToString (SaveOptions.DisableFormatting) + ".");
```

This is the output:

```
<toolbox><handtool>Hammer</handtool><handtool>Rasp</handtool></toolbox>.
<toolbox><handtool>Saw</handtool><powertool>Nailgun</powertool></toolbox>.
<!--Be careful with the nailgun-->.
```

Retrieving elements

The Elements method returns just the child nodes of type XElement:

```
foreach (XElement e in bench.Elements())
    Console.WriteLine (e.Name + "=" + e.Value);    // toolbox=HammerRasp
                                                    // toolbox=SawNailgun
```

The following LINQ query finds the toolbox with the nail gun:

```
IEnumerable<string> query =
    from toolbox in bench.Elements()
    where toolbox.Elements().Any (tool => tool.Value == "Nailgun")
    select toolbox.Value;

RESULT: { "SawNailgun" }
```

The next example uses a SelectMany query to retrieve the hand tools in all toolboxes:

```
IEnumerable<string> query =
    from toolbox in bench.Elements()
    from tool in toolbox.Elements()
    where tool.Name == "handtool"
    select tool.Value;

RESULT: { "Hammer", "Rasp", "Saw" }
```

Elements itself is equivalent to a LINQ query on Nodes. Our preceding query could be started as follows:

```
from toolbox in bench.Nodes().OfType<XElement>()
where ...
```

Elements can also return just the elements of a given name:

```
int x = bench.Elements ("toolbox").Count();    // 2
```

This is equivalent to the following:

```
int x = bench.Elements().Where (e => e.Name == "toolbox").Count(); // 2
```

Elements is also defined as an extension method accepting IEnumerable <XContainer> or, more precisely, it accepts an argument of this type:

```
IEnumerable<T> where T : XContainer
```

This allows it to work with sequences of elements, too. Using this method, we can rewrite the query that finds the hand tools in all toolboxes as follows:

```
from tool in bench.Elements ("toolbox").Elements ("handtool")
select tool.Value;
```

The first call to `Elements` binds to `XContainer`'s instance method; the second call to `Elements` binds to the extension method.

Retrieving a single element

The method `Element` (singular) returns the first matching element of the given name. `Element` is useful for simple navigation, as follows:

```
XElement settings = XElement.Load ("databaseSettings.xml");
string cx = settings.Element ("database").Element ("connectString").Value;
```

`Element` is equivalent to calling `Elements()` and then applying LINQ's `FirstOrDefault` query operator with a name-matching predicate. `Element` returns `null` if the requested element doesn't exist.

 `Element("xyz").Value` will throw a `NullReferenceException` if element xyz does not exist. If you'd prefer a null to an exception, either use the null-conditional operator— `Element("xyz")?.Value`—or cast the `XElement` to a `string` instead of querying its `Value` property. In other words:

```
string xyz = (string) settings.Element ("xyz");
```

This works because `XElement` defines an explicit `string` conversion—just for this purpose!

Retrieving descendants

`XContainer` also provides `Descendants` and `DescendantNodes` methods that return child elements or nodes plus all of their children, and so on (the entire tree). `Descendants` accepts an optional element name. Returning to our earlier example, we can use `Descendants` to find all of the hand tools:

```
Console.WriteLine (bench.Descendants ("handtool").Count());   // 3
```

Both parent and leaf nodes are included, as the following example demonstrates:

```
foreach (XNode node in bench.DescendantNodes())
    Console.WriteLine (node.ToString (SaveOptions.DisableFormatting));
```

Here's the output:

```
<toolbox><handtool>Hammer</handtool><handtool>Rasp</handtool></toolbox>
<handtool>Hammer</handtool>
Hammer
<handtool>Rasp</handtool>
Rasp
<toolbox><handtool>Saw</handtool><powertool>Nailgun</powertool></toolbox>
<handtool>Saw</handtool>
Saw
<powertool>Nailgun</powertool>
Nailgun
<!--Be careful with the nailgun-->
```

The next query extracts all comments anywhere within the X-DOM that contain the word "careful":

```
IEnumerable<string> query =
  from c in bench.DescendantNodes().OfType<XComment>()
  where c.Value.Contains ("careful")
  orderby c.Value
  select c.Value;
```

Parent Navigation

All XNodes have a `Parent` property and `AncestorXXX` methods for parent navigation. A parent is always an XElement:

Return type	Members	Works on
XElement	Parent { get; }	XNode
Enumerable<XElement>	Ancestors()	XNode
	Ancestors (XName)	XNode
	AncestorsAndSelf()	XElement
	AncestorsAndSelf (XName)	XElement

If x is an XElement, the following always prints true:

```
foreach (XNode child in x.Nodes())
  Console.WriteLine (child.Parent == x);
```

However, the same is not the case if x is an XDocument. XDocument is peculiar: it can have children but can never be anyone's parent! To access the XDocument, you instead use the Document property; this works on any object in the X-DOM tree.

Ancestors returns a sequence whose first element is Parent and whose next element is Parent.Parent, and so on, until the root element.

> You can navigate to the root element with the LINQ query AncestorsAndSelf().Last().
>
> Another way to achieve the same thing is to call Document .Root, although this works only if an XDocument is present.

Peer Node Navigation

Return type	Members	Defined in
bool	IsBefore (XNode node)	XNode
	IsAfter (XNode node)	XNode
XNode	PreviousNode { get; }	XNode
	NextNode { get; }	XNode
IEnumerable<XNode>	NodesBeforeSelf()	XNode
	NodesAfterSelf()	XNode
IEnumerable<XElement>	ElementsBeforeSelf()	XNode
	ElementsBeforeSelf (XName name)	XNode
	ElementsAfterSelf()	XNode
	ElementsAfterSelf (XName name)	XNode

With PreviousNode and NextNode (and FirstNode/LastNode), you can traverse nodes with the feel of a linked list. This is noncoincidental: internally, nodes are stored in a linked list.

XNode internally uses a *singly* linked list, so PreviousNode is not performant.

Attribute Navigation

Return type	Members	Defined in
bool	HasAttributes { get; }	XElement
XAttribute	Attribute (XName name)	XElement
	FirstAttribute { get; }	XElement
	LastAttribute { get; }	XElement
IEnumerable<XAttribute>	Attributes()	XElement
	Attributes (XName name)	XElement

In addition, XAttribute defines PreviousAttribute and NextAttribute properties as well as Parent.

The Attributes method that accepts a name returns a sequence with either zero or one element; an element cannot have duplicate attribute names in XML.

Updating an X-DOM

You can update elements and attributes in the following ways:

- Call `SetValue` or reassign the `Value` property.
- Call `SetElementValue` or `SetAttributeValue`.
- Call one of the `RemoveXXX` methods.
- Call one of the `AddXXX` or `ReplaceXXX` methods, specifying fresh content.

You can also reassign the `Name` property on `XElement` objects.

Simple Value Updates

Members	Works on
SetValue (object value)	XElement, XAttribute
Value { get; set }	XElement, XAttribute

The `SetValue` method replaces an element or attribute's content with a simple value. Setting the `Value` property does the same but accepts string data only. We describe both of these functions in detail later in "Working with Values" on page 513. An effect of calling `SetValue` (or reassigning `Value`) is that it replaces all child nodes:

```
XElement settings = new XElement ("settings",
                    new XElement ("timeout", 30)
                );
settings.SetValue ("blah");
Console.WriteLine (settings.ToString());  // <settings>blah</settings>
```

Updating Child Nodes and Attributes

Category	Members	Works on
Add	Add (params object[] content)	XContainer
	AddFirst (params object[] content)	XContainer
Remove	RemoveNodes()	XContainer
	RemoveAttributes()	XElement
	RemoveAll()	XElement
Update	ReplaceNodes (params object[] content)	XContainer
	ReplaceAttributes (params object[] content)	XElement
	ReplaceAll (params object[] content	XElement
	SetElementValue (XName name, object value)	XElement
	SetAttributeValue (XName name, object value)	XElement

The most convenient methods in this group are the last two: SetElementValue and SetAttributeValue. They serve as shortcuts for instantiating an XElement or XAttribute and then Adding it to a parent, replacing any existing element or attribute of that name:

```
XElement settings = new XElement ("settings");
settings.SetElementValue ("timeout", 30);    // Adds child node
settings.SetElementValue ("timeout", 60);    // Update it to 60
```

Add appends a child node to an element or document. AddFirst does the same thing but inserts at the beginning of the collection rather than the end.

You can remove all child nodes or attributes in one hit with RemoveNodes or RemoveAttributes. RemoveAll is equivalent to calling both methods.

The ReplaceXXX methods are equivalent to Removing and then Adding. They take a snapshot of the input, so e.ReplaceNodes(e.Nodes()) works as expected.

Updating Through the Parent

Members	Works on
AddBeforeSelf (params object[] content)	XNode
AddAfterSelf (params object[] content)	XNode
Remove()	XNode, XAttribute
ReplaceWith (params object[] content)	XNode

The methods AddBeforeSelf, AddAfterSelf, Remove, and ReplaceWith don't operate on the node's children. Instead, they operate on the collection in which the node itself is in. This requires that the node have a parent element—otherwise, an exception is thrown. AddBeforeSelf and AddAfterSelf are useful for inserting a node into an arbitrary position:

```
XElement items = new XElement ("items",
                    new XElement ("one"),
                    new XElement ("three")
                );
items.FirstNode.AddAfterSelf (new XElement ("two"));
```

Here's the result:

```
<items><one /><two /><three /></items>
```

Inserting into an arbitrary position within a long sequence of elements is efficient because nodes are stored internally in a linked list.

The Remove method removes the current node from its parent. ReplaceWith does the same and then inserts some other content at the same position:

```
XElement items = XElement.Parse ("<items><one/><two/><three/></items>");
items.FirstNode.ReplaceWith (new XComment ("One was here"));
```

Here's the result:

```
<items><!--one was here--><two /><three /></items>
```

Removing a sequence of nodes or attributes

Thanks to extension methods in System.Xml.Linq, you can also call Remove on a *sequence* of nodes or attributes. Consider this X-DOM:

```
XElement contacts = XElement.Parse (
@"<contacts>
    <customer name='Mary'/>
    <customer name='Chris' archived='true'/>
    <supplier name='Susan'>
      <phone archived='true'>012345678<!--confidential--></phone>
    </supplier>
  </contacts>");
```

The following removes all customers:

```
contacts.Elements ("customer").Remove();
```

The following removes all archived contacts (so *Chris* disappears):

```
contacts.Elements().Where (e => (bool?) e.Attribute ("archived") == true)
                   .Remove();
```

If we replaced Elements() with Descendants(), all archived elements throughout the DOM would disappear, yielding this result:

```
<contacts>
  <customer name="Mary" />
  <supplier name="Susan" />
</contacts>
```

The next example removes all contacts that feature the comment "confidential" anywhere in their tree:

```
contacts.Elements().Where (e => e.DescendantNodes()
                                 .OfType<XComment>()
                                 .Any (c => c.Value == "confidential")
                          ).Remove();
```

This is the result:

```
<contacts>
  <customer name="Mary" />
  <customer name="Chris" archived="true" />
</contacts>
```

Contrast this with the following simpler query, which strips all comment nodes from the tree:

```
contacts.DescendantNodes().OfType<XComment>().Remove();
```

Internally, the Remove method first reads all matching elements into a temporary list and then enumerates over the temporary list to perform the deletions. This prevents errors that could otherwise result from deleting and querying at the same time.

Working with Values

XElement and XAttribute both have a Value property of type string. If an element has a single XText child node, XElement's Value property acts as a convenient shortcut to the content of that node. With XAttribute, the Value property is simply the attribute's value.

Despite the storage differences, the X-DOM provides a consistent set of operations for working with element and attribute values.

Setting Values

There are two ways to assign a value: call SetValue or assign the Value property. SetValue is more flexible because it accepts not just strings but other simple data types, too:

```
var e = new XElement ("date", DateTime.Now);
e.SetValue (DateTime.Now.AddDays(1));
Console.Write (e.Value);          // 2019-10-02T16:39:10.734375+09:00
```

We could have instead just set the element's Value property, but this would mean manually converting the DateTime to a string. This is more complicated than calling ToString—it requires the use of XmlConvert for an XML-compliant result.

When you pass a *value* into XElement or XAttribute's constructor, the same automatic conversion takes place for nonstring types. This ensures that DateTimes are correctly formatted; true is written in lowercase, and double.NegativeInfinity is written as "-INF".

Getting Values

To go the other way around and parse a Value back to a base type, you simply cast the XElement or XAttribute to the desired type. It sounds like it shouldn't work—but it does! For instance:

```
XElement e = new XElement ("now", DateTime.Now);
DateTime dt = (DateTime) e;

XAttribute a = new XAttribute ("resolution", 1.234);
double res = (double) a;
```

An element or attribute doesn't store DateTimes or numbers natively—they're always stored as text and then parsed as needed. It also doesn't "remember" the original type, so you must cast it correctly to prevent a runtime error. To make your code robust, you can put the cast in a try/catch block, catching a Format Exception.

Explicit casts on XElement and XAttribute can parse to the following types:

- All standard numeric types
- string, bool, DateTime, DateTimeOffset, TimeSpan, and Guid
- Nullable<> versions of the aforementioned value types

Casting to a nullable type is useful in conjunction with the Element and Attribute methods, because if the requested name doesn't exist, the cast still works. For instance, if x has no timeout element, the first line generates a runtime error and the second line does not:

```
int timeout = (int) x.Element ("timeout");      // Error
int? timeout = (int?) x.Element ("timeout");     // OK; timeout is null.
```

You can factor away the nullable type in the final result with the ?? operator. The following evaluates to 1.0 if the resolution attribute doesn't exist:

```
double resolution = (double?) x.Attribute ("resolution") ?? 1.0;
```

Casting to a nullable type won't get you out of trouble, though, if the element or attribute *exists* and has an empty (or improperly formatted) value. For this, you must catch a FormatException.

You can also use casts in LINQ queries. The following returns "John":

```
var data = XElement.Parse (
  @"<data>
      <customer id='1' name='Mary' credit='100' />
      <customer id='2' name='John' credit='150' />
      <customer id='3' name='Anne' />
    </data>");

IEnumerable<string> query = from cust in data.Elements()
                            where (int?) cust.Attribute ("credit") > 100
                            select cust.Attribute ("name").Value;
```

Casting to a nullable int prevents a NullReferenceException in the case of Anne, who has no credit attribute. Another solution would be to add a predicate to the where clause:

```
where cust.Attributes ("credit").Any() && (int) cust.Attribute...
```

The same principles apply in querying element values.

Values and Mixed Content Nodes

Given the value of Value, you might wonder when you'd ever need to deal directly with XText nodes. The answer is when you have mixed content. For example:

```
<summary>An XAttribute is <bold>not</bold> an XNode</summary>
```

A simple `Value` property is not enough to capture `summary`'s content. The `summary` element contains three children: an `XText` node, followed by an `XElement`, followed by another `XText` node. Here's how to construct it:

```
XElement summary = new XElement ("summary",
                      new XText ("An XAttribute is "),
                      new XElement ("bold", "not"),
                      new XText (" an XNode")
                   );
```

Interestingly, we can still query `summary`'s `Value`—without getting an exception. Instead, we get a concatenation of each child's value:

```
An XAttribute is not an XNode
```

It's also legal to reassign `summary`'s `Value`, at the cost of replacing all previous children with a single new `XText` node.

Automatic XText Concatenation

When you add simple content to an `XElement`, the X-DOM appends to the existing `XText` child rather than creating a new one. In the following examples, `e1` and `e2` end up with just one child `XText` element whose value is `HelloWorld`:

```
var e1 = new XElement ("test", "Hello"); e1.Add ("World");
var e2 = new XElement ("test", "Hello", "World");
```

If you specifically create `XText` nodes, however, you end up with multiple children:

```
var e = new XElement ("test", new XText ("Hello"), new XText ("World"));
Console.WriteLine (e.Value);            // HelloWorld
Console.WriteLine (e.Nodes().Count());  // 2
```

`XElement` doesn't concatenate the two `XText` nodes, so the nodes' object identities are preserved.

Documents and Declarations

XDocument

As we said previously, an `XDocument` wraps a root `XElement` and allows you to add an `XDeclaration`, processing instructions, a document type, and root-level comments. An `XDocument` is optional and can be ignored or omitted: unlike with the W3C DOM, it does not serve as glue to keep everything together.

An `XDocument` provides the same functional constructors as `XElement`. And because it's based on `XContainer`, it also supports the Add*XXX*, Remove*XXX*, and Replace*XXX* methods. Unlike `XElement`, however, an `XDocument` can accept only limited content:

- A single `XElement` object (the "root")
- A single `XDeclaration` object

- A single XDocumentType object (to reference a document type definition [DTD])

- Any number of XProcessingInstruction objects

- Any number of XComment objects

 Of these, only the root XElement is mandatory in order to have a valid XDocument. The XDeclaration is optional—if omitted, default settings are applied during serialization.

The simplest valid XDocument has just a root element:

```
var doc = new XDocument (
        new XElement ("test", "data")
    );
```

Notice that we didn't include an XDeclaration object. The file generated by calling doc.Save would still contain an XML declaration, however, because one is generated by default.

The next example produces a simple but correct XHTML file, illustrating all the constructs that an XDocument can accept:

```
var styleInstruction = new XProcessingInstruction (
  "xml-stylesheet", "href='styles.css' type='text/css'");

var docType = new XDocumentType ("html",
  "-//W3C//DTD XHTML 1.0 Strict//EN",
  "http://www.w3.org/TR/xhtml1/DTD/xhtml1-strict.dtd", null);

XNamespace ns = "http://www.w3.org/1999/xhtml";
var root =
  new XElement (ns + "html",
    new XElement (ns + "head",
      new XElement (ns + "title", "An XHTML page")),
    new XElement (ns + "body",
      new XElement (ns + "p", "This is the content"))
  );

var doc =
  new XDocument (
    new XDeclaration ("1.0", "utf-8", "no"),
    new XComment ("Reference a stylesheet"),
    styleInstruction,
    docType,
    root);

doc.Save ("test.html");
```

The resultant *test.html* reads as follows:

```
<?xml version="1.0" encoding="utf-8" standalone="no"?>
<!--Reference a stylesheet-->
<?xml-stylesheet href='styles.css' type='text/css'?>
```

```
<!DOCTYPE html PUBLIC "-//W3C//DTD XHTML 1.0 Strict//EN"
                   "http://www.w3.org/TR/xhtml1/DTD/xhtml1-strict.dtd">
<html xmlns="http://www.w3.org/1999/xhtml">
  <head>
    <title>An XHTML page</title>
  </head>
  <body>
    <p>This is the content</p>
  </body>
</html>
```

XDocument has a Root property that serves as a shortcut for accessing a document's single XElement. The reverse link is provided by XObject's Document property, which works for all objects in the tree:

```
Console.WriteLine (doc.Root.Name.LocalName);         // html
XElement bodyNode = doc.Root.Element (ns + "body");
Console.WriteLine (bodyNode.Document == doc);         // True
```

Recall that a document's children have no Parent:

```
Console.WriteLine (doc.Root.Parent == null);          // True
foreach (XNode node in doc.Nodes())
  Console.Write (node.Parent == null);                // TrueTrueTrueTrue
```

An XDeclaration is not an XNode and does not appear in the document's Nodes collection—unlike comments, processing instructions, and the root element. Instead, it's assigned to a dedicated property called Declaration. This is why "True" is repeated four and not five times in the last example.

XML Declarations

A standard XML file starts with a declaration such as the following:

```
<?xml version="1.0" encoding="utf-8" standalone="yes"?>
```

An XML declaration ensures that the file will be correctly parsed and understood by a reader. XElement and XDocument follow these rules in emitting XML declarations:

- Calling Save with a filename always writes a declaration.
- Calling Save with an XmlWriter writes a declaration unless the XmlWriter is instructed otherwise.
- The ToString method never emits an XML declaration.

You can instruct an XmlWriter not to produce a declaration by setting the OmitXmlDeclaration and ConformanceLevel properties of an XmlWriterSettings object when constructing the XmlWriter. We describe this in Chapter 11.

The presence or absence of an XDeclaration object has no effect on whether an XML declaration is written. The purpose of an XDeclaration is instead to *hint the XML serialization*, in two ways:

- What text encoding to use
- What to put in the XML declaration's encoding and standalone attributes (should a declaration be written)

XDeclaration's constructor accepts three arguments, which correspond to the attributes version, encoding, and standalone. In the following example, *test.xml* is encoded in UTF-16:

```
var doc = new XDocument (
            new XDeclaration ("1.0", "utf-16", "yes"),
            new XElement ("test", "data")
          );
doc.Save ("test.xml");
```

 Whatever you specify for the XML version is ignored by the XML writer: it always writes "1.0".

The encoding must use an IETF code such as "utf-16", just as it would appear in the XML declaration.

Writing a declaration to a string

Suppose that we want to serialize an XDocument to a string, including the XML declaration. Because ToString doesn't write a declaration, we'd need to use an XmlWriter instead:

```
var doc = new XDocument (
            new XDeclaration ("1.0", "utf-8", "yes"),
            new XElement ("test", "data")
          );
var output = new StringBuilder();
var settings = new XmlWriterSettings { Indent = true };
using (XmlWriter xw = XmlWriter.Create (output, settings))
  doc.Save (xw);
Console.WriteLine (output.ToString());
```

This is the result:

```
<?xml version="1.0" encoding="utf-16" standalone="yes"?>
<test>data</test>
```

Notice that we have UTF-16 in the output, even though we explicitly requested UTF-8 in an XDeclaration! This might look like a bug, but in fact, XmlWriter is being remarkably smart. Because we're writing to a string and not a file or stream, it's impossible to apply any encoding other than UTF-16—the format in which strings are internally stored. Hence, XmlWriter writes "utf-16" so as not to lie.

This also explains why the ToString method doesn't emit an XML declaration. Imagine that instead of calling Save, you did the following to write an XDocument to a file:

```
File.WriteAllText ("data.xml", doc.ToString());
```

As it stands, *data.xml* would lack an XML declaration, making it incomplete but still parsable (you can infer the text encoding). But if ToString() emitted an XML declaration, *data.xml* would actually contain an *incorrect* declaration (encoding="utf-16"), which might prevent it from being read at all because WriteAllText encodes using UTF-8.

Names and Namespaces

Just as .NET types can have namespaces, so too can XML elements and attributes.

XML namespaces achieve two things. First, rather like namespaces in C#, they help prevent naming collisions. This can become an issue when you merge data from one XML file into another. Second, namespaces assign *absolute* meaning to a name. The name "nil," for instance, could mean anything. Within the *http://www.w3.org/2001/xmlschema-instance* namespace, however, "nil" means something equivalent to null in C# and comes with specific rules on how it can be applied.

Because XML namespaces are a significant source of confusion, we first cover namespaces in general, and then move on to how they're used in LINQ to XML.

Namespaces in XML

Suppose that we want to define a customer element in the namespace OReilly.Nut shell.CSharp. There are two ways to proceed. The first is to use the xmlns attribute:

```
<customer xmlns="OReilly.Nutshell.CSharp"/>
```

xmlns is a special reserved attribute. When used in this manner, it performs two functions:

- It specifies a namespace for the element in question.
- It specifies a default namespace for all descendant elements.

This means that in the following example, address and postcode implicitly reside in the OReilly.Nutshell.CSharp namespace:

```
<customer xmlns="OReilly.Nutshell.CSharp">
  <address>
    <postcode>02138</postcode>
  </address>
</customer>
```

If we want address and postcode to have *no* namespace, we'd need to do this:

```
<customer xmlns="OReilly.Nutshell.CSharp">
  <address xmlns="">
    <postcode>02138</postcode>       <!-- postcode now inherits empty ns -->
  </address>
</customer>
```

Prefixes

The other way to specify a namespace is with a *prefix*. A prefix is an alias that you assign to a namespace to save typing. There are two steps in using a prefix—*defining* the prefix and *using* it. You can do both together:

```
<nut:customer xmlns:nut="OReilly.Nutshell.CSharp"/>
```

Two distinct things are happening here. On the right, xmlns:nut="..." defines a prefix called nut and makes it available to this element and all its descendants. On the left, nut:customer assigns the newly allocated prefix to the customer element.

A prefixed element *does not* define a default namespace for descendants. In the following XML, firstname has an empty namespace:

```
<nut:customer xmlns:nut="OReilly.Nutshell.CSharp">
  <firstname>Joe</firstname>
</customer>
```

To give firstname the OReilly.Nutshell.CSharp prefix, you must do this:

```
<nut:customer xmlns:nut="OReilly.Nutshell.CSharp">
  <nut:firstname>Joe</firstname>
</customer>
```

You can also define a prefix—or prefixes—for the convenience of your descendants, without assigning any of them to the parent element itself. The following defines two prefixes, i and z, while leaving the customer element itself with an empty namespace:

```
<customer xmlns:i="http://www.w3.org/2001/XMLSchema-instance"
          xmlns:z="http://schemas.microsoft.com/2003/10/Serialization/">
  ...
</customer>
```

If this were the root node, the whole document would have i and z at its fingertips. Prefixes are convenient when elements need to draw from multiple namespaces.

Notice that both namespaces in this example are URIs. Using URIs (that you own) is standard practice: it ensures namespace uniqueness. So, in real life, our customer element would more likely be:

```
<customer xmlns="http://oreilly.com/schemas/nutshell/csharp"/>
```

or:

```
<nut:customer xmlns:nut="http://oreilly.com/schemas/nutshell/csharp"/>
```

Attributes

You can assign namespaces to attributes, too. The main difference is that an attribute always requires a prefix. For instance:

```
<customer xmlns:nut="OReilly.Nutshell.CSharp" nut:id="123" />
```

Another difference is that an unqualified attribute always has an empty namespace: it never inherits a default namespace from a parent element.

Attributes tend not to need namespaces because their meaning is usually local to the element. An exception is with general-purpose or metadata attributes such as the nil attribute defined by W3C:

```
<customer xmlns:xsi="http://www.w3.org/2001/XMLSchema-instance">
  <firstname>Joe</firstname>
  <lastname xsi:nil="true"/>
</customer>
```

This indicates unambiguously that lastname is nil (null in C#) and not an empty string. Because we've used the standard namespace, a general-purpose parsing utility could know with certainty our intention.

Specifying Namespaces in the X-DOM

So far in this chapter, we've used just simple strings for XElement and XAttribute names. A simple string corresponds to an XML name with an empty namespace—rather like a .NET type defined in the global namespace.

There are a couple of ways to specify an XML namespace. The first is to enclose it in braces, before the local name:

```
var e = new XElement ("{http://domain.com/xmlspace}customer", "Bloggs");
Console.WriteLine (e.ToString());
```

This yields the resulting XML:

```
<customer xmlns="http://domain.com/xmlspace">Bloggs</customer>
```

The second (and more performant) approach is to use the XNamespace and XName types. Here are their definitions:

```
public sealed class XNamespace
{
  public string NamespaceName { get; }
}

public sealed class XName      // A local name with optional namespace
{
  public string LocalName { get; }
  public XNamespace Namespace { get; }   // Optional
}
```

Both types define implicit casts from string, so the following is legal:

```
XNamespace ns    = "http://domain.com/xmlspace";
XName localName = "customer";
XName fullName  = "{http://domain.com/xmlspace}customer";
```

XNamespace also overloads the + operator, allowing you to combine a namespace and name into an XName without using braces:

```
XNamespace ns = "http://domain.com/xmlspace";
XName fullName = ns + "customer";
Console.WriteLine (fullName);    // {http://domain.com/xmlspace}customer
```

All constructors and methods in the X-DOM that accept an element or attribute name actually accept an XName object rather than a string. The reason you can substitute a string—as in all our examples to date—is because of the implicit cast.

Specifying a namespace is the same whether for an element or an attribute:

```
XNamespace ns = "http://domain.com/xmlspace";
var data = new XElement (ns + "data",
              new XAttribute (ns + "id", 123)
           );
```

The X-DOM and Default Namespaces

The X-DOM ignores the concept of default namespaces until it comes time to actually output XML. This means that when you construct a child XElement, you must give it a namespace explicitly if needed; it *will not* inherit from the parent:

```
XNamespace ns = "http://domain.com/xmlspace";
var data = new XElement (ns + "data",
              new XElement (ns + "customer", "Bloggs"),
              new XElement (ns + "purchase", "Bicycle")
           );
```

The X-DOM does, however, apply default namespaces when reading and outputting XML:

```
Console.WriteLine (data.ToString());

OUTPUT:
  <data xmlns="http://domain.com/xmlspace">
    <customer>Bloggs</customer>
    <purchase>Bicycle</purchase>
  </data>

Console.WriteLine (data.Element (ns + "customer").ToString());

OUTPUT:
    <customer xmlns="http://domain.com/xmlspace">Bloggs</customer>
```

If you construct XElement children without specifying namespaces, in other words:

```
XNamespace ns = "http://domain.com/xmlspace";
var data = new XElement (ns + "data",
              new XElement ("customer", "Bloggs"),
              new XElement ("purchase", "Bicycle")
```

```
         );
  Console.WriteLine (data.ToString());
```

you get this result instead:

```
<data xmlns="http://domain.com/xmlspace">
  <customer xmlns="">Bloggs</customer>
  <purchase xmlns="">Bicycle</purchase>
</data>
```

Another trap is failing to include a namespace when navigating an X-DOM:

```
XNamespace ns = "http://domain.com/xmlspace";
var data = new XElement (ns + "data",
             new XElement (ns + "customer", "Bloggs"),
             new XElement (ns + "purchase", "Bicycle")
           );
XElement x = data.Element (ns + "customer");   // ok
XElement y = data.Element ("customer");         // null
```

If you build an X-DOM tree without specifying namespaces, you can subsequently assign every element to a single namespace, as follows:

```
foreach (XElement e in data.DescendantsAndSelf())
  if (e.Name.Namespace == "")
    e.Name = ns + e.Name.LocalName;
```

Prefixes

The X-DOM treats prefixes just as it treats namespaces: purely as a serialization function. This means that you can choose to completely ignore the issue of prefixes—and get by! The only reason you might want to do otherwise is for efficiency when outputting to an XML file. For example, consider this:

```
XNamespace ns1 = "http://domain.com/space1";
XNamespace ns2 = "http://domain.com/space2";

var mix = new XElement (ns1 + "data",
            new XElement (ns2 + "element", "value"),
            new XElement (ns2 + "element", "value"),
            new XElement (ns2 + "element", "value")
          );
```

By default, XElement will serialize this as follows:

```
<data xmlns="http://domain.com/space1">
  <element xmlns="http://domain.com/space2">value</element>
  <element xmlns="http://domain.com/space2">value</element>
  <element xmlns="http://domain.com/space2">value</element>
</data>
```

As you can see, there's a bit of unnecessary duplication. The solution is *not* to change the way you construct the X-DOM, but instead to hint the serializer prior to writing the XML. Do this by adding attributes defining prefixes that you want to see applied. This is typically done on the root element:

```
mix.SetAttributeValue (XNamespace.Xmlns + "ns1", ns1);
mix.SetAttributeValue (XNamespace.Xmlns + "ns2", ns2);
```

This assigns the prefix "ns1" to our XNamespace variable ns1, and "ns2" to ns2. The X-DOM automatically picks up these attributes when serializing and uses them to condense the resulting XML. Here's the result now of calling ToString on mix:

```
<ns1:data xmlns:ns1="http://domain.com/space1"
          xmlns:ns2="http://domain.com/space2">
  <ns2:element>value</ns2:element>
  <ns2:element>value</ns2:element>
  <ns2:element>value</ns2:element>
</ns1:data>
```

Prefixes don't change the way you construct, query, or update the X-DOM—for these activities, you ignore the presence of prefixes and continue to use full names. Prefixes come into play only when converting to and from XML files or streams.

Prefixes are also honored in serializing attributes. In the following example, we record a customer's date of birth and credit as "nil" using the W3C-standard attribute. The highlighted line ensures that the prefix is serialized without unnecessary namespace repetition:

```
XNamespace xsi = "http://www.w3.org/2001/XMLSchema-instance";
var nil = new XAttribute (xsi + "nil", true);

var cust = new XElement ("customers",
             new XAttribute (XNamespace.Xmlns + "xsi", xsi),
             new XElement ("customer",
               new XElement ("lastname", "Bloggs"),
               new XElement ("dob", nil),
               new XElement ("credit", nil)
             )
           );
```

This is its XML:

```
<customers xmlns:xsi="http://www.w3.org/2001/XMLSchema-instance">
  <customer>
    <lastname>Bloggs</lastname>
    <dob xsi:nil="true" />
    <credit xsi:nil="true" />
  </customer>
</customers>
```

For brevity, we predeclared the nil XAttribute so that we could use it twice in building the DOM. You're allowed to reference the same attribute twice because it's automatically duplicated as required.

Annotations

You can attach custom data to any XObject with an annotation. Annotations are intended for your own private use and are treated as black boxes by X-DOM. If you've ever used the Tag property on a Windows Forms or Windows Presentation

---

Foundation (WPF) control, you'll be familiar with the concept—the difference is that you have multiple annotations, and your annotations can be *privately scoped*. You can create an annotation that other types cannot even see—let alone overwrite.

The following methods on XObject add and remove annotations:

```
public void AddAnnotation (object annotation)
public void RemoveAnnotations<T>()      where T : class
```

The following methods retrieve annotations:

```
public T Annotation<T>()                where T : class
public IEnumerable<T> Annotations<T>() where T : class
```

Each annotation is keyed by its *type*, which must be a reference type. The following adds and then retrieves a string annotation:

```
XElement e = new XElement ("test");
e.AddAnnotation ("Hello");
Console.WriteLine (e.Annotation<string>());    // Hello
```

You can add multiple annotations of the same type and then use the Annotations method to retrieve a *sequence* of matches.

A public type such as string doesn't make a great key, however, because code in other types can interfere with your annotations. A better approach is to use an internal or (nested) private class:

```
class X
{
  class CustomData { internal string Message; }    // Private nested type

  static void Test()
  {
    XElement e = new XElement ("test");
    e.AddAnnotation (new CustomData { Message = "Hello" } );
    Console.Write (e.Annotations<CustomData>().First().Message);  // Hello
  }
}
```

To remove annotations, you must also have access to the key's type:

```
e.RemoveAnnotations<CustomData>();
```

Projecting into an X-DOM

So far, we've shown how to use LINQ to get data *out* of an X-DOM. You can also use LINQ queries to project *into* an X-DOM. The source can be anything over which LINQ can query, such as the following:

- EF Core entity classes
- A local collection
- Another X-DOM

Regardless of the source, the strategy is the same in using LINQ to emit an X-DOM: first write a *functional construction* expression that produces the desired X-DOM shape and then build a LINQ query around the expression.

For instance, suppose that we want to retrieve customers from a database into the following XML:

```
<customers>
  <customer id="1">
    <name>Sue</name>
    <buys>3</buys>
  </customer>
  ...
</customers>
```

We start by writing a functional construction expression for the X-DOM using simple literals:

```
var customers =
  new XElement ("customers",
    new XElement ("customer", new XAttribute ("id", 1),
      new XElement ("name", "Sue"),
      new XElement ("buys", 3)
    )
  );
```

We then turn this into a projection and build a LINQ query around it:

```
var customers =
  new XElement ("customers",
    // We must call AsEnumerable() due to a bug in EF Core.
    from c in dbContext.Customers.AsEnumerable()
    select
      new XElement ("customer", new XAttribute ("id", c.ID),
        new XElement ("name", c.Name),
        new XElement ("buys", c.Purchases.Count)
      )
  );
```

 The call to AsEnumerable is required due to a bug in EF Core (a fix is scheduled for a later release). After the bug is fixed, removing the call to AsEnumerable will improve efficiency by preventing a round-trip with each call to c.Purchases.Count.

Here's the result:

```
<customers>
  <customer id="1">
    <name>Tom</name>
    <buys>3</buys>
  </customer>
  <customer id="2">
    <name>Harry</name>
    <buys>2</buys>
  </customer>
```

```
      ...
    </customers>
```

We can see how this works more clearly by constructing the same query in two steps. First:

```
IEnumerable<XElement> sqlQuery =
  from c in dbContext.Customers.AsEnumerable()
  select
    new XElement ("customer", new XAttribute ("id", c.ID),
      new XElement ("name", c.Name),
      new XElement ("buys", c.Purchases.Count)
    );
```

This inner portion is a normal LINQ query that projects into XElements. Here's the second step:

```
var customers = new XElement ("customers", sqlQuery);
```

This constructs the root XElement. The only thing unusual is that the content, sqlQuery, is not a single XElement but an IQueryable<XElement>, which implements IEnumerable<XElement>. Remember that in the processing of XML content, collections are automatically enumerated. So, each XElement is added as a child node.

Eliminating Empty Elements

Suppose in the preceding example that we also wanted to include details of the customer's most recent high-value purchase. We could do this as follows:

```
var customers =
  new XElement ("customers",
    // The AsEnumerable call can be removed when the EF Core bug is fixed.
    from c in dbContext.Customers.AsEnumerable()
    let lastBigBuy = (from p in c.Purchases
                      where p.Price > 1000
                      orderby p.Date descending
                      select p).FirstOrDefault()
    select
      new XElement ("customer", new XAttribute ("id", c.ID),
        new XElement ("name", c.Name),
        new XElement ("buys", c.Purchases.Count),
        new XElement ("lastBigBuy",
          new XElement ("description", lastBigBuy?.Description),
          new XElement ("price", lastBigBuy?.Price ?? 0m)
        )
    )
  );
```

This emits empty elements, though, for customers with no high-value purchases. (If it were a local query rather than a database query, it would throw a NullReferenceException.) In such cases, it would be better to omit the lastBigBuy node entirely. We can achieve this by wrapping the constructor for the lastBigBuy element in a conditional operator:

```
select
  new XElement ("customer", new XAttribute ("id", c.ID),
    new XElement ("name", c.Name),
    new XElement ("buys", c.Purchases.Count),
    lastBigBuy == null ? null :
      new XElement ("lastBigBuy",
        new XElement ("description", lastBigBuy.Description),
        new XElement ("price", lastBigBuy.Price)
```

For customers with no lastBigBuy, a null is emitted instead of an empty XElement. This is what we want, because null content is simply ignored.

Streaming a Projection

If you're projecting into an X-DOM only to Save it (or call ToString on it), you can improve memory efficiency through an XStreamingElement. An XStreaming Element is a cut-down version of XElement that applies *deferred loading* semantics to its child content. To use it, you simply replace the outer XElements with XStrea mingElements:

```
var customers =
  new XStreamingElement ("customers",
    from c in dbContext.Customers
    select
      new XStreamingElement ("customer", new XAttribute ("id", c.ID),
        new XElement ("name", c.Name),
        new XElement ("buys", c.Purchases.Count)
      )
  );
customers.Save ("data.xml");
```

The queries passed into an XStreamingElement's constructor are not enumerated until you call Save, ToString, or WriteTo on the element; this prevents loading the whole X-DOM into memory at once. The flipside is that the queries are reevaluated, should you re-Save. Also, you cannot traverse an XStreamingElement's child content—it does not expose methods such as Elements or Attributes.

XStreamingElement is not based on XObject—or any other class—because it has such a limited set of members. The only members it has, besides Save, ToString, and WriteTo, are the following:

- An Add method, which accepts content like the constructor
- A Name property

XStreamingElement does not allow you to *read* content in a streamed fashion—for this, you must use an XmlReader in conjunction with the X-DOM. We describe how to do this in "Patterns for Using XmlReader/XmlWriter" on page 539.

11

Other XML and JSON Technologies

In Chapter 10, we covered the LINQ-to-XML API—and XML in general. In this chapter, we explore the low-level `XmlReader`/`XmlWriter` classes and the types for working with JavaScript Object Notation (JSON), which has become a popular alternative to XML.

In the online supplement (*http://www.albahari.com/nutshell*), we describe the tools for working with XML schema and stylesheets.

XmlReader

`XmlReader` is a high-performance class for reading an XML stream in a low-level, forward-only manner.

Consider the following XML file, customer.xml:

```
<?xml version="1.0" encoding="utf-8" standalone="yes"?>
<customer id="123" status="archived">
  <firstname>Jim</firstname>
  <lastname>Bo</lastname>
</customer>
```

To instantiate an `XmlReader`, you call the static `XmlReader.Create` method, passing in a `Stream`, a `TextReader`, or a URI string:

```
using XmlReader reader = XmlReader.Create ("customer.xml");
  ...
```

Because `XmlReader` lets you read from potentially slow sources (`Stream`s and URIs), it offers asynchronous versions of most of its methods so that you can easily write nonblocking code. We cover asynchrony in detail in Chapter 14.

To construct an XmlReader that reads from a string:

```
using XmlReader reader = XmlReader.Create (
  new System.IO.StringReader (myString));
```

You can also pass in an XmlReaderSettings object to control parsing and validation options. The following three properties on XmlReaderSettings are particularly useful for skipping over superfluous content:

```
bool IgnoreComments                // Skip over comment nodes?
bool IgnoreProcessingInstructions  // Skip over processing instructions?
bool IgnoreWhitespace              // Skip over whitespace?
```

In the following example, we instruct the reader not to emit whitespace nodes, which are a distraction in typical scenarios:

```
XmlReaderSettings settings = new XmlReaderSettings();
settings.IgnoreWhitespace = true;

using XmlReader reader = XmlReader.Create ("customer.xml", settings);
  ...
```

Another useful property on XmlReaderSettings is ConformanceLevel. Its default value of Document instructs the reader to assume a valid XML document with a single root node. This is a problem if you want to read just an inner portion of XML, containing multiple nodes:

```
<firstname>Jim</firstname>
<lastname>Bo</lastname>
```

To read this without throwing an exception, you must set ConformanceLevel to Fragment.

XmlReaderSettings also has a property called CloseInput, which indicates whether to close the underlying stream when the reader is closed (there's an analogous property on XmlWriterSettings called CloseOutput). The default value for CloseInput and CloseOutput is false.

Reading Nodes

The units of an XML stream are *XML nodes*. The reader traverses the stream in textual (depth-first) order. The Depth property of the reader returns the current depth of the cursor.

The most primitive way to read from an XmlReader is to call Read. It advances to the next node in the XML stream, rather like MoveNext in IEnumerator. The first call to Read positions the cursor at the first node. When Read returns false, it means the cursor has advanced *past* the last node, at which point the XmlReader should be closed and abandoned.

Two string properties on XmlReader provide access to a node's content: Name and Value. Depending on the node type, either Name or Value (or both) are populated.

In this example, we read every node in the XML stream, outputting each node type as we go:

```
XmlReaderSettings settings = new XmlReaderSettings();
settings.IgnoreWhitespace = true;

using XmlReader reader = XmlReader.Create ("customer.xml", settings);
while (reader.Read())
{
  Console.Write (new string (' ', reader.Depth * 2));  // Write indentation
  Console.Write (reader.NodeType.ToString());

  if (reader.NodeType == XmlNodeType.Element ||
      reader.NodeType == XmlNodeType.EndElement)
  {
    Console.Write (" Name=" + reader.Name);
  }
  else if (reader.NodeType == XmlNodeType.Text)
  {
    Console.Write (" Value=" + reader.Value);
  }
  Console.WriteLine ();
}
```

The output is as follows:

```
XmlDeclaration
Element Name=customer
  Element Name=firstname
    Text Value=Jim
  EndElement Name=firstname
  Element Name=lastname
    Text Value=Bo
  EndElement Name=lastname
EndElement Name=customer
```

> Attributes are not included in Read-based traversal (see "Reading Attributes" on page 535).

NodeType is of type XmlNodeType, which is an enum with these members:

None	Comment	Document
XmlDeclaration	Entity	DocumentType
Element	EndEntity	DocumentFragment
EndElement	EntityReference	Notation
Text	ProcessingInstruction	Whitespace
Attribute	CDATA	SignificantWhitespace

Reading Elements

Often, you already know the structure of the XML document that you're reading. To help with this, XmlReader provides a range of methods that read while *presuming* a particular structure. This simplifies your code as well as performing some validation at the same time.

 XmlReader throws an XmlException if any validation fails. XmlException has LineNumber and LinePosition properties indicating where the error occurred—logging this information is essential if the XML file is large!

ReadStartElement verifies that the current NodeType is Element and then calls Read. If you specify a name, it verifies that it matches that of the current element.

ReadEndElement verifies that the current NodeType is EndElement and then calls Read.

For instance, we could read this:

```
<firstname>Jim</firstname>
```

as follows:

```
reader.ReadStartElement ("firstname");
Console.WriteLine (reader.Value);
reader.Read();
reader.ReadEndElement();
```

The ReadElementContentAsString method does all of this in one hit. It reads a start element, a text node, and an end element, returning the content as a string:

```
string firstName = reader.ReadElementContentAsString ("firstname", "");
```

The second argument refers to the namespace, which is blank in this example. There are also typed versions of this method, such as ReadElementContentAsInt, which parse the result. Returning to our original XML document:

```
<?xml version="1.0" encoding="utf-8" standalone="yes"?>
<customer id="123" status="archived">
  <firstname>Jim</firstname>
  <lastname>Bo</lastname>
  <creditlimit>500.00</creditlimit>    <!-- OK, we sneaked this in! -->
</customer>
```

We could read it in as follows:

```
XmlReaderSettings settings = new XmlReaderSettings();
settings.IgnoreWhitespace = true;

using XmlReader r = XmlReader.Create ("customer.xml", settings);

r.MoveToContent();                   // Skip over the XML declaration
r.ReadStartElement ("customer");
string firstName    = r.ReadElementContentAsString ("firstname", "");
string lastName     = r.ReadElementContentAsString ("lastname", "");
decimal creditLimit = r.ReadElementContentAsDecimal ("creditlimit", "");

r.MoveToContent();        // Skip over that pesky comment
r.ReadEndElement();       // Read the closing customer tag
```

The MoveToContent method is really useful. It skips over all the fluff: XML declarations, whitespace, comments, and processing instructions. You can also instruct the reader to do most of this automatically through the properties on XmlReaderSettings.

Optional elements

In the previous example, suppose that `<lastname>` was optional. The solution to this is straightforward:

```
r.ReadStartElement ("customer");
string firstName    = r. ReadElementContentAsString ("firstname", "");
string lastName     = r.Name == "lastname"
                      ? r.ReadElementContentAsString() : null;
decimal creditLimit = r.ReadElementContentAsDecimal ("creditlimit", "");
```

Random element order

The examples in this section rely on elements appearing in the XML file in a set order. If you need to cope with elements appearing in any order, the easiest solution is to read that section of the XML into an X-DOM. We describe how to do this later in "Patterns for Using XmlReader/XmlWriter" on page 539.

Empty elements

The way that XmlReader handles empty elements presents a horrible trap. Consider the following element:

```
<customerList></customerList>
```

In XML, this is equivalent to the following:

```
<customerList/>
```

And yet, XmlReader treats the two differently. In the first case, the following code works as expected:

```
reader.ReadStartElement ("customerList");
reader.ReadEndElement();
```

In the second case, ReadEndElement throws an exception because there is no separate "end element" as far as XmlReader is concerned. The workaround is to check for an empty element:

```
bool isEmpty = reader.IsEmptyElement;
reader.ReadStartElement ("customerList");
if (!isEmpty) reader.ReadEndElement();
```

In reality, this is a nuisance only when the element in question might contain child elements (such as a customer list). With elements that wrap simple text (such as firstname), you can avoid the entire issue by calling a method such as ReadElementContentAsString. The ReadElement*XXX* methods handle both kinds of empty elements correctly.

Other ReadXXX methods

Table 11-1 summarizes all Read*XXX* methods in XmlReader. Most of these are designed to work with elements. The sample XML fragment shown in bold is the section read by the method described.

Table 11-1. Read methods

Members	Works on NodeType	Sample XML fragment	Input parameters	Data returned
ReadContentAs*XXX*	Text	<a>**x**</a>		x
ReadElement ContentAs*XXX*	Element	**<a>x</a>**		x
ReadInnerXml	Element	**<a>x</a>**		x
ReadOuterXml	Element	**<a>x</a>**		<a>x</a>
ReadStartElement	Element	**<a>**x</a>		
ReadEndElement	Element	<a>x**</a>**		
ReadSubtree	Element	**<a>x</a>**		<a>x</a>
ReadToDescendant	Element	**<a>x<b></b></a>**	"b"	
ReadToFollowing	Element	**<a>x<b></b></a>**	"b"	
ReadToNextSibling	Element	**<a>x</a><b></b>**	"b"	
ReadAttribute Value	Attribute	See "Reading Attributes" on page 535		

The ReadContentAs*XXX* methods parse a text node into type *XXX*. Internally, the XmlConvert class performs the string-to-type conversion. The text node can be within an element or an attribute.

The ReadElementContentAs*XXX* methods are wrappers around corresponding Read ContentAs*XXX* methods. They apply to the *element* node rather than the *text* node enclosed by the element.

ReadInnerXml is typically applied to an element, and it reads and returns an element and all its descendants. When applied to an attribute, it returns the value of the attribute. ReadOuterXml is the same except that it includes rather than excludes the element at the cursor position.

ReadSubtree returns a proxy reader that provides a view over just the current element (and its descendants). The proxy reader must be closed before the original reader can be safely read again. When the proxy reader is closed, the cursor position of the original reader moves to the end of the subtree.

ReadToDescendant moves the cursor to the start of the first descendant node with the specified name/namespace. ReadToFollowing moves the cursor to the start of the first node—regardless of depth—with the specified name/namespace. ReadTo

NextSibling moves the cursor to the start of the first sibling node with the specified name/namespace.

There are also two legacy methods: ReadString and ReadElementString behave like ReadContentAsString and ReadElementContentAsString, except that they throw an exception if there's more than a *single* text node within the element. You should avoid these methods because they throw an exception if an element contains a comment.

Reading Attributes

XmlReader provides an indexer giving you direct (random) access to an element's attributes—by name or position. Using the indexer is equivalent to calling GetAttribute.

Given the XML fragment

```
<customer id="123" status="archived"/>
```

we could read its attributes, as follows:

```
Console.WriteLine (reader ["id"]);          // 123
Console.WriteLine (reader ["status"]);      // archived
Console.WriteLine (reader ["bogus"] == null);  // True
```

The XmlReader must be positioned *on a start element* in order to read attributes. *After* calling ReadStartElement, the attributes are gone forever!

Although attribute order is semantically irrelevant, you can access attributes by their ordinal position. We could rewrite the preceding example as follows:

```
Console.WriteLine (reader [0]);          // 123
Console.WriteLine (reader [1]);          // archived
```

The indexer also lets you specify the attribute's namespace—if it has one.

AttributeCount returns the number of attributes for the current node.

Attribute nodes

To explicitly traverse attribute nodes, you must make a special diversion from the normal path of just calling Read. A good reason to do so is if you want to parse attribute values into other types, via the ReadContentAs*XXX* methods.

The diversion must begin from a *start element*. To make the job easier, the forward-only rule is relaxed during attribute traversal: you can jump to any attribute (forward or backward) by calling MoveToAttribute.

MoveToElement returns you to the start element from any-place within the attribute node diversion.

Returning to our previous example:

```
<customer id="123" status="archived"/>
```

we can do this:

```
reader.MoveToAttribute ("status");
string status = reader.ReadContentAsString();

reader.MoveToAttribute ("id");
int id = reader.ReadContentAsInt();
```

MoveToAttribute returns false if the specified attribute doesn't exist.

You can also traverse each attribute in sequence by calling the MoveToFirstAttri
bute and then the MoveToNextAttribute methods:

```
if (reader.MoveToFirstAttribute())
  do { Console.WriteLine (reader.Name + "=" + reader.Value);  }
  while (reader.MoveToNextAttribute());

// OUTPUT:
id=123
status=archived
```

Namespaces and Prefixes

XmlReader provides two parallel systems for referring to element and attribute
names:

- Name
- NamespaceURI and LocalName

Whenever you read an element's Name property or call a method that accepts a single
name argument, you're using the first system. This works well if no namespaces or
prefixes are present; otherwise, it acts in a crude and literal manner. Namespaces are
ignored, and prefixes are included exactly as they were written; for example:

Sample fragment	Name
<customer ...>	customer
<customer xmlns='blah' ...>	customer
<x:customer ...>	x:customer

The following code works with the first two cases:

```
reader.ReadStartElement ("customer");
```

The following is required to handle the third case:

```
reader.ReadStartElement ("x:customer");
```

The second system works through two *namespace-aware* properties: `NamespaceURI` and `LocalName`. These properties take into account prefixes and default namespaces defined by parent elements. Prefixes are automatically expanded. This means that `NamespaceURI` always reflects the semantically correct namespace for the current element, and `LocalName` is always free of prefixes.

When you pass two name arguments into a method such as `ReadStartElement`, you're using this same system. For example, consider the following XML:

```
<customer xmlns="DefaultNamespace" xmlns:other="OtherNamespace">
  <address>
    <other:city>
    ...
```

We could read this as follows:

```
reader.ReadStartElement ("customer", "DefaultNamespace");
reader.ReadStartElement ("address", "DefaultNamespace");
reader.ReadStartElement ("city",    "OtherNamespace");
```

Abstracting away prefixes is usually exactly what you want. If necessary, you can see what prefix was used through the `Prefix` property and convert it into a namespace by calling `LookupNamespace`.

XmlWriter

`XmlWriter` is a forward-only writer of an XML stream. The design of `XmlWriter` is symmetrical to `XmlReader`.

As with `XmlTextReader`, you construct an `XmlWriter` by calling `Create` with an optional `settings` object. In the following example, we enable indenting to make the output more human-readable and then write a simple XML file:

```
XmlWriterSettings settings = new XmlWriterSettings();
settings.Indent = true;

using XmlWriter writer = XmlWriter.Create ("foo.xml", settings);

writer.WriteStartElement ("customer");
writer.WriteElementString ("firstname", "Jim");
writer.WriteElementString ("lastname", "Bo");
writer.WriteEndElement();
```

This produces the following document (the same as the file we read in the first example of `XmlReader`):

```
<?xml version="1.0" encoding="utf-8"?>
<customer>
  <firstname>Jim</firstname>
  <lastname>Bo</lastname>
</customer>
```

XmlWriter automatically writes the declaration at the top unless you indicate otherwise in XmlWriterSettings by setting OmitXmlDeclaration to true or Con formanceLevel to Fragment. The latter also permits writing multiple root nodes—something that otherwise throws an exception.

The WriteValue method writes a single text node. It accepts both string and non-string types such as bool and DateTime, internally calling XmlConvert to perform XML-compliant string conversions:

```
writer.WriteStartElement ("birthdate");
writer.WriteValue (DateTime.Now);
writer.WriteEndElement();
```

In contrast, if we call

```
WriteElementString ("birthdate", DateTime.Now.ToString());
```

the result would be both non-XML-compliant and vulnerable to incorrect parsing.

WriteString is equivalent to calling WriteValue with a string. XmlWriter automatically escapes characters that would otherwise be illegal within an attribute or element, such as &, < >, and extended Unicode characters.

Writing Attributes

You can write attributes immediately after writing a start element:

```
writer.WriteStartElement ("customer");
writer.WriteAttributeString ("id", "1");
writer.WriteAttributeString ("status", "archived");
```

To write nonstring values, call WriteStartAttribute, WriteValue, and then Write EndAttribute.

Writing Other Node Types

XmlWriter also defines the following methods for writing other kinds of nodes:

```
WriteBase64       // for binary data
WriteBinHex       // for binary data
WriteCData
WriteComment
WriteDocType
WriteEntityRef
WriteProcessingInstruction
WriteRaw
WriteWhitespace
```

WriteRaw directly injects a string into the output stream. There is also a WriteNode method that accepts an XmlReader, echoing everything from the given XmlReader.

Namespaces and Prefixes

The overloads for the `Write*` methods allow you to associate an element or attribute with a namespace. Let's rewrite the contents of the XML file in our previous example. This time we will associate all of the elements with the *http://oreilly.com* namespace, declaring the prefix o at the `customer` element:

```
writer.WriteStartElement ("o", "customer", "http://oreilly.com");
writer.WriteElementString ("o", "firstname", "http://oreilly.com", "Jim");
writer.WriteElementString ("o", "lastname", "http://oreilly.com", "Bo");
writer.WriteEndElement();
```

The output is now as follows:

```
<?xml version="1.0" encoding="utf-8"?>
<o:customer xmlns:o='http://oreilly.com'>
  <o:firstname>Jim</o:firstname>
  <o:lastname>Bo</o:lastname>
</o:customer>
```

Notice how for brevity `XmlWriter` omits the child element's namespace declarations when they are already declared by the parent element.

Patterns for Using XmlReader/XmlWriter

Working with Hierarchical Data

Consider the following classes:

```
public class Contacts
{
  public IList<Customer> Customers = new List<Customer>();
  public IList<Supplier> Suppliers = new List<Supplier>();
}

public class Customer { public string FirstName, LastName; }
public class Supplier { public string Name;              }
```

Suppose that you want to use `XmlReader` and `XmlWriter` to serialize a `Contacts` object to XML, as in the following:

```
<?xml version="1.0" encoding="utf-8"?>
<contacts>
  <customer id="1">
    <firstname>Jay</firstname>
    <lastname>Dee</lastname>
  </customer>
  <customer>                        <!-- we'll assume id is optional -->
    <firstname>Kay</firstname>
    <lastname>Gee</lastname>
  </customer>
  <supplier>
    <name>X Technologies Ltd</name>
  </supplier>
</contacts>
```

The best approach is not to write one big method, but to encapsulate XML functionality in the Customer and Supplier types themselves by writing ReadXml and WriteXml methods on these types. The pattern for doing so is straightforward:

- ReadXml and WriteXml leave the reader/writer at the same depth when they exit.
- ReadXml reads the outer element, whereas WriteXml writes only its inner content.

Here's how we would write the Customer type:

```
public class Customer
{
  public const string XmlName = "customer";
  public int? ID;
  public string FirstName, LastName;

  public Customer () { }
  public Customer (XmlReader r) { ReadXml (r); }

  public void ReadXml (XmlReader r)
  {
    if (r.MoveToAttribute ("id")) ID = r.ReadContentAsInt();
    r.ReadStartElement();
    FirstName = r.ReadElementContentAsString ("firstname", "");
    LastName = r.ReadElementContentAsString ("lastname", "");
    r.ReadEndElement();
  }

  public void WriteXml (XmlWriter w)
  {
    if (ID.HasValue) w.WriteAttributeString ("id", "", ID.ToString());
    w.WriteElementString ("firstname", FirstName);
    w.WriteElementString ("lastname", LastName);
  }
}
```

Notice that ReadXml reads the outer start and end element nodes. If its caller did this job instead, Customer couldn't read its own attributes. The reason for not making WriteXml symmetrical in this regard is twofold:

- The caller might need to choose how the outer element is named.
- The caller might need to write extra XML attributes, such as the element's *subtype* (which could then be used to decide which class to instantiate when reading back the element).

Another benefit of following this pattern is that it makes your implementation compatible with IXmlSerializable (we cover this in "Serialization" in the online supplement at *http://www.albahari.com/nutshell*).

The Supplier class is analogous:

```
public class Supplier
{
  public const string XmlName = "supplier";
  public string Name;

  public Supplier () { }
  public Supplier (XmlReader r) { ReadXml (r); }

  public void ReadXml (XmlReader r)
  {
    r.ReadStartElement();
    Name = r.ReadElementContentAsString ("name", "");
    r.ReadEndElement();
  }

  public void WriteXml (XmlWriter w) =>
    w.WriteElementString ("name", Name);
}
```

With the Contacts class, we must enumerate the customers element in ReadXml, checking whether each subelement is a customer or a supplier. We also need to code around the empty element trap:

```
public void ReadXml (XmlReader r)
{
  bool isEmpty = r.IsEmptyElement;        // This ensures we don't get
  r.ReadStartElement();                   // snookered by an empty
  if (isEmpty) return;                    // <contacts/> element!
  while (r.NodeType == XmlNodeType.Element)
  {
    if (r.Name == Customer.XmlName)     Customers.Add (new Customer (r));
    else if (r.Name == Supplier.XmlName) Suppliers.Add (new Supplier (r));
    else
      throw new XmlException ("Unexpected node: " + r.Name);
  }
  r.ReadEndElement();
}

public void WriteXml (XmlWriter w)
{
  foreach (Customer c in Customers)
  {
    w.WriteStartElement (Customer.XmlName);
    c.WriteXml (w);
    w.WriteEndElement();
  }
  foreach (Supplier s in Suppliers)
  {
    w.WriteStartElement (Supplier.XmlName);
    s.WriteXml (w);
    w.WriteEndElement();
  }
}
```

Here's how to serialize a `Contacts` object populated with `Customers` and `Suppliers` to an XML file:

```
var settings = new XmlWriterSettings();
settings.Indent = true;   // To make visual inspection easier

using XmlWriter writer = XmlWriter.Create ("contacts.xml", settings);

var cts = new Contacts()
// Add Customers and Suppliers...

writer.WriteStartElement ("contacts");
cts.WriteXml (writer);
writer.WriteEndElement();
```

Here's how to deserialize from the same file:

```
var settings = new XmlReaderSettings();
settings.IgnoreWhitespace = true;
settings.IgnoreComments = true;
settings.IgnoreProcessingInstructions = true;

using XmlReader reader = XmlReader.Create("contacts.xml", settings);
reader.MoveToContent();
var cts = new Contacts();
cts.ReadXml(reader);
```

Mixing XmlReader/XmlWriter with an X-DOM

You can fly in an X-DOM at any point in the XML tree where `XmlReader` or `XmlWriter` becomes too cumbersome. Using the X-DOM to handle inner elements is an excellent way to combine X-DOM's ease of use with the low-memory footprint of `XmlReader` and `XmlWriter`.

Using XmlReader with XElement

To read the current element into an X-DOM, you call `XNode.ReadFrom`, passing in the `XmlReader`. Unlike `XElement.Load`, this method is not "greedy" in that it doesn't expect to see a whole document. Instead, it reads just the end of the current subtree.

For instance, suppose that we have an XML logfile structured as follows:

```
<log>
  <logentry id="1">
    <date>...</date>
    <source>...</source>
    ...
  </logentry>
  ...
</log>
```

If there were a million `logentry` elements, reading the entire thing into an X-DOM would waste memory. A better solution is to traverse each `logentry` with an `XmlReader` and then use `XElement` to process the elements individually:

```
XmlReaderSettings settings = new XmlReaderSettings();
settings.IgnoreWhitespace = true;

using XmlReader r = XmlReader.Create ("logfile.xml", settings);

r.ReadStartElement ("log");
while (r.Name == "logentry")
{
  XElement logEntry = (XElement) XNode.ReadFrom (r);
  int id = (int) logEntry.Attribute ("id");
  DateTime date = (DateTime) logEntry.Element ("date");
  string source = (string) logEntry.Element ("source");
  ...
}
r.ReadEndElement();
```

If you follow the pattern described in the previous section, you can slot an XElement into a custom type's ReadXml or WriteXml method without the caller ever knowing you've cheated! For instance, we could rewrite Customer's ReadXml method, as follows:

```
public void ReadXml (XmlReader r)
{
  XElement x = (XElement) XNode.ReadFrom (r);
  ID = (int) x.Attribute ("id");
  FirstName = (string) x.Element ("firstname");
  LastName = (string) x.Element ("lastname");
}
```

XElement collaborates with XmlReader to ensure that namespaces are kept intact, and prefixes are properly expanded—even if defined at an outer level. So, if our XML file reads like this:

```
<log xmlns="http://loggingspace">
  <logentry id="1">
  ...
```

the XElements we constructed at the logentry level would correctly inherit the outer namespace.

Using XmlWriter with XElement

You can use an XElement just to write inner elements to an XmlWriter. The following code writes a million logentry elements to an XML file using XElement—without storing the entire thing in memory:

```
using XmlWriter w = XmlWriter.Create ("logfile.xml");

w.WriteStartElement ("log");
for (int i = 0; i < 1000000; i++)
{
  XElement e = new XElement ("logentry",
              new XAttribute ("id", i),
              new XElement ("date", DateTime.Today.AddDays (-1)),
              new XElement ("source", "test"));
```

```
        e.WriteTo (w);
    }
    w.WriteEndElement ();
```

Using an XElement incurs minimal execution overhead. If we amend this example to use XmlWriter throughout, there's no measurable difference in execution time.

Working with JSON

JSON has become a popular alternative to XML. Although it lacks the advanced features of XML (such as namespaces, prefixes, and schemas), it benefits from being simple and uncluttered, with a format similar to what you would get from converting a JavaScript object to a string.

Historically, .NET had no built-in support for JSON, and you had to rely on third-party libraries—primarily Json.NET. Although this is no longer the case, the Json.NET library is still popular for a number of reasons:

- It's been around since 2011.
- The same API also runs on older .NET platforms.
- It's considered to be more functional (as least in the past) than the Microsoft JSON APIs.

The Microsoft JSON APIs have the advantage of having been designed from the ground up to be simple and extremely efficient. Also, from .NET 6, their functionality has become quite close to that of Json.NET.

In this section, we cover the following:

- The forward-only reader and writer (Utf8JsonReader and Utf8JsonWriter)
- The JsonDocument read-only DOM reader
- The JsonNode read/write DOM reader/writer

In "Serialization," in the online supplement at *http://www.albahari.com/nutshell*, we cover JsonSerializer, which automatically serializes and deserializes JSON to classes.

Utf8JsonReader

System.Text.Json.Utf8JsonReader (*https://oreil.ly/9Fc3E*) is an optimized forward-only reader for UTF-8 encoded JSON text. Conceptually, it's like the XmlReader introduced earlier in this chapter, and is used in much the same way.

Consider the following JSON file named *people.json*:

```
{
  "FirstName":"Sara",
  "LastName":"Wells",
  "Age":35,
  "Friends":["Dylan","Ian"]
}
```

The curly braces indicate a *JSON object* (which contains *properties* such as "First Name" and "LastName"), whereas the square brackets indicate a *JSON array* (which contains repeating elements). In this case, the repeating elements are strings, but they could be objects (or other arrays).

The following code parses the file by enumerating its JSON *tokens*. A token is the beginning or end of an object, the beginning or end of an array, the name of a property, or an array or property value (string, number, true, false, or null):

```
byte[] data = File.ReadAllBytes ("people.json");
Utf8JsonReader reader = new Utf8JsonReader (data);
while (reader.Read())
{
  switch (reader.TokenType)
  {
    case JsonTokenType.StartObject:
      Console.WriteLine ($"Start of object");
      break;
    case JsonTokenType.EndObject:
      Console.WriteLine ($"End of object");
      break;
    case JsonTokenType.StartArray:
      Console.WriteLine();
      Console.WriteLine ($"Start of array");
      break;
    case JsonTokenType.EndArray:
      Console.WriteLine ($"End of array");
      break;
    case JsonTokenType.PropertyName:
      Console.Write ($"Property: {reader.GetString()}");
      break;
    case JsonTokenType.String:
      Console.WriteLine ($" Value: {reader.GetString()}");
      break;
    case JsonTokenType.Number:
      Console.WriteLine ($" Value: {reader.GetInt32()}");
      break;
    default:
      Console.WriteLine ($"No support for {reader.TokenType}");
      break;
  }
}
```

Here's the output:

```
Start of object
Property: FirstName Value: Sara
Property: LastName Value: Wells
Property: Age Value: 35
Property: Friends
Start of array
 Value: Dylan
 Value: Ian
End of array
End of object
```

Because `Utf8JsonReader` works directly with UTF-8, it steps through the tokens without first having to convert the input into UTF-16 (the format of .NET strings). Conversion to UTF-16 takes place only when you call a method such as `Get String()`.

Interestingly, `Utf8JsonReader`'s constructor does not accept a byte array, but rather a `ReadOnlySpan<byte>` (for this reason, `Utf8JsonReader` is defined as a *ref struct*). You can pass in a byte array because there's an implicit conversion from `T[]` to `ReadOnlySpan<T>`. In Chapter 23, we describe how spans work and how you can use them to improve performance by minimizing memory allocations.

JsonReaderOptions

By default, `Utf8JsonReader` requires that the JSON conform strictly to the JSON RFC 8259 standard. You can instruct the reader to be more tolerant by passing an instance of `JsonReaderOptions` to the `Utf8JsonReader` constructor. The options allow the following:

C-Style comments
> By default, comments in JSON cause a `JsonException` to be thrown. Setting the `CommentHandling` property to `JsonCommentHandling.Skip` causes comments to be ignored, whereas `JsonCommentHandling.Allow` causes the reader to recognize them and emit `JsonTokenType.Comment` tokens when they are encountered. Comments cannot appear in the middle of other tokens.

Trailing commas
> Per the standard, the last property of an object and the last element of an array must not have a trailing comma. Setting the `AllowTrailingCommas` property to e relaxes this restriction.

Control over the maximum nesting depth
> By default, objects and arrays can nest to 64 levels. Setting the `MaxDepth` to a different number overrides this setting.

Utf8JsonWriter

`System.Text.Json.Utf8JsonWriter` (*https://oreil.ly/aO3sO*) is a forward-only JSON writer. It supports the following types:

- `String` and `DateTime` (which is formatted as a JSON string)
- The numeric types `Int32`, `UInt32`, `Int64`, `UInt64`, `Single`, `Double`, and `Decimal` (which are formatted as JSON numbers)
- `bool` (formatted as JSON true/false literals)
- JSON null
- Arrays

You can organize these data types into objects in accordance with the JSON standard. It also lets you write comments, which are not part of the JSON standard but are often supported by JSON parsers in practice.

The following code demonstrates its use:

```
var options = new JsonWriterOptions { Indented = true };

using (var stream = File.Create ("MyFile.json"))
using (var writer = new Utf8JsonWriter (stream, options))
{
  writer.WriteStartObject();
  // Property name and value specified in one call
  writer.WriteString ("FirstName", "Dylan");
  writer.WriteString ("LastName", "Lockwood");
  // Property name and value specified in separate calls
  writer.WritePropertyName ("Age");
  writer.WriteNumberValue (46);
  writer.WriteCommentValue ("This is a (non-standard) comment");
  writer.WriteEndObject();
}
```

This generates the following output file:

```
{
  "FirstName": "Dylan",
  "LastName": "Lockwood",
  "Age": 46
  /*This is a (non-standard) comment*/
}
```

From .NET 6, `Utf8JsonWriter` has a `WriteRawValue` method to emit a string or byte array directly into the JSON stream. This is useful in special cases—for instance, if you want a number to be written such that it always includes a decimal point (`1.0` rather than `1`).

In this example, we set the `Indented` property on `JsonWriterOptions` to `true` to improve readability. Had we not done so, the output would be as follows:

```
{"FirstName":"Dylan","LastName":"Lockwood","Age":46...}
```

The JsonWriterOptions also has an Encoder property to control the escaping of strings, and a SkipValidation property to allow structural validation checks to be bypassed (allowing the emission of invalid output JSON).

JsonDocument

System.Text.Json.JsonDocument parses JSON data into a read-only DOM composed of JsonElement instances that are generated on demand. Unlike Utf8Json Reader, JsonDocument lets you access elements randomly.

JsonDocument is one of two DOM-based APIs for working with JSON, the other being JsonNode (which we will cover in the following section). JsonNode was introduced in .NET 6, primarily to satisfy the demand for a writable DOM. However, it's also suitable in read-only scenarios and exposes a somewhat more fluent interface, backed by a traditional DOM that uses classes for JSON values, arrays, and objects. In contrast, JsonDocument is extremely lightweight, comprising just one class of note (JsonDocument) and two lightweight structs (JsonElement and Json Property) that parse the underlying data on demand. The difference is illustrated in Figure 11-1.

 In most real-world scenarios, the performance benefits of JsonDocument over JsonNode are negligible, so you can skip to JsonNode if you prefer to learn just one API.

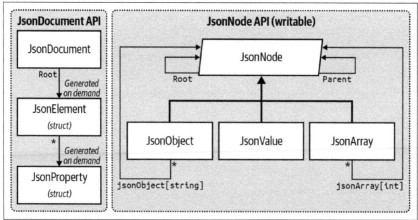

Figure 11-1. JSON DOM APIs

 JsonDocument further improves its efficiency by employing pooled memory to minimize garbage collection. This means that you must dispose the JsonDocument after use; otherwise, its memory will not be returned to the pool. Consequently, when a class stores a JsonDocument in a field, it must also implement IDisposable. Should this be burdensome, consider using JsonNode instead.

The static `Parse` method instantiates a `JsonDocument` from a stream, string, or memory buffer:

```
using JsonDocument document = JsonDocument.Parse (jsonString);
...
```

When calling `Parse`, you can optionally provide a `JsonDocumentOptions` object to control the handling of trailing commas, comments, and the maximum nesting depth (for a discussion on how these options work, see "JsonReaderOptions" on page 546).

From there, you can access the DOM via the `RootElement` property:

```
using JsonDocument document = JsonDocument.Parse ("123");
JsonElement root = document.RootElement;
Console.WriteLine (root.ValueKind);      // Number
```

`JsonElement` can represent a JSON value (string, number, true/false, null), array, or object; the `ValueKind` property indicates which.

The methods that we describe in the following sections throw an exception if the element isn't of the kind expected. If you're not sure of a JSON file's schema, you can avoid such exceptions by checking `ValueKind` first (or by using the `TryGet*` methods).

`JsonElement` also provides two methods that work for any kind of element: `GetRawText()` returns the inner JSON, and `WriteTo` writes that element to a `Utf8JsonWriter`.

Reading simple values

If the element represents a JSON value, you can obtain its value by calling `Get String`, `GetInt32`, `GetBoolean`, etc.):

```
using JsonDocument document = JsonDocument.Parse ("123");
int number = document.RootElement.GetInt32();
```

`JsonElement` also provides methods to parse JSON strings into other commonly used CLR types such as `DateTime` (and even base-64 binary). There are also `TryGet*` versions that avoid throwing an exception if the parse fails.

Reading JSON arrays

If the `JsonElement` represents an array, you can call the following methods:

`EnumerateArray()`
Enumerates all the subitems for a JSON array (as `JsonElements`).

`GetArrayLength()`
Returns the number of elements in the array.

You can also use the indexer to return an element at a specific position:

```
using JsonDocument document = JsonDocument.Parse (@"[1, 2, 3, 4, 5]");
int length = document.RootElement.GetArrayLength();    // 5
int value  = document.RootElement[3].GetInt32();       // 4
```

Reading JSON objects

If the element represents a JSON object, you can call the following methods:

`EnumerateObject()`
  Enumerates all of the object's property names and values.

`GetProperty (string propertyName)`
  Gets a property by name (returning another `JsonElement`). Throws an exception if the name isn't present.

`TryGetProperty (string propertyName, out JsonElement value)`
  Returns an object's property if present.

For example:

```
using JsonDocument document = JsonDocument.Parse (@"{ ""Age"": 32}");
JsonElement root = document.RootElement;
int age = root.GetProperty ("Age").GetInt32();
```

Here's how we could "discover" the Age property:

```
JsonProperty ageProp = root.EnumerateObject().First();
string name = ageProp.Name;              // Age
JsonElement value = ageProp.Value;
Console.WriteLine (value.ValueKind);     // Number
Console.WriteLine (value.GetInt32());    // 32
```

JsonDocument and LINQ

JsonDocument lends itself well to LINQ. Given the following JSON file:

```
[
  {
    "FirstName":"Sara",
    "LastName":"Wells",
    "Age":35,
    "Friends":["Ian"]
  },
  {
    "FirstName":"Ian",
    "LastName":"Weems",
    "Age":42,
    "Friends":["Joe","Eric","Li"]
  },
  {
    "FirstName":"Dylan",
    "LastName":"Lockwood",
    "Age":46,
    "Friends":["Sara","Ian"]
```

```
    }
  ]
```

we can use JsonDocument to query this with LINQ, as follows:

```
using var stream = File.OpenRead (jsonPath);
using JsonDocument document = JsonDocument.Parse (json);

var query =
  from person in document.RootElement.EnumerateArray()
  select new
  {
    FirstName = person.GetProperty ("FirstName").GetString(),
    Age = person.GetProperty ("Age").GetInt32(),
    Friends =
      from friend in person.GetProperty ("Friends").EnumerateArray()
      select friend.GetString()
  };
```

Because LINQ queries are lazily evaluated, it's important to enumerate the query before the document goes out of scope and JsonDocument is implicitly disposed of by virtue of the using statement.

Making updates with a JSON writer

Although JsonDocument is read-only, you can send the content of a JsonElement to a Utf8JsonWriter with the WriteTo method. This provides a mechanism for emitting a modified version of the JSON. Here's how we can take the JSON from the preceding example and write it to a new JSON file that includes only people with two or more friends:

```
using var json = File.OpenRead (jsonPath);
using JsonDocument document = JsonDocument.Parse (json);

var options = new JsonWriterOptions { Indented = true };

using (var outputStream = File.Create ("NewFile.json"))
using (var writer = new Utf8JsonWriter (outputStream, options))
{
  writer.WriteStartArray();
  foreach (var person in document.RootElement.EnumerateArray())
  {
    int friendCount = person.GetProperty ("Friends").GetArrayLength();
    if (friendCount >= 2)
      person.WriteTo (writer);
  }
}
```

If you need the ability to update the DOM, however, JsonNode is a better solution.

JsonNode

JsonNode (in System.Text.Json.Nodes) was introduced in .NET 6, primarily to satisfy the demand for a writable DOM. However, it's also suitable in read-only scenarios and exposes a somewhat more fluent interface, backed by a traditional DOM that uses classes for JSON values, arrays, and objects (see Figure 11-1). Being classes, they incur a garbage-collection cost, but this is likely to be negligible in most real-world scenarios. JsonNode is still highly optimized and can actually be faster than JsonDocument when the same nodes are read repeatedly (because JsonNode, while lazy, caches the results of parsing).

The static Parse method creates a JsonNode from a stream, string, memory buffer, or Utf8JsonReader:

```
JsonNode node = JsonNode.Parse (jsonString);
```

When calling Parse, you can optionally provide a JsonDocumentOptions object to control the handling of trailing commas, comments, and the maximum nesting depth (for a discussion on how these options work, see "JsonReaderOptions" on page 546). Unlike JsonDocument, JsonNode does not require disposal.

 Calling ToString() on a JsonNode returns a human-readable (indented) JSON string. There is also a ToJsonString() method, which returns a compact JSON string.

Parse returns a subtype of JsonNode, which will be JsonValue, JsonObject, or JsonArray. To avoid the clutter of a downcast, JsonNode provides helper methods called AsValue(), AsObject(), and AsArray():

```
var node = JsonNode.Parse ("123");  // Parses to a JsonValue
int number = node.AsValue().GetValue<int>();
// Shortcut for ((JsonValue)node).GetValue<int>();
```

However, you don't usually need to call these methods, because the most commonly used members are exposed on the JsonNode class itself:

```
var node = JsonNode.Parse ("123");
int number = node.GetValue<int>();
// Shortcut for node.AsValue().GetValue<int>();
```

Reading simple values

We just saw that you can extract or parse a simple value by calling GetValue with a type parameter. To make this even easier, JsonNode overloads C#'s explicit cast operators, enabling the following shortcut:

```
var node = JsonNode.Parse ("123");
int number = (int) node;
```

The types for which this works comprise the standard numeric types: char, bool, DateTime, DateTimeOffset, and Guid (and their nullable versions), as well as string.

If you're not sure whether parsing will succeed, the following code is required:

```
if (node.AsValue().TryGetValue<int> (out var number))
  Console.WriteLine (number);
```

Nodes that have been parsed from JSON text are internally
backed by a JsonElement (part of the JsonDocument read-only
JSON API). You can extract the underlying JsonElement as
follows:

```
JsonElement je = node.GetValue<JsonElement>();
```

However, this doesn't work when the node is instantiated
explicitly (as will be the case when we update the DOM).
Such nodes are backed not by a JsonElement but by the actual
parsed value (see "Making updates with JsonNode" on page
554).

Reading JSON arrays

A JsonNode that represents a JSON array will be of type JsonArray.

JsonArray implements IList<JsonNode>, so you can enumerate over it and access
the elements like you would an array or list:

```
var node = JsonNode.Parse (@"[1, 2, 3, 4, 5]");
Console.WriteLine (node.AsArray().Count);        // 5

foreach (JsonNode child in node.AsArray())
{ ... }
```

As a shortcut, you can access the indexer directly from the JsonNode class:

```
Console.WriteLine ((int)node[0]);    // 1
```

Reading JSON objects

A JsonNode that represents a JSON object will be of type JsonObject.

JsonObject implements IDictionary<string,JsonNode>, so you can access a
member via the indexer, as well as enumerating over the dictionary's key/value
pairs.

And as with JsonArray, you can access the indexer directly from the JsonNode class:

```
var node = JsonNode.Parse (@"{ ""Name"":""Alice"", ""Age"": 32}");
string name = (string) node ["Name"];   // Alice
int age = (int) node ["Age"];           // 32
```

Here's how we could "discover" the Name and Age properties:

```
// Enumerate over the dictionary's key/value pairs:
foreach (KeyValuePair<string,JsonNode> keyValuePair in node.AsObject())
{
  string propertyName = keyValuePair.Key;   // "Name" (then "Age")
  JsonNode value = keyValuePair.Value;
}
```

If you're not sure whether a property has been defined, the following pattern also
works:

```
if (node.AsObject().TryGetPropertyValue ("Name", out JsonNode nameNode))
{ ... }
```

Fluent traversal and LINQ

You can reach deep into a hierarchy just with indexers. For example, given the following JSON file:

```
[
  {
    "FirstName":"Sara",
    "LastName":"Wells",
    "Age":35,
    "Friends":["Ian"]
  },
  {
    "FirstName":"Ian",
    "LastName":"Weems",
    "Age":42,
    "Friends":["Joe","Eric","Li"]
  },
  {
    "FirstName":"Dylan",
    "LastName":"Lockwood",
    "Age":46,
    "Friends":["Sara","Ian"]
  }
]
```

we can extract the second person's third friend as follows:

```
string li = (string) node[1]["Friends"][2];
```

Such a file is also easy to query via LINQ:

```
JsonNode node = JsonNode.Parse (File.ReadAllText (jsonPath));

var query =
  from person in node.AsArray()
  select new
  {
    FirstName = (string) person ["FirstName"],
    Age = (int) person ["Age"],
    Friends =
      from friend in person ["Friends"].AsArray()
      select (string) friend
  };
```

Unlike JsonDocument, JsonNode is not disposable, so we don't have to worry about the potential for disposal during lazy enumeration.

Making updates with JsonNode

JsonObject and JsonArray are mutable, so you can update their content.

The easiest way to replace or add properties to a JsonObject is via the indexer. In the following example, we change the Color property's value from "Red" to "White" and add a new property called "Valid":

```
var node = JsonNode.Parse ("{ \"Color\": \"Red\" }");
node ["Color"] = "White";
node ["Valid"] = true;
Console.WriteLine (node.ToJsonString()); // {"Color":"White","Valid":true}
```

The second line in that example is a shortcut for the following:

```
node ["Color"] = JsonValue.Create ("White");
```

Rather than assigning the property a simple value, you can assign it a JsonArray or JsonObject. (We will demonstrate how to construct JsonArray and JsonObject instances in the following section.)

To remove a property, first cast to JsonObject (or call AsObject) and then call the Remove method:

```
node.AsObject().Remove ("Valid");
```

(JsonObject also exposes an Add method, which throws an exception if the property already exists.)

JsonArray also lets you use the indexer to replace items:

```
var node = JsonNode.Parse ("[1, 2, 3]");
node[0] = 10;
```

Calling AsArray exposes the Add/Insert/Remove/RemoveAt methods. In the following example, we remove the first element in the array and add one to the end:

```
var arrayNode = JsonNode.Parse ("[1, 2, 3]");
arrayNode.AsArray().RemoveAt(0);
arrayNode.AsArray().Add (4);
Console.WriteLine (arrayNode.ToJsonString()); // [2,3,4]
```

Constructing a JsonNode DOM programmatically

JsonArray and JsonObject have constructors that support object initialization syntax, which allows you to build an entire JsonNode DOM in one expression:

```
var node = new JsonArray
{
  new JsonObject {
    ["Name"] = "Tracy",
    ["Age"] = 30,
    ["Friends"] = new JsonArray ("Lisa", "Joe")
  },
  new JsonObject {
    ["Name"] = "Jordyn",
    ["Age"] = 25,
    ["Friends"] = new JsonArray ("Tracy", "Li")
  }
};
```

This evaluates to the following JSON:

```
[
  {
    "Name": "Tracy",
    "Age": 30,
    "Friends": ["Lisa", "Joe"]
  },
  {
    "Name": "Jordyn",
    "Age": 25,
    "Friends": ["Tracy","Li"]
  }
]
```

12

Disposal and Garbage Collection

Some objects require explicit tear-down code to release resources such as open files, locks, operating system handles, and unmanaged objects. In .NET parlance, this is called *disposal*, and it is supported through the IDisposable interface. The managed memory occupied by unused objects must also be reclaimed at some point; this function is known as *garbage collection* and is performed by the CLR.

Disposal differs from garbage collection in that disposal is usually explicitly instigated; garbage collection is totally automatic. In other words, the programmer takes care of such things as releasing file handles, locks, and operating system resources, while the CLR takes care of releasing memory.

This chapter discusses both disposal and garbage collection, and also describes C# finalizers and the pattern by which they can provide a backup for disposal. Lastly, we discuss the intricacies of the garbage collector and other memory management options.

IDisposable, Dispose, and Close

.NET defines a special interface for types requiring a tear-down method:

```
public interface IDisposable
{
  void Dispose();
}
```

C#'s using statement provides a syntactic shortcut for calling Dispose on objects that implement IDisposable, using a try/finally block:

```
using (FileStream fs = new FileStream ("myFile.txt", FileMode.Open))
{
  // ... Write to the file ...
}
```

The compiler converts this to the following:

```
FileStream fs = new FileStream ("myFile.txt", FileMode.Open);
try
{
  // ... Write to the file ...
}
finally
{
  if (fs != null) ((IDisposable)fs).Dispose();
}
```

The `finally` block ensures that the `Dispose` method is called even when an exception is thrown or the code exits the block early.

Similarly, the following syntax ensures disposal as soon as `fs` goes out of scope:

```
using FileStream fs = new FileStream ("myFile.txt", FileMode.Open);

// ... Write to the file ...
```

In simple scenarios, writing your own disposable type is just a matter of implementing `IDisposable` and writing the `Dispose` method:

```
sealed class Demo : IDisposable
{
  public void Dispose()
  {
    // Perform cleanup / tear-down.
    ...
  }
}
```

 This pattern works well in simple cases and is appropriate for sealed classes. In "Calling Dispose from a Finalizer" on page 566, we describe a more elaborate pattern that can provide a backup for consumers that forget to call `Dispose`. With unsealed types, there's a strong case for following this latter pattern from the outset—otherwise, it becomes very messy if the subtype wants to add such functionality itself.

Standard Disposal Semantics

.NET follows a de facto set of rules in its disposal logic. These rules are not hardwired to .NET or the C# language in any way; their purpose is to define a consistent protocol to consumers. Here they are:

1. After an object has been disposed, it's beyond redemption. It cannot be reactivated, and calling its methods or properties (other than `Dispose`) throws an `ObjectDisposedException`.

2. Calling an object's `Dispose` method repeatedly causes no error.

3. If disposable object *x* "owns" disposable object *y*, *x*'s `Dispose` method automatically calls *y*'s `Dispose` method—unless instructed otherwise.

These rules are also helpful when writing your own types, though they're not mandatory. Nothing prevents you from writing an "Undispose" method other than, perhaps, the flak you might cop from colleagues!

According to rule 3, a container object automatically disposes its child objects. A good example is a Windows Forms container control such as a `Form` or `Panel`. The container can host many child controls, yet you don't dispose every one of them explicitly; closing or disposing the parent control or form takes care of the whole lot. Another example is when you wrap a `FileStream` in a `DeflateStream`. Disposing the `DeflateStream` also disposes the `FileStream`—unless you instructed otherwise in the constructor.

Close and Stop

Some types define a method called `Close` in addition to `Dispose`. The .NET BCL is not completely consistent on the semantics of a `Close` method, although in nearly all cases it's either of the following:

- Functionally identical to `Dispose`
- A functional *subset* of `Dispose`

An example of the latter is `IDbConnection`: a `Closed` connection can be re-`Opened`; a `Disposed` connection cannot. Another example is a Windows `Form` activated with `ShowDialog`: `Close` hides it; `Dispose` releases its resources.

Some classes define a `Stop` method (e.g., `Timer` or `HttpListener`). A `Stop` method may release unmanaged resources, like `Dispose`, but unlike `Dispose`, it allows for re-`Starting`.

When to Dispose

A safe rule to follow (in nearly all cases) is "if in doubt, dispose." Objects wrapping an unmanaged resource handle will nearly always require disposal in order to free the handle. Examples include file or network streams, network sockets, Windows Forms controls, GDI+ pens, brushes, and bitmaps. Conversely, if a type is disposable, it will often (but not always) reference an unmanaged handle, directly or indirectly. This is because unmanaged handles provide the gateway to the "outside world" of OS resources, network connections, and database locks—the primary means by which objects can create trouble outside of themselves if improperly abandoned.

There are, however, three scenarios for *not* disposing:

- When you don't "own" the object—for example, when obtaining a *shared* object via a static field or property
- When an object's `Dispose` method does something that you don't want

- When an object's `Dispose` method is unnecessary *by design*, and disposing that object would add complexity to your program

The first category is rare. The main cases are in the `System.Drawing` namespace: the GDI+ objects obtained through *static fields or properties* (such as `Brushes.Blue`) must never be disposed because the same instance is used throughout the life of the application. Instances that you obtain through constructors, however (such as `new SolidBrush`), *should* be disposed, as should instances obtained through static *methods* (such as `Font.FromHdc`).

The second category is more common. There are some good examples in the `System.IO` and `System.Data` namespaces:

Type	Disposal function	When not to dispose
`MemoryStream`	Prevents further I/O	When you later need to read/write the stream
`StreamReader`, `StreamWriter`	Flushes the reader/writer and closes the underlying stream	When you want to keep the underlying stream open (you must then call `Flush` on a `StreamWriter` when you're done)
`IDbConnection`	Releases a database connection and clears the connection string	If you need to re-Open it, you should call `Close` instead of `Dispose`
`DbContext` (EF Core)	Prevents further use	When you might have lazily evaluated queries connected to that context

`MemoryStream`'s `Dispose` method disables only the object; it doesn't perform any critical cleanup because a `MemoryStream` holds no unmanaged handles or other such resources.

The third category includes the classes such as `StringReader` and `StringWriter`. These types are disposable under the duress of their base class rather than through a genuine need to perform essential cleanup. If you happen to instantiate and work with such an object entirely in one method, wrapping it in a `using` block adds little inconvenience. But if the object is longer lasting, keeping track of when it's no longer used so that you can dispose of it adds unnecessary complexity. In such cases, you can simply ignore object disposal.

 Ignoring disposal can sometimes incur a performance cost (see "Calling Dispose from a Finalizer" on page 566).

Clearing Fields in Disposal

In general, you don't need to clear an object's fields in its `Dispose` method. However, it is good practice to unsubscribe from events that the object has subscribed to internally over its lifetime (for an example, see "Managed Memory Leaks" on page 576). Unsubscribing from such events prevents receiving unwanted event notifications—and prevents unintentionally keeping the object alive in the eyes of the garbage collector (GC).

 A `Dispose` method itself does not cause (managed) memory to be released—this can happen only in garbage collection.

It's also worth setting a field to indicate that the object is disposed so that you can throw an `ObjectDisposedException` if a consumer later tries to call members on the object. A good pattern is to use a publicly readable automatic property for this:

```
public bool IsDisposed { get; private set; }
```

Although technically unnecessary, it can also be good to clear an object's own event handlers (by setting them to `null`) in the `Dispose` method. This eliminates the possibility of those events firing during or after disposal.

Occasionally, an object holds high-value secrets, such as encryption keys. In these cases, it can make sense to clear such data from fields during disposal (to avoid potential discovery by other processes on the machine when the memory is later released to the operating system). The `SymmetricAlgorithm` class in `System .Security.Cryptography` does exactly this by calling `Array.Clear` on the byte array holding the encryption key.

Anonymous Disposal

Sometimes, it's useful to implement `IDisposable` without having to write a class. For instance, suppose that you want to expose methods on a class that suspend and resume event processing:

```
class Foo
{
  int _suspendCount;

  public void SuspendEvents() => _suspendCount++;
  public void ResumeEvents() => _suspendCount--;

  void FireSomeEvent()
  {
    if (_suspendCount == 0)
      ... fire some event ...
  }
  ...
}
```

Such an API is clumsy to use. Consumers must remember to call `ResumeEvents`. And to be robust, they must do so in a `finally` block (in case an exception is thrown):

```
var foo = new Foo();
foo.SuspendEvents();
try
{
```

```
    ... do stuff ...         // Because an exception could be thrown here
  }
  finally
  {
    foo.ResumeEvents();   // ...we must call this in a finally block
  }
```

A better pattern is to do away with ResumeEvents and have SuspendEvents return
an IDisposable. Consumers can then do this:

```
using (foo.SuspendEvents())
{
  ... do stuff ...
}
```

The problem is that this pushes work onto whoever has to implement the Suspend
Events method. Even with a good effort to reduce whitespace, we end up with this
extra clutter:

```
public IDisposable SuspendEvents()
{
  _suspendCount++;
  return new SuspendToken (this);
}

class SuspendToken : IDisposable
{
  Foo _foo;
  public SuspendToken (Foo foo) => _foo = foo;
  public void Dispose()
  {
    if (_foo != null) _foo._suspendCount--;
    _foo = null;   // Prevent against consumer disposing twice
  }
}
```

The *anonymous disposal* pattern solves this problem. With the following reusable
class:

```
public class Disposable : IDisposable
{
  public static Disposable Create (Action onDispose)
    => new Disposable (onDispose);

  Action _onDispose;
  Disposable (Action onDispose) => _onDispose = onDispose;

  public void Dispose()
  {
    _onDispose?.Invoke();   // Execute disposal action if non-null.
    _onDispose = null;      // Ensure it can't execute a second time.
  }
}
```

we can reduce our `SuspendEvents` method to the following:

```
public IDisposable SuspendEvents()
{
  _suspendCount++;
  return Disposable.Create (() => _suspendCount--);
}
```

Automatic Garbage Collection

Regardless of whether an object requires a `Dispose` method for custom tear-down logic, at some point the memory it occupies on the heap must be freed. The CLR handles this side of it entirely automatically via an automatic GC. You never deallocate managed memory yourself. For example, consider the following method:

```
public void Test()
{
  byte[] myArray = new byte[1000];
  ...
}
```

When `Test` executes, an array to hold 1,000 bytes is allocated on the memory heap. The array is referenced by the variable `myArray`, stored on the local variable stack. When the method exits, this local variable `myArray` pops out of scope, meaning that nothing is left to reference the array on the memory heap. The orphaned array then becomes eligible to be reclaimed in garbage collection.

 In debug mode with optimizations disabled, the lifetime of an object referenced by a local variable extends to the end of the code block to ease debugging. Otherwise, it becomes eligible for collection at the earliest point at which it's no longer used.

Garbage collection does not happen immediately after an object is orphaned. Rather like garbage collection on the street, it happens periodically, although (unlike garbage collection on the street) not to a fixed schedule. The CLR bases its decision on when to collect upon a number of factors, such as the available memory, the amount of memory allocation, and the time since the last collection (the GC self-tunes to optimize for an application's specific memory access patterns). This means that there's an indeterminate delay between an object being orphaned and being released from memory. This delay can range from nanoseconds to days.

 The GC doesn't collect all garbage with every collection. Instead, the memory manager divides objects into *generations*, and the GC collects new generations (recently allocated objects) more frequently than old generations (long-lived objects). We discuss this in more detail in "How the GC Works" on page 569.

Garbage Collection and Memory Consumption

The GC tries to strike a balance between the time it spends doing garbage collection and the application's memory consumption (working set). Consequently, applications can consume more memory than they need, particularly if large temporary arrays are constructed.

You can monitor a process's memory consumption via the Windows Task Manager or Resource Monitor—or programmatically by querying a performance counter:

```
// These types are in System.Diagnostics:
string procName = Process.GetCurrentProcess().ProcessName;
using PerformanceCounter pc = new PerformanceCounter
    ("Process", "Private Bytes", procName);
Console.WriteLine (pc.NextValue());
```

This queries the *private working set*, which gives the best overall indication of your program's memory consumption. Specifically, it excludes memory that the CLR has internally deallocated and is willing to rescind to the OS should another process need it.

Roots

A *root* is something that keeps an object alive. If an object is not directly or indirectly referenced by a root, it will be eligible for garbage collection.

A root is one of the following:

- A local variable or parameter in an executing method (or in any method in its call stack)

- A static variable

- An object on the queue that stores objects ready for finalization (see the next section)

It's impossible for code to execute in a deleted object, so if there's any possibility of an (instance) method executing, its object must somehow be referenced in one of these ways.

Note that a group of objects that reference one another cyclically are considered dead without a root referee (see Figure 12-1). To put it in another way, objects that cannot be accessed by following the arrows (references) from a root object are *unreachable*—and therefore subject to collection.

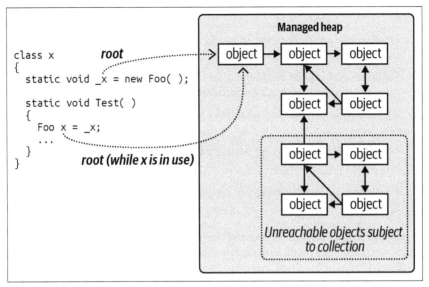

```
class x          root
{
   static void _x = new Foo( );

   static void Test( )
   {
      Foo x = _x;
      ...
   }
}          root (while x is in use)
```

Managed heap

Unreachable objects subject to collection

Figure 12-1. Roots

Finalizers

Prior to an object being released from memory, its *finalizer* runs, if it has one. A finalizer is declared like a constructor, but it is prefixed by the ˜ symbol:

```
class Test
{
   ˜Test()
   {
      // Finalizer logic...
   }
}
```

(Although similar in declaration to a constructor, finalizers cannot be declared as public or static, cannot have parameters, and cannot call the base class.)

Finalizers are possible because garbage collection works in distinct phases. First, the GC identifies the unused objects ripe for deletion. Those without finalizers are deleted immediately. Those with pending (unrun) finalizers are kept alive (for now) and are put onto a special queue.

At that point, garbage collection is complete, and your program continues executing. The *finalizer thread* then kicks in and starts running in parallel to your program, picking objects off that special queue and running their finalization methods. Prior to each object's finalizer running, it's still very much alive—that queue acts as a root object. After it's been dequeued and the finalizer executed, the object becomes orphaned and will be deleted in the next collection (for that object's *generation*).

Finalizers can be useful, but they come with some provisos:

- Finalizers slow the allocation and collection of memory (the GC needs to keep track of which finalizers have run).

- Finalizers prolong the life of the object and any *referred* objects (they must all await the next garbage truck for actual deletion).

- It's impossible to predict in what order the finalizers for a set of objects will be called.

- You have limited control over when the finalizer for an object will be called.

- If code in a finalizer blocks, other objects cannot be finalized.

- Finalizers can be circumvented altogether if an application fails to unload cleanly.

In summary, finalizers are somewhat like lawyers—although there are cases in which you really need them, in general you don't want to use them unless absolutely necessary. If you do use them, you need to be 100% sure you understand what they are doing for you.

Here are some guidelines for implementing finalizers:

- Ensure that your finalizer executes quickly.

- Never block in your finalizer (see "Blocking" on page 612).

- Don't reference other finalizable objects.

- Don't throw exceptions.

 The CLR can call an object's finalizer even if an exception is thrown during construction. For this reason, it pays not to assume that fields are correctly initialized when writing a finalizer.

Calling Dispose from a Finalizer

A popular pattern is to have the finalizer call `Dispose`. This makes sense when cleanup is not urgent and hastening it by calling `Dispose` is more of an optimization than a necessity.

 Keep in mind that with this pattern you couple memory deallocation to resource deallocation—two things with potentially divergent interests (unless the resource is itself memory). You also increase the burden on the finalization thread.

This pattern also serves as a backup for cases when a consumer simply forgets to call `Dispose`. However, it's then a good idea to log the failure so that you can fix the bug.

There's a standard pattern for implementing this, as follows:

```
class Test : IDisposable
{
  public void Dispose()                // NOT virtual
  {
    Dispose (true);
    GC.SuppressFinalize (this);        // Prevent finalizer from running.
  }

  protected virtual void Dispose (bool disposing)
  {
    if (disposing)
    {
      // Call Dispose() on other objects owned by this instance.
      // You can reference other finalizable objects here.
      // ...
    }

    // Release unmanaged resources owned by (just) this object.
    // ...
  }

  ~Test() => Dispose (false);
}
```

Dispose is overloaded to accept a bool disposing flag. The parameterless version is *not* declared as virtual and simply calls the enhanced version with true.

The enhanced version contains the actual disposal logic and is protected and virtual; this provides a safe point for subclasses to add their own disposal logic. The disposing flag means it's being called "properly" from the Dispose method rather than in "last-resort mode" from the finalizer. The idea is that when called with disposing set to false, this method should not, in general, reference other objects with finalizers (because such objects might themselves have been finalized and so be in an unpredictable state). This rules out quite a lot! Here are a couple of tasks that the Dispose method can still perform in last-resort mode, when disposing is false:

- Releasing any *direct references* to OS resources (obtained, perhaps, via a P/Invoke call to the Win32 API)
- Deleting a temporary file created on construction

To make this robust, any code capable of throwing an exception should be wrapped in a try/catch block, and the exception, ideally, logged. Any logging should be as simple and robust as possible.

Notice that we call GC.SuppressFinalize in the parameterless Dispose method—this prevents the finalizer from running when the GC later catches up with it. Technically, this is unnecessary given that Dispose methods must tolerate repeated calls. However, doing so improves performance because it allows the object (and its referenced objects) to be garbage collected in a single cycle.

Resurrection

Suppose a finalizer modifies a living object such that it refers back to the dying object. When the next garbage collection happens (for the object's generation), the CLR will see the previously dying object as no longer orphaned—and so it will evade garbage collection. This is an advanced scenario and is called *resurrection*.

To illustrate, suppose that we want to write a class that manages a temporary file. When an instance of that class is garbage collected, we'd like the finalizer to delete the temporary file. It sounds easy:

```
public class TempFileRef
{
  public readonly string FilePath;
  public TempFileRef (string filePath) { FilePath = filePath; }

  ~TempFileRef() { File.Delete (FilePath); }
}
```

Unfortunately, this has a bug: File.Delete might throw an exception (due to a lack of permissions, perhaps, or the file being in use, or having already been deleted). Such an exception would take down the entire application (as well as preventing other finalizers from running). We could simply "swallow" the exception with an empty catch block, but then we'd never know that anything went wrong. Calling some elaborate error reporting API would also be undesirable because it would burden the finalizer thread, hindering garbage collection for other objects. We want to restrict finalization actions to those that are simple, reliable, and quick.

A better option is to record the failure to a static collection, as follows:

```
public class TempFileRef
{
  static internal readonly ConcurrentQueue<TempFileRef> FailedDeletions
    = new ConcurrentQueue<TempFileRef>();

  public readonly string FilePath;
  public Exception DeletionError { get; private set; }

  public TempFileRef (string filePath) { FilePath = filePath; }

  ~TempFileRef()
  {
    try { File.Delete (FilePath); }
    catch (Exception ex)
    {
      DeletionError = ex;
      FailedDeletions.Enqueue (this);    // Resurrection
    }
  }
}
```

Enqueuing the object to the static FailedDeletions collection gives the object another referee, ensuring that it remains alive until the object is eventually dequeued.

ConcurrentQueue<T> is a thread-safe version of Queue<T> and is defined in System.Collections.Concurrent (see Chapter 22). There are a couple of reasons for using a thread-safe collection. First, the CLR reserves the right to execute finalizers on more than one thread in parallel. This means that when accessing shared state such as a static collection, we must consider the possibility of two objects being finalized at once. Second, at some point we're going to want to dequeue items from FailedDeletions so that we can do something about them. This also must be done in a thread-safe fashion because it could happen while the finalizer is concurrently enqueuing another object.

GC.ReRegisterForFinalize

A resurrected object's finalizer will not run a second time—unless you call GC .ReRegisterForFinalize.

In the following example, we try to delete a temporary file in a finalizer (as in the last example). But if the deletion fails, we reregister the object so as to try again in the next garbage collection:

```
public class TempFileRef
{
  public readonly string FilePath;
  int _deleteAttempt;

  public TempFileRef (string filePath) { FilePath = filePath; }

  ~TempFileRef()
  {
    try { File.Delete (FilePath); }
    catch
    {
      if (_deleteAttempt++ < 3) GC.ReRegisterForFinalize (this);
    }
  }
}
```

After the third failed attempt, our finalizer will silently give up trying to delete the file. We could enhance this by combining it with the previous example—in other words, adding it to the FailedDeletions queue after the third failure.

 Be careful to call ReRegisterForFinalize just once in the finalizer method. If you call it twice, the object will be reregistered twice and will have to undergo two more finalizations!

How the GC Works

The standard CLR uses a generational mark-and-compact GC that performs automatic memory management for objects stored on the managed heap. The GC is considered to be a *tracing* GC in that it doesn't interfere with every access to an object, but rather wakes up intermittently and traces the graph of objects stored on the managed heap to determine which objects can be considered garbage and therefore collected.

The GC initiates a garbage collection upon performing a memory allocation (via the new keyword), either after a certain threshold of memory has been allocated or at other times to reduce the application's memory footprint. This process can also be initiated manually by calling System.GC.Collect. During a garbage collection, all threads can by frozen (more on this in the next section).

The GC begins with its root object references and walks the object graph, marking all the objects it touches as reachable. When this process is complete, all objects that have not been marked are considered unused and are subject to garbage collection.

Unused objects without finalizers are immediately discarded; unused objects with finalizers are enqueued for processing on the finalizer thread after the GC is complete. These objects then become eligible for collection in the next GC for the object's generation (unless resurrected).

The remaining "live" objects are then shifted to the start of the heap (compacted), freeing space for more objects. This compaction serves two purposes: it prevents memory fragmentation, and it allows the GC to employ a very simple strategy when allocating new objects, which is to always allocate memory at the end of the heap. This prevents the potentially time-consuming task of maintaining a list of free memory segments.

If there is insufficient space to allocate memory for a new object after garbage collection and the OS is unable to grant further memory, an OutOfMemoryException is thrown.

 You can obtain information about the current state of the managed heap by calling GC.GetGCMemoryInfo(). From .NET 5, this method has been enhanced to return performance-related data.

Optimization Techniques

The GC incorporates various optimization techniques to reduce the garbage collection time.

Generational collection

The most important optimization is that the GC is generational. This takes advantage of the fact that although many objects are allocated and discarded rapidly, certain objects are long-lived and thus don't need to be traced during every collection.

Basically, the GC divides the managed heap into three generations. Objects that have just been allocated are in *Gen0*, and objects that have survived one collection cycle are in *Gen1*; all other objects are in *Gen2*. Gen0 and Gen1 are known as *ephemeral* (short-lived) generations.

The CLR keeps the Gen0 section relatively small (with a typical size of a few hundred KB to a few MB). When the Gen0 section fills up, the GC instigates a Gen0 collection—which happens relatively often. The GC applies a similar memory threshold to Gen1 (which acts as a buffer to Gen2), and so Gen1 collections are relatively quick and frequent, too. Full collections that include Gen2, however, take much longer and so happen infrequently. Figure 12-2 shows the effect of a full collection.

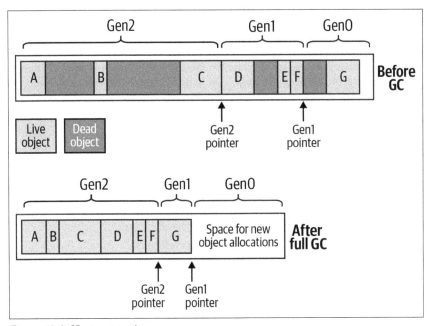

Figure 12-2. Heap generations

To give some very rough ballpark figures, a Gen0 collection might take less than one millisecond, which is not enough to be noticed in a typical application. A full collection, however, might take as long as 100 ms on a program with large object graphs. These figures depend on numerous factors and so can vary considerably—particularly in the case of Gen2, whose size is *unbounded* (unlike Gen0 and Gen1).

The upshot is that short-lived objects are very efficient in their use of the GC. The StringBuilders created in the following method would almost certainly be collected in a fast Gen0:

```
string Foo()
{
  var sb1 = new StringBuilder ("test");
  sb1.Append ("...");
  var sb2 = new StringBuilder ("test");
  sb2.Append (sb1.ToString());
  return sb2.ToString();
}
```

The Large Object Heap

The GC uses a separate heap called the *Large Object Heap* (LOH) for objects larger than a certain threshold (currently 85,000 bytes). This prevents the cost of compacting large objects and prevents excessive Gen0 collections—without the LOH, allocating a series of 16 MB objects might trigger a Gen0 collection after every allocation.

By default, the LOH is not subject to compaction, because moving large blocks of memory during garbage collection would be prohibitively expensive. This has two consequences:

- Allocations can be slower, because the GC can't always simply allocate objects at the end of the heap—it must also look in the middle for gaps, and this requires maintaining a linked list of free memory blocks.[1]
- The LOH is subject to *fragmentation*. This means that the freeing of an object can create a hole in the LOH that can be difficult to fill later. For instance, a hole left by an 86,000-byte object can be filled only by an object of between 85,000 bytes and 86,000 bytes (unless adjoined by another hole).

Should you anticipate a problem with fragmentation, you can instruct the GC to compact the LOH in the next collection, as follows:

```
GCSettings.LargeObjectHeapCompactionMode =
    GCLargeObjectHeapCompactionMode.CompactOnce;
```

Another workaround, if your program frequently allocates large arrays, is to use .NET's array pooling API (see "Array Pooling" on page 575).

The LOH is also nongenerational: all objects are treated as Gen2.

Workstation versus server collection

.NET provides two garbage collection modes: *workstation* and *server*. *Workstation* is the default; you can switch to *server* by adding the following to your application's *.csproj* file:

```
<PropertyGroup>
  <ServerGarbageCollection>true</ServerGarbageCollection>
</PropertyGroup>
```

Upon building your project, this setting is written to the application's *.runtime config.json* file, where's it's read by the CLR:

```
"runtimeOptions": {
  "configProperties": {
    "System.GC.Server": true
    ...
```

---

1 The same thing can occur occasionally in the generational heap due to pinning (see "The fixed Statement" on page 244).

When server collection is enabled, the CLR allocates a separate heap and GC to each core. This speeds up collection but consumes additional memory and CPU resources (because each core requires its own thread). Should the machine be running many other processes with server collection enabled, this can lead to CPU oversubscription, which is particularly harmful on workstations because it makes the OS as a whole feel unresponsive.

Server collection is available only on multicore systems: on single-core devices (or single-core virtual machines), the setting is ignored.

Background collection

In both workstation and server modes, the CLR enables *background collection* by default. You can disable it by adding the following to your application's *.csproj* file:

```
<PropertyGroup>
  <ConcurrentGarbageCollection>false</ConcurrentGarbageCollection>
</PropertyGroup>
```

Upon building, this setting is written to the application's *.runtimeconfig.json* file:

```
"runtimeOptions": {
  "configProperties": {
    "System.GC.Concurrent": false,
    ...
```

The GC must freeze (block) your execution threads for periods during a collection. Background collection minimizes these periods of latency, making your application more responsive. This comes at the expense of consuming slightly more CPU and memory. Hence, by disabling background collection, you accomplish the following:

- Slightly reduce CPU and memory usage
- Increase the pauses (or *latency*) when a garbage collection occurs

Background collection works by allowing your application code to run in parallel with a Gen2 collection. (Gen0 and Gen1 collections are considered sufficiently fast that they don't benefit from this parallelism.)

Background collection is an improved version of what was formerly called *concurrent collection*: it removes a limitation whereby a concurrent collection would cease to be concurrent if the Gen0 section filled up while a Gen2 collection was running. This allows applications that continually allocate memory to be more responsive.

GC notifications

If you disable background collection, you can ask the GC to notify you just before a full (blocking) collection will occur. This is intended for server-farm configurations: the idea is that you divert requests to another server just before a collection. You then instigate the collection immediately and wait for it to complete before rerouting requests back to that server.

To start notification, call `GC.RegisterForFullGCNotification`. Then, start up another thread (see Chapter 14) that first calls `GC.WaitForFullGCApproach`. When this method returns a `GCNotificationStatus` indicating that a collection is near, you can reroute requests to other servers and force a manual collection (see the following section). You then call `GC.WaitForFullGCComplete`: when this method returns, collection is complete, and you can again accept requests. You then repeat the whole cycle.

Forcing Garbage Collection

You can manually force a garbage collection at any time by calling `GC.Collect`. Calling `GC.Collect` without an argument instigates a full collection. If you pass in an integer value, only generations to that value are collected, so `GC.Collect(0)` performs only a fast Gen0 collection.

In general, you get the best performance by allowing the GC to decide when to collect: forcing collection can hurt performance by unnecessarily promoting Gen0 objects to Gen1 (and Gen1 objects to Gen2). It can also upset the GC's *self-tuning* ability, whereby the GC dynamically tweaks the thresholds for each generation to maximize performance as the application executes.

There are exceptions, however. The most common case for intervention is when an application goes to sleep for a while: a good example is a Windows Service that performs a daily activity (checking for updates, perhaps). Such an application might use a `System.Timers.Timer` to initiate the activity every 24 hours. After completing the activity, no further code executes for 24 hours, which means that for this period, no memory allocations are made and so the GC has no opportunity to activate. Whatever memory the service consumed in performing its activity, it will continue to consume for the following 24 hours—even with an empty object graph! The solution is to call `GC.Collect` right after the daily activity completes.

To ensure the collection of objects for which collection is delayed by finalizers, take the additional step of calling `WaitForPendingFinalizers` and re-collecting:

```
GC.Collect();
GC.WaitForPendingFinalizers();
GC.Collect();
```

Often this is done in a loop: the act of running finalizers can free up more objects that themselves have finalizers.

Another case for calling `GC.Collect` is when you're testing a class that has a finalizer.

Tuning Garbage Collection at Runtime

The static `GCSettings.LatencyMode` property determines how the GC balances latency with overall efficiency. Changing this from its default value of `Interactive` to either `LowLatency` or `SustainedLowLatency` instructs the CLR to favor quicker (but more frequent) collections. This is useful if your application needs to respond very quickly to real-time events. Changing the mode to Batch maximizes through-put at the expense of potentially poor responsiveness, which is useful for batch processing.

SustainedLowLatency is not supported if you disable background collection in the *.runtimeconfig.json* file.

You can also tell the CLR to temporarily suspend garbage collection by calling GC.TryStartNoGCRegion, and resume it with GC.EndNoGCRegion.

Memory Pressure

The runtime decides when to initiate collections based on a number of factors, including the total memory load on the machine. If your program allocates unman-aged memory (Chapter 24), the runtime will get an unrealistically optimistic per-ception of its memory usage because the CLR knows only about managed memory. You can mitigate this by instructing the CLR to *assume* that a specified quantity of unmanaged memory has been allocated; you do this by calling GC.AddMemory Pressure. To undo this (when the unmanaged memory is released), call GC.Remove MemoryPressure.

Array Pooling

If your application frequently instantiates arrays, you can avoid most of the garbage collection overhead with *array pooling*. Array pooling was introduced in .NET Core 3 and works by "renting" an array, which you later return to a pool for reuse.

To allocate an array, call the Rent method on the ArrayPool class in the System .Buffers namespace, indicating the size of the array that you'd like:

```
int[] pooledArray = ArrayPool<int>.Shared.Rent (100);  // 100 bytes
```

This allocates an array of (at least) 100 bytes from the global shared array pool. The pool manager might give you an array that's larger than what you asked for (typically, it allocates in powers of 2).

When you've finished with the array, call Return: this releases the array to the pool, allowing the same array to be rented again:

```
ArrayPool<int>.Shared.Return (pooledArray);
```

You can optionally pass in a Boolean value instructing the pool manager to clear the array before returning it to the pool.

 A limitation of array pooling is that nothing prevents you from continuing to (illegally) use an array after it's been returned, so you need to code carefully to avoid this scenario. Keep in mind that you have the power to break not just your own code but other APIs that use array pooling, too, such as ASP.NET Core.

Rather than using the shared array pool, you can create a custom pool and rent from that. This prevents the risk of breaking other APIs, but increases overall memory usage (as it reduces the opportunities for reuse):

```
var myPool = ArrayPool<int>.Create();
int[] array = myPool.Rent (100);
...
```

Managed Memory Leaks

In unmanaged languages such as C++, you must remember to manually deallocate memory when an object is no longer required; otherwise, a *memory leak* will result. In the managed world, this kind of error is impossible due to the CLR's automatic garbage collection system.

Nonetheless, large and complex .NET applications can exhibit a milder form of the same syndrome with the same end result: the application consumes more and more memory over its lifetime, until it eventually must be restarted. The good news is that managed memory leaks are usually easier to diagnose and prevent.

Managed memory leaks are caused by unused objects remaining alive by virtue of unused or forgotten references. A common candidate is event handlers—these hold a reference to the target object (unless the target is a static method). For instance, consider the following classes:

```
class Host
{
  public event EventHandler Click;
}

class Client
{
  Host _host;
  public Client (Host host)
  {
    _host = host;
    _host.Click += HostClicked;
  }

  void HostClicked (object sender, EventArgs e) { ... }
}
```

The following test class contains a method that instantiates 1,000 clients:

```
class Test
{
  static Host _host = new Host();

  public static void CreateClients()
  {
    Client[] clients = Enumerable.Range (0, 1000)
      .Select (i => new Client (_host))
      .ToArray();
```

```
      // Do something with clients ...
    }
  }
```

You might expect that after `CreateClients` finishes executing, the 1,000 `Client` objects will become eligible for collection. Unfortunately, each client has another referee: the _host object whose `Click` event now references each `Client` instance. This can go unnoticed if the `Click` event doesn't fire—or if the `HostClicked` method doesn't do anything to attract attention.

One way to solve this is to make `Client` implement `IDisposable` and, in the `Dispose` method, unhook the event handler:

```
public void Dispose() { _host.Click -= HostClicked; }
```

Consumers of `Client` then dispose of the instances when they're done with them:

```
Array.ForEach (clients, c => c.Dispose());
```

In "Weak References" on page 579, we describe another solution to this problem, which can be useful in environments that tend not to use disposable objects (an example is Windows Presentation Foundation [WPF]). In fact, WPF offers a class called `WeakEventManager` that uses a pattern that employs weak references.

Timers

Forgotten timers can also cause memory leaks (we discuss timers in Chapter 21). There are two distinct scenarios, depending on the kind of timer. Let's first look at the timer in the `System.Timers` namespace. In the following example, the `Foo` class (when instantiated) calls the `tmr_Elapsed` method once every second:

```
using System.Timers;

class Foo
{
  Timer _timer;

  Foo()
  {
    _timer = new System.Timers.Timer { Interval = 1000 };
    _timer.Elapsed += tmr_Elapsed;
    _timer.Start();
  }

  void tmr_Elapsed (object sender, ElapsedEventArgs e) { ... }
}
```

Unfortunately, instances of `Foo` can never be garbage collected! The problem is that the runtime itself holds references to active timers so that it can fire their `Elapsed` events; hence:

- The runtime will keep _timer alive.

- _timer will keep the Foo instance alive, via the tmr_Elapsed event handler.

The solution is obvious when you realize that Timer implements IDisposable. Disposing of the timer stops it and ensures that the runtime no longer references the object:

```
class Foo : IDisposable
{
  ...
  public void Dispose() { _timer.Dispose(); }
}
```

 A good guideline is to implement IDisposable yourself if any field in your class is assigned an object that implements IDisposable.

The WPF and Windows Forms timers behave in the same way with respect to what's just been discussed.

The timer in the System.Threading namespace, however, is special. .NET doesn't hold references to active threading timers; it instead references the callback delegates directly. This means that if you forget to dispose of a threading timer, a finalizer can fire that will automatically stop and dispose of the timer:

```
static void Main()
{
  var tmr = new System.Threading.Timer (TimerTick, null, 1000, 1000);
  GC.Collect();
  System.Threading.Thread.Sleep (10000);    // Wait 10 seconds
}

static void TimerTick (object notUsed) { Console.WriteLine ("tick"); }
```

If this example is compiled in "release" mode (debugging disabled and optimizations enabled), the timer will be collected and finalized before it has a chance to fire even once! Again, we can fix this by disposing of the timer when we're done with it:

```
using (var tmr = new System.Threading.Timer (TimerTick, null, 1000, 1000))
{
  GC.Collect();
  System.Threading.Thread.Sleep (10000);    // Wait 10 seconds
}
```

The implicit call to tmr.Dispose at the end of the using block ensures that the tmr variable is "used" and so not considered dead by the GC until the end of the block. Ironically, this call to Dispose actually keeps the object alive longer!

Diagnosing Memory Leaks

The easiest way to avoid managed memory leaks is to proactively monitor memory consumption as an application is written. You can obtain the current memory consumption of a program's objects as follows (the `true` argument tells the GC to perform a collection first):

```
long memoryUsed = GC.GetTotalMemory (true);
```

If you're practicing test-driven development, one possibility is to use unit tests to assert that memory is reclaimed as expected. If such an assertion fails, you then need examine only the changes that you've made recently.

If you already have a large application with a managed memory leak, the *windbg.exe* tool can assist in finding it. There are also friendlier graphical tools such as Microsoft's CLR Profiler, SciTech's Memory Profiler, and Red Gate's ANTS Memory Profiler.

The CLR also exposes numerous event counters to assist with resource monitoring.

Weak References

Occasionally, it's useful to hold a reference to an object that's "invisible" to the GC in terms of keeping the object alive. This is called a *weak reference* and is implemented by the `System.WeakReference` class.

To use `WeakReference`, construct it with a target object:

```
var sb = new StringBuilder ("this is a test");
var weak = new WeakReference (sb);
Console.WriteLine (weak.Target);      // This is a test
```

If a target is referenced *only* by one or more weak references, the GC will consider the target eligible for collection. When the target is collected, the `Target` property of the `WeakReference` will be null:

```
var weak = GetWeakRef();
GC.Collect();
Console.WriteLine (weak.Target);   // (nothing)

WeakReference GetWeakRef () =>
  new WeakReference (new StringBuilder ("weak"));
```

To prevent the target being collected in between testing for it being null and consuming it, assign the target to a local variable:

```
var sb = (StringBuilder) weak.Target;
if (sb != null) { /* Do something with sb */ }
```

After a target's been assigned to a local variable, it has a strong root and so cannot be collected while that variable's in use.

The following class uses weak references to keep track of all `Widget` objects that have been instantiated, without preventing those objects from being collected:

```
class Widget
{
  static List<WeakReference> _allWidgets = new List<WeakReference>();
```

```
public readonly string Name;

public Widget (string name)
{
  Name = name;
  _allWidgets.Add (new WeakReference (this));
}

public static void ListAllWidgets()
{
  foreach (WeakReference weak in _allWidgets)
  {
    Widget w = (Widget)weak.Target;
    if (w != null) Console.WriteLine (w.Name);
  }
}
}
```

The only proviso with such a system is that the static list will grow over time, accumulating weak references with null targets. So, you need to implement some cleanup strategy.

Weak References and Caching

One use for WeakReference is to cache large object graphs. This allows memory-intensive data to be cached briefly without causing excessive memory consumption:

```
_weakCache = new WeakReference (...);   // _weakCache is a field
...
var cache = _weakCache.Target;
if (cache == null) { /* Re-create cache & assign it to _weakCache */ }
```

This strategy can be only mildly effective in practice because you have little control over when the GC fires and what generation it chooses to collect. In particular, if your cache remains in Gen0, it can be collected within microseconds (and remember that the GC doesn't collect only when memory is low—it collects regularly under normal memory conditions). So, at a minimum, you should employ a two-level cache whereby you start out by holding strong references that you convert to weak references over time.

Weak References and Events

We saw earlier how events can cause managed memory leaks. The simplest solution is to either avoid subscribing in such conditions or implement a Dispose method to unsubscribe. Weak references offer another solution.

Imagine a delegate that holds only weak references to its targets. Such a delegate would not keep its targets alive—unless those targets had independent referees. Of course, this wouldn't prevent a firing delegate from hitting an unreferenced target— in the time between the target being eligible for collection and the GC catching up with it. For such a solution to be effective, your code must be robust in that scenario. Assuming that is the case, you can implement a *weak delegate* class as follows:

```
public class WeakDelegate<TDelegate> where TDelegate : class
{
  class MethodTarget
  {
    public readonly WeakReference Reference;
    public readonly MethodInfo Method;

    public MethodTarget (Delegate d)
    {
      // d.Target will be null for static method targets:
      if (d.Target != null) Reference = new WeakReference (d.Target);
      Method = d.Method;
    }
  }

  List<MethodTarget> _targets = new List<MethodTarget>();

  public WeakDelegate()
  {
    if (!typeof (TDelegate).IsSubclassOf (typeof (Delegate)))
      throw new InvalidOperationException
        ("TDelegate must be a delegate type");
  }

  public void Combine (TDelegate target)
  {
    if (target == null) return;

    foreach (Delegate d in (target as Delegate).GetInvocationList())
      _targets.Add (new MethodTarget (d));
  }

  public void Remove (TDelegate target)
  {
    if (target == null) return;
    foreach (Delegate d in (target as Delegate).GetInvocationList())
    {
      MethodTarget mt = _targets.Find (w =>
        Equals (d.Target, w.Reference?.Target) &&
        Equals (d.Method.MethodHandle, w.Method.MethodHandle));

      if (mt != null) _targets.Remove (mt);
    }
  }

  public TDelegate Target
  {
    get
    {
      Delegate combinedTarget = null;

      foreach (MethodTarget mt in _targets.ToArray())
```

```
        {
          WeakReference wr = mt.Reference;

          // Static target || alive instance target
          if (wr == null || wr.Target != null)
          {
            var newDelegate = Delegate.CreateDelegate (
              typeof(TDelegate), wr?.Target, mt.Method);
            combinedTarget = Delegate.Combine (combinedTarget, newDelegate);
          }
          else
            _targets.Remove (mt);
        }

        return combinedTarget as TDelegate;
      }
      set
      {
        _targets.Clear();
        Combine (value);
      }
    }
  }
}
```

This code illustrates several interesting points in C# and the CLR. First, note that we check that TDelegate is a delegate type in the constructor. This is because of a limitation in C#—the following type constraint is illegal because C# considers System.Delegate a special type for which constraints are not supported:

```
... where TDelegate : Delegate    // Compiler doesn't allow this
```

Instead, we must choose a class constraint and perform a runtime check in the constructor.

In the Combine and Remove methods, we perform the reference conversion from target to Delegate via the as operator rather than the more usual cast operator. This is because C# disallows the cast operator with this type of parameter—because of a potential ambiguity between a *custom conversion* and a *reference conversion*.

We then call GetInvocationList because these methods might be called with multicast delegates—delegates with more than one method recipient.

In the Target property, we build up a multicast delegate that combines all the delegates referenced by weak references whose targets are alive, removing the remaining (dead) references from the list to prevent the _targets list from endlessly growing. (We could improve our class by doing the same in the Combine method; yet another improvement would be to add locks for thread safety [see "Locking and Thread Safety" on page 616].) We also allow delegates without a weak reference at all; these represent delegates whose target is a static method.

The following illustrates how to consume this delegate in implementing an event:

```
public class Foo
{
  WeakDelegate<EventHandler> _click = new WeakDelegate<EventHandler>();

  public event EventHandler Click
  {
    add { _click.Combine (value); } remove { _click.Remove (value); }
  }

  protected virtual void OnClick (EventArgs e)
    => _click.Target?.Invoke (this, e);
}
```

13

Diagnostics

When things go wrong, it's important that information is available to aid in diagnosing the problem. An Integrated Development Environment (IDE) or debugger can assist greatly to this effect—but it is usually available only during development. After an application ships, the application itself must gather and record diagnostic information. To meet this requirement, .NET provides a set of facilities to log diagnostic information, monitor application behavior, detect runtime errors, and integrate with debugging tools if available.

Some diagnostic tools and APIs are Windows specific because they rely on features of the Windows operating system. In an effort to prevent platform-specific APIs from cluttering the .NET BCL, Microsoft has shipped them in separate NuGet packages that you can optionally reference. There are more than a dozen Windows-specific packages, which you can reference all at once with the *Microsoft.Windows.Compatibility* "master" package.

The types in this chapter are defined primarily in the `System.Diagnostics` namespace.

Conditional Compilation

You can conditionally compile any section of code in C# with *preprocessor directives*. Preprocessor directives are special instructions to the compiler that begin with the # symbol (and, unlike other C# constructs, must appear on a line of their own). Logically, they execute before the main compilation takes place (although in practice, the compiler processes them during the lexical parsing phase). The preprocessor directives for conditional compilation are `#if`, `#else`, `#endif`, and `#elif`.

The `#if` directive instructs the compiler to ignore a section of code unless a specified *symbol* has been defined. You can define a symbol in source code by using the `#define` directive (in which case the symbol applies to just that file), or in the *.csproj* file by using a `<DefineConstants>` element (in which case the symbol applies to whole assembly):

```
#define TESTMODE              // #define directives must be at top of file
                             // Symbol names are uppercase by convention.
using System;

class Program
{
  static void Main()
  {
#if TESTMODE
    Console.WriteLine ("in test mode!");     // OUTPUT: in test mode!
#endif
  }
}
```

If we deleted the first line, the program would compile with the `Console.WriteLine` statement completely eliminated from the executable, as though it were commented out.

The `#else` statement is analogous to C#'s `else` statement, and `#elif` is equivalent to `#else` followed by `#if`. The `||`, `&&`, and `!` operators perform *or*, *and*, and *not* operations:

```
#if TESTMODE && !PLAYMODE     // if TESTMODE and not PLAYMODE
  ...
```

Keep in mind, however, that you're not building an ordinary C# expression, and the symbols upon which you operate have absolutely no connection to *variables*—static or otherwise.

You can define symbols that apply to every file in an assembly by editing the *.csproj* file (or in Visual Studio, by going to the Build tab in the Project Properties window). The following defines two constants, TESTMODE and PLAYMODE:

```
<PropertyGroup>
  <DefineConstants>TESTMODE;PLAYMODE</DefineConstants>
</PropertyGroup>
```

If you've defined a symbol at the assembly level and then want to "undefine" it for a particular file, you can do so by using the `#undef` directive.

Conditional Compilation Versus Static Variable Flags

You could instead implement the preceding example with a simple static field:

```
static internal bool TestMode = true;

static void Main()
{
  if (TestMode) Console.WriteLine ("in test mode!");
}
```

This has the advantage of allowing runtime configuration. So, why choose conditional compilation? The reason is that conditional compilation can take you places variable flags cannot, such as the following:

- Conditionally including an attribute

- Changing the declared type of variable

- Switching between different namespaces or type aliases in a `using` directive; for example:

```
using TestType =
  #if V2
     MyCompany.Widgets.GadgetV2;
  #else
     MyCompany.Widgets.Gadget;
  #endif
```

You can even perform major refactoring under a conditional compilation directive, so you can instantly switch between old and new versions, and write libraries that can compile against multiple runtime versions, leveraging the latest features where available.

Another advantage of conditional compilation is that debugging code can refer to types in assemblies that are not included in deployment.

The Conditional Attribute

The `Conditional` attribute instructs the compiler to ignore any calls to a particular class or method, if the specified symbol has not been defined.

To see how this is useful, suppose that you write a method for logging status information as follows:

```
static void LogStatus (string msg)
{
  string logFilePath = ...
  System.IO.File.AppendAllText (logFilePath, msg + "\r\n");
}
```

Now imagine that you want this to execute only if the `LOGGINGMODE` symbol is defined. The first solution is to wrap all calls to `LogStatus` around an `#if` directive:

```
#if LOGGINGMODE
LogStatus ("Message Headers: " + GetMsgHeaders());
#endif
```

This gives an ideal result, but it is tedious. The second solution is to put the `#if` directive inside the `LogStatus` method. This, however, is problematic should `LogStatus` be called as follows:

```
LogStatus ("Message Headers: " + GetComplexMessageHeaders());
```

`GetComplexMessageHeaders` would always be called—which might incur a performance hit.

Diagnostics

We can combine the functionality of the first solution with the convenience of the second by attaching the `Conditional` attribute (defined in `System.Diagnostics`) to the `LogStatus` method:

```
[Conditional ("LOGGINGMODE")]
static void LogStatus (string msg)
{
  ...
}
```

This instructs the compiler to treat calls to `LogStatus` as though they were wrapped in an `#if LOGGINGMODE` directive. If the symbol is not defined, any calls to `Log Status` are eliminated entirely in compilation—including their argument evaluation expressions. (Hence any side-effecting expressions will be bypassed.) This works even if `LogStatus` and the caller are in different assemblies.

 Another benefit of [Conditional] is that the conditionality check is performed when the *caller* is compiled, rather than when the *called method* is compiled. This is beneficial because it allows you to write a library containing methods such as `LogStatus`—and build just one version of that library.

The `Conditional` attribute is ignored at runtime—it's purely an instruction to the compiler.

Alternatives to the Conditional attribute

The `Conditional` attribute is useless if you need to dynamically enable or disable functionality at runtime: instead, you must use a variable-based approach. This leaves the question of how to elegantly circumvent the evaluation of arguments when calling conditional logging methods. A functional approach solves this:

```
using System;
using System.Linq;

class Program
{
  public static bool EnableLogging;

  static void LogStatus (Func<string> message)
  {
    string logFilePath = ...
    if (EnableLogging)
      System.IO.File.AppendAllText (logFilePath, message() + "\r\n");
  }
}
```

A lambda expression lets you call this method without syntax bloat:

```
LogStatus ( () => "Message Headers: " + GetComplexMessageHeaders() );
```

If `EnableLogging` is `false`, `GetComplexMessageHeaders` is never evaluated.

Debug and Trace Classes

Debug and Trace are static classes that provide basic logging and assertion capabilities. The two classes are very similar; the main differentiator is their intended use. The Debug class is intended for debug builds; the Trace class is intended for both debug and release builds. To this effect:

All methods of the Debug class are defined with [Conditional("DEBUG")].
All methods of the Trace class are defined with [Conditional("TRACE")].

This means that all calls that you make to Debug or Trace are eliminated by the compiler unless you define DEBUG or TRACE symbols. (Visual Studio provides checkboxes for defining these symbols in the Build tab of Project Properties, and enables the TRACE symbol by default with new projects.)

Both the Debug and Trace classes provide Write, WriteLine, and WriteIf methods. By default, these send messages to the debugger's output window:

```
Debug.Write     ("Data");
Debug.WriteLine (23 * 34);
int x = 5, y = 3;
Debug.WriteIf   (x > y, "x is greater than y");
```

The Trace class also provides the methods TraceInformation, TraceWarning, and TraceError. The difference in behavior between these and the Write methods depends on the active TraceListeners (we cover this in "TraceListener" on page 590).

Fail and Assert

The Debug and Trace classes both provide Fail and Assert methods. Fail sends the message to each TraceListener in the Debug or Trace class's Listeners collection (see the following section), which by default writes the message to the debug output:

```
Debug.Fail ("File data.txt does not exist!");
```

Assert simply calls Fail if the bool argument is false—this is called *making an assertion* and indicates a bug in the code if violated. Specifying a failure message is optional:

```
Debug.Assert (File.Exists ("data.txt"), "File data.txt does not exist!");
var result = ...
Debug.Assert (result != null);
```

The Write, Fail, and Assert methods are also overloaded to accept a string category in addition to the message, which can be useful in processing the output.

An alternative to assertion is to throw an exception if the opposite condition is true. This is a common practice when validating method arguments:

```
public void ShowMessage (string message)
{
  if (message == null) throw new ArgumentNullException ("message");
  ...
}
```

Such "assertions" are compiled unconditionally and are less flexible in that you can't control the outcome of a failed assertion via `TraceListeners`. And technically, they're not assertions. An assertion is something that, if violated, indicates a bug in the current method's code. Throwing an exception based on argument validation indicates a bug in the *caller*'s code.

TraceListener

The `Trace` class has a static `Listeners` property that returns a collection of `Trace Listener` instances. These are responsible for processing the content emitted by the `Write`, `Fail`, and `Trace` methods.

By default, the `Listeners` collection of each includes a single listener (`Default TraceListener`). The default listener has two key features:

- When connected to a debugger such as Visual Studio, messages are written to the debug output window; otherwise, message content is ignored.
- When the `Fail` method is called (or an assertion fails), the application is terminated.

You can change this behavior by (optionally) removing the default listener and then adding one or more of your own. You can write trace listeners from scratch (by subclassing `TraceListener`) or use one of the predefined types:

- `TextWriterTraceListener` writes to a `Stream` or `TextWriter` or appends to a file.
- `EventLogTraceListener` writes to the Windows event log (Windows only).
- `EventProviderTraceListener` writes to the Event Tracing for Windows (ETW) subsystem (cross-platform support).

`TextWriterTraceListener` is further subclassed to `ConsoleTraceListener`, `DelimitedListTraceListener`, `XmlWriterTraceListener`, and `EventSchemaTrace Listener`.

The following example clears `Trace`'s default listener and then adds three listeners— one that appends to a file, one that writes to the console, and one that writes to the Windows event log:

```
// Clear the default listener:
Trace.Listeners.Clear();

// Add a writer that appends to the trace.txt file:
Trace.Listeners.Add (new TextWriterTraceListener ("trace.txt"));
```

```
// Obtain the Console's output stream, then add that as a listener:
System.IO.TextWriter tw = Console.Out;
Trace.Listeners.Add (new TextWriterTraceListener (tw));

// Set up a Windows Event log source and then create/add listener.
// CreateEventSource requires administrative elevation, so this would
// typically be done in application setup.
if (!EventLog.SourceExists ("DemoApp"))
  EventLog.CreateEventSource ("DemoApp", "Application");

Trace.Listeners.Add (new EventLogTraceListener ("DemoApp"));
```

In the case of the Windows event log, messages that you write with the Write, Fail, or Assert method always display as "Information" messages in the Windows event viewer. Messages that you write via the TraceWarning and TraceError methods, however, show up as warnings or errors.

TraceListener also has a Filter of type TraceFilter that you can set to control whether a message gets written to that listener. To do this, you either instantiate one of the predefined subclasses (EventTypeFilter or SourceFilter), or subclass TraceFilter and override the ShouldTrace method. You could use this to filter by category, for instance.

TraceListener also defines IndentLevel and IndentSize properties for controlling indentation, and the TraceOutputOptions property for writing extra data:

```
TextWriterTraceListener tl = new TextWriterTraceListener (Console.Out);
tl.TraceOutputOptions = TraceOptions.DateTime | TraceOptions.Callstack;
```

TraceOutputOptions are applied when using the Trace methods:

```
Trace.TraceWarning ("Orange alert");

DiagTest.vshost.exe Warning: 0 : Orange alert
    DateTime=2007-03-08T05:57:13.6250000Z
    Callstack=   at System.Environment.GetStackTrace(Exception e, Boolean
needFileInfo)
    at System.Environment.get_StackTrace()     at ...
```

Flushing and Closing Listeners

Some listeners, such as TextWriterTraceListener, ultimately write to a stream that is subject to caching. This has two implications:

- A message might not appear in the output stream or file immediately.

- You must close—or at least flush—the listener before your application ends; otherwise, you lose what's in the cache (up to 4 KB, by default, if you're writing to a file).

The Trace and Debug classes provide static Close and Flush methods that call Close or Flush on all listeners (which in turn calls Close or Flush on any underlying writers and streams). Close implicitly calls Flush, closes file handles, and prevents further data from being written.

As a general rule, call Close before an application ends, and call Flush anytime you want to ensure that current message data is written. This applies if you're using stream- or file-based listeners.

Trace and Debug also provide an AutoFlush property, which, if true, forces a Flush after every message.

 It's a good policy to set AutoFlush to true on Debug and Trace if you're using any file- or stream-based listeners. Otherwise, if an unhandled exception or critical error occurs, the last 4 KB of diagnostic information can be lost.

Debugger Integration

Sometimes, it's useful for an application to interact with a debugger if one is available. During development, the debugger is usually your IDE (e.g., Visual Studio); in deployment, the debugger is more likely to be one of the lower-level debugging tools, such as WinDbg, Cordbg, or MDbg.

Attaching and Breaking

The static Debugger class in System.Diagnostics provides basic functions for interacting with a debugger—namely Break, Launch, Log, and IsAttached.

A debugger must first attach to an application in order to debug it. If you start an application from within an IDE, this happens automatically, unless you request otherwise (by choosing "Start without debugging"). Sometimes, though, it's inconvenient or impossible to start an application in debug mode within the IDE. An example is a Windows Service application or (ironically) a Visual Studio designer. One solution is to start the application normally and then, in your IDE, choose Debug Process. This doesn't allow you to set breakpoints early in the program's execution, however.

The workaround is to call Debugger.Break from within your application. This method launches a debugger, attaches to it, and suspends execution at that point. (Launch does the same, but without suspending execution.) After it's attached, you can log messages directly to the debugger's output window with the Log method. You can verify whether you're attached to a debugger by checking the IsAttached property.

Debugger Attributes

The DebuggerStepThrough and DebuggerHidden attributes provide suggestions to the debugger on how to handle single-stepping for a particular method, constructor, or class.

`DebuggerStepThrough` requests that the debugger step through a function without any user interaction. This attribute is useful in automatically generated methods and in proxy methods that forward the real work to a method somewhere else. In the latter case, the debugger will still show the proxy method in the call stack if a breakpoint is set within the "real" method—unless you also add the `DebuggerHidden` attribute. You can combine these two attributes on proxies to help the user focus on debugging the application logic rather than the plumbing:

```
[DebuggerStepThrough, DebuggerHidden]
void DoWorkProxy()
{
  // setup...
  DoWork();
  // teardown...
}

void DoWork() {...}    // Real method...
```

Processes and Process Threads

We described in the last section of Chapter 6 how to use `Process.Start` to launch a new process. The `Process` class also allows you to query and interact with other processes running on the same or another computer. The `Process` class is part of .NET Standard 2.0, although its features are restricted for the UWP platform.

Examining Running Processes

The `Process.GetProcessXXX` methods retrieve a specific process by name or process ID, or all processes running on the current or nominated computer. This includes both managed and unmanaged processes. Each `Process` instance has a wealth of properties mapping statistics such as name, ID, priority, memory and processor utilization, window handles, and so on. The following sample enumerates all the running processes on the current computer:

```
foreach (Process p in Process.GetProcesses())
using (p)
{
  Console.WriteLine (p.ProcessName);
  Console.WriteLine ("    PID:      " + p.Id);
  Console.WriteLine ("    Memory:   " + p.WorkingSet64);
  Console.WriteLine ("    Threads:  " + p.Threads.Count);
}
```

`Process.GetCurrentProcess` returns the current process.

You can terminate a process by calling its `Kill` method.

Examining Threads in a Process

You can also enumerate over the threads of other processes with the `Process` `.Threads` property. The objects that you get, however, are not `System.Threading`

.Thread objects; they're `ProcessThread` objects and are intended for administrative rather than synchronization tasks. A `ProcessThread` object provides diagnostic information about the underlying thread and allows you to control some aspects of it, such as its priority and processor affinity:

```
public void EnumerateThreads (Process p)
{
  foreach (ProcessThread pt in p.Threads)
  {
    Console.WriteLine (pt.Id);
    Console.WriteLine ("   State:    " + pt.ThreadState);
    Console.WriteLine ("   Priority: " + pt.PriorityLevel);
    Console.WriteLine ("   Started:  " + pt.StartTime);
    Console.WriteLine ("   CPU time: " + pt.TotalProcessorTime);
  }
}
```

StackTrace and StackFrame

The `StackTrace` and `StackFrame` classes provide a read-only view of an execution call stack. You can obtain stack traces for the current thread or an `Exception` object. Such information is useful mostly for diagnostic purposes, though you also can use it in programming (hacks). `StackTrace` represents a complete call stack; `StackFrame` represents a single method call within that stack.

 If you just need to know the name and line number of the calling method, caller info attributes can provide an easier and faster alternative. We cover this topic in "Caller Info Attributes" on page 229.

If you instantiate a `StackTrace` object with no arguments—or with a `bool` argument—you get a snapshot of the current thread's call stack. The `bool` argument, if true, instructs `StackTrace` to read the assembly *.pdb* (project debug) files if they are present, giving you access to filename, line number, and column offset data. Project debug files are generated when you compile with the `/debug` switch. (Visual Studio compiles with this switch unless you request otherwise via *Advanced Build Settings*.)

After you've obtained a `StackTrace`, you can examine a particular frame by calling `GetFrame`—or obtain the whole lot by using `GetFrames`:

```
static void Main() { A (); }
static void A()   { B (); }
static void B()   { C (); }
static void C()
{
  StackTrace s = new StackTrace (true);

  Console.WriteLine ("Total frames:   " + s.FrameCount);
  Console.WriteLine ("Current method: " + s.GetFrame(0).GetMethod().Name);
  Console.WriteLine ("Calling method: " + s.GetFrame(1).GetMethod().Name);
  Console.WriteLine ("Entry method:   " + s.GetFrame
                             (s.FrameCount-1).GetMethod().Name);
```

```
Console.WriteLine ("Call Stack:");
foreach (StackFrame f in s.GetFrames())
  Console.WriteLine (
    " File: "   + f.GetFileName() +
    " Line: "   + f.GetFileLineNumber() +
    " Col: "    + f.GetFileColumnNumber() +
    " Offset: " + f.GetILOffset() +
    " Method: " + f.GetMethod().Name);
}
```

Here's the output:

```
Total frames:   4
Current method: C
Calling method: B
Entry method: Main
Call stack:
  File: C:\Test\Program.cs  Line: 15  Col: 4   Offset: 7  Method: C
  File: C:\Test\Program.cs  Line: 12  Col: 22  Offset: 6  Method: B
  File: C:\Test\Program.cs  Line: 11  Col: 22  Offset: 6  Method: A
  File: C:\Test\Program.cs  Line: 10  Col: 25  Offset: 6  Method: Main
```

 The Intermediate Language (IL) offset indicates the offset of the instruction that will execute *next*—not the instruction that's currently executing. Peculiarly, though, the line and column number (if a *.pdb* file is present) usually indicate the actual execution point.

This happens because the CLR does its best to *infer* the actual execution point when calculating the line and column from the IL offset. The compiler emits IL in such a way as to make this possible—including inserting nop (no-operation) instructions into the IL stream.

Compiling with optimizations enabled, however, disables the insertion of nop instructions, and so the stack trace might show the line and column number of the next statement to execute. Obtaining a useful stack trace is further hampered by the fact that optimization can pull other tricks, including collapsing entire methods.

A shortcut to obtaining the essential information for an entire StackTrace is to call ToString on it. Here's what the result looks like:

```
at DebugTest.Program.C() in C:\Test\Program.cs:line 16
at DebugTest.Program.B() in C:\Test\Program.cs:line 12
at DebugTest.Program.A() in C:\Test\Program.cs:line 11
at DebugTest.Program.Main() in C:\Test\Program.cs:line 10
```

You can also obtain the stack trace for an Exception object (showing what led up to the exception being thrown) by passing the Exception into StackTrace's constructor.

Exception already has a StackTrace property; however, this property returns a simple string—not a StackTrace object. A StackTrace object is far more useful in logging exceptions that occur after deployment—where no *.pdb* files are available —because you can log the *IL offset* in lieu of line and column numbers. With an IL offset and *ildasm*, you can pinpoint where within a method an error occurred.

Windows Event Logs

The Win32 platform provides a centralized logging mechanism, in the form of the Windows event logs.

The Debug and Trace classes we used earlier write to a Windows event log if you register an EventLogTraceListener. With the EventLog class, however, you can write directly to a Windows event log without using Trace or Debug. You can also use this class to read and monitor event data.

 Writing to the Windows event log makes sense in a Windows Service application, because if something goes wrong, you can't pop up a user interface directing the user to some special file where diagnostic information has been written. Also, because it's common practice for services to write to the Windows event log, this is the first place an administrator is likely to look if your service falls over.

There are three standard Windows event logs, identified by these names:

- Application
- System
- Security

The Application log is where most applications normally write.

Writing to the Event Log

To write to a Windows event log:

1. Choose one of the three event logs (usually *Application*).
2. Decide on a *source name* and create it if necessary (create requires administrative permissions).
3. Call EventLog.WriteEntry with the log name, source name, and message data.

The *source name* is an easily identifiable name for your application. You must register a source name before you use it—the CreateEventSource method performs this function. You can then call WriteEntry:

```
const string SourceName = "MyCompany.WidgetServer";

// CreateEventSource requires administrative permissions, so this would
// typically be done in application setup.
if (!EventLog.SourceExists (SourceName))
  EventLog.CreateEventSource (SourceName, "Application");

EventLog.WriteEntry (SourceName,
  "Service started; using configuration file=...",
  EventLogEntryType.Information);
```

EventLogEntryType can be Information, Warning, Error, SuccessAudit, or FailureAudit. Each displays with a different icon in the Windows event viewer. You can also optionally specify a category and event ID (each is a number of your own choosing) and provide optional binary data.

CreateEventSource also allows you to specify a machine name: this is to write to another computer's event log, if you have sufficient permissions.

Reading the Event Log

Diagnostics

To read an event log, instantiate the EventLog class with the name of the log that you want to access and optionally the name of another computer on which the log resides. Each log entry can then be read via the Entries collection property:

```
EventLog log = new EventLog ("Application");

Console.WriteLine ("Total entries: " + log.Entries.Count);

EventLogEntry last = log.Entries [log.Entries.Count - 1];
Console.WriteLine ("Index:   " + last.Index);
Console.WriteLine ("Source:  " + last.Source);
Console.WriteLine ("Type:    " + last.EntryType);
Console.WriteLine ("Time:    " + last.TimeWritten);
Console.WriteLine ("Message: " + last.Message);
```

You can enumerate over all logs for the current (or another) computer via the static method EventLog.GetEventLogs (this requires administrative privileges for full access):

```
foreach (EventLog log in EventLog.GetEventLogs())
  Console.WriteLine (log.LogDisplayName);
```

This normally prints, at a minimum, *Application*, *Security*, and *System*.

Monitoring the Event Log

You can be alerted whenever an entry is written to a Windows event log, via the EntryWritten event. This works for event logs on the local computer, and it fires regardless of what application logged the event.

To enable log monitoring:

1. Instantiate an `EventLog` and set its `EnableRaisingEvents` property to `true`.

2. Handle the `EntryWritten` event.

For example:

```
using (var log = new EventLog ("Application"))
{
  log.EnableRaisingEvents = true;
  log.EntryWritten += DisplayEntry;
  Console.ReadLine();
}

void DisplayEntry (object sender, EntryWrittenEventArgs e)
{
  EventLogEntry entry = e.Entry;
  Console.WriteLine (entry.Message);
}
```

Performance Counters

 Performance Counters are a Windows-only feature and require the NuGet package `System.Diagnostics.Perfor manceCounter`. If you're targeting Linux or macOS, see "Cross-Platform Diagnostic Tools" on page 603 for alternatives.

The logging mechanisms we've discussed to date are useful for capturing information for future analysis. However, to gain insight into the current state of an application (or the system as a whole), a more real-time approach is needed. The Win32 solution to this need is the performance-monitoring infrastructure, which consists of a set of performance counters that the system and applications expose, and the Microsoft Management Console (MMC) snap-ins used to monitor these counters in real time.

Performance counters are grouped into categories such as "System," "Processor," ".NET CLR Memory," and so on. These categories are sometimes also referred to as "performance objects" by the graphical user interface (GUI) tools. Each category groups a related set of performance counters that monitor one aspect of the system or application. Examples of performance counters in the ".NET CLR Memory" category include "% Time in GC," "# Bytes in All Heaps," and "Allocated bytes/sec."

Each category can optionally have one or more instances that can be monitored independently. For example, this is useful in the "% Processor Time" performance counter in the "Processor" category, which allows one to monitor CPU utilization. On a multiprocessor machine, this counter supports an instance for each CPU, allowing you to monitor the utilization of each CPU independently.

The following sections illustrate how to perform commonly needed tasks such as determining which counters are exposed, monitoring a counter, and creating your own counters to expose application status information.

 Reading performance counters or categories might require administrator privileges on the local or target computer, depending on what is accessed.

Enumerating the Available Counters

The following example enumerates over all of the available performance counters on the computer. For those that have instances, it enumerates the counters for each instance:

```
PerformanceCounterCategory[] cats =
  PerformanceCounterCategory.GetCategories();

foreach (PerformanceCounterCategory cat in cats)
{
  Console.WriteLine ("Category: " + cat.CategoryName);

  string[] instances = cat.GetInstanceNames();
  if (instances.Length == 0)
  {
    foreach (PerformanceCounter ctr in cat.GetCounters())
      Console.WriteLine ("  Counter: " + ctr.CounterName);
  }
  else    // Dump counters with instances
  {
    foreach (string instance in instances)
    {
      Console.WriteLine ("  Instance: " + instance);
      if (cat.InstanceExists (instance))
        foreach (PerformanceCounter ctr in cat.GetCounters (instance))
          Console.WriteLine ("    Counter: " + ctr.CounterName);
    }
  }
}
```

 The result is more than 10,000 lines long! It also takes a while to execute because PerformanceCounterCategory.Instance Exists has an inefficient implementation. In a real system, you'd want to retrieve the more detailed information only on demand.

The next example uses LINQ to retrieve just .NET performance counters, writing the result to an XML file:

```
var x =
  new XElement ("counters",
    from PerformanceCounterCategory cat in
         PerformanceCounterCategory.GetCategories()
    where cat.CategoryName.StartsWith (".NET")
    let instances = cat.GetInstanceNames()
```

```
    select new XElement ("category",
      new XAttribute ("name", cat.CategoryName),
      instances.Length == 0
      ?
        from c in cat.GetCounters()
        select new XElement ("counter",
          new XAttribute ("name", c.CounterName))
      :
        from i in instances
        select new XElement ("instance", new XAttribute ("name", i),
          !cat.InstanceExists (i)
          ?
            null
          :
            from c in cat.GetCounters (i)
            select new XElement ("counter",
              new XAttribute ("name", c.CounterName))
        )
    )
  );
x.Save ("counters.xml");
```

Reading Performance Counter Data

To retrieve the value of a performance counter, instantiate a PerformanceCounter object and then call the NextValue or NextSample method. NextValue returns a simple float value; NextSample returns a CounterSample object that exposes a more advanced set of properties, such as CounterFrequency, TimeStamp, BaseValue, and RawValue.

PerformanceCounter's constructor takes a category name, counter name, and optional instance. So, to display the current processor utilization for all CPUs, you would do the following:

```
using PerformanceCounter pc = new PerformanceCounter ("Processor",
                                                      "% Processor Time",
                                                      "_Total");
Console.WriteLine (pc.NextValue());
```

Or to display the "real" (i.e., private) memory consumption of the current process:

```
string procName = Process.GetCurrentProcess().ProcessName;
using PerformanceCounter pc = new PerformanceCounter ("Process",
                                                      "Private Bytes",
                                                      procName);
Console.WriteLine (pc.NextValue());
```

PerformanceCounter doesn't expose a ValueChanged event, so if you want to monitor for changes, you must poll. In the next example, we poll every 200 ms—until signaled to quit by an EventWaitHandle:

```
// need to import System.Threading as well as System.Diagnostics

static void Monitor (string category, string counter, string instance,
                     EventWaitHandle stopper)
```

```
{
  if (!PerformanceCounterCategory.Exists (category))
    throw new InvalidOperationException ("Category does not exist");

  if (!PerformanceCounterCategory.CounterExists (counter, category))
    throw new InvalidOperationException ("Counter does not exist");

  if (instance == null) instance = "";    // "" == no instance (not null!)
  if (instance != "" &&
      !PerformanceCounterCategory.InstanceExists (instance, category))
    throw new InvalidOperationException ("Instance does not exist");

  float lastValue = 0f;
  using (PerformanceCounter pc = new PerformanceCounter (category,
                                                         counter, instance))
    while (!stopper.WaitOne (200, false))
    {
      float value = pc.NextValue();
      if (value != lastValue)          // Only write out the value
      {                                // if it has changed.
        Console.WriteLine (value);
        lastValue = value;
      }
    }
}
```

Here's how we can use this method to simultaneously monitor processor and hard-drive activity:

```
EventWaitHandle stopper = new ManualResetEvent (false);

new Thread (() =>
  Monitor ("Processor", "% Processor Time", "_Total", stopper)
).Start();

new Thread (() =>
  Monitor ("LogicalDisk", "% Idle Time", "C:", stopper)
).Start();

Console.WriteLine ("Monitoring - press any key to quit");
Console.ReadKey();
stopper.Set();
```

Creating Counters and Writing Performance Data

Before writing performance counter data, you need to create a performance category and counter. You must create the performance category along with all the counters that belong to it in one step, as follows:

```
string category = "Nutshell Monitoring";

// We'll create two counters in this category:
string eatenPerMin = "Macadamias eaten so far";
string tooHard = "Macadamias deemed too hard";
```

```
if (!PerformanceCounterCategory.Exists (category))
{
  CounterCreationDataCollection cd = new CounterCreationDataCollection();

  cd.Add (new CounterCreationData (eatenPerMin,
          "Number of macadamias consumed, including shelling time",
          PerformanceCounterType.NumberOfItems32));

  cd.Add (new CounterCreationData (tooHard,
          "Number of macadamias that will not crack, despite much effort",
          PerformanceCounterType.NumberOfItems32));

  PerformanceCounterCategory.Create (category, "Test Category",
    PerformanceCounterCategoryType.SingleInstance, cd);
}
```

The new counters then show up in the Windows performance-monitoring tool when you choose Add Counters. If you later want to define more counters in the same category, you must first delete the old category by calling `Performance CounterCategory.Delete`.

 Creating and deleting performance counters requires administrative privileges. For this reason, it's usually done as part of the application setup.

After you create a counter, you can update its value by instantiating a `Performance Counter`, setting `ReadOnly` to `false`, and setting `RawValue`. You can also use the `Increment` and `IncrementBy` methods to update the existing value:

```
string category = "Nutshell Monitoring";
string eatenPerMin = "Macadamias eaten so far";

using (PerformanceCounter pc = new PerformanceCounter (category,
                                                  eatenPerMin, ""))
{
  pc.ReadOnly = false;
  pc.RawValue = 1000;
  pc.Increment();
  pc.IncrementBy (10);
  Console.WriteLine (pc.NextValue());    // 1011
}
```

The Stopwatch Class

The `Stopwatch` class provides a convenient mechanism for measuring execution times. `Stopwatch` uses the highest-resolution mechanism that the OS and hardware provide, which is typically less than a microsecond. (In contrast, `DateTime.Now` and `Environment.TickCount` have a resolution of about 15 ms.)

To use `Stopwatch`, call `StartNew`—this instantiates a `Stopwatch` and starts it ticking. (Alternatively, you can instantiate it manually and then call `Start`.) The `Elapsed` property returns the elapsed interval as a `TimeSpan`:

```
Stopwatch s = Stopwatch.StartNew();
System.IO.File.WriteAllText ("test.txt", new string ('*', 30000000));
Console.WriteLine (s.Elapsed);        // 00:00:01.4322661
```

`Stopwatch` also exposes an `ElapsedTicks` property, which returns the number of elapsed "ticks" as a `long`. To convert from ticks to seconds, divide by `StopWatch.Frequency`. There's also an `ElapsedMilliseconds` property, which is often the most convenient.

Calling `Stop` freezes `Elapsed` and `ElapsedTicks`. There's no background activity incurred by a "running" `Stopwatch`, so calling `Stop` is optional.

Cross-Platform Diagnostic Tools

In this section, we briefly describe the cross-platform diagnostic tools available to .NET:

dotnet-counters
> Provides an overview of the state of a running application

dotnet-trace
> For more detailed performance and event monitoring

dotnet-dump
> To obtain a memory dump on demand or after a crash

These tools do not require administrative elevation and are suitable for both development and production environments.

dotnet-counters

The *dotnet-counters* tool monitors the memory and CPU usage of a .NET process and writes the data to the console (or a file).

To install the tool, run the following from a command prompt or terminal with *dotnet* in the path:

```
dotnet tool install --global dotnet-counters
```

You can then start monitoring a process, as follows:

```
dotnet-counters monitor System.Runtime --process-id <<ProcessID>>
```

`System.Runtime` means that we want to monitor all counters under the *System.Runtime* category. You can specify either a category or counter name (the dotnet-counters list command lists all available categories and counters).

The output is continually refreshed and looks like this:

```
Press p to pause, r to resume, q to quit.
    Status: Running

[System.Runtime]
    # of Assemblies Loaded                              63
    % Time in GC (since last GC)                         0
    Allocation Rate (Bytes / sec)                  244,864
    CPU Usage (%)                                        6
    Exceptions / sec                                     0
    GC Heap Size (MB)                                    8
    Gen 0 GC / sec                                       0
    Gen 0 Size (B)                                 265,176
    Gen 1 GC / sec                                       0
    Gen 1 Size (B)                                 451,552
    Gen 2 GC / sec                                       0
    Gen 2 Size (B)                                      24
    LOH Size (B)                                 3,200,296
    Monitor Lock Contention Count / sec                  0
    Number of Active Timers                              0
    ThreadPool Completed Work Items / sec               15
    ThreadPool Queue Length                              0
    ThreadPool Threads Count                             9
    Working Set (MB)                                    52
```

Here are all available commands:

Commands	Purpose
list	Displays a list of counter names along with a description of each
ps	Displays a list of dotnet processes eligible for monitoring
monitor	Displays values of selected counters (periodically refreshed)
collect	Saves counter information to a file

The following parameters are supported:

Options/arguments	Purpose
--version	Displays the version of *dotnet-counters*.
-h, --help	Displays help about the program.
-p, --process-id	ID of dotnet process to monitor. Applies to the monitor and collect commands.
--refresh-interval	Sets the desired refresh interval in seconds. Applies to the monitor and collect commands.
-o, --output	Sets the output file name. Applies to the collect command.
--format	Sets the output format. Valid are *csv* or *json*. Applies to the collect command.

dotnet-trace

Traces are timestamped records of events in your program, such as a method being called or a database being queried. Traces can also include performance metrics and custom events, and can contain local context such as the value of local variables. Traditionally, .NET Framework and frameworks such as ASP.NET used ETW. In .NET 5, application traces are written to ETW when running on Windows and LTTng on Linux.

To install the tool, run the following command:

```
dotnet tool install --global dotnet-trace
```

To start recording a program's events, run the following command:

```
dotnet-trace collect --process-id <<ProcessId>>
```

This runs *dotnet-trace* with the default profile, which collects CPU and .NET runtime events and writes to a file called *trace.nettrace*. You can specify other profiles with the `--profile` switch: *gc-verbose* tracks garbage collection and sampled object allocation, and *gc-collect* tracks garbage collection with a low overhead. The `-o` switch lets you specify a different output filename.

The default output is a *.netperf* file, which can be analyzed directly on a Windows machine with the PerfView tool. Alternatively, you can instruct *dotnet-trace* to create a file compatible with Speedscope, which is a free online analysis service at *https://speedscope.app*. To create a Speedscope (*.speedscope.json*) file, use the option `--format speedscope`.

 You can download the latest version of PerfView from *https:// github.com/microsoft/perfview*. The version that ships with Windows 10 might not support *.netperf* files.

The following commands are supported:

Commands	Purpose
collect	Starts recording counter information to a file.
ps	Displays a list of dotnet processes eligible for monitoring.
list-profiles	Lists prebuilt tracing profiles with a description of providers and filters in each.
convert <file>	Converts from the *nettrace* (*.netperf*) format to an alternative format. Currently, *speedscope* is the only target option.

Custom trace events

Your app can emit custom events by defining a custom `EventSource`:

```
[EventSource (Name = "MyTestSource")]
public sealed class MyEventSource : EventSource
{
    public static MyEventSource Instance = new MyEventSource ();
```

Diagnostics

```
MyEventSource() : base (EventSourceSettings.EtwSelfDescribingEventFormat)
{
}

public void Log (string message, int someNumber)
{
  WriteEvent (1, message, someNumber);
}
}
```

The WriteEvent method is overloaded to accept various combinations of simple types (primarily strings and integers). You can then call it as follows:

```
MyEventSource.Instance.Log ("Something", 123);
```

When calling *dotnet-trace*, you must specify the name(s) of any custom event sources that want to record:

```
dotnet-trace collect --process-id <<ProcessId>> --providers MyTestSource
```

dotnet-dump

A *dump*, sometimes called a *core dump*, is a snapshot of the state of a process's virtual memory. You can dump a running process on demand, or configure the OS to generate a dump when an application crashes.

On Ubuntu Linux, the following command enables a core dump upon application crash (the necessary steps can vary between different flavors of Linux):

```
ulimit -c unlimited
```

On Windows, use *regedit.exe* to create or edit the following key in the local machine hive:

```
SOFTWARE\Microsoft\Windows\Windows Error Reporting\LocalDumps
```

Under that, add a key with the same name as your executable (e.g., *foo.exe*), and under that key, add the following keys:

- DumpFolder (REG_EXPAND_SZ), with a value indicating the path to which you want dump files written

- DumpType (REG_DWORD), with a value of 2 to request a full dump

- (Optionally) DumpCount (REG_DWORD), indicating the maximum number of dump files before the oldest is removed

To install the tool, run the following command:

```
dotnet tool install --global dotnet-dump
```

After you've installed it, you can initiate a dump on demand (without ending the process), as follows:

```
dotnet-dump collect --process-id <<YourProcessId>>
```

The following command starts an interactive shell for analyzing a dump file:

```
dotnet-dump analyze <<dumpfile>>
```

If an exception took down the application, you can use the *printexceptions* command (*pe* for short) to display details of that exception. The dotnet-dump shell supports numerous additional commands, which you can list with the *help* command.

14

Concurrency and Asynchrony

Most applications need to deal with more than one thing happening at a time (*concurrency*). In this chapter, we start with the essential prerequisites, namely the basics of threading and tasks, and then describe in detail the principles of asynchrony and C#'s asynchronous functions.

In Chapter 21, we revisit multithreading in greater detail, and in Chapter 22, we cover the related topic of parallel programming.

Introduction

Following are the most common concurrency scenarios:

Writing a responsive user interface
In Windows Presentation Foundation (WPF), mobile, and Windows Forms applications, you must run time-consuming tasks concurrently with the code that runs your user interface to maintain responsiveness.

Allowing requests to process simultaneously
On a server, client requests can arrive concurrently and so must be handled in parallel to maintain scalability. If you use ASP.NET Core or Web API, the runtime does this for you automatically. However, you still need to be aware of shared state (for instance, the effect of using static variables for caching).

Parallel programming
Code that performs intensive calculations can execute faster on multicore/multiprocessor computers if the workload is divided between cores (Chapter 22 is dedicated to this).

Speculative execution
On multicore machines, you can sometimes improve performance by predicting something that might need to be done and then doing it ahead of time. LINQPad uses this technique to speed up the creation of new queries. A variation is to run a number of different algorithms in parallel that all solve the

same task. Whichever one finishes first "wins"—this is effective when you can't know ahead of time which algorithm will execute fastest.

The general mechanism by which a program can simultaneously execute code is called *multithreading*. Multithreading is supported by both the CLR and operating system, and is a fundamental concept in concurrency. Understanding the basics of threading, and in particular the effects of threads on *shared state*, is therefore essential.

Threading

A *thread* is an execution path that can proceed independently of others.

Each thread runs within an operating system process, which provides an isolated environment in which a program runs. With a *single-threaded* program, just one thread runs in the process's isolated environment, and so that thread has exclusive access to it. With a *multithreaded* program, multiple threads run in a single process, sharing the same execution environment (memory, in particular). This, in part, is why multithreading is useful: one thread can fetch data in the background, for instance, while another thread displays the data as it arrives. This data is referred to as *shared state*.

Creating a Thread

A *client* program (Console, WPF, UWP, or Windows Forms) starts in a single thread that's created automatically by the OS (the "main" thread). Here it lives out its life as a single-threaded application, unless you do otherwise, by creating more threads (directly or indirectly).[1]

You can create and start a new thread by instantiating a Thread object and calling its Start method. The simplest constructor for Thread takes a ThreadStart delegate: a parameterless method indicating where execution should begin. Here's an example:

```
// NB: All samples in this chapter assume the following namespace imports:
using System;
using System.Threading;

Thread t = new Thread (WriteY);        // Kick off a new thread
t.Start();                             // running WriteY()

// Simultaneously, do something on the main thread.
for (int i = 0; i < 1000; i++) Console.Write ("x");

void WriteY()
{
  for (int i = 0; i < 1000; i++) Console.Write ("y");
}
```

---

1 The CLR creates other threads behind the scenes for garbage collection and finalization.

```
// Typical Output:
xxxxxxxxxxxxxxxxxxxyyyyyyyyyyyyyyyyyyyyyyyyyyyyyyyyyyyyyyy
xxxxxxxxxxxxxxxxxxxxxxxxxxxxxxxxxxxxxxxxxyyyyyyyyyyyyyy
yyyyyyyyyyyyyyyyyyyyyyyyyyyyyyyyyxxxxxxxxxxxxxxxxxxxxxx
xxxxxxxxxxxxxxxxxxxxxxxxxxxyyyyyyyyyyyyyyyyyyyyyyyyyyyyyy
yyyyyyyyyyyyyxxxxxxxxxxxxxxxxxxxxxxxxxxxxxxxxxxxxxxxxx
...
```

The main thread creates a new thread t on which it runs a method that repeat-edly prints the character *y*. Simultaneously, the main thread repeatedly prints the character *x*, as shown in Figure 14-1. On a single-core computer, the operating system must allocate "slices" of time to each thread (typically 20 ms in Windows) to simulate concurrency, resulting in repeated blocks of *x* and *y*. On a multicore or multiprocessor machine, the two threads can genuinely execute in parallel (subject to competition by other active processes on the computer), although you still get repeated blocks of *x* and *y* in this example because of subtleties in the mechanism by which Console handles concurrent requests.

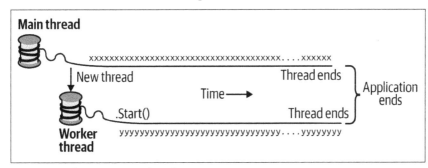

Figure 14-1. Starting a new thread

A thread is said to be *preempted* at the points at which its exe-cution is interspersed with the execution of code on another thread. The term often crops up in explaining why something has gone wrong!

After it's started, a thread's IsAlive property returns true, until the point at which the thread ends. A thread ends when the delegate passed to the Thread's constructor finishes executing. After it's ended, a thread cannot restart.

Each thread has a Name property that you can set for the benefit of debugging. This is particularly useful in Visual Studio because the thread's name is displayed in the Threads Window and Debug Location toolbar. You can set a thread's name just once; attempts to change it later will throw an exception.

The static `Thread.CurrentThread` property gives you the currently executing thread:

```
Console.WriteLine (Thread.CurrentThread.Name);
```

Join and Sleep

You can wait for another thread to end by calling its `Join` method:

```
Thread t = new Thread (Go);
t.Start();
t.Join();
Console.WriteLine ("Thread t has ended!");

void Go() { for (int i = 0; i < 1000; i++) Console.Write ("y"); }
```

This prints "y" 1,000 times, followed by "Thread t has ended!" immediately afterward. You can include a timeout when calling `Join`, either in milliseconds or as a `TimeSpan`. It then returns `true` if the thread ended or `false` if it timed out.

`Thread.Sleep` pauses the current thread for a specified period:

```
Thread.Sleep (TimeSpan.FromHours (1));   // Sleep for 1 hour
Thread.Sleep (500);                      // Sleep for 500 milliseconds
```

`Thread.Sleep(0)` relinquishes the thread's current time slice immediately, voluntarily handing over the CPU to other threads. `Thread.Yield()` does the same thing except that it relinquishes only to threads running on the *same* processor.

> `Sleep(0)` or `Yield` is occasionally useful in production code for advanced performance tweaks. It's also an excellent diagnostic tool for helping to uncover thread safety issues: if inserting `Thread.Yield()` anywhere in your code breaks the program, you almost certainly have a bug.

While waiting on a `Sleep` or `Join`, a thread is blocked.

Blocking

A thread is deemed *blocked* when its execution is paused for some reason, such as when `Sleep`ing or waiting for another to end via `Join`. A blocked thread immediately *yields* its processor time slice, and from then on it consumes no processor time until its blocking condition is satisfied. You can test for a thread being blocked via its `ThreadState` property:

```
bool blocked = (someThread.ThreadState & ThreadState.WaitSleepJoin) != 0;
```

ThreadState is a flags enum, combining three "layers" of data in a bitwise fashion. Most values, however, are redundant, unused, or deprecated. The following extension method strips a ThreadState to one of four useful values: Unstarted, Running, WaitSleepJoin, and Stopped:

```
public static ThreadState Simplify (this ThreadState ts)
{
  return ts & (ThreadState.Unstarted |
               ThreadState.WaitSleepJoin |
               ThreadState.Stopped);
}
```

The ThreadState property is useful for diagnostic purposes but unsuitable for synchronization, because a thread's state can change in between testing ThreadState and acting on that information.

When a thread blocks or unblocks, the OS performs a *context switch*. This incurs a small overhead, typically one or two microseconds.

I/O-bound versus compute-bound

An operation that spends most of its time *waiting* for something to happen is called *I/O-bound*—an example is downloading a web page or calling Console.ReadLine. (I/O-bound operations typically involve input or output, but this is not a hard requirement: Thread.Sleep is also deemed I/O-bound.) In contrast, an operation that spends most of its time performing CPU-intensive work is called *compute-bound*.

Blocking versus spinning

An I/O-bound operation works in one of two ways: it either waits *synchronously* on the current thread until the operation is complete (such as Console.ReadLine, Thread.Sleep, or Thread.Join), or it operates *asynchronously*, firing a callback when the operation finishes in the future (more on this later).

I/O-bound operations that wait synchronously spend most of their time blocking a thread. They can also "spin" in a loop periodically:

```
while (DateTime.Now < nextStartTime)
  Thread.Sleep (100);
```

Leaving aside that there are better ways to do this (such as timers or signaling constructs), another option is that a thread can spin continuously:

```
while (DateTime.Now < nextStartTime);
```

In general, this is very wasteful on processor time: as far as the CLR and OS are concerned, the thread is performing an important calculation and thus is allocated resources accordingly. In effect, we've turned what should be an I/O-bound operation into a compute-bound operation.

There are a couple of nuances with regard to spinning versus blocking. First, spinning *very briefly* can be effective when you expect a condition to be satisfied soon (perhaps within a few microseconds) because it avoids the overhead and latency of a context switch. .NET provides special methods and classes to assist—see the online supplement "SpinLock and SpinWait" (*http://albahari.com/threading*).

Second, blocking does not incur a *zero* cost. This is because each thread ties up around 1 MB of memory for as long as it lives and causes an ongoing administrative overhead for the CLR and OS. For this reason, blocking can be troublesome in the context of heavily I/O-bound programs that need to handle hundreds or thousands of concurrent operations. Instead, such programs need to use a callback-based approach, rescinding their thread entirely while waiting. This is (in part) the purpose of the asynchronous patterns that we discuss later.

Local Versus Shared State

The CLR assigns each thread its own memory stack so that local variables are kept separate. In the next example, we define a method with a local variable and then call the method simultaneously on the main thread and a newly created thread:

```
new Thread (Go).Start();     // Call Go() on a new thread
Go();                        // Call Go() on the main thread

void Go()
{
  // Declare and use a local variable - 'cycles'
  for (int cycles = 0; cycles < 5; cycles++) Console.Write ('?');
}
```

A separate copy of the cycles variable is created on each thread's memory stack, and so the output is, predictably, 10 question marks.

Threads share data if they have a common reference to the same object or variable:

```
bool _done = false;

new Thread (Go).Start();
Go();

void Go()
{
    if (!_done) { _done = true; Console.WriteLine ("Done"); }
}
```

Both threads share the _done variable, so "Done" is printed once instead of twice.

Local variables captured by a lambda expression can also be shared:

```
bool done = false;
ThreadStart action = () =>
```

```
{
  if (!done) { done = true; Console.WriteLine ("Done"); }
};
new Thread (action).Start();
action();
```

More commonly, though, fields are used to share data between threads. In the following example, both threads call Go() on the same ThreadTest instance, so they share the same _done field:

```
var tt = new ThreadTest();
new Thread (tt.Go).Start();
tt.Go();

class ThreadTest
{
  bool _done;

  public void Go()
  {
    if (!_done) { _done = true; Console.WriteLine ("Done"); }
  }
}
```

Static fields offer another way to share data between threads:

```
class ThreadTest
{
  static bool _done;    // Static fields are shared between all threads
                        // in the same process.
  static void Main()
  {
    new Thread (Go).Start();
    Go();
  }

  static void Go()
  {
    if (!_done) { _done = true; Console.WriteLine ("Done"); }
  }
}
```

All four examples illustrate another key concept: that of thread safety (or rather, lack of it!). The output is actually indeterminate: it's possible (though unlikely) that "Done" could be printed twice. If, however, we swap the order of statements in the Go method, the odds of "Done" being printed twice go up dramatically:

```
static void Go()
{
  if (!_done) { Console.WriteLine ("Done"); _done = true; }
}
```

The problem is that one thread can be evaluating the if statement at exactly the same time as the other thread is executing the WriteLine statement—before it's had a chance to set done to true.

Our example illustrates one of many ways that *shared writable state* can introduce the kind of intermittent errors for which multithreading is notorious. Next, we look at how to fix our program by locking; however, it's better to avoid shared state altogether where possible. We see later how asynchronous programming patterns help with this.

Locking and Thread Safety

Locking and thread safety are large topics. For a full discussion, see "Exclusive Locking" on page 866 and "Locking and Thread Safety" on page 874.

We can fix the previous example by obtaining an *exclusive lock* while reading and writing to the shared field. C# provides the lock statement for just this purpose:

```
class ThreadSafe
{
  static bool _done;
  static readonly object _locker = new object();

  static void Main()
  {
    new Thread (Go).Start();
    Go();
  }

  static void Go()
  {
    lock (_locker)
    {
      if (!_done) { Console.WriteLine ("Done"); _done = true; }
    }
  }
}
```

When two threads simultaneously contend a lock (which can be upon any reference-type object; in this case, _locker), one thread waits, or blocks, until the lock becomes available. In this case, it ensures that only one thread can enter its code block at a time, and "Done" will be printed just once. Code that's protected in such a manner—from indeterminacy in a multithreaded context—is called *thread safe*.

Even the act of autoincrementing a variable is not thread safe: the expression x++ executes on the underlying processor as distinct read-increment-write operations. So, if two threads execute x++ at once outside a lock, the variable can end up getting incremented once rather than twice (or worse, x could be *torn*, ending up with a bitwise mixture of old and new content, under certain conditions).

Locking is not a silver bullet for thread safety—it's easy to forget to lock around accessing a field, and locking can create problems of its own (such as deadlocking).

A good example of when you might use locking is around accessing a shared in-memory cache for frequently accessed database objects in an ASP.NET application. This kind of application is simple to get right, and there's no chance of deadlocking. We give an example in "Thread Safety in Application Servers" on page 877 in Chapter 21.

Passing Data to a Thread

Sometimes, you'll want to pass arguments to the thread's startup method. The easiest way to do this is with a lambda expression that calls the method with the desired arguments:

```
Thread t = new Thread ( () => Print ("Hello from t!") );
t.Start();

void Print (string message) => Console.WriteLine (message);
```

With this approach, you can pass in any number of arguments to the method. You can even wrap the entire implementation in a multistatement lambda:

```
new Thread (() =>
{
  Console.WriteLine ("I'm running on another thread!");
  Console.WriteLine ("This is so easy!");
}).Start();
```

An alternative (and less flexible) technique is to pass an argument into Thread's Start method:

```
Thread t = new Thread (Print);
t.Start ("Hello from t!");

void Print (object messageObj)
{
  string message = (string) messageObj;    // We need to cast here
  Console.WriteLine (message);
}
```

This works because Thread's constructor is overloaded to accept either of two delegates:

```
public delegate void ThreadStart();
public delegate void ParameterizedThreadStart (object obj);
```

Lambda expressions and captured variables

As we saw, a lambda expression is the most convenient and powerful way to pass data to a thread. However, you must be careful about accidentally modifying *captured variables* after starting the thread. For instance, consider the following:

```
for (int i = 0; i < 10; i++)
  new Thread (() => Console.Write (i)).Start();
```

The output is nondeterministic! Here's a typical result:

```
0223557799
```

The problem is that the i variable refers to the *same* memory location throughout the loop's lifetime. Therefore, each thread calls Console.Write on a variable whose value can change as it is running! The solution is to use a temporary variable as follows:

```
for (int i = 0; i < 10; i++)
{
  int temp = i;
  new Thread (() => Console.Write (temp)).Start();
}
```

Each of the digits 0 to 9 is then written exactly once. (The *ordering* is still undefined because threads can start at indeterminate times.)

 This is analogous to the problem we described in "Captured Variables" on page 410. The problem is just as much about C#'s rules for capturing variables in for loops as it is about multithreading.

Variable temp is now local to each loop iteration. Therefore, each thread captures a different memory location and there's no problem. We can illustrate the problem in the earlier code more simply with the following example:

```
string text = "t1";
Thread t1 = new Thread ( () => Console.WriteLine (text) );

text = "t2";
Thread t2 = new Thread ( () => Console.WriteLine (text) );

t1.Start(); t2.Start();
```

Because both lambda expressions capture the same text variable, t2 is printed twice.

Exception Handling

Any try/catch/finally blocks in effect when a thread is created are of no relevance to the thread when it starts executing. Consider the following program:

```
try
{
  new Thread (Go).Start();
}
catch (Exception ex)
{
  // We'll never get here!
  Console.WriteLine ("Exception!");
}

void Go() { throw null; }   // Throws a NullReferenceException
```

The try/catch statement in this example is ineffective, and the newly created thread will be encumbered with an unhandled NullReferenceException. This behavior makes sense when you consider that each thread has an independent execution path.

The remedy is to move the exception handler into the Go method:

```
new Thread (Go).Start();

void Go()
{
  try
  {
    ...
    throw null;     // The NullReferenceException will get caught below
    ...
  }
  catch (Exception ex)
  {
    // Typically log the exception and/or signal another thread
    // that we've come unstuck
    ...
  }
}
```

You need an exception handler on all thread entry methods in production applications—just as you do (usually at a higher level, in the execution stack) on your main thread. An unhandled exception causes the whole application to shut down—with an ugly dialog box!

 In writing such exception handling blocks, rarely would you *ignore* the error: typically, you'd log the details of the exception. For a client application, you might display a dialog box allowing the user to automatically submit those details to your web server. You then might choose to restart the application, because it's possible that an unexpected exception might leave your program in an invalid state.

Centralized exception handling

In WPF, UWP, and Windows Forms applications, you can subscribe to "global" exception handling events, Application.DispatcherUnhandledException and Application.ThreadException, respectively. These fire after an unhandled exception in any part of your program that's called via the message loop (this amounts to all code that runs on the main thread while the Application is active). This is useful as a backstop for logging and reporting bugs (although it won't fire for unhandled exceptions on worker threads that you create). Handling these events prevents the program from shutting down, although you may choose to restart the application to avoid the potential corruption of state that can follow from (or that led to) the unhandled exception.

Foreground Versus Background Threads

By default, threads you create explicitly are *foreground threads*. Foreground threads keep the application alive for as long as any one of them is running, whereas *background threads* do not. After all foreground threads finish, the application ends, and any background threads still running abruptly terminate.

 A thread's foreground/background status has no relation to its *priority* (allocation of execution time).

You can query or change a thread's background status using its IsBackground property:

```
static void Main (string[] args)
{
  Thread worker = new Thread ( () => Console.ReadLine() );
  if (args.Length > 0) worker.IsBackground = true;
  worker.Start();
}
```

If this program is called with no arguments, the worker thread assumes foreground status and will wait on the ReadLine statement for the user to press Enter. Meanwhile, the main thread exits, but the application keeps running because a foreground thread is still alive. On the other hand, if an argument is passed to Main(), the worker is assigned background status, and the program exits almost immediately as the main thread ends (terminating the ReadLine).

When a process terminates in this manner, any finally blocks in the execution stack of background threads are circumvented. If your program employs finally (or using) blocks to perform cleanup work such as deleting temporary files, you can avoid this by explicitly waiting out such background threads upon exiting an application, either by joining the thread or with a signaling construct (see "Signaling" on page 621). In either case, you should specify a timeout, so you can abandon a renegade thread should it refuse to finish; otherwise your application will fail to close without the user having to enlist help from the Task Manager (or on Unix, the kill command).

Foreground threads don't require this treatment, but you must take care to avoid bugs that could cause the thread not to end. A common cause for applications failing to exit properly is the presence of active foreground threads.

Thread Priority

A thread's Priority property determines how much execution time it is allotted relative to other active threads in the OS, on the following scale:

```
enum ThreadPriority { Lowest, BelowNormal, Normal, AboveNormal, Highest }
```

This becomes relevant when multiple threads are simultaneously active. You need to take care when elevating a thread's priority because it can starve other threads. If

---

you want a thread to have higher priority than threads in *other* processes, you must also elevate the process priority using the Process class in System.Diagnostics:

```
using Process p = Process.GetCurrentProcess();
p.PriorityClass = ProcessPriorityClass.High;
```

This can work well for non-UI processes that do minimal work and need low latency (the ability to respond very quickly) in the work they do. With compute-hungry applications (particularly those with a user interface), elevating process priority can starve other processes, slowing down the entire computer.

Signaling

Sometimes, you need a thread to wait until receiving notification(s) from other thread(s). This is called *signaling*. The simplest signaling construct is ManualReset Event. Calling WaitOne on a ManualResetEvent blocks the current thread until another thread "opens" the signal by calling Set. In the following example, we start up a thread that waits on a ManualResetEvent. It remains blocked for two seconds until the main thread *signals* it:

```
var signal = new ManualResetEvent (false);

new Thread (() =>
{
  Console.WriteLine ("Waiting for signal...");
  signal.WaitOne();
  signal.Dispose();
  Console.WriteLine ("Got signal!");
}).Start();

Thread.Sleep(2000);
signal.Set();          // "Open" the signal
```

After calling Set, the signal remains open; you can close it again by calling Reset.

ManualResetEvent is one of several signaling constructs provided by the CLR; we cover all of them in detail in Chapter 21.

Threading in Rich Client Applications

In WPF, UWP, and Windows Forms applications, executing long-running operations on the main thread makes the application unresponsive because the main thread also processes the message loop that performs rendering and handles keyboard and mouse events.

A popular approach is to start up "worker" threads for time-consuming operations. The code on a worker thread runs a time-consuming operation and then updates the UI when complete. However, all rich client applications have a threading model whereby UI elements and controls can be accessed only from the thread that created them (typically the main UI thread). Violating this causes either unpredictable behavior or an exception to be thrown.

Hence when you want to update the UI from a worker thread, you must forward the request to the UI thread (the technical term is *marshal*). The low-level way to do this is as follows (later, we discuss other solutions that build on these):

- In WPF, call `BeginInvoke` or `Invoke` on the element's `Dispatcher` object.
- In UWP apps, call `RunAsync` or `Invoke` on the `Dispatcher` object.
- In Windows Forms, call `BeginInvoke` or `Invoke` on the control.

All of these methods accept a delegate referencing the method you want to run. `BeginInvoke`/`RunAsync` work by enqueuing the delegate to the UI thread's *message queue* (the same queue that handles keyboard, mouse, and timer events). `Invoke` does the same thing but then blocks until the message has been read and processed by the UI thread. Because of this, `Invoke` lets you get a return value back from the method. If you don't need a return value, `BeginInvoke`/`RunAsync` are preferable in that they don't block the caller and don't introduce the possibility of deadlock (see "Deadlocks" on page 872).

You can imagine that when you call `Application.Run`, the following pseudo-code executes:

```
while (!thisApplication.Ended)
{
  wait for something to appear in message queue
  Got something: what kind of message is it?
    Keyboard/mouse message -> fire an event handler
    User BeginInvoke message -> execute delegate
    User Invoke message -> execute delegate & post result
}
```

It's this kind of loop that enables a worker thread to marshal a delegate for execution onto the UI thread.

To demonstrate, suppose that we have a WPF window that contains a text box called `txtMessage`, whose content we want a worker thread to update after performing a time-consuming task (which we will simulate by calling `Thread.Sleep`). Here's how we'd do it:

```
partial class MyWindow : Window
{
  public MyWindow()
  {
    InitializeComponent();
    new Thread (Work).Start();
  }

  void Work()
  {
    Thread.Sleep (5000);            // Simulate time-consuming task
    UpdateMessage ("The answer");
  }

  void UpdateMessage (string message)
  {
```

```
    Action action = () => txtMessage.Text = message;
    Dispatcher.BeginInvoke (action);
  }
}
```

Multiple UI Threads

It's possible to have multiple UI threads if they each own different windows. The main scenario is when you have an application with multiple top-level windows, often called a *Single Document Interface* (SDI) application, such as Microsoft Word. Each SDI window typically shows itself as a separate "application" on the taskbar and is mostly isolated, functionally, from other SDI windows. By giving each such window its own UI thread, each window can be made more responsive with respect to the others.

Running this results in a responsive window appearing immediately. Five seconds later, it updates the textbox. The code is similar for Windows Forms, except that we call the (Form's) BeginInvoke method instead:

```
void UpdateMessage (string message)
{
  Action action = () => txtMessage.Text = message;
  this.BeginInvoke (action);
}
```

Synchronization Contexts

In the System.ComponentModel namespace, there's a class called Synchronization Context, which enables the generalization of thread marshaling.

The rich-client APIs for mobile and desktop (UWP, WPF, and Windows Forms) each define and instantiate SynchronizationContext subclasses, which you can obtain via the static property SynchronizationContext.Current (while running on a UI thread). Capturing this property lets you later "post" to UI controls from a worker thread:

```
partial class MyWindow : Window
{
  SynchronizationContext _uiSyncContext;

  public MyWindow()
  {
    InitializeComponent();
    // Capture the synchronization context for the current UI thread:
    _uiSyncContext = SynchronizationContext.Current;
    new Thread (Work).Start();
  }

  void Work()
  {
    Thread.Sleep (5000);         // Simulate time-consuming task
```

```
    UpdateMessage ("The answer");
  }

  void UpdateMessage (string message)
  {
    // Marshal the delegate to the UI thread:
    _uiSyncContext.Post (_ => txtMessage.Text = message, null);
  }
}
```

This is useful because the same technique works with all rich-client user interface APIs.

Calling Post is equivalent to calling BeginInvoke on a Dispatcher or Control; there's also a Send method that is equivalent to Invoke.

The Thread Pool

Whenever you start a thread, a few hundred microseconds are spent organizing such things as a fresh local variable stack. The *thread pool* cuts this overhead by having a pool of pre-created recyclable threads. Thread pooling is essential for efficient parallel programming and fine-grained concurrency; it allows short operations to run without being overwhelmed with the overhead of thread startup.

There are a few things to be wary of when using pooled threads:

- You cannot set the Name of a pooled thread, making debugging more difficult (although you can attach a description when debugging in Visual Studio's Threads window).

- Pooled threads are always *background threads*.

- Blocking pooled threads can degrade performance (see "Hygiene in the thread pool" on page 625).

You are free to change the priority of a pooled thread—it will be restored to normal when released back to the pool.

You can determine whether you're currently executing on a pooled thread via the property Thread.CurrentThread.IsThreadPoolThread.

Entering the thread pool

The easiest way to explicitly run something on a pooled thread is to use Task.Run (we cover this in more detail in the following section):

```
// Task is in System.Threading.Tasks
Task.Run (() => Console.WriteLine ("Hello from the thread pool"));
```

Because tasks didn't exist prior to .NET Framework 4.0, a common alternative is to call ThreadPool.QueueUserWorkItem:

```
ThreadPool.QueueUserWorkItem (notUsed => Console.WriteLine ("Hello"));
```

The following use the thread pool implicitly:

- ASP.NET Core and Web API application servers
- `System.Timers.Timer` and `System.Threading.Timer`
- The parallel programming constructs that we describe in Chapter 22
- The (legacy) `BackgroundWorker` class

Hygiene in the thread pool

The thread pool serves another function, which is to ensure that a temporary excess of compute-bound work does not cause CPU *oversubscription*. Oversubscription is the condition of there being more active threads than CPU cores, with the OS having to time-slice threads. Oversubscription hurts performance because time-slicing requires expensive context switches and can invalidate the CPU caches that have become essential in delivering performance to modern processors.

The CLR prevents oversubscription in the thread pool by queuing tasks and throttling their startup. It begins by running as many concurrent tasks as there are hardware cores, and then tunes the level of concurrency via a hill-climbing algorithm, continually adjusting the workload in a particular direction. If throughput improves, it continues in the same direction (otherwise it reverses). This ensures that it always tracks the optimal performance curve—even in the face of competing process activity on the computer.

The CLR's strategy works best if two conditions are met:

- Work items are mostly short-running (< 250 ms, or ideally < 100 ms) so that the CLR has plenty of opportunities to measure and adjust.
- Jobs that spend most of their time blocked do not dominate the pool.

Blocking is troublesome because it gives the CLR the false idea that it's loading up the CPU. The CLR is smart enough to detect and compensate (by injecting more threads into the pool), although this can make the pool vulnerable to subsequent oversubscription. It also can introduce latency because the CLR throttles the rate at which it injects new threads, particularly early in an application's life (more so on client operating systems where it favors lower resource consumption).

Maintaining good hygiene in the thread pool is particularly relevant when you want to fully utilize the CPU (e.g., via the parallel programming APIs in Chapter 22).

Tasks

A thread is a low-level tool for creating concurrency, and as such, it has limitations, particularly the following:

- Although it's easy to pass data into a thread that you start, there's no easy way to get a "return value" back from a thread that you Join. You need to set up some kind of shared field. And if the operation throws an exception, catching and propagating that exception is equally painful.

- You can't tell a thread to start something else when it's finished; instead you must Join it (blocking your own thread in the process).

These limitations discourage fine-grained concurrency; in other words, they make it difficult to compose larger concurrent operations by combining smaller ones (something essential for the asynchronous programming that we look at in following sections). This in turn leads to greater reliance on manual synchronization (locking, signaling, and so on) and the problems that go with it.

The direct use of threads also has performance implications that we discussed in "The Thread Pool" on page 624. And should you need to run hundreds or thousands of concurrent I/O-bound operations, a thread-based approach consumes hundreds or thousands of megabytes of memory purely in thread overhead.

The Task class helps with all of these problems. Compared to a thread, a Task is higher-level abstraction—it represents a concurrent operation that might or might not be backed by a thread. Tasks are *compositional* (you can chain them together through the use of *continuations*). They can use the *thread pool* to lessen startup latency, and with a TaskCompletionSource, they can employ a callback approach that avoids threads altogether while waiting on I/O-bound operations.

The Task types were introduced in Framework 4.0 as part of the parallel programming library. However, they have since been enhanced (through the use of *awaiters*) to play equally well in more general concurrency scenarios and are backing types for C#'s asynchronous functions.

 In this section, we ignore the features of tasks that are aimed specifically at parallel programming; we cover them instead in Chapter 22.

Starting a Task

The easiest way to start a Task backed by a thread is with the static method Task.Run (the Task class is in the System.Threading.Tasks namespace). Simply pass in an Action delegate:

```
Task.Run (() => Console.WriteLine ("Foo"));
```

Tasks use pooled threads by default, which are background threads. This means that when the main thread ends, so do any tasks that you create. Hence, to run these examples from a console application, you must block the main thread after starting the task (for instance, by Waiting the task or by calling Console.ReadLine):

```
Task.Run (() => Console.WriteLine ("Foo"));
Console.ReadLine();
```

In the book's LINQPad companion samples, Console.Read Line is omitted because the LINQPad process keeps background threads alive.

Calling Task.Run in this manner is similar to starting a thread as follows (except for the thread pooling implications that we discuss shortly):

```
new Thread (() => Console.WriteLine ("Foo")).Start();
```

Task.Run returns a Task object that we can use to monitor its progress, rather like a Thread object. (Notice, however, that we didn't call Start after calling Task.Run because this method creates "hot" tasks; you can instead use Task's constructor to create "cold" tasks, although this is rarely done in practice.)

You can track a task's execution status via its Status property.

Wait

Calling Wait on a task blocks until it completes and is the equivalent of calling Join on a thread:

```
Task task = Task.Run (() =>
{
  Thread.Sleep (2000);
  Console.WriteLine ("Foo");
});
Console.WriteLine (task.IsCompleted);  // False
task.Wait();  // Blocks until task is complete
```

Wait lets you optionally specify a timeout and a cancellation token to end the wait early (see "Cancellation" on page 659).

Long-running tasks

By default, the CLR runs tasks on pooled threads, which is ideal for short-running compute-bound work. For longer-running and blocking operations (such as our preceding example), you can prevent use of a pooled thread as follows:

```
Task task = Task.Factory.StartNew (() => ...,
                            TaskCreationOptions.LongRunning);
```

Running *one* long-running task on a pooled thread won't cause trouble; it's when you run multiple long-running tasks in parallel (particularly ones that block) that performance can suffer. And in that case, there are usually better solutions than `TaskCreationOptions.LongRunning`:

- If the tasks are I/O bound, `TaskCompletionSource` and *asynchronous functions* let you implement concurrency with callbacks (continuations) instead of threads.

- If the tasks are compute bound, a *producer/consumer queue* lets you throttle the concurrency for those tasks, avoiding starvation for other threads and processes (see "Writing a Producer/Consumer Queue" on page 946).

Returning values

`Task` has a generic subclass called `Task<TResult>`, which allows a task to emit a return value. You can obtain a `Task<TResult>` by calling `Task.Run` with a `Func <TResult>` delegate (or a compatible lambda expression) instead of an `Action`:

```
Task<int> task = Task.Run (() => { Console.WriteLine ("Foo"); return 3; });
// ...
```

You can obtain the result later by querying the `Result` property. If the task hasn't yet finished, accessing this property will block the current thread until the task finishes:

```
int result = task.Result;      // Blocks if not already finished
Console.WriteLine (result);    // 3
```

In the following example, we create a task that uses LINQ to count the number of prime numbers in the first three million (+2) integers:

```
Task<int> primeNumberTask = Task.Run (() =>
  Enumerable.Range (2, 3000000).Count (n =>
    Enumerable.Range (2, (int)Math.Sqrt(n)-1).All (i => n % i > 0)));

Console.WriteLine ("Task running...");
Console.WriteLine ("The answer is " + primeNumberTask.Result);
```

This writes "Task running..." and then a few seconds later writes the answer of 216816.

`Task<TResult>` can be thought of as a "future," in that it encapsulates a `Result` that becomes available later in time.

Exceptions

Unlike with threads, tasks conveniently propagate exceptions. So, if the code in your task throws an unhandled exception (in other words, if your task *faults*), that exception is automatically rethrown to whoever calls Wait()—or accesses the Result property of a Task<TResult>:

```
// Start a Task that throws a NullReferenceException:
Task task = Task.Run (() => { throw null; });
try
{
  task.Wait();
}
catch (AggregateException aex)
{
  if (aex.InnerException is NullReferenceException)
    Console.WriteLine ("Null!");
  else
    throw;
}
```

(The CLR wraps the exception in an AggregateException in order to play well with parallel programming scenarios; we discuss this in Chapter 22.)

You can test for a faulted task without rethrowing the exception via the IsFaulted and IsCanceled properties of the Task. If both properties return false, no error occurred; if IsCanceled is true, an OperationCanceledException was thrown for that task (see "Cancellation" on page 918); if IsFaulted is true, another type of exception was thrown, and the Exception property will indicate the error.

Exceptions and autonomous tasks

With autonomous "set-and-forget" tasks (those for which you don't rendezvous via Wait() or Result, or a continuation that does the same), it's good practice to explicitly exception-handle the task code to avoid silent failure, just as you would with a thread.

Ignoring exceptions is fine when an exception solely indicates a failure to obtain a result that you're no longer interested in. For example, if a user cancels a request to download a web page, we wouldn't care if it turns out that the web page didn't exist.

Ignoring exceptions is problematic when an exception indicates a bug in your program, for two reasons:

- The bug may have left your program in an invalid state.

- More exceptions may occur later as a result of the bug, and failure to log the initial error can make diagnosis difficult.

You can subscribe to unobserved exceptions at a global level via the static event TaskScheduler.UnobservedTaskException; handling this event and logging the error can make good sense.

There are a couple of interesting nuances on what counts as unobserved:

- Tasks waited upon with a timeout will generate an unobserved exception if the fault occurs *after* the timeout interval.

- The act of checking a task's Exception property after it has faulted makes the exception "observed."

Continuations

A continuation says to a task, "When you've finished, continue by doing something else." A continuation is usually implemented by a callback that executes once upon completion of an operation. There are two ways to attach a continuation to a task. The first is particularly significant because it's used by C#'s asynchronous functions, as you'll see soon. We can demonstrate it with the prime number counting task that we wrote a short while ago in "Returning values" on page 628:

```
Task<int> primeNumberTask = Task.Run (() =>
  Enumerable.Range (2, 3000000).Count (n =>
    Enumerable.Range (2, (int)Math.Sqrt(n)-1).All (i => n % i > 0)));

var awaiter = primeNumberTask.GetAwaiter();
awaiter.OnCompleted (() =>
{
  int result = awaiter.GetResult();
  Console.WriteLine (result);        // Writes result
});
```

Calling GetAwaiter on the task returns an *awaiter* object whose OnCompleted method tells the *antecedent* task (primeNumberTask) to execute a delegate when it finishes (or faults). It's valid to attach a continuation to an already-completed task, in which case the continuation will be scheduled to execute right away.

 An *awaiter* is any object that exposes the two methods that we've just seen (OnCompleted and GetResult) and a Boolean property called IsCompleted. There's no interface or base class to unify all of these members (although OnCompleted is part of the interface INotifyCompletion). We explain the significance of the pattern in "Asynchronous Functions in C#" on page 639.

If an antecedent task faults, the exception is rethrown when the continuation code calls awaiter.GetResult(). Rather than calling GetResult, we could simply access the Result property of the antecedent. The benefit of calling GetResult is that if the antecedent faults, the exception is thrown directly without being wrapped in AggregateException, allowing for simpler and cleaner catch blocks.

For nongeneric tasks, GetResult() has a void return value. Its useful function is then solely to rethrow exceptions.

If a synchronization context is present, `OnCompleted` automatically captures it and posts the continuation to that context. This is very useful in rich client applications because it bounces the continuation back to the UI thread. In writing libraries, however, it's not usually desirable because the relatively expensive UI-thread-bounce should occur just once upon leaving the library rather than between method calls. Hence, you can defeat it by using the `ConfigureAwait` method:

```
var awaiter = primeNumberTask.ConfigureAwait (false).GetAwaiter();
```

If no synchronization context is present—or you use `ConfigureAwait(false)`—the continuation will (in general) execute on the same thread as the antecedent, avoiding unnecessary overhead.

The other way to attach a continuation is by calling the task's `ContinueWith` method:

```
primeNumberTask.ContinueWith (antecedent =>
{
  int result = antecedent.Result;
  Console.WriteLine (result);        // Writes 123
});
```

`ContinueWith` itself returns a `Task`, which is useful if you want to attach further continuations. However, you must deal directly with `AggregateException` if the task faults, and write extra code to marshal the continuation in UI applications (see "Task Schedulers" on page 939). And in non-UI contexts, you must specify `TaskContinuationOptions.ExecuteSynchronously` if you want the continuation to execute on the same thread; otherwise it will bounce to the thread pool. `Continue With` is particularly useful in parallel programming scenarios; we cover it in detail in Chapter 22.

TaskCompletionSource

We've seen how `Task.Run` creates a task that runs a delegate on a pooled (or non-pooled) thread. Another way to create a task is with `TaskCompletionSource`.

`TaskCompletionSource` lets you create a task out of any operation that completes in the future. It works by giving you a "slave" task that you manually drive—by indicating when the operation finishes or faults. This is ideal for I/O-bound work: you get all the benefits of tasks (with their ability to propagate return values, exceptions, and continuations) without blocking a thread for the duration of the operation.

To use `TaskCompletionSource`, you simply instantiate the class. It exposes a `Task` property that returns a task upon which you can wait and attach continuations—just as with any other task. The task, however, is controlled entirely by the `Task CompletionSource` object via the following methods:

```
public class TaskCompletionSource<TResult>
{
  public void SetResult (TResult result);
```

```
    public void SetException (Exception exception);
    public void SetCanceled();

    public bool TrySetResult (TResult result);
    public bool TrySetException (Exception exception);
    public bool TrySetCanceled();
    public bool TrySetCanceled (CancellationToken cancellationToken);
    ...
}
```

Calling any of these methods *signals* the task, putting it into a completed, faulted, or canceled state (we cover the latter in the section "Cancellation" on page 659). You're supposed to call one of these methods exactly once: if called again, Set Result, SetException, or SetCanceled will throw an exception, whereas the Try* methods return false.

The following example prints 42 after waiting for five seconds:

```
var tcs = new TaskCompletionSource<int>();

new Thread (() => { Thread.Sleep (5000); tcs.SetResult (42); })
  { IsBackground = true }
  .Start();

Task<int> task = tcs.Task;          // Our "slave" task.
Console.WriteLine (task.Result);    // 42
```

With TaskCompletionSource, we can write our own Run method:

```
Task<TResult> Run<TResult> (Func<TResult> function)
{
  var tcs = new TaskCompletionSource<TResult>();
  new Thread (() =>
  {
    try { tcs.SetResult (function()); }
    catch (Exception ex) { tcs.SetException (ex); }
  }).Start();
  return tcs.Task;
}
...
Task<int> task = Run (() => { Thread.Sleep (5000); return 42; });
```

Calling this method is equivalent to calling Task.Factory.StartNew with the Task CreationOptions.LongRunning option to request a nonpooled thread.

The real power of TaskCompletionSource is in creating tasks that don't tie up threads. For instance, consider a task that waits for five seconds and then returns the number 42. We can write this without a thread by using the Timer class, which, with the help of the CLR (and in turn, the OS), fires an event in *x* milliseconds (we revisit timers in Chapter 21):

```
Task<int> GetAnswerToLife()
{
  var tcs = new TaskCompletionSource<int>();
  // Create a timer that fires once in 5000 ms:
```

```
    var timer = new System.Timers.Timer (5000) { AutoReset = false };
    timer.Elapsed += delegate { timer.Dispose(); tcs.SetResult (42); };
    timer.Start();
    return tcs.Task;
}
```

Hence, our method returns a task that completes five seconds later, with a result of 42. By attaching a continuation to the task, we can write its result without blocking *any* thread:

```
var awaiter = GetAnswerToLife().GetAwaiter();
awaiter.OnCompleted (() => Console.WriteLine (awaiter.GetResult()));
```

We could make this more useful and turn it into a general-purpose Delay method by parameterizing the delay time and getting rid of the return value. This means having it return a Task instead of a Task<int>. However, there's no nongeneric version of TaskCompletionSource, which means we can't directly create a nongeneric Task. The workaround is simple: because Task<TResult> derives from Task, we create a TaskCompletionSource<*anything*> and then implicitly convert the Task<*anything*> that it gives you into a Task, like this:

```
var tcs = new TaskCompletionSource<object>();
Task task = tcs.Task;
```

Now we can write our general-purpose Delay method:

```
Task Delay (int milliseconds)
{
  var tcs = new TaskCompletionSource<object>();
  var timer = new System.Timers.Timer (milliseconds) { AutoReset = false };
  timer.Elapsed += delegate { timer.Dispose(); tcs.SetResult (null); };
  timer.Start();
  return tcs.Task;
}
```

 .NET 5 introduces a nongeneric TaskCompletionSource, so if you're targeting .NET 5 or above, you can substitute TaskCompletionSource<object> for TaskCompletionSource.

Here's how we can use it to write "42" after five seconds:

```
Delay (5000).GetAwaiter().OnCompleted (() => Console.WriteLine (42));
```

Our use of TaskCompletionSource without a thread means that a thread is engaged only when the continuation starts, five seconds later. We can demonstrate this by starting 10,000 of these operations at once without error or excessive resource consumption:

```
for (int i = 0; i < 10000; i++)
  Delay (5000).GetAwaiter().OnCompleted (() => Console.WriteLine (42));
```

Timers fire their callbacks on pooled threads, so after five seconds, the thread pool will receive 10,000 requests to call SetResult(null) on a TaskCompletionSource. If the requests arrive faster than they can be processed, the thread pool will respond by enqueuing and then processing them at the optimum level of parallelism for the CPU. This is ideal if the thread-bound jobs are short running, which is true in this case: the thread-bound job is merely the call to SetResult plus either the action of posting the continuation to the synchronization context (in a UI application) or otherwise the continuation itself (Console.WriteLine(42)).

Task.Delay

The Delay method that we just wrote is sufficiently useful that it's available as a static method on the Task class:

```
Task.Delay (5000).GetAwaiter().OnCompleted (() => Console.WriteLine (42));
```

or:

```
Task.Delay (5000).ContinueWith (ant => Console.WriteLine (42));
```

Task.Delay is the *asynchronous* equivalent of Thread.Sleep.

Principles of Asynchrony

In demonstrating TaskCompletionSource, we ended up writing *asynchronous* methods. In this section, we define exactly what asynchronous operations are and explain how this leads to asynchronous programming.

Synchronous Versus Asynchronous Operations

A *synchronous operation* does its work *before* returning to the caller.

An *asynchronous operation* can do (most or all of) its work *after* returning to the caller.

The majority of methods that you write and call are synchronous. An example is List<T>.Add, or Console.WriteLine, or Thread.Sleep. Asynchronous methods are less common and initiate *concurrency*, because work continues in parallel to the caller. Asynchronous methods typically return quickly (or immediately) to the caller; thus, they are also called *nonblocking methods*.

Most of the asynchronous methods that we've seen so far can be described as general-purpose methods:

- Thread.Start

- Task.Run

- Methods that attach continuations to tasks

In addition, some of the methods that we discussed in "Synchronization Contexts" on page 623 (`Dispatcher.BeginInvoke`, `Control.BeginInvoke`, and `Synchroniza tionContext.Post`) are asynchronous, as are the methods that we wrote in "Task-CompletionSource" on page 631, including `Delay`.

What Is Asynchronous Programming?

The principle of asynchronous programming is that you write long-running (or potentially long-running) functions asynchronously. This is in contrast to the conventional approach of writing long-running functions synchronously, and then calling those functions from a new thread or task to introduce concurrency as required.

The difference with the asynchronous approach is that concurrency is initiated *inside* the long-running function rather than from *outside* the function. This has two benefits:

- I/O-bound concurrency can be implemented without tying up threads (as we demonstrate in "TaskCompletionSource" on page 631), improving scalability and efficiency.

- Rich-client applications end up with less code on worker threads, simplifying thread safety.

This, in turn, leads to two distinct uses for asynchronous programming. The first is writing (typically server-side) applications that deal efficiently with a lot of concurrent I/O. The challenge here is not thread *safety* (because there's usually minimal shared state) but thread *efficiency*; in particular, not consuming a thread per network request. So, in this context, it's only I/O-bound operations that benefit from asynchrony.

The second use is to simplify thread-safety in rich-client applications. This is particularly relevant as a program grows in size, because to deal with complexity, we typically refactor larger methods into smaller ones, resulting in chains of methods that call one another (*call graphs*).

With a traditional *synchronous* call graph, if any operation within the graph is long-running, we must run the entire call graph on a worker thread to maintain a responsive UI. Hence, we end up with a single concurrent operation that spans many methods (*coarse-grained concurrency*), and this requires considering thread-safety for every method in the graph.

With an *asynchronous* call graph, we need not start a thread until it's actually needed, typically low in the graph (or not at all in the case of I/O-bound operations). All other methods can run entirely on the UI thread, with much-simplified thread safety. This results in *fine-grained concurrency*—a sequence of small concurrent operations, between which execution bounces to the UI thread.

To benefit from this, both I/O- and compute-bound operations need to be written asynchronously; a good rule of thumb
is to include anything that might take longer than 50 ms.

(On the flipside, *excessively* fine-grained asynchrony can hurt
performance, because asynchronous operations incur an overhead—see "Optimizations" on page 655.)

In this chapter, we focus mostly on the rich-client scenario, which is the more
complex of the two. In Chapter 16, we give two examples that illustrate the I/O-
bound scenario (see "Concurrency with TCP" on page 738 and "Writing an HTTP
Server" on page 731).

The UWP framework encourages asynchronous programming to the point where synchronous versions of some long-
running methods are either not exposed or throw exceptions.
Instead, you must call asynchronous methods that return
tasks (or objects that can be converted into tasks via the
AsTask extension method).

Asynchronous Programming and Continuations

Tasks are ideally suited to asynchronous programming, because they support continuations, which are essential for asynchrony (consider the Delay method that we
wrote in "TaskCompletionSource" on page 631). In writing Delay, we used TaskCom
pletionSource, which is a standard way to implement "bottom-level" I/O-bound
asynchronous methods.

For compute-bound methods, we use Task.Run to initiate thread-bound concurrency. Simply by returning the task to the caller, we create an asynchronous method.
What distinguishes asynchronous programming is that we aim to do so lower in the
call graph so that in rich-client applications, higher-level methods can remain on
the UI thread and access controls and shared state without thread-safety issues. To
illustrate, consider the following method that computes and counts prime numbers,
using all available cores (we discuss ParallelEnumerable in Chapter 22):

```
int GetPrimesCount (int start, int count)
{
  return
    ParallelEnumerable.Range (start, count).Count (n =>
      Enumerable.Range (2, (int)Math.Sqrt(n)-1).All (i => n % i > 0));
}
```

The details of how this works are unimportant; what matters is that it can take a
while to run. We can demonstrate this by writing another method to call it:

```
void DisplayPrimeCounts()
{
  for (int i = 0; i < 10; i++)
    Console.WriteLine (GetPrimesCount (i*1000000 + 2, 1000000) +
      " primes between " + (i*1000000) + " and " + ((i+1)*1000000-1));
  Console.WriteLine ("Done!");
}
```

```
78498 primes between 0 and 999999
70435 primes between 1000000 and 1999999
67883 primes between 2000000 and 2999999
66330 primes between 3000000 and 3999999
65367 primes between 4000000 and 4999999
64336 primes between 5000000 and 5999999
63799 primes between 6000000 and 6999999
63129 primes between 7000000 and 7999999
62712 primes between 8000000 and 8999999
62090 primes between 9000000 and 9999999
```

Now we have a *call graph*, with `DisplayPrimeCounts` calling `GetPrimesCount`. The former uses `Console.WriteLine` for simplicity, although in reality it would more likely be updating UI controls in a rich-client application, as we demonstrate later. We can initiate coarse-grained concurrency for this call graph as follows:

```
Task.Run (() => DisplayPrimeCounts());
```

With a fine-grained asynchronous approach, we instead start by writing an asynchronous version of `GetPrimesCount`:

```
Task<int> GetPrimesCountAsync (int start, int count)
{
  return Task.Run (() =>
    ParallelEnumerable.Range (start, count).Count (n =>
      Enumerable.Range (2, (int) Math.Sqrt(n)-1).All (i => n % i > 0)));
}
```

Why Language Support Is Important

Now we must modify `DisplayPrimeCounts` so that it calls `GetPrimesCountAsync`. This is where C#'s `await` and `async` keywords come into play, because to do so otherwise is trickier than it sounds. If we simply modify the loop as follows:

```
for (int i = 0; i < 10; i++)
{
  var awaiter = GetPrimesCountAsync (i*1000000 + 2, 1000000).GetAwaiter();
  awaiter.OnCompleted (() =>
    Console.WriteLine (awaiter.GetResult() + " primes between... "));
}
Console.WriteLine ("Done");
```

the loop will rapidly spin through 10 iterations (the methods being nonblocking), and all 10 operations will execute in parallel (followed by a premature "Done").

Concurrency and Asynchrony

Executing these tasks in parallel is undesirable in this case because their internal implementations are already parallelized; it will only make us wait longer to see the first results (and muck up the ordering).

There is a much more common reason, however, for needing to *serialize* the execution of tasks, which is that Task B depends on the result of Task A. For example, in fetching a web page, a DNS lookup must precede the HTTP request.

To get them running sequentially, we must trigger the next loop iteration from the continuation itself. This means eliminating the for loop and resorting to a recursive call in the continuation:

```
void DisplayPrimeCounts()
{
  DisplayPrimeCountsFrom (0);
}

void DisplayPrimeCountsFrom (int i)
{
  var awaiter = GetPrimesCountAsync (i*1000000 + 2, 1000000).GetAwaiter();
  awaiter.OnCompleted (() =>
  {
    Console.WriteLine (awaiter.GetResult() + " primes between...");
    if (++i < 10) DisplayPrimeCountsFrom (i);
    else Console.WriteLine ("Done");
  });
}
```

It gets even worse if we want to make DisplayPrimesCount *itself* asynchronous, returning a task that it signals upon completion. To accomplish this requires creating a TaskCompletionSource:

```
Task DisplayPrimeCountsAsync()
{
  var machine = new PrimesStateMachine();
  machine.DisplayPrimeCountsFrom (0);
  return machine.Task;
}

class PrimesStateMachine
{
  TaskCompletionSource<object> _tcs = new TaskCompletionSource<object>();
  public Task Task { get { return _tcs.Task; } }

  public void DisplayPrimeCountsFrom (int i)
  {
    var awaiter = GetPrimesCountAsync (i*1000000+2, 1000000).GetAwaiter();
    awaiter.OnCompleted (() =>
    {
      Console.WriteLine (awaiter.GetResult());
      if (++i < 10) DisplayPrimeCountsFrom (i);
      else { Console.WriteLine ("Done"); _tcs.SetResult (null); }
    });
```

```
    }
}
```

Fortunately, C#'s *asynchronous functions* do all of this work for us. With the `async` and `await` keywords, we need only write this:

```
async Task DisplayPrimeCountsAsync()
{
  for (int i = 0; i < 10; i++)
    Console.WriteLine (await GetPrimesCountAsync (i*1000000 + 2, 1000000) +
      " primes between " + (i*1000000) + " and " + ((i+1)*1000000-1));
  Console.WriteLine ("Done!");
}
```

Consequently, `async` and `await` are essential for implementing asynchrony without excessive complexity. Let's now see how these keywords work.

 Another way of looking at the problem is that imperative looping constructs (`for`, `foreach`, and so on) do not mix well with continuations, because they rely on the *current local state* of the method ("How many more times is this loop going to run?").

Although the `async` and `await` keywords offer one solution, it's sometimes possible to solve it in another way by replacing the imperative looping constructs with the *functional* equivalent (in other words, LINQ queries). This is the basis of *Reactive Extensions* (Rx) and can be a good option when you want to execute query operators over the result—or combine multiple sequences. The price to pay is that to prevent blocking, Rx operates over *push*-based sequences, which can be conceptually tricky.

Asynchronous Functions in C#

The `async` and `await` keywords let you write asynchronous code that has the same structure and simplicity as synchronous code while eliminating the "plumbing" of asynchronous programming.

Awaiting

The `await` keyword simplifies the attaching of continuations. Starting with a basic scenario, the compiler expands this:

```
var result = await expression;
statement(s);
```

into something functionally similar to this:

```
var awaiter = expression.GetAwaiter();
awaiter.OnCompleted (() =>
{
  var result = awaiter.GetResult();
```

```
    statement(s);
});
```

 The compiler also emits code to short-circuit the continuation in case of synchronous completion (see "Optimizations" on page 655) and to handle various nuances that we pick up in later sections.

To demonstrate, let's revisit the asynchronous method that we wrote previously that computes and counts prime numbers:

```
Task<int> GetPrimesCountAsync (int start, int count)
{
  return Task.Run (() =>
    ParallelEnumerable.Range (start, count).Count (n =>
      Enumerable.Range (2, (int)Math.Sqrt(n)-1).All (i => n % i > 0)));
}
```

With the await keyword, we can call it as follows:

```
int result = await GetPrimesCountAsync (2, 1000000);
Console.WriteLine (result);
```

To compile, we need to add the async modifier to the containing method:

```
async void DisplayPrimesCount()
{
  int result = await GetPrimesCountAsync (2, 1000000);
  Console.WriteLine (result);
}
```

The async modifier instructs the compiler to treat await as a keyword rather than an identifier should an ambiguity arise within that method (this ensures that code written prior to C# 5 that might use await as an identifier will still compile without error). The async modifier can be applied only to methods (and lambda expressions) that return void or (as you'll see later) a Task or Task<TResult>.

 The async modifier is similar to the unsafe modifier in that it has no effect on a method's signature or public metadata; it affects only what happens *inside* the method. For this reason, it makes no sense to use async in an interface. However it is legal, for instance, to introduce async when overriding a non-async virtual method, as long as you keep the signature the same.

Methods with the async modifier are called *asynchronous functions*, because they themselves are typically asynchronous. To see why, let's look at how execution proceeds through an asynchronous function.

Upon encountering an await expression, execution (normally) returns to the caller —rather like with yield return in an iterator. But before returning, the runtime attaches a continuation to the awaited task, ensuring that when the task completes, execution jumps back into the method and continues where it left off. If the task faults, its exception is rethrown, otherwise its return value is assigned to the await expression. We can summarize everything we just said by looking at the logical expansion of the asynchronous method we just examined:

```
void DisplayPrimesCount()
{
  var awaiter = GetPrimesCountAsync (2, 1000000).GetAwaiter();
  awaiter.OnCompleted (() =>
  {
    int result = awaiter.GetResult();
    Console.WriteLine (result);
  });
}
```

The expression upon which you await is typically a task; however, any object with a GetAwaiter method that returns an *awaiter* (implementing INotifyComple tion.OnCompleted and with an appropriately typed GetResult method and a bool IsCompleted property) will satisfy the compiler.

Notice that our await expression evaluates to an int type; this is because the expression that we awaited was a Task<int> (whose GetAwaiter().GetResult() method returns an int).

Awaiting a nongeneric task is legal and generates a void expression:

```
await Task.Delay (5000);
Console.WriteLine ("Five seconds passed!");
```

Capturing local state

The real power of await expressions is that they can appear almost anywhere in code. Specifically, an await expression can appear in place of any expression (within an asynchronous function) except for inside a lock expression or unsafe context.

In the following example, we await inside a loop:

```
async void DisplayPrimeCounts()
{
  for (int i = 0; i < 10; i++)
    Console.WriteLine (await GetPrimesCountAsync (i*1000000+2, 1000000));
}
```

Upon first executing GetPrimesCountAsync, execution returns to the caller by virtue of the await expression. When the method completes (or faults), execution resumes where it left off, with the values of local variables and loop counters preserved.

Without the await keyword, the simplest equivalent might be the example we wrote in "Why Language Support Is Important" on page 637. The compiler, however, takes the more general strategy of refactoring such methods into state machines (rather like it does with iterators).

The compiler relies on continuations (via the awaiter pattern) to resume execution after an await expression. This means that if running on the UI thread of a rich client application, the synchronization context ensures execution resumes on the same thread. Otherwise, execution resumes on whatever thread the task finished on. The change of thread does not affect the order of execution and is of little consequence unless you're somehow relying on thread affinity, perhaps through the use of thread-local storage (see "Thread-Local Storage" on page 898). It's like touring a city and hailing taxis to get from one destination to another. With a synchronization context, you'll always get the same taxi; with no synchronization context, you'll usually get a different taxi each time. In either case, though, the journey is the same.

Awaiting in a UI

We can demonstrate asynchronous functions in a more practical context by writing a simple UI that remains responsive while calling a compute-bound method. Let's begin with a synchronous solution:

```
class TestUI : Window
{
  Button _button = new Button { Content = "Go" };
  TextBlock _results = new TextBlock();

  public TestUI()
  {
    var panel = new StackPanel();
    panel.Children.Add (_button);
    panel.Children.Add (_results);
    Content = panel;
    _button.Click += (sender, args) => Go();
  }

  void Go()
  {
    for (int i = 1; i < 5; i++)
      _results.Text += GetPrimesCount (i * 1000000, 1000000) +
        " primes between " + (i*1000000) + " and " + ((i+1)*1000000-1) +
        Environment.NewLine;
  }

  int GetPrimesCount (int start, int count)
  {
    return ParallelEnumerable.Range (start, count).Count (n =>
      Enumerable.Range (2, (int) Math.Sqrt(n)-1).All (i => n % i > 0));
  }
}
```

Upon pressing the "Go" button, the application becomes unresponsive for the time it takes to execute the compute-bound code. There are two steps in asynchronizing this; the first is to switch to the asynchronous version of GetPrimesCount that we used in previous examples:

```
Task<int> GetPrimesCountAsync (int start, int count)
{
  return Task.Run (() =>
    ParallelEnumerable.Range (start, count).Count (n =>
      Enumerable.Range (2, (int) Math.Sqrt(n)-1).All (i => n % i > 0)));
}
```

The second step is to modify Go to call GetPrimesCountAsync:

```
async void Go()
{
  _button.IsEnabled = false;
  for (int i = 1; i < 5; i++)
    _results.Text += await GetPrimesCountAsync (i * 1000000, 1000000) +
      " primes between " + (i*1000000) + " and " + ((i+1)*1000000-1) +
      Environment.NewLine;
  _button.IsEnabled = true;
}
```

This illustrates the simplicity of programming with asynchronous functions: you program as you would synchronously but call asynchronous functions instead of blocking functions and await them. Only the code within GetPrimesCountAsync runs on a worker thread; the code in Go "leases" time on the UI thread. We could say that Go executes *pseudo-concurrently* to the message loop (in that its execution is interspersed with other events that the UI thread processes). With this pseudo-concurrency, the only point at which preemption can occur is during an await. This simplifies thread safety: in our case, the only problem that this could cause is *reentrancy* (clicking the button again while it's running, which we prevent by disabling the button). True concurrency occurs lower in the call stack, inside code called by Task.Run. To benefit from this model, truly concurrent code prevents accessing shared state or UI controls.

To give another example, suppose that instead of calculating prime numbers, we want to download several web pages and sum their lengths. .NET exposes numerous task-returning asynchronous methods, one of which is the WebClient class in System.Net. The DownloadDataTaskAsync method asynchronously downloads a URI to a byte array, returning a Task<byte[]>, so by awaiting it, we get a byte[]. Let's now rewrite our Go method:

```
async void Go()
{
  _button.IsEnabled = false;
  string[] urls = "www.albahari.com www.oreilly.com www.linqpad.net".Split();
  int totalLength = 0;
  try
  {
    foreach (string url in urls)
    {
      var uri = new Uri ("http://" + url);
      byte[] data = await new WebClient().DownloadDataTaskAsync (uri);
      _results.Text += "Length of " + url + " is " + data.Length +
                       Environment.NewLine;
      totalLength += data.Length;
```

```
    }
    _results.Text += "Total length: " + totalLength;
  }
  catch (WebException ex)
  {
    _results.Text += "Error: " + ex.Message;
  }
  finally { _button.IsEnabled = true; }
}
```

Again, this mirrors how we'd write it synchronously—including the use of `catch` and `finally` blocks. Even though execution returns to the caller after the first `await`, the `finally` block does not execute until the method has logically completed (by virtue of all its code executing—or an early `return` or unhandled exception).

It can be helpful to consider exactly what's happening underneath. First, we need to revisit the pseudo-code that runs the message loop on the UI thread:

```
Set synchronization context for this thread to WPF sync context
while (!thisApplication.Ended)
{
    wait for something to appear in message queue
    Got something: what kind of message is it?
      Keyboard/mouse message -> fire an event handler
      User BeginInvoke/Invoke message -> execute delegate
}
```

Event handlers that we attach to UI elements execute via this message loop. When our Go method runs, execution proceeds as far as the `await` expression and then returns to the message loop (freeing the UI to respond to further events). However, the compiler's expansion of `await` ensures that before returning, a continuation is set up such that execution resumes where it left off upon completion of the task. And because we awaited on a UI thread, the continuation posts to the synchronization context, which executes it via the message loop, keeping our entire Go method executing pseudo-concurrently on the UI thread. True (I/O-bound) concurrency occurs within the implementation of DownloadDataTaskAsync.

Comparison to coarse-grained concurrency

Asynchronous programming was difficult prior to C# 5, not only because there was no language support, but because the .NET Framework exposed asynchronous functionality through clumsy patterns called the EAP and the APM (see "Obsolete Patterns" on page 667) rather than task-returning methods.

The popular workaround was coarse-grained concurrency (in fact, there was even a type called BackgroundWorker to help with that). Returning to our original *synchronous* example with GetPrimesCount, we can demonstrate coarse-grained asynchrony by modifying the button's event handler, as follows:

```
...
_button.Click += (sender, args) =>
{
```

```
  _button.IsEnabled = false;
  Task.Run (() => Go());
};
```

(We've chosen to use Task.Run rather than BackgroundWorker because the latter would do nothing to simplify our particular example.) In either case, the end result is that our entire synchronous call graph (Go plus GetPrimesCount) runs on a worker thread. And because Go updates UI elements, we must now litter our code with Dispatcher.BeginInvoke:

```
void Go()
{
  for (int i = 1; i < 5; i++)
  {
    int result = GetPrimesCount (i * 1000000, 1000000);
    Dispatcher.BeginInvoke (new Action (() =>
      _results.Text += result + " primes between " + (i*1000000) +
      " and " + ((i+1)*1000000-1) + Environment.NewLine));
  }
  Dispatcher.BeginInvoke (new Action (() => _button.IsEnabled = true));
}
```

Unlike with the asynchronous version, the loop itself runs on a worker thread. This might seem innocuous, and yet, even in this simple case, our use of multithreading has introduced a race condition. (Can you spot it? If not, try running the program: it will almost certainly become apparent.)

Implementing cancellation and progress reporting creates more possibilities for thread-safety errors, as does any additional code in the method. For instance, suppose that the upper limit for the loop is not hardcoded but comes from a method call:

```
for (int i = 1; i < GetUpperBound(); i++)
```

Now suppose that GetUpperBound() reads the value from a lazily loaded configuration file, which loads from disk upon first call. All of this code now runs on your worker thread, code that's most likely not thread-safe. This is the danger of starting worker threads high in the call graph.

Writing Asynchronous Functions

With any asynchronous function, you can replace the void return type with a Task to make the method itself *usefully* asynchronous (and awaitable). No further changes are required:

```
async Task PrintAnswerToLife()    // We can return Task instead of void
{
  await Task.Delay (5000);
  int answer = 21 * 2;
  Console.WriteLine (answer);
}
```

Notice that we don't explicitly return a task in the method body. The compiler manufactures the task, which it signals upon completion of the method (or upon an unhandled exception). This makes it easy to create asynchronous call chains:

```
async Task Go()
{
  await PrintAnswerToLife();
  Console.WriteLine ("Done");
}
```

And because we've declared Go with a Task return type, Go itself is awaitable.

The compiler expands asynchronous functions that return tasks into code that uses TaskCompletionSource to create a task that it then signals or faults.

Nuances aside, we can expand PrintAnswerToLife into the following functional equivalent:

```
Task PrintAnswerToLife()
{
  var tcs = new TaskCompletionSource<object>();
  var awaiter = Task.Delay (5000).GetAwaiter();
  awaiter.OnCompleted (() =>
  {
    try
    {
      awaiter.GetResult();     // Re-throw any exceptions
      int answer = 21 * 2;
      Console.WriteLine (answer);
      tcs.SetResult (null);
    }
    catch (Exception ex) { tcs.SetException (ex); }
  });
  return tcs.Task;
}
```

Hence, whenever a task-returning asynchronous method finishes, execution jumps back to whatever awaited it (by virtue of a continuation).

In a rich-client scenario, execution bounces at this point back to the UI thread (if it's not already on the UI thread). Otherwise, it continues on whatever thread the continuation came back on. This means that there's no latency cost in bubbling up asynchronous call graphs, other than the first "bounce" if it was UI-thread-initiated.

Returning Task<TResult>

You can return a Task<TResult> if the method body returns TResult:

```
async Task<int> GetAnswerToLife()
{
  await Task.Delay (5000);
  int answer = 21 * 2;
```

```
    return answer;     // Method has return type Task<int> we return int
}
```

Internally, this results in the TaskCompletionSource being signaled with a value rather than null. We can demonstrate GetAnswerToLife by calling it from PrintAnswerToLife (which in turn, called from Go):

```
async Task Go()
{
  await PrintAnswerToLife();
  Console.WriteLine ("Done");
}

async Task PrintAnswerToLife()
{
  int answer = await GetAnswerToLife();
  Console.WriteLine (answer);
}

async Task<int> GetAnswerToLife()
{
  await Task.Delay (5000);
  int answer = 21 * 2;
  return answer;
}
```

In effect, we've refactored our original PrintAnswerToLife into two methods—with the same ease as if we were programming synchronously. The similarity to synchronous programming is intentional; here's the synchronous equivalent of our call graph, for which calling Go() gives the same result after blocking for five seconds:

```
void Go()
{
  PrintAnswerToLife();
  Console.WriteLine ("Done");
}

void PrintAnswerToLife()
{
  int answer = GetAnswerToLife();
  Console.WriteLine (answer);
}

int GetAnswerToLife()
{
  Thread.Sleep (5000);
  int answer = 21 * 2;
  return answer;
}
```

This also illustrates the basic principle of how to design with asynchronous functions in C#:

1. Write your methods synchronously.

2. Replace *synchronous* method calls with *asynchronous* method calls, and await them.

3. Except for "top-level" methods (typically event handlers for UI controls), upgrade your asynchronous methods' return types to Task or Task<TResult> so that they're awaitable.

The compiler's ability to manufacture tasks for asynchronous functions means that for the most part, you need to explicitly instantiate a TaskCompletionSource only in (the relatively rare case of) bottom-level methods that initiate I/O-bound concurrency. (And for methods that initiate compute-bound concurrency, you create the task with Task.Run.)

Asynchronous call graph execution

To see exactly how this executes, it's helpful to rearrange our code as follows:

```
async Task Go()
{
  var task = PrintAnswerToLife();
  await task; Console.WriteLine ("Done");
}

async Task PrintAnswerToLife()
{
  var task = GetAnswerToLife();
  int answer = await task; Console.WriteLine (answer);
}

async Task<int> GetAnswerToLife()
{
  var task = Task.Delay (5000);
  await task; int answer = 21 * 2; return answer;
}
```

Go calls PrintAnswerToLife, which calls GetAnswerToLife, which calls Delay and then awaits. The await causes execution to return to PrintAnswerToLife, which itself awaits, returning to Go, which also awaits and returns to the caller. All of this happens synchronously, on the thread that called Go; this is the brief *synchronous* phase of execution.

Five seconds later, the continuation on Delay fires, and execution returns to Get AnswerToLife on a pooled thread. (If we started on a UI thread, execution now bounces to that thread.) The remaining statements in GetAnswerToLife then run, after which the method's Task<int> completes with a result of 42 and executes the continuation in `PrintAnswerToLife`, which executes the remaining statements in that method. The process continues until Go's task is signaled as complete.

Execution flow matches the synchronous call graph that we showed earlier because we're following a pattern whereby we `await` every asynchronous method immediately after calling it. This creates a sequential flow with no parallelism or overlapping execution within the call graph. Each `await` expression creates a "gap" in execution, after which the program resumes where it left off.

Parallelism

Calling an asynchronous method without awaiting it allows the code that follows to execute in parallel. You might have noticed in earlier examples that we had a button whose event handler called Go, as follows:

```
_button.Click += (sender, args) => Go();
```

Despite Go being an asynchronous method, we didn't await it, and this is indeed what facilitates the concurrency needed to maintain a responsive UI.

We can use this same principle to run two asynchronous operations in parallel:

```
var task1 = PrintAnswerToLife();
var task2 = PrintAnswerToLife();
await task1; await task2;
```

(By awaiting both operations afterward, we "end" the parallelism at that point. Later, we describe how the `WhenAll` task combinator helps with this pattern.)

Concurrency created in this manner occurs whether or not the operations are initiated on a UI thread, although there's a difference in how it occurs. In both cases, we get the same "true" concurrency occurring in the bottom-level operations that initiate it (such as `Task.Delay` or code farmed to `Task.Run`). Methods above this in the call stack will be subject to true concurrency only if the operation was initiated without a synchronization context present; otherwise they will be subject to the pseudo-concurrency (and simplified thread safety) that we talked about earlier, whereby the only place at which we can be preempted is an `await` statement. This lets us, for instance, define a shared field, _x, and increment it in `GetAnswerToLife` without locking:

```
async Task<int> GetAnswerToLife()
{
  _x++;
  await Task.Delay (5000);
  return 21 * 2;
}
```

(We would, though, be unable to assume that _x had the same value before and after the await.)

Asynchronous Lambda Expressions

Just as ordinary *named* methods can be asynchronous:

```
async Task NamedMethod()
{
  await Task.Delay (1000);
  Console.WriteLine ("Foo");
}
```

so can *unnamed* methods (lambda expressions and anonymous methods), if preceded by the async keyword:

```
Func<Task> unnamed = async () =>
{
  await Task.Delay (1000);
  Console.WriteLine ("Foo");
};
```

We can call and await these in the same way:

```
await NamedMethod();
await unnamed();
```

We can use asynchronous lambda expressions when attaching event handlers:

```
myButton.Click += async (sender, args) =>
{
  await Task.Delay (1000);
  myButton.Content = "Done";
};
```

This is more succinct than the following, which has the same effect:

```
myButton.Click += ButtonHandler;
...
async void ButtonHander (object sender, EventArgs args)
{
  await Task.Delay (1000);
  myButton.Content = "Done";
};
```

Asynchronous lambda expressions can also return Task<TResult>:

```
Func<Task<int>> unnamed = async () =>
{
  await Task.Delay (1000);
  return 123;
};
int answer = await unnamed();
```

Asynchronous Streams

With yield return, you can write an iterator; with await, you can write an asynchronous function. *Asynchronous streams* (from C# 8) combine these concepts and let you write an iterator that awaits, yielding elements asynchronously. This support builds on the following pair of interfaces, which are asynchronous counterparts to the enumeration interfaces we described in "Enumeration and Iterators" on page 189:

```
public interface IAsyncEnumerable<out T>
{
  IAsyncEnumerator<T> GetAsyncEnumerator (...);
}

public interface IAsyncEnumerator<out T>: IAsyncDisposable
{
  T Current { get; }
  ValueTask<bool> MoveNextAsync();
}
```

ValueTask<T> is a struct that wraps Task<T> and is behaviorally similar to Task<T> while enabling more efficient execution when the task completes synchronously (which can happen often when enumerating a sequence). See "ValueTask<T>" on page 657 for a discussion of differences. IAsyncDisposable is an asynchronous version of IDisposable; it provides an opportunity to perform cleanup should you choose to manually implement the interfaces:

```
public interface IAsyncDisposable
{
  ValueTask DisposeAsync();
}
```

 The act of fetching each element from the sequence (Move NextAsync) is an asynchronous operation, so asynchronous streams are suitable when elements arrive in a piecemeal fashion (such as when processing data from a video stream). In contrast, the following type is more suitable when the sequence *as a whole* is delayed, but the elements, when they arrive, arrive all together:

```
Task<IEnumerable<T>>
```

To generate an asynchronous stream, you write a method that combines the principles of iterators and asynchronous methods. In other words, your method should include both yield return and await, and it should return IAsyncEnumerable<T>:

```
async IAsyncEnumerable<int> RangeAsync (
  int start, int count, int delay)
{
  for (int i = start; i < start + count; i++)
  {
    await Task.Delay (delay);
    yield return i;
  }
}
```

To consume an asynchronous stream, use the await foreach statement:

```
await foreach (var number in RangeAsync (0, 10, 500))
  Console.WriteLine (number);
```

Note that data arrives steadily, every 500 milliseconds (or, in real life, as it becomes available). Contrast this to a similar construct using Task<IEnumerable<T>> for which no data is returned until the last piece of data is available:

```
static async Task<IEnumerable<int>> RangeTaskAsync (int start, int count,
                                                    int delay)
{
  List<int> data = new List<int>();
  for (int i = start; i < start + count; i++)
  {
    await Task.Delay (delay);
    data.Add (i);
  }

  return data;
}
```

Here's how to consume it with the foreach statement:

```
foreach (var data in await RangeTaskAsync(0, 10, 500))
  Console.WriteLine (data);
```

Querying IAsyncEnumerable<T>

The *System.Linq.Async* NuGet package defines LINQ query operators that operate over IAsyncEnumerable<T>, allowing you to write queries much as you would with IEnumerable<T>.

For instance, we can write a LINQ query over the RangeAsync method that we defined in the preceding section, as follows:

```
IAsyncEnumerable<int> query =
  from i in RangeAsync (0, 10, 500)
  where i % 2 == 0    // Even numbers only.
  select i * 10;      // Multiply by 10.

await foreach (var number in query)
  Console.WriteLine (number);
```

This outputs 0, 20, 40, and so on.

 If you're familiar with Rx, you can benefit from its (more powerful) query operators, too, by calling the ToObservable extension method, which converts an IAsyncEnumerable<T> into an IObservable<T>. A ToAsyncEnumerable extension method is also available, to convert in the reverse direction.

IAsyncEnumerable<T> in ASP.Net Core

ASP.Net Core controller actions can now return IAsyncEnumerable<T>. Such methods must be marked async. For example:

```
[HttpGet]
public async IAsyncEnumerable<string> Get()
{
```

```
using var dbContext = new BookContext();
await foreach (var title in dbContext.Books
                                      .Select(b => b.Title)
                                      .AsAsyncEnumerable())
    yield return title;
}
```

Asynchronous Methods in WinRT

If you're developing UWP applications, you will need to work with the WinRT types defined in the operating system. WinRT's equivalent of `Task` is `IAsyncAction`, and the equivalent of `Task<TResult>` is `IAsyncOperation<TResult>`. And for operations that report progress, the equivalents are `IAsyncActionWithProgress<TProgress>` and `IAsyncOperationWithProgress<TResult, TProgress>`. They are all defined in the `Windows.Foundation` namespace.

You can convert from either into a `Task` or `Task<TResult>` via the `AsTask` extension method:

```
Task<StorageFile> fileTask = KnownFolders.DocumentsLibrary.CreateFileAsync
                                 ("test.txt").AsTask();
```

Or you can await them directly:

```
StorageFile file = await KnownFolders.DocumentsLibrary.CreateFileAsync
                             ("test.txt");
```

 Due to limitations in the COM type system, `IAsyncAction WithProgress<TProgress>` and `IAsyncOperationWithPro gress<TResult, TProgress>` are not based on `IAsyncAction` as you might expect. Instead, both inherit from a common base type called `IAsyncInfo`.

The `AsTask` method is also overloaded to accept a cancellation token (see "Cancellation" on page 659). It can also accept an `IProgress<T>` object when chained to the `WithProgress` variants (see "Progress Reporting" on page 661).

Asynchrony and Synchronization Contexts

We've already seen how the presence of a synchronization context is significant in terms of posting continuations. There are a couple of other more subtle ways in which such synchronization contexts come into play with void-returning asynchronous functions. These are not a direct result of C# compiler expansions, but a function of the `Async*MethodBuilder` types in the `System.CompilerServices` namespace that the compiler uses in expanding asynchronous functions.

Exception posting

It's common practice in rich-client applications to rely on the central exception handling event (`Application.DispatcherUnhandledException` in WPF) to process unhandled exceptions thrown on the UI thread. And in ASP.NET Core applications, a custom `ExceptionFilterAttribute` in the `ConfigureServices` method of *Startup.cs* does a similar job. Internally, they work by invoking UI events (or in ASP.NET Core, the pipeline of page-processing methods) in their own `try/catch` block.

Top-level asynchronous functions complicate this. Consider the following event handler for a button click:

```
async void ButtonClick (object sender, RoutedEventArgs args)
{
  await Task.Delay(1000);
  throw new Exception ("Will this be ignored?");
}
```

When the button is clicked and the event handler runs, execution returns normally to the message loop after the `await` statement, and the exception that's thrown a second later cannot be caught by the `catch` block in the message loop.

To mitigate this problem, `AsyncVoidMethodBuilder` catches unhandled exceptions (in void-returning asynchronous functions) and posts them to the synchronization context if present, ensuring that global exception-handling events still fire.

 The compiler applies this logic only to *void*-returning asynchronous functions. So, if we changed `ButtonClick` to return a `Task` instead of `void`, the unhandled exception would fault the resultant `Task`, which would then have nowhere to go (resulting in an *unobserved* exception).

An interesting nuance is that it makes no difference whether you throw before or after an `await`. Thus, in the following example, the exception is posted to the synchronization context (if present) and never to the caller:

```
async void Foo() { throw null; await Task.Delay(1000); }
```

(If no synchronization context is present, the exception will propagate on the thread pool, which will terminate the application.)

The reason for the exception not being thrown directly back to the caller is to ensure predictability and consistency. In the following example, the `InvalidOper ationException` will always have the same effect of faulting the resultant `Task`— regardless of *someCondition*:

```
async Task Foo()
{
  if (someCondition) await Task.Delay (100);
  throw new InvalidOperationException();
}
```

Iterators work in a similar way:

```
IEnumerable<int> Foo() { throw null; yield return 123; }
```

In this example, an exception is never thrown straight back to the caller: not until the sequence is enumerated is the exception thrown.

OperationStarted and OperationCompleted

If a synchronization context is present, void-returning asynchronous functions also call its `OperationStarted` method upon entering the function, and its `Operation Completed` method when the function finishes.

Overriding these methods is useful if writing a custom synchronization context for unit testing void-returning asynchronous methods. This is discussed on Microsoft's Parallel Programming blog (*https://devblogs.microsoft.com/pfxteam*).

Optimizations

Completing synchronously

An asynchronous function can return *before* awaiting. Consider the following method that caches the downloading of web pages:

```
static Dictionary<string,string> _cache = new Dictionary<string,string>();

async Task<string> GetWebPageAsync (string uri)
{
  string html;
  if (_cache.TryGetValue (uri, out html)) return html;
  return _cache [uri] =
    await new WebClient().DownloadStringTaskAsync (uri);
}
```

Should a URI already exist in the cache, execution returns to the caller with no awaiting having occurred, and the method returns an *already-signaled* task. This is referred to as *synchronous completion*.

When you await a synchronously completed task, execution does not return to the caller and bounce back via a continuation; instead, it proceeds immediately to the next statement. The compiler implements this optimization by checking the `IsCompleted` property on the awaiter; in other words, whenever you await

```
Console.WriteLine (await GetWebPageAsync ("http://oreilly.com"));
```

the compiler emits code to short-circuit the continuation in case of synchronization completion:

```
var awaiter = GetWebPageAsync().GetAwaiter();
if (awaiter.IsCompleted)
  Console.WriteLine (awaiter.GetResult());
else
  awaiter.OnCompleted (() => Console.WriteLine (awaiter.GetResult()));
```

Awaiting an asynchronous function that returns synchronously still incurs a (very) small overhead—maybe 20 nanoseconds on a 2019-era PC.

In contrast, bouncing to the thread pool introduces the cost of a context switch—perhaps one or two microseconds—and bouncing to a UI message loop, at least 10 times that (much longer if the UI thread is busy).

It's even legal to write asynchronous methods that *never* await, although the compiler will generate a warning:

```
async Task<string> Foo() { return "abc"; }
```

Such methods can be useful when overriding virtual/abstract methods, if your implementation doesn't happen to need asynchrony. (An example is MemoryStream's ReadAsync/WriteAsync methods; see Chapter 15.) Another way to achieve the same result is to use Task.FromResult, which returns an already-signaled task:

```
Task<string> Foo() { return Task.FromResult ("abc"); }
```

Our GetWebPageAsync method is implicitly thread safe if called from a UI thread, in that you could invoke it several times in succession (thereby initiating multiple concurrent downloads), and no locking is required to protect the cache. If the series of calls were to the same URI, though, we'd end up initiating multiple redundant downloads, all of which would eventually update the same cache entry (the last one winning). Although not erroneous, it would be more efficient if subsequent calls to the same URI could instead (asynchronously) wait upon the result of the in-progress request.

There's an easy way to accomplish this—without resorting to locks or signaling constructs. Instead of a cache of strings, we create a cache of "futures" (Task<string>):

```
static Dictionary<string,Task<string>> _cache =
  new Dictionary<string,Task<string>>();

Task<string> GetWebPageAsync (string uri)
{
  if (_cache.TryGetValue (uri, out var downloadTask)) return downloadTask;
  return _cache [uri] = new WebClient().DownloadStringTaskAsync (uri);
}
```

(Notice that we don't mark the method as async, because we're directly returning the task we obtain from calling WebClient's method.)

If we call GetWebPageAsync repeatedly with the same URI, we're now guaranteed to get the same Task<string> object back. (This has the additional benefit of minimizing garbage collection load.) And if the task is complete, awaiting it is cheap, thanks to the compiler optimization that we just discussed.

We could further extend our example to make it thread-safe without the protection of a synchronization context, by locking around the entire method body:

```
lock (_cache)
  if (_cache.TryGetValue (uri, out var downloadTask))
    return downloadTask;
  else
    return _cache [uri] = new WebClient().DownloadStringTaskAsync (uri);
}
```

This works because we're not locking for the duration of downloading a page
(which would hurt concurrency); we're locking for the small duration of checking
the cache, starting a new task if necessary, and updating the cache with that task.

ValueTask<T>

 ValueTask<T> is intended for micro-optimization scenarios,
and you might never need to write methods that return this
type. However, it still pays to be aware of the precautions that
we outline in the next section because some .NET methods
return ValueTask<T>, and IAsyncEnumerable<T> makes use
of it, too.

We just described how the compiler optimizes an await expression on a synchronously completed task—by short-circuiting the continuation and proceeding immediately to the next statement. If the synchronous completion is due to caching, we
saw that caching the task itself can provide an elegant and efficient solution.

It's not practical, however, to cache the task in all synchronous completion scenarios. Sometimes, a fresh task must be instantiated, and this creates a (tiny) potential inefficiency. This is because Task and Task<T> are reference types, and so
instantiation requires a heap-based memory allocation and subsequent collection.
An extreme form of optimization is to write code that's allocation-free; in other
words, that does not instantiate any reference types, adding no burden to garbage
collection. To support this pattern, the ValueTask and ValueTask<T> structs have
been introduced, which the compiler allows in place of Task and Task<T>:

```
async ValueTask<int> Foo() { ... }
```

Awaiting ValueTask<T> is allocation-free, *if the operation completes synchronously*:

```
int answer = await Foo();   // (Potentially) allocation-free
```

If the operation doesn't complete synchronously, ValueTask<T> creates an ordinary
Task<T> behind the scenes (to which it forwards the await), and nothing is gained.

You can convert a ValueTask<T> into an ordinary Task<T> by calling the AsTask
method.

There's also a nongeneric version—ValueTask—which is akin to Task.

Precautions when using ValueTask<T>

ValueTask<T> is relatively unusual in that it's defined as a struct *purely* for performance reasons. This means that it's encumbered with *inappropriate* value-type

semantics that can lead to surprises. To avoid incorrect behavior, you must avoid the following:

- Awaiting the same ValueTask<T> multiple times
- Calling .GetAwaiter().GetResult() when the operation hasn't completed

If you need to perform these actions, call .AsTask() and operate instead on the resulting Task.

 The easiest way to avoid these traps is to directly await a method call, for instance:

```
await Foo();    // Safe
```

The door to erroneous behavior opens when you assign the (value) task to a variable:

```
ValueTask<int> valueTask = Foo();   // Caution!
// Our use of valueTask can now lead to errors.
```

which can be mitigated by converting immediately to an ordinary task:

```
Task<int> task = Foo().AsTask();    // Safe
// task is safe to work with.
```

Avoiding excessive bouncing

For methods that are called many times in a loop, you can avoid the cost of repeatedly bouncing to a UI message loop by calling ConfigureAwait. This forces a task not to bounce continuations to the synchronization context, cutting the overhead closer to the cost of a context switch (or much less if the method that you're awaiting completes synchronously):

```
async void A() { ... await B(); ... }

async Task B()
{
  for (int i = 0; i < 1000; i++)
    await C().ConfigureAwait (false);
}

async Task C() { ... }
```

This means that for the B and C methods, we rescind the simple thread-safety model in UI apps whereby code runs on the UI thread and can be preempted only during an await statement. Method A, however, is unaffected and will remain on a UI thread if it started on one.

This optimization is particularly relevant when writing libraries: you don't need the benefit of simplified thread-safety because your code typically does not share state with the caller—and does not access UI controls. (It would also make sense, in our example, for method C to complete synchronously if it knew the operation was likely to be short-running.)

Asynchronous Patterns

Cancellation

It's often important to be able to cancel a concurrent operation after it's started, perhaps in response to a user request. A simple way to implement this is with a cancellation flag, which we could encapsulate by writing a class like this:

```
class CancellationToken
{
  public bool IsCancellationRequested { get; private set; }
  public void Cancel() { IsCancellationRequested = true; }
  public void ThrowIfCancellationRequested()
  {
    if (IsCancellationRequested)
      throw new OperationCanceledException();
  }
}
```

We could then write a cancellable asynchronous method as follows:

```
async Task Foo (CancellationToken cancellationToken)
{
  for (int i = 0; i < 10; i++)
  {
    Console.WriteLine (i);
    await Task.Delay (1000);
    cancellationToken.ThrowIfCancellationRequested();
  }
}
```

When the caller wants to cancel, it calls Cancel on the cancellation token that it passed into Foo. This sets IsCancellationRequested to true, which causes Foo to fault a short time later with an OperationCanceledException (a predefined exception in the System namespace designed for this purpose).

Thread-safety aside (we should be locking around reading/writing IsCancellation Requested), this pattern is effective, and the CLR provides a type called Cancella tionToken that is very similar to what we've just shown. However, it lacks a Cancel method; this method is instead exposed on another type called CancellationToken Source. This separation provides some security: a method that has access only to a CancellationToken object can check for but not *initiate* cancellation.

To get a cancellation token, we first instantiate a CancellationTokenSource:

```
var cancelSource = new CancellationTokenSource();
```

This exposes a Token property, which returns a CancellationToken. Hence, we could call our Foo method, as follows:

```
var cancelSource = new CancellationTokenSource();
Task foo = Foo (cancelSource.Token);
...
```

```
... (sometime later)
cancelSource.Cancel();
```

Most asynchronous methods in the CLR support cancellation tokens, including
Delay. If we modify Foo such that it passes its token into the Delay method, the task
will end immediately upon request (rather than up to a second later):

```
async Task Foo (CancellationToken cancellationToken)
{
  for (int i = 0; i < 10; i++)
  {
    Console.WriteLine (i);
    await Task.Delay (1000, cancellationToken);
  }
}
```

Notice that we no longer need to call ThrowIfCancellationRequested because
Task.Delay is doing that for us. Cancellation tokens propagate nicely down the
call stack (just as cancellation requests cascade *up* the call stack, by virtue of being
exceptions).

 UWP relies on WinRT types, whose asynchronous methods
follow an inferior protocol for cancellation whereby instead of
accepting a CancellationToken, the IAsyncInfo type exposes
a Cancel method. The AsTask extension method is overloaded
to accept a cancellation token, however, bridging the gap.

Synchronous methods can support cancellation, too (such as Task's Wait method).
In such cases, the instruction to cancel will need to come asynchronously (e.g., from
another task). For example:

```
var cancelSource = new CancellationTokenSource();
Task.Delay (5000).ContinueWith (ant => cancelSource.Cancel());
...
```

In fact, you can specify a time interval when constructing CancellationToken
Source to initiate cancellation after a set period of time (just as we demonstrated).
It's useful for implementing timeouts, whether synchronous or asynchronous:

```
var cancelSource = new CancellationTokenSource (5000);
try { await Foo (cancelSource.Token); }
catch (OperationCanceledException ex) { Console.WriteLine ("Cancelled"); }
```

The CancellationToken struct provides a Register method that lets you register a
callback delegate that will be fired upon cancellation; it returns an object that can be
disposed to undo the registration.

Tasks generated by the compiler's asynchronous functions automatically enter a
"Canceled" state upon an unhandled OperationCanceledException (IsCanceled
returns true, and IsFaulted returns false). The same goes for tasks created with
Task.Run for which you pass the (same) CancellationToken to the constructor. The
distinction between a faulted and a canceled task is unimportant in asynchronous
scenarios, in that both throw an OperationCanceledException when awaited; it

matters in advanced parallel programming scenarios (specifically conditional continuations). We pick up this topic in "Canceling Tasks" on page 933.

Progress Reporting

Sometimes, you'll want an asynchronous operation to report back progress as it's running. A simple solution is to pass an `Action` delegate to the asynchronous method, which the method fires whenever progress changes:

```
Task Foo (Action<int> onProgressPercentChanged)
{
  return Task.Run (() =>
  {
    for (int i = 0; i < 1000; i++)
    {
      if (i % 10 == 0) onProgressPercentChanged (i / 10);
      // Do something compute-bound...
    }
  });
}
```

Here's how we could call it:

```
Action<int> progress = i => Console.WriteLine (i + " %");
await Foo (progress);
```

Although this works well in a console application, it's not ideal in rich-client scenarios because it reports progress from a worker thread, causing potential thread-safety issues for the consumer. (In effect, we've allowed a side effect of concurrency to "leak" to the outside world, which is unfortunate given that the method is otherwise isolated if called from a UI thread.)

IProgress<T> and Progress<T>

The CLR provides a pair of types to solve this problem: an interface called `IProgress<T>` and a class that implements this interface called `Progress<T>`. Their purpose, in effect, is to "wrap" a delegate so that UI applications can report progress safely through the synchronization context.

The interface defines just one method:

```
public interface IProgress<in T>
{
  void Report (T value);
}
```

Using `IProgress<T>` is easy; our method hardly changes:

```
Task Foo (IProgress<int> onProgressPercentChanged)
{
  return Task.Run (() =>
  {
    for (int i = 0; i < 1000; i++)
    {
      if (i % 10 == 0) onProgressPercentChanged.Report (i / 10);
```

```
        // Do something compute-bound...
    }
  });
}
```

The `Progress<T>` class has a constructor that accepts a delegate of type `Action<T>` that it wraps:

```
var progress = new Progress<int> (i => Console.WriteLine (i + " %"));
await Foo (progress);
```

(`Progress<T>` also has a `ProgressChanged` event that you can subscribe to instead of [or in addition to] passing an action delegate to the constructor.) Upon instantiating `Progress<int>`, the class captures the synchronization context, if present. When `Foo` then calls `Report`, the delegate is invoked through that context.

Asynchronous methods can implement more elaborate progress reporting by replacing `int` with a custom type that exposes a range of properties.

> If you're familiar with Rx, you'll notice that `IProgress<T>` together with the task returned by the asynchronous function provide a feature set similar to `IObserver<T>`. The difference is that a task can expose a "final" return value *in addition* to (and differently typed to) the values emitted by `IProgress<T>`.
>
> Values emitted by `IProgress<T>` are typically "throwaway" values (e.g., percent complete or bytes downloaded so far), whereas values pushed by `IObserver<T>`'s `OnNext` typically comprise the result itself and are the very reason for calling it.

Asynchronous methods in WinRT also offer progress reporting, although the protocol is complicated by COM's (relatively) primitive type system. Instead of accepting an `IProgress<T>` object, asynchronous WinRT methods that report progress return one of the following interfaces, in place of `IAsyncAction` and `IAsyncOperation<TResult>`:

```
IAsyncActionWithProgress<TProgress>
IAsyncOperationWithProgress<TResult, TProgress>
```

Interestingly, both are based on `IAsyncInfo` (not `IAsyncAction` and `IAsyncOperation<TResult>`).

The good news is that the `AsTask` extension method is also overloaded to accept `IProgress<T>` for the aforementioned interfaces, so as a .NET consumer, you can ignore the COM interfaces and do this:

```
var progress = new Progress<int> (i => Console.WriteLine (i + " %"));
CancellationToken cancelToken = ...
var task = someWinRTobject.FooAsync().AsTask (cancelToken, progress);
```

The Task-Based Asynchronous Pattern

.NET exposes hundreds of task-returning asynchronous methods that you can `await` (mainly related to I/O). Most of these methods (at least partly) follow a pattern called the *Task-Based Asynchronous Pattern* (TAP), which is a sensible formalization of what we have described to date. A TAP method does the following:

- Returns a "hot" (running) `Task` or `Task<TResult>`
- Has an "Async" suffix (except for special cases such as task combinators)
- Is overloaded to accept a cancellation token and/or `IProgress<T>` if it supports cancellation and/or progress reporting
- Returns quickly to the caller (has only a small initial *synchronous phase*)
- Does not tie up a thread if I/O-bound

As we've seen, TAP methods are easy to write with C#'s asynchronous functions.

Task Combinators

A nice consequence of there being a consistent protocol for asynchronous functions (whereby they consistently return tasks) is that it's possible to use and write *task combinators*—functions that usefully combine tasks, without regard for what those specific tasks do.

The CLR includes two task combinators: `Task.WhenAny` and `Task.WhenAll`. In describing them, we'll assume the following methods are defined:

```
async Task<int> Delay1() { await Task.Delay (1000); return 1; }
async Task<int> Delay2() { await Task.Delay (2000); return 2; }
async Task<int> Delay3() { await Task.Delay (3000); return 3; }
```

WhenAny

`Task.WhenAny` returns a task that completes when any one of a set of tasks complete. The following completes in one second:

```
Task<int> winningTask = await Task.WhenAny (Delay1(), Delay2(), Delay3());
Console.WriteLine ("Done");
Console.WriteLine (winningTask.Result);   // 1
```

Because `Task.WhenAny` itself returns a task, we await it, which returns the task that finished first. Our example is entirely nonblocking—including the last line when we access the `Result` property (because `winningTask` will already have finished). Nonetheless, it's usually better to `await` the `winningTask`:

```
Console.WriteLine (await winningTask);   // 1
```

because any exceptions are then rethrown without an `AggregateException` wrapping. In fact, we can perform both `await`s in one step:

```
int answer = await await Task.WhenAny (Delay1(), Delay2(), Delay3());
```

Concurrency and Asynchrony

If a nonwinning task subsequently faults, the exception will go unobserved unless you subsequently await the task (or query its Exception property).

WhenAny is useful for applying timeouts or cancellation to operations that don't otherwise support it:

```
Task<string> task = SomeAsyncFunc();
Task winner = await (Task.WhenAny (task, Task.Delay(5000)));
if (winner != task) throw new TimeoutException();
string result = await task;   // Unwrap result/re-throw
```

Notice that because in this case we're calling WhenAny with differently typed tasks, the winner is reported as a plain Task (rather than a Task<string>).

WhenAll

Task.WhenAll returns a task that completes when *all* of the tasks that you pass to it complete. The following completes after three seconds (and demonstrates the *fork/join* pattern):

```
await Task.WhenAll (Delay1(), Delay2(), Delay3());
```

We could get a similar result by awaiting task1, task2, and task3 in turn rather than using WhenAll:

```
Task task1 = Delay1(), task2 = Delay2(), task3 = Delay3();
await task1; await task2; await task3;
```

The difference (apart from it being less efficient by virtue of requiring three awaits rather than one) is that should task1 fault, we'll never get to await task2/task3, and any of their exceptions will go unobserved.

In contrast, Task.WhenAll doesn't complete until all tasks have completed—even when there's a fault. And if there are multiple faults, their exceptions are combined into the task's AggregateException (this is when AggregateException actually becomes useful—should you be interested in all the exceptions, that is). Awaiting the combined task, however, throws only the first exception, so to see all the exceptions, you need to do this:

```
Task task1 = Task.Run (() => { throw null; } );
Task task2 = Task.Run (() => { throw null; } );
Task all = Task.WhenAll (task1, task2);
try { await all; }
catch
{
   Console.WriteLine (all.Exception.InnerExceptions.Count);   // 2
}
```

Calling WhenAll with tasks of type Task<TResult> returns a Task<TResult[]>, giving the combined results of all the tasks. This reduces to a TResult[] when awaited:

```
Task<int> task1 = Task.Run (() => 1);
Task<int> task2 = Task.Run (() => 2);
int[] results = await Task.WhenAll (task1, task2);   // { 1, 2 }
```

To give a practical example, the following downloads URIs in parallel and sums their total length:

```
async Task<int> GetTotalSize (string[] uris)
{
  IEnumerable<Task<byte[]>> downloadTasks = uris.Select (uri =>
    new WebClient().DownloadDataTaskAsync (uri));

  byte[][] contents = await Task.WhenAll (downloadTasks);
  return contents.Sum (c => c.Length);
}
```

There's a slight inefficiency here, though, in that we're unnecessarily hanging onto the byte arrays that we download until every task is complete. It would be more efficient if we collapsed byte arrays into their lengths immediately after downloading them. This is where an asynchronous lambda comes in handy because we need to feed an await expression into LINQ's Select query operator:

```
async Task<int> GetTotalSize (string[] uris)
{
  IEnumerable<Task<int>> downloadTasks = uris.Select (async uri =>
    (await new WebClient().DownloadDataTaskAsync (uri)).Length);

  int[] contentLengths = await Task.WhenAll (downloadTasks);
  return contentLengths.Sum();
}
```

Custom combinators

It can be useful to write your own task combinators. The simplest "combinator" accepts a single task, such as the following, which lets you await any task with a timeout:

```
async static Task<TResult> WithTimeout<TResult> (this Task<TResult> task,
                                                  TimeSpan timeout)
{
  Task winner = await Task.WhenAny (task, Task.Delay (timeout))
                          .ConfigureAwait (false);
  if (winner != task) throw new TimeoutException();
  return await task.ConfigureAwait (false);   // Unwrap result/re-throw
}
```

Because this is very much a "library method" that doesn't access external shared state, we use ConfigureAwait(false) when awaiting to avoid potentially bouncing to a UI synchronization context. We can further improve efficiency by canceling the Task.Delay when the task completes on time (this avoids the small overhead of a timer hanging around):

```
async static Task<TResult> WithTimeout<TResult> (this Task<TResult> task,
                                                  TimeSpan timeout)
{
```

```
var cancelSource = new CancellationTokenSource();
var delay = Task.Delay (timeout, cancelSource.Token);
Task winner = await Task.WhenAny (task, delay).ConfigureAwait (false);
if (winner == task)
  cancelSource.Cancel();
else
  throw new TimeoutException();
return await task.ConfigureAwait (false);   // Unwrap result/re-throw
}
```

The following lets you "abandon" a task via a CancellationToken:

```
static Task<TResult> WithCancellation<TResult> (this Task<TResult> task,
                                                CancellationToken cancelToken)
{
  var tcs = new TaskCompletionSource<TResult>();
  var reg = cancelToken.Register (() => tcs.TrySetCanceled ());
  task.ContinueWith (ant =>
  {
    reg.Dispose();
    if (ant.IsCanceled)
      tcs.TrySetCanceled();
    else if (ant.IsFaulted)
      tcs.TrySetException (ant.Exception.InnerException);
    else
      tcs.TrySetResult (ant.Result);
  });
  return tcs.Task;
}
```

Task combinators can be complex to write, sometimes requiring the use of signaling constructs, which we cover in Chapter 21. This is actually a good thing, because it keeps concurrency-related complexity out of your business logic and into reusable methods that can be tested in isolation.

The next combinator works like WhenAll, except that if any of the tasks fault, the resultant task faults immediately:

```
async Task<TResult[]> WhenAllOrError<TResult>
  (params Task<TResult>[] tasks)
{
  var killJoy = new TaskCompletionSource<TResult[]>();
  foreach (var task in tasks)
    task.ContinueWith (ant =>
    {
      if (ant.IsCanceled)
        killJoy.TrySetCanceled();
      else if (ant.IsFaulted)
        killJoy.TrySetException (ant.Exception.InnerException);
    });
  return await await Task.WhenAny (killJoy.Task, Task.WhenAll (tasks))
                    .ConfigureAwait (false);
}
```

We begin by creating a `TaskCompletionSource` whose sole job is to end the party if a task faults. Hence, we never call its `SetResult` method, only its `TrySetCanceled` and `TrySetException` methods. In this case, `ContinueWith` is more convenient than `GetAwaiter().OnCompleted` because we're not accessing the tasks' results and wouldn't want to bounce to a UI thread at that point.

Asynchronous Locking

In "Asynchronous semaphores and locks" on page 881, we describe how to use `SemaphoreSlim` to lock or limit concurrency asynchronously.

Obsolete Patterns

.NET employs other patterns for asynchrony, which precede tasks and asynchronous functions. These are rarely required now that task-based asynchrony has become the dominant pattern.

Asynchronous Programming Model

The oldest pattern is called the *Asynchronous Programming Model* (APM) and uses a pair of methods starting in "Begin" and "End" and an interface called `IAsyncResult`. To illustrate, let's take the `Stream` class in `System.IO` and look at its `Read` method. First, the synchronous version:

```
public int Read (byte[] buffer, int offset, int size);
```

You can probably predict what the *task*-based asynchronous version looks like:

```
public Task<int> ReadAsync (byte[] buffer, int offset, int size);
```

Now let's examine the APM version:

```
public IAsyncResult BeginRead (byte[] buffer, int offset, int size,
                               AsyncCallback callback, object state);
public int EndRead (IAsyncResult asyncResult);
```

Calling the `Begin*` method initiates the operation, returning an `IAsyncResult` object that acts as a token for the asynchronous operation. When the operation completes (or faults), the `AsyncCallback` delegate fires:

```
public delegate void AsyncCallback (IAsyncResult ar);
```

Whoever handles this delegate then calls the `End*` method, which provides the operation's return value as well as rethrowing an exception if the operation faulted.

The APM is not only awkward to use but is surprisingly difficult to implement correctly. The easiest way to deal with APM methods is to call the `Task.Factory.FromAsync` adapter method, which converts an APM method pair into a `Task`. Internally, it uses a `TaskCompletionSource` to give you a task that's signaled when an APM operation completes or faults.

The FromAsync method requires the following parameters:

- A delegate specifying a Begin*XXX* method
- A delegate specifying an End*XXX* method
- Additional arguments that will get passed to these methods

FromAsync is overloaded to accept delegate types and arguments that match nearly all the asynchronous method signatures found in .NET. For instance, assuming stream is a Stream and buffer is a byte[], we could do this:

```
Task<int> readChunk = Task<int>.Factory.FromAsync (
    stream.BeginRead, stream.EndRead, buffer, 0, 1000, null);
```

Event-Based Asynchronous Pattern

The *Event-Based Asynchronous Pattern* (EAP) was introduced in 2005 to provide a simpler alternative to the APM, particularly in UI scenarios. It was implemented in only a handful of types, however, most notably WebClient in System.Net. The EAP is just a pattern; no types are provided to assist. Essentially the pattern is this: a class offers a family of members that internally manage concurrency, similar to the following:

```
// These members are from the WebClient class:

public byte[] DownloadData (Uri address);      // Synchronous version
public void DownloadDataAsync (Uri address);
public void DownloadDataAsync (Uri address, object userToken);
public event DownloadDataCompletedEventHandler DownloadDataCompleted;

public void CancelAsync (object userState);  // Cancels an operation
public bool IsBusy { get; }                  // Indicates if still running
```

The *Async methods initiate an operation asynchronously. When the operation completes, the *Completed event fires (automatically posting to the captured synchronization context if present). This event passes back an event arguments object that contains the following:

- A flag indicating whether the operation was canceled (by the consumer calling CancelAsync)
- An Error object indicating an exception that was thrown (if any)
- The userToken object if supplied when calling the Async method

EAP types can also expose a progress reporting event, which fires whenever progress changes (also posted through the synchronization context):

```
public event DownloadProgressChangedEventHandler DownloadProgressChanged;
```

Implementing the EAP requires a large amount of boilerplate code, making the pattern poorly compositional.

BackgroundWorker

BackgroundWorker in System.ComponentModel is a general-purpose implementation of the EAP. It allows rich-client apps to start a worker thread and report completion and percentage-based progress without needing to explicitly capture synchronization context. Here's an example:

```
var worker = new BackgroundWorker { WorkerSupportsCancellation = true };
worker.DoWork += (sender, args) =>
{                                       // This runs on a worker thread
  if (args.Cancel) return;
  Thread.Sleep(1000);
  args.Result = 123;
};
worker.RunWorkerCompleted += (sender, args) =>
{                                       // Runs on UI thread
  // We can safely update UI controls here...
  if (args.Cancelled)
    Console.WriteLine ("Cancelled");
  else if (args.Error != null)
    Console.WriteLine ("Error: " + args.Error.Message);
  else
    Console.WriteLine ("Result is: " + args.Result);
};
worker.RunWorkerAsync();   // Captures sync context and starts operation
```

RunWorkerAsync starts the operation, firing the DoWork event on a pooled worker thread. It also captures the synchronization context, and when the operation completes (or faults), the RunWorkerCompleted event is invoked through that synchronization context (like a continuation).

BackgroundWorker creates coarse-grained concurrency, in that the DoWork event runs entirely on a worker thread. If you need to update UI controls in that event handler (other than posting a percentage-complete message), you must use Dispatcher.BeginInvoke or similar).

We describe BackgroundWorker in more detail at *http://albahari.com/threading*.

15

Streams and I/O

This chapter describes the fundamental types for input and output in .NET, with emphasis on the following topics:

- The .NET stream architecture and how it provides a consistent programming interface for reading and writing across a variety of I/O types
- Classes for manipulating files and directories on disk
- Specialized streams for compression, named pipes, and memory-mapped files.

This chapter concentrates on the types in the System.IO namespace, the home of lower-level I/O functionality.

Stream Architecture

The .NET stream architecture centers on three concepts: backing stores, decorators, and adapters, as shown in Figure 15-1.

A *backing store* is the endpoint that makes input and output useful, such as a file or network connection. Precisely, it is either or both of the following:

- A source from which bytes can be sequentially read
- A destination to which bytes can be sequentially written

A backing store is of no use, though, unless exposed to the programmer. A Stream is the standard .NET class for this purpose; it exposes a standard set of methods for reading, writing, and positioning. Unlike an array, for which all the backing data exists in memory at once, a stream deals with data serially—either one byte at a time or in blocks of a manageable size. Hence, a stream can use a small, fixed amount of memory regardless of the size of its backing store.

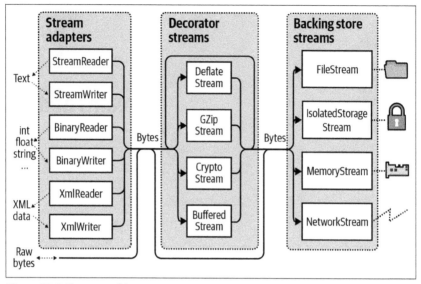

Figure 15-1. Stream architecture

Streams fall into two categories:

Backing store streams
> These are hardwired to a particular type of backing store, such as `FileStream` or `NetworkStream`.

Decorator streams
> These feed off another stream, transforming the data in some way, such as `DeflateStream` or `CryptoStream`.

Decorator streams have the following architectural benefits:

- They liberate backing store streams from needing to implement such features as compression and encryption themselves.
- Streams don't suffer a change of interface when decorated.
- You connect decorators at runtime.
- You can chain decorators together (e.g., a compressor followed by an encryptor).

Both backing store and decorator streams deal exclusively in bytes. Although this is flexible and efficient, applications often work at higher levels, such as text or XML. *Adapters* bridge this gap by wrapping a stream in a class with specialized methods typed to a particular format. For example, a text reader exposes a `ReadLine` method; an XML writer exposes a `WriteAttributes` method.

An adapter wraps a stream, just like a decorator. Unlike a decorator, however, an adapter is not *itself* a stream; it typically hides the byte-oriented methods completely.

To summarize, backing store streams provide the raw data, decorator streams provide transparent binary transformations such as encryption, and adapters offer typed methods for dealing in higher-level types such as strings and XML. Figure 15-1 illustrates their associations. To compose a chain, you simply pass one object into another's constructor.

Using Streams

The abstract `Stream` class is the base for all streams. It defines methods and properties for three fundamental operations: *reading*, *writing*, and *seeking*, as well as for administrative tasks such as closing, flushing, and configuring timeouts (see Table 15-1).

Table 15-1. Stream class members

Category	Members
Reading	`public abstract bool CanRead { get; }`
	`public abstract int Read (byte[] buffer, int offset, int count)`
	`public virtual int ReadByte();`
Writing	`public abstract bool CanWrite { get; }`
	`public abstract void Write (byte[] buffer, int offset, int count);`
	`public virtual void WriteByte (byte value);`
Seeking	`public abstract bool CanSeek { get; }`
	`public abstract long Position { get; set; }`
	`public abstract void SetLength (long value);`
	`public abstract long Length { get; }`
	`public abstract long Seek (long offset, SeekOrigin origin);`
Closing/ flushing	`public virtual void Close();`
	`public void Dispose();`
	`public abstract void Flush();`
Timeouts	`public virtual bool CanTimeout { get; }`
	`public virtual int ReadTimeout { get; set; }`
	`public virtual int WriteTimeout { get; set; }`
Other	`public static readonly Stream Null; // "Null" stream`
	`public static Stream Synchronized (Stream stream);`

There are also asynchronous versions of the Read and Write methods, both of which return Tasks and optionally accept a cancellation token, and overloads that work with Span<T> and Memory<T> types that we describe in Chapter 23.

In the following example, we use a file stream to read, write, and seek:

```
using System;
using System.IO;

// Create a file called test.txt in the current directory:
using (Stream s = new FileStream ("test.txt", FileMode.Create))
{
  Console.WriteLine (s.CanRead);       // True
  Console.WriteLine (s.CanWrite);      // True
  Console.WriteLine (s.CanSeek);       // True

  s.WriteByte (101);
  s.WriteByte (102);
  byte[] block = { 1, 2, 3, 4, 5 };
  s.Write (block, 0, block.Length);    // Write block of 5 bytes

  Console.WriteLine (s.Length);        // 7
  Console.WriteLine (s.Position);      // 7
  s.Position = 0;                      // Move back to the start

  Console.WriteLine (s.ReadByte());    // 101
  Console.WriteLine (s.ReadByte());    // 102

  // Read from the stream back into the block array:
  Console.WriteLine (s.Read (block, 0, block.Length));    // 5

  // Assuming the last Read returned 5, we'll be at
  // the end of the file, so Read will now return 0:
  Console.WriteLine (s.Read (block, 0, block.Length));    // 0
}
```

Reading or writing asynchronously is simply a question of calling ReadAsync/Write Async instead of Read/Write, and awaiting the expression (we must also add the async keyword to the calling method, as we described in Chapter 14):

```
async static void AsyncDemo()
{
  using (Stream s = new FileStream ("test.txt", FileMode.Create))
  {
    byte[] block = { 1, 2, 3, 4, 5 };
    await s.WriteAsync (block, 0, block.Length);     // Write asychronously

    s.Position = 0;                                  // Move back to the start

    // Read from the stream back into the block array:
    Console.WriteLine (await s.ReadAsync (block, 0, block.Length));    // 5
  }
}
```

The asynchronous methods make it easy to write responsive and scalable applications that work with potentially slow streams (particularly network streams), without tying up a thread.

 For the sake of brevity, we'll continue to use synchronous methods for most of the examples in this chapter; however, we recommend the asynchronous Read/Write operations as preferable in most scenarios involving network I/O.

Reading and Writing

A stream can support reading, writing, or both. If CanWrite returns false, the stream is read-only; if CanRead returns false, the stream is write-only.

Read receives a block of data from the stream into an array. It returns the number of bytes received, which is always either less than or equal to the count argument. If it's less than count, it means that either the end of the stream has been reached or the stream is giving you the data in smaller chunks (as is often the case with network streams). In either case, the balance of bytes in the array will remain unwritten, their previous values preserved.

 With Read, you can be certain you've reached the end of the stream only when the method returns 0. So, if you have a 1,000-byte stream, the following code might fail to read it all into memory:

```
// Assuming s is a stream:
byte[] data = new byte [1000];
s.Read (data, 0, data.Length);
```

The Read method could read anywhere from 1 to 1,000 bytes, leaving the balance of the stream unread.

Here's the correct way to read a 1,000-byte stream:

```
byte[] data = new byte [1000];

// bytesRead will always end up at 1000, unless the stream is
// itself smaller in length:

int bytesRead = 0;
int chunkSize = 1;
while (bytesRead < data.Length && chunkSize > 0)
  bytesRead +=
    chunkSize = s.Read (data, bytesRead, data.Length - bytesRead);
```

Fortunately, the `BinaryReader` type provides a simpler way to achieve the same result:

```
byte[] data = new BinaryReader (s).ReadBytes (1000);
```

If the stream is less than 1,000 bytes long, the byte array returned reflects the actual stream size. If the stream is seekable, you can read its entire contents by replacing `1000` with `(int)s.Length`.

We describe the `BinaryReader` type further in "Stream Adapters" on page 687.

The `ReadByte` method is simpler: it reads just a single byte, returning –1 to indicate the end of the stream. `ReadByte` actually returns an `int` rather than a `byte` because the latter cannot return –1.

The `Write` and `WriteByte` methods send data to the stream. If they are unable to send the specified bytes, an exception is thrown.

In the `Read` and `Write` methods, the `offset` argument refers to the index in the `buffer` array at which reading or writing begins, not the position within the stream.

Seeking

A stream is seekable if `CanSeek` returns `true`. With a seekable stream (such as a file stream), you can query or modify its `Length` (by calling `SetLength`) and at any time change the `Position` at which you're reading or writing. The `Position` property is relative to the beginning of the stream; the `Seek` method, however, allows you to move relative to the current position or the end of the stream.

Changing the `Position` on a `FileStream` typically takes a few microseconds. If you're doing this millions of times in a loop, the `MemoryMappedFile` class might be a better choice than a `FileStream` (see "Memory-Mapped Files" on page 712).

With a nonseekable stream (such as an encryption stream), the only way to determine its length is to read it completely through. Furthermore, if you need to reread a previous section, you must close the stream and start afresh with a new one.

Closing and Flushing

Streams must be disposed after use to release underlying resources such as file and socket handles. A simple way to guarantee this is by instantiating streams within `using` blocks. In general, streams follow standard disposal semantics:

- `Dispose` and `Close` are identical in function.
- Disposing or closing a stream repeatedly causes no error.

Closing a decorator stream closes both the decorator and its backing store stream. With a chain of decorators, closing the outermost decorator (at the head of the chain) closes the whole lot.

Some streams internally buffer data to and from the backing store to lessen round-tripping and so improve performance (file streams are a good example of this). This means that data you write to a stream might not hit the backing store immediately; it can be delayed as the buffer fills up. The Flush method forces any internally buffered data to be written immediately. Flush is called automatically when a stream is closed, so you never need to do the following:

```
s.Flush(); s.Close();
```

Timeouts

A stream supports read and write timeouts if CanTimeout returns true. Network streams support timeouts; file and memory streams do not. For streams that support timeouts, the ReadTimeout and WriteTimeout properties determine the desired timeout in milliseconds, where 0 means no timeout. The Read and Write methods indicate that a timeout has occurred by throwing an exception.

The asynchronous ReadAsync/WriteAsync methods do not support timeouts; instead you can pass a cancellation token into these methods.

Thread Safety

As a rule, streams are not thread-safe, meaning that two threads cannot concurrently read or write to the same stream without possible error. The Stream class offers a simple workaround via the static Synchronized method. This method accepts a stream of any type and returns a thread-safe wrapper. The wrapper works by obtaining an exclusive lock around each read, write, or seek, ensuring that only one thread can perform such an operation at a time. In practice, this allows multiple threads to simultaneously append data to the same stream—other kinds of activities (such as concurrent reading) require additional locking to ensure that each thread accesses the desired portion of the stream. We discuss thread safety fully in Chapter 21.

From .NET 6, you can use the RandomAccess class for performant thread-safe file I/O operations. RandomAccess also lets you pass in multiple buffers to improve performance.

Backing Store Streams

Figure 15-2 shows the key backing store streams provided by .NET. A "null stream" is also available via the Stream's static Null field. Null streams can be useful when writing unit tests.

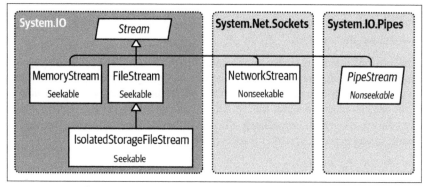

Figure 15-2. Backing store streams

In the following sections, we describe `FileStream` and `MemoryStream`; in the final section in this chapter, we describe `IsolatedStorageStream`. In Chapter 16, we cover `NetworkStream`.

FileStream

Earlier in this section, we demonstrated the basic use of a `FileStream` to read and write bytes of data. Let's now examine the special features of this class.

 If you're using Universal Windows Platform (UWP), you can also do file I/O with the types in `Windows.Storage`. We describe this in the online supplement at *http://www.alba-hari.com/nutshell.*

Constructing a FileStream

The simplest way to instantiate a `FileStream` is to use one of the following static façade methods on the `File` class:

```
FileStream fs1 = File.OpenRead  ("readme.bin");     // Read-only
FileStream fs2 = File.OpenWrite ("writeme.tmp");     // Write-only
FileStream fs3 = File.Create    ("readwrite.tmp");   // Read/write
```

`OpenWrite` and `Create` differ in behavior if the file already exists. `Create` truncates any existing content; `OpenWrite` leaves existing content intact with the stream positioned at zero. If you write fewer bytes than were previously in the file, `OpenWrite` leaves you with a mixture of old and new content.

You can also directly instantiate a `FileStream`. Its constructors provide access to every feature, allowing you to specify a filename or low-level file handle, file creation and access modes, and options for sharing, buffering, and security. The following opens an existing file for read/write access without overwriting it (the `using` keyword ensures it is disposed when `fs` exits scope):

```
using var fs = new FileStream ("readwrite.tmp", FileMode.Open);
```

We look more closely at `FileMode` shortly.

Specifying a filename

A filename can be either absolute (e.g., *c:\temp\test.txt*—or in Unix, */tmp/test.txt*) or relative to the current directory (e.g., *test.txt* or *temp\test.txt*). You can access or change the current directory via the static `Environment.CurrentDirectory` property.

 When a program starts, the current directory might or might not coincide with that of the program's executable. For this reason, you should never rely on the current directory for locating additional runtime files packaged along with your executable.

`AppDomain.CurrentDomain.BaseDirectory` returns the *application base directory*, which in normal cases is the folder containing the program's executable. To specify a filename relative to this directory, you can call `Path.Combine`:

```
string baseFolder = AppDomain.CurrentDomain.BaseDirectory;
string logoPath = Path.Combine (baseFolder, "logo.jpg");
Console.WriteLine (File.Exists (logoPath));
```

Shortcut Methods on the File Class

The following static methods read an entire file into memory in one step:

- `File.ReadAllText` (returns a string)
- `File.ReadAllLines` (returns an array of strings)
- `File.ReadAllBytes` (returns a byte array)

The following static methods write an entire file in one step:

- `File.WriteAllText`
- `File.WriteAllLines`
- `File.WriteAllBytes`
- `File.AppendAllText` (great for appending to a log file)

There's also a static method called `File.ReadLines`: this is like `ReadAllLines` except that it returns a lazily evaluated `IEnumerable<string>`. This is more efficient because it doesn't load the entire file into memory at once. LINQ is ideal for consuming the results; the following calculates the number of lines greater than 80 characters in length:

```
int longLines = File.ReadLines ("filePath")
                     .Count (l => l.Length > 80);
```

You can read and write across a Windows network via a Universal Naming Convention (UNC) path, such as \\JoesPC\PicShare\pic.jpg or \\10.1.1.2\PicShare\pic.jpg. (To access a Windows file share from macOS or Unix, mount it to your filesystem following instructions specific to your OS, and then open it using an ordinary path from C#.)

Specifying a FileMode

All of FileStream's constructors that accept a filename also require a FileMode enum argument. Figure 15-3 shows how to choose a FileMode, and the choices yield results akin to calling a static method on the File class.

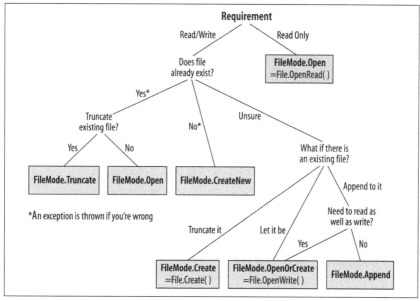

Figure 15-3. Choosing a FileMode

 File.Create and FileMode.Create will throw an exception if used on hidden files. To overwrite a hidden file, you must delete and re-create it:

```
File.Delete ("hidden.txt");
using var file = File.Create ("hidden.txt");
...
```

Constructing a FileStream with just a filename and FileMode gives you (with just one exception) a readable/writable stream. You can request a downgrade if you also supply a FileAccess argument:

```
[Flags]
public enum FileAccess { Read = 1, Write = 2, ReadWrite = 3 }
```

The following returns a read-only stream, equivalent to calling File.OpenRead:

```
using var fs = new FileStream ("x.bin", FileMode.Open, FileAccess.Read);
...
```

FileMode.Append is the odd one out: with this mode, you get a *write-only* stream. To append with read-write support, you must instead use FileMode.Open or File Mode.OpenOrCreate and then seek the end of the stream:

```
using var fs = new FileStream ("myFile.bin", FileMode.Open);

fs.Seek (0, SeekOrigin.End);
...
```

Advanced FileStream features

Here are other optional arguments you can include when constructing a File Stream:

- A FileShare enum describing how much access to grant other processes wanting to dip into the same file before you've finished (None, Read [default], ReadWrite, or Write).

- The size, in bytes, of the internal buffer (default is currently 4 KB).

- A flag indicating whether to defer to the operating system for asynchronous I/O.

- A FileOptions flags enum for requesting operating system encryption (Encryp ted), automatic deletion upon closure for temporary files (DeleteOnClose), and optimization hints (RandomAccess and SequentialScan). There is also a WriteThrough flag that requests that the OS disable write-behind caching; this is for transactional files or logs. Flags not supported by the underlying OS are silently ignored.

Opening a file with FileShare.ReadWrite allows other processes or users to simultaneously read and write to the same file. To avoid chaos, you can all agree to lock specified portions of the file before reading or writing, using these methods:

```
// Defined on the FileStream class:
public virtual void Lock   (long position, long length);
public virtual void Unlock (long position, long length);
```

Lock throws an exception if part or all of the requested file section has already been locked.

MemoryStream

MemoryStream uses an array as a backing store. This partly defeats the purpose of having a stream because the entire backing store must reside in memory at once. MemoryStream is still useful when you need random access to a nonseekable stream. If you know the source stream will be of a manageable size, you can copy it into a MemoryStream as follows:

```
var ms = new MemoryStream();
sourceStream.CopyTo (ms);
```

You can convert a MemoryStream to a byte array by calling ToArray. The GetBuffer method does the same job more efficiently by returning a direct reference to the underlying storage array; unfortunately, this array is usually longer than the stream's real length.

 Closing and flushing a MemoryStream is optional. If you close a MemoryStream, you can no longer read or write to it, but you are still permitted to call ToArray to obtain the underlying data. Flush does absolutely nothing on a memory stream.

You can find further MemoryStream examples in "Compression Streams" on page 695 and in "Overview" on page 851.

PipeStream

PipeStream provides a simple means by which one process can communicate with another through the operating system's *pipes* protocol. There are two kinds of pipe:

Anonymous pipe (faster)
> Allows one-way communication between a parent and child process on the same computer

Named pipe (more flexible)
> Allows two-way communication between arbitrary processes on the same computer or different computers across a network

A pipe is good for interprocess communication (IPC) on a single computer: it doesn't rely on a network transport, which means no network protocol overhead, and it has no issues with firewalls.

 Pipes are stream-based, so one process waits to receive a series of bytes while another process sends them. An alternative is for processes to communicate via a block of shared memory; we describe how to do this in "Memory-Mapped Files" on page 712.

PipeStream is an abstract class with four concrete subtypes. Two are used for anonymous pipes and the other two for named pipes:

Anonymous pipes
> AnonymousPipeServerStream and AnonymousPipeClientStream

Named pipes
> NamedPipeServerStream and NamedPipeClientStream

Named pipes are simpler to use, so we describe them first.

Named pipes

With named pipes, the parties communicate through a pipe of the same name. The protocol defines two distinct roles: the client and server. Communication happens between the client and server as follows:

- The server instantiates a `NamedPipeServerStream` and then calls `WaitFor Connection`.
- The client instantiates a `NamedPipeClientStream` and then calls `Connect` (with an optional timeout).

The two parties then read and write the streams to communicate.

The following example demonstrates a server that sends a single byte (100) and then waits to receive a single byte:

```
using var s = new NamedPipeServerStream ("pipedream");

s.WaitForConnection();
s.WriteByte (100);                   // Send the value 100.
Console.WriteLine (s.ReadByte());
```

Here's the corresponding client code:

```
using var s = new NamedPipeClientStream ("pipedream");

s.Connect();
Console.WriteLine (s.ReadByte());
s.WriteByte (200);                   // Send the value 200 back.
```

Named pipe streams are bidirectional by default, so either party can read or write their stream. This means that the client and server must agree on some protocol to coordinate their actions, so both parties don't end up sending or receiving at once.

There also needs to be agreement on the length of each transmission. Our example was trivial in this regard, because we bounced just a single byte in each direction. To help with messages longer than one byte, pipes provide a *message* transmission mode (Windows only). If this is enabled, a party calling `Read` can know when a message is complete by checking the `IsMessageComplete` property. To demonstrate, we begin by writing a helper method that reads a whole message from a message-enabled `PipeStream`—in other words, reads until `IsMessageComplete` is true:

```
static byte[] ReadMessage (PipeStream s)
{
  MemoryStream ms = new MemoryStream();
  byte[] buffer = new byte [0x1000];     // Read in 4 KB blocks

  do    { ms.Write (buffer, 0, s.Read (buffer, 0, buffer.Length)); }
  while (!s.IsMessageComplete);

  return ms.ToArray();
}
```

(To make this asynchronous, replace "s.Read" with "await s.ReadAsync".)

 You cannot determine whether a PipeStream has finished reading a message simply by waiting for Read to return 0. This is because, unlike most other stream types, pipe streams and network streams have no definite end. Instead, they temporarily "dry up" between message transmissions.

Now we can activate message transmission mode. On the server, this is done by specifying PipeTransmissionMode.Message when constructing the stream:

```
using var s = new NamedPipeServerStream ("pipedream", PipeDirection.InOut,
                                         1, PipeTransmissionMode.Message);

s.WaitForConnection();

byte[] msg = Encoding.UTF8.GetBytes ("Hello");
s.Write (msg, 0, msg.Length);

Console.WriteLine (Encoding.UTF8.GetString (ReadMessage (s)));
```

On the client, we activate message transmission mode by setting ReadMode after calling Connect:

```
using var s = new NamedPipeClientStream ("pipedream");

s.Connect();
s.ReadMode = PipeTransmissionMode.Message;

Console.WriteLine (Encoding.UTF8.GetString (ReadMessage (s)));

byte[] msg = Encoding.UTF8.GetBytes ("Hello right back!");
s.Write (msg, 0, msg.Length);
```

 Message mode is supported only on Windows. Other platforms throw PlatformNotSupportedException.

Anonymous pipes

An anonymous pipe provides a one-way communication stream between a parent and child process. Instead of using a system-wide name, anonymous pipes tune in through a private handle.

As with named pipes, there are distinct client and server roles. The system of communication is a little different, however, and proceeds as follows:

1. The server instantiates an AnonymousPipeServerStream, committing to a Pipe Direction of In or Out.

2. The server calls GetClientHandleAsString to obtain an identifier for the pipe, which it then passes to the client (typically as an argument when starting the child process).

3. The child process instantiates an AnonymousPipeClientStream, specifying the opposite PipeDirection.

4. The server releases the local handle that was generated in Step 2, by calling DisposeLocalCopyOfClientHandle.

5. The parent and child processes communicate by reading/writing the stream.

Because anonymous pipes are unidirectional, a server must create two pipes for bidirectional communication. The following Console program creates two pipes (input and output) and then starts up a child process. It then sends a single byte to the child process and receives a single byte in return:

```
class Program
{
  static void Main (string[] args)
  {
    if (args.Length == 0)
      // No arguments signals server mode
      AnonymousPipeServer();
    else
      // We pass in the pipe handle IDs as arguments to signal client mode
      AnonymousPipeClient (args [0], args [1]);
  }

  static void AnonymousPipeClient (string rxID, string txID)
  {
    using (var rx = new AnonymousPipeClientStream (PipeDirection.In, rxID))
    using (var tx = new AnonymousPipeClientStream (PipeDirection.Out, txID))
    {
      Console.WriteLine ("Client received: " + rx.ReadByte ());
      tx.WriteByte (200);
    }
  }

  static void AnonymousPipeServer ()
  {
    using var tx = new AnonymousPipeServerStream (
                    PipeDirection.Out, HandleInheritability.Inheritable);
    using var rx = new AnonymousPipeServerStream (
                    PipeDirection.In, HandleInheritability.Inheritable);

    string txID = tx.GetClientHandleAsString ();
    string rxID = rx.GetClientHandleAsString ();

    // Create and start up a child process.
    // We'll use the same Console executable, but pass in arguments:
    string thisAssembly = Assembly.GetEntryAssembly().Location;
    string thisExe = Path.ChangeExtension (thisAssembly, ".exe");
    var args = $"{txID} {rxID}";
    var startInfo = new ProcessStartInfo (thisExe, args);

    startInfo.UseShellExecute = false;        // Required for child process
    Process p = Process.Start (startInfo);
```

```
        tx.DisposeLocalCopyOfClientHandle ();   // Release unmanaged
        rx.DisposeLocalCopyOfClientHandle ();   // handle resources.

        tx.WriteByte (100);    // Send a byte to the child process

        Console.WriteLine ("Server received: " + rx.ReadByte ());

        p.WaitForExit ();
    }
}
```

As with named pipes, the client and server must coordinate their sending and receiving and agree on the length of each transmission. Anonymous pipes don't, unfortunately, support message mode, so you must implement your own protocol for message length agreement. One solution is to send, in the first four bytes of each transmission, an integer value defining the length of the message to follow. The BitConverter class provides methods for converting between an integer and an array of four bytes.

BufferedStream

BufferedStream decorates, or wraps, another stream with buffering capability, and it is one of a number of decorator stream types in the .NET, all of which are illustrated in Figure 15-4.

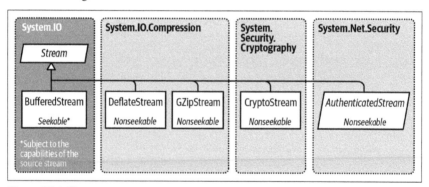

Figure 15-4. Decorator streams

Buffering improves performance by reducing round trips to the backing store. Here's how we wrap a FileStream in a 20 KB BufferedStream:

```
// Write 100K to a file:
File.WriteAllBytes ("myFile.bin", new byte [100000]);

using FileStream fs = File.OpenRead ("myFile.bin");
using BufferedStream bs = new BufferedStream (fs, 20000);  //20K buffer

bs.ReadByte();
Console.WriteLine (fs.Position);           // 20000
```

In this example, the underlying stream advances 20,000 bytes after reading just one byte, thanks to the read-ahead buffering. We could call ReadByte another 19,999 times before the FileStream would be hit again.

Coupling a BufferedStream to a FileStream, as in this example, is of limited value because FileStream already has built-in buffering. Its only use might be in enlarging the buffer on an already-constructed FileStream.

Closing a BufferedStream automatically closes the underlying backing store stream.

Stream Adapters

A Stream deals only in bytes; to read or write data types such as strings, integers, or XML elements, you must plug in an adapter. Here's what .NET provides:

Text adapters (for string and character data)
    TextReader, TextWriter
    StreamReader, StreamWriter
    StringReader, StringWriter

Binary adapters (for primitive types such as int, bool, string, *and* float*)*
    BinaryReader, BinaryWriter

XML adapters (covered in Chapter 11)
    XmlReader, XmlWriter

Figure 15-5 illustrates the relationships between these types.

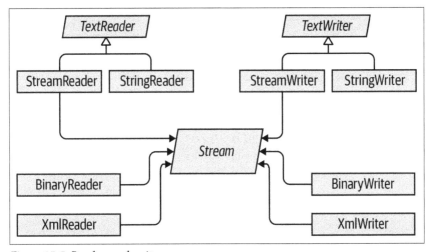

Figure 15-5. Readers and writers

Text Adapters

TextReader and TextWriter are the abstract base classes for adapters that deal exclusively with characters and strings. Each has two general-purpose implementations in .NET:

StreamReader/StreamWriter
> Uses a Stream for its raw data store, translating the stream's bytes into characters or strings

StringReader/StringWriter
> Implements TextReader/TextWriter using in-memory strings

Table 15-2 lists TextReader's members by category. Peek returns the next character in the stream without advancing the position. Both Peek and the zero-argument version of Read return −1 if at the end of the stream; otherwise, they return an integer that can be cast directly to a char. The overload of Read that accepts a char[] buffer is identical in functionality to the ReadBlock method. ReadLine reads until reaching either a CR (character 13) or LF (character 10), or a CR+LF pair in sequence. It then returns a string, discarding the CR/LF characters.

Table 15-2. TextReader members

Category	Members
Reading one char	public virtual int Peek(); // Cast the result to a char
	public virtual int Read(); // Cast the result to a char
Reading many chars	public virtual int Read (char[] buffer, int index, int count);
	public virtual int ReadBlock (char[] buffer, int index, int count);
	public virtual string ReadLine();
	public virtual string ReadToEnd();
Closing	public virtual void Close();
	public void Dispose(); // Same as Close
Other	public static readonly TextReader Null;
	public static TextReader Synchronized (TextReader reader);

Environment.NewLine returns the new-line sequence for the current OS.

On Windows, this is "\r\n" (think "ReturN") and is loosely modeled on a mechanical typewriter: a CR (character 13) followed by an LF (character 10). Reverse the order and you'll get either two new lines or none!

On Unix and macOS, it's simply "\n".

TextWriter has analogous methods for writing, as shown in Table 15-3. The Write and WriteLine methods are additionally overloaded to accept every primitive type, plus the object type. These methods simply call the ToString method on whatever is passed in (optionally through an IFormatProvider specified either when calling the method or when constructing the TextWriter).

Table 15-3. TextWriter members

Category	Members
Writing one char	public virtual void Write (char value);
Writing many chars	public virtual void Write (string value);
	public virtual void Write (char[] buffer, int index, int count);
	public virtual void Write (string format, params object[] arg);
	public virtual void WriteLine (string value);
Closing and flushing	public virtual void Close();
	public void Dispose(); // Same as Close
	public virtual void Flush();
Formatting and encoding	public virtual IFormatProvider FormatProvider { get; }
	public virtual string NewLine { get; set; }
	public abstract Encoding Encoding { get; }
Other	public static readonly TextWriter Null;
	public static TextWriter Synchronized (TextWriter writer);

WriteLine simply appends the given text with Environment.NewLine. You can change this via the NewLine property (this can be useful for interoperability with Unix file formats).

As with Stream, TextReader and TextWriter offer task-based asynchronous versions of their read/write methods.

StreamReader and StreamWriter

In the following example, a `StreamWriter` writes two lines of text to a file, and then a `StreamReader` reads the file back:

```
using (FileStream fs = File.Create ("test.txt"))
using (TextWriter writer = new StreamWriter (fs))
{
  writer.WriteLine ("Line1");
  writer.WriteLine ("Line2");
}

using (FileStream fs = File.OpenRead ("test.txt"))
using (TextReader reader = new StreamReader (fs))
{
  Console.WriteLine (reader.ReadLine());     // Line1
  Console.WriteLine (reader.ReadLine());     // Line2
}
```

Because text adapters are so often coupled with files, the `File` class provides the static methods `CreateText`, `AppendText`, and `OpenText` to shortcut the process:

```
using (TextWriter writer = File.CreateText ("test.txt"))
{
  writer.WriteLine ("Line1");
  writer.WriteLine ("Line2");
}

using (TextWriter writer = File.AppendText ("test.txt"))
  writer.WriteLine ("Line3");

using (TextReader reader = File.OpenText ("test.txt"))
  while (reader.Peek() > -1)
    Console.WriteLine (reader.ReadLine());     // Line1
                                               // Line2
                                               // Line3
```

This also illustrates how to test for the end of a file (viz. `reader.Peek()`). Another option is to read until `reader.ReadLine` returns null.

You can also read and write other types such as integers, but because `TextWriter` invokes `ToString` on your type, you must parse a string when reading it back:

```
using (TextWriter w = File.CreateText ("data.txt"))
{
  w.WriteLine (123);          // Writes "123"
  w.WriteLine (true);         // Writes the word "true"
}

using (TextReader r = File.OpenText ("data.txt"))
{
  int myInt = int.Parse (r.ReadLine());       // myInt == 123
  bool yes = bool.Parse (r.ReadLine());       // yes == true
}
```

Character encodings

`TextReader` and `TextWriter` are by themselves just abstract classes with no connection to a stream or backing store. The `StreamReader` and `StreamWriter` types, however, are connected to an underlying byte-oriented stream, so they must convert between characters and bytes. They do so through an `Encoding` class from the `System.Text` namespace, which you choose when constructing the `StreamReader` or `StreamWriter`. If you choose none, the default UTF-8 encoding is used.

> If you explicitly specify an encoding, `StreamWriter` will, by default, write a prefix to the start of the stream to identity the encoding. This is usually undesirable, and you can prevent it by constructing the encoding as follows:
>
> ```
> var encoding = new UTF8Encoding (
>   encoderShouldEmitUTF8Identifier:false,
>   throwOnInvalidBytes:true);
> ```
>
> The second argument tells the `StreamWriter` (or `Stream Reader`) to throw an exception if it encounters bytes that do not have a valid string translation for their encoding, which matches its default behavior if you do not specify an encoding.

The simplest of the encodings is ASCII because each character is represented by one byte. The ASCII encoding maps the first 127 characters of the Unicode set into its single byte, covering what you see on a US-style keyboard. Most other characters, including specialized symbols and non-English characters, cannot be represented and are converted to the □ character. The default UTF-8 encoding can map all allocated Unicode characters, but it is more complex. The first 127 characters encode to a single byte, for ASCII compatibility; the remaining characters encode to a variable number of bytes (most commonly two or three). Consider the following:

```
using (TextWriter w = File.CreateText ("but.txt"))    // Use default UTF-8
  w.WriteLine ("but-");                                 // encoding.

using (Stream s = File.OpenRead ("but.txt"))
  for (int b; (b = s.ReadByte()) > -1;)
    Console.WriteLine (b);
```

The word "but" is followed not by a stock-standard hyphen, but by the longer em dash (—) character, U+2014. This is the one that won't get you into trouble with your book editor! Let's examine the output:

```
98     // b
117    // u
116    // t
226    // em dash byte 1     Note that the byte values
128    // em dash byte 2     are >= 128 for each part
148    // em dash byte 3     of the multibyte sequence.
13     // <CR>
10     // <LF>
```

Because the em dash is outside the first 127 characters of the Unicode set, it requires more than a single byte to encode in UTF-8 (in this case, three). UTF-8 is efficient with the Western alphabet as most popular characters consume just one byte. It also downgrades easily to ASCII simply by ignoring all bytes above 127. Its disadvantage is that seeking within a stream is troublesome because a character's position does not correspond to its byte position in the stream. An alternative is UTF-16 (labeled just "Unicode" in the Encoding class). Here's how we write the same string with UTF-16:

```
using (Stream s = File.Create ("but.txt"))
using (TextWriter w = new StreamWriter (s, Encoding.Unicode))
  w.WriteLine ("but-");

foreach (byte b in File.ReadAllBytes ("but.txt"))
  Console.WriteLine (b);
```

And here's the output:

```
255    // Byte-order mark 1
254    // Byte-order mark 2
98     // 'b' byte 1
0      // 'b' byte 2
117    // 'u' byte 1
0      // 'u' byte 2
116    // 't' byte 1
0      // 't' byte 2
20     // '--' byte 1
32     // '--' byte 2
13     // <CR> byte 1
0      // <CR> byte 2
10     // <LF> byte 1
0      // <LF> byte 2
```

Technically, UTF-16 uses either two or four bytes per character (there are close to a million Unicode characters allocated or reserved, so two bytes is not always enough). However, because the C# char type is itself only 16 bits wide, a UTF-16 encoding will always use exactly two bytes per .NET char. This makes it easy to jump to a particular character index within a stream.

UTF-16 uses a two-byte prefix to identify whether the byte pairs are written in a "little-endian" or "big-endian" order (the least significant byte first or the most significant byte first). The default little-endian order is standard for Windows-based systems.

StringReader and StringWriter

The StringReader and StringWriter adapters don't wrap a stream at all; instead, they use a string or StringBuilder as the underlying data source. This means no byte translation is required—in fact, the classes do nothing you couldn't easily achieve with a string or StringBuilder coupled with an index variable. Their advantage, though, is that they share a base class with StreamReader/StreamWriter. For instance, suppose that we have a string containing XML and want to parse it with an XmlReader. The XmlReader.Create method accepts one of the following:

- A URI

- A Stream

- A TextReader

So, how do we XML-parse our string? Because `StringReader` is a subclass of `TextReader`, we're in luck. We can instantiate and pass in a `StringReader` as follows:

```
XmlReader r = XmlReader.Create (new StringReader (myString));
```

Binary Adapters

`BinaryReader` and `BinaryWriter` read and write native data types: `bool`, `byte`, `char`, `decimal`, `float`, `double`, `short`, `int`, `long`, `sbyte`, `ushort`, `uint`, and `ulong`, as well as `strings` and arrays of the primitive data types.

Unlike `StreamReader` and `StreamWriter`, binary adapters store primitive data types efficiently because they are represented in memory. So, an `int` uses four bytes; a `double` uses eight bytes. Strings are written through a text encoding (as with `StreamReader` and `StreamWriter`) but are length-prefixed to make it possible to read back a series of strings without needing special delimiters.

Imagine that we have a simple type, defined as follows:

```
public class Person
{
  public string Name;
  public int    Age;
  public double Height;
}
```

We can add the following methods to `Person` to save/load its data to/from a stream using binary adapters:

```
public void SaveData (Stream s)
{
  var w = new BinaryWriter (s);
  w.Write (Name);
  w.Write (Age);
  w.Write (Height);
  w.Flush();          // Ensure the BinaryWriter buffer is cleared.
                      // We won't dispose/close it, so more data
}                     // can be written to the stream.

public void LoadData (Stream s)
{
  var r = new BinaryReader (s);
  Name   = r.ReadString();
  Age    = r.ReadInt32();
  Height = r.ReadDouble();
}
```

BinaryReader can also read into byte arrays. The following reads the entire contents of a seekable stream:

```
byte[] data = new BinaryReader (s).ReadBytes ((int) s.Length);
```

This is more convenient than reading directly from a stream because it doesn't require a loop to ensure that all data has been read.

Closing and Disposing Stream Adapters

You have four choices in tearing down stream adapters:

1. Close the adapter only.
2. Close the adapter and then close the stream.
3. (For writers) Flush the adapter and then close the stream.
4. (For readers) Close just the stream.

> Close and Dispose are synonymous with adapters, just as they are with streams.

Options 1 and 2 are semantically identical because closing an adapter automatically closes the underlying stream. Whenever you nest using statements, you're implicitly taking option 2:

```
using (FileStream fs = File.Create ("test.txt"))
using (TextWriter writer = new StreamWriter (fs))
  writer.WriteLine ("Line");
```

Because the nest disposes from the inside out, the adapter is closed first, and then the stream. Furthermore, if an exception is thrown within the adapter's constructor, the stream still closes. It's hard to go wrong with nested using statements!

> Never close a stream before closing or flushing its writer— you'll amputate any data that's buffered in the adapter.

Options 3 and 4 work because adapters are in the unusual category of *optionally disposable objects*. An example of when you might choose not to dispose an adapter is when you've finished with the adapter but you want to leave the underlying stream open for subsequent use:

```
using (FileStream fs = new FileStream ("test.txt", FileMode.Create))
{
  StreamWriter writer = new StreamWriter (fs);
  writer.WriteLine ("Hello");
  writer.Flush();

  fs.Position = 0;
```

```
        Console.WriteLine (fs.ReadByte());
    }
```

Here, we write to a file, reposition the stream, and then read the first byte before closing the stream. If we disposed the `StreamWriter`, it would also close the underlying `FileStream`, causing the subsequent read to fail. The proviso is that we call `Flush` to ensure that the `StreamWriter`'s buffer is written to the underlying stream.

 Stream adapters—with their optional disposal semantics—do not implement the extended disposal pattern where the finalizer calls `Dispose`. This allows an abandoned adapter to evade automatic disposal when the garbage collector catches up with it.

There's also a constructor on `StreamReader`/`StreamWriter` that instructs it to keep the stream open after disposal. Consequently, we can rewrite the preceding example as follows:

```
using (var fs = new FileStream ("test.txt", FileMode.Create))
{
    using (var writer = new StreamWriter (fs, new UTF8Encoding (false, true),
                                          0x400, true))
        writer.WriteLine ("Hello");

    fs.Position = 0;
    Console.WriteLine (fs.ReadByte());
    Console.WriteLine (fs.Length);
}
```

Compression Streams

Two general-purpose compression streams are provided in the `System.IO.Compres` `sion` namespace: `DeflateStream` and `GZipStream`. Both use a popular compression algorithm similar to that of the ZIP format. They differ in that `GZipStream` writes an additional protocol at the start and end—including a CRC to detect errors. `GZipStream` also conforms to a standard recognized by other software.

.NET also includes `BrotliStream`, which implements the *Brotli* compression algorithm. `BrotliStream` is more than 10 times slower than `DeflateStream` and `GZip` `Stream` but achieves a better compression ratio. (The performance hit applies only to compression—decompression performs very well.)

All three streams allow reading and writing, with the following provisos:

- You always *write* to the stream when compressing.
- You always *read* from the stream when decompressing.

DeflateStream, GZipStream, and BrotliStream are decorators; they compress or decompress data from another stream that you supply in construction. In the following example, we compress and decompress a series of bytes using a FileStream as the backing store:

```
using (Stream s = File.Create ("compressed.bin"))
using (Stream ds = new DeflateStream (s, CompressionMode.Compress))
  for (byte i = 0; i < 100; i++)
    ds.WriteByte (i);

using (Stream s = File.OpenRead ("compressed.bin"))
using (Stream ds = new DeflateStream (s, CompressionMode.Decompress))
  for (byte i = 0; i < 100; i++)
    Console.WriteLine (ds.ReadByte());       // Writes 0 to 99
```

With DeflateStream, the compressed file is 102 bytes; slightly larger than the original (BrotliStream would compress it to 73 bytes). Compression works poorly with "dense," nonrepetitive binary data (and worst of all with encrypted data, which lacks regularity by design). It works well with most text files; in the next example, we compress and decompress a text stream composed of 1,000 words chosen randomly from a small sentence with the *Brotli* algorithm. This also demonstrates chaining a backing store stream, a decorator stream, and an adapter (as depicted at the start of the chapter in Figure 15-1), and the use of asynchronous methods:

```
string[] words = "The quick brown fox jumps over the lazy dog".Split();
Random rand = new Random (0);   // Give it a seed for consistency

using (Stream s = File.Create ("compressed.bin"))
using (Stream ds = new BrotliStream (s, CompressionMode.Compress))
using (TextWriter w = new StreamWriter (ds))
  for (int i = 0; i < 1000; i++)
    await w.WriteAsync (words [rand.Next (words.Length)] + " ");

Console.WriteLine (new FileInfo ("compressed.bin").Length);       // 808

using (Stream s = File.OpenRead ("compressed.bin"))
using (Stream ds = new BrotliStream (s, CompressionMode.Decompress))
using (TextReader r = new StreamReader (ds))
  Console.Write (await r.ReadToEndAsync());  // Output below:
```

```
lazy lazy the fox the quick The brown fox jumps over fox over fox The
brown brown brown over brown quick fox brown dog dog lazy fox dog brown
over fox jumps lazy lazy quick The jumps fox jumps The over jumps dog...
```

In this case, BrotliStream compresses efficiently to 808 bytes—less than one byte per word. (For comparison, DeflateStream compresses the same data to 885 bytes.)

Compressing in Memory

Sometimes, you need to compress entirely in memory. Here's how to use a Memory Stream for this purpose:

```
byte[] data = new byte[1000];          // We can expect a good compression
                                       // ratio from an empty array!
var ms = new MemoryStream();
using (Stream ds = new DeflateStream (ms, CompressionMode.Compress))
  ds.Write (data, 0, data.Length);

byte[] compressed = ms.ToArray();
Console.WriteLine (compressed.Length);     // 11

// Decompress back to the data array:
ms = new MemoryStream (compressed);
using (Stream ds = new DeflateStream (ms, CompressionMode.Decompress))
  for (int i = 0; i < 1000; i += ds.Read (data, i, 1000 - i));
```

The using statement around the DeflateStream closes it in a textbook fashion, flushing any unwritten buffers in the process. This also closes the MemoryStream it wraps—meaning we must then call ToArray to extract its data.

Here's an alternative that avoids closing the MemoryStream and uses the asynchronous read and write methods:

```
byte[] data = new byte[1000];

MemoryStream ms = new MemoryStream();
using (Stream ds = new DeflateStream (ms, CompressionMode.Compress, true))
  await ds.WriteAsync (data, 0, data.Length);

Console.WriteLine (ms.Length);          // 113
ms.Position = 0;
using (Stream ds = new DeflateStream (ms, CompressionMode.Decompress))
  for (int i = 0; i < 1000; i += await ds.ReadAsync (data, i, 1000 - i));
```

The additional flag sent to DeflateStream's constructor instructs it to not follow the usual protocol of taking the underlying stream with it in disposal. In other words, the MemoryStream is left open, allowing us to position it back to zero and reread it.

Unix gzip File Compression

GZipStream's compression algorithm is popular on Unix systems as a file compression format. Each source file is compressed into a separate target file with a *.gz* extension.

The following methods do the work of the Unix command-line gzip and gunzip utilities:

```
async Task GZip (string sourcefile, bool deleteSource = true)
{
  var gzipfile = $"{sourcefile}.gz";
  if (File.Exists (gzipfile))
    throw new Exception ("Gzip file already exists");

  // Compress
  using (FileStream inStream = File.Open (sourcefile, FileMode.Open))
  using (FileStream outStream = new FileStream (gzipfile, FileMode.CreateNew))
```

```
using (GZipStream gzipStream =
  new GZipStream (outStream, CompressionMode.Compress))
  await inStream.CopyToAsync (gzipStream);

if (deleteSource) File.Delete(sourcefile);
}

async Task GUnzip (string gzipfile, bool deleteGzip = true)
{
  if (Path.GetExtension (gzipfile) != ".gz")
    throw new Exception ("Not a gzip file");

  var uncompressedFile = gzipfile.Substring (0, gzipfile.Length - 3);
  if (File.Exists (uncompressedFile))
    throw new Exception ("Destination file already exists");

  // Uncompress
  using (FileStream uncompressToStream =
      File.Open (uncompressedFile, FileMode.Create))
  using (FileStream zipfileStream = File.Open (gzipfile, FileMode.Open))
  using (var unzipStream =
      new GZipStream (zipfileStream, CompressionMode.Decompress))
    await unzipStream.CopyToAsync (uncompressToStream);

  if (deleteGzip) File.Delete (gzipfile);
}
```

The following compresses a file:

```
await GZip ("/tmp/myfile.txt");        // Creates /tmp/myfile.txt.gz
```

And the following decompresses it:

```
await GUnzip ("/tmp/myfile.txt.gz")  // Creates /tmp/myfile.txt
```

Working with ZIP Files

The ZipArchive and ZipFile classes in System.IO.Compression support the ZIP compression format. The advantage of the ZIP format over DeflateStream and GZipStream is that it acts as a container for multiple files and is compatible with ZIP files created with Windows Explorer.

 ZipArchive and ZipFile work in both Windows and Unix; however, the format is most popular in Windows. In Unix, the *.tar* format is more popular as a container for multiple files. You can read/write *.tar* files using a third-party library such as SharpZipLib.

ZipArchive works with streams, whereas ZipFile addresses the more common scenario of working with files. (ZipFile is a static helper class for ZipArchive.)

ZipFile's CreateFromDirectory method adds all the files in a specified directory into a ZIP file:

```
ZipFile.CreateFromDirectory (@"d:\MyFolder", @"d:\archive.zip");
```

ExtractToDirectory does the opposite and extracts a ZIP file to a directory:

```
ZipFile.ExtractToDirectory (@"d:\archive.zip", @"d:\MyFolder");
```

When compressing, you can specify whether to optimize for file size or speed as well as whether to include the name of the source directory in the archive. Enabling the latter option in our example would create a subdirectory in the archive called *MyFolder* into which the compressed files would go.

ZipFile has an Open method for reading/writing individual entries. This returns a ZipArchive object (which you can also obtain by instantiating ZipArchive with a Stream object). When calling Open, you must specify a filename and indicate whether you want to Read, Create, or Update the archive. You can then enumerate existing entries via the Entries property or find a particular file by calling GetEntry:

```
using (ZipArchive zip = ZipFile.Open (@"d:\zz.zip", ZipArchiveMode.Read))

    foreach (ZipArchiveEntry entry in zip.Entries)
        Console.WriteLine (entry.FullName + " " + entry.Length);
```

ZipArchiveEntry also has a Delete method, an ExtractToFile method (this is actually an extension method in the ZipFileExtensions class), and an Open method that returns a readable/writable Stream. You can create new entries by calling CreateEntry (or the CreateEntryFromFile extension method) on the ZipArchive. The following creates the archive *d:\zz.zip*, to which it adds *foo.dll*, under a directory structure within the archive called *bin\X86*:

```
byte[] data = File.ReadAllBytes (@"d:\foo.dll");
using (ZipArchive zip = ZipFile.Open (@"d:\zz.zip", ZipArchiveMode.Update))
    zip.CreateEntry (@"bin\X64\foo.dll").Open().Write (data, 0, data.Length);
```

You could do the same thing entirely in memory by constructing ZipArchive with a MemoryStream.

File and Directory Operations

The System.IO namespace provides a set of types for performing "utility" file and directory operations, such as copying and moving, creating directories, and setting file attributes and permissions. For most features, you can choose between either of two classes, one offering static methods and the other instance methods:

Static classes
  File and Directory

Instance-method classes (constructed with a file or directory name)
  FileInfo and DirectoryInfo

Additionally, there's a static class called Path. This does nothing to files or directories; instead, it provides string manipulation methods for filenames and directory paths. Path also assists with temporary files.

The File Class

File is a static class whose methods all accept a filename. The filename can be either relative to the current directory or fully qualified with a directory. Here are its methods (all public and static):

```
bool Exists (string path);       // Returns true if the file is present

void Delete  (string path);
void Copy    (string sourceFileName, string destFileName);
void Move    (string sourceFileName, string destFileName);
void Replace (string sourceFileName, string destinationFileName,
                                     string destinationBackupFileName);

FileAttributes GetAttributes (string path);
void SetAttributes           (string path, FileAttributes fileAttributes);

void Decrypt (string path);
void Encrypt (string path);

DateTime GetCreationTime   (string path);      // UTC versions are
DateTime GetLastAccessTime (string path);      // also provided.
DateTime GetLastWriteTime  (string path);

void SetCreationTime   (string path, DateTime creationTime);
void SetLastAccessTime (string path, DateTime lastAccessTime);
void SetLastWriteTime  (string path, DateTime lastWriteTime);

FileSecurity GetAccessControl (string path);
FileSecurity GetAccessControl (string path,
                               AccessControlSections includeSections);
void SetAccessControl (string path, FileSecurity fileSecurity);
```

Move throws an exception if the destination file already exists; Replace does not. Both methods allow the file to be renamed as well as moved to another directory.

Delete throws an UnauthorizedAccessException if the file is marked read-only; you can tell this in advance by calling GetAttributes. It also throws that exception if the OS denies delete permission for that file to your process. Here are all the members of the FileAttribute enum that GetAttributes returns:

```
Archive, Compressed, Device, Directory, Encrypted,
Hidden, IntegritySystem, Normal, NoScrubData, NotContentIndexed,
Offline, ReadOnly, ReparsePoint, SparseFile, System, Temporary
```

Members in this enum are combinable. Here's how to toggle a single file attribute without upsetting the rest:

```
string filePath = "test.txt";

FileAttributes fa = File.GetAttributes (filePath);
if ((fa & FileAttributes.ReadOnly) != 0)
{
    // Use the exclusive-or operator (^) to toggle the ReadOnly flag
    fa ^= FileAttributes.ReadOnly;
```

```
    File.SetAttributes (filePath, fa);
}

// Now we can delete the file, for instance:
File.Delete (filePath);
```

FileInfo offers an easier way to change a file's read-only flag:

```
new FileInfo ("test.txt").IsReadOnly = false;
```

Compression and encryption attributes

This feature is Windows-only and requires the NuGet package `System.Management`.

The `Compressed` and `Encrypted` file attributes correspond to the compression and encryption checkboxes on a file or directory's Properties dialog box in Windows Explorer. This type of compression and encryption is *transparent* in that the OS does all the work behind the scenes, allowing you to read and write plain data.

You cannot use `SetAttributes` to change a file's `Compressed` or `Encrypted` attributes—it fails silently if you try! The workaround is simple in the latter case: you instead call the `Encrypt()` and `Decrypt()` methods in the `File` class. With compression, it's more complicated; one solution is to use the Windows Management Instrumentation (WMI) API in `System.Management`. The following method compresses a directory, returning 0 if successful (or a WMI error code if not):

```
static uint CompressFolder (string folder, bool recursive)
{
  string path = "Win32_Directory.Name='" + folder + "'";
  using (ManagementObject dir = new ManagementObject (path))
  using (ManagementBaseObject p = dir.GetMethodParameters ("CompressEx"))
  {
    p ["Recursive"] = recursive;
    using (ManagementBaseObject result = dir.InvokeMethod ("CompressEx",
                                                            p, null))
      return (uint) result.Properties ["ReturnValue"].Value;
  }
}
```

To uncompress, replace `CompressEx` with `UncompressEx`.

Transparent encryption relies on a key seeded from the logged-in user's password. The system is robust to password changes performed by the authenticated user, but if a password is reset via an administrator, data in encrypted files is unrecoverable.

Transparent encryption and compression require special filesystem support. NTFS (used most commonly on hard drives) supports these features; CDFS (on CD-ROMs) and FAT (on removable media cards) do not.

You can determine whether a volume supports compression and encryption with Win32 interop:

```
using System;
using System.IO;
using System.Text;
using System.ComponentModel;
using System.Runtime.InteropServices;

class SupportsCompressionEncryption
{
  const int SupportsCompression = 0x10;
  const int SupportsEncryption = 0x20000;

  [DllImport ("Kernel32.dll", SetLastError = true)]
  extern static bool GetVolumeInformation (string vol, StringBuilder name,
    int nameSize, out uint serialNum, out uint maxNameLen, out uint flags,
    StringBuilder fileSysName, int fileSysNameSize);

  static void Main()
  {
    uint serialNum, maxNameLen, flags;
    bool ok = GetVolumeInformation (@"C:\", null, 0, out serialNum,
                                    out maxNameLen, out flags, null, 0);
    if (!ok)
      throw new Win32Exception();

    bool canCompress = (flags & SupportsCompression) != 0;
    bool canEncrypt = (flags & SupportsEncryption) != 0;
  }
}
```

File security

This feature is Windows-only and requires the NuGet package System.IO.FileSystem.AccessControl.

The FileSecurity class allow you to query and change the OS permissions assigned to users and roles (namespace System.Security.AccessControl).

In this example, we list a file's existing permissions and then assign Write permission to the "Users" group:

```
using System;
using System.IO;
using System.Security.AccessControl;
using System.Security.Principal;

void ShowSecurity (FileSecurity sec)
{
  AuthorizationRuleCollection rules = sec.GetAccessRules (true, true,
                                              typeof (NTAccount));
  foreach (FileSystemAccessRule r in rules.Cast<FileSystemAccessRule>()
```

```
        .OrderBy (rule => rule.IdentityReference.Value))
    {
      // e.g., MyDomain/Joe
      Console.WriteLine ($"  {r.IdentityReference.Value}");
      // Allow or Deny: e.g., FullControl
      Console.WriteLine ($"     {r.FileSystemRights}: {r.AccessControlType}");
    }
  }

  var file = "sectest.txt";
  File.WriteAllText (file, "File security test.");

  var sid = new SecurityIdentifier (WellKnownSidType.BuiltinUsersSid, null);
  string usersAccount = sid.Translate (typeof (NTAccount)).ToString();

  Console.WriteLine ($"User: {usersAccount}");

  FileSecurity sec = new FileSecurity (file,
                          AccessControlSections.Owner |
                          AccessControlSections.Group |
                          AccessControlSections.Access);

  Console.WriteLine ("AFTER CREATE:");
  ShowSecurity(sec); // BUILTIN\Users doesn't have Write permission

  sec.ModifyAccessRule (AccessControlModification.Add,
      new FileSystemAccessRule (usersAccount, FileSystemRights.Write,
                          AccessControlType.Allow),
      out bool modified);

  Console.WriteLine ("AFTER MODIFY:");
  ShowSecurity (sec); // BUILTIN\Users has Write permission
```

We give another example, later, in "Special Folders" on page 707.

The Directory Class

The static Directory class provides a set of methods analogous to those in the File class—for checking whether a directory exists (Exists), moving a directory (Move), deleting a directory (Delete), getting/setting times of creation or last access, and getting/setting security permissions. Furthermore, Directory exposes the following static methods:

```
string GetCurrentDirectory ();
void   SetCurrentDirectory (string path);

DirectoryInfo CreateDirectory  (string path);
DirectoryInfo GetParent        (string path);
string        GetDirectoryRoot (string path);

string[] GetLogicalDrives(); // Gets mount points on Unix

// The following methods all return full paths:
```

```
string[] GetFiles          (string path);
string[] GetDirectories    (string path);
string[] GetFileSystemEntries (string path);

IEnumerable<string> EnumerateFiles           (string path);
IEnumerable<string> EnumerateDirectories     (string path);
IEnumerable<string> EnumerateFileSystemEntries (string path);
```

 The last three methods are potentially more efficient than the Get* variants because they're lazily evaluated—fetching data from the file system as you enumerate the sequence. They're particularly well suited to LINQ queries.

The Enumerate* and Get* methods are overloaded to also accept searchPattern (string) and searchOption (enum) parameters. If you specify SearchOption .SearchAllSubDirectories, a recursive subdirectory search is performed. The *FileSystemEntries methods combine the results of *Files with *Directories.

Here's how to create a directory if it doesn't already exist:

```
if (!Directory.Exists (@"d:\test"))
    Directory.CreateDirectory (@"d:\test");
```

FileInfo and DirectoryInfo

The static methods on File and Directory are convenient for executing a single file or directory operation. If you need to call a series of methods in a row, the FileInfo and DirectoryInfo classes provide an object model that makes the job easier.

FileInfo offers most of the File's static methods in instance form—with some additional properties such as Extension, Length, IsReadOnly, and Directory—for returning a DirectoryInfo object. For example:

```
static string TestDirectory =>
    RuntimeInformation.IsOSPlatform (OSPlatform.Windows)
        ? @"C:\Temp"
        : "/tmp";

Directory.CreateDirectory (TestDirectory);

FileInfo fi = new FileInfo (Path.Combine (TestDirectory, "FileInfo.txt"));

Console.WriteLine (fi.Exists);        // false

using (TextWriter w = fi.CreateText())
    w.Write ("Some text");

Console.WriteLine (fi.Exists);        // false (still)
fi.Refresh();
Console.WriteLine (fi.Exists);        // true

Console.WriteLine (fi.Name);          // FileInfo.txt
Console.WriteLine (fi.FullName);      // c:\temp\FileInfo.txt (Windows)
                                      // /tmp/FileInfo.txt (Unix)
```

```
Console.WriteLine (fi.DirectoryName);  // c:\temp (Windows)
                                       // /tmp (Unix)
Console.WriteLine (fi.Directory.Name); // temp
Console.WriteLine (fi.Extension);      // .txt
Console.WriteLine (fi.Length);         // 9

fi.Encrypt();
fi.Attributes ^= FileAttributes.Hidden;   // (Toggle hidden flag)
fi.IsReadOnly = true;

Console.WriteLine (fi.Attributes);     // ReadOnly,Archive,Hidden,Encrypted
Console.WriteLine (fi.CreationTime);   // 3/09/2019 1:24:05 PM

fi.MoveTo (Path.Combine (TestDirectory, "FileInfoX.txt"));

DirectoryInfo di = fi.Directory;
Console.WriteLine (di.Name);              // temp or tmp
Console.WriteLine (di.FullName);          // c:\temp or /tmp
Console.WriteLine (di.Parent.FullName);   // c:\ or /
di.CreateSubdirectory ("SubFolder");
```

Here's how to use DirectoryInfo to enumerate files and subdirectories:

```
DirectoryInfo di = new DirectoryInfo (@"e:\photos");

foreach (FileInfo fi in di.GetFiles ("*.jpg"))
  Console.WriteLine (fi.Name);

foreach (DirectoryInfo subDir in di.GetDirectories())
  Console.WriteLine (subDir.FullName);
```

Path

The static Path class defines methods and fields for working with paths and filenames.

Assuming this setup code:

```
string dir  = @"c:\mydir";   // or /mydir
string file = "myfile.txt";
string path = @"c:\mydir\myfile.txt";   // or /mydir/myfile.txt

Directory.SetCurrentDirectory (@"k:\demo");   // or /demo
```

we can demonstrate Path's methods and fields with the following expressions:

Expression	Result (Windows, then Unix)
Directory.GetCurrentDirectory()	k:\demo\ or /demo
Path.IsPathRooted (file)	False
Path.IsPathRooted (path)	True
Path.GetPathRoot (path)	c:\ or /
Path.GetDirectoryName (path)	c:\mydir or /mydir

Expression	Result (Windows, then Unix)
`Path.GetFileName (path)`	`myfile.txt`
`Path.GetFullPath (file)`	`k:\demo\myfile.txt` or `/demo/myfile.txt`
`Path.Combine (dir, file)`	`c:\mydir\myfile.txt` or `/mydir/myfile.txt`
File extensions:	
`Path.HasExtension (file)`	`True`
`Path.GetExtension (file)`	`.txt`
`Path.GetFileNameWithoutExtension (file)`	`myfile`
`Path.ChangeExtension (file, ".log")`	`myfile.log`
Separators and characters:	
`Path.DirectorySeparatorChar`	`\` or `/`
`Path.AltDirectorySeparatorChar`	`/`
`Path.PathSeparator`	`;` or `:`
`Path.VolumeSeparatorChar`	`:` or `/`
`Path.GetInvalidPathChars()`	chars 0 to 31 and `"<>|` e or 0
`Path.GetInvalidFileNameChars()`	chars 0 to 31 and `"<>|:*?\/` or 0 and /
Temporary files:	
`Path.GetTempPath()`	*<local user folder>*\Temp or /tmp/
`Path.GetRandomFileName()`	*d2dwuzjf.dnp*
`Path.GetTempFileName()`	*<local user folder>*\Temp*tmp14B.tmp* or /tmp/*tmpubSUYO.tmp*

`Combine` is particularly useful: it allows you to combine a directory and filename—or two directories—without first having to check whether a trailing path separator is present, and it automatically uses the correct path separator for the OS. It provides overloads that accept up to four directory and/or filenames.

`GetFullPath` converts a path relative to the current directory to an absolute path. It accepts values such as ..\..*file.txt*.

`GetRandomFileName` returns a genuinely unique 8.3-character filename, without actually creating any file. `GetTempFileName` generates a temporary filename using an autoincrementing counter that repeats every 65,000 files. It then creates a zero-byte file of this name in the local temporary directory.

You must delete the file generated by `GetTempFileName` when you're done; otherwise, it will eventually throw an exception (after your 65,000th call to `GetTempFileName`). If this is a problem, you can instead Combine `GetTempPath` with `Get RandomFileName`. Just be careful not to fill up the user's hard drive!

Special Folders

One thing missing from `Path` and `Directory` is a means to locate folders such as *My Documents*, *Program Files*, *Application Data*, and so on. This is provided instead by the `GetFolderPath` method in the `System.Environment` class:

```
string myDocPath = Environment.GetFolderPath
  (Environment.SpecialFolder.MyDocuments);
```

`Environment.SpecialFolder` is an enum whose values encompass all special directories in Windows, such as `AdminTools`, `ApplicationData`, `Fonts`, `History`, `SendTo`, `StartMenu`, and so on. Everything is covered here except the .NET runtime directory, which you can obtain as follows:

```
System.Runtime.InteropServices.RuntimeEnvironment.GetRuntimeDirectory()
```

Most of the special folders have no path assigned on Unix systems. The following have paths on Ubuntu Linux 18.04 Desktop: `ApplicationData`, `CommonApplicationData`, `Desktop`, `DesktopDirectory`, `LocalApplicationData`, `MyDocu ments`, `MyMusic`, `MyPictures`, `MyVideos`, `Templates`, and `UserProfile`.

Of particular value on Windows systems is `ApplicationData`, where you can store settings that travel with a user across a network (if roaming profiles are enabled on the network domain); `LocalApplicationData`, which is for nonroaming data (specific to the logged-in user); and `CommonApplicationData`, which is shared by every user of the computer. Writing application data to these folders is considered preferable to using the Windows Registry. The standard protocol for storing data in these folders is to create a subdirectory with the name of your application:

```
string localAppDataPath = Path.Combine (
  Environment.GetFolderPath (Environment.SpecialFolder.ApplicationData),
  "MyCoolApplication");

if (!Directory.Exists (localAppDataPath))
  Directory.CreateDirectory (localAppDataPath);
```

There's a horrible trap when using `CommonApplicationData`: if a user starts your program with administrative elevation and your program then creates folders and files in `CommonApplicationData`, that user might lack permissions to replace those files later, when run under a restricted Windows login. (A similar problem exists when switching between restricted-permission accounts.) You can work around it by creating the desired folder (with permissions assigned to everyone) as part of your setup.

Another place to write configuration and log files is to the application's base directory, which you can obtain with `AppDomain.CurrentDomain.BaseDirectory`. This is not recommended, however, because the OS is likely to deny your application permissions to write to this folder after initial installation (without administrative elevation).

Querying Volume Information

You can query the drives on a computer with the `DriveInfo` class:

```
DriveInfo c = new DriveInfo ("C");        // Query the C: drive.
                                          // On Unix: /

long totalSize = c.TotalSize;             // Size in bytes.
long freeBytes = c.TotalFreeSpace;        // Ignores disk quotas.
long freeToMe  = c.AvailableFreeSpace;    // Takes quotas into account.

foreach (DriveInfo d in DriveInfo.GetDrives())  // All defined drives.
                                                // On Unix: mount points
{
  Console.WriteLine (d.Name);             // C:\
  Console.WriteLine (d.DriveType);        // Fixed
  Console.WriteLine (d.RootDirectory);    // C:\

  if (d.IsReady)    // If the drive is not ready, the following two
                    // properties will throw exceptions:
  {
    Console.WriteLine (d.VolumeLabel);    // The Sea Drive
    Console.WriteLine (d.DriveFormat);    // NTFS
  }
}
```

The static `GetDrives` method returns all mapped drives, including CD-ROMs, media cards, and network connections. `DriveType` is an enum with the following values:

```
Unknown, NoRootDirectory, Removable, Fixed, Network, CDRom, Ram
```

Catching Filesystem Events

The `FileSystemWatcher` class lets you monitor a directory (and optionally, subdirectories) for activity. `FileSystemWatcher` has events that fire when files or subdirectories are created, modified, renamed, and deleted, as well as when their attributes change. These events fire regardless of the user or process performing the change. Here's an example:

```
Watch (GetTestDirectory(), "*.txt", true);

void Watch (string path, string filter, bool includeSubDirs)
{
```

```
using (var watcher = new FileSystemWatcher (path, filter))
{
  watcher.Created += FileCreatedChangedDeleted;
  watcher.Changed += FileCreatedChangedDeleted;
  watcher.Deleted += FileCreatedChangedDeleted;
  watcher.Renamed += FileRenamed;
  watcher.Error   += FileError;

  watcher.IncludeSubdirectories = includeSubDirs;
  watcher.EnableRaisingEvents = true;

  Console.WriteLine ("Listening for events - press <enter> to end");
  Console.ReadLine();
}
// Disposing the FileSystemWatcher stops further events from firing.
}

void FileCreatedChangedDeleted (object o, FileSystemEventArgs e)
  => Console.WriteLine ("File {0} has been {1}", e.FullPath, e.ChangeType);

void FileRenamed (object o, RenamedEventArgs e)
  => Console.WriteLine ("Renamed: {0}->{1}", e.OldFullPath, e.FullPath);

void FileError (object o, ErrorEventArgs e)
  => Console.WriteLine ("Error: " + e.GetException().Message);

string GetTestDirectory() =>
  RuntimeInformation.IsOSPlatform (OSPlatform.Windows)
    ? @"C:\Temp"
    : "/tmp";
```

 Because `FileSystemWatcher` raises events on a separate thread, you must exception-handle the event handling code to prevent an error from taking down the application. For more information, see "Exception Handling" on page 618.

The `Error` event does not inform you of filesystem errors; instead, it indicates that the `FileSystemWatcher`'s event buffer overflowed because it was overwhelmed by `Changed`, `Created`, `Deleted`, or `Renamed` events. You can change the buffer size via the `InternalBufferSize` property.

`IncludeSubdirectories` applies recursively. So, if you create a `FileSystemWatcher` on *C:* with `IncludeSubdirectories` true, its events will fire when a file or directory changes anywhere on the hard drive.

 A trap in using `FileSystemWatcher` is to open and read newly created or updated files before the file has been fully populated or updated. If you're working in conjunction with some other software that's creating files, you might need to consider some strategy to mitigate this, such as creating files with an unwatched extension and then renaming them after they're fully written.

OS Security

All applications are subject to OS restrictions, based on the user's login privileges. These restrictions affect file I/O as well as other capabilities, such as access to the Windows Registry.

In Windows and Unix, there are two types of accounts:

- An administrative/superuser account that imposes no restrictions in accessing the local computer
- A limited permissions account that restricts administrative functions and visibility of other users' data

On Windows, a feature called User Account Control (UAC) means that administrators receive two tokens, or "hats," when logging in: an administrative hat and an ordinary user hat. By default, programs run wearing the ordinary user hat—with restricted permissions—unless the program requests *administrative elevation*. The user must then approve the request in the dialog box that's presented.

On Unix, users typically log in with restricted accounts. That is also true for administrators to lessen the probability of inadvertently damaging the system. When a user needs to run a command that requires elevated permissions, they precede the command with sudo (short for super-user do).

By default, your application will run with restricted user privileges. This means that you must do one of the following:

- Write your application such that it can run without administrative privileges.
- Demand administrative elevation in the application manifest (Windows only), or detect the lack of required privileges and alert the user to restart the application as an administrator/super-user.

The first option is safer and more convenient to the user. Designing your program to run without administrative privileges is easy in most cases.

You can find out whether you're running under an administrative account as follows:

```
[DllImport("libc")]
public static extern uint getuid();

static bool IsRunningAsAdmin()
{
  if (RuntimeInformation.IsOSPlatform (OSPlatform.Windows))
  {
    using var identity = WindowsIdentity.GetCurrent();
    var principal = new WindowsPrincipal (identity);
    return principal.IsInRole (WindowsBuiltInRole.Administrator);
  }
```

```
    return getuid() == 0;
}
```

With UAC enabled on Windows, this returns `true` only if the current process has administrative elevation. On Linux, it returns `true` only if the current process is running as a super-user (e.g., *sudo myapp*).

Running in a Standard User Account

Here are the key things that you *cannot* do in a standard user account:

- Write to the following directories:
  - The OS folder (typically *Windows* or */bin, /sbin, ...*) and subdirectories
  - The program files folder (*Program Files* or */usr/bin, /opt*) and subdirectories
  - The root of the OS drive (e.g., *C:* or */*)
- Write to the HKEY_LOCAL_MACHINE branch of the Registry (Windows)
- Read performance monitoring (WMI) data (Windows)

Additionally, as an ordinary Windows user (or even as an administrator), you might be refused access to files or resources that belong to other users. Windows uses a system of Access Control Lists (ACLs) to protect such resources—you can query and assert your own rights in the ACLs via types in `System.Security.Access Control`. ACLs can also be applied to cross-process wait handles, described in Chapter 21.

If you're refused access to anything as a result of OS security, the CLR detects the failure and throws an `UnauthorizedAccessException` (rather than failing silently).

In most cases, you can deal with standard user restrictions as follows:

- Write files to their recommended locations.
- Avoid using the Registry for information that can be stored in files (aside from the HKEY_CURRENT_USER hive, which you will have read/write access to on Windows only).
- Register ActiveX or COM components during setup (Windows only).

The recommended location for user documents is `SpecialFolder.MyDocuments`:

```
string docsFolder = Environment.GetFolderPath
                    (Environment.SpecialFolder.MyDocuments);

string path = Path.Combine (docsFolder, "test.txt");
```

The recommended location for configuration files that a user might need to modify outside of your application is `SpecialFolder.ApplicationData` (current user only) or `SpecialFolder.CommonApplicationData` (all users). You typically create subdirectories within these folders, based on your organization and product name.

Administrative Elevation and Virtualization

With an *application manifest*, you can request that Windows prompt the user for administrative elevation whenever running your program (Linux ignores this request):

```xml
<?xml version="1.0" encoding="utf-8"?>
<assembly manifestVersion="1.0" xmlns="urn:schemas-microsoft-com:asm.v1">
  <trustInfo xmlns="urn:schemas-microsoft-com:asm.v2">
    <security>
      <requestedPrivileges>
        <requestedExecutionLevel level="requireAdministrator" />
      </requestedPrivileges>
    </security>
  </trustInfo>
</assembly>
```

(We describe application manifests in more detail in Chapter 17.)

If you replace `requireAdministrator` with `asInvoker`, it instructs Windows that administrative elevation is *not* required. The effect is almost the same as not having an application manifest at all—except that *virtualization* is disabled. Virtualization is a temporary measure introduced with Windows Vista to help old applications run correctly without administrative privileges. The absence of an application manifest with a `requestedExecutionLevel` element activates this backward-compatibility feature.

Virtualization comes into play when an application writes to the *Program Files* or *Windows* directory, or the HKEY_LOCAL_MACHINE area of the Registry. Instead of throwing an exception, changes are redirected to a separate location on the hard disk where they can't affect the original data. This prevents the application from interfering with the OS—or other well-behaved applications.

Memory-Mapped Files

Memory-mapped files provide two key features:

- Efficient random access to file data
- The ability to share memory between different processes on the same computer

The types for memory-mapped files reside in the `System.IO.MemoryMappedFiles` namespace. Internally, they work by wrapping the operating system's API for memory-mapped files.

Memory-Mapped Files and Random File I/O

Although an ordinary `FileStream` allows random file I/O (by setting the stream's `Position` property), it's optimized for sequential I/O. As a rough rule of thumb:

- `FileStream`s are approximately 10 times faster than memory-mapped files for sequential I/O.
- Memory-mapped files are approximately 10 times faster than `FileStream`s for random I/O.

Changing a `FileStream`'s `Position` can cost several microseconds—which adds up if done within a loop. A `FileStream` is also unsuitable for multithreaded access—because its position changes as it is read or written.

To create a memory-mapped file:

1. Obtain a `FileStream` as you would ordinarily.
2. Instantiate a `MemoryMappedFile`, passing in the file stream.
3. Call `CreateViewAccessor` on the memory-mapped file object.

The last step gives you a `MemoryMappedViewAccessor` object that provides methods for randomly reading and writing simple types, structures, and arrays (more on this in "Working with View Accessors" on page 715).

The following creates a one million–byte file and then uses the memory-mapped file API to read and then write a byte at position 500,000:

```
File.WriteAllBytes ("long.bin", new byte [1000000]);

using MemoryMappedFile mmf = MemoryMappedFile.CreateFromFile ("long.bin");
using MemoryMappedViewAccessor accessor = mmf.CreateViewAccessor();

accessor.Write (500000, (byte) 77);
Console.WriteLine (accessor.ReadByte (500000));   // 77
```

You can also specify a map name and capacity when calling `CreateFromFile`. Specifying a non-null map name allows the memory block to be shared with other processes (see the following section); specifying a capacity automatically enlarges the file to that value. The following creates a 1,000-byte file:

```
File.WriteAllBytes ("short.bin", new byte [1]);
using (var mmf = MemoryMappedFile.CreateFromFile
                 ("short.bin", FileMode.Create, null, 1000))
    ...
```

Memory-Mapped Files and Shared Memory (Windows)

Under Windows, you can also use memory-mapped files as a means of sharing memory between processes on the same computer. One process creates a shared memory block by calling `MemoryMappedFile.CreateNew`, and then other processes subscribe to that same memory block by calling `MemoryMappedFile.OpenExisting` with the same name. Although it's still referred to as a memory-mapped "file," it resides entirely in memory and has no disk presence.

The following code creates a 500-byte shared memory-mapped file and writes the integer 12345 at position 0:

```
using (MemoryMappedFile mmFile = MemoryMappedFile.CreateNew ("Demo", 500))
using (MemoryMappedViewAccessor accessor = mmFile.CreateViewAccessor())
{
  accessor.Write (0, 12345);
  Console.ReadLine();   // Keep shared memory alive until user hits Enter.
}
```

The following code opens that memory-mapped file and reads that integer:

```
// This can run in a separate executable:
using (MemoryMappedFile mmFile = MemoryMappedFile.OpenExisting ("Demo"))
using (MemoryMappedViewAccessor accessor = mmFile.CreateViewAccessor())
  Console.WriteLine (accessor.ReadInt32 (0));   // 12345
```

Cross-Platform Interprocess Shared Memory

Both Windows and Unix allow multiple processes to memory-map the same file. You must exercise care to ensure appropriate file sharing settings:

```
static void Writer()
{
  var file = Path.Combine (TestDirectory, "interprocess.bin");
  File.WriteAllBytes (file, new byte [100]);

  using FileStream fs =
    new FileStream (file, FileMode.Open, FileAccess.ReadWrite,
                    FileShare.ReadWrite);

  using MemoryMappedFile mmf = MemoryMappedFile
    .CreateFromFile (fs, null, fs.Length, MemoryMappedFileAccess.ReadWrite,
                     HandleInheritability.None, true);
  using MemoryMappedViewAccessor accessor = mmf.CreateViewAccessor();

  accessor.Write (0, 12345);

  Console.ReadLine();   // Keep shared memory alive until user hits Enter.

  File.Delete (file);
}

static void Reader()
{
  // This can run in a separate executable:
  var file = Path.Combine (TestDirectory, "interprocess.bin");
  using FileStream fs =
    new FileStream (file, FileMode.Open, FileAccess.ReadWrite,
                    FileShare.ReadWrite);
  using MemoryMappedFile mmf = MemoryMappedFile
```

```
    .CreateFromFile (fs, null, fs.Length, MemoryMappedFileAccess.ReadWrite,
                     HandleInheritability.None, true);
  using MemoryMappedViewAccessor accessor = mmf.CreateViewAccessor();

  Console.WriteLine (accessor.ReadInt32 (0));    // 12345
}

static string TestDirectory =>
  RuntimeInformation.IsOSPlatform (OSPlatform.Windows)
    ? @"C:\Test"
    : "/tmp";
```

Working with View Accessors

Calling `CreateViewAccessor` on a `MemoryMappedFile` gives you a view accessor that
lets you read/write values at random positions.

The `Read*`/`Write*` methods accept numeric types, bool, and char, as well as arrays
and structs that contain value-type elements or fields. Reference types—and arrays
or structs that contain reference types—are prohibited because they cannot map
into unmanaged memory. So, if you want to write a string, you must encode it into
an array of bytes:

```
byte[] data = Encoding.UTF8.GetBytes ("This is a test");
accessor.Write (0, data.Length);
accessor.WriteArray (4, data, 0, data.Length);
```

Notice that we wrote the length first. This means we know how many bytes to read
back later:

```
byte[] data = new byte [accessor.ReadInt32 (0)];
accessor.ReadArray (4, data, 0, data.Length);
Console.WriteLine (Encoding.UTF8.GetString (data));    // This is a test
```

Here's an example of reading/writing a struct:

```
struct Data { public int X, Y; }
...
var data = new Data { X = 123, Y = 456 };
accessor.Write (0, ref data);
accessor.Read (0, out data);
Console.WriteLine (data.X + " " + data.Y);    // 123 456
```

The `Read` and `Write` methods are surprisingly slow. You can get much better performance by directly accessing the underlying unmanaged memory via a pointer.
Following on from the previous example:

```
unsafe
{
  byte* pointer = null;
  try
  {
    accessor.SafeMemoryMappedViewHandle.AcquirePointer (ref pointer);
    int* intPointer = (int*) pointer;
    Console.WriteLine (*intPointer);            // 123
```

```
      }
      finally
      {
        if (pointer != null)
          accessor.SafeMemoryMappedViewHandle.ReleasePointer();
      }
    }
```

Your project must be configured to allow unsafe code. You can do that by editing your .csproj file:

```
<PropertyGroup>
  <AllowUnsafeBlocks>true</AllowUnsafeBlocks>
</PropertyGroup>
```

The performance advantage of pointers is even more pronounced when working with large structures because they let you work directly with the raw data rather than using Read/Write to *copy* data between managed and unmanaged memory. We explore this further in Chapter 24.

16

Networking

.NET offers a variety of classes in the `System.Net.*` namespaces for communicating via standard network protocols, such as HTTP and TCP/IP. Here's a summary of the key components:

- `HttpClient` for consuming HTTP web APIs and RESTful services
- `HttpListener` for writing an HTTP server
- `SmtpClient` for constructing and sending mail messages via SMTP
- `Dns` for converting between domain names and addresses
- `TcpClient`, `UdpClient`, `TcpListener`, and `Socket` classes for direct access to the transport and network layers

The .NET types in this chapter are in the `System.Net.*` and `System.IO` namespaces.

.NET also provides client-side support for FTP, but only through classes that have been marked as obsolete from .NET 6. If you need to use FTP, your best option is to reach for a NuGet library such as FluentFTP.

Network Architecture

Figure 16-1 illustrates the .NET networking types and the communication layers in which they reside. Most types reside in the *transport layer* or *application layer*. The transport layer defines basic protocols for sending and receiving bytes (TCP and UDP); the application layer defines higher-level protocols designed for specific applications such as retrieving web pages (HTTP), sending mail (SMTP), and converting between domain names and IP addresses (DNS).

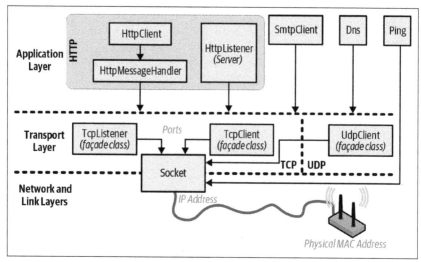

Figure 16-1. Network architecture

It's usually most convenient to program at the application layer; however, there are a couple of reasons why you might want to work directly at the transport layer. One is if you need an application protocol not provided in .NET, such as POP3 for retrieving mail. Another is if you want to invent a custom protocol for a special application such as a peer-to-peer client.

Of the application protocols, HTTP is special in its applicability to general-purpose communication. Its basic mode of operation—"give me the web page with this URL" —adapts nicely to "get me the result of calling this endpoint with these arguments." (In addition to the "get" verb, there is "put," "post," and "delete," allowing for REST-based services.)

HTTP also has a rich set of features that are useful in multitier business applications and service-oriented architectures, such as protocols for authentication and encryption, message chunking, extensible headers and cookies, and the ability to have many server applications share a single port and IP address. For these reasons, HTTP is well supported in .NET—both directly, as described in this chapter, and at a higher level, through such technologies as Web API and ASP.NET Core.

As the preceding discussion makes clear, networking is a field that is awash in acronyms. We list the most common in Table 16-1.

Table 16-1. Network acronyms

Acronym	Expansion	Notes
DNS	Domain Name Service	Converts between domain names (e.g., *ebay.com*) and IP addresses (e.g., 199.54.213.2)
FTP	File Transfer Protocol	Internet-based protocol for sending and receiving files

Acronym	Expansion	Notes
HTTP	Hypertext Transfer Protocol	Retrieves web pages and runs web services
IIS	Internet Information Services	Microsoft's web server software
IP	Internet Protocol	Network-layer protocol below TCP and UDP
LAN	Local Area Network	Most LANs use internet-based protocols such as TCP/IP
POP	Post Office Protocol	Retrieves internet mail
REST	REpresentational State Transfer	A popular web service architecture that uses machine-followable links in responses and that can operate over basic HTTP
SMTP	Simple Mail Transfer Protocol	Sends internet mail
TCP	Transmission and Control Protocol	Transport-layer internet protocol on top of which most higher-layer services are built
UDP	Universal Datagram Protocol	Transport-layer internet protocol used for low-overhead services such as VoIP
UNC	Universal Naming Convention	\\computer\sharename\filename
URI	Uniform Resource Identifier	Ubiquitous resource naming system (e.g., http://www.amazon.com or mailto:joe@bloggs.org)
URL	Uniform Resource Locator	Technical meaning (fading from use): subset of URI; popular meaning: synonym of URI

Addresses and Ports

For communication to work, a computer or device requires an address. The internet uses two addressing systems:

IPv4

Currently the dominant addressing system; IPv4 addresses are 32 bits wide. When string-formatted, IPv4 addresses are written as four dot-separated decimals (e.g., 101.102.103.104). An address can be unique in the world—or unique within a particular *subnet* (such as on a corporate network).

IPv6

The newer 128-bit addressing system. Addresses are string-formatted in hexadecimal with a colon separator (e.g., [3EA0:FFFF:198A:E4A3:4FF2:54fA:41BC:8D31]). .NET requires that you add square brackets around the address.

The IPAddress class in the System.Net namespace represents an address in either protocol. It has a constructor accepting a byte array, and a static Parse method accepting a correctly formatted string:

```
IPAddress a1 = new IPAddress (new byte[] { 101, 102, 103, 104 });
IPAddress a2 = IPAddress.Parse ("101.102.103.104");
Console.WriteLine (a1.Equals (a2));                    // True
```

```
Console.WriteLine (a1.AddressFamily);                    // InterNetwork

IPAddress a3 = IPAddress.Parse
  ("[3EA0:FFFF:198A:E4A3:4FF2:54fA:41BC:8D31]");
Console.WriteLine (a3.AddressFamily);    // InterNetworkV6
```

The TCP and UDP protocols break out each IP address into 65,535 ports, allowing a computer on a single address to run multiple applications, each on its own port. Many applications have standard default port assignments; for instance, HTTP uses port 80; SMTP uses port 25.

 The TCP and UDP ports from 49152 to 65535 are officially unassigned, so they are good for testing and small-scale deployments.

An IP address and port combination is represented in .NET by the IPEndPoint class:

```
IPAddress a = IPAddress.Parse ("101.102.103.104");
IPEndPoint ep = new IPEndPoint (a, 222);           // Port 222
Console.WriteLine (ep.ToString());                 // 101.102.103.104:222
```

 Firewalls block ports. In many corporate environments, only a few ports are open—typically, port 80 (for unencrypted HTTP) and port 443 (for secure HTTP).

URIs

A URI is a specially formatted string that describes a resource on the internet or a LAN, such as a web page, file, or email address. Examples include *http://www.ietf.org*, *ftp://myisp/doc.txt*, and *mailto:joe@bloggs.com*. The exact formatting is defined by the *Internet Engineering Task Force* (*http://www.ietf.org*) (IETF).

A URI can be broken up into a series of elements—typically, *scheme*, *authority*, and *path*. The Uri class in the System namespace performs just this division, exposing a property for each element, as illustrated in Figure 16-2.

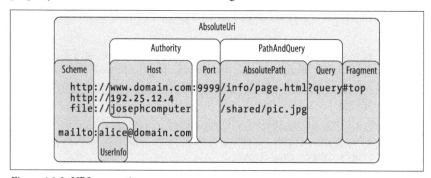

Figure 16-2. URI properties

The Uri class is useful when you need to validate the format of a URI string or to split a URI into its component parts. Otherwise, you can treat a URI simply as a string—most networking methods are overloaded to accept either a Uri object or a string.

You can construct a Uri object by passing any of the following strings into its constructor:

- A URI string, such as *http://www.ebay.com* or *file://janespc/sharedpics/dolphin.jpg*
- An absolute path to a file on your hard disk, such as *c:\myfiles\data.xlsx* or, on Unix, */tmp/myfiles/data.xlsx*
- A UNC path to a file on the LAN, such as *\\janespc\sharedpics\dolphin.jpg*

File and UNC paths are automatically converted to URIs: the "file:" protocol is added, and backslashes are converted to forward slashes. The Uri constructors also perform some basic cleanup on your string before creating the Uri, including converting the scheme and hostname to lowercase and removing default and blank port numbers. If you supply a URI string without the scheme, such as *www.test.com*, a UriFormatException is thrown.

Uri has an IsLoopback property, which indicates whether the Uri references the local host (IP address 127.0.0.1), and an IsFile property, which indicates whether the Uri references a local or UNC (IsUnc) path (IsUnc reports false for a *Samba* share mounted in a *Linux* filesystem). If IsFile returns true, the LocalPath property returns a version of AbsolutePath that is friendly to the local OS (with slashes or backslashes as appropriate to the OS), on which you can call File.Open.

Instances of Uri have read-only properties. To modify an existing Uri, instantiate a UriBuilder object—this has writable properties and can be converted back via its Uri property.

Uri also provides methods for comparing and subtracting paths:

```
Uri info = new Uri ("http://www.domain.com:80/info/");
Uri page = new Uri ("http://www.domain.com/info/page.html");

Console.WriteLine (info.Host);      // www.domain.com
Console.WriteLine (info.Port);      // 80
Console.WriteLine (page.Port);      // 80  (Uri knows the default HTTP port)

Console.WriteLine (info.IsBaseOf (page));        // True
Uri relative = info.MakeRelativeUri (page);
Console.WriteLine (relative.IsAbsoluteUri);      // False
Console.WriteLine (relative.ToString());         // page.html
```

Networking

A relative Uri, such as *page.html* in this example, will throw an exception if you call almost any property or method other than IsAbsoluteUri and ToString(). You can directly instantiate a relative Uri, as follows:

```
Uri u = new Uri ("page.html", UriKind.Relative);
```

 A trailing slash is significant in a URI and makes a difference as to how a server processes a request if a path component is present.

In a traditional web server, for instance, given the URI *http://www.albahari.com/nutshell/*, you can expect an HTTP web server to look in the *nutshell* subdirectory in the site's web folder and return the default document (usually *index.html*).

Without the trailing slash, the web server will instead look for a file called *nutshell* (without an extension) directly in the site's root folder—which is usually not what you want. If no such file exists, most web servers will assume the user mistyped and will return a 301 *Permanent Redirect* error, suggesting the client retry with the trailing slash. A .NET HTTP client, by default, will respond transparently to a 301 in the same way as a web browser—by retrying with the suggested URI. This means that if you omit a trailing slash when it should have been included, your request will still work—but will suffer an unnecessary extra round trip.

The Uri class also provides static helper methods such as EscapeUriString(), which converts a string to a valid URL by converting all characters with an ASCII value greater than 127 to hexadecimal representation. The CheckHostName() and CheckSchemeName() methods accept a string and check whether it is syntactically valid for the given property (although they do not attempt to determine whether a host or URI exists).

HttpClient

The HttpClient class exposes a modern API for HTTP client operations, replacing the old WebClient and WebRequest/WebResponse types (which have since been marked as obsolete).

HttpClient was written in response to the growth of HTTP-based web APIs and REST services, and provides a good experience when dealing with protocols more elaborate than simply fetching a web page. In particular:

- A single HttpClient instance can handle concurrent requests and plays well with features such as custom headers, cookies, and authentication schemes.

- HttpClient lets you write and plug in custom message handlers. This enables mocking in unit tests, and the creation of custom pipelines (for logging, compression, encryption, and so on).

- HttpClient has a rich and extensible type system for headers and content.

 HttpClient does not support progress reporting. For a solution, see "HttpClient with Progress.linq" at *http://www.alba-hari.com/nutshell/code.aspx* or via LINQPad's interactive samples gallery.

The simplest way to use HttpClient is to instantiate it and then call one of its Get* methods, passing in a URI:

```
string html = await new HttpClient().GetStringAsync ("http://linqpad.net");
```

(There's also GetByteArrayAsync and GetStreamAsync.) All I/O-bound methods in HttpClient are asynchronous.

Unlike its WebRequest/WebResponse predecessors, to get the best performance with HttpClient, you *must* reuse the same instance (otherwise things such as DNS resolution can be unnecessarily repeated and sockets are held open longer than necessary). HttpClient permits concurrent operations, so the following is legal and downloads two web pages at once:

```
var client = new HttpClient();
var task1 = client.GetStringAsync ("http://www.linqpad.net");
var task2 = client.GetStringAsync ("http://www.albahari.com");
Console.WriteLine (await task1);
Console.WriteLine (await task2);
```

HttpClient has a Timeout property and a BaseAddress property, which prefixes a URI to every request. HttpClient is somewhat of a thin shell: most of the other properties that you might expect to find here are defined in another class called HttpClientHandler. To access this class, you instantiate it and then pass the instance into HttpClient's constructor:

```
var handler = new HttpClientHandler { UseProxy = false };
var client = new HttpClient (handler);
...
```

In this example, we told the handler to disable proxy support, which can sometimes improve performance by avoiding the cost of automatic proxy detection. There are also properties to control cookies, automatic redirection, authentication, and so on (we describe these in the following sections).

GetAsync and Response Messages

The GetStringAsync, GetByteArrayAsync, and GetStreamAsync methods are convenient shortcuts for calling the more general GetAsync method, which returns a *response message*:

```
var client = new HttpClient();
// The GetAsync method also accepts a CancellationToken.
HttpResponseMessage response = await client.GetAsync ("http://...");
```

```
response.EnsureSuccessStatusCode();
string html = await response.Content.ReadAsStringAsync();
```

HttpResponseMessage exposes properties for accessing the headers (see "Headers" on page 729) and the HTTP StatusCode. An unsuccessful status code such as 404 (not found) doesn't cause an exception to be thrown unless you explicitly call EnsureSuccessStatusCode. Communication or DNS errors, however, do throw exceptions.

HttpContent has a CopyToAsync method for writing to another stream, which is useful in writing the output to a file:

```
using (var fileStream = File.Create ("linqpad.html"))
    await response.Content.CopyToAsync (fileStream);
```

GetAsync is one of four methods corresponding to HTTP's four verbs (the others are PostAsync, PutAsync, and DeleteAsync). We demonstrate PostAsync later in "Uploading Form Data" on page 730.

SendAsync and Request Messages

GetAsync, PostAsync, PutAsync, and DeleteAsync are all shortcuts for calling Send Async, the single low-level method into which everything else feeds. To use this, you first construct an HttpRequestMessage:

```
var client = new HttpClient();
var request = new HttpRequestMessage (HttpMethod.Get, "http://...");
HttpResponseMessage response = await client.SendAsync (request);
response.EnsureSuccessStatusCode();
...
```

Instantiating a HttpRequestMessage object means that you can customize properties of the request, such as the headers (see "Headers" on page 729) and the content itself, allowing you to upload data.

Uploading Data and HttpContent

After instantiating a HttpRequestMessage object, you can upload content by assigning its Content property. The type for this property is an abstract class called HttpContent. .NET includes the following concrete subclasses for different kinds of content (you can also write your own):

- ByteArrayContent

- StringContent

- FormUrlEncodedContent (see "Uploading Form Data" on page 730)

- StreamContent

For example:

```
var client = new HttpClient (new HttpClientHandler { UseProxy = false });
var request = new HttpRequestMessage (
  HttpMethod.Post, "http://www.albahari.com/EchoPost.aspx");
request.Content = new StringContent ("This is a test");
HttpResponseMessage response = await client.SendAsync (request);
response.EnsureSuccessStatusCode();
Console.WriteLine (await response.Content.ReadAsStringAsync());
```

HttpMessageHandler

We said previously that most of the properties for customizing requests are defined not in HttpClient but in HttpClientHandler. The latter is actually a subclass of the abstract HttpMessageHandler class, defined as follows:

```
public abstract class HttpMessageHandler : IDisposable
{
  protected internal abstract Task<HttpResponseMessage> SendAsync
    (HttpRequestMessage request, CancellationToken cancellationToken);

  public void Dispose();
  protected virtual void Dispose (bool disposing);
}
```

The SendAsync method is called from HttpClient's SendAsync method.

HttpMessageHandler is simple enough to subclass easily and offers an extensibility point into HttpClient.

Unit testing and mocking

We can subclass HttpMessageHandler to create a *mocking* handler to assist with unit testing:

```
class MockHandler : HttpMessageHandler
{
  Func <HttpRequestMessage, HttpResponseMessage> _responseGenerator;

  public MockHandler
    (Func <HttpRequestMessage, HttpResponseMessage> responseGenerator)
  {
    _responseGenerator = responseGenerator;
  }

  protected override Task <HttpResponseMessage> SendAsync
    (HttpRequestMessage request, CancellationToken cancellationToken)
  {
    cancellationToken.ThrowIfCancellationRequested();
    var response = _responseGenerator (request);
    response.RequestMessage = request;
    return Task.FromResult (response);
  }
}
```

Its constructor accepts a function that tells the mocker how to generate a response from a request. This is the most versatile approach because the same handler can test multiple requests.

SendAsync is synchronous by virtue of Task.FromResult. We could have maintained asynchrony by having our response generator return a Task<HttpResponseMessage>, but this is pointless given that we can expect a mocking function to be short running. Here's how to use our mocking handler:

```
var mocker = new MockHandler (request =>
  new HttpResponseMessage (HttpStatusCode.OK)
  {
    Content = new StringContent ("You asked for " + request.RequestUri)
  });

var client = new HttpClient (mocker);
var response = await client.GetAsync ("http://www.linqpad.net");
string result = await response.Content.ReadAsStringAsync();
Assert.AreEqual ("You asked for http://www.linqpad.net/", result);
```

(Assert.AreEqual is a method you'd expect to find in a unit-testing framework such as NUnit.)

Chaining handlers with DelegatingHandler

You can create a message handler that calls another (resulting in a chain of handlers) by subclassing DelegatingHandler. You can use this to implement custom authentication, compression, and encryption protocols. The following demonstrates a simple logging handler:

```
class LoggingHandler : DelegatingHandler
{
  public LoggingHandler (HttpMessageHandler nextHandler)
  {
    InnerHandler = nextHandler;
  }

  protected async override Task <HttpResponseMessage> SendAsync
    (HttpRequestMessage request, CancellationToken cancellationToken)
  {
    Console.WriteLine ("Requesting: " + request.RequestUri);
    var response = await base.SendAsync (request, cancellationToken);
    Console.WriteLine ("Got response: " + response.StatusCode);
    return response;
  }
}
```

Notice that we've maintained asynchrony in overriding SendAsync. Introducing the async modifier when overriding a task-returning method is perfectly legal—and desirable in this case.

A better solution than writing to the `Console` would be to have the constructor accept some kind of logging object. Better still would be to accept a couple of `Action<T>` delegates that tell it how to log the request and response objects.

Proxies

A *proxy server* is an intermediary through which HTTP requests can be routed. Organizations sometimes set up a proxy server as the only means by which employees can access the internet—primarily because it simplifies security. A proxy has an address of its own and can demand authentication so that only selected users on the LAN can access the internet.

To use a proxy with `HttpClient`, first create an `HttpClientHandler` and assign its `Proxy` property and then feed that into `HttpClient`'s constructor:

```
WebProxy p = new WebProxy ("192.178.10.49", 808);
p.Credentials = new NetworkCredential ("username", "password", "domain");

var handler = new HttpClientHandler { Proxy = p };
var client = new HttpClient (handler);
...
```

`HttpClientHandler` also has a `UseProxy` property that you can assign to false instead of nulling out the `Proxy` property to defeat autodetection.

If you supply a domain when constructing the `NetworkCredential`, Windows-based authentication protocols are used. To use the currently authenticated Windows user, assign the static `CredentialCache.DefaultNetworkCredentials` value to the proxy's `Credentials` property.

As an alternative to repeatedly setting the `Proxy`, you can set the global default as follows:

```
HttpClient.DefaultWebProxy = myWebProxy;
```

Authentication

You can supply a username and password to an `HttpClient` as follows:

```
string username = "myuser";
string password = "mypassword";

var handler = new HttpClientHandler();
handler.Credentials = new NetworkCredential (username, password);
var client = new HttpClient (handler);
...
```

This works with dialog-based authentication protocols, such as Basic and Digest, and is extensible through the `AuthenticationManager` class. It also supports Windows NTLM and Kerberos (if you include a domain name when constructing the `NetworkCredential` object). If you want to use the currently authenticated

Windows user, you can leave the `Credentials` property null and instead set `Use DefaultCredentials` to true.

When you provide credentials, `HttpClient` automatically negotiates a compatible protocol. In some cases, there can be a choice: if you examine the initial response from a Microsoft Exchange server web mail page, for instance, it might contain the following headers:

```
HTTP/1.1 401 Unauthorized
Content-Length: 83
Content-Type: text/html
Server: Microsoft-IIS/6.0
WWW-Authenticate: Negotiate
WWW-Authenticate: NTLM
WWW-Authenticate: Basic realm="exchange.somedomain.com"
X-Powered-By: ASP.NET
Date: Sat, 05 Aug 2006 12:37:23 GMT
```

The 401 code signals that authorization is required; the "WWW-Authenticate" headers indicate what authentication protocols are understood. If you configure the `HttpClientHandler` with the correct username and password, however, this message will be hidden from you because the runtime responds automatically by choosing a compatible authentication protocol, and then resubmitting the original request with an extra header. Here's an example:

```
Authorization: Negotiate TlRMTVNTUAAABAAAt5II2gjACDArAAACAwACACgAAAAQ
ATmKAAAAD0lVDRdPUksHUq9VUA==
```

This mechanism provides transparency, but generates an extra round trip with each request. You can avoid the extra round trips on subsequent requests to the same URI by setting the `PreAuthenticate` property on the `HttpClientHandler` to true.

CredentialCache

You can force a particular authentication protocol with a `CredentialCache` object. A credential cache contains one or more `NetworkCredential` objects, each keyed to a particular protocol and URI prefix. For example, you might want to avoid the Basic protocol when logging into an Exchange Server because it transmits passwords in plain text:

```
CredentialCache cache = new CredentialCache();
Uri prefix = new Uri ("http://exchange.somedomain.com");
cache.Add (prefix, "Digest",  new NetworkCredential ("joe", "passwd"));
cache.Add (prefix, "Negotiate", new NetworkCredential ("joe", "passwd"));

var handler = new HttpClientHandler();
handler.Credentials = cache;
...
```

An authentication protocol is specified as a string. The valid values include:

```
Basic, Digest, NTLM, Kerberos, Negotiate
```

In this particular situation it will choose `Negotiate`, because the server didn't indicate that it supported `Digest` in its authentication headers. `Negotiate` is a Windows protocol that currently boils down to either Kerberos or NTLM, depending on the capabilities of the server, but ensures forward compatibility of your application when future security standards are deployed.

The static `CredentialCache.DefaultNetworkCredentials` property allows you to add the currently authenticated Windows user to the credential cache without having to specify a password:

```
cache.Add (prefix, "Negotiate", CredentialCache.DefaultNetworkCredentials);
```

Authenticating via headers

Another way to authenticate is to set the authentication header directly:

```
var client = new HttpClient();
client.DefaultRequestHeaders.Authorization =
  new AuthenticationHeaderValue ("Basic",
    Convert.ToBase64String (Encoding.UTF8.GetBytes ("username:password")));
...
```

This strategy also works with custom authentication systems such as OAuth.

Headers

`HttpClient` lets you add custom HTTP headers to a request, as well as enumerate the headers in a response. A header is simply a key/value pair containing metadata, such as the message content type or server software. `HttpClient` exposes strongly typed collections with properties for standard HTTP headers. The `DefaultRequest Headers` property is for headers that apply to every request:

```
var client = new HttpClient (handler);

client.DefaultRequestHeaders.UserAgent.Add (
  new ProductInfoHeaderValue ("VisualStudio", "2022"));

client.DefaultRequestHeaders.Add ("CustomHeader", "VisualStudio/2022");
```

The `Headers` property on the `HttpRequestMessage` class, however, is for headers specific to a request.

Query Strings

A query string is simply a string appended to a URI with a question mark, used to send simple data to the server. You can specify multiple key/value pairs in a query string with the following syntax:

```
?key1=value1&key2=value2&key3=value3...
```

Here's a URI with a query string:

```
string requestURI = "http://www.google.com/search?q=HttpClient&hl=fr";
```

If there's a possibility of your query including symbols or spaces, you can use Uri's EscapeDataString method to create a legal URI:

```
string search = Uri.EscapeDataString ("(HttpClient or HttpRequestMessage)");
string language = Uri.EscapeDataString ("fr");
string requestURI = "http://www.google.com/search?q=" + search +
                    "&hl=" + language;
```

This resultant URI is:

```
http://www.google.com/search?q=(HttpClient%20OR%20HttpRequestMessage)&hl=fr
```

(EscapeDataString is similar to EscapeUriString except that it also encodes characters such as & and =, which would otherwise mess up the query string.)

Uploading Form Data

To upload HTML form data, create and populate the FormUrlEncodedContent object. You can then either pass it into the PostAsync method or assign it to a request's Content property:

```
string uri = "http://www.albahari.com/EchoPost.aspx";
var client = new HttpClient();
var dict = new Dictionary<string,string>
{
    { "Name", "Joe Albahari" },
    { "Company", "O'Reilly" }
};
var values = new FormUrlEncodedContent (dict);
var response = await client.PostAsync (uri, values);
response.EnsureSuccessStatusCode();
Console.WriteLine (await response.Content.ReadAsStringAsync());
```

Cookies

A cookie is a name/value string pair that an HTTP server sends to a client in a response header. A web browser client typically remembers cookies and replays them to the server in each subsequent request (to the same address) until their expiry. A cookie allows a server to know whether it's talking to the same client it was a minute ago—or yesterday—without needing a messy query string in the URI.

By default, HttpClient ignores any cookies received from the server. To accept cookies, create a CookieContainer object and assign it an HttpClientHandler:

```
var cc = new CookieContainer();
var handler = new HttpClientHandler();
handler.CookieContainer = cc;
var client = new HttpClient (handler);
...
```

To replay the received cookies in future requests, simply use the same CookieContainer object again. Alternatively, you can start with a fresh CookieContainer and then add cookies manually, as follows:

```
Cookie c = new Cookie ("PREF",
                       "ID=6b10df1da493a9c4:TM=1179...",
                       "/",
                       ".google.com");
freshCookieContainer.Add (c);
```

The third and fourth arguments indicate the path and domain of the originator. A CookieContainer on the client can house cookies from many different places; HttpClient sends only those cookies whose path and domain match those of the server.

Writing an HTTP Server

If you need to write an HTTP server in .NET 6, an alternative higher-level approach is to use the ASP.NET minimal API. Here's all it takes to get started:

```
var app = WebApplication.CreateBuilder().Build();
app.MapGet ("/", () => "Hello, world!");
app.Run();
```

You can write your own .NET HTTP server with the HttpListener class. The following is a simple server that listens on port 51111, waits for a single client request, and then returns a one-line reply:

```
using var server = new SimpleHttpServer();

// Make a client request:
Console.WriteLine (await new HttpClient().GetStringAsync
  ("http://localhost:51111/MyApp/Request.txt"));

class SimpleHttpServer : IDisposable
{
  readonly HttpListener listener = new HttpListener();

  public SimpleHttpServer() => ListenAsync();
  async void ListenAsync()
  {
    listener.Prefixes.Add ("http://localhost:51111/MyApp/");  // Listen on
    listener.Start();                                         // port 51111

    // Await a client request:
    HttpListenerContext context = await listener.GetContextAsync();

    // Respond to the request:
    string msg = "You asked for: " + context.Request.RawUrl;
    context.Response.ContentLength64 = Encoding.UTF8.GetByteCount (msg);
    context.Response.StatusCode = (int)HttpStatusCode.OK;

    using (Stream s = context.Response.OutputStream)
    using (StreamWriter writer = new StreamWriter (s))
      await writer.WriteAsync (msg);
  }

  public void Dispose() => listener.Close();
```

Networking

```
        }
```

```
    OUTPUT: You asked for: /MyApp/Request.txt
```

On Windows, HttpListener does not internally use .NET Socket objects; it instead calls the Windows HTTP Server API. This allows many applications on a computer to listen on the same IP address and port—as long as each registers different address prefixes. In our example, we registered the prefix *http://localhost/myapp*, so another application would be free to listen on the same IP and port on another prefix such as *http://localhost/anotherapp*. This is of value because opening new ports on corporate firewalls can be politically arduous.

HttpListener waits for the next client request when you call GetContext, returning an object with Request and Response properties. Each is analogous to client request or response, but from the server's perspective. You can read and write headers and cookies, for instance, to the request and response objects, much as you would at the client end.

You can choose how fully to support features of the HTTP protocol, based on your anticipated client audience. At a bare minimum, you should set the content length and status code on each request.

Here's a very simple web page server, written *asynchronously*:

```
using System;
using System.IO;
using System.Net;
using System.Text;
using System.Threading.Tasks;

class WebServer
{
  HttpListener _listener;
  string _baseFolder;        // Your web page folder.

  public WebServer (string uriPrefix, string baseFolder)
  {
    _listener = new HttpListener();
    _listener.Prefixes.Add (uriPrefix);
    _baseFolder = baseFolder;
  }

  public async void Start()
  {
    _listener.Start();
    while (true)
      try
      {
        var context = await _listener.GetContextAsync();
        Task.Run (() => ProcessRequestAsync (context));
      }
      catch (HttpListenerException)      { break; }   // Listener stopped.
      catch (InvalidOperationException) { break; }   // Listener stopped.
  }
```

```
public void Stop() => _listener.Stop();

async void ProcessRequestAsync (HttpListenerContext context)
{
  try
  {
    string filename = Path.GetFileName (context.Request.RawUrl);
    string path = Path.Combine (_baseFolder, filename);
    byte[] msg;
    if (!File.Exists (path))
    {
      Console.WriteLine ("Resource not found: " + path);
      context.Response.StatusCode = (int) HttpStatusCode.NotFound;
      msg = Encoding.UTF8.GetBytes ("Sorry, that page does not exist");
    }
    else
    {
      context.Response.StatusCode = (int) HttpStatusCode.OK;
      msg = File.ReadAllBytes (path);
    }
    context.Response.ContentLength64 = msg.Length;
    using (Stream s = context.Response.OutputStream)
      await s.WriteAsync (msg, 0, msg.Length);
  }
  catch (Exception ex) { Console.WriteLine ("Request error: " + ex); }
}
```

The following code sets things in motion:

```
// Listen on port 51111, serving files in d:\webroot:
var server = new WebServer ("http://localhost:51111/", @"d:\webroot");
try
{
  server.Start();
  Console.WriteLine ("Server running... press Enter to stop");
  Console.ReadLine();
}
finally { server.Stop(); }
```

You can test this at the client end with any web browser; the URI in this case will be *http://localhost:51111/* plus the name of the web page.

 HttpListener will not start if other software is competing for the same port (unless that software also uses the Windows HTTP Server API). Examples of applications that might listen on the default port 80 include a web server or a peer-to-peer program such as Skype.

Our use of asynchronous functions makes this server scalable and efficient. Starting this from a user interface (UI) thread, however, would hinder scalability because for each *request*, execution would bounce back to the UI thread after each await. Incurring such overhead is particularly pointless given that we don't have shared state, so in a UI scenario we'd get off the UI thread, either like this:

```
Task.Run (Start);
```

or by calling `ConfigureAwait(false)` after calling `GetContextAsync`.

Note that we used `Task.Run` to call `ProcessRequestAsync` even though the method was already asynchronous. This allows the caller to process another request *immediately* rather than having to first wait out the synchronous phase of the method (up until the first `await`).

Using DNS

The static `Dns` class encapsulates the DNS, which converts between a raw IP address, such as 66.135.192.87, and a human-friendly domain name, such as *ebay.com*.

The `GetHostAddresses` method converts from domain name to IP address (or addresses):

```
foreach (IPAddress a in Dns.GetHostAddresses ("albahari.com"))
    Console.WriteLine (a.ToString());      // 205.210.42.167
```

The `GetHostEntry` method goes the other way around, converting from address to domain name:

```
IPHostEntry entry = Dns.GetHostEntry ("205.210.42.167");
Console.WriteLine (entry.HostName);                    // albahari.com
```

`GetHostEntry` also accepts an `IPAddress` object, so you can specify an IP address as a byte array:

```
IPAddress address = new IPAddress (new byte[] { 205, 210, 42, 167 });
IPHostEntry entry = Dns.GetHostEntry (address);
Console.WriteLine (entry.HostName);                    // albahari.com
```

Domain names are automatically resolved to IP addresses when you use a class such as `WebRequest` or `TcpClient`. However, if you plan to make many network requests to the same address over the life of an application, you can sometimes improve performance by first using `Dns` to explicitly convert the domain name into an IP address, and then communicating directly with the IP address from that point on. This avoids repeated round-tripping to resolve the same domain name, and it can be of benefit when dealing at the transport layer (via `TcpClient`, `UdpClient`, or `Socket`).

The DNS class also provides awaitable task-based asynchronous methods:

```
foreach (IPAddress a in await Dns.GetHostAddressesAsync ("albahari.com"))
    Console.WriteLine (a.ToString());
```

Sending Mail with SmtpClient

The `SmtpClient` class in the `System.Net.Mail` namespace allows you to send mail messages through the ubiquitous Simple Mail Transfer Protocol, or SMTP. To send a simple text message, instantiate `SmtpClient`, set its `Host` property to your SMTP server address, and then call `Send`:

```
SmtpClient client = new SmtpClient();
client.Host = "mail.myserver.com";
client.Send ("from@adomain.com", "to@adomain.com", "subject", "body");
```

Constructing a `MailMessage` object exposes further options, including the ability to add attachments:

```
SmtpClient client = new SmtpClient();
client.Host = "mail.myisp.net";
MailMessage mm = new MailMessage();

mm.Sender = new MailAddress ("kay@domain.com", "Kay");
mm.From   = new MailAddress ("kay@domain.com", "Kay");
mm.To.Add  (new MailAddress ("bob@domain.com", "Bob"));
mm.CC.Add  (new MailAddress ("dan@domain.com", "Dan"));
mm.Subject = "Hello!";
mm.Body = "Hi there. Here's the photo!";
mm.IsBodyHtml = false;
mm.Priority = MailPriority.High;

Attachment a = new Attachment ("photo.jpg",
                               System.Net.Mime.MediaTypeNames.Image.Jpeg);
mm.Attachments.Add (a);
client.Send (mm);
```

To frustrate spammers, most SMTP servers on the internet will accept connections only from authenticated connections and require communication over SSL:

```
var client = new SmtpClient ("smtp.myisp.com", 587)
{
  Credentials = new NetworkCredential ("me@myisp.com", "MySecurePass"),
  EnableSsl = true
};
client.Send ("me@myisp.com", "someone@somewhere.com", "Subject", "Body");
Console.WriteLine ("Sent");
```

By changing the `DeliveryMethod` property, you can instruct the `SmtpClient` to instead use IIS to send mail messages or simply to write each message to an *.eml* file in a specified directory. This can be useful during development:

```
SmtpClient client = new SmtpClient();
client.DeliveryMethod = SmtpDeliveryMethod.SpecifiedPickupDirectory;
client.PickupDirectoryLocation = @"c:\mail";
```

Using TCP

TCP and UDP constitute the transport layer protocols on top of which most internet—and LAN—services are built. HTTP (version 2 and below), FTP, and SMTP use TCP; DNS and HTTP version 3 use UDP. TCP is connection-oriented and includes reliability mechanisms; UDP is connectionless, has a lower overhead, and supports broadcasting. *BitTorrent* uses UDP, as does Voice over IP (VoIP).

The transport layer offers greater flexibility—and potentially improved performance—over the higher layers, but it requires that you handle such tasks as authentication and encryption yourself.

With TCP in .NET, you have a choice of either the easier-to-use TcpClient and TcpListener façade classes, or the feature-rich Socket class. (In fact, you can mix and match, because TcpClient exposes the underlying Socket object through the Client property.) The Socket class exposes more configuration options and allows direct access to the network layer (IP) and non-internet-based protocols such as Novell's SPX/IPX.

As with other protocols, TCP differentiates a client and server: the client initiates a request, while the server waits for a request. Here's the basic structure for a synchronous TCP client request:

```
using (TcpClient client = new TcpClient())
{
  client.Connect ("address", port);
  using (NetworkStream n = client.GetStream())
  {
    // Read and write to the network stream...
  }
}
```

TcpClient's Connect method blocks until a connection is established (Connect Async is the asynchronous equivalent). The NetworkStream then provides a means of two-way communication, for both transmitting and receiving bytes of data from a server.

A simple TCP server looks like this:

```
TcpListener listener = new TcpListener (<ip address>, port);
listener.Start();

while (keepProcessingRequests)
  using (TcpClient c = listener.AcceptTcpClient())
  using (NetworkStream n = c.GetStream())
  {
    // Read and write to the network stream...
  }

listener.Stop();
```

TcpListener requires the local IP address on which to listen (a computer with two network cards, for instance, can have two addresses). You can use IPAddress.Any to instruct it to listen on all (or the only) local IP addresses. AcceptTcpClient blocks until a client request is received (again, there's also an asynchronous version), at which point we call GetStream, just as on the client side.

When working at the transport layer, you need to decide on a protocol for who talks when and for how long—rather like with a walkie-talkie. If both parties talk or listen at the same time, communication breaks down!

Let's invent a protocol in which the client speaks first, saying "Hello," and then the server responds by saying "Hello right back!" Here's the code:

```
using System;
using System.IO;
using System.Net;
using System.Net.Sockets;
using System.Threading;

new Thread (Server).Start();          // Run server method concurrently.
Thread.Sleep (500);                   // Give server time to start.
Client();

void Client()
{
  using (TcpClient client = new TcpClient ("localhost", 51111))
  using (NetworkStream n = client.GetStream())
  {
    BinaryWriter w = new BinaryWriter (n);
    w.Write ("Hello");
    w.Flush();
    Console.WriteLine (new BinaryReader (n).ReadString());
  }
}

void Server()      // Handles a single client request, then exits.
{
  TcpListener listener = new TcpListener (IPAddress.Any, 51111);
  listener.Start();
  using (TcpClient c = listener.AcceptTcpClient())
  using (NetworkStream n = c.GetStream())
  {
    string msg = new BinaryReader (n).ReadString();
    BinaryWriter w = new BinaryWriter (n);
    w.Write (msg + " right back!");
    w.Flush();                         // Must call Flush because we're not
  }                                    // disposing the writer.
  listener.Stop();
}

// OUTPUT: Hello right back!
```

In this example, we're using the localhost loopback to run the client and server on the same machine. We've arbitrarily chosen a port in the unallocated range (above 49152) and used a BinaryWriter and BinaryReader to encode the text messages. We've avoided closing or disposing the readers and writers in order to keep the underlying NetworkStream open until our conversation completes.

BinaryReader and BinaryWriter might seem like odd choices for reading and writing strings. However, they have a major advantage over StreamReader and Stream Writer: they prefix strings with an integer indicating the length, so a BinaryReader always knows exactly how many bytes to read. If you call StreamReader.ReadToEnd, you might block indefinitely—because a NetworkStream doesn't have an end! As long as the connection is open, the network stream can never be sure that the client isn't going to send more data.

 StreamReader is in fact completely out of bounds with NetworkStream, even if you plan only to call ReadLine. This is because StreamReader has a read-ahead buffer, which can result in it reading more bytes than are currently available, blocking indefinitely (or until the socket times out). Other streams such as FileStream don't suffer this incompatibility with StreamReader because they have a definite *end*—at which point Read returns immediately with a value of 0.

Concurrency with TCP

TcpClient and TcpListener offer task-based asynchronous methods for scalable concurrency. Using these is simply a question of replacing blocking method calls with their *Async versions and awaiting the task that's returned.

In the following example, we write an asynchronous TCP server that accepts requests of 5,000 bytes in length, reverses the bytes, and then sends them back to the client:

```
async void RunServerAsync ()
{
  var listener = new TcpListener (IPAddress.Any, 51111);
  listener.Start ();
  try
  {
    while (true)
      Accept (await listener.AcceptTcpClientAsync ());
  }
  finally { listener.Stop(); }
}

async Task Accept (TcpClient client)
{
  await Task.Yield ();
  try
  {
    using (client)
    using (NetworkStream n = client.GetStream ())
    {
      byte[] data = new byte [5000];

      int bytesRead = 0; int chunkSize = 1;
      while (bytesRead < data.Length && chunkSize > 0)
        bytesRead += chunkSize =
          await n.ReadAsync (data, bytesRead, data.Length - bytesRead);

      Array.Reverse (data);   // Reverse the byte sequence
      await n.WriteAsync (data, 0, data.Length);
    }
  }
}
```

```
  catch (Exception ex) { Console.WriteLine (ex.Message); }
}
```

Such a program is scalable in that it does not block a thread for the duration of a request. So, if 1,000 clients were to connect at once over a slow network connection (so that each request took several seconds from start to finish, for example), this program would not require 1,000 threads for that time (unlike with a synchronous solution). Instead, it leases threads only for the small periods of time required to execute code before and after the await expressions.

Receiving POP3 Mail with TCP

.NET provides no application-layer support for POP3, so you need to write at the TCP layer in order to receive mail from a POP3 server. Fortunately, this is a simple protocol; a POP3 conversation goes like this:

Client	Mail server	Notes
Client connects...	+OK Hello there.	Welcome message
USER joe	+OK Password required.	
PASS password	+OK Logged in.	
LIST	+OK 1 1876 2 5412 3 845 .	Lists the ID and file size of each message on the server
RETR 1	+OK 1876 octets Content of message #1... .	Retrieves the message with the specified ID
DELE 1	+OK Deleted.	Deletes a message from the server
QUIT	+OK Bye-bye.	

Each command and response is terminated by a new line (CR + LF) except for the multiline LIST and RETR commands, which are terminated by a single dot on a separate line. Because we can't use StreamReader with NetworkStream, we can start by writing a helper method to read a line of text in a nonbuffered fashion:

```
string ReadLine (Stream s)
{
  List<byte> lineBuffer = new List<byte>();
  while (true)
  {
    int b = s.ReadByte();
    if (b == 10 || b < 0) break;
    if (b != 13) lineBuffer.Add ((byte)b);
  }
  return Encoding.UTF8.GetString (lineBuffer.ToArray());
}
```

We also need a helper method to send a command. Because we always expect to receive a response starting with +OK, we can read and validate the response at the same time:

```
void SendCommand (Stream stream, string line)
{
  byte[] data = Encoding.UTF8.GetBytes (line + "\r\n");
  stream.Write (data, 0, data.Length);
  string response = ReadLine (stream);
  if (!response.StartsWith ("+OK"))
    throw new Exception ("POP Error: " + response);
}
```

With these methods written, the job of retrieving mail is easy. We establish a TCP connection on port 110 (the default POP3 port) and then start talking to the server. In this example, we write each mail message to a randomly named file with an *.eml* extension, before deleting the message off the server:

```
using (TcpClient client = new TcpClient ("mail.isp.com", 110))
using (NetworkStream n = client.GetStream())
{
  ReadLine (n);                         // Read the welcome message.
  SendCommand (n, "USER username");
  SendCommand (n, "PASS password");
  SendCommand (n, "LIST");              // Retrieve message IDs
  List<int> messageIDs = new List<int>();
  while (true)
  {
    string line = ReadLine (n);         // e.g.,  "1 1876"
    if (line == ".") break;
    messageIDs.Add (int.Parse (line.Split (' ')[0] ));   // Message ID
  }

  foreach (int id in messageIDs)        // Retrieve each message.
  {
    SendCommand (n, "RETR " + id);
    string randomFile = Guid.NewGuid().ToString() + ".eml";
    using (StreamWriter writer = File.CreateText (randomFile))
      while (true)
      {
        string line = ReadLine (n);     // Read next line of message.
        if (line == ".") break;         // Single dot = end of message.
        if (line == "..") line = ".";   // "Escape out" double dot.
        writer.WriteLine (line);        // Write to output file.
      }
    SendCommand (n, "DELE " + id);      // Delete message off server.
  }
  SendCommand (n, "QUIT");
}
```

 You can find open source POP3 libraries on NuGet that provide support for protocol aspects such as authentication TLS/SSL connections, MIME parsing, and more.

17

Assemblies

An *assembly* is the basic unit of deployment in .NET and is also the container for all types. An assembly contains compiled types with their Intermediate Language (IL) code, runtime resources, and information to assist with versioning and referencing other assemblies. An assembly also defines a boundary for type resolution. In .NET, an assembly comprises a single file with a *.dll* extension.

When you build an executable application in .NET, you end up with two files: an assembly (*.dll*) and an executable launcher (*.exe*) appropriate to the platform you're targeting.

This differs from what happens in .NET Framework, which generates a *portable executable* (PE) assembly. A PE has an *.exe* extension and acts both as an assembly and an application launcher. A PE can simultaneously target 32- and 64-bit versions of Windows.

Most of the types in this chapter come from the following namespaces:

```
System.Reflection
System.Resources
System.Globalization
```

What's in an Assembly

An assembly contains four kinds of things:

An assembly manifest
Provides information to the CLR, such as the assembly's name, version, and other assemblies that it references

An application manifest
Provides information to the operating system, such as how the assembly should be deployed and whether administrative elevation is required

Compiled types
    The compiled IL code and metadata of the types defined within the assembly

Resources
    Other data embedded within the assembly, such as images and localizable text

Of these, only the *assembly manifest* is mandatory, although an assembly nearly always contains compiled types (unless it's a resource assembly. See "Resources and Satellite Assemblies" on page 752).

The Assembly Manifest

The assembly manifest serves two purposes:

- It describes the assembly to the managed hosting environment.
- It acts as a directory to the modules, types, and resources in the assembly.

Assemblies are thus *self-describing*. A consumer can discover all of an assembly's data, types, and functions—without needing additional files.

 An assembly manifest is not something you add explicitly to an assembly—it's automatically embedded into an assembly as part of compilation.

Here's a summary of the functionally significant data stored in the manifest:

- The simple name of the assembly
- A version number (`AssemblyVersion`)
- A public key and signed hash of the assembly, if strongly named
- A list of referenced assemblies, including their version and public key
- A list of types defined in the assembly
- The culture it targets, if a satellite assembly (`AssemblyCulture`)

The manifest can also store the following informational data:

- A full title and description (`AssemblyTitle` and `AssemblyDescription`)
- Company and copyright information (`AssemblyCompany` and `AssemblyCopyright`)
- A display version (`AssemblyInformationalVersion`)
- Additional attributes for custom data

Some of this data is derived from arguments given to the compiler, such as the list of referenced assemblies or the public key with which to sign the assembly. The rest comes from assembly attributes, indicated in parentheses.

You can view the contents of an assembly's manifest with the .NET tool *ildasm.exe*. In Chapter 18, we describe how to use reflection to do the same programmatically.

Specifying assembly attributes

Commonly used assembly attributes can be specified in Visual Studio on the project's Properties page, on the Package tab. The settings on that tab are added to the project file (*.csproj*).

To specify attributes not supported by the Package tab, or if not working with a *.csproj* file, you can specify assembly attributes in source code (this is often done in a file called called *AssemblyInfo.cs*).

A dedicated attributes file contains only `using` statements and assembly attribute declarations. For example, to expose internally scoped types to a unit test project, you would do this:

```
using System.Runtime.CompilerServices;

[assembly:InternalsVisibleTo("MyUnitTestProject")]
```

The Application Manifest (Windows)

An application manifest is an XML file that communicates information about the assembly to the OS. An application manifest is embedded into the startup executable as a Win32 resource during the build process. If present, the manifest is read and processed before the CLR loads the assembly—and can influence how Windows launches the application's process.

A .NET application manifest has a root element called `assembly` in the XML namespace `urn:schemas-microsoft-com:asm.v1`:

```
<?xml version="1.0" encoding="utf-8"?>
<assembly manifestVersion="1.0" xmlns="urn:schemas-microsoft-com:asm.v1">
  <!-- contents of manifest -->
</assembly>
```

The following manifest instructs the OS to request administrative elevation:

```
<?xml version="1.0" encoding="utf-8"?>
<assembly manifestVersion="1.0" xmlns="urn:schemas-microsoft-com:asm.v1">
  <trustInfo xmlns="urn:schemas-microsoft-com:asm.v2">
    <security>
      <requestedPrivileges>
        <requestedExecutionLevel level="requireAdministrator" />
      </requestedPrivileges>
    </security>
  </trustInfo>
</assembly>
```

(UWP applications have a far more elaborate manifest, described in the *Package .appxmanifest* file. This includes a declaration of the program's capabilities, which determine permissions granted by the OS. The easiest way to edit this file is with Visual Studio, which displays a dialog when you double-click the manifest file.)

Deploying an application manifest

You can add an application manifest to a .NET project in Visual Studio by right-clicking your project in Solution Explorer, selecting Add, then New Item, and then choosing Application Manifest File. Upon building, the manifest will be embedded into the output assembly.

 The .NET tool *ildasm.exe* is blind to the presence of an embedded application manifest. Visual Studio, however, indicates whether an embedded application manifest is present if you double-click the assembly in Solution Explorer.

Modules

The contents of an assembly are actually packaged within an intermediate container, called a *module*. A module corresponds to a file containing the contents of an assembly. The reason for this extra layer of containership is to allow an assembly to span multiple files, a feature present in .NET Framework but absent in .NET 5 and .NET Core. Figure 17-1 illustrates the relationship.

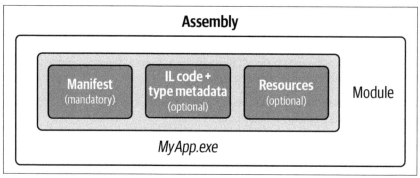

Figure 17-1. Single-file assembly

Although .NET does not support multifile assemblies, at times you need to be aware of the extra level of containership that modules impose. The main scenario is with reflection (see "Reflecting Assemblies" on page 802 and "Emitting Assemblies and Types" on page 815).

The Assembly Class

The Assembly class in System.Reflection is a gateway to accessing assembly metadata at runtime. There are a number of ways to obtain an assembly object: the simplest is via a Type's Assembly property:

```
Assembly a = typeof (Program).Assembly;
```

You can also obtain an `Assembly` object by calling one of `Assembly`'s static methods:

`GetExecutingAssembly`
Returns the assembly of the type that defines the currently executing function

`GetCallingAssembly`
Does the same as `GetExecutingAssembly` but for the function that called the currently executing function

`GetEntryAssembly`
Returns the assembly defining the application's original entry method

After you have an `Assembly` object, you can use its properties and methods to query the assembly's metadata and reflect upon its types. Table 17-1 shows a summary of these functions.

Table 17-1. Assembly members

Functions	Purpose	See the section...
`FullName`, `GetName`	Returns the fully qualified name or an `AssemblyName` object	"Assembly Names" on page 747
`CodeBase`, `Location`	Location of the assembly file	"Loading, Resolving, and Isolating Assemblies" on page 759
`Load`, `LoadFrom`, `LoadFile`	Manually loads an assembly into memory	"Loading, Resolving, and Isolating Assemblies" on page 759
`GetSatelliteAssembly`	Locates the satellite assembly of a given culture	"Resources and Satellite Assemblies" on page 752
`GetType`, `GetTypes`	Returns a type, or all types, defined in the assembly	"Reflecting and Activating Types" on page 782
`EntryPoint`	Returns the application's entry method, as a `MethodInfo`	"Reflecting and Invoking Members" on page 789
`GetModule`, `GetModules`, `ManifestModule`	Returns all modules, or the main module, of an assembly	"Reflecting Assemblies" on page 802
`GetCustomAttribute`, `GetCustomAttributes`	Returns the assembly's attributes	"Working with Attributes" on page 803

Assemblies

Strong Names and Assembly Signing

Strongly naming an assembly was important in .NET Framework for two reasons:

- It allowed the assembly to be loaded into the "Global assembly cache."
- It allowed the assembly to by referenced by other strongly named assemblies.

Strong naming is much less important in .NET 5 and .NET Core, because these runtimes do not have a global assembly cache, nor do they impose the second restriction.

A *strongly named* assembly has a unique identity. It works by adding two bits of metadata to the manifest:

- A *unique number* that belongs to the authors of the assembly
- A *signed hash* of the assembly, proving that the unique number holder produced the assembly

This requires a public/private key pair. The *public key* provides the unique identifying number, and the *private key* facilitates signing.

Strong-name-signing is not the same as *Authenticode*-signing. We cover Authenticode later in this chapter.

The public key is valuable in guaranteeing the uniqueness of assembly references: a strongly named assembly incorporates the public key into its identity.

In .NET Framework, the private key protects your assembly from tampering, in that without your private key, no one can release a modified version of the assembly without the signature breaking. In practice, this is of use when loading an assembly into .NET Framework's global assembly cache. In .NET 5 and .NET Core, the signature is of little use because it's never checked.

Adding a strong name to a previously "weak" named assembly changes its identity. For this reason, it pays to strong-name an assembly from the outset if you think the assembly might need a strong name in the future.

How to Strongly Name an Assembly

To give an assembly a strong name, first generate a public/private key pair with the *sn.exe* utility:

```
sn.exe -k MyKeyPair.snk
```

Visual Studio installs a shortcut called *Developer Command Prompt for VS*, which starts a command prompt whose PATH contains development tools such as *sn.exe*.

This manufactures a new key pair and stores it to a file called *MyKeyPair.snk*. If you subsequently lose this file, you will permanently lose the ability to recompile your assembly with the same identity.

You can sign an assembly with this file by updating your project file. From Visual Studio, go to the Project Properties window, and then, on the *Signing* tab, select the "Sign the assembly" checkbox and select your *.snk* file.

The same key pair can sign multiple assemblies—they'll still have distinct identities if their simple names differ.

Assembly Names

An assembly's "identity" comprises four pieces of metadata from its manifest:

- Its simple name
- Its version ("0.0.0.0" if not present)
- Its culture ("neutral" if not a satellite)
- Its public key token ("null" if not strongly named)

The simple name comes not from any attribute, but from the name of the file to which it was originally compiled (less any extension). So, the simple name of the *System.Xml.dll* assembly is "System.Xml." Renaming a file doesn't change the assembly's simple name.

The version number comes from the `AssemblyVersion` attribute. It's a string divided into four parts as follows:

```
major.minor.build.revision
```

You can specify a version number as follows:

```
[assembly: AssemblyVersion ("2.5.6.7")]
```

The culture comes from the `AssemblyCulture` attribute and applies to satellite assemblies, described later in the section "Resources and Satellite Assemblies" on page 752.

The public key token comes from the strong name supplied at compile time, as we discussed in the preceding section.

Fully Qualified Names

A fully qualified assembly name is a string that includes all four identifying components, in this format:

```
simple-name, Version=version, Culture=culture, PublicKeyToken=public-key
```

Assemblies

For example, the fully qualified name of *System.Private.CoreLib.dll* is *System.Private.CoreLib, Version=4.0.0.0, Culture=neutral, PublicKeyToken=7cec85d7bea7798e*.

If the assembly has no `AssemblyVersion` attribute, the version appears as `0.0.0.0`. If it is unsigned, its public key token appears as `null`.

An `Assembly` object's `FullName` property returns its fully qualified name. The compiler always uses fully qualified names when recording assembly references in the manifest.

A fully qualified assembly name does not include a directory path to assist in locating it on disk. Locating an assembly residing in another directory is an entirely separate matter that we pick up in "Loading, Resolving, and Isolating Assemblies" on page 759.

The AssemblyName Class

`AssemblyName` is a class with a typed property for each of the four components of a fully qualified assembly name. `AssemblyName` has two purposes:

- It parses or builds a fully qualified assembly name.
- It stores some extra data to assist in resolving (finding) the assembly.

You can obtain an `AssemblyName` object in any of the following ways:

- Instantiate an `AssemblyName`, providing a fully qualified name.
- Call `GetName` on an existing `Assembly`.
- Call `AssemblyName.GetAssemblyName`, providing the path to an assembly file on disk.

You can also instantiate an `AssemblyName` object without any arguments and then set each of its properties to build a fully qualified name. An `AssemblyName` is mutable when constructed in this manner.

Here are its essential properties and methods:

```
string      FullName    { get; }         // Fully qualified name
string      Name        { get; set; }    // Simple name
Version     Version     { get; set; }    // Assembly version
CultureInfo CultureInfo { get; set; }    // For satellite assemblies
string      CodeBase    { get; set; }    // Location

byte[]      GetPublicKey();              // 160 bytes
void        SetPublicKey (byte[] key);
byte[]      GetPublicKeyToken();         // 8-byte version
void        SetPublicKeyToken (byte[] publicKeyToken);
```

`Version` is itself a strongly typed representation, with properties for `Major`, `Minor`, `Build`, and `Revision` numbers. `GetPublicKey` returns the full cryptographic public key; `GetPublicKeyToken` returns the last eight bytes used in establishing identity.

To use `AssemblyName` to obtain the simple name of an assembly:

```
Console.WriteLine (typeof (string).Assembly.GetName().Name);
// System.Private.CoreLib
```

To get an assembly version:

```
string v = myAssembly.GetName().Version.ToString();
```

Assembly Informational and File Versions

Two further assembly attributes are available for expressing version-related information. Unlike `AssemblyVersion`, the following two attributes do not affect an assembly's identity and so have no effect on what happens at compile-time or at runtime:

`AssemblyInformationalVersion`
> The version as displayed to the end user. This is visible in the Windows File Properties dialog box as Product Version. Any string can go here, such as "5.1 Beta 2." Typically, all of the assemblies in an application would be assigned the same informational version number.

`AssemblyFileVersion`
> This is intended to refer to the build number for that assembly. This is visible in the Windows File Properties dialog box as File Version. As with `AssemblyVersion`, it must contain a string consisting of up to four numbers separated by periods.

Authenticode Signing

Authenticode is a code-signing system whose purpose is to prove the identity of the publisher. Authenticode and *strong-name* signing are independent: you can sign an assembly with either or both systems.

Although strong-name signing can prove that assemblies A, B, and C came from the same party (assuming the private key hasn't been leaked), it can't tell you who that party was. To know that the party was Joe Albahari—or Microsoft Corporation—you need Authenticode.

Authenticode is useful when downloading programs from the internet, because it provides assurance that a program came from whoever was named by the Certificate Authority and was not modified in transit. It also prevents the "Unknown Publisher" warning when running a downloaded application for the first time. Authenticode signing is also a requirement when submitting apps to the Windows Store.

Authenticode works with not only .NET assemblies, but also unmanaged executables and binaries such as *.msi* deployment files. Of course, Authenticode doesn't guarantee that a program is free from malware—although it does make it less likely. A person or entity has been willing to put its name (backed by a passport or company document) behind the executable or library.

 The CLR does not treat an Authenticode signature as part of an assembly's identity. However, it can read and validate Authenticode signatures on demand, as you'll see soon.

Signing with Authenticode requires that you contact a *Certificate Authority* (CA) with evidence of your personal identity or company's identity (articles of incorporation, etc.). After the CA has checked your documents, it will issue an X.509 code-signing certificate that is typically valid for one to five years. This enables you to sign assemblies with the *signtool* utility. You can also make a certificate yourself with the *makecert* utility; however, it will be recognized only on computers on which the certificate is explicitly installed.

The fact that (non-self-signed) certificates can work on any computer relies on public key infrastructure. Essentially, your certificate is signed with another certificate belonging to a CA. The CA is trusted because all CAs are loaded into the OS. (To see them, go to the Windows Control Panel and then, in the search box, type `certificate`. In the Administrative Tools section, click "Manage computer certificates." This launches the Certificate Manager. Open the node Trusted Root Certification Authorities and click Certificates.) A CA can revoke a publisher's certificate if leaked, so verifying an Authenticode signature requires periodically asking the CA for an up-to-date list of certification revocations.

Because Authenticode uses cryptographic signing, an Authenticode signature is invalid if someone subsequently tampers with the file. We discuss cryptography, hashing, and signing in Chapter 20.

How to Sign with Authenticode

Obtaining and installing a certificate

The first step is to obtain a code-signing certificate from a CA (see the sidebar that follows). You can then either work with the certificate as a password-protected file or load the certificate into the computer's certificate store. The benefit of doing the latter is that you can sign without needing to specify a password. This is advantageous because it prevents having a password visible in automated build scripts or batch files.

To load a certificate into the computer's certificate store, open the Certificate Manager as described earlier. Open the Personal folder, right-click its Certificates folder, and then pick All Tasks/Import. An import wizard guides you through the process. After the import is complete, click the View button on the certificate, go to the Details tab, and copy the certificate's *thumbprint*. This is the SHA-256 hash that you'll subsequently need to identify the certificate when signing.

If you also want to strong-name-sign your assembly, you must do so *before* Authenticode signing. This is because the CLR knows about Authenticode signing, but not vice versa. So, if you strong-name-sign an assembly *after* Authenticode-signing it, the latter will see the addition of the CLR's strong name as an unauthorized modification and consider the assembly tampered.

Signing with signtool.exe

You can Authenticode-sign your programs with the *signtool* utility that comes with Visual Studio (look in the *Microsoft SDKs\ClickOnce\SignTool* folder under *Program Files*). The following signs a file called *LINQPad.exe* with the certificate located in the computer's *My Store* called "Joseph Albahari," using the secure SHA256 hashing algorithm:

```
signtool sign /n "Joseph Albahari" /fd sha256 LINQPad.exe
```

You can also specify a description and product URL with /d and /du:

```
... /d LINQPad /du http://www.linqpad.net
```

In most cases, you will also want to specify a *time-stamping server*.

Time stamping

After your certificate expires, you'll no longer be able to sign programs. However, programs that you signed *before* its expiry will still be valid—if you specified a *time-stamping server* with the /tr switch when signing. The CA will provide you with a URI for this purpose: the following is for Comodo (or K Software):

```
... /tr http://timestamp.comodoca.com/authenticode /td SHA256
```

Verifying that a program has been signed

The easiest way to view an Authenticode signature on a file is to view the file's properties in Windows Explorer (look in the Digital Signatures tab). The *signtool* utility also provides an option for this.

Resources and Satellite Assemblies

An application typically contains not only executable code, but also content such as text, images, or XML files. Such content can be represented in an assembly through a *resource*. There are two overlapping use cases for resources:

- Incorporating data that cannot go into source code, such as images
- Storing data that might need translation in a multilingual application

An assembly resource is ultimately a byte stream with a name. You can think of an assembly as containing a dictionary of byte arrays keyed by string. You can see this in *ildasm* if you disassemble an assembly that contains a resource called *banner.jpg* and a resource called *data.xml*:

```
.mresource public banner.jpg
{
  // Offset: 0x00000F58 Length: 0x000004F6
}
.mresource public data.xml
{
  // Offset: 0x00001458 Length: 0x0000027E
}
```

In this case, *banner.jpg* and *data.xml* were included directly in the assembly—each as its own embedded resource. This is the simplest way to work.

.NET also lets you add content through intermediate *.resources* containers. These are designed for holding content that might require translation into different languages. Localized *.resources* can be packaged as individual satellite assemblies that are automatically picked up at runtime, based on the user's OS language.

Figure 17-2 illustrates an assembly that contains two directly embedded resources, plus a *.resources* container called *welcome.resources*, for which we've created two localized satellites.

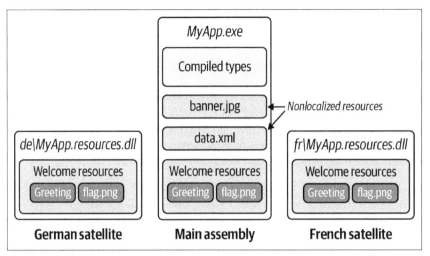

Figure 17-2. Resources

Directly Embedding Resources

 Embedding resources into assemblies is not supported in Windows Store apps. Instead, add any extra files to your deployment package, and access them by reading from your application StorageFolder (Package.Current .InstalledLocation).

To directly embed a resource using Visual Studio:

- Add the file to your project.
- Set its build action to Embedded Resource.

Visual Studio always prefixes resource names with the project's default namespace, plus the names of any subfolders in which the file is contained. So, if your project's default namespace was Westwind.Reports and your file was called *banner.jpg* in the folder *pictures*, the resource name would be *Westwind.Reports.pictures.banner.jpg*.

 Resource names are case sensitive. This makes project subfolder names in Visual Studio that contain resources effectively case sensitive.

To retrieve a resource, you call GetManifestResourceStream on the assembly containing the resource. This returns a stream, which you can then read as any other:

```
Assembly a = Assembly.GetEntryAssembly();

using (Stream s = a.GetManifestResourceStream ("TestProject.data.xml"))
using (XmlReader r = XmlReader.Create (s))
  ...
```

Assemblies

```
System.Drawing.Image image;
using (Stream s = a.GetManifestResourceStream ("TestProject.banner.jpg"))
    image = System.Drawing.Image.FromStream (s);
```

The stream returned is seekable, so you can also do this:

```
byte[] data;
using (Stream s = a.GetManifestResourceStream ("TestProject.banner.jpg"))
    data = new BinaryReader (s).ReadBytes ((int) s.Length);
```

If you've used Visual Studio to embed the resource, you must remember to include the namespace-based prefix. To help avoid error, you can specify the prefix in a separate argument, using a *type*. The type's namespace is used as the prefix:

```
using (Stream s = a.GetManifestResourceStream (typeof (X), "data.xml"))
```

X can be any type with the desired namespace of your resource (typically, a type in the same project folder).

Setting a project item's build action in Visual Studio to Resource within a Windows Presentation Foundation (WPF) application is *not* the same as setting its build action to Embedded Resource. The former actually adds the item to a *.resources* file called *<AssemblyName>.g.resources*, whose content you access through WPF's Application class, using a URI as a key.

To add to the confusion, WPF further overloads the term "resource." *Static resources* and *dynamic resources* are both unrelated to assembly resources!

GetManifestResourceNames returns the names of all resources in the assembly.

.resources Files

.resources files are containers for potentially localizable content. A *.resources* file ends up as an embedded resource within an assembly—just like any other kind of file. The difference is that you must do the following:

- Package your content into the *.resources* file to begin with

- Access its content through a ResourceManager or *pack URI* rather than a Get ManifestResourceStream

.resources files are structured in binary and so are not human-editable; therefore, you must rely on tools provided by .NET and Visual Studio to work with them. The standard approach with strings or simple data types is to use the *.resx* format, which can be converted to a *.resources* file either by Visual Studio or the resgen tool. The *.resx* format is also suitable for images intended for a Windows Forms or ASP.NET application.

In a WPF application, you must use Visual Studio's "Resource" build action for images or similar content needing to be referenced by URI. This applies whether localization is needed or not.

We describe how to do each of these in the following sections.

.resx Files

A *.resx* file is a design-time format for producing *.resources* files. A *.resx* file uses XML and is structured with name/value pairs as follows:

```
<root>
  <data name="Greeting">
    <value>hello</value>
  </data>
  <data name="DefaultFontSize" type="System.Int32, mscorlib">
    <value>10</value>
  </data>
</root>
```

To create a *.resx* file in Visual Studio, add a project item of type Resources File. The rest of the work is done automatically:

- The correct header is created.
- A designer is provided for adding strings, images, files, and other kinds of data.
- The *.resx* file is automatically converted to the *.resources* format and embedded into the assembly upon compilation.
- A class is written to help you access the data later on.

 The resource designer adds images as typed Image objects (*System.Drawing.dll*) rather than as byte arrays, making them unsuitable for WPF applications.

Reading .resources files

 If you create a *.resx* file in Visual Studio, a class of the same name is generated automatically with properties to retrieve each of its items.

The ResourceManager class reads *.resources* files embedded within an assembly:

```
ResourceManager r = new ResourceManager ("welcome",
                                  Assembly.GetExecutingAssembly());
```

(The first argument must be namespace-prefixed if the resource was compiled in Visual Studio.)

You can then access what's inside by calling GetString or GetObject with a cast:

```
string greeting = r.GetString ("Greeting");
int fontSize = (int) r.GetObject ("DefaultFontSize");
Image image = (Image) r.GetObject ("flag.png");
```

To enumerate the contents of a .*resources* file:

```
ResourceManager r = new ResourceManager (...);
ResourceSet set = r.GetResourceSet (CultureInfo.CurrentUICulture,
                                    true, true);
foreach (System.Collections.DictionaryEntry entry in set)
  Console.WriteLine (entry.Key);
```

Creating a pack URI resource in Visual Studio

In a WPF application, XAML files need to be able to access resources by URI. For instance:

```
<Button>
  <Image Height="50" Source="flag.png"/>
</Button>
```

Or, if the resource is in another assembly:

```
<Button>
  <Image Height="50" Source="UtilsAssembly;Component/flag.png"/>
</Button>
```

(Component is a literal keyword.)

To create resources that can be loaded in this manner, you cannot use .*resx* files. Instead, you must add the files to your project and set their build action to Resource (not Embedded Resource). Visual Studio then compiles them into a .*resources* file called <*AssemblyName*>.*g.resources*—also the home of compiled XAML (.*baml*) files.

To load a URI-keyed resource programmatically, call Application.GetResource Stream:

```
Uri u = new Uri ("flag.png", UriKind.Relative);
using (Stream s = Application.GetResourceStream (u).Stream)
```

Notice we used a relative URI. You can also use an absolute URI in exactly the following format (the three commas are not a typo):

```
Uri u = new Uri ("pack://application:,,,/flag.png");
```

If you'd rather specify an Assembly object, you can retrieve content instead with a ResourceManager:

```
Assembly a = Assembly.GetExecutingAssembly();
ResourceManager r = new ResourceManager (a.GetName().Name + ".g", a);
using (Stream s = r.GetStream ("flag.png"))
   ...
```

A ResourceManager also lets you enumerate the content of a .*g.resources* container within a given assembly.

Satellite Assemblies

Data embedded in *.resources* is localizable.

Resource localization is relevant when your application runs on a version of Windows built to display everything in a different language. For consistency, your application should use that same language, too.

A typical setup is as follows:

- The main assembly contains *.resources* for the default, or *fallback*, language.
- Separate *satellite assemblies* contain localized *.resources* translated to different languages.

When your application runs, .NET examines the language of the current OS (from CultureInfo.CurrentUICulture). Whenever you request a resource using ResourceManager, the runtime looks for a localized satellite assembly. If one's available—and it contains the resource key you requested—it's used in place of the main assembly's version.

This means that you can enhance language support simply by adding new satellites—without changing the main assembly.

 A satellite assembly cannot contain executable code, only resources.

Satellite assemblies are deployed in subdirectories of the assembly's folder, as follows:

```
programBaseFolder\MyProgram.exe
              \MyLibrary.exe
              \XX\MyProgram.resources.dll
              \XX\MyLibrary.resources.dll
```

XX refers to the two-letter language code (such as "de" for German) or a language and region code (such as "en-GB" for English in Great Britain). This naming system allows the CLR to find and load the correct satellite assembly automatically.

Building satellite assemblies

Recall our previous *.resx* example, which included the following:

```
<root>
  ...
  <data name="Greeting"
    <value>hello</value>
  </data>
</root>
```

We then retrieved the greeting at runtime as follows:

```
ResourceManager r = new ResourceManager ("welcome",
                                Assembly.GetExecutingAssembly());
Console.Write (r.GetString ("Greeting"));
```

Suppose that we want this to instead write "hallo" if running on the German version of Windows. The first step is to add another *.resx* file named *welcome.de.resx* that substitutes *hello* for *hallo*:

```
<root>
  <data name="Greeting">
    <value>hallo<value>
  </data>
</root>
```

In Visual Studio, this is all you need to do—when you rebuild, a satellite assembly called *MyApp.resources.dll* is automatically created in a subdirectory called *de*.

Testing satellite assemblies

To simulate running on an OS with a different language, you must change the CurrentUICulture using the Thread class:

```
System.Threading.Thread.CurrentThread.CurrentUICulture
  = new System.Globalization.CultureInfo ("de");
```

CultureInfo.CurrentUICulture is a read-only version of the same property.

 A useful testing strategy is to ɫoȼɑɫ̄ɪzə into words that can still be read as English but do not use the standard Roman Unicode characters.

Visual Studio designer support

The designers in Visual Studio provide extended support for localizing components and visual elements. The WPF designer has its own workflow for localization; other Component-based designers use a design-time-only property to make it appear that a component or Windows Forms control has a Language property. To customize for another language, simply change the Language property and then start modifying the component. All properties of controls that are attributed as Localizable will be saved to a *.resx* file for that language. You can switch between languages at any time just by changing the Language property.

Cultures and Subcultures

Cultures are split into cultures and subcultures. A culture represents a particular language; a subculture represents a regional variation of that language. The .NET runtime follows the RFC1766 standard, which represents cultures and subcultures with two-letter codes. Here are the codes for English and German cultures:

```
En
de
```

Here are the codes for the Australian English and Austrian German subcultures:

```
en-AU
de-AT
```

A culture is represented in .NET with the `System.Globalization.CultureInfo` class. You can examine the current culture of your application, as follows:

```
Console.WriteLine (System.Threading.Thread.CurrentThread.CurrentCulture);
Console.WriteLine (System.Threading.Thread.CurrentThread.CurrentUICulture);
```

Running this on a computer localized for Australia illustrates the difference between the two:

```
en-AU
en-US
```

`CurrentCulture` reflects the regional settings of the Windows Control Panel, whereas `CurrentUICulture` reflects the language of the OS.

Regional settings include such things as time zone and the formatting of currency and dates. `CurrentCulture` determines the default behavior of such functions as `DateTime.Parse`. Regional settings can be customized to the point where they no longer resemble any particular culture.

`CurrentUICulture` determines the language in which the computer communicates with the user. Australia doesn't need a separate version of English for this purpose, so it just uses the US one. If I spent a couple of months working in Austria, I would go to the Control Panel and change my `CurrentCulture` to Austrian-German. However, given that I can't speak German, my `CurrentUICulture` would remain US English.

`ResourceManager`, by default, uses the current thread's `CurrentUICulture` property to determine the correct satellite assembly to load. `ResourceManager` uses a fallback mechanism when loading resources. If a subculture assembly is defined, that one is used; otherwise, it falls back to the generic culture. If the generic culture is not present, it falls back to the default culture in the main assembly.

Loading, Resolving, and Isolating Assemblies

Loading an assembly from a known location is a relatively simple process. We refer to this as *assembly loading*.

More commonly, however, you (or the CLR) will need to load an assembly knowing only its full (or simple) name. This is called *assembly resolution*. Assembly resolution differs from loading in that the assembly must first be located.

Assembly resolution is triggered in two scenarios:

- By the CLR, when it needs to resolve a dependency
- Explicitly, when you call a method such as `Assembly.Load(AssemblyName)`

Assemblies

To illustrate the first scenario, consider an application comprising a main assembly plus a set of statically referenced library assemblies (dependencies), as shown in this example:

```
AdventureGame.dll    // Main assembly
Terrain.dll          // Referenced assembly
UIEngine.dll         // Referenced assembly
```

By "statically referenced," we mean that *AdventureGame.dll* was compiled with references to *Terrain.dll* and *UIEngine.dll*. The compiler itself does not need to perform assembly resolution, because it's told (either explicitly or by MSBuild) where to find *Terrain.dll* and *UIEngine.dll*. During compilation, it writes the *full names* of the Terrain and UIEngine assemblies into the metadata of *AdventureGame.dll* but no information on where to find them. So, at runtime, the Terrain and UIEngine assemblies must be *resolved*.

Assembly loading and resolution is handled by an *assembly load context* (ALC); specifically, an instance of the `AssemblyLoadContext` class in `System.Run time.Loader`. Because *AdventureGame.dll* is the main assembly for the application, the CLR uses the *default ALC* (`AssemblyLoadContext.Default`) to resolve its dependencies. The default ALC resolves dependencies first by looking for and examining a file called *AdventureGame.deps.json* (which describes where to find dependencies), or if not present, it looks in the application base folder, where it will find *Terrain.dll* and *UIEngine.dll*. (The default ALC also resolves the .NET runtime assemblies.)

As a developer, you can dynamically load additional assemblies during the execution of your program. For example, you might want to package optional features in assemblies that you deploy only when those features have been purchased. In such a case, you could load the extra assemblies, when present, by calling `Assembly.Load(AssemblyName)`.

A more complex example would be implementing a plug-in system whereby the user can provide third-party assemblies that your application detects and loads at runtime to extend your application's functionality. The complexity arises because each plug-in assembly might have its own dependencies that must also be resolved.

By subclassing `AssemblyLoadContext` and overriding its assembly resolution method (`Load`), you can control how a plug-in finds its dependencies. For example, you might decide that each plug-in should reside in its own folder, and its dependencies should also reside in that folder.

ALCs have another purpose: by instantiating a separate `AssemblyLoadContext` for each (plug-in + dependencies), you can keep each isolated, ensuring that their dependencies load in parallel and do not interfere with one another (nor the host application). Each, for instance, can have its own version of JSON.NET. Hence, in addition to *loading* and *resolution*, ALCs also provide a mechanism for *isolation*. Under certain conditions, ALCs can even be *unloaded*, freeing their memory.

In this section, we elaborate on each of these principles and describe the following:

- How ALCs handle loading and resolution
- The role of the default ALC
- `Assembly.Load` and contextual ALCs
- How to use `AssemblyDependencyResolver`
- How to load and resolve unmanaged libraries
- Unloading ALCs
- The legacy assembly loading methods

Then, we put the theory to work and demonstrate how to write a plug-in system with ALC isolation.

 The `AssemblyLoadContext` class is new to .NET 5 and .NET Core. In .NET Framework, ALCs were present but restricted and hidden: the only way to create and interact with them was indirectly via the `LoadFile(string)`, `LoadFrom(string)`, and `Load(byte[])` static methods on the `Assembly` class. Compared to the ALC API, these methods are inflexible, and their use can lead to surprises (particularly when handling dependencies). For this reason, it's best to favor explicit use of the `AssemblyLoadContext` API in .NET 5 and .NET Core.

Assembly Load Contexts

As we just discussed, the `AssemblyLoadContext` class is responsible for loading and resolving assemblies as well as providing a mechanism for isolation.

Every .NET `Assembly` object belongs to exactly one `AssemblyLoadContext`. You can obtain the ALC for an assembly, as follows:

```
Assembly assem = Assembly.GetExecutingAssembly();
AssemblyLoadContext context = AssemblyLoadContext.GetLoadContext (assem);
Console.WriteLine (context.Name);
```

Conversely, you can think of an ALC as "containing" or "owning" assemblies, which you can obtain via its `Assemblies` property. Following on from the previous example:

```
foreach (Assembly a in context.Assemblies)
  Console.WriteLine (a.FullName);
```

The `AssemblyLoadContext` class also has a static `All` property that enumerates all ALCs.

You can create a new ALC just by instantiating `AssemblyLoadContext` and providing a name (the name is helpful when debugging), although more commonly, you'd first subclass `AssemblyLoadContext` so that you can implement logic to *resolve* dependencies; in other words, load an assembly from its *name*.

Loading assemblies

`AssemblyLoadContext` provides the following methods to explicitly load an assembly into its context:

```
public Assembly LoadFromAssemblyPath (string assemblyPath);
public Assembly LoadFromStream (Stream assembly, Stream assemblySymbols);
```

The first method loads an assembly from a file path, whereas the second method loads it from a `Stream` (which can come directly from memory). The second parameter is optional and corresponds to the contents of the project debug (*.pdb*) file, which allows stack traces to include source code information when code executes (useful in exception reporting).

With both of these methods, no *resolution* takes place.

The following loads the assembly *c:\temp\foo.dll* into its own ALC:

```
var alc = new AssemblyLoadContext ("Test");
Assembly assem = alc.LoadFromAssemblyPath (@"c:\temp\foo.dll");
```

If the assembly is valid, loading will always succeed, subject to one important rule: an assembly's *simple name* must be unique within its ALC. This means that you cannot load multiple versions of the same-named assembly into a single ALC; to do this, you must create additional ALCs. We could load another copy of *foo.dll*, as follows:

```
var alc2 = new AssemblyLoadContext ("Test 2");
Assembly assem2 = alc2.LoadFromAssemblyPath (@"c:\temp\foo.dll");
```

Note that types that originate from different `Assembly` objects are incompatible even if the assemblies are otherwise identical. In our example, the types in `assem` are incompatible with the types in `assem2`.

After an assembly is loaded, it cannot be unloaded except by unloading its ALC (see "Unloading ALCs" on page 773). The CLR maintains a lock of the file for the duration that it's loaded.

You can avoid locking the file by loading the assembly via a byte array:

```
bytes[] bytes = File.ReadAllBytes (@"c:\temp\foo.dll");
var ms = new MemoryStream (bytes);
var assem = alc.LoadFromStream (ms);
```

This has two drawbacks:

- The assembly's `Location` property will end up blank. Sometimes, it's useful to know where an assembly was loaded from (and some APIs rely on it being populated).

- Private memory consumption must increase immediately to accommodate the full size of the assembly. If you instead load from a filename, the CLR uses a memory-mapped file, which enables lazy loading and process sharing. Also, should memory run low, the OS can release its memory and reload as required without writing to a page file.

LoadFromAssemblyName

`AssemblyLoadContext` also provides the following method, which loads an assembly by *name*:

```
public Assembly LoadFromAssemblyName (AssemblyName assemblyName);
```

Unlike the two methods just discussed, you don't pass in any information to indicate where the assembly is located; instead you're instructing the ALC to *resolve* the assembly.

Resolving assemblies

The preceding method triggers *assembly resolution*. The CLR also triggers assembly resolution when loading dependencies. For example, suppose that assembly A statically references assembly B. To resolve reference B, the CLR triggers assembly resolution on whichever *ALC assembly A was loaded into.*

The CLR resolves dependencies by triggering assembly resolution—whether the triggering assembly is in the default or a custom ALC. The difference is that with the default ALC, the resolution rules are hardcoded, whereas with a custom ALC, you write the rules yourself.

Here's what then happens:

1. The CLR first checks whether an identical resolution has already taken place in that ALC (with a matching full assembly name); if so, it returns the `Assembly` it returned before.

2. Otherwise, it calls the ALC's (virtual protected) `Load` method, which does the work of locating and loading the assembly. The default ALC's `Load` method

applies the rules we describe in "The Default ALC" on page 766. With a custom ALC, it's entirely up to you how you locate the assembly. For instance, you might look in some folder and then call `LoadFromAssemblyPath` when you find the assembly. It's also perfectly legal to return an already-loaded assembly from the same or another ALC (we demonstrate this in "Writing a Plug-In System" on page 775).

3. If Step 2 returns null, the CLR then calls the `Load` method on the default ALC (this serves as a useful "fallback" for resolving .NET runtime and common application assemblies).

4. If Step 3 returns null, the CLR then fires the `Resolving` events on both ALCs—first, on the default ALC and then on the original ALC.

5. (For compatibility with .NET Framework): If the assembly still hasn't been resolved, the `AppDomain.CurrentDomain.AssemblyResolve` event fires.

After this process completes, the CLR does a "sanity check" to ensure that whatever assembly was loaded has a name that's compatible with what was requested. The simple name must match; the public key token must match *if specified*. The version need not match—it can be higher or lower than what was requested.

From this, we can see that there are two ways to implement assembly resolution in a custom ALC:

- Override the ALC's `Load` method. This gives your ALC "first say" over what happens, which is usually desirable (and essential when you need isolation).

- Handle the ALC's `Resolving` event. This fires only *after* the default ALC has failed to resolve assembly.

If you attach multiple event handlers to the `Resolving` event, the first to return a non-null value wins.

To illustrate, let's assume that we want to load an assembly that our main application knew nothing about at compile time, called *foo.dll*, located in *c:\temp* (which is different from our application folder). We'll also assume that *foo.dll* has a private dependency on *bar.dll*. We want to ensure that when we load *c:\temp\foo.dll* and execute its code, *c:\temp\bar.dll* can correctly resolve. We also want to ensure that foo and its private dependency, bar, do not interfere with the main application.

Let's begin by writing a custom ALC that overrides `Load`:

```
using System.IO;
using System.Runtime.Loader;

class FolderBasedALC : AssemblyLoadContext
```

```
  {
    readonly string _folder;
    public FolderBasedALC (string folder) => _folder = folder;

    protected override Assembly Load (AssemblyName assemblyName)
    {
      // Attempt to find the assembly:
      string targetPath = Path.Combine (_folder, assemblyName.Name + ".dll");

      if (File.Exists (targetPath))
        return LoadFromAssemblyPath (targetPath);   // Load the assembly

      return null;     // We can't find it: it could be a .NET runtime assembly
    }
  }
```

Notice that in the Load method, we return null if the assembly file is not present. This check is important because *foo.dll* will also have dependencies on the .NET BCL assemblies; hence, the Load method will be called on assemblies such as System.Runtime. By returning null, we allow the CLR to fall back to the default ALC, which will correctly resolve these assemblies.

 Notice that we didn't attempt to load the .NET runtime BCL assemblies into our own ALC. These system assemblies are not designed to run outside the default ALC, and attempts to load them into your own ALC can result in incorrect behavior, performance degradation, and unexpected type incompatibility.

Here's how we could use our custom ALC to load the *foo.dll* assembly in *c:\temp*:

```
var alc = new FolderBasedALC (@"c:\temp");
Assembly foo = alc.LoadFromAssemblyPath (@"c:\temp\foo.dll");
...
```

When we subsequently begin calling code in the foo assembly, the CLR will at some point need to resolve the dependency on *bar.dll*. This is when the custom ALC's Load method will fire and successfully locate the *bar.dll* assembly in *c:\temp*.

In this case, our Load method is also capable of resolving *foo.dll*, so we could simplify our code to this:

```
var alc = new FolderBasedALC (@"c:\temp");
Assembly foo = alc.LoadFromAssemblyName (new AssemblyName ("foo"));
...
```

Now, let's consider an alternative solution: instead of subclassing AssemblyLoad Context and overriding Load, we could instantiate a plain AssemblyLoadContext and handle its Resolving event:

```
var alc = new AssemblyLoadContext ("test");
alc.Resolving += (loadContext, assemblyName) =>
{
  string targetPath = Path.Combine (@"c:\temp", assemblyName.Name + ".dll");
```

```
    return alc.LoadFromAssemblyPath (targetPath);    // Load the assembly
};
Assembly foo = alc.LoadFromAssemblyName (new AssemblyName ("foo"));
```

Notice now that we don't need to check whether the assembly exists. Because the Resolving event fires *after* the default ALC has had a chance to resolve the assembly (and only when it fails), our handler won't fire for the .NET BCL assemblies. This makes this solution simpler, although there's a disadvantage. Remember that in our scenario, the main application knew nothing about *foo.dll* or *bar.dll* at compile time. This means that it's possible for the main application to itself depend on assemblies called *foo.dll* or *bar.dll*. If this were to occur, the Resolving event would never fire, and the application's foo and bar assemblies would load instead. In other words, we would fail to achieve *isolation*.

Our FolderBasedALC class is good for illustrating the concept of assembly resolution, but it's of less use in real life because it cannot handle platform-specific and (for library projects) development-time NuGet dependencies. In "AssemblyDependencyResolver" on page 772, we describe the solution to this problem, and in "Writing a Plug-In System" on page 775, we give a detailed example.

The Default ALC

When an application starts, the CLR assigns a special ALC to the static Assembly LoadContext.Default property. The default ALC is where your startup assembly loads, along with its statically referenced dependencies and the .NET runtime BCL assemblies.

The default ALC looks first in the *default probing* paths to automatically resolve assemblies (see "Default probing" on page 767); this normally equates to the locations indicated in the application's *.deps.json* and *.runtimeconfig.json* files.

If the ALC cannot find an assembly in its default probing paths, its Resolving event fires. Handling this event lets you load the assembly from other locations, which means that you can deploy an application's dependencies to additional locations, such as subfolders, shared folders, or even as a binary resource inside the host assembly:

```
AssemblyLoadContext.Default.Resolving += (loadContext, assemblyName) =>
{
    // Try to locate assemblyName, returning an Assembly object or null.
    // Typically you'd call LoadFromAssemblyPath after finding the file.
    // ...
};
```

The Resolving event in the default ALC also fires when a custom ALC fails to resolve (in other words, when its Load method returns null) and the default ALC is unable to resolve the assembly.

You can also load assemblies into the default ALC from outside the Resolving event. Before proceeding, however, you should first determine whether you can solve the problem better by using a separate ALC or with the approaches we describe in the following section (which use the *executing* and *contextual* ALCs). Hardcoding to the default ALC makes your code brittle because it cannot as a whole be isolated (for instance, by unit testing frameworks or by LINQPad).

If you still want to proceed, it's preferable to call a *resolution method* (i.e., LoadFrom AssemblyName) rather than a *loading method* (such as LoadFromAssemblyPath)— especially if your assembly is statically referenced. This is because it's possible that the assembly might already be loaded, in which case LoadFromAssemblyName will return the already-loaded assembly, whereas LoadFromAssemblyPath will throw an exception.

(With LoadFromAssemblyPath, you can also run the risk of loading the assembly from a place that's inconsistent with where the ALC's default resolution mechanism would find it.)

If the assembly is in a place where the ALC won't automatically find it, you can still follow this procedure and additionally handle the ALC's Resolving event.

Note that when calling LoadFromAssemblyName, you don't need to provide the full name; the simple name will do (and is valid even if the assembly is strongly named):

```
AssemblyLoadContext.Default.LoadFromAssemblyName ("System.Xml");
```

However, if you include the public key token in the name, it must match with what's loaded.

Default probing

The default probing paths normally comprise the following:

- Paths specified in *AppName.deps.json* (where *AppName* is the name of your application's main assembly). If this file is not present, the application base folder is used instead.

- Folders containing the .NET runtime system assemblies (if your application is Framework-dependent).

MSBuild automatically generates a file called *AppName.deps.json*, which describes where to find all of its dependencies. These include platform-agnostic assemblies, which are placed in the application base folder, and platform-specific assemblies, which are placed in the *runtimes* subdirectory under a subfolder such as *win* or *unix*.

The paths specified in the generated *.deps.json* file are relative to the application base folder—or any additional folders that you specify in the additionalProbingPaths section of the *AppName.runtimeconfig.json* and/or *AppName.runtimeconfig.dev.json* configuration files (the latter is intended only for the development environment).

The "Current" ALC

In the preceding section, we cautioned against explicitly loading assemblies into the default ALC. What you usually want, instead, is to load/resolve into the "current" ALC.

In most cases, the "current" ALC is the one containing the currently executing assembly:

```
var executingAssem = Assembly.GetExecutingAssembly();
var alc = AssemblyLoadContext.GetLoadContext (executingAssem);

Assembly assem = alc.LoadFromAssemblyName (...);   // to resolve by name
          // OR: = alc.LoadFromAssemblyPath (...);   // to load by path
```

Here's a more flexible and explicit way to obtain the ALC:

```
var myAssem = typeof (SomeTypeInMyAssembly).Assembly;
var alc = AssemblyLoadContext.GetLoadContext (myAssem);
...
```

Sometimes, it's impossible to infer the "current" ALC. For example, suppose that you were responsible for writing the .NET binary serializer (we describe serialization in the online supplement at *http://www.albahari.com/nutshell*). A serializer such as this writes the full names of the types that it serializes (including their assembly names), which must be *resolved* during deserialization. The question is, which ALC should you use? The problem with relying on the executing assembly is that it will return whatever assembly contains the deserializer, not the assembly that's *calling* the deserializer.

The best solution is not to guess but to ask:

```
public object Deserialize (Stream stream, AssemblyLoadContext alc)
{
   ...
}
```

Being explicit maximizes flexibility and minimizes the chance of making mistakes. The caller can now decide what should count as the "current" ALC:

```
var assem = typeof (SomeTypeThatIWillBeDeserializing).Assembly;
var alc = AssemblyLoadContext.GetLoadContext (assem);
var object = Deserialize (someStream, alc);
```

Assembly.Load and Contextual ALCs

To help with the common case of loading an assembly into the currently executing ALC; that is:

```
var executingAssem = Assembly.GetExecutingAssembly();
var alc = AssemblyLoadContext.GetLoadContext (executingAssem);
Assembly assem = alc.LoadFromAssemblyName (...);
```

Microsoft has defined the following method in the Assembly class:

```
public static Assembly Load (string assemblyString);
```

as well as a functionally identical version that accepts an `AssemblyName` object:

```
public static Assembly Load (AssemblyName assemblyRef);
```

(Don't confuse these methods with the legacy `Load(byte[])` method, which behaves in a totally different manner—see "The Legacy Loading Methods" on page 774.)

As with `LoadFromAssemblyName`, you have a choice of specifying the assembly's simple, partial, or full name:

```
Assembly a = Assembly.Load ("System.Private.Xml");
```

This loads the `System.Private.Xml` assembly into whatever ALC the *executing code's assembly* is loaded in.

In this case, we specified a simple name. The following strings would also be valid, and all would have the same result in .NET:

```
"System.Private.Xml, PublicKeyToken=cc7b13ffcd2ddd51"
"System.Private.Xml, Version=4.0.1.0"
"System.Private.Xml, Version=4.0.1.0, PublicKeyToken=cc7b13ffcd2ddd51"
```

If you choose to specify a public key token, it must match with what's loaded.

The Microsoft Developer Network (MSDN) cautions against loading an assembly from a partial name, recommending that you specify the exact version and public key token. Their rationale is based on factors relevant to .NET Framework, such as the effects of the Global Assembly Cache and Code Access Security. In .NET 5 and .NET Core, these factors aren't present, and it's generally safe to load from a simple or partial name.

Both of these methods are strictly for *resolution*, so you cannot specify a file path. (If you populate the `CodeBase` property in the `AssemblyName` object, it will be ignored.)

Don't fall into the trap of using `Assembly.Load` to load a statically referenced assembly. All you need do in this case is refer to a type in the assembly and obtain the assembly from that:

```
Assembly a = typeof (System.Xml.Formatting).Assembly;
```

Or, you could even do this:

```
Assembly a = System.Xml.Formatting.Indented.GetType().Assembly;
```

This prevents hardcoding the assembly name (which you might change in the future) while triggering assembly resolution on the *executing code's* ALC (as would happen with `Assembly.Load`).

If you were to write the `Assembly.Load` method yourself, it would (almost) look like this:

```
[MethodImpl(MethodImplOptions.NoInlining)]
Assembly Load (string name)
```

```
{
  Assembly callingAssembly = Assembly.GetCallingAssembly();
  var callingAlc = AssemblyLoadContext.GetLoadContext (callingAssembly);
  return callingAlc.LoadFromAssemblyName (new AssemblyName (name));
}
```

EnterContextualReflection

Assembly.Load's strategy of using the calling assembly's ALC context fails when Assembly.Load is called via an intermediary, such as a deserializer or unit test runner. If the intermediary is defined in a different assembly, the intermediary's load context is used instead of the caller's load context.

We described this scenario earlier, when we talked about how you might write a deserializer. In such cases, the ideal solution is to force the caller to specify an ALC rather than inferring it with Assembly.Load(string).

But because .NET 5 and .NET Core evolved from .NET Framework—where isolation was accomplished with application domains rather than ALCs—the ideal solution is not prevalent, and Assembly.Load(string) is sometimes used inappropriately in scenarios in which the ALC cannot be reliably inferred. An example is the .NET binary serializer.

To allow Assembly.Load to still work in such scenarios, Microsoft has added a method to AssemblyLoadContext called EnterContextualReflection. This assigns an ALC to AssemblyLoadContext.CurrentContextualReflectionContext. Although this is a static property, its value is stored in an AsyncLocal variable, so it can hold separate values on different threads (but still be preserved throughout asynchronous operations).

If this property is non-null, Assembly.Load automatically uses it in preference to the calling ALC:

```
Method1();

var myALC = new AssemblyLoadContext ("test");
using (myALC.EnterContextualReflection())
{
    Console.WriteLine (
      AssemblyLoadContext.CurrentContextualReflectionContext.Name);  // test

    Method2();
}

// Once disposed, EnterContextualReflection() no longer has an effect.
Method3();

void Method1() => Assembly.Load ("...");   // Will use calling ALC
void Method2() => Assembly.Load ("...");   // Will use myALC
void Method3() => Assembly.Load ("...");   // Will use calling ALC
```

We previously demonstrated how you could write a method that's functionally similar to Assembly.Load. Here's a more accurate version that takes the contextual reflection context into account:

```
[MethodImpl(MethodImplOptions.NoInlining)]
Assembly Load (string name)
{
  var alc = AssemblyLoadContext.CurrentContextualReflectionContext
    ?? AssemblyLoadContext.GetLoadContext (Assembly.GetCallingAssembly());

  return alc.LoadFromAssemblyName (new AssemblyName (name));
}
```

Even though the contextual reflection context can be useful in allowing legacy code to run, a more robust solution (as we described earlier) is to modify the code that calls Assembly.Load so that it instead calls LoadFromAssemblyName on an ALC that's passed in by the caller.

 .NET Framework has no equivalent of EnterContextualReflection—and does not need it—despite having the same Assembly.Load methods. This is because with .NET Framework, isolation is accomplished primarily with *application domains* rather than ALCs. Application domains provide a stronger isolation model whereby each application domain has its own default load context, so isolation can still work even when only the default load context is used.

Loading and Resolving Unmanaged Libraries

ALCs can also load and resolve native libraries. Native resolution is triggered when you call an external method that's marked with the [DllImport] attribute:

```
[DllImport ("SomeNativeLibrary.dll")]
static extern int SomeNativeMethod (string text);
```

Because we didn't specify a full path in the [DllImport] attribute, calling SomeNativeMethod triggers a resolution in whatever ALC contains the assembly in which SomeNativeMethod is defined.

The virtual *resolving* method in the ALC is called LoadUnmanagedDll, and the *loading* method is called LoadUnmanagedDllFromPath:

```
protected override IntPtr LoadUnmanagedDll (string unmanagedDllName)
{
  // Locate the full path of unmanagedDllName...
  string fullPath = ...
  return LoadUnmanagedDllFromPath (fullPath);    // Load the DLL
}
```

If you're unable to locate the file, you can return IntPtr.Zero. The CLR will then fire the ALC's ResolvingUnmanagedDll event.

Interestingly, the `LoadUnmanagedDllFromPath` method is protected, so you won't usually be able to call it from a `ResolvingUnmanagedDll` event handler. However, you can achieve the same result by calling the static `NativeLibrary.Load`:

```
someALC.ResolvingUnmanagedDll += (requestingAssembly, unmanagedDllName) =>
{
  return NativeLibrary.Load ("(full path to unmanaged DLL)");
};
```

Although native libraries are typically resolved and loaded by ALCs, they don't "belong" to an ALC. After it's loaded, a native library stands on its own and takes responsibility for resolving any transitive dependencies that it might have. Furthermore, native libraries are global to the process, so it's not possible to load two different versions of a native library if they have the same filename.

AssemblyDependencyResolver

In "Default probing" on page 767, we said that the default ALC reads the *.deps.json* and *.runtimeconfig.json* files, if present, in determining where to look to resolve platform-specific and development-time NuGet dependencies.

If you want to load an assembly into a custom ALC that has platform-specific or NuGet dependencies, you'll need to somehow reproduce this logic. You could accomplish this by parsing the configuration files and carefully following the rules on platform-specific monikers, but doing so is not only difficult, but the code that you write will break if the rules change in a later version of .NET.

The `AssemblyDependencyResolver` class solves this problem. To use it, you instantiate it with the path of the assembly whose dependencies you want to probe:

```
var resolver = new AssemblyDependencyResolver (@"c:\temp\foo.dll");
```

Then, to find the path of a dependency, you call the `ResolveAssemblyToPath` method:

```
string path = resolver.ResolveAssemblyToPath (new AssemblyName ("bar"));
```

In the absence of a *.deps.json* file (or if the *.deps.json* doesn't contain anything relevant to *bar.dll*), this will evaluate to *c:\temp\bar.dll*.

You can similarly resolve unmanaged dependencies by calling `ResolveUnmanaged DllToPath`.

A great way to illustrate a more complex scenario is to create a new Console project called `ClientApp` and then add a NuGet reference to *Microsoft.Data.SqlClient*. Add the following class:

```
using Microsoft.Data.SqlClient;

namespace ClientApp
{
  public class Program
  {
    public static SqlConnection GetConnection() => new SqlConnection();
```

```
    static void Main() => GetConnection();    // Test that it resolves
  }
}
```

Now build the application and look in the output folder: you'll see a file called *Microsoft.Data.SqlClient.dll*. However, this file *never loads* when run, and attempting to explicitly load it throws an exception. The assembly that actually loads is located in the *runtimes\win* (or *runtimes/unix*) subfolder; the default ALC knows to load it because it parses the *ClientApp.deps.json* file.

If you were to try to load the *ClientApp.dll* assembly from another application, you'd need to write an ALC that can resolve its dependency, *Microsoft.Data.SqlClient.dll*. In doing so, it would be insufficient to merely look in the folder where *ClientApp.dll* is located (as we did in "Resolving assemblies" on page 763). Instead, you'd need to use `AssemblyDependencyResolver` to determine where that file is located for the platform in use:

```
string path = @"C:\source\ClientApp\bin\Debug\netcoreapp3.0\ClientApp.dll";
var resolver = new AssemblyDependencyResolver (path);
var sqlClient = new AssemblyName ("Microsoft.Data.SqlClient");
Console.WriteLine (resolver.ResolveAssemblyToPath (sqlClient));
```

On a Windows machine, this outputs the following:

```
C:\source\ClientApp\bin\Debug\netcoreapp3.0\runtimes\win\lib\netcoreapp2.1
\Microsoft.Data.SqlClient.dll
```

We give a complete example in "Writing a Plug-In System" on page 775.

Unloading ALCs

In simple cases, it's possible to unload a nondefault `AssemblyLoadContext`, freeing memory and releasing file locks on the assemblies it loaded. For this to work, the ALC must have been instantiated with the `isCollectible` parameter `true`:

```
var alc = new AssemblyLoadContext ("test", isCollectible:true);
```

You can then call the `Unload` method on the ALC to initiate the unload process.

The unload model is cooperative rather than preemptive. If any methods in any of the ALC's assemblies are executing, the unload will be deferred until those methods finish.

The actual unload takes place during garbage collection; it will not take place if anything from outside the ALC has any (nonweak) reference to anything inside the ALC (including objects, types, and assemblies). It's not uncommon for APIs (including those in the .NET BCL) to cache objects in static fields or dictionaries— or subscribe to events—and this makes it easy to create references that will prevent an unload, especially if code in the ALC uses APIs outside its ALC in a nontrivial way. Determining the cause of a failed unload is difficult and requires the use of tools such as WinDbg.

The Legacy Loading Methods

If you're still using .NET Framework (or writing a library that targets .NET Standard and want to support .NET Framework), you won't be able to use the `Assembly LoadContext` class. Loading is accomplished instead by using the following methods:

```
public static Assembly LoadFrom (string assemblyFile);
public static Assembly LoadFile (string path);
public static Assembly Load (byte[] rawAssembly);
```

`LoadFile` and `Load(byte[])` provide isolation, whereas `LoadFrom` does not.

Resolution is accomplished by handling the application domain's `AssemblyResolve` event, which works like the default ALC's `Resolving` event.

The `Assembly.Load(string)` method is also available to trigger resolution and works in a similar way.

LoadFrom

`LoadFrom` loads an assembly from a given path into the default ALC. It's a bit like calling `AssemblyLoadContext.Default.LoadFromAssemblyPath` except for the following:

- If an assembly with the same simple name is already present in the default ALC, `LoadFrom` returns that assembly rather than throwing an exception.

- If an assembly with the same simple name is *not* already present in the default ALC and a load takes place, the assembly is given a special "LoadFrom" status. This status affects the default ALC's resolution logic, in that should that assembly have any dependencies in the *same folder*, those dependencies will resolve automatically.

 .NET Framework has a *Global Assembly Cache* (GAC). If the assembly is present in the GAC, the CLR will always load from there instead. This applies to all three loading methods.

`LoadFrom`'s ability to automatically resolve transitive same-folder dependencies can be convenient—until it loads an assembly that it shouldn't. Because such scenarios can be difficult to debug, it can be better to use `Load(string)` or `LoadFile` and resolve transitive dependencies by handling the application domain's `AssemblyRe solve` event. This gives you the power to decide how to resolve each assembly and allows for debugging (by creating a breakpoint inside the event handler).

LoadFile and Load(byte[])

`LoadFile` and `Load(byte[])` load an assembly from a given file path or byte array into a new ALC. Unlike `LoadFrom`, these methods provide isolation and let you load multiple versions of the same assembly. However, there are two caveats:

- Calling `LoadFile` again with the identical path will return the previously loaded assembly.

- In .NET Framework, both methods first check the GAC and load from there instead if the assembly is present.

With `LoadFile` and `Load(byte[])`, you end up with a separate ALC per assembly (caveats aside). This enables isolation, although it can make it more awkward to manage.

To resolve dependencies, you handle the `AppDomain`'s `Resolving` event, which fires on all ALCs:

```
AppDomain.CurrentDomain.AssemblyResolve += (sender, args) =>
{
  string fullAssemblyName = args.Name;
  // return an Assembly object or null
  ...
};
```

The `args` variable also includes a property called `RequestingAssembly`, which tells you which assembly triggered the resolution.

After locating the assembly, you can then call `Assembly.LoadFile` to load it.

 You can enumerate all of the assemblies that have been loaded into the current application domain with `AppDomain.Current Domain.GetAssemblies()`. This works in .NET 5, too, where it's equivalent to the following:

```
AssemblyLoadContext.All.SelectMany (a => a.Assemblies)
```

Writing a Plug-In System

To fully demonstrate the concepts that we've covered in this section, let's write a plug-in system that uses unloadable ALCs to isolate each plug-in.

Our demo system will initially comprise three .NET projects:

Plugin.Common (library)
Defines an interface that plug-ins will implement

Capitalizer (library)
A plug-in that capitalizes text

Plugin.Host (console application)
Locates and invokes plug-ins

Let's assume that the projects reside in the following directories:

```
c:\source\PluginDemo\Plugin.Common
c:\source\PluginDemo\Capitalizer
c:\source\PluginDemo\Plugin.Host
```

All projects will reference the Plugin.Common library, and there will be no other interproject references.

> If Plugin.Host were to reference Capitalizer, we wouldn't be writing a plug-in system; the central idea is that the plug-ins are written by third parties after Plugin.Host and Plugin.Common have been published.
>
> If you're using Visual Studio, it can be convenient to put all three projects into a single solution for the sake of this demo. If you do so, right-click the Plugin.Host project, choose Build Dependencies > Project Dependencies, and then tick the Capitalizer project. This forces Capitalizer to build when you run the Plugin.Host project, without adding a reference.

Plugin.Common

Let's begin with Plugin.Common. Our plug-ins will perform a very simple task, which is to transform a string. Here's how we'll define the interface:

```
namespace Plugin.Common
{
  public interface ITextPlugin
  {
    string TransformText (string input);
  }
}
```

That's all there is to Plugin.Common.

Capitalizer (plug-in)

Our Capitalizer plug-in will reference Plugin.Common and contain a single class. For now, we'll keep the logic simple so that the plug-in has no extra dependencies:

```
public class CapitalizerPlugin : Plugin.Common.ITextPlugin
{
  public string TransformText (string input) => input.ToUpper();
}
```

If you build both projects and look in Capitalizer's output folder, you'll see the following two assemblies:

```
Capitalizer.dll      // Our plug-in assembly
Plugin.Common.dll    // Referenced assembly
```

Plugin.Host

Plugin.Host is a console application with two classes. The first class is a custom ALC to load the plug-ins:

```
class PluginLoadContext : AssemblyLoadContext
{
  AssemblyDependencyResolver _resolver;
```

```
public PluginLoadContext (string pluginPath, bool collectible)
  // Give it a friendly name to help with debugging:
  : base (name: Path.GetFileName (pluginPath), collectible)
{
  // Create a resolver to help us find dependencies.
  _resolver = new AssemblyDependencyResolver (pluginPath);
}

protected override Assembly Load (AssemblyName assemblyName)
{
  // See below
  if (assemblyName.Name == typeof (ITextPlugin).Assembly.GetName().Name)
    return null;

  string target = _resolver.ResolveAssemblyToPath (assemblyName);

  if (target != null)
    return LoadFromAssemblyPath (target);

  // Could be a BCL assembly. Allow the default context to resolve.
  return null;
}

protected override IntPtr LoadUnmanagedDll (string unmanagedDllName)
{
  string path = _resolver.ResolveUnmanagedDllToPath (unmanagedDllName);

  return path == null
    ? IntPtr.Zero
    : LoadUnmanagedDllFromPath (path);
}
}
```

In the constructor, we pass in the path to the main plug-in assembly as well as a flag to indicate whether we'd like the ALC to be collectible (so that it can be unloaded).

The Load method is where we handle dependency resolution. All plug-ins must reference Plugin.Common so that they can implement ITextPlugin. This means that the Load method will fire at some point to resolve Plugin.Common. We need to be careful because the plug-in's output folder is likely to contain not only *Capitalizer.dll* but also its own copy of *Plugin.Common.dll*. If we were to load this copy of *Plugin.Common.dll* into the PluginLoadContext, we'd end up with two copies of the assembly: one in the host's default context and one in the plug-in's PluginLoadContext. The assemblies would be incompatible, and the host would complain that the plug-in does not implement ITextPlugin!

To solve this, we check explicitly for this condition:

```
if (assemblyName.Name == typeof (ITextPlugin).Assembly.GetName().Name)
  return null;
```

Returning null allows the host's default ALC to instead resolve the assembly.

Instead of returning null, we could return typeof(ITextPlu gin).Assembly, and it would also work correctly. How can we be certain that ITextPlugin will resolve on the host's ALC and not on our PluginLoadContext? Remember that our PluginLoadContext class is defined in the Plugin.Host assembly. Therefore, any types that you statically reference from this class will trigger an assembly resolution on the ALC into which *its assembly*, Plugin.Host, was loaded.

After checking for the common assembly, we use AssemblyDependencyResolver to locate any private dependencies that the plug-in might have. (Right now, there will be none.)

Notice that we also override the LoadUnamangedDll method. This ensures that if the plug-in has any unmanaged dependencies, these will load correctly, too.

The second class to write in Plugin.Host is the main program itself. For simplicity, let's hardcode the path to our Capitalizer plug-in (in real life, you might discover the paths of plug-ins by looking for DLLs in known locations or reading from a configuration file):

```
class Program
{
  const bool UseCollectibleContexts = true;

  static void Main()
  {
    const string capitalizer = @"C:\source\PluginDemo\"
      + @"Capitalizer\bin\Debug\netcoreapp3.0\Capitalizer.dll";

    Console.WriteLine (TransformText ("big apple", capitalizer));
  }

  static string TransformText (string text, string pluginPath)
  {
    var alc = new PluginLoadContext (pluginPath, UseCollectibleContexts);
    try
    {
      Assembly assem = alc.LoadFromAssemblyPath (pluginPath);

      // Locate the type in the assembly that implements ITextPlugin:
      Type pluginType = assem.ExportedTypes.Single (t =>
                        typeof (ITextPlugin).IsAssignableFrom (t));

      // Instantiate the ITextPlugin implementation:
      var plugin = (ITextPlugin)Activator.CreateInstance (pluginType);

      // Call the TransformText method
      return plugin.TransformText (text);
    }
    finally
    {
      if (UseCollectibleContexts) alc.Unload();     // unload the ALC
    }
```

```
      }
   }
```

Let's look at the `TransformText` method. We first instantiate a new ALC for our plug-in and then ask it to load the main plug-in assembly. Next, we use Reflection to locate the type that implements `ITextPlugin` (we cover this in detail in Chapter 18). Then, we instantiate the plug-in, call the `TransformText` method, and unload the ALC.

 If you needed to call the `TransformText` method repeatedly, a better approach would be to cache the ALC rather than unloading it after each call.

Here's the output:

```
BIG APPLE
```

Adding dependencies

Our code is fully capable of resolving and isolating dependencies. To illustrate, let's first add a NuGet reference to *Humanizer.Core*, version 2.6.2. You can do this via the Visual Studio UI or by adding the following element to the *Capitalizer.csproj* file:

```
<ItemGroup>
  <PackageReference Include="Humanizer.Core" Version="2.6.2" />
</ItemGroup>
```

Now, modify `CapitalizerPlugin`, as follows:

```
using Humanizer;
namespace Capitalizer
{
  public class CapitalizerPlugin : Plugin.Common.ITextPlugin
  {
    public string TransformText (string input) => input.Pascalize();
  }
}
```

If you rerun the program, the output will now be this:

```
BigApple
```

Next, we create another plug-in called Pluralizer. Create a new .NET library project and add a NuGet reference to *Humanizer.Core*, version 2.7.9:

```
<ItemGroup>
  <PackageReference Include="Humanizer.Core" Version="2.7.9" />
</ItemGroup>
```

Now, add a class called `PluralizerPlugin`. This will be similar to `Capitalizer PlugIn`, but we call the `Pluralize` method instead:

```
using Humanizer;
namespace Pluralizer
{
  public class PluralizerPlugin : Plugin.Common.ITextPlugin
```

```
  {
    public string TransformText (string input) => input.Pluralize();
  }
}
```

Finally, we need to add code to the Plugin.Host's `Main` method to load and run the Pluralizer plug-in:

```
static void Main()
{
  const string capitalizer = @"C:\source\PluginDemo\"
    + @"Capitalizer\bin\Debug\netcoreapp3.0\Capitalizer.dll";

  Console.WriteLine (TransformText ("big apple", capitalizer));

  const string pluralizer = @"C:\source\PluginDemo\"
    + @"Pluralizer\bin\Debug\netcoreapp3.0\Pluralizer.dll";

  Console.WriteLine (TransformText ("big apple", pluralizer));
}
```

The output will now be like this:

```
BigApple
big apples
```

To fully see what's going on, change the `UseCollectibleContexts` constant to false and add the following code to the `Main` method to enumerate the ALCs and their assemblies:

```
foreach (var context in AssemblyLoadContext.All)
{
  Console.WriteLine ($"Context: {context.GetType().Name} {context.Name}");

  foreach (var assembly in context.Assemblies)
    Console.WriteLine ($"  Assembly: {assembly.FullName}");
}
```

In the output, you can see two different versions of Humanizer, each loaded into its own ALC:

```
Context: PluginLoadContext Capitalizer.dll
  Assembly: Capitalizer, Version=1.0.0.0, Culture=neutral, PublicKeyToken=...
  Assembly: Humanizer, Version=2.6.0.0, Culture=neutral, PublicKeyToken=...
Context: PluginLoadContext Pluralizer.dll
  Assembly: Pluralizer, Version=1.0.0.0, Culture=neutral, PublicKeyToken=...
  Assembly: Humanizer, Version=2.7.0.0, Culture=neutral, PublicKeyToken=...
Context: DefaultAssemblyLoadContext Default
  Assembly: System.Private.CoreLib, Version=4.0.0.0, Culture=neutral,...
  Assembly: Host, Version=1.0.0.0, Culture=neutral, PublicKeyToken=null
  ...
```

Even if both plug-ins were to use the same version of Humanizer, the isolation of separate assemblies can still be beneficial because each will have its own static variables.

18

Reflection and Metadata

As we saw in Chapter 17, a C# program compiles into an assembly that includes metadata, compiled code, and resources. Inspecting the metadata and compiled code at runtime is called *reflection*.

The compiled code in an assembly contains almost all of the content of the original source code. Some information is lost, such as local variable names, comments, and preprocessor directives. However, reflection can access pretty much everything else, even making it possible to write a decompiler.

Many of the services available in .NET and exposed via C# (such as dynamic binding, serialization, and data binding) depend on the presence of metadata. Your own programs can also take advantage of this metadata and even extend it with new information using custom attributes. The System.Reflection namespace houses the reflection API. It is also possible at runtime to dynamically create new metadata and executable instructions in Intermediate Language (IL) via the classes in the System.Reflection.Emit namespace.

The examples in this chapter assume that you import the System and System.Reflection as well as System.Reflection.Emit namespaces.

 When we use the term "dynamically" in this chapter, we mean using reflection to perform some task whose type safety is enforced only at runtime. This is similar in principle to *dynamic binding* via C#'s dynamic keyword, although the mechanism and functionality is different.

Dynamic binding is much easier to use and employs the Dynamic Language Runtime (DLR) for dynamic language interoperability. Reflection is relatively clumsy to use, but it is more flexible in terms of what you can do with the CLR. For instance, reflection lets you obtain lists of types and members, instantiate an object whose name comes from a string, and build assemblies on the fly.

Reflecting and Activating Types

In this section, we examine how to obtain a `Type`, inspect its metadata, and use it to dynamically instantiate an object.

Obtaining a Type

An instance of `System.Type` represents the metadata for a type. Because `Type` is widely used, it lives in the `System` namespace rather than the `System.Reflection` namespace.

You can get an instance of a `System.Type` by calling `GetType` on any object or with C#'s `typeof` operator:

```
Type t1 = DateTime.Now.GetType();    // Type obtained at runtime
Type t2 = typeof (DateTime);         // Type obtained at compile time
```

You can use `typeof` to obtain array types and generic types, as follows:

```
Type t3 = typeof (DateTime[]);          // 1-d Array type
Type t4 = typeof (DateTime[,]);         // 2-d Array type
Type t5 = typeof (Dictionary<int,int>); // Closed generic type
Type t6 = typeof (Dictionary<,>);       // Unbound generic type
```

You can also retrieve a `Type` by name. If you have a reference to its `Assembly`, call `Assembly.GetType` (we describe this further in the section "Reflecting Assemblies" on page 802):

```
Type t = Assembly.GetExecutingAssembly().GetType ("Demos.TestProgram");
```

If you don't have an `Assembly` object, you can obtain a type through its *assembly qualified name* (the type's full name followed by the assembly's fully or partially qualified name). The assembly implicitly loads as if you called `Assembly.Load(string)`:

```
Type t = Type.GetType ("System.Int32, System.Private.CoreLib");
```

After you have a `System.Type` object, you can use its properties to access the type's name, assembly, base type, visibility, and so on:

```
Type stringType = typeof (string);
string name      = stringType.Name;        // String
Type baseType    = stringType.BaseType;     // typeof(Object)
Assembly assem   = stringType.Assembly;     // System.Private.CoreLib
bool isPublic    = stringType.IsPublic;     // true
```

A `System.Type` instance is a window into the entire metadata for the type—and the assembly in which it's defined.

> `System.Type` is abstract, so the `typeof` operator must actually give you a subclass of `Type`. The subclass that the CLR uses is internal to .NET and is called `RuntimeType`.

TypeInfo

Should you target .NET Core 1.x (or an older Windows Store profile), you'll find most of Type's members are missing. These missing members are exposed instead on a class called TypeInfo, which you obtain by calling GetTypeInfo. So, to get our previous example to run, you would do this:

```
Type stringType = typeof(string);
string name = stringType.Name;
Type baseType = stringType.GetTypeInfo().BaseType;
Assembly assem = stringType.GetTypeInfo().Assembly;
bool isPublic = stringType.GetTypeInfo().IsPublic;
```

TypeInfo also exists in .NET Core 2 and 3, and .NET 5+ (and .NET Framework 4.5+ and all .NET Standard versions), so the preceding code works almost universally. TypeInfo also includes additional properties and methods for reflecting over members.

Obtaining array types

As we just saw, typeof and GetType work with array types. You can also obtain an array type by calling MakeArrayType on the *element* type:

```
Type simpleArrayType = typeof (int).MakeArrayType();
Console.WriteLine (simpleArrayType == typeof (int[]));    // True
```

You can create multidimensional arrays by passing an integer argument to Make ArrayType:

```
Type cubeType = typeof (int).MakeArrayType (3);      // cube shaped
Console.WriteLine (cubeType == typeof (int[,,]));    // True
```

GetElementType does the reverse: it retrieves an array type's element type:

```
Type e = typeof (int[]).GetElementType();    // e == typeof (int)
```

GetArrayRank returns the number of dimensions of a rectangular array:

```
int rank = typeof (int[,,]).GetArrayRank();    // 3
```

Obtaining nested types

To retrieve nested types, call GetNestedTypes on the containing type:

```
foreach (Type t in typeof (System.Environment).GetNestedTypes())
  Console.WriteLine (t.FullName);

OUTPUT: System.Environment+SpecialFolder
```

or:

```
foreach (TypeInfo t in typeof (System.Environment).GetTypeInfo()
                                         .DeclaredNestedTypes)
  Debug.WriteLine (t.FullName);
```

The one caveat with nested types is that the CLR treats a nested type as having special "nested" accessibility levels:

```
Type t = typeof (System.Environment.SpecialFolder);
Console.WriteLine (t.IsPublic);             // False
Console.WriteLine (t.IsNestedPublic);       // True
```

Type Names

A type has Namespace, Name, and FullName properties. In most cases, FullName is a composition of the former two:

```
Type t = typeof (System.Text.StringBuilder);

Console.WriteLine (t.Namespace);    // System.Text
Console.WriteLine (t.Name);         // StringBuilder
Console.WriteLine (t.FullName);     // System.Text.StringBuilder
```

There are two exceptions to this rule: nested types and closed generic types.

 Type also has a property called AssemblyQualifiedName, which returns FullName followed by a comma and then the full name of its assembly. This is the same string that you can pass to Type.GetType, and it uniquely identifies a type within the default loading context.

Nested type names

With nested types, the containing type appears only in FullName:

```
Type t = typeof (System.Environment.SpecialFolder);

Console.WriteLine (t.Namespace);    // System
Console.WriteLine (t.Name);         // SpecialFolder
Console.WriteLine (t.FullName);     // System.Environment+SpecialFolder
```

The + symbol differentiates the containing type from a nested namespace.

Generic type names

Generic type names are suffixed with the ' symbol, followed by the number of type parameters. If the generic type is unbound, this rule applies to both Name and FullName:

```
Type t = typeof (Dictionary<,>); // Unbound
Console.WriteLine (t.Name);       // Dictionary'2
Console.WriteLine (t.FullName);   // System.Collections.Generic.Dictionary'2
```

If the generic type is closed, however, FullName (only) acquires a substantial extra appendage. Each type parameter's full *assembly qualified name* is enumerated:

```
Console.WriteLine (typeof (Dictionary<int,string>).FullName);

// OUTPUT:
System.Collections.Generic.Dictionary`2[[System.Int32,
```

```
System.Private.CoreLib, Version=4.0.0.0, Culture=neutral,
PublicKeyToken=7cec85d7bea7798e],[System.String, System.Private.CoreLib,
Version=4.0.0.0, Culture=neutral, PublicKeyToken=7cec85d7bea7798e]]
```

This ensures that `AssemblyQualifiedName` (a combination of the type's full name and assembly name) contains enough information to fully identify both the generic type and its type parameters.

Array and pointer type names

Arrays present with the same suffix that you use in a `typeof` expression:

```
Console.WriteLine (typeof ( int[]  ).Name);     // Int32[]
Console.WriteLine (typeof ( int[,] ).Name);     // Int32[,]
Console.WriteLine (typeof ( int[,] ).FullName); // System.Int32[,]
```

Pointer types are similar:

```
Console.WriteLine (typeof (byte*).Name);     // Byte*
```

ref and out parameter type names

A `Type` describing a `ref` or out parameter has an & suffix:

```
public void RefMethod (ref int p)
{
  Type t = MethodInfo.GetCurrentMethod().GetParameters()[0].ParameterType;
  Console.WriteLine (t.Name);     // Int32&
}
```

More on this later, in the section "Reflecting and Invoking Members" on page 789.

Base Types and Interfaces

Type exposes a `BaseType` property:

```
Type base1 = typeof (System.String).BaseType;
Type base2 = typeof (System.IO.FileStream).BaseType;

Console.WriteLine (base1.Name);     // Object
Console.WriteLine (base2.Name);     // Stream
```

The `GetInterfaces` method returns the interfaces that a type implements:

```
foreach (Type iType in typeof (Guid).GetInterfaces())
  Console.WriteLine (iType.Name);

IFormattable
IComparable
IComparable'1
IEquatable'1
```

Reflection provides three dynamic equivalents to C#'s static `is` operator:

`IsInstanceOfType`
    Accepts a type and instance

`IsAssignableFrom` *and (from .NET 5)* `IsAssignableTo`
   Accepts two types

Here's an example of the first:

```
object obj  = Guid.NewGuid();
Type target = typeof (IFormattable);

bool isTrue   = obj is IFormattable;          // Static C# operator
bool alsoTrue = target.IsInstanceOfType (obj);   // Dynamic equivalent
```

`IsAssignableFrom` is more versatile:

```
Type target = typeof (IComparable), source = typeof (string);
Console.WriteLine (target.IsAssignableFrom (source));      // True
```

The `IsSubclassOf` method works on the same principle as `IsAssignableFrom` but excludes interfaces.

Instantiating Types

There are two ways to dynamically instantiate an object from its type:

- Call the static `Activator.CreateInstance` method

- Call `Invoke` on a `ConstructorInfo` object obtained from calling `GetConstruc` `tor` on a `Type` (advanced scenarios)

`Activator.CreateInstance` accepts a `Type` and optional arguments that it passes to the constructor:

```
int i = (int) Activator.CreateInstance (typeof (int));

DateTime dt = (DateTime) Activator.CreateInstance (typeof (DateTime),
                                  2000, 1, 1);
```

`CreateInstance` lets you specify many other options, such as the assembly from which to load the type and whether to bind to a nonpublic constructor. A `Missing` `MethodException` is thrown if the runtime can't find a suitable constructor.

Calling `Invoke` on a `ConstructorInfo` is necessary when your argument values can't disambiguate between overloaded constructors. For example, suppose that class X has two constructors: one accepting a parameter of type `string` and another accepting a parameter of type `StringBuilder`. The target is ambiguous should you pass a `null` argument into `Activator.CreateInstance`. This is when you need to use a `ConstructorInfo` instead:

```
// Fetch the constructor that accepts a single parameter of type string:
ConstructorInfo ci = typeof (X).GetConstructor (new[] { typeof (string) });

// Construct the object using that overload, passing in null:
object foo = ci.Invoke (new object[] { null });
```

Or, if you're targeting .NET Core 1, an older Windows Store profile:

```
ConstructorInfo ci = typeof (X).GetTypeInfo().DeclaredConstructors
  .FirstOrDefault (c =>
    c.GetParameters().Length == 1 &&
    c.GetParameters()[0].ParameterType == typeof (string));
```

To obtain a nonpublic constructor, you need to specify BindingFlags—see "Accessing Nonpublic Members" on page 798 within the section "Reflecting and Invoking Members" on page 789.

 Dynamic instantiation adds a few microseconds onto the time taken to construct the object. This is quite a lot in relative terms because the CLR is ordinarily very fast in instantiating objects (a simple new on a small class takes in the region of tens of nanoseconds).

To dynamically instantiate arrays based on just element type, first call MakeArray Type. You can also instantiate generic types: we describe this in the next section.

To dynamically instantiate a delegate, call Delegate.CreateDelegate. The following example demonstrates instantiating both an instance delegate and a static delegate:

```
class Program
{
  delegate int IntFunc (int x);

  static int Square (int x) => x * x;        // Static method
  int        Cube   (int x) => x * x * x;    // Instance method

  static void Main()
  {
    Delegate staticD = Delegate.CreateDelegate
      (typeof (IntFunc), typeof (Program), "Square");

    Delegate instanceD = Delegate.CreateDelegate
      (typeof (IntFunc), new Program(), "Cube");

    Console.WriteLine (staticD.DynamicInvoke (3));    // 9
    Console.WriteLine (instanceD.DynamicInvoke (3));  // 27
  }
}
```

You can invoke the Delegate object that's returned by calling DynamicInvoke, as we did in this example, or by casting to the typed delegate:

```
IntFunc f = (IntFunc) staticD;
Console.WriteLine (f(3));        // 9 (but much faster!)
```

You can pass a MethodInfo into CreateDelegate instead of a method name. We describe MethodInfo shortly, in "Reflecting and Invoking Members" on page 789, along with the rationale for casting a dynamically created delegate back to the static delegate type.

Generic Types

A `Type` can represent a closed or unbound generic type. Just as at compile time, a closed generic type can be instantiated, whereas an unbound type cannot:

```
Type closed = typeof (List<int>);
List<int> list = (List<int>) Activator.CreateInstance (closed);  // OK

Type unbound  = typeof (List<>);
object anError = Activator.CreateInstance (unbound);     // Runtime error
```

The `MakeGenericType` method converts an unbound into a closed generic type. Simply pass in the desired type arguments:

```
Type unbound = typeof (List<>);
Type closed = unbound.MakeGenericType (typeof (int));
```

The `GetGenericTypeDefinition` method does the opposite:

```
Type unbound2 = closed.GetGenericTypeDefinition();  // unbound == unbound2
```

The `IsGenericType` property returns `true` if a `Type` is generic, and the `IsGeneric TypeDefinition` property returns `true` if the generic type is unbound. The following tests whether a type is a nullable value type:

```
Type nullable = typeof (bool?);
Console.WriteLine (
  nullable.IsGenericType &&
  nullable.GetGenericTypeDefinition() == typeof (Nullable<>));  // True
```

`GetGenericArguments` returns the type arguments for closed generic types:

```
Console.WriteLine (closed.GetGenericArguments()[0]);     // System.Int32
Console.WriteLine (nullable.GetGenericArguments()[0]);   // System.Boolean
```

For unbound generic types, `GetGenericArguments` returns pseudotypes that represent the placeholder types specified in the generic type definition:

```
Console.WriteLine (unbound.GetGenericArguments()[0]);      // T
```

> At runtime, all generic types are either *unbound* or *closed*. They're unbound in the (relatively unusual) case of an expression such as `typeof(Foo<>)`; otherwise, they're closed. There's no such thing as an *open* generic type at runtime: all open types are closed by the compiler. The method in the following class always prints `False`:
>
> ```
> class Foo<T>
> {
>   public void Test()
>     => Console.Write (GetType().IsGenericTypeDefinition);
> }
> ```

Reflecting and Invoking Members

The `GetMembers` method returns the members of a type. Consider the following class:

```
class Walnut
{
  private bool cracked;
  public void Crack() { cracked = true; }
}
```

We can reflect on its public members, as follows:

```
MemberInfo[] members = typeof (Walnut).GetMembers();
foreach (MemberInfo m in members)
  Console.WriteLine (m);
```

This is the result:

```
Void Crack()
System.Type GetType()
System.String ToString()
Boolean Equals(System.Object)
Int32 GetHashCode()
Void .ctor()
```

When called with no arguments, `GetMembers` returns all the public members for a type (and its base types). `GetMember` retrieves a specific member by name—although it still returns an array because members can be overloaded:

```
MemberInfo[] m = typeof (Walnut).GetMember ("Crack");
Console.WriteLine (m[0]);                                    // Void Crack()
```

`MemberInfo` also has a property called `MemberType` of type `MemberTypes`. This is a flags enum with these values:

All	Custom	Field	NestedType	TypeInfo
Constructor	Event	Method	Property	

When calling `GetMembers`, you can pass in a `MemberTypes` instance to restrict the kinds of members that it returns. Alternatively, you can restrict the result set by calling `GetMethods`, `GetFields`, `GetProperties`, `GetEvents`, `GetConstructors`, or `GetNestedTypes`. There are also singular versions of each of these to home in on a specific member.

 It pays to be as specific as possible when retrieving a type member so that your code doesn't break if additional members are added later. If you're retrieving a method by name, specifying all parameter types ensures that your code will still work if the method is later overloaded (we provide examples shortly, in "Method Parameters" on page 796).

Reflecting Members with TypeInfo

`TypeInfo` exposes a different (and somewhat simpler) protocol for reflecting over members. Using this API is optional (except in .NET Core 1 and older Windows Store apps given that there's no exact equivalent to the `GetMembers` method).

Instead of exposing methods like `GetMembers` that return arrays, `TypeInfo` exposes *properties* that return `IEnumerable<T>`, upon which you typically run LINQ queries. The broadest is `DeclaredMembers`:

```
IEnumerable<MemberInfo> members =
  typeof(Walnut).GetTypeInfo().DeclaredMembers;
```

Unlike with `GetMembers()`, the result excludes inherited members:

```
Void Crack()
Void .ctor()
Boolean cracked
```

There are also properties for returning specific kinds of members (`DeclaredProper ties`, `DeclaredMethods`, `DeclaredEvents`, and so on) and methods for returning a specific member by name (e.g., `GetDeclaredMethod`). The latter cannot be used on overloaded methods (because there's no way to specify parameter types). Instead, you run a LINQ query over `DeclaredMethods`:

```
MethodInfo method = typeof (int).GetTypeInfo().DeclaredMethods
  .FirstOrDefault (m => m.Name == "ToString" &&
                   m.GetParameters().Length == 0);
```

A `MemberInfo` object has a `Name` property and two `Type` properties:

`DeclaringType`
: Returns the `Type` that defines the member

`ReflectedType`
: Returns the `Type` upon which `GetMembers` was called

The two differ when called on a member that's defined in a base type: `Declaring Type` returns the base type, whereas `ReflectedType` returns the subtype. The following example highlights this:

```
// MethodInfo is a subclass of MemberInfo; see Figure 18-1.

MethodInfo test = typeof (Program).GetMethod ("ToString");
MethodInfo obj  = typeof (object) .GetMethod ("ToString");

Console.WriteLine (test.DeclaringType);    // System.Object
Console.WriteLine (obj.DeclaringType);     // System.Object

Console.WriteLine (test.ReflectedType);    // Program
Console.WriteLine (obj.ReflectedType);     // System.Object

Console.WriteLine (test == obj);           // False
```

Because they have different `ReflectedTypes`, the `test` and `obj` objects are not equal. Their difference, however, is purely a fabrication of the reflection API; our `Program` type has no distinct `ToString` method in the underlying type system. We can verify that the two `MethodInfo` objects refer to the same method in either of two ways:

```
Console.WriteLine (test.MethodHandle == obj.MethodHandle);    // True

Console.WriteLine (test.MetadataToken == obj.MetadataToken    // True
                   && test.Module == obj.Module);
```

A `MethodHandle` is unique to each (genuinely distinct) method within a process; a `MetadataToken` is unique across all types and members within an assembly module.

`MemberInfo` also defines methods to return custom attributes (see "Retrieving Attributes at Runtime" on page 807).

 You can obtain the `MethodBase` of the currently executing method by calling `MethodBase.GetCurrentMethod`.

Member Types

`MemberInfo` itself is light on members because it's an abstract base for the types shown in Figure 18-1.

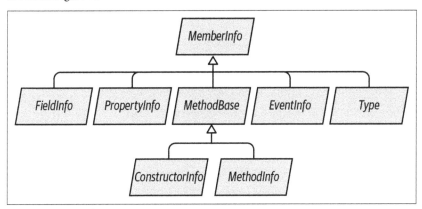

Figure 18-1. Member types

You can cast a `MemberInfo` to its subtype, based on its `MemberType` property. If you obtained a member via `GetMethod`, `GetField`, `GetProperty`, `GetEvent`, `GetConstructor`, or `GetNestedType` (or their plural versions), a cast isn't necessary. Table 18-1 summarizes what methods to use for each kind of C# construct.

Table 18-1. Retrieving member metadata

C# construct	Method to use	Name to use	Result
Method	GetMethod	(method name)	MethodInfo
Property	GetProperty	(property name)	PropertyInfo
Indexer	GetDefaultMembers		MemberInfo[] (containing PropertyInfo objects if compiled in C#)
Field	GetField	(field name)	FieldInfo
Enum member	GetField	(member name)	FieldInfo
Event	GetEvent	(event name)	EventInfo
Constructor	GetConstructor		ConstructorInfo
Finalizer	GetMethod	"Finalize"	MethodInfo
Operator	GetMethod	"op_" + operator name	MethodInfo
Nested type	GetNestedType	(type name)	Type

Each MemberInfo subclass has a wealth of properties and methods, exposing all aspects of the member's metadata. This includes such things as visibility, modifiers, generic type arguments, parameters, return type, and custom attributes.

Here is an example of using GetMethod:

```
MethodInfo m = typeof (Walnut).GetMethod ("Crack");
Console.WriteLine (m);                  // Void Crack()
Console.WriteLine (m.ReturnType);       // System.Void
```

All *Info instances are cached by the reflection API on first use:

```
MethodInfo method = typeof (Walnut).GetMethod ("Crack");
MemberInfo member = typeof (Walnut).GetMember ("Crack") [0];

Console.Write (method == member);       // True
```

As well as preserving object identity, caching improves the performance of what is otherwise a fairly slow API.

C# Members Versus CLR Members

The preceding table illustrates that some of C#'s functional constructs don't have a 1:1 mapping with CLR constructs. This makes sense because the CLR and reflection API were designed with all .NET languages in mind—you can use reflection even from Visual Basic.

Some C# constructs—namely indexers, enums, operators, and finalizers—are contrivances as far as the CLR is concerned. Specifically:

- A C# indexer translates to a property accepting one or more arguments, marked as the type's [DefaultMember].
- A C# enum translates to a subtype of System.Enum with a static field for each member.
- A C# operator translates to a specially named static method, starting in "op_"; for example, "op_Addition".
- A C# finalizer translates to a method that overrides Finalize.

Another complication is that properties and events actually comprise two things:

- Metadata describing the property or event (encapsulated by PropertyInfo or EventInfo)
- One or two backing methods

In a C# program, the backing methods are encapsulated within the property or event definition. But when compiled to IL, the backing methods present as ordinary methods that you can call like any other. This means that GetMethods returns property and event backing methods alongside ordinary methods:

```
class Test { public int X { get { return 0; } set {} } }

void Demo()
{
  foreach (MethodInfo mi in typeof (Test).GetMethods())
    Console.Write (mi.Name + "  ");
}

// OUTPUT:
get_X  set_X  GetType  ToString  Equals  GetHashCode
```

You can identify these methods through the IsSpecialName property in Method Info. IsSpecialName returns true for property, indexer, and event accessors, as well as operators. It returns false only for conventional C# methods—and the Finalize method if a finalizer is defined.

Here are the backing methods that C# generates:

C# construct	Member type	Methods in IL
Property	Property	get_*XXX* and set_*XXX*
Indexer	Property	get_Item and set_Item
Event	Event	add_*XXX* and remove_*XXX*

Each backing method has its own associated `MethodInfo` object. You can access these as follows:

```
PropertyInfo pi = typeof (Console).GetProperty ("Title");
MethodInfo getter = pi.GetGetMethod();          // get_Title
MethodInfo setter = pi.GetSetMethod();          // set_Title
MethodInfo[] both = pi.GetAccessors();          // Length==2
```

`GetAddMethod` and `GetRemoveMethod` perform a similar job for `EventInfo`.

To go in the reverse direction—from a `MethodInfo` to its associated `PropertyInfo` or `EventInfo`—you need to perform a query. LINQ is ideal for this job:

```
PropertyInfo p = mi.DeclaringType.GetProperties()
                    .First (x => x.GetAccessors (true).Contains (mi));
```

Init-only properties

Init-only properties, introduced in C# 9, can be set via an object initializer but are subsequently treated as read-only by the compiler. From the CLR's perspective, an `init` accessor is just like an ordinary `set` accessor but with a special flag applied to the `set` method's return type (which means something to the compiler).

Curiously, this flag is not encoded as a convention attribute. Instead, it uses a relatively obscure mechanism called a *modreq*, which ensures that previous versions of the C# compiler (which don't recognize the new modreq) ignore the accessor rather than treat the property as writable.

The modreq for init-only accessors is called `IsExternalInit`, and you can query for it as follows:

```
bool IsInitOnly (PropertyInfo pi) => pi
  .GetSetMethod().ReturnParameter.GetRequiredCustomModifiers()
  .Any (t => t.Name == "IsExternalInit");
```

NullabilityContextInfo

From .NET 6, you can use the NullabilityInfoContext class to obtain information about the nullability annotations for a field, property, event or parameter:

```
void PrintPropertyNullability (PropertyInfo pi)
{
  var info = new NullabilityInfoContext().Create (pi);
  Console.WriteLine (pi.Name + " read " + info.ReadState);
  Console.WriteLine (pi.Name + " write " + info.WriteState);
  // Use info.Element to get nullability info for array elements
}
```

Generic Type Members

You can obtain member metadata for both unbound and closed generic types:

```
PropertyInfo unbound = typeof (IEnumerator<>)  .GetProperty ("Current");
PropertyInfo closed = typeof (IEnumerator<int>).GetProperty ("Current");
```

```
Console.WriteLine (unbound);    // T Current
Console.WriteLine (closed);     // Int32 Current

Console.WriteLine (unbound.PropertyType.IsGenericParameter);  // True
Console.WriteLine (closed.PropertyType.IsGenericParameter);   // False
```

The MemberInfo objects returned from unbound and closed generic types are
always distinct, even for members whose signatures don't feature generic type
parameters:

```
PropertyInfo unbound = typeof (List<>)  .GetProperty ("Count");
PropertyInfo closed = typeof (List<int>).GetProperty ("Count");

Console.WriteLine (unbound);    // Int32 Count
Console.WriteLine (closed);     // Int32 Count

Console.WriteLine (unbound == closed);   // False

Console.WriteLine (unbound.DeclaringType.IsGenericTypeDefinition); // True
Console.WriteLine (closed.DeclaringType.IsGenericTypeDefinition); // False
```

Members of unbound generic types cannot be *dynamically invoked*.

Dynamically Invoking a Member

 Dynamically invoking a member can be accomplished more
easily using the Uncapsulator open source library (available
on NuGet and GitHub). Uncapsulator was written by the
author, and provides a fluent API for invoking public and
non-public members via reflection, using a custom dynamic
binder.

After you have a MethodInfo, PropertyInfo, or FieldInfo object, you can dynamically call it or get/set its value. This is called *late binding* because you choose which
member to invoke at runtime rather than compile time.

To illustrate, the following uses ordinary *static binding*:

```
string s = "Hello";
int length = s.Length;
```

Here's the same thing performed dynamically with late binding:

```
object s = "Hello";
PropertyInfo prop = s.GetType().GetProperty ("Length");
int length = (int) prop.GetValue (s, null);              // 5
```

GetValue and SetValue get and set the value of a PropertyInfo or FieldInfo. The
first argument is the instance, which can be null for a static member. Accessing
an indexer is just like accessing a property called "Item," except that you provide
indexer values as the second argument when calling GetValue or SetValue.

To dynamically call a method, call Invoke on a MethodInfo, providing an array of
arguments to pass to that method. If you get any of the argument types wrong,

an exception is thrown at runtime. With dynamic invocation, you lose compile-time type safety, but you still have runtime type safety (just as with the dynamic keyword).

Method Parameters

Suppose that we want to dynamically call string's Substring method. Statically, we would do this as follows:

```
Console.WriteLine ("stamp".Substring(2));                    // "amp"
```

Here's the dynamic equivalent with reflection and late binding:

```
Type type = typeof (string);
Type[] parameterTypes = { typeof (int) };
MethodInfo method = type.GetMethod ("Substring", parameterTypes);

object[] arguments = { 2 };
object returnValue = method.Invoke ("stamp", arguments);
Console.WriteLine (returnValue);                            // "amp"
```

Because the Substring method is overloaded, we had to pass an array of parameter types to GetMethod to indicate which version we wanted. Without the parameter types, GetMethod would throw an AmbiguousMatchException.

The GetParameters method, defined on MethodBase (the base class for MethodInfo and ConstructorInfo), returns parameter metadata. We can continue our previous example, as follows:

```
ParameterInfo[] paramList = method.GetParameters();
foreach (ParameterInfo x in paramList)
{
  Console.WriteLine (x.Name);                    // startIndex
  Console.WriteLine (x.ParameterType);           // System.Int32
}
```

Dealing with ref and out parameters

To pass ref or out parameters, call MakeByRefType on the type before obtaining the method. For instance, you can dynamically execute this code

```
int x;
bool successfulParse = int.TryParse ("23", out x);
```

as follows:

```
object[] args = { "23", 0 };
Type[] argTypes = { typeof (string), typeof (int).MakeByRefType() };
MethodInfo tryParse = typeof (int).GetMethod ("TryParse", argTypes);
bool successfulParse = (bool) tryParse.Invoke (null, args);

Console.WriteLine (successfulParse + " " + args[1]);        // True 23
```

This same approach works for both ref and out parameter types.

Retrieving and invoking generic methods

Explicitly specifying parameter types when calling GetMethod can be essential in disambiguating overloaded methods. However, it's impossible to specify generic parameter types. For instance, consider the System.Linq.Enumerable class, which overloads the Where method, as follows:

```
public static IEnumerable<TSource> Where<TSource>
  (this IEnumerable<TSource> source, Func<TSource, bool> predicate);

public static IEnumerable<TSource> Where<TSource>
  (this IEnumerable<TSource> source, Func<TSource, int, bool> predicate);
```

To retrieve a specific overload, we must retrieve all methods and then manually find the desired overload. The following query retrieves the former overload of Where:

```
from m in typeof (Enumerable).GetMethods()
where m.Name == "Where" && m.IsGenericMethod
let parameters = m.GetParameters()
where parameters.Length == 2
let genArg = m.GetGenericArguments().First()
let enumerableOfT = typeof (IEnumerable<>).MakeGenericType (genArg)
let funcOfTBool = typeof (Func<,>).MakeGenericType (genArg, typeof (bool))
where parameters[0].ParameterType == enumerableOfT
   && parameters[1].ParameterType == funcOfTBool
select m
```

Calling .Single() on this query gives the correct MethodInfo object with unbound type parameters. The next step is to close the type parameters by calling MakeGener icMethod:

```
var closedMethod = unboundMethod.MakeGenericMethod (typeof (int));
```

In this case, we've closed TSource with int, allowing us to call Enumerable.Where with a source of type IEnumerable<int> and a predicate of type Func<int,bool>:

```
int[] source = { 3, 4, 5, 6, 7, 8 };
Func<int, bool> predicate = n => n % 2 == 1;   // Odd numbers only
```

We can now invoke the closed generic method:

```
var query = (IEnumerable<int>) closedMethod.Invoke
  (null, new object[] { source, predicate });

foreach (int element in query) Console.Write (element + "|");  // 3|5|7|
```

If you're using the System.Linq.Expressions API to dynamically build expressions (Chapter 8), you don't need to go to this trouble to specify a generic method. The Expression .Call method is overloaded to let you specify the closed type arguments of the method that you want to call:

```
int[] source = { 3, 4, 5, 6, 7, 8 };
Func<int, bool> predicate = n => n % 2 == 1;

var sourceExpr = Expression.Constant (source);
var predicateExpr = Expression.Constant (predicate);

var callExpression = Expression.Call (
  typeof (Enumerable), "Where",
  new[] { typeof (int) },  // Closed generic arg type.
  sourceExpr, predicateExpr);
```

Using Delegates for Performance

Dynamic invocations are relatively inefficient, with an overhead typically in the few-microseconds region. If you're calling a method repeatedly in a loop, you can shift the per-call overhead into the nanoseconds region by instead calling a dynamically instantiated delegate that targets your dynamic method. In the next example, we dynamically call string's Trim method a million times without significant overhead:

```
MethodInfo trimMethod = typeof (string).GetMethod ("Trim", new Type[0]);
var trim = (StringToString) Delegate.CreateDelegate
                             (typeof (StringToString), trimMethod);
for (int i = 0; i < 1000000; i++)
  trim ("test");

delegate string StringToString (string s);
```

This is faster because the costly late binding (shown in bold) happens just once.

Accessing Nonpublic Members

All of the methods on types used to probe metadata (e.g., GetProperty, GetField, etc.) have overloads that take a BindingFlags enum. This enum serves as a metadata filter and allows you to change the default selection criteria. The most common use for this is to retrieve nonpublic members (this works only in desktop apps).

For instance, consider the following class:

```
class Walnut
{
  private bool cracked;
  public void Crack() { cracked = true; }

  public override string ToString() { return cracked.ToString(); }
}
```

We can *uncrack* the walnut as follows:

```
Type t = typeof (Walnut);
Walnut w = new Walnut();
```

```
w.Crack();
FieldInfo f = t.GetField ("cracked", BindingFlags.NonPublic |
                                      BindingFlags.Instance);
f.SetValue (w, false);
Console.WriteLine (w);          // False
```

Using reflection to access nonpublic members is powerful, but it is also dangerous because you can bypass encapsulation, creating an unmanageable dependency on the internal implementation of a type.

The BindingFlags enum

BindingFlags is intended to be bitwise-combined. To get any matches at all, you need to start with one of the following four combinations:

```
BindingFlags.Public    | BindingFlags.Instance
BindingFlags.Public    | BindingFlags.Static
BindingFlags.NonPublic | BindingFlags.Instance
BindingFlags.NonPublic | BindingFlags.Static
```

NonPublic includes internal, protected, protected internal, and private.

The following example retrieves all the public static members of type object:

```
BindingFlags publicStatic = BindingFlags.Public | BindingFlags.Static;
MemberInfo[] members = typeof (object).GetMembers (publicStatic);
```

The following example retrieves all the nonpublic members of type object, both static and instance:

```
BindingFlags nonPublicBinding =
  BindingFlags.NonPublic | BindingFlags.Static | BindingFlags.Instance;

MemberInfo[] members = typeof (object).GetMembers (nonPublicBinding);
```

The DeclaredOnly flag excludes functions inherited from base types, unless they are overridden.

> The DeclaredOnly flag is somewhat confusing in that it
> *restricts* the result set (whereas all the other binding flags
> *expand* the result set).

Generic Methods

You cannot directly invoke generic methods; the following throws an exception:

```
class Program
{
  public static T Echo<T> (T x) { return x; }

  static void Main()
  {
    MethodInfo echo = typeof (Program).GetMethod ("Echo");
    Console.WriteLine (echo.IsGenericMethodDefinition);   // True
    echo.Invoke (null, new object[] { 123 } );            // Exception
```

```
        }
    }
```

An extra step is required, which is to call `MakeGenericMethod` on the `MethodInfo`, specifying concrete generic type arguments. This returns another `MethodInfo`, which you can then invoke, as follows:

```
MethodInfo echo = typeof (Program).GetMethod ("Echo");
MethodInfo intEcho = echo.MakeGenericMethod (typeof (int));
Console.WriteLine (intEcho.IsGenericMethodDefinition);     // False
Console.WriteLine (intEcho.Invoke (null, new object[] { 3 } )); // 3
```

Anonymously Calling Members of a Generic Interface

Reflection is useful when you need to invoke a member of a generic interface and you don't know the type parameters until runtime. In theory, the need for this arises rarely if types are perfectly designed; of course, types are not always perfectly designed.

For instance, suppose that we want to write a more powerful version of `ToString` that could expand the result of LINQ queries. We could start out as follows:

```
public static string ToStringEx <T> (IEnumerable<T> sequence)
{
  ...
}
```

This is already quite limiting. What if sequence contained *nested* collections that we also want to enumerate? We'd need to overload the method to cope:

```
public static string ToStringEx <T> (IEnumerable<IEnumerable<T>> sequence)
```

And then what if sequence contained groupings, or *projections* of nested sequences? The static solution of method overloading becomes impractical—we need an approach that can scale to handle an arbitrary object graph, such as the following:

```
public static string ToStringEx (object value)
{
  if (value == null) return "<null>";
  StringBuilder sb = new StringBuilder();

  if (value is List<>)                                      // Error
    sb.Append ("List of " + ((List<>) value).Count + " items"); // Error

  if (value is IGrouping<,>)                                // Error
    sb.Append ("Group with key=" + ((IGrouping<,>) value).Key); // Error

  // Enumerate collection elements if this is a collection,
  // recursively calling ToStringEx()
  // ...

  return sb.ToString();
}
```

Unfortunately, this won't compile: you cannot invoke members of an *unbound* generic type such as List<> or IGrouping<>. In the case of List<>, we can solve the problem by using the nongeneric IList interface instead:

```
if (value is IList)
    sb.AppendLine ("A list with " + ((IList) value).Count + " items");
```

 We can do this because the designers of List<> had the foresight to implement IList classic (as well as IList *generic*). The same principle is worthy of consideration when writing your own generic types: having a nongeneric interface or base class upon which consumers can fall back can be extremely valuable.

The solution is not as simple for IGrouping<,>. Here's how the interface is defined:

```
public interface IGrouping <TKey,TElement> : IEnumerable <TElement>,
                                             IEnumerable
{
    TKey Key { get; }
}
```

There's no nongeneric type we can use to access the Key property, so here we must use reflection. The solution is not to invoke members of an unbound generic type (which is impossible) but to invoke members of a *closed* generic type, whose type arguments we establish at runtime.

 In the following chapter, we solve this more simply with C#'s dynamic keyword. A good indication for dynamic binding is when you would otherwise need to perform *type gymnastics*— as we are doing right now.

The first step is to determine whether value implements IGrouping<,> and, if so, obtain its closed generic interface. We can do this most easily by executing a LINQ query. Then, we retrieve and invoke the Key property:

```
public static string ToStringEx (object value)
{
    if (value == null) return "<null>";
    if (value.GetType().IsPrimitive) return value.ToString();

    StringBuilder sb = new StringBuilder();

    if (value is IList)
        sb.Append ("List of " + ((IList)value).Count + " items: ");

    Type closedIGrouping = value.GetType().GetInterfaces()
        .Where (t => t.IsGenericType &&
                    t.GetGenericTypeDefinition() == typeof (IGrouping<,>))
        .FirstOrDefault();

    if (closedIGrouping != null)    // Call the Key property on IGrouping<,>
    {
        PropertyInfo pi = closedIGrouping.GetProperty ("Key");
```

```
      object key = pi.GetValue (value, null);
      sb.Append ("Group with key=" + key + ": ");
    }

    if (value is IEnumerable)
      foreach (object element in ((IEnumerable)value))
        sb.Append (ToStringEx (element) + " ");

    if (sb.Length == 0) sb.Append (value.ToString());

    return "\r\n" + sb.ToString();
  }
```

This approach is robust: it works whether IGrouping<,> is implemented implicitly or explicitly. The following demonstrates this method:

```
Console.WriteLine (ToStringEx (new List<int> { 5, 6, 7 } ));
Console.WriteLine (ToStringEx ("xyyzzz".GroupBy (c => c) ));

List of 3 items: 5 6 7

Group with key=x: x
Group with key=y: y y
Group with key=z: z z z
```

Reflecting Assemblies

You can dynamically reflect an assembly by calling GetType or GetTypes on an Assembly object. The following retrieves from the current assembly the type called TestProgram in the Demos namespace:

```
Type t = Assembly.GetExecutingAssembly().GetType ("Demos.TestProgram");
```

You can also obtain an assembly from an existing type:

```
typeof (Foo).Assembly.GetType ("Demos.TestProgram");
```

The next example lists all the types in the assembly *mylib.dll* in *e:\demo*:

```
Assembly a = Assembly.LoadFile (@"e:\demo\mylib.dll");

foreach (Type t in a.GetTypes())
  Console.WriteLine (t);
```

or:

```
Assembly a = typeof (Foo).GetTypeInfo().Assembly;

foreach (Type t in a.ExportedTypes)
  Console.WriteLine (t);
```

GetTypes and ExportedTypes return only top-level and not nested types.

Modules

Calling `GetTypes` on a multimodule assembly returns all types in all modules. As a result, you can ignore the existence of modules and treat an assembly as a type's container. There is one case, though, for which modules are relevant—and that's when dealing with metadata tokens.

A metadata token is an integer that uniquely refers to a type, member, string, or resource within the scope of a module. IL uses metadata tokens, so if you're parsing IL, you'll need to be able to resolve them. The methods for doing this are defined in the `Module` type and are called `ResolveType`, `ResolveMember`, `ResolveString`, and `ResolveSignature`. We revisit this in the final section of this chapter, on writing a disassembler.

You can obtain a list of all the modules in an assembly by calling `GetModules`. You can also access an assembly's main module directly via its `ManifestModule` property.

Working with Attributes

The CLR allows additional metadata to be attached to types, members, and assemblies through attributes. This is the mechanism by which many CLR functions such as serialization and security are directed, making attributes an indivisible part of an application.

A key characteristic of attributes is that you can write your own and then use them just as you would any other attribute to "decorate" a code element with additional information. This additional information is compiled into the underlying assembly and can be retrieved at runtime using reflection to build services that work declaratively, such as automated unit testing.

Attribute Basics

There are three kinds of attributes:

- Bit-mapped attributes
- Custom attributes
- Pseudocustom attributes

Of these, only *custom attributes* are extensible.

 The term "attribute" by itself can refer to any of the three, although in the C# world, it most often refers to custom attributes or pseudocustom attributes.

Bit-mapped attributes (our terminology) map to dedicated bits in a type's metadata. Most of C#'s modifier keywords, such as `public`, `abstract`, and `sealed`, compile to bit-mapped attributes. These attributes are very efficient because they consume minimal space in the metadata (usually just one bit), and the CLR can locate them

with little or no indirection. The reflection API exposes them via dedicated properties on `Type` (and other `MemberInfo` subclasses), such as `IsPublic`, `IsAbstract`, and
`IsSealed`. The `Attributes` property returns a flags enum that describes most of
them in one hit:

```
static void Main()
{
  TypeAttributes ta = typeof (Console).Attributes;
  MethodAttributes ma = MethodInfo.GetCurrentMethod().Attributes;
  Console.WriteLine (ta + "\r\n" + ma);
}
```

Here's the result:

```
AutoLayout, AnsiClass, Class, Public, Abstract, Sealed, BeforeFieldInit
PrivateScope, Private, Static, HideBySig
```

In contrast, *custom attributes* compile to a blob that hangs off the type's main metadata table. All custom attributes are represented by a subclass of `System.Attribute`
and, unlike bit-mapped attributes, are extensible. The blob in the metadata identifies the attribute class and also stores the values of any positional or named
argument that was specified when the attribute was applied. Custom attributes
that you define yourself are architecturally identical to those defined in the .NET
libraries.

Chapter 4 described how to attach custom attributes to a type or member in C#.
Here, we attach the predefined `Obsolete` attribute to the `Foo` class:

```
[Obsolete] public class Foo {...}
```

This instructs the compiler to incorporate an instance of `ObsoleteAttribute` into
the metadata for `Foo`, which then can be reflected at runtime by calling `GetCustom`
`Attributes` on a `Type` or `MemberInfo` object.

Pseudocustom attributes look and feel just like standard custom attributes. They are
represented by a subclass of `System.Attribute` and are attached in the standard
manner:

```
[Serializable] public class Foo {...}
```

The difference is that the compiler or CLR internally optimizes pseudocustom
attributes by converting them to bit-mapped attributes. Examples include [`Serial`
`izable`], `StructLayout`, `In`, and `Out` (Chapter 24). Reflection exposes pseudocustom attributes through dedicated properties such as `IsSerializable`, and in many
cases they are also returned as `System.Attribute` objects when you call `GetCustom`
`Attributes` (`SerializableAttribute` included). This means that you can (almost)
ignore the difference between pseudo- and non-pseudocustom attributes (a notable
exception is when using `Reflection.Emit` to generate types dynamically at runtime;
see "Emitting Assemblies and Types" on page 815).

The AttributeUsage Attribute

`AttributeUsage` is an attribute applied to attribute classes. It instructs the compiler on how the target attribute should be used:

```
public sealed class AttributeUsageAttribute : Attribute
{
  public AttributeUsageAttribute (AttributeTargets validOn);

  public bool AllowMultiple      { get; set; }
  public bool Inherited          { get; set; }
  public AttributeTargets ValidOn { get; }
}
```

`AllowMultiple` controls whether the attribute being defined can be applied more than once to the same target; `Inherited` controls whether an attribute applied to a base class also applies to derived classes (or in the case of methods, whether an attribute applied to a virtual method also applies to overriding methods). `ValidOn` determines the set of targets (classes, interfaces, properties, methods, parameters, etc.) to which the attribute can be attached. It accepts any combination of values from the `AttributeTargets` enum, which has the following members:

All	Delegate	GenericParameter	Parameter
Assembly	Enum	Interface	Property
Class	Event	Method	ReturnValue
Constructor	Field	Module	Struct

To illustrate, here's how the authors of .NET have applied `AttributeUsage` to the `Serializable` attribute:

```
[AttributeUsage (AttributeTargets.Delegate |
                 AttributeTargets.Enum     |
                 AttributeTargets.Struct   |
                 AttributeTargets.Class,     Inherited = false)
]
public sealed class SerializableAttribute : Attribute { }
```

This is, in fact, almost the complete definition of the `Serializable` attribute. Writing an attribute class that has no properties or special constructors is this simple.

Defining Your Own Attribute

Here's how to write your own attribute:

1. Derive a class from `System.Attribute` or a descendent of `System.Attribute`. By convention, the class name should end with the word "Attribute," although this isn't required.

2. Apply the `AttributeUsage` attribute, described in the preceding section.

If the attribute requires no properties or arguments in its constructor, the job is done.

3. Write one or more public constructors. The parameters to the constructor define the positional parameters of the attribute and will become mandatory when using the attribute.

4. Declare a public field or property for each named parameter you wish to support. Named parameters are optional when using the attribute.

 Attribute properties and constructor parameters must be of the following types:

- A sealed primitive type: in other words, bool, byte, char, double, float, int, long, short, or string
- The Type type
- An enum type
- A one-dimensional array of any of these

When an attribute is applied, it must also be possible for the compiler to statically evaluate each of the properties or constructor arguments.

The following class defines an attribute for assisting an automated unit-testing system. It indicates that a method should be tested, the number of test repetitions, and a message in case of failure:

```
[AttributeUsage (AttributeTargets.Method)]
public sealed class TestAttribute : Attribute
{
  public int     Repetitions;
  public string  FailureMessage;

  public TestAttribute () : this (1)     { }
  public TestAttribute (int repetitions) { Repetitions = repetitions; }
}
```

Here's a Foo class with methods decorated in various ways with the Test attribute:

```
class Foo
{
  [Test]
  public void Method1() { ... }

  [Test(20)]
  public void Method2() { ... }

  [Test(20, FailureMessage="Debugging Time!")]
  public void Method3() { ... }
}
```

Retrieving Attributes at Runtime

There are two standard ways to retrieve attributes at runtime:

- Call `GetCustomAttributes` on any `Type` or `MemberInfo` object
- Call `Attribute.GetCustomAttribute` or `Attribute.GetCustomAttributes`

These latter two methods are overloaded to accept any reflection object that corresponds to a valid attribute target (`Type`, `Assembly`, `Module`, `MemberInfo`, or `ParameterInfo`).

 You can also call `GetCustomAttributesData()` on a type or member to obtain attribute information. The difference between this and `GetCustomAttributes()` is that the former lets you know you *how* the attribute was instantiated: it reports the constructor overload that was used, and the value of each constructor argument and named parameter. This is useful when you want to emit code or IL to reconstruct the attribute to the same state (see "Emitting Type Members" on page 818).

Here's how we can enumerate each method in the preceding `Foo` class that has a `TestAttribute`:

```
foreach (MethodInfo mi in typeof (Foo).GetMethods())
{
  TestAttribute att = (TestAttribute) Attribute.GetCustomAttribute
    (mi, typeof (TestAttribute));

  if (att != null)
    Console.WriteLine ("Method {0} will be tested; reps={1}; msg={2}",
                       mi.Name, att.Repetitions, att.FailureMessage);
}
```

or:

```
foreach (MethodInfo mi in typeof (Foo).GetTypeInfo().DeclaredMethods)
...
```

Here's the output:

```
Method Method1 will be tested; reps=1; msg=
Method Method2 will be tested; reps=20; msg=
Method Method3 will be tested; reps=20; msg=Debugging Time!
```

To complete the illustration on how we could use this to write a unit-testing system, here's the same example expanded so that it actually calls the methods decorated with the `Test` attribute:

```
foreach (MethodInfo mi in typeof (Foo).GetMethods())
{
  TestAttribute att = (TestAttribute) Attribute.GetCustomAttribute
    (mi, typeof (TestAttribute));
```

```
    if (att != null)
      for (int i = 0; i < att.Repetitions; i++)
        try
        {
          mi.Invoke (new Foo(), null);      // Call method with no arguments
        }
        catch (Exception ex)        // Wrap exception in att.FailureMessage
        {
          throw new Exception ("Error: " + att.FailureMessage, ex);
        }
  }
```

Returning to attribute reflection, here's an example that lists the attributes present on a specific type:

```
object[] atts = Attribute.GetCustomAttributes (typeof (Test));
foreach (object att in atts) Console.WriteLine (att);

[Serializable, Obsolete]
class Test
{
}
```

And, here's the output:

```
System.ObsoleteAttribute
System.SerializableAttribute
```

Dynamic Code Generation

The System.Reflection.Emit namespace contains classes for creating metadata and IL at runtime. Generating code dynamically is useful for certain kinds of programming tasks. An example is the regular expressions API, which emits performant types tuned to specific regular expressions. Another example is Entity Framework Core, which uses Reflection.Emit to generate proxy classes to enable lazy loading.

Generating IL with DynamicMethod

The DynamicMethod class is a lightweight tool in the System.Reflection.Emit namespace for generating methods on the fly. Unlike TypeBuilder, it doesn't require that you first set up a dynamic assembly, module, and type in which to contain the method. This makes it suitable for simple tasks—as well as serving as a good introduction to Reflection.Emit.

> A DynamicMethod and the associated IL are garbage-collected when no longer referenced. This means you can repeatedly generate dynamic methods without filling up memory. (To do the same with dynamic *assemblies*, you must apply the AssemblyBuilderAccess.RunAndCollect flag when creating the assembly.)

Here is a simple use of `DynamicMethod` to create a method that writes `Hello world` to the console:

```
public class Test
{
  static void Main()
  {
    var dynMeth = new DynamicMethod ("Foo", null, null, typeof (Test));
    ILGenerator gen = dynMeth.GetILGenerator();
    gen.EmitWriteLine ("Hello world");
    gen.Emit (OpCodes.Ret);
    dynMeth.Invoke (null, null);                    // Hello world
  }
}
```

`OpCodes` has a static read-only field for every IL opcode. Most of the functionality is exposed through various opcodes, although `ILGenerator` also has specialized methods for generating labels and local variables and for exception handling. A method always ends in `Opcodes.Ret`, which means "return," or some kind of branching/throwing instruction. The `EmitWriteLine` method on `ILGenerator` is a shortcut for `Emit`ting a number of lower-level opcodes. We would get the same result if we replaced the call to `EmitWriteLine` with this:

```
MethodInfo writeLineStr = typeof (Console).GetMethod ("WriteLine",
                          new Type[] { typeof (string) });
gen.Emit (OpCodes.Ldstr, "Hello world");    // Load a string
gen.Emit (OpCodes.Call, writeLineStr);      // Call a method
```

Note that we passed `typeof(Test)` into `DynamicMethod`'s constructor. This gives the dynamic method access to the nonpublic methods of that type, allowing us to do this:

```
public class Test
{
  static void Main()
  {
    var dynMeth = new DynamicMethod ("Foo", null, null, typeof (Test));
    ILGenerator gen = dynMeth.GetILGenerator();

    MethodInfo privateMethod = typeof(Test).GetMethod ("HelloWorld",
      BindingFlags.Static | BindingFlags.NonPublic);

    gen.Emit (OpCodes.Call, privateMethod);     // Call HelloWorld
    gen.Emit (OpCodes.Ret);

    dynMeth.Invoke (null, null);                // Hello world
  }

  static void HelloWorld()        // private method, yet we can call it
  {
    Console.WriteLine ("Hello world");
  }
}
```

Understanding IL requires a considerable investment of time. Rather than understand all the opcodes, it's much easier to compile a C# program and then examine,
copy, and tweak the IL. LINQPad displays the IL for any method or code snippet
that you type, and assembly viewing tools such ILSpy are useful for examining
existing assemblies.

The Evaluation Stack

Central to IL is the concept of the *evaluation stack*. To call a method with arguments, you first push ("load") the arguments onto the evaluation stack and then
call the method. The method then pops the arguments it needs from the evaluation
stack. We demonstrated this previously, in calling Console.WriteLine. Here's a
similar example with an integer:

```
var dynMeth = new DynamicMethod ("Foo", null, null, typeof(void));
ILGenerator gen = dynMeth.GetILGenerator();
MethodInfo writeLineInt = typeof (Console).GetMethod ("WriteLine",
                                     new Type[] { typeof (int) });

// The Ldc* op-codes load numeric literals of various types and sizes.

gen.Emit (OpCodes.Ldc_I4, 123);      // Push a 4-byte integer onto stack
gen.Emit (OpCodes.Call, writeLineInt);

gen.Emit (OpCodes.Ret);
dynMeth.Invoke (null, null);          // 123
```

To add two numbers together, you first load each number onto the evaluation stack
and then call Add. The Add opcode pops two values from the evaluation stack and
pushes the result back on. The following adds 2 and 2, and then writes the result
using the writeLine method obtained previously:

```
gen.Emit (OpCodes.Ldc_I4, 2);        // Push a 4-byte integer, value=2
gen.Emit (OpCodes.Ldc_I4, 2);        // Push a 4-byte integer, value=2
gen.Emit (OpCodes.Add);              // Add the result together
gen.Emit (OpCodes.Call, writeLineInt);
```

To calculate 10 / 2 + 1, you can do either this:

```
gen.Emit (OpCodes.Ldc_I4, 10);
gen.Emit (OpCodes.Ldc_I4, 2);
gen.Emit (OpCodes.Div);
gen.Emit (OpCodes.Ldc_I4, 1);
gen.Emit (OpCodes.Add);
gen.Emit (OpCodes.Call, writeLineInt);
```

or this:

```
gen.Emit (OpCodes.Ldc_I4, 1);
gen.Emit (OpCodes.Ldc_I4, 10);
gen.Emit (OpCodes.Ldc_I4, 2);
gen.Emit (OpCodes.Div);
gen.Emit (OpCodes.Add);
gen.Emit (OpCodes.Call, writeLineInt);
```

Passing Arguments to a Dynamic Method

The Ldarg and Ldarg_*XXX* opcodes load an argument passed into a method onto the stack. To return a value, leave exactly one value on the stack upon finishing. For this to work, you must specify the return type and argument types when calling Dynamic Method's constructor. The following creates a dynamic method that returns the sum of two integers:

```
DynamicMethod dynMeth = new DynamicMethod ("Foo",
    typeof (int),                            // Return type = int
    new[] { typeof (int), typeof (int) },    // Parameter types = int, int
    typeof (void));

ILGenerator gen = dynMeth.GetILGenerator();

gen.Emit (OpCodes.Ldarg_0);     // Push first arg onto eval stack
gen.Emit (OpCodes.Ldarg_1);     // Push second arg onto eval stack
gen.Emit (OpCodes.Add);         // Add them together (result on stack)
gen.Emit (OpCodes.Ret);         // Return with stack having 1 value

int result = (int) dynMeth.Invoke (null, new object[] { 3, 4 } );   // 7
```

 When you exit, the evaluation stack must have exactly 0 or 1 item (depending on whether your method returns a value). If you violate this, the CLR will refuse to execute your method. You can remove an item from the stack without processing it by emitting OpCodes.Pop.

Rather than calling Invoke, it can be more convenient to work with a dynamic method as a typed delegate. The CreateDelegate method achieves just this. In our case, the delegate that we need has two integer parameters and an integer return type. We can use the Func<int, int, int> delegate for this purpose. The last line of our preceding example then becomes the following:

```
var func = (Func<int,int,int>) dynMeth.CreateDelegate
                          (typeof (Func<int,int,int>));
int result = func (3, 4);  // 7
```

 A delegate also eliminates the overhead of dynamic method invocation—saving a few microseconds per call.

We demonstrate how to pass by reference in "Emitting Type Members" on page 818.

Generating Local Variables

You can declare a local variable by calling DeclareLocal on an ILGenerator. This returns a LocalBuilder object, which you can use in conjunction with opcodes such as Ldloc (load a local variable) or Stloc (store a local variable). Ldloc pushes the evaluation stack; Stloc pops it. For example, consider the following C# code:

```
int x = 6;
int y = 7;
x *= y;
Console.WriteLine (x);
```

The following generates the preceding code dynamically:

```
var dynMeth = new DynamicMethod ("Test", null, null, typeof (void));
ILGenerator gen = dynMeth.GetILGenerator();

LocalBuilder localX = gen.DeclareLocal (typeof (int));   // Declare x
LocalBuilder localY = gen.DeclareLocal (typeof (int));   // Declare y

gen.Emit (OpCodes.Ldc_I4, 6);        // Push literal 6 onto eval stack
gen.Emit (OpCodes.Stloc, localX);    // Store in localX
gen.Emit (OpCodes.Ldc_I4, 7);        // Push literal 7 onto eval stack
gen.Emit (OpCodes.Stloc, localY);    // Store in localY

gen.Emit (OpCodes.Ldloc, localX);    // Push localX onto eval stack
gen.Emit (OpCodes.Ldloc, localY);    // Push localY onto eval stack
gen.Emit (OpCodes.Mul);              // Multiply values together
gen.Emit (OpCodes.Stloc, localX);    // Store the result to localX

gen.EmitWriteLine (localX);          // Write the value of localX
gen.Emit (OpCodes.Ret);

dynMeth.Invoke (null, null);         // 42
```

Branching

In IL, there are no while, do, and for loops; it's all done with labels and the equivalent of goto and conditional goto statements. These are the branching opcodes, such as Br (branch unconditionally), Brtrue (branch if the value on the evaluation stack is true), and Blt (branch if the first value is less than the second value).

To set a branch target, first call DefineLabel (this returns a Label object), and then call MarkLabel at the place where you want to anchor the label. For example, consider the following C# code:

```
int x = 5;
while (x <= 10) Console.WriteLine (x++);
```

We can emit this as follows:

```
ILGenerator gen = ...

Label startLoop = gen.DefineLabel();                     // Declare labels
Label endLoop = gen.DefineLabel();

LocalBuilder x = gen.DeclareLocal (typeof (int));        // int x
gen.Emit (OpCodes.Ldc_I4, 5);                            //
gen.Emit (OpCodes.Stloc, x);                             // x = 5
gen.MarkLabel (startLoop);
  gen.Emit (OpCodes.Ldc_I4, 10);                         // Load 10 onto eval stack
  gen.Emit (OpCodes.Ldloc, x);                           // Load x onto eval stack
```

```
gen.Emit (OpCodes.Blt, endLoop);              // if (x > 10) goto endLoop

gen.EmitWriteLine (x);                        // Console.WriteLine (x)

gen.Emit (OpCodes.Ldloc, x);                  // Load x onto eval stack
gen.Emit (OpCodes.Ldc_I4, 1);                 // Load 1 onto the stack
gen.Emit (OpCodes.Add);                       // Add them together
gen.Emit (OpCodes.Stloc, x);                  // Save result back to x

  gen.Emit (OpCodes.Br, startLoop);           // return to start of loop
gen.MarkLabel (endLoop);

gen.Emit (OpCodes.Ret);
```

Instantiating Objects and Calling Instance Methods

The IL equivalent of new is the Newobj opcode. This takes a constructor and loads
the constructed object onto the evaluation stack. For instance, the following constructs a StringBuilder:

```
var dynMeth = new DynamicMethod ("Test", null, null, typeof (void));
ILGenerator gen = dynMeth.GetILGenerator();

ConstructorInfo ci = typeof (StringBuilder).GetConstructor (new Type[0]);
gen.Emit (OpCodes.Newobj, ci);
```

After loading an object onto the evaluation stack, you can use the Call or Callvirt
opcode to invoke the object's instance methods. Extending this example, we'll query
the StringBuilder's MaxCapacity property by calling the property's get accessor
and then write out the result:

```
gen.Emit (OpCodes.Callvirt, typeof (StringBuilder)
                      .GetProperty ("MaxCapacity").GetGetMethod());

gen.Emit (OpCodes.Call, typeof (Console).GetMethod ("WriteLine",
                              new[] { typeof (int) } ));
gen.Emit (OpCodes.Ret);
dynMeth.Invoke (null, null);          // 2147483647
```

To emulate C# calling semantics:

- Use Call to invoke static methods and value type instance methods.

- Use Callvirt to invoke reference type instance methods (whether or not
  they're declared virtual).

In our example, we used Callvirt on the StringBuilder instance—even though
MaxProperty is not virtual. This doesn't cause an error: it simply performs a nonvirtual call instead. Always invoking reference type instance methods with Callvirt
avoids risking the opposite condition: invoking a virtual method with Call. (The
risk is real. The author of the target method may later *change* its declaration.)
Callvirt also has the benefit of checking that the receiver is non-null.

Invoking a virtual method with `Call` bypasses virtual calling semantics and calls that method directly. This is rarely desirable and, in effect, violates type safety.

In the following example, we construct a `StringBuilder` passing in two arguments, append `", world!"` to the `StringBuilder`, and then call `ToString` on it:

```
// We will call:   new StringBuilder ("Hello", 1000)

ConstructorInfo ci = typeof (StringBuilder).GetConstructor (
                    new[] { typeof (string), typeof (int) } );

gen.Emit (OpCodes.Ldstr, "Hello");     // Load a string onto the eval stack
gen.Emit (OpCodes.Ldc_I4, 1000);       // Load an int onto the eval stack
gen.Emit (OpCodes.Newobj, ci);         // Construct the StringBuilder

Type[] strT = { typeof (string) };
gen.Emit (OpCodes.Ldstr, ", world!");
gen.Emit (OpCodes.Call, typeof (StringBuilder).GetMethod ("Append", strT));
gen.Emit (OpCodes.Callvirt, typeof (object).GetMethod ("ToString"));
gen.Emit (OpCodes.Call, typeof (Console).GetMethod ("WriteLine", strT));
gen.Emit (OpCodes.Ret);
dynMeth.Invoke (null, null);           // Hello, world!
```

For fun we called `GetMethod` on `typeof(object)` and then used `Callvirt` to perform a virtual method call on `ToString`. We could have gotten the same result by calling `ToString` on the `StringBuilder` type itself:

```
gen.Emit (OpCodes.Callvirt, typeof (StringBuilder).GetMethod ("ToString",
                                                   new Type[0] ));
```

(The empty type array is required in calling `GetMethod` because `StringBuilder` overloads `ToString` with another signature.)

Had we called `object`'s `ToString` method nonvirtually like this:

```
gen.Emit (OpCodes.Call,
          typeof (object).GetMethod ("ToString"));
```

the result would have been `System.Text.StringBuilder`. In other words, we would have circumvented `StringBuilder`'s `ToString` override and called `object`'s version directly.

Exception Handling

`ILGenerator` provides dedicated methods for exception handling. Thus, the translation for this C# code:

```
try                                 { throw new NotSupportedException(); }
catch (NotSupportedException ex)    { Console.WriteLine (ex.Message);    }
finally                             { Console.WriteLine ("Finally");     }
```

is this:

```
MethodInfo getMessageProp = typeof (NotSupportedException)
                                  .GetProperty ("Message").GetGetMethod();

MethodInfo writeLineString = typeof (Console).GetMethod ("WriteLine",
                                         new[] { typeof (object) } );
gen.BeginExceptionBlock();
  ConstructorInfo ci = typeof (NotSupportedException).GetConstructor (
                                                  new Type[0] );
  gen.Emit (OpCodes.Newobj, ci);
  gen.Emit (OpCodes.Throw);
gen.BeginCatchBlock (typeof (NotSupportedException));
  gen.Emit (OpCodes.Callvirt, getMessageProp);
  gen.Emit (OpCodes.Call, writeLineString);
gen.BeginFinallyBlock();
  gen.EmitWriteLine ("Finally");
gen.EndExceptionBlock();
```

Just as in C#, you can include multiple catch blocks. To rethrow the same exception, emit the Rethrow opcode.

 ILGenerator provides a helper method called ThrowExcep
tion. This contains a bug, however, preventing it from being
used with a DynamicMethod. It works only with a Method
Builder (see the next section).

Emitting Assemblies and Types

Although DynamicMethod is convenient, it can generate only methods. If you need to emit any other construct—or a complete type—you need to use the full "heavyweight" API. This means dynamically building an assembly and module. The assembly need not have a disk presence (in fact, it cannot, because .NET 5+ and .NET Core do not let you save generated assemblies to disk).

Let's assume that we want to dynamically build a type. Because a type must reside in a module within an assembly, we first must create the assembly and module before we can create the type. This is the job of the AssemblyBuilder and ModuleBuilder types:

```
AssemblyName aname = new AssemblyName ("MyDynamicAssembly");

AssemblyBuilder assemBuilder =
  AssemblyBuilder.DefineDynamicAssembly (aname, AssemblyBuilderAccess.Run);

ModuleBuilder modBuilder = assemBuilder.DefineDynamicModule ("DynModule");
```

 You can't add a type to an existing assembly, because an
assembly is immutable after it's created.

Dynamic assemblies are not garbage-collected and remain in
memory until the process ends, unless you specify Assembly
BuilderAccess.RunAndCollect when defining the assembly.
Various restrictions apply to collectible assemblies (see *http://
albahari.com/dynamiccollect*).

Reflection
and Metadata

After we have a module in which the type can reside, we can use `TypeBuilder` to create the type. The following defines a class called `Widget`:

```
TypeBuilder tb = modBuilder.DefineType ("Widget", TypeAttributes.Public);
```

The `TypeAttributes` flags enum supports the CLR type modifiers you see when disassembling a type with *ildasm*. As well as member visibility flags, this includes type modifiers such as `Abstract` and `Sealed`—and `Interface` for defining a .NET interface. It also includes `Serializable`, which is equivalent to applying the `[Serializable]` attribute in C#, and `Explicit`, which is equivalent to applying `[StructLayout(LayoutKind.Explicit)]`. We describe how to apply other kinds of attributes later in this chapter, in "Attaching Attributes" on page 823.

The `DefineType` method also accepts an optional base type:

- To define a struct, specify a base type of `System.Value Type`.

- To define a delegate, specify a base type of `System.Multi castDelegate`.

- To implement an interface, use the constructor that accepts an array of interface types.

- To define an interface, specify `TypeAttributes.Inter face | TypeAttributes.Abstract`.

Defining a delegate type requires a number of extra steps. In his blog, Joel Pobar demonstrates how this is done in his article titled "Creating delegate types via Reflection.Emit" (*http:// www.albahari.com/joelpob*).

We can now create members within the type:

```
MethodBuilder methBuilder = tb.DefineMethod ("SayHello",
                                             MethodAttributes.Public,
                                             null, null);
ILGenerator gen = methBuilder.GetILGenerator();
gen.EmitWriteLine ("Hello world");
gen.Emit (OpCodes.Ret);
```

We're now ready to create the type, which finalizes its definition:

```
Type t = tb.CreateType();
```

After the type is created, we can use ordinary reflection to inspect and perform late binding:

```
object o = Activator.CreateInstance (t);
t.GetMethod ("SayHello").Invoke (o, null);       // Hello world
```

The Reflection.Emit Object Model

Figure 18-2 illustrates the essential types in `System.Reflection.Emit`. Each type describes a CLR construct and is based on a counterpart in the `System.Reflection` namespace. This allows you to use emitted constructs in place of normal constructs when building a type. For example, we previously called `Console.WriteLine`, as follows:

```
MethodInfo writeLine = typeof(Console).GetMethod ("WriteLine",
                                   new Type[] { typeof (string) });
gen.Emit (OpCodes.Call, writeLine);
```

We could just as easily call a dynamically generated method by calling `gen.Emit` with a `MethodBuilder` instead of a `MethodInfo`. This is essential—otherwise, you couldn't write one dynamic method that called another in the same type.

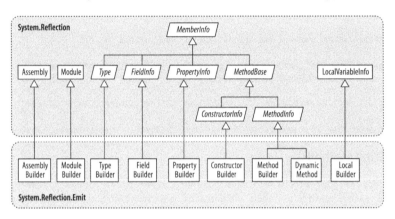

Figure 18-2. System.Reflection.Emit

Recall that you must call `CreateType` on a `TypeBuilder` when you've finished populating it. Calling `CreateType` seals the `TypeBuilder` and all its members—so nothing more can be added or changed—and gives you back a real `Type` that you can instantiate.

Before you call `CreateType`, the `TypeBuilder` and its members are in an "uncreated" state. There are significant restrictions on what you can do with uncreated constructs. In particular, you cannot call any of the members that return `Member Info` objects, such as `GetMembers`, `GetMethod`, or `GetProperty`—these all throw an exception. If you want to refer to members of an uncreated type, you must use the original emissions:

```
TypeBuilder tb = ...

MethodBuilder method1 = tb.DefineMethod ("Method1", ...);
MethodBuilder method2 = tb.DefineMethod ("Method2", ...);

ILGenerator gen1 = method1.GetILGenerator();

// Suppose we want method1 to call method2:
```

```
gen1.Emit (OpCodes.Call, method2);              // Right
gen1.Emit (OpCodes.Call, tb.GetMethod ("Method2"));    // Wrong
```

After calling CreateType, you can reflect on and activate not only the Type returned but also the original TypeBuilder object. The TypeBuilder, in fact, morphs into a proxy for the real Type. You'll see why this feature is important in "Awkward Emission Targets" on page 825.

Emitting Type Members

All the examples in this section assume a TypeBuilder, tb, has been instantiated, as follows:

```
AssemblyName aname = new AssemblyName ("MyEmissions");

AssemblyBuilder assemBuilder = AssemblyBuilder.DefineDynamicAssembly (
  aname, AssemblyBuilderAccess.Run);

ModuleBuilder modBuilder = assemBuilder.DefineDynamicModule ("MainModule");

TypeBuilder tb = modBuilder.DefineType ("Widget", TypeAttributes.Public);
```

Emitting Methods

You can specify a return type and parameter types when calling DefineMethod, in the same manner as when instantiating a DynamicMethod. For instance, the following method:

```
public static double SquareRoot (double value) => Math.Sqrt (value);
```

can be generated like this:

```
MethodBuilder mb = tb.DefineMethod ("SquareRoot",
  MethodAttributes.Static | MethodAttributes.Public,
  CallingConventions.Standard,
  typeof (double),                    // Return type
  new[] { typeof (double) } );        // Parameter types

mb.DefineParameter (1, ParameterAttributes.None, "value");  // Assign name

ILGenerator gen = mb.GetILGenerator();
gen.Emit (OpCodes.Ldarg_0);                       // Load 1st arg
gen.Emit (OpCodes.Call, typeof(Math).GetMethod ("Sqrt"));
gen.Emit (OpCodes.Ret);

Type realType = tb.CreateType();
double x = (double) tb.GetMethod ("SquareRoot").Invoke (null,
                                  new object[] { 10.0 });
Console.WriteLine (x);   // 3.16227766016838
```

Calling DefineParameter is optional and is typically done to assign the parameter a name. The number 1 refers to the first parameter (0 refers to the return value). If you call DefineParameter, the parameter is implicitly named __p1, __p2, and so on.

Assigning names makes sense if you will write the assembly to disk; it makes your methods friendly to consumers.

 `DefineParameter` returns a `ParameterBuilder` object upon which you can call `SetCustomAttribute` to attach attributes (see "Attaching Attributes" on page 823).

To emit pass-by-reference parameters, such as in the following C# method:

```
public static void SquareRoot (ref double value)
  => value = Math.Sqrt (value);
```

call `MakeByRefType` on the parameter type(s):

```
MethodBuilder mb = tb.DefineMethod ("SquareRoot",
  MethodAttributes.Static | MethodAttributes.Public,
  CallingConventions.Standard,
  null,
  new Type[] { typeof (double).MakeByRefType() } );

mb.DefineParameter (1, ParameterAttributes.None, "value");

ILGenerator gen = mb.GetILGenerator();
gen.Emit (OpCodes.Ldarg_0);
gen.Emit (OpCodes.Ldarg_0);
gen.Emit (OpCodes.Ldind_R8);
gen.Emit (OpCodes.Call, typeof (Math).GetMethod ("Sqrt"));
gen.Emit (OpCodes.Stind_R8);
gen.Emit (OpCodes.Ret);

Type realType = tb.CreateType();
object[] args = { 10.0 };
tb.GetMethod ("SquareRoot").Invoke (null, args);
Console.WriteLine (args[0]);                  // 3.16227766016838
```

The opcodes here were copied from a disassembled C# method. Notice the difference in semantics for accessing parameters passed by reference: `Ldind` and `Stind` mean "load indirectly" and "store indirectly," respectively. The R8 suffix means an eight-byte floating-point number.

The process for emitting out parameters is identical, except that you call `Define Parameter`, as follows:

```
mb.DefineParameter (1, ParameterAttributes.Out, "value");
```

Generating instance methods

To generate an instance method, specify `MethodAttributes.Instance` when calling `DefineMethod`:

```
MethodBuilder mb = tb.DefineMethod ("SquareRoot",
  MethodAttributes.Instance | MethodAttributes.Public
  ...
```

With instance methods, argument zero is implicitly this; the remaining arguments start at 1. So, Ldarg_0 loads this onto the evaluation stack; Ldarg_1 loads the first real method argument.

Overriding methods

Overriding a virtual method in a base class is easy: simply define a method with an identical name, signature, and return type, specifying MethodAttributes .Virtual when calling DefineMethod. The same applies when implementing interface methods.

TypeBuilder also exposes a method called DefineMethodOverride that overrides a method with a different name. This makes sense only with explicit interface implementation; in other scenarios, use DefineMethod.

HideBySig

If you're subclassing another type, it's nearly always worth specifying MethodAttrib utes.HideBySig when defining methods. HideBySig ensures that C#-style method-hiding semantics are applied, which is that a base method is hidden only if a subtype defines a method with an identical *signature*. Without HideBySig, method hiding considers only the *name*, so Foo(string) in the subtype will hide Foo() in the base type, which is generally undesirable.

Emitting Fields and Properties

To create a field, you call DefineField on a TypeBuilder, specifying the desired field name, type, and visibility. The following creates a private integer field called "length":

```
FieldBuilder field = tb.DefineField ("length", typeof (int),
                                      FieldAttributes.Private);
```

Creating a property or indexer requires a few more steps. First, call DefineProperty on a TypeBuilder, providing it with the name and type of the property:

```
PropertyBuilder prop = tb.DefineProperty (
                    "Text",                     // Name of property
                    PropertyAttributes.None,
                    typeof (string),            // Property type
                    new Type[0]                 // Indexer types
                );
```

(If you're writing an indexer, the final argument is an array of indexer types.) Note that we haven't specified the property visibility: this is done individually on the accessor methods.

The next step is to write the get and set methods. By convention, their names are prefixed with "get_" or "set_". You then attach them to the property by calling SetGetMethod and SetSetMethod on the PropertyBuilder.

To give a complete example, let's take the following field and property declaration:

```
string _text;
public string Text
{
  get          => _text;
  internal set => _text = value;
}
```

and generate it dynamically:

```
FieldBuilder field = tb.DefineField ("_text", typeof (string),
                                FieldAttributes.Private);
PropertyBuilder prop = tb.DefineProperty (
                    "Text",                         // Name of property
                    PropertyAttributes.None,
                    typeof (string),                // Property type
                    new Type[0]);                   // Indexer types

MethodBuilder getter = tb.DefineMethod (
  "get_Text",                                       // Method name
  MethodAttributes.Public | MethodAttributes.SpecialName,
  typeof (string),                                  // Return type
  new Type[0]);                                     // Parameter types

ILGenerator getGen = getter.GetILGenerator();
getGen.Emit (OpCodes.Ldarg_0);        // Load "this" onto eval stack
getGen.Emit (OpCodes.Ldfld, field);   // Load field value onto eval stack
getGen.Emit (OpCodes.Ret);            // Return

MethodBuilder setter = tb.DefineMethod (
  "set_Text",
  MethodAttributes.Assembly | MethodAttributes.SpecialName,
  null,                                             // Return type
  new Type[] { typeof (string) } );                 // Parameter types

ILGenerator setGen = setter.GetILGenerator();
setGen.Emit (OpCodes.Ldarg_0);        // Load "this" onto eval stack
setGen.Emit (OpCodes.Ldarg_1);        // Load 2nd arg, i.e., value
setGen.Emit (OpCodes.Stfld, field);   // Store value into field
setGen.Emit (OpCodes.Ret);            // return

prop.SetGetMethod (getter);           // Link the get method and property
prop.SetSetMethod (setter);           // Link the set method and property
```

We can test the property as follows:

```
Type t = tb.CreateType();
object o = Activator.CreateInstance (t);
t.GetProperty ("Text").SetValue (o, "Good emissions!", new object[0]);
string text = (string) t.GetProperty ("Text").GetValue (o, null);

Console.WriteLine (text);             // Good emissions!
```

Notice that in defining the accessor MethodAttributes, we included SpecialName. This instructs compilers to disallow direct binding to these methods when statically referencing the assembly. It also ensures that the accessors are handled appropriately by reflection tools and Visual Studio's IntelliSense.

 You can emit events in a similar manner, by calling DefineEvent on a TypeBuilder. You then write explicit event accessor methods and attach them to the EventBuilder by calling SetAddOnMethod and SetRemoveOnMethod.

Emitting Constructors

You can define your own constructors by calling DefineConstructor on a type builder. You're not obliged to do so—a default parameterless constructor is automatically provided if you don't. The default constructor calls the base class constructor if subtyping, just like in C#. Defining one or more constructors displaces this default constructor.

If you need to initialize fields, the constructor's a good spot. In fact, it's the only spot: C#'s field initializers don't have special CLR support—they are simply a syntactic shortcut for assigning values to fields in the constructor.

So, to reproduce this:

```
class Widget
{
  int _capacity = 4000;
}
```

you would define a constructor, as follows:

```
FieldBuilder field = tb.DefineField ("_capacity", typeof (int),
                                     FieldAttributes.Private);
ConstructorBuilder c = tb.DefineConstructor (
  MethodAttributes.Public,
  CallingConventions.Standard,
  new Type[0]);                       // Constructor parameters

ILGenerator gen = c.GetILGenerator();

gen.Emit (OpCodes.Ldarg_0);           // Load "this" onto eval stack
gen.Emit (OpCodes.Ldc_I4, 4000);      // Load 4000 onto eval stack
gen.Emit (OpCodes.Stfld, field);      // Store it to our field
gen.Emit (OpCodes.Ret);
```

Calling base constructors

If subclassing another type, the constructor we just wrote would *circumvent the base class constructor*. This is unlike C#, in which the base class constructor is always called, whether directly or indirectly. For instance, given the following code:

```
class A    { public A() { Console.Write ("A"); } }
class B : A { public B() {} }
```

the compiler, in effect, will translate the second line into this:

```
class B : A { public B() : base() {} }
```

This is not the case when generating IL: you must explicitly call the base constructor if you want it to execute (which nearly always, you do). Assuming the base class is called A, here's how to do it:

```
gen.Emit (OpCodes.Ldarg_0);
ConstructorInfo baseConstr = typeof (A).GetConstructor (new Type[0]);
gen.Emit (OpCodes.Call, baseConstr);
```

Calling constructors with arguments is just the same as with methods.

Attaching Attributes

You can attach custom attributes to a dynamic construct by calling `SetCustomAttribute` with a `CustomAttributeBuilder`. For example, suppose that we want to attach the following attribute declaration to a field or property:

```
[XmlElement ("FirstName", Namespace="http://test/", Order=3)]
```

This relies on the `XmlElementAttribute` constructor that accepts a single string. To use `CustomAttributeBuilder`, we must retrieve this constructor as well as the two additional properties that we want to set (`Namespace` and `Order`):

```
Type attType = typeof (XmlElementAttribute);

ConstructorInfo attConstructor = attType.GetConstructor (
  new Type[] { typeof (string) } );

var att = new CustomAttributeBuilder (
  attConstructor,                       // Constructor
  new object[] { "FirstName" },         // Constructor arguments
  new PropertyInfo[]
  {
    attType.GetProperty ("Namespace"),  // Properties
    attType.GetProperty ("Order")
  },
  new object[] { "http://test/", 3 }    // Property values
);

myFieldBuilder.SetCustomAttribute (att);
// or propBuilder.SetCustomAttribute (att);
// or typeBuilder.SetCustomAttribute (att);  etc
```

Emitting Generic Methods and Types

All the examples in this section assume that `modBuilder` has been instantiated as follows:

```
AssemblyName aname = new AssemblyName ("MyEmissions");

AssemblyBuilder assemBuilder = AssemblyBuilder.DefineDynamicAssembly (
  aname, AssemblyBuilderAccess.Run);
```

```
ModuleBuilder modBuilder = assemBuilder.DefineDynamicModule ("MainModule");
```

Defining Generic Methods

To emit a generic method:

1. Call `DefineGenericParameters` on a `MethodBuilder` to obtain an array of `GenericTypeParameterBuilder` objects.

2. Call `SetSignature` on a `MethodBuilder` using these generic type parameters.

3. Optionally, name the parameters as you would otherwise.

For example, the following generic method:

```
public static T Echo<T> (T value)
{
  return value;
}
```

can be emitted like this:

```
TypeBuilder tb = modBuilder.DefineType ("Widget", TypeAttributes.Public);

MethodBuilder mb = tb.DefineMethod ("Echo", MethodAttributes.Public |
                                            MethodAttributes.Static);
GenericTypeParameterBuilder[] genericParams
  = mb.DefineGenericParameters ("T");

mb.SetSignature (genericParams[0],     // Return type
                null, null,
                genericParams,         // Parameter types
                null, null);

mb.DefineParameter (1, ParameterAttributes.None, "value");   // Optional

ILGenerator gen = mb.GetILGenerator();
gen.Emit (OpCodes.Ldarg_0);
gen.Emit (OpCodes.Ret);
```

The `DefineGenericParameters` method accepts any number of string arguments—these correspond to the desired generic type names. In this example, we needed just one generic type called T. `GenericTypeParameterBuilder` is based on `System.Type`, so you can use it in place of a `TypeBuilder` when emitting opcodes.

`GenericTypeParameterBuilder` also lets you specify a base type constraint:

```
genericParams[0].SetBaseTypeConstraint (typeof (Foo));
```

and interface constraints:

```
genericParams[0].SetInterfaceConstraints (typeof (IComparable));
```

To replicate this:

```
public static T Echo<T> (T value) where T : IComparable<T>
```

you would write:

```
genericParams[0].SetInterfaceConstraints (
  typeof (IComparable<>).MakeGenericType (genericParams[0]) );
```

For other kinds of constraints, call SetGenericParameterAttributes. This accepts
a member of the GenericParameterAttributes enum, which includes the following
values:

```
DefaultConstructorConstraint
NotNullableValueTypeConstraint
ReferenceTypeConstraint
Covariant
Contravariant
```

The last two are equivalent to applying the out and in modifiers to the type
parameters.

Defining Generic Types

You can define generic types in a similar fashion. The difference is that you call
DefineGenericParameters on the TypeBuilder rather than the MethodBuilder. So,
to reproduce this:

```
public class Widget<T>
{
  public T Value;
}
```

you would do the following:

```
TypeBuilder tb = modBuilder.DefineType ("Widget", TypeAttributes.Public);

GenericTypeParameterBuilder[] genericParams
  = tb.DefineGenericParameters ("T");

tb.DefineField ("Value", genericParams[0], FieldAttributes.Public);
```

Generic constraints can be added, just as with a method.

Awkward Emission Targets

All of the examples in this section assume that a modBuilder has been instantiated
as in previous sections.

Uncreated Closed Generics

Suppose that you want to emit a method that uses a closed generic type:

```
public class Widget
{
  public static void Test() { var list = new List<int>(); }
}
```

The process is fairly straightforward:

```
TypeBuilder tb = modBuilder.DefineType ("Widget", TypeAttributes.Public);

MethodBuilder mb = tb.DefineMethod ("Test", MethodAttributes.Public |
                                            MethodAttributes.Static);
ILGenerator gen = mb.GetILGenerator();

Type variableType = typeof (List<int>);

ConstructorInfo ci = variableType.GetConstructor (new Type[0]);

LocalBuilder listVar = gen.DeclareLocal (variableType);
gen.Emit (OpCodes.Newobj, ci);
gen.Emit (OpCodes.Stloc, listVar);
gen.Emit (OpCodes.Ret);
```

Now suppose that instead of a list of integers, we want a list of widgets:

```
public class Widget
{
    public static void Test() { var list = new List<Widget>(); }
}
```

In theory, this is a simple modification; all we do is replace this line:

```
Type variableType = typeof (List<int>);
```

with this one:

```
Type variableType = typeof (List<>).MakeGenericType (tb);
```

Unfortunately, this causes a NotSupportedException to be thrown when we then call GetConstructor. The problem is that you cannot call GetConstructor on a generic type closed with an uncreated type builder. The same goes for GetField and GetMethod.

The solution is unintuitive. TypeBuilder provides three static methods:

```
public static ConstructorInfo GetConstructor (Type, ConstructorInfo);
public static FieldInfo       GetField       (Type, FieldInfo);
public static MethodInfo      GetMethod      (Type, MethodInfo);
```

Although it doesn't appear so, these methods exist specifically to obtain members of generic types closed with uncreated type builders! The first parameter is the closed generic type; the second parameter is the member that you want on the *unbound* generic type. Here's the corrected version of our example:

```
MethodBuilder mb = tb.DefineMethod ("Test", MethodAttributes.Public |
                                            MethodAttributes.Static);
ILGenerator gen = mb.GetILGenerator();

Type variableType = typeof (List<>).MakeGenericType (tb);

ConstructorInfo unbound = typeof (List<>).GetConstructor (new Type[0]);
ConstructorInfo ci = TypeBuilder.GetConstructor (variableType, unbound);

LocalBuilder listVar = gen.DeclareLocal (variableType);
gen.Emit (OpCodes.Newobj, ci);
```

```
gen.Emit (OpCodes.Stloc, listVar);
gen.Emit (OpCodes.Ret);
```

Circular Dependencies

Suppose that you want to build two types that reference each other, such as these:

```
class A { public B Bee; }
class B { public A Aye; }
```

You can generate this dynamically, as follows:

```
var publicAtt = FieldAttributes.Public;

TypeBuilder aBuilder = modBuilder.DefineType ("A");
TypeBuilder bBuilder = modBuilder.DefineType ("B");

FieldBuilder bee = aBuilder.DefineField ("Bee", bBuilder, publicAtt);
FieldBuilder aye = bBuilder.DefineField ("Aye", aBuilder, publicAtt);

Type realA = aBuilder.CreateType();
Type realB = bBuilder.CreateType();
```

Notice that we didn't call CreateType on aBuilder or bBuilder until we populated both objects. The principle is this: first hook everything up, and then call Create Type on each type builder.

Interestingly, the realA type is valid but *dysfunctional* until you call CreateType on bBuilder. (If you started using aBuilder prior to this, an exception would be thrown when you tried to access field Bee.)

You might wonder how bBuilder knows to "fix up" realA after creating realB. The answer is that it doesn't: realA can fix *itself* the next time it's used. This is possible because after calling CreateType, a TypeBuilder morphs into a proxy for the real runtime type. So, realA, with its references to bBuilder, can easily obtain the metadata it needs for the upgrade.

This system works when the type builder demands simple information of the unconstructed type—information that can be *predetermined*—such as type, member, and object references. In creating realA, the type builder doesn't need to know, for instance, how many bytes realB will eventually occupy in memory. This is just as well because realB has not yet been created! But now imagine that realB was a struct. The final size of realB is now critical information in creating realA.

If the relationship is noncyclical; for instance:

```
struct A { public B Bee; }
struct B {                 }
```

you can solve this by first creating struct B and then struct A. But consider this:

```
struct A { public B Bee; }
struct B { public A Aye; }
```

We won't try to emit this because it's nonsensical to have two structs contain each other (C# generates a compile-time error if you try). But the following variation is both legal and useful:

```
public struct S<T> { ... }    // S can be empty and this demo will work.

class A { S<B> Bee; }
class B { S<A> Aye; }
```

In creating A, a TypeBuilder now needs to know the memory footprint of B, and vice versa. To illustrate, let's assume that struct S is defined statically. Here's the code to emit classes A and B:

```
var pub = FieldAttributes.Public;

TypeBuilder aBuilder = modBuilder.DefineType ("A");
TypeBuilder bBuilder = modBuilder.DefineType ("B");

aBuilder.DefineField ("Bee", typeof(S<>).MakeGenericType (bBuilder), pub);
bBuilder.DefineField ("Aye", typeof(S<>).MakeGenericType (aBuilder), pub);

Type realA = aBuilder.CreateType();    // Error: cannot load type B
Type realB = bBuilder.CreateType();
```

CreateType now throws a TypeLoadException no matter in which order you go:

- Call aBuilder.CreateType first, and it says "cannot load type B".
- Call bBuilder.CreateType first, and it says "cannot load type A"!

To solve this, you must allow the type builder to create realB partway through creating realA. You do this by handling the TypeResolve event on the AppDomain class just before calling CreateType. So, in our example, we replace the last two lines with this:

```
TypeBuilder[] uncreatedTypes = { aBuilder, bBuilder };

ResolveEventHandler handler = delegate (object o, ResolveEventArgs args)
{
  var type = uncreatedTypes.FirstOrDefault (t => t.FullName == args.Name);
  return type == null ? null : type.CreateType().Assembly;
};

AppDomain.CurrentDomain.TypeResolve += handler;

Type realA = aBuilder.CreateType();
Type realB = bBuilder.CreateType();

AppDomain.CurrentDomain.TypeResolve -= handler;
```

The TypeResolve event fires during the call to aBuilder.CreateType, at the point when it needs you to call CreateType on bBuilder.

Handling the `TypeResolve` event as in this example is also necessary when defining a nested type, when the nested and parent types refer to each other.

Parsing IL

You can obtain information about the content of an existing method by calling `GetMethodBody` on a `MethodBase` object. This returns a `MethodBody` object that has properties for inspecting a method's local variables, exception handling clauses, stack size, and the raw IL. Rather like the reverse of `Reflection.Emit`!

Inspecting a method's raw IL can be useful in profiling code. A simple use would be to determine which methods in an assembly have changed when an assembly is updated.

To illustrate parsing IL, we'll write an application that disassembles IL in the style of *ildasm*. This could be used as the starting point for a code analysis tool or a higher-level language disassembler.

Remember that in the reflection API, all of C#'s functional constructs are either represented by a `MethodBase` subtype or (in the case of properties, events, and indexers) have `Method Base` objects attached to them.

Writing a Disassembler

Here is a sample of the output that our disassembler will produce:

```
IL_00EB:  ldfld      Disassembler._pos
IL_00F0:  ldloc.2
IL_00F1:  add
IL_00F2:  ldelema    System.Byte
IL_00F7:  ldstr      "Hello world"
IL_00FC:  call       System.Byte.ToString
IL_0101:  ldstr      " "
IL_0106:  call       System.String.Concat
```

To obtain this output, we must parse the binary tokens that make up the IL. The first step is to call the `GetILAsByteArray` method on `MethodBody` to obtain the IL as a byte array. To make the rest of the job easier, we will write this into a class as follows:

```
public class Disassembler
{
  public static string Disassemble (MethodBase method)
    => new Disassembler (method).Dis();

  StringBuilder _output;    // The result to which we'll keep appending
  Module _module;           // This will come in handy later
  byte[] _il;               // The raw byte code
  int _pos;                 // The position we're up to in the byte code
```

```
Disassembler (MethodBase method)
{
  _module = method.DeclaringType.Module;
  _il = method.GetMethodBody().GetILAsByteArray();
}

string Dis()
{
  _output = new StringBuilder();
  while (_pos < _il.Length) DisassembleNextInstruction();
  return _output.ToString();
}
}
```

The static `Disassemble` method will be the only public member of this class. All
other members will be private to the disassembly process. The `Dis` method contains
the "main" loop where we process each instruction.

With this skeleton in place, all that remains is to write `DisassembleNextInstruc`
`tion`. But before doing so, it will help to load all the opcodes into a static dictionary
so that we can access them by their 8- or 16-bit value. The easiest way to accomplish
this is to use reflection to retrieve all the static fields whose type is `OpCode` in the
`OpCodes` class:

```
static Dictionary<short,OpCode> _opcodes = new Dictionary<short,OpCode>();

static Disassembler()
{
  Dictionary<short, OpCode> opcodes = new Dictionary<short, OpCode>();
    foreach (FieldInfo fi in typeof (OpCodes).GetFields
                              (BindingFlags.Public | BindingFlags.Static))
      if (typeof (OpCode).IsAssignableFrom (fi.FieldType))
      {
        OpCode code = (OpCode) fi.GetValue (null);    // Get field's value
        if (code.OpCodeType != OpCodeType.Nternal)
          _opcodes.Add (code.Value, code);
      }
}
```

We've written it in a static constructor so that it executes just once.

Now we can write `DisassembleNextInstruction`. Each IL instruction consists of a
one- or two-byte opcode, followed by an operand of zero, one, two, four, or eight
bytes. (An exception is inline switch opcodes, which are followed by a variable
number of operands.) So, we read the opcode and then the operand, and then we
write out the result:

```
void DisassembleNextInstruction()
{
  int opStart = _pos;

  OpCode code = ReadOpCode();
  string operand = ReadOperand (code);
```

```
    _output.AppendFormat ("IL_{0:X4}:  {1,-12} {2}",
                           opStart, code.Name, operand);
    _output.AppendLine();
}
```

To read an opcode, we advance one byte and see whether we have a valid instruction. If not, we advance another byte and look for a two-byte instruction:

```
OpCode ReadOpCode()
{
  byte byteCode = _il [_pos++];
  if (_opcodes.ContainsKey (byteCode)) return _opcodes [byteCode];

  if (_pos == _il.Length)  throw new Exception ("Unexpected end of IL");

  short shortCode = (short) (byteCode * 256 + _il [_pos++]);

  if (!_opcodes.ContainsKey (shortCode))
    throw new Exception ("Cannot find opcode " + shortCode);

  return _opcodes [shortCode];
}
```

To read an operand, we first must establish its length. We can do this based on
the operand type. Because most operands are four bytes long, we can filter out the
exceptions fairly easily in a conditional clause.

The next step is to call FormatOperand, which attempts to format the operand:

```
string ReadOperand (OpCode c)
{
  int operandLength =
    c.OperandType == OperandType.InlineNone
      ? 0 :
    c.OperandType == OperandType.ShortInlineBrTarget ||
    c.OperandType == OperandType.ShortInlineI ||
    c.OperandType == OperandType.ShortInlineVar
      ? 1 :
    c.OperandType == OperandType.InlineVar
      ? 2 :
    c.OperandType == OperandType.InlineI8 ||
    c.OperandType == OperandType.InlineR
      ? 8 :
    c.OperandType == OperandType.InlineSwitch
      ? 4 * (BitConverter.ToInt32 (_il, _pos) + 1) :
      4;  // All others are 4 bytes

  if (_pos + operandLength > _il.Length)
    throw new Exception ("Unexpected end of IL");

  string result = FormatOperand (c, operandLength);
  if (result == null)
  {                             // Write out operand bytes in hex
    result = "";
    for (int i = 0; i < operandLength; i++)
      result += _il [_pos + i].ToString ("X2") + " ";
```

```
    }
    _pos += operandLength;
    return result;
}
```

If the result of calling `FormatOperand` is `null`, it means the operand needs no special formatting, so we simply write it out in hexadecimal. We could test the disassembler at this point by writing a `FormatOperand` method that always returns `null`. Here's what the output would look like:

```
IL_00A8:  ldfld       98 00 00 04
IL_00AD:  ldloc.2
IL_00AE:  add
IL_00AF:  ldelema     64 00 00 01
IL_00B4:  ldstr       26 04 00 70
IL_00B9:  call        B6 00 00 0A
IL_00BE:  ldstr       11 01 00 70
IL_00C3:  call        91 00 00 0A
...
```

Although the opcodes are correct, the operands are not much use. Instead of hexadecimal numbers, we want member names and strings. The `FormatOperand` method, when it's written, will address this—identifying the special cases that benefit from such formatting. These comprise most four-byte operands and the short branch instructions:

```
string FormatOperand (OpCode c, int operandLength)
{
    if (operandLength == 0) return "";

    if (operandLength == 4)
        return Get4ByteOperand (c);
    else if (c.OperandType == OperandType.ShortInlineBrTarget)
        return GetShortRelativeTarget();
    else if (c.OperandType == OperandType.InlineSwitch)
        return GetSwitchTarget (operandLength);
    else
        return null;
}
```

There are three kinds of four-byte operands that we treat specially. The first is references to members or types—with these, we extract the member or type name by calling the defining module's `ResolveMember` method. The second case is strings —these are stored in the assembly module's metadata and can be retrieved by calling `ResolveString`. The final case is branch targets, where the operand refers to a byte offset in the IL. We format these by working out the absolute address *after* the current instruction (+ four bytes):

```
string Get4ByteOperand (OpCode c)
{
    int intOp = BitConverter.ToInt32 (_il, _pos);

    switch (c.OperandType)
    {
```

```
        case OperandType.InlineTok:
        case OperandType.InlineMethod:
        case OperandType.InlineField:
        case OperandType.InlineType:
          MemberInfo mi;
          try   { mi = _module.ResolveMember (intOp); }
          catch { return null; }
          if (mi == null) return null;

          if (mi.ReflectedType != null)
            return mi.ReflectedType.FullName + "." + mi.Name;
          else if (mi is Type)
            return ((Type)mi).FullName;
          else
            return mi.Name;

        case OperandType.InlineString:
          string s = _module.ResolveString (intOp);
          if (s != null) s = "'" + s + "'";
          return s;

        case OperandType.InlineBrTarget:
          return "IL_" + (_pos + intOp + 4).ToString ("X4");

        default:
          return null;
      }
    }
```

The point where we call ResolveMember is a good window for
a code analysis tool that reports on method dependencies.

For any other four-byte opcode, we return null (this will cause ReadOperand to
format the operand as hex digits).

The final kinds of operand that need special attention are short branch targets and
inline switches. A short branch target describes the destination offset as a single
signed byte, as at the end of the current instruction (i.e., + one byte). A switch target
is followed by a variable number of four-byte branch destinations:

```
string GetShortRelativeTarget()
{
  int absoluteTarget = _pos + (sbyte) _il [_pos] + 1;
  return "IL_" + absoluteTarget.ToString ("X4");
}

string GetSwitchTarget (int operandLength)
{
  int targetCount = BitConverter.ToInt32 (_il, _pos);
  string [] targets = new string [targetCount];
  for (int i = 0; i < targetCount; i++)
  {
    int ilTarget = BitConverter.ToInt32 (_il, _pos + (i + 1) * 4);
    targets [i] = "IL_" + (_pos + ilTarget + operandLength).ToString ("X4");
```

Reflection
and Metadata

```
    }
    return "(" + string.Join (", ", targets) + ")";
  }
```

This completes the disassembler. We can test it by disassembling one of its own methods:

```
MethodInfo mi = typeof (Disassembler).GetMethod (
  "ReadOperand", BindingFlags.Instance | BindingFlags.NonPublic);

Console.WriteLine (Disassembler.Disassemble (mi));
```

19

Dynamic Programming

Chapter 4 explained how dynamic binding works in the C# language. In this chapter, we look briefly at the *Dynamic Language Runtime* (DLR) and then explore the following dynamic programming patterns:

- Numeric type unification
- Dynamic member overload resolution
- Custom binding (implementing dynamic objects)
- Dynamic language interoperability

 In Chapter 24, we describe how `dynamic` can improve COM interoperability.

The types in this chapter reside in the `System.Dynamic` namespace, except for `CallSite<>`, which resides in `System.Runtime.CompilerServices`.

The Dynamic Language Runtime

C# relies on the DLR to perform dynamic binding.

Contrary to its name, the DLR is not a dynamic version of the CLR. Rather, it's a library that sits atop the CLR—just like any other library such as *System.Xml.dll*. Its primary role is to provide runtime services to *unify* dynamic programming—in both statically and dynamically typed languages. Hence, languages such as C#, Visual Basic, IronPython, and IronRuby all use the same protocol for calling functions dynamically. This allows them to share libraries and call code written in other languages.

The DLR also makes it relatively easy to write new dynamic languages in .NET. Instead of having to emit Intermediate Language (IL), dynamic language authors work at the level of *expression trees* (the same expression trees in System.Linq.Expressions that we talked about in Chapter 8).

The DLR further ensures that all consumers get the benefit of *call-site caching*, an optimization whereby the DLR prevents unnecessarily repeating the potentially expensive member resolution decisions made during dynamic binding.

Numeric Type Unification

Chapter 4 explained how dynamic lets us write a single method that works across all numeric types:

```
static dynamic Mean (dynamic x, dynamic y) => (x + y) / 2;

static void Main()
{
  int x = 3, y = 5;
  Console.WriteLine (Mean (x, y));
}
```

What Are Call Sites?

When the compiler encounters a dynamic expression, it has no idea who will evaluate that expression at runtime. For instance, consider the following method:

```
public dynamic Foo (dynamic x, dynamic y)
{
  return x / y;   // Dynamic expression
}
```

The x and y variables could be any CLR object, a COM object, or even an object hosted in a dynamic language. The compiler cannot, therefore, take its usual static approach of emitting a call to a known method of a known type. Instead, the compiler emits code that eventually results in an expression tree that describes the operation, managed by a *call site* that the DLR will bind at runtime. The call site essentially acts as an intermediary between caller and callee.

A call site is represented by the CallSite<> class in *System.Core.dll*. We can see this by disassembling the preceding method—the result is something like this:

```
static CallSite<Func<CallSite,object,object,object>> divideSite;

[return: Dynamic]
public object Foo ([Dynamic] object x, [Dynamic] object y)
{
  if (divideSite == null)
    divideSite =
      CallSite<Func<CallSite,object,object,object>>.Create (
        Microsoft.CSharp.RuntimeBinder.Binder.BinaryOperation (
          CSharpBinderFlags.None,
          ExpressionType.Divide,
          /* Remaining arguments omitted for brevity */ ));

  return divideSite.Target (divideSite, x, y);
}
```

As you can see, the call site is cached in a static field to avoid the cost of re-creating it on each call. The DLR further caches the result of the binding phase and the actual method targets. (There can be multiple targets depending on the types of x and y.)

The actual dynamic call then happens by calling the site's Target (a delegate), passing in the x and y operands.

Notice that the Binder class is specific to C#. Every language with support for dynamic binding provides a language-specific binder to help the DLR interpret expressions in a manner specific to that language, so as not to surprise the programmer. For instance, if we called Foo with integer values of 5 and 2, the C# binder would ensure that we got back 2. In contrast, a VB.NET binder would give us 2.5.

It's a humorous reflection on C# that the keywords static and dynamic can appear adjacently! The same applies to the keywords internal and extern.

However, this (unnecessarily) sacrifices static type safety. The following compiles without error but then fails at runtime:

```
string s = Mean (3, 5);   // Runtime error!
```

We can fix this by introducing a generic type parameter and then casting to dynamic within the calculation itself:

```
static T Mean<T> (T x, T y)
{
  dynamic result = ((dynamic) x + y) / 2;
  return (T) result;
}
```

Notice that we *explicitly* cast the result back to T. If we omitted this cast, we'd be relying on an implicit cast, which might at first appear to work correctly. The implicit cast would fail at runtime, though, upon calling the method with an 8- or 16-bit integral type. To understand why, consider what happens with ordinary static typing when you sum two 8-bit numbers together:

```
byte b = 3;
Console.WriteLine ((b + b).GetType().Name);  // Int32
```

We get an Int32—because the compiler "promotes" 8- or 16-bit numbers to Int32 prior to performing arithmetic operations. For consistency, the C# binder instructs the DLR to do exactly the same thing, and we end up with an Int32 that requires an explicit cast to the smaller numeric type. Of course, this could create the possibility of overflow if we were, say, summing rather than averaging the values.

Dynamic binding incurs a small performance hit—even with call-site caching. You can mitigate this by adding statically typed overloads that cover just the most commonly used types. For example, if subsequent performance profiling showed that calling Mean with doubles was a bottleneck, you could add the following overload:

```
static double Mean (double x, double y) => (x + y) / 2;
```

The compiler will favor that overload when Mean is called with arguments that are known at compile time to be of type double.

Dynamic Member Overload Resolution

Calling a statically known method with dynamically typed arguments defers member overload resolution from compile time to runtime. This is useful in simplifying certain programming tasks—such as simplifying the *Visitor* design pattern. It's also useful in working around limitations imposed by C#'s static typing.

Simplifying the Visitor Pattern

In essence, the *Visitor* pattern allows you to "add" a method to a class hierarchy without altering existing classes. Although useful, this pattern in its static incarnation is subtle and unintuitive compared to most other design patterns. It also requires that visited classes be made "visitor-friendly" by exposing an Accept method, which can be impossible if the classes are not under your control.

With dynamic binding, you can achieve the same goal more easily—and without needing to modify existing classes. To illustrate, consider the following class hierarchy:

```
class Person
{
  public string FirstName { get; set; }
  public string LastName  { get; set; }

  // The Friends collection may contain Customers & Employees:
  public readonly IList<Person> Friends = new Collection<Person> ();
}

class Customer : Person { public decimal CreditLimit { get; set; } }
class Employee : Person { public decimal Salary      { get; set; } }
```

Suppose that we want to write a method that programmatically exports a Person's details to an XML XElement. The most obvious solution is to write a virtual method called ToXElement() in the Person class that returns an XElement populated with a Person's properties. We would then override it in Customer and Employee classes such that the XElement was also populated with CreditLimit and Salary. This pattern can be problematic, however, for two reasons:

- You might not own the Person, Customer, and Employee classes, making it impossible to add methods to them. (And extension methods wouldn't give polymorphic behavior.)

- The Person, Customer, and Employee classes might already be quite big. A frequent antipattern is the "God Object," in which a class such as Person attracts so much functionality that it becomes a nightmare to maintain. A good antidote is to avoid adding functions to Person that don't need to access Person's private state. A ToXElement method might be an excellent candidate.

With dynamic member overload resolution, we can write the ToXElement functionality in a separate class, without resorting to ugly switches based on type:

```
class ToXElementPersonVisitor
{
  public XElement DynamicVisit (Person p) => Visit ((dynamic)p);

  XElement Visit (Person p)
  {
    return new XElement ("Person",
      new XAttribute ("Type", p.GetType().Name),
      new XElement ("FirstName", p.FirstName),
      new XElement ("LastName", p.LastName),
      p.Friends.Select (f => DynamicVisit (f))
    );
  }

  XElement Visit (Customer c)   // Specialized logic for customers
  {
    XElement xe = Visit ((Person)c);   // Call "base" method
    xe.Add (new XElement ("CreditLimit", c.CreditLimit));
    return xe;
  }

  XElement Visit (Employee e)   // Specialized logic for employees
  {
    XElement xe = Visit ((Person)e);   // Call "base" method
    xe.Add (new XElement ("Salary", e.Salary));
    return xe;
  }
}
```

The DynamicVisit method performs a dynamic dispatch—calling the most specific version of Visit as determined at runtime. Notice the line in boldface, in which we call DynamicVisit on each person in the Friends collection. This ensures that if a friend is a Customer or Employee, the correct overload is called.

We can demonstrate this class, as follows:

```
var cust = new Customer
{
  FirstName = "Joe", LastName = "Bloggs", CreditLimit = 123
};
cust.Friends.Add (
  new Employee { FirstName = "Sue", LastName = "Brown", Salary = 50000 }
);

Console.WriteLine (new ToXElementPersonVisitor().DynamicVisit (cust));
```

Here's the result:

```
<Person Type="Customer">
  <FirstName>Joe</FirstName>
  <LastName>Bloggs</LastName>
  <Person Type="Employee">
    <FirstName>Sue</FirstName>
    <LastName>Brown</LastName>
    <Salary>50000</Salary>
  </Person>
  <CreditLimit>123</CreditLimit>
</Person>
```

Variations

If you plan more than one visitor class, a useful variation is to define an abstract base class for visitors:

```
abstract class PersonVisitor<T>
{
  public T DynamicVisit (Person p) { return Visit ((dynamic)p); }

  protected abstract T Visit (Person p);
  protected virtual T Visit (Customer c) { return Visit ((Person) c); }
  protected virtual T Visit (Employee e) { return Visit ((Person) e); }
}
```

Subclasses then don't need to define their own DynamicVisit method: all they do is override the versions of Visit whose behavior they want to specialize. This also has the advantages of centralizing the methods that encompass the Person hierarchy and allowing implementers to call base methods more naturally:

```
class ToXElementPersonVisitor : PersonVisitor<XElement>
{
  protected override XElement Visit (Person p)
  {
    return new XElement ("Person",
      new XAttribute ("Type", p.GetType().Name),
      new XElement ("FirstName", p.FirstName),
      new XElement ("LastName", p.LastName),
      p.Friends.Select (f => DynamicVisit (f))
    );
  }

  protected override XElement Visit (Customer c)
  {
    XElement xe = base.Visit (c);
    xe.Add (new XElement ("CreditLimit", c.CreditLimit));
    return xe;
  }

  protected override XElement Visit (Employee e)
  {
    XElement xe = base.Visit (e);
    xe.Add (new XElement ("Salary", e.Salary));
    return xe;
```

```
    }
  }
```

You then can even subclass ToXElementPersonVisitor itself.

Anonymously Calling Members of a Generic Type

The strictness of C#'s static typing is a double-edged sword. On the one hand, it enforces a degree of correctness at compile time. On the other hand, it occasionally makes certain kinds of code difficult or impossible to express, at which point you must resort to reflection. In these situations, dynamic binding is a cleaner and faster alternative to reflection.

An example is when you need to work with an object of type G<T> where T is unknown. We can illustrate this by defining the following class:

```
public class Foo<T> { public T Value; }
```

Suppose that we then write a method as follows:

```
static void Write (object obj)
{
  if (obj is Foo<>)                          // Illegal
    Console.WriteLine (((Foo<>) obj).Value); // Illegal
}
```

This method won't compile: you can't invoke members of *unbound* generic types.

Dynamic binding offers two means by which we can work around this. The first is to access the Value member dynamically as follows:

```
static void Write (dynamic obj)
{
  try { Console.WriteLine (obj.Value); }
  catch (Microsoft.CSharp.RuntimeBinder.RuntimeBinderException) {...}
}
```

Multiple Dispatch

C# and the CLR have always supported a limited form of dynamism in the form of virtual method calls. This differs from C#'s dynamic binding in that for virtual method calls, the compiler must commit to a particular virtual member at compile time—based on the name and signature of a member you called. This means that:

- The calling expression must be fully understood by the compiler (e.g., it must decide at compile time whether a target member is a field or property).

- Overload resolution must be completed entirely by the compiler, based on the compile-time argument types.

A consequence of that last point is that the ability to perform virtual method calls is known as *single dispatch*. To see why, consider the following method call (in which Walk is a virtual method):

```
animal.Walk (owner);
```

The runtime decision of whether to invoke a dog's Walk method or a cat's Walk method depends only on the type of the *receiver*, animal (hence, "single"). If many overloads of Walk accept different kinds of owner, an overload will be selected at compile time without regard to the actual runtime type of the owner object. In other words, only the runtime type of the *receiver* can vary which method gets called.

In contrast, a dynamic call defers overload resolution until runtime:

```
animal.Walk ((dynamic) owner);
```

The final choice of which Walk method to call now depends on the types of both animal and owner—this is called *multiple dispatch* because the runtime types of arguments, in addition to the receiver type, contribute to the determination of which Walk method to call.

This has the (potential) advantage of working with any object that defines a Value field or property. However, there are a couple of problems. First, catching an exception in this manner is somewhat messy and inefficient (and there's no way to ask the DLR in advance, "Will this operation succeed?"). Second, this approach wouldn't work if Foo were an interface (say, IFoo<T>) and either of the following conditions were true:

- Value was implemented explicitly.

- The type that implemented IFoo<T> was inaccessible (more on this soon).

A better solution is to write an overloaded helper method called GetFooValue and to call it using *dynamic member overload resolution*:

```
static void Write (dynamic obj)
{
  object result = GetFooValue (obj);
  if (result != null) Console.WriteLine (result);
}

static T GetFooValue<T> (Foo<T> foo) => foo.Value;
static object GetFooValue (object foo) => null;
```

Notice that we overloaded GetFooValue to accept an object parameter, which acts as a fallback for any type. At runtime, the C# dynamic binder will pick the best overload when calling GetFooValue with a dynamic argument. If the object in question is not based on Foo<T>, it will choose the object-parameter overload instead of throwing an exception.

 An alternative is to write just the first GetFooValue overload and then catch the RuntimeBinderException. The advantage is that it distinguishes the case of foo.Value being null. The disadvantage is that it incurs the performance overhead of throwing and catching an exception.

In Chapter 18, we solved the same problem with an interface using reflection—with a lot more effort (see "Anonymously Calling Members of a Generic Interface" on page 800). The example we used was to design a more powerful version of ToString() that could understand objects such as IEnumerable and IGrouping<,>. Here's the same example solved more elegantly using dynamic binding:

```
static string GetGroupKey<TKey,TElement> (IGrouping<TKey,TElement> group)
  => "Group with key=" + group.Key + ": ";

static string GetGroupKey (object source) => null;

public static string ToStringEx (object value)
{
  if (value == null) return "<null>";
  if (value is string s) return s;
  if (value.GetType().IsPrimitive) return value.ToString();

  StringBuilder sb = new StringBuilder();

  string groupKey = GetGroupKey ((dynamic)value);   // Dynamic dispatch
  if (groupKey != null) sb.Append (groupKey);

  if (value is IEnumerable)
    foreach (object element in ((IEnumerable)value))
      sb.Append (ToStringEx (element) + " ");

  if (sb.Length == 0) sb.Append (value.ToString());

  return "\r\n" + sb.ToString();
}
```

Here it is in action:

```
Console.WriteLine (ToStringEx ("xyyzzz".GroupBy (c => c) ));

Group with key=x: x
Group with key=y: y y
Group with key=z: z z z
```

Notice that we used dynamic *member overload resolution* to solve this problem. If we instead did the following:

```
dynamic d = value;
try { groupKey = d.Value); }
catch (Microsoft.CSharp.RuntimeBinder.RuntimeBinderException) {...}
```

it would fail because LINQ's GroupBy operator returns a type implementing IGrouping<,>, which itself is internal and therefore inaccessible:

```
internal class Grouping : IGrouping<TKey,TElement>, ...
{
  public TKey Key;
  ...
}
```

Even though the Key property is declared public, its containing class caps it at internal, making it accessible only via the IGrouping<,> interface. And as is explained in Chapter 4, there's no way to instruct the DLR to bind to that interface when invoking the Value member dynamically.

Implementing Dynamic Objects

An object can provide its binding semantics by implementing IDynamicMetaObject Provider—or more easily by subclassing DynamicObject, which provides a default implementation of this interface. This is demonstrated briefly in Chapter 4 via the following example:

```
dynamic d = new Duck();
d.Quack();              // Quack method was called
d.Waddle();             // Waddle method was called

public class Duck : DynamicObject
{
  public override bool TryInvokeMember (
    InvokeMemberBinder binder, object[] args, out object result)
  {
    Console.WriteLine (binder.Name + " method was called");
    result = null;
    return true;
  }
}
```

DynamicObject

In the preceding example, we overrode TryInvokeMember, which allows the consumer to invoke a method on the dynamic object—such as a Quack or Waddle. DynamicObject exposes other virtual methods that enable consumers to use other programming constructs as well. The following correspond to constructs that have representations in C#:

Method	Programming construct
TryInvokeMember	Method
TryGetMember, TrySetMember	Property or field
TryGetIndex, TrySetIndex	Indexer
TryUnaryOperation	Unary operator such as !
TryBinaryOperation	Binary operator such as ==
TryConvert	Conversion (cast) to another type
TryInvoke	Invocation on the object itself—e.g., d("foo")

These methods should return `true` if successful. If they return `false`, the DLR will fall back to the language binder, looking for a matching member on the `Dynamic Object` (subclass) itself. If this fails, a `RuntimeBinderException` is thrown.

We can illustrate `TryGetMember` and `TrySetMember` with a class that lets us dynamically access an attribute in an `XElement` (`System.Xml.Linq`):

```
static class XExtensions
{
  public static dynamic DynamicAttributes (this XElement e)
    => new XWrapper (e);

  class XWrapper : DynamicObject
  {
    XElement _element;
    public XWrapper (XElement e) { _element = e; }

    public override bool TryGetMember (GetMemberBinder binder,
                                       out object result)
    {
      result = _element.Attribute (binder.Name).Value;
      return true;
    }

    public override bool TrySetMember (SetMemberBinder binder,
                                       object value)
    {
      _element.SetAttributeValue (binder.Name, value);
      return true;
    }
  }
}
```

Here's how to use it:

```
XElement x = XElement.Parse (@"<Label Text=""Hello"" Id=""5""/>");
dynamic da = x.DynamicAttributes();
Console.WriteLine (da.Id);          // 5
da.Text = "Foo";
Console.WriteLine (x.ToString());   // <Label Text="Foo" Id="5" />
```

The following does a similar thing for `System.Data.IDataRecord`, making it easier to use data readers:

```
public class DynamicReader : DynamicObject
{
  readonly IDataRecord _dataRecord;
  public DynamicReader (IDataRecord dr) { _dataRecord = dr; }

  public override bool TryGetMember (GetMemberBinder binder,
                                     out object result)
  {
    result = _dataRecord [binder.Name];
    return true;
  }
```

```
  }
  ...
using (IDataReader reader = someDbCommand.ExecuteReader())
{
  dynamic dr = new DynamicReader (reader);
  while (reader.Read())
  {
    int id = dr.ID;
    string firstName = dr.FirstName;
    DateTime dob = dr.DateOfBirth;
    ...
  }
}
```

The following demonstrates TryBinaryOperation and TryInvoke:

```
dynamic d = new Duck();
Console.WriteLine (d + d);           // foo
Console.WriteLine (d (78, 'x'));     // 123

public class Duck : DynamicObject
{
  public override bool TryBinaryOperation (BinaryOperationBinder binder,
                                           object arg, out object result)
  {
    Console.WriteLine (binder.Operation);   // Add
    result = "foo";
    return true;
  }

  public override bool TryInvoke (InvokeBinder binder,
                                  object[] args, out object result)
  {
    Console.WriteLine (args[0]);     // 78
    result = 123;
    return true;
  }
}
```

DynamicObject also exposes some virtual methods for the benefit of dynamic languages. In particular, overriding GetDynamicMemberNames allows you to return a list of all member names that your dynamic object provides.

> Another reason to implement GetDynamicMemberNames is that Visual Studio's debugger makes use of this method to display a view of a dynamic object.

ExpandoObject

Another simple application of DynamicObject would be to write a dynamic class that stored and retrieved objects in a dictionary, keyed by string. However, this functionality is already provided via the ExpandoObject class:

```
dynamic x = new ExpandoObject();
x.FavoriteColor = ConsoleColor.Green;
x.FavoriteNumber = 7;
Console.WriteLine (x.FavoriteColor);    // Green
Console.WriteLine (x.FavoriteNumber);   // 7
```

ExpandoObject implements IDictionary<string,object>—so we can continue our example and do this:

```
var dict = (IDictionary<string,object>) x;
Console.WriteLine (dict ["FavoriteColor"]);    // Green
Console.WriteLine (dict ["FavoriteNumber"]);   // 7
Console.WriteLine (dict.Count);                // 2
```

Interoperating with Dynamic Languages

Although C# supports dynamic binding via the dynamic keyword, it doesn't go as far as allowing you to execute an expression described in a string at runtime:

```
string expr = "2 * 3";
// We can't "execute" expr
```

This is because the code to translate a string into an expression tree requires a lexical and semantic parser. These features are built into the C# compiler and are not available as a runtime service. At runtime, C# merely provides a *binder*, which instructs the DLR how to interpret an already-built expression tree.

True dynamic languages such as IronPython and IronRuby do allow you to execute an arbitrary string, and this is useful in tasks such as scripting, dynamic configuration, and implementing dynamic rules engines. So, although you can write most of your application in C#, it can be useful to call out to a dynamic language for such tasks. In addition, you might want to use an API that is written in a dynamic language where no equivalent functionality is available in a .NET library.

The Roslyn scripting NuGet package *Microsoft.CodeAnalysis.CSharp.Scripting* provides an API that lets you execute a C# string, although it does so by first compiling your code into a program. The compilation overhead makes it slower than Python interop, unless you intend to execute the same expression repeatedly.

In the following example, we use IronPython to evaluate an expression created at runtime from within C#. You could use the following script to write a calculator.

To run this code, add the NuGet packages *DynamicLanguageRuntime* (not to be confused with the *System.Dynamic.Runtime* package) and *IronPython* to your application.

```
using System;
using IronPython.Hosting;
using Microsoft.Scripting;
using Microsoft.Scripting.Hosting;
```

```
int result = (int) Calculate ("2 * 3");
Console.WriteLine (result);              // 6

object Calculate (string expression)
{
  ScriptEngine engine = Python.CreateEngine();
  return engine.Execute (expression);
}
```

Because we're passing a string into Python, the expression will be evaluated according to Python's rules and not C#'s. It also means that we can use Python's language features, such as lists:

```
var list = (IEnumerable) Calculate ("[1, 2, 3] + [4, 5]");
foreach (int n in list) Console.Write (n);  // 12345
```

Passing State Between C# and a Script

To pass variables from C# to Python, a few more steps are required. The following example illustrates those steps and could be the basis of a rules engine:

```
// The following string could come from a file or database:
string auditRule = "taxPaidLastYear / taxPaidThisYear > 2";

ScriptEngine engine = Python.CreateEngine ();

ScriptScope scope = engine.CreateScope ();
scope.SetVariable ("taxPaidLastYear", 20000m);
scope.SetVariable ("taxPaidThisYear", 8000m);

ScriptSource source = engine.CreateScriptSourceFromString (
                        auditRule, SourceCodeKind.Expression);

bool auditRequired = (bool) source.Execute (scope);
Console.WriteLine (auditRequired);   // True
```

You can also get variables back by calling GetVariable:

```
string code = "result = input * 3";

ScriptEngine engine = Python.CreateEngine();

ScriptScope scope = engine.CreateScope();
scope.SetVariable ("input", 2);

ScriptSource source = engine.CreateScriptSourceFromString (code,
                            SourceCodeKind.SingleStatement);
source.Execute (scope);
Console.WriteLine (scope.GetVariable ("result"));   // 6
```

Notice that we specified SourceCodeKind.SingleStatement in the second example (rather than Expression) to inform the engine that we want to execute a statement.

Types are automatically marshaled between the .NET and Python worlds. You can even access members of .NET objects from the scripting side:

```
string code = @"sb.Append (""World"")";

ScriptEngine engine = Python.CreateEngine ();

ScriptScope scope = engine.CreateScope ();
var sb = new StringBuilder ("Hello");
scope.SetVariable ("sb", sb);

ScriptSource source = engine.CreateScriptSourceFromString (
                        code, SourceCodeKind.SingleStatement);
source.Execute (scope);
Console.WriteLine (sb.ToString());    // HelloWorld
```

20

Cryptography

In this chapter, we discuss the major cryptography APIs in .NET:

- Windows Data Protection API (DPAPI)
- Hashing
- Symmetric encryption
- Public key encryption and signing

The types covered in this chapter are defined in the following namespaces:

```
System.Security;
System.Security.Cryptography;
```

Overview

Table 20-1 summarizes the cryptography options in .NET. In the remaining sections, we explore each of these.

Table 20-1. Encryption and hashing options in .NET

Option	Keys to manage	Speed	Strength	Notes
File.Encrypt	0	Fast	Depends on user's password	Protects files transparently with filesystem support. A key is derived implicitly from the logged-in user's credentials. Windows only.
Windows Data Protection	0	Fast	Depends on user's password	Encrypts and decrypts byte arrays using an implicitly derived key.
Hashing	0	Fast	High	One-way (irreversible) transformation. Used for storing passwords, comparing files, and checking for data corruption.

Option	Keys to manage	Speed	Strength	Notes
Symmetric Encryption	1	Fast	High	For general-purpose encryption/decryption. The same key encrypts and decrypts. Can be used to secure messages in transit.
Public Key Encryption	2	Slow	High	Encryption and decryption use different keys. Used for exchanging a symmetric key in message transmission and for digitally signing files.

.NET also provides more specialized support for creating and validating XML-based signatures in `System.Security.Cryptography.Xml` and types for working with digital certificates in `System.Security.Cryptography.X509Certificates`.

Windows Data Protection

Windows Data Protection is available on Windows only, and throws a `PlatformNotSupportedException` on other operating systems.

In the section "File and Directory Operations" on page 699, we described how you could use `File.Encrypt` to request that the operating system transparently encrypt a file:

```
File.WriteAllText ("myfile.txt", "");
File.Encrypt ("myfile.txt");
File.AppendAllText ("myfile.txt", "sensitive data");
```

The encryption in this case uses a key derived from the logged-in user's password. You can use this same implicitly derived key to encrypt a byte array with the Windows Data Protection API (DPAPI). The DPAPI is exposed through the `ProtectedData` class—a simple type with two static methods:

```
public static byte[] Protect
  (byte[] userData, byte[] optionalEntropy, DataProtectionScope scope);

public static byte[] Unprotect
  (byte[] encryptedData, byte[] optionalEntropy, DataProtectionScope scope);
```

Whatever you include in `optionalEntropy` is added to the key, thereby increasing its security. The `DataProtectionScope` enum argument allows two options: `Current User` or `LocalMachine`. With `CurrentUser`, a key is derived from the logged-in user's credentials; with `LocalMachine`, a machine-wide key is used, common to all users. This means that with the `CurrentUser` scope, data encrypted by one user cannot be decrypted by another. A `LocalMachine` key provides less protection but works under a Windows Service or a program needing to operate under a variety of accounts.

Here's a simple encryption and decryption demonstration:

```
byte[] original = {1, 2, 3, 4, 5};
DataProtectionScope scope = DataProtectionScope.CurrentUser;

byte[] encrypted = ProtectedData.Protect (original, null, scope);
byte[] decrypted = ProtectedData.Unprotect (encrypted, null, scope);
// decrypted is now {1, 2, 3, 4, 5}
```

Windows Data Protection provides moderate security against an attacker with full access to the computer, depending on the strength of the user's password. With LocalMachine scope, it's effective only against those with restricted physical and electronic access.

Hashing

A *hashing algorithm* distills a potentially large number of bytes into a small fixed-length *hashcode*. Hashing algorithms are designed such that a single-bit change anywhere in the source data results in a significantly different hashcode. This makes it suitable for comparing files or detecting accidental (or malicious) corruption to a file or data stream.

Hashing also acts as one-way encryption, because it's difficult to impossible to convert a hashcode back into the original data. This makes it ideal for storing passwords in a database, because should your database become compromised, you don't want the attacker to gain access to plain-text passwords. To authenticate, you simply hash what the user types in and compare it to the hash that's stored in the database.

To hash, you call ComputeHash on one of the HashAlgorithm subclasses, such as SHA1 or SHA256:

```
byte[] hash;
using (Stream fs = File.OpenRead ("checkme.doc"))
  hash = SHA1.Create().ComputeHash (fs);   // SHA1 hash is 20 bytes long
```

The ComputeHash method also accepts a byte array, which is convenient for hashing passwords (we describe a more secure technique in "Hashing Passwords" on page 854):

```
byte[] data = System.Text.Encoding.UTF8.GetBytes ("stRhong%pword");
byte[] hash = SHA256.Create().ComputeHash (data);
```

 The GetBytes method on an Encoding object converts a string to a byte array; the GetString method converts it back. An Encoding object cannot, however, convert an encrypted or hashed byte array to a string, because scrambled data usually violates text encoding rules. Instead, use Convert.ToBase64String and Convert.FromBase64String: these convert between any byte array and a legal (and XML- or JSON-friendly) string.

Hash Algorithms in .NET

SHA1 and SHA256 are two of the HashAlgorithm subtypes provided by .NET. Here are all the major algorithms, in ascending order of security (and hash length, in bytes):

```
MD5(16) → SHA1(20) → SHA256(32) → SHA384(48) → SHA512(64)
```

MD5 and SHA1 are currently the fastest algorithms, although the other algorithms are not more than (roughly) two times slower in their current implementations. To give a ballpark figure, you can expect a performance of more than 100 MB per second with any of these algorithms on today's typical desktop or server. The longer hashes decrease the possibility of *collision* (two distinct files yielding the same hash).

 Use *at least* SHA256 when hashing passwords or other security-sensitive data. MD5 and SHA1 are considered insecure for this purpose and are suitable to protect only against accidental corruption, not deliberate tampering.

Hashing Passwords

The longer SHA algorithms are suitable as a basis for password hashing, if you enforce a strong password policy to mitigate a *dictionary attack*—a strategy whereby an attacker builds a password lookup table by hashing every word in a dictionary.

A standard technique, when hashing passwords, is to incorporate "salt"—a long series of bytes that you initially obtain via a random number generator and then combine with each password before hashing. This frustrates hackers in two ways:

- They must also know the salt bytes.

- They cannot use *rainbow tables* (publicly available *precomputed* databases of passwords and their hashcodes), although a dictionary attack might still be possible with sufficient computing power.

You can further strengthen security by "stretching" your password hashes—repeatedly rehashing to obtain more computationally intensive byte sequences. If you rehash 100 times, a dictionary attack that might otherwise take one month would take eight years. The KeyDerivation, Rfc2898DeriveBytes, and PasswordDerive Bytes classes perform exactly this kind of stretching while also allowing for convenient salting. Of these, KeyDerivation.Pbkdf2 offers the best hashing:

```
byte[] encrypted = KeyDerivation.Pbkdf2 (
    password: "stRhong%pword",
    salt: Encoding.UTF8.GetBytes ("j78Y#p)/saREN!y3@"),
    prf: KeyDerivationPrf.HMACSHA512,
    iterationCount: 100,
    numBytesRequested: 64);
```

KeyDerivation.Pbkdf2 requires the NuGet package Micro soft.AspNetCore.Cryptography.KeyDerivation. Though it's in the ASP.NET Core namespace, any .NET application can use it.

Symmetric Encryption

Symmetric encryption uses the same key for encryption as for decryption. The .NET BCL provides four symmetric algorithms, of which Rijndael (pronounced "Rhine Dahl" or "Rain Doll") is the premium; the other algorithms are intended mainly for compatibility with older applications. Rijndael is both fast and secure and has two implementations:

- The Rijndael class
- The Aes class

The two are almost identical, except that Aes does not let you weaken the cipher by changing the block size. Aes is recommended by the CLR's security team.

Rijndael and Aes allow symmetric keys of length 16, 24, or 32 bytes: all are currently considered secure. Here's how to encrypt a series of bytes as they're written to a file, using a 16-byte key:

```
byte[] key = {145,12,32,245,98,132,98,214,6,77,131,44,221,3,9,50};
byte[] iv  = {15,122,132,5,93,198,44,31,9,39,241,49,250,188,80,7};

byte[] data = { 1, 2, 3, 4, 5 };   // This is what we're encrypting.

using (SymmetricAlgorithm algorithm = Aes.Create())
using (ICryptoTransform encryptor = algorithm.CreateEncryptor (key, iv))
using (Stream f = File.Create ("encrypted.bin"))
using (Stream c = new CryptoStream (f, encryptor, CryptoStreamMode.Write))
  c.Write (data, 0, data.Length);
```

The following code decrypts the file:

```
byte[] key = {145,12,32,245,98,132,98,214,6,77,131,44,221,3,9,50};
byte[] iv  = {15,122,132,5,93,198,44,31,9,39,241,49,250,188,80,7};

byte[] decrypted = new byte[5];

using (SymmetricAlgorithm algorithm = Aes.Create())
using (ICryptoTransform decryptor = algorithm.CreateDecryptor (key, iv))
using (Stream f = File.OpenRead ("encrypted.bin"))
using (Stream c = new CryptoStream (f, decryptor, CryptoStreamMode.Read))
  for (int b; (b = c.ReadByte()) > -1;)
    Console.Write (b + " ");                        // 1 2 3 4 5
```

In this example, we made up a key of 16 randomly chosen bytes. If the wrong key was used in decryption, CryptoStream would throw a CryptographicException. Catching this exception is the only way to test whether a key is correct.

As well as a key, we made up an IV, or *Initialization Vector*. This 16-byte sequence forms part of the cipher—much like the key—but is not considered *secret*. If you're transmitting an encrypted message, you would send the IV in plain text (perhaps in a message header) and then *change it with every message*. This would render each encrypted message unrecognizable from any previous one—even if their unencrypted versions were similar or identical.

 If you don't need—or want—the protection of an IV, you can defeat it by using the same 16-byte value for both the key and the IV. Sending multiple messages with the same IV, though, weakens the cipher and might even make it possible to crack.

The cryptography work is divided among the classes. `Aes` is the mathematician; it applies the cipher algorithm, along with its `encryptor` and `decryptor` transforms. `CryptoStream` is the plumber; it takes care of stream plumbing. You can replace `Aes` with a different symmetric algorithm yet still use `CryptoStream`.

`CryptoStream` is *bidirectional*, meaning you can read or write to the stream depending on whether you choose `CryptoStreamMode.Read` or `CryptoStreamMode.Write`. Both encryptors and decryptors are read *and* write savvy, yielding four combinations—the choice can have you staring at a blank screen for a while! It can be helpful to model reading as "pulling" and writing as "pushing." If in doubt, start with `Write` for encryption and `Read` for decryption; this is often the most natural.

To generate a random key or IV, use `RandomNumberGenerator` in `System.Cryptography`. The numbers it produces are genuinely unpredictable, or *cryptographically strong* (the `System.Random` class does not offer the same guarantee). Here's an example:

```
byte[] key = new byte [16];
byte[] iv  = new byte [16];
RandomNumberGenerator rand = RandomNumberGenerator.Create();
rand.GetBytes (key);
rand.GetBytes (iv);
```

Or, from .NET 6:

```
byte[] key = RandomNumberGenerator.GetBytes (16);
byte[] iv = RandomNumberGenerator.GetBytes (16);
```

If you don't specify a key and IV, cryptographically strong random values are generated automatically. You can query these through the `Aes` object's `Key` and `IV` properties.

Encrypting in Memory

From .NET 6, you can utilize the `EncryptCbc` and `DecryptCbc` methods to shortcut the process of encrypting and decrypting byte arrays:

```
public static byte[] Encrypt (byte[] data, byte[] key, byte[] iv)
{
  using Aes algorithm = Aes.Create();
```

```
    algorithm.Key = key;
    return algorithm.EncryptCbc (data, iv);
  }

  public static byte[] Decrypt (byte[] data, byte[] key, byte[] iv)
  {
    using Aes algorithm = Aes.Create();
    algorithm.Key = key;
    return algorithm.DecryptCbc (data, iv);
  }
```

Here's an equivalent that works in all .NET versions:

```
  public static byte[] Encrypt (byte[] data, byte[] key, byte[] iv)
  {
    using (Aes algorithm = Aes.Create())
    using (ICryptoTransform encryptor = algorithm.CreateEncryptor (key, iv))
      return Crypt (data, encryptor);
  }

  public static byte[] Decrypt (byte[] data, byte[] key, byte[] iv)
  {
    using (Aes algorithm = Aes.Create())
    using (ICryptoTransform decryptor = algorithm.CreateDecryptor (key, iv))
      return Crypt (data, decryptor);
  }

  static byte[] Crypt (byte[] data, ICryptoTransform cryptor)
  {
    MemoryStream m = new MemoryStream();
    using (Stream c = new CryptoStream (m, cryptor, CryptoStreamMode.Write))
      c.Write (data, 0, data.Length);
    return m.ToArray();
  }
```

Here, CryptoStreamMode.Write works best for both encryption and decryption, since in both cases we're "pushing" into a fresh memory stream.

Here are overloads that accept and return strings:

```
  public static string Encrypt (string data, byte[] key, byte[] iv)
  {
    return Convert.ToBase64String (
      Encrypt (Encoding.UTF8.GetBytes (data), key, iv));
  }

  public static string Decrypt (string data, byte[] key, byte[] iv)
  {
    return Encoding.UTF8.GetString (
      Decrypt (Convert.FromBase64String (data), key, iv));
  }
```

The following demonstrates their use:

```
  byte[] key = new byte[16];
  byte[] iv = new byte[16];
```

```
var cryptoRng = RandomNumberGenerator.Create();
cryptoRng.GetBytes (key);
cryptoRng.GetBytes (iv);

string encrypted = Encrypt ("Yeah!", key, iv);
Console.WriteLine (encrypted);                  // R1/5gYvcxyR2vzPjnT7yaQ==

string decrypted = Decrypt (encrypted, key, iv);
Console.WriteLine (decrypted);                  // Yeah!
```

Chaining Encryption Streams

CryptoStream is a decorator, meaning that you can chain it with other streams. In the following example, we write compressed encrypted text to a file and then read it back:

```
byte[] key = new byte [16];
byte[] iv = new byte [16];

var cryptoRng = RandomNumberGenerator.Create();
cryptoRng.GetBytes (key);
cryptoRng.GetBytes (iv);

using (Aes algorithm = Aes.Create())
{
  using (ICryptoTransform encryptor = algorithm.CreateEncryptor(key, iv))
  using (Stream f = File.Create ("serious.bin"))
  using (Stream c = new CryptoStream (f, encryptor, CryptoStreamMode.Write))
  using (Stream d = new DeflateStream (c, CompressionMode.Compress))
  using (StreamWriter w = new StreamWriter (d))
    await w.WriteLineAsync ("Small and secure!");

  using (ICryptoTransform decryptor = algorithm.CreateDecryptor(key, iv))
  using (Stream f = File.OpenRead ("serious.bin"))
  using (Stream c = new CryptoStream (f, decryptor, CryptoStreamMode.Read))
  using (Stream d = new DeflateStream (c, CompressionMode.Decompress))
  using (StreamReader r = new StreamReader (d))
    Console.WriteLine (await r.ReadLineAsync());       // Small and secure!
}
```

(As a final touch, we make our program asynchronous by calling WriteLineAsync and ReadLineAsync and awaiting the result.)

In this example, all one-letter variables form part of a chain. The mathematicians—algorithm, encryptor, and decryptor—are there to assist CryptoStream in the cipher work, as illustrated in Figure 20-1.

Chaining streams in this manner demands little memory, regardless of the ultimate stream sizes.

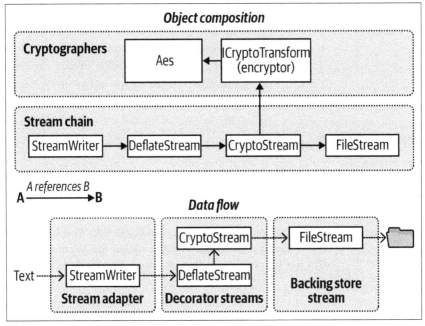

Figure 20-1. Chaining encryption and compression streams

Disposing Encryption Objects

Disposing a `CryptoStream` ensures that its internal cache of data is flushed to the underlying stream. Internal caching is necessary for encryption algorithms because they process data in blocks, rather than one byte at a time.

`CryptoStream` is unusual in that its `Flush` method does nothing. To flush a stream (without disposing it) you must call `FlushFinalBlock`. In contrast to `Flush`, you can call `FlushFinalBlock` only once, and then no further data can be written.

We also disposed the mathematicians—the `Aes` algorithm and `ICryptoTransform` objects (`encryptor` and `decryptor`). When the Rijndael transforms are disposed, they wipe the symmetric key and related data from memory, preventing subsequent discovery by other software running on the computer (we're talking malware). You can't rely on the garbage collector for this job, because it merely flags sections of memory as available; it doesn't write zeros over every byte.

The easiest way to dispose an `Aes` object outside of a `using` statement is to call `Clear`. Its `Dispose` method is hidden via explicit implementation (to signal its unusual disposal semantics, whereby it clears memory rather than releasing unmanaged resources).

You can further reduce your application's vulnerability to leaking secrets via released memory by doing the following:

- Avoiding strings for security information (being immutable, a string's value can never be cleared once created)
- Overwriting buffers as soon as they're no longer needed (for instance, by calling `Array.Clear` on a byte array)

Key Management

Key management is a critical element of security: if your keys are exposed, so is your data. You need to consider who should have access to keys and how to back them up in case of hardware failure while storing them in a manner that prevents unauthorized access.

It is inadvisable to hardcode encryption keys because popular tools exist to decompile assemblies with little expertise required. A better option (on Windows) is to manufacture a random key for each installation, storing it securely with Windows Data Protection.

For applications deployed to the cloud, Microsoft Azure and Amazon Web Services (AWS) offer key-management systems with additional features that can be useful in an enterprise environment, such as audit trails.

If you're encrypting a message stream, public-key encryption still provides the best option.

Public-Key Encryption and Signing

Public-key cryptography is *asymmetric*, meaning that encryption and decryption use different keys.

Unlike symmetric encryption, for which any arbitrary series of bytes of appropriate length can serve as a key, asymmetric cryptography requires specially crafted key pairs. A key pair contains a *public key* and *private key* component that work together as follows:

- The public key encrypts messages.
- The private key decrypts messages.

The party "crafting" a key pair keeps the private key secret while distributing the public key freely. A special feature of this type of cryptography is that you cannot calculate a private key from a public key. So, if the private key is lost, encrypted data cannot be recovered; conversely, if a private key is leaked, the encryption system becomes useless.

A public key handshake allows two computers to communicate securely over a public network, with no prior contact and no existing shared secret. To see how this works, suppose that computer *Origin* wants to send a confidential message to computer *Target*:

1. *Target* generates a public/private key pair and then sends its public key to *Origin*.

2. *Origin* encrypts the confidential message using *Target*'s public key and then sends it to *Target*.

3. *Target* decrypts the confidential message using its private key.

An eavesdropper will see the following:

- *Target*'s public key

- The secret message, encrypted with *Target*'s public key

But without *Target*'s private key, the message cannot be decrypted.

 This doesn't prevent against a man-in-the-middle attack: in other words, *Origin* cannot know that *Target* isn't some malicious party. To authenticate the recipient, the originator needs to already know the recipient's public key or be able to validate its key through a *digital site certificate*.

Because public key encryption is relatively slow and its message size limited, the secret message sent from *Origin* to *Target* typically contains a fresh key for subsequent *symmetric* encryption. This allows public key encryption to be abandoned for the remainder of the session, in favor of a symmetric algorithm capable of handling larger messages. This protocol is particularly secure if a fresh public/private key pair is generated for each session because no keys then need to be stored on either computer.

 The public key encryption algorithms rely on the message being smaller than the key. This makes them suitable for encrypting only small amounts of data, such as a key for subsequent symmetric encryption. If you try to encrypt a message much larger than half the key size, the provider will throw an exception.

The RSA Class

.NET provides a number of asymmetric algorithms, of which RSA is the most popular. Here's how to encrypt and decrypt with RSA:

```
byte[] data = { 1, 2, 3, 4, 5 };   // This is what we're encrypting.

using (var rsa = new RSACryptoServiceProvider())
{
  byte[] encrypted = rsa.Encrypt (data, true);
  byte[] decrypted = rsa.Decrypt (encrypted, true);
}
```

Because we didn't specify a public or private key, the cryptographic provider automatically generated a key pair, using the default length of 1,024 bits; you can request longer keys in increments of eight bytes, through the constructor. For security-critical applications, it's prudent to request 2,048 bits:

```
var rsa = new RSACryptoServiceProvider (2048);
```

Generating a key pair is computationally intensive—taking perhaps 100 ms. For this reason, the RSA implementation delays this until a key is actually needed, such as when calling Encrypt. This gives you the chance to load in an existing key—or key pair, should it exist.

The methods ImportCspBlob and ExportCspBlob load and save keys in byte array format. FromXmlString and ToXmlString do the same job in a string format, the string containing an XML fragment. A bool flag lets you indicate whether to include the private key when saving. Here's how to manufacture a key pair and save it to disk:

```
using (var rsa = new RSACryptoServiceProvider())
{
  File.WriteAllText ("PublicKeyOnly.xml", rsa.ToXmlString (false));
  File.WriteAllText ("PublicPrivate.xml", rsa.ToXmlString (true));
}
```

Because we didn't provide existing keys, ToXmlString forced the manufacture of a fresh key pair (on the first call). In the next example, we read back these keys and use them to encrypt and decrypt a message:

```
byte[] data = Encoding.UTF8.GetBytes ("Message to encrypt");

string publicKeyOnly = File.ReadAllText ("PublicKeyOnly.xml");
string publicPrivate = File.ReadAllText ("PublicPrivate.xml");

byte[] encrypted, decrypted;

using (var rsaPublicOnly = new RSACryptoServiceProvider())
{
  rsaPublicOnly.FromXmlString (publicKeyOnly);
  encrypted = rsaPublicOnly.Encrypt (data, true);

  // The next line would throw an exception because you need the private
  // key in order to decrypt:
  // decrypted = rsaPublicOnly.Decrypt (encrypted, true);
}

using (var rsaPublicPrivate = new RSACryptoServiceProvider())
{
  // With the private key we can successfully decrypt:
  rsaPublicPrivate.FromXmlString (publicPrivate);
  decrypted = rsaPublicPrivate.Decrypt (encrypted, true);
}
```

Digital Signing

You also can use public key algorithms to digitally sign messages or documents. A signature is like a hash, except that its production requires a private key and so cannot be forged. The public key is used to verify the signature. Here's an example:

```
byte[] data = Encoding.UTF8.GetBytes ("Message to sign");
byte[] publicKey;
byte[] signature;
object hasher = SHA1.Create();        // Our chosen hashing algorithm.

// Generate a new key pair, then sign the data with it:
using (var publicPrivate = new RSACryptoServiceProvider())
{
  signature = publicPrivate.SignData (data, hasher);
  publicKey = publicPrivate.ExportCspBlob (false);    // get public key
}

// Create a fresh RSA using just the public key, then test the signature.
using (var publicOnly = new RSACryptoServiceProvider())
{
  publicOnly.ImportCspBlob (publicKey);
  Console.Write (publicOnly.VerifyData (data, hasher, signature)); // True

  // Let's now tamper with the data and recheck the signature:
  data[0] = 0;
  Console.Write (publicOnly.VerifyData (data, hasher, signature)); // False

  // The following throws an exception as we're lacking a private key:
  signature = publicOnly.SignData (data, hasher);
}
```

Signing works by first hashing the data and then applying the asymmetric algorithm to the resultant hash. Because hashes are of a small fixed size, large documents can be signed relatively quickly (public key encryption is much more CPU-intensive than hashing). If you want, you can do the hashing yourself and then call SignHash instead of SignData:

```
using (var rsa = new RSACryptoServiceProvider())
{
  byte[] hash = SHA1.Create().ComputeHash (data);
  signature = rsa.SignHash (hash, CryptoConfig.MapNameToOID ("SHA1"));
  ...
}
```

SignHash still needs to know what hash algorithm you used; CryptoConfig.Map NameToOID provides this information in the correct format from a friendly name such as "SHA1".

RSACryptoServiceProvider produces signatures whose size matches that of the key. Currently, no mainstream algorithm produces secure signatures significantly smaller than 128 bytes (suitable for product activation codes, for instance).

For signing to be effective, the recipient must know, and trust, the sender's public key. This can happen via prior communication, preconfiguration, or a site certificate. A site certificate is an electronic record of the originator's public key and name—itself signed by an independent trusted authority. The namespace `System.Security.Cryptography.X509Certif icates` defines the types for working with certificates.

21

Advanced Threading

We started Chapter 14 with the basics of threading as a precursor to tasks and asynchrony. Specifically, we showed how to start and configure a thread, and covered essential concepts such as thread pooling, blocking, spinning, and synchronization contexts. We also introduced locking and thread safety, and demonstrated the simplest signaling construct, ManualResetEvent.

This chapter picks up where Chapter 14 left off on the topic of threading. In the first three sections, we flesh out synchronization, locking, and thread safety in greater detail. We then cover:

- Nonexclusive locking (Semaphore and reader/writer locks)
- All signaling constructs (AutoResetEvent, ManualResetEvent, Countdown Event, and Barrier)
- Lazy initialization (Lazy<T> and LazyInitializer)
- Thread-local storage (ThreadStaticAttribute, ThreadLocal<T>, and GetData/ SetData)
- Timers

Threading is such a vast topic that we've put additional material online to complete the picture. Visit *http://albahari.com/threading* for a discussion on the following, more arcane, topics:

- Monitor.Wait and Monitor.Pulse for specialized signaling scenarios
- Nonblocking synchronization techniques for micro-optimization (Interlocked, memory barriers, volatile)
- SpinLock and SpinWait for high-concurrency scenarios

Synchronization Overview

Synchronization is the act of coordinating concurrent actions for a predictable outcome. Synchronization is particularly important when multiple threads access the same data; it's surprisingly easy to run aground in this area.

The simplest and most useful synchronization tools are arguably the continuations and task combinators described in Chapter 14. By formulating concurrent programs into asynchronous operations strung together with continuations and combinators, you lessen the need for locking and signaling. However, there are still times when the lower-level constructs come into play.

The synchronization constructs can be divided into three categories:

Exclusive locking
> Exclusive locking constructs allow just one thread to perform some activity or execute a section of code at a time. Their primary purpose is to let threads access shared writing state without interfering with one another. The exclusive locking constructs are lock, Mutex, and SpinLock.

Nonexclusive locking
> Nonexclusive locking lets you *limit* concurrency. The nonexclusive locking constructs are Semaphore(Slim) and ReaderWriterLock(Slim).

Signaling
> These allow a thread to block until receiving one or more notifications from other thread(s). The signaling constructs include ManualResetEvent(Slim), AutoResetEvent, CountdownEvent, and Barrier. The former three are referred to as *event wait handles*.

It's also possible (and tricky) to perform certain concurrent operations on shared state without locking through the use of *nonblocking synchronization constructs*. These are Thread.MemoryBarrier, Thread.VolatileRead, Thread.VolatileWrite, the volatile keyword, and the Interlocked class. We cover this topic online (*http://albahari.com/threading*), along with Monitor's Wait/Pulse methods, which you can use to write custom signaling logic.

Exclusive Locking

There are three exclusive locking constructs: the lock statement, Mutex, and SpinLock. The lock construct is the most convenient and widely used, whereas the other two target niche scenarios:

- Mutex lets you span multiple processes (computer-wide locks).
- SpinLock implements a micro-optimization that can lessen context switches in high-concurrency scenarios (see *http://albahari.com/threading*).

The lock Statement

To illustrate the need for locking, consider the following class:

```
class ThreadUnsafe
{
  static int _val1 = 1, _val2 = 1;

  static void Go()
  {
    if (_val2 != 0) Console.WriteLine (_val1 / _val2);
    _val2 = 0;
  }
}
```

This class is not thread-safe: if Go were called by two threads simultaneously, it would be possible to get a division-by-zero error because _val2 could be set to zero in one thread right as the other thread was in between executing the if statement and Console.WriteLine. Here's how lock fixes the problem:

```
class ThreadSafe
{
  static readonly object _locker = new object();
  static int _val1 = 1, _val2 = 1;

  static void Go()
  {
    lock (_locker)
    {
      if (_val2 != 0) Console.WriteLine (_val1 / _val2);
      _val2 = 0;
    }
  }
}
```

Only one thread can lock the synchronizing object (in this case, _locker) at a time, and any contending threads are blocked until the lock is released. If more than one thread contends the lock, they are queued on a "ready queue" and granted the lock on a first-come, first-served basis.[1] Exclusive locks are sometimes said to enforce *serialized* access to whatever's protected by the lock because one thread's access cannot overlap with that of another. In this case, we're protecting the logic inside the Go method as well as the fields _val1 and _val2.

Monitor.Enter and Monitor.Exit

C#'s lock statement is in fact a syntactic shortcut for a call to the methods Monitor.Enter and Monitor.Exit, with a try/finally block. Here's (a simplified version of) what's actually happening within the Go method of the preceding example:

---

[1] Nuances in the behavior of Windows and the CLR mean that the fairness of the queue can sometimes be violated.

```
Monitor.Enter (_locker);
try
{
  if (_val2 != 0) Console.WriteLine (_val1 / _val2);
  _val2 = 0;
}
finally { Monitor.Exit (_locker); }
```

Calling `Monitor.Exit` without first calling `Monitor.Enter` on the same object throws an exception.

The lockTaken overloads

The code that we just demonstrated has a subtle vulnerability. Consider the (unlikely) event of an exception being thrown between the call to `Monitor.Enter` and the `try` block (due, perhaps, to an `OutOfMemoryException` or, in .NET Framework, if the thread is aborted). In such a scenario, the lock might or might not be taken. If the lock *is* taken, it won't be released—because we'll never enter the `try`/`finally` block. This will result in a leaked lock. To avoid this danger, `Monitor.Enter` defines the following overload:

```
public static void Enter (object obj, ref bool lockTaken);
```

`lockTaken` is false after this method if (and only if) the `Enter` method throws an exception and the lock was not taken.

Here's the more robust pattern of use (which is exactly how C# translates a `lock` statement):

```
bool lockTaken = false;
try
{
  Monitor.Enter (_locker, ref lockTaken);
  // Do your stuff...
}
finally { if (lockTaken) Monitor.Exit (_locker); }
```

TryEnter

`Monitor` also provides a `TryEnter` method that allows a timeout to be specified, either in milliseconds or as a `TimeSpan`. The method then returns `true` if a lock was obtained, or `false` if no lock was obtained because the method timed out. `TryEnter` can also be called with no argument, which "tests" the lock, timing out immediately if the lock can't be obtained immediately. As with the `Enter` method, `TryEnter` is overloaded to accept a `lockTaken` argument.

Choosing the Synchronization Object

You can use any object visible to each of the partaking threads as a synchronizing object, subject to one hard rule: it must be a reference type. The synchronizing object is typically private (because this helps to encapsulate the locking logic) and

---

is typically an instance or static field. The synchronizing object can double as the object it's protecting, as the _list field does in the following example:

```
class ThreadSafe
{
  List <string> _list = new List <string>();

  void Test()
  {
    lock (_list)
    {
      _list.Add ("Item 1");
      ...
```

A field dedicated for the purpose of locking (such as _locker, in the example prior) allows precise control over the scope and granularity of the lock. You can also use the containing object (this) as a synchronization object:

```
lock (this) { ... }
```

Or even its type:

```
lock (typeof (Widget)) { ... }    // For protecting access to statics
```

The disadvantage of locking in this way is that you're not encapsulating the locking logic, so it becomes more difficult to prevent deadlocking and excessive blocking.

You can also lock on local variables captured by lambda expressions or anonymous methods.

Locking doesn't restrict access to the synchronizing object itself in any way. In other words, x.ToString() will not block because another thread has called lock(x); both threads must call lock(x) in order for blocking to occur.

When to Lock

As a basic rule, you need to lock around accessing *any writable shared field*. Even in the simplest case—an assignment operation on a single field—you must consider synchronization. In the following class, neither the Increment nor the Assign method is thread-safe:

```
class ThreadUnsafe
{
  static int _x;
  static void Increment() { _x++; }
  static void Assign()    { _x = 123; }
}
```

Here are thread-safe versions of Increment and Assign:

```
static readonly object _locker = new object();
static int _x;
```

```
static void Increment() { lock (_locker) _x++; }
static void Assign()    { lock (_locker) _x = 123; }
```

Without locks, two problems can arise:

- Operations such as incrementing a variable (or even reading/writing a variable, under certain conditions) are not atomic.

- The compiler, CLR, and processor are entitled to reorder instructions and cache variables in CPU registers to improve performance—as long as such optimizations don't change the behavior of a *single*-threaded program (or a multithreaded program that uses locks).

Locking mitigates the second problem because it creates a *memory barrier* before and after the lock. A memory barrier is a "fence" through which the effects of reordering and caching cannot penetrate.

 This applies not just to locks but to all synchronization constructs. So, if your use of a *signaling* construct, for instance, ensures that just one thread reads/writes a variable at a time, you don't need to lock. Hence, the following code is thread-safe without locking around x:

```
var signal = new ManualResetEvent (false);
int x = 0;
new Thread (() => { x++; signal.Set(); }).Start();
signal.WaitOne();
Console.WriteLine (x);    // 1 (always)
```

In "Nonblocking Synchronization" (*http://albahari.com/threading*), we explain how this need arises and how the memory barriers and the Interlocked class can provide alternatives to locking in these situations.

Locking and Atomicity

If a group of variables are always read and written within the same lock, you can say that the variables are read and written *atomically*. Let's suppose that fields x and y are always read and assigned within a lock on object locker:

```
lock (locker) { if (x != 0) y /= x; }
```

We can say that x and y are accessed atomically because the code block cannot be divided or preempted by the actions of another thread in such a way that it will change x or y and *invalidate its outcome*. You'll never get a division-by-zero error, provided that x and y are always accessed within this same exclusive lock.

The atomicity provided by a lock is violated if an exception is thrown within a lock block (whether or not multithreading is involved). For example, consider the following:

```
decimal _savingsBalance, _checkBalance;

void Transfer (decimal amount)
{
  lock (_locker)
  {
    _savingsBalance += amount;
    _checkBalance -= amount + GetBankFee();
  }
}
```

If an exception were thrown by GetBankFee(), the bank would lose money. In this case, we could avoid the problem by calling GetBankFee earlier. A solution for more complex cases is to implement "rollback" logic within a catch or finally block.

Instruction atomicity is a different, albeit analogous, concept: an instruction is atomic if it executes indivisibly on the underlying processor.

Nested Locking

A thread can repeatedly lock the same object in a nested (*reentrant*) fashion:

```
lock (locker)
  lock (locker)
    lock (locker)
    {
        // Do something...
    }
```

Alternatively:

```
Monitor.Enter (locker); Monitor.Enter (locker);  Monitor.Enter (locker);
// Do something...
Monitor.Exit (locker);  Monitor.Exit (locker);    Monitor.Exit (locker);
```

In these scenarios, the object is unlocked only when the outermost lock statement has exited—or a matching number of Monitor.Exit statements have executed.

Nested locking is useful when one method calls another from within a lock:

```
object locker = new object();

lock (locker)
{
  AnotherMethod();
  // We still have the lock - because locks are reentrant.
}

void AnotherMethod()
{
  lock (locker) { Console.WriteLine ("Another method"); }
}
```

A thread can block on only the first (outermost) lock.

Deadlocks

A deadlock happens when two threads each wait for a resource held by the other, so neither can proceed. The easiest way to illustrate this is with two locks:

```
object locker1 = new object();
object locker2 = new object();

new Thread (() => {
                    lock (locker1)
                    {
                      Thread.Sleep (1000);
                      lock (locker2);        // Deadlock
                    }
                  }).Start();
lock (locker2)
{
  Thread.Sleep (1000);
  lock (locker1);                            // Deadlock
}
```

You can create more elaborate deadlocking chains with three or more threads.

 The CLR, in a standard hosting environment, is not like SQL Server and does not automatically detect and resolve deadlocks by terminating one of the offenders. A threading deadlock causes participating threads to block indefinitely, unless you've specified a locking timeout. (Under the SQL CLR integration host, however, deadlocks *are* automatically detected, and a [catchable] exception is thrown on one of the threads.)

Deadlocking is one of the most difficult problems in multithreading—especially when there are many interrelated objects. Fundamentally, the hard problem is that you can't be sure what locks your *caller* has taken out.

So, you might lock private field a within your class x, unaware that your caller (or caller's caller) has already locked field b within class y. Meanwhile, another thread is doing the reverse—creating a deadlock. Ironically, the problem is exacerbated by (good) object-oriented design patterns, because such patterns create call chains that are not determined until runtime.

The popular advice "lock objects in a consistent order to prevent deadlocks," although helpful in our initial example, is difficult to apply to the scenario just described. A better strategy is to be wary of locking around calls to methods in objects that might have references back to your own object. Also, consider whether you really need to lock around calls to methods in other classes (often you do—as you'll see in "Locking and Thread Safety" on page 874—but sometimes there are other options). Relying more on higher-level synchronization options such as task continuations/combinators, data parallelism and immutable types (later in this chapter) can lessen the need for locking.

 Here is an alternative way to perceive the problem: when you call out to other code while holding a lock, the encapsulation of that lock subtly *leaks*. This is not a fault in the CLR; it's a fundamental limitation of locking in general. The problems of locking are being addressed in various research projects, including *Software Transactional Memory*.

Another deadlocking scenario arises when calling `Dispatcher.Invoke` (in a WPF application) or `Control.Invoke` (in a Windows Forms application) while in possession of a lock. If the user interface happens to be running another method that's waiting on the same lock, a deadlock will happen right there. You often can fix this simply by calling `BeginInvoke` instead of `Invoke` (or relying on asynchronous functions that do this implicitly when a synchronization context is present). Alternatively, you can release your lock before calling `Invoke`, although this won't work if your *caller* took out the lock.

Performance

Locking is fast: you can expect to acquire and release a lock in less than 20 nanoseconds on a 2020-era computer if the lock is uncontended. If it is contended, the consequential context switch moves the overhead closer to the microsecond region, although it can be longer before the thread is actually rescheduled.

Mutex

A `Mutex` is like a C# `lock`, but it can work across multiple processes. In other words, `Mutex` can be *computer-wide* as well as *application-wide*. Acquiring and releasing an uncontended `Mutex` takes around half a microsecond—more than 20 times slower than a `lock`.

With a `Mutex` class, you call the `WaitOne` method to lock and `ReleaseMutex` to unlock. Just as with the `lock` statement, a `Mutex` can be released only from the same thread that obtained it.

 If you forget to call `ReleaseMutex` and simply call `Close` or `Dispose`, an `AbandonedMutexException` will be thrown upon anyone else waiting upon that mutex.

A common use for a cross-process `Mutex` is to ensure that only one instance of a program can run at a time. Here's how it's done:

```
// Naming a Mutex makes it available computer-wide. Use a name that's
// unique to your company and application (e.g., include your URL).

using var mutex = new Mutex (true, @"Global\oreilly.com OneAtATimeDemo");
// Wait a few seconds if contended, in case another instance
// of the program is still in the process of shutting down.
```

```
if (!mutex.WaitOne (TimeSpan.FromSeconds (3), false))
{
  Console.WriteLine ("Another instance of the app is running. Bye!");
  return;
}
try { RunProgram(); }
finally { mutex.ReleaseMutex (); }

void RunProgram()
{
  Console.WriteLine ("Running. Press Enter to exit");
  Console.ReadLine();
}
```

If you're running under Terminal Services or in separate Unix consoles, a computer-wide Mutex is ordinarily visible only to applications in the same session. To make it visible to all terminal server sessions, prefix its name with *Global*, as shown in the example.

Locking and Thread Safety

A program or method is thread-safe if it can work correctly in any multithreading scenario. Thread safety is achieved primarily with locking and by reducing the possibilities for thread interaction.

General-purpose types are rarely thread-safe in their entirety, for the following reasons:

- The development burden in full thread safety can be significant, particularly if a type has many fields (each field is a potential for interaction in an arbitrarily multithreaded context).

- Thread safety can entail a performance cost (payable, in part, whether or not the type is actually used by multiple threads).

- A thread-safe type does not necessarily make the program using it thread-safe, and often the work involved in the latter makes the former redundant.

Thread safety is thus usually implemented just where it needs to be in order to handle a specific multithreading scenario.

There are, however, a few ways to "cheat" and have large and complex classes run safely in a multithreaded environment. One is to sacrifice granularity by wrapping large sections of code—even access to an entire object—within a single exclusive lock, enforcing serialized access at a high level. This tactic is, in fact, essential if you want to use thread-unsafe third-party code (or most .NET types, for that matter) in a multithreaded context. The trick is simply to use the same exclusive lock to protect access to all properties, methods, and fields on the thread-unsafe object. The solution works well if the object's methods all execute quickly (otherwise, there will be a lot of blocking).

Primitive types aside, few .NET types, when instantiated, are thread-safe for anything more than concurrent read-only access. The onus is on the developer to superimpose thread safety, typically with exclusive locks. (The collections in System.Collections.Concurrent that we cover in Chapter 22 are an exception.)

Another way to cheat is to minimize thread interaction by minimizing shared data. This is an excellent approach and is used implicitly in "stateless" middle-tier application and web-page servers. Because multiple client requests can arrive simultaneously, the server methods they call must be thread-safe. A stateless design (popular for reasons of scalability) intrinsically limits the possibility of interaction because classes do not save data between requests. Thread interaction is then limited just to the static fields that you might choose to create, for such purposes as caching commonly used data in memory and in providing infrastructure services such as authentication and auditing.

Yet another solution (in rich-client applications) is to run code that accesses shared state on the UI thread. As we saw in Chapter 14, asynchronous functions make this easy.

Thread Safety and .NET Types

You can use locking to convert thread-unsafe code into thread-safe code. A good application of this is .NET: nearly all of its nonprimitive types are not thread-safe (for anything more than read-only access) when instantiated, and yet you can use them in multithreaded code if all access to any given object is protected via a lock. Here's an example in which two threads simultaneously add an item to the same List collection and then enumerate the list:

```
class ThreadSafe
{
  static List <string> _list = new List <string>();

  static void Main()
  {
    new Thread (AddItem).Start();
    new Thread (AddItem).Start();
  }

  static void AddItem()
  {
    lock (_list) _list.Add ("Item " + _list.Count);

    string[] items;
    lock (_list) items = _list.ToArray();
    foreach (string s in items) Console.WriteLine (s);
  }
}
```

In this case, we're locking on the _list object itself. If we had two interrelated lists, we would need to choose a common object upon which to lock (we could nominate one of the lists, or better: use an independent field).

Enumerating .NET collections is also thread-unsafe in the sense that an exception is thrown if the list is modified during enumeration. Rather than locking for the duration of enumeration, in this example, we first copy the items to an array. This avoids holding the lock excessively if what we're doing during enumeration is potentially time-consuming. (Another solution is to use a reader/writer lock; see "Reader/Writer Locks" on page 882.)

Locking around thread-safe objects

Sometimes, you also need to lock around accessing thread-safe objects. To illustrate, imagine that .NET's List class was, indeed, thread-safe, and we want to add an item to a list:

```
if (!_list.Contains (newItem)) _list.Add (newItem);
```

Regardless of whether the list was thread-safe, this statement is certainly not! The whole if statement would need to be wrapped in a lock to prevent preemption in between testing for containership and adding the new item. This same lock would then need to be used everywhere we modified that list. For instance, the following statement would also need to be wrapped in the identical lock to ensure that it did not preempt the former statement:

```
_list.Clear();
```

In other words, we would need to lock exactly as with our thread-unsafe collection classes (making the List class's hypothetical thread safety redundant).

 Locking around accessing a collection can cause excessive blocking in highly concurrent environments. To this end, .NET provides a thread-safe queue, stack, and dictionary, which we discuss in Chapter 22.

Static members

Wrapping access to an object around a custom lock works only if all concurrent threads are aware of—and use—the lock. This might not be the case if the object is widely scoped. The worst case is with static members in a public type. For instance, imagine if the static property on the DateTime struct, DateTime.Now, was not thread-safe and that two concurrent calls could result in garbled output or an exception. The only way to remedy this with external locking might be to lock the type itself—lock(typeof(DateTime))—before calling DateTime.Now. This would work only if all programmers agreed to do this (which is unlikely). Furthermore, locking a type creates problems of its own.

For this reason, static members on the DateTime struct have been carefully programmed to be thread-safe. This is a common pattern throughout .NET: *static members are thread-safe; instance members are not*. Following this pattern also makes sense when writing types for public consumption, so as not to create impossible thread-safety conundrums. In other words, by making static methods thread-safe, you're programming so as not to *preclude* thread safety for consumers of that type.

 Thread safety in static methods is something that you must explicitly code: it doesn't happen automatically by virtue of the method being static!

Read-only thread safety

Making types thread-safe for concurrent read-only access (where possible) is advantageous because it means that consumers can avoid excessive locking. Many .NET types follow this principle: collections, for instance, are thread-safe for concurrent readers.

Following this principle yourself is simple: if you document a type as being thread-safe for concurrent read-only access, don't write to fields within methods that a consumer would expect to be read-only (or lock around doing so). For instance, in implementing a ToArray() method in a collection, you might begin by compacting the collection's internal structure. However, this would make it thread-unsafe for consumers that expected this to be read-only.

Read-only thread safety is one of the reasons that enumerators are separate from "enumerables": two threads can simultaneously enumerate over a collection because each gets a separate enumerator object.

 In the absence of documentation, it pays to be cautious in assuming whether a method is read-only in nature. A good example is the Random class: when you call Random.Next(), its internal implementation requires that it update private seed values. Therefore, you must either lock around using the Ran dom class or maintain a separate instance per thread.

Thread Safety in Application Servers

Application servers need to be multithreaded to handle simultaneous client requests. ASP.NET Core and Web API applications are implicitly multithreaded. This means that when writing code on the server side, you must consider thread safety if there's any possibility of interaction among the threads processing client requests. Fortunately, such a possibility is rare; a typical server class is either stateless (no fields) or has an activation model that creates a separate object instance for each client or each request. Interaction usually arises only through static fields, sometimes used for caching in memory parts of a database to improve performance.

For example, suppose that you have a RetrieveUser method that queries a database:

```
// User is a custom class with fields for user data
internal User RetrieveUser (int id) { ... }
```

If this method were called frequently, you could improve performance by caching the results in a static `Dictionary`. Here's a conceptually simple solution that takes thread safety into account:

```
static class UserCache
{
  static Dictionary <int, User> _users = new Dictionary <int, User>();

  internal static User GetUser (int id)
  {
    User u = null;

    lock (_users)
      if (_users.TryGetValue (id, out u))
        return u;

    u = RetrieveUser (id);          // Method to retrieve from database;
    lock (_users) _users [id] = u;
    return u;
  }
}
```

We must, at a minimum, lock around reading and updating the dictionary to ensure thread safety. In this example, we choose a practical compromise between simplicity and performance in locking. Our design creates a small potential for inefficiency: if two threads simultaneously called this method with the same previously unretrieved `id`, the `RetrieveUser` method would be called twice—and the dictionary would be updated unnecessarily. Locking once across the whole method would prevent this, but it would create a worse inefficiency: the entire cache would be locked up for the duration of calling `RetrieveUser`, during which time other threads would be blocked in retrieving *any* user.

For an ideal solution, we need to use the strategy we described in "Completing synchronously" on page 655. Instead of caching `User`, we cache `Task<User>`, which the caller then awaits:

```
static class UserCache
{
  static Dictionary <int, Task<User>> _userTasks =
    new Dictionary <int, Task<User>>();

  internal static Task<User> GetUserAsync (int id)
  {
    lock (_userTasks)
      if (_userTasks.TryGetValue (id, out var userTask))
        return userTask;
      else
        return _userTasks [id] = Task.Run (() => RetrieveUser (id));
  }
}
```

Notice that we now have a single lock that covers the entire method's logic. We can do this without hurting concurrency because all we're doing inside the lock is accessing the dictionary and (potentially) *initiating* an asynchronous operation (by calling `Task.Run`). Should two threads call this method at the same time with the same ID, they'll both end up awaiting the *same task*, which is exactly the outcome we want.

Immutable Objects

An immutable object is one whose state cannot be altered—externally or internally. The fields in an immutable object are typically declared read-only and are fully initialized during construction.

Immutability is a hallmark of functional programming—where instead of *mutating* an object, you create a new object with different properties. LINQ follows this paradigm. Immutability is also valuable in multithreading in that it avoids the problem of shared writable state—by eliminating (or minimizing) the writable.

One pattern is to use immutable objects to encapsulate a group of related fields, to minimize lock durations. To take a very simple example, suppose that we had two fields, as follows:

```
int _percentComplete;
string _statusMessage;
```

Now let's assume that we want to read and write them atomically. Rather than locking around these fields, we could define the following immutable class:

```
class ProgressStatus      // Represents progress of some activity
{
  public readonly int PercentComplete;
  public readonly string StatusMessage;

  // This class might have many more fields...

  public ProgressStatus (int percentComplete, string statusMessage)
  {
    PercentComplete = percentComplete;
    StatusMessage = statusMessage;
  }
}
```

Then we could define a single field of that type, along with a locking object:

```
readonly object _statusLocker = new object();
ProgressStatus _status;
```

We can now read and write values of that type without holding a lock for more than a single assignment:

```
var status = new ProgressStatus (50, "Working on it");
// Imagine we were assigning many more fields...
// ...
lock (_statusLocker) _status = status;     // Very brief lock
```

To read the object, we first obtain a copy of the object reference (within a lock). Then, we can read its values without needing to hold onto the lock:

```
ProgressStatus status;
lock (_statusLocker) status = _status;    // Again, a brief lock
int pc = status.PercentComplete;
string msg = status.StatusMessage;
...
```

Nonexclusive Locking

The nonexclusive locking constructs serve to *limit* concurrency. In this section, we cover semaphores and read/writer locks, and also illustrate how the SemaphoreSlim class can limit concurrency with asynchronous operations.

Semaphore

A semaphore is like a nightclub: it has a certain capacity, enforced by a bouncer. When the club is full, no more people can enter, and a queue builds up outside. Then, for each person who leaves, one person enters. The constructor requires a minimum of two arguments: the number of places currently available in the nightclub and the club's total capacity.

A semaphore with a capacity of one is similar to a Mutex or lock, except that the semaphore has no "owner"—it's *thread agnostic*. Any thread can call Release on a Semaphore, whereas with Mutex and lock, only the thread that obtained the lock can release it.

There are two functionally similar versions of this class: Semaphore and SemaphoreSlim. The latter has been optimized to meet the low-latency demands of parallel programming. It's also useful in traditional multithreading because it lets you specify a cancellation token when waiting (see "Cancellation" on page 659), and it exposes a WaitAsync method for asynchronous programming. You cannot use it, however, for interprocess signaling.

Semaphore incurs about one microsecond in calling WaitOne and Release; SemaphoreSlim incurs about one-tenth of that.

Semaphores can be useful in limiting concurrency—preventing too many threads from executing a particular piece of code at once. In the following example, five threads try to enter a nightclub that allows only three threads in at once:

```
class TheClub       // No door lists!
{
  static SemaphoreSlim _sem = new SemaphoreSlim (3);     // Capacity of 3

  static void Main()
  {
    for (int i = 1; i <= 5; i++) new Thread (Enter).Start (i);
  }

  static void Enter (object id)
  {
```

```
    Console.WriteLine (id + " wants to enter");
    _sem.Wait();
    Console.WriteLine (id + " is in!");          // Only three threads
    Thread.Sleep (1000 * (int) id);              // can be here at
    Console.WriteLine (id + " is leaving");      // a time.
    _sem.Release();
  }
}

1 wants to enter
1 is in!
2 wants to enter
2 is in!
3 wants to enter
3 is in!
4 wants to enter
5 wants to enter
1 is leaving
4 is in!
2 is leaving
5 is in!
```

A Semaphore, if named, can span processes in the same way as a Mutex (named Semaphores are available only on Windows, whereas named Mutex also work on Unix platforms).

Asynchronous semaphores and locks

It is illegal to lock across an await statement:

```
lock (_locker)
{
  await Task.Delay (1000);    // Compilation error
  ...
}
```

Doing so would make no sense, because locks are held by a thread, which typically changes when returning from an await. Locking also *blocks*, and blocking for a potentially long period of time is exactly what you're *not* trying to achieve with asynchronous functions.

It's still sometimes desirable, however, to make asynchronous operations execute sequentially—or limit the parallelism such that not more than *n* operations execute at once. For example, consider a web browser: it needs to perform asynchronous downloads in parallel, but it might want to impose a limit such that a maximum of 10 downloads happen at a time. We can achieve this by using a SemaphoreSlim:

```
SemaphoreSlim _semaphore = new SemaphoreSlim (10);

async Task<byte[]> DownloadWithSemaphoreAsync (string uri)
{
    await _semaphore.WaitAsync();
    try { return await new WebClient().DownloadDataTaskAsync (uri); }
```

```
      finally { _semaphore.Release(); }
  }
```

Reducing the semaphore's initialCount to 1 reduces the maximum parallelism to 1, turning this into an asynchronous lock.

Writing an EnterAsync extension method

The following extension method simplifies the asynchronous use of SemaphoreSlim by using the Disposable class that we wrote in "Anonymous Disposal" on page 561:

```
public static async Task<IDisposable> EnterAsync (this SemaphoreSlim ss)
{
  await ss.WaitAsync().ConfigureAwait (false);
  return Disposable.Create (() => ss.Release());
}
```

With this method, we can rewrite our DownloadWithSemaphoreAsync method as follows:

```
async Task<byte[]> DownloadWithSemaphoreAsync (string uri)
{
  using (await _semaphore.EnterAsync())
    return await new WebClient().DownloadDataTaskAsync (uri);
}
```

Parallel.ForEachAsync

From .NET 6, another approach to limit asynchronous concurrency is to use the Parallel.ForEachAsync method. Assuming uris in an array of URIs that you wish to download, here's how to download them in parallel, while limiting the concurrency to a maximum of 10 parallel downloads:

```
await Parallel.ForEachAsync (uris,
  new ParallelOptions { MaxDegreeOfParallelism = 10 },
  async (uri, cancelToken) =>
  {
    var download = await new HttpClient().GetByteArrayAsync (uri);
    Console.WriteLine ($"Downloaded {download.Length} bytes");
  });
```

The other methods in the Parallel class are intended for (compute-bound) parallel programming scenarios, which we describe in Chapter 22.

Reader/Writer Locks

Quite often, instances of a type are thread-safe for concurrent read operations, but not for concurrent updates (nor for a concurrent read and update). This can also be true with resources such as a file. Although protecting instances of such types with a simple exclusive lock for all modes of access usually does the trick, it can unreasonably restrict concurrency if there are many readers and just occasional updates. An example of where this could occur is in a business application server, for which commonly used data is cached for fast retrieval in static fields. The

`ReaderWriterLockSlim` class is designed to provide maximum-availability locking in just this scenario.

> `ReaderWriterLockSlim` is a replacement for the older "fat" `ReaderWriterLock` class. The latter is similar in functionality, but it is several times slower and has an inherent design fault in its mechanism for handling lock upgrades.
>
> When compared to an ordinary `lock` (`Monitor.Enter/Exit`), `ReaderWriterLockSlim` is still twice as slow, though. The trade-off is less contention (when there's a lot of reading and minimal writing).

With both classes, there are two basic kinds of lock—a read lock and a write lock:

- A write lock is universally exclusive.
- A read lock is compatible with other read locks.

So, a thread holding a write lock blocks all other threads trying to obtain a read *or* write lock (and vice versa). But if no thread holds a write lock, any number of threads may concurrently obtain a read lock.

`ReaderWriterLockSlim` defines the following methods for obtaining and releasing read/write locks:

```
public void EnterReadLock();
public void ExitReadLock();
public void EnterWriteLock();
public void ExitWriteLock();
```

Additionally, there are "Try" versions of all `EnterXXX` methods that accept timeout arguments in the style of `Monitor.TryEnter` (timeouts can occur quite easily if the resource is heavily contended). `ReaderWriterLock` provides similar methods, named `AcquireXXX` and `ReleaseXXX`. These throw an `ApplicationException` if a timeout occurs, rather than returning `false`.

The following program demonstrates `ReaderWriterLockSlim`. Three threads continually enumerate a list, while two further threads append a random number to the list every 100 ms. A read lock protects the list readers, and a write lock protects the list writers:

```
class SlimDemo
{
  static ReaderWriterLockSlim _rw = new ReaderWriterLockSlim();
  static List<int> _items = new List<int>();
  static Random _rand = new Random();

  static void Main()
  {
    new Thread (Read).Start();
    new Thread (Read).Start();
    new Thread (Read).Start();
```

```
      new Thread (Write).Start ("A");
      new Thread (Write).Start ("B");
    }

    static void Read()
    {
      while (true)
      {
        _rw.EnterReadLock();
        foreach (int i in _items) Thread.Sleep (10);
        _rw.ExitReadLock();
      }
    }

    static void Write (object threadID)
    {
      while (true)
      {
        int newNumber = GetRandNum (100);
        _rw.EnterWriteLock();
        _items.Add (newNumber);
        _rw.ExitWriteLock();
        Console.WriteLine ("Thread " + threadID + " added " + newNumber);
        Thread.Sleep (100);
      }
    }

    static int GetRandNum (int max) { lock (_rand) return _rand.Next(max); }
  }
```

 In production code, you'd typically add try/finally blocks to ensure that locks were released if an exception were thrown.

Here's the result:

```
Thread B added 61
Thread A added 83
Thread B added 55
Thread A added 33
...
```

ReaderWriterLockSlim allows more concurrent Read activity than a simple lock. We can illustrate this by inserting the following line in the Write method, at the start of the while loop:

```
Console.WriteLine (_rw.CurrentReadCount + " concurrent readers");
```

This nearly always prints "3 concurrent readers" (the Read methods spend most of their time inside the foreach loops). As well as CurrentReadCount, ReaderWriter LockSlim provides the following properties for monitoring locks:

```
public bool IsReadLockHeld               { get; }
public bool IsUpgradeableReadLockHeld { get; }
public bool IsWriteLockHeld              { get; }

public int  WaitingReadCount      { get; }
public int  WaitingUpgradeCount   { get; }
public int  WaitingWriteCount     { get; }

public int  RecursiveReadCount    { get; }
public int  RecursiveUpgradeCount { get; }
public int  RecursiveWriteCount   { get; }
```

Upgradeable locks

Sometimes, it's useful to swap a read lock for a write lock in a single atomic operation. For instance, suppose that you want to add an item to a list only if the item wasn't already present. Ideally, you'd want to minimize the time spent holding the (exclusive) write lock, so you might proceed as follows:

1. Obtain a read lock.

2. Test whether the item is already present in the list; if so, release the lock and return.

3. Release the read lock.

4. Obtain a write lock.

5. Add the item.

The problem is that another thread could sneak in and modify the list (e.g., adding the same item) between Steps 3 and 4. ReaderWriterLockSlim addresses this through a third kind of lock called an *upgradeable lock*. An upgradeable lock is like a read lock except that it can later be promoted to a write lock in an atomic operation. Here's how you use it:

1. Call EnterUpgradeableReadLock.

2. Perform read-based activities (e.g., test whether the item is already present in the list).

3. Call EnterWriteLock (this converts the upgradeable lock to a write lock).

4. Perform write-based activities (e.g., add the item to the list).

5. Call ExitWriteLock (this converts the write lock back to an upgradeable lock).

6. Perform any other read-based activities.

7. Call ExitUpgradeableReadLock.

From the caller's perspective, it's rather like nested or recursive locking. Functionally, though, in Step 3, ReaderWriterLockSlim releases your read lock and obtains a fresh write lock, atomically.

There's another important difference between upgradeable locks and read locks. Although an upgradeable lock can coexist with any number of *read* locks, only one upgradeable lock can itself be taken out at a time. This prevents conversion deadlocks by *serializing* competing conversions—just as update locks do in SQL Server:

SQL Server	ReaderWriterLockSlim
Share lock	Read lock
Exclusive lock	Write lock
Update lock	Upgradeable lock

We can demonstrate an upgradeable lock by changing the Write method in the preceding example such that it adds a number to the list only if it's not already present:

```
while (true)
{
  int newNumber = GetRandNum (100);
  _rw.EnterUpgradeableReadLock();
  if (!_items.Contains (newNumber))
  {
    _rw.EnterWriteLock();
    _items.Add (newNumber);
    _rw.ExitWriteLock();
    Console.WriteLine ("Thread " + threadID + " added " + newNumber);
  }
  _rw.ExitUpgradeableReadLock();
  Thread.Sleep (100);
}
```

 ReaderWriterLock can also do lock conversions—but unreliably because it doesn't support the concept of upgradeable locks. This is why the designers of ReaderWriterLockSlim had to start afresh with a new class.

Lock recursion

Ordinarily, nested or recursive locking is prohibited with ReaderWriterLockSlim. Hence, the following throws an exception:

```
var rw = new ReaderWriterLockSlim();
rw.EnterReadLock();
rw.EnterReadLock();
rw.ExitReadLock();
rw.ExitReadLock();
```

It runs without error, however, if you construct ReaderWriterLockSlim as follows:

```
var rw = new ReaderWriterLockSlim (LockRecursionPolicy.SupportsRecursion);
```

This ensures that recursive locking can happen only if you plan for it. Recursive locking can create undesired complexity because it's possible to acquire more than one kind of lock:

```
rw.EnterWriteLock();
rw.EnterReadLock();
Console.WriteLine (rw.IsReadLockHeld);    // True
Console.WriteLine (rw.IsWriteLockHeld);   // True
rw.ExitReadLock();
rw.ExitWriteLock();
```

The basic rule is that after you've acquired a lock, subsequent recursive locks can be less, but not greater, on the following scale:

Read Lock→Upgradeable Lock→Write Lock

A request to promote an upgradeable lock to a write lock, however, is always legal.

Signaling with Event Wait Handles

The simplest kind of signaling constructs are called *event wait handles* (unrelated to C# events). Event wait handles come in three flavors: AutoResetEvent, Manual ResetEvent(Slim), and CountdownEvent. The former two are based on the common EventWaitHandle class from which they derive all their functionality.

AutoResetEvent

An AutoResetEvent is like a ticket turnstile: inserting a ticket lets exactly one person through. The "auto" in the class's name refers to the fact that an open turnstile automatically closes or "resets" after someone steps through. A thread waits, or blocks, at the turnstile by calling WaitOne (wait at this "one" turnstile until it opens), and a ticket is inserted by calling the Set method. If a number of threads call WaitOne, a queue[2] builds up behind the turnstile. A ticket can come from any thread; in other words, any (unblocked) thread with access to the AutoResetEvent object can call Set on it to release one blocked thread.

You can create an AutoResetEvent in two ways. The first is via its constructor:

```
var auto = new AutoResetEvent (false);
```

(Passing true into the constructor is equivalent to immediately calling Set upon it.) The second way to create an AutoResetEvent is as follows:

```
var auto = new EventWaitHandle (false, EventResetMode.AutoReset);
```

---

2 As with locks, the fairness of the queue can sometimes be violated due to nuances in the operating system.

In the following example, a thread is started whose job is simply to wait until signaled by another thread (see Figure 21-1):

```
class BasicWaitHandle
{
  static EventWaitHandle _waitHandle = new AutoResetEvent (false);

  static void Main()
  {
    new Thread (Waiter).Start();
    Thread.Sleep (1000);                  // Pause for a second...
    _waitHandle.Set();                    // Wake up the Waiter.
  }

  static void Waiter()
  {
    Console.WriteLine ("Waiting...");
    _waitHandle.WaitOne();                // Wait for notification
    Console.WriteLine ("Notified");
  }
}

// Output:
Waiting... (pause) Notified.
```

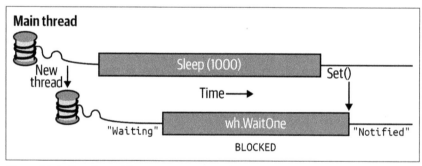

Figure 21-1. Signaling with an EventWaitHandle

If Set is called when no thread is waiting, the handle stays open for as long as it takes until some thread calls WaitOne. This behavior helps prevent a race between a thread heading for the turnstile and a thread inserting a ticket ("Oops, inserted the ticket a microsecond too soon; now you'll have to wait indefinitely!"). However, calling Set repeatedly on a turnstile at which no one is waiting doesn't allow an entire party through when they arrive: only the next single person is let through, and the extra tickets are "wasted."

Calling Reset on an AutoResetEvent closes the turnstile (should it be open) without waiting or blocking.

WaitOne accepts an optional timeout parameter, returning false if the wait ended because of a timeout rather than obtaining the signal.

Calling WaitOne with a timeout of 0 tests whether a wait handle is "open," without blocking the caller. Keep in mind, though, that doing this resets the AutoResetEvent if it's open.

Two-way signaling

Suppose that we want the main thread to signal a worker thread three times in a row. If the main thread simply calls Set on a wait handle several times in rapid succession, the second or third signal can become lost because the worker might take time to process each signal.

The solution is for the main thread to wait until the worker's ready before signaling it. We can do this by using another AutoResetEvent, as follows:

```
class TwoWaySignaling
{
  static EventWaitHandle _ready = new AutoResetEvent (false);
  static EventWaitHandle _go = new AutoResetEvent (false);
  static readonly object _locker = new object();
  static string _message;

  static void Main()
  {
    new Thread (Work).Start();

    _ready.WaitOne();                 // First wait until worker is ready
    lock (_locker) _message = "ooo";
    _go.Set();                        // Tell worker to go

    _ready.WaitOne();
    lock (_locker) _message = "ahhh"; // Give the worker another message
    _go.Set();

    _ready.WaitOne();
```

```
      lock (_locker) _message = null;    // Signal the worker to exit
      _go.Set();
    }

    static void Work()
    {
      while (true)
      {
        _ready.Set();                     // Indicate that we're ready
        _go.WaitOne();                    // Wait to be kicked off...
        lock (_locker)
        {
          if (_message == null) return;   // Gracefully exit
          Console.WriteLine (_message);
        }
      }
    }
  }
}

// Output:
ooo
ahhh
```

Figure 21-2 shows this process.

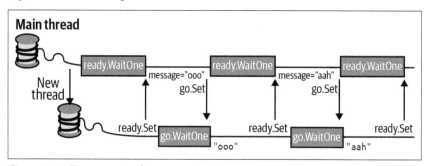

Figure 21-2. Two-way signaling

Here, we're using a null message to indicate that the worker should end. With threads that run indefinitely, it's important to have an exit strategy!

ManualResetEvent

As we described in Chapter 14, a ManualResetEvent functions like a simple gate. Calling Set opens the gate, allowing *any* number of threads calling WaitOne to be let through. Calling Reset closes the gate. Threads that call WaitOne on a closed gate will block; when the gate is next opened, they will be released all at once. Apart from these differences, a ManualResetEvent functions like an AutoResetEvent.

As with AutoResetEvent, you can construct a ManualResetEvent in two ways:

```
var manual1 = new ManualResetEvent (false);
var manual2 = new EventWaitHandle (false, EventResetMode.ManualReset);
```

There's another version of `ManualResetEvent` called `ManualRe` `setEventSlim`. The latter is optimized for short waiting times —with the ability to opt into spinning for a set number of iterations. It also has a more efficient managed implementation and allows a `Wait` to be canceled via a `CancellationToken`. `ManualResetEventSlim` doesn't subclass `WaitHandle`; however, it exposes a `WaitHandle` property that returns a `WaitHandle`-based object when called (with the performance profile of a traditional wait handle).

Signaling Constructs and Performance

A `ManualResetEvent` is useful in allowing one thread to unblock many other threads. The reverse scenario is covered by `CountdownEvent`.

CountdownEvent

`CountdownEvent` lets you wait on more than one thread. The class has an efficient, fully managed implementation. To use the class, instantiate it with the number of threads, or "counts," that you want to wait on:

```
var countdown = new CountdownEvent (3);  // Initialize with "count" of 3.
```

Calling `Signal` decrements the "count"; calling `Wait` blocks until the count goes down to zero:

```
new Thread (SaySomething).Start ("I am thread 1");
new Thread (SaySomething).Start ("I am thread 2");
new Thread (SaySomething).Start ("I am thread 3");

countdown.Wait();   // Blocks until Signal has been called 3 times
Console.WriteLine ("All threads have finished speaking!");

void SaySomething (object thing)
{
  Thread.Sleep (1000);
  Console.WriteLine (thing);
  countdown.Signal();
}
```

You can sometimes more easily solve problems for which CountdownEvent is effective by using the *structured parallelism* constructs that we describe in Chapter 22 (PLINQ and the Parallel class).

You can reincrement a CountdownEvent's count by calling AddCount. However, if it has already reached zero, this throws an exception: you can't "unsignal" a Count downEvent by calling AddCount. To prevent the possibility of an exception being thrown, you can instead call TryAddCount, which returns false if the countdown is zero.

To unsignal a countdown event, call Reset: this both unsignals the construct and resets its count to the original value.

Like ManualResetEventSlim, CountdownEvent exposes a WaitHandle property for scenarios in which some other class or method expects an object based on WaitHandle.

Creating a Cross-Process EventWaitHandle

EventWaitHandle's constructor allows a "named" EventWaitHandle to be created, capable of operating across multiple processes. The name is simply a string, and it can be any value that doesn't unintentionally conflict with someone else's! If the name is already in use on the computer, you get a reference to the same underlying EventWaitHandle; otherwise, the OS creates a new one. Here's an example:

```
EventWaitHandle wh = new EventWaitHandle (false, EventResetMode.AutoReset,
                              @"Global\MyCompany.MyApp.SomeName");
```

If two applications each ran this code, they would be able to signal each other: the wait handle would work across all threads in both processes.

Named event wait handles are available only on Windows.

Wait Handles and Continuations

Rather than waiting on a wait handle (and blocking your thread), you can attach a "continuation" to it by calling ThreadPool.RegisterWaitForSingleObject. This method accepts a delegate that is executed when a wait handle is signaled:

```
var starter = new ManualResetEvent (false);

RegisteredWaitHandle reg = ThreadPool.RegisterWaitForSingleObject
  (starter, Go, "Some Data", -1, true);

Thread.Sleep (5000);
Console.WriteLine ("Signaling worker...");
starter.Set();
Console.ReadLine();
reg.Unregister (starter);    // Clean up when we're done.

void Go (object data, bool timedOut)
```

```
{
  Console.WriteLine ("Started - " + data);
  // Perform task...
}

// Output:
(5 second delay)
Signaling worker...
Started - Some Data
```

When the wait handle is signaled (or a timeout elapses), the delegate runs on a pooled thread. You are then supposed to call `Unregister` to release the unmanaged handle to the callback.

In addition to the wait handle and delegate, `RegisterWaitForSingleObject` accepts a "black box" object that it passes to your delegate method (rather like `Parameteri zedThreadStart`) as well as a timeout in milliseconds (`-1` meaning no timeout) and a Boolean flag indicating whether the request is a one-off rather than recurring.

> You can reliably call `RegisterWaitForSingleObject` only once per wait handle. Calling this method again on the same wait handle causes an intermittent failure, whereby an unsignaled wait handle fires a callback as though it were signaled.
>
> This limitation makes (the nonslim) wait handles poorly suited to asynchronous programming.

WaitAny, WaitAll, and SignalAndWait

In addition to the `Set`, `WaitOne`, and `Reset` methods, there are static methods on the `WaitHandle` class to crack more complex synchronization nuts. The `WaitAny`, `WaitAll`, and `SignalAndWait` methods perform signaling and waiting operations on multiple handles. The wait handles can be of differing types (including `Mutex` and `Semaphore` given that these also derive from the abstract `WaitHandle` class). `ManualResetEventSlim` and `CountdownEvent` can also partake in these methods via their `WaitHandle` properties.

> `WaitAll` and `SignalAndWait` have a weird connection to the legacy COM architecture: these methods require that the caller be in a multithreaded apartment, the model least suitable for interoperability. The main thread of a WPF or Windows Forms application, for example, is unable to interact with the clipboard in this mode. We discuss alternatives shortly.

`WaitHandle.WaitAny` waits for any one of an array of wait handles; `Wait Handle.WaitAll` waits on all of the given handles, atomically. This means that if you wait on two `AutoResetEvents`:

- `WaitAny` will never end up "latching" both events.

- `WaitAll` will never end up "latching" only one event.

`SignalAndWait` calls `Set` on one `WaitHandle` and then calls `WaitOne` on another `WaitHandle`. After signaling the first handle, it will jump to the head of the queue in waiting on the second handle; this helps it succeed (although the operation is not truly atomic). You can think of this method as "swapping" one signal for another, and use it on a pair of `EventWaitHandle`s to set up two threads to rendezvous, or "meet," at the same point in time. Either `AutoResetEvent` or `ManualResetEvent` will do the trick. The first thread executes the following:

```
WaitHandle.SignalAndWait (wh1, wh2);
```

The second thread does the opposite:

```
WaitHandle.SignalAndWait (wh2, wh1);
```

Alternatives to WaitAll and SignalAndWait

`WaitAll` and `SignalAndWait` won't run in a single-threaded apartment. Fortunately, there are alternatives. In the case of `SignalAndWait`, it's rare that you need its queue-jumping semantics: in our rendezvous example, for instance, it would be valid simply to call `Set` on the first wait handle, and then `WaitOne` on the other, if wait handles were used solely for that rendezvous. In the following section, we explore yet another option for implementing a thread rendezvous.

In the case of `WaitAny` and `WaitAll`, if you don't need atomicity, you can use the code we wrote in the previous section to convert the wait handles to tasks and then use `Task.WhenAny` and `Task.WhenAll` (Chapter 14).

If you need atomicity, you can take the lowest-level approach to signaling and write the logic yourself with `Monitor`'s `Wait` and `Pulse` methods. We describe `Wait` and `Pulse` in detail in *http://albahari.com/threading*.

The Barrier Class

The `Barrier` class implements a *thread execution barrier*, allowing many threads to rendezvous at a point in time (not to be confused with `Thread.MemoryBarrier`). The class is very fast and efficient, and is built upon `Wait`, `Pulse`, and spinlocks.

To use this class:

1. Instantiate it, specifying how many threads should partake in the rendezvous (you can change this later by calling `AddParticipants`/`RemoveParticipants`).
2. Have each thread call `SignalAndWait` when it wants to rendezvous.

Instantiating `Barrier` with a value of 3 causes `SignalAndWait` to block until that method has been called three times. It then starts over: calling `SignalAndWait` again blocks until called another three times. This keeps each thread "in step" with every other thread.

In the following example, each of three threads writes the numbers 0 through 4 while keeping in step with the other threads:

```
var barrier = new Barrier (3);

new Thread (Speak).Start();
new Thread (Speak).Start();
new Thread (Speak).Start();

void Speak()
{
  for (int i = 0; i < 5; i++)
  {
    Console.Write (i + " ");
    barrier.SignalAndWait();
  }
}
```

```
OUTPUT:  0 0 0 1 1 1 2 2 2 3 3 3 4 4 4
```

A really useful feature of Barrier is that you can also specify a *post-phase action* when constructing it. This is a delegate that runs after SignalAndWait has been called *n* times, but *before* the threads are unblocked (as shown in the shaded area in Figure 21-3). In our example, if we instantiate our barrier as follows:

```
static Barrier _barrier = new Barrier (3, barrier => Console.WriteLine());
```

the output is this:

```
0 0 0
1 1 1
2 2 2
3 3 3
4 4 4
```

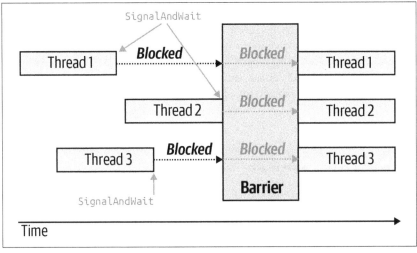

Figure 21-3. Barrier

A post-phase action can be useful for coalescing data from each of the worker threads. It doesn't need to worry about preemption, because all workers are blocked while it does its thing.

Lazy Initialization

A frequent problem in threading is how to lazily initialize a shared field in a thread-safe fashion. The need arises when you have a field of a type that's expensive to construct:

```
class Foo
{
  public readonly Expensive Expensive = new Expensive();
  ...
}
class Expensive {  /* Suppose this is expensive to construct */  }
```

The problem with this code is that instantiating Foo incurs the performance cost of instantiating Expensive—regardless of whether the Expensive field is ever accessed. The obvious answer is to construct the instance *on demand*:

```
class Foo
{
  Expensive _expensive;
  public Expensive Expensive          // Lazily instantiate Expensive
  {
    get
    {
      if (_expensive == null) _expensive = new Expensive();
      return _expensive;
    }
  }
  ...
}
```

The question then arises, is this thread-safe? Aside from the fact that we're accessing _expensive outside a lock without a memory barrier, consider what would happen if two threads accessed this property at once. They could both satisfy the if statement's predicate and each thread end up with a *different* instance of Expensive. Because this can lead to subtle errors, we would say, in general, that this code is not thread-safe.

The solution to the problem is to lock around checking and initializing the object:

```
Expensive _expensive;
readonly object _expenseLock = new object();

public Expensive Expensive
{
  get
  {
    lock (_expenseLock)
    {
```

```
        if (_expensive == null) _expensive = new Expensive();
        return _expensive;
      }
    }
  }
```

Lazy<T>

The Lazy<T> class is available to help with lazy initialization. If instantiated with an argument of true, it implements the thread-safe initialization pattern just described.

 Lazy<T> actually implements a micro-optimized version of this pattern, called *double-checked locking*. Double-checked locking performs an additional volatile read to avoid the cost of obtaining a lock if the object is already initialized.

To use Lazy<T>, instantiate the class with a value factory delegate that tells it how to initialize a new value, and the argument true. Then, access its value via the Value property:

```
Lazy<Expensive> _expensive = new Lazy<Expensive>
  (() => new Expensive(), true);

public Expensive Expensive { get { return _expensive.Value; } }
```

If you pass false into Lazy<T>'s constructor, it implements the thread-unsafe lazy initialization pattern that we described at the beginning of this section—this makes sense when you want to use Lazy<T> in a single-threaded context.

LazyInitializer

LazyInitializer is a static class that works exactly like Lazy<T> except:

- Its functionality is exposed through a static method that operates directly on a field in your own type. This prevents a level of indirection, improving performance in cases where you need extreme optimization.

- It offers another mode of initialization in which multiple threads can race to initialize.

To use LazyInitializer, call EnsureInitialized before accessing the field, passing a reference to the field and the factory delegate:

```
Expensive _expensive;
public Expensive Expensive
{
  get           // Implement double-checked locking
  {
    LazyInitializer.EnsureInitialized (ref _expensive,
                                       () => new Expensive());
    return _expensive;
  }
}
```

You can also pass in another argument to request that competing threads *race* to initialize. This sounds similar to our original thread-unsafe example except that the first thread to finish always wins—and so you end up with only one instance. The advantage of this technique is that it's even faster (on multicores) than double-checked locking because it can be implemented entirely without locks using advanced techniques that we describe in "Nonblocking Synchronization" and "Lazy Initialization" at *http://albahari.com/threading*. This is an extreme (and rarely needed) optimization that comes at a cost:

- It's slower when more threads race to initialize than you have cores.
- It potentially wastes CPU resources performing redundant initialization.
- The initialization logic must be thread-safe (in this case, it would be thread-unsafe if Expensive's constructor wrote to static fields, for instance).
- If the initializer instantiates an object requiring disposal, the "wasted" object won't be disposed without additional logic.

Thread-Local Storage

Much of this chapter has focused on synchronization constructs and the issues arising from having threads concurrently access the same data. Sometimes, however, you want to keep data isolated, ensuring that each thread has a separate copy. Local variables achieve exactly this, but they are useful only with transient data.

The solution is *thread-local storage*. You might be hard-pressed to think of a requirement: data you'd want to keep isolated to a thread tends to be transient by nature. Its main application is for storing "out-of-band" data—that which supports the execution path's infrastructure, such as messaging, transaction, and security tokens. Passing such data around in method parameters can be clumsy and can alienate all but your own methods; storing such information in ordinary static fields means sharing it among all threads.

Thread-local storage can also be useful in optimizing parallel code. It allows each thread to exclusively access its own version of a thread-unsafe object without needing locks—and without needing to reconstruct that object between method calls.

There are four ways to implement thread-local storage. We take a look at them in the following subsections.

[ThreadStatic]

The easiest approach to thread-local storage is to mark a static field with the ThreadStatic attribute:

```
[ThreadStatic] static int _x;
```

Each thread then sees a separate copy of _x.

Unfortunately, [ThreadStatic] doesn't work with instance fields (it simply does nothing); nor does it play well with field initializers—they execute only *once* on the thread that's running when the static constructor executes. If you need to work with instance fields—or start with a nondefault value—ThreadLocal<T> provides a better option.

ThreadLocal<T>

ThreadLocal<T> provides thread-local storage for both static and instance fields, and allows you to specify default values.

Here's how to create a ThreadLocal<int> with a default value of 3 for each thread:

```
static ThreadLocal<int> _x = new ThreadLocal<int> (() => 3);
```

You then use _x's Value property to get or set its thread-local value. A bonus of using ThreadLocal is that values are lazily evaluated: the factory function evaluates on the first call (for each thread).

ThreadLocal<T> and instance fields

ThreadLocal<T> is also useful with instance fields and captured local variables. For example, consider the problem of generating random numbers in a multithreaded environment. The Random class is not thread-safe, so we have to either lock around using Random (limiting concurrency) or generate a separate Random object for each thread. ThreadLocal<T> makes the latter easy:

```
var localRandom = new ThreadLocal<Random>(() => new Random());
Console.WriteLine (localRandom.Value.Next());
```

Our factory function for creating the Random object is a bit simplistic, though, in that Random's parameterless constructor relies on the system clock for a random number seed. This may be the same for two Random objects created within ~10 ms of each other. Here's one way to fix it:

```
var localRandom = new ThreadLocal<Random>
  ( () => new Random (Guid.NewGuid().GetHashCode()) );
```

We use this in Chapter 22 (see the parallel spellchecking example in "PLINQ" on page 911).

GetData and SetData

The third approach is to use two methods in the Thread class: GetData and SetData. These store data in thread-specific "slots." Thread.GetData reads from a thread's isolated data store; Thread.SetData writes to it. Both methods require a Local DataStoreSlot object to identify the slot. You can use the same slot across all threads and they'll still get separate values. Here's an example:

```
class Test
{
  // The same LocalDataStoreSlot object can be used across all threads.
  LocalDataStoreSlot _secSlot = Thread.GetNamedDataSlot ("securityLevel");

  // This property has a separate value on each thread.
  int SecurityLevel
  {
    get
    {
      object data = Thread.GetData (_secSlot);
      return data == null ? 0 : (int) data;     // null == uninitialized
    }
    set { Thread.SetData (_secSlot, value); }
  }
  ...
```

In this instance, we called `Thread.GetNamedDataSlot`, which creates a named slot—this allows sharing of that slot across the application. Alternatively, you can control a slot's scope yourself with an unnamed slot, obtained by calling `Thread.Allocate DataSlot`:

```
class Test
{
  LocalDataStoreSlot _secSlot = Thread.AllocateDataSlot();
  ...
```

`Thread.FreeNamedDataSlot` will release a named data slot across all threads, but only once all references to that `LocalDataStoreSlot` have dropped out of scope and have been garbage-collected. This ensures that threads don't have data slots pulled out from under their feet, as long as they keep a reference to the appropriate `LocalDataStoreSlot` object while the slot is needed.

AsyncLocal<T>

The approaches to thread-local storage that we've discussed so far are incompatible with asynchronous functions, because after an `await`, execution can resume on a different thread. The `AsyncLocal<T>` class solves this by preserving its value across an `await`:

```
static AsyncLocal<string> _asyncLocalTest = new AsyncLocal<string>();

async void Main()
{
  _asyncLocalTest.Value = "test";
  await Task.Delay (1000);
  // The following works even if we come back on another thread:
  Console.WriteLine (_asyncLocalTest.Value);   // test
}
```

`AsyncLocal<T>` is still able to keep operations started on separate threads apart, whether initiated by `Thread.Start` or `Task.Run`. The following writes "one one" and "two two":

```
static AsyncLocal<string> _asyncLocalTest = new AsyncLocal<string>();

void Main()
{
  // Call Test twice on two concurrent threads:
  new Thread (() => Test ("one")).Start();
  new Thread (() => Test ("two")).Start();
}

async void Test (string value)
{
  _asyncLocalTest.Value = value;
  await Task.Delay (1000);
  Console.WriteLine (value + " " + _asyncLocalTest.Value);
}
```

AsyncLocal<T> has an interesting and unique nuance: if an AsyncLocal<T> object already has a value when a thread is started, the new thread will "inherit" that value:

```
static AsyncLocal<string> _asyncLocalTest = new AsyncLocal<string>();

void Main()
{
  _asyncLocalTest.Value = "test";
  new Thread (AnotherMethod).Start();
}

void AnotherMethod() => Console.WriteLine (_asyncLocalTest.Value);   // test
```

The new thread, however, gets a *copy* of the value, so any changes that it makes will not affect the original:

```
static AsyncLocal<string> _asyncLocalTest = new AsyncLocal<string>();

void Main()
{
  _asyncLocalTest.Value = "test";
  var t = new Thread (AnotherMethod);
  t.Start(); t.Join();
  Console.WriteLine (_asyncLocalTest.Value);    // test  (not ha-ha!)
}

void AnotherMethod() => _asyncLocalTest.Value = "ha-ha!";
```

Keep in mind that the new thread gets a *shallow* copy of the value. So, if you were to replace Async<string> with Async<StringBuilder> or Async<List<string>>, the new thread could clear the StringBuilder or add/remove items to the List<string>, and this would affect the original.

Timers

If you need to execute some method repeatedly at regular intervals, the easiest way is with a *timer*. Timers are convenient and efficient in their use of memory and resources—compared with techniques such as the following:

```
new Thread (delegate() {
                        while (enabled)
                        {
                          DoSomeAction();
                          Thread.Sleep (TimeSpan.FromHours (24));
                        }
                }).Start();
```

Not only does this permanently tie up a thread resource, but without additional coding, DoSomeAction will happen at a later time each day. Timers solve these problems.

.NET provides five timers. Two of these are general-purpose multithreaded timers:

- System.Threading.Timer
- System.Timers.Timer

The other two are special-purpose single-threaded timers:

- System.Windows.Forms.Timer (Windows Forms timer)
- System.Windows.Threading.DispatcherTimer (WPF timer)

The multithreaded timers are more powerful, accurate, and flexible; the single-threaded timers are safer and more convenient for running simple tasks that update Windows Forms controls or WPF elements.

Finally, from .NET 6, there's the PeriodicTimer, which we will cover first.

PeriodicTimer

PeriodicTimer is not really a timer; it's a class to help with asynchronous looping. It's important to consider that since the advent of async and await, traditional timers are not usually necessary. Instead, the following pattern works nicely:

```
StartPeriodicOperation();

async void StartPeriodicOperation()
{
  while (true)
  {
    await Task.Delay (1000);
    Console.WriteLine ("Tick");     // Do some action
  }
}
```

 If you call StartPeriodicOperation from a UI thread, it will behave as a single-threaded timer, because the await will always return on the same synchronization context.

You can make it behave as a multithreaded timer simply by adding .ConfigureAwait(false) to the await.

`PeriodicTimer` is a class to simplify this pattern:

```
var timer = new PeriodicTimer (TimeSpan.FromSeconds (1));
StartPeriodicOperation();
// Optionally dispose timer when you want to stop looping.

async void StartPeriodicOperation()
{
  while (await timer.WaitForNextTickAsync())
    Console.WriteLine ("Tick");    // Do some action
}
```

PeriodicTimer also allows you to stop the timer by disposing the timer instance. This results in WaitForNextTickAsync returning false, allowing the loop to end.

Multithreaded Timers

Advanced Threading

`System.Threading.Timer` is the simplest multithreaded timer: it has just a constructor and two methods (a delight for minimalists, as well as book authors!). In the following example, a timer calls the `Tick` method, which writes "tick..." after five seconds have elapsed, and then every second after that, until the user presses Enter:

```
using System;
using System.Threading;

// First interval = 5000ms; subsequent intervals = 1000ms
Timer tmr = new Timer (Tick, "tick...", 5000, 1000);
Console.ReadLine();
tmr.Dispose();          // This both stops the timer and cleans up.

void Tick (object data)
{
  // This runs on a pooled thread
  Console.WriteLine (data);       // Writes "tick..."
}
```

 See "Timers" on page 577 for a discussion on disposing multithreaded timers.

You can change a timer's interval later by calling its `Change` method. If you want a timer to fire just once, specify `Timeout.Infinite` in the constructor's last argument.

.NET provides another timer class of the same name in the `System.Timers` namespace. This simply wraps the `System.Threading.Timer`, providing additional convenience while using the identical underlying engine. Here's a summary of its added features:

- An `IComponent` implementation, allowing it to be sited in Visual Studio's Designer's component tray
- An `Interval` property instead of a `Change` method
- An `Elapsed` *event* instead of a callback delegate

- An Enabled property to start and stop the timer (its default value being false)

- Start and Stop methods in case you're confused by Enabled

- An AutoReset flag for indicating a recurring event (default value is true)

- A SynchronizingObject property with Invoke and BeginInvoke methods for safely calling methods on WPF elements and Windows Forms controls

Here's an example:

```
using System;
using System.Timers;          // Timers namespace rather than Threading

var tmr = new Timer();        // Doesn't require any args
tmr.Interval = 500;
tmr.Elapsed += tmr_Elapsed;   // Uses an event instead of a delegate
tmr.Start();                  // Start the timer
Console.ReadLine();
tmr.Stop();                   // Stop the timer
Console.ReadLine();
tmr.Start();                  // Restart the timer
Console.ReadLine();
tmr.Dispose();                // Permanently stop the timer

void tmr_Elapsed (object sender, EventArgs e)
  => Console.WriteLine ("Tick");
```

Multithreaded timers use the thread pool to allow a few threads to serve many timers. This means that the callback method or Elapsed event can fire on a different thread each time it is called. Furthermore, the Elapsed event always fires (approximately) on time—regardless of whether the previous Elapsed event finished executing. Hence, callbacks or event handlers must be thread-safe.

The precision of multithreaded timers depends on the OS, and is typically in the 10- to 20-millisecond region. If you need greater precision, you can use native interop and call the Windows multimedia timer. This has precision down to one millisecond, and it is defined in *winmm.dll*. First call timeBeginPeriod to inform the OS that you need high timing precision, and then call timeSetEvent to start a multimedia timer. When you're done, call timeKillEvent to stop the timer and timeEndPeriod to inform the OS that you no longer need high timing precision. Chapter 24 demonstrates calling external methods with P/Invoke. You can find complete examples on the internet that use the multimedia timer by searching for the keywords *dllimport winmm.dll timesetevent*.

Single-Threaded Timers

.NET provides timers designed to eliminate thread-safety issues for WPF and Windows Forms applications:

- `System.Windows.Threading.DispatcherTimer` (WPF)
- `System.Windows.Forms.Timer` (Windows Forms)

 The single-threaded timers are not designed to work outside their respective environments. If you use a Windows Forms timer in a Windows Service application, for instance, the `Timer` event won't fire!

Both are like `System.Timers.Timer` in the members that they expose—`Interval`, `Start`, and `Stop` (and `Tick`, which is equivalent to `Elapsed`)—and are used in a similar manner. However, they differ in how they work internally. Instead of firing timer events on pooled threads, they post the events to the WPF or Windows Forms message loop. This means that the `Tick` event always fires on the same thread that originally created the timer—which, in a normal application, is the same thread used to manage all user interface elements and controls. This has a number of benefits:

- You can forget about thread safety.
- A fresh `Tick` will never fire until the previous `Tick` has finished processing.
- You can update user interface elements and controls directly from `Tick` event handling code without calling `Control.BeginInvoke` or `Dispatcher.Begin Invoke`.

Thus, a program employing these timers is not really multithreaded: you end up with the same kind of pseudo-concurrency that's described in Chapter 14 with asynchronous functions that execute on a UI thread. One thread serves all timers as well as the processing UI events, which means that the `Tick` event handler must execute quickly, otherwise the UI becomes unresponsive.

This makes the WPF and Windows Forms timers suitable for small jobs, typically updating some aspect of the UI (e.g., a clock or countdown display).

In terms of precision, the single-threaded timers are similar to the multithreaded timers (tens of milliseconds), although they are typically less *accurate* because they can be delayed while other UI requests (or other timer events) are processed.

22

Parallel Programming

In this chapter, we cover the multithreading APIs and constructs aimed at leveraging multicore processors:

- Parallel LINQ, or *PLINQ*
- The `Parallel` class
- The *task parallelism* constructs
- The *concurrent collections*

These constructs are collectively known (loosely) as *Parallel Framework* (PFX). The `Parallel` class together with the task parallelism constructs is called the *Task Parallel Library* (TPL).

You'll need to be comfortable with the fundamentals in Chapter 14 before reading this chapter—particularly locking, thread safety, and the `Task` class.

> .NET offers a number of additional specialized APIs to help with parallel and asynchronous programming:
>
> - `System.Threading.Channels.Channel` is a high-performance asynchronous producer/consumer queue, introduced in .NET Core 3.
>
> - *Microsoft Dataflow* (in the `System.Threading.Tasks` `.Dataflow` namespace) is a sophisticated API for creating networks of buffered *blocks* that execute actions or data transformations in parallel, with a semblance to actor/agent programming.
>
> - *Reactive Extensions* implements LINQ over `IObservable` (an alternative abstraction to `IAsyncEnumerable`) and excels at combining asynchronous streams. Reactive extensions ships in the *System.Reactive* NuGet package.

Why PFX?

Over the past 15 years, CPU manufacturers have shifted from single-core to multi-core processors. This is problematic for us as programmers because single-threaded code does not automatically run faster as a result of those extra cores.

Utilizing multiple cores is easy for most server applications, where each thread can independently handle a separate client request, but it's more difficult on the desktop because it typically requires that you take your computationally intensive code and do the following:

1. *Partition* it into small chunks.

2. Execute those chunks in parallel via multithreading.

3. *Collate* the results as they become available, in a thread-safe and performant manner.

Although you can do all of this with the classic multithreading constructs, it's awkward—particularly the steps of partitioning and collating. A further problem is that the usual strategy of locking for thread safety causes a lot of contention when many threads work on the same data at once.

The PFX libraries have been designed specifically to help in these scenarios.

 Programming to leverage multicores or multiple processors is called *parallel programming*. This is a subset of the broader concept of multithreading.

PFX Concepts

There are two strategies for partitioning work among threads: *data parallelism* and *task parallelism*.

When a set of tasks must be performed on many data values, we can parallelize by having each thread perform the (same) set of tasks on a subset of values. This is called *data parallelism* because we are partitioning the *data* between threads. In contrast, with *task parallelism* we partition the *tasks*; in other words, we have each thread perform a different task.

In general, data parallelism is easier and scales better to highly parallel hardware because it reduces or eliminates shared data (thereby reducing contention and thread-safety issues). Also, data parallelism exploits the fact that there are often more data values than discrete tasks, increasing the parallelism potential.

Data parallelism is also conducive to *structured parallelism*, which means that parallel work units start and finish in the same place in your program. In contrast, task parallelism tends to be unstructured, meaning that parallel work units may start and finish in places scattered across your program. Structured parallelism is simpler and less error prone and allows you to farm the difficult job of partitioning and thread coordination (and even result collation) out to libraries.

PFX Components

PFX comprises two layers of functionality, as shown in Figure 22-1. The higher layer consists of two *structured data parallelism* APIs: PLINQ and the `Parallel` class. The lower layer contains the task parallelism classes—plus a set of additional constructs to help with parallel programming activities.

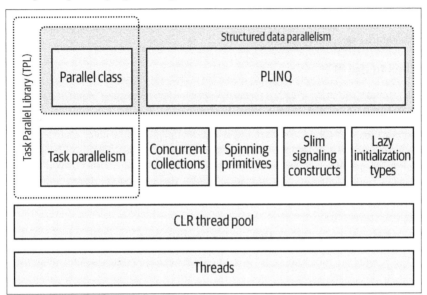

Figure 22-1. PFX components

PLINQ offers the richest functionality: it automates all the steps of parallelization—including partitioning the work into tasks, executing those tasks on threads, and collating the results into a single output sequence. It's called *declarative*—because you simply declare that you want to parallelize your work (which you structure as a LINQ query) and let the runtime take care of the implementation details. In contrast, the other approaches are *imperative*, in that you need to explicitly write code to partition or collate. As the following synopsis shows, in the case of the `Parallel` class, you must collate results yourself; with the task parallelism constructs, you must partition the work yourself, too:

	Partitions work	Collates results
PLINQ	Yes	Yes
The `Parallel` class	Yes	No
PFX's task parallelism	No	No

The concurrent collections and spinning primitives help you with lower-level parallel programming activities. These are important because PFX has been designed to work not only with today's hardware but also with future generations of processors with far more cores. If you want to move a pile of chopped wood and you have 32 workers to do the job, the biggest challenge is moving the wood without the workers getting in one another's way. It's the same with dividing an algorithm among 32 cores: if ordinary locks are used to protect common resources, the resultant blocking can mean that only a fraction of those cores are ever actually busy at once. The concurrent collections are tuned specifically for highly concurrent access, with the focus on minimizing or eliminating blocking. PLINQ and the Parallel class themselves rely on the concurrent collections and on spinning primitives for efficient management of work.

When to Use PFX

The primary use case for PFX is *parallel programming*: leveraging multicore processors to speed up computationally intensive code.

A challenge in parallel programming is Amdahl's law, which states that the maximum performance improvement from parallelization is governed by the portion of the code that must execute sequentially. For instance, if only two-thirds of an algorithm's execution time is parallelizable, you can never exceed a threefold performance gain—even with an infinite number of cores.

Other Uses for PFX

The parallel programming constructs are useful not only for leveraging multicores but in other scenarios as well:

- The concurrent collections are sometimes appropriate when you want a thread-safe queue, stack, or dictionary.
- BlockingCollection provides an easy means to implement producer/consumer structures, and is a good way to *limit* concurrency.
- Tasks are the basis of asynchronous programming, as we saw in Chapter 14.

So, before proceeding, it's worth verifying that the bottleneck is in parallelizable code. It's also worth considering whether your code *needs* to be computationally intensive—optimization is often the easiest and most effective approach. There's a trade-off, though, in that some optimization techniques can make it more difficult to parallelize code.

The easiest gains come with what's called *embarrassingly parallel* problems—this is when a job can be easily divided into tasks that efficiently execute on their own (structured parallelism is very well suited to such problems). Examples include many image-processing tasks, ray tracing, and brute-force approaches in mathematics or cryptography. An example of a non-embarrassingly parallel problem is implementing an optimized version of the quicksort algorithm—a good result takes some thought and might require unstructured parallelism.

PLINQ

PLINQ automatically parallelizes local LINQ queries. PLINQ has the advantage of being easy to use in that it offloads the burden of both work partitioning and result collation to .NET.

To use PLINQ, simply call AsParallel() on the input sequence and then continue the LINQ query as usual. The following query calculates the prime numbers between 3 and 100,000, making full use of all cores on the target machine:

```
// Calculate prime numbers using a simple (unoptimized) algorithm.

IEnumerable<int> numbers = Enumerable.Range (3, 100000-3);

var parallelQuery =
  from n in numbers.AsParallel()
  where Enumerable.Range (2, (int) Math.Sqrt (n)).All (i => n % i > 0)
  select n;

int[] primes = parallelQuery.ToArray();
```

AsParallel is an extension method in System.Linq.ParallelEnumerable. It wraps the input in a sequence based on ParallelQuery<TSource>, which causes the LINQ query operators that you subsequently call to bind to an alternate set of extension methods defined in ParallelEnumerable. These provide parallel implementations of each of the standard query operators. Essentially, they work by partitioning the input sequence into chunks that execute on different threads, collating the results back into a single output sequence for consumption, as depicted in Figure 22-2.

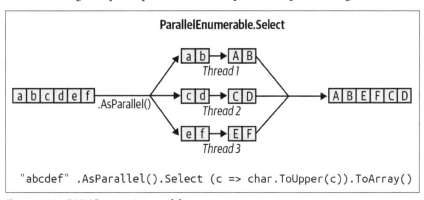

Figure 22-2. PLINQ execution model

Calling AsSequential() unwraps a ParallelQuery sequence so that subsequent query operators bind to the standard query operators and execute sequentially. This is necessary before calling methods that have side effects or are not thread-safe.

For query operators that accept two input sequences (Join, GroupJoin, Concat, Union, Intersect, Except, and Zip), you must apply AsParallel() to both input sequences (otherwise, an exception is thrown). You don't, however, need to keep applying `AsParallel` to a query as it progresses, because PLINQ's query operators output another `ParallelQuery` sequence. In fact, calling `AsParallel` again introduces inefficiency in that it forces merging and repartitioning of the query:

```
mySequence.AsParallel()         // Wraps sequence in ParallelQuery<int>
      .Where (n => n > 100)     // Outputs another ParallelQuery<int>
      .AsParallel()             // Unnecessary - and inefficient!
      .Select (n => n * n)
```

Not all query operators can be effectively parallelized. For those that cannot (see "PLINQ Limitations" on page 914), PLINQ implements the operator sequentially, instead. PLINQ might also operate sequentially if it suspects that the overhead of parallelization will actually slow a particular query.

PLINQ is only for local collections: it doesn't work with Entity Framework, for instance, because in those cases the LINQ translates into SQL, which then executes on a database server. However, you *can* use PLINQ to perform additional local querying on the result sets obtained from database queries.

 If a PLINQ query throws an exception, it's rethrown as an `AggregateException` whose `InnerExceptions` property contains the real exception (or exceptions). For more details, see "Working with AggregateException" on page 940.

Parallel Execution Ballistics

Like ordinary LINQ queries, PLINQ queries are lazily evaluated. This means that execution is triggered only when you begin consuming the results—typically via a `foreach` loop (although it can also be via a conversion operator such as `ToArray` or an operator that returns a single element or value).

As you enumerate the results, though, execution proceeds somewhat differently from that of an ordinary sequential query. A sequential query is powered entirely by the consumer in a "pull" fashion: each element from the input sequence is fetched exactly when required by the consumer. A parallel query ordinarily uses independent threads to fetch elements from the input sequence slightly *ahead* of when they're needed by the consumer (rather like a teleprompter for newsreaders). It then processes the elements in parallel through the query chain, holding the results in a small buffer so that they're ready for the consumer on demand. If the consumer pauses or breaks out of the enumeration early, the query processor also pauses or stops so as not to waste CPU time or memory.

You can tweak PLINQ's buffering behavior by calling With MergeOptions after AsParallel. The default value of AutoBuf fered generally gives the best overall results. NotBuffered disables the buffer and is useful if you want to see results as soon as possible; FullyBuffered caches the entire result set before presenting it to the consumer (the OrderBy and Reverse operators naturally work this way, as do the element, aggregation, and conversion operators).

PLINQ and Ordering

A side effect of parallelizing the query operators is that when the results are collated, it's not necessarily in the same order that they were submitted (see Figure 22-2). In other words, LINQ's normal order-preservation guarantee for sequences no longer holds.

If you need order preservation, you can force it by calling AsOrdered() after AsParallel():

```
myCollection.AsParallel().AsOrdered()...
```

Calling AsOrdered incurs a performance hit with large numbers of elements because PLINQ must keep track of each element's original position.

You can negate the effect of AsOrdered later in a query by calling AsUnordered: this introduces a "random shuffle point," which allows the query to execute more efficiently from that point on. So, if you wanted to preserve input-sequence ordering for just the first two query operators, you'd do this:

```
inputSequence.AsParallel().AsOrdered()
  .QueryOperator1()
  .QueryOperator2()
  .AsUnordered()         // From here on, ordering doesn't matter
  .QueryOperator3()
  ...
```

AsOrdered is not the default because for most queries, the original input ordering doesn't matter. In other words, if AsOrdered were the default, you'd need to apply AsUnordered to the majority of your parallel queries to get the best performance, which would be burdensome.

PLINQ Limitations

There are practical limitations on what PLINQ can parallelize. The following query operators prevent parallelization by default unless the source elements are in their original indexing position:

> The indexed versions of Select, SelectMany, and ElementAt

Most query operators change the indexing position of elements (including those that remove elements, such as Where). This means that if you want to use the preceding operators, they'll usually need to be at the start of the query.

The following query operators are parallelizable but use an expensive partitioning strategy that can sometimes be slower than sequential processing:

> Join, GroupBy, GroupJoin, Distinct, Union, Intersect, and Except

The Aggregate operator's *seeded* overloads in their standard incarnations are not parallelizable—PLINQ provides special overloads to deal with this (see "Optimizing PLINQ" on page 919).

All other operators are parallelizable, although use of these operators doesn't guarantee that your query will be parallelized. PLINQ might run your query sequentially if it suspects that the overhead of parallelization will slow down that particular query. You can override this behavior and force parallelism by calling the following after AsParallel():

```
.WithExecutionMode (ParallelExecutionMode.ForceParallelism)
```

Example: Parallel Spellchecker

Suppose that we want to write a spellchecker that runs quickly with very large documents by utilizing all available cores. By formulating our algorithm into a LINQ query, we can very easily parallelize it.

The first step is to download a dictionary of English words into a HashSet for efficient lookup:

```
if (!File.Exists ("WordLookup.txt")    // Contains about 150,000 words
  File.WriteAllText ("WordLookup.txt",
    await new HttpClient().GetStringAsync (
      "http://www.albahari.com/ispell/allwords.txt")));

var wordLookup = new HashSet<string> (
  File.ReadAllLines ("WordLookup.txt"),
  StringComparer.InvariantCultureIgnoreCase);
```

We then use our word lookup to create a test "document" comprising an array of a million random words. After we build the array, let's introduce a couple of spelling mistakes:

```
var random = new Random();
string[] wordList = wordLookup.ToArray();

string[] wordsToTest = Enumerable.Range (0, 1000000)
  .Select (i => wordList [random.Next (0, wordList.Length)])
  .ToArray();

wordsToTest [12345] = "woozsh";    // Introduce a couple
wordsToTest [23456] = "wubsie";    // of spelling mistakes.
```

Now we can perform our parallel spellcheck by testing wordsToTest against wordLookup. PLINQ makes this very easy:

```
var query = wordsToTest
  .AsParallel()
  .Select ((word, index) => new IndexedWord { Word=word, Index=index })
  .Where  (iword => !wordLookup.Contains (iword.Word))
  .OrderBy (iword => iword.Index);

foreach (var mistake in query)
  Console.WriteLine (mistake.Word + " - index = " + mistake.Index);

// OUTPUT:
// woozsh - index = 12345
// wubsie - index = 23456
```

IndexedWord is a custom struct that we define as follows:

```
struct IndexedWord { public string Word; public int Index; }
```

The wordLookup.Contains method in the predicate gives the query some "meat" and makes it worth parallelizing.

We could simplify the query slightly by using an anonymous type instead of the IndexedWord struct. However, this would degrade performance because anonymous types (being classes and therefore reference types) incur the cost of heap-based allocation and subsequent garbage collection.

The difference might not be enough to matter with sequential queries, but with parallel queries, favoring stack-based allocation can be quite advantageous. This is because stack-based allocation is highly parallelizable (as each thread has its own stack), whereas all threads must compete for the same heap—managed by a single memory manager and garbage collector.

Using ThreadLocal<T>

Let's extend our example by parallelizing the creation of the random test-word list itself. We structured this as a LINQ query, so it should be easy. Here's the sequential version:

```
string[] wordsToTest = Enumerable.Range (0, 1000000)
  .Select (i => wordList [random.Next (0, wordList.Length)])
  .ToArray();
```

Unfortunately, the call to random.Next is not thread-safe, so it's not as simple as inserting AsParallel() into the query. A potential solution is to write a function that locks around random.Next; however, this would limit concurrency. The better option is to use ThreadLocal<Random> (see "Thread-Local Storage" on page 898) to create a separate Random object for each thread. We then can parallelize the query, as follows:

```
var localRandom = new ThreadLocal<Random>
  ( () => new Random (Guid.NewGuid().GetHashCode()) );

string[] wordsToTest = Enumerable.Range (0, 1000000).AsParallel()
  .Select (i => wordList [localRandom.Value.Next (0, wordList.Length)])
  .ToArray();
```

In our factory function for instantiating a Random object, we pass in a Guid's hash-code to ensure that if two Random objects are created within a short period of time, they'll yield different random number sequences.

When to Use PLINQ

It's tempting to search your existing applications for LINQ queries and experiment with parallelizing them. This is usually unproductive, because most problems for which LINQ is obviously the best solution tend to execute very quickly and so don't benefit from parallelization. A better approach is to find a CPU-intensive bottleneck and then consider whether it can be expressed as a LINQ query. (A welcome side effect of such restructuring is that LINQ typically makes code smaller and more readable.)

PLINQ is well suited to embarrassingly parallel problems. It can be a poor choice for imaging, however, because collating millions of pixels into an output sequence creates a bottleneck. Instead, it's better to write pixels directly to an array or unmanaged memory block and use the `Parallel` class or task parallelism to manage the multithreading. (It is possible, however, to defeat result collation using `ForAll`—we discuss this in "Optimizing PLINQ" on page 919. Doing so makes sense if the image-processing algorithm naturally lends itself to LINQ.)

Functional Purity

Because PLINQ runs your query on parallel threads, you must be careful not to perform thread-unsafe operations. In particular, writing to variables is *side-effecting* and therefore thread-unsafe:

```
// The following query multiplies each element by its position.
// Given an input of Enumerable.Range(0,999), it should output squares.
int i = 0;
var query = from n in Enumerable.Range(0,999).AsParallel() select n * i++;
```

We could make incrementing `i` thread-safe by using locks, but the problem would still remain that `i` won't necessarily correspond to the position of the input element. And adding `AsOrdered` to the query wouldn't fix the latter problem, because `AsOrdered` ensures only that the elements are output in an order consistent with them having been processed sequentially—it doesn't actually *process* them sequentially.

The correct solution is to rewrite our query to use the indexed version of `Select`:

```
var query = Enumerable.Range(0,999).AsParallel().Select ((n, i) => n * i);
```

For best performance, any methods called from query operators should be thread-safe by virtue of not writing to fields or properties (non-side-effecting, or *functionally pure*). If they're thread-safe by virtue of *locking*, the query's parallelism potential will be limited by the duration of the lock divided by the total time spent in that function.

Setting the Degree of Parallelism

By default, PLINQ chooses an optimum degree of parallelism for the processor in use. You can override it by calling `WithDegreeOfParallelism` after `AsParallel`:

```
...AsParallel().WithDegreeOfPallelism(4)...
```

An example of when you might increase the parallelism beyond the core count is with I/O-bound work (downloading many web pages at once, for instance). However, task combinators and asynchronous functions provide a similarly easy and more *efficient* solution (see "Task Combinators" on page 663). Unlike with `Tasks`, PLINQ cannot perform I/O-bound work without blocking threads (and *pooled* threads, to make matters worse).

Changing the degree of parallelism

You can call WithDegreeOfParallelism only once within a PLINQ query. If you need to call it again, you must force merging and repartitioning of the query by calling AsParallel() again within the query:

```
"The Quick Brown Fox"
  .AsParallel().WithDegreeOfParallelism (2)
  .Where (c => !char.IsWhiteSpace (c))
  .AsParallel().WithDegreeOfParallelism (3)    // Forces Merge + Partition
  .Select (c => char.ToUpper (c))
```

Cancellation

Canceling a PLINQ query whose results you're consuming in a foreach loop is easy: simply break out of the foreach, and the query will be automatically canceled as the enumerator is implicitly disposed.

For a query that terminates with a conversion, element, or aggregation operator, you can cancel it from another thread via a *cancellation token* (see "Cancellation" on page 659). To insert a token, call WithCancellation after calling AsParallel, passing in the Token property of a CancellationTokenSource object. Another thread can then call Cancel on the token source, which throws an OperationCanceled Exception on the query's consumer:

```
IEnumerable<int> million = Enumerable.Range (3, 1000000);

var cancelSource = new CancellationTokenSource();

var primeNumberQuery =
  from n in million.AsParallel().WithCancellation (cancelSource.Token)
  where Enumerable.Range (2, (int) Math.Sqrt (n)).All (i => n % i > 0)
  select n;

new Thread (() => {
                    Thread.Sleep (100);      // Cancel query after
                    cancelSource.Cancel();   // 100 milliseconds.
                  }
           ).Start();
try
{
  // Start query running:
  int[] primes = primeNumberQuery.ToArray();
  // We'll never get here because the other thread will cancel us.
}
catch (OperationCanceledException)
{
  Console.WriteLine ("Query canceled");
}
```

Upon cancellation, PLINQ waits for each worker thread to finish with its current element before ending the query. This means that any external methods that the query calls will run to completion.

Optimizing PLINQ

Output-side optimization

One of PLINQ's advantages is that it conveniently collates the results from parallelized work into a single output sequence. Sometimes, though, all that you end up doing with that sequence is running some function once over each element:

```
foreach (int n in parallelQuery)
  DoSomething (n);
```

If this is the case—and you don't care about the order in which the elements are processed—you can improve efficiency with PLINQ's ForAll method.

The ForAll method runs a delegate over every output element of a ParallelQuery. It hooks directly into PLINQ's internals, bypassing the steps of collating and enumerating the results. Here's a trivial example:

```
"abcdef".AsParallel().Select (c => char.ToUpper(c)).ForAll (Console.Write);
```

Figure 22-3 shows the process.

 Collating and enumerating results is not a massively expensive operation, so the ForAll optimization yields the greatest gains when there are large numbers of quickly executing input elements.

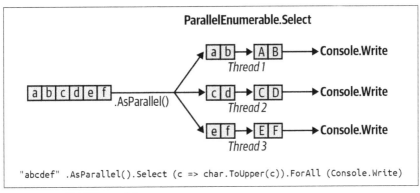

Figure 22-3. PLINQ ForAll

Input-side optimization

PLINQ has three partitioning strategies for assigning input elements to threads:

Strategy	Element allocation	Relative performance
Chunk partitioning	Dynamic	Average
Range partitioning	Static	Poor to excellent
Hash partitioning	Static	Poor

For query operators that require comparing elements (GroupBy, Join, GroupJoin, Intersect, Except, Union, and Distinct), you have no choice: PLINQ always uses *hash partitioning*. Hash partitioning is relatively inefficient in that it must precalculate the hashcode of every element (so that elements with identical hashcodes can be processed on the same thread). If you find this to be too slow, your only option is to call AsSequential to disable parallelization.

For all other query operators, you have a choice as to whether to use range or chunk partitioning. By default:

- If the input sequence is *indexable* (if it's an array or implements IList<T>), PLINQ chooses *range partitioning*.
- Otherwise, PLINQ chooses *chunk partitioning*.

In a nutshell, range partitioning is faster with long sequences for which every element takes a similar amount of CPU time to process. Otherwise, chunk partitioning is usually faster.

To force range partitioning:

- If the query starts with Enumerable.Range, replace that method with Parallel Enumerable.Range.
- Otherwise, simply call ToList or ToArray on the input sequence (obviously, this incurs a performance cost in itself, which you should take into account).

 ParallelEnumerable.Range is not simply a shortcut for calling Enumerable.Range(...).AsParallel(). It changes the performance of the query by activating range partitioning.

To force chunk partitioning, wrap the input sequence in a call to Partitioner .Create (in System.Collection.Concurrent), as follows:

```
int[] numbers = { 3, 4, 5, 6, 7, 8, 9 };
var parallelQuery =
  Partitioner.Create (numbers, true).AsParallel()
  .Where (...)
```

The second argument to Partitioner.Create indicates that you want to *load-balance* the query, which is another way of saying that you want chunk partitioning.

Chunk partitioning works by having each worker thread periodically grab small "chunks" of elements from the input sequence to process (see Figure 22-4). PLINQ starts by allocating very small chunks (one or two elements at a time). It then increases the chunk size as the query progresses: this ensures that small sequences are effectively parallelized and large sequences don't cause excessive round-tripping. If a worker happens to get "easy" elements (that process quickly), it will end up getting more chunks. This system keeps every thread equally busy (and the cores "balanced"); the only downside is that fetching elements from the shared input sequence requires synchronization (typically an exclusive lock)—and this can result in some overhead and contention.

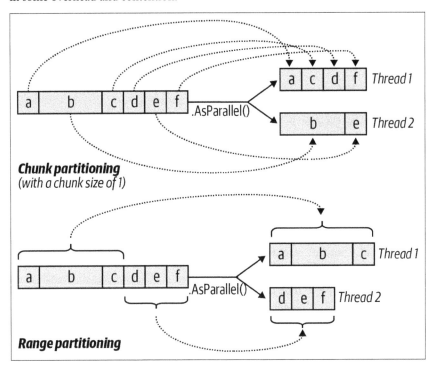

Figure 22-4. Chunk versus range partitioning

Range partitioning bypasses the normal input-side enumeration and preallocates an equal number of elements to each worker, avoiding contention on the input sequence. But if some threads happen to get easy elements and finish early, they sit idle while the remaining threads continue working. Our earlier prime number calculator might perform poorly with range partitioning. An example of when range partitioning would do well is in calculating the sum of the square roots of the first 10 million integers:

```
ParallelEnumerable.Range (1, 10000000).Sum (i => Math.Sqrt (i))
```

`ParallelEnumerable.Range` returns a `ParallelQuery<T>`, so you don't need to subsequently call `AsParallel`.

 Range partitioning doesn't necessarily allocate element ranges in *contiguous* blocks—it might instead choose a "striping" strategy. For instance, if there are two workers, one worker might process odd-numbered elements while the other processes even-numbered elements. The `TakeWhile` operator is almost certain to trigger a striping strategy to avoid unnecessarily processing elements later in the sequence.

Optimizing custom aggregations

PLINQ parallelizes the `Sum`, `Average`, `Min`, and `Max` operators efficiently without additional intervention. The `Aggregate` operator, though, presents special challenges for PLINQ. As described in Chapter 9, `Aggregate` performs custom aggregations. For example, the following sums a sequence of numbers, mimicking the `Sum` operator:

```
int[] numbers = { 1, 2, 3 };
int sum = numbers.Aggregate (0, (total, n) => total + n);   // 6
```

We also saw in Chapter 9 that for *unseeded* aggregations, the supplied delegate must be associative and commutative. PLINQ will give incorrect results if this rule is violated, because it draws *multiple seeds* from the input sequence in order to aggregate several partitions of the sequence simultaneously.

Explicitly seeded aggregations might seem like a safe option with PLINQ, but unfortunately these ordinarily execute sequentially because of the reliance on a single seed. To mitigate this, PLINQ provides another overload of `Aggregate` that lets you specify multiple seeds—or rather, a *seed factory function*. For each thread, it executes this function to generate a separate seed, which becomes a *thread-local* accumulator into which it locally aggregates elements.

You must also supply a function to indicate how to combine the local and main accumulators. Finally, this `Aggregate` overload (somewhat gratuitously) expects a delegate to perform any final transformation on the result (you can achieve this as easily by running some function on the result yourself afterward). So, here are the four delegates, in the order they are passed:

seedFactory
> Returns a new local accumulator

updateAccumulatorFunc
> Aggregates an element into a local accumulator

combineAccumulatorFunc
> Combines a local accumulator with the main accumulator

resultSelector
> Applies any final transformation on the end result

> In simple scenarios, you can specify a *seed value* instead of a seed factory. This tactic fails when the seed is a reference type that you want to mutate, because the same instance will then be shared by each thread.

To give a very simple example, the following sums the values in a `numbers` array:

```
numbers.AsParallel().Aggregate (
  () => 0,                              // seedFactory
  (localTotal, n) => localTotal + n,    // updateAccumulatorFunc
```

```
      (mainTot, localTot) => mainTot + localTot,    // combineAccumulatorFunc
      finalResult => finalResult)                    // resultSelector
```

This example is contrived in that we could get the same answer just as efficiently using simpler approaches (such as an unseeded aggregate, or better, the Sum operator). To give a more realistic example, suppose that we want to calculate the frequency of each letter in the English alphabet in a given string. A simple sequential solution might look like this:

```
string text = "Let's suppose this is a really long string";
var letterFrequencies = new int[26];
foreach (char c in text)
{
  int index = char.ToUpper (c) - 'A';
  if (index >= 0 && index < 26) letterFrequencies [index]++;
};
```

 An example of when the input text might be very long is in gene sequencing. The "alphabet" would then consist of the letters *a, c, g,* and *t*.

To parallelize this, we could replace the foreach statement with a call to Paral lel.ForEach (which we cover in the following section), but this will leave us to deal with concurrency issues on the shared array. And locking around accessing that array would all but kill the potential for parallelization.

Aggregate offers a tidy solution. The accumulator, in this case, is an array just like the letterFrequencies array in our preceding example. Here's a sequential version using Aggregate:

```
int[] result =
  text.Aggregate (
    new int[26],                  // Create the "accumulator"
    (letterFrequencies, c) =>     // Aggregate a letter into the accumulator
    {
      int index = char.ToUpper (c) - 'A';
      if (index >= 0 && index < 26) letterFrequencies [index]++;
      return letterFrequencies;
    });
```

And now the parallel version, using PLINQ's special overload:

```
int[] result =
  text.AsParallel().Aggregate (
    () => new int[26],            // Create a new local accumulator

    (localFrequencies, c) =>      // Aggregate into the local accumulator
    {
      int index = char.ToUpper (c) - 'A';
      if (index >= 0 && index < 26) localFrequencies [index]++;
      return localFrequencies;
    },
                                  // Aggregate local->main accumulator
    (mainFreq, localFreq) =>
```

```
            mainFreq.Zip (localFreq, (f1, f2) => f1 + f2).ToArray(),

    finalResult => finalResult      // Perform any final transformation
  );                                // on the end result.
```

Notice that the local accumulation function *mutates* the localFrequencies array. This ability to perform this optimization is important—and is legitimate because localFrequencies is local to each thread.

The Parallel Class

PFX provides a basic form of structured parallelism via three static methods in the Parallel class:

Parallel.Invoke
:   Executes an array of delegates in parallel

Parallel.For
:   Performs the parallel equivalent of a C# for loop

Parallel.ForEach
:   Performs the parallel equivalent of a C# foreach loop

All three methods block until all work is complete. As with PLINQ, after an unhandled exception, remaining workers are stopped after their current iteration, and the exception (or exceptions) are thrown back to the caller—wrapped in an AggregateException (see "Working with AggregateException" on page 940).

Parallel.Invoke

Parallel.Invoke executes an array of Action delegates in parallel and then waits for them to complete. The simplest version of the method is defined as follows:

```
public static void Invoke (params Action[] actions);
```

Just as with PLINQ, the Parallel.* methods are optimized for compute-bound and not I/O-bound work. However, downloading two web pages at once provides a simple way to demonstrate Parallel.Invoke:

```
Parallel.Invoke (
  () => new WebClient().DownloadFile ("http://www.linqpad.net", "lp.html"),
  () => new WebClient().DownloadFile ("http://microsoft.com", "ms.html"));
```

On the surface, this seems like a convenient shortcut for creating and waiting on two thread-bound Task objects. But there's an important difference: Parallel .Invoke still works efficiently if you pass in an array of a million delegates. This is because it *partitions* large numbers of elements into batches that it assigns to a handful of underlying Tasks rather than creating a separate Task for each delegate.

As with all of Parallel's methods, you're on your own when it comes to collating the results. This means that you need to keep thread safety in mind. The following, for instance, is thread-unsafe:

```
var data = new List<string>();
Parallel.Invoke (
  () => data.Add (new WebClient().DownloadString ("http://www.foo.com")),
  () => data.Add (new WebClient().DownloadString ("http://www.far.com")));
```

Locking around adding to the list would resolve this, although locking would create
a bottleneck if you had a much larger array of quickly executing delegates. A better
solution is to use the thread-safe collections, which we cover in later sections—
ConcurrentBag would be ideal in this case.

Parallel.Invoke is also overloaded to accept a ParallelOptions object:

```
public static void Invoke (ParallelOptions options,
                           params Action[] actions);
```

With ParallelOptions, you can insert a cancellation token, limit the maximum
concurrency, and specify a custom task scheduler. A cancellation token is relevant
when you're executing (roughly) more tasks than you have cores: upon cancellation,
any unstarted delegates will be abandoned. Any already executing delegates will,
however, continue to completion. See "Cancellation" on page 918 for an example of
how to use cancellation tokens.

Parallel.For and Parallel.ForEach

Parallel.For and Parallel.ForEach perform the equivalent of a C# for and
foreach loop but with each iteration executing in parallel instead of sequentially.
Here are their (simplest) signatures:

```
public static ParallelLoopResult For (
  int fromInclusive, int toExclusive, Action<int> body)
```

```
public static ParallelLoopResult ForEach<TSource> (
  IEnumerable<TSource> source, Action<TSource> body)
```

This sequential for loop:

```
for (int i = 0; i < 100; i++)
  Foo (i);
```

is parallelized like this:

```
Parallel.For (0, 100, i => Foo (i));
```

or more simply:

```
Parallel.For (0, 100, Foo);
```

And this sequential foreach:

```
foreach (char c in "Hello, world")
  Foo (c);
```

is parallelized like this:

```
Parallel.ForEach ("Hello, world", Foo);
```

To give a practical example, if we import the `System.Security.Cryptography` namespace, we can generate six public/private keypair strings in parallel, as follows:

```
var keyPairs = new string[6];

Parallel.For (0, keyPairs.Length,
              i => keyPairs[i] = RSA.Create().ToXmlString (true));
```

As with `Parallel.Invoke`, we can feed `Parallel.For` and `Parallel.ForEach` a large number of work items and they'll be efficiently partitioned onto a few tasks.

 The latter query could also be done with PLINQ:

```
string[] keyPairs =
  ParallelEnumerable.Range (0, 6)
  .Select (i => RSA.Create().ToXmlString (true))
  .ToArray();
```

Outer versus inner loops

`Parallel.For` and `Parallel.ForEach` usually work best on outer rather than inner loops. This is because with the former, you're offering larger chunks of work to parallelize, diluting the management overhead. Parallelizing both inner and outer loops is usually unnecessary. In the following example, we'd typically need more than 100 cores to benefit from the inner parallelization:

```
Parallel.For (0, 100, i =>
{
  Parallel.For (0, 50, j => Foo (i, j));   // Sequential would be better
});                                        // for the inner loop.
```

Indexed Parallel.ForEach

Sometimes, it's useful to know the loop iteration index. With a sequential `foreach`, it's easy:

```
int i = 0;
foreach (char c in "Hello, world")
  Console.WriteLine (c.ToString() + i++);
```

Incrementing a shared variable, however, is not thread-safe in a parallel context. You must instead use the following version of `ForEach`:

```
public static ParallelLoopResult ForEach<TSource> (
  IEnumerable<TSource> source, Action<TSource,ParallelLoopState,long> body)
```

We'll ignore `ParallelLoopState` (which we cover in the following section). For now, we're interested in `Action`'s third type parameter of type `long`, which indicates the loop index:

```
Parallel.ForEach ("Hello, world", (c, state, i) =>
{
  Console.WriteLine (c.ToString() + i);
});
```

To put this into a practical context, let's revisit the spellchecker that we wrote with PLINQ. The following code loads up a dictionary along with an array of a million words to test:

```
if (!File.Exists ("WordLookup.txt"))     // Contains about 150,000 words
  new WebClient().DownloadFile (
    "http://www.albahari.com/ispell/allwords.txt", "WordLookup.txt");

var wordLookup = new HashSet<string> (
  File.ReadAllLines ("WordLookup.txt"),
  StringComparer.InvariantCultureIgnoreCase);

var random = new Random();
string[] wordList = wordLookup.ToArray();

string[] wordsToTest = Enumerable.Range (0, 1000000)
  .Select (i => wordList [random.Next (0, wordList.Length)])
  .ToArray();

wordsToTest [12345] = "woozsh";       // Introduce a couple
wordsToTest [23456] = "wubsie";       // of spelling mistakes.
```

We can perform the spellcheck on our wordsToTest array using the indexed version of Parallel.ForEach, as follows:

```
var misspellings = new ConcurrentBag<Tuple<int,string>>();

Parallel.ForEach (wordsToTest, (word, state, i) =>
{
  if (!wordLookup.Contains (word))
    misspellings.Add (Tuple.Create ((int) i, word));
});
```

Notice that we had to collate the results into a thread-safe collection: having to do this is the disadvantage when compared to using PLINQ. The advantage over PLINQ is that we avoid the cost of applying an indexed Select query operator—which is less efficient than an indexed ForEach.

ParallelLoopState: Breaking early out of loops

Because the loop body in a parallel For or ForEach is a delegate, you can't exit the loop early with a break statement. Instead, you must call Break or Stop on a ParallelLoopState object:

```
public class ParallelLoopState
{
  public void Break();
  public void Stop();

  public bool IsExceptional { get; }
  public bool IsStopped { get; }
  public long? LowestBreakIteration { get; }
  public bool ShouldExitCurrentIteration { get; }
}
```

Obtaining a `ParallelLoopState` is easy: all versions of For and ForEach are over-loaded to accept loop bodies of type `Action<TSource,ParallelLoopState>`. So, to parallelize this:

```
foreach (char c in "Hello, world")
  if (c == ',')
    break;
  else
    Console.Write (c);
```

do this:

```
Parallel.ForEach ("Hello, world", (c, loopState) =>
{
  if (c == ',')
    loopState.Break();
  else
    Console.Write (c);
});
```

```
// OUTPUT: Hlloe
```

You can see from the output that loop bodies can complete in a random order. Aside from this difference, calling `Break` yields *at least* the same elements as execut-ing the loop sequentially: this example will always output *at least* the letters *H, e, l, l,* and *o* in some order. In contrast, calling `Stop` instead of `Break` forces all threads to finish immediately after their current iteration. In our example, calling `Stop` could give us a subset of the letters *H, e, l, l,* and *o* if another thread were lagging behind. Calling `Stop` is useful when you've found something that you're looking for—or when something has gone wrong and you won't be looking at the results.

> The `Parallel.For` and `Parallel.ForEach` methods return a `ParallelLoopResult` object that exposes properties called `IsCompleted` and `LowestBreakIteration`. These tell you whether the loop ran to completion; if it didn't, it indicates at what cycle the loop was broken.
>
> If `LowestBreakIteration` returns null, it means that you called `Stop` (rather than `Break`) on the loop.

If your loop body is long, you might want other threads to break partway through the method body in case of an early `Break` or `Stop`. You can do this by polling the `ShouldExitCurrentIteration` property at various places in your code; this property becomes true immediately after a `Stop`—or soon after a `Break`.

> `ShouldExitCurrentIteration` also becomes true after a can-cellation request—or if an exception is thrown in the loop.

`IsExceptional` lets you know whether an exception has occurred on another thread. Any unhandled exception will cause the loop to stop after each thread's current iteration: to avoid this, you must explicitly handle exceptions in your code.

Optimization with local values

`Parallel.For` and `Parallel.ForEach` each offer a set of overloads that feature a generic type argument called `TLocal`. These overloads are designed to help you optimize the collation of data with iteration-intensive loops. The simplest is this:

```
public static ParallelLoopResult For <TLocal> (
  int fromInclusive,
  int toExclusive,
  Func <TLocal> localInit,
  Func <int, ParallelLoopState, TLocal, TLocal> body,
  Action <TLocal> localFinally);
```

These methods are rarely needed in practice because their target scenarios are covered mostly by PLINQ (which is fortunate because these overloads are somewhat intimidating!).

Essentially, the problem is this: suppose that we want to sum the square roots of the numbers 1 through 10,000,000. Calculating 10 million square roots is easily parallelizable, but summing their values is troublesome because we must lock around updating the total:

```
object locker = new object();
double total = 0;
Parallel.For (1, 10000000,
              i => { lock (locker) total += Math.Sqrt (i); });
```

The gain from parallelization is more than offset by the cost of obtaining 10 million locks—plus the resultant blocking.

The reality, though, is that we don't actually *need* 10 million locks. Imagine a team of volunteers picking up a large volume of litter. If all workers shared a single trash can, the travel and contention would make the process extremely inefficient. The obvious solution is for each worker to have a private or "local" trash can, which is occasionally emptied into the main bin.

The `TLocal` versions of `For` and `ForEach` work in exactly this way. The volunteers are internal worker threads, and the *local value* represents a local trash can. For `Parallel` to do this job, you must feed it two additional delegates that indicate the following:

1. How to initialize a new local value

2. How to combine a local aggregation with the master value

Additionally, instead of the body delegate returning `void`, it should return the new aggregate for the local value. Here's our example refactored:

```
object locker = new object();
double grandTotal = 0;

Parallel.For (1, 10000000,

  () => 0.0,                     // Initialize the local value.
```

```
        (i, state, localTotal) =>          // Body delegate. Notice that it
            localTotal + Math.Sqrt (i),     // returns the new local total.

        localTotal =>                                    // Add the local value
            { lock (locker) grandTotal += localTotal; }  // to the master value.
    );
```

We must still lock, but only around aggregating the local value to the grand total.
This makes the process dramatically more efficient.

As stated earlier, PLINQ is often a good fit in these scenarios.
Our example could be parallelized with PLINQ like this:

```
ParallelEnumerable.Range (1, 10000000)
               .Sum (i => Math.Sqrt (i))
```

(Notice that we used `ParallelEnumerable` to force *range partitioning*: this improves performance in this case because all
numbers will take equally long to process.)

In more complex scenarios, you might use LINQ's `Aggregate`
operator instead of `Sum`. If you supplied a local seed factory,
the situation would be somewhat analogous to providing a
local value function with `Parallel.For`.

Task Parallelism

Task parallelism is the lowest-level approach to parallelization with PFX. The classes
for working at this level are defined in the `System.Threading.Tasks` namespace
and comprise the following:

Class	Purpose
Task	For managing a unit for work
Task<TResult>	For managing a unit for work with a return value
TaskFactory	For creating tasks
TaskFactory<TResult>	For creating tasks and continuations with the same return type
TaskScheduler	For managing the scheduling of tasks
TaskCompletionSource	For manually controlling a task's workflow

We covered the basics of tasks in Chapter 14; in this section, we look at advanced
features of tasks that are aimed at parallel programming:

- Tuning a task's scheduling
- Establishing a parent/child relationship when one task is started from another
- Advanced use of continuations
- `TaskFactory`

The Task Parallel Library lets you create hundreds (or even thousands) of tasks with minimal overhead. But if you want to create millions of tasks, you'll need to partition those tasks into larger work units to maintain efficiency. The Parallel class and PLINQ do this automatically.

Visual Studio provides a window for monitoring tasks (Debug→Window→Parallel Tasks). This is equivalent to the Threads window, but for tasks. The Parallel Stacks window also has a special mode for tasks.

Creating and Starting Tasks

As described in Chapter 14, Task.Run creates and starts a Task or Task<TResult>. This method is actually a shortcut for calling Task.Factory.StartNew, which allows greater flexibility through additional overloads.

Specifying a state object

Task.Factory.StartNew lets you specify a *state* object that is passed to the target. The target method's signature must then comprise a single object-type parameter:

```
var task = Task.Factory.StartNew (Greet, "Hello");
task.Wait();  // Wait for task to complete.

void Greet (object state) { Console.Write (state); }   // Hello
```

This avoids the cost of the closure required for executing a lambda expression that calls Greet. This is a micro-optimization and is rarely necessary in practice, so we can put the *state* object to better use, which is to assign a meaningful name to the task. We can then use the AsyncState property to query its name:

```
var task = Task.Factory.StartNew (state => Greet ("Hello"), "Greeting");
Console.WriteLine (task.AsyncState);   // Greeting
task.Wait();

void Greet (string message) { Console.Write (message); }
```

Visual Studio displays each task's AsyncState in the Parallel Tasks window, so having a meaningful name here can ease debugging considerably.

TaskCreationOptions

You can tune a task's execution by specifying a TaskCreationOptions enum when calling StartNew (or instantiating a Task). TaskCreationOptions is a flags enum with the following (combinable) values:

```
LongRunning, PreferFairness, AttachedToParent
```

LongRunning suggests that the scheduler dedicate a thread to the task, and as we described in Chapter 14, this is beneficial for I/O-bound tasks and for long-running tasks that might otherwise force short-running tasks to wait an unreasonable amount of time before being scheduled.

PreferFairness instructs the scheduler to try to ensure that tasks are scheduled in the order in which they were started. It might ordinarily do otherwise because it internally optimizes the scheduling of tasks using local work-stealing queues—an optimization that allows the creation of *child* tasks without incurring the contention overhead that would otherwise arise with a single work queue. A child task is created by specifying AttachedToParent.

Child tasks

When one task starts another, you can optionally establish a parent-child relationship:

```
Task parent = Task.Factory.StartNew (() =>
{
  Console.WriteLine ("I am a parent");

  Task.Factory.StartNew (() =>        // Detached task
  {
    Console.WriteLine ("I am detached");
  });

  Task.Factory.StartNew (() =>        // Child task
  {
    Console.WriteLine ("I am a child");
  }, TaskCreationOptions.AttachedToParent);
});
```

A child task is special in that when you wait for the *parent* task to complete, it waits for any children, as well. At which point any child exceptions bubble up:

```
TaskCreationOptions atp = TaskCreationOptions.AttachedToParent;
var parent = Task.Factory.StartNew (() =>
{
  Task.Factory.StartNew (() =>    // Child
  {
    Task.Factory.StartNew (() => { throw null; }, atp);    // Grandchild
  }, atp);
});

// The following call throws a NullReferenceException (wrapped
// in nested AggregateExceptions):
parent.Wait();
```

This can be particularly useful when a child task is a continuation, as you'll see shortly.

Waiting on Multiple Tasks

We saw in Chapter 14 that you can wait on a single task either by calling its Wait method or accessing its Result property (if it's a Task<TResult>). You can also wait on multiple tasks at once—via the static methods `Task.WaitAll` (waits for all the specified tasks to finish) and `Task.WaitAny` (waits for just one task to finish).

`WaitAll` is similar to waiting out each task in turn, but is more efficient in that it requires (at most) just one context switch. Also, if one or more of the tasks throw an unhandled exception, `WaitAll` still waits out every task. It then rethrows an `AggregateException` that accumulates the exceptions from each faulted task (this is where `AggregateException` is genuinely useful). It's equivalent to doing this:

```
// Assume t1, t2 and t3 are tasks:
var exceptions = new List<Exception>();
try { t1.Wait(); } catch (AggregateException ex) { exceptions.Add (ex); }
try { t2.Wait(); } catch (AggregateException ex) { exceptions.Add (ex); }
try { t3.Wait(); } catch (AggregateException ex) { exceptions.Add (ex); }
if (exceptions.Count > 0) throw new AggregateException (exceptions);
```

Calling `WaitAny` is equivalent to waiting on a `ManualResetEventSlim` that's signaled by each task as it finishes.

As well as a timeout, you can also pass in a *cancellation token* to the `Wait` methods: this lets you cancel the wait—*not the task itself.*

Canceling Tasks

You can optionally pass in a cancellation token when starting a task. Then, if cancellation occurs via that token, the task itself enters the "Canceled" state:

```
var cts = new CancellationTokenSource();
CancellationToken token = cts.Token;
cts.CancelAfter (500);

Task task = Task.Factory.StartNew (() =>
{
  Thread.Sleep (1000);
  token.ThrowIfCancellationRequested();  // Check for cancellation request
}, token);

try { task.Wait(); }
catch (AggregateException ex)
{
  Console.WriteLine (ex.InnerException is TaskCanceledException);  // True
  Console.WriteLine (task.IsCanceled);                            // True
  Console.WriteLine (task.Status);                                // Canceled
}
```

`TaskCanceledException` is a subclass of `OperationCanceledException`. If you want to explicitly throw an `OperationCanceledException` (rather than calling `token.ThrowIfCancellationRequested`), you must pass the cancellation token into `OperationCanceledException`'s constructor. If you fail to do this, the task won't end up with a `TaskStatus.Canceled` status and won't trigger `OnlyOnCanceled` continuations.

If the task is canceled before it has started, it won't get scheduled—an OperationCan
celedException will instead be thrown on the task immediately.

Because cancellation tokens are recognized by other APIs, you can pass them into
other constructs, and cancellations will propagate seamlessly:

```
var cancelSource = new CancellationTokenSource();
CancellationToken token = cancelSource.Token;

Task task = Task.Factory.StartNew (() =>
{
  // Pass our cancellation token into a PLINQ query:
  var query = someSequence.AsParallel().WithCancellation (token)...
  ... enumerate query ...
});
```

Calling Cancel on cancelSource in this example will cancel the PLINQ query,
which will throw an OperationCanceledException on the task body, which will
then cancel the task.

 The cancellation tokens that you can pass into methods such
as Wait and CancelAndWait allow you to cancel the *wait* operation and not the task itself.

Continuations

The ContinueWith method executes a delegate immediately after a task ends:

```
Task task1 = Task.Factory.StartNew (() => Console.Write ("antecedant.."));
Task task2 = task1.ContinueWith (ant => Console.Write ("..continuation"));
```

As soon as task1 (the *antecedent*) completes, fails, or is canceled, task2 (the *continuation*) starts. (If task1 had completed before the second line of code ran, task2
would be scheduled to execute immediately.) The ant argument passed to the continuation's lambda expression is a reference to the antecedent task. ContinueWith
itself returns a task, making it easy to add further continuations.

By default, antecedent and continuation tasks may execute on different threads.
You can force them to execute on the same thread by specifying TaskContinuation
Options.ExecuteSynchronously when calling ContinueWith: this can improve per-
formance in very fine-grained continuations by lessening indirection.

Continuations and Task<TResult>

Just like ordinary tasks, continuations can be of type Task<TResult> and return
data. In the following example, we calculate Math.Sqrt(8*2) using a series of
chained tasks and then write out the result:

```
Task.Factory.StartNew<int> (() => 8)
  .ContinueWith (ant => ant.Result * 2)
  .ContinueWith (ant => Math.Sqrt (ant.Result))
  .ContinueWith (ant => Console.WriteLine (ant.Result));    // 4
```

Our example is somewhat contrived for simplicity; in real life, these lambda expressions would call computationally intensive functions.

Continuations and exceptions

A continuation can know whether an antecedent faulted by querying the antecedent task's Exception property—or simply by invoking Result / Wait and catching the resultant AggregateException. If an antecedent faults and the continuation does neither, the exception is considered *unobserved*, and the static TaskScheduler.Unob servedTaskException event fires when the task is later garbage collected.

A safe pattern is to rethrow antecedent exceptions. As long as the continuation is Waited upon, the exception will be propagated and rethrown to the Waiter:

```
Task continuation = Task.Factory.StartNew      (() => { throw null; })
                                     .ContinueWith (ant =>
  {
    ant.Wait();
    // Continue processing...
  });

continuation.Wait();     // Exception is now thrown back to caller.
```

Another way to deal with exceptions is to specify different continuations for exceptional versus nonexceptional outcomes. This is done with TaskContinuation Options:

```
Task task1 = Task.Factory.StartNew (() => { throw null; });

Task error = task1.ContinueWith (ant => Console.Write (ant.Exception),
                          TaskContinuationOptions.OnlyOnFaulted);

Task ok = task1.ContinueWith (ant => Console.Write ("Success!"),
                          TaskContinuationOptions.NotOnFaulted);
```

This pattern is particularly useful in conjunction with child tasks, as you'll see very soon.

The following extension method "swallows" a task's unhandled exceptions:

```
public static void IgnoreExceptions (this Task task)
{
  task.ContinueWith (t => { var ignore = t.Exception; },
    TaskContinuationOptions.OnlyOnFaulted);
}
```

(This could be improved by adding code to log the exception.) Here's how it would be used:

```
Task.Factory.StartNew (() => { throw null; }).IgnoreExceptions();
```

Continuations and child tasks

A powerful feature of continuations is that they kick off only when all child tasks have completed (see Figure 22-5). At that point, any exceptions thrown by the children are marshaled to the continuation.

In the following example, we start three child tasks, each throwing a `NullRef erenceException`. We then catch all of them in one fell swoop via a continuation on the parent:

```
TaskCreationOptions atp = TaskCreationOptions.AttachedToParent;
Task.Factory.StartNew (() =>
{
  Task.Factory.StartNew (() => { throw null; }, atp);
  Task.Factory.StartNew (() => { throw null; }, atp);
  Task.Factory.StartNew (() => { throw null; }, atp);
})
.ContinueWith (p => Console.WriteLine (p.Exception),
               TaskContinuationOptions.OnlyOnFaulted);
```

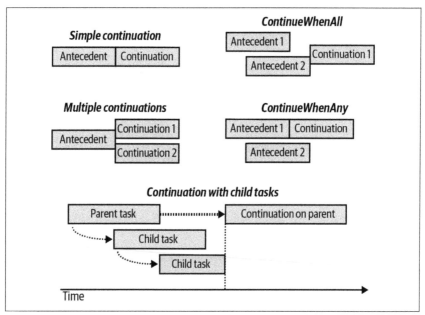

Figure 22-5. Continuations

Conditional continuations

By default, a continuation is scheduled *unconditionally*, whether the antecedent completes, throws an exception, or is canceled. You can alter this behavior via a set of (combinable) flags included within the `TaskContinuationOptions` enum. Following are the three core flags that control conditional continuation:

```
NotOnRanToCompletion = 0x10000,
NotOnFaulted = 0x20000,
NotOnCanceled = 0x40000,
```

These flags are subtractive in the sense that the more you apply, the less likely the continuation is to execute. For convenience, there are also the following precombined values:

```
OnlyOnRanToCompletion = NotOnFaulted | NotOnCanceled,
OnlyOnFaulted = NotOnRanToCompletion | NotOnCanceled,
OnlyOnCanceled = NotOnRanToCompletion | NotOnFaulted
```

(Combining all the Not* flags [NotOnRanToCompletion, NotOnFaulted, NotOn Canceled] is nonsensical because it would result in the continuation always being canceled.)

"RanToCompletion" means that the antecedent succeeded without cancellation or unhandled exceptions.

"Faulted" means that an unhandled exception was thrown on the antecedent.

"Canceled" means one of two things:

- The antecedent was canceled via its cancellation token. In other words, an OperationCanceledException was thrown on the antecedent, whose Cancella tionToken property matched that passed to the antecedent when it was started.

- The antecedent was implicitly canceled because *it* didn't satisfy a conditional continuation predicate.

It's essential to grasp that when a continuation doesn't execute by virtue of these flags, the continuation is not forgotten or abandoned—it's canceled. This means that any continuations on the continuation itself *will then run* unless you predicate them with NotOnCanceled. For example, consider this:

```
Task t1 = Task.Factory.StartNew (...);

Task fault = t1.ContinueWith (ant => Console.WriteLine ("fault"),
                          TaskContinuationOptions.OnlyOnFaulted);

Task t3 = fault.ContinueWith (ant => Console.WriteLine ("t3"));
```

As it stands, t3 will always get scheduled—even if t1 doesn't throw an exception (see Figure 22-6). This is because if t1 succeeds, the fault task will be canceled, and with no continuation restrictions placed on t3, t3 will then execute unconditionally.

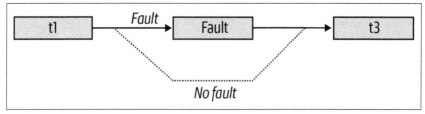

Figure 22-6. Conditional continuations

If we want t3 to execute only if fault actually runs, we must instead do this:

```
Task t3 = fault.ContinueWith (ant => Console.WriteLine ("t3"),
                            TaskContinuationOptions.NotOnCanceled);
```

(Alternatively, we could specify OnlyOnRanToCompletion; the difference is that t3 would not then execute if an exception were thrown within fault.)

Continuations with multiple antecedents

You can schedule continuation to execute based on the completion of multiple antecedents with the ContinueWhenAll and ContinueWhenAny methods in the Task Factory class. These methods have become redundant, however, with the introduction of the task combinators discussed in Chapter 14 (WhenAll and WhenAny). Specifically, given the following tasks:

```
var task1 = Task.Run (() => Console.Write ("X"));
var task2 = Task.Run (() => Console.Write ("Y"));
```

we can schedule a continuation to execute when both complete as follows:

```
var continuation = Task.Factory.ContinueWhenAll (
  new[] { task1, task2 }, tasks => Console.WriteLine ("Done"));
```

Here's the same result with the WhenAll task combinator:

```
var continuation = Task.WhenAll (task1, task2)
                     .ContinueWith (ant => Console.WriteLine ("Done"));
```

Multiple continuations on a single antecedent

Calling ContinueWith more than once on the same task creates multiple continuations on a single antecedent. When the antecedent finishes, all continuations will start together (unless you specify TaskContinuationOptions.ExecuteSynchronously, in which case the continuations will execute sequentially).

The following waits for one second and then writes either XY or YX:

```
var t = Task.Factory.StartNew (() => Thread.Sleep (1000));
t.ContinueWith (ant => Console.Write ("X"));
t.ContinueWith (ant => Console.Write ("Y"));
```

Task Schedulers

A *task scheduler* allocates tasks to threads and is represented by the abstract Task Scheduler class. .NET provides two concrete implementations: the *default scheduler* that works in tandem with the CLR thread pool, and the *synchronization context scheduler*. The latter is designed (primarily) to help you with the threading model of WPF and Windows Forms, which requires that user interface elements and controls are accessed only from the thread that created them (see "Threading in Rich Client Applications" on page 621). By capturing it, we can instruct a task or a continuation to execute on this context:

```
// Suppose we are on a UI thread in a Windows Forms / WPF application:
_uiScheduler = TaskScheduler.FromCurrentSynchronizationContext();
```

Assuming Foo is a compute-bound method that returns a string and lblResult is a WPF or Windows Forms label, we could then safely update the label after the operation completes, as follows:

```
Task.Run (() => Foo())
  .ContinueWith (ant => lblResult.Content = ant.Result, _uiScheduler);
```

Of course, C#'s asynchronous functions would more commonly be used for this kind of thing.

It's also possible to write our own task scheduler (by subclassing TaskScheduler), although this is something you'd do only in very specialized scenarios. For custom scheduling, you'd more commonly use TaskCompletionSource.

TaskFactory

When you call Task.Factory, you're calling a static property on Task that returns a default TaskFactory object. The purpose of a task factory is to create tasks; specifically, three kinds of tasks:

- "Ordinary" tasks (via StartNew)
- Continuations with multiple antecedents (via ContinueWhenAll and Continue WhenAny)
- Tasks that wrap methods that follow the defunct APM (via FromAsync; see "Obsolete Patterns" on page 667)

Another way to create tasks is to instantiate Task and call Start. However, this lets you create only "ordinary" tasks, not continuations.

Creating your own task factories

`TaskFactory` is not an *abstract* factory: you can actually instantiate the class, and this is useful when you want to repeatedly create tasks using the same (nonstandard) values for `TaskCreationOptions`, `TaskContinuationOptions`, or `TaskScheduler`. For example, if we want to repeatedly create long-running *parented* tasks, we could create a custom factory, as follows:

```
var factory = new TaskFactory (
    TaskCreationOptions.LongRunning | TaskCreationOptions.AttachedToParent,
    TaskContinuationOptions.None);
```

Creating tasks is then simply a matter of calling `StartNew` on the factory:

```
Task task1 = factory.StartNew (Method1);
Task task2 = factory.StartNew (Method2);
...
```

The custom continuation options are applied when calling `ContinueWhenAll` and `ContinueWhenAny`.

Working with AggregateException

As we've seen, PLINQ, the `Parallel` class, and `Task`s automatically marshal exceptions to the consumer. To see why this is essential, consider the following LINQ query, which throws a `DivideByZeroException` on the first iteration:

```
try
{
  var query = from i in Enumerable.Range (0, 1000000)
              select 100 / i;
  ...
}
catch (DivideByZeroException)
{
  ...
}
```

If we asked PLINQ to parallelize this query and it ignored the handling of exceptions, a `DivideByZeroException` would probably be thrown on a *separate thread*, bypassing our `catch` block and causing the application to die.

Hence, exceptions are automatically caught and rethrown to the caller. But unfortunately, it's not quite as simple as catching a `DivideByZeroException`. Because these libraries utilize many threads, it's actually possible for two or more exceptions to be thrown simultaneously. To ensure that all exceptions are reported, exceptions are therefore wrapped in an `AggregateException` container, which exposes an `Inner Exceptions` property containing each of the caught exception(s):

```
try
{
  var query = from i in ParallelEnumerable.Range (0, 1000000)
              select 100 / i;
  // Enumerate query
  ...
}
catch (AggregateException aex)
{
  foreach (Exception ex in aex.InnerExceptions)
    Console.WriteLine (ex.Message);
}
```

 Both PLINQ and the Parallel class end the query or loop execution upon encountering the first exception—by not processing any further elements or loop bodies. More exceptions might be thrown, however, before the current cycle is complete. The first exception in AggregateException is visible in the InnerException property.

Flatten and Handle

The AggregateException class provides a couple of methods to simplify exception handling: Flatten and Handle.

Flatten

AggregateExceptions will quite often contain other AggregateExceptions. An example of when this might happen is if a child task throws an exception. You can eliminate any level of nesting to simplify handling by calling Flatten. This method returns a new AggregateException with a simple flat list of inner exceptions:

```
catch (AggregateException aex)
{
  foreach (Exception ex in aex.Flatten().InnerExceptions)
    myLogWriter.LogException (ex);
}
```

Handle

Sometimes, it's useful to catch only specific exception types and have other types rethrown. The Handle method on AggregateException provides a shortcut for doing this. It accepts an exception predicate, which it runs over every inner exception:

```
public void Handle (Func<Exception, bool> predicate)
```

If the predicate returns true, it considers that exception "handled." After the delegate has run over every exception, the following happens:

- If all exceptions were "handled" (the delegate returned true), the exception is not rethrown.

- If there were any exceptions for which the delegate returned `false` ("unhandled"), a new `AggregateException` is built up containing those exceptions and is rethrown.

For instance, the following ends up rethrowing another `AggregateException` that contains a single `NullReferenceException`:

```
var parent = Task.Factory.StartNew (() =>
{
  // We'll throw 3 exceptions at once using 3 child tasks:

  int[] numbers = { 0 };

  var childFactory = new TaskFactory
    (TaskCreationOptions.AttachedToParent, TaskContinuationOptions.None);

  childFactory.StartNew (() => 5 / numbers[0]);    // Division by zero
  childFactory.StartNew (() => numbers [1]);       // Index out of range
  childFactory.StartNew (() => { throw null; });   // Null reference
});

try { parent.Wait(); }
catch (AggregateException aex)
{
  aex.Flatten().Handle (ex =>    // Note that we still need to call Flatten
  {
    if (ex is DivideByZeroException)
    {
      Console.WriteLine ("Divide by zero");
      return true;                       // This exception is "handled"
    }
    if (ex is IndexOutOfRangeException)
    {
      Console.WriteLine ("Index out of range");
      return true;                       // This exception is "handled"
    }
    return false;     // All other exceptions will get rethrown
  });
}
```

Concurrent Collections

.NET offers thread-safe collections in the `System.Collections.Concurrent` namespace:

Concurrent collection	Nonconcurrent equivalent
ConcurrentStack<T>	Stack<T>
ConcurrentQueue<T>	Queue<T>
ConcurrentBag<T>	(none)
ConcurrentDictionary<TKey,TValue>	Dictionary<TKey,TValue>

The concurrent collections are optimized for high-concurrency scenarios; however, they can also be useful whenever you need a thread-safe collection (as an alternative to locking around an ordinary collection). There are some caveats, though:

- The conventional collections outperform the concurrent collections in all but highly concurrent scenarios.

- A thread-safe collection doesn't guarantee that the code using it will be thread-safe (see "Locking and Thread Safety" on page 874).

- If you enumerate over a concurrent collection while another thread is modifying it, no exception is thrown—instead, you get a mixture of old and new content.

- There's no concurrent version of List<T>.

- The concurrent stack, queue, and bag classes are implemented internally with linked lists. This makes them less memory-efficient than the nonconcurrent Stack and Queue classes, but better for concurrent access because linked lists are conducive to lock-free or low-lock implementations. (This is because inserting a node into a linked list requires updating just a couple of references, whereas inserting an element into a List<T>-like structure might require moving thousands of existing elements.)

In other words, these collections are not merely shortcuts for using an ordinary collection with a lock. To demonstrate, if we execute the following code on a *single* thread:

```
var d = new ConcurrentDictionary<int,int>();
for (int i = 0; i < 1000000; i++) d[i] = 123;
```

it runs three times more slowly than this:

```
var d = new Dictionary<int,int>();
for (int i = 0; i < 1000000; i++) lock (d) d[i] = 123;
```

(*Reading* from a ConcurrentDictionary, however, is fast because reads are lock-free.)

The concurrent collections also differ from conventional collections in that they expose special methods to perform atomic test-and-act operations, such as Try Pop. Most of these methods are unified via the IProducerConsumerCollection<T> interface.

IProducerConsumerCollection<T>

A producer/consumer collection is one for which the two primary use cases are:

- Adding an element ("producing")
- Retrieving an element while removing it ("consuming")

The classic examples are stacks and queues. Producer/consumer collections are significant in parallel programming because they're conducive to efficient lock-free implementations.

The IProducerConsumerCollection<T> interface represents a thread-safe producer/consumer collection. The following classes implement this interface:

```
ConcurrentStack<T>
ConcurrentQueue<T>
ConcurrentBag<T>
```

IProducerConsumerCollection<T> extends ICollection, adding the following methods:

```
void CopyTo (T[] array, int index);
T[] ToArray();
bool TryAdd (T item);
bool TryTake (out T item);
```

The TryAdd and TryTake methods test whether an add/remove operation can be performed; if so, they perform the add/remove. The testing and acting are atomically performed, eliminating the need to lock as you would around a conventional collection:

```
int result;
lock (myStack) if (myStack.Count > 0) result = myStack.Pop();
```

TryTake returns false if the collection is empty. TryAdd always succeeds and returns true in the three implementations provided. If you wrote your own concurrent collection that prohibited duplicates, however, you'd make TryAdd return false if the element already existed (an example would be if you wrote a concurrent *set*).

The particular element that TryTake removes is defined by the subclass:

- With a stack, TryTake removes the most recently added element.
- With a queue, TryTake removes the least recently added element.
- With a bag, TryTake removes whatever element it can remove most efficiently.

The three concrete classes mostly implement the TryTake and TryAdd methods explicitly, exposing the same functionality through more specifically named public methods such as TryDequeue and TryPop.

ConcurrentBag<T>

ConcurrentBag<T> stores an *unordered* collection of objects (with duplicates permitted). ConcurrentBag<T> is suitable in situations for which you *don't care* which element you get when calling Take or TryTake.

The benefit of ConcurrentBag<T> over a concurrent queue or stack is that a bag's Add method suffers almost *no* contention when called by many threads at once. In contrast, calling Add in parallel on a queue or stack incurs *some* contention (although a lot less than locking around a *nonconcurrent* collection). Calling `Take` on a concurrent bag is also very efficient—as long as each thread doesn't take more elements than it `Added`.

Inside a concurrent bag, each thread gets its own private linked list. Elements are added to the private list that belongs to the thread calling `Add`, eliminating contention. When you enumerate over the bag, the enumerator travels through each thread's private list, yielding each of its elements in turn.

When you call `Take`, the bag first looks at the current thread's private list. If there's at least one element,[1] it can complete the task easily and without contention. But if the list is empty, it must "steal" an element from another thread's private list and incur the potential for contention.

So, to be precise, calling `Take` gives you the element added most recently on that thread; if there are no elements on that thread, it gives you the element added most recently on another thread, chosen at random.

Concurrent bags are ideal when the parallel operation on your collection mostly comprises `Adding` elements—or when the `Adds` and `Takes` are balanced on a thread. We saw an example of the former previously, when using `Parallel.ForEach` to implement a parallel spellchecker:

```
var misspellings = new ConcurrentBag<Tuple<int,string>>();

Parallel.ForEach (wordsToTest, (word, state, i) =>
{
  if (!wordLookup.Contains (word))
    misspellings.Add (Tuple.Create ((int) i, word));
});
```

A concurrent bag would be a poor choice for a producer/consumer queue because elements are added and removed by *different* threads.

BlockingCollection<T>

If you call `TryTake` on any of the producer/consumer collections we discussed in the previous section, `ConcurrentStack<T>`, `ConcurrentQueue<T>`, and `Concurrent Bag<T>`, and the collection is empty, the method returns `false`. Sometimes, it would be more useful in this scenario to *wait* until an element is available.

Rather than overloading the `TryTake` methods with this functionality (which would have caused a blowout of members after allowing for cancellation tokens and timeouts), PFX's designers encapsulated this functionality into a wrapper class called `BlockingCollection<T>`. A blocking collection wraps any collection that

---

1 Due to an implementation detail, there actually needs to be at least two elements to avoid contention entirely.

implements `IProducerConsumerCollection<T>` and lets you `Take` an element from the wrapped collection—blocking if no element is available.

A blocking collection also lets you limit the total size of the collection, blocking the *producer* if that size is exceeded. A collection limited in this manner is called a *bounded blocking collection*.

To use `BlockingCollection<T>`:

1. Instantiate the class, optionally specifying the `IProducerConsumerCollection<T>` to wrap, and the maximum size (bound) of the collection.

2. Call `Add` or `TryAdd` to add elements to the underlying collection.

3. Call `Take` or `TryTake` to remove (consume) elements from the underlying collection.

If you call the constructor without passing in a collection, the class will automatically instantiate a `ConcurrentQueue<T>`. The producing and consuming methods let you specify cancellation tokens and timeouts. `Add` and `TryAdd` may block if the collection size is bounded; `Take` and `TryTake` block while the collection is empty.

Another way to consume elements is to call `GetConsumingEnumerable`. This returns a (potentially) infinite sequence that yields elements as they become available. You can force the sequence to end by calling `CompleteAdding`: this method also prevents further elements from being enqueued.

`BlockingCollection` also provides static methods called `AddToAny` and `TakeFromAny`, which let you add or take an element while specifying several blocking collections. The action is then honored by the first collection able to service the request.

Writing a Producer/Consumer Queue

A producer/consumer queue is a useful structure, both in parallel programming and general concurrency scenarios. Here's how it works:

- A queue is set up to describe work items—or data upon which work is performed.

- When a task needs executing, it's enqueued, and the caller gets on with other things.

- One or more worker threads plug away in the background, picking off and executing queued items.

A producer/consumer queue gives you precise control over how many worker threads execute at once, which is useful in limiting not only CPU consumption but other resources as well. If the tasks perform intensive disk I/O, for instance, you can limit concurrency to avoid starving the operating system and other applications. You can also dynamically add and remove workers throughout the queue's life. The CLR's thread pool itself is a kind of producer/consumer queue, optimized for short-running compute-bound jobs.

A producer/consumer queue typically holds items of data upon which (the same) task is performed. For example, the items of data may be filenames, and the task might be to encrypt those files. By making the item a delegate, however, you can write a more general-purpose producer/consumer queue where each item can do anything.

At *http://albahari.com/threading*, we show how to write a producer/consumer queue from scratch using an AutoResetEvent (and later, using Monitor's Wait and Pulse). However, writing a producer/consumer from scratch is unnecessary because most of the functionality is provided by BlockingCollection<T>. Here's how to use it:

```
public class PCQueue : IDisposable
{
  BlockingCollection<Action> _taskQ = new BlockingCollection<Action>();

  public PCQueue (int workerCount)
  {
    // Create and start a separate Task for each consumer:
    for (int i = 0; i < workerCount; i++)
      Task.Factory.StartNew (Consume);
  }

  public void Enqueue (Action action) { _taskQ.Add (action); }

  void Consume()
  {
    // This sequence that we're enumerating will block when no elements
    // are available and will end when CompleteAdding is called.

    foreach (Action action in _taskQ.GetConsumingEnumerable())
      action();       // Perform task.
  }

  public void Dispose() { _taskQ.CompleteAdding(); }
}
```

Because we didn't pass anything into BlockingCollection's constructor, it instanti-ated a concurrent queue automatically. Had we passed in a ConcurrentStack, we'd have ended up with a producer/consumer stack.

Using Tasks

The producer/consumer that we just wrote is inflexible in that we can't track work items after they've been enqueued. It would be nice if we could do the following:

- Know when a work item has completed (and `await` it)
- Cancel a work item
- Deal elegantly with any exceptions thrown by a work item

An ideal solution would be to have the `Enqueue` method return some object giving us the functionality just described. The good news is that a class already exists to do exactly this—the `Task` class, which we can generate either with a `TaskCompletion Source` or by instantiating directly (creating an unstarted or *cold* task):

```
public class PCQueue : IDisposable
{
  BlockingCollection<Task> _taskQ = new BlockingCollection<Task>();

  public PCQueue (int workerCount)
  {
    // Create and start a separate Task for each consumer:
    for (int i = 0; i < workerCount; i++)
      Task.Factory.StartNew (Consume);
  }

  public Task Enqueue (Action action, CancellationToken cancelToken
                                    = default (CancellationToken))
  {
    var task = new Task (action, cancelToken);
    _taskQ.Add (task);
    return task;
  }

  public Task<TResult> Enqueue<TResult> (Func<TResult> func,
            CancellationToken cancelToken = default (CancellationToken))
  {
    var task = new Task<TResult> (func, cancelToken);
    _taskQ.Add (task);
    return task;
  }

  void Consume()
  {
    foreach (var task in _taskQ.GetConsumingEnumerable())
      try
      {
          if (!task.IsCanceled) task.RunSynchronously();
      }
      catch (InvalidOperationException) { }  // Race condition
  }

  public void Dispose() { _taskQ.CompleteAdding(); }
}
```

In Enqueue, we enqueue and return to the caller a task that we create but don't start.

In Consume, we run the task synchronously on the consumer's thread. We catch an InvalidOperationException to handle the unlikely event that the task is canceled in between checking whether it's canceled and running it.

Here's how we can use this class:

```
var pcQ = new PCQueue (2);      // Maximum concurrency of 2
string result = await pcQ.Enqueue (() => "That was easy!");
...
```

Hence, we have all the benefits of tasks—with exception propagation, return values, and cancellation—while taking complete control over scheduling.

23

Span<T> and Memory<T>

The Span<T> and Memory<T> structs act as low-level façades over an array, string, or any contiguous block of managed or unmanaged memory. Their main purpose is to help with certain kinds of micro-optimization—in particular, writing *low-allocation* code that minimizes managed memory allocations (thereby reducing the load on the garbage collector) without having to duplicate your code for different kinds of input. They also enable *slicing*—working with a portion of an array, string, or memory block without creating a copy.

Span<T> and Memory<T> are particularly useful in performance hotspots, such as the ASP.NET Core processing pipeline or a JSON parser that serves an object database.

Should you come across these types in an API and not need or care for their potential performance advantages, you can deal with them easily as follows:

- When calling a method that expects a Span<T>, ReadOnly Span<T>, Memory<T>, or ReadOnlyMemory<T>, pass in an array instead; that is, T[]. (This works thanks to implicit conversion operators.)

- To convert from a span/memory *to* an array, call the ToArray method. And if T is char, ToString will convert the span/memory into a string.

Specifically, Span<T> does two things:

- It provides a common array-like interface over managed arrays, strings, and pointer-backed memory. This gives you the freedom to employ stack-allocated and unmanaged memory to avoid garbage collection, without having to duplicate code or mess with pointers.

- It allows "slicing": exposing reusable subsections of the span without making copies.

 Span<T> comprises just two fields, a pointer and a length. For this reason, it can represent only contiguous blocks of memory. (Should you need to work with noncontiguous memory, the ReadOnlySequence<T> class is available to serve as a linked list.)

Because Span<T> can wrap stack-allocated memory, there are restrictions on how you can store or pass around instances (imposed, in part, by Span<T> being a *ref struct*). Memory<T> acts as a span without those restrictions, but it cannot wrap stack-allocated memory. Memory<T> still provides the benefit of slicing.

Each struct comes with a read-only counterpart (ReadOnlySpan<T> and ReadOnly Memory<T>). As well as preventing unintentional change, the read-only counterparts further improve performance by allowing the compiler and runtime additional freedom for optimization.

.NET itself (and ASP.NET Core) use these types to improve efficiency with I/O, networking, string handling, and JSON parsing.

 Span<T> and Memory<T>'s ability to perform array slicing make the old ArraySegment<T> class redundant. To help with any transition, there are implicit conversion operators from Array Segment<T> to all of the span/memory structs, and from Mem ory<T> and ReadOnlyMemory<T> to ArraySegment<T>.

Spans and Slicing

Suppose that you're writing a method to sum an array of integers. A micro-optimized implementation would avoid LINQ in favor of a foreach loop:

```
int Sum (int[] numbers)
{
  int total = 0;
  foreach (int i in numbers) total += i;
  return total;
}
```

Now imagine that you want to sum just a *portion* of the array. You have two options:

- First copy the portion of the array that you want to sum into another array.
- Add additional parameters (offset and count).

The first option is inefficient; the second option adds clutter and complexity (which worsens with methods that need to accept more than one array).

Spans solve this nicely. All you need to do is to change the parameter type from int[] to ReadOnlySpan<int> (everything else stays the same):

```
int Sum (ReadOnlySpan<int> numbers)
{
  int total = 0;
  foreach (int i in numbers) total += i;
  return total;
}
```

 We used ReadOnlySpan<T> rather than Span<T> because we don't need to modify the array. There's an implicit conversion from Span<T> to ReadOnlySpan<T>, so you can pass a Span<T> into a method that expects a ReadOnlySpan<T>.

We can test this method, as follows:

```
var numbers = new int [1000];
for (int i = 0; i < numbers.Length; i++) numbers [i] = i;

int total = Sum (numbers);
```

We can call Sum with an array because there's an implicit conversion from T[] to Span<T> and ReadOnlySpan<T>. Another option is to use the AsSpan extension method:

```
var span = numbers.AsSpan();
```

The indexer for ReadOnlySpan<T> uses C#'s ref readonly feature to reach directly into the underlying data: this allows our method to perform almost as well as the original example that used an array. But what we've gained is that we can now "slice" the array and sum just a portion of the elements as follows:

```
// Sum the middle 500 elements (starting from position 250):
int total = Sum (numbers.AsSpan (250, 500));
```

If you already have a Span<T> or ReadOnlySpan<T>, you can slice it by calling the Slice method:

```
Span<int> span = numbers;
int total = Sum (span.Slice (250, 500));
```

You can also use C#'s *indices* and *ranges* (from C# 8):

```
Span<int> span = numbers;
Console.WriteLine (span [^1]);             // Last element
Console.WriteLine (Sum (span [..10]));     // First 10 elements
Console.WriteLine (Sum (span [100..]));    // 100th element to end
Console.WriteLine (Sum (span [^5..]));     // Last 5 elements
```

Although Span<T> doesn't implement IEnumerable<T> (it can't implement interfaces by virtue of being a ref struct), it does implement the pattern, which allows C#'s foreach statement to work (see "Enumeration" on page 189).

CopyTo and TryCopyTo

The CopyTo method copies elements from one span (or Memory<T>) to another. In the following example, we copy all of the elements from span x into span y:

```
Span<int> x = new[] { 1, 2, 3, 4 };
Span<int> y = new int[4];
x.CopyTo (y);
```

Slicing makes this method much more useful. In the next example, we copy the first half of span x into the second half of span y:

```
Span<int> x = new[] { 1,  2,  3,  4 };
Span<int> y = new[] { 10, 20, 30, 40 };
x[..2].CopyTo (y[2..]);                    // y is now { 10, 20, 1, 2 }
```

If there's not enough space in the destination to complete the copy, CopyTo throws an exception, whereas TryCopyTo returns false (without copying any elements).

The span structs also expose methods to Clear and Fill the span as well as an IndexOf method to search for an element in the span.

Working with Text

Spans are designed to work well with strings, which are treated as ReadOnly Span<char>. The following method counts whitespace characters:

```
int CountWhitespace (ReadOnlySpan<char> s)
{
  int count = 0;
  foreach (char c in s)
    if (char.IsWhiteSpace (c))
      count++;
  return count;
}
```

You can call such a method with a string (thanks to an implicit conversion operator):

```
int x = CountWhitespace ("Word1 Word2");   // OK
```

or with a substring:

```
int y = CountWhitespace (someString.AsSpan (20, 10));
```

The ToString() method converts a ReadOnlySpan<char> back to a string.

Extension methods ensure that some of the commonly used methods on the string class are also available to ReadOnlySpan<char>:

```
var span = "This ".AsSpan();              // ReadOnlySpan<char>
Console.WriteLine (span.StartsWith ("This"));  // True
Console.WriteLine (span.Trim().Length);    // 4
```

(Note that methods such as StartsWith use *ordinal* comparison, whereas the corresponding methods on the string class use culture-sensitive comparison by default.)

Methods such as ToUpper and ToLower are available, but you must pass in a destination span with the correct length (this allows you to decide how and where to allocate the memory).

Some of string's methods are unavailable, such as Split (which splits a string into an array of words). It's actually impossible to write the direct equivalent of string's Split method because you cannot create an array of spans.

> This is because spans are defined as *ref structs*, which can exist only on the stack.
>
> (By "exist only on the stack," we mean that the struct itself can exist only on the stack. The content that the span *wraps* can—and does, in this case—exist on the heap.)

The System.Buffers.Text namespace contains additional types to help you work with span-based text, including the following:

- Utf8Formatter.TryFormat does the equivalent of calling ToString on built-in and simple types such as decimal, DateTime, and so on but writes to a span instead of a string.

- Utf8Parser.TryParse does the reverse and parses data from a span into a simple type.

- The Base64 type provides methods for reading/writing base-64 data.

Fundamental CLR methods such as int.Parse have also been overloaded to accept ReadOnlySpan<char>.

Memory<T>

Span<T> and ReadOnlySpan<T> are defined as *ref structs* to maximize their optimization potential as well as allowing them to work safely with stack-allocated memory (as you'll see in the next section). However, they also impose limitations. In addition to being array-unfriendly, they cannot be used as fields in a class (this would put them on the heap). This, in turn, prevents them from appearing in lambda expressions—and as parameters in asynchronous methods, iterators, and asynchronous streams:

```
async void Foo (Span<int> notAllowed)    // Compile-time error!
```

(Remember that the compiler processes asynchronous methods and iterators by writing a private *state machine*, which means that any parameters and local variables end up as fields. The same applies to lambda expressions that close over variables: these also end up as fields in a *closure*.)

The Memory<T> and ReadOnlyMemory<T> structs work around this, acting as spans that cannot wrap stack-allocated memory, allowing their use in fields, lambda expressions, asynchronous methods, and so on.

You can obtain a Memory<T> or ReadOnlyMemory<T> from an array via an implicit conversion or the AsMemory() extension method:

```
Memory<int> mem1 = new int[] { 1, 2, 3 };
var mem2 = new int[] { 1, 2, 3 }.AsMemory();
```

You can easily "convert" a Memory<T> or ReadOnlyMemory<T> into a Span<T> or ReadOnlySpan<T> via its Span property so that you can interact with it as though it were a span. The conversion is efficient in that it doesn't perform any copying:

```
async void Foo (Memory<int> memory)
{
  Span<int> span = memory.Span;
  ...
}
```

(You can also directly slice a Memory<T> or ReadOnlyMemory<T> via its Slice method or a C# range, and access its length via its Length property.)

 Another way to obtain a Memory<T> is to rent it from a *pool*, using the System.Buffers.MemoryPool<T> class. This works just like array pooling (see "Array Pooling" on page 575) and offers another strategy for reducing the load on the garbage collector.

We said in the previous section that you cannot write the direct equivalent of string.Split for spans, because you cannot create an array of spans. This limitation does not apply to ReadOnlyMemory<char>:

```
// Split a string into words:
IEnumerable<ReadOnlyMemory<char>> Split (ReadOnlyMemory<char> input)
{
  int wordStart = 0;
  for (int i = 0; i <= input.Length; i++)
    if (i == input.Length || char.IsWhiteSpace (input.Span [i]))
    {
      yield return input [wordStart..i];   // Slice with C# range operator
      wordStart = i + 1;
    }
}
```

This is more efficient than string's Split method: instead of creating new strings for each word, it returns *slices* of the original string:

```
foreach (var slice in Split ("The quick brown fox jumps over the lazy dog"))
{
  // slice is a ReadOnlyMemory<char>
}
```

 You can easily convert a Memory<T> into a Span<T> (via the Span property), but not vice versa. For this reason, it's better to write methods that accept Span<T> than Memory<T> when you have a choice.

For the same reason, it's better to write methods that accept ReadOnlySpan<T> than Span<T>.

Forward-Only Enumerators

In the preceding section, we employed ReadOnlyMemory<char> as a solution to implementing a string-style Split method. But by giving up on ReadOnly Span<char>, we lost the ability to slice spans backed by unmanaged memory. Let's revisit ReadOnlySpan<char> to see whether we can find another solution.

One possible option would be to write our Split method so that it returns *ranges*:

```
Range[] Split (ReadOnlySpan<char> input)
{
  int pos = 0;
  var list = new List<Range>();
  for (int i = 0; i <= input.Length; i++)
    if (i == input.Length || char.IsWhiteSpace (input [i]))
    {
      list.Add (new Range (pos, i));
      pos = i + 1;
    }
  return list.ToArray();
}
```

The caller could then use those ranges to slice the original span:

```
ReadOnlySpan<char> source = "The quick brown fox";
foreach (Range range in Split (source))
{
  ReadOnlySpan<char> wordSpan = source [range];
  ...
}
```

This is an improvement, but it's still imperfect. One of the reasons for using spans in the first place is to avoid memory allocations. But notice that our Split method creates a List<Range>, adds items to it, and then converts the list into an array. This incurs *at least* two memory allocations as well a memory-copy operation.

The solution to this is to eschew the list and array in favor of a forward-only enumerator. An enumerator is clumsier to work with, but it can be made allocation-free with the use of structs:

```
// We must define this as a ref struct, because _input is a ref struct.
public readonly ref struct CharSpanSplitter
{
  readonly ReadOnlySpan<char> _input;
  public CharSpanSplitter (ReadOnlySpan<char> input) => _input = input;
  public Enumerator GetEnumerator() => new Enumerator (_input);

  public ref struct Enumerator    // Forward-only enumerator
  {
    readonly ReadOnlySpan<char> _input;
    int _wordPos;
    public ReadOnlySpan<char> Current { get; private set; }

    public Rator (ReadOnlySpan<char> input)
```

```
  {
    _input = input;
    _wordPos = 0;
    Current = default;
  }

  public bool MoveNext()
  {
    for (int i = _wordPos; i <= _input.Length; i++)
      if (i == _input.Length || char.IsWhiteSpace (_input [i]))
      {
        Current = _input [_wordPos..i];
        _wordPos = i + 1;
        return true;
      }
    return false;
  }
 }
}

public static class CharSpanExtensions
{
  public static CharSpanSplitter Split (this ReadOnlySpan<char> input)
    => new CharSpanSplitter (input);

  public static CharSpanSplitter Split (this Span<char> input)
    => new CharSpanSplitter (input);
}
```

Here's how you would call it:

```
var span = "the quick brown fox".AsSpan();
foreach (var word in span.Split())
{
  // word is a ReadOnlySpan<char>
}
```

By defining a `Current` property and a `MoveNext` method, our enumerator can work with C#'s `foreach` statement (see "Enumeration" on page 189). We don't have to implement the `IEnumerable<T>`/`IEnumerator<T>` interfaces (in fact, we can't; ref structs can't implement interfaces). We're sacrificing abstraction for micro-optimization.

Working with Stack-Allocated and Unmanaged Memory

Another effective micro-optimization technique is to reduce the load on the garbage collector by minimizing heap-based allocations. This means making greater use of stack-based memory—or even unmanaged memory.

Unfortunately, this normally requires that you rewrite code to use pointers. In the case of our previous example that summed elements in an array, we would need to write another version as follows:

```
unsafe int Sum (int* numbers, int length)
{
  int total = 0;
  for (int i = 0; i < length; i++) total += numbers [i];
  return total;
}
```

so that we could do this:

```
int* numbers = stackalloc int [1000]; // Allocate array on the stack
int total = Sum (numbers, 1000);
```

Spans solve this problem: you can construct a Span<T> or ReadOnlySpan<T> directly from a pointer:

```
int* numbers = stackalloc int [1000];
var span = new Span<int> (numbers, 1000);
```

Or in one step:

```
Span<int> numbers = stackalloc int [1000];
```

(Note that this doesn't require the use of unsafe.) Recall the Sum method that we wrote previously:

```
int Sum (ReadOnlySpan<int> numbers)
{
  int total = 0;
  int len = numbers.Length;
  for (int i = 0; i < len; i++) total += numbers [i];
  return total;
}
```

This method works equally well for a stack-allocated span. We have gained on three counts:

- The same method works with both arrays and stack-allocated memory.

- We can use stack-allocated memory with minimal use of pointers.

- The span can be sliced.

The compiler is smart enough to prevent you from writing a method that allocates memory on the stack and returns it to the caller via a Span<T> or ReadOnlySpan<T>.

(In other scenarios, however, you can legally return a Span<T> or ReadOnlySpan<T>.)

You can also use spans to wrap memory that you allocate from the unmanaged heap. In the following example, we allocate unmanaged memory using the Marshal.AllocHGlobal function, wrap it in a Span<char>, and then copy a string into the unmanaged memory. Finally, we employ the CharSpanSplitter struct that we wrote in the preceding section to split the unmanaged string into words:

```
var source = "The quick brown fox".AsSpan();
var ptr = Marshal.AllocHGlobal (source.Length * sizeof (char));
try
{
  var unmanaged = new Span<char> ((char*)ptr, source.Length);
  source.CopyTo (unmanaged);
  foreach (var word in unmanaged.Split())
    Console.WriteLine (word.ToString());
}
finally { Marshal.FreeHGlobal (ptr); }
```

A nice bonus is that Span<T>'s indexer performs bounds-checking, preventing a buffer overrun. This protection applies if you correctly instantiate Span<T>: in our example, you would lose this protection if you wrongly obtained the span:

```
var span = new Span<char> ((char*)ptr, source.Length * 2);
```

There's also no protection from the equivalent of a dangling pointer, so you must take care not to access the span after releasing its unmanaged memory with Marshal.FreeHGlobal.

24

Native and COM Interoperability

This chapter describes how to integrate with native (unmanaged) Dynamic-Link Libraries (DLLs) and Component Object Model (COM) components. Unless otherwise stated, the types mentioned in this chapter exist in either the System or the System.Runtime.InteropServices namespace.

Calling into Native DLLs

P/Invoke, short for *Platform Invocation Services*, allows you to access functions, structs, and callbacks in unmanaged DLLs (*shared libraries* on Unix).

For example, consider the MessageBox function, defined in the Windows DLL *user32.dll*, as follows:

```
int MessageBox (HWND hWnd, LPCTSTR lpText, LPCTSTR lpCaption, UINT uType);
```

You can call this function directly by declaring a static method of the same name, applying the extern keyword, and adding the DllImport attribute:

```
using System;
using System.Runtime.InteropServices;

MessageBox (IntPtr.Zero,
            "Please do not press this again.", "Attention", 0);

[DllImport("user32.dll")]
static extern int MessageBox (IntPtr hWnd, string text, string caption,
                              int type);
```

The MessageBox classes in the System.Windows and System.Windows.Forms namespaces themselves call similar unmanaged methods.

Here's a `DllImport` example for Ubuntu Linux:

```
Console.WriteLine ($"User ID: {getuid()}");

[DllImport("libc")]
static extern uint getuid();
```

The CLR includes a marshaler that knows how to convert parameters and return values between .NET types and unmanaged types. In the Windows example, the `int` parameters translate directly to four-byte integers that the function expects, and the string parameters are converted into null-terminated arrays of Unicode characters (encoded in UTF-16). `IntPtr` is a struct designed to encapsulate an unmanaged handle; it's 32 bits wide on 32-bit platforms and 64 bits wide on 64-bit platforms. A similar translation happens on Unix. (From C# 9, you can also use the `nint` type, which maps to `IntPtr`.)

Type and Parameter Marshaling

Marshaling Common Types

On the unmanaged side, there can be more than one way to represent a given data type. A string, for instance, can contain single-byte ANSI characters or UTF-16 Unicode characters, and can be length prefixed, null terminated, or of fixed length. With the `MarshalAs` attribute, you can specify to the CLR marshaler the variation in use, so it can provide the correct translation. Here's an example:

```
[DllImport("...")]
static extern int Foo ( [MarshalAs (UnmanagedType.LPStr)] string s );
```

The `UnmanagedType` enumeration includes all the Win32 and COM types that the marshaler understands. In this case, the marshaler was told to translate to `LPStr`, which is a null-terminated single-byte ANSI string.

On the .NET side, you also have some choice as to what data type to use. Unmanaged handles, for instance, can map to `IntPtr`, `int`, `uint`, `long`, or `ulong`.

 Most unmanaged handles encapsulate an address or pointer and so must be mapped to `IntPtr` for compatibility with both 32- and 64-bit operating systems. A typical example is HWND.

Quite often with Win32 and POSIX functions, you come across an integer parameter that accepts a set of constants, defined in a C++ header file such as *WinUser.h*. Rather than defining these as simple C# constants, you can define them within an enum instead. Using an enum can make for tidier code as well as increase static type safety. We provide an example in "Shared Memory" on page 971.

When installing Microsoft Visual Studio, be sure to install the C++ header files—even if you choose nothing else in the C++ category. This is where all the native Win32 constants are defined. You can then locate all header files by searching for *.h in the Visual Studio program directory.

On Unix, the POSIX standard defines names of constants, but individual implementations of POSIX-compliant Unix systems may assign different numeric values to these constants. You must use the correct numeric value for your operating system of choice. Similarly, POSIX defines a standard for structs used in interop calls. The ordering of fields in the struct is not fixed by the standard, and a Unix implementation might add additional fields. C++ header files defining functions and types are often installed in */usr/include* or */usr/local/include*.

Receiving strings from unmanaged code back to .NET requires that some memory management take place. The marshaler automatically performs this work if you declare the external method with a `StringBuilder` rather than a `string`, as follows:

```
StringBuilder s = new StringBuilder (256);
GetWindowsDirectory (s, 256);
Console.WriteLine (s);

[DllImport("kernel32.dll")]
static extern int GetWindowsDirectory (StringBuilder sb, int maxChars);
```

On Unix, it works similarly. The following calls `getcwd` to return the current directory:

```
var sb = new StringBuilder (256);
Console.WriteLine (getcwd (sb, sb.Capacity));

[DllImport("libc")]
static extern string getcwd (StringBuilder buf, int size);
```

Although `StringBuilder` is convenient to use, it's somewhat inefficient in that the CLR must perform additional memory allocations and copying. In performance hotspots, you can avoid this overhead by using `char[]` instead:

```
[DllImport ("kernel32.dll", CharSet = CharSet.Unicode)]
static extern int GetWindowsDirectory (char[] buffer, int maxChars);
```

Notice that you must specify a `CharSet` in the `DllImport` attribute. You must also trim the output string to length after calling the function. You can achieve this while minimizing memory allocations with the use of array pooling (see "Array Pooling" on page 575), as follows:

```
string GetWindowsDirectory()
{
  var array = ArrayPool<char>.Shared.Rent (256);
  try
  {
    int length = GetWindowsDirectory (array, 256);
```

```
    return new string (array, 0, length).ToString();
  }
  finally { ArrayPool<char>.Shared.Return (array); }
}
```

(Of course, this example is contrived in that you can obtain the Windows directory via the built-in `Environment.GetFolderPath` method.)

 If you are unsure how to call a particular Win32 or Unix method, you will usually find an example on the internet if you search for the method name and *DllImport*. For Windows, the site *http://www.pinvoke.net* is a wiki that aims to document all Win32 signatures.

Marshaling Classes and Structs

Sometimes, you need to pass a struct to an unmanaged method. For example, `GetSystemTime` in the Win32 API is defined as follows:

```
void GetSystemTime (LPSYSTEMTIME lpSystemTime);
```

LPSYSTEMTIME conforms to this C struct:

```
typedef struct _SYSTEMTIME {
  WORD wYear;
  WORD wMonth;
  WORD wDayOfWeek;
  WORD wDay;
  WORD wHour;
  WORD wMinute;
  WORD wSecond;
  WORD wMilliseconds;
} SYSTEMTIME, *PSYSTEMTIME;
```

To call `GetSystemTime`, we must define a .NET class or struct that matches this C struct:

```
using System;
using System.Runtime.InteropServices;

[StructLayout(LayoutKind.Sequential)]
class SystemTime
{
  public ushort Year;
  public ushort Month;
  public ushort DayOfWeek;
  public ushort Day;
  public ushort Hour;
  public ushort Minute;
  public ushort Second;
  public ushort Milliseconds;
}
```

The StructLayout attribute instructs the marshaler how to map each field to its unmanaged counterpart. LayoutKind.Sequential means that we want the fields aligned sequentially on *pack-size* boundaries (you'll see what this means shortly), just as they would be in a C struct. The field names here are irrelevant; it's the ordering of fields that's important.

Now we can call GetSystemTime:

```
SystemTime t = new SystemTime();
GetSystemTime (t);
Console.WriteLine (t.Year);

[DllImport("kernel32.dll")]
static extern void GetSystemTime (SystemTime t);
```

Similarly, on Unix:

```
Console.WriteLine (GetSystemTime());

static DateTime GetSystemTime()
{
  DateTime startOfUnixTime =
    new DateTime(1970, 1, 1, 0, 0, 0, 0, System.DateTimeKind.Utc);

  Timespec tp = new Timespec();
  int success = clock_gettime (0, ref tp);
  if (success != 0) throw new Exception ("Error checking the time.");
  return startOfUnixTime.AddSeconds (tp.tv_sec).ToLocalTime();
}

[DllImport("libc")]
static extern int clock_gettime (int clk_id, ref Timespec tp);

[StructLayout(LayoutKind.Sequential)]
struct Timespec
{
  public long tv_sec;    /* seconds */
  public long tv_nsec;   /* nanoseconds */
}
```

In both C and C#, fields in an object are located at *n* number of bytes from the address of that object. The difference is that in a C# program, the CLR finds this offset by looking it up using the field token; C field names are compiled directly into offsets. For instance, in C, wDay is just a token to represent whatever is at the address of a SystemTime instance plus 24 bytes.

For access speed, each field is placed at an offset that is a multiple of the field's size. That multiplier, however, is restricted to a maximum of *x* bytes, where *x* is the *pack size*. In the current implementation, the default pack size is 8 bytes, so a struct comprising an sbyte followed by an (8-byte) long occupies 16 bytes, and the 7 bytes following the sbyte are wasted. You can lessen or eliminate this wastage by specifying a *pack size* via the Pack property of the StructLayout attribute: this makes the fields align to offsets that are multiples of the specified pack size. So, with a pack size of 1, the struct just described would occupy just 9 bytes. You can specify pack sizes of 1, 2, 4, 8, or 16 bytes.

The `StructLayout` attribute also lets you specify explicit field offsets (see "Simulating a C Union" on page 970).

In and Out Marshaling

In the previous example, we implemented `SystemTime` as a class. We could have instead chosen a struct—provided that `GetSystemTime` was declared with a `ref` or `out` parameter:

```
[DllImport("kernel32.dll")]
static extern void GetSystemTime (out SystemTime t);
```

In most cases, C#'s directional parameter semantics work the same with external methods. Pass-by-value parameters are copied in, C# `ref` parameters are copied in/out, and C# `out` parameters are copied out. However, there are some exceptions for types that have special conversions. For instance, array classes and the `String Builder` class require copying when coming out of a function, so they are in/out. It is occasionally useful to override this behavior, with the `In` and `Out` attributes. For example, if an array should be read-only, the `in` modifier indicates to copy only the array going into the function, not coming out of it:

```
static extern void Foo ( [In] int[] array);
```

Calling Conventions

Unmanaged methods receive arguments and return values via the stack and (optionally) CPU registers. Because there's more than one way to accomplish this, a number of different protocols have emerged. These protocols are known as *calling conventions*.

The CLR currently supports three calling conventions: StdCall, Cdecl, and ThisCall.

By default, the CLR uses the *platform default* calling convention (the standard convention for that platform). On Windows, it's StdCall, and on Linux x86, it's Cdecl.

Should an unmanaged method not follow this default, you can explicitly state its calling convention as follows:

```
[DllImport ("MyLib.dll", CallingConvention=CallingConvention.Cdecl)]
static extern void SomeFunc (...)
```

The somewhat misleadingly named `CallingConvention.WinApi` refers to the platform default.

Callbacks from Unmanaged Code

C# also allows external functions to call C# code, via callbacks. There are two ways to accomplish callbacks:

- Via function pointers (from C# 9)
- Via delegates

To illustrate, we will call the following Windows function in *User32.dll*, which enumerates all top-level window handles:

```
BOOL EnumWindows (WNDENUMPROC lpEnumFunc, LPARAM lParam);
```

WNDENUMPROC is a callback that is fired with the handle of each window in sequence (or until the callback returns `false`). Here is its definition:

```
BOOL CALLBACK EnumWindowsProc (HWND hwnd, LPARAM lParam);
```

Callbacks with Function Pointers

From C# 9, the simplest and most performant option—when your callback is a static method—is to use a *function pointer*. In the case of the WNDENUMPROC callback, we can use the following function pointer:

```
delegate*<IntPtr, IntPtr, bool>
```

This denotes a function that accepts two `IntPtr` arguments and returns a `bool`. You can then use the & operator to feed it a static method:

```
using System;
using System.Runtime.InteropServices;

unsafe
{
  EnumWindows (&PrintWindow, IntPtr.Zero);

  [DllImport ("user32.dll")]
  static extern int EnumWindows (
    delegate*<IntPtr, IntPtr, bool> hWnd, IntPtr lParam);

  static bool PrintWindow (IntPtr hWnd, IntPtr lParam)
  {
    Console.WriteLine (hWnd.ToInt64());
    return true;
  }
}
```

With function pointers, the callback must be a static method (or a static local function, as in this example).

UnmanagedCallersOnly

You can improve performance by applying the unmanaged keyword to the function pointer declaration, and the [UnmanagedCallersOnly] attribute to the callback method:

```
using System;
using System.Runtime.CompilerServices;
using System.Runtime.InteropServices;

unsafe
{
  EnumWindows (&PrintWindow, IntPtr.Zero);

  [DllImport ("user32.dll")]
  static extern int EnumWindows (
    delegate* unmanaged <IntPtr, IntPtr, byte> hWnd, IntPtr lParam);

  [UnmanagedCallersOnly]
  static byte PrintWindow (IntPtr hWnd, IntPtr lParam)
  {
    Console.WriteLine (hWnd.ToInt64());
    return 1;
  }
}
```

This attribute flags the PrintWindow method such that it can be called *only* from unmanaged code, allowing the runtime to take shortcuts. Notice that we've also changed the method's return type from bool to byte: this is because methods to which you apply [UnmanagedCallersOnly] can use only *blittable* value types in the signature. Blittable types are those that don't require any special marshalling logic because they're represented identically in the managed and unmanaged worlds. These include the primitive integral types, float, double, and structs that contain only blittable types. The char type is also blittable, if part of a struct with a Struct Layout attribute specifying CharSet.Unicode:

```
[StructLayout (LayoutKind.Sequential, CharSet=CharSet.Unicode)]
```

Nondefault calling conventions

By default, the compiler assumes that the unmanaged callback follows the platform-default calling convention. Should this not be so, you can explicitly state its calling convention via the CallConvs parameter of the [UnmanagedCallersOnly] attribute:

```
[UnmanagedCallersOnly (CallConvs = new[] { typeof (CallConvStdcall) })]
static byte PrintWindow (IntPtr hWnd, IntPtr lParam) ...
```

You must also update the function pointer type by inserting a special modifier after the unmanaged keyword:

```
delegate* unmanaged[Stdcall] <IntPtr, IntPtr, byte> hWnd, IntPtr lParam);
```

The compiler lets you put any identifier (such as XYZ) inside the square brackets, as long as there's a .NET type called CallConvXYZ (that's understood by the runtime and matches what you specified when applying the [UnmanagedCallersOnly] attribute). This makes it easier for Microsoft to add new calling conventions in the future.

In this case, we specified StdCall, which is the platform default for Windows (Cdecl is the default for Linux x86). Here are all the options that are currently supported:

Name	unmanaged modifier	Supporting type
Stdcall	unmanaged[Stdcall]	CallConvStdcall
Cdecl	unmanaged[Cdecl]	CallConvCdecl
ThisCall	unmanaged[Thiscall]	CallConvThiscall

Callbacks with Delegates

Unmanaged callbacks can also be accomplished with delegates. This approach works in all versions of C#, and allows for callbacks that reference instance methods.

To proceed, first declare a delegate type with a signature that matches the callback. Then you can pass a delegate instance to the external method:

```
class CallbackFun
{
  delegate bool EnumWindowsCallback (IntPtr hWnd, IntPtr lParam);

  [DllImport("user32.dll")]
  static extern int EnumWindows (EnumWindowsCallback hWnd, IntPtr lParam);

  static bool PrintWindow (IntPtr hWnd, IntPtr lParam)
  {
    Console.WriteLine (hWnd.ToInt64());
    return true;
  }
  static readonly EnumWindowsCallback printWindowFunc = PrintWindow;

  static void Main() => EnumWindows (printWindowFunc, IntPtr.Zero);
}
```

Using delegates for unmanaged callbacks is ironically unsafe, because it's easy to fall into the trap of allowing a callback to occur after the delegate instance falls out of scope (at which point the delegate becomes eligible for garbage collection). This can result in the worst kind of runtime exception—one with no useful stack trace. In the case of static method callbacks, you can avoid this by assigning the delegate instance to a read-only static field (as we did in this example). With instance method callbacks, this pattern won't help, so you must code carefully to ensure that you maintain at least one reference to the delegate instance for the duration of any potential callback. Even then, if there's a bug on the unmanaged side—whereby it invokes a callback after you've told it not to—you may still have to deal with an untraceable exception. A workaround is to define a unique delegate type per unmanaged function: this helps diagnostically because the delegate type is reported in the exception.

You can change the callback's calling convention from the platform default by applying the [UnmanagedFunctionPointer] attribute to the delegate:

```
[UnmanagedFunctionPointer (CallingConvention.Cdecl)]
delegate void MyCallback (int foo, short bar);
```

Simulating a C Union

Each field in a struct is given enough room to store its data. Consider a struct containing one int and one char. The int is likely to start at an offset of 0 and is guaranteed at least four bytes. So, the char would start at an offset of at least 4. If, for some reason, the char started at an offset of 2, you'd change the value of the int if you assigned a value to the char. Sounds like mayhem, doesn't it? Strangely enough, the C language supports a variation on a struct called a *union* that does exactly this. You can simulate this in C# by using LayoutKind.Explicit and the FieldOffset attribute.

It might be challenging to think of a case in which this would be useful. However, suppose that you want to play a note on an external synthesizer. The Windows Multimedia API provides a function for doing just this via the MIDI protocol:

```
[DllImport ("winmm.dll")]
public static extern uint midiOutShortMsg (IntPtr handle, uint message);
```

The second argument, message, describes what note to play. The problem is in constructing this 32-bit unsigned integer: it's divided internally into bytes, representing a MIDI channel, note, and velocity at which to strike. One solution is to shift and mask via the bitwise <<, >>, &, and | operators to convert these bytes to and from the 32-bit "packed" message. Far simpler, though, is to define a struct with explicit layout:

```
[StructLayout (LayoutKind.Explicit)]
public struct NoteMessage
{
  [FieldOffset(0)] public uint PackedMsg;     // 4 bytes long

  [FieldOffset(0)] public byte Channel;       // FieldOffset also at 0
  [FieldOffset(1)] public byte Note;
  [FieldOffset(2)] public byte Velocity;
}
```

The Channel, Note, and Velocity fields deliberately overlap with the 32-bit packed message. This allows you to read and write using either. No calculations are required to keep other fields in sync:

```
NoteMessage n = new NoteMessage();
Console.WriteLine (n.PackedMsg);    // 0
```

```
n.Channel = 10;
n.Note = 100;
n.Velocity = 50;
Console.WriteLine (n.PackedMsg);     // 3302410

n.PackedMsg = 3328010;
Console.WriteLine (n.Note);          // 200
```

Shared Memory

Memory-mapped files, or *shared memory*, is a feature in Windows that allows multi-ple processes on the same computer to share data. Shared memory is extremely fast and, unlike pipes, offers *random* access to the shared data. We saw in Chapter 15 how you can use the `MemoryMappedFile` class to access memory-mapped files; bypassing this and calling the Win32 methods directly is a good way to demonstrate P/Invoke.

The Win32 `CreateFileMapping` function allocates shared memory. You tell it how many bytes you need and the name with which to identify the share. Another application can then subscribe to this memory by calling `OpenFileMapping` with the same name. Both methods return a *handle*, which you can convert to a pointer by calling `MapViewOfFile`.

Here's a class that encapsulates access to shared memory:

```
using System;
using System.Runtime.InteropServices;
using System.ComponentModel;

public sealed class SharedMem : IDisposable
{
  // Here we're using enums because they're safer than constants

  enum FileProtection : uint      // constants from winnt.h
  {
    ReadOnly = 2,
    ReadWrite = 4
  }

  enum FileRights : uint          // constants from WinBASE.h
  {
    Read = 4,
    Write = 2,
    ReadWrite = Read + Write
  }

  static readonly IntPtr NoFileHandle = new IntPtr (-1);

  [DllImport ("kernel32.dll", SetLastError = true)]
  static extern IntPtr CreateFileMapping (IntPtr hFile,
                                          int lpAttributes,
                                          FileProtection flProtect,
```

```
                                uint dwMaximumSizeHigh,
                                uint dwMaximumSizeLow,
                                string lpName);

[DllImport ("kernel32.dll", SetLastError=true)]
static extern IntPtr OpenFileMapping (FileRights dwDesiredAccess,
                                      bool bInheritHandle,
                                      string lpName);

[DllImport ("kernel32.dll", SetLastError = true)]
static extern IntPtr MapViewOfFile (IntPtr hFileMappingObject,
                                    FileRights dwDesiredAccess,
                                    uint dwFileOffsetHigh,
                                    uint dwFileOffsetLow,
                                    uint dwNumberOfBytesToMap);

[DllImport ("Kernel32.dll", SetLastError = true)]
static extern bool UnmapViewOfFile (IntPtr map);

[DllImport ("kernel32.dll", SetLastError = true)]
static extern int CloseHandle (IntPtr hObject);

IntPtr fileHandle, fileMap;

public IntPtr Root => fileMap;

public SharedMem (string name, bool existing, uint sizeInBytes)
{
  if (existing)
    fileHandle = OpenFileMapping (FileRights.ReadWrite, false, name);
  else
    fileHandle = CreateFileMapping (NoFileHandle, 0,
                                    FileProtection.ReadWrite,
                                    0, sizeInBytes, name);
  if (fileHandle == IntPtr.Zero)
    throw new Win32Exception();

  // Obtain a read/write map for the entire file
  fileMap = MapViewOfFile (fileHandle, FileRights.ReadWrite, 0, 0, 0);

  if (fileMap == IntPtr.Zero)
    throw new Win32Exception();
}

public void Dispose()
{
  if (fileMap != IntPtr.Zero) UnmapViewOfFile (fileMap);
  if (fileHandle != IntPtr.Zero) CloseHandle (fileHandle);
  fileMap = fileHandle = IntPtr.Zero;
}
}
```

In this example, we set `SetLastError=true` on the `DllImport` methods that use the `SetLastError` protocol for emitting error codes. This ensures that the `Win32Excep tion` is populated with details of the error when that exception is thrown. (It also allows you to query the error explicitly by calling `Marshal.GetLastWin32Error`.)

To demonstrate this class, we need to run two applications. The first one creates the shared memory, as follows:

```
using (SharedMem sm = new SharedMem ("MyShare", false, 1000))
{
  IntPtr root = sm.Root;
  // I have shared memory!

  Console.ReadLine();        // Here's where we start a second app...
}
```

The second application subscribes to the shared memory by constructing a `Share dMem` object of the same name, with the `existing` argument `true`:

```
using (SharedMem sm = new SharedMem ("MyShare", true, 1000))
{
  IntPtr root = sm.Root;
  // I have the same shared memory!
  // ...
}
```

The net result is that each program has an `IntPtr`—a pointer to the same unmanaged memory. The two applications now need somehow to read and write to memory via this common pointer. One approach is to write a class that encapsulates all the shared data and then serialize (and deserialize) the data to the unmanaged memory using an `UnmanagedMemoryStream`. This is inefficient, however, if there's a lot of data. Imagine if the shared memory class had a megabyte of data, and just one integer needed to be updated. A better approach is to define the shared data construct as a struct and then map it directly into shared memory. We discuss this in the following section.

Mapping a Struct to Unmanaged Memory

You can directly map a struct with a `StructLayout` of `Sequential` or `Explicit` into unmanaged memory. Consider the following struct:

```
[StructLayout (LayoutKind.Sequential)]
unsafe struct MySharedData
{
  public int Value;
  public char Letter;
  public fixed float Numbers [50];
}
```

The `fixed` directive allows us to define fixed-length value-type arrays inline, and it is what takes us into the `unsafe` realm. Space in this struct is allocated inline for 50 floating-point numbers. Unlike with standard C# arrays, Numbers is not a *reference* to an array—it *is* the array. If we run the following:

```
static unsafe void Main() => Console.WriteLine (sizeof (MySharedData));
```

the result is 208: 50 four-byte floats, plus the four bytes for the Value integer, plus two bytes for the Letter character. The total, 206, is rounded to 208 due to the floats being aligned on four-byte boundaries (four bytes being the size of a float).

We can demonstrate MySharedData in an unsafe context, most simply, with stack-allocated memory:

```
MySharedData d;
MySharedData* data = &d;          // Get the address of d

data->Value = 123;
data->Letter = 'X';
data->Numbers[10] = 1.45f;
```

or:

```
// Allocate the array on the stack:
MySharedData* data = stackalloc MySharedData[1];

data->Value = 123;
data->Letter = 'X';
data->Numbers[10] = 1.45f;
```

Of course, we're not demonstrating anything that couldn't otherwise be achieved in a managed context. Suppose, however, that we want to store an instance of MySharedData on the *unmanaged heap*, outside the realm of the CLR's garbage collector. This is where pointers become really useful:

```
MySharedData* data = (MySharedData*)
    Marshal.AllocHGlobal (sizeof (MySharedData)).ToPointer();

data->Value = 123;
data->Letter = 'X';
data->Numbers[10] = 1.45f;
```

Marshal.AllocHGlobal allocates memory on the unmanaged heap. Here's how to later free the same memory:

```
Marshal.FreeHGlobal (new IntPtr (data));
```

(The result of forgetting to free the memory is a good old-fashioned memory leak.)

 From .NET 6, you can instead use the new NativeMemory class for allocating and freeing unmanaged memory. NativeMemory uses a newer (and better) underlying API than AllocHGlobal and also includes methods for performing aligned allocations.

In keeping with its name, here we use MySharedData in conjunction with the Share dMem class we wrote in the preceding section. The following program allocates a block of shared memory, and then maps the MySharedData struct into that memory:

```
static unsafe void Main()
{
  using (SharedMem sm = new SharedMem ("MyShare", false,
                        (uint) sizeof (MySharedData)))
  {
    void* root = sm.Root.ToPointer();
    MySharedData* data = (MySharedData*) root;

    data->Value = 123;
    data->Letter = 'X';
    data->Numbers[10] = 1.45f;
    Console.WriteLine ("Written to shared memory");

    Console.ReadLine();

    Console.WriteLine ("Value is " + data->Value);
    Console.WriteLine ("Letter is " + data->Letter);
    Console.WriteLine ("11th Number is " + data->Numbers[10]);
    Console.ReadLine();
  }
}
```

 You can use the built-in MemoryMappedFile class instead of
SharedMem, as follows:

```
using (MemoryMappedFile mmFile =
        MemoryMappedFile.CreateNew ("MyShare", 1000))
using (MemoryMappedViewAccessor accessor =
        mmFile.CreateViewAccessor())
{
  byte* pointer = null;
  accessor.SafeMemoryMappedViewHandle.AcquirePointer
  (ref pointer);
  void* root = pointer;
  ...
}
```

Here's a second program that attaches to the same shared memory, reading the
values written by the first program (it must be run while the first program is waiting
on the ReadLine statement because the shared memory object is disposed upon
leaving its using statement):

```
static unsafe void Main()
{
  using (SharedMem sm = new SharedMem ("MyShare", true,
                        (uint) sizeof (MySharedData)))
  {
    void* root = sm.Root.ToPointer();
    MySharedData* data = (MySharedData*) root;

    Console.WriteLine ("Value is " + data->Value);
    Console.WriteLine ("Letter is " + data->Letter);
    Console.WriteLine ("11th Number is " + data->Numbers[10]);

    // Our turn to update values in shared memory!
    data->Value++;
    data->Letter = '!';
```

```
    data->Numbers[10] = 987.5f;
    Console.WriteLine ("Updated shared memory");
    Console.ReadLine();
  }
}
```

The output from each of these programs is as follows:

```
// First program:

Written to shared memory
Value is 124
Letter is !
11th Number is 987.5

// Second program:

Value is 123
Letter is X
11th Number is 1.45
Updated shared memory
```

Don't be put off by the pointers: C++ programmers use them throughout whole applications and are able to get everything working. At least most of the time! This sort of usage is fairly simple by comparison.

As it happens, our example is unsafe—quite literally—for another reason. We've not considered the thread-safety (or more precisely, process-safety) issues that arise with two programs accessing the same memory at once. To use this in a production application, we'd need to add the volatile keyword to the Value and Letter fields in the MySharedData struct to prevent fields from being cached by the Just-in-Time (JIT) compiler (or by the hardware in CPU registers). Furthermore, as our interaction with the fields grew beyond the trivial, we would most likely need to protect their access via a cross-process Mutex, just as we would use lock statements to protect access to fields in a multithreaded program. We discussed thread safety in detail in Chapter 21.

fixed and fixed {...}

One limitation of mapping structs directly into memory is that the struct can contain only unmanaged types. If you need to share string data, for instance, you must use a fixed-character array instead. This means manual conversion to and from the string type. Here's how to do it:

```
[StructLayout (LayoutKind.Sequential)]
unsafe struct MySharedData
{
  ...
  // Allocate space for 200 chars (i.e., 400 bytes).
  const int MessageSize = 200;
  fixed char message [MessageSize];

  // One would most likely put this code into a helper class:
```

```
public string Message
{
  get { fixed (char* cp = message) return new string (cp); }
  set
  {
    fixed (char* cp = message)
    {
      int i = 0;
      for (; i < value.Length && i < MessageSize - 1; i++)
        cp [i] = value [i];

      // Add the null terminator
      cp [i] = '\0';
    }
  }
}
```

 There's no such thing as a reference to a fixed array; instead, you get a pointer. When you index into a fixed array, you're actually performing pointer arithmetic!

With the first use of the fixed keyword, we allocate space, inline, for 200 characters in the struct. The same keyword (somewhat confusingly) has a different meaning when used later in the property definition. It instructs the CLR to *pin* an object so that should it decide to perform a garbage collection inside the fixed block, it will not move the underlying struct about on the memory heap (because its contents are being iterated via direct memory pointers). Looking at our program, you might wonder how MySharedData could ever shift in memory, given that it resides not on the heap but in the unmanaged world, where the garbage collector has no jurisdiction. The compiler doesn't know this, however, and is concerned that we *might* use MySharedData in a managed context, so it insists that we add the fixed keyword to make our unsafe code safe in managed contexts. And the compiler does have a point—here's all it would take to put MySharedData on the heap:

```
object obj = new MySharedData();
```

This results in a boxed MySharedData—on the heap and eligible for transit during garbage collection.

This example illustrates how a string can be represented in a struct mapped to unmanaged memory. For more complex types, you also have the option of using existing serialization code. The one proviso is that the serialized data must never exceed, in length, its allocation of space in the struct; otherwise, the result is an unintended union with subsequent fields.

COM Interoperability

The .NET runtime provides special support for COM, enabling COM objects to be used from .NET, and vice versa. COM is available only on Windows.

The Purpose of COM

COM is an acronym for Component Object Model, a binary standard for interfacing with libraries, released by Microsoft in 1993. The motivation for inventing COM was to enable components to communicate with each other in a language-independent and version-tolerant manner. Before COM, the approach in Windows was to publish DLLs that declared structures and functions using the C programming language. Not only is this approach language specific, but it's also brittle. The specification of a type in such a library is inseparable from its implementation: even updating a structure with a new field means breaking its specification.

The beauty of COM was to separate the specification of a type from its underlying implementation through a construct known as a *COM interface*. COM also allowed for the calling of methods on stateful *objects*—rather than being limited to simple procedure calls.

 In a way, the .NET programming model is an evolution of the principles of COM programming: the .NET platform also facilitates cross-language development and allows binary components to evolve without breaking applications that depend on them.

The Basics of the COM Type System

The COM type system revolves around interfaces. A COM interface is rather like a .NET interface, but it's more prevalent because a COM type exposes its functionality *only* through an interface. In the .NET world, for instance, we could declare a type simply, as follows:

```
public class Foo
{
  public string Test() => "Hello, world";
}
```

Consumers of that type can use Foo directly. And if we later changed the *implementation* of Test(), calling assemblies would not require recompilation. In this respect, .NET separates interface from implementation—without requiring interfaces. We could even add an overload without breaking callers:

```
public string Test (string s) => $"Hello, world {s}";
```

In the COM world, Foo exposes its functionality through an interface to achieve this same decoupling. So, in Foo's type library, an interface such as this would exist:

```
public interface IFoo { string Test(); }
```

(We've illustrated this by showing a C# interface—not a COM interface. The principle, however, is the same—although the plumbing is different.)

Callers would then interact with IFoo rather than Foo.

When it comes to adding the overloaded version of Test, life is more complicated with COM than with .NET. First, we would avoid modifying the IFoo interface because this would break binary compatibility with the previous version (one of the principles of COM is that interfaces, once published, are *immutable*). Second, COM doesn't allow method overloading. The solution is to instead have Foo implement a *second interface*:

```
public interface IFoo2 { string Test (string s); }
```

(Again, we've transliterated this into a .NET interface for familiarity.)

Supporting multiple interfaces is of key importance in making COM libraries versionable.

IUnknown and IDispatch

All COM interfaces are identified with a Globally Unique Identifier (GUID).

The root interface in COM is IUnknown—all COM objects must implement it. This interface has three methods:

- AddRef
- Release
- QueryInterface

AddRef and Release are for lifetime management given that COM uses reference counting rather than automatic garbage collection (COM was designed to work with unmanaged code, where automatic garbage collection isn't feasible). The Query Interface method returns an object reference that supports that interface, if it can do so.

To enable dynamic programming (e.g., scripting and automation), a COM object can also implement IDispatch. This enables dynamic languages such as VBScript to call COM objects in a late-bound manner—rather like dynamic in C# (although only for simple invocations).

Calling a COM Component from C#

The CLR's built-in support for COM means that you don't work directly with IUnknown and IDispatch. Instead, you work with CLR objects, and the runtime marshals your calls to the COM world via Runtime-Callable Wrappers (RCWs). The runtime also handles lifetime management by calling AddRef and Release (when the .NET object is finalized) and takes care of the primitive type conversions between the two worlds. Type conversion ensures that each side sees, for example, the integer and string types in their familiar forms.

Additionally, there needs to be some way to access RCWs in a statically typed fashion. This is the job of *COM interop types*. COM interop types are automatically generated proxy types that expose a .NET member for each COM member. The type library importer tool (*tlbimp.exe*) generates COM interop types from the command line, based on a COM library that you choose, and compiles them into a *COM interop assembly.*

> If a COM component implements multiple interfaces, the *tlbimp.exe* tool generates a single type that contains a union of members from all interfaces.

You can create a COM interop assembly in Visual Studio by going to the Add Reference dialog box and choosing a library from the COM tab. For example, if you have Microsoft Excel installed, adding a reference to the Microsoft Excel Object Library allows you to interoperate with Excel's COM classes. Here's the C# code to create and show a workbook, and then populate a cell in that workbook:

```
using System;
using Excel = Microsoft.Office.Interop.Excel;

var excel = new Excel.Application();
excel.Visible = true;
Excel.Workbook workBook = excel.Workbooks.Add();
((Excel.Range)excel.Cells[1, 1]).Font.FontStyle = "Bold";
((Excel.Range)excel.Cells[1, 1]).Value2 = "Hello World";
workBook.SaveAs (@"d:\temp.xlsx");
```

> It is currently necessary to embed interop types in your application (otherwise, the runtime won't locate them at runtime). Either click the COM reference in Visual Studio's Solution Explorer and set the Embed Interop Types property to true in the Properties window, or open your *.csproj* file and add the following line (in boldface):
>
> ```
> <ItemGroup>
>   <COMReference Include="Microsoft.Office.Excel.dll">
>     ...
>     <EmbedInteropTypes>true</EmbedInteropTypes>
>   </COMReference>
> </ItemGroup>
> ```

The `Excel.Application` class is a COM interop type whose runtime type is an RCW. When we access the `Workbooks` and `Cells` properties, we get back more interop types.

Optional Parameters and Named Arguments

Because COM APIs don't support function overloading, it's very common to have functions with numerous parameters, many of which are optional. For instance, here's how you might call an Excel workbook's `Save` method:

```
var missing = System.Reflection.Missing.Value;

workBook.SaveAs (@"d:\temp.xlsx", missing, missing, missing, missing,
  missing, Excel.XlSaveAsAccessMode.xlNoChange, missing, missing,
  missing, missing, missing);
```

The good news is that the C#'s support for optional parameters is COM-aware, so we can just do this:

```
workBook.SaveAs (@"d:\temp.xlsx");
```

(As we stated in Chapter 3, optional parameters are "expanded" by the compiler into the full verbose form.)

Named arguments allow you to specify additional arguments, regardless of their position:

```
workBook.SaveAs (@"c:\test.xlsx", Password:"foo");
```

Implicit ref Parameters

Some COM APIs (Microsoft Word, in particular) expose functions that declare *every* parameter as pass-by-reference—whether or not the function modifies the parameter value. This is because of the perceived performance gain from not copying argument values (the *real* performance gain is negligible).

Historically, calling such methods from C# has been clumsy because you must specify the ref keyword with every argument, and this prevents the use of optional parameters. For instance, to open a Word document, we used to have to do this:

```
object filename = "foo.doc";
object notUsed1 = Missing.Value;
object notUsed2 = Missing.Value;
object notUsed3 = Missing.Value;
...
Open (ref filename, ref notUsed1, ref notUsed2, ref notUsed3, ...);
```

Thanks to implicit ref parameters, you can omit the ref modifier on COM function calls, allowing the use of optional parameters:

```
word.Open ("foo.doc");
```

The caveat is that you will get neither a compile-time nor a runtime error if the COM method you're calling actually does mutate an argument value.

Indexers

The ability to omit the ref modifier has another benefit: it makes COM indexers with ref parameters accessible via ordinary C# indexer syntax. This would otherwise be forbidden because ref/out parameters are not supported with C# indexers.

You can also call COM properties that accept arguments. In the following example, Foo is a property that accepts an integer argument:

```
myComObject.Foo [123] = "Hello";
```

Writing such properties yourself in C# is still prohibited: a type can expose an indexer only on itself (the "default" indexer). Therefore, if you wanted to write code in C# that would make the preceding statement legal, Foo would need to return another type that exposed a (default) indexer.

Dynamic Binding

There are two ways that dynamic binding can help when calling COM components.

The first way is in allowing access to a COM component without a COM interop type. To do this, call `Type.GetTypeFromProgID` with the COM component name to obtain a COM instance, and then use dynamic binding to call members from then on. Of course, there's no IntelliSense, and compile-time checks are impossible:

```
Type excelAppType = Type.GetTypeFromProgID ("Excel.Application", true);
dynamic excel = Activator.CreateInstance (excelAppType);
excel.Visible = true;
dynamic wb = excel.Workbooks.Add();
excel.Cells [1, 1].Value2 = "foo";
```

(The same thing can be achieved, much more clumsily, with reflection instead of dynamic binding.)

 A variation of this theme is calling a COM component that supports *only* `IDispatch`. Such components are quite rare, however.

Dynamic binding can also be useful (to a lesser extent) in dealing with the COM `variant` type. For reasons due more to poor design than necessity, COM API functions are often peppered with this type, which is roughly equivalent to `object` in .NET. If you enable "Embed Interop Types" in your project (more on this soon), the runtime will map `variant` to `dynamic`, instead of mapping `variant` to `object`, avoiding the need for casts. For instance, you could legally do

```
excel.Cells [1, 1].Font.FontStyle = "Bold";
```

instead of:

```
var range = (Excel.Range) excel.Cells [1, 1];
range.Font.FontStyle = "Bold";
```

The disadvantage of working in this way is that you lose autocompletion, so you must know that a property called `Font` happens to exist. For this reason, it's usually easier to *dynamically* assign the result to its known interop type:

```
Excel.Range range = excel.Cells [1, 1];
range.Font.FontStyle = "Bold";
```

As you can see, this saves only five characters over the old-fashioned approach!

The mapping of `variant` to `dynamic` is the default, and is a function of enabling Embed Interop Types on a reference.

Embedding Interop Types

We said previously that C# ordinarily calls COM components via interop types that are generated by calling the *tlbimp.exe* tool (directly or via Visual Studio).

Historically, your only option was to *reference* interop assemblies just as you would with any other assembly. This could be troublesome because interop assemblies can get quite large with complex COM components. A tiny add-in for Microsoft Word, for instance, requires an interop assembly that is orders of magnitude larger than itself.

Rather than *referencing* an interop assembly, you have the option of embedding the portions that you use. The compiler analyzes the assembly to work out precisely the types and members that your application requires, and embeds definitions for (just) those types and members directly in your application. This avoids bloat as well as the need to ship an additional file.

To enable this feature, either select the COM reference in Visual Studio's Solution Explorer and then set Embed Interop Types to true in the Properties window, or edit your *.csproj* file as we described earlier (see "Calling a COM Component from C#" on page 979).

Type Equivalence

The CLR supports *type equivalence* for linked interop types. This means that if two assemblies each link to an interop type, those types will be considered equivalent if they wrap the same COM type. This holds true even if the interop assemblies to which they linked were generated independently.

Type equivalence relies on the `TypeIdentifierAttribute` attribute in the `System.Runtime.InteropServices` namespace. The compiler automatically applies this attribute when you link to interop assemblies. COM types are then considered equivalent if they have the same GUID.

Exposing C# Objects to COM

Native and
COM Inter-
operability

It's also possible to write classes in C# that can be consumed in the COM world. The CLR makes this possible through a proxy called a *COM-Callable Wrapper* (CCW). A CCW marshals types between the two worlds (as with an RCW) and implements IUnknown (and optionally IDispatch) as required by the COM protocol. A CCW is lifetime-controlled from the COM side via reference counting (rather than through the CLR's garbage collector).

You can expose any public class to COM (as an "in-proc" server). To do so, first create an interface, assign it a unique GUID (in Visual Studio, you can use Tools > Create GUID), declare it visible to COM, and then set the interface type:

```
namespace MyCom
{
  [ComVisible(true)]
  [Guid ("226E5561-C68E-4B2B-BD28-25103ABCA3B1")]  // Change this GUID
  [InterfaceType (ComInterfaceType.InterfaceIsIUnknown)]
  public interface IServer
  {
```

```
    int Fibonacci();
  }
}
```

Next, provide an implementation of your interface, assigning a unique GUID to that implementation:

```
namespace MyCom
{
  [ComVisible(true)]
  [Guid ("09E01FCD-9970-4DB3-B537-0EC555967DD9")]  // Change this GUID
  public class Server
  {
    public ulong Fibonacci (ulong whichTerm)
    {
      if (whichTerm < 1) throw new ArgumentException ("...");
      ulong a = 0;
      ulong b = 1;
      for (ulong i = 0; i < whichTerm; i++)
      {
        ulong tmp = a;
        a = b;
        b = tmp + b;
      }
      return a;
    }
  }
}
```

Edit your *.csproj* file, adding the following line (in boldface):

```
<PropertyGroup>
  <TargetFramework>netcoreapp3.0</TargetFramework>
  <EnableComHosting>true</EnableComHosting>
</PropertyGroup>
```

Now, when you build your project, an additional file is generated, *MyCom .comhost.dll*, which can be registered for COM interop. (Keep in mind that the file will always be 32 bit or 64 bit depending on your project configuration: there's no such thing as "Any CPU" in this scenario.) From an *elevated* command prompt, switch to the directory holding your DLL and run *regsvr32 MyCom.comhost.dll*.

You can then consume your COM component from most COM-capable languages. For example, you can create this Visual Basic Script in a text editor and run it by double-clicking the file in Windows Explorer, or by starting it from a command prompt as you would a program:

```
REM Save file as ComClient.vbs
Dim obj
Set obj = CreateObject("MyCom.Server")

result = obj.Fibonacci(12)
Wscript.Echo result
```

Note that .NET Framework cannot be loaded into the same process as .NET 5+ or .NET Core. Therefore, a .NET 5+ COM server cannot be loaded into a .NET Framework COM client process, or vice versa.

Enabling Registry-Free COM

Traditionally, COM adds type information to the registry. Registry-free COM uses a manifest file instead of the registry to control object activation. To enable this feature, add the following line (in boldface) to your *.csproj* file:

```
<PropertyGroup>
  <TargetFramework>netcoreapp3.0</TargetFramework>
  <EnableComHosting>true</EnableComHosting>
  <EnableRegFreeCom>true</EnableRegFreeCom>
</PropertyGroup>
```

Your build will then generate *MyCom.X.manifest*.

 There is no support in .NET 5+ for generating a COM type library (*.tlb). You can manually write an IDL (Interface Definition Language) file or C++ header for the native declarations in your interface.

25

Regular Expressions

The regular expressions language identifies character patterns. The .NET types supporting regular expressions are based on Perl 5 regular expressions and support both search and search/replace functionality.

Regular expressions are used for tasks such as:

- Validating text input such as passwords and phone numbers
- Parsing textual data into more structured forms (e.g., a NuGet version string)
- Replacing patterns of text in a document (e.g., whole words only)

This chapter is split into both conceptual sections teaching the basics of regular expressions in .NET, and reference sections describing the regular expressions language.

All regular expression types are defined in `System.Text.RegularExpressions`.

 The samples in this chapter are all preloaded into LINQ-Pad, which also includes an interactive RegEx tool (press Ctrl+Shift+F1). An online tool is available at *http://regex storm.net/tester*.

Regular Expression Basics

One of the most common regular expression operators is a *quantifier*. ? is a quantifier that matches the preceding item 0 or 1 time. In other words, ? means *optional*. An item is either a single character or a complex structure of characters in square brackets. For example, the regular expression `"colou?r"` matches color and colour, but not colouur:

```
Console.WriteLine (Regex.Match ("color",   @"colou?r").Success); // True
Console.WriteLine (Regex.Match ("colour",  @"colou?r").Success); // True
Console.WriteLine (Regex.Match ("colouur", @"colou?r").Success); // False
```

Regex.Match searches within a larger string. The object that it returns has properties for the Index and Length of the match as well as the actual Value matched:

```
Match m = Regex.Match ("any colour you like", @"colou?r");

Console.WriteLine (m.Success);      // True
Console.WriteLine (m.Index);        // 4
Console.WriteLine (m.Length);       // 6
Console.WriteLine (m.Value);        // colour
Console.WriteLine (m.ToString());   // colour
```

You can think of Regex.Match as a more powerful version of the string's IndexOf method. The difference is that it searches for a *pattern* rather than a literal string.

The IsMatch method is a shortcut for calling Match and then testing the Success property.

The regular expressions engine works from left to right by default, so only the leftmost match is returned. You can use the NextMatch method to return more matches:

```
Match m1 = Regex.Match ("One color? There are two colours in my head!",
                        @"colou?rs?");
Match m2 = m1.NextMatch();
Console.WriteLine (m1);      // color
Console.WriteLine (m2);      // colours
```

The Matches method returns all matches in an array. We can rewrite the preceding example, as follows:

```
foreach (Match m in Regex.Matches
        ("One color? There are two colours in my head!", @"colou?rs?"))
    Console.WriteLine (m);
```

Another common regular expressions operator is the *alternator*, expressed with a vertical bar, |. An alternator expresses alternatives. The following matches "Jen", "Jenny", and "Jennifer":

```
Console.WriteLine (Regex.IsMatch ("Jenny", "Jen(ny|nifer)?"));  // True
```

The brackets around an alternator separate the alternatives from the rest of the expression.

 You can specify a timeout when matching regular expressions. If a match operation takes longer than the specified TimeSpan, a RegexMatchTimeoutException is thrown. This can be useful if your program processes arbitrary regular expressions (for instance, in an advanced search dialog box) because it prevents malformed regular expressions from infinitely spinning.

Compiled Regular Expressions

In some of the preceding examples, we called a static RegEx method repeatedly with the same pattern. An alternative approach in these cases is to instantiate a Regex object with the pattern and RegexOptions.Compiled and then call instance methods:

```
Regex r = new Regex (@"sausages?", RegexOptions.Compiled);
Console.WriteLine (r.Match ("sausage"));    // sausage
Console.WriteLine (r.Match ("sausages"));   // sausages
```

RegexOptions.Compiled instructs the RegEx instance to use lightweight code generation (DynamicMethod in Reflection.Emit) to dynamically build and compile code tailored to that particular regular expression. This results in faster matching, at the expense of an initial compilation cost.

You can also instantiate a Regex object without using RegexOptions.Compiled. A Regex instance is immutable.

 The regular expressions engine is fast. Even without compilation, a simple match typically takes less than a microsecond.

RegexOptions

The RegexOptions flags enum lets you tweak matching behavior. A common use for RegexOptions is to perform a case-insensitive search:

```
Console.WriteLine (Regex.Match ("a", "A", RegexOptions.IgnoreCase)); // a
```

This applies the current culture's rules for case equivalence. The CultureInvariant flag lets you request the invariant culture instead:

```
Console.WriteLine (Regex.Match ("a", "A", RegexOptions.IgnoreCase
                     | RegexOptions.CultureInvariant));
```

You can activate most of the RegexOptions flags within a regular expression itself, using a single-letter code, as follows:

```
Console.WriteLine (Regex.Match ("a", @"(?i)A"));                    // a
```

You can turn options on and off throughout an expression:

```
Console.WriteLine (Regex.Match ("AAAa", @"(?i)a(?-i)a"));          // Aa
```

Another useful option is IgnorePatternWhitespace or (?x). This allows you to insert whitespace to make a regular expression more readable—without the whitespace being taken literally.

Table 25-1 lists all RegExOptions values along with their single-letter codes.

Table 25-1. Regular expression options

Enum value	Regular expressions code	Description
None		
IgnoreCase	i	Ignores case (by default, regular expressions are case sensitive)
Multiline	m	Changes ^ and $ so that they match the start/end of a line instead of start/end of the string
ExplicitCapture	n	Captures only explicitly named or explicitly numbered groups (see "Groups" on page 996)
Compiled		Forces compilation to IL (see "Compiled Regular Expressions" on page 989)
Singleline	s	Makes . match every character (instead of matching every character except \n)
IgnorePatternWhitespace	x	Eliminates unescaped whitespace from the pattern
RightToLeft	r	Searches from right to left; can't be specified midstream
ECMAScript		Forces ECMA compliance (by default, the implementation is not ECMA compliant)
CultureInvariant		Turns off culture-specific behavior for string comparisons

Character Escapes

Regular expressions have the following metacharacters, which have a special rather than literal meaning:

        \ * + ? | { [( ) ^ $. #

To use a metacharacter literally, you must prefix, or *escape*, the character with a backslash. In the following example, we escape the ? character to match the string "what?":

```
Console.WriteLine (Regex.Match ("what?", @"what\?")); // what? (correct)
Console.WriteLine (Regex.Match ("what?", @"what?"));  // what  (incorrect)
```

 If the character is inside a *set* (square brackets), this rule does not apply, and the metacharacters are interpreted literally. We discuss sets in the following section.

The Regex's Escape and Unescape methods convert a string containing regular expression metacharacters by replacing them with escaped equivalents, and vice versa:

```
Console.WriteLine (Regex.Escape   (@"?"));    // \?
Console.WriteLine (Regex.Unescape (@"\?"));   // ?>
```

All the regular expression strings in this chapter are expressed with the C# @ literal. This is to bypass C#'s escape mechanism, which also uses the backslash. Without the @, a literal backslash would require four backslashes:

```
Console.WriteLine (Regex.Match ("\\", "\\\\"));    // \
```

Unless you include the (?x) option, spaces are treated literally in regular expressions:

```
Console.Write (Regex.IsMatch ("hello world", @"hello world"));  // True
```

Character Sets

Character sets act as wildcards for a particular set of characters.

Expression	Meaning	Inverse ("not")
[abcdef]	Matches a single character in the list.	[^abcdef]
[a-f]	Matches a single character in a *range*.	[^a-f]
\d	Matches anything in the Unicode *digits* category. In ECMAScript mode, [0-9].	\D
\w	Matches a *word* character (by default, varies according to CultureInfo.CurrentCulture; for example, in English, same as [a-zA-Z_0-9]).	\W
\s	Matches a whitespace character; that is, anything for which char.IsWhiteSpace returns true (including Unicode spaces). In ECMAScript mode, [\n\r\t\f\v].	\S
\p{*category*}	Matches a character in a specified *category*.	\P
.	(Default mode) Matches any character except \n.	\n
.	(SingleLine mode) Matches any character.	\n

To match exactly one of a set of characters, put the character set in square brackets:

```
Console.Write (Regex.Matches ("That is that.", "[Tt]hat").Count);   // 2
```

To match any character *except* those in a set, put the set in square brackets with a ^ symbol before the first character:

```
Console.Write (Regex.Match ("quiz qwerty", "q[^aeiou]").Index);    // 5
```

You can specify a range of characters by using a hyphen. The following regular expression matches a chess move:

```
Console.Write (Regex.Match ("b1-c4", @"[a-h]\d-[a-h]\d").Success);  // True
```

\d indicates a digit character, so \d will match any digit. \D matches any nondigit character.

\w indicates a word character, which includes letters, numbers, and the underscore. \W matches any nonword character. These work as expected for non-English letters, too, such as Cyrillic.

. matches any character except \n (but allows \r).

\p matches a character in a specified category, such as {Lu} for uppercase letter or {P} for punctuation (we list the categories in the reference section later in the chapter):

```
Console.Write (Regex.IsMatch ("Yes, please", @"\p{P}"));   // True
```

We will find more uses for \d, \w, and . when we combine them with *quantifiers*.

Quantifiers

Quantifiers match an item a specified number of times.

Quantifier	Meaning
*	Zero or more matches
+	One or more matches
?	Zero or one match
{*n*}	Exactly *n* matches
{*n*,}	At least *n* matches
{*n*,*m*}	Between *n* and *m* matches

The * quantifier matches the preceding character or group zero or more times. The following matches *cv.docx*, along with any numbered versions of the same file (e.g., *cv2.docx*, *cv15.docx*):

```
Console.Write (Regex.Match ("cv15.docx", @"cv\d*\.docx").Success);  // True
```

Notice that we must escape the period in the file extension using a backslash.

The following allows anything between *cv* and *.docx* and is equivalent to dir cv*.docx:

```
Console.Write (Regex.Match ("cvjoint.docx", @"cv.*\.docx").Success); // True
```

The + quantifier matches the preceding character or group one or more times. For example:

```
Console.Write (Regex.Matches ("slow! yeah slooow!", "slo+w").Count);  // 2
```

The {} quantifier matches a specified number (or range) of repetitions. The following matches a blood pressure reading:

```
Regex bp = new Regex (@"\d{2,3}/\d{2,3}");
Console.WriteLine (bp.Match ("It used to be 160/110"));  // 160/110
Console.WriteLine (bp.Match ("Now it's only 115/75"));   // 115/75
```

Greedy Versus Lazy Quantifiers

By default, quantifiers are *greedy*, as opposed to *lazy*. A greedy quantifier repeats as *many* times as it can before advancing. A lazy quantifier repeats as *few* times as it can before advancing. You can make any quantifier lazy by suffixing it with the ? symbol. To illustrate the difference, consider the following HTML fragment:

```
string html = "<i>By default</i> quantifiers are <i>greedy</i> creatures";
```

Suppose that we want to extract the two phrases in italics. If we execute the following

```
foreach (Match m in Regex.Matches (html, @"<i>.*</i>"))
  Console.WriteLine (m);
```

the result is not two matches, but a *single* match:

```
<i>By default</i> quantifiers are <i>greedy</i>
```

The problem is that our * quantifier greedily repeats as many times as it can before matching `</i>`. So, it passes right by the first `</i>`, stopping only at the final `</i>` (the *last point* at which the rest of the expression can still match).

If we make the quantifier lazy, the * bails out at the *first* point at which the rest of the expression can match:

```
foreach (Match m in Regex.Matches (html, @"<i>.*?</i>"))
  Console.WriteLine (m);
```

Here's the result:

```
<i>By default</i>
<i>greedy</i>
```

Zero-Width Assertions

The regular expressions language lets you place conditions on what should occur *before* or *after* a match, through *lookbehind*, *lookahead*, *anchors*, and *word boundaries*. These are called *zero-width* assertions because they don't increase the width (or length) of the match itself.

Lookahead and Lookbehind

The (?=*expr*) construct checks whether the text that follows matches *expr*, without including expr in the result. This is called *positive lookahead*. In the following example, we look for a number followed by the word "miles":

```
Console.WriteLine (Regex.Match ("say 25 miles more", @"\d+\s(?=miles)"));
```

OUTPUT: 25

Notice that the word "miles" was not returned in the result, even though it was required to *satisfy* the match.

After a successful *lookahead*, matching continues as though the sneak preview never took place. So, if we append .* to our expression like this:

```
Console.WriteLine (Regex.Match ("say 25 miles more", @"\d+\s(?=miles).*"));
```

the result is 25 miles more.

Lookahead can be useful in enforcing rules for a strong password. Suppose that a password must be at least six characters and contain at least one digit. With a lookup, we could achieve this, as follows:

```
string password = "...";
bool ok = Regex.IsMatch (password, @"(?=.*\d).{6,}");
```

This first performs a *lookahead* to ensure that a digit occurs somewhere in the string. If satisfied, it returns to its position before the sneak preview began and matches six or more characters. (In "Cookbook Regular Expressions" on page 999, we include a more substantial password validation example.)

The opposite is the *negative lookahead* construct, (?!*expr*). This requires that the match *not* be followed by *expr*. The following expression matches "good"—unless "however" or "but" appears later in the string:

```
string regex = "(?i)good(?!.*(however|but))";
Console.WriteLine (Regex.IsMatch ("Good work! But...", regex));  // False
Console.WriteLine (Regex.IsMatch ("Good work! Thanks!", regex));  // True
```

The (?<=*expr*) construct denotes *positive lookbehind* and requires that a match be *preceded* by a specified expression. The opposite construct, (?<!*expr*), denotes *negative lookbehind* and requires that a match *not be preceded* by a specified expression. For example, the following matches "good"—unless "however" appears *earlier* in the string:

```
string regex = "(?i)(?<!however.*)good";
Console.WriteLine (Regex.IsMatch ("However good, we...", regex)); // False
Console.WriteLine (Regex.IsMatch ("Very good, thanks!", regex));  // True
```

We could improve these examples by adding *word boundary assertions*, which we introduce shortly.

Anchors

The anchors ^ and $ match a particular *position*. By default:

^

Matches the *start* of the string

$

Matches the *end* of the string

^ has two context-dependent meanings: an *anchor* and a *character class negator*.

$ has two context-dependent meanings: an *anchor* and a *replacement group denoter*.

For example:

```
Console.WriteLine (Regex.Match ("Not now", "^[Nn]o"));   // No
Console.WriteLine (Regex.Match ("f = 0.2F", "[Ff]$"));   // F
```

When you specify `RegexOptions.Multiline` or include (`?m`) in the expression:

- ^ matches the start of the string or *line* (directly after a \n).
- $ matches the end of the string or *line* (directly before a \n).

There's a catch to using $ in multiline mode: a new line in Windows is nearly always denoted with \r\n rather than just \n. This means that for $ to be useful for Windows files, you must usually match the \r, as well, with a *positive lookahead*:

```
(?=\r?$)
```

The *positive lookahead* ensures that \r doesn't become part of the result. The following matches lines that end in ".txt":

```
string fileNames = "a.txt" + "\r\n" + "b.docx" + "\r\n" + "c.txt";
string r = @".+\.txt(?=\r?$)";
foreach (Match m in Regex.Matches (fileNames, r, RegexOptions.Multiline))
  Console.Write (m + " ");

OUTPUT: a.txt c.txt
```

The following matches all empty lines in string s:

```
MatchCollection emptyLines = Regex.Matches (s, "^(?=\r?$)",
                                       RegexOptions.Multiline);
```

The following matches all lines that are either empty or contain only whitespace:

```
MatchCollection blankLines = Regex.Matches (s, "^[ \t]*(?=\r?$)",
                                       RegexOptions.Multiline);
```

Because an anchor matches a position rather than a character, specifying an anchor on its own matches an empty string:

```
Console.WriteLine (Regex.Match ("x", "$").Length);   // 0
```

Word Boundaries

The word boundary assertion \b matches where word characters (\w) adjoin either:

- Nonword characters (\W)
- The beginning/end of the string (^ and $)

\b is often used to match whole words:

```
foreach (Match m in Regex.Matches ("Wedding in Sarajevo", @"\b\w+\b"))
  Console.WriteLine (m);

Wedding
in
Sarajevo
```

The following statements highlight the effect of a word boundary:

```
int one = Regex.Matches ("Wedding in Sarajevo", @"\bin\b").Count;  // 1
int two = Regex.Matches ("Wedding in Sarajevo", @"in").Count;     // 2
```

The next query uses *positive lookahead* to return words followed by "(sic)":

```
string text = "Don't loose (sic) your cool";
Console.Write (Regex.Match (text, @"\b\w+\b\s(?=\(sic\))"));  // loose
```

Groups

Sometimes, it's useful to separate a regular expression into a series of subexpressions, or *groups*. For instance, consider the following regular expression that represents a US phone number such as 206-465-1918:

```
\d{3}-\d{3}-\d{4}
```

Suppose that we want to separate this into two groups: area code and local number. We can achieve this by using parentheses to *capture* each group:

```
(\d{3})-(\d{3}-\d{4})
```

We then retrieve the groups programmatically:

```
Match m = Regex.Match ("206-465-1918", @"(\d{3})-(\d{3}-\d{4})");

Console.WriteLine (m.Groups[1]);  // 206
Console.WriteLine (m.Groups[2]);  // 465-1918
```

The zeroth group represents the entire match. In other words, it has the same value as the match's Value:

```
Console.WriteLine (m.Groups[0]);  // 206-465-1918
Console.WriteLine (m);            // 206-465-1918
```

Groups are part of the regular expressions language itself. This means that you can refer to a group within a regular expression. The \n syntax lets you index the group by group number n within the expression. For example, the expression (\w)ee\1 matches deed and peep. In the following example, we find all words in a string starting and ending in the same letter:

```
foreach (Match m in Regex.Matches ("pop pope peep", @"\b(\w)\w+\1\b"))
  Console.Write (m + " ");  // pop peep
```

The brackets around the \w instruct the regular expressions engine to store the submatch in a group (in this case, a single letter) so that it can be used later. We refer to that group later using \1, meaning the first group in the expression.

Named Groups

In a long or complex expression, it can be easier to work with groups by *name* rather than index. Here's a rewrite of the previous example, using a group that we name 'letter':

```
string regEx =
    @"\b"                + // word boundary
    @"(?'letter'\w)"     + // match first letter, and name it 'letter'
    @"\w+"               + // match middle letters
    @"\k'letter'"        + // match last letter, denoted by 'letter'
    @"\b";                 // word boundary

foreach (Match m in Regex.Matches ("bob pope peep", regEx))
    Console.Write (m + " ");  // bob peep
```

Here's how to name a captured group:

```
(?'group-name'group-expr)   or   (?<group-name>group-expr)
```

And here's how to refer to a group:

```
\k'group-name'   or   \k<group-name>
```

The following example matches a simple (non-nested) XML/HTML element by looking for start and end nodes with a matching name:

```
string regFind =
    @"<(?'tag'\w+?).*>" + // lazy-match first tag, and name it 'tag'
    @"(?'text'.*?)"     + // lazy-match text content, name it 'text'
    @"</\k'tag'>";        // match last tag, denoted by 'tag'

Match m = Regex.Match ("<h1>hello</h1>", regFind);
Console.WriteLine (m.Groups ["tag"]);     // h1
Console.WriteLine (m.Groups ["text"]);    // hello
```

Allowing for all possible variations in XML structure, such as nested elements, is more complex. The .NET regular expressions engine has a sophisticated extension called "matched balanced constructs" that can assist with nested tags—information on this is available on the internet and in *Mastering Regular Expressions* (O'Reilly) by Jeffrey E. F. Friedl.

Replacing and Splitting Text

The RegEx.Replace method works like string.Replace except that it uses a regular expression.

The following replaces "cat" with "dog". Unlike with `string.Replace`, "catapult" won't change into "dogapult", because we match on word boundaries:

```
string find = @"\bcat\b";
string replace = "dog";
Console.WriteLine (Regex.Replace ("catapult the cat", find, replace));

OUTPUT: catapult the dog
```

The replacement string can reference the original match with the `$0` substitution construct. The following example wraps numbers within a string in angle brackets:

```
string text = "10 plus 20 makes 30";
Console.WriteLine (Regex.Replace (text, @"\d+", @"<$0>"));

OUTPUT: <10> plus <20> makes <30>
```

You can access any captured groups with `$1`, `$2`, `$3`, and so on, or `${name}` for a named group. To illustrate how this can be useful, consider the regular expression in the previous section that matched a simple XML element. By rearranging the groups, we can form a replacement expression that moves the element's content into an XML attribute:

```
string regFind =
    @"<(?'tag'\w+?).*>" +    // lazy-match first tag, and name it 'tag'
    @"(?'text'.*?)"    +     // lazy-match text content, name it 'text'
    @"</\k'tag'>";           // match last tag, denoted by 'tag'

string regReplace =
    @"<${tag}"      +  // <tag
    @"value="""     +  // value="
    @"${text}"      +  // text
    @"""/>";           // "/>

Console.Write (Regex.Replace ("<msg>hello</msg>", regFind, regReplace));
```

Here's the result:

```
<msg value="hello"/>
```

MatchEvaluator Delegate

`Replace` has an overload that takes a `MatchEvaluator` delegate, which is invoked per match. This allows you to delegate the content of the replacement string to C# code when the regular expressions language isn't expressive enough:

```
Console.WriteLine (Regex.Replace ("5 is less than 10", @"\d+",
                   m => (int.Parse (m.Value) * 10).ToString()) );

OUTPUT: 50 is less than 100
```

In "Cookbook Regular Expressions" on page 999, we show how to use a `Match Evaluator` to escape Unicode characters appropriately for HTML.

Splitting Text

The static `Regex.Split` method is a more powerful version of the `string.Split` method, with a regular expression denoting the separator pattern. In this example, we split a string, where any digit counts as a separator:

```
foreach (string s in Regex.Split ("a5b7c", @"\d"))
  Console.Write (s + " ");     // a b c
```

The result, here, doesn't include the separators themselves. You can include the separators, however, by wrapping the expression in a *positive lookahead*. The following splits a camel-case string into separate words:

```
foreach (string s in Regex.Split ("oneTwoThree", @"(?=[A-Z])"))
  Console.Write (s + " ");     // one Two Three
```

Cookbook Regular Expressions

Recipes

Matching US Social Security number/phone number

```
string ssNum = @"\d{3}-\d{2}-\d{4}";

Console.WriteLine (Regex.IsMatch ("123-45-6789", ssNum));       // True

string phone = @"(?x)
  ( \d{3}[-\s] | \(\d{3}\)\s? )
    \d{3}[-\s]?
    \d{4}";

Console.WriteLine (Regex.IsMatch ("123-456-7890",   phone));    // True
Console.WriteLine (Regex.IsMatch ("(123) 456-7890", phone));    // True
```

Extracting "name = value" pairs (one per line)

Note that this starts with the *multiline* directive (?m):

```
string r = @"(?m)^\s*(?'name'\w+)\s*=\s*(?'value'.*)\s*(?=\r?$)";

string text =
  @"id = 3
    secure = true
    timeout = 30";

foreach (Match m in Regex.Matches (text, r))
  Console.WriteLine (m.Groups["name"] + " is " + m.Groups["value"]);
id is 3 secure is true timeout is 30
```

Strong password validation

The following checks whether a password has at least six characters and whether it contains a digit, symbol, or punctuation mark:

```
string r = @"(?x)^(?=.* ( \d | \p{P} | \p{S} )).{6,}";

Console.WriteLine (Regex.IsMatch ("abc12", r));    // False
Console.WriteLine (Regex.IsMatch ("abcdef", r));   // False
Console.WriteLine (Regex.IsMatch ("ab88yz", r));   // True
```

Lines of at least 80 characters

```
string r = @"(?m)^.{80,}(?=\r?$)";

string fifty = new string ('x', 50);
string eighty = new string ('x', 80);

string text = eighty + "\r\n" + fifty + "\r\n" + eighty;

Console.WriteLine (Regex.Matches (text, r).Count);   // 2
```

Parsing dates/times (N/N/N H:M:S AM/PM)

This expression handles a variety of numeric date formats—and works whether the year comes first or last. The (?x) directive improves readability by allowing white-space; the (?i) switches off case sensitivity (for the optional AM/PM designator). You can then access each component of the match through the Groups collection:

```
string r = @"(?x)(?i)
(\d{1,4}) [./-]
(\d{1,2}) [./-]
(\d{1,4}) [\sT]
(\d+):(\d+):(\d+) \s? (A\.?M\.?|P\.?M\.?)?";

string text = "01/02/2008 5:20:50 PM";

foreach (Group g in Regex.Match (text, r).Groups)
  Console.WriteLine (g.Value + " ");
01/02/2008 5:20:50 PM 01 02 2008 5 20 50 PM
```

(Of course, this doesn't verify that the date/time is correct.)

Matching Roman numerals

```
string r =
  @"(?i)\bm*"          +
  @"(d?c{0,3}|c[dm])"  +
  @"(l?x{0,3}|x[lc])"  +
  @"(v?i{0,3}|i[vx])"  +
  @"\b";

Console.WriteLine (Regex.IsMatch ("MCMLXXXIV", r));   // True
```

Removing repeated words

Here, we capture a named group called dupe:

```csharp
string r = @"(?'dupe'\w+)\W\k'dupe'";

string text = "In the the beginning...";
Console.WriteLine (Regex.Replace (text, r, "${dupe}"));
```

In the beginning

Word count

```csharp
string r = @"\b(\w|[-'])+\b";

string text = "It's all mumbo-jumbo to me";
Console.WriteLine (Regex.Matches (text, r).Count);    // 5
```

Matching a GUID

```csharp
string r =
  @"(?i)\b"               +
  @"[0-9a-fA-F]{8}\-" +
  @"[0-9a-fA-F]{4}\-" +
  @"[0-9a-fA-F]{4}\-" +
  @"[0-9a-fA-F]{4}\-" +
  @"[0-9a-fA-F]{12}" +
  @"\b";

string text = "Its key is {3F2504E0-4F89-11D3-9A0C-0305E82C3301}.";
Console.WriteLine (Regex.Match (text, r).Index);              // 12
```

Parsing an XML/HTML tag

Regex is useful for parsing HTML fragments—particularly when the document might be imperfectly formed:

```csharp
string r =
  @"<(?'tag'\w+?).*>"  +  // lazy-match first tag, and name it 'tag'
  @"(?'text'.*?)"      +  // lazy-match text content, name it 'textd'
  @"</\k'tag'>";          // match last tag, denoted by 'tag'

string text = "<h1>hello</h1>";

Match m = Regex.Match (text, r);

Console.WriteLine (m.Groups ["tag"]);      // h1
Console.WriteLine (m.Groups ["text"]);     // hello
```

Splitting a camel-cased word

This requires a *positive lookahead* to include the uppercase separators:

```csharp
string r = @"(?=[A-Z])";

foreach (string s in Regex.Split ("oneTwoThree", r))
  Console.Write (s + " ");    // one Two Three
```

Obtaining a legal filename

```
string input = "My \"good\" <recipes>.txt";

char[] invalidChars = System.IO.Path.GetInvalidFileNameChars();
string invalidString = Regex.Escape (new string (invalidChars));

string valid = Regex.Replace (input, "[" + invalidString + "]", "");
Console.WriteLine (valid);

My good recipes.txt
```

Escaping Unicode characters for HTML

```
string htmlFragment = "© 2007";

string result = Regex.Replace (htmlFragment, @"[\u0080-\uFFFF]",
            m => @"&#" + ((int)m.Value[0]).ToString() + ";");

Console.WriteLine (result);        // &#169; 2007
```

Unescaping characters in an HTTP query string

```
string sample = "C%23 rocks";

string result = Regex.Replace (
    sample,
    @"%[0-9a-f][0-9a-f]",
    m => ((char) Convert.ToByte (m.Value.Substring (1), 16)).ToString(),
    RegexOptions.IgnoreCase
);

Console.WriteLine (result);    // C# rocks
```

Parsing Google search terms from a web stats log

You should use this in conjunction with the previous example to unescape characters in the query string:

```
string sample =
    "http://google.com/search?hl=en&q=greedy+quantifiers+regex&btnG=Search";

Match m = Regex.Match (sample, @"(?<=google\..+search\?.*q=).+?(?=(&|$))");

string[] keywords = m.Value.Split (
    new[] { '+' }, StringSplitOptions.RemoveEmptyEntries);

foreach (string keyword in keywords)
    Console.Write (keyword + " ");        // greedy quantifiers regex
```

Regular Expressions Language Reference

Tables 25-2 through 25-12 summarize the regular expressions grammar and syntax supported in the .NET implementation.

Table 25-2. Character escapes

Escape code sequence	Meaning	Hexadecimal equivalent
\a	Bell	\u0007
\b	Backspace	\u0008
\t	Tab	\u0009
\r	Carriage return	\u000A
\v	Vertical tab	\u000B
\f	Form feed	\u000C
\n	Newline	\u000D
\e	Escape	\u001B
\nnn	ASCII character nnn as octal (e.g., \n052)	
\xnn	ASCII character nn as hex (e.g., \x3F)	
\cl	ASCII control character l (e.g., \cG for Ctrl-G)	
\unnnn	Unicode character nnnn as hex (e.g., \u07DE)	
\symbol	A nonescaped symbol	

Special case: within a regular expression, \b means word boundary, except in a [ ] set, in which \b means the backspace character.

Table 25-3. Character sets

Expression	Meaning	Inverse ("not")
[abcdef]	Matches a single character in the list	[^abcdef]
[a-f]	Matches a single character in a *range*	[^a-f]
\d	Matches a decimal digit Same as [0-9]	\D
\w	Matches a *word* character (by default, varies according to CultureInfo.CurrentCulture; for example, in English, same as [a-zA-Z_0-9])	\W
\s	Matches a whitespace character Same as [\n\r\t\f\v]	\S
\p{category}	Matches a character in a specified *category* (see Table 25-4)	\P
.	(Default mode) Matches any character except \n	\n
.	(SingleLine mode) Matches any character	\n

Table 25-4. Character categories

Quantifier	Meaning
\p{L}	Letters
\p{Lu}	Uppercase letters
\p{Ll}	Lowercase letters
\p{N}	Numbers
\p{P}	Punctuation
\p{M}	Diacritic marks
\p{S}	Symbols
\p{Z}	Separators
\p{C}	Control characters

Table 25-5. Quantifiers

Quantifier	Meaning
*	Zero or more matches
+	One or more matches
?	Zero or one match
{n}	Exactly n matches
{n,}	At least n matches
{n,m}	Between n and m matches

The ? suffix can be applied to any of the quantifiers to make them *lazy* rather than *greedy*.

Table 25-6. Substitutions

Expression	Meaning
$0	Substitutes the matched text
$group-number	Substitutes an indexed *group-number* within the matched text
${group-name}	Substitutes a text *group-name* within the matched text

Substitutions are specified only within a replacement pattern.

Table 25-7. Zero-width assertions

Expression	Meaning
^	Start of string (or line in *multiline* mode)
$	End of string (or line in *multiline* mode)
\A	Start of string (ignores *multiline* mode)

Expression	Meaning
\z	End of string (ignores *multiline* mode)
\Z	End of line or string
\G	Where search started
\b	On a word boundary
\B	Not on a word boundary
(?=*expr*)	Continue matching only if expression *expr* matches on right (*positive lookahead*)
(?!*expr*)	Continue matching only if expression *expr* doesn't match on right (*negative lookahead*)
(?<=*expr*)	Continue matching only if expression *expr* matches on left (*positive lookbehind*)
(?<!*expr*)	Continue matching only if expression *expr* doesn't match on left (*negative lookbehind*)
(?>*expr*)	Subexpression *expr* is matched once and not backtracked

Table 25-8. Grouping constructs

Syntax	Meaning
(*expr*)	Capture matched expression *expr* into indexed group
(?*number*)	Capture matched substring into a specified group *number*
(?'*name*')	Capture matched substring into group *name*
(?'*name1-name2*')	Undefine *name2* and store interval and current group into *name1*; if *name2* is undefined, matching backtracks
(?:*expr*)	Noncapturing group

Table 25-9. Back references

Parameter syntax	Meaning
index	Reference a previously captured group by *index*
\k<*name*>	Reference a previously captured group by *name*

Table 25-10. Alternation

Expression syntax	Meaning
|	Logical *or*
(?(*expr*)yes|no)	Matches *yes* if expression matches; otherwise, matches *no* (*no* is optional)
(?(*name*)yes|no)	Matches *yes* if named group has a match; otherwise, matches *no* (*no* is optional)

Table 25-11. Miscellaneous constructs

Expression syntax	Meaning
(?#*comment*)	Inline comment
#*comment*	Comment to end of line (works only in IgnorePatternWhitespace mode)

Table 25-12. Regular expression options

Option	Meaning
(?i)	Case-insensitive match ("ignore" case)
(?m)	Multiline mode; changes ^ and $ so that they match beginning and end of any line
(?n)	Captures only explicitly named or numbered groups
(?c)	Compiles to Intermediate Language
(?s)	Single-line mode; changes meaning of "." so that it matches every character
(?x)	Eliminates unescaped whitespace from the pattern
(?r)	Searches from right to left; can't be specified midstream

Index

automatic properties, 107
autonomous tasks, 629
AutoResetEvent, 887-890
Average operator, 491
AVL tree, 387
await expressions, 639-645
    awaiting in a UI, 642-644
    capturing local state, 641
    locking and, 881
AWS (Amazon Web Services), 860

B

b (word boundary assertion), 995
background garbage collection, 573
background threads, 620
BackgroundWorker class, 669
backing fields, 228
backing store streams, 677
backslash (\)
    in regular expressions, 990
    preceding escape sequences, 51
banker's rounding, 311
Barrier class, 894-896
base class library (BCL), 4
base constructors, 822
base keyword, 122
base types and interfaces, 785
base-class constraint, 150
BaseType property, 785
Basic Multilingual Plane (BMP), 284
BCL (base class library), 4
BigInteger struct, 316
binary adapters, 693
binary operators, 71
BinaryReader, 737
BinaryWriter, 737
binding
    dynamic binding, 232-239
    static versus dynamic, 232
BindingFlags enum, 799
bit-mapped attributes, 803
BitArray class, 370
BitConverter, 313
bitwise operators, 46
blocking
    spinning versus, 613
    threads, 612
BlockingCollection<T>, 945-949

using tasks, 948-949
    writing a producer/consumer queue,
        946-949
BMP (Basic Multilingual Plane), 284
bool (Boolean) type and operators, 31,
    49-51
    conditional operators, 50
    equality and comparison operators, 49
bounds checking, 58
boxing, 126
    copying semantics, 127
    interfaces and, 138
    nullable values, 195
braces ({})
    enclosing expressions in interpolated
        strings, 276
    enclosing statement blocks, 26, 76
    in if statements, 78
    in regular expressions, 992
branching, 812
break statement, 85
broadcaster type, 167
BrotliStream, 695
BufferedStream class, 686
builder class, 386
built-in types, 31
byte arrays, 283
byte type, 47

C

C# (generally)
    brief history of features introduced
        from C# 2.0 through C# 9.0, 7-24
    language basics, 25-94
    memory management, 3, 4
        (see also garbage collection[GC])
    niche runtimes, 7
    object orientation, 1
    platform support, 3
    simple program, 25-27
    syntax, 28-30
    type safety, 2
C# 10
    applying attributes to lambda expres-
        sions, 228
    CallerArgumentExpression, 231
    constant interpolated strings, 54
    file-scoped namespaces, 88

public keyword, 33
symmetry of predefined/custom types, 32
customizable collections and proxies, 378-384
    Collection<T> and CollectionBase, 379-381
    KeyedCollection<TKey,TItem> and DictionaryBase, 381-383
    ReadOnlyCollection<T>, 383

D

data members, 32
data parallelism, 908
data transfer object (DTO), 460
dates and times, 284-297
    dates and time zones, 292-297
    DateTime and DateTimeOffset, 286-291
    parsing with regular expressions, 1000
    TimeSpan, 284
DateTime, 286-291
    constructing, 287
    DateTimeOffset versus, 286
    daylight saving time and, 296
    format strings, 307-309
    formatting/parsing datetimes, 290
    null values, 291
    parsing/misparsing, 308
    returning current date/time with, 289
    time zones and, 292
    working with dates and times, 290
DateTime.MinValue, 291
DateTimeFormatInfo, 300
DateTimeOffset, 286-291, 325
    constructing, 288
    DateTime versus, 286
    format strings, 307-309
    formatting/parsing datetimes, 291
    null values, 291
    returning current date/time with, 289
    time zones and, 293
    working with dates and times, 290
DateTimeStyles, 309
daylight saving time, 296
DbContext, 431-437
    change tracking, 437
    configuring the connection, 431

configuring the model, 432
creating the database, 434
disposing, 436
object tracking, 435
using, 435
Debug and Trace classes, 589-592
    Fail and Assert methods, 589
    flushing and closing listeners, 591
    TraceListener, 590
Debugger class, 592
    attaching and breaking, 592
    attributes, 592
DebuggerHidden attribute, 592
DebuggerStepThrough attribute, 592
decimal conversions, 44
declaration statements, 76
declarative parallelism, 909
Deconstruct method, 102, 225
deconstructing assignment, 103
deconstructors, 102-103
decorator sequence, 411
decrement operator (--), 45
deep cloning, 504
default keyword, 61, 149
default scheduler, 939
DefaultIfEmpty operator, 490
deferred execution
    captured variables, 410
    chaining decorators, 412
    EF Core queries, 440
    how queries are executed, 413
    LINQ queries, 408-414
    mechanism of operation, 411
    reevaluation, 409
    subqueries and, 417
deferred loading, 528
#define directive, 585
DefineMethodOverride, 820
definite assignment policy, 60
DeflateStream, 695-697
delegate type, 159
Delegate.CreateDelegate, 787
delegates, 159-167
    callbacks with, 969
    calling dynamically instantiated delegates, 798
    compatibility, 165-167
    dynamically instantiating, 787
    Func and Action delegates, 164

SQL LIKE comparisons in EF Core,
453
Take and Skip, 454
TakeWhile and SkipWhile, 455
Where, 452-455
WHERE x IN (...,...,...) in EF Core,
454
finalizer (~), 112
calling Dispose from, 566
GC and, 565-569
GC.ReRegisterForFinalize, 569
resurrection, 568-569
finally blocks, 184, 193
fine-grained concurrency, 635
First operator, 488
FirstNode function, 505
FirstOrDefault operator, 489
fixed keyword, 976
fixed statement, 244
fixed-size buffers, 245
Flags attribute, 142
Flatten method, 941
floating-point types, 42
conversions, 44
special float and double values, 47
fluent syntax, 397-403
chaining query operators, 397-400
composing lambda expressions,
400-402
importance of extension methods, 399
joining in, 471
mixed-syntax queries, 407
natural ordering, 402
query syntax versus, 407
for loops, 83
foreach loops, 84
foreground threads, 620
form data, uploading, 730
format item, 276
formatting and parsing, 297-309
BitConverter, 313
composite formatting, 300
Convert class, 310-312
custom numeric format strings, 304
Date/Time format strings, 307-309
DateTimeFormatInfo, 300
DateTimeStyles, 309
enum format strings, 309
enums, 320-323

equality comparison, 324-335
format providers, 298-302
format providers and CultureInfo, 299
format string, 276
globalization, 314
Guid struct, 323
IFormatProvider and ICustomFormat-
ter, 301
NumberFormatInfo, 300
NumberStyles, 305
numeric format strings, 303
parsing with format providers, 301
standard format strings and parsing
flags, 303
ToString and Parse methods, 297
type converters, 313
working with numbers, 315-319
XmlConvert, 312
FormatTransitionTime, 296
forward slash (/)
as division operator, 44
trailing in URIs, 722
forward slash, double (//), 25, 30
forward-only enumerators, 957-958
frameworks, 4
(see also runtimes)
friend assemblies, 133
fully qualified names, 747
Func delegate, 164, 401
function pointers, 248, 967
functional construction, 502
functional programming, 384

G

garbage collection (GC), 563-564
array pooling, 575
automatic, 563-564
background collection, 573
defined, 557
finalizers, 565-569
forcing, 574
generational collection, 570
Large Object Heap, 572
managed memory leaks, 576-579
memory consumption and, 564
memory pressure, 575
notifications, 573
optimization, 570-574

void pointer (void*), 246
volume information, querying, 708

W

wait handles (see event wait handles)
Wait method, 627
WaitAll method, 893
WaitAny method, 893
#warning preprocessor directive, 250
weak references
    caching and, 580
    events and, 580-583
    GC and, 579-583
Where clause, 452-455
    Enumerable.Where implementation, 452
    indexed filtering, 453
WHERE x IN (...,...,...), 454
while loops, 83
wildcards (character sets), 991
Windows
    application manifest, 743
    memory-mapped files and shared memory, 713
    OS security, 710
Windows Data Protection API (DPAPI), 852
Windows Desktop application layer, 267
Windows event logs, 596-598
    monitoring, 597
    reading, 597
    writing to, 596
Windows Forms, 267
Windows Management Instrumentation (WMI) API, 701
Windows Presentation Foundation (WPF), 267
Windows Runtime (WinRT)
    asynchronous methods in, 653
WithDegreeOfParallelism, 917
WithMergeOptions, 913
WMI (Windows Management Instrumentation) API, 701
word boundary assertions, 995
WPF (Windows Presentation Foundation), 267
write locks, 882-887

X

x++ (incrementing), 616
X-DOM (see XML DOM)
XAML (Extensible Application Markup Language) files, 313, 756
XAttribute, 500
XContainer, 500
XDeclaration object, 515
XDocument, 500, 515-519
XElement, 498-502
    using XmlReader with, 542
    using XmlWriter with, 543
XML declarations, 517
XML documentation, 252-255
    standard tags, 253-254
    type or member cross-references, 255
    user-defined tags, 255
XML DOM (X-DOM), 498
    attribute navigation, 509
    automatic deep cloning, 504
    automatic XText concatenation, 515
    child node navigation, 505
    content specification, 503
    default namespaces, 522
    functional construction, 502
    getting values, 513
    instantiating, 502-504
    loading and parsing, 500
    mixing XmlReader/XmlWriter with, 542
    namespace specification, 521
    navigating and querying, 504-509
    overview, 498-502
    parent navigation, 508
    peer node navigation, 509
    prefixes, 523
    projecting into, 525-528
    removing a sequence of nodes or attributes, 512
    retrieving a single element, 507
    retrieving descendants, 507
    retrieving elements, 506
    saving and serializing, 501
    setting values, 513
    simple value updates, 510
    updating, 510-513
    updating child nodes and attributes, 511

About the Authors

Joseph Albahari is the author of *C# 9.0 in a Nutshell*, *C# 10 Pocket Reference*, and *LINQ Pocket Reference*. He also wrote LINQPad—the popular code scratchpad and LINQ querying utility.

Colophon

The animal on the cover of *C# 10 in a Nutshell* is a numidian crane. The numidian crane (*Grus virgo*) is also called the demoiselle crane because of its grace and symmetry. This species of crane is native to Europe and Asia and migrates to India, Pakistan, and northeast Africa in the winter.

Though numidian cranes are the smallest cranes, they defend their territories as aggressively as other crane species, using their loud voices to warn others of trespassing. If necessary, they will fight. Numidian cranes nest in uplands rather than wetlands and will even live in the desert if there is water within 200 to 500 meters. They sometimes make nests out of pebbles in which to lay their eggs, though more often they will lay eggs directly on the ground, protected only by vegetation.

Numidian cranes are considered a symbol of good luck in some countries and are sometimes even protected by law. Many of the animals on O'Reilly covers are endangered; all of them are important to the world.

The cover illustration is by Karen Montgomery, based on a black-and-white engraving from *Wood's Illustrated Natural History*. The cover fonts are Gilroy Semibold and Guardian Sans. The text font is Adobe Minion Pro, the heading font is Adobe Myriad Condensed, and the code font is Dalton Maag's Ubuntu Mono.

Lightning Source UK Ltd.
Milton Keynes UK
UKHW030948090222
398390UK00001B/1